Entertainment Law
and Practice

Entertainment Law
and Practice

THIRD EDITION

Jon M. Garon
PROFESSOR OF LAW
NOVA SOUTHEASTERN UNIVERSITY
SHEPARD BROAD COLLEGE OF LAW

CAROLINA ACADEMIC PRESS
Durham, North Carolina

ISBN 978-1-5310-1843-6
eISBN 978-1-5310-1844-3
LCCN 2020930523

Carolina Academic Press
700 Kent Street
Durham, North Carolina 27701
Telephone (919) 489-7486
Fax (919) 493-5668
www.cap-press.com

Printed in the United States of America

*For my family
Avery, Alec Sasha (z"l), Noah,
and Stacy Blumberg Garon.*

Summary of Contents

Contents

Table of Principal Cases

Preface to the Third Edition

The third edition to Entertainment Law & Practice illustrates the continuing transformation triggered by the digital revolution to all media formats covered by the book. The music industry had been impacted first, going back to the turn of the twenty-first century. Since then, the publication and distribution of books has been redefined by Amazon.com; the way the public watches television has been upended by Netflix and Amazon Prime; the ability to make and upload films and videos has created a new industry on YouTube; the ubiquity of social media has changed marketing and retail; and the video game industry has entered an entirely new era as a result of the rise of esports and the expansion of the viewer audience on Twitch.

The changes in these industries have resulted in continued expansion of the case law in the areas of trademark and publicity rights. Each of these topics now has its own chapter. The statutory and case law for online digital media have also continued to evolve. The chapters on television and cable have been revised to reflect that "television" is now a metaphor for broadcast, cable, satellite, and over the top video streaming. It is viewed on traditional television sets, but it is also viewed on computers, tablets, phones, watches, and other mobile devices. Instead of separate chapters for television and for cable, the third edition has a chapter focused on television content production and television regulation.

Other important changes are slowly making their way through the entertainment industries, and these are also reflected in the new edition. The chapter on ethics has been expanded to include a focus on the gender and race disparities prevalent in aspects of the entertainment industries. Although there is little case law, these materials highlight the need for continued inclusion in the industry and the role that lawyers can play in fostering these efforts.

The design of the book is fashioned to serve as a capstone for many bar tested subjects, a seminar on sophisticated legal doctrine, or a workshop on practicing law. The third edition includes more introductory material to provide context for each of the entertainment industries. Questions, hypotheticals, notes, statutes, and historical materials continue to provide a robust context in which to explore the entertainment industries and develop a sophisticated understanding of these critically important and highly complex materials. Each chapter retains the bibliography to encourage additional research on the themes of the chapter.

All questions, comments, and inquiries should be directed to me at Nova Southeastern University Shepard Broad College of Law, email: garon@nova.edu; phone: (954) 262-6229.

Jon M. Garon, editor
Ft. Lauderdale, FL

Preface to the Second Edition

Although I have endeavored to update the first edition of Entertainment Law & Practice every other year with a supplement, technological change and court decisions required that I publish a new edition of the casebook itself. In industries such as publishing, the central debates challenging the industry a decade ago have been entirely replaced as new economic realities reshape the relationships within the industry. The casebook also has a great many more Supreme Court decisions than the prior edition because the concerns of the entertainment industries have become profound enough to warrant the time of the Court.

From a substantive law perspective, copyright has undergone the greatest transformation in the past decade. Once a primarily commercial body of law involving disputes between creators and distributors of content, or on rare occasion a dispute between copyright industries and commercial industries which utilized copyrighted works, most of the new cases reproduced in the second edition focus on consumers and the public rather than commercial defendants. This change in the role of the law may explain a good deal about how the entertainment industries have been transformed in the past decade.

The transformation is well underway, but still has miles to go. As these changes affect the lives of more and more individuals, the concerns covered in the casebook will increasingly become the focus of public debate. I hope the second edition provides a helpful tool to facilitate that debate in a thoughtful, well-informed manner. Entertainment has always been fun. Today it is more important than ever.

All questions, comments, and inquiries should be directed to me, Jon M. Garon, Director, NKU Chase Law + Informatics Institute and Professor of Law, Northern Kentucky University Chase College of Law.

Jon M. Garon, editor
Highland Heights, KY

Preface to the First Edition

In choosing to write, publish, adopt, or study a casebook, the threshold question to be answered is Why this book? The editorial structure of this casebook is an extension of my work attempting to demonstrate that entertainment law is more than a series of generally applicable laws that can be applied to the fun and exciting world of entertainers. Entertainment law has evolved into a discrete body of law whereby other legal doctrines take on unique interpretations. (See, Jon M. Garon, *Entertainment Law*, 76 Tulane L. Rev. 559 (2002).) Broad areas of law such as copyright, privacy, and free speech have been transformed by or translated through the entertainment industries. This casebook reflects more of the unified or thematic approach to entertainment law than others previously published.

The unified approach to entertainment, however, does not tell the complete story. There are other areas of entertainment practice that are governed by laws specifically written to regulate these industries. There are also historical practices — some centuries old — that dictate the relationships between parties and the structure of the industry. In many situations, these practices bear no relation to entertainment as a whole, but instead focus on practices highly concentrated on one particular industry, such as professional theatre, music publishing, or commercial film. As a result, the practice of entertainment is an equally important aspect of study for any serious student of entertainment law.

The law and practice sections of the book reflect the broad dichotomy between those areas where entertainment has reshaped general law and those areas where the entertainment practice is specific to a particular industry or industries. Admittedly, this dichotomy may sometimes be subtle or artificial. The organization is my preferred structure, but each subchapter stands as a complete module, so that each instructor may design the course to fit his or her pedagogy and objectives.

The thematic structure of the casebook may help to explain why the topics covered are sometimes quite different than other books on the topic. One example may help illustrate the approach. Every entertainment law casebook has some discussion of trademark principles and how these concepts apply to film titles and professional credits. This book also includes a specific review of trademark analysis and partnership law as it applies to the ownership of a band's name. Although this topic is central to practitioners' texts and arguably the most valuable asset owned by a musical performer, the unique intersection of trademark, publicity, free speech and partnership law has not previously been addressed in any of the commercially available casebooks.

Useful teaching materials are more likely to come from those developed in the classroom than those created in isolation, and I have been very fortunate to have built this casebook over time as my students worked through the materials selected and provided me with feedback and insight. When teaching Entertainment Law or either of my breakout courses, Law of Motion Pictures and the Performing Arts and Music Management & Licensing, my teaching objectives are to develop the students' problem-solving skills using issues related to the entertainment industry and business planning; to familiarize students with the intellectual property rights and contractual relationships between the media producers, distributors and authors in these industries and to introduce the deal-making aspects of practice in the entertainment industry; and to track the legal and business structure of the entertainment industries.

The included notes, questions, and problems help focus the reading on the problem solving skills of the students. To this end, some materials are included to illustrate tensions in the law and limitations imposed by legal rules, collective bargaining restrictions, or practical consequences. Other materials simply illustrate industry practice. In addition, the range of cases promotes traditional critical reading and reasoning skills.

Depending on the course hours available, many professors may elect to assign less than the entire text. Part I can be considered sufficient to teach an entire survey course. Alternatively, selected sections of Part II can be integrated with Part I to focus on music, film, television, or theatre, depending on the interests of the course and the instructor.

The entertainment industries rely heavily on copyright, trademark, First Amendment, antitrust, labor law, and telecommunications law. The casebook provides introductions to explain the relevant principles in the context of entertainment law. Questions, hypotheticals, notes, statutes, and historical materials provide a robust context in which to explore the entertainment industries and develop a sophisticated understanding of these critically important and highly complex materials.

Each subchapter provides sufficient context that it can be read without regard to the chapter as a whole. Helpful historical cases and materials are typically left to the notes so that the student can identify the current law or practice instead of tracking the growth of a doctrine or custom through voluminous reading.

Each chapter has a bibliography focused on the general themes of the chapter. Most sections have notes and questions that help focus and refine the topics under consideration. In addition, most sections have a problem—always focused on Bryce, the client who comes to students for advice throughout the book. As Bryce's career moves through the various entertainment fields and chapters of the book, Bryce's concerns become more sophisticated, creating an opportunity to integrate the topics being explored. These problems move beyond the materials of the section, often highlighting the intersection of various themes in the book and serving as potential research topics or areas for further study.

To make the student assignments manageable in length, it is necessary to heavily shorten most of the materials. Deletions of textual material are generally noted with ellipses (…), except for footnotes and citations, which are not noted. In addition, some central footnotes have been moved directly into the text where the note would otherwise have been placed. The remaining footnotes are renumbered. Insertions and any editorial changes are placed in brackets ([ ]). Where necessary, paragraph breaks have also been added or deleted without notation.

Finally, I have endeavored to edit the cases in a manner that allows the students to see the interrelation between multiple causes of action. Many cases involve a copyright, trademark, unfair competition, and publicity rights cause of action for the same alleged misconduct. The First Amendment is sometimes invoked as a defense to all of these. As a result, fewer but longer cases may better inform students regarding the relationship between the doctrinal legal boxes taught elsewhere. I have attempted to keep the book capable of longer or shorter reading assignments to provide flexibility for instructors who seek to emphasize some topics, but not others.

Like any casebook, particularly one where the area of law and practice is in such a state of transformation, the book is constantly evolving. I appreciate all feedback and suggestions.

Jon M. Garon, editor
St. Paul, MN 2004

Acknowledgments

This book has been a continual outgrowth of my practice and academic work in the area of entertainment law. I have benefited from the assistance of colleagues at each of the five law schools where parts of this work were developed: Western State University College of Law, Franklin Pierce Law Center (now University of New Hampshire School of Law), Hamline University School of Law, Northern Kentucky University Salmon P. Chase College of Law, and Nova Southeastern University Shepard Broad College of Law. Among my colleagues who assisted, I would like to thank Maryann Jones, Susan Richey, Sophie Sparrow, Tom Field, Larry Bakken, Carol Swanson, Dennis Honabach, Kevin Kirby, Susan Stephan, and Debra Moss Vollweiler. I also appreciate the assistance of attorneys with whom I have worked at the firms of Hawes & Fisher and Gallagher, Callahan, & Gartrell.

My thanks go out to Stacy Blumberg Garon for her editing on this book and many of my articles, Lena Abdin, Andrea Pontecorvi, and Cherie Gannet who worked on the third edition of the casebook, Luke (Walter) Bubenzer who has worked on the second edition of the casebook as well as the 2012 Supplement, Matthew Ryan for his work on the second edition, and Jacqueline A. Olson, my research assistant on the 2010 supplement. I also wish to thank Lindsey Jaeger and Laurie Darwish, who have worked extensively with me at the NKU Chase Law + Informatics Institute and who have made it possible for me to complete the second edition.

I must also acknowledge the reliance I have made on the casebooks I have used throughout my teaching as models and guides for this book. Robert Gorman and Jane Ginsburg, *Copyright Cases and Materials* and Eugene Volokh, *The First Amendment—Law, Cases, Problems, and Policy Arguments* both served as models for me in determining what should be included and omitted from this book.

From the first edition, I would like to recognize the assistance provided by Ed Kroening, my old friend and editor at that time; by Carol Swanson, my Associate Dean for Academic Affairs at Hamline; and to Hamline Law Students Shelley Ryan, Corinna Venters, Amanda Leonhardt, Kristin Luckenbill, Chris Viloria, and Chris Rogers, for their assistance with editing, proofing, and adjusting the text. Of course, all responsibility for the content is solely my own.

About the Author

Jon M. Garon is a professor of law and the immediate past dean of Nova Southeastern University Shepard Broad College of Law. He is a nationally recognized authority on technology law and intellectual property, particularly copyright law, entertainment and information privacy. A tenured member of the law faculty, Dean Garon teaches Information Privacy Law, Cyberspace Law, Copyright Law, Entertainment Law, and related courses. He is the author of more than 50 books, book chapters, and articles, and he has presented at more than 200 programs across the U.S. A Minnesota native, he received his bachelor's degree from the University of Minnesota in 1985 and his juris doctor degree from Columbia University School of Law in 1988.

Prior to joining Nova Southeastern University in 2014, Garon was the inaugural director of the Northern Kentucky University Salmon P. Chase College of Law, Law + Informatics Institute from 2011–2014. The Law + Informatics Institute serves to integrate the specialized programming on technology and information systems as they apply across legal disciplines. He also served as dean and professor of law at Hamline University School of Law in St. Paul, Minnesota and interim dean of the Graduate School of Management from 2005 to 2006. Before Hamline, Dean Garon taught Entertainment Law and Copyright at Franklin Pierce Law Center in Concord, New Hampshire and Western State University College of Law in Orange County, California.

Among his publications on intellectual property, Dean Garon has written the following books, book chapters and law review articles:

Books

Author, ENTERTAINMENT LAW & PRACTICE (Third Edition 2020) (with Teacher's Manual), (Second Edition, Carolina Academic Press, June 2014) (First Edition 2005).

Author, ENTERTAINMENT LAW & PRACTICE SUPPLEMENTS (Carolina Academic Press, 2012, 2010, and 2007).

Author, BURN RATE (Manegiare Publications, 2019) (novel focused on cybersecurity and cyberwar risks).

Author, THE ENTREPRENEUR'S INTELLECTUAL PROPERTY & BUSINESS HANDBOOK (Manegiare Publications, August 2018) (First edition: OWN IT—THE LAW & BUSINESS GUIDE TO LAUNCHING A NEW BUSINESS THROUGH INNOVATION, EXCLUSIVITY AND RELEVANCE (Carolina Academic Press, September 2007)).

Author, POP CULTURE BUSINESS HANDBOOK FOR CONS AND FESTIVALS (Manegiare Publications, 2017).

Author, The Independent Filmmaker's Law & Business Guide—Financing, Shooting, and Distributing Independent and Digital Films (Second Edition, A Cappella Books/Chicago Review Press, June 2009) (First Edition 2002).

Author, Own It—The Law & Business Guide to Launching a New Business through Innovation, Exclusivity and Relevance (Carolina Academic Press, September 2007).

Book Chapters

Author, *Chapter 6: White v. Samsung Elecs. Am., Inc., 971 F.2d 1395 (9th Cir. 1992)*, Feminist Judgments: Rewritten Property Opinions (Eloisa C. Rodriguez-Dod and Elena Maria Marty-Nelson, eds., Cambridge University Press 2020 (forthcoming)).

Author, *How AI Affects Traditional Laws and Regulations*, The Law of Artificial Intelligence and Smart Machines (Ted Claypoole, ed., American Bar Association 2019).

Author, *Reordering the chaos of the virtual arena: harmonizing law and framing collective bargaining for avatar actors and digital athletes*, The Law of Virtual and Augmented Reality (Edward Elgar Publishing 2018).

Author, *Forecasting the Role of Social Media Law for Sports in a Global Context*, in Handbook of American Sports Law (Michael McCann ed., Oxford University Press 2017).

Author, *Copyright at the Crossroads of Commerce, Culture and Creativity*, in Estudos Avançados em Direito de Autor (*Copyright Advanced Studies*) (Leonardo Machado Pontes, ed., Elsevier 2014).

Author, *The Band—Artistic, legal and financial structures which shape modern music*, in Music and Law (Mathieu Deflem ed., Emerald Group Publishing 2013).

Author, *Legal Issues for Database Protection in the US and Abroad*, in Bioinformatics Law: Legal Issues for Computational Biology in the Post-Genome Era (Jorge Contreras ed., American Bar Association 2013).

Author, *Copyright, Trademark, Trade Secret and Publicity Rights Concerns*, in Emerging Legal Issues in RFID and Other Contactless Data Exchange Systems: What Lawyers Should Know (Sarah Jane Hughes ed., American Bar Association 2012).

Author, *Localism as a Production Imperative: An Alternative Framework for Promoting, Intangible Cultural Heritage*, in Transnational Culture in the Internet Age (Sean A. Pager & Adam Candeub eds., Elgar Publishing 2012).

Author, *Google, Fairness and the Battle of the Books*, in The 2010 IP Book (Midwest Intellectual Property Institute 2010).

Contributor, Annual Review of Intellectual Property Law Developments 2006–2008 (George Jordan ed., ABA Section of Intellectual Property Law 2009).

Author, Theater Law: Cases and Materials (Robert Jarvis, *et al.*, Carolina Academic Press, July 2004) (with Teacher's Manual).

Law Review Articles

Article, *The Empires Strike Back: Reassertion of Territorial Regulation in Cyberspace*, 3 J.L. & TECH. AT TEXAS 1 (2019).

Article, *Cyber-World War III: Origins*, 7 J.L. & CYBER WARFARE 1 (2018).

Article, *Ownership of University Intellectual Property*, 36 CARDOZO ARTS & ENT. L.J. 635 (2018).

Article, *The Once and Future Profession: Autonomy, Intellectualism, and Obligation*, 48 TOLEDO L. REV. 253 (2017).

Article, *Seeking to Promote Security over Privacy and Achieving Neither*, 19 SMU SCI. & TECH. L. REV. 351 (2016).

Article, *Hidden Hands that Shaped the Marketplace of Ideas: Television's early transformation from Medium to Genre*, 18 U. DENVER SPORTS & ENT. L.J. 29 (2016).

Article, *The Lawyer's Role in Promoting the Use of Fair Use*, 6 J. INT'L MEDIA & ENT. L. 101 (2016) (Biederman Institute at Southwestern Law School in association with the ABA Forum on Communication Law and Forum on the Entertainment and Sports Industries).

Journal Introduction, *Finding Purpose in a Journal of Sports and Entertainment Law*, 1 J. ENT. & SPORTS L. 1 (2015) (Karnataka State Law University).

Article, *To Promote the Progress: Incentives, Exclusives, and Values to Build a more Perfect Creative Culture*, 40 OHIO N. L. REV. 467 (2014).

Article, *Commercializing the Digital Canvas: Renewing Rights of Attribution for Artists in the Networked Economy*, 1 TEX. A&M LAW. REV. 837 (2014).

Article, *Tidying up the Internet: Take Down of Unauthorized Content under Copyright, Trademark and Defamation Law*, 41 CAPITAL U. L. REV. 513 (2013).

Article, *Digital Hollywood2.0: Reimagining Film, Music, Television and Publishing Distribution as a Global Artist Collaborative*, 21 MICH. ST. INT'L L. REV. 563 (2013) *reprinted* Entertainment, Publishing and the Arts Handbook (West 2014); reprinted 1 J. ENT. & SPORTS L. 32 (2015) (Karnataka State Law University).

Article, *Legal Education in Disruption: The Headwinds and Tailwinds of Technology*, 45 CONN. L. REV. 1165 (2013).

Article, *Beyond the First Amendment: Shaping the Contours of Commercial Speech in Video Games, Virtual Worlds and Social Media*, 2012 UTAH L. REV. 607 (2012), *reprinted* ENTERTAINMENT, PUBLISHING AND THE ARTS HANDBOOK (West 2013).

Article, *Mortgaging the Meme: Financing and Managing Disruptive Innovation*, 10 NW. J. TECH. & INTEL. PROP. 441 (2012).

Article, *The Heart of the Deal: Intellectual Property Aspects in the Law & Business of Entertainment*, 17 J. INT. PROP. L. 443 (2012).

Article, *Revolutions and Expatriates: Social Networking, Ubiquitous Media and the Disintermediation of the State*, 11 J. INT. BUS. L. 293 (2012).

Article, *Technology Requires Reboot of Professionalism and Ethics for Practitioners*, 16 J. INTERNET L. 3 (2012).

Article (Co-authored with Elaine Ziff), *The Work for Hire Doctrine Revisited: Startup and Technology Employees and the Use of Contracts in a Hiring Relationship*, 12 Minn. J.L. Sci. & Tech. 489 (2011) (republished 2012 Intellectual Property Law Review (Thomson Reuters)).

Article, *Content, Control and the Socially Networked Film*, 48 U. Louisville L. Rev. 771 (2010), *reprinted* Entertainment, Publishing and the Arts Handbook (West 2011).

Article, *Searching Inside Google: Cases, Controversies and the Future of the World's Most Provocative Company*, 30 Loyola L.A. Ent. L. Rev. 429 (2010).

Article, *The Implications of Informatics on Data Policy*, 1 Media L. Rev. 16 (2010) (NALSAR University of Law, Hyderabad, India).

Article, *Wiki Authorship, Social Media and the Curatorial Audience*, 1 Harv. J. Sports & Ent. L. 95 (2010).

Article, *Reintermediation*, 2 Int. J. of Private Law 227 (2009) (republished in Synergies and Conflicts in Cyberlaw (2008) (Sylvia Kierkegaard, Ed.).

Article, *Playing in the Virtual Arena: Avatars, Publicity and Identity Reconceptualized through Virtual Worlds and Computer Games*, 11 Chapman L. Rev. 465 (2008).

Article, *What if DRM Fails?: Seeking Patronage in the iWasteland and the Virtual O*, 2008 Mich. State L. Rev. 103 (2008).

Article, *To Make a Difference: Dean as Producer*, 39 U. Tol. L. Rev. 297 (2008).

Article, *Take Back the Night: Why an Association of Regional Law Schools will Return Core Values to Legal Education and Provide an Alternative to Tiered Rankings*, 38 U. Tol. L. Rev. 517 (2007).

Article, *Acquiring and Managing Identity Interests*, 1 Fla. Ent. L. Rev. 39 (2006).

Article, *Normative Copyright: A Conceptual Framework for Copyright Philosophy & Ethics*, 88 Cornell L. Rev. 101 (2003).

Article, *Entertainment Law*, 76 Tulane L. Rev. 559 (2002).

Article, *The Electronic Jungle: The Application of Intellectual Property Law to Distance Education*, 4 Vand. J. Ent. L. & Prac. 146 (2002).

Article, *Media and Monopoly in the Information Age: Slowing the Convergence at the Marketplace of Ideas*, 17 Cardozo Arts & Ent. L.J. 491 (1999).

Article, *Star Wars: Film Permitting, Prior Restraint and Government's Role in the Entertainment Industry*, 17 Loyola Entertainment L.J. 1 (1996). Reprinted, Robert Thorne & John David Viera, Ed., Entertainment, Publishing & the Arts Handbook, 1997–1998 Edition (West Group 1997).

Article, *Charity Begins at Home: Alternatives in Nonprofit Regulation*, 2 W. St. U. Consumer L.J. 1 (1993).

Note, *The Director's Choice: The Fine Line Between Interpretation and Infringement of an Author's Work*, 12 Colum.-VLA J.L. & Arts 277 (1988).

Part I

Legal Issues in the Entertainment Industries

Chapter 1

The Nature of Entertainment Law

A. Overview

Entertainment law covers the legal disciplines of copyright, publicity, privacy, trademark law, antitrust, contracts, First Amendment, and labor law. The creative content industries have trade, custom, usage, and other unique attributes that make the practice of entertainment law unique, even for those who practice within a single doctrinal discipline within a particular industry.

The entertainment industries are changing more rapidly today than ever before. Video games, including the casual games for cell phones and the massive online gaming experiences, have emerged as a dominant entertainment industry generating as much as the other entertainment media combined. The expansion of over-the-top media are bypassing broadcast television, cable, and satellite communications. Streaming services have significantly reduced the expectation that consumers purchase music as LPs, CDs or digital downloads. Publishing has been reimagined as an online experience, and though print remains an important part of economy, chain bookstores have been nearly eliminated. Moreover, despite the rapidity of these changes in the past two decades, the speed of change continues to increase.

1. First Amendment History

The cases below are designed to introduce the sweep of Supreme Court jurisprudence with regard to Entertainment Law. In 1911, in *Kalem Company v. Harper Brothers*, the Court first recognized the potential for a silent film to infringe the copyright in a written book, carrying forward a line of cases in which each new entertainment medium had been incorporated into the sweep of legal protection. In *Joseph Burstyn, Inc. v. Wilson*, the Court acknowledged for the first time that motion picture licensing has First Amendment implications. Then, in *Zacchini v. Scripps-Howard Broadcasting Co.*, the Court addressed the right of an entertainer to have a publicity interest in his performance. As recently as 2011, the Court was again required to assert that entertainment media should receive the same protections as other speech. In *Brown v. Entertainment Merchants Association*, the Court forcefully reminded the litigants that video games are entitled to the same level of First Amendment protection as provided to print and broadcast. In each case, the Court articulates its own history of struggling with the role of entertainment against the concepts of copyright, free speech, and privacy law—the areas most systemically changed by the influences of the entertainment industry.

Kalem Company v. Harper Brothers
222 U.S. 55 (1911)

Mr. Justice Holmes delivered the opinion of the court.

This is an appeal from a decree restraining an alleged infringement of the copyright upon the late General Lew Wallace's book 'Ben Hur.' The case was heard on the pleadings and an agreed statement of facts, and the only issue is whether those facts constitute an infringement of the copyright upon the book....

[T]he question that has the most general importance is whether the public exhibition of these moving pictures infringed any rights under the copyright law. As amended by the act of March 3, 1891, authors have the exclusive right to dramatize any of their works. So, if the exhibition was or was founded on a dramatizing of Ben Hur this copyright was infringed. We are of opinion that Ben Hur was dramatized by what was done. Whether we consider the purpose of this clause of the statute, or the etymological history and present usages of language, drama may be achieved by action as well as by speech. Action can tell a story, display all the most vivid relations between men, and depict every kind of human emotion, without the aid of a word. It would be impossible to deny the title of drama to pantomime as played by masters of the art. But if a pantomime of Ben Hur would be a dramatizing of Ben Hur, it would be none the less so that it was exhibited to the audience by reflection from a glass and not by direct vision of the figures—as sometimes has been done in order to produce ghostly or inexplicable effects. The essence of the matter in the case last supposed is not the mechanism employed but that we see the event or story lived. The moving pictures are only less vivid than reflections from a mirror. With the former as with the latter our visual impression—what we see—is caused by the real pantomime of real men through the medium of natural forces, although the machinery is different and more complex. How it would be if the illusion of motion were produced from paintings instead of from photographs of the real thing may be left open until the question shall arise.

It is said that pictures of scenes in a novel may be made and exhibited without infringing the copyright and that they may be copyrighted themselves. Indeed it was conceded by the Circuit Court of Appeals that these films could be copyrighted and, we may assume, could be exhibited as photographs. Whether this concession is correct or not, in view of the fact that they are photographs of an unlawful dramatization of the novel, we need not decide. We will assume that it is. But it does not follow that the use of them in motion does not infringe the author's rights. The most innocent objects, such as the mirror in the other case that we have supposed, may be used for unlawful purposes. And if, as we have tried to show, moving pictures may be used for dramatizing a novel, when the photographs are used in that way they are used to infringe a right which the statute reserves.

But again it is said that the defendant did not produce the representations, but merely sold the films to jobbers, and on that ground ought not to be held. In some cases where an ordinary article of commerce is sold nice questions may arise as to the point at which the seller becomes an accomplice in a subsequent illegal use by the buyer. It has been held that mere indifferent supposition or knowledge on the part of the seller that the buyer of spirituous liquor is contemplating such unlawful use is not enough to connect him with the possible unlawful consequences, was made with a view to the illegal resale the price could not be recovered. But no such niceties are involved here. The defendant not only expected but invoked by advertisement the use of its films for dramatic reproduction of the story. That was the most conspicuous purpose for which they could be used, and the one for which especially they were made. If the defendant did not contribute to the infringement, it is impossible to do so except by taking part in the final act. It is liable on principles recognized in every part of the law.

It is argued that the law construed as we have construed it goes beyond the power conferred upon Congress by the Constitution, to secure to authors for a limited time the exclusive right to their writings. Art. I, §8, cl. 8. It is suggested that to extend the copyright to a case like this is to extend it to the ideas as distinguished from the words in which those ideas are clothed. But there is no attempt to make a monopoly of the ideas expressed. The law confines itself to a particular, cognate and well known form of reproduction. If to that extent a grant of monopoly is thought a proper way to secure the right to the writings this court cannot say that Congress was wrong. Decree affirmed.

Joseph Burstyn, Inc. v. Wilson
343 U.S. 495 (1952)

Mr. Justice Clark delivered the opinion of the Court.

The issue here is the constitutionality, under the First and Fourteenth Amendments, of a New York statute which permits the banning of motion picture films on the ground that they are "sacrilegious." That statute makes it unlawful "to exhibit, or to sell, lease or lend for exhibition at any place of amusement for pay or in connection with any business in the state of New York, any motion picture film or reel [with specified exceptions not relevant here], unless there is at the time in full force and effect a valid license or permit therefore of the education department...." The statute further provides:

> The director of the [motion picture] division [of the education department] or, when authorized by the regents, the officers of a local office or bureau shall cause to be promptly examined every motion picture film submitted to them as herein required, and unless such film or a part thereof is obscene, indecent, immoral, inhuman, sacrilegious, or is of such a character that its exhibition would tend to corrupt morals or incite to crime, shall issue a license therefore. If such director or, when so authorized, such officer shall

not license any film submitted, he shall furnish to the applicant therefore a written report of the reasons for his refusal and a description of each rejected part of a film not rejected in toto.

Appellant is a corporation engaged in the business of distributing motion pictures. It owns the exclusive rights to distribute throughout the United States a film produced in Italy entitled "The Miracle." On November 30, 1950, after having examined the picture, the motion picture division of the New York education department, acting under the statute quoted above, issued to appellant a license authorizing exhibition of "The Miracle," with English subtitles, as one part of a trilogy called "Ways of Love." Thereafter, for a period of approximately eight weeks, "Ways of Love" was exhibited publicly in a motion picture theater in New York City under an agreement between appellant and the owner of the theater whereby appellant received a stated percentage of the admission price.

During this period, the New York State Board of Regents, which by statute is made the head of the education department, received "hundreds of letters, telegrams, post cards, affidavits and other communications" both protesting against and defending the public exhibition of "The Miracle." The Chancellor of the Board of Regents requested three members of the Board to view the picture and to make a report to the entire Board. After viewing the film, this committee reported to the Board that in its opinion there was basis for the claim that the picture was "sacrilegious." Thereafter, on January 19, 1951, the Regents directed appellant to show cause, at a hearing to be held on January 30, why its license to show "The Miracle" should not be rescinded on that ground. Appellant appeared at this hearing, which was conducted by the same three-member committee of the Regents which had previously viewed the picture, and challenged the jurisdiction of the committee and of the Regents to proceed with the case. With the consent of the committee, various interested persons and organizations submitted to it briefs and exhibits bearing upon the merits of the picture and upon the constitutional and statutory questions involved. On February 16, 1951, the Regents, after viewing "The Miracle," determined that it was "sacrilegious" and for that reason ordered the Commissioner of Education to rescind appellant's license to exhibit the picture. The Commissioner did so.

Appellant brought the present action in the New York courts to review the determination of the Regents. Among the claims advanced by appellant were (1) that the statute violates the Fourteenth Amendment as a prior restraint upon freedom of speech and of the press; (2) that it is invalid under the same Amendment as a violation of the guaranty of separate church and state and as a prohibition of the free exercise of religion; and, (3) that the term "sacrilegious" is so vague and indefinite as to offend due process. The Appellate Division rejected all of appellant's contentions and upheld the Regents' determination. On appeal the New York Court of Appeals, two judges dissenting, affirmed the order of the Appellate Division.

As we view the case, we need consider only appellant's contention that the New York statute is an unconstitutional abridgment of free speech and a free press. In

Mutual Film Corp. v. Industrial Comm'n, 236 U.S. 230 (1915), a distributor of motion pictures sought to enjoin the enforcement of an Ohio statute which required the prior approval of a board of censors before any motion picture could be publicly exhibited in the state, and which directed the board to approve only such films as it adjudged to be "of a moral, educational or amusing and harmless character." The statute was assailed in part as an unconstitutional abridgment of the freedom of the press guaranteed by the First and Fourteenth Amendments. The District Court rejected this contention, stating that the first eight Amendments were not a restriction on state action. On appeal to this Court, plaintiff in its brief abandoned this claim and contended merely that the statute in question violated the freedom of speech and publication guaranteed by the Constitution of Ohio. In affirming the decree of the District Court denying injunctive relief, this Court stated:

> It cannot be put out of view that the exhibition of moving pictures is a business pure and simple, originated and conducted for profit, like other spectacles, not to be regarded, nor intended to be regarded by the Ohio constitution, we think, as part of the press of the country or as organs of public opinion....

It cannot be doubted that motion pictures are a significant medium for the communication of ideas. They may affect public attitudes and behavior in a variety of ways, ranging from direct espousal of a political or social doctrine to the subtle shaping of thought which characterizes all artistic expression. The importance of motion pictures as an organ of public opinion is not lessened by the fact that they are designed to entertain as well as to inform. As was said in *Winters v. New York*, 333 U.S. 507, 510 (1948):

> The line between the informing and the entertaining is too elusive for the protection of that basic right [a free press]. Everyone is familiar with instances of propaganda through fiction. What is one man's amusement, teaches another's doctrine.

It is urged that motion pictures do not fall within the First Amendment's aegis because their production, distribution, and exhibition is a large-scale business conducted for private profit. We cannot agree. That books, newspapers, and magazines are published and sold for profit does not prevent them from being a form of expression whose liberty is safeguarded by the First Amendment. We fail to see why operation for profit should have any different effect in the case of motion pictures.

It is further urged that motion pictures possess a greater capacity for evil, particularly among the youth of a community, than other modes of expression. Even if one were to accept this hypothesis, it does not follow that motion pictures should be disqualified from First Amendment protection. If there be capacity for evil it may be relevant in determining the permissible scope of community control, but it does not authorize substantially unbridled censorship such as we have here. For the foregoing reasons, we conclude that expression by means of motion pictures is included within the free speech and free press guaranty of the First and Fourteenth Amendments. To the extent that language in the opinion in *Mutual Film Corp. v. Industrial Comm'n, supra,* is out of harmony with the views here set forth, we no longer adhere to it. To hold that liberty of expression by means of motion pictures is guaranteed by the First and Fourteenth Amendments, however, is not the end of our problem. It does not follow that the Constitution requires absolute freedom to exhibit every motion picture of every kind at all times and all places. That much is evident from the series of decisions of this Court with respect to other media of communication of ideas. Nor does it follow that motion pictures are necessarily subject to the precise rules governing any other particular method of expression. Each method tends to present its own peculiar problems. But the basic principles of freedom of speech and the press, like the First Amendment's command, do not vary. Those principles, as they have frequently been enunciated by this Court, make freedom of expression the rule. There is no justification in this case for making an exception to that rule.

The statute involved here does not seek to punish, as a past offense, speech or writing falling within the permissible scope of subsequent punishment. On the contrary, New York requires that permission to communicate ideas be obtained in advance from state officials who judge the content of the words and pictures sought to be communicated. This Court recognized many years ago that such a previous restraint is a form of infringement upon freedom of expression to be especially condemned. *Near v. Minnesota ex rel. Olson*, 283 U.S. 697 (1931). The Court there recounted the history which indicates that a major purpose of the First Amendment guaranty of a free press was to prevent prior restraints upon publication, although it was carefully pointed out that the liberty of the press is not limited to that protection. It was further stated that "the protection even as to previous restraint is not absolutely unlimited. But the limitation has been recognized only in exceptional cases." In the light of the First Amendment's history and of the *Near* decision, the State has a heavy burden to demonstrate that the limitation challenged here presents such an exceptional case.

New York's highest court says there is "nothing mysterious" about the statutory provision applied in this case: "It is simply this: that no religion, as that word is understood by the ordinary, reasonable person, shall be treated with contempt, mockery, scorn and ridicule...." This is far from the kind of narrow exception to freedom of expression which a state may carve out to satisfy the adverse demands of other interests of society.... Since the term "sacrilegious" is the sole standard under attack here, it is not necessary for us to decide, for example, whether a state may censor motion pictures under a clearly drawn statute designed and applied to prevent the showing of obscene films. That is a very different question from the one now before us. We hold only that under the First and Fourteenth Amendments a state may not ban a film on the basis of a censor's conclusion that it is "sacrilegious."

Reversed.

Zacchini v. Scripps-Howard Broadcasting Co.

433 U.S. 562 (1977)

MR. JUSTICE WHITE delivered the opinion of the Court.

Petitioner, Hugo Zacchini, is an entertainer. He performs a "human cannonball" act in which he is shot from a cannon into a net some 200 feet away. Each performance occupies some 15 seconds. In August and September 1972, petitioner was engaged to perform his act on a regular basis at the Geauga County Fair in Burton, Ohio. He performed in a fenced area, surrounded by grandstands, at the fair grounds. Members of the public attending the fair were not charged a separate admission fee to observe his act.

On August 30, a free-lance reporter for Scripps-Howard Broadcasting Co., the operator of a television broadcasting station and respondent in this case, attended the fair. He carried a small movie camera. Petitioner noticed the reporter and asked him not to film the performance. The reporter did not do so on that day; but on the instructions of the producer of respondent's daily newscast, he returned the following day and videotaped the entire act. This film clip, approximately 15 seconds in length, was shown on the 11 o'clock news program that night, together with favorable commentary.

Petitioner then brought this action for damages, alleging that he is "engaged in the entertainment business," that the act he performs is one "invented by his father and … performed only by his family for the last fifty years," that respondent "showed and commercialized the film of his act without his consent," and that such conduct was an "unlawful appropriation of plaintiff's professional property." Respondent answered and moved for summary judgment, which was granted by the trial court.

The Court of Appeals of Ohio reversed. The majority held that petitioner's complaint stated a cause of action for conversion and for infringement of a common-law copyright, and one judge concurred in the judgment on the ground that the complaint stated a cause of action for appropriation of petitioner's "right of publicity" in the film of his act. All three judges agreed that the First Amendment did not privilege the press to show the entire performance on a news program without compensating petitioner for any financial injury he could prove at trial.

Like the concurring judge in the Court of Appeals, the Supreme Court of Ohio rested petitioner's cause of action under state law on his "right to publicity value of his performance." The opinion syllabus, to which we are to look for the rule of law used to decide the case, declared first that one may not use for his own benefit the name or likeness of another, whether or not the use or benefit is a commercial one, and second that respondent would be liable for the appropriation, over petitioner's objection and in the absence of license or privilege, of petitioner's right to the publicity value of his performance. The court nevertheless gave judgment for respondent because, in the words of the syllabus:

A TV station has a privilege to report in its newscasts matters of legitimate public interest which would otherwise be protected by an individual's right of publicity, unless the actual intent of the TV station was to appropriate the benefit of the publicity for some non-privileged private use, or unless the actual intent was to injure the individual.

We granted certiorari to consider an issue unresolved by this Court: whether the First and Fourteenth Amendments immunized respondent from damages for its alleged infringement of petitioner's state-law "right of publicity." Insofar as the Ohio Supreme Court held that the First and Fourteenth Amendments of the United States Constitution required judgment for respondent, we reverse the judgment of that court.

If the judgment below rested on an independent and adequate state ground, the writ of certiorari should be dismissed as improvidently granted, for "[o]ur only power over state judgments is to correct them to the extent that they incorrectly adjudge federal rights...." We are confident, however, that the judgment below did not rest on an adequate and independent state ground and that we have jurisdiction to decide the federal issue presented in this case.

There is no doubt that petitioner's complaint was grounded in state law and that the right of publicity which petitioner was held to possess was a right arising under Ohio law. It is also clear that respondent's claim of constitutional privilege was sustained. The source of this privilege was not identified in the syllabus. It is clear enough from the opinion of the Ohio Supreme Court, which we are permitted to consult for understanding of the syllabus, that in adjudicating the crucial question of whether respondent had a privilege to film and televise petitioner's performance, the court placed principal reliance on *Time, Inc. v. Hill*, 385 U.S. 374 (1967), a case involving First Amendment limitations on state tort actions. It construed the principle of that case, along with that of *New York Times Co. v. Sullivan*, 376 U.S. 254 (1964), to be that "the press has a privilege to report matters of legitimate public interest even though such reports might intrude on matters otherwise private," and concluded, therefore, that the press is also "privileged when an individual seeks to publicly exploit his talents while keeping the benefits private." The privilege thus exists in cases "where appropriation of a right of publicity is claimed." The court's opinion also referred to Draft 21 of the relevant portion of Restatement (Second) of Torts (1975), which was understood to make room for reasonable press appropriations by limiting the reach of the right of privacy rather than by creating a privileged invasion. The court preferred the notion of privilege over the Restatement's formulation, however, reasoning that "since the gravamen of the issue in this case is not whether the degree of intrusion is reasonable, but whether First Amendment principles require that the right of privacy give way to the public right to be informed of matters of public interest and concern, the concept of privilege seems the more useful and appropriate one." ...

The Ohio Supreme Court held that respondent is constitutionally privileged to include in its newscasts matters of public interest that would otherwise be protected by the right of publicity, absent an intent to injure or to appropriate for some non-privileged purpose. If under this standard respondent had merely reported that petitioner was performing at the fair and described or commented on his act, with or without showing his picture on television, we would have a very different case. But petitioner is not contending that his appearance at the fair and his performance could not be reported by the press as newsworthy items. His complaint is that respondent filmed his entire act and displayed that film on television for the public to see and enjoy. This, he claimed, was an appropriation of his professional property. The Ohio Supreme Court agreed that petitioner had "a right of publicity" that gave him "personal control over commercial display and exploitation of his personality and the exercise of his talents." This right of "exclusive control over the publicity given to his perform-ances" was said to be such a "valuable part of the benefit which may be attained by his talents and efforts" that it was entitled to legal protection. It was also observed, or at least expressly assumed, that petitioner had not abandoned his rights by per-forming under the circumstances present at the Geauga County Fair Grounds.

The Ohio Supreme Court nevertheless held that the challenged invasion was priv-ileged, saying that the press "must be accorded broad latitude in its choice of how much it presents of each story or incident, and of the emphasis to be given to such presentation. No fixed standard which would bar the press from reporting or depicting either an entire occurrence or an entire discrete part of a public performance can be formulated which would not unduly restrict the 'breathing room' in reporting which freedom of the press requires." Under this view, respondent was thus constitutionally free to film and display petitioner's entire act.

The Ohio Supreme Court relied heavily on *Time, Inc. v. Hill*, 385 U.S. 374 (1967), but that case does not mandate a media privilege to televise a performer's entire act without his consent....

The differences between these two torts are important. First, the State's interests in providing a cause of action in each instance are different. "The interest protected" in permitting recovery for placing the plaintiff in a false light "is clearly that of rep-utation, with the same overtones of mental distress as in defamation." By contrast, the State's interest in permitting a "right of publicity" is in protecting the proprietary interest of the individual in his act in part to encourage such entertainment. As we later note, the State's interest is closely analogous to the goals of patent and copyright law, focusing on the right of the individual to reap the reward of his endeavors and having little to do with protecting feelings or reputation. Second, the two torts differ in the degree to which they intrude on dissemination of information to the public. In "false light" cases the only way to protect the interests involved is to attempt to minimize publication of the damaging matter, while in "right of publicity" cases the only question is who gets to do the publishing. An entertainer such as petitioner usu-ally has no objection to the widespread publication of his act as long as he gets the commercial benefit of such publication. Indeed, in the present case petitioner did not seek to enjoin the broadcast of his act; he simply sought compensation for the broadcast in the form of damages....

It is evident, and there is no claim here to the contrary, that petitioner's state-law right of publicity would not serve to prevent respondent from reporting the newsworthy facts about petitioner's act. Wherever the line in particular situations is to be drawn between media reports that are protected and those that are not, we are quite sure that the First and Fourteenth Amendments do not immunize the media when they broadcast a performer's entire act without his consent. The Constitution no more prevents a State from requiring respondent to compensate petitioner for broadcasting his act on television than it would privilege respondent to film and broadcast a copyrighted dramatic work without liability to the copyright owner, where the promoters or the participants had other plans for publicizing the event. There are ample reasons for reaching this conclusion.

The broadcast of a film of petitioner's entire act poses a substantial threat to the economic value of that performance. As the Ohio court recognized, this act is the product of petitioner's own talents and energy, the end result of much time, effort, and expense. Much of its economic value lies in the "right of exclusive control over the publicity given to his performance"; if the public can see the act free on television, it will be less willing to pay to see it at the fair. The effect of a public broadcast of the performance is similar to preventing petitioner from charging an admission fee. "The rationale for [protecting the right of publicity] is the straight-forward one of preventing unjust enrichment by the theft of good will. No social purpose is served by having the defendant get free some aspect of the plaintiff that would have market value and for which he would normally pay." Moreover, the broadcast of petitioner's entire performance, unlike the unauthorized use of another's name for purposes of trade or the incidental use of a name or picture by the press, goes to the heart of petitioner's ability to earn a living as an entertainer. Thus, in this case, Ohio has recognized what may be the strongest case for a "right of publicity"—involving, not the appropriation of an entertainer's reputation to enhance the attractiveness of a commercial product, but the appropriation of the very activity by which the entertainer acquired his reputation in the first place.

Of course, Ohio's decision to protect petitioner's right of publicity here rests on more than a desire to compensate the performer for the time and effort invested in his act; the protection provides an economic incentive for him to make the investment required to produce a performance of interest to the public.... There is no doubt that entertainment, as well as news, enjoys First Amendment protection. It is also true that entertainment itself can be important news. But it is important to note that neither the public nor respondent will be deprived of the benefit of petitioner's performance as long as his commercial stake in his act is appropriately recognized. Petitioner does not seek to enjoin the broadcast of his performance; he simply wants to be paid for it.... We conclude that although the State of Ohio may as a matter of its own law privilege the press in the circumstances of this case, the First and Fourteenth Amendments do not require it to do so.

Reversed.

Brown v. Entertainment Merchants Ass'n
564 U.S. 786 (2011)

JUSTICE SCALIA delivered the opinion of the Court.

We consider whether a California law imposing restrictions on violent video games comports with the First Amendment. California Assembly Bill 1179 (2005), Cal. Civ.Code Ann. §§ 1746–1746.5 (West 2009) (Act), prohibits the sale or rental of "violent video games" to minors, and requires their packaging to be labeled "18." The Act covers games "in which the range of options available to a player includes killing, maiming, dismembering, or sexually assaulting an image of a human being, if those acts are depicted" in a manner that "[a] reasonable person, considering the game as a whole, would find appeals to a deviant or morbid interest of minors," that is "patently offensive to prevailing standards in the community as to what is suitable for minors," and that "causes the game, as a whole, to lack serious literary, artistic, political, or scientific value for minors." Violation of the Act is punishable by a civil fine of up to $1,000.

California correctly acknowledges that video games qualify for First Amendment protection. The Free Speech Clause exists principally to protect discourse on public matters, but we have long recognized that it is difficult to distinguish politics from entertainment, and dangerous to try. "Everyone is familiar with instances of propaganda through fiction. What is one man's amusement, teaches another's doctrine." *Winters v. New York*, 333 U.S. 507, 510 (1948). Like the protected books, plays, and movies that preceded them, video games communicate ideas — and even social messages — through many familiar literary devices (such as characters, dialogue, plot, and music) and through features distinctive to the medium (such as the player's interaction with the virtual world). That suffices to confer First Amendment protection. Under our Constitution, "esthetic and moral judgments about art and literature ... are for the individual to make, not for the Government to decree, even with the mandate or approval of a majority." *United States v. Playboy Entertainment Group, Inc.,* 529 U.S. 803, 818 (2000). And whatever the challenges of applying the Constitution to ever-advancing technology, "the basic principles of freedom of speech and the press, like the First Amendment's command, do not vary" when a new and different medium for communication appears. *Joseph Burstyn, Inc. v. Wilson,* 343 U.S. 495, 503 (1952).

Last Term, in *United States v. Stevens,* 559 U.S. ___, 130 S. Ct. 1577, 1584 (2010) we held that new categories of unprotected speech may not be added to the list by a legislature that concludes certain speech is too harmful to be tolerated. *Stevens* concerned a federal statute purporting to criminalize the creation, sale, or possession of certain depictions of animal cruelty. . . . California has tried to make violent-speech regulation look like obscenity regulation by appending a saving clause required for the latter. That does not suffice. Our cases have been clear that the obscenity exception to the First Amendment does not cover whatever a legislature finds shocking, but only depictions of "sexual conduct." . . .

[California] wishes to create a wholly new category of content-based regulation that is permissible only for speech directed at children. That is unprecedented and mistaken. "[M]inors are entitled to a significant measure of First Amendment protection, and only in relatively narrow and well-defined circumstances may government bar public dissemination of protected materials to them." *Erznoznik v. Jacksonville*, 422 U.S. 205, 212–213 (1975).... Certainly the *books* we give children to read—or read to them when they are younger—contain no shortage of gore. Grimm's Fairy Tales, for example, are grim indeed. As her just deserts for trying to poison Snow White, the wicked queen is made to dance in red hot slippers "till she fell dead on the floor, a sad example of envy and jealousy." Cinderella's evil stepsisters have their eyes pecked out by doves. And Hansel and Gretel (children!) kill their captor by baking her in an oven.... As for the argument that video games enable participation in the violent action, that seems to us more a matter of degree than of kind.

Because the Act imposes a restriction on the content of protected speech, it is invalid unless California can demonstrate that it passes strict scrutiny—that is, unless it is justified by a compelling government interest and is narrowly drawn to serve that interest. California cannot meet that standard.... As a means of protecting children from portrayals of violence, the legislation is seriously underinclusive, not only because it excludes portrayals other than video games, but also because it permits a parental or avuncular veto. And as a means of assisting concerned parents it is seriously overinclusive because it abridges the First Amendment rights of young people whose parents (and aunts and uncles) think violent video games are a harmless pastime. And the overbreadth in achieving one goal is not cured by the underbreadth in achieving the other. Legislation such as this, which is neither fish nor fowl, cannot survive strict scrutiny.

We affirm the judgment below.

Notes and Questions

a. The history of protection for entertainment media has been one of slow but realistic responses to technology and popular culture. Congress added musical compositions to copyright law in 1831. It added photographs in 1865, public performances of plays in 1868, and fine art (including painting, drawing, chromo, and statuary) in 1872. Fine art was ultimately determined to be a form of work rather than an aesthetic standard when the Supreme Court reversed lower court holdings and allowed copyright protection for a circus poster in *Bleistein v. Donaldson Lithographing Co.*, 188 U.S. 239 (1903).

In 1897, Congress added public performances of musical works to those defined as protected performances. This amendment captured the popularity of player pianos and introduction of the phonograph. Player piano rolls, however, received no copyright protection because they had no written notation. Congress extended the protection to the musical composer's work embodied in the phonorecord or piano roll in 1909, when it fundamentally revised the Copyright Act. Sound recordings, the phonorecord equivalents of the piano rolls, were not themselves federally protected by copyright until 1972. Limited protection for the digital performance of a sound recording was added in 1995.

b. Initially not protected by the First Amendment, film and theatrical licensing remained common throughout most of the twentieth century and residual issues remain today. This is true for anti-obscenity licensing schemes, use of public theatrical venues, and the intersection between First Amendment and intellectual property protections. This tension is explored for various media throughout the chapters of the book.

c. Since 1992, Congress has been a much more active participant in the regulation and balancing of the competing interests in the entertainment industries, enacting more legislation affecting copyright, media, consumer electronics, and international trade than in any prior period in history. At the state level, many regulatory provisions exist that specifically regulate various aspects of the entertainment industry. These include the New York Theatrical Syndication Financing Act, N.Y. Arts & Cult. Aff. Law 23.01 (McKinney 2006), which regulates the financing of Broadway productions; family law, such as Cal. Fam. Code § 6750 (Deering 2003), protecting child performers from the unscrupulous or wasteful actions of their parents or financial guardians; talent agency licensing statutes, Cal. Lab. Code §§ 1700–1700.47 (Deering 2003); or film permit ordinances, such as Newport Beach, Cal. Mun. Ordinance ch. 5.46, 10 (2009).

d. In *Matal v. Tam*, 582 U.S. ___, 137 S. Ct. 1744 (2017), the Court again extended First Amendment rights to restrict longstanding federal regulation of trademark registration. The Court struck down the statutory basis for denying trademarks that may "disparage ... or bring ... into contemp[t] or disrepute" any "persons, living or dead." 15 U.S.C. § 1052(a). Has a new exuberance for the First Amendment transformed the constitutional phrase that "Congress shall make no law ..."?

e. The First Amendment limitations sometimes take on interesting forms. To what extent can anti-counterfeiting laws prohibit the creation of movie-money to serve as real looking props for films? *See Regan v. Time, Inc.*, 468 U.S. 641 (1984).

f. Another of the rapidly changing areas for the entertainment industry is the convergence between commercial speech and marketing of products and services. Expansion of First Amendment protection for commercial speech has led to increasing conflict when names, photographs, or clips are used without the permission of the publicity rights owner, trademark owner, or copyright owner. As the California Supreme Court explained:

> Nor does the fact that expression takes a form of nonverbal, visual representation remove it from the ambit of First Amendment protection. In *Bery v. City of New York*, 97 F.3d 689 (2d Cir. 1996) the court overturned an ordinance requiring visual artists—painters, printers, photographers, sculptors, etc.—to obtain licenses to sell their work in public places, but exempted the vendors of books, newspapers or other written matter. As the court stated: "Both the [district] court and the City demonstrate an unduly restricted view

of the First Amendment and of visual art itself. Such myopic vision not only overlooks case law central to First Amendment jurisprudence but fundamentally misperceives the essence of visual communication and artistic expression. Visual art is as wide ranging in its depiction of ideas, concepts and emotions as any book, treatise, pamphlet or other writing, and is similarly entitled to full First Amendment protection.... One cannot look at Winslow Homer's paintings on the Civil War without seeing, in his depictions of the boredom and hardship of the individual soldier, expressions of anti-war sentiments, the idea that war is not heroic."

Comedy III Prods., Inc. v. Gary Saderup, Inc., 25 Cal. 4th 387, 398–99, 21 P.3d 797, 804 (Cal. 2001).

g. Does the state's interest in particular artistic formats have First Amendment implications? A New Orleans municipal ordinance regulating street artists in the French Quarter limited vendor licenses to those who "manually paint, sketch or draw on plain surfaces only...." Artist Marc Trebert retouches digital photographs with pastels, in violation of the ordinance. With some incredulity, the court explained the New Orleans position: "The City argues that Trebert's digital photographs are not entitled to First Amendment protection because they are not 'art.' ... The question is not whether plaintiff's work is art, but whether it is 'speech' within the protection of the First Amendment." Ignoring the "art" question, the court found the photographs to be speech and the ordinance to be inconsistent with the First Amendment. *Trebert v. City of New Orleans,* No. 04-1349, 2005 U.S. Dist. LEXIS 1560 (E.D. La. Feb. 1, 2005) (featured opinion in *infra* Chapter XVII).

Problem 1-A

Meet Bryce. Bryce is a talented, up-and-coming artist — a hyphenate actor, writer, singer, director, and producer — in other words, a fairly typical young talent. Throughout the course of the textbook, Bryce will engage in transactions involving the development of new ideas into film, music, television, theatre, and computer-game projects.

As a student using this casebook, you are placed in the role of a senior associate in the firm of Story, Marshall & Cardozo, a national law firm with offices in New York, London, Newport Beach, California, and your own home town.

Sitting down with Bryce for an initial meeting, explain to Bryce what types of legal issues with which your law firm can assist Bryce and how to go about developing a long-term strategy for professional success.

2. Sources of Regulation and Management

Although there are a myriad of municipal, state, and federal laws and regulations, the intellectual property regulations of copyright, trademark, and trade secret are among the most important. The collective bargaining for union workers regulated under the National Labor Relations Act provide another significant source of law and regulation. While not exhaustive, these statutes provide a useful federal framework for many of the topics which follow throughout the case book.

- Children's Online Privacy Protection Act of 1998, 15 U.S.C. §§ 6501–6506 (2001); Children's Online Privacy Protection Rule ("COPPA"), 16 C.F.R. § 312 (2001)
- Children's Internet Protection Act (CIPA), 20 U.S.C. § 9134 and 47 U.S.C. § 254(h)
- Communications Act of 1934, 47 U.S.C. § 151 et seq.
- Communications Decency Act of 1996, 47 U.S.C. § 230 (1996)
- Copyright Act of 1976, 17 U.S.C. § 101 et seq.
- Digital Millennium Copyright Act, 17 U.S.C. §§ 512, 1201–1205
- Federal Trade Commission Act, 15 U.S.C. § 45 et seq.
- Lanham Act (Trademark Act of 1946), 15 U.S.C. § 1051 et seq.
- Music Modernization Act, 17 U.S.C. §§ 114, 115
- National Labor Relations Act (Wagner Act), 29 U.S.C. §§ 151–169
- Securities Act of 1933 15 U.S.C. § 77a; Securities and Exchange Act of 1934, 15 U.S.C. § 78a et seq.
- Stop Enabling Sex Traffickers Act (SESTA) and Allow States and Victims to Fight Online Sex Trafficking Act (FOSTA), 18 U.S.C. § 2421A.

True regulation comes from many sources. For the entertainment industries, one of the most important sources of regulation is the agreed-upon rules established through collective bargaining. The collective bargaining agreements establish minimum wages, structure the provision of professional credits, and determine membership control in each trade and industry. More importantly, the collective bargaining agreements provide a framework for working conditions in each industry and supplement state and federal law on issues such as the intersection of copyright and rights of publicity. These are a few of the key unions and trade associations:

- **Actors' Equity Association** (AEA), founded in 1913, is the labor union representing actors and stage managers in the legitimate theatre in the United States.
- **Alliance of Motion Picture and Television Producers** (AMPTP) is the entertainment industry's official collective bargaining representative for producers, negotiating 58 industry-wide collective bargaining agreements on behalf of hundreds of motion picture and television producers.
- **American Federation of Musicians** (AFM) negotiates, administers, and enforces contract agreements for musicians touring with theatrical musicals, etc.
- **Broadway League** is the national trade association for the Broadway and live theatrical industry. The League members include theatre owners and operators, producers, presenters, and general managers in North American cities, as well as suppliers of goods and services to the commercial theatre industry.
- **Directors' Guild of America** (DGA) represents Film and Television Directors, Unit Production Managers, First Asst. Directors, Second Asst. Directors, Tech-

nical Coordinators and Tape Associate Directors, Stage Managers and Production Associates.

- **Dramatists Guild of America** (DG) is not a union, but it provides advocacy and standardized industry agreements for playwrights, composers and lyricists writing for the living stage.
- **International Alliance of Theatrical and Stage Employees** (IATSE) is the labor union representing technicians, artisans and craftspersons in the entertainment industry, including live theatre, film and television production, and trade shows.
- **Screen Actors Guild** (SAG) represents and coordinates the activities of the various persons engaged or employed as performers in the motion picture industry. Now merged with SAG, the **American Federation of Television and Radio Artists** (AFTRA) represented its members in four major areas: 1) news and broadcasting; 2) entertainment programming; 3) the recording business; and 4) commercials and non-broadcast, industrial and educational media.
- **Writers Guild of America (WGA)** is the labor union representing writers in the motion picture, broadcast, cable and new technologies industries.

B. Transactions in Ideas

1. Overview

Every new work begins with a single idea. The work of writers, directors, artists, musicians, producers, designers, and the many other professionals involved in the entertainment industry may be summarized simply as translating that idea into expression which can be enjoyed by audiences.

The subject matter clause of the Copyright Act of 1976 differentiates those works which have transformed from mere ideas into fully protected expressive works.

17 U.S.C. § 102. Subject matter of copyright: In general

(a) Copyright protection subsists, in accordance with this title, in original works of authorship fixed in any tangible medium of expression, now known or later developed, from which they can be perceived, reproduced, or otherwise communicated, either directly or with the aid of a machine or device. Works of authorship include the following categories:

(1) literary works;

(2) musical works, including any accompanying words;

(3) dramatic works, including any accompanying music;

(4) pantomimes and choreographic works;

(5) pictorial, graphic, and sculptural works;

(6) motion pictures and other audiovisual works;

(7) sound recordings; and

(8) architectural works.

(b) In no case does copyright protection for an original work of authorship extend to any idea, procedure, process, system, method of operation, concept, principle, or discovery, regardless of the form in which it is described, explained, illustrated, or embodied in such work.

In separating out the ideas from the copyrightable expression, copyright policy attempts to encourage multiple authors to explore themes and ideas. "Boy meets girl" plots, "war between the sexes" battles, "coming of age" stories, "spy thrillers," "buddy pictures," and other themes are the ideas that underlie each particular novel, lyric, play, or screenplay.

Nonetheless, while ideas may be too abstract to be protected by copyright, they still have particular economic value. The idea of a shark which terrorizes a local community gave rise to the valuable expression created by Peter Benchley in his novel *Jaws* and in Steven Spielberg's movie of the same name. Even the idea to translate an existing piece of expression from one medium to another may have value to a producer looking for the next hot project. Since copyright is unavailable to protect such interests, however, courts struggle to frame the legal rights available for the sale of such ideas.

2. Source of Ideas

Whether the medium is film, television, theatre, print, video games, or music, the first step for creating a literary work is to begin with the premise and slowly aggregate the necessary legal interests and technical skills essential to complete the work. Only once this is done can the work be exploited in the marketplace.

Most projects start with authorship. Authors include playwrights, novelists, journalists, composers, lyricists, film directors, and music producers, to name just a few. The combination of these skills results in a literary work, the first step in creating entertainment. On occasion, however, identifying the author is somewhat difficult.

Who, in the absence of contract, can be considered an author of a movie? The word is traditionally used to mean the originator or the person who causes something to come into being, or even the first cause, as when Chaucer refers to the "Author of Nature." For a movie, that might be the producer who raises the money. Eisenstein thought the author of a movie was the editor. The "auteur" theory suggests that it might be the director, at least if the director is able to impose his artistic judgments on the film. Traditionally, by analogy to books, the author was regarded as the person who writes the screenplay, but often a movie reflects the work of many screenwriters. [Richard] Grenier suggests that the person with creative control tends to be the person in whose name the money is raised, perhaps a star, perhaps the director, perhaps the producer, with control gravitating to the star as the financial investment in scenes already shot grows.[1] Where the visual aspect of

---

1. *See* Richard Grenier, Capturing the Culture, 206–07 (1991).

the movie is especially important, the chief cinematographer might be regarded as the author. And for, say, a Disney animated movie like "The Jungle Book," it might perhaps be the animators and the composers of the music....

The Supreme Court dealt with the problem of defining "author" in new media in *Burrow-Giles Lithographic Co. v. Sarony*, [111 U.S. 53, 61 (1884)]. The question there was, who is the author of a photograph: the person who sets it up and snaps the shutter, or the person who makes the lithograph from it. Oscar Wilde, the person whose picture was at issue, doubtless offered some creative advice as well. The Court decided that the photographer was the author, quoting various English authorities: "the person who has superintended the arrangement, who has actually formed the picture by putting the persons in position, and arranging the place where the people are to be — the man who is the effective cause of that"; "'author' involves originating, making, producing, as the inventive or master mind, the thing which is to be protected"; "the man who really represents, creates, or gives effect to the idea, fancy, or imagination." The Court said that an "author," in the sense that the Founding Fathers used the term in the Constitution, was "'he to whom anything owes its origin; originator; maker; one who completes a work of science or literature.'"

Aalmuhammed v. Lee, 202 F.3d 1227, 1232 (9th Cir. 1999) (quoting *Burrow-Giles Lithographic Co. v. Sarony*, 111 U.S. 53, 61 (1884)).

The key distinction noted by the Ninth Circuit in *Aalmuhammed* is the difference between projects based on an agreement and those based on federal or state law. Contracts, collective bargaining agreements, and other binding arrangements allow the entertainment industries to operate smoothly despite legal doctrines that are often under-developed and stunningly at odds with the industry customs and trade they purport to regulate. Despite a long tradition of handshake agreements, the entertainment industry operates through written, oral, and implied agreements that do far more to regulate the daily business life than any other body of law. The law of the deal, therefore, is as important as any other legal doctrine.

Blaustein v. Burton

9 Cal. App. 3d 161, 88 Cal. Rptr. 319 (1970)

Plaintiff, on November 14, 1967, filed his complaint against the defendants Richard Burton, Elizabeth Taylor Burton, and Franco Zeffirelli, wherein he sought damages for (1) breach of contract, (2) unjust enrichment, (3) breach of confidential relationship and (4) services rendered and benefits conferred. Answer to the complaint was filed by the Burtons on January 16, 1968, and no other defendant was served or appeared in the action....

The functions of a producer of a motion picture are to (1) generate the enthusiasm of the various creative elements as well as to bring them together: (2) search out viable locations which would be proper for the artistic side of the production and would be proper from the logistic physical production side; (3) create a budget that would be acceptable from the physical point of view as well as satisfactory from the point of view of implementing the requirements of the script; (4) make arrangements with foreign government where the photography would take place; (5) supervise the execution of the script, the implementation of it onto film; (6) supervise the editing of all the production work down through the dubbing process and the release printing process, at least through the answer print process with Technicolor in this case; (7) the obligation of consulting with the United Artists people on advertising and publicity; (8) arrange casting; (9) engage the interests of the kind of star or stars that they (the United Artists' people) would find sufficiently attractive to justify an investment, and (10) develop the interest of a proper director.

During 1964, appellant conceived an idea consisting of a number of constituent elements including the following: (a) the idea of producing a motion picture based upon William Shakespeare's play "the Taming of the Shrew"; (b) the idea of casting respondents Richard Burton and Elizabeth Taylor Burton as the stars of this motion picture; (c) the idea of using as the director of the motion picture Franco Zeffirelli, a stage director, who at that time had never directed a motion picture and who was relatively unknown in the United States; (d) the idea of eliminating from the film version of the play the so-called "frame" (i.e., the play within a play device which Shakespeare employed), and beginning the film with the main body of the story; (e) the idea of including in the film version the two key scenes (i.e., the wedding scene and the wedding night scene) which in Shakespeare's play occur offstage and are merely described by a character on stage; (f) the idea of filming the picture in Italy, in the actual Italian settings described by Shakespeare.

[The Court next discusses a series of meetings and correspondence between Blaustein and various defendants as well as the introduction of the eventual director, Franco Zeffirelli to the project. During those conversations Blaustein's role as producer was called into question. Eventually Columbia Pictures produced a motion picture without Blaustein's participation.] ...

Thereafter, a motion picture based upon William Shakespeare's play "The Taming of the Shrew" was produced and exhibited commencing in or about March 1967. The motion picture stars respondents Richard Burton and Elizabeth Taylor Burton, and is directed by Franco Zeffirelli.... The motion picture as completed utilizes the following ideas disclosed by appellant to respondents: (1) It is based upon the Shakespearean play "The Taming of the Shrew"; (2) it stars Elizabeth Taylor Burton and Richard Burton in the roles of Katherine and Petruchio, respectively; (3) the director is Franco Zeffirelli; (4) it eliminates the "frame," i.e., the play within a play device found in the original Shakespearean play, and begins with the main body of the story; and (5) it includes an enactment of the two key scenes previously referred to by appellant which in Shakespeare's play occur off-stage.

In addition, the film was photographed in Italy, although not in the actual locales in Italy described by Shakespeare. Respondents have paid no monies to appellant, nor have they accorded him any screen or advertising credit.

...

Appellant urges that (1) there are triable issues of fact as to whether a contract was entered into between appellant and respondents pursuant to which appellant is entitled to compensation by reason of respondents' utilization of the idea disclosed to them by appellant; (2) there are triable issues of fact as to whether appellant is entitled to recover from respondents under quasi-contract for services rendered and benefits conferred, and (3) there are triable issues of fact as to whether appellant is entitled to recover from respondents for breach of a confidential relationship.

Respondents urge that ... respondents were not unjustly enriched at appellant's expense, nor did respondents breach any confidential relationship such as to require the law to impose a quasi-contractual obligation upon respondents to pay any sums to appellant....

The rights of an idea discloser to recover damages from an idea recipient under an express or implied contract to pay for the idea in event the idea recipient uses such idea after disclosure is discussed in *Desny v. Wilder*, 46 Cal.2d 715, 731–739 [299 P.2d 257], as follows:

> "The Law Pertaining to Ideas. Generally speaking, ideas are as free as the air and as speech and the senses, and as potent or weak, interesting or drab, as the experiences, philosophies, vocabularies, and other variables of speaker and listener may combine to produce, to portray, or to comprehend. But there can be circumstances when neither air nor ideas may be acquired without cost. The diver who goes deep in the sea, even as the pilot who ascends high in the troposphere, knows full well that for life itself he, or someone on his behalf, must arrange for air (or its respiration-essential element, oxygen) to be specially provided at the time and place of need. The theatrical producer likewise may be dependent for his business life on the procurement of ideas from other persons as well as the dressing up and portrayal of his self-conceptions; he may not find his own sufficient for survival. As counsel for the Writers Guild aptly say, ideas 'are not freely usable by the entertainment media until the latter are made aware of them.' The producer may think up the idea himself, dress it and portray it; or he may purchase either the conveyance of the idea alone or a manuscript embodying the idea in the author's concept of a literary vehicle giving it form, adaptation and expression. It cannot be doubted that some ideas are of value of a producer.

> "An idea is usually not regarded as property, because all sentient beings may conceive and evolve ideas throughout the gamut of their powers of cerebration and because our concept of property implies something which may be owned and possessed to the exclusion of all other persons. We quote as an accurate statement of the law in this respect the following language of

Mr. Justice Brandeis, dissenting in *International News Service v. Associated Press*, 248 U.S. 215, 250 (1918), 'An essential element of individual property is the legal right to exclude others from enjoying it. If the property is private, the right of exclusion may be absolute; if the property is affected with a public interest, the right of exclusion is qualified. But the fact that a product of the mind has cost its producer money and labor, and has a value for which others are willing to pay, is not sufficient to ensure to it this legal attribute of property. The general rule of law is, that the noblest of human productions—knowledge, truths ascertained, conceptions, and ideas—become, after voluntary communication to others, free as the air to common use.' Of similar import, but stated negatively: 'The doctrine that an author has a property right in his ideas and is entitled to demand for them the same protection which the law accords to the proprietor of personal property generally finds no recognition either in the common law or in the statutes of any civilized country.'...

"An eminent writer says that 'The elements requisite for an informal contract ... are identical whether they are expressly stated or implied in fact,'... 'A "contract implied in fact" requires a meeting of the minds, an agreement, just as much as an "express contract"; the difference between the two being largely in the character of the evidence by which they are established.' The same author describes quasi contracts by declaring that 'as quasi contractual obligations are imposed by the law for the purpose of bringing about justice without reference to the intention of the parties, the only apparent restriction upon the power of the law to create such obligations is that they must be of such a sort as would have been appropriately enforced under common-law procedure by a contractual action. Indeed even this limitation is too narrow, for a bill in equity or a libel in admiralty might be the appropriate means of enforcing some quasi contractual obligations. As the law may impose any obligations that justice requires, the only limit in the last analysis to the category of quasi contracts is that the obligation in question more closely resembles those created by contract than those created by tort. On the other hand, a true contract cannot exist, however desirable it might be to have one, unless there is a manifestation of assent to the making of a promise. Furthermore, the measure of damages appropriate to contractual obligations differs from that applicable to quasi contracts ... It is also true that quasi contractual obligations are not so universally based on unjust enrichment or benefit as is sometimes supposed. There are many cases where the law enforces in a contractual action a duty to restore the plaintiff to a former status—not merely to surrender the benefit which the defendant has received.'...

"From what has been shown respecting the law of ideas and of contracts we conclude that conveyance of an idea can constitute valuable consideration and can be bargained for before it is disclosed to the proposed purchaser, but once it is conveyed, i.e., disclosed to him and he has grasped, it, it is henceforth his own and he may work with it and use it as he sees fit. In the field of entertainment the producer may properly and validly agree that he will pay for the service of conveying to him ideas which are valuable and which he can put to profitable use. Furthermore, where an idea has been conveyed with the expectation by the purveyor that compensation will be paid if the idea is used, there is no reason why the producer who has been the beneficiary of the conveyance of such an idea, and who finds if valuable and is profiting by it, may not then for the first time, although he is not at that time under any legal obligation so to do, promise to pay a reasonable compensation for that idea — that is, for the past service of furnishing it to him — and thus create a valid obligation...." (*Desny v. Wilder, supra,* 46 Cal.2d 715, 731–739.)

It is held that "... if a producer obligates himself to pay for the disclosure of an idea, whether it is for protectible or unprotectible material, in return for a disclosure thereof he should be compelled to hold to his promise." There is nothing unreasonable in the assumption that a producer would obligate himself to pay for the disclosure of an idea which he would otherwise be legally free to use, but which in fact, he would be unable to use but for the disclosure.

"The producer and the writer should be free to make any contract they desire to make with reference to the buying of the ideas of the writer; the fact that the producer may later determine, with a little thinking, that he could have had the same ideas and could thereby have saved considerable money for himself, is no defense against the claim of the writer. This is so even though the material to be purchased is abstract and unprotected material." An idea which can be the subject matter of a contract need not be novel or concrete.

It may be noted here that the law of the State of New York no longer requires that an idea be "novel" in order to be the subject of contract protection. As stated in *Frederick Chusid & Co. v. Marshall Leeman & Co.,* 279 F. Supp. 913, 917 (S.D.N.Y. 1968): "Under New York law the parties have the right by contract to prevent disclosure of such materials, even though they are not secret or confidential and may indeed be a matter of public knowledge." The court in *Krisel v. Duran,* 258 F. Supp. 845, 860 (S.D.N.Y. 1966) stated: "Under New York law, an idea, if valuable, even though it does not contain novel, secret or confidential material, may be protected by such an agreement. This doctrine applies even when the subject matter of the idea is common or open to public knowledge."

We are of the opinion that appellant's idea of the filming of Shakespeare's play "The Taming of the Shrew" is one which may be protected by contract.

Express or implied contracts both are based upon the intention of the parties and are distinguishable only in the manifestation of assent. The making of an agreement may be inferred by proof of conduct as well as by proof of the use of words. Whether or not the appellant and respondents here, by their oral declarations and conduct, as shown by the depositions and affidavits, entered into a contract whereby respondents agreed to compensate appellant in the event respondents used appellant's idea, is a question of fact which may not be properly resolved in a summary judgment proceeding, but must be resolved upon a trial of the issue. Even where a question of interpretation of contractual provisions is involved on a motion for summary judgment, it is settled that, if the opposing interpretations are both reasonable, a question of fact is raised which precludes summary judgment....

Confidential Relationship. Respondents urge that the record is devoid of any evidence tending to establish the fact that they breached a duty of confidence owed to appellant.

Appellant, in his affidavit, stated: "Because I knew Mr. French to be a highly reputable agent, had had prior dealings with him, had the same firm of attorneys as the Burtons and had been the recipient of an invitation, constantly renewed, to disclose my ideas and render services on the project, I reposed trust and confidence in the Burtons and their representatives and expected that my ideas would be kept in confidence by them. I did not expect or intend that defendants would go forward with production of "Shrew" and make use of my ideas without my participation."

Under the rules governing the granting of a summary judgment, the foregoing declaration on the part of appellant, made in opposition to the motion for summary judgment, is sufficient to raise a triable issue of fact as to whether the disclosure of his idea to respondents was made in confidence, and was accepted by respondents upon the understanding that they would not use it without the consent of appellant. The judgment is reversed.

Faris v. Enberg

97 Cal. App. 3d 309 (Cal. App. 2d 1979)

The developer of an idea for a television sports quiz show (Edgar C. Faris) sued a television sports announcer (Richard Enberg) and others in two separate actions for appropriating his idea and producing a sports quiz show based upon it. This appeal follows the granting of defendants' motion for summary judgment in the trial court. We affirm the judgment....

Faris conceived a sports quiz show idea in 1964, and prepared and registered a format of the idea. A few days before June 4, 1970, Faris called KTLA studios and told a secretary that he had created a sports television show that would interest Mr. Enberg. He left his name and number. The next day Enberg telephoned Faris, who told Enberg that he "... had a sports oriented TV show that I intended to produce and that I desired to talk to him about participating in the show as the master of ceremonies." Faris told Enberg the format of the show and gave Enberg a copy, which Enberg read through at the meeting, and again expressed interest. Enberg asked for a copy, and Faris said it was his "creation" and "literary property." "I discussed with Mr. Enberg his prospects as to both being an MC for the show or, if he desired, actually participating with me in the production of the show and could participate then as a part owner thereof. At all times I discussed my show and Mr. Enberg's participation as a business proposal or offer to Mr. Enberg and I mentioned to him that, if he came with me, we would both make money on the show." Enberg told Faris he was going to talk the next week with some KTLA producers about a sports show. He asked Faris to leave a copy of the format for further review....

At some time following this meeting, the "Sports Challenge" show appeared on television with Enberg as master of ceremonies, and produced by defendant Gross. There were certain differences and similarities between the show and plaintiff's idea. Although Gross claimed the production of the show was well under way before Faris met Enberg, we cannot in this appeal assume such to be true, nor do we consider any facts in conflict with plaintiff's version of events....

In *Desny v. Wilder*, 46 Cal.2d 715 [299 P.2d 257 (1956)], plaintiff submitted to Billy Wilder's secretary a story based on the life of cave explorer Floyd Collins. The Supreme Court found that there were triable issues of fact, and reversed the lower court's order granting summary judgment to defendant. In doing so, the court carefully explained the subject of implied-in-fact contracts. Plaintiff called Billy Wilder on the telephone, and was told by a secretary that, because Wilder was so busy, plaintiff would have to present a synopsis for Wilder to read. Plaintiff told the secretary that he would have to be paid if they used it. His purpose was to sell the story. Plaintiff prepared the synopsis, read it to the secretary over the phone, and later Wilder produced a film which appeared to be similar to plaintiff's work. The work was not protected on any theory other than a contract express or implied from the facts....

For an implied-in-fact contract one must show: that he or she prepared the work; that he or she disclosed the work to the offeree for sale; under all circumstances attending disclosure it can be concluded that the offeree voluntarily accepted the disclosure knowing the conditions on which it was tendered (i.e., the offeree must have the opportunity to reject the attempted disclosure if the conditions were unacceptable); and the reasonable value of the work.

Applying these elements to the instant case, we find that the trial court correctly determined that there was no triable issue of fact on a cause of action for an implied-in-fact contract. The trial judge correctly concluded that "Enberg ... is entitled to summary judgment, since there is no evidence to support an implied-in-fact contract for the services of revealing plaintiff's format to him. All the evidence is to the contrary. Both participants to the conversation agreed that the format was submitted to Enberg in connection with an inquiry as to whether Enberg would act as master of ceremonies for plaintiff's television show.... There is absolutely no evidence that plaintiff expected, or indicated his expectation of receiving compensation for the service of revealing the format to Enberg. To the contrary, the sole evidence is that plaintiff voluntarily submitted it to Enberg for the sole purpose of enabling Enberg to make a determination of his willingness to enter into a future business relationship with plaintiff."

So far as the record before us reveals, plaintiff never thought of selling his sports quiz show idea to anyone—including Enberg. He appears at all times to have intended to produce it himself, and sought out Enberg, as a master of ceremonies. He obviously hoped to make his idea more marketable by hiring a gifted sports announcer as his master of ceremonies. Not only did Faris seek to induce Enberg to join him by showing him the product, but also sought to entice him by promises of a "piece" of the enterprise for his involvement. Plaintiff never intended to submit the property for sale and did not tell Enberg that he was submitting it for sale. There is no reason to think that Enberg, or anyone else with whom Enberg spoke, would have believed that Faris' submission was an offer to sell something, which if used would oblige the user to pay.

Based on the clear holding of *Desny* an obligation to pay could not be inferred from the mere fact of submission on a theory that everyone knows that the idea man expects to be paid. Nor could it be inferred from the comment by Faris that the format was his "creation" and "literary property." ...

Baer v. Chase
392 F.3d 609 (3d Cir. 2004)

Entertainment law covers the legal disciplines of copyright, publicity, privacy, trademark law, antitrust, contracts, First Amendment, and labor law. The creative content industries have trade, custom, usage, and other unique attributes that make practice of entertainment law unique, even for those who practice within a single doctrinal discipline within a particular industry.

This matter comes on before this court on Robert V. Baer's ("Baer") appeal from an order of the district court entered February 20, 2004, granting summary judgment to the defendants, David Chase and DC Enterprises, Inc. (together called "Chase"), pursuant to Federal Rule of Civil Procedure 56(c). This dispute centers on the creation and development of the well-known television series, The Sopranos. Through this action, Baer seeks compensation for what he perceives was his role in the creation and development of the popular and financially successful television series....

Baer predicates his contract claim on this appeal on an implied-in-fact contract rather than on the oral agreement he reached with Chase. The issue with respect to the implied-in-fact contract claim concerns whether Chase and Baer entered into an enforceable contract for services Baer rendered that aided in the creation and production of The Sopranos. In the district court Baer offered two alternative theories in which a purported contract was formed: the "oral agreement/success contingency" and an implied-in-fact contract.

The parties agree for purposes of the summary judgment motion that there was a contingent oral agreement providing for Chase to compensate Baer, depending on Chase's "success," in exchange for the aid Baer provided in the creation and production of The Sopranos. As we noted above, the parties reached the oral agreement in three exchanges in which Baer proposed: "that I would perform the services while assuming the risk that if the show failed [Chase] would owe me nothing. If, however, the show succeeded he would remunerate me in a manner commensurate to the true value of my services." As we have indicated, for purposes of the summary judgment motion only, Chase accepts this version of the events so we will regard the existence of the oral agreement as not in dispute....

New Jersey law deems the price term, i.e., the amount of compensation, an essential term of any contract. An agreement lacking definiteness of price, however, is not unenforceable if the parties specify a practicable method by which they can determine the amount. However, in the absence of an agreement as to the manner or method of determining compensation the purported agreement is invalid. Additionally, the duration of the contract is deemed an essential term and therefore any agreement must be sufficiently definitive to allow a court to determine the agreed upon length of the contractual relationship.

The New Jersey Supreme Court explicitly has held that an implied-in-fact contract "must be sufficiently definite [so] that the performance to be rendered by each party can be ascertained with reasonable certainty." *Weichert* [*Co. Realtors v. Ryan*], 608 A.2d at 284 [(N.J. 1992)] (citations and internal quotations omitted). If possible, courts will "attach a sufficiently definite meaning to the terms of a bargain to make it enforceable[,]" *Paley v. Barton Sav. and Loan Ass'n,* 82 N.J.Super. 75, 196 A.2d 682, 686 (1964), and in doing so may refer to "commercial practice or other usage or custom." *Lynch v. New Deal Delivery Serv. Inc.,* 974 F. Supp. 441, 458 (D.N.J.1997). But the courts recognize that a contract is "unenforceable for vagueness when its terms are too indefinite to allow a court to determine with reasonable certainty what each party has promised to do." *Id.* at 457.

Baer premises his argument on his view that New Jersey should disregard the well-established requirement of definiteness in its contract law when the subject-matter of the contract is an "idea submission." He cites extensively to a string of cases from various jurisdictions which he urges support his contention. *See, e.g., Wrench L.L.C v. Taco Bell Corp.,* 256 F.3d 446 (6th Cir.2001); *Nadel v. Play-by-Play Toys & Novelties, Inc.,* 208 F.3d 368 (2d Cir.2000); *Duffy* [*v. Charles Schwab & Co.*, 123 F. Supp. 2d 802 (2001)]. Baer contends that these cases support the proposition that "[e]very Circuit that has published on the issue, has upheld implied contract claims where price and duration were absent and a price term was implied as the reasonable value of the ideas conveyed."

Baer's argument is inaccurate and misleading. He attempts to transform cases where the issues raised pertain to adequacy of consideration and discrepancies over the use of submitted facts, into the proposition that implied-in-fact contracts involving idea submissions need not be sufficiently definite. For example: *Wrench,* 256 F.3d at 459–63, reversed a summary judgment disposition that held that novelty was required to prove consideration and sustain an implied-in-fact contract claim; *Duffy,* 123 F.Supp.2d at 816–19, held that a plaintiff must prove that an idea disclosed to the defendant was novel in order to find consideration for the alleged contract and denied summary judgment because a material issue existed over novelty and use; *Nadel,* 208

F.3d at 374, reversed a summary judgment granted "only on ground that [the plaintiff's] idea lacked general novelty and thus would not suffice as consideration" and remanded for the district court to determine "whether the other elements necessary to find a valid express or implied-in-fact contract are present here." *Id.* at 382. None of the cases Baer cites holds that there is not a definiteness requirement necessary to create an enforceable contract in idea submission cases. *Duffy*'s holding is helpful in summarizing the actual law to be derived from the above cited cases: "The existence of novelty to the buyer only addresses the element of consideration necessary for the formation of a contract. Thus, apart from consideration, the formation of a contract will depend upon the presence of other elements." *Duffy*, 123 F.Supp.2d at 818 (citing *Nadel*, 208 F.3d at 377 n. 5).

New Jersey precedent does not support Baer's attempt to carve out an exception to traditional principles of contract law for submission-of-idea cases. The New Jersey courts have not provided even the slightest indication that they intend to depart from their well-established requirement that enforceability of a contract requires definiteness with respect to the essential terms of that contract. Accordingly, we will not relax the need for Baer to demonstrate definiteness as to price and duration with respect to the contract he entered into with Chase.

The final question with respect to the Baer's contract claim, therefore, is whether his contract is enforceable in light of the traditional requirement of definitiveness in New Jersey contract law for a contract to be enforceable. A contract may be expressed in writing, or orally, or in acts, or partly in one of these ways and partly in others. In this case, even when all of the parties' verbal and non-verbal actions are aggregated and viewed most favorably to Baer, we cannot find a contract that is distinct and definitive enough to be enforceable.

Nothing in the record indicates that the parties agreed on how, how much, where, or for what period Chase would compensate Baer. The parties did not discuss who would determine the "true value" of Baer's services, when the "true value" would be calculated, or what variables would go into such a calculation. There was no discussion or agreement as to the meaning of "success" of The Sopranos. There was no discussion how "profits" were to be defined. There was no contemplation of dates of commencement or termination of the contract. And again, nothing in Baer's or Chase's conduct, or the surrounding circumstances of the relationship, shed light on, or answers, any of these questions. The district court was correct in its description of the contract between the parties: "The contract as articulated by the Plaintiff lacks essential terms, and is vague, indefinite and uncertain; no version of the alleged agreement contains sufficiently precise terms to constitute an enforceable contract." We therefore will affirm the district court's rejection of Baer's claim to recover under a theory of implied-in-fact contract.

. . .

Notes and Questions

a. California has been more explicit about what constitutes a contract for ideas than many other states, likely owing to *Desny v. Wilder*, 46 Cal.2d 715 (1956). In *Klekas v. EMI Films, Inc.*, 150 Cal. App. 3d 1102 (Cal. Ct. App. 1984), the court explained that in order to establish an implied-in-fact contract in the entertainment context, the following was required:

> [Plaintiff must establish] that he or she prepared the work; that he or she disclosed the work to an offeree for sale; that under all circumstances attending disclosure it can be concluded that the offeree voluntarily accepted the disclosure knowing the conditions on which it was tendered (i.e., the offeree must have the opportunity to reject the attempted disclosure if the conditions were unacceptable); and the reasonable value of the work.

b. There is an increasing tension between the theft of ideas and the ever-expanding understanding of the First Amendment. Parties seeking to stop the theft of ideas often use their superior economic positions to economically intimidate former employees and small competitors. To address this, a number of states have adopted "anti-SLAPP statutes." A SLAPP suit is a "strategic lawsuit against public participation." The anti-SLAPP statutes are intended to promote public participation through First Amendment protected activities. The Anti-SLAPP statutes provide early termination of lawsuits that are likely to result in eventual dismissal on First Amendment grounds. Although most anti-SLAPP statutes involve defamation and other tortious conduct, they may also have an impact on breach of contract lawsuits. *See Jordan-Benel v. Universal City Studios, Inc.*, 859 F.3d 1184, 1187 (9th Cir. 2017) (involving allegations that have since been settled over the authorship of the film series *The Purge*).

c. The issue of novelty and originality continues to be a controversial element of the law pertaining to transactions of ideas. There is a significant amount of confusion between claims for breach of contract and claims for misappropriation of an idea. Over time, it is likely that most misappropriation claims will be preempted by copyright. Properly distinguished, contract claims should survive preemption. *See Orson, Inc. v. Miramax Film Corp.*, 189 F.3d 377, 382 (3d Cir. 1999) (en banc) (discussing the various types of preemption in the copyright setting).

d. A screenwriter reads an obituary of a soldier from World War I who recently died. The obituary was written and paid for by the children of the soldier. The sixty-word obituary refers to a particular act of bravery by the soldier when he was stationed in Germany after the war, when he stopped a gang of hooligans from beating and possibly killing a young man named Adolph Hitler. The screenwriter uses the idea to write a screenplay which is made into a successful motion picture. In an action by the family against the screenwriter and the motion picture studio, what is the appropriate result and why? *See*, for example, *Desny v. Wilder*, 46 Cal.2d 715, 299 P.2d 257 (1956).

e. How can a client develop a work as a producer or in a similar capacity without the risk of that effort being stolen? Are there bodies of law beyond copyright, trademark and contract to provide protection? Should such protection even be available?

f. The general industry practice regarding submission of treatment is to use releases to waive all claims other than copyright infringement. At a minimum, defendants should retain the releases. *See Sims v. Viacom, Inc.,* 2009 U.S. Dist. LEXIS 107938 (E.D. Pa. Nov. 17, 2009).

g. In *Baer v. Chase,* Baer also attempted to claim a breach of confidentiality under New Jersey law.

> The court in *Flemming* [*v. Ronson Corp.,* 107 N.J. Super. 311, 258 A.2d 153, 156–57 (1969)] articulated the test for determining whether the law will imply an obligation to pay for a confidentially submitted idea: When "a person communicates a novel idea to another with the intention that the latter may use the idea and compensate him for such use, the other party is liable for such use and must pay compensation if ... (1) the idea was novel; (2) it was made in confidence [to the defendant]; and (3) it was adopted and made use of [by the defendant in connection with his own activities]."

Flemming, 258 A.2d at 156–57 (citations omitted). The decisions do not explain what ideas can be novel, merely that "even an otherwise novel idea would lose its novelty if it was 'in the domain of public knowledge' before the defendant used it." *Baer v. Chase,* 392 F.3d 609, 628 (3d Cir. 2004), quoting *Flemming,* 258 A.2d at 157–58.

Problem 1-B

Bryce has met with you for the first time since signing a representation agreement with Story, Marshall & Cardozo[2] as legal counsel. Bryce has the idea to create a multimedia project based on an original story idea. Bryce has already composed songs for the project. What are the steps that Bryce and you must take to protect the work before it is shown to potential investors or producers? Identify the legal mechanisms available to help protect Bryce, as well as the limitations Bryce might face.

C. Written Submission Agreements

Nadel v. Play-By-Play Toys

208 F.3d 368 (2d Cir. 2000)

Plaintiff-appellant Craig P. Nadel ("Nadel") brought this action against defendant-appellee Play-By-Play Toys & Novelties, Inc. ("Play-By-Play") for breach of contract,

---

2. *See* Chapter 3 regarding the questions of the lawyer's ethical issues. What unique provisions might be needed in the law firm representation (or retainer) agreement?

quasi contract, and unfair competition. The thrust of Nadel's complaint was that Play-By-Play took his idea for an upright, sound-emitting, spinning plush toy and that, contrary to industry custom, Play-By-Play used the idea in its "Tornado Taz" product without paying him compensation. Play-By-Play also filed several counter-claims against Nadel, alleging that Nadel falsely told other members of the toy industry that Play-By-Play had stolen his idea, thereby harming its ability to receive toy concepts from toy industry members.

For the reasons that follow, we vacate that part of the district court's order granting Play-By-Play's motion for summary judgment and dismissing Nadel's complaint and affirm that part of the district court's order dismissing Play-By-Play's counterclaims.

Nadel is a toy idea man. Toy companies regularly do business with independent inventors such as Nadel in order to develop and market new toy concepts as quickly as possible. To facilitate the exchange of ideas, the standard custom and practice in the toy industry calls for companies to treat the submission of an idea as confidential. If the company subsequently uses the disclosed idea, industry custom provides that the company shall compensate the inventor, unless, of course, the disclosed idea was already known to the company.

In 1996, Nadel developed the toy concept at issue in this case. He transplanted the "eccentric mechanism" found in several hanging Halloween toys then on the mar-ket—such as "Spooky Skull" and "Shaking Mutant Pumpkin"—and placed the mech-anism inside of a plush toy monkey skin to develop the prototype for a new table-top monkey toy. This plush toy figure sat upright, emitted sound, and spun when placed on a flat surface.

In October 1996, Nadel met with Neil Wasserman, an executive at Play-By-Play who was responsible for the development of its plush toy line. According to Nadel, he showed his prototype monkey toy to Wasserman, who expressed interest in adapting the concept to a non-moving, plush Tazmanian Devil toy that Play-By-Play was already producing under license from Warner Bros. Nadel contends that, consistent with industry custom, any ideas that he disclosed to Wasserman during their October 1996 meeting were subject to an agreement by Play-By-Play to keep such ideas con-fidential and to compensate Nadel in the event of their use.

Nadel claims that he sent his prototype monkey toy to Wasserman as a sample and awaited the "Taz skin" and voice tape, which Wasserman allegedly said he would send, so that Nadel could make a sample spinning/laughing Tazmanian Devil toy for Play-By-Play. Wasserman never provided Nadel with the Taz skin and voice tape, however, and denies ever having received the prototype monkey toy from Nadel.

Notwithstanding Wasserman's denial, his secretary, Melissa Rodriguez, testified that Nadel's prototype monkey toy remained in Wasserman's office for several months. According to Ms. Rodriguez, the monkey toy was usually kept in a glass cabinet behind Wasserman's desk, but she remembered that on one occasion she had seen it on a table in Wasserman's office. Despite Nadel's multiple requests, Wasserman did not return Nadel's prototype monkey toy until February 1997, after Play-By-Play introduced its "Tornado Taz" product at the New York Toy Fair.

The parties do not dispute that "Tornado Taz" has the same general characteristics as Nadel's prototype monkey toy. Like Nadel's toy, Tornado Taz is a plush toy that emits sounds (including "screaming," "laughing," "snarling," and "grunting"), sits upright, and spins by means of an internal eccentric vibration mechanism.

Nadel claims that, in violation of their alleged agreement, Play-By-Play used his idea without paying him compensation. Play-By-Play contends, however, that it independently developed the Tornado Taz product concept and that Nadel is therefore not entitled to any compensation. Specifically, Play-By-Play maintains that, as early as June or July of 1996, two of its officers—Wasserman and Slattery—met in Hong Kong and began discussing ways to create a spinning or vibrating Tazmanian Devil, including the possible use of an eccentric mechanism. Furthermore, Play-By-Play claims that in late September or early October 1996, it commissioned an outside manufacturing agent—Barter Trading of Hong Kong—to begin developing Tornado Taz.

Play-By-Play also argues that, even if it did use Nadel's idea to develop Tornado Taz, Nadel is not entitled to compensation because Nadel's concept was unoriginal and non-novel to the toy industry in October 1996. In support of this argument, Play-By-Play has submitted evidence of various toys, commercially available prior to October 1996, which used eccentric motors and allegedly contained the same characteristics as Nadel's prototype monkey toy....

Nadel's factual allegations present a familiar submission-of-idea case: (1) the parties enter into a pre-disclosure confidentiality agreement; (2) the idea is subsequently disclosed to the prospective buyer; (3) there is no post-disclosure contract for payment based on use; and (4) plaintiff sues defendant for allegedly using the disclosed idea under either a contract-based or property-based theory. For the reasons that follow, we conclude that a finding of novelty as to Play-By-Play can suffice to provide consideration for Nadel's contract claims against Play-By-Play. Accordingly, because we also find that there exists a genuine issue of material fact as to whether Nadel's idea was novel to Play-By-Play at the time of his October 1996 disclosure, we vacate the district court's grant of summary judgment on Nadel's contract claims. With respect to Nadel's misappropriation claim, we similarly vacate the district court's grant of summary judgment and remand for further proceedings to determine whether Nadel's idea was original or novel generally.

A. Submission-of-Idea Cases under New York Law.

Our analysis begins with the New York Court of Appeals' most recent discussion of the law governing idea submission cases, *Apfel v. Prudential-Bache Securities, Inc.*, 81 N.Y.2d 470 (1993). In *Apfel*, the Court of Appeals discussed the type of novelty an idea must have in order to sustain a contract-based or property-based claim for its uncompensated use. Specifically, *Apfel* clarified an important distinction between the requirement of "novelty to the buyer" for contract claims, on the one hand, and "originality" (or novelty generally) for misappropriation claims, on the other hand.

Under the facts of *Apfel*, the plaintiff disclosed his idea to the defendant pursuant to a confidentiality agreement and, subsequent to disclosure, entered into another agreement wherein the defendant agreed to pay a stipulated price for the idea's use. The defendant used the idea but refused to pay plaintiff pursuant to the post-disclosure agreement on the asserted ground that "no contract existed between the parties because the sale agreement lacked consideration." The defendant argued that an idea could not constitute legally sufficient consideration unless it was original or novel generally and that, because plaintiff's idea was not original or novel generally (it had been in the public domain at the time of the post-disclosure agreement), the idea provided insufficient consideration to support the parties' post-disclosure contract.

In rejecting defendant's argument, the Court of Appeals held that there was sufficient consideration to support plaintiff's contract claim because the idea at issue had value to the defendant at the time the parties concluded their post-disclosure agreement. The *Apfel* court noted that "traditional principles of contract law" provide that parties "are free to make their bargain, even if the consideration exchanged is grossly unequal or of dubious value," and that, so long as the "defendant received something of value" under the contract, the contract would not be void for lack of consideration.

The *Apfel* court explicitly rejected defendant's contention that the court should carve out "an exception to traditional principles of contract law" for submission-of-idea cases by requiring that an idea must also be original or novel generally in order to constitute valid consideration. In essence, the defendant sought to impose a requirement that an idea be novel in absolute terms, as opposed to only the defendant buyer, in order to constitute valid consideration for the bargain. In rejecting this argument, the *Apfel* court clarified the standards for both contract-based and property-based claims in submission-of-idea cases. That analysis guides our decision here.

The *Apfel* court first noted that "novelty as an element of an idea seller's claim" is a distinct element of proof with respect to both (1) "a claim based on a property theory" and (2) "a claim based on a contract theory." The court then proceeded to discuss how the leading submission-of-idea case—*Downey v. General Foods Corp.*, 31 N.Y.2d 56 (1972)—treated novelty with respect to property-based and contract-based claims. First, the Apfel court explained that the plaintiff's property based claims for misappropriation were dismissed in *Downey* because "the elements of novelty and originality [were] absent," i.e., the ideas were so common as to be unoriginal and known generally. Second, the *Apfel* court explained that the plaintiff's contract claims in *Downey* had been dismissed on the separate ground that the "defendant possessed plaintiff's ideas prior to plaintiff's disclosure [and thus], the ideas could have no value to defendant and could not supply consideration for any agreement between the parties."

By distinguishing between the two types of claims addressed in *Downey* and the different bases for rejecting each claim, the New York Court of Appeals clarified that the novelty requirement in submission-of-idea cases is different for misappropriation of property and breach of contract claims. The Court of Appeals underscored this important distinction by citing *Ferber v. Sterndent Corp.*, 51 N.Y.2d 782 (1980), which also refers to the two different types of novelty, i.e., novelty to the buyer and novelty generally....

Thus, the *Apfel* court refused to read *Downey* and "similar decisions" as requiring originality or novelty generally in all cases involving disclosure of ideas. Rather, the *Apfel* court clarified that the longstanding requirement that an idea have originality or general novelty in order to support a misappropriation claim does not apply to contract claims. For contract-based claims in submission-of-idea cases, a showing of novelty to the buyer will supply sufficient consideration to support a contract.

Moreover, *Apfel* made clear that the "novelty to the buyer" standard is not limited to cases involving an express post-disclosure contract for payment based on an idea's use. The *Apfel* court explicitly discussed the pre-disclosure contract scenario present in the instant case, where "the buyer and seller contract for disclosure of the idea with payment based on use, but no separate post-disclosure contract for the use of the idea has been made." In such a scenario, a seller might, as Nadel did here, bring an action against a buyer who allegedly used his ideas without payment, claiming both misappropriation of property and breach of an express or implied-in-fact contract. The *Apfel* court recognized that these cases present courts with the difficult problem of determining "whether the idea the buyer was using was, in fact, the seller's." Specifically, the court noted that, with respect to a misappropriation of property claim, it is difficult to "prove that the buyer obtained the idea from [the seller] and nowhere else." With respect to a breach of contract claim, the court noted that it would be inequitable to enforce a contract if "it turns out upon disclosure that the buyer already possessed the idea." The court then concluded that, with respect to these cases, "[a] showing of novelty, at least novelty as to the buyer" should address these problems.

We note, moreover, that the "novelty to the buyer" standard comports with traditional principles of contract law. While an idea may be unoriginal or non-novel in a general sense, it may have substantial value to a particular buyer who is unaware of it and therefore willing to enter into contract to acquire and exploit it. *See* Robert Unikel, *Bridging the "Trade Secret" Gap: Protecting "Confidential Information" Not Rising to the Level of Trade Secrets*, 29 Loy. U. Chi. L.J. 841, 877 n. 151 (1998) (noting that, if a valuable idea is already known to an industry but has not yet been acquired by a prospective buyer, one of two circumstances may exist: "(1) the person[] ha[s] not identified the potential value of the easily acquired information; or (2) the person[] ha[s] not identified the means, however easy or proper, for obtaining the valuable information"). As the *Apfel* court emphasized, "the buyer may reap benefits from such a contract in a number of ways—for instance, by not having to expend resources pursuing the idea through other channels or by having a profit-making idea implemented sooner rather than later."

In fact, the notion that an unoriginal idea may still be novel (and valuable) to a particular buyer is not itself a novel proposition. In *Keller v. American Chain Co.*, 255 N.Y. 94, 174 N.E. 74 (1930)—which is cited by *Apfel*—the parties entered into a verbal pre-disclosure contract whereby the plaintiff allegedly agreed to disclose money-saving information to the defendant in exchange for one-third of the savings realized. The disclosed idea—that the defendant could use a more favorable freight rate classification for his auto chains—was not original or novel to the industry, as several railroads already adhered to the lower rate. Nonetheless, the *Keller* court stated that, where the defendant used and benefited from information otherwise unknown to it, there can be sufficient consideration to enforce the parties' pre-disclosure contract.

In contrast to contract-based claims, a misappropriation claim can only arise from the taking of an idea that is original or novel in absolute terms, because the law of property does not protect against the misappropriation or theft of that which is free and available to all. *See Murray v. National Broad. Co.,* 844 F.2d 988, 993 (2d Cir. 1988) ("Since ... non-novel ideas are not protectible as property, they cannot be stolen.")....

Finally, although the legal requirements for contract-based claims and property-based claims are well-defined, we note that the determination of novelty in a given case is not always clear. The determination of whether an idea is original or novel depends upon several factors, including, inter alia, the idea's specificity or generality (is it a generic concept or one of specific application?), its commonality (how many people know of this idea?), its uniqueness (how different is this idea from generally known ideas?), and its commercial availability (how widespread is the idea's use in the industry?). *Cf. Murray,* 844 F.2d at 993 ("In assessing whether an idea is in the public domain, the central issue is the uniqueness of the creation."). Thus, for example, a once original or novel idea may become so widely disseminated over the course of time that it enters the body of common knowledge. When this occurs, the idea ceases to be novel or original. *See, e.g., Murray,* 844 F.2d at 989, 991–92 (affirming district court's finding that plaintiff's idea for a television sitcom "The Cosby Show" about "black American family life" was not novel or original because it "merely combined two ideas which had been circulating in the industry for a number of years—namely, the family situation comedy, which was a standard formula, and the casting of black actors in non-stereotypical roles," even though "the portrayal of a non-stereo-typical black family on television was indeed a breakthrough").

Moreover, in assessing the interrelationship between originality and novelty to the buyer, we note that in some cases an idea may be so unoriginal or lacking in novelty that its obviousness bespeaks widespread and public knowledge of the idea, and such knowledge is therefore imputed to the buyer. In such cases, a court may conclude, as a matter of law, that the idea lacks both the originality necessary to support a misappropriation claim and the novelty to the buyer necessary to support a contract claim.

In the first of two post-*Apfel* decisions in New York—*Oasis Music, Inc. v. 900 U.S.A., Inc.,* 614 N.Y.S.2d 878 (1994)—the plaintiff alleged that the defendant misappropriated its ideas for an interactive telephone game in violation of a pre-disclosure confidentiality agreement. The *Oasis Music* court correctly began its contract analysis by reciting *Apfel*'s "novelty as to the buyer" standard. But after concluding that the various aspects of plaintiff's ideas already existed in the public domain, the court appeared to dismiss plaintiff's claims for lack of novelty generally. In light of *Apfel*, we read the *Oasis Music* opinion to hold that, because plaintiff's ideas had such a high degree of commonality, the ideas were so unoriginal that, as a matter of law, they were non-novel to the buyer.

In the other post-*Apfel* decision in New York—*Marraccini v. Bertelsmann Music Group, Inc.*, 221 A.D.2d 95 (3d Dep't 1996)—the plaintiff alleged that the defendant breached their pre-disclosure agreement and misappropriated his idea for a "Pop TV" music channel. On appeal from the Supreme Court, New York's Appellate Division reiterated *Downey*'s statement that, "[w]hen there is no postdisclosure agreement for the use of an idea, 'no promise to pay for its use may be implied, and no asserted agreement enforced, if the elements of novelty and originality are absent, since the property right in an idea is based upon these two elements.'" We agree with the *Marraccini* court's statement that "*Downey* ... and its progeny remain[] intact," insofar as that line of cases was clarified by *Apfel*, but we conclude that the *Marraccini* court's reliance on *Downey*'s language for the proposition that the consideration for the contract in contract-based claims must consist of originality or novelty generally—as opposed to just novelty to the buyer—has been foreclosed by *Apfel*. We do not understand *Apfel*'s holding to be limited only to situations where there is an express post-disclosure contract between the parties.

In sum, we find that New York law in submission-of-idea cases is governed by the following principles: Contract-based claims require only a showing that the disclosed idea was novel to the buyer in order to find consideration. Such claims involve a fact-specific inquiry that focuses on the perspective of the particular buyer. By contrast, misappropriation claims require that the idea at issue be original and novel in absolute terms. This is so because unoriginal, known ideas have no value as property and the law does not protect against the use of that which is free and available to all. Finally, an idea may be so unoriginal or lacking in novelty generally that, as a matter of law, the buyer is deemed to have knowledge of the idea. In such cases, neither a property-based nor a contract-based claim for uncompensated use of the idea may lie.

[B.] Nadel's Contract Claims.

Mindful that, under New York law, a finding of novelty as to Play-By-Play will provide sufficient consideration to support Nadel's contract claims, we next consider whether the record exhibits a genuine issue of material fact on this point.

Reading the record in a light most favorable to Nadel, we conclude that there exists a genuine issue of material fact as to whether Nadel's idea was, at the time he disclosed it to Wasserman in early October 1996, novel to Play-By-Play. Notably, the timing of Play-By-Play's development and release of Tornado Taz in relation to Nadel's October 1996 disclosure is, taken alone, highly probative. Moreover, although custom in the toy industry provides that a company shall promptly return all samples if it already possesses (or does not want to use) a disclosed idea, Play-By-Play in this case failed to return Nadel's prototype monkey toy for several months, despite Nadel's multiple requests for its return. According to Wasserman's secretary, Melissa Rodriguez, Nadel's sample was not returned until after the unveiling of "Tornado Taz" at the

New York Toy Fair in February 1997. Ms. Rodriguez testified that from October 1996 through February 1997, Nadel's sample was usually kept in a glass cabinet behind Wasserman's desk, and on one occasion, she remembered seeing it on a table in Wasserman's office. These facts give rise to the reasonable inference that Play-By-Play may have used Nadel's prototype as a model for the development of Tornado Taz....

We therefore conclude that there exists a genuine issue of material fact as to whether Nadel's idea was, at the time he disclosed it to Wasserman in early October 1996, novel to Play-By-Play. As to whether the other elements necessary to find a valid express or implied-in-fact contract are present here, e.g., mutual assent, legal capacity, legal subject matter, we leave that determination to the district court to address, if necessary, on remand.

FASA Corp. v. Playmates Toys Inc.
892 F. Supp. 1061 (N.D. Ill. 1995)

Plaintiff FASA Corporation ("FASA") is the creator, developer, publisher, promoter and distributor of various fictional universes, including but not limited to BAT-TLETECH, which form the basis for board games, role-playing games, novels, game systems and other game supplements which it licenses to third parties for the development of location-based interactive entertainment games and centers, disk-based computer games, cartridge-based computer games, models, miniatures, merchandise, movies, television programming, toys and other items. Defendant Playmates Toys, Inc. ("Playmates"), is a distributor of toys supplied by a related company, Playmates Toys (Hong Kong) Ltd. ("Playmates HK"), including TEENAGE MUTANT NINJA TURTLES, STAR TREK, ADDAMS FAMILY and various Disney characters.

The lawsuit centers on Playmates' alleged infringement of FASA's intellectual property and proprietary rights in BATTLETECH by designing and marketing the Ex-oSquad toy line. In late 1991, Robert Allen, a Cincinnati, Ohio, toy designer, asked FASA for the opportunity to interest toy companies in the BATTLETECH property. Although Allen and FASA never reached agreement on the nature and scope of Allen's role, FASA did permit Allen to make at least three presentations to toy companies regarding a BATTLETECH toy line.

When Allen arrived at Playmates on December 11, 1991, to present BATTLETECH, Playmates presented Allen with an untitled document that Playmates represented as its standard "New Product Submission Form." This New Product Submission Form reads as follows:

> It is the policy of Playmates Toys, Inc. not to review or consider any unsolicited proposals of any kind. You have advised us that you have an "idea" which you believe may be of interest to us. We are prepared to consider your idea only upon the following terms:
>
> 1. You will expressly waive any and all claims of any kind whatsoever, past, present or future, known or unknown against Playmates Toys, Inc. in any way relating to or connected to the "idea".

2. In consideration for such waiver, Playmates Toys, Inc., will review your "idea" in written form. We will return all materials submitted in connection therewith within two weeks after submission.

3. At our sole and complete discretion, we may then enter into negotiations with you for a contractual agreement regarding the idea.

4. Except as to any future agreement entered into under Paragraph 3, we shall have no obligation of any kind toward you in connection with the proposed idea. The disclosed matter relates to: [handwritten] (1) "BATTLETECH" (2) "WENDY & HER WAGON" (3) "SPEEDBALLS".

Allen had signed nondisclosure or new product submission forms before which did not require or include waivers of either copyright or trademark infringement claims or of other future unknown claims by the owner of the property. Playmates knew that Allen was not an employee of FASA. Although Playmates had never dealt with FASA in the past, Playmates made no effort to verify Allen's authority. At no time did Playmates attempt to contact FASA. There was no communication of any type between Playmates and FASA until this lawsuit was filed, and FASA did not explicitly authorize Allen to waive any of its intellectual property rights in BATTLETECH.

While the Court finds that many toy companies use nondisclosure or new product submission forms—the Court finds that such companies do not require, as a standard practice, a waiver of all the intellectual property rights held by the inventor. In this regard, the Court notes that Playmates' own experts testified that it is not typical in the toy industry for a toy company to require an inventor to waive all rights to the invention in order to submit it for review. Moreover, even Playmates' president testified that he did not understand the waiver provision in Playmates' new product submission form to include a waiver of copyright, trademark, or patent claims.

Under the California Civil Code, "[a]n agent has such authority as the principal, actually or ostensibly, confers upon him," Cal. Civil Code § 2315, and "[a]n agent represents his principal for all purposes within the scope of his actual or ostensible authority." Cal. Civ. Code § 2330. Only those liabilities "which would accrue to the agent from transactions within [his actual or ostensible authority], if they had been entered into on his own account, accrue to the principal."

Because FASA did not confer authority on Allen to waive its intellectual property rights in BATTLETECH, and because Allen did not believe that he had authority to waive FASA's intellectual property rights, the Court finds that Allen did not have actual authority to waive FASA's intellectual property rights.

Having determined that FASA cannot be bound by Allen's purported waiver of its intellectual property rights, our inquiry could be at an end. However, we proceed to offer an alternate basis for our holding that FASA is not bound by Allen's purported waiver—namely, that Playmates' waiver form is unenforceable as a matter of law. This issue, as the parties concede, seems to be one of first impression.

As a threshold consideration in assessing the enforceability of the purported waiver, we must address what law governs this issue. Playmates contends that since the underlying claims at issue are federal claims, federal law controls. And, in this limited sense, they are correct....

In the instant case, we find that federal authority, as well as that of Illinois and California converge on the conclusion that Playmates' waiver form is unenforceable because it purports to require the signor to waive unknown future claims. Such a waiver is void as against public policy.

The California Civil Code provides that "A general release does not extend to claims which the creditor does not know or suspect to exist in his favor at the time of executing the release...." Cal. Civ. Code § 1542. Thus, we believe that California recognizes the general proposition that a waiver of future unknown claims is unenforceable. Similarly, under Illinois caselaw, "A general release is inapplicable to an unknown claim." The Court finds no federal authority supporting Playmates' position that waiver of future unknown claims is valid....

In the Securities context a waiver, like the waiver sought to be enforced by Playmates, is explicitly precluded by statute. Similarly, in the antitrust context, Judge Shadur even in the absence of a statutory prohibition has nevertheless refused to enforce a waiver that purported to bar a lawsuit based on anticompetitive events arising after the signing of the waiver.... [S]uch a waiver could itself become a contract in restraint of trade.

In the instant case, we are persuaded that a purported waiver of future, unknown federal intellectual property rights is unenforceable and void as against public policy. Such a waiver would permit a party to violate another's intellectual property rights with impunity in contravention of the clear and long standing public policies underlying the trademark, copyright and patent laws. Giving force to such waivers would invariably stifle creativity and inventiveness and inhibit inventors from presenting their creations to others. Thus, even if we were not to look at state law as a guide we would reach the same conclusion: The waiver of unknown future claims is unenforceable.

Playmates' New Product Form violates public policy because it allows Playmates to violate federal intellectual property law with impunity. Playmates' New Product Form also violates California law to which this Court may look in fashioning federal common law.

Conclusion. For all of the reasons set forth herein the Court finds that Playmates' New Product Form is legally unenforceable under the facts and circumstances of this case. The Court therefore finds that defendant Playmates has not met its burden of establishing its affirmative defense of waiver.

Notes and Questions

a. One of the most significant and potentially misleading cases on the topic of waiver comes from the Second Circuit. In *Murray v. National Broadcasting Company, Inc.*, 844 F.2d 988 (2d Cir. 1988), the court determined that a staff writer's submission describing a modern *Dick Van Dyke Show*, to star Bill Cosby in an upper class African-American household with five children, was not protected against NBC when that network contracted with Carsey-Werner for the creation of *The Cosby Show*. The court found for NBC after determining that the idea had to be novel. Subsequent decisions, however, seem to have rejected this analysis.

Instead of novelty, the New York Court of Appeals explains that in a contract dispute, the idea need merely be unknown to the purchaser. Under this alternative, NBC still would have won the dispute because Bill Cosby himself had first proposed the show two decades earlier. Murray's idea was known to NBC. The Second Circuit recognized this, reporting Cosby's earlier statement that this *Dick Van Dyke*-style show "'will be radically different. Everyone in it will be a Negro.'... Nearly twenty years later, on September 20, 1984, Cosby's dream for a 'color-blind' family series materialized with the premier of *The Cosby Show*—a situation comedy about a family known as the Huxtables." *Id.* at 989. One final irony of the decision is that Carsey-Werner was paid for the idea rather than Bill Cosby.

b. Every large media company regularly receives thousands of suggestions for new projects, both unsolicited and solicited. What steps would you suggest that a media company take to protect itself from expensive litigation brought by third parties?

c. Given the invalidity of the submission agreement in *FASA*, what terms should be included and excluded in a contractual submission agreement in order to make such an agreement enforceable?

d. As a practical matter, a strongly worded waiver provision may discourage claims against entertainment entities. As an attorney for such an entity, what ethical rules, or rules of professional conduct, limit participation in writing an agreement like that used in *FASA*? As the attorney for an originator of an idea, to what extent can you counsel your client to sign the agreement because it is not likely to be binding?

e. A written submission agreement can take two forms. The first requires the submitting party to waive any rights to the ideas or contract. The submitting party must rely exclusively on copyright protections, as applicable. In the context of unsolicited material, this should be the expectation of both parties. The second form may be used in the context of solicited material, through adoption of a nondisclosure agreement. Heavily utilized in some entertainment industries such as software and videogames, these are far less common in the film, television, and publishing industries. Nonetheless, the purposes and effectiveness are the same. Here are sample provisions of the key provisions:

1. *Confidentiality.* Recipient shall not directly or indirectly disclose, disseminate, publish, or use for its business advantage or for any other purpose, at any time during or after the term of this Agreement, any information received from Creator deemed confidential by the other party ("Confidential Information") without the express written permission of Creator for a period of five (5) years following the date of receipt of the Confidential Information.

a. *Definitions.* For purposes of this Agreement, Confidential Information shall be defined as any information not generally known in the industry about Creator's ideas, concepts, products, designs, intellectual property, trade secrets, services, or any combination thereof, whether or not such information would be recognized as proprietary absent this Agreement, including but not limited to information related to the Property developed by Creator.

b. *Limitations.* Notwithstanding any other provision of this Agreement, Recipient shall not be liable for disclosing, disseminating, publishing or using information which (i) was already known prior to the receipt of the Confidential Information; (ii) is now or becomes public information through no wrongful act of the Recipient; (iii) is independently developed or acquired by Recipient without any use of the Confidential Information in such development; or (iv) is required to be disclosed by law.

2. *Documents and Materials.* The documents and materials of Creator (including but not limited to all scripts, scenarios, treatments, data, reports, projections, records, notes, lists, specifications and designs) are furnished in accordance of this Agreement and shall remain the sole property of Creator. This information (collectively known as "Evaluation Material") shall upon the termination of this Agreement be promptly returned to Creator, including all copies thereof, which are in the possession or control of Recipient, its agents, and its representatives.

Problem 1-C

You have spoken with an acquaintance, Angel, an investor, who might be willing to finance a multimedia project for an up-and-coming talent like Bryce. Angel is a classic "angel" investor, someone who is willing to invest in high-risk entertainment projects because the investor believes in developing new talent and enjoys the vicarious thrill of participating. Neither you nor your firm provides legal representation to Angel.

Bryce remains quite concerned that the project's concept will be stolen, if not by Angel directly, then by someone with whom Angel shares the information. Can a contract be drafted that accommodates Bryce's concerns and does not discourage Angel from learning more about the project? Since Angel considers dozens of potential projects for each one that receives any funds, any agreement must be sufficiently narrow that it does not unduly burden Angel. Identify the primary terms of such an agreement and how you would accommodate the needs of both Bryce and Angel. Also consider what issues, if any, are raised by your role in introducing Bryce to Angel.

Entertainment industries must greatly control the access to potential projects in order to avoid claims of access to copyrighted material. Unsolicited materials are returned unread. Only agents or lawyers are permitted to submit materials. Contracts explicitly waiving the right for compensation are sometimes required. These steps are necessary to protect the creators of copyrighted works from claims of copyright infringement, breach of contract, and theft of ideas.

D. Bibliography and Links

Treatises to Be Used throughout the Course

Alexander Lindey & Michael Landau, Lindey on Entertainment, Publishing and the Arts (West) (looseleaf).

David Nimmer & Melville Nimmer, Nimmer on Copyright (Matthew Bender) (looseleaf).

Law Review Articles for Chapter I

Samantha Barbas, *How the Movies Became Speech*, 64 Rutgers L. Rev. 665 (2012).

Benjamin R. Barber, *Free Speech and Community: The Market as Censor: Freedom of Expression in a World of Consumer Totalism*, 29 Ariz. St. L.J. 501 (1997) (discussing the contextualized meaning of entertainment media and First Amendment principles).

Clay Calvert & Robert D. Richards, *Mediated Images of Violence and the First Amendment: From Video Games to the Evening News*, 57 Me. L. Rev. 91 (2005).

Michael Coblenz, *Not for Entertainment Only: Fair Use and Fiction as Social Commentary*, 16 UCLA Ent. L. Rev. 265 (2009).

Robert C. Denicola, *The New Law of Ideas*, 28 Harv. J.L. & Tech. 195 (2014).

Christine Haight Farley, *Judging Art*, 79 Tul. L. Rev. 805 (2005).

Jon M. Garon, *The Heart of the Deal: Intellectual Property Aspects in the Law & Business of Entertainment*, 17 J. Int. Prop. L. 443 (2012).

William O. Knox, *The Role of Novelty in a California Idea Submission Case*, 11 UCLA Ent. L. Rev. 27 (2004).

Glen L. Kulik, *Copyright Preemption: Is This the End of Desny v. Wilder?*, 21 Loy. L.A. Ent. L.J. 1 (2000).

Joseph P. Liu, *The New Public Domain*, 2013 U. Ill. L. Rev. 1395 (2013).

Gary Myers, *Trademarks & the First Amendment After Matal v. Tam* 26 J. Intell. Prop. L. 67 (2019).

David Nimmer, *The Moral Imperative Against Academic Plagiarism (Without a Moral Right Against Reverse Passing Off)*, 54 DePaul L. Rev. 1 (2004).

Lisa P. Ramsey, *Free Speech Challenges to Trademark Law After Matal v. Tam*, 56 Hous. L. Rev. 401 (2018).

Frederick Schauer, *Harm(s) and the First Amendment*, 2011 S. Ct. Rev. 81 (2011).

Rebecca Tushnet, *Copyright as a Model for Free Speech Law: What Copyright has in Common with Anti-Pornography Laws, Campaign Finance Reform, and Telecommunications Regulation*, 42 B.C. L. Rev. 1 (2000).

Rebecca Tushnet, *Performance Anxiety: Copyright Embodied and Disembodied,* 60 J. Copyright Socy. U.S.A. 209 (2013).

Daniel E. Wanat, *Entertainment Law: An Analysis of Judicial Decision-Making in Cases where a Celebrity's Publicity Right is in Conflict with a User's First Amendment Right,* 67 Alb. L. Rev. 251 (2003).

Mary W. S. Wong, *Toward an Alternative Normative Framework for Copyright: From Private Property to Human Rights,* 26 Cardozo Arts & Ent. L.J. 775 (2009).

Websites

ABANetwork Forum on Ent. & Sports Ind., www.abanet.org/forums/entsports/home.html

Hollywood Reporter, www.hollywoodreporter.com/

Los Angeles Times — Entertainment Business, www.latimes.com/business/custom/cotown/

Loyola of Los Angeles Entertainment Law Journal, https://digitalcommons.lmu.edu/elr/

United States Copyright Office, www.copyright.gov

United States Federal Communications Commission, www.fcc.gov

United States Patent and Trademark Office, www.uspto.gov

Variety, http://variety.com/

Chapter 2

Copyright for Entertainment Law

A. Overview

Copyright Protection

from *Jon M. Garon, Pop Culture Business Handbook for Cons and Festivals*[1]

While the First Amendment is designed to protect all speakers, the constitutional right to copyright protection is designed to protect authors and creators of literary works. By providing these authors, inventors, and artists exclusive protection over their works, they invest their time and effort, expanding the scope of human knowledge and the breadth of our arts, literature, and culture. These values have received significant criticism in the past two decades and sometimes conflict with the technological benefits of easy access to content and information, but they are essential to maintain a vibrant society.

A. Copyright Attributes — Authorship, Scope, Duration, and Formalities

At its heart, copyright protects authors and artists by granting them a strong property interest in their works. The Copyright Office provides a helpful working definition of copyright as follows:

> [Copyright is a] form of protection provided by the laws of the United States for "original works of authorship" including literary, dramatic, musical, architectural, cartographic, choreographic, pantomimic, pictorial, graphic, sculptural, and audiovisual creations. "Copyright" literally means the right to copy, but has come to mean that body of exclusive rights granted by law to copyright owners for protection of their work.[2]

This summary captures three essential aspects of copyright: the role of the author and other owners in creating the work; the range or scope of the copyright; and the steps needed to secure and protect the copyright.

---

1. (2017 Manegiare Publications) (reproduced with permission).

2. 17 U.S.C. § 101 (2012) (U.S. Copyright Definitions are also available at http://www.copyright.gov/help/faq/definitions.html).

i. Authorship, Including Joint Authors

The term "author" is not actually defined in the Copyright Act. Instead, court decisions help explain that the author for copyright purposes is the person who created the work. In most instances, authorship is self-evident. A novelist is the author of her novel, the playwright is the author of his play, the graphic artist who wrote and illustrated her comic book is the author of that comic book, and the musician who composed the music and wrote the lyrics to a song is the author of the song.

In certain situations, one person may be the author and the person assisting is not credited as an author. For example, the film director is generally the author of the movie. Although the cinematographer helps choose camera and lighting angles, these tasks are done under the supervision and control of the director. Since the director has control over the subordinate staff, she remains the author for purposes of copyright. Similarly, a sculptor who has help in creating a mold and pouring bronze for a large sculpture remains the sole author of that work and no other parties are recognized as authors of that sculpture.

In other situations, the law does recognize joint authors. A work by co-authors is "a work prepared by two or more authors with the intention that their contributions be merged into inseparable or interdependent parts of a unitary whole."[3] In many circuits, there is an express requirement that each of the contributions can itself be protected by copyright. Using the examples above, a team comprised of a composer and lyricist would be joint authors provided they wrote with the intention that the finished songs be interdependent parts of a single song.

In contrast, ten different musicians each writing one song for an album would not likely be joint authors because the songs can be singles as well as part of the album. The album will be considered a compilation of songs rather than a unitary work. Short story authors in a magazine are part of a compilation, not joint authors in a larger, unified publication.

If the contributions can be part of a unified or interdependent work, then the law will recognize the authors as joint authors if there is evidence establishing that the authors intended this result. If instead, the authors intended that their works remain separate, then their intent will govern as well. A written agreement is the most effective way to demonstrate this intent. In the absence of a signed, written agreement, intent can be inferred from the authors' conduct and less formal correspondence.

While there is no legal requirement that their understanding be put into a signed agreement, it is a very good idea to do so. Without an agreement, memories and events often change the parties' recollection about their intent at the time the work was created. An agreement can also explain whether the authors intend to have equal interests regarding the authority over the copyright and the revenue from the new work or whether they plan to vary their ownership because their contributions or reputations require a different split.

---

3. 17 U.S.C. § 101.

There is one additional form of authorship that affects many works used in the creative industries as well as in business more generally. This third category of authorship is known as "work for hire." An employer will be the author of "work for hire" if the work is made by an employee within the scope of that employee's employment. For example, the software written by the employees of a software company vests directly in the employer rather than in the hundreds of employees contributing to that software. Most of the comic books created during the post-war period were made as works for hire because the artists and authors fell within the definition of work for hire at that time.

A second category of work for hire also is recognized by the Copyright Act. When a purchaser chooses to contract with the creators of a work as a "specially commissioned work," then the purchaser will be treated like the employer, and earn the legal designation as the author of the work. Two conditions must be met. First, the commissioned work must fall into one of nine narrow categories of works that include motion pictures, translations, and collective works.[4] Second, the work will only be treated as a specially commissioned work for hire if both parties expressly agree to those conditions in a signed writing.

ii. Scope of Copyright

The Copyright Act provides a list for the categories of works covered by copyright:

(a) Copyright protection subsists ... in original works of authorship fixed in any tangible medium of expression, now known or later developed.... Works of authorship include the following categories:

(1) literary works;

(2) musical works, including any accompanying words;

(3) dramatic works, including any accompanying music;

(4) pantomimes and choreographic works;

(5) pictorial, graphic, and sculptural works;

(6) motion pictures and other audiovisual works;

---

4. 17 U.S.C. §101
A "work made for hire" is—
(1) a work prepared by an employee within the scope of his or her employment; or
(2) a work specially ordered or commissioned for use as a contribution to a collective work, as a part of a motion picture or other audiovisual work, as a translation, as a supplementary work, as a compilation, as an instructional text, as a test, as answer material for a test, or as an atlas, if the parties expressly agree in a written instrument signed by them that the work shall be considered a work made for hire. For the purpose of the foregoing sentence, a "supplementary work" is a work prepared for publication as a secondary adjunct to a work by another author for the purpose of introducing, concluding, illustrating, explaining, revising, commenting upon, or assisting in the use of the other work, such as forewords, afterwords, pictorial illustrations, maps, charts, tables, editorial notes, musical arrangements, answer material for tests, bibliographies, appendixes, and indexes, and an "instructional text" is a literary, pictorial, or graphic work prepared for publication and with the purpose of use in systematic instructional activities.

(7) sound recordings; and

(8) architectural works.[5]

The categories of copyright protection are broadly defined. For example, software is protected by copyright under the category of literary works. Before the law was amended to include motion pictures, films were still covered as compilations of pictorial works.

The more important aspect of the definition are the two limitations on the categories of protected works. First, the work must be "fixed in a tangible form," meaning that the work must be written or recorded in some permanent manner. Notation systems work for music and choreography. Taping a live lecture will provide the fixation for the content of the lecture. Without some form of authorized fixation, however, the work will be outside the scope of copyright.

Second, copyright has limits. It only protects specific expression rather than ideas. It does not protect the facts or information behind the information, so no author can stop another from using a procedure or discovery using copyright. The functional aspects of a copyrighted work are excluded from copyright protection. There is no protection for "any idea, procedure, process, system, method of operation, concept, principle, or discovery, regardless of the form in which it is described, explained, illustrated, or embodied in such work."[6] Patent law may apply in some of these situations, but copyright is not available. The law makes this limitation very specific and both the Copyright Office and the courts enforce this distinction aggressively.

Although less clear from the law, the Copyright Office rules and court opinions also exclude "names, titles, short phrases, slogans, familiar symbols, mere variations of typographic ornamentation, lettering, coloring, and listings of contents or ingredients."[7] In some cases, these are excluded because there is not enough original authorship upon which to base copyright protection, in other cases, the rule is essentially historical in origin. For example, most street clothes are not protected by copyright because clothes are functional. In contrast, costumes are protected by copyright to the extent they go beyond typical clothing. Animal costumes, superhero costumes, and similar works are created for their aesthetic value rather than to wear to the grocery store, so these works will typically be protectable by copyright.

iii. Securing and Protecting the Copyright

Under the modern copyright law, the protection of copyright begins as soon as a work is fixed in a tangible form. Merely saving to a computer file or snapping a photograph is sufficient to make a copyright-protected work. At that point, the work is fully protected by copyright, or "copyrighted." (Note that the term is not "copywritten.") A work does not need to be published in order to have protection. Similarly,

---

5. 17 U.S.C. § 102.

6. 17 U.S.C. § 102.

7. 17 U.S.C. § 101 (U.S. Copyright Definitions are also available at http://www.copyright.gov/help/faq/definitions.html).

there is no need to register any work with the Copyright Office. Still, there are three primary advantages to registration. First, copyright registration is generally required before a person can bring an infringement action in court. Second, the registration provides some evidence regarding the sufficiency of the copyrighted work. And third, there is a broader range of remedies available to the successful owner of a copyrighted work if the work was registered prior to the infringement.[8]

When a person files a registration with the Copyright Office, the person must upload or mail the work being registered. Often, this version of the work is not the published version of the work. Separate from the opportunity to register the work is the legal obligation to provide the Library of Congress with two copies of the published edition of the work.

If a dispute arises regarding the content that was protected by copyright, the material deposited with the Copyright Office should be available to establish this record. As an alternative, the Writers Guild of America West (https://www.wgawregistry.org/) has long maintained a legal system for registering a copy of the work in a secure manner that serves to prove precisely what content had been created by the owner at the time of the WGAW deposit. This is a very cost-effective and practical service that provides great benefit, particularly for those who are distributing unpublished manuscripts for possible comment or purchase.

B. Copyright Ownership, Transfer, and Termination

i. Ownership

Copyright initially vests in the author of the work as the owner of the copyright. If there are two or more joint authors, then the joint authors are co-owners of the copyright. On the other hand, if the copyright was created as a work for hire, then the employer is the initial owner of the copyright and treated as the exclusive author of the work.

The copyright owner is free to use the copyright or to transfer the copyright interests in whole or in part. In practice, this means that the rights in the copyright can be separated along a number of different lines.

ii. Transfers

First, transfers of copyright can be for very narrow aspects of the copyright. For example, the owner of the copyright in a comic book could license the reproduction and distribution rights of the comic to a comic book publisher and separately license the adaptation right to a motion picture company to make a film version of the comic book. That same author could separate the rights, so that a book publishing company is sold the rights to make a non-graphic novel out of the comic book story. The paperback book rights could be sold separately for English language publications, French publications, Spanish publications, and every other language. Each of the licensees

---

8. Circular 50, Copyright Registration for Musical Compositions, Copyright Office, https://www.copyright.gov/circs/circ50.pdf.

would have the right to reproduce and distribute its particular market of the work, and none of the licensees would have permission to compete in the other markets.

Similarly, the exclusive rights may be licensed for specific periods of time. A theater company may have the exclusive right to stage a play for six months. After that time, the owner of the play can license the exclusive right to stage that play to another company. Copyright interests can also be separated by geographic territory, at the country-by-country level or even by markets within the United States.

Generally speaking, licenses are for a set duration that is shorter than the life of the copyright. In contrast, if the entire copyright is transferred, then that would be called an assignment of the copyright because no rights are retained by the original copyright owner.

Secondly, transfers of the copyright may be either exclusive or non-exclusive. An exclusive transfer must be evidenced with a writing signed by the transferring party. The new owner has the power to enforce the copyright by bringing a court action to stop infringement or any other power that was held by the original copyright owners so long as the enforcement falls within the scope of the exclusive license.

A non-exclusive license is less formal than an exclusive license and provides much less authority to the licensee. The non-exclusive license gives the licensee permission to use the work in the manner specified by the owner, but not the right to stop anyone else from using the work.... Similarly, when a play publisher licenses public performance rights in a play to high schools and community theaters, they license them on a non-exclusive basis so that in any given year there might be hundreds of productions of that play across the country. Unless there is an express agreement to make a copyright license exclusive, the license will be considered non-exclusive.

A non-exclusive license can be established by a signed writing, by an oral agreement, or just by the conduct between the parties.... Nonetheless, it is always the best practice to get permission to use another's copyright in writing in order to avoid disputes in the future.

iii. Term and Termination

For works created after January 1, 1978, the copyright generally lasts for the life of the author plus 70 years. In the case of joint authors, the term is 70 years from the date of the last-surviving author's death. "In the case of an anonymous work, a pseudonymous work, or a work made for hire, the copyright endures for a term of 95 years from the year of its first publication, or a term of 120 years from the year of its creation, whichever expires first."[9]

For works created before January 1, 1978, the length of the copyright term is much harder to calculate. Works published in the United States prior to January 1, 1923, are in the public domain. Public domain works have no copyright protection and can be used for any purpose. Similarly, works that were published prior to January

9. 17 U.S.C. § 302(c).

1, 1978, without copyright notice and copyright registration are typically in the public domain. When looking at a particular work, however, it is important to realize that there may have been multiple versions published. Merely finding one version without the notice does not mean that the work has lost its copyright protection. Each such use must be investigated carefully.

Any work published after January 1, 1923, and before January 1, 1964, has a term of 95 years from the date of the work's publication, provided the copyright in the work was renewed with the Copyright Office in the 28th year of the copyright. An untold number of movies, songs, books, comics, and other works were not renewed and are available in the public domain. One must be careful, however, not to rely just on the dates.

Many works were not actually "published" as that term was defined under the Copyright Act.[10] For example, a public performance of a work does not result in publishing that work. Given that the public exhibition of a film or play is a public performance rather than a publication of the work, even a widely distributed show will not have been published under the 1909 Copyright Act. In contrast, if the works were sold as DVDs or published scripts to the public, then the offers for sale would have triggered publication. Since the duty to renew a work does not apply to unpublished works, the implications of the 1909 definition of publication continue to matter for the protection of some works. The point is really that copyright is not as simple as it would appear.

For works created after January 1, 1978, there is no longer any obligation to renew. To keep the structure of a two-term copyright, however, the law now allows for the original authors to terminate certain grants after 35 years. For the works which are not made as work for hire, the Copyright Act provides the original author a right to terminate licenses and assignments. The termination period runs from after the 35th year for a period of five years following the date of the license or assignment for most works.[11] The mechanics of this law are quite technical and even experienced lawyers are struggling to follow the complex language and mechanical hoops in the law. For authors who created works that continue to have lasting value 35 years later, this has become a very generous reward under the law.

C. Copyright's Limits, Including Fair Use

There are many limitations on the exclusive rights of copyright holders. Just as owners of real estate must give easements to public utilities and be subject to zoning and other use restrictions, intellectual property rights owners are subject to certain limitations over their exclusive rights in their works. These rules seek to balance the

---

10. 17 U.S.C. §9 (1909) (superseded)
    SEC. 9. That any person entitled thereto by this Act may secure copyright for his work by publication thereof with the notice of copyright required by this Act; and such notice shall be affixed to each copy thereof published or offered for sale in the United States by authority of the copyright proprietor....
11. 17 U.S.C. §203.

needs of the copyright holder to control the use of the work and to earn revenue from the effort with the public need to interact with the works in a common sense fashion.

i. The Range of Copyright Limitations

Copyright provides the exclusive rights to the owner of the copyrighted work, but the exclusive rights are subject to many statutory and other limitations. Sections 107–122 of the Copyright Act list a myriad of limitations that restrict the exclusive rights of the copyright owner. Here are just a few:

- The "first sale doctrine," which gives the owner of a particular copy of a work the right to resell, give-away, burn, or otherwise dispose of that copy, with some limits as the rule applies to digital files, music, and software.
- Rights for libraries and archives to make back-up and restoration copies.
- Rights of musicians to make cover recordings of previously released songs by paying a statutory license.
- Rights to use certain materials in the classroom without needing a license.
- Rights of religious organizations to perform music without needing a license.
- Rights of charities to perform certain works without needing a license when done without charge.
- Rights of software owners to make back-up copies.
- Rights of small stores and restaurants to rebroadcast radio and television without obtaining a public performance license.

ii. Fair Use

The single most well-known and most powerful exception to copyright is the concept of fair use.[12] Fair use is a highly flexible and constantly shifting doctrine. Initially developed by the courts and later codified in the Copyright Act, fair use rules tend to fall into two broad categories: consumer fair use and creative fair use. In the consumer fair use category, fair use provides consumers a greater latitude in what they do with the copies of the works to which they have access or they have purchased. In the category of creative fair use, the rule promotes commentary, criticism, parody, and cultural references essential as part of the general creative process.

The distinction between consumer fair use and creative fair use is not based on any law or specific case. It serves as a useful framework, however, to understand the context for these two rather distinct groups of cases, and explains a great deal about how fair use has evolved in the past thirty years.

The Supreme Court embraced the concept of consumer fair use in the famous "Betamax" case of *Sony Corp. v. Universal City Studios*,[13] where the decision embraced the concept that a consumer who had a lawful right to watch a television show must

---

12. 17 U.S.C. § 107.
13. Sony Corp. of America v. Universal City Studios, Inc., 464 U.S. 417 (1984).

also have the ability to "time-shift" that show to temporary videocassette recording for later play-back and then erasure. Although the consumer was making a copy without permission, the consumer was assumed to be doing it for the temporary purpose of watching at a more convenient time.

The concept of time shifting later extended to "space-shifting," so that a consumer who owned a copy of a song could move that song from a CD onto their portable music player without being required to purchase a second copy of the song.

The expansion of the digital economy has made this consumer exception increasingly important, and it has begun to extend well beyond its earlier origins. For example, without an exemption, making a back-up copy of software or data would require a separate license for each back-up copy. The law, instead, provides that a single back-up copy is permitted. Generally accepted practice suggests utilizing multiple back-up copies of all critical software and data, so the practice has created an exception to the interpretation of the law.

Increasingly, fair use decisions that once permitted consumers to make broader use of their technology are now permitting companies such as Google to make these conveniences on behalf of the public. Google's ability to scan millions of books into its database and then show large snippets of those works on its search results was permitted because of the significant consumer benefit derived from the database. The decision to label Google's conduct fair use focused on the consumer use of the database rather than the massive scope of the unauthorized copying.

Creative fair use is the older and more complex version of the rule. The cases often pit one creative artist against another and one publisher against another publisher. Since every quote or close paraphrase relies on fair use, authors and other creative artists rely on fair use regularly. Most of these situations are taken for granted, but in other cases the line between fair use and copyright infringement is harder to determine.

As the Copyright Act explains, "the fair use of a copyrighted work ... for purposes such as criticism, comment, news reporting, teaching (including multiple copies for classroom use), scholarship, or research, is not an infringement of copyright."[14] This general statement is then interpreted through a broad, four-factor test that looks at the following:

- the purpose and character to which the work was used by the unauthorized user;
- the nature of the work, meaning the extent to which the work was a highly creative work or a more narrowly-protected factual work;
- the quantitative and qualitative amount of the work taken; and
- most importantly, the effect on the actual or potential marketplace for the work used without authorization.[15]

---

14. 17 U.S.C. § 107.

15. 17 U.S.C. § 107. *Pop Culture Business Handbook for Cons and Festivals* provides a paraphrase of the four factors from the actual test, which are: (1) the purpose and character of the use, including

When analyzing the first factor, the Supreme Court has explained that the purpose to which the unauthorized user is making of the work has two different dimensions. One meaning of this question is the extent to which the unauthorized use is a commercial one, as contrasted with an educational use or a use for comment and criticism. The second meaning is the extent to which the use is transformative, making something substantially new or different than that made by the copyright owner. These are hard questions to answer and the determination is often subjective in close calls.

The second factor regarding the nature of the work is much simpler. Copyright gives very thin protection to works that are highly factual, since copyright does not protect the facts and instead only protects the expression about the facts. Highly expressive works are granted more fulsome copyright protection, so the nature of the copyright owner's work will impact the scope of the protection.

The third factor goes to the amount actually taken. The court decisions often recite that a person relying on fair use should take no more than is necessary to achieve the purpose of the copying, such as comment, criticism or parody. A book review can include short passages to illustrate the review, but it cannot copy whole chapters because copying on such a grand scale is not needed for the review. In the consumer setting, copying whole works is permitted, but in the creative fair use context, this is much less common and generally permitted only where the work is too small to be subdivided.

The fourth factor focuses on the effect on the market for the original work. If the unauthorized copy can replace the copyright owner's work in the marketplace, then that market should be left to the original owner. On the other hand, if the unauthorized use does not provide a substitute, then there is little actual harm in letting the second person build upon the work of the first author. This same rule works, with a bit more interpretation, for the potential market as well. An unauthorized adaptation of an author's novel into a movie does not directly substitute for the novel, but the opportunity to adapt the book into the novel is an expected part of the adaptation right of the original author, so an unauthorized movie of this kind would be an infringement of the potential market. This is a very pragmatic analysis of the harm caused by the fair use, so this factor often has the most sway. If the use causes harm, it probably should not be allowed. If there is no harm in the copying, then the court is much less likely to stop it.

In practice, most fair use cases are not as difficult as the court opinions suggest. This makes sense, because only the most difficult cases need to go to trial. Using passages from published books to write reviews is fair use. Showing short clips from movies to provide movie reviews is fair use. Showing the entire movie is not fair use, even if the person exhibiting the movie then provides an extensive critique.

---

whether such use is of a commercial nature or is for nonprofit educational purposes; (2) the nature of the copyrighted work; (3) the amount and substantiality of the portion used in relation to the copyrighted work as a whole; and (4) the effect of the use upon the potential market for or value of the copyrighted work.

Reproducing copyright protected artwork on T-shirts, mugs, and posters is not fair use. Changing the medium to a lunchbox or other commercial product does not transform the work. But a comic book mash-up of characters from various literary works could be a fair use, provided the amount taken from any work was kept to a reasonable amount (which may be somewhat more than the minimum necessary to achieve the purpose of the new work).

It is worth noting, however, that many commercial parodies and mash-ups do not rely on fair use. Instead, permission is sought in advance. The reason for this is quite practical—the legal costs to defend fair use can be very high, so the safer choice is to get a license. This is particularly true for commercial projects that tend to have a high visibility. Highly visible commercial projects also tend to have a greater marketplace impact, so the fourth factor is less helpful to the author seeking to utilize fair use.

. . .

Notes and Questions

a. Treatment of work for hire reflects general United States agency concepts that work done for an employer belongs to that employer, making the employer the statutory author of the work. The status of authorship is higher than that of mere owner. Ownership under copyright as a work for hire changes the term of the copyright and eliminates the reversionary rights otherwise incorporated into assignments of copyright as a matter of law. Where the employer is a corporation (or other non-natural person), this makes complete sense. The life-plus-seventy term of copyright is inapplicable to a corporation which has a perpetual existence, and since the corporation can only act through its employee-agents, its assertion of copyright can only exist through either an assignment of copyright by its employees or a legal assumption that a transfer has occurred.

b. Although there are two different categories of work for hire, the use of the same term for both species of work for hire often leads to undue confusion. To be considered work for hire in the traditional employment setting, the employee must be within the employ of the employer and providing services within the general scope of that employee's employment. While the Supreme Court in *Community for Creative Non-Violence v. Reid*, 490 U.S. 730 (1989), required that traditional agency factors be reviewed, most cases turn on more narrow employment criteria such as the tax and benefit status of the person. A corporate employer is hard-pressed to treat a person as an independent contractor for tax purposes while claiming employment status for copyright purposes. *See Aymes v. Bonelli*, 980 F.2d 857, 863 (2d Cir. 1992) ("[E]very case since *Reid* that has applied the test has found the hired party to be an independent contractor where the hiring party failed to extend benefits or pay social security taxes."). *See also Hi-Tech Video Prods. v. Capital Cities/ABC*, 58 F.3d 1093 (6th Cir. 1995) (invalidating the copyright in the plaintiff's video because the registration as a work for hire was incorrect and invalid). In addition to the creator of the work being an employee based on agency principles, the employee's work must fall within the scope of the person's employment. Under this requirement, all the reports, brochures, or other written material a person normally creates at work will be covered under the work for hire doctrine, vesting the copyright in the employer. A novel written after hours would not be made within the scope of the person's employment and not owned by the employer.

Questions arise if the expressive works are created in unique situations. Would photographs taken on behalf of the company be work for hire, if the photographer had never been asked to take pictures at any other time and the subject matter of the photographs was unrelated to the employee's normal duties?

Academic employees creating syllabi, tests, and teaching materials fit within the general definition of work for hire, while scholarly writings and creative projects relevant to faculty tenure but not under economic control of their home institutions may be outside the scope of an academic employee's work product. To what extent is this distinction consistent with *Reid* and the definition in § 101? Regardless of the answer, the default rule provided by the work for hire doctrine can be varied by the parties, so academic employees generally look to faculty handbooks and collective bargaining agreements for the particular terms of their employment.

c. The second category of work for hire regards specially commissioned works. For this category, the work must both fall within one of the nine categories listed in the statute[16] and be evidenced by a writing signed by both parties. This writing requirement is the most stringent required under copyright law.

The nine enumerated categories are also significant in the context of the music industry. Sound recordings were briefly added to the enumerated categories as a technical amendment, but when the musicians' unions and others learned of the change, Congress not only retreated from the position, but also eliminated the amendment retroactively. This is a strong indication that sound recordings should not be treated as falling within the work for hire subject matter for specially commissioned works. Nonetheless, audiovisual works are within the nine categories, and the expansion of digital media makes it increasingly easy to integrate images and other audiovisual content into what the consumer considers to be music. As a result, some sound recordings still fall within the definition.

d. Regardless of the work for hire definition, other problems remain — particularly for specially commissioned works. Outside the United States, the concept of works for hire is generally rejected. As a result, contractual provisions providing for such results may be declared void. To avoid this result, contracting parties should incorporate assignment of copyright language as an alternative to work for hire language

16. 17 U.S.C. § 101 provides that a work for hire includes "a work specially ordered or commissioned for use as a contribution to a collective work, as a part of a motion picture or other audiovisual work, as a translation, as a supplementary work, as a compilation, as an instructional text, as a test, as answer material for a test, or as an atlas, if the parties expressly agree in a written instrument signed by them that the work shall be considered a work made for hire."

as a matter of course. This may also avoid many of the interpretative problems by further evidencing the intent of the parties.

e. In recent years, the rights of authors to terminate prior licenses and grants have taken on financial significance as these rights begin to vest. Section 203 of the Copyright Act governs transfers made on or after January 1, 1978, while §304(c) governs those transfers made prior to that date. In addition, §304(d) governs grants made of a copyright's final twenty year lifespan in cases where other termination provisions were not exercised. The implications of these sections are only now being explored by the courts. *See Baldwin v. EMI Feist Catalog, Inc.*, 805 F.3d 18 (2d Cir. 2015) (Under the 1976 Copyright Act, while further grant, or agreement to make further grant, of any right covered by terminated grant is valid only if it is made after effective date of the termination; under the "existing-grantee exception," an agreement for further grant may be made between the author or his statutory heirs and the original grantee after the notice of termination has been served).

f. For works transferred after Jan. 1, 1978, §203 of the Copyright Act governs. "Termination of the grant may be effected at any time during a period of five years beginning at the end of thirty-five years from the date of execution of the grant; or, if the grant covers the right of publication of the work, the period begins at the end of thirty-five years from the date of publication of the work under the grant or at the end of forty years from the date of execution of the grant, whichever term ends earlier." 17 U.S.C. §203(a)(3). The party terminating the grant must provide at least two years (nor more than ten years) notice. For example, the rights to publish a novel sold in 1978 may be terminated beginning in 2013. Notices successfully terminating such grants are now being enforced.

Problem 2-A

Bryce has been approached by St. James Corporation, a privately owned insurance company, to produce a training program (known in the business as an "industrial") to introduce corporate employees to the issues dealing with client privacy. The industrial is to be used in a variety of media, primarily through video tutorials and self-run computer-based simulations. St. James is interested in producing an industrial video of approximately twenty minutes in length, a computer simulation using text and streaming video content, and a written manual. St. James will provide the primary manual content and the most important talking points for the industrial video and computer simulation. Bryce has been asked to write a script, produce and direct the video, produce the computer simulation, and incorporate music already written by Bryce for the opening and ending credits.

You are assigned the task of writing the deal memorandum and agreement between Bryce and St. James. St. James insists that the work be treated as a work for hire to the "greatest extent allowed by law," and that it "retain the rights to modify the material or update it from time to time, as needed." Bryce is willing to part with ownership and control, but insists on "credit in all the materials, the right to use copies as examples of prior work, and the retention of copyright in all music used in the work."

Outline the key terms of the understanding (leaving blanks for delivery date and payment details). Identify other possible provisions that might be needed in such an agreement.

B. Comparison between Works—Ideas & Abstractions

Nichols v. Universal Pictures Co.

45 F.2d 119 (2d Cir. 1930)

L. HAND, Circuit Judge.

The plaintiff is the author of a play, "Abie's Irish Rose," which it may be assumed was properly copyrighted under section five, subdivision (d), of the Copyright Act, 17 USCA § 5(d). The defendant produced publicly a motion picture play, "The Cohens and The Kellys," which the plaintiff alleges was taken from it. As we think the defendant's play too unlike the plaintiff's to be an infringement, we may assume, arguendo, that in some details the defendant used the plaintiff's play, as will subsequently appear, though we do not so decide. It therefore becomes necessary to give an outline of the two plays.

"Abie's Irish Rose" presents a Jewish family living in prosperous circumstances in New York. The father, a widower, is in business as a merchant, in which his son and only child helps him. The boy has philandered with young women, who to his father's great disgust have always been Gentiles, for he is obsessed with a passion that his daughter-in-law shall be an orthodox Jewess. When the play opens the son, who has been courting a young Irish Catholic girl, has already married her secretly before a Protestant minister, and is concerned to soften the blow for his father, by securing a favorable impression of his bride, while concealing her faith and race. To accomplish this he introduces her to his father at his home as a Jewess, and lets it appear that he is interested in her, though he conceals the marriage. The girl somewhat reluctantly falls in with the plan; the father takes the bait, becomes infatuated with the girl, concludes that they must marry, and assumes that of course they will, if he so decides. He calls in a rabbi, and prepares for the wedding according to the Jewish rite.

Meanwhile the girl's father, also a widower, who lives in California, and is as intense in his own religious antagonism as the Jew, has been called to New York, supposing that his daughter is to marry an Irishman and a Catholic. Accompanied by a priest, he arrives at the house at the moment when the marriage is being celebrated, but too late to prevent it, and the two fathers, each infuriated by the proposed union of his child to a heretic, fall into unseemly and grotesque antics. The priest and the rabbi become friendly, exchange trite sentiments about religion, and agree that the match is good. Apparently out of abundant caution, the priest celebrates the marriage for a third time, while the girl's father is inveigled away. The second act closes with each father, still outraged, seeking to find some way by which the union, thus trebly insured, may be dissolved.

The last act takes place about a year later, the young couple having meanwhile been abjured by each father, and left to their own resources. They have had twins, a boy and a girl, but their fathers know no more than that a child has been born. At Christmas each, led by his craving to see his grandchild, goes separately to the young folks' home, where they encounter each other, each laden with gifts, one for a boy, the other for a girl. After some slapstick comedy, depending upon the insistence of each that he is right about the sex of the grandchild, they become reconciled when they learn the truth, and that each child is to bear the given name of a grandparent. The curtain falls as the fathers are exchanging amenities, and the Jew giving evidence of an abatement in the strictness of his orthodoxy.

"The Cohens and The Kellys" presents two families, Jewish and Irish, living side by side in the poorer quarters of New York in a state of perpetual enmity. The wives in both cases are still living, and share in the mutual animosity, as do two small sons, and even the respective dogs. The Jews have a daughter, the Irish a son; the Jewish father is in the clothing business; the Irishman is a policeman. The children are in love with each other, and secretly marry, apparently after the play opens. The Jew, being in great financial straits, learns from a lawyer that he has fallen heir to a large fortune from a great-aunt, and moves into a great house, fitted luxuriously. Here he and his family live in vulgar ostentation, and here the Irish boy seeks out his Jewish bride, and is chased away by the angry father. The Jew then abuses the Irishman over the telephone, and both become hysterically excited. The extremity of his feelings makes the Jew sick, so that he must go to Florida for a rest, just before which the daughter discloses her marriage to her mother.

On his return the Jew finds that his daughter has borne a child; at first he suspects the lawyer, but eventually learns the truth and is overcome with anger at such a low alliance. Meanwhile, the Irish family who have been forbidden to see the grandchild, go to the Jew's house, and after a violent scene between the two fathers in which the Jew disowns his daughter, who decides to go back with her husband, the Irishman takes her back with her baby to his own poor lodgings. The lawyer, who had hoped to marry the Jew's daughter, seeing his plan foiled, tells the Jew that his fortune really belongs to the Irishman, who was also related to the dead woman, but offers to conceal his knowledge, if the Jew will share the loot. This the Jew repudiates, and, leaving the astonished lawyer, walks through the rain to his enemy's house to surrender the property. He arrives in great dejection, tells the truth, and abjectly turns to leave. A reconciliation ensues, the Irishman agreeing to share with him equally. The Jew shows some interest in his grandchild, though this is at most a minor motive in the reconciliation, and the curtain falls while the two are in their cups, the Jew insisting that in the firm name for the business, which they are to carry on jointly, his name shall stand first.

It is of course essential to any protection of literary property, whether at common-law or under the statute, that the right cannot be limited literally to the text, else a plagiarist would escape by immaterial variations. That has never been the law, but, as soon as literal appropriation ceases to be the test, the whole matter is necessarily at large, so that, as was recently well said by a distinguished judge, the decisions cannot help much in a new case. When plays are concerned, the plagiarist may excise a separate scene Then the question is whether the part so taken is "substantial," and therefore not a "fair use" of the copyrighted work; it is the same question as arises in the case of any other copyrighted work. But when the plagiarist does not take out a block in situ, but an abstract of the whole, decision is more troublesome. Upon any work, and especially upon a play, a great number of patterns of increasing generality will fit equally well, as more and more of the incident is left out. The last may perhaps be no more than the most general statement of what the play is about, and at times might consist only of its title; but there is a point in this series of abstractions where they are no longer protected, since otherwise the playwright could prevent the use of his "ideas," to which, apart from their expression, his property is never extended. Nobody has ever been able to fix that boundary, and nobody ever can. In some cases the question has been treated as though it were analogous to lifting a portion out of the copyrighted work; but the analogy is not a good one, because, though the skeleton is a part of the body, it pervades and supports the whole. In such cases we are rather concerned with the line between expression and what is expressed. As respects plays, the controversy chiefly centers upon the characters and sequence of incident, these being the substance.

We did not in *Dymow v. Bolton*, 11 F.(2d) 690, hold that a plagiarist was never liable for stealing a plot; that would have been flatly against our rulings in *Dam v. Kirk La Shelle Co.*, 175 F. 902, 41 L.R.A. (N.S.) 1002, 20 Ann. Cas. 1173, and *Stodart v. Mutual Film Co.*, 249 F. 513, affirming my decision in (D.C.) 249 F. 507; neither of which we meant to overrule. We found the plot of the second play was too different to infringe, because the most detailed pattern, common to both, eliminated so much from each that its content went into the public domain; and for this reason we said, "this mere subsection of a plot was not susceptible of copyright." But we do not doubt that two plays may correspond in plot closely enough for infringement. How far that correspondence must go is another matter. Nor need we hold that the same may not be true as to the characters, quite independently of the "plot" proper, though, as far as we know, such a case has never arisen. If Twelfth Night were copyrighted, it is quite possible that a second comer might so closely imitate Sir Toby Belch or Malvolio as to infringe, but it would not be enough that for one of his characters he cast a riotous knight who kept wassail to the discomfort of the household, or a vain and foppish steward who became amorous of his mistress. These would be no more than Shakespeare's "ideas" in the play, as little capable of monopoly as Einstein's Doctrine of Relativity, or Darwin's theory of the Origin of Species. It follows that the less developed the characters, the less they can be copyrighted; that is the penalty an author must bear for marking them too indistinctly.

In the two plays at bar we think both as to incident and character, the defendant took no more assuming that it took anything at all than the law allowed. The stories are quite different. One is of a religious zealot who insists upon his child's marrying no one outside his faith; opposed by another who is in this respect just like him, and is his foil. Their difference in race is merely an obbligato to the main theme, religion. They sink their differences through grandparental pride and affection. In the other, zealotry is wholly absent; religion does not even appear. It is true that the parents are hostile to each other in part because they differ in race; but the marriage of their son to a Jew does not apparently offend the Irish family at all, and it exacerbates the existing animosity of the Jew, principally because he has become rich, when he learns it. They are reconciled through the honesty of the Jew and the generosity of the Irishman; the grandchild has nothing whatever to do with it. The only matter common to the two is a quarrel between a Jewish and an Irish father, the marriage of their children, the birth of grandchildren and a reconciliation.

If the defendant took so much from the plaintiff, it may well have been because her amazing success seemed to prove that this was a subject of enduring popularity. Even so, granting that the plaintiff's play was wholly original, and assuming that novelty is not essential to a copyright, there is no monopoly in such a background. Though the plaintiff discovered the vein, she could not keep it to herself; so defined, the theme was too generalized an abstraction from what she wrote. It was only a part of her "ideas."

Nor does she fare better as to her characters. It is indeed scarcely credible that she should not have been aware of those stock figures, the low comedy Jew and Irishman. The defendant has not taken from her more than their prototypes have contained for many decades. If so, obviously so to generalize her copyright, would allow her to cover what was not original with her. But we need not hold this as matter of fact, much as we might be justified. Even though we take it that she devised her figures out of her brain de novo, still the defendant was within its rights.

There are but four characters common to both plays, the lovers and the fathers. The lovers are so faintly indicated as to be no more than stage properties. They are loving and fertile; that is really all that can be said of them, and anyone else is quite within his rights if he puts loving and fertile lovers in a play of his own, wherever he gets the cue. The plaintiff's Jew is quite unlike the defendant's. His obsession is his religion, on which depends such racial animosity as he has. He is affectionate, warm and patriarchal. None of these fit the defendant's Jew, who shows affection for his daughter only once, and who has none but the most superficial interest in his grandchild. He is tricky, ostentatious and vulgar, only by misfortune redeemed into honesty. Both are grotesque, extravagant and quarrelsome; both are fond of display; but these common qualities make up only a small part of their simple pictures, no more than any one might lift if he chose. The Irish fathers are even more unlike; the plaintiff's a mere symbol for religious fanaticism and patriarchal pride, scarcely a character at all. Neither quality appears in the defendant's, for while he goes to get his grandchild, it is rather out of a truculent determination not to be forbidden, than from pride in his progeny. For the rest he is only a grotesque hobbledehoy, used for low comedy of the most conventional sort, which any one might borrow, if he chanced not to know the exemplar. . . .

[T]he case confined to the actual issues; that is, whether the copyrighted work was original, and whether the defendant copied it, so far as the supposed infringement is identical.

The defendant, "the prevailing party," was entitled to a reasonable attorney's fee.

Decree affirmed.

Sheldon v. Metro-Goldwyn Pictures Corp.

81 F.2d 49 (2d Cir. 1936)

L. Hand, Circuit Judge.

The suit is to enjoin the performance of the picture play, "Letty Lynton," as an infringement of the plaintiffs' copyrighted play, "Dishonored Lady." The plaintiffs' title is conceded, so too the validity of the copyright; the only issue is infringement. The defendants say that they did not use the play in any way to produce the picture; the plaintiffs discredit this denial because of the negotiations between the parties for the purchase of rights in the play, and because the similarities between the two are too specific and detailed to have resulted from chance. The judge thought that, so far as the defendants had used the play, they had taken only what the law allowed, that is, those general themes, motives, or ideas in which there could be no copyright. Therefore he dismissed the bill.

[The detailed comparison between the public trial on which the play and novel were based and each of these works is better summarized in a later proceeding before the Supreme Court:

> Petitioners' complaint charged infringement of their play 'Dishonored Lady' by respondents' motion picture 'Letty Lynton', and sought an injunction and an accounting of profits. The Circuit Court of Appeals, reversing the District Court, found and enjoined the infringement and directed an accounting.... Petitioners' play 'Dishonored Lady' was based upon the trial in Scotland, in 1857, of Madeleine Smith for the murder of her lover,—a *cause celebre* included in the series of 'Notable British Trials' which was published in 1927. The play was copyrighted as an unpublished work in 1930, and was produced here and abroad. Respondents took the title of their motion picture 'Letty Lynton' from a novel of that name written by an English author, Mrs. Belloc Lowndes, and published in 1930. That novel was also based upon the story of Madeleine Smith and the motion picture rights were bought by respondents. There had been negotiations for the motion picture rights in petitioners' play, and the price had been fixed at $30,000, but these negotiations fell through.
>
> As the Court of Appeals found, respondents in producing the motion picture in question worked over old material; 'the general skeleton was already in the public demesne. A wanton girl kills her lover to free herself for a better match; she is brought to trial for the murder and escapes'. But not content with the mere use of that basic plot, respondents resorted to petitioners'

copyrighted play. They were not innocent offenders. From comparison and analysis, the Court of Appeals concluded that they had 'deliberately lifted the play'; their 'borrowing was a deliberate plagiarism'....

Sheldon v. Metro-Goldwyn Pictures Corp., 309 U.S. 390, 396–97 (1940).] ...

The defendants, who are engaged in producing speaking films on a very large scale in Hollywood, California, had seen the play and wished to get the rights. They found, however, an obstacle in an association of motion picture producers presided over by Mr. Will Hays, who thought the play obscene; not being able to overcome his objections, they returned the copy of the manuscript which they had had. That was in the spring of 1930, but in the autumn they induced the plaintiffs to get up a scenario, which they hoped might pass moral muster. Although this did not suit them after the plaintiffs prepared it, they must still have thought in the spring of 1931 that they could satisfy Mr. Hays, for they then procured an offer from the plaintiffs to sell their rights for $30,000. These negotiations also proved abortive because the play continued to be objectionable, and eventually they cried off on the bargain. Mrs. Lowndes' novel was suggested to Thalberg, one of the vice-presidents of the Metro-Goldwyn Company, in July, 1931, and again in the following November, and he bought the rights to it in December....

We are to remember that it makes no difference how far the play was anticipated by works in the public demesne which the plaintiffs did not use.... At times, in discussing how much of the substance of a play the copyright protects, courts have indeed used language which seems to give countenance to the notion that, if a plot were old, it could not be copyrighted. But we understand by this no more than that in its broader outline a plot is never copyrightable, for it is plain beyond peradventure that anticipation as such cannot invalidate a copyright. Borrowed the work must indeed not be, for a plagiarist is not himself *pro tanto* an "author"; but if by some magic a man who had never known it were to compose anew Keats's Ode on a Grecian Urn, he would be an "author," and, if he copyrighted it, others might not copy that poem, though they might of course copy Keats's. But though a copyright is for this reason less vulnerable than a patent, the owner's protection is more limited, for just as he is no less an "author" because others have preceded him, so another who follows him, is not a tort-feasor unless he pirates his work. If the copyrighted work is therefore original, the public demesne is important only on the issue of infringement; that is, so far as it may break the force of the inference to be drawn from likenesses between the work and the putative piracy. If the defendant has had access to other material which would have served him as well, his disclaimer becomes more plausible.

In the case at bar there are then two questions: First, whether the defendants actually used the play; second, if so, whether theirs was a "fair use." The judge did not make any finding upon the first question, as we said at the outset, because he thought the defendants were in any case justified; in this following our decision in *Nichols v. Universal Pictures Corporation*, 45 F.2d 119 (2d Cir. 1930). The plaintiffs challenge that opinion because we said that "copying" might at times be a "fair use"; but it is convenient to define such a use by saying that others may "copy" the "theme," or "ideas," or the like, of a work, though not its "expression." At any rate so long as it is clear what is meant, no harm is done. In the case at bar the distinction is not so important as usual, because so much of the play was borrowed from the story of Madeleine Smith, and the plaintiffs' originality is necessarily limited to the variants they introduced. Nevertheless, it is still true that their whole contribution may not be protected; for the defendants were entitled to use, not only all that had gone before, but even the plaintiffs' contribution itself, if they drew from it only the more general patterns; that is, if they kept clear of its "expression." We must therefore state in detail those similarities which seem to us to pass the limits of "fair use." ...

We have often decided that a play may be pirated without using the dialogue.... Were it not so, there could be no piracy of a pantomime, where there cannot be any dialogue; yet nobody would deny to pantomime the name of drama. Speech is only a small part of a dramatist's means of expression; he draws on all the arts and compounds his play from words and gestures and scenery and costume and from the very looks of the actors themselves. Again and again a play may lapse into pantomime at its most poignant and significant moments; a nod, a movement of the hand, a pause, may tell the audience more than words could tell. To be sure, not all this is always copyrighted, though there is no reason why it may not be, for those decisions do not forbid which hold that mere scenic tricks will not be protected. The play is the sequence of the confluents of all these means, bound together in an inseparable unity; it may often be most effectively pirated by leaving out the speech, for which a substitute can be found, which keeps the whole dramatic meaning. That as it appears to us is exactly what the defendants have done here; the dramatic significance of the scenes we have recited is the same, almost to the letter. True, much of the picture owes nothing to the play; some of it is plainly drawn from the novel; but that is entirely immaterial; it is enough that substantial parts were lifted; no plagiarist can excuse the wrong by showing how much of his work he did not pirate. We cannot avoid the conviction that, if the picture was not an infringement of the play, there can be none short of taking the dialogue.

The decree will be reversed and an injunction will go against the picture together with a decree for damages and an accounting. The plaintiffs will be awarded an attorney's fee in this court and in the court below, both to be fixed by the District Court upon the final decree.

Decree reversed.

Twentieth Century-Fox Film Corp. v. MCA, Inc.
715 F.2d 1327 (9th Cir. 1983)

Appellants claim that their copyrighted production of the book and motion picture "Star Wars" was infringed by appellees' production "Battlestar: Galactica." The district court granted appellees' motion for partial summary judgment. We reverse and remand.

In 1977, Twentieth Century-Fox produced and distributed the motion picture "Star Wars." The commercial success of that venture did not go unnoticed. The following year "Battlestar: Galactica" was released as both a motion picture and television series. Universal Studios, Inc., a subsidiary of MCA, Inc., produced and owned the rights to Battlestar, and ABC televised the Battlestar space saga.

In June 1978, Fox commenced this action against MCA, Universal, and ABC, alleging copyright infringement. Subsequently, Fox's amended complaint joined Lucasfilm, Ltd. as co-plaintiff, and alleged that defendants had also infringed Lucasfilm's copyright in its 1976 Star Wars book.

Defendants moved for partial summary judgment on the copyright claims. In connection with that motion, the trial judge reviewed a videotape montage of prior science fiction works, the Star Wars film and book, and a videotape of the first television episode of Battlestar. Defendants did not contest the validity of plaintiffs' Star Wars copyrights. Further, for purposes of the motion, defendants admitted access to plaintiffs' works.

The only issue raised in the motion was whether defendants' Battlestar: Galactica production was so dissimilar to plaintiffs' Star Wars works, as to both ideas and expression of those ideas, that no material issue of fact existed on the question of substantial similarity, and the question could be decided as a matter of law. The trial court granted defendants' motion for partial summary judgment. This appeal ensued.

The law relating to a grant of summary judgment is clear. Only if no genuine issue of material fact exists will the moving party be entitled to prevail as a matter of law.

On appeal, the question whether summary judgment was properly granted below is one of law. That is, this court must view the evidence and inferences therefrom in the light most favorable to the nonmoving party, herein plaintiffs-appellants Fox and Lucasfilm (collectively referred to as "Fox"). Defendants-appellees MCA, Universal and ABC (collectively referred to as "MCA") may prevail only if no genuine issue of material fact exists on the questions of substantial similarity of idea and idea expression.

After viewing the Star Wars and Battlestar motion pictures, we conclude that the films do in fact raise genuine issues of material fact as to whether only the Star Wars idea or the expression of that idea was copied. At a minimum, it is a close enough question that it should be resolved by way of a trial. We intimate no opinion whether the films are substantially similar as to either idea or expression, but state only that reasonable minds could differ on those key factual issues. Thus, a grant of summary judgment was improvident.

Appellant Fox argued in its brief that a comparison of the two works discloses at least 34 similarities. For illustrative purposes only, we list 13 of the alleged similarities:

(1) The central conflict of each story is a war between the galaxy's democratic and totalitarian forces.

(2) In Star Wars the young hero's father had been a leader of the democratic forces, and the present leader of the democratic forces is a father figure to the young hero. In Battlestar the young hero's father is a leader of the democratic forces.

(3) The leader of the democratic forces is an older man, displaying great wisdom, and symbolizing goodness and leadership, with a mysterious mystical ability to dominate a leader of the totalitarian forces.

(4) An entire planet, central to the existence of the democratic forces, is destroyed.

(5) The heroine is imprisoned by the totalitarian forces.

(6) A leading character returns to the family home to find it destroyed.

(7) The search by the totalitarians and the liberation attempt by the democratic forces are depicted in alternating sequences between the totalitarian and democratic camps.

(8) There is a romance between the hero's friend (the cynical fighter pilot) and the daughter of one of the leaders of the democratic forces.

(9) A friendly robot, who aids the democratic forces is severely injured (Star Wars) or destroyed (Battlestar) by the totalitarian forces.

(10) There is a scene in a cantina (Star Wars) or casino (Battlestar), in which musical entertainment is offered by bizarre, non-human creatures.

(11) Space vehicles, although futuristic, are made to look used and old, contrary to the stereo-typical sleek, new appearance of space age equipment.

(12) The climax consists of an attack by the democratic fighter pilots on the totalitarian headquarters.

(13) Each work ends with an awards ceremony in honor of the democratic heroes.

Since substantial similarity is usually an extremely close question of fact, summary judgment has traditionally been disfavored in copyright litigation. While that may be, we emphasize that summary judgment determinations result from close factual analyses, and are inherently peculiar to each case. Further, if Rule 56 is to be of any effect, summary judgment must be granted in certain situations.

REVERSED and REMANDED.

Gaiman v. McFarlane

360 F.3d 644 (7th Cir. 2004)

Posner, Circuit Judge.

Neil Gaiman brought suit under the Copyright Act against Todd McFarlane and corporations controlled by him that we can ignore, seeking a declaration that he (Gaiman) owns copyrights jointly with McFarlane in certain comic-book characters.... The case was tried to a jury, which brought in a verdict for Gaiman.... Gaiman and McFarlane are both celebrated figures in the world of comic books, but they play different though overlapping roles. Gaiman just writes scripts; McFarlane writes scripts too, but he also illustrates and publishes the comic books. In 1992, shortly after forming his own publishing house, McFarlane began publishing a series of comic books entitled Spawn, which at first he wrote and illustrated himself. "Spawn," more precisely

"Hellspawn," are officers in an army of the damned commanded by a devil named Malebolgia, who hopes one day to launch his army against Heaven. The leading character in the series is a man named Al Simmons, who is dead but has returned to the world of the living as a Hellspawn....

The early issues in the series were criticized for bad writing, so McFarlane decided to invite four top writers each to write the script for one issue of Spawn. One of those invited was Gaiman. He accepted the invitation and wrote the script for Spawn issue No. 9. Their contract, made in 1992, was oral. There was no mention of copyright, nor, for that matter, of how Gaiman would be compensated for his work, beyond McFarlane's assuring Gaiman that he would treat him "better than the big guys" did. The reference was to the two leading comic book publishers, Marvel Comics (not to be confused with Gaiman's company, Marvels and Miracles) and DC Comics, for which Gaiman and other writers write on a "work made for hire" basis. This means that the publishers own the copyrights on their work. § 201(b).

It might seem that when McFarlane told Gaiman that he would treat Gaiman "better than the big guys" did, he just meant he'd compensate him more generously for work made for hire. But McFarlane rightly does not argue this. Gaiman's work for him was not work made for hire. It was neither (1) work created by an employee within the scope of his employment nor (2) "a work specially ordered or commissioned for use as a contribution to a collective work, as a part of a motion picture or other audiovisual work, as a translation, as a supplementary work, as a compilation, as an instructional text, as a test, as answer material for a test, or as an atlas, if the parties expressly agree in a written instrument signed by them that the work shall be considered a work made for hire." 17 U.S.C. § 101. There was no written agreement between Gaiman and McFarlane, and Gaiman was not an employee of McFarlane....

In his script for Spawn No. 9, Gaiman introduced three new characters—Medieval Spawn (as he was later called by McFarlane—Gaiman had not named it and in the issue he is just referred to as a Spawn, with no further identifier), Angela (no last name), and Count Nicholas Cogliostro. Gaiman described, named, and wrote the dialogue for them, but McFarlane drew them. Gaiman contends that he and McFarlane are joint owners of the copyrights on the three characters by reason of their respective contributions to joint (indivisible) work. McFarlane concedes Gaiman's joint ownership of Angela, but not of the other two.... Spawn No. 9 was a huge success, selling more than a million copies. McFarlane paid Gaiman $100,000 for his work on it. Gaiman testified that this was about what he would have expected to receive from DC Comics had he written the script of Spawn No. 9 for that company as a work made for hire.

Because Angela was a big hit with Spawn's readers, McFarlane asked Gaiman to do a "mini-series" of three issues starring her, which he did. He also wrote several pages for Spawn No. 26 to form a bridge to the Angela series; because Angela hadn't appeared in Spawn Nos. 10 through 25, Gaiman was concerned that readers would not realize that Angela was an offshoot of Spawn. McFarlane paid Gaiman $3,300 for his contribution to Spawn No. 26 and more than $30,000 (the exact amount is not in the record) for the Angela series. Only one of these four issues (the second Angela) contains a copyright notice; the notice is similar to the one in Spawn No. 9....

McFarlane makes two arguments for why Gaiman does not have copyright in Medieval Spawn (the name that McFarlane settled on for Olden Days Spawn) or Cogliostro. The first is that all that Gaiman contributed was the idea for the characters, and ideas are not copyrightable, only expression is and the expression was due to McFarlane's drawing of the characters. It is true that people who contribute merely nonexpressive elements to a work are not copyright owners. As we said in *Seshadri v. Kasraian*, 130 F.3d 798, 803 (7th Cir.1997) "the assistance that a research assistant or secretary or draftsman or helpfully commenting colleague provides in the preparation of a scholarly paper does not entitle the helper to claim the status of a joint author." There has to be some original expression contributed by anyone who claims to be a co-author, and the rule (we'll consider an exception momentarily) is that his contribution must be independently copyrightable. Had someone merely remarked to McFarlane one day, "you need a medieval Spawn" or "you need an old guy to move the story forward," and McFarlane had carried it from there, and if later a copyeditor had made some helpful editorial changes, neither the suggester nor the editor would be a joint owner. Otherwise almost every expressive work would be a jointly authored work, and copyright would explode.

But where two or more people set out to create a character jointly in such mixed media as comic books and motion pictures and succeed in creating a copyrightable character, it would be paradoxical if though the result of their joint labors had more than enough originality and creativity to be copyrightable, no one could claim copyright. That would be peeling the onion until it disappeared. The decisions that say, rightly in the generality of cases, that each contributor to a joint work must make a contribution that if it stood alone would be copyrightable weren't thinking of the case in which it couldn't stand alone because of the nature of the particular creative process that had produced it.

McFarlane's second argument against the copyrightability of Medieval Spawn and Cogliostro appeals to the confusingly named doctrine of "scènes à faire" (literally "scenes for action," a theatrical term meaning the climactic scene in a play or opera, which is not the legal meaning). Related to the fundamental idea-expression dichotomy that we've already mentioned, the doctrine teaches that "a copyright owner can't prove infringement by pointing to features of his work that are found in the defendant's work as well but that are so rudimentary, commonplace, standard, or unavoidable that they do not serve to distinguish one work within a class of works from another." If standard features could be used to prove infringement, not only would there be great confusion because it would be hard to know whether the alleged infringer had copied the feature from a copyrighted work or from the public domain, but the net of liability would be cast too wide; authors would find it impossible to write without obtaining a myriad of copyright permissions.... If a drunken old bum were a copyrightable character, so would be a drunken suburban housewife, a gesticulating

Frenchman, a fire-breathing dragon, a talking cat, a Prussian officer who wears a monocle and clicks his heels, a masked magician, and, in Learned Hand's memorable paraphrase of Twelfth Night, "a riotous knight who kept wassail to the discomfort of the household, or a vain and foppish steward who became amorous of his mistress." It would be difficult to write successful works of fiction without negotiating for dozens or hundreds of copyright licenses, even though such stereotyped characters are the products not of the creative imagination but of simple observation of the human comedy.

McFarlane argues that even as dolled up by the penciler, the inker, and the colorist, Cogliostro is too commonplace to be copyrightable. Gaiman could not copyright a character described merely as an unexpectedly knowledgeable old wino, that is true; but that is not his claim. He claims to be the joint owner of the copyright on a character that has a specific name and a specific appearance. Cogliostro's age, obviously phony title ("Count"), what he knows and says, his name, and his faintly Mosaic facial features combine to create a distinctive character. No more is required for a character copyright. As long as the character is distinctive, other authors can use the stock character out of which it may have been built without fear (well, without too much fear) of being accused as infringers.

We are mindful that the Ninth Circuit denied copyrightability to Dashiell Hammett's famously distinctive detective character *Sam Spade* in *Warner Bros. Pictures, Inc. v. Columbia Broadcasting System, Inc.*, 216 F.2d 945 (9th Cir.1954). That decision is wrong, though perhaps understandable on the "legal realist" ground that Hammett was not claiming copyright in Sam Spade—on the contrary, he wanted to reuse his own character but to be able to do so he had to overcome Warner Brothers' claim to own the copyright. The Ninth Circuit has killed the decision, *see Olson v. National Broadcasting Co.*, 855 F.2d 1446, 1452 and n. 7 (9th Cir.1988); *Walt Disney Productions v. Air Pirates*, 581 F.2d 755, n. 11 (9th Cir.1978), though without the usual obsequies, but even if the decision were correct and were binding authority in this circuit, it would not rule this case. The reason is the difference between literary and graphic expression....

Although Gaiman's verbal description of Cogliostro may well have been of a stock character, once he was drawn and named and given speech he became sufficiently distinctive to be copyrightable. Gaiman's contribution may not have been copyrightable by itself, but his contribution had expressive content without which Cogliostro wouldn't have been a character at all, but merely a drawing. The expressive work that is the comic-book character Count Nicholas Cogliostro was the joint work of Gaiman and McFarlane—their contributions strike us as quite equal—and both are entitled to ownership of the copyright.

Medieval Spawn may seem to present a closer case than Cogliostro so far as copyrightability is concerned, because he has no name in Spawn No. 9. In fact he has never been named—"Medieval Spawn" is a description, not a proper name. But the Lone Ranger doesn't have a proper name either (at least not one known to most of his audience—actually he does have a proper name, John Reid), so that can't be critical. A more telling objection to copyrightability is that the identifier, "Medieval Spawn," was added by McFarlane in subsequent issues of Spawn to which Gaiman did not contribute. Only his costume and manner of speech, together with the medieval background, distinguish him in Spawn No. 9 from other Hellspawn.

But that is enough expressive content for copyrightability, because Spawn itself (the original Spawn, né Al Simmons) is not a stock character (McFarlane would have a heart attack if we said he was). Spawn is copyrightable, and the question is simply whether Medieval Spawn is sufficiently distinct from Spawn also to be copyrightable as a derivative work. The purpose of requiring that a derivative work to be copyrightable be significantly different from the copyrighted original is twofold: to avoid the confusion that would be created if two indistinguishable works were copyrighted and to prevent a copyright owner from extending his copyright beyond the statutory period by making an identical work as the statutory period was nearing its end, calling it a derivative work, and copyrighting it....

To summarize, we find no error in the district court's decision, and since the decision gave Gaiman all the relief he sought, there is no need to consider the cross-appeal.

AFFIRMED.

Notes and Questions

a. For a review of the use of parody as a defense to both literal copying, and arguably copying the total concept and feel of a work, see *Warner Bros. v. American Broad. Cos.*, 720 F.2d 231 (2d Cir. 1983) (*infra* at Section 13-C).

b. In *Gaiman v. McFarlane*, 360 F.3d 644, 659 (7th Cir. 2004), the Seventh Circuit explained one of the important concepts that limit evidence of copyright infringement. The term "scènes à faire" provides that:

> a copyright owner can't prove infringement by pointing to features of his work that are found in the defendant's work as well but that are so rudimentary, commonplace, standard, or unavoidable that they do not serve to distinguish one work within a class of works from another. (citations omitted.) If standard features could be used to prove infringement, not only would there be great confusion because it would be hard to know whether the alleged infringer had copied the feature from a copyrighted work or from the public domain, but the net of liability would be cast too wide; authors would find it impossible to write without obtaining a myriad of copyright permissions.

c. It is very difficult to find reported victories over the Hollywood studios regarding theft of screenplays, yet the fear of having a screenplay plagiarized or copied remains a prominent aspect of the screenwriter's profession. It may be that the plots, ideas, and occasionally protected expression embodied in screenplays are taken, but generally without corporate authority. When a credible claim of copyright infringement occurs, the studios are likely to enter into an agreement to satisfy the parties and to insist on confidentiality regarding that settlement. On rare occasions, however, there is a record. *See Jordan-Benel v. Universal City Studios, Inc.*, 859 F.3d 1184, 1187 (9th Cir. 2017) (asserting theft of screenplay and breach of contract in a case subsequently settled).

d. In the television context, complaints that a television premise has been stolen will come either from the general public or from insiders who regularly work on television projects. Outsiders have a challenge in establishing studio access to their work, so they typically do not fare well with their copyright infringement claims. The more important cases are those brought by television insiders—writers or other production staff who claim that a project originally developed has been credited to someone else. These cases, in turn, fall into two categories: those claims brought under a signed, express contract, and those brought under copyright infringement and an implied contract. In both cases, the issue often flows from whether the television series which ultimately airs is "based upon" the plaintiff's work or whether such work is substantially similar. If the two works are substantially similar under copyright law, then the plaintiff will win in either situation. If the work is based upon the plaintiff's work, but not similar enough to meet the substantial similarity test of copyright, then the written contract claim may survive while the copyright claim and implied contract claim will fail.

e. In *Metcalf v. Bochco*, 294 F.3d 1069 (9th Cir. 2002), Jerome and Laurie Metcalf ("the Metcalfs") sued television producer Steven Bochco over the series "City of Angels." Access was conceded because the Metcalfs had pitched the show three times to Bochco and other defendants. The Ninth Circuit allowed the plaintiffs to avoid summary judgment by analyzing the copyright claim in the sequence, order, and arrangement of the material submitted, including the *scènes à faire* and other unprotectable elements. As a result, Judge Kozinski was reluctant to ignore the similarities:

> Bochco correctly argues that copyright law protects a writer's expression of ideas, but not the ideas themselves. General plot ideas are not protected by copyright law; they remain forever the common property of artistic mankind. Nor does copyright law protect "scenes a faire," or scenes that flow naturally from unprotectable basic plot premises. Instead, protectable expression includes the specific details of an author's rendering of ideas, or the actual concrete elements that make up the total sequence of events and the relationships between the major characters. Here, the similarities proffered by the Metcalfs are not protectable when considered individually; they are either too generic or constitute "scenes a faire." One cannot copyright the idea of an idealistic young professional choosing between financial and emotional reward, or of love triangles among young professionals that eventually become strained, or of political forces interfering with private action.
>
> However, the presence of so many generic similarities and the common patterns in which they arise do help the Metcalfs satisfy the extrinsic test. The particular sequence in which an author strings a significant number of unprotectable elements can itself be a protectable element. Each note in a scale, for example, is not protectable, but a pattern of notes in a tune may

earn copyright protection. A common "pattern [that] is sufficiently concrete … warrants a finding of substantial similarity."

Id. at 1074 (citations omitted).

Against this backdrop, the decision in *Murray Hill Publ'ns, Inc. v. Twentieth Century Fox Film Corp.*, 361 F.3d 312 (6th Cir. 2003), providing for judgment as a matter of law, becomes more significant. Fox was able to convince the appellate court that it was entitled to judgment as a matter of law, denying any copyright infringement between its film *Jingle All the Way* and the screenplay entitled *Could This be Christmas.* Although Fox had the treatments to both films at the same time, the *Jingle* treatment had been completed and submitted to Fox prior to its receiving the Christmas screenplay.

The Sixth Circuit reviewed the various abstraction-filtration-comparison schemes used by the Second, Ninth and D.C. Circuits to explain why even copyrightable elements may be filtered out for comparison between the works. The court explained that "elements of a copyright defendant's work that were created prior to access to a plaintiff's work are to be filtered out at the first stage of substantial-similarity analysis," which eliminated all the common elements between *Jingle* and *Christmas.* Of the twenty-four similarities between the two scripts, eighteen were found in the *Jingle All the Way* treatment that the court determined had been completed before access to the plaintiff's script could have occurred. In what the Sixth Circuit said was an issue of first impression, it determined it should filter out those occurrences before determining substantial similarity, and it found the remaining six similarities superficial.

The necessity of filtering out a defendant's own prior material appears self-evident. Access is irrelevant for portions of a plaintiff's work that could not have been drawn from the plaintiff. The interesting question is whether any such material had existed in *Metcalf v. Bochco*, or whether all the development had occurred by plaintiffs, rather than independently but at the same time as Bocho's own production activities. As a legal standard, the Sixth Circuit's gloss that copyrightable elements of a defendant's work will be filtered out if it predates the plaintiff's work helps separate copying from common elements and will likely seep into the jurisprudence of the other circuits.

Problem 2-B

Bryce is struggling to finish the industrial video for St. James Corporation (*see* Problem 2-A, above). The concept of the project is to parallel a famous film featuring privacy issues and work that theme into the corporate setting. Bryce considered *All the President's Men,* by having an employee use corporate records to ferret out political misconduct; *Fatal Attraction,* by showing how an employee could illegally "stalk" another through the misuse of corporate records; and even *Alien,* by having the corporate records searched to prove that a client was really an android working for the company.

The executives at the St. James Corporation have raised concerns that the parallels between Bryce's suggestions and commercial films could give rise to adverse claims against the company. Bryce has called you for legal and practical advice. Specifically, St. James will allow Bryce to use such a script idea (i) if you can provide a legal opinion letter that the work is not an infringement of copyright for the motion pictures described; and (ii) if Bryce agrees to indemnify the St. James Corporation for all costs, including attorneys' fees, in the event that any third party objects to the use of the plots, characters, dialogue or ideas from any of these commercial films.

Consult with the partners in your firm to confirm whether you can provide such an opinion letter and what advice you would give to Bryce.

C. Other Uses of Copyrighted Works

Ringgold v. Black Entertainment Television, Inc.

126 F.3d 70 (2d Cir. 1997)

This appeal primarily concerns the scope of copyright protection for a poster of an artistic work that was used as set decoration for a television program. Faith Ringgold appeals from the September 24, 1996, judgment of the District Court for the Southern District of New York dismissing, on motion for summary judgment, her copyright infringement suit against Black Entertainment Television, Inc. ("BET") and Home Box Office, Inc. ("HBO"). The District Court sustained defendants' defense of fair use. We conclude that summary judgment was not warranted, and we therefore reverse and remand for further consideration of plaintiff's claim.

Faith Ringgold is a successful contemporary artist who created, and owns the copyright in, a work of art entitled "Church Picnic Story Quilt" (sometimes hereafter called "Church Picnic" or "the story quilt"). "Church Picnic" is an example of a new form of artistic expression that Ringgold has created. She calls the form a "story quilt design." These designs consist of a painting, a handwritten text, and quilting fabric, all three of which Ringgold unites to communicate parables.... Since 1988 the High Museum has held a non-exclusive license to reproduce "Church Picnic" as a poster ("'Church Picnic' poster" or "the poster"), and to sell those reproductions. The "Church Picnic" poster sells for $20.00 a copy and was not produced as a limited edition. Thousands of copies of the poster have been sold since 1988. Although the license to reproduce poster copies of "Church Picnic" has terminated, copies of the poster remain available for sale.

Below the portion of the poster that displays "Church Picnic" are several identifying words. "High Museum of Art" appears in letters 1 1/4 inches high. Below these words is the phrase "Faith Ringgold, Church Picnic Story Quilt, 1988, gift of Don and Jill Childress" in letters 1/8 inch high. Below this line, in smaller type, appears "Courtesy Bernice Steinbaum Galley, New York City. Poster 1988 High Museum of Art, Atlanta."

2. The alleged infringing use.

HBO Independent Productions, a division of HBO, produced "ROC," a television "sitcom" series concerning a middle-class African-American family living in Baltimore. Some time prior to 1992, HBO Independent Productions produced an episode of ROC in which a "Church Picnic" poster, presumably sold by the High Museum, was used as part of the set decoration.... The "Church Picnic" poster was used as a wall-hanging in the church hall....

In the scene, at least a portion of the poster is shown a total of nine times. In some of those instances, the poster is at the center of the screen, although nothing in the dialogue, action, or camera work particularly calls the viewer's attention to the poster. The nine sequences in which a portion of the poster is visible range in duration from 1.86 to 4.16 seconds. The aggregate duration of all nine sequences is 26.75 seconds....

The copy of the poster used in the episode was framed without the identifying wording that appears beneath the artwork. As framed, the poster includes a notice of copyright, but the type is too small to be discernible to a television viewer.

A broadcast television network first televised the episode in 1992, and in October 1994 BET aired the episode for the first time on cable television. In January 1995, Ringgold happened to watch the episode on BET (apparently a repeat showing), and at that time became aware of the defendants' use of the poster as part of the set decoration.

Ringgold sued the defendants, alleging infringement of her copyright in "Church Picnic Story Quilt," in violation of 17 U.S.C. § 106 (1994), because of the unauthorized use of the poster as part of the set decoration for the episode of "ROC." ... Prior to discovery, the defendants moved for summary judgment, contending (i) that they were not liable for copyright infringement, because their use of the story quilt was either *de minimis* or a fair use....

The Copyright Act grants certain exclusive rights to the owner of a copyright, including the right to make and distribute copies and derivative works based on the copyrighted work, and the right to display the copyrighted work publicly. In the absence of defenses, these exclusive rights normally give a copyright owner the right to seek royalties from others who wish to use the copyrighted work. Ringgold contends that the defendants violated this licensing right by using the "Church Picnic" poster to decorate the set of their sitcom without her authorization.

The caselaw provides little illumination concerning claims that copyright in a visual work has been infringed by including it within another visual work. The Nimmer treatise posits the problem of a motion picture in which an actor is reading a magazine of which the cover picture is observable, and acknowledges that "the answer is by no means certain." The treatise observes, with uncharacteristic ambivalence, that a fair use defense might be supported on the ground that "the entire work does not supplant the function of the plaintiff's work," yet also points out that "ordinarily" the copying of a magazine cover into another medium "will constitute infringement, and not fair use."

HBO and BET defend their use of the poster on two separate, though related grounds: (a) that their use of the poster was *de minimis*, and (b) that, as Judge Martin ruled, their use of the poster was a permissible "fair use."

I. De minimis

The *de minimis* Concept in Copyright Law.

The legal maxim "*de minimis non curat lex*" (sometimes rendered, "the law does not concern itself with trifles") insulates from liability those who cause insignificant violations of the rights of others. In the context of copyright law, the concept of *de minimis* has significance in three respects, which, though related, should be considered separately.

First, *de minimis* in the copyright context can mean what it means in most legal contexts: a technical violation of a right so trivial that the law will not impose legal consequences. Understandably, fact patterns are rarely litigated illustrating this use of the phrase, for, as Judge Leval has observed, such circumstances would usually involve "questions that never need to be answered." He offers the example of a New Yorker cartoon put up on a refrigerator.[17] In *Knickerbocker Toy Co. v. Azrak-Hamway International, Inc.*, 668 F.2d 699, 703 (2d Cir. 1982), we relied on the *de minimis* doctrine to reject a toy manufacturer's claim based on a photograph of its product in an office copy of a display card of a competitor's product where the display card was never used.

Second, *de minimis* can mean that copying has occurred to such a trivial extent as to fall below the quantitative threshold of substantial similarity, which is always a required element of actionable copying. In applying the maxim for this purpose, care must be taken to recognize that the concept of "substantial similarity" itself has unfortunately been used to mean two different things. On the one hand, it has been used as the threshold to determine the degree of similarity that suffices, once access has been shown, as indirect proof of copying; on the other hand, "substantial similarity" is more properly used, after the fact of copying has been established, as the threshold for determining that the degree of similarity suffices to demonstrate actionable infringement. Professor Latman helpfully suggested that when "substantial similarity" is used to mean the threshold for copying as a factual matter, the better term is "probative similarity," and that "substantial similarity" should mean only the threshold for actionable copying. *See* Alan Latman, *"Probative Similarity" as Proof of Copying: Toward Dispelling Some Myths in Copyright Infringement*, 90 Colum. L. Rev. 1187, 1204 (1990). The Nimmer treatise endorses and has implemented the Latman taxonomy, as has this Court.

In the pending case, there is no dispute about copying as a factual matter: the "Church Picnic" poster itself, not some poster that was similar in some respects to it, was displayed on the set of defendants' television program. What defendants dispute when they assert that their use of the poster was *de minimis* is whether the admitted copying occurred to an extent sufficient to constitute actionable copying, i.e., infringe-

---

17. Presumably, Judge Leval has in mind the posting of a photocopy of the cartoon; photocopying the cartoon, if not insulated by the doctrine *of de minimis*, or subject to some recognized defense, might violate the copyright proprietor's right to reproduce a copy of the work, *see* 17 U.S.C. § 106(1), though if the original page of the magazine was posted, the work would not have been "displayed ... publicly," *id.* § 106(5).

ment. That requires "substantial similarity" in the sense of actionable copying, and it is that sense of the phrase to which the concept of *de minimis* is relevant.

At first glance, it might seem odd to pursue an inquiry as to "substantial similarity" even after copying as a factual matter has been established. However, the superficial anomaly reflects only a lack of appreciation of the difference between factual copying and actionable copying. The former (probative similarity) requires only the fact that the infringing work copies something from the copyrighted work; the latter (substantial similarity) requires that the copying is quantitatively and qualitatively sufficient to support the legal conclusion that infringement (actionable copying) has occurred. The qualitative component concerns the copying of expression, rather than ideas, a distinction that often turns on the level of abstraction at which the works are compared. The quantitative component generally concerns the amount of the copyrighted work that is copied, a consideration that is especially pertinent to exact copying.[18] In cases involving visual works, like the pending one, the quantitative component of substantial similarity also concerns the observability of the copied work — the length of time the copied work is observable in the allegedly infringing work and such factors as focus, lighting, camera angles, and prominence. Thus, as in this case, a copyrighted work might be copied as a factual matter, yet a serious dispute might remain as to whether the copying that occurred was actionable. Since "substantial similarity," properly understood, includes a quantitative component, it becomes apparent why the concept of *de minimis* is relevant to a defendant's contention that an indisputably copied work has not been infringed.

Third, *de minimis* might be considered relevant to the defense of fair use. One of the statutory factors to be assessed in making the fair use determination is "the amount and substantiality of the portion used in relation to the copyrighted work as a whole." A defendant might contend, as the District Court concluded in this case, that the portion used was minimal and the use was so brief and indistinct as to tip the third fair use factor decisively against the plaintiff.[19]

Though the concept of *de minimis* is useful in insulating trivial types of copying from liability (the photocopied cartoon on the refrigerator) and in marking the quantitative threshold for actionable copying, the concept is an inappropriate one to be enlisted in fair use analysis. The third fair use factor concerns a quantitative continuum. Like all the fair use factors, it has no precise threshold below which the factor

---

18. The Nimmer treatise helpfully refers to exact copying of a portion of a work as "fragmented literal similarity," *see Nimmer*, § 13.03[A][2], in contrast to "comprehensive nonliteral similarity," which refers to an alleged copy that is qualitatively but not exactly similar to a copyrighted work, *id.* § 13.03[A][1]. We have endorsed that taxonomy. *See* Twin Peaks Prods., Inc. v. Publ'ns Int'l, Ltd., 996 F.2d 1366, 1372 n.1 (2d Cir. 1993); Arica Inst., Inc. v. Palmer, 970 F.2d 1067, 1073 (2d Cir. 1992).

19. Whether a use of a copyrighted work that surpasses the de minimis threshold of "substantial similarity" for purposes of actionable copying can nevertheless be de minimis for purposes of the third fair use factor is an inquiry in the class of angelic terpsichore on heads of pins. Perhaps that is why the Supreme Court has quoted approvingly Professor Latman's reference to "the partial marriage between the doctrine of fair use and the legal maxim *de minimis non curat lex.*" *See* Sony Corp. of America v. Universal Studios, Inc., 464 U.S. 417, 451 n.34, 78 L. Ed. 2d 574, 104 S. Ct. 774 (1984).

is accorded decisive significance. If the amount copied is very slight in relation to the work as a whole, the third factor might strongly favor the alleged infringer, but that will not always be the case. More important, the fair use defense involves a careful examination of many factors, often confronting courts with a perplexing task. If the allegedly infringing work makes such a quantitatively insubstantial use of the copyrighted work as to fall below the threshold required for actionable copying, it makes more sense to reject the claim on that basis and find no infringement, rather than undertake an elaborate fair use analysis in order to uphold a defense.

B. The *de minimis* Concept Applied to Defendants' Copying.

Defendants contend that the nine instances in their television program in which portions of the poster were visible, individually and in the aggregate, were *de minimis*, in the sense that the quantity of copying (or at least the quantity of observable copying) was below the threshold of actionable copying. The parties appear to agree on the durational aspects of the copying. The segments of the program in which the poster was visible to any degree lasted between 1.86 and 4.16 seconds. The aggregate duration of all nine segments was 26.75 seconds....

A helpful analogy in determining whether the purpose and duration of the segments should be regarded as de minimis is the regulation issued by the Librarian of Congress providing for royalties to be paid by public broadcasting entities for the use of published pictorial and visual works. The Librarian appoints the Register of Copyrights, who serves as the director of the Copyright Office. The Librarian's regulation distinguishes between a "featured" and a "background" display, setting a higher royalty rate for the former. Obviously the Librarian has concluded that use of a copyrighted visual work even as "background" in a television program normally requires payment of a license fee. Moreover, the Librarian has defined a "featured" display as "a full-screen or substantially full screen display for more than three seconds," and a "background" display as "any display less than full-screen or substantially full-screen, or full-screen for three seconds or less," If defendants' program were to be shown on public television, plaintiff would appear to be entitled to a "background" license fee for a "less than full-screen" display.

From the standpoint of a quantitative assessment of the segments, the principal four-to-five-second segment in which almost all of the poster is clearly visible, albeit in less than perfect focus, reenforced by the briefer segments in which smaller portions are visible, all totaling 26 to 27 seconds, are not *de minimis* copying.

Defendants further contend that the segments showing any portion of the poster are *de minimis* from the standpoint of qualitative sufficiency and therefore not actionable copying because no protectable aspects of plaintiff's expression are discernible. In defendants' view, the television viewer sees no more than "some vague stylized [sic] painting that includes black people," and can discern none of Ringgold's particular expression of her subjects. That is about like saying that a videotape of the Mona Lisa shows only a painting of a woman with a wry smile. Indeed, it seems disingenuous for the defendant HBO, whose production staff evidently thought that the poster was well suited as a set decoration for the African-American church scene of a ROC episode, now to contend that no visually significant aspect of the poster is discernible. In some circumstances, a visual work, though selected by production staff for thematic relevance, or at least for its decorative value, might ultimately be filmed at such a distance and so out of focus that a typical program viewer would not discern any decorative effect that the work of art contributes to the set. But that is not this case. The painting component of the poster is recognizable as a painting, and with sufficient observable detail for the "average lay observer," to discern African-Americans in Ringgold's colorful, virtually two-dimensional style. The *de minimis* threshold for actionable copying of protected expression has been crossed.

II. Fair Use

The District Court upheld the defendants' fair use defense after considering the four non-exclusive factors identified in 17 U.S.C. §107. Concerning the first factor—purpose and character of the use—the Court acknowledged that defendants' use was commercial, but thought this circumstance was "undercut" by the fact that the defendants did not use the poster to encourage viewers to watch the ROC episode and did not try to "exploit" Ringgold's work. The Court acknowledged that the second factor—nature of the copyrighted work—favored Ringgold in view of the imaginative nature of her artwork.

The Court considered the third factor—amount and substantiality of the portion used in relation to the entire work—to favor the defendants because the segments of the program in which the poster is visible are brief, in some only a portion is seen, and in those showing nearly all the poster, it is not in exact focus.

The Court considered the fourth factor—effect of the use upon the potential market for the work—also to favor the defendants. Noting that the television episode cannot be considered a substitute for the poster, Judge Martin predicted "little likelihood" of any adverse impact on poster sales. In addition, he observed that Ringgold did not claim that her ability to license the poster "has been negatively impacted by the defendants' use in the four years" since the episode was aired. Concluding that defendants' use "had little or no effect on Ringgold's potential market for her work," he granted summary judgment in their favor, sustaining their fair use defense.

In reviewing the grant of summary judgment, we note preliminarily that the District Court gave no explicit consideration to whether the defendants' use was within any of the categories that the preamble to section 107 identifies as illustrative of a fair use, or even whether it was similar to such categories. Though the listed categories—criticism, comment, news reporting, teaching, scholarship, and research,—have an "'illustrative and not limitative'" function, and the four factors should be considered even if a challenged use is not within any of these categories, the illustrative nature of the categories should not be ignored. As the Supreme Court's recent and significant fair use opinion in *Campbell* [v. *Acuff-Rose Music, Inc.,* 510 U.S. 569 (1994),] observes, "The enquiry [concerning the first fair use factor] may be guided by the examples given in the preamble to § 107, looking to whether the use is for criticism, or comment, or news reporting, and the like...."

First factor.

Considering the first fair use factor with the preamble illustrations as a "guide[ ],"we observe that the defendants' use of Ringgold's work to decorate the set for their television episode is not remotely similar to any of the listed categories. In no sense is the defendants' use " 'transformative.' " In *Campbell*, Justice Souter explained a "transformative" use that would tip the first factor toward a defendant:

> The central purpose of this investigation is to see, in Justice Story's words, whether the new work merely "supersedes the objects" of the original creation, or instead adds something new, with a further purpose or different character, altering the first with new expression, meaning, or message....

The defendants have used Ringgold's work for precisely a central purpose for which it was created — to be decorative. Even if the thematic significance of the poster and its relevance to the ROC episode are not discernible, the decorative effect is plainly evident. Indeed, the poster is the only decorative artwork visible in the church hall scene. Nothing that the defendants have done with the poster "supplants" the original or "adds something new." The defendants have used the poster to decorate their set to make it more attractive to television viewers precisely as a poster purchaser would use it to decorate a home.

In considering whether a visual work has been "supplanted" by its use in a movie or a television program, care must be taken not to draw too close an analogy to copying of written works. When all or a substantial portion of text that contains protectable expression is included in another work, solely to convey the original text to the reader without adding any comment or criticism, the second work may be said to have supplanted the original because a reader of the second work has little reason to buy a copy of the original. Although some books and other writings are profitably reread, their basic market is the one-time reader. By contrast, visual works are created, and sold or licensed, usually for repetitive viewing. Thus, the fact that the episode of ROC does not supplant the need or desire of a television viewer to see and appreciate the poster (or the original) again and again does not mean that the defendants' use is of a "purpose and character" that favors fair use. Indeed, unauthorized displays of a visual work might often increase viewers' desire to see the work again. Nevertheless, where, as here, the purpose of the challenged use is, at a minimum, the same decorative purpose for which the poster is sold, the defendants' use has indeed "superseded the objects" of the original, and does not favor fair use. Of course, no one would buy a videotape of the ROC episode as a substitute for the poster, but the challenged use need not supplant the original itself, only, as Justice Story said, the "objects" of the original.

It is not difficult to imagine a television program that uses a copyrighted visual work for a purpose that heavily favors fair use. If a TV news program produced a feature on Faith Ringgold and included camera shots of her story quilts, the case for a fair use defense would be extremely strong.[20] The same would be true of a news feature on the High Museum that included a shot of "Church Picnic." However, it must be recognized that visual works are created, in significant part, for their decorative value, and, just as members of the public expect to pay to obtain a painting or a poster to decorate their homes, producers of plays, films, and television programs should generally expect to pay a license fee when they conclude that a particular work of copyrighted art is an appropriate component of the decoration of a set.

The District Court's consideration of the first fair use factor was legally flawed in its failure to assess the decorative purpose for which defendants used the plaintiff's work. Instead, the Court tipped the first factor against the plaintiff because the presence of the poster was "incidental" to the scene and the defendants did not use the poster to encourage viewers to watch the ROC episode. The first point could be said of virtually all set decorations, thereby expanding fair use to permit wholesale appropriation of copyrighted art for movies and television. The second point uses a test that makes it far too easy for a defendant to invoke the fair use defense.

Second factor.

The District Court accepted the plaintiff's contention that the second fair use factor weighs in her favor because of the creative nature of her work.

Third factor.

Though we have earlier noted that the *de minimis* concept is inappropriate for a fair use analysis, since a copying that is *de minimis* incurs no liability, without the need for an elaborate fair use inquiry, the third fair use factor obliges a court to consider the amount and substantiality of the portion used, whenever that portion crosses the *de minimis* threshold for actionable copying. The District Court properly considered the brevity of the intervals in which the poster was observable and the fact that in some segments only a portion of the poster and the nearly full view was not in precise focus. Our own viewing of the episode would incline us to weight the third factor less strongly toward the defendants than did Judge Martin, but we are not the fact-finders, and the fact-finding pertinent to each fair use factor, under proper legal standards, is for the District Court, although the ultimate conclusion is a mixed question of law and fact.

Even if the third factor favors the defendants, courts considering the fair use defense in the context of visual works copied or displayed in other visual works must be careful not to permit this factor too easily to tip the aggregate fair use assessment in favor of those whom the other three factors do not favor. Otherwise, a defendant

20. We hesitate to say "conclusive" because even existing technological advances, much less those in the future, create extraordinary possibilities. For example, if the news program included a direct shot of an entire story quilt (whether original or poster reproduction), well lit and in clear focus, a viewer so inclined could tape the newscast at home, scan the tape, and with digital photographic technology, produce a full size copy of the original, thereby securing an attractive "poster"-like wall-hanging without paying the $20 poster fee. A news program that recommended this technique would be a weak candidate for fair use.

who uses a creative work in a way that does not serve any of the purposes for which the fair use defense is normally invoked and that impairs the market for licensing the work will escape liability simply by claiming only a small infringement.

Fourth factor.

The fourth fair use factor is "the effect of the use upon the potential market for or value of the copyrighted work." "It requires courts to consider not only the extent of market harm caused by the alleged infringer, but also 'whether unrestricted and widespread conduct of the sort engaged in by the defendant … would result in substantially adverse impact on the potential market for the original.'" Ringgold contends that there is a potential market for licensing her story quilts, and stated in an affidavit that in 1995 she earned $31,500 from licensing her various artworks and that she is often asked to license her work for films and television. Specifically, she avers that in 1992 she was asked to license use of the "Church Picnic" poster by the producers of another TV sitcom and declined because of an inadequate price and inadequate artist's credit.

We have recognized the danger of circularity in considering whether the loss of potential licensing revenue should weight the fourth factor in favor of a plaintiff. Since the issue is whether the copying should be compensable, the failure to receive licensing revenue cannot be determinative in the plaintiff's favor. We have endeavored to avoid the vice of circularity by considering "only traditional, reasonable, or likely to be developed markets" when considering a challenged use upon a potential market. Ringgold's affidavit clearly raises a triable issue of fact concerning a market for licensing her work as set decoration. She is not alleging simply loss of the revenue she would have earned from a compensated copying; she is alleging an "exploitation of the copyrighted material without paying the customary price."[21]

The District Court's assessment of the fourth factor in favor of the defendants was legally flawed. The Court relied primarily on the fact that the ROC episode had little likelihood of adversely affecting poster sales and that Ringgold had not claimed that her ability to license the poster had been "negatively impacted." The first consideration deserves little weight against a plaintiff alleging appropriation without payment of a customary licensing fee. The second consideration confuses lack of one item of specific damages with lack of adverse impact on a potential market. Ringgold is not required to show a decline in the number of licensing requests for the "Church Picnic" poster since the ROC episode was aired. The fourth factor will favor her if she can show a "traditional, reasonable, or likely to be developed" market for licensing her work as set decoration. Certainly "unrestricted and widespread conduct of the sort engaged in by the defendants … would result in substantially adverse impact on the potential market for [licensing of] the original." Particularly in view of what Ringgold has

---

21. The amicus curiae brief for the Artists Rights Society, Inc. and the Picasso Administration strongly indicates evidence of licensing of artistic works for film and television set decoration, evidence that plaintiff is entitled to present at trial.

averred and is prepared to prove, the record on the fourth fair use factor is inadequate to permit summary judgment for the defendants.

Conclusion

For all of these reasons, plaintiff's copyright infringement claim must be returned to the District Court to afford an opportunity for further development of the record and a sensitive aggregate assessment by the fact-finder of the fair use factors in light of the applicable legal principles....

The judgment of the District Court is reversed, and the case is remanded.

Leigh v. Warner Bros., Inc.

212 F.3d 1210 (11th Cir. 2000)

This appeal concerns the scope of a photographer's copyright and trademark rights in his work, the role of the court in determining whether images are "substantially similar" for purposes of copyright, and the power of the court to rule on dispositive motions without first allowing broad discovery. Jack Leigh took the now-famous photograph of the Bird Girl statue in Savannah's Bonaventure Cemetery that appears on the cover of the best-selling novel *Midnight in the Garden of Good and Evil*. Warner Brothers made a film version of the novel and used images of the Bird Girl both in promotional materials and in the movie itself. Leigh sued Warner Brothers, asserting that it infringed his copyright and trademark rights in the Bird Girl photograph. The district court granted summary judgment for Warner Brothers on all claims, except one that the parties now have settled, and Leigh appeals.

The district court correctly ascertained the elements of Leigh's photograph protected by copyright and determined that the Warner Brothers film sequences are not substantially similar to those protected elements. Copyright infringement is generally a question of fact for the jury to decide, however, and the court erred in holding as a matter of law that no reasonable jury could find that the Warner Brothers promotional single-frame images were substantially similar to the aspects of Leigh's work protected by copyright....

In 1993, Random House commissioned Jack Leigh to take a photograph for the cover of *Midnight in the Garden of Good and Evil* ("*Midnight*"), a novel by John Berendt. After reading a manuscript of the novel, Leigh explored appropriate settings in Savannah and ultimately selected a photograph of a sculpture in the Bonaventure Cemetery known as the Bird Girl. Sylvia Shaw Judson had sculpted the Bird Girl in 1938, and she produced three copies of the statue. The Trosdal family had purchased one of the statues and placed it in their plot at Bonaventure Cemetery. The novel does not mention the Bird Girl statue. Leigh granted Random House permission to use the photo, but retained ownership and registered his claim of copyright.

In 1997, Warner Brothers produced a movie based on *Midnight* and decided to use the Bird Girl statue on promotional materials and at the beginning and end of the movie. Because the Trosdals had removed the statue from their cemetery plot after the book's publication, Warner Brothers made a replica of the Bird Girl with the permission of Sylvia Shaw Judson's heir. The company then took photographs and film footage of the replica in a new location in Bonaventure Cemetery. Those images are the subject of this lawsuit.

Three segments of film footage depict the Bird Girl statue. One is a promotional clip, and the others appear at the beginning and end of the Warner Brothers movie. Six still images feature the Bird Girl: a promotional photograph and nearly identical picture on the "goodandevil" web site, a movie poster, a newspaper advertisement, the cover for the movie's soundtrack, and an internet icon. Leigh alleges that these images infringed his copyright and trademark rights in his Bird Girl photograph. The district court granted Warner Brothers' motion to stay all discovery, and later granted summary judgment for Warner Brothers on all claims except a copyright claim pertaining to the internet icon. The parties subsequently settled all claims pertaining to that Internet icon.

We review the district court's grant of summary judgment *de novo,* construing all evidence in the light most favorable to the non-moving party. Summary judgment is only proper when there are no genuine issues of material fact. We review the court's decision to rule on the summary judgment motion without allowing the plaintiff to complete desired discovery for abuse of discretion.

To establish a claim of copyright infringement, a plaintiff must prove, first, that he owns a valid copyright in a work and, second, that the defendant copied original elements of that work. The plaintiff can prove copying either directly or indirectly, by establishing that the defendant had access, and produced something "substantially similar," to the copyrighted work. Substantial similarity, in this sense, "exists where an average lay observer would recognize the alleged copy as having been appropriated from the copyrighted work."

"Substantial similarity" also is important in a second, more focused way. No matter how the copying is proved, the plaintiff also must establish specifically that the allegedly infringing work is substantially similar to the plaintiff's work *with regard to its protected elements.* Even in the rare case of a plaintiff with direct evidence that a defendant attempted to appropriate his original expression, there is no infringement unless the defendant succeeded to a meaningful degree.

For the purposes of its motion for summary judgment and this appeal, Warner Brothers does not contest Leigh's ownership of a valid copyright in the Bird Girl photograph. Leigh, on the other hand, takes issue both with the district court's view of the scope of his copyright and with the court's analysis of the similarities between the Bird Girl images.

Leigh's copyright does not cover the appearance of the statue itself or of Bonaventure Cemetery, for Leigh has no rights in the statue or its setting. Nor does the copyright protect the association of the statue with the *Midnight* story. Leigh may have been the first to think of the statue as evocative of the novel's mood and as an appropriate symbol of the book's themes, but copyright law protects only original expression, not ideas.

Thus, the district court correctly identified the elements of artistic craft protected by Leigh's copyright as the selection of lighting, shading, timing, angle, and film. Leigh suggests that the court also should have considered the overall combination of these protected elements as well as the mood they convey. The court determined that the "eerie," "spiritual" mood was *scenes faire,* expression commonly associated with the subject matter (cemeteries) and thus non-original and unprotectable. Leigh contests the notion that cemeteries are typically portrayed in an eerie, spiritual manner, but there is no need to determine whether *scenes faire* applies in this case.

Analyzing relatively amorphous characteristics of the picture as a whole (such as the "mood" or "combination of elements") creates a danger of unwittingly extending copyright protection to unoriginal aspects of the work. This danger is especially acute in a case such as this, in which the unprotected elements of the plaintiff's work — the haunting pose and expression of the Bird Girl and the cemetery setting — are so significant.

Although some cases have evaluated the "mood" of a work independently, in this case it is safest to focus on the more concrete elements of the photographer's craft. Even as Leigh describes it, the mood is not so much an independent aspect of his photograph protected by copyright, as the effect created by the lighting, shading, timing, angle, and film. The same holds true for the overall combination of elements in the photograph. As long as the analysis is not overly detached and technical, it can adequately address both the effect of the protected, original elements of Leigh's photograph on the viewer and the contribution of those elements to the work as a whole.

In its order granting summary judgment, the court methodically and accurately details a number of differences in the compositional elements between Leigh's photograph and the Warner Brothers images. This circuit has noted, however, that lists of similarities between works are inherently subjective and unreliable, and the same can be true of lists of distinguishing characteristics.

The court was correct to hold as a matter of law that the film sequences featuring the Bird Girl statue are not substantially similar to the protected elements of Leigh's photograph. In one sequence, the cemetery is shrouded in fog, revealing only the Bird Girl and a Celtic cross, a decoration absent from Leigh's photograph. The camera frame also crops the head of the Bird Girl statue. A second sequence is shot at least partly in color and in broad daylight. The statue's plinth is never shown, and as the camera pans up it shows only the upper portions of the statue on the left side of the screen. In the final sequence, the camera rotates around the statue, beginning with a side shot, and captures only the head and shoulders before panning back to show the Bird Girl's torso. Again, the statue is on the left side of the screen and the sequence is shot in daylight. The film sequences were not shot in the same section of the Bonaventure Cemetery as Leigh's photograph, so the surrounding gravestones and greenery are different. These film sequences have nothing substantial in common with Leigh's photograph except the statue itself.

The same cannot be said for Warner Brothers' photographic images. There are, undeniably, significant differences between the pictures. The statue is smaller and more distant in most of the Warner Brothers pictures than in Leigh's photograph, and as a result the vegetation and headstones in the foreground are more prominent. The Bird Girl is approximately the same size only on the soundtrack cover. Although both the Leigh photograph and the soundtrack cover have diffuse light that "glows" about the statue, the lighting contrast is more extreme in most of the Warner Brothers pictures, with beams of light piercing the tree canopy like spotlights. The shafts of light and surrounding shadows obscure details of the statue and the cemetery setting. Finally, Warner Brothers has added elements to some of its images that are absent from Leigh's photo: some have a green or orange tint; some prominently feature a Celtic cross and tree; and the movie poster includes pictures of the cast along its left side.

Although it may be easy to identify differences between the Warner Brothers still shots and Leigh's photograph, however, the Warner Brothers images also have much in common with the elements protected by Leigh's copyright. All of the photographs are taken from a low position, angled up slightly at the Bird Girl so that the contents of the bowls in her hands remain hidden. Hanging Spanish moss borders the tops of all the photographs except the soundtrack cover. The statue is close to centered in all of the pictures except one newspaper advertisement for the movie, which places the Bird Girl in the left third of the frame. Light shines down and envelopes the statue in all of the images, leaving the surrounding cemetery in relative darkness. All of the photographs are monochromatic.

These expressive elements all make the pictures more effective. The Spanish moss provides a top border to the images. The location of the statue and the lighting in the pictures together draw the viewer's attention. The lighting also lends a spiritual air to the Bird Girl. Finally, by keeping the contents of the Bird Girl's bowls hidden, the angle contributes to the mystery and symbolic meaning of the images.

A jury ultimately may conclude that the similarities between the protected elements of the Leigh photograph and the Warner Brothers still shots are not "substantial." The similarities are significant enough, however, to preclude summary judgment. "Substantial similarity" is a question of fact, and summary judgment is only appropriate if no reasonable jury could differ in weighing the evidence....

We AFFIRM the grant of summary judgment for the Defendant on Leigh's trademark claims and the copyright claim as it relates to the film sequences. We REVERSE the grant of summary judgment for the Defendant on Leigh's copyright claim as it relates to Warner Brothers' single-frame images, and we REMAND for proceedings consistent with this decision.

Notes and Questions

a. One of the most significant factors of fair use is the effect unauthorized use has on the marketplace for the plaintiff's work. The more the use supplants or replaces the existing or potential market for plaintiff's work, the more likely the court is to find the defendant's activities objectionable. A fine example of this is *Campbell v. Acuff-Rose Music, Inc.*, 510 U.S. 569 (1994), where 2 Live Crew not only generated significant mechanical royalties for Roy Orbison, but put those royalties in trust so that Orbison could have dropped his objection and earned the market rate for his songs. By putting the funds in trust, the band moved itself from the category of marketplace infringers to that of First Amendment champions, taking the ethical high ground in the dispute. Applying this to *Ringgold*, to what extent did the preexisting system of compensating the copyright holders of television decorations weigh on the court in determining that the use of the poster was not a fair use based on the nature of the broadcast?

b. Copyrighted works often appear in many public arenas that we take for granted. Does a motion picture producer need a license if a character wears a t-shirt with copyrighted artwork on the front or back? Does a television entertainment program have the same obligation? Does a network news program have the same obligation? If not, where under copyright law can one defend different results based on the nature of the broadcast?

c. The use of another's copyright can interfere with that work's economic value in two very different ways. As recognized by § 107, the use can replace the original work in the marketplace—stealing the economic opportunity. The second form of economic interference occurs when the defendant's work destroys the perceived value of the plaintiff's work. A vicious but accurate review of a book may quote the plaintiff's work extensively for the purpose of criticizing every aspect of it. The result may be to reduce sales substantially, but this economic destruction does not supplant the original work in the marketplace and, therefore, should not be considered when weighing the fair use factors. In fact, the more the criticism impacts the market, the more likely the criticism is a fair use, as provided by the Section 107 preamble and the history of fair use litigation.

d. In *Dr. Seuss Enters., L.P. v. ComicMix L.L.C.*, 372 F. Supp. 3d 1101 (S.D. Cal. 2019), the court found that a satirical use of the Dr. Seuss book "Oh, The Places You'll Go!" with the Star Trek inspired work, "Oh, the Places You'll Boldly Go!" constituted fair use. The court first found the defendant's work to be a transformative use of the Dr. Seuss book. But because "Oh, The Places You'll Go!" is such a popular graduation present, there remained a question regarding the fourth fair use factor regarding the impact on the market. The court, however, used the finding on the transformative nature of the first fair use factor to shift the burden of persuasion on the fourth factor:

> [I]f the Court concludes that Boldly is transformative, the burden is on Plaintiff to demonstrate a likelihood of future market harm. Not only must Plaintiff introduce evidence of substantial harm to it, but Plaintiff must make this showing by a preponderance of the evidence. Given that this factor is often treated as the single most important element of fair use, the parties hotly contest the inferences that can be drawn from the developed record. Plaintiff, on the one hand, contends that Boldly was intended to compete with, and thus supplant, Go! in the market for graduation gifts, and, given the enduring popularity of Star Trek over the last 50 years, it is reasonable to assume that some prospective Go! buyers would instead buy Boldly because

the purchaser or the gift recipient is a Star Trek fan.... Defendants, on the other hand, counter that Plaintiff shows only that it has a market for its works, not that Boldly would affect that market....

Even viewing the undisputed evidence most favorably to Plaintiff, the Court concludes that Plaintiff has failed to sustain its burden to demonstrate by a preponderance of the evidence that Boldly is likely substantially to harm the market for Go! or licensed derivatives of Go! Instead, the potential harm to Plaintiff's market remains hypothetical. (Internal quotations and citations omitted.)

e. Architectural works pose unique problems. Architectural designs for building designs enjoy copyright protection under § 106, but those rights are significantly limited under § 120. Under the limitation, "[t]he copyright in an architectural work that has been constructed does not include the right to prevent the making, distributing, or public display of pictures, paintings, photographs, or other pictorial representations of the work...." Despite the limitation, building owners and copyright holders sometimes try to extend their property interests into the copyright of the building or the building's silhouette as a trademark for goods or services. *See Leicester v. Warner Bros.*, 232 F.3d 1212 (9th Cir. 2000).

f. Although not an absolute barrier to copyright infringement, authors of factual works have a much narrower interest in their writings than those of fictional writers. Filmmakers, television producers, musicians, and others may freely research the ideas published by other authors. One interesting conflict arises when creative theories are published as fact: do these speculative works receive the broader protection of fiction or the narrower protection of fact? *See Nash v. CBS, Inc.*, 899 F.2d 1537 (7th Cir. 1990).

g. Filmmakers are often challenged to "clear" or obtain copyright releases for all objects that might be filmed in the background of a scene. Such copyrighted materials include not only artwork on walls, but also more useful objects, such as t-shirts, product labels, and objects with copyrighted images or graphics incorporated into their design. In *Gottlieb Dev. L.L.C. v. Paramount Pictures Corp.*, 590 F. Supp. 2d 625 (S.D.N.Y. 2008), the court found brief glimpses of copyrighted designs in a pinball machine to be *de minimis* as a matter of law.

h. Clearance continues to be a challenge for content producers, particularly those making documentary projects. It is also a significant issue for those involved in online video production and collaborative authorship. The Center for Media & Social Media, a project of American University's School of Communication, has provided a wealth of best practices materials to assist both lawyers and creative artists.

i. Other decisions challenge the notion that every use of an image must be licensed outside of a non-documentary context, though the risks of litigation are present even if the use is *de minimis* or fair use. *See SOFA Entm't, Inc. v. Dodger Prods.*, 709 F.3d 1273 (9th Cir. 2013), regarding a short television clip from the Ed Sullivan show in a theatrical production, and *Seltzer v. Green Day, Inc.*, 725 F.3d 1170 (9th Cir. 2013), regarding the use of an image on a music concert video screen.

Problem 2-C

In preparing the St. James Corporation industrial and computer program, Bryce planned to do a great deal of filming of the exterior and interior of the St. James corporate headquarters. The St. James headquarters was designed and constructed in 1995; a commissioned statue stands in the front of the building; and a number of famous modern and classical paintings adorn the halls.

Bryce needs information on the type of location permission required. While St. James intends to use the industrial video and computer simulation exclusively for its own employees, a provision of the production agreement states that Bryce has "obtained all necessary copyright and other clearances to complete the work." St. James has not granted any copyright permission to Bryce, nor does it claim copyright in any of the artwork or sculptures. Advise Bryce on how to proceed. If additional permission is needed to film some or all of the art, identify from whom such permission should be obtained and what should be included in the written release.

D. Scope of Contractually Acquired Rights

Welles v. Turner Entm't Co.

503 F.3d 728 (9th Cir. 2007)

GOULD, Circuit Judge.

Beatrice Welles, the daughter of screenwriter, filmmaker, and actor Orson Welles, filed suit against Turner Entertainment Co., Entertainment Acquisition Co., and other persons not parties to this appeal (collectively, "the defendants"), seeking a declaratory judgment that Beatrice Welles owns the copyright and home video rights to the motion picture *Citizen Kane* and seeking an accounting of the royalties she alleges she is owed from the profits of the motion picture. The district court granted summary judgment for the defendants. Because there are triable issues of fact, we vacate in part and remand.

Several separate contracts between Orson Welles, Mercury Productions, Inc. (a production company owned by Orson Welles), and RKO Radio Pictures, Inc. are integral to this case. On July 22, 1939, Orson Welles, Mercury, and RKO signed two agreements. The first agreement, between Mercury and RKO (the "Production Agreement"), provided that "[RKO] hereby engages [Mercury] to produce, direct and write the screenplay for the two (2) motion pictures hereinafter described, which are herein referred to as 'the Pictures.'"

Section 13 of the Production Agreement determines who owns the fruits of the RKO–Mercury Production Agreement. That section begins:

> [RKO] shall own the negative and positive prints of each of the Pictures and all rights of every kind and nature in and to each Picture, and all parts thereof and all material, tangible and intangible, used therein, as soon as such rights

come into existence, including, but not being limited to, the exclusive rights of distribution, exploitation, manufacture, recordation, broadcasting, televising (other than in connection with the advertising or exploitation of a commercial product or service), and reproduction by any art or method, and the literary, dramatic, musical and other works included in such Picture.... [Mercury] agrees that it will have no interest of any kind in either of the Pictures, except as in this agreement expressly provided.

Section 13 concludes with what the parties call the "original story" provision. The provision states:

In case of any original story written by [Mercury] or any of its employees and used as the basis of either Picture, however, [RKO] shall acquire the motion picture and television rights in such story for such Picture only. [RKO] shall not remake any such Picture unless [Mercury] produces or directs the same or unless [RKO] buys the remake rights from [Mercury] at a price satisfactory to both parties. [Mercury] shall own the publication, radio, dramatic and other rights in any such story but shall not use the same in any way to compete with or injure the distribution of the Picture based on such story.

The second agreement entered into on July 22, 1939, between Orson Welles and RKO (the "Actor Agreement"), provided that Orson Welles would play the leading male role in the two motion pictures produced pursuant to the Production Agreement and that Orson Welles would receive compensation of $30,000 plus a percentage of the net profits of the two motion pictures.... RKO released *Citizen Kane* on May 1, 1941. By December 15, 1944, *Citizen Kane* had not turned a profit, the second film produced under the Production Agreement, entitled *It's All True,* was not finished, and production had not commenced on the third film described in the supplemental agreement. To end their business relationship, Mercury, Orson Welles, and RKO entered into an agreement that terminated the Production and Actor Agreements and their amendments (the "Exit Agreement").

Signed on December 15, 1944, the Exit Agreement first outlined the prior agreements between the parties. It then stated:

All fixed compensation payable to Mercury or Welles for services in connection with the first two motion pictures has been paid in full. Welles under the agreements of the parties is entitled, as contingent compensation, to twenty per cent (20%) of the net profits of the first two pictures as a unit. No net profits resulted from the sale and distribution of the first picture produced under the title "CITIZEN KANE", and accordingly Welles is entitled to no contingent compensation.

It is now the mutual desire of the parties to terminate and cancel each and all of the existing agreements between [RKO] and Mercury and between [RKO] and Welles, and to mutually release and discharge each party to each of said agreements from all rights, duties, liabilities and obligations thereunder and from all claims, demands and causes of action of every kind and nature of each party as against the other party.

The Exit Agreement also gave Orson Welles the option to purchase from RKO for $200,000 all of the film recorded for It's All True.

Beatrice Welles first argues that there is a genuine issue of material fact about who owns the right to distribute Citizen Kane on home video.... Her complaint sought a declaration that she "alone owns all publication, radio, dramatic, home video and other rights in the story of Citizen Kane" and "that Mercury did not grant to RKO any right to exploit through home video devices sold to the public, the story of *Citizen Kane* as expressed in the screenplay and as embodied in the motion picture produced by Mercury of the same name." *Citizen Kane* was an "original story" written by Mercury. Thus, whether RKO or Beatrice Welles owns the home video rights to *Citizen Kane* turns on an interpretation of Section 13 of the Production Agreement.

In interpreting the Production Agreement, we first determine whether its language is ambiguous or reasonably susceptible to more than one interpretation. If the language is unambiguous, we give effect to its plain meaning. If the language is ambiguous, or susceptible to more than one reasonable interpretation, we may consider extrinsic evidence in interpreting the agreement. The interpretation of a contract is a question of law that we may decide unless the interpretation depends on the credibility of extrinsic evidence, in which case the interpretation of the contract is the task of the factfinder.

To display publicly or distribute *Citizen Kane,* the defendants need two rights: First, the defendants need the right to display the motion picture. Second, because a motion picture is derived from its underlying screenplay, the defendants need the right to exploit the screenplay.

In this case, the first paragraph of Section 13 deals with the first right the defendants need to distribute *Citizen Kane* on home video — the right to display the motion picture. Section 13 gives RKO "all rights of every kind and nature.... including, but not being limited to, the exclusive rights of distribution, exploitation, manufacture, recordation.... and reproduction by any art or method" in the motion pictures produced under the Production Agreement. This tells us that, as a general matter, the defendants, as successors to RKO, have the right to exploit in any manner the motion pictures produced pursuant to the Production Agreement, including *Citizen Kane.*

However, to distribute *Citizen Kane* on home video, the defendants still need the right to exploit the screenplay from which the *Citizen Kane* motion picture was derived. The original story provision deals with this issue. As noted above, the provision states that Mercury retained the rights to any screenplay written by Mercury or its employees. So, in order to allow RKO to display motion pictures derived from those screenplays, the Production Agreement provided RKO with certain rights in the "original stories" on which those motion pictures were based. Specifically, RKO acquired "the motion picture and television rights in such stor[ies] for such Picture[s] only," and Mercury reserved ownership of "the publication, radio, dramatic and other rights" in those original stories.

Thus, the question before us is whether the defendants' "motion picture and television" rights in the *Citizen Kane* screenplay encompass the right to distribute the *Citizen Kane* screenplay on home video. On one hand, a reasonable argument can be made that distributing a motion picture on home video is simply an exploitation of the defendants' "motion picture" rights in the *Citizen Kane* screenplay. On the other hand, such a broad interpretation would render the additional grant of "television rights" to the defendants superfluous because if "motion picture" rights encompassed home video rights, "motion picture" rights could also be argued to encompass the right to display *Citizen Kane* on television. Thus, it seems to us unclear whether the parties would have intended RKO's motion picture and television rights in the *Citizen Kane* screenplay to include the right to exploit the *Citizen Kane* screenplay in home video form.

We dealt with a similar situation in *Cohen v. Paramount Pictures Corp.*, 845 F.2d 851 (9th Cir.1988). In that case, in 1969, a composer granted a license to the producer of a motion picture to use the composer's copyrighted music "for: (a) The exhibition of said motion picture.... to audiences in motion picture theatres and other places of public entertainment where motion pictures are customarily exhibited" and "(b) The exhibition of said motion picture.... by means of television...., including 'pay television', 'subscription television' and 'closed circuit into homes' television." The license reserved to the composer "all rights and uses in and to said musical composition, except those herein granted to the Licensee." The district court had granted summary judgment to the producer, concluding that the license's grant of the right to exhibit the picture "by means of television" included the right to distribute the picture on home video, but we reversed. We emphasized that "VCRs for home use were not invented or known in 1969, when the license was executed" and noted the dissimilarities between display of a motion picture on television and distribution of a motion picture on home video, and we also pointed out that the license did not directly address which party owned the right to exploit music in media that had not yet been invented.

This case is similar to *Cohen*. Home video was not invented when the parties signed the Production Agreement in 1939, the right to distribute *Citizen Kane* on home video is quite different from the right to display *Citizen Kane* on television, and the Production Agreement does not specify who owns the right to exploit original story screenplays in media that had not been invented in 1939. Perhaps most importantly, the rights RKO acquired by license in the *Citizen Kane* screenplay were quite narrow, encompassing only motion picture and television rights, just as the producer in *Cohen* obtained the right to use the composer's music only in theaters and on television. Mercury, on the other hand, retained broad rights in the screenplay: publication, radio, and residual "other rights," just as the composer in *Cohen* retained "all rights" not granted to the producer. Had Mercury granted RKO sweeping rights in the screenplay and only retained minimal rights for itself, we might be able to distinguish *Cohen* and conclude that, had RKO and Mercury thought about the matter of home video rights, they would have vested those rights in RKO. But, in light of the narrow scope of rights granted to RKO and the broad reservation of rights by Mercury, we cannot conclude with certainty that the parties would have given RKO home video rights had they contemplated the issue. We hold that the contract is ambiguous regarding which party owns the right to exploit the *Citizen Kane* screenplay on home video.

In so holding, we do not adopt a presumption against applying a grant of rights in "motion pictures" to new technologies. Instead, we simply interpret the written contract of the parties in this case, as our precedent instructs. *See also Boosey & Hawkes Music Publishers v. Walt Disney Co.,* 145 F.3d 481, 487 (2d Cir.1998) (holding that "new-use analysis should rely on neutral principles of contract interpretation" and that "the language of the contract" governs).

In some cases, a contract might permit the licensee to exploit the work in a new medium without a future technologies clause. For example, in *Maljack Productions,* [*Inc. v. GoodTimes Home Video Corp.,* 81 F.3d 881 (9th Cir. 1996),] we held that a licensee obtained the right to exploit certain music in a motion picture in a new medium when the license had no future technologies clause but granted the licensee "any and all worldwide rights under copyright and otherwise.... to the music and musical composition recorded or contained upon the sound track of the Picture." However, in this case, the Production Agreement, in addition to having no future technologies clause, granted RKO only motion picture and television rights in the *Citizen Kane* screenplay while granting Mercury broad, residual rights in the screenplay. It is thus not clear to us to whom the parties would have intended to grant the right to exploit the screenplay in new mediums.

Because we cannot discern, from the Production Agreement alone, what the parties in this case would have agreed upon had they known that some day *Citizen Kane* would be distributed on home video, we turn to extrinsic evidence to aid our interpretation of the contract.... We vacate the district court's summary judgment on Beatrice Welles's claim for profit participation and remand the claim for further proceedings.

Notes and Questions

a. The New York courts continue to struggle to interpret older contracts and the language used to address new technologies. In *Popovich v. Sony Music Ent., Inc.,* 508 F.3d 348, 357–58 (6th Cir. 2007), the court analyzed whether Sony owed a contractual duty to include the logo of a music producer on works it released for the artist Meatloaf, including "Bat Out of Hell," on Internet downloads.

> Popovich appeals the district court's decision on summary judgment finding that the 1998 Agreement unambiguously did not cover internet downloads. The district court held that the language "manufactured by Sony Music after September 1, 1998" precludes items not "manufactured" by Sony. In the words of the district court, "while Sony 'manufactures' albums, CDs, and cassettes, asserting that Sony 'manufactures' Internet downloads or streaming audio requires a liberal interpretation of 'manufacture.' Such an

interpretation is simply too great a stretch for this court to conclude that there is ambiguity in the language."

Popovich contends that the "all forms and configurations" language was intended to cover future music formats such as internet downloads, and the "manufactured by Sony Music after September 1, 1998" language merely provides Sony a grace period to comply with its obligations.

The relevant question for this Court is whether the sentence "all forms and configurations ... manufactured by Sony" includes internet downloads. Neither party has cited to, nor have we been able to find, a case holding that internet downloads may be "manufactured." As the district court noted, had the parties included the words "distributed by," the agreement would have lent itself to the interpretation that internet downloads were meant to be included in the logo obligation. As a result, we do not believe the district court erred in its holding that it is an unreasonable interpretation of the language of the agreement to conclude it covers internet downloads.

Popovich raises the doctrine of "new use" in his appeal. According to Popovich, New York courts have held that where one party wants contractual language governing a work's distribution to be broadly construed to govern use in a new medium, and the other party attempts to limit the application of the agreement, the burden of excluding the right to the new use will rest with the party attempting to limit the application, in his case, Sony. The Second Circuit applied the new-use doctrine in *Boosey & Hawkes Music Publishers, Ltd. v. Walt Disney Co.,* 145 F.3d 481, 486–87 (2d Cir.1998). In doing so, the court stated that the words of the contract govern, and a court should not favor one party over the other. "If the contract is more reasonably read to convey one meaning, the party benefitted by that reading should be able to rely on it; the party seeking exception or deviation from the meaning reasonably conveyed by the words of the contract should bear the burden of negotiating for language that would express the limitation or deviation. This principle favors neither licensors nor licensees. It follows simply from the words of the contract." The New York Court of Appeals affirmed the Second Circuit's reasoning in *Greenfield v. Philles Records, Inc.,* 98 N.Y.2d 562, 750 N.Y.S.2d 565, 780 N.E.2d 166, 171–72 (2002). The New York court held that the reasonable interpretation of the contract governs.

It is important to remember that the new-use doctrine has only been applied in the licensing arena and has not been applied to the factual situation in the present case. Regardless, taking into account the new-use doctrine's requirement that the language of the contract must be more reasonably read to include the new-use being proposed—here, internet downloads—the language "all forms and configurations ... manufactured by Sony" is not more reasonably read to include internet downloads than to exclude internet downloads.

Popovich v. Sony Music Ent., Inc., 508 F.3d 348, 357–58 (6th Cir. 2007).

b. In *Boosey & Hawkes Music Publ'rs., Ltd. v. Walt Disney Co.,* the Second Circuit dismisses the importance of two specific clauses, a "future technologies clause" and a "reservation clause." 145 F.3d 481 (2d Cir. 1998). Notwithstanding the court's comment, these clauses can have an important impact. First, an express grant for "all uses now known or hereafter created" leaves no ambiguity that nothing was retained by the grantor and can readily be enforced. *See Platinum Record Co. v. Lucasfilm, Ltd.,* 566 F. Supp. 226 (D.N.J. 1983). In the alternative, a statement that licenses only expressly listed uses similarly eliminates any ambiguities.

c. Given today's rapid technological changes, the parties could also agree to limit the exploitation of a work to those media from which revenues of not less than $10,000 were generated during the first five years of the license. This rather awkward concept essentially provides that from the date of the license, a set time period will begin to run during which either the grantee will exploit the work in that market or lose that market. Markets not yet existing and markets existing but not exploited would both lapse and those rights would vest in the licensor.

d. As noted in *Welles v. Turner Ent. Co.,* there are two discrete grant clauses in each agreement for the use of an underlying work. 503 F.3d 728 (9th Cir. 2007). The first right needed is the right to exploit the work, meaning the right to adapt, derive, and modify the licensed material. The second is the right to reproduce, distribute, display, and perform the work in various media. For example, a novel may be licensed to be adapted into a motion picture. A license which provides that the motion picture may be performed in any media may fail to provide the rights to adapt the novel into a stage play, television production, or video game. *See Goodis v. United Artists Television, Inc.,* 425 F.2d 397, 403 (2d Cir. 1970). Occasionally this may be the intent of the parties; more often it is the failure to anticipate the sheer length of time and change of circumstance that the license agreements must regulate.

e. What is the meaning of the following Lucasfilm music synchronization clause for the film *American Graffiti*?

> Subject to our performance of the terms and conditions herein contained, you agree that we have the right to record, dub and synchronize the above mentioned master recordings, or portions thereof, into and with our motion picture and trailers therefor, and to exhibit, distribute, exploit, market and perform said motion picture, its air, screen and television trailers, perpetually throughout the world by any means or methods now or hereafter known.

Platinum Record Co. v. Lucasfilm, Ltd., 566 F. Supp. 226, 227 (D.N.J. 1983). Does the scope of the license apply to the use of the songs in any media, the exploitation of the motion picture—including the songs—in any media, both, or neither? In what way could the language be improved?

f. At other times, the problem of licensing translates into enforcement of the simplest of contract provisions—payment for services rendered. Courts require copyright provisions to be enforced, however, and will not rely on informal industry practice to modify the statute. *See Effects Assoc., Inc. v. Cohen*, 908 F.2d 555 (9th Cir. 1990) (interpreting the transfer of a special effect for the motion picture *The Stuff*).

g. As the technology for publishing continues to change, the struggle to control reprints and print-on-demand continues. When publishing giant Simon & Schuster attempted to sweep the board by retaining all rights in their published works regardless of level of prints sold, the Authors Guild stepped in to fight a public relations war so the authors could continue the practice of retaining their out-of-print or out-of-mind works. *See* Motoko Rich, *Publisher and Authors Parse a Term: Out of Print*, N.Y. Times, May 18, 2007, at C3.[22]

h. The Supreme Court decision in *eBay, Inc. v. MercExchange, L.L.C.*, 547 U.S. 388 (2006), has been extended to copyright decisions, requiring that irreparable injury may not be presumed for copyright infringement actions. In *Salinger v. Colting*, 607 F.3d 68, 78 (2d Cir. 2010), the court explained "that the Supreme Court did not view patent and copyright injunctions as different in kind, or as requiring different standards." As a result, it reversed and remanded the grant of a preliminary injunction involving the unauthorized sequel to J.D. Salinger's *Catcher in the Rye*.

> [P]laintiffs must show that, on the facts of their case, the failure to issue an injunction would actually cause irreparable harm.... But as the Supreme Court has suggested, a copyright holder might also have a First Amendment interest in *not* speaking. The defendant to a copyright suit likewise has a property interest in his or her work to the extent that work does not infringe the plaintiff's copyright. And a defendant also has a core First Amendment interest in the freedom to express him or herself, so long as that expression does not infringe the plaintiff's copyright.... Harm might be irremediable, or irreparable, for many reasons, including that a loss is difficult to replace or difficult to measure, or that it is a loss that one should not be expected to suffer.... After *eBay*, however, courts must not simply presume irreparable harm.

Id.

Problem 2-D

As author of the musical compositions and sound recordings that will be incorporated into the industrial film and computer program being completed for the St. James Corporation, Bryce has learned to carefully document all transactions. Bryce has asked you to draft a non-exclusive license agreement that provides St. James with the rights needed for the completion of the project, but which will ensure Bryce retains as much ownership and control of the musical compositions and sound recordings as possible. On the expectation that St. James will demand a much broader grant of rights, also prepare a much more inclusive license from Bryce to St. James that will still allow Bryce to retain ownership of the musical works and sound recordings, while limiting St. James' use of the music to that of the project.

---

22. Available at https://www.nytimes.com/2007/05/18/books/18books.html?searchResultPosition=1.

E. Bibliography and Links

Gregory Duhl, *Old Lyrics, Knock-Offs Videos, and Copycat Comic Books: The Fourth Fair Use Factor in U.S. Copyright Law*, 54 Syracuse L. Rev. 665 (2004).

Barbara Friedman, *From Deontology to Dialogue: The Cultural Consequences of Copyright*, 13 Cardozo Arts & Ent. L.J. 157 (1994).

Jon M. Garon, *Reintermediation*, 2 Int'l J. Priv. L. 227 (2009).

Jane C. Ginsburg, *A Tale of Two Copyrights: Literary Property in Revolutionary France and America*, 64 Tul. L. Rev. 991 (1990).

Peter Jaszi, *Fixing Copyright: Copyright, Fair Use and Motion Pictures*, 2007 Utah L. Rev. 715 (2007).

Jon O. Newman, *New Lyrics for an Old Melody: The Idea/Expression Dichotomy in the Computer Age*, 17 Cardozo Arts & Ent. L.J. 691 (1999).

David Nimmer, *Codifying Copyright Comprehensibly*, 51 UCLA L. Rev. 1233 (2004).

William F. Patry & Richard A. Posner, *Fair Use and Statutory Reform in the Wake of Eldred*, 92 Cal. L. Rev. 1639 (2004).

R. Anthony Reese, *What Copyright Owes the Future*, 50 Hous. L. Rev. 287 (2012).

Darren M. Richard, *Music Licensing 101 A Nuts and Bolts Guide for Filmmakers, Television Producers, Music Publishers, and Songwriters*, 29 Ent. & Sports Law. 12 (2012).

Douglas L. Rogers, *Increasing Access to Knowledge Through Fair Use—Analyzing the Google Litigation to Unleash Developing Countries*, 10 Tul. J. Tech. & Intell. Prop. 1 (2007).

Russ VerSteeg, *Defining "Author" for Purposes of Copyright*, 45 Am. U.L. Rev. 1323 (1996).

Chapter 3

Ethical and Equitable Issues: Agents, Lawyers, and Treatment of Minors, Women, and Minorities

A. Agent Regulation

Statutory Regulations

a. CAL. LAB. CODE § 1700.5. Necessity and posting of license. No person shall engage in or carry on the occupation of a talent agency without first procuring a license therefor from the Labor Commissioner.

b. N.Y. GEN. BUS. LAW § 172. License required. No person shall open, keep, maintain, own, operate or carry on any employment agency unless such person shall have first procured a license therefor as provided in this article.... [Section 171 provides:] "Theatrical employment agency" means any person ... who procures or attempts to procure employment or engagements for circus, vaudeville, the variety field, the legitimate theater, motion pictures, radio, television, phonograph recordings, transcriptions, opera, concert, ballet, modeling or other entertainments or exhibitions or performances, but such term does not include the business of managing such entertainments, exhibitions or performances, or the artists or attractions constituting the same, where such business only incidentally involves the seeking of employment therefor. "Theatrical engagement" means any engagement or employment of a person as an actor, performer or entertainer in employment described in ... this section.

Yoo v. Robi

126 Cal. App. 4th 1089 (Cal. Ct. App. 2005)

Howard Wolf brought this action to recover a commission allegedly due him under a personal management contract with Paul Robi, one of the original members of the legendary singing group The Platters. The trial court awarded judgment to Robi. Wolf and Robi both filed timely appeals. The principal issues in Wolf's appeal are whether Wolf violated the Talent Agencies Act (Cal. Lab. Code § 1700 *et seq.*) by procuring performance engagements for Robi without being licensed as a talent agency and, if so, whether such violation of the Act bars Wolf's recovery of a commission for procuring a recording engagement for Robi—an activity which the Act specifically exempts from the license requirement....

We conclude substantial evidence supports the trial court's finding Wolf procured performance engagements for Robi in violation of the Act thus rendering his contracts with Robi void and barring his recovery of a commission for procuring a recording contract for Robi. We further conclude an appeal from a determination by the Labor Commissioner of a controversy arising under the Act may be filed either in a pending action between the parties to the controversy or in a separate, independent action.

In April 1986 Robi entered into a contract with Jango Records to record a Platters record album in exchange for consideration including royalties based on the number of albums sold. The Platters recorded the album in June and July of 1986 but Jango never released it.

At the time Robi and The Platters recorded the album for Jango, Robi also had a contract with Wolf under which Wolf was to perform certain services for Robi. This contract covered the period November 1985 to November 1986 and was one of a series of one-year contracts with identical terms spanning the period November 1983 to February 1988.

Under these contracts Wolf agreed to: "[A]dvise and counsel in the selection of literary and artistic material; advise and counsel in any and all matters pertaining to public relations; advise and counsel with relation to the adoption of proper formats for presentation of [Robi's] artistic talents [and] in the determination of proper style, mood, setting, business and characterization in keeping with [Robi's] talents; advise and counsel the selection of artistic talent to assist, accompany or embellish [Robi's] artistic presentation; and advise and counsel with regard to general practices in the entertainment industry and with respect to such matters of which [Wolf] may have knowledge concerning compensation and privileges extended for similar artistic values."

As compensation for his services Wolf was to receive "a sum equal to 10% of any and all gross monies or other considerations which [Robi] may receive as a result of [his] activities in and throughout the entertainment, amusement and publishing industries...." Paragraph 8 of the contracts further provided Robi would pay Wolf "a similar sum following the expiration of the term [of the contract] upon and with respect to any and all engagements, contracts and agreements entered into or substantially negotiated during the term hereof relating to any of the foregoing...."

In entering into the contracts with Wolf, Robi acknowledged: "You [i.e., Wolf] have specifically advised me [i.e., Robi] that you are not a 'talent agent' but active [sic] solely as a personal manager, and that you are not licensed as a 'talent agent' under the Labor Code of the State of California; you have at all times advised me that you are not licensed to seek or obtain employment or engagements for me and that you do not agree to do so, and you have made no representations to me, either oral or written, to the contrary."

Following Robi's death Martha Robi, his widow and successor in interest, licensed the manufacture of two record albums utilizing the recordings Robi and the Platters made for Jango Records.

Wolf filed this action alleging Paragraph 8 of his contract, quoted above, entitled him to a commission of 10 percent of the gross amount Robi earned from the sale of those albums. Robi filed a demurrer to the complaint which the trial court sustained and we overruled. Robi then answered the complaint raising numerous affirmative defenses. Robi's answer, however, did not include as an affirmative defense a claim Wolf's contract with Robi was void and invalid because Wolf acted under the contract to procure employment or engagements for Robi without a license to do so in violation of the Act.[1]

Although Robi did not raise the invalidity of the contract as an affirmative defense, while this action was pending in the superior court Robi did raise the invalidity issue in a Petition to Determine Controversy filed with the California Labor Commissioner pursuant to Labor Code, section 1700.44....

[T]he trial court found during each of the years 1983 through 1988 Wolf, acting without a talent agency license, procured and attempted to procure employment and engagements for Robi as an artist in violation of Labor Code, section 1700.5. Wolf contends these findings are not supported by substantial evidence....

Leaving aside Wolf's admission in his opening brief he "work[ed] through regional agents all over America to procure work for [Robi]," the record is replete with illustrations of Wolf's procurement activities on Robi's behalf.

Robi's widow, Martha, testified Robi had no contracts with talent agents in 1986 and that Wolf handled the negotiations for Robi's appearances. She recalled, for example, Wolf obtained an engagement for Robi at the Santa Clara County fair in August 1986. Donnie Brooks, a talent agent, testified he represented Santa Clara in negotiating with Wolf over Robi's appearance at the fair. Brooks also testified he negotiated with Wolf to have Robi perform for one of Brooks' clients in Bristol Connecticut in April 1986. The evidence showed other occasions in 1986 in which Wolf procured or attempted to procure performance engagements for Robi. In addition, Wolf testified he sent out promotional packages "in order to solicit" engagements for Robi and negotiated the details of potential performance contracts offered to him as Robi's agent by other talent agents.

The evidence also showed Wolf negotiated the Jango Records contract on behalf of Robi.

Wolf contends sending out promotional packages and negotiating performance contracts do not constitute "procuring" or "attempting to procure" employment

---

1. Labor Code section 1700.4, subdivision (a) defines a talent agency as "a person or corporation who engages in the occupation of procuring, offering, promising, or attempting to procure employment or engagements for an artist." Labor Code section 1700.5 states: "No person shall engage in or carry on the occupation of a talent agency without first procuring a license therefore from the Labor Commissioner." (All future statutory references are to the Labor Code unless otherwise noted.

within the meaning of Labor Code, section 1700.4, subdivision (a). If promoting an artist requires a talent agency license, Wolf argues, then public relations firms, publicists and advertising agencies all would have to be licensed as talent agencies. Wolf further maintains when personal managers negotiate performance contracts on behalf of their artist clients they are merely acting as spokespersons for the artists so the artists can concentrate on their artistry and not have to spend their time conversing with booking agents.

We need not decide in this case whether public relations firms, publicists and advertising agencies should be required to register as talent agencies because Wolf does not contend he is any of these. We note, however, a rational distinction can be drawn between promoting an artist to the public generally and "[t]he talent agent's primary function [of marketing] the artist's talent to buyers within the entertainment industry." ...

There is also a distinction between being the spokesperson for a client on a contract and being the negotiator for a client on a contract. The spokesperson merely passes on the client's desires or demands to the person who is contemplating engaging the client....

California courts have uniformly held a contract under which an unlicensed party procures or attempts to procure employment for an artist in violation of the Act is void *ab initio* and the party procuring the employment is barred from recovering commissions for *any* activities under the contract. This rule applies even if, as in the present case, the contract does not call for the procuring of employment or contains an affirmative statement the party seeking compensation has not agreed to obtain employment for the artist....

If negotiating the recording contract with Jango Records in 1986 was the only employment procurement Wolf engaged in on behalf of Robi this case would have to be decided differently because, as Wolf correctly points out, procuring recording contracts does not require a talent agency license. But the evidence shows Wolf engaged in numerous other employment procurement activities on behalf of Robi during the term of the 1986 contract. The fact procuring recording contracts without a license does not in itself violate public policy is not determinative. The same thing could be said about numerous other activities personal managers engage in which do not require a license such as counseling artists in the development of their professional careers, selecting material for their performances, managing their money, and the like. Engaging in those activities without a talent agency license does not violate public policy but those activities are nevertheless noncompensable if they are mixed in with activities which do require a license because of the overriding public policy of deterring unlicensed activities....

Marathon Entertainment, Inc. v. Blasi

42 Cal.4th 974 (2008)

In Hollywood, talent—the actors, directors, and writers, the Jimmy Stewarts, Frank Capras, and Billy Wilders who enrich our daily cultural lives—is represented by two groups of people: agents and managers. Agents procure roles; they put artists on the screen, on the stage, behind the camera; indeed, by law, only they may do so. Managers coordinate everything else; they counsel and advise, take care of business arrangements, and chart the course of an artist's career.

This division largely exists only in theory. The reality is not nearly so neat. The line dividing the functions of agents, who must be licensed, and of managers, who need not be, is often blurred and sometimes crossed. Agents sometimes counsel and advise; managers sometimes procure work. Indeed, the occasional procurement of employment opportunities may be standard operating procedure for many managers and an understood goal when not-yet-established talents, lacking access to the few licensed agents in Hollywood, hire managers to promote their careers.

We must decide what legal consequences befall a manager who steps across the line and solicits or procures employment without a talent agency license. We hold that (1) contrary to the arguments of personal manager Marathon Entertainment, Inc. (Marathon), the strictures of the Talent Agencies Act (Lab. Code, § 1700 et seq.) (Act) apply to managers as well as agents; (2) contrary to the arguments of actress Rosa Blasi (Blasi), while the Labor Commissioner has the authority to void manager-talent contracts *ab initio* for unlawful procurement, she also has discretion to apply the doctrine of severability to partially enforce these contracts; and (3) in this case, a genuine dispute of material fact exists over whether severability might apply to allow partial enforcement of the parties' contract. Accordingly, we affirm the Court of Appeal.

FACTUAL AND PROCEDURAL BACKGROUND

In 1998, Marathon and Blasi entered into an oral contract for Marathon to serve as Blasi's personal manager. Marathon was to counsel Blasi and promote her career; in exchange, Blasi was to pay Marathon 15 percent of her earnings from entertainment employment obtained during the course of the contract. During the ensuing three years, Blasi's professional appearances included a role in a film, *Noriega: God's Favorite*, and a lead role as Dr. Luisa Delgado on the television series *Strong Medicine*.

According to Marathon, Blasi reneged on her agreement to pay Marathon its 15 percent commission from her *Strong Medicine* employment contract. In the summer of 2001, she unilaterally reduced payments to 10 percent. Later that year, she ceased payment altogether and terminated her Marathon contract, stating that her licensed talent agent, John Kelly, who had served as her agent throughout the term of the management contract with Marathon, was going to become her new personal manager.

Marathon sued Blasi for breach of oral contract, quantum meruit, false promise, and unfair business practices, seeking to recover unpaid *Strong Medicine* commissions. Marathon alleged that it had provided Blasi with lawful personal manager services by providing the down payment on her home, paying the salary of her business manager, providing her with professional and personal advice, and paying her travel expenses.

After obtaining a stay of the action, Blasi filed a petition with the Labor Commissioner alleging that Marathon had violated the Act by soliciting and procuring employment for Blasi without a talent agency license. The Labor Commissioner agreed. The commissioner found Marathon had procured various engagements for Blasi, including a role in the television series *Strong Medicine*. Concluding that one or more acts of solicitation and procurement by Marathon violated the Act, the commissioner voided the parties' contract *ab initio* and barred Marathon from recovery.

Marathon appealed the Labor Commissioner's ruling to the superior court for a trial *de novo*.... The trial court granted Blasi's motion for summary judgment and invalidated Marathon's personal management contract as an illegal contract for unlicensed talent agency services in violation of the Act....

The Court of Appeal reversed in part. It agreed with the trial court that the Act applied to personal managers. However, it concluded that under the law of severability of contracts (Civ. Code, § 1599), because the parties' agreement had the lawful purpose of providing personal management services that are unregulated by the Act, and because Blasi had not established that her *Strong Medicine* employment contract was procured illegally, the possibility existed that Blasi's obligation to pay Marathon a commission on that contract could be severed from any unlawful parts of the parties' management agreement....

We granted review to address the applicability of the Act to personal managers and the availability of severance under the Act.

DISCUSSION

I. *Background*

A. *Agents and Managers*

In Hollywood, talent agents act as intermediaries between the buyers and sellers of talent. While formally artists are agents' clients, in practice a talent agent's livelihood depends on cultivating valuable connections on both sides of the artistic labor market. Generally speaking, an agent's focus is on the deal: on negotiating numerous short-term, project-specific engagements between buyers and sellers.

Agents are effectively subject to regulation by the various guilds that cover most of the talent available in the industry: most notably, the Screen Actors Guild, American Federation of Television and Radio Artists, Directors Guild of America, Writers Guild of America, and American Federation of Musicians. Artists may informally agree to use only agents who have been "franchised" by their respective guilds; in turn, as a condition of franchising, the guilds may require agents to agree to a code of conduct and restrictions on terms included in agent-talent contracts. Most significantly, those restrictions typically include a cap on the commission charged (generally 10 percent), a cap on contract duration, and a bar on producing one's client's work and obtaining a producer's fee. These restrictions create incentives to establish a high volume clientele, offer more limited services, and focus on those lower risk artists with established track records who can more readily be marketed to talent buyers.

Personal managers, in contrast, are not franchised by the guilds. They typically accept a higher risk clientele and offer a much broader range of services, focusing on advising and counseling each artist with an eye to making the artist as marketable and attractive to talent buyers as possible, as well as managing the artist's personal and professional life in a way that allows the artist to focus on creative productivity. Given this greater degree of involvement and risk, managers typically have a smaller client base and charge higher commissions than agents (as they may, in the absence of guild price caps); managers may also produce their clients' work and thus receive compensation in that fashion.

B. *The Talent Agencies Act*

Aside from guild regulation, the representation of artists is principally governed by the Act. (§§ 1700–1700.47.) ... In its present incarnation, the Act requires anyone who solicits or procures artistic employment or engagements for artists[2] to obtain a talent agency license. (§§ 1700.4, 1700.5.) In turn, the Act establishes detailed requirements for how licensed talent agencies conduct their business, including a code of conduct, submission of contracts and fee schedules to the state, maintenance of a client trust account, posting of a bond, and prohibitions against discrimination, kickbacks, and certain conflicts of interest. (§§ 1700.23–1700.47.) No separate analogous licensing or regulatory scheme extends to personal managers.

With this background in mind, we turn to two questions not previously addressed by this court: whether the Act in fact applies to personal managers, as the Courts of Appeal and Labor Commissioner have long assumed, and if so, how.

II. *The Scope of the Talent Agencies Act: Application to Managers*

...

We begin with the language of the Act. Section 1700.5 provides in relevant part: "No *person* shall engage in or carry on the occupation of a *talent agency* without first procuring a license therefor from the Labor Commissioner." (Italics added.) In turn, "person" is expressly defined to include "any individual, company, society, firm, partnership, association, corporation, limited liability company, *manager*, or their agents or employees" (§ 1700, italics added), and "'[t]alent agency' means a person or corporation who engages in the occupation of procuring, offering, promising, or attempting to procure employment or engagements for an artist or artists ..." other than recording contracts. (§ 1700.4, subd. (a).)

The Act establishes its scope through a functional, not a titular, definition. It regulates *conduct*, not labels; it is the act of procuring (or soliciting), not the title of one's business, that qualifies one as a talent agency and subjects one to the Act's licensure and related requirements. (§ 1700.4, subd. (a).) Any person who procures employment — any individual, any corporation, any manager — is a talent agency

---

2. "'Artists' means actors and actresses rendering services on the legitimate stage and in the production of motion pictures, radio artists, musical artists, musical organizations, directors of legitimate stage, motion picture and radio productions, musical directors, writers, cinematographers, composers, lyricists, arrangers, models, and other artists and persons rendering professional services in motion picture, theatrical, radio, television and other entertainment enterprises" (§ 1700.4 subd. (b).)

subject to regulation. (§§ 1700, 1700.4, subd. (a).) Consequently, as the Courts of Appeal have unanimously held, a personal manager who solicits or procures employment for his artist-client is subject to and must abide by the Act.

As to the further question whether even a single act of procurement suffices to bring a manager under the Act, we note that the Act references the "occupation" of procuring employment and serving as a talent agency. (§§ 1700.4, subd. (a), 1700.5.) Considering this in isolation, one might interpret the statute as applying only to those who regularly, and not merely occasionally, procure employment. However, as we have previously acknowledged in dicta, "[t]he weight of authority is that even the incidental or occasional provision of such services requires licensure." (*Styne v. Stevens*, [26 Cal.4th 42, 51 (2001)].) In agreement with these decisions, the Labor Commissioner has uniformly interpreted the Act as extending to incidental procurement. The Labor Commissioner's views are entitled to substantial weight if not clearly erroneous; accordingly, we likewise conclude the Act extends to individual incidents of procurement....

III. *Sanctions for Solicitation and Procurement Under the Act*

A. *Marathon's Procurement*

We note we are not called on to decide, and do not decide, what precisely constitutes "procurement" under the Act. The Act contains no definition, and the Labor Commissioner has struggled over time to better delineate which actions involve mere general assistance to an artist's career and which stray across the line to illicit procurement. Here, however, the Labor Commissioner concluded Marathon had engaged in various instances of procurement, the trial court concluded there was no material dispute that Marathon had done so, and Marathon has not further challenged that conclusion. We thus take it as a given that Marathon has engaged in one or more acts of procurement and that (as the parties also agree) Marathon has no talent agency license to do so.

We also take as a given, at least at this stage, that Marathon's unlicensed procurement did not include the procurement specifically of Blasi's *Strong Medicine* role....

B. *The Applicability of the Doctrine of Severability to Manager-Talent Contracts*

We turn to the key question in Blasi's appeal: What is the artist's remedy for a violation of the Act? In particular, when a manager has engaged in unlawful procurement, is the manager always barred from any recovery of outstanding fees from the artist or may the court or Labor Commissioner apply the doctrine of severability (Civ. Code, § 1599) to allow partial recovery of fees owed for legally provided services?

Again, we begin with the language of the Act. On this question, it offers no assistance. The Act is silent—completely silent—on the subject of the proper remedy for illegal procurement.

On the other hand, the text of Civil Code section 1599 is clear. Adopted in 1872, it codifies the common law doctrine of severability of contracts: "Where a contract has several distinct objects, of which one at least is lawful, and one at least is unlawful, in whole or in part, the contract is void as to the latter and valid as to the rest." (*Ibid.*) By its terms, it applies even—indeed, only—when the parties have contracted, in part, for something illegal. Notwithstanding any such illegality, it preserves and enforces any lawful portion of a parties' contract that feasibly may be severed.

Under ordinary rules of interpretation, we must read Civil Code section 1599 and the Act so as to, to the extent possible, give effect to both. The two are not in conflict. The Act defines conduct, and hence contractual arrangements, that are illegal: An unlicensed talent agency may not contract with talent to provide procurement services. The Act provides no remedy for its violation, but neither does it repudiate the generally applicable and long-standing rule of severability. Hence, that rule applies absent other persuasive evidence that the Legislature intended to reject the rule in disputes under the Act.

The conclusion that the rule applies is consistent with those Labor Commissioner decisions that recognize severability principles may apply to disputes under the Act. In *Almendarez v. Unico Talent Management, Inc.* (Cal. Lab. Com., Aug. 26, 1999) TAC No. 55-97, a radio personality sought a determination that his personal manager had acted as an unlicensed talent agency. The Labor Commissioner concluded the manager had engaged in unlawful procurement—indeed, that procuring employment was the manager's primary role—but stopped short of voiding all agreements between the parties in their entirety....

Until two years ago, Court of Appeal decisions under the Act had neither accepted nor repudiated the general applicability of the severability doctrine. In 2005, in *Yoo v. Robi, supra,* 126 Cal. App. 4th 1089 [(Cal. Ct. App. 2005),] however, the Court of Appeal considered whether to apply Civil Code section 1599 to allow a personal manager to seek commissions for lawfully provided services. It noted, correctly, that severance is not mandatory and its application in an individual case must be informed by equitable considerations. Civil Code section 1599 grants courts the power, not the duty, to sever contracts in order to avoid an inequitable windfall or preserve a contractual relationship where doing so would not condone illegality. The *Yoo* Court of Appeal concluded the windfall for the artist, Robi, was not so great as to warrant severance.

In *Chiba v. Greenwald* 156 Cal. App. 4th 71 [(2007)], the Court of Appeal also considered whether severance was available for an unlicensed manager/agent who in that case alleged she had had a *Marvin* agreement[3] with her deceased musician client/ partner. Acknowledging she had acted without a license, the manager relinquished any claim to commissions, and the Court of Appeal thus was not presented with the question whether severance might apply to any management services that required no license. In light of the facts as pleaded, the Court of Appeal concluded equity did

---

3. Marvin v. Marvin, 18 Cal.3d 660 [134 Cal. Rptr. 815, 557 P.2d 106] (1976).

not require severance of any lawful portions of the *Marvin* agreement from the un-lawful agreement to provide unlicensed talent agency services.

Neither *Chiba* nor *Yoo v. Robi*, stands for the proposition that severance is never available under the Act. In contrast, the Court of Appeal here expressly concluded, as we do, that it is available....

[T]he Legislature has not seen fit to specify the remedy for violations of the Act. Ordinary rules of interpretation suggest Civil Code section 1599 applies fully to disputes under the Act; nothing in the Act's text, its history, or the decisions inter-preting it justifies the opposite conclusion. We conclude the full voiding of the par-ties' contract is available, but not mandatory; likewise, severance is available, but not mandatory.

C. *Application of the Severability Doctrine*

Finally, we turn to application of the severability doctrine to the facts of this case, insofar as those facts are established by the summary judgment record. Given the procedural posture, our inquiry is narrow: On this record, has Blasi established as a matter of law that there is no basis for severance? ...

Blasi argues that once a personal manager solicits or procures employment, all his services — advice, counseling, and the like — become those of an unlicensed talent agency and are thus uncompensable. We are not persuaded. In this regard, the conduct-driven definitions of the Act cut both ways. A personal manager who spends 99 percent of his time engaged in counseling a client and organizing the client's affairs is not insulated from the Act's strictures if he spends 1 percent of his time procuring or soliciting; conversely, however, the 1 percent of the time he spends soliciting and procuring does not thereby render illegal the 99 percent of the time spent in conduct that requires no license and that may involve a level of personal service and attention far beyond what a talent agency might have time to provide. Courts are empowered under the severability doctrine to consider the central pur-poses of a contract; if they determine in a given instance that the parties intended for the representative to function as an unlicensed talent agency or that the repre-sentative engaged in substantial procurement activities that are inseparable from managerial services, they may void the entire contract. For the personal manager who truly acts as a personal manager, however, an isolated instance of procurement does not automatically bar recovery for services that could lawfully be provided without a license.

Inevitably, no verbal formulation can precisely capture the full contours of the range of cases in which severability properly should be applied, or rejected. The doctrine is equitable and fact specific, and its application is appropriately directed to the sound discretion of the Labor Commissioner and trial courts in the first in-stance. As the Legislature has not seen fit to preclude categorically this case-by-case consideration of the doctrine in disputes under the Act, we may not do so either.

. . .

For the foregoing reasons, we affirm the Court of Appeal's judgment and remand this case for further proceedings consistent with this opinion.

Notes and Questions

a. California continues to remind attorneys that their work to negotiate talent agreements does not waive the exclusive licensing requirements of the Talent Agencies Act. *See Doughty v. Hess*, No. TAC 39547 (Cal. Lab. Comm'r 2017). Because agreements to pay unlicensed talent agents are void, the risk is that the manager or unlicensed talent agent will lose all income that might have resulted from the arrangement—even if the relationship goes sour well after the time of the procurement. In *Park v. Deftones*, 71 Cal. App. 4th 1465 (Cal. Ct. App. 1999), Park, the band manager, was fired after arranging for the recording agreement. Because his activity was void and illegal, he has no basis to complain of any mistreatment.

b. In addition to licensing talent agencies, states such as New York and California also regulate the terms of the talent agency agreement. These regulations do not automatically set the fees a talent agency may charge, but they do tend to disapprove of excessive fees. The New York regulations are representative:

§ 37.03. Theatrical employment; contracts

Every licensed person who shall procure for or offer to an applicant a theatrical engagement shall have executed in duplicate a contract or deliver to the parties as herein set forth a statement containing the name and address of the applicant; the name and address of the employer of the applicant and of the person acting for such employer in employing such applicant; the time and duration of such engagement; the amount to be paid to such applicant; the character of entertainment to be given or services to be rendered; the number of performances per day or per week that are to be given by said applicant; if a vaudeville engagement, the name of the person by whom the transportation is to be paid, and if by the applicant, either the cost of transportation between the places where said entertainment or services are to be given or rendered, or the average cost of transportation between the places where such services are to be given or rendered; and if a dramatic engagement, the cost of transportation to the place where the services begin, if paid by the applicant; and the gross commission or fees to be paid by said applicant and to whom. Such contracts or statements shall contain no other conditions and provisions except such as are equitable between the parties thereto and do not constitute an unreasonable restriction of business. Forms of such contract and statement in blank shall be first approved by the commissioner and his determination shall be reviewable by certiorari. One of such duplicate contracts or of such statements shall be delivered to the person engaging the applicant and the other shall be retained by the applicant. The licensed person procuring such engagement for such applicant shall keep on file or enter in a book provided for that purpose a copy of such contract or statement.

N.Y. ARTS & CULT. AFF. § 37.03 (2013).

c. In addition to the regulation provided by statute, the fees for various industry talent agencies often are controlled under the regulatory auspices of collective bargaining agreements and the trade unions which negotiate them. For example, it is the Screen Actors Guild which prohibits talent agents from charging more than ten percent of their client's salaries as the talent agent fee. Members must limit themselves to licensed agencies that have submitted themselves to the union's review and approval. This serves as the primary regulatory mechanism for the market.

d. One of the ongoing ethical issues involved in entertainment licensing arises from the scale of the corporate organizations. In 1999, David Duchovny, co-star of "The X-Files" television series, sued 20th Century Fox for licensing the series to Fox outlets and subsidiary cable network FX at a price far below market rates, giving rise to claims for breach of contract, breach of good faith, and conspiracy. While that claim was ultimately settled, a similar claim is proceeding. *See Scholastic Entm't, Inc. v. Fox Entm't Group, Inc.,* 336 F.3d 982 (9th Cir. 2003). To what extent does the attorney involved in the subsequent licensing transaction have an ethical duty not to create an intentionally ambiguous contract or to proceed with a transaction knowing it is based on a breach of good faith in another proceeding? Does a third party have a claim for tortious interference of contract against the attorneys if they are aware of the pre-existing agreements?

e. Does the agent representing a film producer owe any fiduciary duty to the screenwriter submitting a script? *See A Slice of Pie Prods. v. Wayans Bros. Entm't,* 392 F. Supp. 2d 297 (D. Conn. 2005).

Problem 3-A

Bryce's talent is starting to be noticed. Bryce has received an offer for representation from Diablo Jones, who styles himself a local film and music agent/manager. Jones provided Bryce a form contract which specifies a fifteen percent fee for management services and a fifteen percent fee for procuring employment "in any entertainment field or media." The term of the proposed form agreement was three years. Jones retained the power to assign the agreement. Jones told Bryce "all his clients signed the agreement in this form because it was standard in the industry."

Thankfully, Bryce has come to you for advice prior to signing the form agreement. Explain to Bryce what terms are reasonable for a talent agent agreement and for a management agreement, describing the difference(s) between the two roles.

B. Regulation of Attorneys

Blanks v. Seyfarth Shaw L.L.P.

171 Cal. App. 4th 336 (2009)

In this legal-malpractice based lawsuit, plaintiff and respondent Billy Blanks (Blanks) won a multi-million dollar judgment against his former attorneys, defendants and appellants William H. Lancaster (Lancaster) and Seyfarth Shaw, LLP (Seyfarth Shaw), jointly Seyfarth.

... We are ... called upon to discuss the effect of Seyfarth's failure to file a petition with the Commissioner within the Act's one-year statute of limitation (Lab. Code, § 1700.44, subd. (c)), and the doctrine of severability of contracts applied to the TAA as addressed in *Marathon Entertainment, Inc. v. Blasi* 42 Cal.4th 974 (2008)....

Blanks is a celebrity karate champion. He developed Tae Bo, a fitness routine combining calisthenics, karate, dance, and push-ups. The routine was ideal for weight control, organized exercise classes, and training. Blanks developed an enthusiastic following and established the Billy Blanks World Karate Center where people lined up around the block to take classes. Radio and television programs spotlighted the Tae Bo craze. Blanks was in demand for film projects and public appearances. The first mass marketed Tae Bo videotape was a huge success.

In 1991 or 1992, certified public accountant Jeffrey Greenfield (Greenfield) came into Blanks's studio as a client. Soon thereafter, Greenfield became Blanks's accountant.... In December 1997, Blanks hired licensed talent agent Suzy Unger (Unger) at the William Morris Agency. While Blanks was represented by the William Morris Agency, Greenfield arranged a number of movie and television appearances in 1998 and 1999. However, Greenfield's inept actions also harmed Blanks. For example, Greenfield's negotiations relating to a television action project called "Tae Bo Squad" did not result in an agreement. The project fizzled during the contract stage. In 1999, Greenfield's mishandling of the negotiations for a television series called "Battle Dome" resulted in Blanks being paid only as a consultant and at a sum far below Blanks's worth. Greenfield did not return telephone messages from those seeking to hire Blanks, resulting in lost opportunities....

The TAA requires all agents to be licensed. If an agent procures work for an artist and is unlicensed, the Act permits the Labor Commissioner to void ab initio all contracts between the parties and order the unlicensed agent to disgorge funds earned for those services. Such requests for affirmative relief first must be made by filing a claim with the Labor Commissioner, who has original jurisdiction over TAA claims. The TAA has a one-year statute of limitations, which the parties agree begins to run from the date the payment is made to the unlicensed agent. (Lab. Code, § 1700.44.) Generally, there is no right to conduct discovery in TAA matters before the Commissioner....

[Despite the exclusive jurisdiction of the Labor Commissioner, Seyfarth pursued a civil cause of action without first filing with the Labor Commissioner and failed to file before the TAA statute of limitations expired.]

While Seyfarth was handling Blanks's case against Greenfield, Blanks paid Seyfarth approximately $400,000. According to Seyfarth, Blanks still owed approximately $46,000....

On March 11, 2002, the Labor Commissioner issued a formal determination of controversy finding that Greenfield was operating as an unlicensed talent agent and had violated the TAA at least twice (once for "Tae Bo Squad" and once for "Battle Dome"). The Commissioner further ruled that Blanks's petition was untimely because Blanks had not satisfied the one-year TAA statute of limitations and thus, the Commissioner could not order Greenfield to disgorge monies he had received from Blanks....

In this case premised upon a claim of legal malpractice, Blanks accuses Seyfarth of losing his right to seek redress from Greenfield because Seyfarth failed to timely file a petition with the Labor Commissioner.

"In civil malpractice cases, the elements of a cause of action for professional negligence are: '(1) the duty of the attorney to use such skill, prudence and diligence as members of the profession commonly possess; (2) a breach of that duty; (3) a proximate causal connection between the breach and the resulting injury; and (4) actual loss or damage." (*Wiley v. County of San Diego*, 19 Cal.4th 532, 536 (1998).)

"In addressing breach of duty, 'the crucial inquiry is whether [the attorney's] advice was so legally deficient when it was given that he [or she] may be found to have failed to use "such skill, prudence, and diligence as lawyers of ordinary skill and capacity commonly possess and exercise in the performance of the tasks which they undertake."

With regard to causation and damages, the plaintiff is required to prove that but for the defendant's negligent acts or omissions, "the plaintiff would have obtained a more favorable judgment or settlement in the action in which the malpractice allegedly occurred." (*Viner v. Sweet*, 30 Cal.4th 1232, 1241 (2003).) As such, a determination of the underlying case is required. This method of presenting a legal malpractice lawsuit is commonly called a trial within a trial....

The Labor Commissioner is given exclusive original jurisdiction over controversies colorably arising under the TAA, which must be brought within one year.

Labor Code section 1700.44, subdivision (c) details the TAA limitation period. It provides that "[n]o action or proceeding shall be brought pursuant to [the Act] with respect to any violation which is alleged to have occurred more than one year prior to commencement of the action or proceeding." As we held in *Greenfield v. Superior Court, supra*, 106 Cal.App.4th 743, filing a complaint in the superior court does not satisfy Labor Code section 1700.44's filing requirement as it is not an "action or proceeding[]" as envisioned in the Act. Rather, a petition must be filed with the Commissioner....

Generally, there is no due process right to discovery in TAA hearings before the Commissioner. Rather, the scope of discovery is governed by statute and the Commissioner's discretion.

After the issues are first addressed by the Commissioner, both parties have the right to a trial de novo. "De novo" review "means that the appealing party is entitled to a complete new hearing—a complete new trial—in the superior court that is in no way a review of the prior proceeding." (*Buchwald v. Katz* 8 Cal.3d 493, 502 (1972).) If an artist seeking to recover funds paid to an unlicensed agent prematurely files a civil lawsuit prior to filing with the Commissioner, the superior court proceedings are stayed until the remedies before the Commissioner are exhausted....

The civil lawsuit filed by Seyfarth on behalf of Blanks on November 4, 1999, identified 17 causes of action, *all* premised upon the allegation that Greenfield must return the $10.6 million paid to him because Greenfield had acted as an agent without first procuring a license as required by the Labor Code. One cause of action alleged a violation of Business and Professions Code section 17200, the Unfair Competition Law (UCL). It alleged that Greenfield had engaged in an unlawful business practice because he did not have the required licensure under the TAA....

Seyfarth argues that even if it was negligent in allowing the TAA statute to expire prior to filing with the Labor Commissioner, such negligence did not harm Blanks because the statute of limitations for Blanks's UCL cause of action had not expired and that cause of action would have yielded the same recovery as alleged in the first cause of action for violating the TAA. Therefore, Seyfarth argues, as a matter of law, Blanks could not prove causation and damages required by the trial-within-a-trial methodology. We hold that by this argument, Seyfarth unpersuasively seeks to circumvent the comprehensive statutory scheme in which the Legislature has given exclusive original jurisdiction to the Labor Commissioner with regard to TAA claims.

... Unlike other statutes that might be used as the basis for a UCL cause of action, the TAA mandates that cases colorably arising under the TAA *must first* be filed with the Commissioner within the one-year statute of limitation period. This is a procedural predicate-filing requirement that cannot be circumvented by recasting a TAA cause of action as a UCL cause of action. Persons, such as Blanks, seeking affirmative relief under the TAA may not invoke the jurisdiction of the Superior Court until after the Commissioner has issued a ruling. This is not a matter of judicial discretion, but is a fundamental rule of procedure.

There can be no argument here that the essence of the underlying case involves a dispute as to whether the relationship between Blanks and Greenfield was controlled by the TAA. The only possible way to satisfy the broad jurisdictional boundaries of the TAA is to require that this issue first be examined by the Commissioner, who would determine if Greenfield procured employment for Blanks. This, and many other issues involved in the *Blanks v. Greenfield* case, including whether or not severance (discussed *infra*) is appropriate, are the precise types of issues that the TAA demands initially be examined by the Commissioner, who has special competence in rendering such decisions. Seyfarth may not plead around the TAA by stating the requested relief alternatively as a UCL cause of action....

Seyfarth [also] contends that the contract between Blanks and Greenfield was subject to the doctrine of severability. This contention is persuasive and because the instructions did not comport with the law in this regard, reversal of the judgment is required.

Blanks's legal malpractice lawsuit against Seyfarth was based upon the theory that he would have been successful in the underlying case against Greenfield had Seyfarth not placed its interests above Blanks's. Blanks argued that had Seyfarth timely filed a petition with the Labor Commissioner rather than delaying the filing of the TAA petition to inflate attorney's fees, Blanks would have been entitled to recover all sums Blanks paid Greenfield because Greenfield was not a licensed talent agent, *i.e.*, had Seyfarth timely filed with the Commissioner, Blanks would have obtained a disgorgement award from the Commissioner of approximately $10.6 million dollars.

Seyfarth did not concede liability. However, it argued that even *if* the Blanks/Greenfield arrangement was tainted with illegality because Greenfield was not a licensed talent agent, and even *if* a TAA petition had been timely filed, the doctrine of severability of contracts applied and Blanks was not entitled to disgorgement of *all* sums paid. In making this argument, Seyfarth noted that Greenfield rendered many non-agent services. Thus, according to Seyfarth, even *if* it was liable, Greenfield's agent-activities (which would have been illegal) had to be severed from the non-agent-activities (which did not violate the TAA), and any recovery to Blanks in the legal malpractice case was limited to those sums attributable to Greenfield's agent-activities....

Marathon recognized that it is often unclear as to whether a person is acting as an artist's agent or in some other capacity, such as a manager. *Marathon* held, however, that the doctrine of severability of contracts, as codified in Civil Code section 1599, applies to contracts involving such arrangements. Thus, if an unlicensed person renders procurement services that require a license under the TAA and also renders non-procurement services, that person may be entitled to compensation for those acts that did not involve unlawful procurement. In such cases, the Labor Commissioner hearing the dispute "is empowered to void contracts in their entirety," however, she is not "obligated to do so.... [Rather, the Labor Commissioner has] the ability to apply equitable doctrines such as severance to achieve a more measured and appropriate remedy where the facts so warrant." (*Id.* at p. 995.)

"In deciding whether severance is available, [*Marathon* has] explained '[t]he overarching inquiry is whether "'the interests of justice ... would be furthered'" by severance.' 'Courts are to look to the various purposes of the contract. If the central purpose of the contract is tainted with illegality, then the contract as a whole cannot be enforced. If the illegality is collateral to the main purpose of the contract, and the illegal provision can be extirpated from the contract by means of severance or restriction, then such severance and restriction are appropriate.'" The analysis is case specific. Further, the doctrine of severability can apply even if the unlicensed person "receives an undifferentiated right to a certain percentage of the client's income stream." (*Id.* at 996–98.) ...

The parties did not fully address whether it was equitable or feasible to sever Greenfield's unlicensed procurement activities from the lawful, non-procurement ones. They did not discuss if the income Greenfield derived was attributable to the central purpose of the Blanks/Greenfield agreement, or if Greenfield's talent agent activities permeated all other services rendered. The parties did not discuss the relevance of the fact that Greenfield was entitled to a percentage of Blanks's total income and how this undifferentiated income affects the severability question.

Lastly, it appears the jury accepted Blanks's all-or-nothing approach because the jury awarded Blanks the exact amount he had paid to Greenfield—$10,634,542—thereby finding that had Seyfarth timely filed a petition with the Commissioner, the Commissioner would have awarded Blanks that sum.

Thus, the trial court's instructional error relating to the doctrine of severability infected the entire trial and the judgment must be reversed....

Todd W. Musburger, Ltd. v. Meier
394 Ill. App. 3d 781 (2009)

A jury returned a verdict in favor of plaintiff Todd W. Musburger, Ltd., a law firm, against defendant Garry Meier, awarding $68,750 in damages on count II of plaintiff's verified complaint for services rendered under a theory of quantum meruit.... We affirm for the reasons set forth below.

According to the complaint in the case at bar, plaintiff "is an entertainment law firm that focuses on negotiating and drafting personal services contracts for broadcasters, writers, performers and directors, as well as negotiating and drafting contracts for entertainment projects in development." Todd Musburger is the president of plaintiff law firm, and has been licensed as an Illinois attorney since 1973. Brian Musburger is Todd Musburger's son and is not an attorney and is employed by plaintiff law firm. Brian develops presentations, prepares industry analyses, keeps abreast of the media industry, and assists with negotiations between clients and their media employers, and has been employed with plaintiff law firm since 1998....

The complaint in the case at bar alleges that on or about sometime in January 1998, defendant orally requested plaintiff to "serve as [defendant's] agent and exclusive legal representative for the negotiating and drafting of [defendant's] multi-million dollar agreements with the entertainment fields of radio and television." On February 6, 1998, plaintiff and defendant entered into a written agreement (1998 Agreement) where plaintiff agreed "to provide its services as [defendant's] exclusive representative for negotiating and drafting of [defendant's] agreements in the entertainment fields of radio and television." The complaint further alleges that plaintiff also agreed to provide advice and counseling "as needed," and to use its best efforts to locate other broadcast outlets that would be interested in defendant's services. Under the 1998 Agreement, defendant agreed to pay "the sum of 5% of the gross amount of the contract negotiated by [p]laintiff on [defendant's] behalf," and all expenses incurred on behalf of defendant....

The complaint then alleges that from September 2002 until September 2003, plaintiff "spent well over [200] hours aggressively and effectively negotiating with WLS and other radio stations for a renewal contract that was satisfactory to [defendant]." ... In particular, WLS offered defendant a 10-year renewal contract whereby defendant would be paid over $12 million.

The complaint alleges that on September 11, 2003, defendant instructed plaintiff to cease all negotiations for a one-week period and to terminate all efforts during

114 3 · ETHICAL AND EQUITABLE ISSUES

that time period. On September 22, 2003, defendant executed a letter addressed to plaintiff terminating plaintiff as defendant's agent and legal representative.

On January 23, 2004, plaintiff executed a letter addressed to defendant including a bill for the work performed by plaintiff on defendant's behalf in 2002 and 2003. The bill provided for 170 hours at a billing rate of $475 per hour for the work performed by Todd Musburger, and 40 hours at a rate of $300 per hour for the work performed by Brian Musburger, for a total of $92,750. The bill was not itemized. Defendant refused to pay any portion of the bill.

Plaintiff filed its verified complaint against defendant on April 1, 2004, which included three counts alleging causes of action for breach of contract, quantum meruit, and unjust enrichment, respectively. Counts I and III of the complaint alleging breach of contract and unjust enrichment, respectively, dismissed by the trial court prior to trial because the counts did not state a cause of action, are not before this court. Only the alleged cause of action for quantum meruit is before this court....

This quantum meruit action was brought by plaintiff to collect fees for services performed for defendant between September 2002 and September 2003. A discharged attorney, in this case more accurately, a law firm, is entitled to recover the reasonable value of services performed.

As the trial court recognized, plaintiff law firm could only pursue an action for quantum meruit (and could not pursue a cause of action for breach of contract) because it was representing defendant on a contingent basis and was discharged in the midst of that representation. A client may discharge her attorney at any time, with or without cause. In quantum meruit recovery, the former client is liable for the reasonable value of the services received during the attorney's employment. Quantum meruit is based on the implied promise of a recipient of services to pay for valuable services because otherwise the recipient would be unjustly enriched. In some cases, it is possible for a client to receive services and yet not be enriched in a tangible way....

An attorney representing a client on a contingent basis who is discharged prior to the consummation of a transaction is entitled to recover the reasonable value of her services rendered. The attorney is not, however, entitled to enforce a contractual fee agreement or collect on the contingency. That would unreasonably interfere with a client's right to discharge her attorney at any time. Based on these principals, plaintiff pursued an action in quantum meruit and the jury returned a verdict in its favor....

Section 1 of the [Employment Agency] Act requires employment agencies to procure a license to operate from the Department of Labor. 225 ILCS 515/1 (West 2006). It requires them to file a schedule of fees with the Department and provides that "[i]t shall be unlawful for any employment agency to collect or attempt to collect any compensation for any service not specified in the schedule of fees filed with the department." 225 ILCS 515/1 (West 2006). The term "employment agency" is defined in section 11 of the Act as follows:

> "Any person engaged for gain or profit in the business of securing or attempting to secure employment for persons seeking employment or employ-

ees for employers. However, the term 'employment agency' shall not include any person engaged in the business of consulting or recruiting, and who in the course of such business is compensated solely by any employer to identify, appraise, or recommend an individual or individuals who are at least 18 years of age or who hold a high school diploma for consideration for a position, provided that in no instance is the individual who is identified, appraised, or recommended for consideration for such position charged a fee directly or indirectly in connection with such identification, appraisal, or recommendation, or for preparation of any resume, or on account of any other personal service performed by the person engaged in the business of consulting or recruiting; but this exclusion is not applicable to theatrical employment agencies or domestic service employment agencies." 225 ILCS 515/11 (West 2006).

The Act was enacted to provide regulation for the recruiting and placement industry, which otherwise lacked safeguards to ensure the ethical conduct of businesses and individuals who provided recruiting and placement services. *T.E.C. & Associates, Inc. v. Alberto-Culver Co.,* 131 Ill.App.3d 1085, 1096, 87 Ill. Dec. 220, 476 N.E.2d 1212 (1985). The Act governs the conduct of employment agencies and addresses the ability of an employment agency to recover fees for the placement of a job applicant with an employer.

In *National Talent Associates, Inc. v. Holland,* 76 Ill.App.3d 556, 32 Ill.Dec. 195, 395 N.E.2d 142 (1979), this court examined the scope of the Act. The *National Talent* court found that an agency that photographed children and submitted their photographs to booking agencies for consideration in placing children in advertising commercials was not an "employment agency." The purpose of the Act was central to the *National Talent* court's decision. The court first noted "the general rule that statutes which are regulatory and penal in nature generally require strict construction." *National Talent Associates, Inc.* 76 Ill.App.3d at 562, 32 Ill. Dec. 195, 395 N.E.2d 142. Further the court noted that, "the primary purpose of statutory construction is to ascertain and give effect to the intention of the legislature, and in so doing, courts should consider not only the language used but also the evil to be remedied." *National Talent Associates, Inc.,* 76 Ill.App.3d at 562, 32 Ill.Dec. 195, 395 N.E.2d 142. According to the court:

"The evils incident to private employment agencies, which statutes such as the [Act] were enacted to correct, were summarized in a report published by the United States Bureau of Labor in October 1912 (United States Bureau of Labor Bulletin, No. 109, p. 36), as quoted in *Adams v. Tanner* [244 U.S. 590, 601–02, (1917)] (Brandeis, J., dissenting), as follows:

1. Charging a fee and failing to make any effort to find work for the applicant.

2. Sending applicants where no work exists.

3. Sending applicants to distant points where no work or where unsatisfactory work exists, but whence the applicant will not return on account of the expense involved.

4. Collusion between the agent and employer, whereby the applicant is given a few days' work and then discharged to make way for new workmen, the agent and employer dividing the fee.

5. Charging exorbitant fees, or giving jobs to such applicants as contribute extra fees, presents, etc.

6. Inducing workers, particularly girls, who have been placed, to leave, pay another fee, and get a 'better job.'

Other evils charged against employment agents are the congregating of persons for gambling or other evil practices, collusion with keepers of immoral houses, and the sending of women applicants to houses of prostitution; sometimes employment offices are maintained in saloons, with the resulting evils."

The [Act] ... consists primarily of regulations to remedy such abuses." *National Talent Associates, Inc.,* 76 Ill.App.3d at 563, 32 Ill. Dec. 195, 395 N.E.2d 142.

Defendant's claim that plaintiff's failure to comply with the licensing requirements of the Act bars it action to seek recovery for fees related to its representation of defendant in 2002 and 2003 is not persuasive. Plaintiff was not providing recruiting or placement services for defendant. Rather, plaintiff was engaged in negotiating and drafting the terms of defendant's contracts and providing legal counsel on the contract negotiations. Plaintiff law firm represented defendant as his legal counsel and was not sending defendant out to employers to apply for work. Plaintiff was working on a renewal of an existing contract while exploring the industry for a more lucrative contract from other radio and television stations. The services provided by plaintiff to defendant were vastly different than the recruiting and placement services governed by the Act.

The purpose of the Act is clear when all of the sections of the Act are read together in context. The Act is intended to apply to recruiting and placement agencies. An application of the Act's record-keeping requirements to an attorney-client relationship such as that between plaintiff and defendant does not follow logically. The Act requires every licensed private employment agency:

"[T]o keep a complete record in the English language of all orders for employees which are received from prospective employers. Upon request of the Department, a licensee shall verify the date when the order was received, the name of the person recording the job order, the name and address of the employer seeking the services of an employee, the name of the person placing the order, the kind of employee requested, the qualifications required in the employee, the salary or wages to be paid if known, and the possible duration of the job. Prior to the placement of any job advertisement, an employment agency must have a current, bona fide job order, and must maintain a copy of both the advertisement and the job order in a register established specially for that purpose." 225 ILCS 515/3 (West 2006).

Plaintiff was not taking orders for jobs from anyone on defendant's behalf. Defendant was not "applying" for work; he was already employed by WLS. Defendant had an existing contract and retained plaintiff to assist in negotiating a more favorable renewal agreement when the contract was set to expire in 2004. Plaintiff was not "placing a job advertisement." It was hired to negotiate the terms of a renewal contract with defendant's then-employer, WLS, or a new contract with others in the same industry.

For the foregoing reasons, we cannot say that the trial court abused its discretion by denying defendant's motion for leave to file a fifth affirmative defense seeking to assert that plaintiff could not receive payment for its 2002 and 2003 services because it was not licensed to act as an employment agency pursuant to the Act....

Solis v. Blancarte

No. TAC-27089 (Cal. Lab. Comm'r 2013)

... This proceeding arises out of the Petition to Determine Controversy filed by [Petitioner Mario Solis (hereinafter "Petitioner")] with the Labor Commissioner on April 30, 2012. The petition alleges that respondent entered into a representation agreement with petitioner, pursuant to which respondent agreed to act and acted as an unlicensed talent agent in violation of Labor Code section 1700.5, a provision of the Talent Agencies Act (TAA), Labor Code section 1700 et seq. The petition seeks a declaration that the contract is void and unenforceable, and that respondent is therefore barred from seeking any recovery under the terms of the contract....

Petitioner is a sports reporter and news anchor for a Los Angeles television station, KNBC Channel 4. Apart from his talents and activities as a broadcast journalist, petitioner's artistic pursuits include acting, script writing, voice overs, and performing as an entertainer. Respondent is a duly licensed attorney who is admitted by the state bar to practice law in the State of California.

Prior to July, 2002, when the parties entered into the engagement contract described below, respondent had on certain occasions provided legal services to the petitioner. In addition, according to petitioner, respondent had provided management type services to petitioner in connection with petitioner's interest in breaking into network television; specifically, respondent advised petitioner that he would keep his eye open for opportunities for petitioner to work in television. Sometime prior to July 8, 2002, KNBC approached petitioner and expressed an interest in hiring petitioner to work for the station as a sports reporter, news anchor, commentator, and analyst, as well as in other roles related to the entertainment programming offered by the station.

Following this expression of interest by KNBC, petitioner contacted respondent and asked him to represent petitioner in handling the negotiation of the terms of his employment with the station. Respondent was receptive to the proposal, and on July 8, 2002 the parties entered into a written engagement contract set out in the form of an engagement letter from respondent to petitioner. At the outset the letter states: "We appreciate your asking us to represent you in connection with your broadcasting and entertainment career, including without limitation, contract negotiations with KNBC Channel 4."

The engagement contract provided that respondent would be paid a five percent (5%) commission on all net monies paid to petitioner under the contract to be negotiated by respondent with KNBC. According to petitioner, respondent wanted to be paid a commission instead of a one-time fee because of the follow-up work he would do on the contract and because he would be acting as petitioner's representative and agent....

[T]hrough the end of 2007, respondent received his 5% share of petitioner's net monthly income under the employment agreement, representing the commissions due pursuant to the engagement contract. Thereafter, petitioner made no further commission payments to respondent....

On December 30, 2011, respondent filed a civil action against petitioner in the Los Angeles County Superior Court, Central District — *Blancarte v. Solis*, Case No. BC476169. The complaint sought to recover the commissions due under the engagement contract based on the net monies paid to petitioner between January 1, 2008 and August 31, 2009 pursuant to the employment agreement with KNBC.

After filing an answer to the complaint, which included an affirmative defense based on the TAA, petitioner filed the instant petition with the Labor Commissioner seeking a determination that the engagement contract was entered into is violation of the TAA and was therefore void and unenforceable....

[P]etitioner was a person rendering artistic and professional services in the medium of television for purposes of entertaining the public. Thus, it is clear petitioner was an artist within the meaning of section 1700.4, subdivision (b). The next, and crucial question, is whether respondent was engaged in the occupation of a talent agency, that is to say, whether he was engaged in procuring or in offering, promising, or attempting to procure employment or engagements for petitioner.

The principal and dominant activities that respondent performed on behalf of petitioner pursuant to the engagement contract involved the negotiation of the compensation and other terms of the agreements for the employment of petitioner by KNBC. The Labor Commissioner has long recognized that the acts undertaken in the course of negotiating an agreement for the employment of an artist constitute "procuring ... or attempting to procure employment" within the meaning of section 1700.4, subdivision (a).

> The term "procure," as used in Labor Code § 1700.4(a), means "to get possession of: obtain, acquire, to cause to happen or be done: bring about." *Wachs v. Curry* 13 Cal.App.4th 616, 628 (1993). Thus, "procuring employment" under the Talent Agencies Act is not limited to initiating discussions with potential purchasers of the artist's professional services or otherwise soliciting employment; rather, "procurement" includes any active participation

in a communication with a potential purchaser of the artist's services aimed at obtaining employment for the artist, regardless of who initiated the communication The Labor Commissioner has long held that "procurement" includes the process of negotiating an agreement for an artist's services. Significantly, the Talent Agencies Act specifically provides that an unlicensed person may nevertheless participate in negotiating an employment contract for an artist, provided he or she does so "in conjunction with, and at the request of a licensed talent agent." Labor Code § 1700.44(d). This limited exception to the licensing requirement would be unnecessary if negotiating an employment contract for an artist did not require a license in the first place.

(*Danielewski v. Agon Investment Company* (Cal.Lab.Com., October 28, 2005) TAC No. 41-03, pages 15–16.)

The negotiation of petitioner's employment agreements with KNBC represented the bulk of the activities that respondent engaged in on behalf of petitioner under the engagement contract. Indeed, the contract was entered into for the purpose of having respondent conduct such negotiations, and respondent carried out the contract by effectuating and accomplishing that purpose. By negotiating the KNBC agreements on petitioner's behalf, respondent attempted to procure and procured employment for petitioner. As a consequence, respondent engaged in and carried out the occupation of a talent agency; because he did so without having first obtained a talent agency license from the Labor Commissioner, respondent violated the provision of Labor Code section 1700.5.

Respondent contends that because he is a duly licensed attorney, his activities in negotiating the KNBC agreements on behalf of petitioner should be treated as exempt from the licensing requirements of section 1700.5. The provisions of the TAA do not contain or recognize any such exemption. Moreover, respondent has provided no authority that would support the propriety of applying or creating such an exemption.

The applicable scope of the TAA has been delineated by the Supreme Court:

> The Act establishes its scope through a functional, not a titular, definition. It regulates conduct, not labels; it is the act of procuring (or soliciting), not the title of one's business, that qualifies one as a talent agency and subjects one to the Act's licensure and related requirements. (§ 1700.4, subd. (a).) Any person who procures employment—any individual, any corporation, any manager—is a talent agency subject to regulation. (§§ 1700.4, subd. (a).)

(*Marathon Entertainment, Inc. v. Blasi* 42 Cal.4th 974, 986 (2008).) As the foregoing makes perfectly clear, anyone who procures or solicits engagements for an artist is carrying on the occupation of a talent agency and must be licensed.

It is evident that the functional scope of the TAA admits of no exceptions and encompasses the procurement activities of respondent, even though he is an attorney. In this regard, it is of no moment that some of the skills respondent may have brought to the negotiations on behalf of petitioner are the result of skills for which he has been licensed as an attorney. As Labor Code section 1700.44 makes unequivocally clear, when someone who is not licensed under the TAA wishes to bring such skills to bear on the negotiation of an artist's contract, he must do so "in conjunction with, and at the request of, a licensed talent agency." Here, respondent acted entirely on his own and without a talent agency license; consequently, his conduct constituted a clear violation of the licensure requirements of section 1700.5.

The consequences that flow from a violation of the TAA are well settled. When a person contracts to act as a talent agent without first having obtained a talent agency license as required by the TAA, the contract that has been entered into is illegal, void, and unenforceable. "Since the clear object of the Act is to prevent improper persons from becoming [talent agents] and to regulate such activity for the protection of the public, a contract between an unlicensed [talent agent] and an artist is void." *(Buchwald v. Superior Court* 254 Cal.App. 2d 347, 351(1967).).

As recognized in *Marathon Entertainment, Inc. v. Blasi, supra,* in some cases there may be a basis for severing the illegal portions of a contract violative of the TAA's licensure requirements from the other parts of the contract. However, this will be permissible only where there are both illegal and legal aspects to the contract and where the two aspects can be properly severed in accordance with the legal standards governing application of the severance doctrine.

There is no basis for applying the doctrine of severability in the circumstances of this case. It is established law that if the central purpose of a contract is illegal, the entire contract is void and will not be enforced. In the present case, the central purpose of the engagement contract was to enable respondent to act as petitioners' unlicensed talent agent. This illegal purpose contaminated the entire contract, and rendered it void and unenforceable. In addition, in this case respondent is seeking to preserve his right to recover certain commissions under the engagement contract; the commissions that he seeks to protect are based on the income that respondent generated for petitioner through his illegal procurement activities. Plainly, respondent cannot capitalize on and gain a benefit from illegal conduct under a contract; in these circumstances, the illegality permeates the entire engagement contract and renders it void and unenforceable. In light of these conclusions, it is unnecessary to consider whether, in rendering services under the engagement contract, respondent engaged in other conduct violative of the TAA.

In sum, for the reasons stated above, it is determined that' in entering into the engagement contract with petitioner, and in performing under that contract, respondent engaged in the occupation of a talent agency without having obtained a license from the Labor Commissioner. Because it was pervaded by illegality, the entire contract is found to be void and unenforceable....

The contract between petitioner and respondent is declared to be illegal, void and unenforceable, and respondent is barred from enforcing or seeking to enforce the contract against petitioner in any manner.

Notes and Questions

a. Lawyers who provide services other than traditional legal services, or who change their relationship with clients during the course of the representation, run the risk of violating rules of professional responsibility as well as the Talent Agencies Act. Nonetheless, these additional services are not uncommon among lawyers. What steps might an attorney take to protect against claims of any breach of ethical or legal duties?

b. Not every claim filed against the lawyer results in liability or the barring of attorneys' fees. For a claim upholding the one-third contingency fee earned for successfully challenging the royalty residuals owed to members of Lynyrd Skynyrd, see *King v. Fox*, No. 97 Civ. 4134, 2004 U.S. Dist. LEXIS 462 (S.D.N.Y. Jan. 16, 2004).

c. The one-year statute of limitations under the Talent Agency Act impacts the ability of artists to recover from payments made in violation of the act brought more than a year after the payment. To what extent does entering into a void talent agent agreement violate other attorney's obligations that might extend the statute of limitations?

Problem 3-B

Having avoided signing with a representative purporting to be both talent agent and manager, Bryce receives an opportunity to run a motion picture company in a state which has no specific talent agency law. Bryce is told to seek local legal counsel to negotiate the agreement if Bryce plans to relocate to the home of the production company. The attorney Bryce calls offers to negotiate the contract for a five percent commission on Bryce's earnings (from any source) during the term of the employment agreement, including any extensions to that agreement. The retainer letter provides that local law applies to the engagement letter, so California law does not apply.

Explain to Bryce what terms are reasonable for a talent agent agreement and for a management agreement, describing the difference(s) between the two roles.

C. Enforcement of Contracts for Minors

Expansion of Coogan Laws

Federal employment law does not govern the wages or working conditions for minors in the entertainment industry. Under 29 U.S.C. § 213(c)(1)(C)(3) of the Fair Labor Standards Act, federal employment law "relating to child labor shall not apply to any child employed as an actor or performer in motion pictures or theatrical productions, or in radio or television productions." The exclusion regarding child media productions shifts all legislation to the states.

In the area of minors' contracts, the laws have improved since the first Coogan Law was passed in 1939. California updated its law in 2000 and New York adopted a Coogan Law for the first time in 2003. Jackie Coogan, who starred with Charlie

Chaplin in *The Kid* at the age of four, never saw any of his childhood fortune because the adults who were supposed to be protecting him spent it.

> In California a law designed to protect the earnings of child actors, known as the Coogan Law was enacted in 1939. The law was named for child actor Jackie Coogan, who filed suit against his parents to recover the $4 million fortune he had made as a popular child actor. However the law was ineffective and the Screen Actors Guild lobbied to have it amended. California's new Coogan Law (SB 1162) became effective on January 1, 2000 and it ensures that every time young performers work under an entertainment contract, 15% of the gross earnings will be set aside for them until they reach legal majority. The bill also makes it clear that the earnings of a minor are the legal property of the minor and not his parents.

Alliance of Canadian Cinema, Television and Radio Artists, Minor's Trust Frequently Asked Questions.[4]

> Coogan Accounts (a.k.a. Blocked Trust Accounts and Trust Accounts) are required by the State of California, New York, Louisiana and New Mexico. In most instances, you will have to supply proof of a trust account prior to receiving a work permit. 15% of the minor's gross wages are required to be withheld by the employer and deposited into the Coogan account within 15 days of employment. The parent must supply the Coogan account number to the employer.[5]

California Family Code § 6750

(a) This chapter applies to the following contracts entered into between an unemancipated minor and any third party or parties on or after January 1, 2000:

(1) A contract pursuant to which a minor is employed or agrees to render artistic or creative services, either directly or through a third party, including, but not limited to, a personal services corporation (loan-out company), or through a casting agency. "Artistic or creative services" includes, but is not limited to, services as an actor, actress, dancer, musician, comedian, singer, stunt-person, voice-over artist, or other performer or entertainer, or as a songwriter, musical producer or arranger, writer, director, producer, production executive, choreographer, composer, conductor, or designer.

(2) A contract pursuant to which a minor agrees to purchase, or otherwise secure, sell, lease, license, or otherwise dispose of literary, musical, or dramatic properties, or use of a person's likeness, voice recording, performance, or story of or incidents in his or her life, either tangible or intangible, or any rights therein for use in motion pictures, television, the production of sound recordings in any format now known or hereafter devised, the legitimate or living stage, or otherwise in the entertainment field.

4. https://www.actra.ca/prs/minors-trust/minors-trust-faq/.
5. https://www.sagaftra.org/membership-benefits/young-performers/coogan-law.

(3) A contract pursuant to which a minor is employed or agrees to render services as a participant or player in a sport.

(b) (1) If a minor is employed or agrees to render services directly for any person or entity, that person or entity shall be considered the minor's employer for purposes of this chapter.

(2) If a minor's services are being rendered through a third-party individual or personal services corporation (loan-out company), the person to whom or entity to which that third party is providing the minor's services shall be considered the minor's employer for purposes of this chapter.

(3) If a minor renders services as an extra, background performer, or in a similar capacity through an agency or service that provides one or more of those performers for a fee (casting agency), the agency or service shall be considered the minor's employer for the purposes of this chapter.

(c) (1) For purposes of this chapter, the minor's "gross earnings" shall mean the total compensation payable to the minor under the contract or, if the minor's services are being rendered through a third-party individual or personal services corporation (loan-out company), the total compensation payable to that third party for the services of the minor.

(2) Notwithstanding paragraph (1), with respect to contracts pursuant to which a minor is employed or agrees to render services as a musician, singer, songwriter, musical producer, or arranger only, for purposes of this chapter, the minor's "gross earnings" shall mean the total amount paid to the minor pursuant to the contract, including the payment of any advances to the minor pursuant to the contract, but excluding deductions to offset those advances or other expenses incurred by the employer pursuant to the contract, or, if the minor's services are being rendered through a third-party individual or personal services corporation (loan-out company), the total amount payable to that third party for the services of the minor.

New York Arts and Cultural Affairs Law § 35.03. Judicial approval of certain contracts for services of infants; effect of approval; guardianship of savings

1. A contract made by an infant or made by a parent or guardian of an infant, or a contract proposed to be so made, under which (a) the infant is to perform or render services as an actor, actress, dancer, musician, vocalist or other performing artist, or as a participant or player in professional sports, or (b) a person is employed to render services to the infant in connection with such services of the infant or in connection with contracts therefor, may be approved by the supreme court or the surrogate's court as provided in this section where the infant is a resident of this state or the services of the infant are to be performed or rendered in this state. If the contract is so approved the infant may not, either during his minority or upon reaching his majority, disaffirm the contract on the ground of infancy or assert that the parent or guardian lacked authority to make the contract. A contract modified, amended or assigned after its approval under this section shall be deemed a new contract....

California Labor Code § 2855. Enforcement of contract to render personal service; time limit

(a) ... [A] contract to render personal service, ... may not be enforced against the employee beyond seven years from the commencement of service under it. Any contract, otherwise valid, to perform or render service of a special, unique, unusual, extraordinary, or intellectual character, which gives it peculiar value and the loss of which can not be reasonably or adequately compensated in damages in an action at law, may nevertheless be enforced against the person contracting to render the service, for a term not to exceed seven years from the commencement of service under it. If the employee voluntarily continues to serve under it beyond that time, the contract may be referred to as affording a presumptive measure of the compensation.

(b) Notwithstanding subdivision (a):

(1) Any employee who is a party to a contract to render personal service in the production of phonorecords in which sounds are first fixed, as defined in Section 101 of Title 17 of the United States Code, may not invoke the provisions of subdivision (a) without first giving written notice to the employer in accordance with Section 1020 of the Code of Civil Procedure, specifying that the employee from and after a future date certain specified in the notice will no longer render service under the contract by reason of subdivision (a).

(2) Any party to such a contract shall have the right to recover damages for a breach of the contract occurring during its term in an action commenced during or after its term, but within the applicable period prescribed by law.

(3) In the event a party to such a contract is, or could contractually be, required to render personal service in the production of a specified quantity of the phonorecords and fails to render all of the required service prior to the date specified in the notice provided in paragraph (1), the party damaged by the failure shall have the right to recover damages for each phonorecord as to which that party has failed to render service in an action which, notwithstanding paragraph (2), shall be commenced within 45 days after the date specified in the notice.

Scott Eden Management v. Kavovit

563 N.Y.S.2d 1001 (Sup. Ct. 1990)

In this case of first impression, an infant actor has disaffirmed a personal services contract. He thereby seeks to avoid responsibility to his manager for commissions due in the future on income from performance contracts already obtained for him by the manager.

The salient facts are not in dispute. In 1984, when defendant Andrew M. Kavovit was 12 years of age, he and his defendant parents entered into a contract with plaintiffs (Scott Eden) whereby Scott Eden became the exclusive personal manager to supervise and promote Andrew's career in the entertainment industry. This agreement ran from February 8, 1984 to February 8, 1986 with an extension for another three years to February 8, 1989. It provided that Scott Eden was entitled to a 15% commission on Andrew's gross compensation. "With respect to contracts entered into by [Andrew] ... during the term of this agreement ... [Scott Eden] shall be entitled to [its] commission from the residuals or royalties of such contracts, the full term of such contracts, including all extensions or renewals thereof, notwithstanding the earlier termination of this agreement."

In 1986, Andrew signed an agency contract with the Andreadis Agency, a licensed agent selected by Scott Eden pursuant to industry requirements. This involved an additional 10% commission. Thereafter, Andrew signed several contracts for his services. The most important contract, from a financial and career point of view, secured a role for Andrew on "As the World Turns," a long-running television soap opera. Income from this employment contract appears to have commenced on December 28, 1987 and continues through December 28, 1990, with a strong possibility for renewal.

One week before the contract with Scott Eden was to expire, Andrew's attorney notified Scott Eden that his "clients hereby disaffirm the contract on the grounds [sic] of infancy". Up until then, the Andreadis Agency had been forwarding Scott Eden its commissions, but by letter of February 4, 1989, Andrew's father, David Kavovit, advised Andreadis that Andrew's salary would go directly to Andrew and that he would send Andreadis its 10%. Needless to say, no further commissions were sent to Scott Eden.

The complaint seeks money damages for (1) all sums due plaintiffs for commissions relating to Andrew's personal appearances prior to February 8, 1989, the date of disaffirmance, (2) all sums due plaintiff for commissions with respect to contracts entered into by Andrew in the entertainment or promotion fields during the term of his contract with plaintiffs, "i.e., commissions from the residuals or royalties of such contracts — the full term of such contracts — including all extensions or renewals thereof", and (3) $50,000 for tortious interference with the relationship between plaintiff and the Andreadis Agency....

An infant's contract is voidable and the infant has an absolute right to disaffirm. This aspect of the law of contracts was well entrenched in the common law as early as the 15th century. In bringing this action, and defending the motion, plaintiffs fully recognize the principle of law involved here and in no way challenge the infant's right to disaffirm. Rather, plaintiffs rely upon a corollary to the main rule, which also evolved early in the common law

> "After disaffirmance, the infant is not entitled to be put in a position superior to such a one as he would have occupied if he had never entered into his voidable agreement. He is not entitled to retain an advantage from a transaction which he repudiates. 'The privilege of infancy is to be used as a shield and not as a sword.'"

As stated differently by the same court in an earlier case involving an infant's disaffirmance:

"The theory of a rescission is that the party proceeded against shall be restored to his original position. The plaintiff cannot rescind if he retains in himself or withholds through another any fruit of the contract."

The restoration of consideration requirement found voice in CPLR 3004 which states that the infant need not tender restoration of benefits received prior to disaffirmance "but the court may make a tender of restoration a condition of its judgment, and may otherwise in its judgment so adjust the equities between the parties that unjust enrichment is avoided." The restoration of consideration principle, as interpreted by the courts, has resulted in the infant being responsible for wear and tear on the goods returned by him. In the event that the minor cannot return the benefits obtained, he is effectively precluded from disaffirming the contract in order to get back the consideration he has given. In *Vichnes v Transcontinental & W. Air* (173 Misc 631) the infant paid the air fare from New York to Los Angeles. On returning to New York she demanded the return of her money. Appellate Term granted summary judgment to defendant because "there is no basis for rescission here in view of the concession that the reasonable value of the transportation was the sum paid by plaintiff."

The parties have not cited, nor has the court found, a case dealing with the exact issue at bar, i.e., whether disaffirmance may void the contractual obligation to pay agents' commissions without any concomitant exchange being made. However, an analogy may be drawn from the case of *Mutual Milk & Cream Co. v Prigge* (112 App Div 652). There, a minor had entered the employ of the plaintiff as a milk wagon driver and had signed a contract which included a restrictive covenant wherein the minor agreed not to solicit plaintiff's customers within three years after leaving plaintiff's employ. Several months after entering into the contract, the minor quit, pursuant to the terms of the contract, but then went to work for plaintiff's rival and solicited business from plaintiff's customers.

The Appellate Division affirmed the issuance of an injunction against the minor, who had pleaded infancy in avoidance of the contractual obligations. The court considered that the issue was not one of liability of an infant for a breach of his contract, but whether an infant should be allowed to repudiate his contract without restoring what he had received and, if restoration could not be made, without being enjoined from making use of the information he had gained from his employment by the plaintiff to the latter's damage. The court held that the infant should be enjoined "from making use of that information in violation of his agreement made at the time when he desired and obtained employment and upon the faith of which he obtained the information and acquaintance." The court further noted that "No man would engage the services of an infant if he could not impose the same condition for his own protection against the use of his formulas, trade secrets, and lists of customers that he could exact of an adult."

The rationale of the *Mutual Milk* case is applicable to this case. The work a personal manager does for and with his client is preparatory to the performance contract. Once a performance contract has been signed, the personal manager is entitled to his percentage fee, subject only to the condition subsequent that the client performs and earns his fee. This is clearly the understanding in the industry, unlike, for example, the standard in the insurance field where the initial commission is disproportionately high and the subsequent, smaller commissions are viewed as consideration for continued efforts in keeping the insurance contract current. When the client signs a performance contract, it is with the understanding that the gross amount to be paid is not solely for him. It is the expectation of all parties—the agent, the performer and, in this case, the soap opera production company, that 15% of that gross amount belongs to the personal manager. To the extent that the performer obtains that 15% for himself, he is unjustly enriched.

Here, the position adopted by defendants is no different than that advanced on behalf of the infant who had taken the airplane ride and wanted her money back or the truck driver who had milked his employer's efforts and tutelage and then refused to honor his reciprocal commitment. In each case, the infant consumed the fruits of the contract and refused to pay for that fruit, to the clear prejudice of the other party. In this case, the infant will continue to reap the benefits of his contract with plaintiff but is using his infancy as an excuse not to honor the promise made in return for that benefit.

If the argument asserted by defendants were adopted by the court, the infant would be put in a position superior to that which he would have occupied had he never entered into the contract with plaintiff. He would be retaining an advantage from the repudiated transaction, i.e., using the privilege of infancy as a sword rather than a shield. Not only is this manifestly unfair, but it would undermine the policy underlying the rule allowing disaffirmance. If the infant may rescind the contract with the manager immediately after a lucrative performance contract is signed, yet still retain the benefits of the performance contract, no reputable manager will expend any efforts on behalf of an infant.

In this case, adjustment of the equities so as to prevent unjust enrichment, as suggested by CPLR 3004, leads to the conclusion that defendants must continue to pay to plaintiffs all commissions to which plaintiffs would be entitled under their contract, as they become due. Thus, on the first two causes of action summary judgment is denied to defendants and is granted to plaintiffs to the extent that they shall be restored to their original condition. Moreover, inasmuch as plaintiffs will no longer be involved in the day-to-day personal management of the infant, they will be entitled to periodic statements regarding Andrew's income and the sources thereof and they shall have the right to annual inspections of the books and records kept with regard to Andrew's income.

The third cause of action is dismissed. Plaintiffs have come forward with no proof to buttress their conclusory claim that defendants have tortiously interfered with their business relationship with the Andreadis Agency.

The court notes that this entire situation may have arisen due to a misreading of a statute which is related to the problem at hand but irrelevant to its determination. The affidavit of David J. Kavovit makes reference to Arts and Cultural Affairs Law

§ 35.03 as a bar to this action and that "I am advised that the agreement was void at its inception by reason of the fact that its term, including options to extend, exceeded a three year period of time."

Section 35.03 provides for judicial approval of infants' contracts in order to avoid later disaffirmance. However, no such contract may be approved if it extends for a period of more than three years, whether by option or otherwise. However, the purpose of the statute was to limit the infant's right to disaffirm. If there is no judicial approval, for whatever reason, then the statute has no effect upon the infant's contract or upon his right to disaffirm.

Berg v. Traylor

148 Cal. App. 4th 809 (Cal. Ct. App. 2007)

Appellants Meshiel Cooper Traylor (Meshiel) and her minor son Craig Lamar Traylor (Craig) appeal the judgment confirming an arbitration award in favor of Craig's former personal manager, respondent Sharyn Berg (Berg), for unpaid commissions under a contract between Berg, Meshiel and Craig and unrepaid loans from Berg. Because we find that Craig had the statutory right as a minor to disaffirm both the original contract and the arbitration award, we reverse the judgment against Craig. We affirm the judgment against Meshiel.

On January 18, 1999, Berg entered into a two-page "Artist's Manager's Agreement" (agreement) with Meshiel and Craig, who was then 10 years old. Meshiel signed the agreement and wrote Craig's name on the signature page where he was designated "Artist." Craig did not sign the agreement. Pursuant to the agreement, Berg was to act as Craig's exclusive personal manager in exchange for a commission of 15 percent of all gross monies or other consideration paid to him as an artist during the three-year term of the agreement, as well as income from merchandising or promotional efforts or offers of employment made during the term of the agreement, regardless of when Craig received such monies. The agreement expressly provided that any action Craig "may take in the future pertaining to disaffirmance of this agreement, whether successful or not," would not affect Meshiel's liability for any commissions due Berg. The agreement also provided that any disputes concerning payment or interpretation of the agreement would be determined by arbitration in accordance with the rules of Judicial Arbitration and Mediation Services, Inc. (JAMS).

On or about June 13, 2001, Craig obtained a recurring acting role on the Fox Television Network show "Malcolm in the Middle" (show). On September 11, 2001, four months prior to the expiration of the agreement, Meshiel sent a certified letter to Berg stating that while she and Craig appreciated her advice and guidance, they no longer needed her management services and could no longer afford to pay Berg her 15 percent commission because they owed a "huge amount" of taxes. On September 28, 2001, Berg responded, informing appellants that they were in breach of the agreement.

In 2004, Berg filed suit against Meshiel and Craig for breach of the agreement, breach of the implied covenant of good faith and fair dealing, breach of an oral loan agreement, conversion and declaratory relief....

Because appellants had failed to pay their share of the arbitration fees, Berg did not anticipate their appearance and did not retain a court reporter. Though Meshiel and Craig's counsel failed to appear at the hearing, Meshiel personally appeared with Craig's talent agent, Steven Rice. Craig did not appear. According to Meshiel, the arbitrator denied her request for a two-week continuance. The arbitrator permitted Meshiel to use Rice's assistance and advice in presenting her case. Rice asserted that the agreement was invalid because Craig was a minor at the time it was executed and there had been no court approval of the agreement....

The arbitrator awarded Berg commissions and interest of $154,714.15, repayment of personal loans and interest of $5,094, and attorney fees and costs of $13,762. He also awarded Berg $405,000 "for future earnings projected on a minimum of 6 years for national syndication earnings," and stated that this part of the award would "vest and become final, as monies earned after February 7, 2005, become due and payable." On February 20, 2005, the arbitrator served a clarification of the award, stating that "all monies earned by Craig Traylor, pursuant to the contract with Ms. Berg, are paid directly to Ms. Berg.... After deduction of fees and commissions, etc., the balance of the funds shall be forwarded to the client." ...

On July 8, 2005, Berg served a petition to confirm the arbitration award, which was filed on July 12, 2005.... Appellants then filed a motion to vacate the judgment pursuant to Code of Civil Procedure section 473. While the motion was pending, appellants filed a notice of appeal from the judgment. In a January 2006 order, the trial court determined that it had no jurisdiction to rule on the matter in light of the appeal and ordered the motion off calendar.

Simply stated, one who provides a minor with goods and services does so at her own risk. The agreement here expressly contemplated this risk, requiring that Meshiel remain obligated for commissions due under the agreement regardless of whether Craig disaffirmed the agreement. Thus, we have no difficulty in reaching the conclusion that Craig is permitted to and did disaffirm the agreement and any obligations stemming therefrom, while Meshiel remains liable under the agreement and resulting judgment. Where our difficulty lies is in understanding how counsel, the arbitrator and the trial court repeatedly and systematically ignored Craig's interests in this matter. From the time Meshiel signed the agreement, her interests were not aligned with Craig's. That no one—counsel, the arbitrator or the trial court—recognized this conflict and sought appointment of a guardian ad litem for Craig is nothing short of stunning. It is the court's responsibility to protect the rights of a minor who is a litigant in court.

Our review of an arbitrator's award is generally limited. In *Aguilar v. Lerner* 32 Cal.4th 974, 981–982 (2004), the Supreme Court stated: "When parties choose to forgo the traditional court system and arbitrate their claims, it is assumed they wish to have a final and conclusive resolution of their dispute. The Legislature has recognized this underlying assumption of finality and has, by statute, limited the grounds for judicial review of an arbitrator's award. (Code Civ. Proc., § 1286.2.) Consistent with this legislative intent, we recognized the general rule that 'an arbitrator's decision cannot be reviewed for errors of fact or law.' (*Moncharsh v. Heily & Blase* 3 Cal.4th 1, 11 (1992).) We explained that because the Legislature has provided certain statutory grounds to overturn or modify an arbitrator's decision, courts should not subject such decisions to standard judicial review. In addition, however, to the statutory grounds for vacating an arbitrator's award, we explained in *Moncharsh* " 'that there may be some limited and exceptional circumstances justifying judicial review of an arbitrator's decision.... Such cases would include those in which granting finality to an arbitrator's decision would be inconsistent with the protection of a party's *statutory rights.*'"...

The trial court denied appellants' petition to vacate the arbitration award on the ground that it was untimely. Code of Civil Procedure section 1288 provides that a petition to vacate or correct an arbitration award must be served and filed no later than 100 days after the date of service of a signed copy of the award on the petitioner. Code of Civil Procedure section 1290.6 provides that a response to a petition to confirm an award must be served and filed within 10 days after service of the petition. Here, the arbitration award was served on February 14, 2005 and the clarification of the award was served on February 20, 2005. Berg's petition to confirm the award was served on July 8, 2005 and filed on July 12, 2005. It is undisputed that by the time appellants' fourth and current counsel substituted into the action and thereafter filed a petition to vacate the arbitration award and response to the petition to confirm it on August 18, 2005, both of these statutory deadlines had passed.

Appellants contend that despite the lapse of these deadlines, Craig had the statutory right as a minor to disaffirm both the original agreement with Berg containing the arbitration provision and the arbitration award itself. We agree. Craig's minority status entitled him to disaffirm the agreement and his minority status coupled with the absence of the appointment of guardian ad litem entitled him to disaffirm the arbitration award and judgment even after the statutory deadline for moving to vacate the arbitration award had passed.

"As a general proposition, parental consent is required for the provision of services to minors for the simple reason that minors may disaffirm their own contracts to acquire such services." (*Ballard v. Anderson* 4 Cal.3d 873, 878 (1971).) According to Family Code section 6700, "a minor may make a contract in the same manner as an adult, subject to the power of disaffirmance" provided by Family Code section 6710. In turn, Family Code section 6710 states: "Except as otherwise provided by statute, a contract of a minor may be disaffirmed by the minor before majority or within a reasonable time afterwards or, in case of the minor's death within that period, by the minor's heirs or personal representative." Sound policy considerations support this provision: "The law shields minors from their lack of judgment and experience and under certain conditions vests in them the right to disaffirm their contracts. Although in many instances such disaffirmance may be a hardship upon those who deal with an infant, the right to avoid his contracts is conferred by law upon a minor 'for his protection against his own improvidence and the designs of others.' It is the policy of the law to protect a minor against himself and his indiscretions and immaturity as well as against the machinations of other people and to discourage adults from contracting with an infant. Any loss occasioned by the disaffirmance of a minor's contract might have been avoided by declining to enter into the contract." (*Niemann v. Deverich* 98 Cal.App.2d 787, 793 (1950).)

Berg offers two reasons why the plain language of Family Code section 6710 is inapplicable, neither of which we find persuasive. First, she argues that a minor may not disaffirm an agreement signed by a parent. She relies on two cases to support her position, both of which are inapposite because they address discrete public policy concerns not at issue here [*e.g.,* a healthcare contract containing an arbitration provision signed by the minor's father and a liability release signed by a parent relating to a minor's participation in a school program]. Further, because there is a statutory procedure governing contracts in which minors agree to render artistic or creative services, there is no danger that talent managers will decline to contract with minors absent their parents contracting on their behalf. (*See* Fam.Code, §§ 6750, 6751, subd. (a).)[6]

Second, Berg argues that Craig cannot disaffirm the agreement because it was for his and his family's necessities. Family Code section 6712 provides that a valid contract cannot be disaffirmed by a minor if all of the following requirements are met: the contract is to pay the reasonable value of things necessary for the support of the minor or the minor's family, the things have actually been furnished to the minor or the minor's family, and the contract is entered into by the minor when not under the care of a parent or guardian able to provide for the minor or the minor's family. These requirements are not met here. The agreement was not a contract to pay for the necessities of life for Craig or his family.... Family Code section 6712 does not bar the minor's disaffirmance of the contract....

We find that Craig was entitled to and did disaffirm the agreement which, among other things, required him to arbitrate his disputes with Berg. On this basis alone, therefore, the judgment confirming the arbitration award must be reversed.

Although it is unnecessary to our disposition, we further find that Craig was entitled to and did disaffirm the arbitration award because he was never represented by an appointed guardian ad litem.

Code of Civil Procedure section 372, subdivision (a) requires that a minor who is a party to a lawsuit "shall appear either by a guardian or conservator of the estate or by a guardian ad litem appointed by the court in which the action or proceeding is pending, or by a judge thereof, in each case." As aptly explained in *Keane v. Penha*

---

6. While we recognize that the agreement here does not fall within the parameters of the contracts specified by Family Code section 6750, subdivision (a), which generally involve the employment of a minor to render artistic services, there was evidence below that parties to agreements for the provision of personal management services in the entertainment industry routinely seek court approval for the protection of all involved.

76 Cal.App.2d 693, 696 (1946): "It is the general rule that an omission to cause the appointment of a guardian if there be none is fatal to all subsequent steps taken in the action.... Unless a minor is 'duly represented as provided by law' at the time a judgment is entered against him his right to disaffirm such judgment 'continues until barred by laches after the minor has attained the age of majority.' Such a judgment is voidable and may be disaffirmed. The right of disaffirmance by a minor of a judgment rendered voidable by the fact that he was not represented by a guardian in the action is absolute, and such right continues throughout his minority."

Berg contends that no appointment of a guardian ad litem was necessary because Meshiel functioned as Craig's "guardian." She relies on a declaration submitted in support of appellants' petition to vacate the arbitration award in which Meshiel averred that she was "the natural mother and guardian of Craig." Meshiel's self-characterization in no way obviated the need for the appointment of a guardian ad litem to represent Craig's interests. Code of Civil Procedure, section 372, subdivision (a) provides that "[a] guardian ad litem may be appointed in any case when it is deemed by the court in which the action or proceeding is prosecuted, or by a judge thereof, expedient to appoint a guardian ad litem to represent the minor, ... notwithstanding that the person may have a guardian or conservator of the estate and may have appeared by the guardian or conservator of the estate."

Such an appointment was required here due to the inherent conflict of interest between Craig and Meshiel. The agreement expressly provided that if even Craig disaffirmed, Meshiel would remain liable for commissions due Berg. It was therefore not in Meshiel's interest to have Craig disaffirm the agreement because Berg would look to her, personally, for satisfaction of Craig's obligations under the agreement. As such, Meshiel's interests in the lawsuit were in direct conflict with those of her son's. It is clear that Meshiel, as Craig's guardian, could not adequately represent his interests. "'When there is a potential conflict between a perceived parental responsibility and an obligation to assist the court in achieving a just and speedy determination of the action,' a court has the right to select a guardian ad litem who is not a parent if that guardian would best protect the child's interests." (*Williams v. Superior Court, supra.* 147 Cal.App.4th at 49.) As such, it was necessary for Craig to have a guardian ad litem appointed to separately represent his interest with respect to Berg's claims....

Appellants do not generally distinguish their arguments between mother and son, apparently assuming that if Craig disaffirms the agreement and judgment, Meshiel would be permitted to escape liability as well. But a disaffirmance of an agreement by a minor does not operate to terminate the contractual obligations of the parent who signed the agreement. The agreement Meshiel signed provided that Craig's disaffirmance would not serve to void or avoid Meshiel's obligations under the agreement and that Meshiel remained liable for commissions due Berg regardless of Craig's disaffirmance. Accordingly, we find no basis for Meshiel to avoid her independent obligations under the agreement.

Appellants remaining challenges to the arbitration award do not mandate reversal of the judgment as to Meshiel. They argue that the award must be vacated because the arbitrator refused to postpone the hearing despite sufficient cause being shown. (Code Civ. Proc., § 1286.2, subd. (a)(5).) They also raise the defense that the agreement was unenforceable because Berg was allegedly performing the acts of an unlicensed agent in violation of the Talent Agencies Act (Lab. Code, § 1700 et seq.) (the Act), an issue not raised at the arbitration.[7] But Meshiel fails to explain how these issues can be considered after she stipulated to the finality of the arbitration award. More importantly, her failure to file a timely petition to vacate the arbitration award bars her from challenging the judgment confirming the award on appeal.

While we conclude that Craig nevertheless had the right to disaffirm the arbitration award and the subsequent judgment as an unrepresented minor, Meshiel has not provided us with any authority that would permit her now to challenge the award against her. Accordingly, the judgment confirming the arbitration award is affirmed as to Meshiel. The judgment is reversed as to Craig and affirmed as to Meshiel. The parties to bear their own costs on appeal.

Notes and Questions

a. California has a similar statutory provision to that discussed above.

A minor cannot disaffirm a contract, otherwise valid, entered into during minority, either during the actual minority of the minor entering into such contract or at any time thereafter, with a duly licensed talent agency as defined in Section 1700.4 to secure him engagements to render artistic or creative services in motion pictures, television, the production of phonograph records, the legitimate or living stage, or otherwise in the entertainment field including, but without being limited to, services as an actor, actress, dancer, musician, comedian, singer, or other performer or entertainer, or as a writer, director, producer, production executive, choreographer, composer, conductor or designer, the blank form of which has been approved by the Labor Commissioner pursuant to Section 1700.23, where such contract has been approved by the superior court of the county where such minor resides or is employed.

CAL. LAB. CODE § 1700.37 (2003).

b. The language in both California Labor Code section 1700.37 and New York Arts and Cultural Affairs Law section 35.03 provides that a court approved contract involving a minor cannot be disaffirmed. After *Scott Eden Management v. Kavovit*, is there any remaining need to seek court approval for manager contracts or talent agency contracts? So long as the talented minor enters into a role prior to the disaffirmance, the *Scott Eden Management* decision suggests the manager remains entitled

---

7. In its amicus curiae brief, SAG raises for the first time the issue that this defense must be resolved by the California Labor Commissioner, who has exclusive authority to hear disputes arising under the Act.... Appellants never raised this issue below and we decline to consider it. "California courts refuse to consider arguments raised by amicus curiae when those arguments are not presented in the trial court, and are not urged by the parties on appeal...."

to that income stream in perpetuity despite the lack of any judicial approval. Would a California court give this same construction to the meaning of its statute?

Problem 3-C

Bryce stops by your office holding a folded-up contract. Bryce explains that last year, at the age of seventeen, Bryce agreed to a three-year contract to appear in direct-to-video films being shot in California. Bryce appeared in the first of the films, an adult-oriented comedy. Although Bryce was not featured in any of the film's scenes that involved nudity or more mature content, Bryce feels the film was terrible and embarrassing both personally and professionally. Bryce has recently been asked to appear in the second film. Even though Bryce had not appeared nude in the first film, the signed contract included a nudity rider, specifically authorizing the filmmakers to photograph Bryce nude in the film. The contract was signed in California, the same state where Bryce had acted in the first film.

Bryce wants to repudiate the contract, get out of any future filming obligation, and ideally have Bryce's name removed from any future copies of the first film. Bryce is not asking to enjoin the distribution of the first film or to have the film re-edited.

Inform Bryce of the basis for terminating the agreement or disaffirming the obligations under the agreement and whether the California courts would allow the disaffirmance.

D. Racial and Gender Disparity Issues

1. Introduction

The entertainment industries have long been identified with contributing to the pay and power disparities in American society. Salaries for male stars are generally much higher than for their female counterparts, the number of women and minorities in the decision-making positions continues to be underrepresented, and the content created as a result often reinforces stereotypes and prejudices.

There have been few, if any, major examples of litigation that have changed these outcomes. Nonetheless, the research and consequences are well-understood, creating an ethical imperative for lawyers to conduct their business in a manner that advances equality as part of their obligations to their clients. The Center for the Study of Women in Television & Film at San Diego State University provides annual reports on both the representation of women and minorities within the entertainment content and on their employment within the industry.

In 2019, the USC Annenberg Inclusion Initiative published the study, *Latinos in Film: Erasure on Screen & Behind the Camera Across 1,200 Popular Movies.*[8] After doc-

---

8. Stacy Smith, et al., USC Annenberg Inclusion Initiative, Latinos in Film: Erasure on Screen & Behind the Camera Across 1,200 Popular Movies, https://www.nalip.org/about (pub-

umenting the systemic lack of Hispanic and Latino representation in acting roles and production across the entertainment industry, "[t]he report includes several suggestions that individuals, organizations, and companies can use to increase the opportunities for Latino actors and content creators to work in Hollywood."[9] The report provides a summary of the statistics:

#1 The Prevalence of Latino Leading Actors Is Vastly Out of Step with U.S. Population

- Across the 100 top grossing movies from 2007–2018, only 3% of films featured leads or co leads with Latino actors.
- Females represented 49% (n=17) of the leads or co leads. However, 5 of those 17 roles went to one female actress (Cameron Diaz).
- Summing across protagonist types (leads, co leads, actors driving ensemble casts), the most frequently hired Latino actors were Cameron Diaz, Jennifer Lopez, Eugenio Derbez, and Jessica Alba.
- Only 8 male and 2 female leads, co leads or members of an ensemble cast that were 45 years of age or older at the time of theatrical release. Both female leads were played by Jennifer Lopez.
- Only 4.5% of all speaking characters were Latino. This is 13.8 percentage points below U.S. Census. Despite all of the talk about diversity and inclusion in Hollywood and the popular press, these findings represent no change in depictions of the largest ethnic group in America, who also comprise 39% of the population of the state of California, and 49% of Los Angeles' population.
- 77% of 50 U.S. states and 2 territories have populations with a higher percentage of Latinos than what we currently see in Hollywood films (4.5%).

#2 Erasure, Not Inclusion, is the Norm for Latinos on Screen

- Forty-seven percent of the 1,200 movies in the sample completely erased Latino speaking characters.
- Out of 1,200 movies, a total of 688 erased males from the Latino community and 828 erased females. The degree of invisibility between 2007 and 2018 seems to be decreasing for Latinas on screen. Though, more films erased Latinas in 2018 (70) than 2017 (64).
- A mere 5 films out of 500 showed a Latino character from the LGBT community between 2014 and 2018.
- A total of 387 of 400 movies were missing Latino characters with a disability.

#3 Poor, Isolated, Criminal: Latino Stereotypes in Film

- A qualitative analysis of 200 top films from 2017–2018 revealed that 82% of these movies assessed only featured one top billed Latino, 11% two, and 5%

lished in association with the National Association of Latino Independent Producers and Wise Entertainment) (last visited Oct. 25, 2019).

9. *Id.*

three. Across 200 movies, only one featured 5 Latino actors across all 5 top billed slots.

- Every film with a Latino in a top billed role was analyzed for stereotypes across all Latino speaking characters.

- One of the most frequent portrayals on screen involved stripping Latino characters of their culture or community. A full 36% of all Latino speaking characters and 60% of top billed Latinos were depicted without any cultural artifacts, symbols, or references to the characters' ethnic group.

- Just under a quarter (24%) of all of Latino speaking characters and 28% of top billed Latino talent were depicted as law breakers across a range of violent and non-violent crimes. Over half (61.9%) of all characters shown engaged in illegal activity were part of an organized crime group such as gang members or drug dealers. Thirty-eight percent of criminals were depicted committing fraud, thievery, murder, or having previously been in prison for reasons not made clear in the film.

- One-sixth (17%) of all top billed Latino talent and one-eighth (13%) of all Latino speaking characters were shown poor or impoverished on screen.

- Of the 52% of Latino characters depicted with a job, 54% were shown holding an occupation that did not require college education (e.g., salesperson, construction worker, and farmer). Thirty-one percent were shown in law enforcement (e.g., police officers, members of the military).

- Only 4% of jobs were high level occupations involving STEM careers and 9 depicted high level/educated professionals (i.e., 3 reporters, 3 individuals running a family corporation, 1 medical doctor, 1 judge, and 1 lawyer).

#4 Hollywood Employs Few Latino Content Creators Behind the Camera

- Of the 3,616 Produced by credits, only 3% were held by Latinos. Seventy-eight of those credits were held by Latinos and 19 were held by Latinas; this is a gender ratio of 4 male producers to every 1 female.

- Only 4% of directors were Latinos out of the 1,335 holding top jobs. Forty-eight of those directors were male and 1 was female (i.e., Patricia Riggen). A total of 28 individual or unique Latino directors worked across the 1,200 top films studied.

- Twenty-nine percent of the 28 directors were U.S. filmmakers and 71% are international filmmakers.

- A full 48% of directors were clients of William Morris Endeavor (WME). Twenty-six percent were represented by Creative Artists Agency and 17% by United Talent Agency.

- Sundance Film Festival submissions in 2017 and 2018 were assessed. In terms of U.S. dramatic submissions, a full 7% of directors were identified as Latino with 88% male, 11% female, and 1% gender non conforming.

- Of international feature submissions, a full 13% of directors were Latino. Of those, 81% were male, 19% female, and <1% gender non conforming.

- Only 3% of the casting directors across the sample of 1,200 films were Latino.

- When a Latino director was attached to a film, the percentage of Latino characters on screen increased from 4% to 13%.

- Similar increases were observed when a Latino producer worked on a movie — the percentage of Latino characters on screen climbed from 4% to 9%. Finally, when a Latino casting director was attached, the on screen prevalence of Latino characters improved from 4% to 10%.[10]

The Center for the Study of Women in Television and Media has tracked women's employment for over two decades. It reports that "[in] 2018, women comprised 20% of all directors, writers, producers, executive producers, editors, and cinematographers working on the top 250 domestic grossing films. This represents an increase of 2 percentage points from 18% in 2017."[11] Despite this modest annual improvement, however, "only 1% of films employed 10 or more women in the above roles. In contrast, 74% of films employed 10 or more men."[12] The data were consistently low in each professional job category. "Women accounted for 8% of directors working on the top 250 films in 2018, down 3 percentage points from 11% in 2017. This is 1 percentage point below the 9% achieved in 1998."[13]

The challenges are similar regarding racial diversity as well as gender diversity within the entertainment fields, and particularly problematic for women of color.

> Despite the fact that changing demographics in the United States reflect more racial and ethnic diversity than ever before, the film workforce, along with the films they produce, continues to fall short of mirroring the diverse population it serves. Even though this is a reality, the film workforce continues to play a leading role in shaping the American culture in unique ways by producing films that allow its audience to escape, dream, imagine the impossible, as well as create their own ending to a story within a 2-hour timeframe or less....
>
> In 2016, the lack of diversity represented in the film industry reached a boiling point when several African American and White actors such as Brad Pitt, Will Smith, Jada Pinkett Smith, Spike Lee, Viola Davis, George Clooney, Don Cheadle, Reese Witherspoon, and Chris Rock, along with President

10. *Id.*
11. Martha M. Lauzen, The Celluloid Ceiling: Behind-the-Scenes Employment of Women on the Top 100, 250, and 500 Films of 2018, https://womenintvfilm.sdsu.edu/wp-content/uploads/2019/01/2018_Celluloid_Ceiling_Report.pdf (last visited June 28, 2019) ("It is the longest-running and most comprehensive study of women's behind-the-scenes employment in film available. This annual study is sponsored by the Center for the Study of Women in Television and Film, San Diego State University, San Diego, CA 92182, lauzen@mail.sdsu.edu.").
12. *Id.*
13. *Id.*

Obama, called on the film industry publicly to diversify its workforce and actors.[14]

For example, in the field of journalism, the gender inequality has been well documented:

> **Women in (Washington) Journalism**: Women in journalism already face structural inequalities that reflect a constellation of complex "historical, material and cultural/social conditions".... Gender can be explored through analysis of byline disparities, promotion and retention patterns, beat assignments, source selection, and gender representation in news coverage. In 2015, The Global Media Monitoring Project found "persistent and emerging gaps in gender portrayal and representation in not only traditional (print and broadcast) media, but in new electronic media forms" in research across 114 countries. Gendered practices emerge in the routines and rituals of news work, often with the curious pattern of women denying the importance of gender to their work while simultaneously expressing frustration about how male journalists fail to treat them as equals.[15]

A study focusing on the gender bias in Ireland highlighted the patterns in the television industry:

> Media production work cultures were also gendered in the sense that there was 'considerable evidence that gendered identities at work were being constructed in traditional ways, drawing in particular on women's perceived "soft skills."' Bias in the perception of women's skills and their appropriateness for the workplace sometimes led to women being given particular assignments or types of production jobs. Being female was a salient issue when it came to commissioning. One female director recounted that 'the interviewer said "we really should have a woman direct this", and it really struck me that he was looking at me and seeing a woman, not seeing my work ...' (Respondent B). One cameraperson noted 'Going out to certain stories, a victim of some incident, a murder or a rape, you would be chosen to go because you were female' (Respondent J).
>
> More frequently, the gendering of skills worked to disadvantage women. For more than half of the respondents, negative bias in perceptions of their skills was gender based. A presenter commented 'A producer told me that the documentary would be taken more seriously with a male voice over' (Respondent I). A female cameraperson noted 'I've gone for interviews ... and men with one third of the experience I have were given the job' (Respondent

---

14. Chaunda L. Scott, *Under-Representation of Diversity in the Scientific, Technical, and Film Workforce*, *in* Diversity in the Workforce: Current Issues and Emerging Trends (Marilyn Y. Byrd & Chaunda L. Scott eds., 2d ed., 2018).

15. Nikki Usher, Jesse Holcomb & Justin Littman, *Twitter Makes It Worse: Political Journalists, Gendered Echo Chambers, and the Amplification of Gender Bias*, 23 Int'l J. Press/Pols. 324 (2018) (internal citations omitted).

C). A female director was equally blunt about perceptions of women's skills: 'a financier, without meeting me, vetoed my appointment ... it was because the financier said that "You're not going to get the material, you're not going to get the emotion, because it's a boy's story"' (Respondent B). A producer noted that while women often had good people skills, these were undervalued in the industry (Respondent O)....

Within the media industry there was also a clear sense that men were perceived to be more suitable to senior or management roles than women.... A producer commented 'There was automatically higher reverence for men' (Respondent O). Women were simply not presumed to be in charge, even when they were. 'I was the senior producer-director on a documentary, but at every meeting people would immediately address their comments to a male associate producer ...' (Respondent D). As well as gendered presumptions regarding status and skills women also faced outright gender discrimination....

In these ways women in media work are structurally disadvantaged by a gendered work culture. But a further problem is that the networked nature of production work makes it difficult for women to assert their rights, for fear of gaining a reputation within industry networks for being 'difficult' or 'troublesome' and thereby risking future work.[16]

Just as there is a pervasive underrepresentation in the profession, there is an underrepresentation and stereotyping in the entertainment content.

To tackle the underrepresentation of women in movies in 1985, the cartoonist Alison Bechdel published a test in her comic strip *Dykes to Watch Out For* to assess how fairly women are presented in media. The Bechdel-Wallace test (denoted as the Bechdel test) has three rules that a movie has to pass to be considered "women friendly":

1. It has to have at least two women in it.

2. The women have to talk to each other.

3. The women must talk about something besides a man.

Only 57% of current movies pass this test. To Bechdel's surprise, the media adopted her joke, and today it is a standard for female representation in movies....

The state of women in the film industry is similar to other domains: women are underrepresented and badly portrayed. The *Boxed In 2017–18* report observed a 2% decline in female major characters across all platforms, compared to the previous year.[17]

---

16. Anne O'Brien, *'Men Own Television': Why Women Leave Media Work*, 36 Media, Culture & Soc'y 1207, 1202–14, (2017–18) (internal citations omitted).

17. Dima Kagan, Thomas Chesney & Michael Firez, *Using Data Science to Understand the Film Industry's Gender Gap*, https://arxiv.org/abs/1903.06469 (last revised Mar. 24, 2019) (citing A. Bechdel, The Rule, Dykes to Watch for (1985); other internal citations omitted).

2. Riders

The obligation of a SAG-AFTRA performer to perform simulated sex acts, to appear nude or to appear partially nude must be agreed to by the performer separately from the standard contract. The rider is designed to protect the performer by restricting the set only to necessary personnel, limiting the use of the footage shot, providing approvals for the actors of the footage used (if the actor is of sufficient stature and bargaining leverage), and specifying the details of the shoot. SAG-AFTRA explains the purpose of the rider as follows:

> The nudity rider should include a detailed description of the scene(s), the type of nudity or physical contact required, limitations on use of the footage and production stills (if any), and any other conditions that you and a producer have agreed upon. Remember, even if you have signed a nudity rider, you have the right to withdraw consent at any time prior to filming of the scene.

Despite the explanation of the union, an example of the nudity rider required by Central Casting for the HBO series Westworld caught the public's attention. The rider provided for background performers was explicit in highlighting the demands on the cast, but provided none of the other protections recommended by SAG-AFTRA:

> You are being given this Disclosure & Consent to Work because you have knowingly and freely accepted an assignment as a background actor on the project Westworld ("the Project") and understand and accept the nature of the assignment as described below. This document serves to inform you that this project will require you to be fully nude and/or witness others fully nude and participate in graphic sexual situations. By accepting this Project assignment, you may be required to do any of the following: appear fully nude; wear a pubic hair patch; perform genital-to-genital touching; have your genitals painted; simulate oral sex with hand-to-genital touching; contort to form a table-like shape while being fully nude; pose on all fours while others who are fully nude ride on your back; ride on someone's back while you are both fully nude; and other assorted acts the Project may require ("Various Acts"), The Project will also include language and sexual situations that some may consider personally objectionable or uncomfortable ("Project Environment"). If you object to or are not comfortable with working on the Project for any reason, including the graphic nature, required Various Acts, and/or the Project Environment described in this Disclosure & Consent, you will not be able to work on the Project.

In addition to the potential for coercion when filming nudity, there are many other considerations that should be taken into account. Increasingly, it is difficult for production companies to stop unauthorized filming on sets or the leaks of footage from the production houses. To protect the cast members, some nudity riders require that clothing and reflective tape be used to limit the extent to which the cast member is exposed. Production companies must also be very sure that the actors performing in nude scenes are at least eighteen years old.

In Canada, for example, the collective bargaining agreement is more protective of the performers:

> Nude scenes can be anything from a performer taking a leisurely bubble bath to a violent sexual attack and everything in between. The rider must define the tone, the flavor, the exact nature of the nude scene. You may be comfortable with a gentle love scene but not an explicitly aggressive one. Having this clearly defined in the rider eliminates the possibility of the director making changes to the nude scene or making demands on you during a scene without your prior written consent. Take a look at clause A2402 in the IPA. It states: Performers may refuse to do anything not specified in the Performer's contract without liability or forfeiture of any portion of the Contracted Fee.

> [The nudity rider should include all] the stuff you talked about with your agent and the director: the maximum degree of nudity required; if you are to be shot from the front or back or side only. Perhaps you are to be shot only from the waist up or maybe you agree to full frontal nudity. A description of the clothing if you are to appear semi-nude (see-through clothing for example). Body suit, modesty patches, tape etc. Maybe you have specific lighting requirements or you want to be sure you will be robed between takes. You can specify who will be allowed on a closed set and indicate the maximum number of persons allowed on set during the final rehearsal and filming of the nude scene. You could also have it state the number of days you will be required to be nude.[18]

A second kind of rider is also becoming a political force in Hollywood. Known as an "Inclusion Rider," designed to require the production company to take specific, concrete steps to increase diversity and inclusion on a production or throughout the company.

> A handful of high-profile actors and directors, including Brie Larson, Matt Damon, Ben Affleck and Paul Feig, have expressed varying commitments to using inclusion riders. But advocates have repeatedly argued that powerful studios could have a much greater impact by adopting company-wide policies. WarnerMedia, the parent company of HBO and Warner Bros, did not provide details of its policy in the announcement, saying in a statement that in the "early stages of the production process, we will engage with our writers, producers and directors to create a plan for implementing this commitment to diversity and inclusion on our projects, with the goal of providing opportunities for individuals from under-represented groups at all levels."

> Stacy L. Smith, founder of the Annenberg Inclusion Initiative at the University of Southern California, first outlined inclusion riders in a 2016 speech and has argued that an effective way to improve representation for women,

18. ACTRA, Nudity in Film Survival Guide 7, http://www.ubcp.com/wp-content/uploads/ACTRA_Nudity_Survival_Guide.pdf (last visited June 28, 2019).

people of color, LGBT people and other marginalized groups is to make proactive commitments in contracts.... WarnerMedia said it would issue an annual report on its progress.[19]

3. Representation

The following 1981 case from Tennessee involving Loretta Lynn provides an unfortunately common story of bad representation, weak statutory safeguards, and years of abuse and neglect. Consistent with the lack of participation in the industry, it reflects on the systemic mismanagement and tendency to take advantage of those in the industry who lack representation and power. It does not develop additional case law on managers and agents, but should serve to remind lawyers that they need to protect their clients from the fiduciaries who surround them.

Wil-Helm Agency v. Lynn
618 S.W.2d 748 (Tenn. Ct. App. 1981)

The Wil-Helm Agency sues for damages due to the breach of a theatrical agency contract entered into between the agency and Loretta Lynn, an artist. Loretta Lynn filed a counterclaim wherein she avers that the agency breached the contract and, therefore, owes her damages and she further alleges that the agency released her from the contract. The chancellor found that the agency had breached the contract and, in addition, had released Loretta Lynn from the contract. The chancellor further held that the amounts due each party offset each other and allowed no monetary award to either party.

The agency appeals insisting that the chancellor erred in finding: (1) that the agency breached the contract; (2) that the agency released Loretta Lynn from the contract; and (3) that the damages due the parties offset each other....

Loretta Lynn was born in the area of Van Leer, Kentucky, and at the age of fourteen years married O.V. Lynn of that same area. A few months after the marriage, O.V. Lynn went to the state of Washington and obtained employment as an agricultural laborer. Later Loretta joined him at Custer, Washington. Loretta began singing at local gatherings and formed a band which soon became fully booked in the area at various local places of entertainment. She appeared on the Buck Owens show and entered into a recording contract under the Zero label. Loretta wrote and recorded the song "I'm a Honky Tonk Girl," appeared on various radio shows, appeared as a guest performer on the Grand Ole Opry, and was becoming recognized as a budding young artist.

In 1961 she and her husband moved to Nashville, Tennessee. In that year she entered into her first two-year contract with the Wil-Helm Agency. Thereafter, she en-

---

19. Sam Levin, *Warner Bros to launch 'inclusion rider' diversity policy with Michael B Jordan film*, GUARDIAN, Sept. 8, 2018, https://www.theguardian.com/film/2018/sep/05/warner-bros-adopts-company-wide-inclusion-policy-to-boost-diversity.

tered into another five-year contract with that agency. On April 12, 1966, she and the agency entered into the contract now under consideration. This contract provides in pertinent part as follows:

WITNESSETH

1. The Artist hereby engages the Agent as his sole and exclusive personal representative and adviser in the radio, television, recording and personal appearances field of entertainment throughout the world and in outer space for a period of Twenty years (20 years)

2. The Agent's duties hereunder shall be as follows: To use all reasonable efforts to procure employment for the artist in any branch of the field of entertainment in which the Artist notifies the Agent that his services are or will be available. In addition, at the Artist's request to:

(a) Assist the Artist in negotiating with respect to all forms of advertising and commercial tie-ups in all fields, wherever the Artist's name, business likeness or voice may be used, including but not limited to the radio, television, recording and personal appearances field of entertainment.

(b) Counsel and advise the Artist in matters which concern his professional interest in the radio, television, recording and personal appearances field of entertainment.

3. The Agent hereby accepts this engagement and agrees to perform the services specified herein. The Agent shall have the right to render his services to other persons, either in a capacity in which he is hereby engaged or otherwise. However, the Artist agrees not to engage any other person to act for him in the capacity for which the Agent has been engaged. The Artist hereby represents and warrants that he is wholly free to enter into this agreement and has no contract or obligations which will conflict with it.

An Amendment of the same date was attached to the contract which provides in part as follows:

(3) This Amendment and the Agreement shall be null and void in the event there is a change of ownership in the Agency. It being the Artist (demands) that she be associated only with current management.

The contract and the amendment were signed by Smiley Wilson for the agency and by Loretta Lynn.

The Wil-Helm Agency apparently was a partnership composed of the four Wilburn brothers: Doyle, Teddy, Leslie and Lester. As we view the lawsuit, it is immaterial whether there was a change in the ownership of the agency, and the amendment to the contract will not be further considered.

The parties enjoyed several years of successful association. Loretta's popularity grew, and she is now recognized as an outstanding star in the field of country music. From 1961 through the latter part of the 1960s, the agency assisted Loretta and played an important part in her rise to stardom. Teddy Wilburn worked closely with Loretta.

When the 1966 contract was signed, he was spending several hours almost daily with Loretta. He assisted her in rewriting her songs and advised her on costumes, mannerisms, and lines. Loretta was very fond of Teddy Wilburn; she sought his counsel and followed his advice. She appeared as the only female artist on the Wilburn Brothers Show. The agency obtained a recording contract for Loretta with Decca Records. She made appearances on national television and followed a hard-working road show schedule.

In about 1967, Doyle Wilburn began to drink alcohol in excessive amounts. When drinking or drunk, he was extremely abusive and boorish. This conduct by Doyle resulted in Teddy Wilburn leaving the show in 1968. Teddy moved to California and returned to Nashville only to do certain television work. It appears that Smiley Wilson then became the member of the agency upon whom Loretta depended. Wilson did his job and aided the artist; however, she missed the expertise and experience of Teddy Wilburn. It seems that Teddy did relent and return to the show, only to leave again in 1971 for the same reason as previously stated.

With Teddy gone, it appears that Doyle Wilburn took it upon himself to be more closely identified with Loretta and her work. The record is replete with instances which reveal almost constant misconduct on the part of Doyle Wilburn acting as the agent of Loretta. Some of the more glaring instances of misconduct are: (1) insulting the producer of the Johnny Carson Show while there to close a deal for Loretta to appear on that show; (2) drunkenness on the part of Doyle Wilburn while on the stage acting as master of ceremonies; (3) actually disturbing Loretta during performances; (4) the telling of sacrilegious jokes on Loretta's show in Boston, Massachusetts; (5) drunken vomiting on the dinner table at a post-performance party given for patrons, promoters, disc jockeys and their wives; (6) drunkenness throughout most of a tour in England; (7) drunkenness during the time Loretta was preparing jingles for the Coca Cola ads; (8) getting drunk and passing out during the signing of the Glo-coat contract; (9) being so drunk while emceeing Loretta's performance at a rodeo that he fell off the stage; (10) drunkenness when taping Loretta on the Ed Sullivan Show; (11) insulting the black musicians while on the David Frost Show; (12) being drunk on practically every road trip, interfering with Loretta's need for rest on the bus, ignoring instructions of airline personnel while on flights, and generally being an obnoxious drunk in the presence of people upon whom the success of the artist depended. This conduct was carried on while Doyle Wilburn was acting as the representative of the agency with whom Loretta had contracted. This conduct was known to all members of the agency; some effort was made to reason with Doyle, but to no avail.

In about October 1970 Smiley Wilson left the agency. He was replaced by Mr. Brumley who was then replaced by Leslie Hart. Hart advised Loretta that she was being woefully mismanaged and recommended that she see an attorney. Up to this time Loretta had not received independent advice on anything. The agency kept her books, handled her financing, and referred her to the agency's lawyer for any personal legal advice. Upon the advice of Hart, Loretta employed an attorney. Upon investigating the situation, the attorney wrote a letter dated April 1, 1971, to the agency saying the agency had breached the contract, and Loretta would not further abide by it. Further negotiations between the lawyers resulted in certain letters which the chancellor found constitute a release of the contract by the agency. As we view the situation, it is of no import whether the agency released Loretta from the contract; we hold that the contract was breached by the agency.

We agree with the chancellor that the conduct of Doyle Wilburn as the representative of the agency was entirely inconsistent with the duty owed the artist under the contract. The agreement is a bilateral contract wherein each party was obligated to the other to render certain performances, the carrying out of which by each party was essential to the realization of benefits under the contract. Each party to the contract was under an implied obligation to restrain from doing any act that would delay or prevent the other party's performance of the contract. Each party had the right to proceed free of hinderance by the other party, and if such other party interfered, hindered, or prevented the performance to such an extent as to render the performance difficult and diminish the benefits to be received, the first party could treat the contract as broken and was not bound to proceed under the added burdens.

There is ample material evidence that the agency, by the conduct of its representative, committed a substantial breach of its contract with Loretta Lynn. The chancellor is affirmed in this respect.

Damages.

The chancellor referred the question of damages to the clerk and master, but, after the taking of considerable proof, that official passed the issue back to the chancellor without making a finding of any kind. Thereupon, the chancellor found as follows:

> After sifting through the proof and after reviewing the previous Memorandum and the orders based on it, the Court concludes that the claims of the parties off-set each other and should be dismissed. The plaintiff Agency claims $178,556.72 due on the contract up until the date of termination with allowances for dates already booked to November of 1971. The defendant counter-claimed for damages for breach of the management agreement. The proof shows that the defendant was being booked at a fee of $2,500.00 to $4,000.00 per appearance up until the date of termination of the agreement while an artist of her stature should have commanded a much higher figure.

> A simple calculation based on the number of dates she worked in a few years prior to 1971 shows how much of a loss that was. In addition, the failure to expose her to national television and the stress of the conditions under which she worked result in damages that are reasonably certain and should off-set the plaintiff's claim. The Court declines to speculate on the amount of damages the plaintiff would be entitled to if the decision had been otherwise.

We accept the figure of $178,556.72 as the amount due the agency under the contract up until the date of termination with allowances for dates already booked to November 1971. The artist claims that this amount can not be awarded to the plaintiff agency because the plaintiff breached the contract and is not entitled to any amount thereunder. We disagree with the artist in this respect.

The record reveals that the plaintiff agency committed a substantial breach of the contract. The defendant artist did not commit any breach of the contract. Therefore, if the plaintiff is to recover at all, it must do so upon the theory that it has rendered a part performance of value, that it has done more good than harm to the artist, and that the artist will be unjustly enriched and the plaintiff unjustly penalized if the artist is allowed to retain the beneficial part performance without paying anything in return. By the same token, the plaintiff is the wrongdoer, and it must not be allowed to profit from its own wrong. Therefore, allowance must be made to the defendant artist in damages for the full extent of the injury that the plaintiff's breach has caused her. Under the facts of this bilateral contract, whereby each party agreed to carry out certain performances in return for performances by the other party, we conclude that the plaintiff agency is entitled to its commissions based upon its part performance less the amount of the injury to the artist caused by the breach. Having accepted the figure of $178,556.72 as the amount due the agency for its part performance, it must now be determined in what amount, if any, the artist was damaged by the breach.

The defendant artist averred by counterclaim that due to the conduct of Doyle Wilburn, she had been deprived of engagements as an artist, that she had suffered physical and emotional distress and had been rendered unable to perform to her capacity, and that subsequent to the breach and the termination of the contract, the agency had held itself out as the sole and exclusive agent of the artist thereby depriving her of engagements and the resulting revenues therefrom. By amendment to the counterclaim, the artist averred that over the years the agency had booked her for engagements at a price below that to which she was entitled and had entered into a recording contract for her at a rate substantially less than her professional ability demanded, all to her financial detriment and in breach of the agency's duties under the contract.

As noted, the chancellor found (1) that the artist was booked at a fee below that which an artist of her stature should have commanded, and (2) that the stress of the conditions under which she was forced to work resulted in damages that are reasonably certain.

There is competent and material evidence that Loretta Lynn won more awards, had a larger following, and was more sought after than any other artist in her field of entertainment. There is competent and material evidence that artists of less ability, following, and demand were drawing from $5,000 to $7,500 for a performance during the late 1960s and up to 1971. There is ample proof that Loretta Lynn should have been drawing those amounts instead of the $2,500 to $4,000 range in which she was booked. The plaintiff agency presented proof (Exhibit 53) which purported to list every performance of Loretta Lynn for which the agency claimed a commission. From a review of the number of those performances and an application of a reasonable average fee at which the artist should have been booked, the chancellor concluded that the damage she suffered from having been "underbooked" for several years more than offset the amount proved by the agency as owing to it.

The chancellor properly held that strain and stress unnecessarily suffered by the actress due to the conduct of the agency representatives resulted in damages for which the artist could recover. There is ample material evidence to sustain the finding that the conditions under which she had to work, rendered the artist nervous, uncertain, dismayed, and embarrassed, all to her professional detriment through no fault of her own.

Although not ruled on by the chancellor, we find another element of damage to the artist based upon the recording contract it entered into for the artist with Decca Records. It seems that in the early years of the recording industry a recording company suffered substantial losses due to records being broken while in transit to the buyers. As a result, a custom built up that when contracting with an artist the recording company would deduct 10% from the sales figures to take care of this breakage, and the artist was paid a royalty based upon 90% of the sales figure. Later records were made of plastic or some other material not subject to the breakage previously sustained. The proof establishes that as of 1966, when Decca contracted to record Loretta, all recording contracts being renewed and all new contracts being entered into provided for a royalty based upon the 100% figure. This was done at the mere request of the artist or agent. However, the plaintiff agency booked Loretta at a royalty based upon the 90% figure. In 1972, after the parties had gone their separate ways, Decca voluntarily changed the contract so as to pay royalties on the 100% figure. There is material evidence that the loss suffered by the artist because of this breach of duty on the part of the agency amounted to approximately $200,000 during the period from 1966 to 1971.

We, therefore, agree with the chancellor that the damages suffered by the artist more than offset those amounts claimed by the agency for its part performance of the contract. Admittedly, neither the chancellor nor this court fix the actual amount of damages to which the artist is entitled due to the breach of the contract by the agency. We have, however, fully satisfied ourselves that the damages thus suffered exceed the amount due the plaintiff agency. The artist did not appeal. We conclude that under all the circumstances of this lawsuit, the chancellor's decree is supported by a preponderance of the evidence, and that decree is affirmed.

The cost in this court is adjudged against the appellant, Wil-Helm Agency, for which execution may issue, if necessary.

Notes and Questions

a. There are a myriad of discriminatory acts, large and small, that shape the entertainment industry. The nature of talent representation reflects one of the areas where women and minorities have received the worst treatment. As the entertainment industries have finally begun to recognize their lack of diversity, these industries are also beginning to recognize the excessive influence and revenue of the talent agencies, and their over-reach in booking fees and with production demands.

b. Although the context for rights of publicity and the preemption issues involving publicity rights and copyrights are addressed in later chapters, the gender issues of *KNB Enterprises v. Matthews*, 78 Cal. App. 4th 362 (2000), are worth noting in the context of this section. Rather than enforcing its lawful copyright in erotic photographs through a federal copyright action, the sexually explicit photography company used its licenses with its models to bring a statutory right of publicity claim in California state court. Despite the explanation in *Fleet v. CBS, Inc.*, the court found that the nude images were commercial products within the statute, avoiding the preemption required under *Fleet*. Later decisions have rejected this approach, albeit without exploring whether the nature of the images as explicit photographs somehow recharacterized the images into commercial products.

Problem 3-D

In the prior problem, Bryce provided you the three-year agreement to perform in direct-to-video films that included nudity. Those productions are not subject to the SAG-AFTRA agreements, because the production company is not a signatory and Bryce is not a member. Therefore, the contractual protections are not available to Bryce from the collective bargaining agreement. Bryce has been offered a new agreement by a different company for an upcoming film, but again, the film would include scenes requiring full frontal nudity and simulated sex acts. Bryce is willing to participate in the scenes but requires that the contract be drafted to include the equivalent of a nudity rider that minimizes the use of the filmed scenes to the one sex scene in the script that Bryce is willing to do. Provide a provision for the contract that limits the scope of the producer's ability to film Bryce and helps assure that the scene will be shot only as described in the current script.

E. Bibliography and Links

Donald E. Biederman, *Agents v. Managers Revisited*, 1 Vand. J. Ent. L. & Prac. 5 (1999).

William A. Birdthistle, *A Contested Ascendancy: Problems with Personal Managers Acting as Producers*, 20 Loy. L.A. Ent. L. Rev. 493 (2000).

Christopher C. Cianci, *Entertainment or Exploitation?: Reality Television and the Inadequate Protection of Child Participants Under the Law*, 18 S. Cal. Interdisc. L.J. 363 (2009).

Saira Din, *Review of Selected 2003 California Legislation: Family Chapter 667: Instituting Proper Trust Funds and Safeguarding the Earnings of Child Performers from Dissipation by Parents, Guardians and Trustees*, 35 McGeorge L. Rev. 473 (2004).

Shayne J. Heller, *Legislative Updates: The Price of Celebrity: When a Child's Star-Studded Career Amounts to Nothing*, 10 DePaul-LCA J. Art & Ent. L. 161 (1999).

Erin M. Jacobson, *360 Deals and the California Talent Agencies Act Are Record Labels Procuring Employment?*, 29 Ent. & Sports Law. 9 (2011).

Edwin F. McPherson, *The Talent Agencies Act: Time for a Change*, 19 HASTINGS COMM. & ENT. L.J. 899 (1997).

Kimberlianne Podlas, *Does Exploiting a Child Amount to Employing a Child? The FLSA's Child Labor Provisions and Children on Reality Television*, 17 UCLA ENT. L. REV. 39 (2010).

Maria A. Sanders, *Singing Machines: Boy Bands and the Struggle for Artistic Legitimacy*, 20 CARDOZO ARTS & ENT. L.J. 525 (2002).

Matthew H. Schwartz, *Beaten to "Submissions": Talent Agents Score a Victory over Managers on Submissions of Motion Picture Screenplays*, 22 J. NAT'L ASS'N ADMIN L. JUDGES 145 (2002).

Koh Siok Tian Wilson, *Symposium Selected Issues in Labor Relations in the Motion Picture and Television Industries: Talent Agents as Producers: A Historical Perspective of Screen Actors Guild Regulation and the Rising Conflict with Managers*, 21 LOY. L.A. ENT. L.J. 401 (2001).

Symposium: The Uniform Athlete Agents Act, 13 SETON HALL J. SPORTS L. 345 (2003).

Chapter 4

First Amendment Aspects of the Entertainment Industry

A. First Amendment Recognition of the Entertainment Industries

Mutual Film Corp. v. Ohio Industrial Comm.

236 U.S. 230 (1915)

Mr. Justice McKenna, after stating the case as above, delivered the opinion of the court:

Complainant directs its argument to three propositions: (1) The statute in controversy imposes an unlawful burden on interstate commerce; (2) it violates the freedom of speech and publication guaranteed by § 11, art. 1, of the Constitution of the state of Ohio;[1] and (3) it attempts to delegate legislative power to censors and to other boards to determine whether the statute offends in the particulars designated.

It is necessary to consider only §§ 3, 4, and 5. Section 3 makes it the duty of the board to examine and censor motion picture films to be publicly exhibited and displayed in the state of Ohio. The films are required to be exhibited to the board before they are delivered to the exhibitor for exhibition, for which a fee is charged.

Section 4. "Only such films as are, in the judgment and discretion of the board of censors, of a moral, educational, or amusing and harmless character shall be passed and approved by such board." The films are required to be stamped or designated in a proper manner.

Section 5. The board may work in conjunction with censor boards of other states as a censor congress, and the action of such congress in approving or rejecting films shall be considered as the action of the state board, and all films passed, approved, stamped, and numbered by such congress, when the fees therefore are paid, shall be considered approved by the board.

---

1. Section 11. Every citizen may freely speak, write, and publish his sentiments on all subjects, being responsible for the abuse of the right; and no law shall be passed to restrain or abridge the liberty of speech, or of the press. In all criminal prosecutions for libel the truth may be given in evidence to the jury, and if it shall appear to the jury that the matter charged as libelous is true, and was published with good motives and for justifiable ends, the party shall be acquitted.

By § 7 a penalty is imposed for each exhibition of films without the approval of the board, and by § 8 any person dissatisfied with the order of the board is given the same rights and remedies for hearing and reviewing, amendment or vacation of the order "as is provided in the case of persons dissatisfied with the orders of the Industrial Commission."

The censorship, therefore, is only of films intended for exhibition in Ohio, and we can immediately put to one side the contention that it imposes a burden on interstate commerce. It is true that, according to the allegations of the bill, some of the films of complainant are shipped from Detroit, Michigan, but they are distributed to exhibitors, purchasers, renters, and lessors in Ohio, for exhibition in Ohio, and this determines the application of the statute. In other words, it is only films which are "to be publicly exhibited and displayed in the state of Ohio" which are required to be examined and censored. It would be straining the doctrine of original packages to say that the films retain that form and composition even when unrolling and exhibiting to audiences, or, being ready for renting for the purpose of exhibition within the state, could not be disclosed to the state officers. If this be so, whatever the power of the state to prevent the exhibition of films not approved,—and for the purpose of this contention we must assume the power is otherwise plenary,—films brought from another state, and only because so brought, would be exempt from the power, and films made in the state would be subject to it. There must be some time when the films are subject to the law of the state, and necessarily when they are in the hands of the exchanges, ready to be rented to exhibitors, or have passed to the latter, they are in consumption, and mingled as much as from their nature they can be with other property of the state.

It is true that the statute requires them to be submitted to the board before they are delivered to the exhibitor, but we have seen that the films are shipped to "exchanges" and by them rented to exhibitors, and the "exchanges" are described as "nothing more or less than circulating libraries or clearing houses." And one film "serves in many theaters from day to day until it is worn out."

The next contention is that the statute violates the freedom of speech and publication guaranteed by the Ohio Constitution. In its discussion counsel have gone into a very elaborate description of moving picture exhibitions and their many useful purposes as graphic expressions of opinion and sentiments, as exponents of policies, as teachers of science and history, as useful, interesting, amusing, educational, and moral. And a list of the "campaigns," as counsel call them, which may be carried on, is given. We may concede the praise. It is not questioned by the Ohio statute, and under its comprehensive description, "campaigns" of an infinite variety may be conducted. Films of a "moral, educational, or amusing and harmless character shall be passed and approved," are the words of the statute. No exhibition, therefore, or "campaign" of complainant will be prevented if its pictures have those qualities. Therefore, however missionary of opinion films are or may become, however educational or entertaining, there is no impediment to their value or effect in the Ohio statute. But they may be used for evil, and against that possibility the statute was enacted. Their power of amusement, and, it may be, education, the audiences they assemble, not of women alone nor of men alone, but together, not of adults only, but of children, make them the more insidious in corruption by a pretense of worthy purpose or if they should degenerate from worthy purpose. Indeed, we may go beyond that possibility. They take their attraction from the general interest, eager and wholesome it may be, in their subjects, but a prurient interest may be excited and appealed to. Besides, there are some things which should not have pictorial representation in public places and to all audiences. And not only the state of Ohio, but other states, have considered it to be in the interest of the public morals and welfare to supervise moving picture exhibitions. We would have to shut our eyes to the facts of the world to regard the precaution unreasonable or the legislation to effect it a mere wanton interference with personal liberty.

We do not understand that a possibility of an evil employment of films is denied, but a freedom from the censorship of the law and a precedent right of exhibition are asserted, subsequent responsibility only, it is contended, being incurred for abuse. In other words, as we have seen, the Constitution of Ohio is invoked, and an exhibition of films is assimilated to the freedom of speech, writing, and publication assured by that instrument, and for the abuse of which only is there responsibility, and, it is insisted, that as no law may be passed "to restrain the liberty of speech or of the press," no law may be passed to subject moving pictures to censorship before their exhibition.

We need not pause to dilate upon the freedom of opinion and its expression, and whether by speech, writing, or printing. They are too certain to need discussion—of such conceded value as to need no supporting praise. Nor can there be any doubt of their breadth, nor that their underlying safeguard is, to use the words of another, "that opinion is free, and that conduct alone is amenable to the law."

Are moving pictures within the principle, as it is contended they are? They, indeed, may be mediums of thought, but so are many things. So is the theater, the circus, and all other shows and spectacles, and their performances may be thus brought by the like reasoning under the same immunity from repression or supervision as the public press,—made the same agencies of civil liberty.

Counsel have not shrunk from this extension of their contention, and cite a case in this court where the title of drama was accorded to pantomime; and such and other spectacles are said by counsel to be publications of ideas, satisfying the definition of the dictionaries,—that is, and we quote counsel, a means of making or announcing publicly something that otherwise might have remained private or unknown,—and this being peculiarly the purpose and effect of moving pictures, they come directly, it is contended, under the protection of the Ohio constitution.

The first impulse of the mind is to reject the contention. We immediately feel that the argument is wrong or strained which extends the guaranties of free opinion and speech to the multitudinous shows which are advertised on the billboards of our cities and towns, and which regards them as emblems of public safety, to use the words of Lord Camden, quoted by counsel, and which seeks to bring motion pictures and other spectacle into practical and legal similitude to a free press and liberty of opinion.

The judicial sense supporting the common sense of the country is against the contention.... The exercise of the power upon moving picture exhibitions has been sustained.... It cannot be put out of view that the exhibition of moving pictures is a business, pure and simple, originated and conducted for profit, like other spectacles, not to be regarded, nor intended to be regarded by the Ohio Constitution, we think, as part of the press of the country, or as organs of public opinion. They are mere representations of events, of ideas and sentiments published and known; vivid, useful, and entertaining, no doubt, but, as we have said, capable of evil, having power for it, the greater because of their attractiveness and manner of exhibition. It was this capability and power, and it may be in experience of them, that induced the state of Ohio, in addition to prescribing penalties for immoral exhibitions, as it does in its Criminal Code, to require censorship before exhibition, as it does by the act under review. We cannot regard this as beyond the power of government.

It does not militate against the strength of these considerations that motion pictures may be used to amuse and instruct in other places than theaters, — in churches, for instance, and in Sunday schools and public schools. Nor are we called upon to say on this record whether such exceptions would be within the provisions of the statute, nor to anticipate that it will be so declared by the state courts, or so enforced by the state officers....

[The Court also finds the legislation is a proper exercise of state authority.]

Joseph Burstyn, Inc. v. Wilson

343 U.S. 495 (1952)

[The decision overturning The Mutual is presented in Chapter 1, *supra*, where the Supreme Court extends First Amendment protections to all forms of speech, including entertainment.]

Interstate Circuit v. City of Dallas

390 U.S. 676 (1968)

Mr. Justice Marshall delivered the opinion of the Court.

Appellants are an exhibitor and the distributor of a motion picture named "Viva Maria," which, pursuant to a city ordinance, the Motion Picture Classification Board of the appellee City of Dallas classified as "not suitable for young persons." A county court upheld the Board's determination and enjoined exhibition of the film without acceptance by appellants of the requirements imposed by the restricted classification. The Texas Court of Civil Appeals affirmed, and we noted probable jurisdiction, to consider the First and Fourteenth Amendment issues raised by appellants with respect to appellee's classification ordinance.

That ordinance, adopted in 1965, may be summarized as follows. It establishes a Motion Picture Classification Board, composed of nine appointed members, all of whom serve without pay. The Board classifies films as "suitable for young persons" or as "not suitable for young persons," young persons being defined as children who have not reached their 16th birthday. An exhibitor must be specially licensed to show "not suitable" films.

The ordinance requires the exhibitor, before any initial showing of a film, to file with the Board a proposed classification of the film together with a summary of its plot and similar information. The proposed classification is approved if the Board affirmatively agrees with it, or takes no action upon it within five days of its filing.

If a majority of the Board is dissatisfied with the proposed classification, the exhibitor is required to project the film before at least five members of the Board at the earliest practicable time. At the showing, the exhibitor may also present testimony or other support for his proposed classification. Within two days the Board must issue its classification order. Should the exhibitor disagree, he must file within two days a notice of nonacceptance. The Board is then required to go to court within three days to seek a temporary injunction, and a hearing is required to be set on that application within five days thereafter; if the exhibitor agrees to waive notice and requests a hearing on the merits of a permanent injunction, the Board is required to waive its application for a temporary injunction and join in the exhibitor's request. If an injunction does not issue within 10 days of the exhibitor's notice of nonacceptance, the Board's classification order is suspended. The ordinance does not define the scope of judicial review of the Board's determination, but the Court of Civil Appeals held that *de novo* review in the trial court was required. If an injunction issues and the exhibitor seeks appellate review, or if an injunction is refused and the Board appeals, the Board must waive all statutory notices and times, and join a request of the exhibitor, to advance the case on the appellate court's docket, *i.e.*, do everything it can to assure a speedy determination.

The ordinance is enforced primarily by a misdemeanor penalty: an exhibitor is subject to a fine of up to $200 if he exhibits a film that is classified "not suitable for young persons" without advertisements clearly stating its classification or without the classification being clearly posted, exhibits on the same program a suitable and a not suitable film, knowingly admits a youth under age 16 to view the film without his guardian or spouse accompanying him, makes any false or willfully misleading statement in submitting a film for classification, or exhibits a not suitable film without having a valid license therefor.

The same penalty is applicable to a youth who obtains admission to a not suitable film by falsely giving his age as 16 years or over, and to any person who sells or gives to a youth under 16 a ticket to a not suitable film, or makes any false statements to enable such a youth to gain admission.

Other means of enforcement, as against the exhibitor, are provided. Repeated violations of the ordinance, or persistent failure "to use reasonable diligence to determine whether those seeking admittance to the exhibition of a film classified "not suitable for young persons" are below the age of sixteen," may be the basis for revocation of a license to show not suitable films. Such a persistent failure, or exhibition of a not suitable film by an exhibitor with three convictions under the ordinance, *inter alia*, are defined as "public nuisances," which the Board may seek to restrain by a suit for injunctive relief.

The substantive standards governing classification are as follows:

"Not suitable for young persons" means:

(1) Describing or portraying brutality, criminal violence or depravity in such a manner as to be, in the judgment of the Board, likely to incite or encourage crime or delinquency on the part of young persons; or

(2) Describing or portraying nudity beyond the customary limits of candor in the community, or sexual promiscuity or extra-marital or abnormal sexual relations in such a manner as to be, in the judgment of the Board, likely to incite or encourage delinquency or sexual promiscuity on the part of young persons or to appeal to their prurient interest.

A film shall be considered "likely to incite or encourage" crime delinquency or sexual promiscuity on the part of young persons, if, in the judgment of the Board, there is a substantial probability that it will create the impression on young persons that such conduct is profitable, desirable, acceptable, respectable, praiseworthy or commonly accepted. A film shall be considered as appealing to "prurient interest" of young persons, if in the judgment of the Board, its calculated or dominant effect on young persons is substantially to arouse sexual desire. In determining whether a film is "not suitable for young persons," the Board shall consider the film as a whole, rather than isolated portions, and shall determine whether its harmful effects outweigh artistic or educational values such film may have for young persons."

Appellants attack those standards as unconstitutionally vague. We agree. Motion pictures are, of course, protected by the First Amendment, and thus we start with the premise that "precision of regulation must be the touchstone." And while it is true that this Court refused to strike down, against a broad and generalized attack, a prior restraint requirement that motion pictures be submitted to censors in advance of exhibition, there has been no retreat in this area from rigorous insistence upon procedural safeguards and judicial superintendence of the censor's action.

In *Winters v. New York,* 333 U.S. 507 (1948), this Court struck down as vague and indefinite a statutory standard interpreted by the state court to be "criminal news or stories of deeds of bloodshed or lust, so massed as to become vehicles for inciting violent and depraved crimes...." In *Joseph Burstyn, Inc. v. Wilson, supra,* the Court dealt with a film licensing standard of "sacrilegious," which was found to have such an all-inclusive definition as to result in "substantially unbridled censorship." Following *Burstyn,* the Court held the following film licensing standards to be unconstitutionally vague: "of such character as to be prejudicial to the best interests of the people of said City," *Gelling v. Texas,* 343 U.S. 960 (1952); "moral, educational or amusing and harmless," *Superior Films, Inc. v. Department of Education,* 346 U.S. 587 (1954); "immoral," and "tend to corrupt morals," *Commercial Pictures Corp. v. Regents,* 346 U.S. 587 (1954); "approve such films ... [as] are moral and proper; ... disapprove such as are cruel, obscene, indecent or immoral, or such as tend to debase or corrupt morals," *Holmby Productions, Inc. v. Vaughn*, 350 U.S. 870 (1955).

The vice of vagueness is particularly pronounced where expression is sought to be subjected to licensing. It may be unlikely that what Dallas does in respect to the licensing of motion pictures would have a significant effect upon film makers in Hollywood or Europe. But what Dallas may constitutionally do, so many other cities and States. Indeed, we are told that this ordinance is being used as a model for legislation in other localities. Thus, one who wishes to convey his ideas through that medium, which of course includes one who is interested not so much in expression as in making money, must consider whether what he proposes to film, and how he proposes to film it, is within the terms of classification schemes such as this. If he is unable to determine what the ordinance means, he runs the risk of being foreclosed, in practical effect, from a significant portion of the movie-going public. Rather than run that risk, he might choose nothing but the innocuous, perhaps save for the so-called "adult" picture. Moreover, a local exhibitor who cannot afford to risk losing the youthful audience when a film may be of marginal interest to adults — perhaps a "Viva Maria" — may contract to show only the totally inane. The vast wasteland that some have described in reference to another medium might be a verdant paradise in comparison. The First Amendment interests here are, therefore, broader than merely those of the film maker, distributor, and exhibitor, and certainly broader than those of youths under 16.

Of course, as the Court said in *Joseph Burstyn, Inc. v. Wilson*, "it does not follow that the Constitution requires absolute freedom to exhibit every motion picture of every kind at all times and all places." What does follow at the least, as the cases above illustrate, is that the restrictions imposed cannot be so vague as to set "the censor ... adrift upon a boundless sea...." In short, as Justice Frankfurter said, "legislation must not be so vague, the language so loose, as to leave to those who have to apply it too wide a discretion...," one reason being that "where licensing is rested, in the first instance, in an administrative agency, the available judicial review is in effect rendered inoperative [by vagueness]." Thus, to the extent that vague standards do not sufficiently guide the censor, the problem is not cured merely by affording *de novo* judicial review. Vague standards, unless narrowed by interpretation, encourage erratic administration whether the censor be administrative or judicial; "individual impressions become the yardstick of action, and result in regulation in accordance with the beliefs of the individual censor rather than regulation by law."

The dangers inherent in vagueness are strikingly illustrated in these cases. Five members of the Board viewed "Viva Maria." Eight members voted to classify it as "not suitable for young persons," the ninth member not voting. The Board gave no reasons for its determination. Appellee alleged in its petition for an injunction that the classification was warranted because the film portrayed "sexual promiscuity in such a manner as to be in the judgment of the Board likely to incite or encourage delinquency or sexual promiscuity on the part of young persons or to appeal to their prurient interests." Two Board members, a clergyman and a lawyer, testified at the hearing. Each adverted to several scenes in the film which, in their opinion, portrayed male-female relationships in a way contrary to "acceptable and approved behavior." Each acknowledged, in reference to scenes in which clergymen were involved in violence, most of which was farcical, that "sacrilege" might have entered into the Board's determination. And both conceded that the asserted portrayal of "sexual promiscuity" was implicit rather than explicit, *i.e.*, that it was a product of inference by, and imagination of, the viewer.

So far as "judicial superintendence" and *de novo* review are concerned, the trial judge, after viewing the film and hearing argument, stated merely: "Oh, I realize you gentlemen might be right. There are two or three features in this picture that look to me would be unsuitable to young people.... So I enjoin the exhibitor ... from exhibiting it." Nor did the Court of Civil Appeals provide much enlightenment or a narrowing definition of the ordinance.

United Artists argued that the obscenity standards similar to those set forth in *Roth v. United States,* 354 U.S. 476 (1957), and other decisions of this Court ought to be controlling. The majority of the Court of Civil Appeals held, alternatively, (1) that such cases were not applicable because the legislation involved in them resulted in suppression of the offending expression rather than its classification; (2) that if obscenity standards were applicable then "Viva Maria" was obscene as to adults (a patently untenable conclusion) and therefore entitled to no constitutional protection; and (3) that if obscenity standards were modified as to children, the film was obscene as to them, a conclusion which was not in terms given as a narrowing interpretation of any specific provision of the ordinance. In regard to the last alternative holding, we must conclude that the court in effect ruled that the "portrayal ... of sexual promiscuity as acceptable," is in itself obscene as to children. The court also held that the standards of the ordinance were "sufficiently definite."

Thus, we are left merely with the film and directed to the words of the ordinance. The term "sexual promiscuity" is not there defined and was not interpreted in the state courts. It could extend, depending upon one's moral judgment, from the obvious to any sexual contacts outside a marital relationship. The determinative manner of the "describing or portraying" of the subjects covered by the ordinance, including "sexual promiscuity," is defined as "such a manner as to be, in the judgment of the Board, likely to incite or encourage delinquency or sexual promiscuity on the part of young persons." A film is so " 'likely to incite or encourage' crime delinquency or sexual promiscuity on the part of young persons, if, in the judgment of the Board, there is a substantial probability that it will create the impression on young persons that such conduct is profitable, desirable, acceptable, respectable, praiseworthy or commonly accepted." It might be excessive literalism to insist, as do appellants, that because those last six adjectives are stated in the disjunctive, they represent separate and alternative subtle determinations the Board is to make, any of which results in a not suitable classification. Nonetheless, "what may be to one viewer the glorification of an idea as being 'desirable, acceptable or proper' may to the notions of another be entirely devoid of such a teaching. The only limits on the censor's discretion is his understanding of what is included within the term 'desirable, acceptable or proper.' This is nothing less than a roving commission...."

Vagueness and the attendant evils we have earlier described are not rendered less objectionable because the regulation of expression is one of classification rather than direct suppression. Nor is it an answer to an argument that a particular regulation of expression is vague to say that it was adopted for the salutary purpose of protecting children. The permissible extent of vagueness is not directly proportional to, or a function of, the extent of the power to regulate or control expression with respect to children. As Chief Judge Fuld has said:

> "It is ... essential that legislation aimed at protecting children from allegedly harmful expression—no less than legislation enacted with respect to adults— be clearly drawn and that the standards adopted be reasonably precise so that those who are governed by the law and those that administer it will understand its meaning and application."

The vices—the lack of guidance to those who seek to adjust their conduct and to those who seek to administer the law, as well as the possible practical curtailing of the effectiveness of judicial review—are the same.

It is not our province to draft legislation. Suffice it to say that we have recognized that some believe "motion pictures possess a greater capacity for evil, particularly among the youth of a community, than other modes of expression," and we have indicated more generally that because of its strong and abiding interest in youth, a State may regulate the dissemination to juveniles of, and their access to, material objectionable as to them, but which a State clearly could not regulate as to adults. Here we conclude only that "the absence of narrowly drawn, reasonable and definite standards for the officials to follow," is fatal.

Appellants also assert that the city ordinance violates the teachings of *Freedman v. Maryland* [380 U.S. 51, 58 (1965),] because it does not secure prompt state appellate review. The assurance of a "prompt final judicial decision" is made here, we think, by the guaranty of a speedy determination in the trial court (in this case nine days after the Board's classification). Nor is *Freedman* violated by the requirement that the exhibitor file a notice of nonacceptance of the Board's classification. To be sure, it is emphasized in *Freedman* that "only a procedure requiring a judicial determination suffices to impose a valid final restraint" and here if the exhibitor chooses not to file the notice of nonacceptance, the Board's determination is final without judicial approval. But we are not constrained to view that procedure as invalid in the absence of a showing that it has any significantly greater effect than would the exhibitor's decision not to contest in court the Board's suit for a temporary injunction. The ordinance provides that the Board has the burden of going to court to seek a temporary injunction, once the exhibitor has indicated his nonacceptance, and there it has the burden of sustaining its classification.

The judgment of the Texas Court of Civil Appeals is reversed and the cases are remanded for further proceedings not inconsistent with this opinion.

Southeastern Promotions, Ltd. v. Conrad

420 U.S. 546 (1975)

Mr. Justice Blackmun delivered the opinion of the Court.

The issue in this case is whether First Amendment rights were abridged when respondents denied petitioner the use of a municipal facility in Chattanooga, Tenn., for the showing of the controversial rock musical "Hair." It is established, of course, that the Fourteenth Amendment has made applicable to the States the First Amendment's guarantee of free speech.

Petitioner, Southeastern Promotions, Ltd., is a New York corporation engaged in the business of promoting and presenting theatrical productions for profit. On October 29, 1971, it applied for the use of the Tivoli, a privately owned Chattanooga theater under long-term lease to the city, to present "Hair" there for six days beginning November 23. This was to be a road company showing of the musical that had played for three years on Broadway, and had appeared in over 140 cities in the United States.

Twice previously, petitioner informally had asked permission to use the Tivoli, and had been refused. In other cities, it had encountered similar resistance and had successfully sought injunctions ordering local officials to permit use of municipal facilities. The musical had been presented in two Tennessee cities, Memphis and Nashville.

Respondents are the directors of the Chattanooga Memorial Auditorium, a municipal theater. Shortly after receiving Southeastern's application, the directors met, and, after a brief discussion, voted to reject it. None of them had seen the play or read the script, but they understood from outside reports that the musical, as produced elsewhere, involved nudity and obscenity on stage. Although no conflicting engagement was scheduled for the Tivoli, respondents determined that the production would not be "in the best interest of the community." Southeastern was so notified but no written statement of reasons was provided.

On November 1 petitioner, alleging that respondents' action abridged its First Amendment rights, sought a preliminary injunction from the United States District Court for the Eastern District of Tennessee. Respondents did not then file an answer to the complaint. A hearing was held on November 4. The District Court took evidence as to the play's content, and respondent Conrad gave the following account of the board's decision:

> "We use the general terminology in turning down the request for its use that we felt it was not in the best interest of the community and I can't speak beyond that. That was the board's determination.
>
> "Now, I would have to speak for myself, the policy to which I would refer, as I mentioned, basically indicates that we will, as a board, allow those productions which are clean and healthful and culturally uplifting, or words to

that effect. They are quoted in the original dedication booklet of the Memorial Auditorium."[2]

The court denied preliminary relief, concluding that petitioner had failed to show that it would be irreparably harmed pending a final judgment since scheduling was "purely a matter of financial loss or gain" and was compensable.

Southeastern some weeks later pressed for a permanent injunction permitting it to use the larger auditorium, rather than the Tivoli, on Sunday, April 9, 1972. The District Court held three days of hearings beginning April 3. On the issue of obscenity vel non, presented to an advisory jury, it took evidence consisting of the full script and libretto, with production notes and stage instructions, a recording of the musical numbers, a souvenir program, and the testimony of seven witnesses who had seen the production elsewhere. The jury returned a verdict that "Hair" was obscene. The District Court agreed. It concluded that conduct in the production—group nudity and simulated sex—would violate city ordinances and state statutes making public nudity and obscene acts criminal offenses. This criminal conduct, the court reasoned, was neither speech nor symbolic speech, and was to be viewed separately from the musical's speech elements. Being pure conduct, comparable to rape or murder, it was not entitled to First Amendment protection. Accordingly, the court denied the injunction.

On appeal, the United States Court of Appeals for the Sixth Circuit, by a divided vote, affirmed. The majority relied primarily on the lower court's reasoning. Neither the judges of the Court of Appeals nor the District Court saw the musical performed. Because of the First Amendment overtones, we granted certiorari.

Petitioner urges reversal on the grounds that (1) respondents' action constituted an unlawful prior restraint, (2) the courts below applied an incorrect standard for the determination of the issue of obscenity vel non, and (3) the record does not support a finding that "Hair" is obscene. We do not reach the latter two contentions, for we agree with the first. We hold that respondents' rejection of petitioner's application to use this public forum accomplished a prior restraint under a system lacking in constitutionally required minimal procedural safeguards. Accordingly, on this narrow ground, we reverse.

---

2. The Memorial Auditorium, completed in 1924, was dedicated to the memory of Chattanooga citizens who had "offered their lives" in World War I. The booklet referred to is entitled Souvenir of Dedication of Soldiers & Sailors Auditorium Chattanooga, Tenn. It contains the following:

"It will be [the board's] endeavor to make [the auditorium] the community center of Chattanooga; where civic, educational, religious, patriotic and charitable organizations and associations may have a common meeting place to discuss and further the upbuilding and general welfare of the city and surrounding territory.

"It will not be operated for profit, and no effort to obtain financial returns above the actual operating expenses will be permitted. Instead its purpose will be devoted for cultural advancement, and for clean, healthful, entertainment which will make for the upbuilding of a better citizenship."

Respondents' action here is indistinguishable in its censoring effect from the official actions consistently identified as prior restraints in a long line of this Court's decisions. In these cases, the plaintiffs asked the courts to provide relief where public officials had forbidden the plaintiffs the use of public places to say what they wanted to say. The restraints took a variety of forms, with officials exercising control over different kinds of public places under the authority of particular statutes. All, however, had this in common: they gave public officials the power to deny use of a forum in advance of actual expression.

Invariably, the Court has felt obliged to condemn systems in which the exercise of such authority was not bounded by precise and clear standards. The reasoning has been, simply, that the danger of censorship and of abridgment of our precious First Amendment freedoms is too great where officials have unbridled discretion over a forum's use. Our distaste for censorship — reflecting the natural distaste of a free people — is deep-written in our law.

In each of the cited cases the prior restraint was embedded in the licensing system itself, operating without acceptable standards. In *Shuttlesworth* [*v. Birmingham*, 394 U.S. 147, 150–151 (1969),] the Court held unconstitutional a Birmingham ordinance which conferred upon the city commission virtually absolute power to prohibit any "parade," "procession," or "demonstration" on streets or public ways. It ruled that "a law subjecting the exercise of First Amendment freedoms to the prior restraint of a license, without narrow, objective, and definite standards to guide the licensing authority, is unconstitutional." In *Hague v. CIO*, 307 U.S. 496 (1939), a Jersey City ordinance that forbade public assembly in the streets or parks without a permit from the local director of safety, who was empowered to refuse the permit upon his opinion that he would thereby prevent " 'riots, disturbances or disorderly assemblage,' " was held void on its face.

In *Cantwell v. Connecticut*, 310 U.S. 296 (1940), a unanimous Court held invalid an act which proscribed the solicitation of money or any valuable thing for "any alleged religious, charitable or philanthropic cause" unless that cause was approved by the secretary of the public welfare council. The elements of the prior restraint were clearly set forth:

> "It will be noted, however, that the Act requires an application to the secretary of the public welfare council of the State; that he is empowered to determine whether the cause is a religious one, and that the issue of a certificate depends upon his affirmative action. If he finds that the cause is not that of religion, to solicit for it becomes a crime. He is not to issue a certificate as a matter of course. His decision to issue or refuse it involves appraisal of facts, the exercise of judgment, and the formation of an opinion."

The elements of prior restraint identified in *Cantwell* and other cases were clearly present in the system by which the Chattanooga board regulated the use of its theaters. One seeking to use a theater was required to apply to the board. The board was empowered to determine whether the applicant should be granted permission — in effect, a license or permit—on the basis of its review of the content of the proposed production. Approval of the application depended upon the board's affirmative action. Approval was not a matter of routine; instead, it involved the "appraisal of facts, the exercise of judgment, and the formation of an opinion" by the board.

The board's judgment effectively kept the musical off stage. Respondents did not permit the show to go on and rely on law enforcement authorities to prosecute for anything illegal that occurred. Rather, they denied the application in anticipation that the production would violate the law.

Respondents' action was no less a prior restraint because the public facilities under their control happened to be municipal theaters. The Memorial Auditorium and the Tivoli were public forums designed for and dedicated to expressive activities. There was no question as to the usefulness of either facility for petitioner's production. There was no contention by the board that these facilities could not accommodate a production of this size. None of the circumstances qualifying as an established exception to the doctrine of prior restraint was present. Petitioner was not seeking to use a facility primarily serving a competing use. Nor was rejection of the application based on any regulation of time, place, or manner related to the nature of the facility or applications from other users.

Whether petitioner might have used some other, privately owned, theater in the city for the production is of no consequence. There is reason to doubt on this record whether any other facility would have served as well as these, since none apparently had the seating capacity, acoustical features, stage equipment, and electrical service that the show required. Even if a privately owned forum had been available, that fact alone would not justify an otherwise impermissible prior restraint. "[One] is not to have the exercise of his liberty of expression in appropriate places abridged on the plea that it may be exercised in some other place."

Thus, it does not matter for purposes of this case that the board's decision might not have had the effect of total suppression of the musical in the community. Denying use of the municipal facility under the circumstances present here constituted the prior restraint. That restraint was final. It was no mere temporary bar while necessary judicial proceedings were under way.

Also important, though unessential to our conclusion, are the classificatory aspects of the board's decision. A licensing system need not effect total suppression in order to create a prior restraint. In *Interstate Circuit v. Dallas*, 390 U.S. 676, 688 (1968), it was observed that the evils attendant on prior restraint "are not rendered less objectionable because the regulation of expression is one of classification rather than direct suppression." In that case, the Court held that a prior restraint was created by a system whereby an administrative board in Texas classified films as "suitable for young persons" or "not suitable for young persons." The "not suitable" films were not suppressed, but exhibitors were required to have special licenses and to advertise their classification in order to show them. Similarly, in *Bantam Books, Inc. v. Sullivan*, 372 U.S. 58 (1963), the Court held that a system of "informal censorship" working by exhortation and advice sufficiently inhibited expression to constitute a prior restraint and warrant injunctive relief. There, the Court held unconstitutional a system in which a commission was charged with reviewing material "manifestly tending to the corruption of the youth"; it did not have direct regulatory or suppressing functions, but operated by persuasion and intimidation, and these informal methods were found effective.

In the present case, the board classified the musical as unfit for showing in municipal facilities. It did not make a point of publicizing its finding that "Hair" was not in the "best interest" of the public, but the classification stood as a warning to all concerned, private theater owners and general public alike. There is little in the record to indicate the extent to which the board's action may have affected petitioner's ability to obtain a theater and attract an audience. The board's classification, whatever the magnitude of its effect, was not unlike that in *Interstate Circuit* and *Bantam Books*.

Only if we were to conclude that live drama is unprotected by the First Amendment—or subject to a totally different standard from that applied to other forms of expression—could we possibly find no prior restraint here. Each medium of expression, of course, must be assessed for First Amendment purposes by standards suited to it, for each may present its own problems. By its nature, theater usually is the acting out—or singing out—of the written word, and frequently mixes speech with live action or conduct. But that is no reason to hold theater subject to a drastically different standard. For, as was said in *Burstyn, supra*, at 503, when the Court was faced with the question of what First Amendment standard applies to films:

> "[The] basic principles of freedom of speech and the press, like the First Amendment's command, do not vary. Those principles, as they have frequently been enunciated by this Court, make freedom of expression the rule. There is no justification in this case for making an exception to that rule."

Labeling respondents' action a prior restraint does not end the inquiry. Prior restraints are not unconstitutional *per se*. We have rejected the contention that the First Amendment's protection "includes complete and absolute freedom to exhibit, at least once, any and every kind of motion picture ... even if this film contains the basest type of pornography, or incitement to riot, or forceful overthrow of orderly government...."

Any system of prior restraint, however, "comes to this Court bearing a heavy presumption against its constitutional validity." The presumption against prior restraints is heavier—and the degree of protection broader—than that against limits on expression imposed by criminal penalties. Behind the distinction is a theory deeply etched in our law: a free society prefers to punish the few who abuse rights of speech *after* they break the law than to throttle them and all others beforehand. It is always difficult to know in advance what an individual will say, and the line between legitimate and illegitimate speech is often so finely drawn that the risks of freewheeling censorship are formidable.

In order to be held lawful, respondents' action, first, must fit within one of the narrowly defined exceptions to the prohibition against prior restraints, and, second, must have been accomplished with procedural safeguards that reduce the danger of suppressing constitutionally protected speech. We do not decide whether the performance of "Hair" fits within such an exception or whether, as a substantive matter, the board's standard for resolving that question was correct, for we conclude that the standard, whatever it may have been, was not implemented by the board under a system with appropriate and necessary procedural safeguards.

The settled rule is that a system of prior restraint "avoids constitutional infirmity only if it takes place under procedural safeguards designed to obviate the dangers of a censorship system." *Freedman v. Maryland,* 380 U.S. 51, 58 (1965). In *Freedman* the Court struck down a state scheme for the licensing of motion pictures, holding "that, because only a judicial determination in an adversary proceeding ensures the necessary sensitivity to freedom of expression, only a procedure requiring a judicial determination suffices to impose a valid final restraint." We held in *Freedman,* and we reaffirm here, that a system of prior restraint runs afoul of the First Amendment if it lacks certain safeguards: *First,* the burden of instituting judicial proceedings, and of proving that the material is unprotected, must rest on the censor. Second, any restraint prior to judicial review can be imposed only for a specified brief period and only for the purpose of preserving the status quo. Third, a prompt final judicial determination must be assured....

The theory underlying the requirement of safeguards is applicable here with equal if not greater force. An administrative board assigned to screening stage productions — and keeping off stage anything not deemed culturally uplifting or healthful — may well be less responsive than a court, an independent branch of government, to constitutionally protected interests in free expression. And if judicial review is made unduly onerous, by reason of delay or otherwise, the board's determination in practice may be final.

Insistence on rigorous procedural safeguards under these circumstances is "but a special instance of the larger principle that the freedoms of expression must be ringed about with adequate bulwarks." Because the line between unconditionally guaranteed speech and speech that may be legitimately regulated is a close one, the "separation of legitimate from illegitimate speech calls for ... sensitive tools." The perils of prior restraint are well illustrated by this case, where neither the Board nor the lower courts could have known precisely the extent of nudity or simulated sex in the musical, or even that either would appear, before the play was actually performed.

Procedural safeguards were lacking here in several respects. The board's system did not provide a procedure for prompt judicial review. Although the District Court commendably held a hearing on petitioner's motion for a preliminary injunction within a few days of the board's decision, it did not review the merits of the decision at that time. The question at the hearing was whether petitioner should receive *preliminary* relief, *i.e.,* whether there was likelihood of success on the merits and whether petitioner would suffer irreparable injury pending full review. Effective review on the merits was not obtained until more than five months later. Throughout, it was petitioner, not the board, that bore the burden of obtaining judicial review. It was petitioner that had the burden of persuasion at the preliminary hearing if not at the later stages of the litigation. Respondents did not file a formal answer to the complaint for five months after petitioner sought review. During the time prior to judicial determination, the restraint altered the status quo. Petitioner was forced to forgo the initial dates planned for the engagement and to seek to schedule the performance at a later date. The delay and uncertainty inevitably discouraged use of the forum.

The procedural shortcomings that form the basis for our decision are unrelated to the standard that the board applied. Whatever the reasons may have been for the board's exclusion of the musical, it could not escape the obligation to afford appropriate procedural safeguards. We need not decide whether the standard of obscenity applied by respondents or the courts below was sufficiently precise or substantively correct, or whether the production is in fact obscene. The standard, whatever it may be, must be implemented under a system that assures prompt judicial review with a minimal restriction of First Amendment rights necessary under the circumstances. *Reversed.*

Ward v. Rock Against Racism
491 U.S. 781 (1989)

JUSTICE KENNEDY delivered the opinion of the Court.

In the southeast portion of New York City's Central Park, about 10 blocks upward from the park's beginning point at 59th Street, there is an amphitheater and stage structure known as the Naumberg Acoustic Bandshell. The bandshell faces west across the remaining width of the park. In close proximity to the bandshell, and lying within the directional path of its sound, is a grassy open area called the Sheep Meadow. The city has designated the Sheep Meadow as a quiet area for passive recreations like reclining, walking, and reading. Just beyond the park, and also within the potential sound range of the bandshell, are the apartments and residences of Central Park West.

This case arises from the city's attempt to regulate the volume of amplified music at the bandshell so the performances are satisfactory to the audience without intruding upon those who use the Sheep Meadow or live on Central Park West and in its vicinity.

The city's regulation requires bandshell performers to use sound-amplification equipment and a sound technician provided by the city. The challenge to this volume control technique comes from the sponsor of a rock concert. The trial court sustained the noise control measures, but the Court of Appeals for the Second Circuit reversed. We granted certiorari to resolve the important First Amendment issues presented by the case.

Rock Against Racism, respondent in this case, is an unincorporated association which, in its own words, is "dedicated to the espousal and promotion of antiracist views." Each year from 1979 through 1986, RAR has sponsored a program of speeches and rock music at the bandshell. RAR has furnished the sound equipment and sound technician used by the various performing groups at these annual events.

Over the years, the city received numerous complaints about excessive sound amplification at respondent's concerts from park users and residents of areas adjacent to the park. On some occasions RAR was less than cooperative when city officials asked that the volume be reduced; at one concert, police felt compelled to cut off the power to the sound system, an action that caused the audience to become unruly and hostile.

Before the 1984 concert, city officials met with RAR representatives to discuss the problem of excessive noise. It was decided that the city would monitor sound levels at the edge of the concert ground, and would revoke respondent's event permit if specific volume limits were exceeded. Sound levels at the concert did exceed acceptable levels for sustained periods of time, despite repeated warnings and requests that the volume be lowered. Two citations for excessive volume were issued to respondent during the concert. When the power was eventually shut off, the audience became abusive and disruptive.

The following year, when respondent sought permission to hold its upcoming concert at the bandshell, the city declined to grant an event permit, citing its problems with noise and crowd control at RAR's previous concerts. The city suggested some other city-owned facilities as alternative sites for the concert. RAR declined the invitation and filed suit in United States District Court against the city, its mayor, and various police and parks department officials, seeking an injunction directing issuance of an event permit. After respondent agreed to abide by all applicable regulations, the parties reached agreement and a permit was issued.

The city then undertook to develop comprehensive New York City Parks Department Use Guidelines for the Naumberg Bandshell. A principal problem to be addressed by the guidelines was controlling the volume of amplified sound at bandshell events. A major concern was that at some bandshell performances the event sponsors had been unable to "provide the amplification levels required and 'crowds unhappy with the sound became disappointed or unruly.'" The city found that this problem had several causes, including inadequate sound equipment, sound technicians who were either unskilled at mixing sound outdoors or unfamiliar with the acoustics of the bandshell and its surroundings, and the like. Because some performers compensated for poor sound mix by raising volume, these factors tended to exacerbate the problem of excess noise.

The amplified sound heard at a rock concert consists of two components, volume and mix. Sound produced by the various instruments and performers on stage is picked up by microphones and fed into a central mixing board, where it is combined into one signal and then amplified through speakers to the audience. A sound technician is at the mixing board to select the appropriate mix, or balance, of the various sounds produced on stage, and to add other effects as desired by the performers. In addition to controlling the sound mix, the sound technician also controls the overall volume of sound reaching the audience. During the course of a performance, the sound technician is continually manipulating various controls on the mixing board to provide the desired sound mix and volume. The sound technician thus plays an important role in determining the quality of the amplified sound that reaches the audience.

The city considered various solutions to the sound-amplification problem. The idea of a fixed decibel limit for all performers using the bandshell was rejected because the impact on listeners of a single decibel level is not constant, but varies in response to changes in air temperature, foliage, audience size, and like factors. The city also rejected the possibility of employing a sound technician to operate the equipment provided by the various sponsors of bandshell events, because the city's technician might have had difficulty satisfying the needs of sponsors while operating unfamiliar, and perhaps inadequate, sound equipment. Instead, the city concluded that the most effective way to achieve adequate but not excessive sound amplification would be for the city to furnish high quality sound equipment and retain an independent, experienced sound technician for all performances at the bandshell. After an extensive search the city hired a private sound company capable of meeting the needs of all the varied users of the bandshell.

The Use Guidelines were promulgated on March 21, 1986. After learning that it would be expected to comply with the guidelines at its upcoming annual concert in May 1986, respondent returned to the District Court and filed a motion for an injunction against the enforcement of certain aspects of the guidelines. The District Court preliminarily enjoined enforcement of the sound-amplification rule on May 1, 1986. Under the protection of the injunction, and alone among users of the bandshell in the 1986 season, RAR was permitted to use its own sound equipment and technician, just as it had done in prior years. RAR's 1986 concert again generated complaints about excessive noise from park users and nearby residents.

After the concert, respondent amended its complaint to seek damages and a declaratory judgment striking down the guidelines as facially invalid. After hearing five days of testimony about various aspects of the guidelines, the District Court issued its decision upholding the sound-amplification guideline. The court found that the city had been "motivated by a desire to obtain top-flight sound equipment and experienced operators" in selecting an independent contractor to provide the equipment and technician for bandshell events, and that the performers who did use the city's sound system in the 1986 season, in performances "which ran the full cultural gamut from grand opera to salsa to reggae," were uniformly pleased with the quality of the sound provided.

Although the city's sound technician controlled both sound volume and sound mix by virtue of his position at the mixing board, the court found that "[t]he City's practice for events at the Bandshell is to give the sponsor autonomy with respect to the sound mix: balancing treble with bass, highlighting a particular instrument or voice, and the like," and that the city's sound technician "does all he can to accommodate the sponsor's desires in those regards." Even with respect to volume control, the city's practice was to confer with the sponsor before making any decision to turn the volume down. In some instances, as with a New York Grand Opera performance, the sound technician accommodated the performers' unique needs by integrating special microphones with the city's equipment. The court specifically found that "[t]he City's implementation of the Bandshell guidelines provides for a sound amplification system capable of meeting RAR's technical needs and leaves control of the sound 'mix' in the hands of RAR." Applying this Court's three-part test for judging the constitutionality of government regulation of the time, place, or manner of protected speech, the court found the city's regulation valid.

The Court of Appeals reversed. After recognizing that "[c]ontent neutral time, place and manner regulations are permissible so long as they are narrowly tailored to serve a substantial government interest and do not unreasonably limit alternative avenues of expression," the court added the proviso that "the method and extent of such regulation must be reasonable, that is, it must be the least intrusive upon the freedom of expression as is reasonably necessary to achieve a legitimate purpose of the regulation." Applying this test, the court determined that the city's guideline was valid only to the extent necessary to achieve the city's legitimate interest in controlling excessive volume, but found there were various alternative means of controlling volume without also intruding on respondent's ability to control the sound mix. For example, the city could have directed respondent's sound technician to keep the volume below specified levels. Alternatively, a volume-limiting device could have been installed; and as a "last resort," the court suggested, "the plug can be pulled on the sound to enforce the volume limit." In view of the potential availability of these seemingly less restrictive alternatives, the Court of Appeals concluded that the sound-amplification guideline was invalid because the city had failed to prove that its regulation "was the least intrusive means of regulating the volume."

We granted certiorari to clarify the legal standard applicable to governmental regulation of the time, place, or manner of protected speech. Because the Court of Appeals erred in requiring the city to prove that its regulation was the least intrusive means of furthering its legitimate governmental interests, and because the ordinance is valid on its face, we now reverse.

Music is one of the oldest forms of human expression. From Plato's discourse in the Republic to the totalitarian state in our own times, rulers have known its capacity to appeal to the intellect and to the emotions, and have censored musical compositions to serve the needs of the state. The Constitution prohibits any like attempts in our own legal order. Music, as a form of expression and communication, is protected under the First Amendment. In the case before us the performances apparently consisted of remarks by speakers, as well as rock music, but the case has been presented as one in which the constitutional challenge is to the city's regulation of the musical aspects of the concert; and, based on the principle we have stated, the city's guideline must meet the demands of the First Amendment. The parties do not appear to dispute that proposition.

We need not here discuss whether a municipality which owns a bandstand or stage facility may exercise, in some circumstances, a proprietary right to select performances and control their quality. Though it did demonstrate its own interest in the effort to insure high quality performances by providing the equipment in question, the city justifies its guideline as a regulatory measure to limit and control noise. Here the bandshell was open, apparently, to all performers; and we decide the case as one in which the bandshell is a public forum for performances in which the government's right to regulate expression is subject to the protections of the First Amendment. Our cases make clear, however, that even in a public forum the government may impose reasonable restrictions on the time, place, or manner of protected speech, provided the restrictions "are justified without reference to the content of the regulated speech, that they are narrowly tailored to serve a significant governmental interest, and that they leave open ample alternative channels for communication of the information." We consider these requirements in turn.

The principal inquiry in determining content neutrality, in speech cases generally and in time, place, or manner cases in particular, is whether the government has adopted a regulation of speech because of disagreement with the message it conveys. The government's purpose is the controlling consideration. A regulation that serves purposes unrelated to the content of expression is deemed neutral, even if it has an incidental effect on some speakers or messages but not others. Government regulation of expressive activity is content neutral so long as it is "*justified* without reference to the content of the regulated speech."

The principal justification for the sound-amplification guideline is the city's desire to control noise levels at bandshell events, in order to retain the character of the Sheep Meadow and its more sedate activities, and to avoid undue intrusion into residential areas and other areas of the park. This justification for the guideline "ha[s] nothing to do with content," and it satisfies the requirement that time, place, or manner regulations be content neutral.

The only other justification offered below was the city's interest in "ensur[ing] the quality of sound at Bandshell events." Respondent urges that this justification is not content neutral because it is based upon the quality, and thus the content, of the speech being regulated. In respondent's view, the city is seeking to assert artistic control over performers at the bandshell by enforcing a bureaucratically determined, value-laden conception of good sound. That all performers who have used the city's sound equipment have been completely satisfied is of no moment, respondent argues, because "[t]he First Amendment does not permit and cannot tolerate state control of artistic expression merely because the State claims that [its] efforts will lead to 'top-quality' results."

While respondent's arguments that the government may not interfere with artistic judgment may have much force in other contexts, they are inapplicable to the facts of this case. The city has disclaimed in express terms any interest in imposing its own view of appropriate sound mix on performers. To the contrary, as the District Court found, the city requires its sound technician to defer to the wishes of event sponsors concerning sound mix. On this record, the city's concern with sound quality extends only to the clearly content-neutral goals of ensuring adequate sound amplification and avoiding the volume problems associated with inadequate sound mix. Any governmental attempt to serve purely esthetic goals by imposing subjective standards of acceptable sound mix on performers would raise serious First Amendment concerns, but this case provides us with no opportunity to address those questions. As related above, the District Court found that the city's equipment and its sound technician could meet all of the standards requested by the performers, including RAR.

Respondent argues further that the guideline, even if not content based in explicit terms, is nonetheless invalid on its face because it places unbridled discretion in the hands of city officials charged with enforcing it. According to respondent, there is nothing in the language of the guideline to prevent city officials from selecting wholly inadequate sound equipment or technicians, or even from varying the volume and quality of sound based on the message being conveyed by the performers.

As a threshold matter, it is far from clear that respondent should be permitted to bring a facial challenge to this aspect of the regulation. Our cases permitting facial challenges to regulations that allegedly grant officials unconstrained authority to regulate speech have generally involved licensing schemes that "ves[t] unbridled discretion in a government official over whether to permit or deny expressive activity." The grant of discretion that respondent seeks to challenge here is of an entirely different, and lesser, order of magnitude, because respondent does not suggest that city officials enjoy unfettered discretion to deny bandshell permits altogether. Rather, respondent contends only that the city, by exercising what is concededly its right to regulate amplified sound, could choose to provide inadequate sound for performers based on the content of their speech. Since respondent does not claim that city officials enjoy unguided discretion to deny the right to speak altogether, it is open to question whether respondent's claim falls within the narrow class of permissible facial challenges to allegedly unconstrained grants of regulatory authority.

We need not decide, however, whether the "extraordinary doctrine" that permits facial challenges to some regulations of expression should be extended to the circumstances of this case, for respondent's facial challenge fails on its merits. The city's guideline states that its goals are to "provide the best sound for all events" and to "insure appropriate sound quality balanced with respect for nearby residential neighbors and the mayorally decreed quiet zone of [the] Sheep Meadow." While these standards are undoubtedly flexible, and the officials implementing them will exercise considerable discretion, perfect clarity and precise guidance have never been required even of regulations that restrict expressive activity. By its own terms the city's sound-amplification guideline must be interpreted to forbid city officials purposely to select inadequate sound systems or to vary the sound quality or volume based on the message being delivered by performers. The guideline is not vulnerable to respondent's facial challenge.

Even if the language of the guideline were not sufficient on its face to withstand challenge, our ultimate conclusion would be the same, for the city has interpreted the guideline in such a manner as to provide additional guidance to the officials charged with its enforcement. The District Court expressly found that the city's policy is to defer to the sponsor's desires concerning sound quality. With respect to sound volume, the city retains ultimate control, but city officials "mak[e] it a practice to confer with the sponsor if any questions of excessive sound arise, before taking any corrective action." The city's goal of ensuring that "the sound amplification [is] sufficient to reach all listeners within the defined concertground," serves to limit further the discretion of the officials on the scene. Administrative interpretation and implementation of a regulation are, of course, highly relevant to our analysis, for "[i]n evaluating a facial challenge to a state law, a federal court must ... consider any limiting construction that a state court or enforcement agency has proffered." Any inadequacy on the face of the guideline would have been more than remedied by the city's narrowing construction.

The city's regulation is also "narrowly tailored to serve a significant governmental interest." Despite respondent's protestations to the contrary, it can no longer be doubted that government "ha[s] a substantial interest in protecting its citizens from unwelcome noise." This interest is perhaps at its greatest when government seeks to protect "'the well-being, tranquility, and privacy of the home,'" but it is by no means limited to that context, for the government may act to protect even such traditional public forums as city streets and parks from excessive noise.

We think it also apparent that the city's interest in ensuring the sufficiency of sound amplification at bandshell events is a substantial one. The record indicates that inadequate sound amplification has had an adverse effect on the ability of some audiences to hear and enjoy performances at the bandshell. The city enjoys a substantial interest in ensuring the ability of its citizens to enjoy whatever benefits the city parks have to offer, from amplified music to silent meditation.... Lest any confusion on the point remain, we reaffirm today that a regulation of the time, place, or manner of protected speech must be narrowly tailored to serve the government's legitimate, content-neutral interests but that it need not be the least restrictive or least intrusive means of doing so.

Rather, the requirement of narrow tailoring is satisfied "so long as the ... regulation promotes a substantial government interest that would be achieved less effectively absent the regulation." To be sure, this standard does not mean that a time, place, or manner regulation may burden substantially more speech than is necessary to further the government's legitimate interests. Government may not regulate expression in such a manner that a substantial portion of the burden on speech does not serve to advance its goals. So long as the means chosen are not substantially broader than necessary to achieve the government's interest, however, the regulation will not be invalid simply because a court concludes that the government's interest could be adequately served by some less-speech-restrictive alternative. "The validity of [time, place, or manner] regulations does not turn on a judge's agreement with the responsible decisionmaker concerning the most appropriate method for promoting significant government interests" or the degree to which those interests should be promoted....

The court squarely rejected respondent's claim that the city's "technician is not able properly to implement a sponsor's instructions as to sound quality or mix," finding that "[n]o evidence to that effect was offered at trial; as noted, the evidence is to the contrary." In view of these findings, which were not disturbed by the Court of Appeals, we must conclude that the city's guideline has no material impact on any performer's ability to exercise complete artistic control over sound quality. Since the guideline allows the city to control volume without interfering with the performer's desired sound mix, it is not "substantially broader than necessary" to achieve the city's legitimate ends, and thus it satisfies the requirement of narrow tailoring.

The final requirement, that the guideline leave open ample alternative channels of communication, is easily met. Indeed, in this respect the guideline is far less restrictive than regulations we have upheld in other cases, for it does not attempt to ban any particular manner or type of expression at a given place or time. Rather, the guideline continues to permit expressive activity in the bandshell, and has no effect on the quantity or content of that expression beyond regulating the extent of amplification. That the city's limitations on volume may reduce to some degree the potential audience for respondent's speech is of no consequence, for there has been no showing that the remaining avenues of communication are inadequate.

The city's sound-amplification guideline is narrowly tailored to serve the substantial and content-neutral governmental interests of avoiding excessive sound volume and providing sufficient amplification within the bandshell concert ground, and the guideline leaves open ample channels of communication. Accordingly, it is valid under the First Amendment as a reasonable regulation of the place and manner of expression. The judgment of the Court of Appeals is *Reversed.*

United States v. Stevens
559 U.S. 460 (2010)

CHIEF JUSTICE ROBERTS delivered the opinion of the Court.

Congress enacted 18 U.S.C. § 48 to criminalize the commercial creation, sale, or possession of certain depictions of animal cruelty. The statute does not address underlying acts harmful to animals, but only portrayals of such conduct. The question presented is whether the prohibition in the statute is consistent with the freedom of speech guaranteed by the First Amendment.

Section 48 establishes a criminal penalty of up to five years in prison for anyone who knowingly "creates, sells, or possesses a depiction of animal cruelty," if done "for commercial gain" in interstate or foreign commerce. § 48(a). A depiction of "animal cruelty" is defined as one "in which a living animal is intentionally maimed, mutilated, tortured, wounded, or killed," if that conduct violates federal or state law where "the creation, sale, or possession takes place." § 48(c)(1). In what is referred to as the "exceptions clause," the law exempts from prohibition any depiction "that has serious religious, political, scientific, educational, journalistic, historical, or artistic value."

The legislative background of § 48 focused primarily on the interstate market for "crush videos." According to the House Committee Report on the bill, such videos feature the intentional torture and killing of helpless animals, including cats, dogs, monkeys, mice, and hamsters. Crush videos often depict women slowly crushing animals to death "with their bare feet or while wearing high heeled shoes," sometimes while "talking to the animals in a kind of dominatrix patter" over "[t]he cries and squeals of the animals, obviously in great pain." Apparently these depictions "appeal to persons with a very specific sexual fetish who find them sexually arousing or otherwise exciting." The acts depicted in crush videos are typically prohibited by the animal cruelty laws enacted by all 50 States and the District of Columbia. But crush videos rarely disclose the participants' identities, inhibiting prosecution of the underlying conduct.

This case, however, involves an application of § 48 to depictions of animal fighting. Dogfighting, for example, is unlawful in all 50 States and the District of Columbia, and has been restricted by federal law since 1976. . . .

The Government's primary submission is that § 48 necessarily complies with the Constitution because the banned depictions of animal cruelty, as a class, are categorically unprotected by the First Amendment. We disagree.

The First Amendment provides that "Congress shall make no law . . . abridging the freedom of speech." "[A]s a general matter, the First Amendment means that government has no power to restrict expression because of its message, its ideas, its subject matter, or its content." *Ashcroft v. American Civil Liberties Union*, 535 U.S. 564, 573, (2002) (internal quotation marks omitted). Section 48 explicitly regulates expression based on content: The statute restricts "visual [and] auditory depiction[s]," such as photographs, videos, or sound recordings, depending on whether they depict conduct in which a living animal is intentionally harmed. As such, § 48 is " 'presumptively invalid,' and the Government bears the burden to rebut that presumption." *United States v. Playboy Entertainment Group, Inc.*, 529 U.S. 803, 817, (2000).

From 1791 to the present, however, the First Amendment has permitted restrictions upon the content of speech in a few limited areas, and has never included a freedom to disregard these traditional limitations. These historic and traditional categories long familiar to the bar,—including obscenity, defamation, fraud, incitement, and speech integral to criminal conduct,—are well-defined and narrowly limited classes of speech, the prevention and punishment of which have never been thought to raise any Constitutional problem. [Internal quotations and citation omitted.]

The Government argues that "depictions of animal cruelty" should be added to the list. It contends that depictions of "illegal acts of animal cruelty" that are "made, sold, or possessed for commercial gain" necessarily "lack expressive value," and may accordingly "be regulated as *unprotected* speech." The claim is not just that Congress may regulate depictions of animal cruelty subject to the First Amendment, but that these depictions are outside the reach of that Amendment altogether — that they fall into a " 'First Amendment Free Zone.' " *Board of Airport Comm'rs of Los Angeles v. Jews for Jesus, Inc.*, 482 U.S. 569, 574 (1987). . . .

The Government thus proposes that a claim of categorical exclusion should be considered under a simple balancing test: "Whether a given category of speech enjoys First Amendment protection depends upon a categorical balancing of the value of the speech against its societal costs."

As a free-floating test for First Amendment coverage, that sentence is startling and dangerous. The First Amendment's guarantee of free speech does not extend only to categories of speech that survive an ad hoc balancing of relative social costs and benefits. The First Amendment itself reflects a judgment by the American people that the benefits of its restrictions on the Government outweigh the costs. Our Constitution forecloses any attempt to revise that judgment simply on the basis that some speech is not worth it. The Constitution is not a document "prescribing limits, and declaring that those limits may be passed at pleasure." *Marbury v. Madison,* 1 Cranch 137, 178 (1803).

To be fair to the Government, its view did not emerge from a vacuum. As the Government correctly notes, this Court has often *described* historically unprotected categories of speech as being "'of such slight social value as a step to truth that any benefit that may be derived from them is clearly outweighed by the social interest in order and morality.'" *R.A.V.* [*v. St. Paul,* 505 U.S. 377 (1992)], *supra,* at 383. In *New York v. Ferber,* 458 U.S. 747 (1982), we noted that within these categories of unprotected speech, "the evil to be restricted so overwhelmingly outweighs the expressive interests, if any, at stake, that no process of case-by-case adjudication is required," because "the balance of competing interests is clearly struck." The Government derives its proposed test from these descriptions in our precedents.

But such descriptions are just that — descriptive. They do not set forth a test that may be applied as a general matter to permit the Government to imprison any speaker so long as his speech is deemed valueless or unnecessary, or so long as an ad hoc calculus of costs and benefits tilts in a statute's favor.

When we have identified categories of speech as fully outside the protection of the First Amendment, it has not been on the basis of a simple cost-benefit analysis. In *Ferber,* for example, we classified child pornography as such a category. We noted that the State of New York had a compelling interest in protecting children from abuse, and that the value of using children in these works (as opposed to simulated conduct or adult actors) was *de minimis.* But our decision did not rest on this "balance of competing interests" alone. We made clear that *Ferber* presented a special case: The market for child pornography was "intrinsically related" to the underlying abuse, and was therefore "an integral part of the production of such materials, an activity illegal throughout the Nation."

Our decisions in *Ferber* and other cases cannot be taken as establishing a freewheeling authority to declare new categories of speech outside the scope of the First Amendment. Maybe there are some categories of speech that have been historically unprotected, but have not yet been specifically identified or discussed as such in our case law. But if so, there is no evidence that "depictions of animal cruelty" is among them. We need not foreclose the future recognition of such additional categories to reject the Government's highly manipulable balancing test as a means of identifying them....

To succeed in a typical facial attack, Stevens would have to establish "that no set of circumstances exists under which [§ 48] would be valid," *United States v. Salerno,*

481 U.S. 739, 745, (1987), or that the statute lacks any "plainly legitimate sweep," *Washington v. Glucksberg*, 521 U.S. 702, 740, n. 7, (1997). Which standard applies in a typical case is a matter of dispute that we need not and do not address, and neither *Salerno* nor *Glucksberg* is a speech case. Here the Government asserts that Stevens cannot prevail because § 48 is plainly legitimate as applied to crush videos and animal fighting depictions. Deciding this case through a traditional facial analysis would require us to resolve whether these applications of § 48 are in fact consistent with the Constitution.

In the First Amendment context, however, this Court recognizes "a second type of facial challenge," whereby a law may be invalidated as overbroad if "a substantial number of its applications are unconstitutional, judged in relation to the statute's plainly legitimate sweep." *Washington State Grange v. Washington State Republican Party*, 552 U.S. 442, 449, n. 6, (2008). Stevens argues that § 48 applies to common depictions of ordinary and lawful activities, and that these depictions constitute the vast majority of materials subject to the statute. The Government makes no effort to defend such a broad ban as constitutional. Instead, the Government's entire defense of § 48 rests on interpreting the statute as narrowly limited to specific types of "extreme" material. As the parties have presented the issue, therefore, the constitutionality of § 48 hinges on how broadly it is construed. It is to that question that we now turn.

As we explained two Terms ago, "[t]he first step in overbreadth analysis is to construe the challenged statute; it is impossible to determine whether a statute reaches too far without first knowing what the statute covers." *United States v. Williams*, 553 U.S. 285, 293 (2008). Because § 48 is a federal statute, there is no need to defer to a state court's authority to interpret its own law.

We read § 48 to create a criminal prohibition of alarming breadth. To begin with, the text of the statute's ban on a "depiction of animal cruelty" nowhere requires that the depicted conduct be cruel. That text applies to "any ... depiction" in which "a living animal is intentionally maimed, mutilated, tortured, wounded, or killed." § 48(c)(1). "[M]aimed, mutilated, [and] tortured" convey cruelty, but "wounded" or "killed" do not suggest any such limitation....

[T]he phrase "wounded ... or killed" at issue here contains little ambiguity. The Government's opening brief properly applies the ordinary meaning of these words, stating for example that to " 'kill' is 'to deprive of life.' " We agree that "wounded" and "killed" should be read according to their ordinary meaning. Nothing about that meaning requires cruelty.

While not requiring cruelty, § 48 does require that the depicted conduct be "illegal." But this requirement does not limit § 48 along the lines the Government suggests. There are myriad federal and state laws concerning the proper treatment of animals, but many of them are not designed to guard against animal cruelty. Protections of endangered species, for example, restrict even the humane "wound[ing] or kill[ing]" of "living animal[s]." § 48(c)(1). Livestock regulations are often designed to protect the health of human beings, and hunting and fishing rules (seasons, licensure, bag limits, weight requirements) can be designed to raise revenue, preserve animal populations, or prevent accidents. The text of § 48(c) draws no distinction based on the reason the intentional killing of an animal is made illegal, and includes, for example, the humane slaughter of a stolen cow.

What is more, the application of § 48 to depictions of illegal conduct extends to conduct that is illegal in only a single jurisdiction. Under subsection (c)(1), the depicted conduct need only be illegal in "the State in which the creation, sale, or possession takes place, regardless of whether the ... wounding ... or killing took place in [that] State." A depiction of entirely lawful conduct runs afoul of the ban if that depiction later finds its way into another State where the same conduct is unlawful. This provision greatly expands the scope of § 48, because although there may be "a broad societal consensus" against cruelty to animals, there is substantial disagreement on what types of conduct are properly regarded as cruel. Both views about cruelty to animals and regulations having no connection to cruelty vary widely from place to place.

In the District of Columbia, for example, all hunting is unlawful. Other jurisdictions permit or encourage hunting, and there is an enormous national market for hunting-related depictions in which a living animal is intentionally killed. Hunting periodicals have circulations in the hundreds of thousands or millions, and hunting television programs, videos, and Web sites are equally popular....

The only thing standing between defendants who sell such depictions and five years in federal prison—other than the mercy of a prosecutor—is the statute's exceptions clause. Subsection (b) exempts from prohibition "any depiction that has serious religious, political, scientific, educational, journalistic, historical, or artistic value." The Government argues that this clause substantially narrows the statute's reach: News reports about animal cruelty have "journalistic" value; pictures of bullfights in Spain have "historical" value; and instructional hunting videos have "educational" value. Thus, the Government argues, § 48 reaches only crush videos, depictions of animal fighting (other than Spanish bullfighting), and perhaps other depictions of "extreme acts of animal cruelty." ...

Quite apart from the requirement of "serious" value in § 48(b), the excepted speech must also fall within one of the enumerated categories. Much speech does not. Most hunting videos, for example, are not obviously instructional in nature, except in the sense that all life is a lesson. According to Safari Club International and the Congressional Sportsmen's Foundation, many popular videos "have primarily entertainment value" and are designed to "entertai[n] the viewer, marke[t] hunting equipment, or increas[e] the hunting community." The National Rifle Association agrees that "much of the content of hunting media ... is merely *recreational* in nature." The Government offers no principled explanation why these depictions of hunting or depictions of Spanish bullfights would be *inherently* valuable while those of Japanese dogfights are not....

The Government explains that the language of § 48(b) was largely drawn from our opinion in *Miller v. California*, 413 U.S. 15 (1973), which excepted from its definition of obscenity any material with "serious literary, artistic, political, or scientific value." According to the Government, this incorporation of the *Miller* standard into § 48 is therefore surely enough to answer any First Amendment objection.

In *Miller* we held that "serious" value shields depictions of sex from regulation as obscenity. Limiting *Miller*'s exception to "serious" value ensured that "'[a] quotation from Voltaire in the flyleaf of a book [would] not constitutionally redeem an otherwise obscene publication.'" We did not, however, determine that serious value could be used as a general precondition to protecting *other* types of speech in the first place. *Most* of what we say to one another lacks "religious, political, scientific, educational, journalistic, historical, or artistic value" (let alone serious value), but it is still sheltered from government regulation.... Thus, the protection of the First Amendment presumptively extends to many forms of speech that do not qualify for the serious-value exception of § 48(b), but nonetheless fall within the broad reach of § 48(c).

Not to worry, the Government says: The Executive Branch construes § 48 to reach only "extreme" cruelty, and it "neither has brought nor will bring a prosecution for anything less," The Government hits this theme hard, invoking its prosecutorial discretion several times. But the First Amendment protects against the Government; it does not leave us at the mercy of *noblesse oblige*. We would not uphold an unconstitutional statute merely because the Government promised to use it responsibly....

Our construction of § 48 decides the constitutional question; the Government makes no effort to defend the constitutionality of § 48 as applied beyond crush videos and depictions of animal fighting. It argues that those particular depictions are intrinsically related to criminal conduct or are analogous to obscenity (if not themselves obscene), and that the ban on such speech is narrowly tailored to reinforce restrictions on the underlying conduct, prevent additional crime arising from the depictions, or safeguard public mores. But the Government nowhere attempts to extend these arguments to depictions of any other activities—depictions that are presumptively protected by the First Amendment but that remain subject to the criminal sanctions of § 48.

Nor does the Government seriously contest that the presumptively impermissible applications of § 48 (properly construed) far outnumber any permissible ones.... We therefore need not and do not decide whether a statute limited to crush videos or other depictions of extreme animal cruelty would be constitutional. We hold only that § 48 is not so limited but is instead substantially overbroad, and therefore invalid under the First Amendment.

JUSTICE ALITO, dissenting.

The Court strikes down in its entirety a valuable statute, 18 U.S.C. § 48, that was enacted not to suppress speech, but to prevent horrific acts of animal cruelty—in particular, the creation and commercial exploitation of "crush videos," a form of depraved entertainment that has no social value. The Court's approach, which has the practical effect of legalizing the sale of such videos and is thus likely to spur a resumption of their production, is unwarranted. Respondent was convicted under § 48 for selling videos depicting dogfights.... Instead of applying the doctrine of overbreadth, I would vacate the decision below and instruct the Court of Appeals on remand to decide whether the videos that respondent sold are constitutionally protected. If the question of overbreadth is to be decided, however, I do not think the present record supports the Court's conclusion that §48 bans a substantial quantity of protected speech....

In holding that §48 violates the overbreadth rule, the Court declines to decide whether, as the Government maintains, §48 is constitutional as applied to two broad categories of depictions that exist in the real world: crush videos and depictions of deadly animal fights....

[I]f the hunting of wild animals were otherwise covered by §48(a), I would hold that hunting depictions fall within the exception in §48(b) for depictions that have "serious" (*i.e.*, not "trifling") "scientific," "educational," or "historical" value. While there are certainly those who find hunting objectionable, the predominant view in this country has long been that hunting serves many important values, and it is clear that Congress shares that view.

I do not have the slightest doubt that Congress, in enacting §48, had no intention of restricting the creation, sale, or possession of depictions of hunting. Proponents of the law made this point clearly....

[W]e have a duty to interpret §48 so as to avoid serious constitutional concerns, and §48 may reasonably be construed not to reach almost all, if not all, of the depictions that the Court finds constitutionally protected. Thus, §48 does not appear to have a large number of unconstitutional applications....

In sum, §48 may validly be applied to at least two broad real-world categories of expression covered by the statute: crush videos and dogfighting videos.... Accordingly, I would reject respondent's claim that §48 is facially unconstitutional under the overbreadth doctrine.

Brown v. Entertainment Merchants Association

564 U.S. 786 (2011)

[The decision following *Stevens* related to regulation of violent video games is presented in Chapter 1, where the Supreme Court extends First Amendment protections to video games as a medium of speech and reiterates the holding of *Stevens* that there can be no additional categories of unprotected speech.]

Notes and Questions

a. The twin First Amendment rules that arise from *Southeastern Promotions, Ltd. v. Conrad* and *Ward v. Rock Against Racism* result in First Amendment interpretation that bars public or governmental facilities from banning shows from government-owned facilities because of questions of taste. *See Marilyn Manson, Inc. v. New Jersey Sports & Exposition Auth.*, 971 F. Supp. 875 (D.N.J. 1997).

b. Perhaps the only area where First Amendment rights have not been expanded involve the criminalization of child pornography. Following a report of the Attorney General's Commission on Pornography published in 1986, Congress enacted the Child Protection and Obscenity Enforcement Act, 18 U.S.C. §2257 (2006), which imposed identification, record-keeping, labeling, and inspection requirements on producers of adult media. The act has faced numerous constitutional challenges, but very few of its provisions have been found unconstitutional. *See Free Speech Coal., Inc. v. Attorney Gen. United States*, 825 F.3d 149 (3d Cir. 2016), on remand at *Free Speech Coal., Inc. v. Sessions*, 314 F. Supp. 3d 678 (E.D. Pa. 2018) (invalidating portions of the inspection provisions).

c. The scope of First Amendment protection is not limited to questions of prior restraint. In *Iota Xi Chapter of Sigma Chi Fraternity v. George Mason Univ.*, 993 F.2d 386, 390–91 (4th Cir. 1993), the Fourth Circuit affirmed a district court decision annulling punishment meted out by a public university against a fraternity chapter for an "'ugly woman contest' with racist and sexist overtones." The decision is a good reminder of the difference between the power to encourage taste and community rather than the power to prohibit or punish speech. The Court stated:

> The involved Fraternity members appeared in the contest dressed as caricatures of different types of women, including one member dressed as an offensive caricature of a black woman. He was painted black and wore stringy, black hair decorated with curlers, and his outfit was stuffed with pillows to exaggerate a woman's breasts and buttocks. He spoke in slang to parody African-Americans.... The Fraternity, which later apologized to the University officials for the presentation, conceded during the litigation that the contest was sophomoric and offensive.

> Following the contest, a number of students protested to the University that the skit had been objectionably sexist and racist. Two hundred forty-seven students, many of them members of the foreign or minority student body, executed a petition, which stated: "We are condemning the racist and sexist implications of this event in which male members dressed as women. One man in particular wore a black face, portraying a negative stereotype of black women."

The Court explained that even tasteless programs are protected by the First Amendment. "First Amendment principles governing live entertainment are relatively clear: short of obscenity, it is generally protected.... [T]he low quality of entertainment does not necessarily weigh in the First Amendment inquiry. It would seem, therefore, that the Fraternity's skit, even as low-grade entertainment, was inherently expressive and thus entitled to First Amendment protection."

d. Similar limitations have curbed the license schemes for the sale of artwork. *See Bery v. City of New York*, 97 F.3d 689 (2d Cir. N.Y. 1996). The City of New York could not enforce its licensing for artwork sold on the streets because it failed to meet the standards of *Ward v. Rock Against Racism*. But the scope of the *Bery* injunction prohibiting enforcement of the licensing law against vendors of "paintings, photographs, prints and/or sculpture" has been substantially narrowed "to the narrowest definitions of those terms, as understood by 'plain meaning and normal usage.... '" *People v. Ndiaye*, 887 N.Y.S.2d 832, 839–40 (N.Y.Crim.Ct. 2009).

> [Under *Ndiaye*,] there are three categories of merchandise for purposes of determining whether the License Law may be validly applied to its sale. First, newspapers, periodicals, books, pamphlets or other similar written matter are expressly exempt by [statute]. Second, paintings, photographs, prints and sculpture, narrowly defined, are exempt by the terms of the *Bery* injunction. And third, everything else, including jewelry, may constitutionally be made subject to licensure as a reasonable time, place or manner restriction.

e. Most of the court decisions determining the scope of reasonable time, place, and manner restrictions in the entertainment context involve nude dancing, which is afforded some degree of First Amendment protection as a form of expression. That discussion is beyond the scope of this book.

f. For issues of venue access, the First Amendment protections apply only to state action, generally requiring that the property be owned by the government or under the control of the government, and that it be generally available for public use either as an open public forum, or in some more limited forum. To what extent, if any, do these rules affect private property?

g. To what extent do the Federal Trade Commission's regulation of endorsements and prohibitions against astroturfing run afoul of the First Amendment rights of media companies and political organizations? *Compare Rezec v. Sony Pictures Entm't, Inc.*, 116 Cal. App. 4th 135, 10 Cal. Rptr. 3d 333 (2004), *with FilmOn.com, Inc. v. DoubleVerify, Inc.*, 439 P.3d 1156 (Cal. 2019) ("Nothing in the [anti-Strategic Lawsuit Against Public Participation (anti-SLAPP)] statute elides the potential relevance of [the statement's] commercial character in deciding whether speech merits protection under the [statute's] catchall provision. Instead, courts must consider whether a statement—including the identity of its speaker, for example, or the audience sought— contributes to or furthers the public conversation on an issue of public interest.").

Problem 4-A

Bryce is interested in the development of a new project. Bryce has written a script set in a junior high school and is interested in developing it into both a stage play and an independent film screenplay. Working with a company of local, non-union actors, Bryce plans to stage the play at the State Theatre, a city-owned auditorium, and to film the video at Abraham Lincoln Junior High School.

Unfortunately, because of the subject matter of the play, Bryce has received some negative feedback. The play, titled *Juliet Prescott*, is a modern adaptation of *Romeo & Juliet*. Romeo comes from a Catholic Mexican-American family, while Juliet's parents are white and Protestant. Pregnant by Romeo, Juliet's family is encouraging her to have an abortion. Adding fuel to the fire, Bryce has conceived the cleric who secretly marries the couple as an African-American Baptist minister. Bryce assures you that the marriage ceremony is a musical extravaganza that rivals "the church scene in *Blues Brothers*."

Although neither the State Theatre nor the junior high school had originally requested a copy of the script when first approached, both are now demanding a copy. Bryce believes that a write-up in the local weekly arts magazine overstated the risqué and controversial nature of the play, which depicts no nudity. Concerned local citizens mailed the article to members of the city council and school board to complain about the proposed production. The school is threatening to cancel the location agreement it had signed. The State Theatre has not cancelled yet, but it is demanding a copy of the script, written permission slips from the parents of each minor cast member, and a bond or advance payment. The State Theatre's complaint is based on the highly controversial subject matter, the inclusion of minors in the cast, and the semi-comic tone used through much of the production. (Like *Romeo & Juliet*, however, the script ends tragically.)

Bryce wants the production to go forward and is hoping that the controversy will boost sales. Nonetheless, the costs of the bond and difficulties caused by losing the school for filming could derail the project. Advise Bryce on the legal issues involved in using the theatre and school, as well as how best to proceed.

B. Claims for Injuries Caused by Media Content

James v. Meow Media, Inc.
300 F.3d 683 (6th Cir. 2002)

On December 1, 1997, Michael Carneal walked into the lobby of Heath High School in Paducah, Kentucky, and shot several of his fellow students, killing three and wounding many others. The parents and estate administrators of Carneal's victims—Jessica James, Kayce Steger, and Nicole Hadley—(hereinafter collectively referred to as "James") appeal the judgment of the district court dismissing, for failing to state claims on which relief could be granted, their actions against several video game, movie production, and internet content-provider firms. According to James's complaint, Carneal regularly played video games, watched movies, and viewed internet sites produced by the defendant firms. These activities, James argues, "desensitized" Carneal to violence and "caused" him to kill the students of Heath High School. James claims that the distribution of this material to impressionable youth like Carneal constitutes actionable negligence under Kentucky law, entitling James to recover wrongful death damages from the distributing firms. Moreover, James contends that the defendant firms purveyed defective "products," namely the content of video games, movies, and internet sites, triggering strict product liability under Kentucky law.

The defendant firms argue that they owe no duty to protect third parties from how players, watchers or viewers process the ideas and images presented in their video games, movies, and internet sites. Specifically, the defendants contend that

Carneal's actions were not sufficiently foreseeable to trigger the defendants' liability. Even if they were to owe such a duty to protect third parties from the consumers of their ideas and images, the defendants argue that Carneal's independent decision to kill his fellow students constitutes a superseding cause of the claimed damages and defeats the proximate cause element of James's *prima facie* case. The defendants further contend that tort liability for the non-defamatory ideas and images communicated in their respective media would raise significant First Amendment questions that ought to be avoided. Finally, the defendants note that James's theory of product liability is flawed as they have not distributed "products" under Kentucky law.

For the reasons set forth below, we affirm the district court's dismissal of James's actions....

Carneal regularly played "Doom," "Quake," "Castle Wolfenstein," "Redneck Rampage," "Nightmare Creatures," "Mech Warrior," "Resident Evil," and "Final Fantasy," which are interactive computer games that, in various ways, all involve the player shooting virtual opponents. Carneal also possessed a video tape containing the movie, "The Basketball Diaries," in a few minutes of which the high-school-student protagonist dreams of killing his teacher and several of his fellow classmates. Investigators examined Carneal's computer and discovered that he had visited "www.persiankitty.com," which appears to catalogue and link to sites with sexually-suggestive material. It also appeared that through "www.adultkey.com," a site operated by Network Authentication Systems and designed to restrict access to certain websites to viewers over certain ages, Carneal was granted age verification sufficient to visit many other pornographic sites....

First, James alleged that the defendants had been negligent in that they either knew or should have known that the distribution of their material to Carneal and other young people created an unreasonable risk of harm to others. James alleged that exposure to the defendants' material made young people insensitive to violence and more likely to commit violent acts. But for Carneal's steady diet of the defendants' material, James contended, Carneal would not have committed his violent acts.

Second, James asserted that the video game cartridges, movie cassettes, and internet transmissions that the defendants produced and distributed were "products" for purposes of Kentucky product liability law. According to James, the violent features of the movie, games, and internet sites were product defects. The defendants, as producers and distributors of the "products," are strictly liable under Kentucky law for damages caused by such product defects....

The legal questions under review in this case are questions of Kentucky law. When faced with the resolution of these state law issues, our inquiry is in part hypothetical. Specifically, we are charged to decide these questions of Kentucky state law as Kentucky state courts would....

James contends that the defendants in this case acted negligently, perhaps in producing, but at least in distributing to young people, their materials. It was this negligence, according to James, that caused Carneal to undertake his violent actions and that thereby caused the deaths of the plaintiffs' daughters. In order to establish an actionable tort under Kentucky law, the plaintiff must establish that the defendant owed a duty of care to the plaintiff, that the defendant breached that duty of care, and that the *defendant's breach* was the proximate cause of the plaintiff's damages.

A. The Existence of a Duty of Care

The district court held that James's allegations, even if assumed to be true, failed to establish the first element of the *prima facie* case. Specifically, the district court determined that the defendants were under no duty to protect James, Steger, and Hadley from Carneal's actions. James argues that the district court erred as a matter of Kentucky law in this regard....

Kentucky courts have held that the determination of whether a duty of care exists is whether the harm to the plaintiff resulting from the defendant's negligence was "foreseeable." Foreseeability is an often invoked, but not terribly well defined, concept in the common law of tort. Some common law tort regimes use foreseeability as the standard for determining proximate causation. Kentucky's particular use of foreseeability in the duty inquiry finds its roots in perhaps the most famous application of the foreseeability principle. In *Palsgraf v. Long Island Railroad Co.*, 248 N.Y. 339 (N.Y. 1928), then-Judge Cardozo determined that the defendant's duty is to avoid "risks reasonably to be perceived." ... Cardozo determined that the railroad simply did not owe a duty to Palsgraf to protect against *the injury that she suffered*. For Cardozo, the harm that Palsgraf suffered was not sufficiently probable that the railroad employees could have been expected to anticipate it occurring from their actions. Cardozo's reasoning, although implying that Palsgraf was the unforeseeable plaintiff, rested on the improbability of the *harm* that she suffered arising from the defendant's particular actions. For Cardozo too, the existence of a duty of care was a creature of circumstance....

Kentucky courts have struggled with the formless nature of this inquiry. At bottom, Kentucky courts have conceded, deciding the existence of a duty of care is "essentially a policy determination." Rather than the sophisticated weighing of probabilities, the content of that policy determination "is but a conclusion of whether a plaintiff's interests are entitled to legal protection against the defendant's conduct."

Thus, we are called, as best we can, to implement Kentucky's duty of care analysis in this case. Our inquiry is whether the deaths of James, Steger, and Hadley were the reasonably foreseeable result of the defendants' creation and distribution of their games, movie, and internet sites. Whether an event was reasonably foreseeable is not for us to determine with the assistance of hindsight. The mere fact that the risk may have materialized does little to resolve the foreseeability question.

Kentucky courts, in resolving foreseeability questions, have consistently inquired into the relative likelihood of the injuries produced. Of particular interest in this case are cases in which plaintiffs have sought to hold defendants liable for the actions of third parties, allegedly enabled or encouraged by the defendants. A line of cases in this vein concerns dram shops. In *Grayson* [*Fraternal Order of Eagles v. Claywell*, 736 S.W.2d 328 (Ky 1987),] the Kentucky Supreme Court held that an automobile accident injuring third parties was a reasonably foreseeable result of the negligent act of serving alcohol to an intoxicated individual. In contrast, the court later held that an intoxicated patron fighting with and shooting a fellow customer was simply not a foreseeable result of continuing to serve the patron alcohol. According to the court, the violent fighting and shooting was so much less likely a result from the serving of alcohol than the negligent operation of a motor vehicle that it was not reasonably foreseeable. Accordingly, the court held that dram shops, although negligent in serving alcohol to the obviously intoxicated, do not have a duty to protect third parties from the intentional violent acts of their intoxicated patrons.

Intentional violence is less likely to result from intoxication than negligent operation of a motor vehicle. Yet, the Kentucky Supreme Court never makes clear how unlikely is too unlikely for a particular type of harm to be unforeseeable. The cases do not create a principle, portable to the context of this case, for evaluating the probability of harm.

This court has encountered this foreseeability inquiry under Kentucky law before in a situation similar to this case. In *Watters v. TSR, Inc.,* 904 F.2d 378 (6th Cir. 1990), the mother of a suicide victim sued TSR for manufacturing the game "Dungeons and Dragons." The suicide victim regularly played the game. The mother contended that the game's violent content "desensitized" the victim to violence and caused him to undertake the violent act of shooting himself in the head. We held that the boy's suicide was simply not a reasonably foreseeable result of producing the game, notwithstanding its violent content. To have held otherwise would have been "to stretch the concepts of foreseeability and ordinary care to lengths that would deprive them of all normal meaning."

Foreseeability, however, is a slippery concept. Indeed, it could be argued that we ourselves confused it with some concept of negligence. We noted in *Watters*: "The defendant cannot be faulted, obviously, for putting its game on the market without attempting to ascertain the mental condition of each and every prospective player." We almost appeared to say that the costs of acquiring such knowledge would so outweigh the social benefits that it would not be negligent to abstain from such an investigation. We can put the *foreseeability* point a little more precisely, however. It appears simply impossible to predict that these games, movie, and internet sites (alone, or in what combinations) would incite a young person to violence. Carneal's reaction to the games and movies at issue here, assuming that his violent actions were such a reaction, was simply too idiosyncratic to expect the defendants to have anticipated it. We find that it is simply too far a leap from shooting characters on a video screen (an activity undertaken by millions) to shooting people in a classroom (an activity undertaken by a handful, at most) for Carneal's actions to have been reasonably foreseeable to the manufacturers of the media that Carneal played and viewed.

At first glance, our conclusion also appears to be little more than an assertion. Mental health experts could quite plausibly opine about the manner in which violent movies and video games affect viewer behavior. We need not stretch to imagine some mixture of impressionability and emotional instability that might unnaturally react with the violent content of the "Basketball Diaries" or "Doom." Of course, Carneal's reaction was not a normal reaction. Indeed, Carneal is not a normal person, but it is not utter craziness to predict that someone like Carneal is out there.

We return, however, to the Kentucky court's observation that the existence of a duty of care reflects a judicial policy judgment at bottom. From the Kentucky cases on foreseeability, we can discern two relevant policies that counsel against finding that Carneal's violent actions were the reasonably foreseeable result of defendants' distribution of games, movies, and internet material.

1. The Duty to Protect Against Intentional Criminal Actions

First, courts have held that, except under extraordinary circumstances, individuals are generally entitled to assume that third parties will not commit intentional criminal acts. The reasons behind this general rule are simple enough. The first reason is a probabilistic judgment that foreseeability analysis requires. Individuals generally are significantly deterred from undertaking intentional criminal conduct given the sanctions that can follow. The threatened sanctions make the third-party intentional criminal conduct sufficiently less likely that, under normal circumstances, we do not require the putative tort defendant to anticipate it. Indeed, this statistical observation explains the distinction drawn by Kentucky courts in the dram shop liability cases.

The second reason is structural. The system of criminal liability has concentrated responsibility for an intentional criminal act in the primary actor, his accomplices, and his co-conspirators. By imposing liability on those who did not endeavor to accomplish the intentional criminal undertaking, tort liability would diminish the responsibility placed on the criminal defendant. The normative message of tort law in these situations would be that the defendant is not entirely responsible for his intentional criminal act.

Does this case involve the extraordinary circumstances under which we would require the defendants to anticipate a third party's intentional criminal act? Kentucky courts have found such circumstances when the tort defendant had previously developed "a special relationship" with the victim of a third-party intentional criminal act. This duty to protect can be triggered by placing the putative plaintiff in custody or by taking other affirmative steps that disable the plaintiff from protecting himself against third-party intentional criminal acts. Of course, a special relationship can be created by a contract between the plaintiff and the defendant. Finally, some states have imposed a duty to protect others from third-party intentional criminal acts on members of discrete professions who become aware of the third-party's intention to engage in criminal conduct against a specific person. We can find nothing close to a "special relationship" in this case. The defendants did not even know James, Steger, and Hadley prior to Carneal's actions, much less take any affirmative steps that disabled them from protecting themselves.

Courts have held, under extremely limited circumstances, that individuals, notwithstanding their relationship with the victims of third-party violence, can be liable when their affirmative actions "create a high degree of risk of [the third party's] intentional misconduct." Generally, such circumstances are limited to cases in which the defendant has given a young child access to ultra-hazardous materials such as blasting caps or firearms. Even in those cases, courts have relied on the third party's severely diminished capacity to handle the ultra-hazardous materials. With older third parties, courts have found liability only where defendants have vested a particular person, under circumstances that made his nefarious plans clear, with the tools that he then quickly used to commit the criminal act. Arguably, the defendants' games, movie, and internet sites gave Carneal the ideas and emotions, the "psychological tools," to commit three murders. However, this case lacks such crucial features of our jurisprudence in this area. First, the defendants in this case had no idea Carneal even existed, much less the particular idiosyncrasies of Carneal that made their products particularly dangerous in his hands. In every case that this court has discovered in which defendants have been held liable for negligently creating an unreasonably high risk of third-party criminal conduct, the defendants have been specifically aware of the peculiar tendency of a particular person to commit a criminal act with the defendants' materials.

Second, no court has ever held that ideas and images can constitute the tools for a criminal act under this narrow exception. Beyond their intangibility, such ideas and images are at least one step removed from the implements that can be used in the criminal act itself. In the cases supporting this exception, the item that the defendant has given to the third-party criminal actor has been the direct instrument of harm.

2. First Amendment Problems

Moreover, we are loath to hold that ideas and images can constitute the tools for a criminal act under this exception, or even to attach tort liability to the dissemination of ideas. We agree with the district court that attaching tort liability to the effect that such ideas have on a criminal actor would raise significant constitutional problems under the First Amendment that ought to be avoided. Although the plaintiffs' contentions in this case do not concern the absolute proscription of the defendants' conduct, courts have made clear that attaching tort liability to protected speech can violate the First Amendment.

The first inquiry is whether the defendants' activity constitutes protected speech under the First Amendment. One thing is perfectly clear to this court: the plaintiffs' argument does not seek to attach liability to the cassettes and cartridges distributed by the defendants, but the ideas and images communicated to Carneal by those products. Although the defendants' products may be a mixture of expressive and inert content, the plaintiffs' theory of liability isolates the expressive content of the defendants' products.

Expression, to be constitutionally protected, need not constitute the reasoned discussion of the public affairs, but may also be for purposes of entertainment. Clearly, the various media distributed in this case fall along a spectrum of expressive content. It is long settled that movies can constitute protected speech. Of more recent, but no less definitive, resolution is that internet sites are similarly entitled to protection. The constitutional status of video games has been less litigated in federal courts. Yet most federal courts to consider the issue have found video games to be constitutionally protected.

Extending First Amendment protection to video games certainly presents some thorny issues. After all, there are features of video games which are not terribly communicative, such as the manner in which the player controls the game. The plaintiffs in this case, however, complain about none of those non-expressive features. Instead, they argue that the video game, somehow, communicated to Carneal a disregard for human life and an endorsement of violence that persuaded him to commit three murders. Because the plaintiffs seek to attach tort liability to the communicative aspect of the video games produced by the defendants, we have little difficulty in holding that the First Amendment protects video games in the sense uniquely relevant to this lawsuit. Our decision here today should not be interpreted as a broad holding on the protected status of video games, but as a recognition of the particular manner in which James seeks to regulate them through tort liability.

To say that the features of the defendants' products of which the plaintiffs complain are protected by the First Amendment is not necessarily to say that attaching tort liability to those features raises significant constitutional problems. The plaintiffs' argument is more nuanced: they do not seek to hold the defendants responsible merely for distributing their materials to anyone, but to young, impressionable children or, even more specifically, to Carneal. The protections of the First Amendment have always adapted to the audience intended for the speech. Specifically, we have recognized certain speech, while fully protected when directed to adults, may be restricted when directed towards minors. We have also required, however, that such regulations be narrowly tailored to protecting minors from speech that may improperly influence them and not effect an "unnecessarily broad suppression of speech" appropriate for adults.

Of course, the measure here intended to protect minors from the improper influence of otherwise protected speech is quite different from the regulations that we have countenanced in the past. Those regulations were the product of the reasoned deliberation of democratically elected legislative bodies, or at least regulatory agencies exercising authority delegated by such bodies. It was legislative bodies that had demarcated what otherwise protected speech was inappropriate for children and that had outlined in advance the measures that speakers were required to take in order to protect children from the speech.

. . .

With the movie and video game defendants, James contends that their material is excessively violent and constitutes obscene, non-protected speech. We decline to extend our obscenity jurisprudence to violent, instead of sexually explicit, material. Even if we were to consider such an expansion, James's arguments are not conceptually linked to our obscenity jurisprudence. The concept of obscenity was designed to permit the regulation of "offensive" material, that is, material that people find "disgusting" or "degrading." James's argument, on the other hand, is that the violent content of these video games and the movie shapes behavior and causes its consumers to commit violent acts. This is a different claim than the obscenity doctrine, which is a limit on the extent to which the community's sensibilities can be shocked by speech, not a protection against the behavior that the speech creates.

This is not to say that protecting people from the violence that speech might incite is a completely impermissible purpose for regulating speech. However, we have generally handled that endeavor under a different category of our First Amendment jurisprudence, excluding from constitutional protection those communicated ideas and images that incite others to violence. Speech that falls within this category of incitement is not entitled to First Amendment protection. The Court firmly set out the test for whether speech constitutes unprotected incitement to violence in *Brandenburg v. Ohio*, 395 U.S. 444 (1969). In protecting against the propensity of expression to cause violence, states may only regulate that speech which is "*directed to* inciting or producing *imminent* lawless action and *is likely to incite* or produce such action."

The violent material in the video games and *The Basketball Diaries* falls well short of this threshold. First, while the defendants in this case may not have exercised exquisite care regarding the persuasive power of the violent material that they disseminated, they certainly did not "intend" to produce violent actions by the consumers, as is required by the *Brandenburg* test. Second, the threat of a person like Carneal reacting to the violent content of the defendants' media was not "imminent." Even the theory of causation in this case is that persistent exposure to the defendants' media gradually undermined Carneal's moral discomfort with violence to the point that he solved his social disputes with a gun. This glacial process of personality development is far from the temporal imminence that we have required to satisfy the *Brandenburg* test. Third, it is a long leap from the proposition that Carneal's actions were foreseeable to the *Brandenburg* requirement that the violent content was "likely" to cause Carneal to behave this way....

B. Proximate Causation

Even if this court were to find that the defendants owed a duty to protect James, Steger, and Hadley from Carneal's violent actions, the plaintiffs likely have not alleged sufficient facts to establish the third element of a *prima facie* tort case: proximate causation.... Our determination regarding the idiosyncratic nature of Carneal's reaction to the defendants' media would likely compel us to hold that his action constitutes a superseding cause. We, however, need not reach this question because we have determined that the defendants did not owe a duty to protect the decedents.

James also contends that the district court erred in dismissing his products liability claims.... James has failed to demonstrate a prior requirement, that the video games, movies, and internet sites are "products" for purposes of strict liability. This was the basis on which the district court dismissed James's products liability claims, holding that the video games, movie, and internet transmissions were not "products," at least in the sense that James sought to attach liability to them.

This court has already substantially resolved the question of Kentucky law presented. In *Watters v. TSR*, 904 F.2d 378 (6th Cir. 1990), this court held that "words and pictures" contained in a board game could not constitute "products" for purposes of maintaining a strict liability action. We cannot find any intervening Kentucky authority that persuades us that *Watters* no longer correctly states Kentucky law. James's theory of liability, that the ideas conveyed by the video games, movie cassettes and internet transmissions, caused Carneal to kill his victims, attempts to attach product liability in a nearly identical way.... The video game cartridges, movie cassette, and internet transmissions are not sufficiently "tangible" to constitute products in the sense of their communicative content.

For all the foregoing reasons, we AFFIRM the district court's dismissal of all James's claims.

Waller v. Osbourne

763 F. Supp. 1144 (M.D. Ga. 1991) *aff'd*, 958 F.2d 1084 (11th Cir. 1992)

Plaintiffs Thomas and Myra Waller in the above captioned action allege that the defendants proximately caused the wrongful death of their son Michael Jeffery Waller by inciting him to commit suicide through the music, lyrics, and subliminal messages contained in the song "Suicide Solution" on the album "Blizzard of Oz." Defendants deny all allegations of wrongdoing on their part and now have pending before the court a joint motion for summary judgment.

Plaintiffs filed their original complaint in this case on April 28, 1988, following the death of their son Michael Jeffery Waller on May 3, 1986, as the result of a self-inflicted pistol wound to his head. In that original complaint, plaintiffs alleged that their son's suicide occurred after he had repeatedly listened to an Ozzy Osbourne cassette tape which contained audible and perceptible lyrics that directed Michael Waller to take his own life.[3]

Defendants Ozzy Osbourne, CBS Inc., and CBS RECORDS Inc., responded to the plaintiffs' complaint by moving the court to dismiss the complaint pursuant to Federal Rule of Civil Procedure 12(b)(6) because it failed to state a claim upon which relief could be granted. Before the court acted on the motion to dismiss, however, plaintiffs filed a motion to amend their complaint which the court authorized.

---

3. The alleged lyrics that were audible and perceptible during a twenty-eight second interlude in the song "Suicide Solution" on the album titled "Blizzard of Oz" went as follows:

> Ah know people
> You really know where it's at
> You got it
> Why try, why try
> Get the gun and try it
> Shoot, shoot, shoot.

The modified complaint discarded the claim that the lyrics which allegedly incited their son to commit suicide were audible and perceptible and instead charged that those same lyrics represent a subliminal message that is consciously intelligible only when the music is electronically adjusted. The amended complaint further alleges that as a result of the dissemination of the music, lyrics, and subliminal message in the song "Suicide Solution" on the album "Blizzard of Oz," defendants are liable to the plaintiffs for causing the pain and suffering of their deceased son; inciting his wrongful death; encouraging persons to physically harm themselves or commit suicide; and engaging in fraud, invasion of privacy, and nuisance....

In determining whether or not the court should grant the joint summary judgment motion of the defendants in this case, the court must initially resolve the issue of whether, as a matter of law, the song "Suicide Solution" on the album "Blizzard of Oz" contains subliminal messages as alleged by plaintiffs. The court finds this step necessary because it is convinced that the presence of a subliminal message, whose surreptitious nature makes it more akin to false and misleading commercial speech and other forms of speech extremely limited in their social value, would relegate the music containing such to a class worthy of little, if any, first amendment constitutional protection.

Plaintiffs attempt to establish the presence of subliminal messages in the song "Suicide Solution" contained on the "Blizzard of Oz" album primarily through the deposition testimony of two expert witnesses. Plaintiffs' expert, Mr. Hall, however, fails to create an issue of fact concerning the existence of a subliminal message when his specific finding is that since the lyrics in question in this case are audible, they cannot be a subliminal message as plaintiffs allege.

Plaintiffs' other expert, Ms. Evans, is equally unsuccessful in creating a genuine issue of fact since she contends that the lyrics in question are a subliminal message precisely because they are barely heard but not decipherable. While the court was unable to find a precise legal definition of a subliminal message, it is clear from the definition of subliminal that lyrics which are audible enough to make one consciously aware of their presence, though they may not necessarily be intelligible, do not qualify as a subliminal message.

According to *Webster's Ninth New Collegiate Dictionary*, (1985 Edition), subliminal is actually defined as "inadequate to produce a sensation or perception" and "existing or functioning below the threshold of conscious awareness." *Random House Dictionary* (1987 Edition) defines subliminal as "existing or operating below the threshold of consciousness; being or employing stimuli insufficiently intense to produce a discrete sensation but often being or designed to be intense enough to influence the mental processes or the behavior of the individual." If, as defined, a subliminal message must exist below the threshold of conscious awareness then it must follow that lyrics distinct enough to be heard and reacted to — even though garbled or unclear, are not a subliminal message. The most important character of a subliminal message is that it sneaks into the brain while the listener is completely unaware that he has heard anything at all. If the message is heard to any extent, even if garbled and unintelligible, the listener consciously attempts to discern a meaning from that which he hears. One is then dealing, not with a subliminal message, but rather the interpretation of an abstract medium which is akin to spotting objects in cloud formations.

Possibly a visual subliminal message such as the words "eat popcorn" on a reel of movie film can be proved more easily than an audio one such as the one alleged here. If the film is stopped and one holds each frame up to the light somewhere there must be at least one frame that says "eat popcorn." Here, there is nothing that says what the plaintiffs contend unless one uses his imagination. Therefore, despite her desire to label the lyrics contained in the twenty eight second interlude on the song "Suicide Solution" a subliminal message, the fact that Ms. Evans found that those lyrics are audible means that she has proved just the opposite—that the lyrics are not a subliminal message.

Furthermore, honoring Ms. Evans definition of subliminal message would mean that all rock music, or any music for that matter, which contains unintelligible lyrics could be found to contain a subliminal message, thereby, subjecting an endless number of performers and producers to possible law suits. It would be an understatement to say such a ruling would open the flood gates of litigation....

The court noted in its order denying defendants' motion to dismiss that the plaintiffs would be hard-pressed to avoid summary judgment in this action absent the presence of a subliminal message in the music of the defendants. Such is the case because music in the form of entertainment represents a type of speech that is generally afforded first amendment constitutional protection.

The first amendment protection that shields those who produce, perform, and distribute music is not however absolute. Music legally classified as obscene or defamatory, or that which represents fighting words or incites imminent lawless activity is either entitled to diminished first amendment constitutional protection or none at all. Therefore, even though the court has found that defendants' music does not contain subliminal messages, plaintiffs can strip away the first amendment protection defendants now stand behind if they can demonstrate that defendants music fits into one of the above categories.

Plaintiffs contend that the song "Suicide Solution" on the album "Blizzard of Oz" is properly categorized as speech which incites imminent lawless activity thereby depriving defendants of any legitimate claim to first amendment protection. The removal of first amendment protection from defendants' music on such a basis is contingent on a finding that it was "directed to inciting or producing imminent lawless action and is likely to incite or produce such action." Subsequent Supreme Court decisions have further indicated that in making such a finding the primary focus of the court should be on the imminence of the threat.

In *Hess* [*v. Indiana*, 414 U.S. 105 (1973)], the Court was forced to decide whether an antiwar demonstrator's first amendment rights were violated when the state of Indiana arrested him for shouting, "We'll take the fucking street later [or again]," to a crowd the police were attempting to disperse. In upholding the demonstrator's first amendment right to make that statement the court concluded that:

> Since the uncontroverted evidence showed that Hess' statement was not directed to any person or group of persons, it cannot be said that he was advocating, in the normal sense, any action. And since there was no evidence or rational inference from the import of the language, that his words were intended to produce, and likely to produce, *imminent* disorder, those words could not be punished by the state on the ground that they had "a tendency to lead to violence."

A careful examination of the defendants' music in accordance with the test developed in *Brandenburg* and refined in *Hess* leads this court to conclude that the defendants did not engage in culpable incitement. There is no indication whatsoever that defendants' music was directed toward any particular person or group of persons. Moreover, there is no evidence that defendants' music was intended to produce acts of suicide, and likely to cause *imminent* acts of suicide; nor could one rationally infer such a meaning from the lyrics. There, in fact, is no evidence nor even any allegations in this case that Michael Jeffery Waller committed suicide immediately after listening to defendants' music.

Viewing the facts in a light most favorable to the plaintiffs, the song "Suicide Solution" can be perceived as asserting in a philosophical sense that suicide may be a viable option one should consider in certain circumstances. And a strong argument can certainly be made that in light of the almost epidemic proportion of teenage suicides now occurring in this country it is irresponsible and callous for a musician with a large teenage following such as Ozzy Osbourne to portray suicide in any manner other than a tragic occurrence. Nevertheless, an abstract discussion of the moral propriety or even moral necessity for a resort to suicide, is not the same as indicating to someone that he should commit suicide and encouraging him to take such action. That, however, is what the law requires the plaintiffs to demonstrate in order to hold the defendants liable for inciting their son to commit suicide through the dissemination of their music. Plaintiffs have made no such showing and have failed to demonstrate any manner in which defendants' music can be categorized as speech which incites imminent lawless activity. Accordingly, the court finds as a matter of law that defendants are protected by the first amendment from liability for culpable incitement.

Absent the allegation that defendants' music represents speech that incites imminent lawless activities, plaintiffs have no other plausible basis in this case upon which they can overcome the broad first amendment protection generally afforded speech in the form of music. Plaintiffs put forth other theories of liability such as negligence, nuisance, fraud, and invasion of privacy. However, all of those tort based theories, as asserted by plaintiffs, fail to overcome the defendants' imposition of a valid first amendment defense.

Numerous courts have pointed out that any attempt to impose tort liability on persons engaged in the dissemination of protected speech involves too great a risk of seriously chilling all free speech....

Plaintiffs failed to demonstrate the existence of a subliminal message or that defendants' music incites imminent lawless activity, and were thereby left with the difficult task of attempting to impose liability on the defendants based on their dissemination of speech fully protected by the first amendment. It was a task plaintiffs were unable to accomplish.

Having ruled on the matter before the court, this order cannot be signed without an expression of sympathy for the parents of Michael Jeffery Waller who have shown their devotion to his memory by the filing and prosecution of this lawsuit. The court has no doubt as to the sincerity of their motives in following through with what must be an extremely painful course of action. The death of anyone before he has had a full measure of life is tragic and especially so if the person is a much loved teenaged son. If the death is by suicide the pain and grief to those left behind is almost unbearable. Although the court must render all its decisions without regard to sympathy, that does not mean it loses its capacity to experience that emotion.

Winter v. G.P. Putnam's Sons
938 F.2d 1033 (9th Cir. 1991)

Plaintiffs are mushroom enthusiasts who became severely ill from picking and eating mushrooms after relying on information in *The Encyclopedia of Mushrooms*, a book published by the defendant. Plaintiffs sued the publisher and sought damages under various theories. The district court granted summary judgment for the defendant. We affirm.

The Encyclopedia of Mushrooms is a reference guide containing information on the habitat, collection, and cooking of mushrooms. It was written by two British authors and originally published by a British publishing company. Defendant Putnam, an American book publisher, purchased copies of the book from the British publisher and distributed the finished product in the United States. Putnam neither wrote nor edited the book.

Plaintiffs purchased the book to help them collect and eat wild mushrooms. In 1988, plaintiffs went mushroom hunting and relied on the descriptions in the book in determining which mushrooms were safe to eat. After cooking and eating their harvest, plaintiffs became critically ill. Both have required liver transplants.

Plaintiffs allege that the book contained erroneous and misleading information concerning the identification of the most deadly species of mushrooms. In their suit against the book publisher, plaintiffs allege liability based on products liability, breach of warranty, negligence, negligent misrepresentation, and false representations. Defendant moved for summary judgment asserting that plaintiffs' claims failed as a matter of law because 1) the information contained in a book is not a product for the purposes of strict liability under products liability law; and 2) defendant is not liable under any remaining theories because a publisher does not have a duty to investigate the accuracy of the text it publishes. The district court granted summary judgment for the defendant. Plaintiffs appeal. We affirm.

A book containing Shakespeare's sonnets consists of two parts, the material and print therein, and the ideas and expression thereof. The first may be a product, but the second is not. The latter, were Shakespeare alive, would be governed by copyright laws; the laws of libel, to the extent consistent with the First Amendment; and the laws of misrepresentation, negligent misrepresentation, negligence, and mistake. These doctrines applicable to the second part are aimed at the delicate issues that arise with respect to intangibles such as ideas and expression. Products liability law is geared to the tangible world.

A. *Products Liability*

The language of products liability law reflects its focus on tangible items. In describing the scope of products liability law, the Restatement (Second) of Torts lists examples of items that are covered. All of these are tangible items, such as tires, automobiles, and insecticides. The American Law Institute clearly was concerned with including all physical items but gave no indication that the doctrine should be expanded beyond that area.

The purposes served by products liability law also are focused on the tangible world and do not take into consideration the unique characteristics of ideas and expression. Under products liability law, strict liability is imposed on the theory that "the costs of damaging events due to defectively dangerous products can best be borne by the enterprisers who make and sell these products." *Prosser & Keeton on The Law of Torts*, §98, at 692–93 (W. Keeton ed. 5th ed. 1984). Strict liability principles have been adopted to further the "cause of accident prevention ... [by] the elimination of the necessity of proving negligence." Additionally, because of the difficulty of establishing fault or negligence in products liability cases, strict liability is the appropriate legal theory to hold manufacturers liable for defective products. Thus, the seller is subject to liability "even though he has exercised all possible care in the preparation and sale of the product." It is not a question of fault but simply a determination of how society wishes to assess certain costs that arise from the creation and distribution of products in a complex technological society in which the consumer thereof is unable to protect himself against certain product defects.

Although there is always some appeal to the involuntary spreading of costs of injuries in any area, the costs in any comprehensive cost/benefit analysis would be quite different were strict liability concepts applied to words and ideas. We place a high priority on the unfettered exchange of ideas. We accept the risk that words and ideas have wings we cannot clip and which carry them we know not where. The threat of liability without fault (financial responsibility for our words and ideas in the absence of fault or a special undertaking or responsibility) could seriously inhibit those who wish to share thoughts and theories. As a New York court commented, with the specter of strict liability, "would any author wish to be exposed ... for writing on a topic which might result in physical injury? *e.g.* How to cut trees; How to keep bees?" One might add: "Would anyone undertake to guide by ideas expressed in words either a discrete group, a nation, or humanity in general?"

Strict liability principles even when applied to products are not without their costs. Innovation may be inhibited. We tolerate these losses. They are much less disturbing than the prospect that we might be deprived of the latest ideas and theories.

Plaintiffs suggest, however, that our fears would be groundless were strict liability rules applied only to books that give instruction on how to accomplish a physical activity and that are intended to be used as part of an activity that is inherently dangerous. We find such a limitation illusory. Ideas are often intimately linked with proposed action, and it would be difficult to draw such a bright line. While "How To" books are a special genre, we decline to attempt to draw a line that puts "How To Live A Good Life" books beyond the reach of strict liability while leaving "How To Exercise Properly" books within its reach.

Plaintiffs' argument is stronger when they assert that *The Encyclopedia of Mushrooms* should be analogized to aeronautical charts. Several jurisdictions have held that charts which graphically depict geographic features or instrument approach information for airplanes are "products" for the purpose of products liability law. Plaintiffs suggest that *The Encyclopedia of Mushrooms* can be compared to aeronautical charts because both items contain representations of natural features and both are intended to be used while engaging in a hazardous activity. We are not persuaded.

Aeronautical charts are highly technical tools. They are graphic depictions of technical, mechanical data. The best analogy to an aeronautical chart is a compass. Both may be used to guide an individual who is engaged in an activity requiring certain knowledge of natural features. Computer software that fails to yield the result for which it was designed may be another. In contrast, *The Encyclopedia of Mushrooms* is like a book on how to use a compass or an aeronautical chart. The chart itself is like a physical "product" while the "How to Use" book is pure thought and expression.[4]

---

4. In reversing a lower court opinion that aeronautical charts are not products, the *Fluor court* made the following comments:

> [The trial court] explained that it believed strict liability principles are applicable only to items whose physical properties render them innately dangerous, e.g., mechanical devices, explosives, combustible or flammable materials, etc. This belief was erroneous.... Although a sheet of paper might not be dangerous, per se, it would be difficult indeed to conceive of a salable commodity with more inherent lethal potential than an aid to aircraft navigation that, contrary to its own design standards, fails to list the highest land mass immediately surrounding a landing site.

Fluor Corp. v. Jeppesen & Co., 170 Cal. App. 3d 468, 475–76, 216 Cal. Rptr. 68, 71–72 (1985). Plaintiffs argue that this language shows that California courts would not draw a line between physical products and intangible ideas.

The *Fluor* language, however, cannot be stretched that far. The court was simply discussing the

Given these considerations, we decline to expand products liability law to embrace the ideas and expression in a book. We know of no court that has chosen the path to which the plaintiffs point.

B. *The Remaining Theories*

As discussed above, plaintiffs must look to the doctrines of copyright, libel, misrepresentation, negligent misrepresentation, negligence, and mistake to form the basis of a claim against the defendant publisher. Unless it is assumed that the publisher is a guarantor of the accuracy of an author's statements of fact, plaintiffs have made no case under any of these theories other than possibly negligence. Guided by the First Amendment and the values embodied therein, we decline to extend liability under this theory to the ideas and expression contained in a book.

In order for negligence to be actionable, there must be a legal duty to exercise due care. The plaintiffs urge this court that the publisher had a duty to investigate the accuracy of *The Encyclopedia of Mushrooms'* contents. We conclude that the defendants have no duty to investigate the accuracy of the contents of the books it publishes. A publisher may of course assume such a burden, but there is nothing inherent in the role of publisher or the surrounding legal doctrines to suggest that such a duty should be imposed on publishers. Indeed the cases uniformly refuse to impose such a duty. Were we tempted to create this duty, the gentle tug of the First Amendment and the values embodied therein would remind us of the social costs.

Finally, plaintiffs ask us to find that a publisher should be required to give a warning 1) that the information in the book is not complete and that the consumer may not fully rely on it or 2) that this publisher has not investigated the text and cannot guarantee its accuracy. With respect to the first, a publisher would not know what warnings, if any, were required without engaging in a detailed analysis of the factual contents of the book. This would force the publisher to do exactly what we have said he has no duty to do—that is, independently investigate the accuracy of the text. We will not introduce a duty we have just rejected by renaming it a "mere" warning label. With respect to the second, such a warning is unnecessary given that *no* publisher has a duty as a guarantor.

For the reasons outlined above, the decision of the district court is AFFIRMED.

Anthony v. Buena Vista Home Entertainment Inc.

2016 WL 6836950 (C.D. Cal. Sept. 28, 2016)

Plaintiffs Christine Anthony et al. ("Plaintiffs") bring this putative consumer class action against Defendants Buena Vista Home Entertainment Inc. et al. ("Defendants"

---

fact that under products liability law, the injury does not have to be caused by impact from the physical properties of the item. In other words, the injury does not have to result because a compass explodes in your hand, but can result because the compass malfunctions and leads you over a cliff. This is quite different from saying that liability can be imposed for such things as ideas which have no physical properties at all.

or "Studios"). Presently before the Court are Defendants' motion to dismiss pursuant to Federal Rule of Civil procedure 12(b)(6) and motion to strike pursuant to California's anti-SLAPP statute. For the reasons stated below, the Court GRANTS Defendants' motions. Plaintiffs are consumers who are deaf or hard of hearing and require captioning or subtitling to understand words or lyrics in movies and TV shows.

Motion to Dismiss

Plaintiffs allege that Defendants produced and distributed (1) DVDs enclosed in packaging with language advertising the DVDs as subtitled, (2) movies advertised as captioned, and (3) movies or TV shows advertised as subtitled via online streaming services. Plaintiffs allege that these movies and TV shows were advertised with language such as "captioned, English subtitles, or subtitles for the Deaf and Hard of Hearing." However, Plaintiffs contend that despite being advertised as captioned or subtitled (collectively "subtitled"), the movies and TV shows were not fully subtitled. In particular, the movies and TV shows did not include subtitles for music and song lyrics. Plaintiffs contend that music and song lyrics are often used to explain the premise or theme of a movie or TV show, and can sometimes be crucial to developing a plot (e.g., musicals).

Plaintiffs' claims can be grouped into three categories: (1) misrepresentation claims, (2) warranty claims, and (3) Unruh Act claim. To state a claim under Plaintiffs' misrepresentation claims, Plaintiffs must allege a misrepresentation that would be likely to deceive a reasonable consumer. Plaintiffs allege that Defendants' advertisement of movies and TV shows as subtitled or captioned would be likely to deceive a reasonable consumer to believe that all song lyrics would be captioned. However, Plaintiffs fail to allege that this alleged misrepresentation would be likely to deceive a reasonable consumer; rather, Plaintiffs only allege that content advertised as subtitled "should include the DVD feature presentation, special features, and music/song lyrics."

However, whether such content *should* include subtitled song lyrics is quite distinct from whether consumers expect it to. Plaintiffs argue that reasonable consumers may rely on the notion that certain Studios would differ in the amount of subtitling or captioning and include captioned song lyrics, or they may expect the Studios' practice to change over time. Such arguments fall far short of demonstrating that reasonable consumers would actually be *deceived* as to the amount of subtitled content provided, as there are no representations whatsoever that all song lyrics would be captioned, or even that the content would be "fully" captioned. Instead, they merely demonstrate that the Plaintiffs hopes that the industry practice would change were not fulfilled. In fact, as to Plaintiffs specifically, it is unclear whether Plaintiffs allege they were deceived by the advertisement that the movies and TV shows were subtitled. Plaintiffs allege that "the practice of not subtitling song/music lyrics is frustratingly widespread," and they each purchased or rented "numerous DVDs" in which the content "including music lyrics, was not subtitled or captioned." Thus, taken together, Plaintiffs allegations not only fail to allege that reasonable consumers would be likely to be deceived by the alleged misrepresentation, but also fail to allege that they were even deceived by the alleged misrepresentation.

For the same reasons discussed above, Plaintiffs fail to adequately allege reliance on the alleged misrepresentation. Plaintiffs contend that they relied on an understanding that the movie would be fully captioned, including song lyrics, when they made the purchases of the shows or movies. Additionally, Plaintiffs further allege that they check to see whether a movie or show is represented as "captioned or subtitled," prior to purchase or rental, and that this representation should include song lyrics.

However, other portions of the Complaint and Opposition brief demonstrate that they did not truly rely on the alleged misrepresentations. For instance, the Plaintiffs state that if they want to watch a movie or show, they must buy the captioned versions produced by the Defendants, as there are no alternatives with captioned song lyrics. Opp. at 7, 10. In effect, the Plaintiffs are conceding that they would buy or rent the products even without full captioning and subtitling, as there are no better alternatives available to them. Therefore, the Plaintiffs have not relied on the alleged misrepresentation, as they concede they would buy the movies regardless of whether the song lyrics were subtitled. Because the Plaintiffs have failed to properly allege a misrepresentation that would be likely to deceive a reasonable consumer and have failed to properly allege reliance on that misrepresentation, the Motion to Dismiss with respect to the misrepresentation claims (Counts One, Four, and Six) is GRANTED.

The Plaintiffs also assert causes of action for a breach of implied warranty of fitness and a breach of implied warranty of merchantability under California's Song-Beverly Consumer Warranty Act, Cal. Civ. Code §§ 1791.1, 1792, 1792.1 ("Song-Beverly Act"). The Plaintiffs allege that the Defendants had reason to know that the Plaintiffs were relying on Defendants' skill and judgment in producing and distributing movies with captions and subtitles that would meet the needs of the deaf and hard of hearing communities, and that they breached this warranty by producing and distributing movies and shows with song and music lyrics that were inaccessible to the members of that community. Additionally, the Plaintiffs allege a breach of the warranty of merchantability because the movies and shows were not fit for the ordinary purposes for which those goods are used. The warranties asserted by the Plaintiffs apply to "sale[s] of consumer goods." Courts commonly distinguish between the expressive content of movies and other intellectual property with the tangible media that conveys that content, finding that only the tangible products are subject to product liability regulations.

The Court finds that the Plaintiffs have failed to allege either a sale or a consumer good as required by the Beverly-Song Act. The Plaintiffs claims involve the video content of the DVDs, streaming services, or live movies, and therefore it is that content that must have been sold in order to be subject to the regulations of the Act. However, Plaintiffs do not sufficiently allege that such a sale took place. In the case of DVDs and streaming services, the title to the video content remains with the copyright owner. The consumer may purchase title to the physical DVD, but only purchases a license to view the expressive content. As a result, while a sale occurs with respect to the physical DVD, there has been no sale with respect to the expressive video content because title has not been passed. If there has been no "sale" of the relevant good, the Beverly-Song Act does not apply by its own terms.

The Plaintiffs' only response to this argument is that DVDs are a consumer good. This is undoubtedly true, as the Defendants concede that a scratched DVD could be subject to warranty law. However, the Plaintiffs do not demonstrate how the expressive content of the movies or shows constitute a consumer good. Therefore, any claims involving the content of the movies and shows, including the claims in this case, do not involve a consumer good and consequently are not subject to the regulations of the Beverly-Song Act. As a result, the Plaintiffs have failed to adequately allege a sale of a consumer good, and the Motion to Dismiss with respect to the warranty claims (Counts Two and Three) is GRANTED.

Finally, the Plaintiffs' fifth cause of action is a violation of California's Unruh Civil Rights Act, Cal. Civ. Code § 51 *et seq.* ("Unruh Act"), which guarantees equal access for people with disabilities to the accommodations, advantages, facilities, privileges, and services of all business establishments. The Plaintiffs argue that the Defendants have violated the Unruh Act because they have provided services (access to music and song lyrics) to certain users but not to users who are deaf or hard of hearing, such as the Plaintiffs.

To establish an Unruh Act violation, a plaintiff "must plead and prove intentional discrimination in public accommodations in violation of the terms of the Act." *Greater L.A. Agency on Deafness v. Cable News Network, Inc.*, 742 F.3d 414, 426–27 (9th Cir. 2014) ("*GLAAD*"). Plaintiffs "must allege more than the disparate impact of a facially neutral policy on a particular group" to state a claim for intentional discrimination.

The Plaintiff's Unruh Act cause of action fails under the controlling authority set by the Ninth Circuit in the *GLAAD* case. In that case, the Ninth Circuit found that CNN's policy of not captioning online video programming did not violate the Unruh Act. Specifically, CNN's policy applied equally to all CNN.com visitors whether they were healing impaired or not, and therefore could not possibly constitute "willful, affirmative misconduct" or intentional discrimination as required by the Unruh Act. The allegations asserted by the Plaintiffs are essentially the same as the ones at issue in *GLAAD*. The captioning and subtitling of the movies and shows are available equally to all consumers. In fact, the Defendants provide captioning and subtitling for a large portion of the video content despite not being required to do so, as the Plaintiffs only allege that some music and song lyrics are not captioned. Therefore, the Plaintiffs' Complaint fails to allege intentional discrimination for the reasons stated in the *GLAAD* case. That hearing-impaired individuals bear the brunt of the Studios' neutral policy with respect to captioning and subtitling is insufficient to support an Unruh Act claim as a matter of law.

Anti-SLAPP Motion to Strike

In addition to their motion to dismiss. Defendants filed a special motion to strike Plaintiffs' complaint pursuant to California's anti-Strategic Lawsuits Against Public

Participation ("anti-SLAPP") statute, California Code of Civil Procedure § 425.16. While Defendants prevailed on their motion to dismiss, the Court must still consider the anti-SLAPP motion because a successful anti-SLAPP motion results in the award of fees.

A. Legal Standard—The anti-SLAPP statute provides that "[a] cause of action against a person arising from any act of that person in furtherance of the person's right of petition or free speech under the United States Constitution or the California Constitution in connection with a public issue shall be subject to a special motion to strike, unless the court determines that the plaintiff has established that there is a probability that the plaintiff will prevail on the claim." Cal. Code Civ. P. § 425.16(b). The statute is to "be construed broadly." Cal. Code Civ. P. § 425.16(a).

An anti-SLAPP motion involves a two-step analysis. "First, the defendant must make a prima facie showing that the plaintiffs suit arises from an act in furtherance of the defendant's rights of petition or free speech. Second, once the defendant has made a prima facie showing, the burden shifts to the plaintiff to demonstrate a probability of prevailing on the challenged claims." The defendant "need not show that the plaintiffs' suit was brought with the intention to chill the defendant's speech or that any speech was actually chilled."

1. Protected Activity in Connection with a Public Issue—Determining whether a cause of action arises from protected speech or petitioning activity requires a focus on the principal thrust or gravamen of the cause of action. Where a cause of action alleges both protected and unprotected activity, the cause of action will be subject to section 425.15 unless the protected activity is 'merely incidental' to the unprotected conduct. A court must generally presume the validity of the claimed constitutional right in the first step of the anti-SLAPP analysis, and then permit the parties to address the issue in the second step of the analysis, if necessary.

The Plaintiffs concede that movies involve free speech. They acknowledge that the *GLAAD* case addressed captioning and subtitling as related to videos and found that the captioning of videos constitutes protected speech and is therefore subject to the anti-SLAPP provision. The Plaintiffs attempt to distinguish the present case from the *GLAAD* case by arguing that the *GLAAD* case did not involve advertising and other "statements" regarding the captioning of the videos, and instead solely involved the captions themselves. This case, Plaintiffs argue, involves such statements and advertisements and therefore involves "commercial speech," which is not covered by the anti-SLAPP statute because it does not connect to the public interest. However, the Plaintiffs' argument does not at all distinguish the Plaintiffs' warranty and Unruh Act claims from the holding in *GLAAD* because the "principal thrust" of both the warranty and Unruh Act claims is clearly the captions and subtitles themselves, not the labeling on the box.

Additionally, the cause of action under the Unruh Act similarly focuses on the captioning itself rather than the statements or advertising related to the captioning. The Plaintiffs' Unruh Act claim alleges that the Plaintiffs and other class members have not been provided services that are provided to other customers, as they have been denied access to the music and song lyrics that are not captioned. Again, this claim is essentially unrelated to the labeling of the movies and shows, as the conduct at issue in this claim is clearly the subtitles and captions themselves. A change in the labelling would not provide the relief sought by the Plaintiffs as it would not provide the access to the content of the movies and shows that is sought by the Plaintiffs. As a result, the Court finds that the Plaintiffs' warranty and Unruh Act causes of action primarily involve the captioning of the movies and shows, and therefore fall under the *GLAAD* precedent, which found that captioning of videos involves a protected activity in connection with a public issue. Thus, the first prong of the anti-SLAPP analysis is satisfied with regards to Claims Two. Three, and Five.

The first prong of the anti-SLAPP analysis of the Plaintiffs' misrepresentation claims is more complex, as the "principal thrust" of those claims is clearly the advertising and labeling of the content rather than the captions and subtitles themselves. Therefore, the Plaintiffs' argument that their claims involve purely commercial speech rather than protected content carries more weight for their misrepresentation claims than it does for the warranty and Unruh Act claims. However, the Court finds that even the Plaintiffs' misrepresentation claims satisfy the first prong of the anti-SLAPP analysis because the advertisements and labeling constitute acts that are "in furtherance" of the Defendants' right of free speech and are in connection with a public issue, and therefore fall under the coverage of the anti-SLAPP statute. As a result, the representations and advertisements of the captioned content is not purely "commercial speech" that is not covered by the anti-SLAPP statute, but rather is a mechanism by which protected speech is disseminated to the target consumers.

2. Likelihood of Prevailing—Once the Court finds the anti-SLAPP movant has established covered conduct, the burden shifts to the plaintiff to demonstrate "a probability of prevailing on the claim." In denying a motion to strike on the ground that the plaintiff has established the requisite probability of success, ... the trial court necessarily concludes that the plaintiff has substantiated a legally tenable claim through a facially sufficient evidentiary showing."

For the same reasons that the Court granted Defendants' motion to dismiss Plaintiffs' claims for failure to state a claim upon which relief may be granted, the Court does not find Plaintiffs can establish a legally tenable claim. For those reasons, the Court finds that the Plaintiffs have failed to demonstrate a probability of prevailing on the claim, thereby satisfying the second prong of the anti-SLAPP analysis.

In addition, even assuming Plaintiffs stated legally sufficient claims, they have failed to substantiate their claims with admissible evidence. In opposing an anti-SLAPP motion, the plaintiff cannot rely on the allegations of the complaint, but must produce evidence that would be admissible at trial. The Plaintiffs' Opposition to the motion to strike does not point to any substantiated facts that could sustain a judgment on the merits in the Plaintiffs' favor, but rather restates the allegations contained in the Complaint and the Opposition to the Motion to Dismiss.

Since both prongs of the anti-SLAPP statute have been satisfied for each of the Plaintiffs' claims, the Court GRANTS the Defendants' Motion to Strike pursuant to California's anti-SLAPP statute for all causes of action.

Notes and Questions

a. The court, in *James v. Meow Media, Inc.*, explained that "Learned Hand's famous conception of negligence would hold conduct negligent if the harm that the conduct threatens to create, discounted by the *ex ante* probability of the harm's non-occurrence, outweighs the utility created by the conduct." *James v. Meow Media, Inc.* (citing *United States v. Carroll Towing Co.,* 159 F.2d 169 (2d Cir. 1947)). Assuming the probability-utility formula, does the utility of free speech outweigh the low-risk but extremely high cost of incidents such as the murders at Columbine High School in Colorado and Heath High School in Paducah, Kentucky? Can the answer for general free speech be reframed for violence-based content?

b. Although only briefly discussed by the courts, another question exists as to whether there is a sufficiently direct, causal link between the objectionable content and the violent, criminal activity. While there are numerous studies indicating a correlation, legally sufficient causation is much less likely to be established.

c. Although an unpublished opinion, *Anthony v. Buena Vista Home Entertainment Inc.* provides some key distinctions for tort liability of entertainment media. The decision anticipates an important copyright distinction between the ownership of a copy of a work (the DVD) from the underlying copyrighted work (the film) for purposes of warranty policies, transfer rights, and ownership. The decision also provides a very clear, useful explanation of the California anti-SLAPP legislation that triggers significant fee-shifting consequences if a court determines a lawsuit interferes with the speech rights of the defendant.

Problem 4-B

Bryce has been diligently working on the set for *Juliet Prescott*. Since Bryce is not an expert at set design, Bryce purchased a detailed manual entitled *Set Construction for Amateur and Professional Theatre* written by a local university professor. Bryce carefully followed the instructions for the design of a moving wall. Unfortunately, the drawing in the book had been transposed and by following the directions in the text, Bryce failed to put the proper bracing on the set. The set piece crashed during rehearsal, injuring one of the actors.

Bryce calls you for advice. Bryce wishes to interplead the book author, bookstore, and book publisher in the event Bryce is sued for the injury. Explain what liability, if any, the various participants in the authoring and sale of the book might have to the injured party.

C. Limits on First Amendment Deference
National Endowment for the Arts v. Finley
524 U.S. 569 (1998)

JUSTICE O'CONNOR delivered the opinion of the Court.

The National Foundation on the Arts and Humanities Act, as amended in 1990, requires the Chairperson of the National Endowment for the Arts (NEA) to ensure that "artistic excellence and artistic merit are the criteria by which [grant] applications are judged, taking into consideration general standards of decency and respect for the diverse beliefs and values of the American public." In this case, we review the Court of Appeals' determination that §954(d)(1), on its face, impermissibly discriminates on the basis of viewpoint and is void for vagueness under the First and Fifth Amendments. We conclude that §954(d)(1) is facially valid, as it neither inherently interferes with First Amendment rights nor violates constitutional vagueness principles.

With the establishment of the NEA in 1965, Congress embarked on a "broadly conceived national policy of support for the ... arts in the United States," pledging federal funds to "help create and sustain not only a climate encouraging freedom of thought, imagination, and inquiry but also the material conditions facilitating the release of ... creative talent." The enabling statute vests the NEA with substantial discretion to award grants; it identifies only the broadest funding priorities, including "artistic and cultural significance, giving emphasis to American creativity and cultural diversity," "professional excellence," and the encouragement of "public knowledge, education, understanding, and appreciation of the arts."

Applications for NEA funding are initially reviewed by advisory panels composed of experts in the relevant field of the arts. Under the 1990 Amendments to the enabling statute, those panels must reflect "diverse artistic and cultural points of view" and include "wide geographic, ethnic, and minority representation," as well as "lay individuals who are knowledgeable about the arts." The panel's report to the 26-member National Council on the Arts (Council), which, in turn, advises the NEA Chairperson. The Chairperson has the ultimate authority to award grants but may not approve an application as to which the Council has made a negative recommendation.

Since 1965, the NEA has distributed over three billion dollars in grants to individuals and organizations, funding that has served as a catalyst for increased state, corporate, and foundation support for the arts. Congress has recently restricted the availability of federal funding for individual artists, confining grants primarily to qualifying organizations and state arts agencies, and constraining sub-granting. By far the largest portion of the grants distributed in fiscal year 1998 were awarded directly to state arts agencies. In the remaining categories, the most substantial grants were allocated to symphony orchestras, fine arts museums, dance theater foundations, and opera associations.

Throughout the NEA's history, only a handful of the agency's roughly 100,000 awards have generated formal complaints about misapplied funds or abuse of the public's trust. Two provocative works, however, prompted public controversy in 1989 and led to congressional revaluation of the NEA's funding priorities and efforts to increase oversight of its grant-making procedures. The Institute of Contemporary Art at the University of Pennsylvania had used $30,000 of a visual arts grant it received from the NEA to fund a 1989 retrospective of photographer Robert Mapplethorpe's work. The exhibit, entitled *The Perfect Moment*, included homoerotic photographs that several Members of Congress condemned as pornographic. Members also denounced artist Andres Serrano's work *Piss Christ*, a photograph of a crucifix immersed in urine. Serrano had been awarded a $15,000 grant from the Southeast Center for Contemporary Art, an organization that received NEA support.

When considering the NEA's appropriations for fiscal year 1990, Congress reacted to the controversy surrounding the Mapplethorpe and Serrano photographs by eliminating $45,000 from the agency's budget, the precise amount contributed to the two exhibits by NEA grant recipients. Congress also enacted an amendment providing that no NEA funds "may be used to promote, disseminate, or produce materials which in the judgment of [the NEA] may be considered obscene, including but not limited to, depictions of sadomasochism, homoeroticism, the sexual exploitation of children, or individuals engaged in sex acts and which, when taken as a whole, do not have serious literary, artistic, political, or scientific value." The NEA implemented Congress' mandate by instituting a requirement that all grantees certify in writing that they would not utilize federal funding to engage in projects inconsistent with the criteria in the 1990 appropriations bill. That certification requirement was subsequently invalidated as unconstitutionally vague by a Federal District Court, and the NEA did not appeal the decision....

Ultimately, Congress adopted the Williams/Coleman Amendment, a bipartisan compromise between Members opposing any funding restrictions and those favoring some guidance to the agency. In relevant part, the Amendment became § 954(d)(1), which directs the Chairperson, in establishing procedures to judge the artistic merit of grant applications, to "take into consideration general standards of decency and respect for the diverse beliefs and values of the American public."[5]

The NEA has not promulgated any official interpretation of the provision, but in December 1990, the Council unanimously adopted a resolution to implement § 954(d)(1) merely by ensuring that the members of the advisory panels that conduct

---

5. Title 20 U.S.C. § 954(d) provides in full that:

"No payment shall be made under this section except upon application therefor which is submitted to the National Endowment for the Arts in accordance with regulations issued and procedures established by the Chairperson. In establishing such regulations and procedures, the Chairperson shall ensure that—

"(1) artistic excellence and artistic merit are the criteria by which applications are judged, taking into consideration general standards of decency and respect for the diverse beliefs and values of the American public; and

"(2) applications are consistent with the purposes of this section. Such regulations and procedures shall clearly indicate that obscenity is without artistic merit, is not protected speech, and shall not be funded."

the initial review of grant applications represent geographic, ethnic, and aesthetic diversity. John Frohnmayer, then Chairperson of the NEA, also declared that he would "count on [the] procedures" ensuring diverse membership on the peer review panels to fulfill Congress' mandate.

The four individual respondents in this case, Karen Finley, John Fleck, Holly Hughes, and Tim Miller, are performance artists who applied for NEA grants before § 954(d)(1) was enacted. An advisory panel recommended approval of respondents' projects, both initially and after receiving Frohnmayer's request to reconsider three of the applications. A majority of the Council subsequently recommended disapproval, and in June 1990, the NEA informed respondents that they had been denied funding. Respondents filed suit, alleging that the NEA had violated their First Amendment rights by rejecting the applications on political grounds, had failed to follow statutory procedures by basing the denial on criteria other than those set forth in the NEA's enabling statute, and had breached the confidentiality of their grant applications through the release of quotations to the press, in violation of the Privacy Act of 1974. Respondents sought restoration of the recommended grants or reconsideration of their applications, as well as damages for the alleged Privacy Act violations. When Congress enacted § 954(d)(1), respondents, now joined by the National Association of Artists' Organizations (NAAO), amended their complaint to challenge the provision as void for vagueness and impermissibly viewpoint based....

Respondents raise a facial constitutional challenge to § 954(d)(1), and consequently they confront "a heavy burden" in advancing their claim. Facial invalidation "is, manifestly, strong medicine" that "has been employed by the Court sparingly and only as a last resort." To prevail, respondents must demonstrate a substantial risk that application of the provision will lead to the suppression of speech.

Respondents argue that the provision is a paradigmatic example of viewpoint discrimination because it rejects any artistic speech that either fails to respect mainstream values or offends standards of decency. The premise of respondents' claim is that § 954(d)(1) constrains the agency's ability to fund certain categories of artistic expression. The NEA, however, reads the provision as merely hortatory, and contends that it stops well short of an absolute restriction. Section 954(d)(1) adds "considerations" to the grant-making process; it does not preclude awards to projects that might be deemed "indecent" or "disrespectful," nor place conditions on grants, or even specify that those factors must be given any particular weight in reviewing an application. Indeed, the agency asserts that it has adequately implemented § 954(d)(1) merely by ensuring the representation of various backgrounds and points of view on the advisory panels that analyze grant applications. *See* Declaration of Randolph McAusland, Deputy Chairman for Programs at the NEA, (stating that the NEA implements the provision "by ensuring that the peer review panels represent a variety of geographical areas, aesthetic views, professions, areas of expertise, races and ethnic groups, and gender, and include a lay person"). We do not decide whether the NEA's view—that the formulation of diverse advisory panels is sufficient to comply with

Congress' command—is in fact a reasonable reading of the statute. It is clear, however, that the text of § 954(d)(1) imposes no categorical requirement. The advisory language stands in sharp contrast to congressional efforts to prohibit the funding of certain classes of speech. When Congress has in fact intended to affirmatively constrain the NEA's grant-making authority, it has done so in no uncertain terms.

Furthermore, like the plain language of § 954(d), the political context surrounding the adoption of the "decency and respect" clause is inconsistent with respondents' assertion that the provision compels the NEA to deny funding on the basis of viewpoint discriminatory criteria. The legislation was a bipartisan proposal introduced as a counterweight to amendments aimed at eliminating the NEA's funding or substantially constraining its grant-making authority. The Independent Commission had cautioned Congress against the adoption of distinct viewpoint-based standards for funding, and the Commission's report suggests that "additional criteria for selection, if any, should be incorporated as part of the selection process (perhaps as part of a definition of 'artistic excellence'), rather than isolated and treated as exogenous considerations." In keeping with that recommendation, the criteria in § 954(d)(1) inform the assessment of artistic merit, but Congress declined to disallow any particular viewpoints. As the sponsors of § 954(d)(1) noted in urging rejection of the Rohrabacher Amendment, "if we start down that road of prohibiting categories of expression, categories which are indeed constitutionally protected speech, where do we end? Where one Member's aversions end, others with different sensibilities and with different values begin." ([the Court cites a] statement of Rep. Williams) (arguing that the Rohrabacher Amendment would prevent the funding of Jasper Johns' flag series, "The Merchant of Venice," "Chorus Line," "Birth of a Nation," and the "Grapes of Wrath"). In contrast, before the vote on § 954(d)(1), one of its sponsors stated: "If we have done one important thing in this amendment, it is this. We have maintained the integrity of freedom of expression in the United States."

That § 954(d)(1) admonishes the NEA merely to take "decency and respect" into consideration, and that the legislation was aimed at reforming procedures rather than precluding speech, undercut respondents' argument that the provision inevitably will be utilized as a tool for invidious viewpoint discrimination. In cases where we have struck down legislation as facially unconstitutional, the dangers were both more evident and more substantial. In *R.A.V. v. St. Paul*, 505 U.S. 377 (1992), for example, we invalidated on its face a municipal ordinance that defined as a criminal offense the placement of a symbol on public or private property "'which one knows or has reasonable grounds to know arouses anger, alarm, or resentment in others on the basis of race, color, creed, religion, or gender.'" That provision set forth a clear penalty, proscribed views on particular "disfavored subjects," and suppressed "distinctive ideas, conveyed by a distinctive message."

In contrast, the "decency and respect" criteria do not silence speakers by expressly "threatening censorship of ideas." Thus, we do not perceive a realistic danger that § 954(d)(1) will compromise First Amendment values. As respondents' own arguments demonstrate, the considerations that the provision introduces, by their nature, do not engender the kind of directed viewpoint discrimination that would prompt this Court to invalidate a statute on its face. Respondents assert, for example, that "one would be hard-pressed to find two people in the United States who could agree on what the 'diverse beliefs and values of the American public' are, much less on whether a particular work of art 'respects' them"; and they claim that "'decency' is likely to mean something very different to a septuagenarian in Tuscaloosa and a teenager in Las Vegas." The NEA likewise views the considerations enumerated in § 954(d)(1) as susceptible to multiple interpretations. Accordingly, the provision does not introduce considerations that, in practice, would effectively preclude or punish the expression of particular views. Indeed, one could hardly anticipate how "decency" or "respect" would bear on grant applications in categories such as funding for symphony orchestras.

Respondents' claim that the provision is facially unconstitutional may be reduced to the argument that the criteria in § 954(d)(1) are sufficiently subjective that the agency could utilize them to engage in viewpoint discrimination. Given the varied interpretations of the criteria and the vague exhortation to "take them into consideration," it seems unlikely that this provision will introduce any greater element of selectivity than the determination of "artistic excellence" itself. And we are reluctant, in any event, to invalidate legislation "on the basis of its hypothetical application to situations not before the Court."

The NEA's enabling statute contemplates a number of indisputably constitutional applications for both the "decency" prong of § 954(d)(1) and its reference to "respect for the diverse beliefs and values of the American public." Educational programs are central to the NEA's mission. Permissible applications of the mandate to consider "respect for the diverse beliefs and values of the American public" are also apparent. In setting forth the purposes of the NEA, Congress explained that "it is vital to democracy to honor and preserve its multicultural artistic heritage." The agency expressly takes diversity into account, giving special consideration to "projects and productions ... that reach, or reflect the culture of, a minority, inner city, rural, or tribal community," as well as projects that generally emphasize "cultural diversity." Respondents do not contend that the criteria in § 954(d)(1) are impermissibly applied when they may be justified, as the statute contemplates, with respect to a project's intended audience.

We recognize, of course, that reference to these permissible applications would not alone be sufficient to sustain the statute against respondents' First Amendment challenge. But neither are we persuaded that, in other applications, the language of § 954(d)(1) itself will give rise to the suppression of protected expression. Any content-based considerations that may be taken into account in the grant-making process are a consequence of the nature of arts funding. The NEA has limited resources and it must deny the majority of the grant applications that it receives, including many that propose "artistically excellent" projects. The agency may decide to fund particular projects for a wide variety of reasons, "such as the technical proficiency of the artist, the creativity of the work, the anticipated public interest in or appreciation of the work, the work's contemporary relevance, its educational value, its suitability for or appeal to special audiences (such as children or the disabled), its service to a rural or isolated community, or even simply that the work could increase public knowledge of an art form."

As the dissent below noted, it would be "impossible to have a highly selective grant program without denying money to a large amount of constitutionally protected expression." The "very assumption" of the NEA is that grants will be awarded according to the "artistic worth of competing applications," and absolute neutrality is simply "inconceivable."

Respondent's reliance on our decision in *Rosenberger v. Rector and Visitors of Univ. of Va.,* 515 U.S. 819 (1995), is therefore misplaced. In *Rosenberger,* a public university declined to authorize disbursements from its Student Activities Fund to finance the printing of a Christian student newspaper. We held that by subsidizing the Student Activities Fund, the University had created a limited public forum, from which it impermissibly excluded all publications with religious editorial viewpoints. Although the scarcity of NEA funding does not distinguish this case from *Rosenberger,* the competitive process according to which the grants are allocated does. In the context of arts funding, in contrast to many other subsidies, the Government does not indiscriminately "encourage a diversity of views from private speakers." The NEA's mandate is to make aesthetic judgments, and the inherently content-based "excellence" threshold for NEA support sets it apart from the subsidy at issue in *Rosenberger*—which was available to all student organizations that were "'related to the educational purpose of the University,'"—and from comparably objective decisions on allocating public benefits, such as access to a school auditorium or a municipal theater, or the second class mailing privileges available to "'all newspapers and other periodical publications.'"

Respondents do not allege discrimination in any particular funding decision. (In fact, after filing suit to challenge § 954(d)(1), two of the individual respondents received NEA grants. Thus, we have no occasion here to address an as-applied challenge in a situation where the denial of a grant may be shown to be the product of invidious viewpoint discrimination. If the NEA were to leverage its power to award subsidies on the basis of subjective criteria into a penalty on disfavored viewpoints, then we would confront a different case. We have stated that, even in the provision of subsidies, the Government may not "aim at the suppression of dangerous ideas," and if a subsidy were "manipulated" to have a "coercive effect," then relief could be appropriate. In addition, as the NEA itself concedes, a more pressing constitutional question would arise if government funding resulted in the imposition of a disproportionate burden calculated to drive "certain ideas or viewpoints from the marketplace." Unless and until § 954(d)(1) is applied in a manner that raises concern about the suppression of disfavored viewpoints, however, we uphold the constitutionality of the provision.

Finally, although the First Amendment certainly has application in the subsidy context, we note that the Government may allocate competitive funding according to criteria that would be impermissible were direct regulation of speech or a criminal penalty at stake. So long as legislation does not infringe on other constitutionally protected rights, Congress has wide latitude to set spending priorities....

The lower courts also erred in invalidating §954(d)(1) as unconstitutionally vague. Under the First and Fifth Amendments, speakers are protected from arbitrary and discriminatory enforcement of vague standards. The terms of the provision are undeniably opaque, and if they appeared in a criminal statute or regulatory scheme, they could raise substantial vagueness concerns. It is unlikely, however, that speakers will be compelled to steer too far clear of any "forbidden area" in the context of grants of this nature.... In the context of selective subsidies, it is not always feasible for Congress to legislate with clarity. Indeed, if this statute is unconstitutionally vague, then so too are all government programs awarding scholarships and grants on the basis of subjective criteria such as "excellence." ... Section 954(d)(1) merely adds some imprecise considerations to an already subjective selection process. It does not, on its face, impermissibly infringe on First or Fifth Amendment rights. Accordingly, the judgment of the Court of Appeals is reversed and the case is remanded for further proceedings consistent with this opinion. *It is so ordered.*

JUSTICE SOUTER, dissenting.

The question here is whether the italicized segment of this statute is unconstitutional on its face: "artistic excellence and artistic merit are the criteria by which applications [for grants from the National Endowment for the Arts] are judged, *taking into consideration general standards of decency and respect for the diverse beliefs and values of the American public.*" It is. The decency and respect proviso mandates viewpoint-based decisions in the disbursement of government subsidies, and the Government has wholly failed to explain why the statute should be afforded an exemption from the fundamental rule of the First Amendment that viewpoint discrimination in the exercise of public authority over expressive activity is unconstitutional....

Notes and Questions

a. Following *National Endowment for the Arts v. Finley*, the Supreme Court addressed application of the controversial decision in *Agency for Int'l Dev. v. All. for Open Soc'y Int'l, Inc.*, 570 U.S. 205 (2013). There, the Supreme Court addressed a more restrictive version of the government's speech requirements:

> In the United States Leadership Against HIV/AIDS, Tuberculosis, and Malaria Act of 2003 (Leadership Act), 22 U.S.C. §7601 et seq., Congress has authorized the appropriation of billions of dollars to fund efforts by non-governmental organizations to combat HIV/AIDS worldwide. The Act imposes two related conditions: (1) No funds "may be used to promote or advocate the legalization or practice of prostitution," §7631(e); and (2) no funds may be used by an organization "that does not have a policy explicitly opposing prostitution," §7631(f). To enforce the second condition, known as the Policy Requirement, the Department of Health and Human Services (HHS) and the United States Agency for International Development (USAID) require funding recipients to agree in their award documents that they oppose prostitution....

The Policy Requirement mandates that recipients of Leadership Act funds explicitly agree with the Government's policy to oppose prostitution and sex trafficking. It is, however, a basic First Amendment principle that "freedom of speech prohibits the government from telling people what they must say." *Rumsfeld v. Forum for Academic and Institutional Rights, Inc.*, 547 U.S. 47, 61 (2006). Were it enacted as a direct regulation of speech, the Policy Requirement would plainly violate the First Amendment. The question is whether the Government may nonetheless impose that requirement as a condition on the receipt of federal funds....

As a general matter, if a party objects to a condition on the receipt of federal funding, its recourse is to decline the funds. This remains true when the objection is that a condition may affect the recipient's exercise of its First Amendment rights. At the same time, however, we have held that the Government "may not deny a benefit to a person on a basis that infringes his constitutionally protected ... freedom of speech even if he has no entitlement to that benefit." ... By requiring recipients to profess a specific belief, the Policy Requirement goes beyond defining the limits of the federally funded program to defining the recipient.... The Policy Requirement compels as a condition of federal funding the affirmation of a belief that by its nature cannot be confined within the scope of the Government program. In so doing, it violates the First Amendment and cannot be sustained.

b. One recurring issue of state-sponsored discrimination occurs in the context of school facilities that are made available for some, but not all, outside groups. These restrictions may range from prohibitions of religious content to restrictions of plays or film productions based on the content of the activity. *See Lamb's Chapel v. Ctr. Moriches Union Free Sch. Dist.*, 508 U.S. 384, 386 (1993); *Se. Promotions, Ltd. v. Conrad*, 420 U.S. 546, 555 (1975).

c. Another of the state activities declared unconstitutional was the so-called "Son of Sam" legislation, which attempted to bar a convicted felon of the profits earned by selling the book or film rights. *See Simon & Schuster, Inc. v. Members of N.Y. State Crime Victims Bd.*, 502 U.S. 105 (1991). Despite the unconstitutionality of such legislation, states may generally provide legislation for victim restitution and may expand the time-period of such payments to include income earned while in prison from all activities—including the sale of film or book rights. So long as the legislation does not single out the expressive activities, such legislation should be constitutional.

d. Despite the public assumptions regarding the First Amendment, the ability of the government to selectively fund speech, to protect minors, to ban obscenity, and to regulate broadcast media continues to give the government a significant role in the shape of content. Because the broadcast industries, the music industries, and the motion picture industry also rely heavily on the government to promote international trade and copyright policies abroad, these industries are particularly sensitive to the political concerns of elected officials. Voluntary rating systems and other industry self-regulation often stem from the need to appear responsive to the political power that is not shielded by the First Amendment.

The motion picture rating system operated by the Motion Picture Association of America provides guidance for the public—primarily designed to inform parents about the adult nature of motion pictures. With the expansion of the adult or "X" rated film and the attempt by the motion picture industry to market adult films that were adult in tone rather than merely pornographic, the MPAA created the NC-17 rating.

One of the reasons for this change is the policy enforced by most daily newspapers not to advertise films that are either unrated or rated X. Most television stations have a similar policy. As a result, marketing such films successfully is nearly impossible. The advertising ban does not appear to extend to "uncut" versions of previously rated films on DVD. As a result, such uncut DVDs have become a new submarket in recent years.

e. Compare the voluntary rating system employed by the Motion Picture Association and the Association of Broadcasters to the statutes at issue in *Interstate Circuit*. How has the voluntary ratings system changed the availability and content of films available?

f. Because the advertising in mass transportation systems is in a designated public forum, the transportation authority has limited discretion in which advertising to reject. Faced with challenges to a marijuana ad and a religious ad, which ad would be more likely to withstand the refusal to be displayed? *See Ridley v. Mass. Bay Transp. Auth.*, 390 F.3d 65 (1st Cir. 2004).

Problem 4-C

Bryce is interested to know whether the play, *Juliet Prescott*, can be the subject of a grant application from the National Endowment for the Arts, the National Endowment for the Humanities, or the two similar state agencies. Bryce is particularly concerned that the play would have to be revised as a condition of accepting such funding. Advise Bryce as to whether the granting agencies could require Bryce to edit the play as a condition of receiving these funds.

D. Bibliography and Links

David A. Anderson, *First Amendment Limitations on Tort Law*, 69 Brook. L. Rev. 755 (2004).

Marc Jonathan Blitz, *A First Amendment for Second Life: What Virtual Worlds Mean for the Law of Video Games*, 11 Vand. J. Ent. & Tech. L. 779 (2009).

Clay Calvert, *The First Amendment, the Media and the Culture Wars: Eight Important Lessons from 2004 About Speech, Censorship, Science and Public Policy*, 41 Cal. W. L. Rev. 325 (2005).

Clay Calvert & Robert D. Richards, *Violence and Video Games 2006: Legislation and Litigation*, 8 Tex. Rev. Ent. & Sports L. 49 (2007).

Peter DiCola, *Copyright Equality: Free Speech, Efficiency, and Regulatory Parity in Distribution*, 93 B.U.L. Rev. 1837, 1838 (2013).

Michelle Freeman, *Administrative Law Discussion Forum: First Amendment Protection for the Arts After NEA v. Finley*, 38 Brandeis L.J. 405 (2000).

Patrick M. Garry, *The First Amendment and Non-Political Speech: Exploring a Constitutional Model That Focuses on the Existence of Alternative Channels of Communication*, 72 Mo. L. Rev. 477 (2007).

Gregory K. Laughlin, *Playing Games with the First Amendment: Are Video Games Speech and May Minors' Access to Graphically Violent Video Games Be Restricted?*, 40 U. Rich. L. Rev. 481 (2006).

William E. Lee, *Books, Video Games, and Foul-Mouthed Hollywood Glitteratae: The Supreme Court and the Technology-Neutral Interpretation of the First Amendment*, 14 Colum. Sci. & Tech. L. Rev. 295 (2013).

Lisa P. Ramsey, *Increasing First Amendment Scrutiny of Trademark Law*, 61 SMU L. Rev. 381 (2008).

Robert D. Richards & Clay Calvert, *Columbine Fallout: The Long-Term Effects on Free Expression Take Hold in Public Schools*, 83 B.U.L. Rev. 1089 (2003).

Kevin W. Saunders, *Regulating Youth Access to Violent Video Games: Three Responses to First Amendment Concerns*, 2003 L. Rev. M.S.U.-D.C.L. 51 (2003).

Chapter 5

Attention to Non-Literary Rights

A. Defamation

1. Introduction[1]

Defamation is a false statement of fact that injures a person's reputation in the manner defined by statute or case law. A false statement becomes defamatory if "it tends so to harm the reputation of another as to lower him in the estimation of the community or to deter third persons from associating or dealing with him."[2] At common law, a defamatory statement is a false statement of fact that exposes a person to hatred, ridicule, or contempt, causes him to be shunned, or injures him in his business or trade. This more graphic description of the defamatory statement may still be found in some jurisdictions.

According to the Restatement (Second) of Torts § 558, the elements of the defamation cause of action are:

(a) a false and defamatory statement concerning another;

(b) an unprivileged publication to a third party;

(c) fault amounting at least to negligence on the part of the publisher; and

(d) either actionability of the statement irrespective of special harm or the existence of special harm caused by the publication.[3]

Each element of the claim must be proven by the plaintiff, including the falsity of the statement.

To be defamatory in the U.S., the person alleging the defamation must prove that the statement is false as well as that it is harmful, that it pertains to the person suing,

---

1. Adapted from Jon M. Garon, The Independent Filmmaker's Law and Business Guide: Financing, Shooting, and Distributing Independent and Digital Films (2007).
2. Restatement (Second) Torts § 559 (1977). Under California law, "libel is a false and unprivileged publication by writing ... which exposes any person to hatred, contempt, ridicule, or obloquy, or which causes him to be shunned or avoided, or which has a tendency to injure him in his occupation." Cal. Civ. Code § 45 (West 2019).
3. Restatement (Second) of Torts § 558.

and that it has been published to someone other than the plaintiff, and that the defendant published the statement with the requisite level of negligence or intentional conduct.

Once a person has died, his heirs may not pursue the claim. Any publication to a third person, such as through publication in a script, on a website, or through sending a letter or email, will give rise to liability if the publication is a false defamatory statement of or concerning the defamed person. Under common law, republishing a false defamatory statement will give rise to a new claim for defamation. As a result, a filmmaker is responsible for any defamatory material in the work he creates, licenses, or borrows.

In *New York Times Co. v. Sullivan*, the Supreme Court addressed the relationship between free speech and defamation. "The constitutional guarantees [of free speech] require, we think, a federal rule that prohibits a public official from recovering damages for a defamatory falsehood relating to his official conduct unless he proves that the statement was made with 'actual malice'—that is, with knowledge that it was false or with reckless disregard of whether it was false or not."[4] Unless a statement is defamatory, it is protected by the First Amendment, which means the courts, as a governmental entity, will not impose liability on the speaker. "We hold today that the Constitution delimits a State's power to award damages for libel in actions brought by public officials against critics of their official conduct."[5] In an extension of the Actual Malice standard, the Supreme Court extended the rule from just public officials to all public figures.[6] The Court reasoned "that public figures are less deserving of protection than private persons because public figures, like public officials, have voluntarily exposed themselves to increased risk of injury from defamatory falsehood concerning them."[7] "For the most part those who attain [public figure] status have assumed roles of especial prominence in the affairs of society. Some occupy positions of such persuasive power and influence that they are deemed public figures for all purposes. More commonly, those classed as public figures have thrust themselves to the forefront of particular public controversies in order to influence the resolution of the issues involved."[8]

> In *Gertz v. Robert Welch, Inc.*, [the] Court held that a person may become a public figure for a limited range of issues if he "voluntarily injects himself or is drawn into a particular public controversy." Such a person, the Court reasoned, resembles a public official in that he typically enjoys "significantly greater access to the channels of effective communication" and knowingly

---

4. New York Times Co. v. Sullivan, 376 U.S. 254, 279–80 (1964).
5. *Id*. at 283.
6. Gertz v. Robert Welch, Inc., 418 U.S. 323, 344 (1974).
7. Wolston v. Reader's Digest Ass'n, Inc., 443 U.S. 157, 164 (1979) (quoting *Gertz*) (internal quotation marks omitted).
8. *Gertz*, 418 U.S., at 345.

"runs the risk of closer public scrutiny" than would have been true had he remained in private life. The passage of time, I believe, often will be relevant in deciding whether a person possesses these two public-figure characteristics. First, a lapse of years between a controversial event and a libelous utterance may diminish the defamed party's access to the means of counterargument....

This analysis implies, of course, that one may be a public figure for purposes of contemporaneous reporting of a controversial event, yet not be a public figure for purposes of historical commentary on the same occurrence. Historians, consequently, may well run a greater risk of liability for defamation. Yet this result, in my view, does no violence to First Amendment values. While historical analysis is no less vital to the marketplace of ideas than reporting current events, historians work under different conditions than do their media counterparts. A reporter trying to meet a deadline may find it totally impossible to check thoroughly the accuracy of his sources. A historian writing sub specie aeternitatis has both the time for reflection and the opportunity to investigate the veracity of the pronouncements he makes.[9]

If the publication is about a private individual involving some matter of public interest, then the filmmaker can be liable merely by being negligent in failing to ascertain the truth[10] or in the manner in which the truth was altered to fit the dramatic needs of the project.[11] Nonetheless, the party suing the filmmaker for defamation must prove that the statements or depictions are defamatory. Unless the jury determines the depiction is inaccurate, the filmmaker will not lose the lawsuit.

One particularly insidious form of libel is to falsely attribute quotes to a person. The Supreme Court has held that otherwise unobjectionable statements could be deemed libelous when they were transformed into quotes attributed to the victim.[12] Attributing dialogue to a character in a film can easily achieve this effect. When a film character is based on a living person, the dialogue may include statements that were originally made by critics of that person, but are now portrayed as self-deprecating comments made by the character. This increases the amount of material included in a documentary to which objections may be made.

Fictionalization may also result in the creation of composite characters—fictional characters that embody attributes of a number of live individuals. Because of the requirement that the statement be of or concerning the person claiming defamation, a common practice is to create fictional characters to stand in for unsavory conduct that may have been undertaken by real people. If the fictional character or composite character is identifiable as a real person involved in the situation, then the fictionalization

---

9. Wolston v. Reader's Digest Ass'n, Inc., 443 U.S. 157, 170–71 (Justice Blackmun, with whom Mr. Justice Marshall joined, concurring).

10. *Gertz*, 418 at 344 (1974).

11. Davis v. Costa-Gavras, 654 F. Supp. 653, 655 (S.D.N.Y. 1987).

12. Masson v. New Yorker Magazine, 501 U.S. 496, 522 (1991).

adds to the potential for liability.[13] This appears to occur most frequently when the fictional character's name bears some resemblance to the living person's name.

Fortunately for filmmakers, courts tend to disfavor defamation awards. This may be a result of the strong respect held by the courts for the First Amendment. It may also reflect respect for the detailed investigative process that major motion picture studios and television networks go through for their docudramas and fact-based works. Needless to say, the institutional respect for filmmakers will not extend to guerilla filmmakers and individuals shooting on-the-fly films on shoestring budgets. For this reason, it is vital that when producing a fact-based story, the filmmaker document every step taken to verify the truth of the story before creating the script and shooting the film. As discussed below, having the actual people who are depicted or identified sign agreements will reduce the risk that those people will sue for defamation, but unless every character depicted in a fact-based story has signed a release, the risk of a defamation claim remains.

2. Expansion of the *N.Y. Times* Standard

Excerpt from Gertz v. Robert Welch, Inc.

418 U.S. 323 (1974)

Three years after *New York Times*, a majority of the Court agreed to extend the constitutional privilege to defamatory criticism of "public figures." This extension was announced in *Curtis Publishing Co. v. Butts* [388 U.S. 130 (1967),] and its companion, *Associated Press v. Walker*, 388 U.S. 130, 162 (1967). The first case involved the Saturday Evening Post's charge that Coach Wally Butts of the University of Georgia had conspired with Coach "Bear" Bryant of the University of Alabama to fix a football game between their respective schools. Walker involved an erroneous Associated Press account of former Major General Edwin Walker's participation in a University of Mississippi campus riot. Because Butts was paid by a private alumni association and Walker had resigned from the Army, neither could be classified as a "public official" under *New York Times*. Although Mr. Justice Harlan announced the result in both cases, a majority of the Court agreed with Mr. Chief Justice Warren's conclusion that the New York Times test should apply to criticism of "public figures" as well as "public officials." The Court extended the constitutional privilege announced in that case to protect defamatory criticism of nonpublic persons who "are nevertheless intimately involved in the resolution of important public questions or, by reason of their fame, shape events in areas of concern to society at large."

New York Times and later cases explicated the meaning of the new standard. In *New York Times* the Court held that under the circumstances the newspaper's failure to check the accuracy of the advertisement against news stories in its own files did not establish reckless disregard for the truth. In *St. Amant v. Thompson*, 390 U.S. 727,

---

13. Springer v. Viking Press, 90 A.D.2d 315, 457 N.Y.S.2d 246 (1st Dept. 1982) *aff'd*, 60 N.Y.2d 916, 470 N.Y.S.2d 579 (1983).

731 (1968), the Court equated reckless disregard of the truth with subjective awareness of probable falsity: "There must be sufficient evidence to permit the conclusion that the defendant in fact entertained serious doubts as to the truth of his publication."

In *Beckley Newspapers Corp. v. Hanks,* 389 U.S. 81 (1967), the Court emphasized the distinction between the New York Times test of knowledge of falsity or reckless disregard of the truth and "actual malice" in the traditional sense of ill-will.

Garrison v. Louisiana, 379 U.S. 64 125 (1964), made plain that the new standard applied to criminal libel laws as well as to civil actions and that it governed criticism directed at "anything which might touch on an official's fitness for office."

Finally, in *Rosenblatt v. Baer,* 383 U.S. 75, 85 (1966), the Court stated that "the 'public official' designation applies at the very least to those among the hierarchy of government employees who have, or appear to the public to have, substantial responsibility for or control over the conduct or governmental affairs."

In *Time, Inc. v. Hill,* 385 U.S. 374 (1967), the Court applied the *New York Times* standard to actions under an unusual state statute. The statute did not create a cause of action for libel. Rather, it provided a remedy for unwanted publicity. Although the law allowed recovery of damages for harm caused by exposure to public attention rather than by factual inaccuracies, it recognized truth as a complete defense. Thus, nondefamatory factual errors could render a publisher liable for something akin to invasion of privacy. The Court ruled that the defendant in such an action could invoke the *New York Times* privilege regardless of the fame or anonymity of the plaintiff. Speaking for the Court, Mr. Justice Brennan declared that this holding was not an extension of *New York Times* but rather a parallel line of reasoning applying that standard to this discrete context:

> This is neither a libel action by a private individual nor a statutory action by a public official. Therefore, although the First Amendment principles pronounced in New York Times guide our conclusion, we reach that conclusion only by applying these principles in this discrete context. It therefore serves no purpose to distinguish the facts here from those in *New York Times*. Were this a libel action, the distinction which has been suggested between the relative opportunities of the public official and the private individual to rebut defamatory charges might be germane. And the additional state interest in the protection of the individual against damage to his reputation would be involved.

Huckabee v. Time Warner Entertainment Co., L.P.
19 S.W.3d 413 (Tex. 2000)

We must decide whether a media defendant sued for defamation by a public official is entitled on the facts of this record to summary judgment on the issue of actual malice. Because the defendant produced evidence negating actual malice as a matter of law, and because the plaintiff did not produce controverting evidence raising a fact issue, we affirm the summary judgment granted by the court of appeals.

When this claim arose, Charles Dean Huckabee was presiding judge of the 247th District Court of Harris County, which by statute gives preference to family law matters. Judge Huckabee claims that Respondent, HBO, defamed him by broadcasting the documentary *Women on Trial* on its premium cable channel. This hour-long program chronicled four southeast Texas cases in which family courts granted custody of a child to the father after the mother accused the father of child abuse. Three of these cases arose in Harris County, and Judge Huckabee presided over two of them. Judge Huckabee principally claims that the documentary defamed him in its report on his decision regarding the custody of four-year-old Wayne Hebert. See *In re the Marriage of Sandra Hebert and Michael Hebert* ... ("*Hebert*").

The *Hebert* case began in 1988, when Sandra Hebert discovered that Wayne had sustained an injury to his penis. The day before, Wayne had returned from visiting Michael Hebert, his father and Sandra's ex-husband. Wayne had gone with Michael to visit his grandmother's home in Louisiana. Believing that Michael caused Wayne's injury, Sandra consulted with her friend Sherry Turner, a Houston police officer who specialized in sexual abuse cases. Turner, interviewing Wayne alone, videotaped Wayne's statement that Michael had injured him while taking a bath. In two other videotaped interviews, Wayne also told social worker Cheryl Bennett and Child Protective Services caseworker Wilma Smith that Michael caused the injury. After investigating further, Smith concluded that Wayne had been abused, but that the abuser could not be identified. Because Michael was a Houston police officer, the Houston Police Department's Internal Affairs Department also investigated the incident and likewise determined that the abuser could not be identified.

Alleging that Michael had abused Wayne, Sandra moved to modify the custody order to restrict Michael's visitation rights. After a three-day hearing in March 1988, Judge Huckabee rendered a temporary order that not only made Michael rather than Sandra the managing conservator of Wayne, but went on to deny Sandra all access to her child, even though Michael had not sought either of these changes. Sandra unsuccessfully sought a writ of mandamus from the court of appeals to overturn the temporary order. She did not seek a subsequent modification of the order, and it was still in effect when *Women on Trial* was broadcast in 1992.

In late 1990, Lee Grant, the director of *Women on Trial*, first began work on a documentary about divorce. Hoping to examine how once happily married couples later ended up in bitter divorces, Grant secured her husband's production company, Joseph Feury Productions (JFP), to produce the film. Grant assigned JFP employee Virginia Cotts to find suitable stories for the program. In March 1991, Cotts met in Houston with Joleen Reynolds, the leader of Citizens Organized for Divorce Ethics and Solutions (CODES), a support group for men and women who felt that the Houston family courts had treated them unfairly. Reynolds discussed a number of cases with Cotts, including the *Hebert* case. After meeting with Reynolds, Cotts wrote a three-page summary of Sandra Hebert's situation.

Sandra Hebert's story was included along with several others submitted by Cotts and Grant to HBO in April 1991. In her summary of the Hebert story, Cotts included the following bullet points: (1) "Police ex-husband abused son"; (2) "Corrupt Judge gave custody to father/abuser"; (3) and "Sandy lost all rights to see her child." Sandra Hebert's story particularly impressed the HBO executives. After reading it, HBO vice-president Sheila Nevins wrote on her copy: "Great story. Do at once." Nevins's assistant, Cis Wilson, wrote: "Great, sad story." After considering the proposal, HBO agreed to purchase the film. Throughout the rest of the film's production, Cotts and Grant regularly met with Wilson and Nevins.

Cotts and Grant both came to Houston to film interviews. In addition to Joleen Reynolds, Sandra Hebert, and her current and former attorneys, they also interviewed Ivy Raschke, another woman who had been denied access to her children by Judge Huckabee after accusing the children's father of abuse. Cotts also continued her research into other allegations of impropriety in the Harris County family courts, including those reported by local print and broadcast media.

In September 1991, JFP delivered a "rough cut" of the film to HBO. Cotts's contemporaneous status report revealed tension between Lee Grant and Sheila Nevins over the film's direction. Grant apparently wanted to present a broad picture of divorce that showed both the fathers' and the mothers' perspectives, but Nevins wanted a narrower piece that focused on mothers who believed the family court system had treated them unfairly. Nothing in the status report, however, indicated that Grant, Cotts, or anyone at HBO believed anything in the documentary to be false or entertained serious doubts about the truth of any of the film's allegations.

In November 1991, Grant and Cotts returned to Houston and videotaped Judge Huckabee. While Judge Huckabee stated that he could not talk specifically about the *Hebert* case because it was pending in his court, he did agree to talk about it in "hypothetical" terms. He then explained that all of his decisions in this and other cases were based on the best interests of the children. HBO did not include these statements in the final version. Instead, it aired this response by Judge Huckabee to a question about a "hypothetical" version of the *Hebert* case:

> I have to do what's best for the child. If someone, is, uh, brainwashing the a [sic] child to the same extent that it causes psychological and emotional problems with the child, especially coupled with some physical abuse, in my opinion the child has to be removed from that situation.

The broadcast also aired Judge Huckabee's explanation of his criteria for determining when a mother in that situation could see her children again:

> Well, if its [sic] a person who has mental health problems, they're going to have to seek mental health, uh, care. If its [sic] a person sexually abusing a child, they're probably going to have to seek mental health care.

Finally, the broadcast aired Judge Huckabee's statement that he took the decision to deny access to a parent very seriously, but that he was satisfied that he had made the correct decision in every case in which he had done so.

The filmmakers also interviewed Dr. Kit Harrison, a psychologist appointed by Judge Huckabee in *Hebert* and in many other cases. Four months after Judge Huckabee rendered the temporary order denying Sandra Hebert access to Wayne, Dr. Harrison issued a report concluding that Michael had not caused Wayne's injury. Rather, the report concluded that Wayne's older brother John committed the abuse while Wayne was in Sandra's custody. Based on this belief, Dr. Harrison agreed with Judge Huckabee's decision to transfer Wayne to his father's custody and deny Sandra access to the child. Although the final version mentioned Dr. Harrison's recommendation approving of the judge's order, it did not detail Dr. Harrison's reasons.

Finally, Cotts and Grant interviewed Houston attorney Randy Burton, an outspoken critic of the Houston family courts. Among other things, Burton accused the Harris County family court judges of practicing cronyism and disregarding the best interests of the children before them.

After these interviews, Cotts and Grant recut the film to include some of the new footage. From April to September 1991, HBO and JFP's lawyers reviewed the film, finally allowing the film to air in October 1991. HBO also agreed to indemnify JFP should a judgment arise from the film in excess of JFP's errors-and-omissions insurance coverage.

Women on Trial aired on October 28, 1992. In addition to the Sandra Hebert and Ivy Raschke segments, the film included two other stories. In one, another Harris County family district court judge, Allen Daggett, had transferred custody of Mary Frances Parker's child to her ex-husband, a convicted rapist, even though she claimed that he was abusing the child. In the other, Sherry Nance was convicted of murdering her ex-husband and his father after a Bee County jury awarded custody of her son to the ex-husband. Nance claimed that she killed her ex-husband to save her son from continuing sexual abuse. The documentary did not name the judge in the Bee County case....

To recover for defamation, a public figure or public official, such as Judge Huckabee, must prove that the defendant published a false and defamatory statement with actual malice. As we resolve this case solely on the issue of whether HBO negated actual malice as a matter of law, we assume without deciding that the documentary either expressly or implicitly made false statements about Judge Huckabee. We also do not reach the issue of whether any of these statements, even if false, were not defamatory because the documentary's overall portrayal of Judge Huckabee was substantially true.

Actual malice in a defamation case is a term of art. Unlike common-law malice, it does not include ill-will, spite, or evil motive. Rather, to establish actual malice, a plaintiff must prove that the defendant made the statement "with knowledge that it was false or with reckless disregard of whether it was true or not." Reckless disregard is also a term of art. To establish reckless disregard, a public official or public figure must prove that the publisher "entertained serious doubts as to the truth of his publication." Finally, to prevail at trial, a plaintiff must establish actual malice by clear and convincing evidence.

In Texas, under our traditional summary judgment procedure, defendants can obtain summary judgment only if they conclusively negate one of the elements of the plaintiff's claim. A libel defendant can negate actual malice as a matter of law by presenting evidence that he or she did not publish the statement with knowledge of its falsity or reckless disregard for its truth. Once the defendant has produced evidence negating actual malice as a matter of law, the burden shifts to the plaintiff to present controverting proof raising a genuine issue of material fact....

HBO supported its motion for summary judgment with affidavits from Lee Grant, Sheila Nevins, Cis Wilson, and Virginia Cotts. Grant's affidavit stated that she neither believed the film to have contained a false statement nor entertained any doubts about the truth of any statement regarding Judge Huckabee. Her sources for the Sandra Hebert story included the transcript of the March 1988 hearing, information from Sandra's current and former lawyers, and research by Virginia Cotts.

Sheila Nevins's affidavit stated that as vice-president for documentaries and family programming for HBO, she relied on the favorable reputations for accuracy and truthfulness of both Grant and JFP and her own favorable personal experience with their earlier work. She was aware of Grant and Cotts's efforts to ensure the film's accuracy, and she neither believed any statement in the documentary to be untrue nor harbored any doubts about the film's truthfulness. Cis Wilson's affidavit contained similar statements.

HBO presented two extensive affidavits from Virginia Cotts. In her first affidavit, Cotts explained the steps she took in researching the stories presented in *Women on Trial*. To ensure that the film's account of the *Hebert* case was accurate, she (1) reviewed the transcript from the March 1988 hearing, (2) interviewed Sandra and her attorneys, (3) viewed all three videotapes of Wayne Hebert, (4) reviewed articles in the Houston press describing problems in the family courts, and (5) read Dr. Harrison's deposition in the *Hebert* case. In all, Cotts reviewed over two thousand pages of documents in connection with the Texas cases. From this extensive review, Cotts stated that she believed that the film's depiction of the *Hebert* case was accurate and that she had no doubts regarding this account.

Cotts's second affidavit detailed her reasons for doubting Dr. Harrison's conclusion that Wayne's brother was the abuser, such as (1) her own viewing of the videotapes in which Wayne identified his father as the abuser; (2) the improbability of Harrison's theory that Wayne's older brother John had injured him using a favorite toy; (3) the fact that Wayne's initial description of events was similar to stories that John had told Cotts about abuse from his father; (4) Dr. Harrison's own statement in a scholarly paper that children often recant after disclosing sexual abuse; and (5) the fact that Wayne had sustained a similar injury once before. Cotts buttressed her conclusion by attaching her own notes from the Harrison interview, indicating that she did not believe his explanation even as the interview was in progress.

Because these affidavits are from interested witnesses, they will negate actual malice as a matter of law only if they are "clear, positive, and direct, otherwise credible and free from contradictions and inconsistencies, and [able to be] readily controverted." In actual malice cases, such affidavits must establish the defendant's belief in the challenged statements' truth and provide a plausible basis for this belief. As all four of HBO's affidavits satisfied the Rule 166a(c) requirements, HBO negated actual malice as a matter of law.

Thus, the burden shifted to Judge Huckabee to present evidence to raise a fact issue. He offered six categories of allegedly controverting evidence: (1) HBO and JFP's alleged desire to portray him in an unflattering light; (2) editorial choices by HBO and JFP that left a false impression of events; (3) the filmmakers' disregard for Judge Huckabee's and Dr. Harrison's explanations for Judge Huckabee's order; (4) JFP's and HBO's alleged purposeful avoidance of the truth; (5) HBO's extensive legal review of the film, the film's many rewrites, and the indemnification agreement between HBO and JFP; and (6) HBO's and JFP's decision to air the film despite the knowledge that it contained inaccurate statements. In determining whether the evidence presents a fact issue, we assume that all facts favorable to the nonmovant are true and indulge all reasonable inferences in that party's favor. Even under this lenient standard, we are persuaded that Judge Huckabee has not raised a genuine issue of material fact on any of his categories.

1. HBO's desire to portray Judge Huckabee in an unflattering light.

In claiming that JFP and HBO intended to portray him unfairly, Judge Huckabee first points to Virginia Cotts's three-page summary of the *Hebert* case describing him to HBO executives Sheila Nevins and Cis Wilson as a "corrupt judge." He also points to Cotts's September 1991 status report regarding the disagreement between Grant and Nevins over the film's artistic direction. Neither of these documents, however, indicates actual malice. While Cotts's original memo might suggest personal ill-will toward Judge Huckabee, nothing in either of these documents suggests that Cotts or Grant had any doubts about the truth of the broadcast.

Likewise, Nevins's insistence that the filmmakers focus on divorce from the women's perspective is no evidence of actual malice. Without more, mere evidence of pressure to produce stories from a particular point of view, even when they are hard-hitting or sensationalistic, is no evidence of actual malice. Although evidence that HBO directed Grant to produce a sensational story *without regard for its truth* would raise a fact question, Judge Huckabee has not produced any such evidence.

2. Editorial choices.

Next, Judge Huckabee complains of HBO's choice of material for the documentary. His principal complaint is that *Women on Trial* did not discuss much of the evidence presented at the 1988 *Hebert* hearing, including (1) Wayne's initial treating physician's testimony that Wayne had denied that his father caused the injury; (2) Child Protective Services case worker Wilma Smith's testimony that in his videotaped interview Wayne said that his mother told him to say that his father had abused him (although Wayne still maintained that such abuse occurred); (3) Smith's further testimony that in a subsequent interview with Wayne, he told her that his father had not abused him during the Christmas holidays, but that his father had touched his private area in July 1987; (4) Smith and social worker Cheryl Bennett's testimony that Wayne and his brother John often fought after Wayne returned from Michael; (5) Bennett's testimony that Sandra told her that she preferred that Michael not be allowed visitation rights and had inquired about what was necessary to terminate them; and (6) Wayne's grandmother's testimony that Michael had not bathed Wayne during their visit to her home. By failing to include this evidence, Judge Huckabee claims that HBO intentionally made it look like he was presented with an open-and-shut case against Michael Hebert, when in fact much of the evidence justified his order.

Further, Judge Huckabee complains about the film's failure to clarify two facts: first, that his statements in the interview with Grant came in response to questions about a "hypothetical" case; and second, that Sandra did not move to modify the temporary order in the three years after the court of appeals denied her petition for mandamus. Because of all these omissions, Judge Huckabee claims that the viewers saw him falsely as a judge who flouted his legal duty to render decisions in the best interests of children.

A broadcaster's omission of facts may be actionable if it so distorts the viewers' perception that they receive a substantially false impression of the event. As a public official, however, Judge Huckabee may recover for such an omission only by making the familiar showing that the publisher selected the material with actual malice, *i.e.*, the awareness that the omission could create a substantially false impression. This standard does not, therefore, prevent liability if a media organization selectively omits facts from the record to portray falsely a judge's opinion as arbitrary and unreasonable. Even if a defamation defendant is not persuaded by the evidence which supports a judge's decision, he or she may not deliberately omit all reference to this evidence in order to portray the decision as arbitrary, when in fact it was not. But in the absence of evidence that the defendant selected the material to portray the judge's record falsely, the First Amendment protects the organization's choice of which material to include in its broadcast.

In this case, there is no evidence that HBO chose its material for the broadcast with actual malice. We recognize that an omission may be so glaring and may result in such a gross distortion that by itself it constitutes some evidence of actual malice. For example, when an article reported that an FBI memorandum mentioned plaintiff several times in connection with Jimmy Hoffa's disappearance, the newspaper's decision not to report that the memorandum also cleared plaintiff of wrongdoing was held to be evidence of actual malice. In such a case, the omission so changes the character of the story that one could infer that the defendant knew, or at least suspected, that the omission would convey a false impression. Here, HBO's omissions did not change the character of the story to such an extent. Although the facts omitted might or might not have led a reasonable viewer to suspend judgment or even to reach an opposite conclusion regarding Judge Huckabee's order, their omission did not grossly distort the story. At most, HBO's failure to capture accurately all the story's details suggests an error in judgment, which is no evidence of actual malice. Moreover, the broadcasters did acknowledge Judge Huckabee's explanation for his decision when they aired the portion of the interview responding to questions about the "hypothetical" *Hebert* case. Although the documentary did not convey Judge Huckabee's position as strongly as it could have, the law did not require it to do so....

[3]. Purposeful avoidance.

Next, Judge Huckabee contends that the filmmakers purposefully avoided discovering the truth about the *Hebert* case. Under *Harte-Hanks* [*Communications, Inc. v. Connaughton*, 491 U.S. 657 (1989)], evidence showing that HBO purposefully avoided the truth would be some evidence of actual malice. In *Harte-Hanks*, a newspaper published a story claiming that Daniel Connaughton, a candidate for municipal judge, had promised two sisters, Alice Thompson and Patsy Stephens, jobs and vacations in return for making allegations of corruption against the incumbent judge's court administrator. The newspaper's only source for this story was Thompson. Before the newspaper published the story, Connaughton produced five witnesses who were present when Thompson claimed that Connaughton offered her and Stephens the gifts. All the witnesses denied Thompson's story. Connaughton also produced a tape recording of the conversation in which Thompson accused the administrator of corruption. The newspaper failed to listen to this recording even though it would have confirmed or denied many of Thompson's claims, such as her claims that Connaughton had selectively turned the recorder on and off during various parts of the interview and that her allegations of corruption against the court administrator had come in response to leading questions from him. More importantly, the newspaper failed to interview Stephens, the one person not associated with Connaughton who could have confirmed or denied Thompson's allegations against Connaughton. According to the Court, the newspaper's failure to consult the two sources that could have objectively verified the story was evidence that the newspaper purposefully avoided learning facts that would have shown the story to be false. Upholding a jury verdict against the newspaper, the Court held that this purposeful avoidance of the truth was enough to suggest that the newspaper doubted the story's accuracy, and hence was evidence of actual malice.

Judge Huckabee has not presented a purposeful avoidance case. Unlike *Harte-Hanks*, in which the newspaper based its story on the testimony of a single unreliable source, here the summary judgment evidence reveals that the filmmakers interviewed several people on both sides of the story, including Judge Huckabee and Dr. Harrison. They also read, among other documents, the transcript of the *Hebert* hearing. Such extensive research precludes a finding of purposeful avoidance....

[4]. Legal Review, Rewrites, and Indemnification

Next, we turn to the evidence that Judge Huckabee believes established "institutional doubt" on the part of HBO regarding the truth of *Women on Trial*. According to Judge Huckabee, HBO's extensive legal review of the film, the editorial rewrites that accompanied this review, and the indemnification agreement between HBO and JFP all suggest that HBO entertained serious doubts about the film's content. We disagree.

That the film underwent a lengthy legal review does not by itself provide evidence of actual malice. HBO could have wished merely to confirm the film's controversial and potentially damaging allegations before its release. This same conclusion also applies to the indemnification agreement. Judge Huckabee can point to no evidence that JFP and HBO entered into the agreement because they entertained serious doubts about the film's truthfulness. Individuals and business organizations enter into indemnification agreements for various reasons; doing so, without more, simply presents no evidence of actual malice....

Virginia Citizens Defense League v. Couric

910 F.3d 780 (4th Cir. 2018)

This case arises from the creation and publication of Under the Gun, a documentary film on gun violence in America. Aggrieved at their portrayal in the film, appellants—Virginia Citizens Defense League and two of its members, Daniel L. Hawes, and Patricia Webb—filed this action. They alleged defamation by the film's creators, appellees Katie Couric, Stephanie Soechtig, Atlas Films L.L.C., and Studio 3 Partners, L.L.C. (doing business as Epix Entertainment L.L.C.). The district court dismissed their complaint, and appellants appeal. For the reasons that follow, we affirm.

In 2016, journalist Couric and filmmaker Soechtig released a documentary titled Under the Gun. The documentary concerns gun policy in America, and it takes a perspective favoring regulation. Couric narrated the film, interviewed participants, and served as an executive producer. Soechtig directed and edited the film, which Atlas Films produced and Epix distributed.

Although the film advocates for gun control, its creators assertedly sought to present viewpoints from organizations that opposed measures like universal background checks. To that end, a producer employed by Atlas Films contacted the Virginia Citizens Defense League ("VCDL"), a non-profit gun-rights organization, and set up an interview with members of the VCDL. Nine members, including Hawes and Webb, agreed to participate.

The final cut of the film includes portions of Couric's interview with these VCDL members. The segment lasts just over three minutes. At its outset, Couric thanks the VCDL members for participating, noting that they "have a specific point of view on this issue and some of the issues that we're tackling." Couric then poses a series of questions on gun policy. She asks about the appeal of owning a gun, and whether a person should have to pass a background check to purchase a gun. She also asks whether anyone in the group feared that the government would take their guns. These questions prompt detailed responses from the panel members, which are included in the film. Apart from the filmmakers' lighting choices, appellants do not object to this portion of the interview.

Instead, this suit centers on a twelve-second clip at the close of the three-minute VCDL interview. In it, Couric asks the following question: "If there are no background checks for gun purchasers, how do you prevent felons or terrorists from purchasing a gun?" Approximately nine seconds of silence follow, during which the VCDL members, including Webb, a gun store owner, and Hawes, an attorney, sit in silence and shift uncomfortably in their seats, averting their eyes. The film cuts to a revolver chamber closing. Couric then says: "The background check is considered the first line of defense, and 90% of Americans agree it's a good thing." Neither the VCDL nor its members are mentioned again in the 105-minute film.

Although the film accurately portrays most of the interview with VCDL members, the twelve-second clip described above did not transpire as depicted. In the unedited footage, Couric's background check question prompted approximately six minutes of responses from the VCDL members. Hawes responded by suggesting that the government cannot, consistent with the Constitution, prevent crimes through prior restraint. Webb commented that background checks are unlikely to prevent motivated criminals from obtaining guns or committing crimes. These responses were followed by approximately three minutes of related discussion between Couric and the panel. Rather than use these responses, the filmmakers spliced in b-roll footage taken prior to the interview in which Couric asked the VCDL interviewees to sit in silence while technicians calibrated the recording equipment.

Shortly after the film's showing at various film festivals, the VCDL released unedited audio of the interview. In the public backlash that followed, Couric issued a statement admitting that the edited version of the film did "not accurately represent [the VCDL members'] response" and that the segment was "misleading." Believing the misleading segment to be defamatory, the VCDL and two of its featured members, Hawes and Webb, brought this action. The district court dismissed their complaint for failure to state a claim, reasoning that the film was neither false nor defamatory and that, as to claims brought by the VCDL, the film was not "of and concerning" the organization. This appeal followed.

To state a claim for defamation under Virginia law, a plaintiff must plead three elements: (1) publication of (2) an actionable statement with (3) the requisite intent. The first and third elements are not at issue here. The parties dispute only whether the statement—in this case, footage edited to convey silence—is actionable. To be "actionable," a statement must be "both false and defamatory." To recover, the VCDL must also establish that the alleged defamatory statement was "of and concerning" the organization.

"Defamatory words are those tending so to harm the reputation of another as to lower him in the estimation of the community or to deter third persons from associating or dealing with him. The Supreme Court of Virginia has held that actionable defamatory language is that which "tends to injure one's reputation in the common estimation of mankind, to throw contumely, shame, or disgrace upon him, or which tends to hold him up to scorn, ridicule, or contempt, or which is calculated to render him infamous, odious, or ridiculous." In contrast, "language that is insulting, offensive, or otherwise inappropriate, but constitutes no more than 'rhetorical hyperbole,' not actionable."

Applying Virginia law, a court "must decide as a threshold matter of law whether a statement is reasonably capable of defamatory meaning before allowing the matter to be presented to a finder of fact." This "reasonable capability" test recognizes that defamatory meaning is often implied.

Virginia law requires that when "determining whether the words and statements complained of ... are reasonably capable of the meaning ascribed to them by innuendo, every fair inference that may be drawn from the pleadings must be resolved in the plaintiff's favor." ... There must be a "nexus between the content of the defamatory statement and the skills or character required to carry out the particular occupation of the plaintiff."

Turning first to Hawes, appellants argue that because Hawes "is an attorney whose practice focuses on firearms and self-defense," the edited footage "is reasonably capable of being understood" as suggesting "that Hawes lacks the required competencies and abilities for his profession, including oral advocacy skills." But ... the questions posed to Hawes had nothing to do with his legal practice or expertise.... Accepting Hawes' defamation per se claim would require us to extend mere silence into professional ineptitude. Thus, his claim fails.

Similarly, the film is not reasonably capable of suggesting that Webb is unfit to own a gun store. Arguing otherwise, Webb contends that her "business requires her to be knowledgeable ... about the right of individuals to purchase firearms," and that the edited footage suggests that "she lacks knowledge regarding integral aspects of her business." But of course, no part of Webb's job as a gun store owner requires her to have nuanced views on gun policy. Had the film suggested that Webb did not know, for instance, whether a gun store owner must perform a background check, this might be a different case. But as the district court explained, "[n]ot having an answer to a specific question about effective alternatives to background checks does not imply anything about fitness to own a gun store and to sell guns." ...

Having resolved appellants' per se claim, we consider their contention that the film implied other actionable defamatory meanings. Appellants maintain that the edited footage suggests that the VCDL and its members have no basis for opposing background checks or are otherwise uninformed in their areas of expertise. This claim fails because it divorces the twelve-second clip from the film as a whole. The disputed segment comes on the heels of several other questions concerning background checks, and the panelists' answers to all of those questions are included in the film.

To be sure, the film gives the impression that Couric's final question stumped the panelists. But at worst, the plain, ordinary meaning of this edit conveys that these particular members of the VCDL, after answering a series of related questions, did not have a ready-made answer to a nuanced policy question. Even with the benefit of every inference, the edited footage is not reasonably capable of suggesting that the VCDL and its members are, as they contend on appeal, "ignorant and incompetent on the subject to which they have dedicated their organizational mission."

In arguing to the contrary, appellants ... ask us to focus on this single word, at the expense of those surrounding it, eschewing ordinary interpretive principles. Reading the term "ridiculous" in context with the descriptive words preceding it — i.e., language that "tends to hold [one] up to scorn, ridicule, or contempt, or which is calculated to render [one] infamous, odious, or ridiculous," … Virginia law makes abundantly clear [that] simple insults are not "actionable" in Virginia.

Davis v. Costa-Gavras
654 F. Supp. 653 (S.D.N.Y. 1987)

This is a libel case brought by a public figure which presently is before the Court on a motion by the defendants for summary judgment in their favor pursuant to Rule 56 of the Federal Rules of Civil Procedure.

Following the submission of affidavits and deposition testimony on the motion, the Court determined that an oral evidentiary hearing was needed under Rule 43(e) of the Federal Rules of Civil Procedure to aid in determining with a fair degree of specificity what plaintiff is able to present at a trial that is provable, clear and convincing affirmative evidence of actual malice on the part of the defendants in publishing the alleged defamation.

Absent such evidence, the action cannot be maintained as a matter of law, and the existence of such evidence is appropriately determined on a motion for summary judgment. The only remaining defamation charged in the complaint is that in their film, "Missing," defendants allegedly portrayed with actual malice that plaintiff, the Commander of the United States Military Group and Chief of the United States Mission to Chile at the time of the 1973 coup in Chile, ordered or approved a Chilean order to kill Charles Horman, an American residing in Chile.

It is now clear that this is a case devoid of any evidence of actual malice. There is no evidence thereof to be considered; no prima facie case at all is supplied on any standard of proof on the requirement of actual malice, be it a preponderance or clear and convincing.

Summary judgment should be granted when the evidence propounded is "of insufficient caliber or quality to allow a rational finder of fact to find actual malice by clear and convincing evidence;" there then is "no genuine issue." A jury could not properly return a verdict herein in plaintiff's favor; the evidence is so one-sided that defendants must prevail as a matter of law.

Actual malice is established in a public figure defamation litigation only where defendant publishes a statement "with knowledge that it was false or with reckless disregard of whether it was false or not." Reckless disregard in such a case means that a defendant published after he "in fact entertained serious doubts as to the truth of his publication."

The paper record on this motion consists of an enormous mass of words. The Rule 43(e) hearing was ordered to permit plaintiff to present or designate any clear and convincing evidence of actual malice detached from the obscure and semantic allusions thereto in the moving papers, and so as to allow the Court to assess the record expeditiously and accurately.

At the Rule 43(e) hearing, the plaintiff conceded that he had no evidence to offer on the requisite standard beyond what was contained in the papers and depositions submitted in opposition to the motion—plaintiff called no witnesses. A prolix and cloudy paper response will not suffice to defeat a motion for summary judgment to dismiss a public figure libel claim. The Rules obligated the nonmoving party to designate "specific facts showing that there is a genuine issue for trial." No such facts have been furnished.

Designated Evidence Offered by Plaintiff

Plaintiff alleges that there are four general categories of purported evidence in the paper defense to the motion from which to find actual malice on behalf of defendants: (1) that defendants' "entire purpose in making 'Missing' was to show plaintiff as responsible for Charles Horman's death"; (2) that defendants' reliance on Thomas Hauser's book *The Execution of Charles Horman* ("*Execution*") was unreasonable; (3) that defendants never consulted with plaintiff on the facts presented in the film; and (4) that "Missing" contains scenes portraying certain episodes which defendants knew were embroidered.

An analysis of the record shows that to accept the plaintiff's opposition to summary judgment would require a distortion of the proofs, deviation from applicable law, and wrenching of the film out of its plain context.

A. *The Thesis of the Film*

Plaintiff has produced no evidence in his papers to substantiate his assertion that the purpose of "Missing" was to make a non-fictional film establishing that Ray Davis, the plaintiff, was responsible for Charles Horman's death. To the contrary, the papers unalterably establish that the film is not a non-fictional documentary or aimed at Ray Davis as an individual, and that it cannot be understood as other than a dramatization of a true story. The film includes fictional characters and a composite portrayal of the American military presence in Chile at the time of the uprising and Allende coup.

The theme of the film is the search for a missing man by his father and his wife. The man who disappeared is finally found to have been executed by the Chilean military. The film is *based upon* a true story. It is only in that setting that the composite conduct of the American governmental representatives in Chile at the time and the degree of their assistance in that search comes under scrutiny and criticism. There is no person named Ray Davis referred to in the film at any time. Ray Tower, with whom the plaintiff associates himself, is a symbolic fictional composite of the entire American political and military entourage in Chile.

The film derives from and is solidly documented and supported by the stories relied on by the filmmakers, taken from the acts and statements of the concerned father and the anguished wife set forth in detail in Thomas Hauser's book, *Execution*. Those sources are shown to have been heavily investigated and confirmed by the filmmakers, who entertained no serious doubts of their truth or knowledge to the contrary of what they portrayed....

B. *Defendants' Reliance on Hauser's Book*

"Missing" is a dramatic portrayal of events and interpretations detailed in Thomas Hauser's book, *Execution*. The substance of the movie's scenes is extracted directly from *Execution*. To meet those facts, plaintiff purports to suggest that defendants' reliance on Hauser's book was unreasonable and that Hauser's credentials would have disclosed him to be "suspect" had a good faith search by defendants been made.

As a matter of law, to prevail on a defamation claim against a public official a plaintiff must do more than propound potential avenues of investigation that a defendant might have pursued. "Mere proof of failure to investigate, without more, cannot establish reckless disregard for the truth." "Rather, a public figure defamation plaintiff must show either that the publisher actually entertained serious doubts about the veracity of the publication, or that there are *obvious* reasons to doubt the veracity of the informant or the accuracy of his reports."

There is nothing in the record tending to show that the filmmakers questioned Hauser's credentials or his book in any respect at the time "Missing" was made. The record is to the contrary. The filmmakers met with Hauser, went over his investigation and sources, supplied him with drafts of the script under preparation and were satisfied that there was no reason to doubt his work. No evidence whatever challenges those facts. Certainly the filmmakers obtained no knowledge contradicting the veracity or accuracy of Hauser's book and the stories of the Hormans as told to them and reflected in the book. There is no suggestion to the contrary from any provable sources. Indeed, nothing in plaintiff's papers demonstrates that either Hauser's credentials or his book, which was nominated for a Pulitzer Prize, are in fact "suspect" in any way.

The filmmakers knew that Hauser was a lawyer who had served as a judicial clerk in the Chambers of a Federal Judge and then worked for a prestigious Wall Street law firm. They knew that Hauser interviewed Captain Ray Davis, as well as other United States officials in Chile and numerous other persons when preparing *Execution*. The filmmakers also knew that no legal action whatsoever was taken against the book in the approximately four years since its publication. In an August 1980 meeting where Costa-Gavras, the film's director, and Stewart, the co-scriptwriter, met with Hauser to verify the accuracy of his book, Hauser described his meticulous research methods and broad inquiries. There is no evidence to the contrary.

The filmmakers then met with Charles Horman's parents, his wife, and one Terry Simon, a close friend who was in Chile with Charles around the time of his disappearance. Each of these individuals made clear to Costa-Gavras and Stewart that Hauser's book accurately and reliably depicted events as they knew and believed them. There is no evidence that any of defendants' further research and review of documents regarding Horman and events in Chile during the coup caused them to doubt the veracity of Hauser's book.

Plaintiff argues that an effective search of Hauser's background would have disclosed "fraudulent letters" sent by Hauser to political figures and The New York Times. This allusion is to Hauser's political satires where he had written on public issues to officials in the voice of a nine-year old boy, "Martin Bear." The New York Times, in fact, solicited from Hauser and published on its "op-ed" page one of these satirical pieces, which can hardly be reason to "suspect" the veracity of his book.

In any event, plaintiff has neither presented nor designated specific facts suggesting or from which it could be reasonably inferred and found that defendants entertained serious doubts as to Hauser's account or that there were obvious reasons to doubt the veracity or accuracy of Hauser's book. Absent such evidence, reliance on *Execution* is not evidence of actual malice.

C. *Failure to Consult Plaintiff Prior to Making Film*

Plaintiff argues that defendant's failure to consult plaintiff personally prior to presentation of the film is evidence of actual malice. However, plaintiff cannot prove actual malice merely by asserting that a publisher failed to contact the subject of his work. The actual malice standard cannot be satisfied by evidence of a failure to check with third parties prior to publication without proof that a publisher knew his publication was false, entertained serious doubts as to its truth, or had obvious reasons to doubt the veracity or accuracy of the source of published information.

While "verification of facts" of a story with its subjects and with others is a desirable and responsible practice and "an important reporting standard, a reporter, without a 'high degree of awareness of their probable falsity,' may rely on statements made by a single source even though they reflect only one side of the story without fear of libel prosecution...." Plaintiff has not designated specific facts suggesting an awareness or even suspicion by defendants of probable falsity of their source material.

D. *Scenes in "Missing" as Evidence of Actual Malice*

Plaintiff enumerates nine scenes in "Missing" which the filmmakers allegedly created, or in which they distorted the context, or made baseless suggestions. None of these scenes provides or contributes to the requisite evidence of actual malice.

It should be made clear that "Missing" is not a documentary, but a dramatization of the Horman disappearance and search. The film does not purport to depict a chronology of the events precisely as they actually occurred; it opens with the prologue: "This film is *based on* a true story. The incidents and facts are documented. Some of the names have been changed to protect the innocent and also to protect the film." No one challenged the accuracy and veracity of Hauser's book to the knowledge of defendants. Defendants concede that although the substance of the film's scenes is extracted almost directly from Thomas Hauser's book, not everything in their film is literally faithful to the actual historical record as if in a documentary. That is not to say that which was not historical was set out in bad faith, portrayed with actual malice, or established or increased the defamatory impact.

The film is not a documentary. A documentary is a non-fictional story or series of historical events portrayed in their actual location; a film of real people and real events as they occur. A documentary maintains strict fidelity to fact.

"Missing," on the other hand, is an art form sometimes described as "Docu-Drama." The line separating a documentary from a docudrama is not always sharply defined, but is nonetheless discernible. Both forms are necessarily selective, given the time constraints of movies and the attention span of the viewing audience. The docudrama is a dramatization of an historical event or lives of real people, using actors or actresses.

Docudramas utilize simulated dialogue, composite characters, and a telescoping of events occurring over a period into a composite scene or scenes. This treatment is singularly appropriate and unexceptionable if the context is not distorted when dealing with public and political figures.

Self-evidently a docudrama partakes of author's license—it is a creative interpretation of reality—and if alterations of fact in scenes portrayed are not made with serious doubts of truth of the essence of the telescoped composite, such scenes do not ground a charge of actual malice.

Each scene questioned by the plaintiff is a telescoped composite of events, personalities, and of the American representatives in Chile who are involved therein. Each uses permissible literary license to fit historical detail into a suitable dramatic context. Such dramatic embellishments as are made do not distort the fundamental story being told—the frantic search by his family for a missing man who has suddenly disappeared, their emotions, anxieties, impatience, frustration, and doubts of assistance from American officialdom. The scenes are thus a hybrid of fact and fiction which however do not materially distort the analysis. Always to be remembered is that they fairly represent the source materials for the film believed to be true by the filmmakers. Leeway is properly afforded to an author who thus attempts to recount a true event.

As a matter of law, the dramatic overlay supplied by the film does not serve to increase the impact of what plaintiff charges as defamatory since it fairly and reasonably portrays the unassailable beliefs of the Hormans, the record thereof in the Hauser book, and the corroborative results of the authors' inquiries. In docudrama, minor fictionalization cannot be considered evidence or support for the requirement of actual malice.

The nine scenes selected by plaintiff as support for the requirement of actual malice do no such thing. Each is related solely and unquestionably to the theme of this film. The movie's Ray Tower character is a fictional composite of the American presence operating in Chile at the time. He is a symbolic figure. The artistic input in the scenes questioned is found in permissible syntheses and composite treatment in the film. Although in actuality particular individuals were not physically present when certain dialogue occurred, in the movie scene the composite character portrayed was.

The content of the film reflects what happened according to the book, the persons who complained, and the sources relied on by defendants. While the actual persons involved in the events portrayed do not appear in on-scene interviews to describe their experiences, actions, and motivations, the real names of some individuals are employed. But the name Ray Davis is never mentioned. Real life personalities are accordingly represented by telescoped composites in many instances.

The cases on point demonstrate that the First Amendment protects such dramatizations and does not demand literal truth in every episode depicted; publishing a dramatization is not of itself evidence of actual malice. In *Street v. National Broad-*

casting Co., 645 F.2d 1227 (6th Cir.), *cert. granted,* 454 U.S. 815, *cert. dismissed,* 454 U.S. 1095, (1981), the Court of Appeals affirmed a ruling on a directed verdict that the dramatization embodied in defendant's broadcast program on the Scottsboro rape trial was protected by the *New York Times v. Sullivan* standard, and not chargeable with actual malice. While the dramatization contained certain literal falsehoods, including undocumented statements and conversations, *Street,* the movie was based "in all material respects" on the Judge's findings in the Scottsboro case, and a book by a historian documenting the Scottsboro trial. *See also Reader's Digest Association v. Superior Court,* 37 Cal. 3d 244, 264, 690 P.2d 610, 623, 208 Cal. Rptr. 137, 150 (1984) (summary judgment granted, and no triable issue of actual malice presented where published material "falls within an acceptable range of literary license."); *Leopold v. Levin,* 45 Ill. 2d 434, 259 N.E.2d 250, 256 (1970) (insufficient evidence of actual malice to overcome summary judgment where fictionalized episodes could be "traced in a substantial way" to a recorded source).

Similarly, in *Meeropol v. Nizer,* 381 F. Supp. 29 (S.D.N.Y. 1974), *aff'd,* 560 F.2d 1061 (2d Cir. 1977), *cert. denied,* 434 U.S. 1013 (1978), summary judgment was granted for a defendant sued for defamation of a public figure based on plaintiff's inability to designate specific evidence of actual malice. Defendant had written a book based on letters written by Ethel and Julius Rosenberg, convicted spies. The book contained "minor fictionalizations or approximations of conversations." The court held that these do not supply the requisite specific evidence of actual malice:

> Such techniques do not rise to the constitutional level of clear and convincing showing of reckless disregard.... Deviations from or embellishments upon the information obtained from the primary sources relied upon were miniscule and can be attributed to the leeway afforded an author who attempts to recount and popularize an historic event.

Hotchner v. Castillo-Puche, 551 F.2d 910 (2d Cir.), *cert. denied,* 434 U.S. 834 (1977), was an appeal of a judgment entered after a jury verdict for plaintiff. Defendant published a book which purported to quote derogatory remarks by Ernest Hemingway about plaintiff. Defendant did not print the literal words used by Hemingway, and "was fictionalizing to some extent." The Court of Appeals held that such fictionalization or dramatization does not satisfy the requirement of clear and convincing evidence from which a jury might reasonably find that defendant published the alleged libel with actual malice. Actual malice could not be inferred because "the change did not increase the defamatory impact or alter the substantive content" of Hemingway's original statement which defendants relied upon.

The issue on the motion is not the truth of whether Davis (qua Ray Tower) ordered or approved a Chilean order to kill Charles Horman because he "knew too much" about alleged American involvement in the Chilean coup; the issue is whether the filmmakers intentionally portrayed such a defamatory suggestion, knowing that it was false or with serious doubts of its truth. There is no doubt that Ed Horman, the father of the missing man, asserted such a theory and that assertion is documented in Hauser's book. Plaintiff has not presented evidence that defendants knew the theory of the father was false, or entertained serious doubts as to its truth. There is no evidence that defendants acted with actual malice or disbelieved what the Hormans thought and said or what Hauser wrote.

In sum, returning to the *ratio decidendi*; no provable, clear and convincing, affirmative evidence nor specific facts showing actual malice on the part of the defendants in publishing the alleged defamation have been shown, and the complaint by plaintiff, a public figure, falls as not sustainable under the law....

Pippen v. NBCUniversal Media L.L.C.
734 F.3d 610 (2013)

Scottie Pippen, who won six championship rings with the Chicago Bulls and was named in 1996 to the National Basketball Association's list of the 50 greatest players in its history, has encountered financial reverses since his playing days ended in 2004. He has lost through bad investments a large portion of the fortune he amassed during his playing days. In an effort to recoup some of these losses, he has pursued multiple lawsuits against former financial and legal advisors who he believes led him astray. The media caught wind of Pippen's woes, and several news organizations reported that he had filed for bankruptcy. This is false; he has not.

Pippen contends that the false reports have impaired his ability to earn a living through product endorsements and personal appearances. He filed this suit against multiple defendants under the diversity jurisdiction in the Northern District of Illinois, contending that he was defamed and cast in a false light. The district court dismissed the complaint. It found that the falsehoods did not fit within any of the categories of statements recognized by Illinois law to be so innately harmful that damages may be presumed. The district court also concluded that the complaint did not plausibly allege that the defendants had published the falsehoods with actual malice—a term that looks as if it might mean "ill will" but in fact means knowledge the statement is false or reckless disregard of whether it is false. Demonstrating actual malice is a requirement for a public figure such as Pippen to recover damages for defamation, and to make out a claim of false light under Illinois law.

There are two types of action for defamation. The first, called defamation *per quod*, requires a plaintiff to show that the false statements caused him harm. Some statements, however, expose the subject to such great obloquy that they are actionable without proof of injury. This is defamation *per se*. Let us begin with the latter type.

Illinois recognizes five categories of defamation *per se*, but only two are of interest here: (1) statements that suggest that the subject can't perform his job because of lack of ability or want of integrity, and (2) statements that prejudice the subject in the pursuit of his trade or profession. The difference between the two is subtle. The former seems to imply some sort of on-the-job malfeasance; the latter covers suitability for a trade or profession. Pippen argues that this court has already established in *Giant Screen Sports v. Canadian Imperial Bank of Commerce*, 553 F.3d 527 (7th Cir.2009), that false accusations of bankruptcy fit into one of these categories.

But the statements at issue in *Giant Screen Sports* were not about bankruptcy; instead, they repeated false accusations that a company willfully defaulted on a credit agreement it was not a party to. The statements depicted the company as one that shirked its contractual obligations; a reader might reasonably think twice about doing business with the company. A similar taint does not attach to the reputation of people who go bankrupt. Many innocent reasons lead to financial distress. Readers of the defendants' statements who mistakenly believe that Pippen is insolvent readily could conclude that his advisers bear the blame.

What's more, Pippen was reported to be personally bankrupt. To succeed under Illinois law without the need to prove injury, he must show that he was falsely accused of lacking ability in his trade or of doing something bad while performing his job. Pippen has been employed since he retired from basketball as a goodwill ambassador for the Chicago Bulls, a basketball analyst, and a celebrity product endorser. Bankruptcy does not imply that he lacks the competence or integrity to perform any of these jobs.

Sometimes personal and professional ability or integrity are linked. When the subject of the false statements is employed in an occupation (schoolteacher for example) that requires certain personal traits, such as trustworthiness, accusations of being a scam artist or an inveterate liar could lead to unemployment. Pippen does not contend that his is such a situation. His post-retirement employability derives from his pre-retirement stardom (for his endorsement and appearance work) and basketball knowledge (for his work as an analyst), not his financial prudence or investment savvy. Reports of personal bankruptcy would not so impugn his job performance that they necessarily constitute defamation.

This leaves the second type of defamation (*per quod*).... The district court dismissed these claims after concluding that Pippen had failed to allege special damages in sufficient detail. We think this a mistake.... Pippen's complaint alleges that his endorsement and personal-appearance opportunities dwindled as a result of the defendants' false reports. In a proposed amended complaint, Pippen itemized losses that in his view flowed from defendants' statements; he identified specific business opportunities that had been available to him earlier but that, following the defendants' statements, were available no more. This is more than a general allegation of economic loss; it is an allegation that third parties have ceased to do business with him because of the defendants' actions. This contention may be substantively inadequate. It appears to be an example of the *post hoc ergo propter hoc* fallacy: since Pippen's opportunities diminished after the statements were made, he believes they must have diminished *because* the statements were made. This theory of causation is weak for professional athletes, whose earnings related to past stardom drop as time passes since their playing days. But, as a matter of pleading, Pippen did enough.

The district court had a second reason, however, and it is stronger. The judge observed that Pippen is a public figure, which he concedes. Thus he must show that the defendants published the defamatory statements with actual malice—in other words, that the defendants either knew the statements to be false or were recklessly indifferent to whether they are true or false. States of mind may be pleaded generally, but a plaintiff still must point to details sufficient to render a claim plausible.

Defendants had many ways to learn whether Pippen had filed for bankruptcy. For example, all bankruptcy court dockets can be searched simultaneously through the federal courts' PACER service. And then there's the tried-and-true journalistic practice of asking a story's subject. If rather than relying on the rumor mill the defendants had conducted even a cursory investigation, they would have discovered that Pippen had not declared bankruptcy—and they concede this. But failure to investigate is precisely what the Supreme Court has said is insufficient to establish reckless disregard for the truth.

The Supreme Court also has said that actual malice cannot be inferred from a publisher's failure to retract a statement once it learns it to be false. Thus the fact that Pippen alerted the defendants by email *after* publication that he had not entered bankruptcy does not help him establish actual malice at the time of publication. And Illinois has adopted the Uniform Single Publication Act, 740 ILCS 165/1, which provides that a claim for relief for defamation is complete at the time of first publication; later circulation of the original publication does not trigger fresh claims. The Act protects speakers and writers from repeated litigation arising from a single, but mass-produced, defamatory publication.

Pippen argues that the Act does not apply to statements on the Internet, where all defendants made their reportage available. Online publishers do not face the same logistical hurdles or costs in correcting a false statement as their old-media counterparts. Print publishers would need to hunt down every physical copy of a book, magazine, or newspaper in circulation, while Internet publishers can alter their sites with relative ease. In Pippen's view, then, every day that an unaltered defamatory statement remains online after a publisher learns of its falsity constitutes an actionable republication.

Illinois courts have not yet considered how the single-publication rule applies to Internet publications, so our job is to predict how the state's highest court would answer the question if asked. In the absence of any Illinois authority on the question, decisions from other jurisdictions may prove instructive. We conclude that, if presented with the opportunity, the Supreme Court of Illinois would deem the single-publication rule applicable to the Internet.

Every state court that has considered the question applies the single-publication rule to information online. And those federal courts that have addressed the topic have concluded that the relevant state supreme court would agree. Pippen does not alert us to any authority supporting his view, and we have found none.

The theme of these decisions is that excluding the Internet from the single-publication rule would eviscerate the statute of limitations and expose online publishers to potentially limitless liability. This same concern previously led courts to apply the single-publication rule to books. They did so despite the fact that book publishers have greater post-publication control over the circulation of their content than do newspaper publishers. All copies of a single newspaper edition are made available to the public on one day; in contrast, book publishers hold stock in reserve and release batches to the public over months or years. In Pippen's view, the single-publication rule ought not have been extended to book publishers because they could pulp the books they kept in stock, while newspaper publishers had no leftover stock to destroy. But no court saw it that way, and no court has been persuaded that the even greater control that Internet publishers have over their content — and the much lower cost of editing or deleting that content — is a reason to exclude them from the Act's coverage. Indeed, courts have drawn the opposite conclusion: the Internet's greater reach comes with an "even greater potential for endless retriggering of the statute of limitations, multiplicity of suits and harassment of defendants." *Firth* [*v. State,*] 98 N.Y.2d 365, 370 (2002)]; the more reason that the single-publication rule should apply.

A publisher's degree of control over its content does not matter to Illinois's test for whether redistribution of a defamatory statement amounts to a republication. Instead, courts must ask whether the "act of the defendant [was] a conscious independent one." *Winrod v. Time Inc.*, 334 Ill.App. 59 (1948). Courts have grappled with what degree of affirmative act constitutes a republication. The defendants in those cases changed the URL where the statements were posted but left the statements unaltered. In *Firth*, the defendants added an unrelated story to the web page hosting the allegedly defamatory statement. None of those acts was sufficient to count as a republication. Pippen does not contend that the defendants took any action beyond initially posting the stories to their web sites, and we conclude that Illinois would deem the passive maintenance of a web site not a republication.

Notes and Questions

a. The standards for defamation are quite clear in the abstract, but very difficult to adapt to the world of novelization, motion pictures, and dramatic license. Even the less controversial characters are sometimes put into question. In the film *The Hurricane*, former middleweight champion Joey Giardello sued for the allegedly false portrayal of his title fight against Rubin Hurricane Carter. The case was eventually settled, reportedly with changes to the DVD version of the movie, including a voice-over by director Norman Jewison which alludes to an admission that the fight scene in the movie was inaccurate. *See* Matthew Stohl, *False Light Invasion of Privacy in Docudramas: The Oxymoron Which Must Be Solved*, 35 AKRON L. REV. 251 (2002). Similar issues occurred with *Boys Don't Cry*, *Erin Brockovich*, *The Perfect Storm*, and many other stories based on true events.

b. In Matthew Stohl's account of the controversy involving Joey Giardello, the descriptions are not likely to meet the actual malice standard. As former middleweight champion, it is likely that Giardello would have been treated as a public figure and therefore unable to prove his case. Unlike Giardello, minor characters who claim defamation are not typically public figures or public officials. As private figures, plaintiffs need only prove negligence to have a claim — something much more likely to occur during the constant change of editing or filmmaking.

c. What role does a film's disclaimer serve to limit tort liability? In *Davis v. Costa-Gavras*, the district court put a good deal of stock in the "based upon" language of the film's description — assuming that the public understood what a dramatization implies about specific incidents. Other books, plays, and motion pictures use much broader disclaimers. One such formulation, from the book *Rush*, provides that the book "is a work of fiction. Any resemblance its characters may have to persons living or dead is purely coincidental."

d. The motion picture *Harry Potter and the Sorcerer's Stone* uses a fittingly more British approach: "The story, all names, characters & incidents portrayed in this production are fictitious. No identification with actual persons, places, buildings & products is intended or should be inferred." The *Harry Potter* disclaimer is interesting in its expansive scope. To what extent do the disclaimers impact the outcome of litigation or attempts to bring litigation? Does the addition of buildings and places suggest new potential claims for invasion of legal interests? Will such a disclaimer serve to avoid trademark issues or concerns about product disparity?

e. Defamation remains in the eye of the beholder. Described by the Ninth Circuit as a "compliment," famed daredevil Evel Knievel did not appreciate ESPN's form of attention. As the court explained,

> Famed motorcycle stuntman Evel Knievel and his wife Krystal were photographed when they attended ESPN's Action Sports and Music Awards in 2001. The photograph depicted Evel, who was wearing a motorcycle jacket and rose-tinted sunglasses, with his right arm around Krystal and his left arm around another young woman. ESPN published the photograph on its "extreme sports" website with a caption that read "Evel Knievel proves that you're never too old to be a pimp."

Knievel v. ESPN, 393 F.3d 1068, 1070 (9th Cir. 2005). The court reminded Knievel that an assessment of defamation must take the context of the website into account, and the remainder of the website used an "overwhelming presence of slang and non-literal language," along with such terms as "hardcore" and "scoping," and slang phrases such as "throwing down a pose," "put a few back," and "hottie of the year...." *Id.* at 1077.

f. What is based upon a true story? Given the facts and standards of the dispute between Little League volunteer Robert Muzikowski and Paramount Pictures, the standard is evidently very low. In a bitterly contested defamation claim, the plaintiff objected to the conversion of the "nonfiction novel" *Hardball: A Season in the Projects* into the fictional movie *Hardball*. *Muzikowski v. Paramount Pictures Corp.*, 477 F.3d 899 (7th Cir. 2007). Having denied that Muzikowski is represented in any fashion in the fictionalization — to avoid the claims of defamation — Paramount claims the movie is based on the true story of the baseball team.

> Muzikowski claimed that Paramount's promotion of the *Hardball* movie as "inspired by a true story" was false because of the extent to which Muzikowski's life story was changed in the film. The district court concluded that these theories failed too, because Muzikowski had neither demonstrated

that Paramount's advertisement was false nor that consumers who viewed the advertisements had been deceived.

In order to establish a claim of false or deceptive advertising under § 43(a) of the Lanham Act, a plaintiff must show that the defendant made a material false statement of fact in a commercial advertisement and that the false statement deceived or had the tendency to deceive a substantial segment of its audience. The district court held, and we have previously assumed without deciding, that this analysis also applies to Illinois false advertising claims. Because Muzikowski does not argue to the contrary, we assume the same in this case.

In granting summary judgment to Paramount on the false advertising claims, the district court reasoned that Paramount's statement "inspired by a true story" is "literally true," observing that neither party disputes the veracity of the statement. Paramount insists that its advertisement represents the film as "the story of ... the [Little League] team featured in Coyle's book." Muzikowski, on the other hand, contends that the advertisements "lead viewers to believe that the story is his." Since Muzikowski does not in any event contest the district court's conclusion that Paramount's advertising for *Hardball* did not contain a false statement of fact, we conclude that he has waived both this argument and his false advertising claims generally.

Id. at 907–08.

Eighteen affidavits did little to convince the judge that a substantial portion of the viewers knew about Muzikowski or cared that it was based upon a true story, making enforcement of the "based on a true story" pronouncement much less likely. *See id.*

g. To what extent can the use of images to illustrate a story be defamatory of those depicted in the photographs if they are not related to the story itself? *See Stanton v. Metro Corp.*, 438 F.3d 119 (1st Cir. 2006) (depicting teens at a high school party in an unrelated story about teenage promiscuity).

Problem 5-A

Angered and frustrated by the response to Bryce's *Juliet Prescott* (*see* Problem 4-A), Bryce tried to strike back. Bryce added a scene to the script set in the city hall depicting characters whose first names were those of actual local city officials. Other than in the matter of first names, none of Bryce's characterizations bear any direct relation or resemblance to the city council members. Bryce never performed any background research on the city council members. The play's new city council characters are generally depicted as racist and illiterate. At the end of the scene, the city council voted to "deport Romeo—at least to New Mexico." Bryce has shown you the scene (which you acknowledge is a clever satire of the city council) to ask your advice. Advise Bryce regarding the extent to which the scene is actionable as defamatory.

B. Parody and Satire

Hustler Magazine v. Falwell

485 U.S. 46 (1988)

CHIEF JUSTICE REHNQUIST delivered the opinion of the Court.

Petitioner Hustler Magazine, Inc., is a magazine of nationwide circulation. Respondent Jerry Falwell, a nationally known minister who has been active as a commentator on politics and public affairs, sued petitioner and its publisher, petitioner Larry Flynt, to recover damages for invasion of privacy, libel, and intentional infliction of emotional distress. The District Court directed a verdict against respondent on the privacy claim, and submitted the other two claims to a jury. The jury found for petitioners on the defamation claim, but found for respondent on the claim for intentional infliction of emotional distress and awarded damages. We now consider whether this award is consistent with the First and Fourteenth Amendments of the United States Constitution.

The inside front cover of the November 1983 issue of Hustler Magazine featured a "parody" of an advertisement for Campari Liqueur that contained the name and picture of respondent and was entitled "Jerry Falwell talks about his first time." This parody was modeled after actual Campari ads that included interviews with various celebrities about their "first times." Although it was apparent by the end of each interview that this meant the first time they sampled Campari, the ads clearly played on the sexual double entendre of the general subject of "first times." Copying the form and layout of these Campari ads, Hustler's editors chose respondent as the featured celebrity and drafted an alleged "interview" with him in which he states that his "first time" was during a drunken incestuous rendezvous with his mother in an outhouse. The Hustler parody portrays respondent and his mother as drunk and immoral, and suggests that respondent is a hypocrite who preaches only when he is drunk. In small print at the bottom of the page, the ad contains the disclaimer, "ad parody—not to be taken seriously." The magazine's table of contents also lists the ad as "Fiction; Ad and Personality Parody." . . .

This case presents us with a novel question involving First Amendment limitations upon a State's authority to protect its citizens from the intentional infliction of emotional distress. We must decide whether a public figure may recover damages for emotional harm caused by the publication of an ad parody offensive to him, and doubtless gross and repugnant in the eyes of most. Respondent would have us find that a State's interest in protecting public figures from emotional distress is sufficient to deny First Amendment protection to speech that is patently offensive and is intended to inflict emotional injury, even when that speech could not reasonably have been interpreted as stating actual facts about the public figure involved. This we decline to do. . . .

We conclude that public figures and public officials may not recover for the tort of intentional infliction of emotional distress by reason of publications such as the one here at issue without showing in addition that the publication contains a false statement of fact which was made with "actual malice," i.e., with knowledge that the statement was false or with reckless disregard as to whether or not it was true. This is not merely a "blind application" of the *New York Times* standard, see *Time, Inc. v. Hill*, 385 U.S. 374, 390, (1967), it reflects our considered judgment that such a standard is necessary to give adequate "breathing space" to the freedoms protected by the First Amendment.

Here it is clear that respondent Falwell is a "public figure" for purposes of First Amendment law. The jury found against respondent on his libel claim when it decided that the Hustler ad parody could not "reasonably be understood as describing actual facts about [respondent] or actual events in which [he] participated." The Court of Appeals interpreted the jury's finding to be that the ad parody "was not reasonably believable," and in accordance with our custom we accept this finding. Respondent is thus relegated to his claim for damages awarded by the jury for the intentional infliction of emotional distress by "outrageous" conduct. But for reasons heretofore stated this claim cannot, consistently with the First Amendment, form a basis for the award of damages when the conduct in question is the publication of a caricature such as the ad parody involved here. The judgment of the Court of Appeals is accordingly Reversed.

Farah v. Esquire Magazine

736 F.3d 528 (2013)

This case is principally a defamation action based on the publication of an article by journalist Mark Warren on *Esquire Magazine*'s Politics Blog. The article was posted one day after the release of a book entitled "*Where's the Birth Certificate? The Case that Barack Obama is not Eligible to Be President,*" written by Jerome Corsi and published by Joseph Farah's WND Books. Farah's website, WorldNetDaily, announced the book launch with the headline, "**It's out! The book that proves Obama's ineligible:** Today's the day Corsi is unleashed to tell all about that 'birth certificate'" (emphasis in original). Approximately three weeks earlier, President Obama had released his long-form birth certificate showing that he was born in Hawaii. Warren's article was entitled "**BREAKING: Jerome Corsi's Birther Book Pulled from Shelves!**" (emphasis in original). It stated, in part: "In a stunning development one day after the release of [the Corsi book], [Farah] has announced plans to recall and pulp the entire 200,000 first printing run of the book, as well as announcing an offer to refund the purchase price to anyone who has already bought … the book." Approximately ninety minutes later, *Esquire* published an "update" on its blog "for those who didn't figure it out," that Warren's article was "satire"; the "update" clarified that the article was untrue and referenced other "serious" *Esquire* articles on the birth certificate issue. Farah observed the same day that he thought the blog post was a "poorly executed parody." Also that day, Warren told *The Daily Caller* that he had no regrets about publishing the fictitious article and expressed his negative view of the book's author; his statements were published on *The Daily Caller* website that day and the following day.

Farah and Corsi filed suit for compensatory and punitive damages alleging defamation.… *Esquire* for all defendants moved to dismiss on several grounds, and the district court dismissed the complaint.... Upon *de novo* review, we hold that the complaint was properly dismissed pursuant to Federal Rule of Civil Procedure 12(b)(6) for failure to state a claim because the blog post was fully protected political satire and the "update" and Warren's statements are protected opinion. The complaint also fails to state a claim for violation of the Lanham Act. Accordingly, we affirm the dismissal of the complaint....

Esquire published an online article by Mark Warren entitled "**BREAKING: Jerome Corsi's Birther Book Pulled from Shelves!**" The article contained "false and misleading facts" about Corsi's book. The article, on "The Politics Blog," was accompanied by a copy of the "Drudge Siren" above an image of the book's cover. It read in full:

> **In a stunning development** one day after the release of *Where's the Birth Certificate? The Case that Barack Obama is not Eligible to be President,* by Dr. Jerome Corsi, World Net Daily Editor and Chief Executive Officer Joseph Farah has announced plans to recall and pulp the entire 200,000 first printing run of the book, as well as announcing an offer to refund the purchase price to anyone who has already bought either a hard copy or electronic download of the book.
>
> In an exclusive interview, a reflective Farah, who wrote the book's foreword and also published Corsi's earlier best-selling work, *Unfit for Command: Swift Boat Veterans Speak out Against John Kerry* and *Capricorn One: NASA, JFK, and the Great "Moon Landing" Cover-Up,* said that after much serious reflection, he could not go forward with the project. "I believe with all my heart that Barack Obama is destroying this country, and I will continue to stand against his administration at every turn, but in light of recent events, this book has become problematic, and contains what I now believe to be factual inaccuracies," he said this morning. "I cannot in good conscience publish it and expect anyone to believe it."
>
> When asked if he had any plans to publish a corrected version of the book, he said cryptically, "There is no book." Farah declined to comment on his discussions of the matter with Corsi.
>
> A source at WND, who requested that his name be withheld, said that Farah was "rip-shit" when, on April 27, President Obama took the extraordinary step of personally releasing his "long-form" birth certificate, thus resolving the matter of Obama's legitimacy for "anybody with a brain."
>
> "He called up Corsi and really tore him a new one," says the source. "I mean, we'll do anything to hurt Obama, and erase his memory, but we don't want to look like fucking idiots, you know? Look, at the end of the day, bullshit is bullshit."
>
> Corsi, who graduated from Harvard and is a professional journalist, could not be reached for comment.

According to the complaint, "[i]mmediately" after the blog posting, "news organizations, readers of WorldNetDaily, purchasers and distributors of WND Books and others began contacting [] Farah for confirmation of the story and comment." Also, "consumers began requesting refunds[,] ... book supporters began attacking Farah and Corsi[,] [and] [b]ook stores ... began pulling the book from their shelves, or not offering it for sale at all." Only after Farah "issued a statement saying he was exploring legal options against *Esquire* and Warren did they purport to issue a disclaimer." This "so-called disclaimer" was "as false[] [and] misleading ... as the initial story that was published" on the website. *Id.* It read in full:

> DEVELOPING ...
>
> *UPDATE, 12:25 p.m., for those who didn't figure it out yet, and the many on Twitter for whom it took a while:* We committed satire this morning to point out the problems with selling and marketing a book that has had its core premise and reason to exist gutted by the news cycle, several weeks in advance of publication. Are its author and publisher chastened? Well, no. They double down, and accuse the President of the United States of perpetrating a fraud on the world by having released a forged birth certificate. Not because this claim is in any way based on reality, but to hold their terribly gullible audience captive to their lies, and to sell books. This is despicable, and deserves only ridicule. That's why we committed satire in the matter of the Corsi book. Hell, even the president has a sense of humor about it all. Some more serious reporting from us on this whole "birther" phenomenon here, here, and here.
>
> **Tags:** birther book, jerome corsi, where's the birth certificate, drudge without context, birthers, wingnuts, humor

... On June 28, 2011, Farah and Corsi sued Esquire Magazine, Inc., Hearst Communications, Inc., and Warren (together "*Esquire*") for defamation, ... The complaint sought in excess of $100 million for actual and compensatory damages, and punitive damages in excess of $20 million....

To meet the requirements for defamation under District of Columbia law, a plaintiff must prove (1) that he was the subject of a false and defamatory statement; (2) that the statement was published to a third party; (3) that publishing the statement was at least negligent; and (4) that the plaintiff suffered either actual or legal harm. A statement is "defamatory" if it tends to injure the plaintiff in his trade, profession or community standing, or to lower him in the estimation of the community. This court, in reviewing the dismissal of the complaint, "must assume, as the complaint alleges, the falsity of any express or implied factual statements made" in the publications at issue. The court must also assume that *Esquire* made such statements with the requisite state of mind. And, "[i]n determining whether a complaint states a claim, the court may consider the facts alleged in the complaint, documents attached thereto or incorporated therein, and matters of which it may take judicial notice." *Abhe & Svoboda, Inc. v. Chao*, 508 F.3d 1052, 1059 (D.C.Cir.2007) Judicial notice is properly taken of publicly available historical articles such as were attached to *Esquire*'s motions to dismiss....

Esquire maintains that Farah and Corsi have no cognizable defamation claim because the blog post is fully protected satire. "Satire" is a long-established artistic form that uses means such as "ridicule, derision, burlesque, irony, parody, [or] caricature" to censure the "vices, follies, abuses, or shortcomings" of an individual or society. *Satire*, Encyc. Britannica Online, http://www.britannica.com/EBchecked/topic/524958/ satire (last visited Nov. 1, 2013). Although satire has been employed since the time of Ancient Greece, it remains "one of the most imprecise" of all literary designations—a notoriously broad and complex genre whose "forms are as varied as its victims." *Id.* Sometimes satire is funny. *See, e.g., Saturday Night Live* (NBC television broadcast); The Onion, http://www.theonion.com (last visited Nov. 1, 2013). Other times it may seem cruel and mocking, attacking the core beliefs of its target. And sometimes it is absurd, as in the classic example of Jonathan Swift's proposal to "solve" the problem of Irish poverty by killing and eating Irish children. *See* Jonathan Swift, A Modest Proposal (1729). Satire's unifying element is the use of wit "to expose something foolish or vicious to criticism." *Satire*, Encyc. Britannica Online. A "parody" is to the same effect: the style of an individual or work is closely imitated for comic effect or in ridicule. *See* Merriam Webster's Collegiate Dictionary at 846 (10th ed.1993) ("parody"); *see id.* at 1038 ("satire").

Despite its literal falsity, satirical speech enjoys First Amendment protection. Consistent with the "actual facts" requirement, "the 'statement' that the plaintiff must prove false ... is not invariably the literal phrase published but rather what a reasonable reader would have understood the author to have said." *Milkovich* [*v. Lorain Journal Co.*, 497 U.S. 1, 23–24 (1990)]. Thus, a satire or parody must be assessed in the appropriate context; it is not actionable if it "cannot reasonably be interpreted as stating actual facts about an individual." *Milkovich,* 497 U.S. at 20. In light of the special characteristics of satire, of course, "what a reasonable reader would have understood" is more informed by an assessment of her well-considered view than by her immediate yet transitory reaction. Without First Amendment protection, there is a risk that public debate would "suffer for lack of 'imaginative expression'" and "the 'rhetorical hyperbole' which has traditionally added much to the discourse of our Nation." *Id.* (quoting *Hustler Magazine,* 485 U.S. at 53–55).

Farah and Corsi do not suggest that satire, as a genre, lacks constitutional protection. Rather, in their view *Esquire's particular attempt* at satire is not protected because reasonable readers would take the fictitious blog post literally. They point to the inquiries they received following the blog post, as well as to *Esquire's* own "update" clarifying that the post was satire, as evidence that many actual readers were misled by *Esquire's* story. But it is the nature of satire that not everyone "gets it" immediately. For example, when Daniel Defoe first published *The Shortest Way with the Dissenters,* an anonymous satirical pamphlet against religious persecution, it was initially welcomed by the church establishment Defoe sought to ridicule. Similarly, Benjamin Franklin's "Speech of Miss Polly Baker," a fictitious news story mocking New England's harsh treatment of unwed mothers, was widely republished in both England and the United States as actual news.

Indeed, satire is effective as social commentary precisely because it is often grounded in truth. In a similar case involving a satirical news article, the Texas Supreme Court observed that satire works by "distort[ing] ... the familiar with the pretense of reality in order to convey an underlying critical message." *New Times v. Isaacks,* 146 S.W.3d 144, 151 (Tex.2004). Here, too, *Esquire*'s story conveyed its message by layering fiction upon fact. The test, however, is not whether some actual readers were misled, but whether the hypothetical reasonable reader could be (after time for reflection). And to the extent Farah and Corsi rely on *Esquire*'s "update" to demonstrate reader confusion, *Esquire* can hardly be penalized for attempting to set the record straight and *avoid* confusion by those readers who did not at first "get" the satirical nature of Warren's article.

Considering the blog post in its context, the reasonable reader could not understand Warren's article to be conveying "real news" about Farah and Corsi. The article's primary intended audience—that is, readers of "The Politics Blog"—would have been familiar with *Esquire*'s history of publishing satirical stories, with recent topics ranging from Osama Bin Laden's television-watching habits to "Sex Tips from Donald Rumsfeld." At the same time, followers of "The Politics Blog" were politically informed readers. The "update" notes that *Esquire*.com had previously featured several "serious" reports on the birth certificate issue. Farah and Corsi acknowledge that they were well-known leaders of the movement questioning President Obama's eligibility, and admit that readers of *Esquire*.com would have been familiar with WorldNetDaily and its positions,. The postings on Farah's own website show that he has been writing on the issue for years, and Corsi's then-forthcoming book had recently received publicity on the Drudge Report. It defies common sense to suppose that readers of "The Politics Blog" were unaware of the birth certificate controversy or the heated debate it had provoked.

With that baseline of knowledge, reasonable readers of "The Politics Blog" would recognize the prominent indicia of satire in the Warren article. Most notably, the very substance of the story would alert the reasonable reader to the possibility that the post was satirical. The essence of the fictitious story was that Farah, a self-described leader (along with Corsi) of the movement to challenge President Obama's eligibility to serve, had suddenly and without any warning decided to recall and "pulp" the Corsi book the very day after it was released. The supposed basis for this decision was President Obama's earlier release of his long-form birth certificate; yet that release occurred three weeks before Corsi's book was published, and, as Farah acknowledges, he and Corsi remained (and still remain) committed to the book even after that event. *After* the release of the birth certificate, Farah appeared on MSNBC and published more than 40 articles on WorldNetDaily continuing to promote the book. The day of the Corsi book's release— the day before *Esquire* posted its fictitious story—WorldNetDaily announced the publication on its website with an article entitled, "**It's out! The book that proves Obama's ineligible:** Today's the day Corsi is unleashed to tell all about that 'birth certificate.'" It is inconceivable that Farah would reverse course so abruptly, as *Esquire*'s fictitious story claimed. Readers of "The Politics Blog" would have recognized that the article was "reporting" events and statements that were totally inconsistent with Farah's and Corsi's well-publicized views, and could not reasonably have taken the story literally.

A number of humorous or outlandish details in the blog post also betray its satirical nature. The story attributes to Corsi an obviously fictitious book entitled, *Capricorn One: NASA, JFK, and the Great "Moon Landing" Cover-Up.* Of all prominent cover-ups featured in the news in recent years, a moon cover-up — much less "the Great 'Moon Landing' Cover-Up" — was not among them. Further, the story includes incredible counter-factual statements like, "[Farah] said cryptically, 'There is no book.'" Farah had published and released the book and then confirmed the next day to *The Daily Caller* that the book "was selling briskly. I am 100 percent behind it." The story repeatedly attributes to a "source at WND" quotes that are highly unorthodox for a real news story, such as Farah was "rip-shit," "bullshit is bullshit," and "we don't want to look like fucking idiots, you know?" ...

Even if none of these elements standing alone — the story's substance, outlandish and humorous details, stylistic elements — would convince the reasonable reader that the blog post was satirical, taken in context and as a whole they could lead to no other conclusion. Farah immediately recognized the blog post as a "parody," although he told *The Daily Caller* that in his view it was "a very poorly executed" one. Admittedly, apart from its headline, the article did not employ the sort of imitation and exaggerated mimicry that are typical of parody. But satire is a far broader concept than parody, incorporating a variety of literary forms and devices. And poorly executed or not, the reasonable reader would have to suspend virtually all that he or she knew to be true of Farah's and Corsi's views on the issue of President Obama's eligibility to serve in order to conclude the story was reporting true facts.

Because the reasonable reader could not, in context, understand *Esquire's* blog post to be conveying "real news" — that is, actual facts about Farah and Corsi — the blog post was not actionable defamation. To the contrary, almost everything about the story and the nature of the issue itself showed it was political speech aimed at critiquing Farah's and Corsi's public position on the issue of President Obama's eligibility to hold office even after he had released his long-form birth certificate showing he was born in Hawaii. Farah and Corsi were entitled to express their opinion that its delayed release signaled it was a forgery, but they could not then sue for defamation because *Esquire* conveyed its contrary view by using satire, rather than straightforward attack. Because the blog post was entitled to First Amendment protection, the district court properly dismissed the defamation count as to the blog post for failure to state a claim.

Notes and Questions

a. *Hustler v. Falwell* was preceded by two other decisions which together help frame the parody analysis of defamation law. *See Greenbelt Cooperative Publishing Assn., Inc. v. Bresler*, 398 U.S. 6 (1970) (rhetorical hyperbole should not be construed as factual assertions); *Letter Carriers v. Austin*, 418 U.S. 264 (1974) (false representation of fact required for defamation so opinion or hyperbole not actionable).

b. *Mink v. Knox* summarized the *Greenbelt, Letter Carriers,* and *Falwell* line of cases as follows:

As to the constitutional limits on the *type* of speech which may be the subject of state defamation actions, the line of cases provides protection for statements, such as parody, fantasy, rhetorical hyperbole, and imaginative expressions, that cannot reasonably [be] interpreted as stating actual facts' about an individual. Because no reasonable person would take these types of speech as true, they simply cannot impair one's good name. This provides assurance that public debate will not suffer for lack of 'imaginative expression' or the 'rhetorical hyperbole' which has traditionally added much to the discourse of our Nation."

Mink v. Knox, 613 F.3d 995, 1005 (10th Cir. 2010) (internal quotations and citations omitted).

c. Do satire and parody apply differently to private individuals rather than public officials or regarding matters that are not of public concern? With social media allowing any person to publish content available to large groups of people, topics that are non-public involving private individuals are commonly published. How should parody be viewed? *See Pring v. Penthouse Intern., Ltd.*, 695 F.2d 438, 443 (10th Cir. 1982).

Problem 5-B

Like many artists, Bryce maintains a significant presence on social media. Bryce publishes information about upcoming events, future projects, and personal musings. Some of these posts talk about the many artists with whom Bryce collaborates. Frustrated late one evening, Bryce wrote a fictional dialogue between Bryce's producer and distributor. The essence of the discussion was how funny the producer and distributor thought it was to watch artists dedicate their lives to content that would be sold for pennies and what little money was paid by the distributor to the producer would be kept far away from the artists. The dialogue was written in Seussian Rhyme. Bryce's producer has threatened to bring a lawsuit for defamation and demanded a significant financial settlement, an apology, and the removal of the post. Please advise Bryce regarding the best strategy to address the problem.

C. Privacy

Time, Inc. v. Hill

385 U.S. 374 (1967)

Mr. Justice Brennan delivered the opinion of the Court.

The question in this case is whether appellant, publisher of Life Magazine, was denied constitutional protections of speech and press by the application by the New York courts of §§ 50–51 of the New York Civil Rights Law[14] to award appellee damages

---

14. The complete text of the New York Civil Rights Law §§ 50–51 is as follows:

§ 50. Right of privacy

A person, firm or corporation that uses for advertising purposes, or for the purposes of on allegations that Life falsely reported that a new play portrayed an experience suffered by appellee and his family.

The article appeared in Life in February 1955. It was entitled "True Crime Inspires Tense Play," with the subtitle, "The ordeal of a family trapped by convicts gives Broadway a new thriller, 'The Desperate Hours.'" The text of the article reads as follows:

Three years ago Americans all over the country read about the desperate ordeal of the James Hill family, who were held prisoners in their home outside Philadelphia by three escaped convicts. Later they read about it in Joseph Hayes's novel, *The Desperate Hours*, inspired by the family's experience. Now they can see the story re-enacted in Hayes's Broadway play based on the book, and next year will see it in his movie, which has been filmed but is being held up until the play has a chance to pay off.

The play, directed by Robert Montgomery and expertly acted, is a heart-stopping account of how a family rose to heroism in a crisis. Life photographed the play during its Philadelphia tryout, transported some of the actors to the actual house where the Hills were besieged. On the next page scenes from the play are re-enacted on the site of the crime.

The pictures on the ensuing two pages included an enactment of the son being "roughed up" by one of the convicts, entitled "brutish convict," a picture of the daughter biting the hand of a convict to make him drop a gun, entitled "daring daughter," and one of the father throwing his gun through the door after a "brave try" to save his family is foiled.

---

trade, the name, portrait or picture of any living person without having first obtained the written consent of such person, or if a minor of his or her parent or guardian, is guilty of a misdemeanor.

§ 51. Action for injunction and for damages

Any person whose name, portrait or picture is used within this state for advertising purposes or for the purposes of trade without the written consent first obtained as above provided may maintain an equitable action in the supreme court of this state against the person, firm or corporation so using his name, portrait or picture, to prevent and restrain the use thereof; and may also sue and recover damages for any injuries sustained by reason of such use and if the defendant shall have knowingly used such person's name, portrait or picture in such manner as is forbidden or declared to be unlawful by the last section, the jury, in its discretion, may award exemplary damages. But nothing contained in this act shall be so construed as to prevent any person, firm or corporation, practicing the profession of photography, from exhibiting in or about his or its establishment specimens of the work of such establishment, unless the same is continued by such person, firm or corporation after written notice objecting thereto has been given by the person portrayed; and nothing contained in this act shall be so construed as to prevent any person, firm or corporation from using the name, portrait or picture of any manufacturer or dealer in connection with the goods, wares and merchandise manufactured, produced or dealt in by him which he has sold or disposed of with such name, portrait or picture used in connection therewith; or from using the name, portrait or picture of any author, composer or artist in connection with his literary, musical or artistic productions which he has sold or disposed of with such name, portrait or picture used in connection therewith.

The James Hill referred to in the article is the appellee. He and his wife and five children involuntarily became the subjects of a front-page news story after being held hostage by three escaped convicts in their suburban, Whitemarsh, Pennsylvania, home for 19 hours on September 11–12, 1952. The family was released unharmed. In an interview with newsmen after the convicts departed, appellee stressed that the convicts had treated the family courteously, had not molested them, and had not been at all violent. The convicts were thereafter apprehended in a widely publicized encounter with the police which resulted in the killing of two of the convicts. Shortly thereafter the family moved to Connecticut. The appellee discouraged all efforts to keep them in the public spotlight through magazine articles or appearances on television.

In the spring of 1953, Joseph Hayes' novel, The Desperate Hours, was published. The story depicted the experience of a family of four held hostage by three escaped convicts in the family's suburban home. But, unlike Hill's experience, the family of the story suffer violence at the hands of the convicts; the father and son are beaten and the daughter subjected to a verbal sexual insult.

The book was made into a play, also entitled The Desperate Hours, and it is Life's article about the play which is the subject of appellee's action. The complaint sought damages under §§ 50–51 on allegations that the Life article was intended to, and did, give the impression that the play mirrored the Hill family's experience, which, to the knowledge of defendant "… was false and untrue." Appellant's defense was that the article was "a subject of legitimate news interest," "a subject of general interest and of value and concern to the public" at the time of publication, and that it was "published in good faith without any malice whatsoever…." A motion to dismiss the complaint for substantially these reasons was made at the close of the case and was denied by the trial judge on the ground that the proofs presented a jury question as to the truth of the article.

The jury awarded appellee $50,000 compensatory and $25,000 punitive damages. On appeal the Appellate Division of the Supreme Court ordered a new trial as to damages but sustained the jury verdict of liability. The court said as to liability:

> Although the play was fictionalized, *Life's* article portrayed it as a re-enactment of the Hills' experience. It is an inescapable conclusion that this was done to advertise and attract further attention to the play, and to increase present and future magazine circulation as well. It is evident that the article cannot be characterized as a mere dissemination of news, nor even an effort to supply legitimate newsworthy information in which the public had, or might have a proper interest.

At the new trial on damages, a jury was waived and the court awarded $30,000 compensatory damages without punitive damages.

The New York Court of Appeals affirmed the Appellate Division "on the majority and concurring opinions at the Appellate Division," two judges dissenting. We noted probable jurisdiction of the appeal to consider the important constitutional questions of freedom of speech and press involved. After argument last Term, the case was restored to the docket for reargument, We reverse and remand the case to the Court of Appeals for further proceedings not inconsistent with this opinion....

Although "Right of Privacy" is the caption of §§ 50–51, the term nowhere appears in the text of the statute itself. The text of the statute appears to proscribe only ... the appropriation and use in advertising or to promote the sale of goods, of another's name, portrait or picture without his consent. An application of that limited scope would present different questions of violation of the constitutional protections for speech and press.

The New York courts have, however, construed the statute to operate much more broadly. In *Spahn* [v. *Julian Messner, Inc.,* 18 N.Y.2d 324, 221 N.E.2d 543 (1966)], the Court of Appeals stated that "Over the years since the statute's enactment in 1903, its social desirability and remedial nature have led to its being given a liberal construction consonant with its over-all purpose...." Specifically, it has been held in some circumstances to authorize a remedy against the press and other communications media which publish the names, pictures, or portraits of people without their consent. Reflecting the fact, however, that such applications may raise serious questions of conflict with the constitutional protections for speech and press, decisions under the statute have tended to limit the statute's application. "Ever mindful that the written word or picture is involved, courts have engrafted exceptions and restrictions onto the statute to avoid any conflict with the free dissemination of thoughts, ideas, newsworthy events, and matters of public interest."

In the light of questions that counsel were asked to argue on reargument, it is particularly relevant that the Court of Appeals made crystal clear in the *Spahn* opinion that truth is a complete defense in actions under the statute based upon reports of newsworthy people or events. The opinion states: "The factual reporting of newsworthy persons and events is in the public interest and is protected." Constitutional questions which might arise if truth were not a defense are therefore of no concern....

We find applicable here the standard of knowing or reckless falsehood, not through blind application of *New York Times Co. v. Sullivan*, relating solely to libel actions by public officials, but only upon consideration of the factors which arise in the particular context of the application of the New York statute in cases involving private individuals. This is neither a libel action by a private individual nor a statutory action by a public official. Therefore, although the First Amendment principles pronounced in *New York Times* guide our conclusion, we reach that conclusion only by applying these principles in this discrete context....

II.

Turning to the facts of the present case, the proofs reasonably would support either a jury finding of innocent or merely negligent misstatement by Life, or a finding that Life portrayed the play as a re-enactment of the Hill family's experience reckless of the truth or with actual knowledge that the portrayal was false. The relevant testimony is as follows:

Joseph Hayes, author of the book, also wrote the play. The story theme was inspired by the desire to write about "true crime" and for years before writing the book, he collected newspaper clippings of stories of hostage incidents. His story was not shaped by any single incident, but by several, including incidents which occurred in California, New York, and Detroit. He said that he did not consciously portray any member of the Hill family, or the Hill family's experience, although admitting that "in a very direct way" the Hill experience "triggered" the writing of the book and the play.

The Life article was prepared at the direction and under the supervision of its entertainment editor, Prideaux. He learned of the production of the play from a news story. The play's director, Robert Montgomery, later suggested to him that its interesting stage setting would make the play a worthwhile subject for an article in Life. At about the same time, Prideaux ran into a friend of author Hayes, a free-lance photographer, who told Prideaux in casual conversation that the play had a "substantial connection with a true-life incident of a family being held by escaped convicts near Philadelphia." As the play was trying out in Philadelphia, Prideaux decided to contact the author. Hayes confirmed that an incident somewhat similar to the play had occurred in Philadelphia, and agreed with Prideaux to find out whether the former Hill residence would be available for the shooting of pictures for a Life article. Prideaux then met with Hayes in Philadelphia where he saw the play and drove with Hayes to the former Hill residence to test its suitability for a picture story. Neither then nor thereafter did Prideaux question Hayes about the extent to which the play was based on the Hill incident. "A specific question of that nature was never asked, but a discussion of the play itself, what the play was about, in the light of my own knowledge of what the true incident was about, confirmed in my mind beyond any doubt that there was a relationship, and Mr. Hayes' presence at this whole negotiation was tacit proof of that."

Prideaux sent photographers to the Hill residence for location photographs of scenes of the play enacted in the home, and proceeded to construct the text of the article. In his "story file" were several news clippings about the Hill incident which revealed its nonviolent character, and a New York Times article by Hayes in which he stated that the play "was based on various news stories," mentioning incidents in New York, California, Detroit and Philadelphia.

Prideaux's first draft made no mention of the Hill name except for the caption of one of the photographs. The text related that a true story of a suburban Philadelphia family had "sparked off" Hayes to write the novel, that the play was a "somewhat fictionalized" account of the family's heroism in time of crisis. Prideaux's research assistant, whose task it was to check the draft for accuracy, put a question mark over the words "somewhat fictionalized." Prideaux testified that the question mark "must have been" brought to his attention, although he did not recollect having seen it. The draft was also brought before the copy editor, who, in the presence of Prideaux, made several changes in emphasis and substance. The first sentence was changed to focus on the Hill incident, using the family's name; the novel was said to have been "inspired" by that incident, and the play was referred to as a "re-enactment." The words "somewhat fictionalized" were deleted.

Prideaux labeled as "emphatically untrue" defense counsel's suggestion during redirect examination that from the beginning he knew that the play had no relationship to the Hill incident apart from being a hostage incident. Prideaux admitted that he knew the play was "between a little bit and moderately fictionalized," but stated that he thought beyond doubt that the important quality, the "heart and soul" of the play, was the Hill incident.

The jury might reasonably conclude from this evidence—particularly that the New York Times article was in the story file, that the copy editor deleted "somewhat fictionalized" after the research assistant questioned its accuracy, and that Prideaux admitted that he knew the play was "between a little bit and moderately fictionalized"—that Life knew the falsity of, or was reckless of the truth in, stating in the article that "the story re-enacted" the Hill family's experience. On the other hand, the jury might reasonably predicate a finding of innocent or only negligent misstatement on the testimony that a statement was made to Prideaux by the free-lance photographer that linked the play to an incident in Philadelphia, that the author Hayes cooperated in arranging for the availability of the former Hill home, and that Prideaux thought beyond doubt that the "heart and soul" of the play was the Hill incident.

We do not think, however, that the instructions confined the jury to a verdict of liability based on a finding that the statements in the article were made with knowledge of their falsity or in reckless disregard of the truth. The jury was instructed that liability could not be found under §§ 50–51 "merely because of some incidental mistake of fact, or some incidental incorrect statement," and that a verdict of liability could rest only on findings that (1) Life published the article, "not to disseminate news, but was using plaintiffs' names, in connection with a fictionalized episode as to plaintiffs' relationship to The Desperate Hours"; the Court variously restated this "fictionalization" requirement in terms such as whether appellant "altered or changed the true facts concerning plaintiffs' relationship to The Desperate Hours, so that the article, as published, constituted substantially fiction or a fictionalized version...," whether the article constituted "fiction," or was "fictionalized"; and that (2) the article was published to advertise the play or "for trade purposes." This latter purpose was variously defined as one "to amuse, thrill, astonish or move the reading public so as to increase the circulation of the magazine or for some other material benefit," "to increase circulation or enhance the standing of the magazine with its readers," and "for the publisher's profits through increased circulation, induced by exploitation of the plaintiffs."

The court also instructed the jury that an award of punitive damages was justified if the jury found that the appellant falsely connected appellee to the play "knowingly or through failure to make a reasonable investigation," adding "You do not need to find that there was any actual ill will or personal malice toward the plaintiffs if you find a reckless or wanton disregard of the plaintiffs' rights."

Appellee argues that the instructions to determine whether Life "altered or changed" the true facts, and whether, apart from incidental errors, the article was a "substantial fiction" or a "fictionalized version" were tantamount to instructions that the jury must find that Life knowingly falsified the facts. We do not think that the instructions bear that interpretation, particularly in light of the marked contrast in the instructions on compensatory and punitive damages. The element of "knowingly" is mentioned only in the instruction that punitive damages must be supported by a finding that Life falsely connected the Hill family with the play "knowingly or through failure to make a reasonable investigation."

Moreover, even as to punitive damages, the instruction that such damages were justified on the basis of "failure to make a reasonable investigation" is an instruction that proof of negligent misstatement is enough, and we have rejected the test of negligent misstatement as inadequate. Next, the trial judge plainly did not regard his instructions as limiting the jury to a verdict of liability based on a finding of knowing or reckless falsity; he denied appellant's motion to dismiss after the close of the evidence because he perceived that it was for the jury to find "whether the Life article was true or whether an inference could be obtained from reading it that it was not true." This implies a view that "fictionalization" was synonymous with "falsity" without regard to knowledge or even negligence, except for the purpose of an award of punitive damages. Finally, nothing in the New York cases decided at the time of trial limited liability to cases of knowing or reckless falsity and *Spahn*, decided since, has left the question in doubt.

The requirement that the jury also find that the article was published "for trade purposes," as defined in the charge, cannot save the charge from constitutional infirmity. "That books, newspapers, and magazines are published and sold for profit does not prevent them from being a form of expression whose liberty is safeguarded by the First Amendment." ...

The judgment of the Court of Appeals is set aside and the case is remanded for further proceedings not inconsistent with this opinion.

Polydoros v. Twentieth Century Fox Film Corp.

67 Cal. App. 4th 318 (Ct. App. 2d 1997)

In 1993, respondents released The Sandlot, a comedic coming-of-age story set in the San Fernando Valley in the 1960s. The film's protagonists are a motley group of boys on a sandlot baseball team who, in the course of one summer, overcome various adversaries, including a disdainful, well-funded opposing team and a gigantic, ferocious dog that has taken possession of the team's baseballs and secreted them in a neighboring yard. One of the boys on the sandlot team is a character named Michael Palledorous, nicknamed "Squints." The Palledorous character is one of the team's leaders, and spearheads the team's valiant efforts to reclaim a baseball autographed by Babe Ruth from the slavering canine next door.

Appellant Michael Polydoros grew up in a setting similar to that described in the film. Appellant was a schoolmate of respondent David Mickey Evans. Evans wrote and directed The Sandlot. A photograph of appellant dating from the 1960s is similar to a photograph of the Palledorous character in the movie, right down to appellant's eyeglasses and the color and design of his shirt. Appellant played baseball with friends on a sandlot when he was a child, swam in a community pool like the one shown in the movie, and was somewhat obstreperous, like the "Squints" character. Other than the similarity in names and attire, the enjoyment of baseball and swimming, and the brash nature of the "Squints" character, appellant cannot point to any other aspects in which the film accurately depicts his life. Appellant concedes that the work is fiction. He also concedes that he has not been financially damaged by the motion picture.

Piqued by the similarities in name and by the physical likeness of the "Squints" character to himself as a child, appellant filed suit in March of 1994. The operative pleading asserts causes of action for commercial appropriation of identity, invasion of privacy, negligence and defamation. Appellant alleges that the nickname "Squints" used in the film "is a blatantly derogatory moniker derived from the thick glasses the character wears throughout the film" and that people began teasing appellant by calling him "Squints." Appellant felt "embarrassed and humiliated" by the nickname. To make matters worse, in appellant's view, respondents used the "Squints" Palledorous character as their principal advertising image for the film....

Invasion of privacy claims have been rejected by the courts when there is merely alleged to be some resemblance between an actual person and a character in a work of fiction. In *Aguilar* [*v. Universal City Studios, Inc.*, 174 Cal. App. 3d 384, 219 Cal. Rptr. 891 (1985)], for example, the plaintiff alleged that the movie Zoot Suit (Universal Pictures 1981) invaded her privacy by exposing "unsavory incidents" from her adolescence through the use of a character who shared plaintiff's surname. The court observed that the plaintiff, a grown woman, was not the 13-year-old person shown in the movie, although plaintiff was 13 at the time of the historical incident recreated in the movie. Because there was no consonance between the plaintiff's present age and the movie character's age or physical appearance, and because plaintiff's actual experiences diverged in many respects from those of the character who shared her name, no trier of fact could reasonably draw a connection between the two.

We find particularly compelling the reasoning in the New York case of *People v. Charles Scribner's Sons*, 205 Misc. 818 [130 N.Y.S.2d 514] (1954), which involved the interpretation of a commercial appropriation of likeness statute. The complainant in that case, Joseph A. Maggio, served in the United States Army in Hawaii in the early 1940s in the same Army company as James Jones. Jones thereafter authored a successful book entitled, From Here to Eternity (1951) which was made into a motion picture. The book tells a story about Army personnel stationed in Hawaii in the early 1940s. One of the characters portrayed in the book and film is called "Angelo Maggio" or "Maggio." Despite the obvious similarities in name and his former contact with the author, Maggio did not claim that the story portrayed acts performed by him: "Except for the alleged identity of name, none of the things which the character 'Angelo Maggio' does in the book, nor any of the details of the background and life of 'Angelo Maggio' as set forth in the book, are claimed by the complainant to be a portrayal of him or of his life and do not in any wise point to or identify him as the person intended or referred to." As the court noted, if the author had not chosen the name "Maggio" for his fictional character, "the complainant could not by any stretch of the imagination have implied any identity of the character with himself."

The court rejected the misappropriation of name charge made against the book publisher and the motion picture company. It wrote,

> It is generally understood that novels are written out of the background and experiences of the novelist. The characters portrayed are fictional, but very often they grow out of real persons the author has met or observed. This is so also with respect to the places which are the setting of the novel. The end result may be so fictional as to seem wholly imaginary, but the acorn of fact is usually the progenitor of the oak, which when fully grown no longer has any resemblance to the acorn. In order to disguise the acorn and to preserve the fiction, the novelist disguises the names of the actual persons who inspired the characters in his book. Since a novel is not biography, the details of the character's life and deeds usually have, beyond possible faint outlines, no resemblance to the life and deeds of the actual person known to the author. Thus, the public has come to accept novels as pure fiction and does not attribute their characters to real life.

For the reasons cited in *Aguilar* and *Maggio*, the cases above, appellant cannot state a claim that respondents invaded his privacy by appropriating his name or likeness for commercial purposes. First, there was a marked difference in age and appearance between our appellant, the 40-year-old Michael Polydoros, and the 10-year-old character of Squints Palledorous. No person seeing this film could confuse the two. Second, the rudimentary similarities in locale and boyhood activities do not make The Sandlot a film about appellant's life. This is a universal theme and a concededly fictional film. The faint outlines appellant has seized upon do not transform the fiction into fact.

Film is a "significant medium for the communication of ideas" and, whether exhibited in theaters or on television, is protected by constitutional guarantees of free expression. Popular entertainment is entitled to the same constitutional protection as the exposition of political ideas: "It is clear that works of fiction are constitutionally protected in the same manner as political treatises and topical news stories."

The plaintiff in *Guglielmi* [*v. Spelling-Goldberg Productions*, 25 Cal. 3d 860, 160 Cal. Rptr. 352, 603 P.2d 454 (1979),] was the nephew of deceased silent picture star Rudolph Valentino and had a proprietary interest in the commercial use of Valentino's name and likeness. He sued the defendants after they exhibited a film purporting to recreate a portion of the life of Valentino using Valentino's name, likeness and personality. Plaintiff alleged that the film did not truthfully portray Valentino's life and that Valentino's name and likeness were used to sell or commercially exploit the film for defendants' profit.

At the heart of *Guglielmi* was the fictional nature of the film exhibited by the defendants. Four justices of the Supreme Court agreed that plaintiff was protected by the common law right of publicity. Nevertheless, the context and nature of the defendants' use of Valentino's name and likeness in a *fictional* work of art, even if created *for financial gain*, was protected by the constitutional right to free expression, the justices concluded. They observed, "The First Amendment is not limited to those who publish without charge. Whether the activity involves newspaper publication or motion picture production, it does not lose its constitutional protection because it is undertaken for profit. The fact that respondents sought to profit from the production and exhibition of a film utilizing Valentino's name and likeness is not constitutionally significant."

Guglielmi unequivocally prevents appellant from proceeding on his claim for commercial appropriation of identity. There is no question that The Sandlot is a fanciful work of fiction and imagination. In the movie, the dog next door to the sandlot assumes the proportions of a grizzly bear (having been magnified by the boys' fear); baseball hero Babe Ruth appears and offers advice (notwithstanding Ruth's death some 20 years before the movie takes place); the dog's owner just happens to be a former teammate of Babe Ruth; the "Squints" character fakes his own drowning death in order to sneak a kiss from the pretty female lifeguard, and so on. Appellant does not attempt to suggest that any of this is true or actually happened to him. Because the film is obvious fantasy, appellant could not reasonably suffer injury to his feelings or his peace of mind. This film is not a portrait of appellant's life and reveals no private facts about appellant: His name and former physical appearance are not private facts.

Appellant is especially vexed because respondents used photographs of "his" character in particular to advertise and promote public viewing of The Sandlot. This issue is addressed in *Guglielmi*. A filmmaker's use of photographs of an actor resembling an actual personage to promote a fictional work is "merely an adjunct to the exhibition of the film." "Having established that any interest in financial gain in producing the film did not affect the constitutional stature of respondents' undertaking, it is of no moment that the advertisements may have increased the profitability of the film. It would be illogical to allow respondents to exhibit the film but effectively preclude any advance discussion or promotion of their lawful enterprise. Since the use of Valentino's name and likeness in the film was not an actionable infringement of Valentino's right of publicity, the use of his identity in advertisements for the film is similarly not actionable."

In sum, appellant is not entitled to recover under a commercial appropriation of name or likeness theory merely because respondents used a name that sounds like appellant's name or employed an actor who resembles appellant at the age of 10. Because respondents were creating a fictionalized artistic work, their endeavor is constitutionally protected. This right was not diminished when respondents advertised then sold their work as mass public entertainment. . . .

The judgment is affirmed.

Notes and Questions

a. One of the preliminary questions that must be asked in a defamation or invasion of privacy case is whether the plaintiff was in fact the party depicted, or put another way, whether a reasonable person viewing the work would understand the character depicted was the plaintiff. In *Aguilar v. Universal City Studios, Inc.*, 174 Cal. App. 3d 384, 388 (1985), the California Court of Appeals explained this preliminary step.

> Plaintiff, Bertha Aguilar, claims she is the character "Bertha" and that she is falsely portrayed in the film ["Zoot Suit"] as "a fornicating woman of loose morals." The motion picture "Zoot Suit" is a work of fiction based on the sensational 1942 Sleepy Lagoon murder case and the ensuing "zoot suit" riots.... The screen play was adapted by Luis Valdez from his play of the same name.... The gist of Ms. Aguilar's libel complaint is that the character "Bertha" is depicted as unchaste. This allegation is based on a single reference to "Bertha" which implies she had had sexual relations with another character in the back seat of a car. Ms. Aguilar also contends the film invaded her privacy by exposing "unsavory incidents" from her past....
>
> In order to succeed on any of her causes of action, Ms. Aguilar must first establish she is portrayed in the film "Zoot Suit." The test is whether a reasonable person, viewing the motion picture, would understand the character "Bertha" was, in actual fact, Bertha Aguilar conducting herself as described....
>
> In support of her argument summary judgment was improper Ms. Aguilar makes three points relating to the issue of identity. The film uses the name "Bertha"; Ms. Aguilar was a participant in the Sleepy Lagoon incident; and other persons have concluded she is the character "Bertha." [T]his evidence is insufficient to raise a triable issue as to whether Ms. Aguilar is portrayed in the film....
>
> [A]s a matter of law, mere similarity or even identity of names is insufficient to establish a work of fiction is of and concerning a real person....

There Is No Similarity Between Ms. Aguilar and "Bertha" in Terms of Age or Physical Appearance.

> ... Ms. Aguilar was 13 years of age at the time of the Sleepy Lagoon incident. "Bertha" is not a 13 year-old-girl. Even Ms. Aguilar admits she is "much older than 13." She also admits at the time of the Sleepy Lagoon incident she did not look or dress like "Bertha." ...
>
> Ms. Aguilar's Involvement in the Sleepy Lagoon Incident Bears No Resemblance to the Involvement of "Bertha." Close parallels between real and fictional events may establish a reasonable belief in identity despite the author's efforts to hide the real person through alteration of name or physical appearance....
>
> Finally, there is the uncontradicted testimony of the author, Luis Valdez, he had never heard of Ms. Aguilar until after the play was written. The similarity in names appears to have been purely coincidental....

b. The four distinct privacy torts give rise to a variety of claims. For a discussion on the limited right to be free from prying videotape cameras, see *Sanders v. American Broadcasting Companies,* 20 Cal. 4th 907, 85 Cal. Rptr. 2d 909, 978 P.2d 67 (1999). A key issue in these cases is the newsworthiness of the event being publicly broadcast or presented. The offshoot of privacy torts that has evolved into the right of publicity is treated separately in Chapter 7.

c. Notwithstanding the broad First Amendment protection afforded to novelizations and dramatizations, what steps should be taken by authors, producers, and distributors of these works? How would you recommend a client proceed to develop a fictionalized version of a true story?

d. The courts continue to struggle with the application of the *N.Y. Times v. Sullivan* actual malice standard to intentionally fictionalized material. It is axiomatic that intentionally fictionalized material is knowingly false. If that intentional fictionalization is defamatory about a person, it will be actionable. As *Time v. Hill* and other cases demonstrate, however, many intentional falsehoods are not defamatory, but remain objectionable. To what extent does *N.Y. Times v. Sullivan* continue to shield authors, producers, and distributors from "false light invasion of privacy" when the material is knowingly false? Can Michael Polydoros' claims be reconciled with *Time v. Hill*, or is there a broader shield provided by the First Amendment than that articulated in *Time v. Hill* and *N.Y. Times v. Sullivan*?

e. False light invasion of privacy is often subsumed by defamation analysis. In some states, however, the cause of action remains discrete. With local news stations seeking to make stories more newsworthy than the facts provide, the lead-ins to those stories may be grounds for liability even though the story is more factually accurate. *See Grogan v. KOKH, L.L.C.*, 256 P.3d 1021, 1029 (Okla. App. Div. 2 2011), where a misunderstanding between students and a coach escalated to a lead-in on local television tying the story to terrorism. Such a stretch was capable of creating a false light invasion of privacy.

f. In *Jews For Jesus, Inc. v. Rapp*, 997 So. 2d 1098, 1105 (Fla. 2008), the Florida Supreme Court rejected the tort of false light invasion of privacy as actionable in Florida. It explained that "courts rejecting false light have expressed the following two primary concerns: (1) it is largely duplicative of defamation, both in the conduct alleged and the interests protected, and creates the potential for confusion because many of its parameters, in contrast to defamation, have yet to be defined; and (2) without many of the First Amendment protections attendant to defamation, it has the potential to chill speech without any appreciable benefit to society." In contrast, "Tennessee recognizes the claim of false light invasion of privacy as a cause of action separate and distinct from defamation, to protect the rights of plaintiffs who 'have had attributed to them certain qualities, characteristics, or beliefs that, while not injurious to their reputation, place those persons in an undesirable light.'" *S.E. v. Chmerkovskiy*, 221 F. Supp. 3d 980, 985 (M.D. Tenn. 2016) (quoting *West v. Media Gen. Convergence, Inc.*, 53 S.W.3d 640, 645 (Tenn. 2001)).

g. Notwithstanding constitutional protection, most publishers and producers go to extensive efforts to eliminate risk of litigation by checking names and locations for any possible connections with real persons and by purchasing the right to portray persons involved in the story. While the case law suggests that these portrayal agreements are not necessary, prudence and risk management suggest that motion picture companies, in particular, are often better served by acquiring the releases of those portrayed rather than to rely solely on the constitutional privilege of portraying the events.

Problem 5-C

Bryce stops by your office. (By now you know the problem is worse if Bryce stops in rather than merely calls.) Bryce acknowledges that the idea for *Juliet Prescott*, the Romeo & Juliet concept project, came to Bryce after learning that a sixteen-year-old classmate, Julie, had become pregnant by a boy of another race. Only a few students knew of Julie's pregnancy; Bryce only found out accidentally while waiting at the doctor's office. Bryce does not want to cancel or rewrite the play but is concerned about being liable to Julie. Please advise Bryce regarding the legal implications of the play for Julie and any legal recourse she may have.

D. Communications Decency Act Changes to Common Law Privacy and Defamation

The Communications Decency Act of 1996 (CDA) was an attempt by Congress to censor the Internet regarding its obscene and pornographic content. In *Reno v. ACLU*, 521 U.S. 844 (1997), most of these regulations were found to be unconstitutional.

The most important provision of the CDA that survived constitutional challenge is 47 U.S.C. §230, which was designed to provide civil immunity for private blocking and screening of offensive material. Section 230(c) provides the following:

(c) **Protection for "Good Samaritan" blocking and screening of offensive material**

(1) Treatment of publisher or speaker—No provider or user of an interactive computer service shall be treated as the publisher or speaker of any information provided by another information content provider.

(2) Civil liability—No provider or user of an interactive computer service shall be held liable on account of—(A) any action voluntarily taken in good faith to restrict access to or availability of material that the provider or user considers to be obscene, lewd, lascivious, filthy, excessively violent, harassing, or otherwise objectionable, whether or not such material is constitutionally protected; or (B) any action taken to enable or make available to information content providers or others the technical means to restrict access to material described [in subparagraph A]....

(e) **Effect on other laws**

(1) No effect on criminal law—Nothing in this section shall be construed to impair the enforcement of section 223 or 231 of this title, chapter 71 (relating to obscenity) or 110 (relating to sexual exploitation of children) of Title 18, or any other Federal criminal statute.

(2) No effect on intellectual property law—Nothing in this section shall be construed to limit or expand any law pertaining to intellectual property.

(3) State law—Nothing in this section shall be construed to prevent any State from enforcing any State law that is consistent with this section. No cause of action may be brought and no liability may be imposed under any State or local law that is inconsistent with this section.

47 U.S.C. § 230(c), (e) (2018).

Section 230(c)(1) has the purpose of reversing the common law rule regarding the republication of a defamatory statement or a statement that would result in an invasion of privacy. Based on the purpose of promoting the quickly growing Internet economy, Congress did not wish to see these new platforms overwhelmed with litigation costs related to content posted by third parties. "Absent § 230, a person who published or distributed speech over the Internet could be held liable for defamation even if he or she was not the author of the defamatory text, and, indeed, at least with regard to publishers, even if unaware of the statement." *Batzel v. Smith*, 333 F.3d 1018, 1026–30 (9th Cir. 2003) (superseded on other grounds, *Breazeale v. Victim Services, Inc.*, 878 F.3d 759 (9th Cir. 2017)).

Section 230(c)(2) was designed to give these ISPs the ability to utilize professional editorial discretion to remove harmful content without being liable to the parties who posted the material for trying to self-police the content posted online. Section 230(c)(2) is furthered by end user license agreements and terms of service agreements that give the ISPs wide latitude regarding the nature of the content they choose to allow on their systems.

> The statute does not use ISP. Instead it uses the defined term, interactive computer service. The term "interactive computer service" means any information service, system, or access software provider that provides or enables computer access by multiple users to a computer server, including specifically a service or system that provides access to the Internet and such systems operated or services offered by libraries or educational institutions.

47 U.S.C. § 230(f)(2).

The content host loses its immunity from tort liability if it publishes the content that is the subject of the litigation as the information content provider—or author—of the content. "The term "information content provider" means any person or entity that is responsible, in whole or in part, for the creation or development of information provided through the Internet or any other interactive computer service." 47 U.S.C. § 230(f)(3).

> In passing section 230, Congress sought to spare interactive computer services this grim choice by allowing them to perform some editing on user-generated content without thereby becoming liable for all defamatory or otherwise unlawful messages that they didn't edit or delete. In other words, Congress sought to immunize the removal of user-generated content, not the creation of content ... One of the specific purposes of this section is to overrule *Strat-*

ton Oakmont v. Prodigy[15] and any other similar decisions which have treated such providers ... as publishers or speakers of content that is not their own because they have restricted access to objectionable material.

Fair Hous. Council of San Fernando Valley v. Roommates.Com, L.L.C., 521 F.3d 1157, 1163 (9th Cir. 2008) (quoting H.R. REP. No. 104-458 (1996) (Conf. Rep.), reprinted in 1996 U.S.C.C.A.N. 10).

The purpose of § 230 has been readily recognized by courts, and it is generally afforded a broad interpretation to discourage litigation. Nonetheless, the tension between the service provider's role as content host and its role as author or developer of online content creates an inherent tension for some services.

> A website operator can simultaneously act as both a service provider and a content provider. If a website displays content that is created entirely by third parties, then it is only a service provider with respect to that content — and thus is immune from claims predicated on that content. But if a website operator is in part responsible for the creation or development of content, then it is an information content provider as to that content — and is not immune from claims predicated on it. Thus, a website may be immune from liability for some of the third-party content it publishes but be subject to liability for the content that it is responsible for as a creator or developer. In short, immunity under the CDA depends on the pedigree of the content at issue. Aware of this limit on § 230 immunity, courts have recognized that § 230 bars a claim if (1) the defendant asserting immunity is an interactive computer service provider, (2) the particular information at issue was provided by another information content provider, and (3) the claim seeks to treat the defendant as a publisher or speaker of that information. By contrast, a defendant is not entitled to protection from claims based on the publication of information if the defendant is "responsible, in whole or in part, for the creation or development of [the] information." 47 U.S.C. § 230(f)(3).

Jones v. Dirty World Entm't Recordings L.L.C., 755 F.3d 398, 406–09 (6th Cir. 2014).

Because the statute provides immunity from liability, there is no statutory scheme that requires a service provider to request the removal of offensive content. This stands in contrast to content that a copyright owner believes has been posted in a manner that infringes the copyright of the work. Section 230(e)(2) specifically exempts intellectual property claims from the scope of the CDA's immunity.

Nonetheless, service provides do need to address violations of criminal law and violations of intellectual property laws. There are also strong business reasons for taking advantage of the Good Samaritan aspects of § 230(c)(2) to remove offensive content, so many service providers employ mechanisms that allows those who may have been harmed by third party content to request that it be removed. Most of these processes

---

15. Stratton Oakmont, Inc. v. Prodigy Servs. Co., 1995 WL 323710 (N.Y. Sup. Ct. May 24, 1995).

follow the rules provided under copyright law, so the steps for removing content are similar to those provided under § 512 of the Digital Millennium Copyright Act.

Notes and Questions

a. On the site TheDirty.com, submissions are uploaded directly by third-party users. Under this depiction of the site, does it retain immunity under § 230?

> The content submission form instructs users to "Tell us what's happening. Remember to tell us who, what, when, where, why." The content submission form requires users to submit a title and category for their submission as well as their city or college for indexing. Submissions appear on the website as though they were authored by a single, anonymous author—"THE DIRTY ARMY." This eponymous introduction is automatically added to every post that Richie receives from a third-party user. Many, but not all, of the submissions and commentaries appearing on the website relate to stories, news, and gossip about local individuals who are not public figures. The site receives thousands of new submissions each day. Richie or his staff selects and edits approximately 150 to 200 submissions for publication each day. The editing done to published submissions only consists of deletion. Richie or his staff briefly reviews each submission selected for publication to ensure that nudity, obscenity, threats of violence, profanity, and racial slurs are removed. Richie typically adds a short, one-line comment about the post with "some sort of humorous or satirical observation." Richie, however, does not materially change, create, or modify any part of the user-generated submission, nor does he fact-check submissions for accuracy.

Jones, 755 F.3d at 402–03.

b. Other courts have looked at how submission forms create editorial control. In a case where the defendant was accused of creating a rental market screening system that violated state and federal fair housing laws, the court explained the process:

> [T]he part of the profile that is alleged to offend the Fair Housing Act and state housing discrimination laws—the information about sex, family status and sexual orientation—is provided by subscribers in response to [Romate.com's] questions, which they cannot refuse to answer if they want to use defendant's services. By requiring subscribers to provide the information as a condition of accessing its service, and by providing a limited set of pre-populated answers, Roommate becomes much more than a passive transmitter of information provided by others; it becomes the developer, at least in part, of that information.

Fair Hous. Council of San Fernando Valley v. Roommates.Com, L.L.C., 521 F.3d 1157, 1166 (9th Cir. 2008).

c. The Supreme Court has upheld a long tradition of adding First Amendment protection to anonymous speech. At the same time, the protections of the CDA, when combined with protections for anonymous speech, would result in defamation and invasion of privacy that has the potential to be intentional, harmful and false. As a result, courts have to balance the competing interests of a speaker's right to speak anonymously with an individual's right to privacy and to be free from tortious defamation. Tests on whether to allow a subpoena of a service provider range from a simple good faith test to complex, multi-part procedural requirements and substantive evidence of success on the merits. *Solers, Inc. v. Doe*, 977 A.2d 941, 954 (D.C. 2009), provides such an example:

> When presented with a motion to quash (or to enforce) a subpoena which seeks the identity of an anonymous defendant, the court should: (1) ensure that the plaintiff has adequately pleaded the elements of the defamation claim, (2) require reasonable efforts to notify the anonymous defendant that the complaint has been filed and the subpoena has been served, (3) delay further action for a reasonable time to allow the defendant an opportunity to file a motion to quash, (4) require the plaintiff to proffer evidence creating a genuine issue of material fact on each element of the claim that is within its control, and (5) determine that the information sought is important to enable the plaintiff to proceed with his lawsuit.

See Thomson v. Doe, 189 Wash. App. 45, 52, 356 P.3d 727, 731 (Wash. Ct. App. 2015); *Doe No. 1 v. Cahill*, 884 A.2d 451, 456 (Del. 2005); *Dendrite Int'l, Inc. v. Doe No. 3*, 342 N.J. Super. 134, 140, 775 A.2d 756 (2001).

d. More than two decades after the CDA rewrote the common law of defamation and privacy, perhaps one or the other of the regimes is in need of updating. Why should a physical bookstore chain have a different obligation to police its shelves than an online service provider? For example, to what extent should content deemed outside the First Amendment (such as content already determined by a court to be defamatory or an invasion of privacy) be subject to a takedown requirement?

Problem 5-D

Bryce calls you at your office. An unknown person has posted on Facebook and Instagram statements about the upcoming play that allege Bryce is involved only to steal money from the cast members and the public. These statements are untrue and deeply hurtful to Bryce. Members of the cast are considering pulling out of the production. Bryce does not know who posted the statements. What are Bryce's options to have the offending content removed from the service providers? In addition, to what extent can Bryce bring a defamation action against the service providers or the individuals who posted the offending content?

E. Bibliography and Links

Josh Blackman, *Omniveillance, Google, Privacy in Public, and the Right to Your Digital Identity: A Tort for Recording and Disseminating an Individual's Image Over the Internet*, 49 SANTA CLARA L. REV. 313 (2009).

David A. Elder, *Truth, Accuracy and Neutral Reportage: Beheading the Media Jabberwock's Attempts to Circumvent New York Times v. Sullivan*, 9 VAND. J. ENT. & TECH. L. 551 (2007).

Lawrence M. Friedman, *The One-Way Mirror: Law, Privacy, and the Media*, 82 WASH. U. L.Q. 319 (2004).

Jon M. Garon, *Tidying up the Internet: Take Down of Unauthorized Content under Copyright, Trademark and Defamation Law*, 41 CAPITAL U. L. REV. 513 (2013).

Jon M. Garon, *Star Wars: Film Permitting, Prior Restraint and Government's Role in the Entertainment Industry*, 17 LOYOLA ENT. L. J. 1 (1996).

Joseph H. King, *Defamation Claims Based on Parody and Other Fanciful Communications Not Intended to Be Understood As Fact*, 2008 UTAH L. REV. 875 (2008).

David Kohler, *Forty Years after New York Times v. Sullivan: The Good, the Bad, and the Ugly*, 83 OR. L. REV. 1203 (2004).

Laura E. Little, *Just A Joke: Defamatory Humor and Incongruity's Promise*, 21 S. CAL. INTERDISC. L.J. 95 (2011).

William L. Prosser, *Privacy*, 48 CAL. L. REV. 383 (1960) (articulating the four distinct branches of privacy).

George P. Smith, *The Extent of Protection of the Individual's Personality against Commercial Use: Toward a New Property Right*, 54 S.C.L. REV. 1 (Fall 2002).

Samuel D. Warren & Louis D. Brandeis, *The Right to Privacy*, 4 HARV. L. REV. 193 (1890) (the law review article which originated or discovered the right of privacy).

Websites

Federal Communications Commission, www.fcc.gov

Media Watch, www.mediawatch.com (a website dedicated to fighting censorship in the media, discusses current cases against the media)

Privacy Rights.Org, www.privacyrights.org

Chapter 6

Trademarks

A. Overview[1]

1. Subject Matter of Trademark Law

Trademarks are the most visible form of intellectual property used by businesses, dating back to the origins of commercial trade. In both Europe and Asia, archeologists have identified the practices of artisans, smiths, and others identifying the source of their goods with marks or engraved names. Through these marks, consumers knew who was responsible for the quality of a product. A successful vendor could expand his business through his reputation. In the alternative, the family members of a blacksmith's unfortunate customer could seek appropriate revenge if a poorly forged sword broke in battle and led to its owner's untimely demise. Throughout the law, business and this text, the word "mark" encompasses all forms of trademarks, service marks, collective marks, and certification marks.

From their origins, trademarks are fundamentally different than patents or copyrights because trademarks were conceived as protecting the public rather than the user of the trademark. Although this distinction has blurred under modern American jurisprudence, the fundamental difference in emphasis explains a great deal about the evolution of trademark law and protection.

"A trademark is a brand name. A trademark or service mark includes any word, name, symbol, device, or any combination, used or intended to be used to identify and distinguish the goods/services of one seller or provider from those of others, and to indicate the source of the goods/services."[2] A trademark is very context-specific. For example, "apple" is the generic name for a fruit but also serves as a valid trademark for a grocery store chain, a record label, and a computer manufacturer. The grocery store chain has nothing to do with the computer company, which illustrates that the scope of a trademark is shaped by public perceptions of the trademark and the scope of the company's activities.

---

1. Adapted from JON M. GARON, THE ENTREPRENEUR'S INTELLECTUAL PROPERTY AND BUSINESS HANDBOOK (Manegiare Pub. 2018).

2. *Trademark Basics*, U.S. PATENT & TRADEMARK OFFICE, https://www.uspto.gov/trademarks-getting-started/trademark-basics (last visited July 10, 2018).

The laws of trademark block third parties from using a trademark in a manner that interferes with the public's interest not to be confused regarding the source of goods or services. Trademarks differ from copyrights and patents because they are not considered personal property. For example, if a new company selected the name Apple Software, it would be likely to confuse the public, so Apple (the computer and consumer electronics company) would be successful if it were to bring a lawsuit against this new company. In contrast, if a tree nursery was to adopt the name Apple Fruit Trees, then Apple would be unlikely to prove the public was confused by the association with the word apple.

The explanation that treats trademarks as having no personal property rights attached tends to understate the property interests companies have in their trademarks. Changes in U.S. law that permit applications to protect trademarks before they are used, along with state and federal law protecting the trademark from dilution, disparagement, or tarnishment, all reflect the property interests held by the trademark holder. As a result, trademarks are better considered to have both property and consumer protection aspects, rather than to be wholly lumped into one category or another.

2. Sources of Legal Protection from Both State and Federal Law

The U.S. Constitution provides federal power for copyright and patent legislation because such laws need to be uniform throughout the country. Congress, nearly a century after providing federal protection for copyright and patent legislation, provided the same protections for trademarks. The initial effort failed. In 1879, an attempt to create national trademark laws was struck down as beyond the power of Congress.[3] Congress responded by restructuring the law to focus on goods in interstate commerce, an area that it had constitutional authority to regulate. This resulted in the first successful federal law to be enacted in 1881, but which regulated only interstate use of trademarks and left states free to regulate trademarks used exclusively within a state.

The result of this trademark history is a two-tiered system of trademark protection. State law can protect trademarks used only within that state, while federal law protects the interstate use of trademarks. In recent years, however, the Internet has undermined the core of this distinction, causing geographically diverse and highly local businesses to run into customer confusion on the Internet.

In addition, because trademark protection relies primarily on the use in commerce of the trademark, actual usage is more important than registration at either the state or federal level. To assert trademark priority, a business must show it used the trademark first.

---

3. *In re* Trade-Mark Cases, 100 U.S. 82 (1879).

3. Benefits of Federal Trademark Registration

The registration and filing processes reinforce the central axiom that the business which first uses a trademark in commerce has priority to use that trademark and to stop others from making use of that trademark in a manner likely to confuse the public. In this way, the federal trademark system builds upon the common law and state law system to create a national clearinghouse for trademarks used in the United States.

To encourage use of the federal system, Congress has created incentives for participation in the federal regime. Federal trademark protection is preferable to state trademark protection because it has a much broader geographic scope. The USPTO lists other benefits as well:

- A legal presumption of your ownership of the mark and your exclusive right to use the mark nationwide ...;
- Public notice of your claim of ownership of the mark;
- Listing in the USPTO's online databases;
- The ability to record the U.S. registration with U.S. Customs and Border Protection to prevent importation of infringing foreign goods;
- The right to use the federal registration symbol "®";
- The ability to bring an action concerning the mark in federal court; and
- The use of U.S. registration as a basis to obtain registration in foreign countries.[4]

The benefits are procedural in nature. The existence of trademark protection flows from the use of a mark in commerce rather than a particular state or federal filing.

4. A Trademark Must Be Distinctive

At the heart of trademark is the obligation that the trademark be distinctive. The very definition of a trademark provides that the purpose of the use of the mark is "to identify and distinguish his or her goods, including a unique product, from those manufactured or sold by others and to indicate the source of the goods, even if that source is unknown."[5]

The distinctiveness or distinguishing characteristic of the trademark must establish a one-to-one relationship between the manufacturer and the product. If two companies both use the same trademark on similar products, then the public will not know which company provided the good, and the mark cannot be used. The level of distinctiveness turns on the creativity of the mark adopted and the association made by the public.

---

4. *Basic Facts About Trademarks: Protecting Your Trademark, Enhancing Your Rights Through Federal Registration* 11 U.S. PATENT & TRADEMARK OFFICE (May 2016), https://www.uspto.gov/sites/default/files/documents/BasicFacts.pdf.

5. 15 U.S.C. § 1127 (2018).

Under longstanding law and tradition, there are "four different categories of terms with respect to trademark protection.... These classes are (1) generic, (2) descriptive, (3) suggestive and (4) arbitrary or fanciful."[6] Generic terms can never be trademarks, while arbitrary or fanciful marks with few exceptions can always be used as trademarks. Suggestive, arbitrary, or fanciful marks are entitled to trademark protection without direct evidence that the public associate the trademark with particular goods. For example, "squirrel" is an arbitrary name for computer software and thus would be available to use as a product name unless it is in use by another party. In contrast, "squirrel" would be generic for squirrel cages, just as "software" would be generic for software. A fanciful mark is different than an arbitrary mark because it is invented by the owner. Alternatively, "squirrel" might be suggestive of a children's toy collection of plastic nuts.

As one leading court opinion observed,

> [t]he category of "suggestive" marks was spawned by the felt need to accord protection to marks that were neither exactly descriptive on the one hand nor truly fanciful on the other.... A term is suggestive if it requires imagination, thought and perception to reach a conclusion as to the nature of goods. A term is descriptive if it forthwith conveys an immediate idea of the ingredients, qualities or characteristics of the goods....[7]

The goal of companies launching new products is to have a trademark that associates the product with the attributes that the manufacturer hopes will promote the item, making the item more relevant to consumers. Suggestive marks are often selected to reinforce the attribute that the seller is hoping to promote. For example, the trademark "Sleep Comfort Adjustable Beds" provides a rather descriptive appellation of the feature that such a mattress should provide. Tempur-Pedic, a registered trademark, alludes to the temperature control attribute and orthopedic benefits of the bed. The USPTO did not find the name Tempur-Pedic too descriptive for trademark registration. Another competitor, Angelbeds, uses an even more suggestive allusion to the bed's lightness of the touch.

5. Secondary Meaning and Acquired Distinctiveness

If a mark is not distinctive when first used, it may become distinctive by its association with the goods over time. Generic words, however, can never become trademarks. "Bed" could never be used as the trademark for a bed. Descriptive words, in contrast, may become distinctive through ongoing usage, if the usage is "exclusive and continuous" for a period of five years. So, if only one company is using a descriptive word or phrase for its product, then that company may gain trademark rights over it.

A term which is descriptive ... may, through usage by one producer with reference to his product, acquire a special significance so that to the consuming public the

---

6. Abercrombie & Fitch Co. v. Hunting World, Inc., 537 F.2d 4, 9–10 (2d Cir. 1976).
7. *Id.* at 10–11 (internal quotations and citations omitted).

word has come to mean that the product is produced by that particular manufacturer.... This is what is known as secondary meaning.

The crux of the secondary meaning doctrine is that the mark comes to identify not only the goods but the source of those goods. To establish secondary meaning, it must be shown that the *primary* significance of the term in the minds of the consuming public is not the product but the producer (citations omitted). This may be an anonymous producer, since consumers often buy goods without knowing the personal identity or actual name of the manufacturer.[8]

To establish that a mark has acquired distinctiveness in the marketplace and is no longer merely descriptive, the business using the mark may rely on evidence of acquired distinctiveness by showing the consumer's knowledge of the mark as well as by verifying the substantially exclusive and continuous use of the mark for a period of five years. In addition, the existence of federal trademark registration of the mark for other goods sold by the business may substantiate the claim of distinctiveness.

Survey evidence, market research and consumer reaction studies may be useful in showing the acquired distinctiveness of a mark. Other factors demonstrating distinctiveness of a mark include the length of time the mark has been used, the advertising expenditures invested in promoting the mark, the care in which the words were used as a trademark, affidavits and declarations by knowledgeable individuals regarding the use of the mark, and other evidence that helps establish the mark's role as a unique, exclusive identifier of the goods. These rules parallel the manner in which a business should promote and manage its trademarks.

6. A Trademark Owner Must Be First in Priority

Because trademark law was historically based on actual usage, the party using the mark in association with the goods has priority over other users. But a priority does not equate to a monopoly. Businesses may often select the same marks, totally unaware of other users of the name in other markets.

To set national notice standards, the federal application process provides a single, national registry. If a company federally registers its trademark, then the entire country is put on constructive notice of the registration. With a federally registered trademark, no one can rely on their lack of knowledge about a potential competitor's use of the same trademark. The "innocent user" defense is blocked from the date of application on the federal register. As a result, the registrant of a federal trademark cannot find itself facing a claim that another company began using the trademark in another state after the date of the federal registration.

A federal trademark registration can only be made if the registration does not interfere with the rights of other trademark holders. A company cannot receive federal

---

8. U.S. Patent & Trademark Office, Trademark Manual of Examination Procedures § 1212 (Oct. 2017), https://tmep.uspto.gov/RDMS/TMEP/current#/current/TMEP-1200d1e10316.html (quoting Ralston Purina Co. v. Thomas J. Lipton, Inc., 341 F. Supp. 129, 133 (S.D.N.Y. 1972)).

trademark registration for a mark that resembles another mark—whether registered or not—that is likely to cause consumer confusion, cause mistake, or otherwise deceive the public. This limitation of consumer confusion is at the heart of trademark practice.

The examination process of the federal trademark application is designed to assure the examiner that the use of the requested mark does not infringe the use of any other trademark holder, so as to eliminate the likelihood of consumer confusion.

Once a trademark is used, particularly if it is federally registered, the trademark owner has an obligation to enforce the trademark against others using the mark. In most situations, when a third party adopts aspects of a company's trademark, it is done without the company realizing the situation. Once the two companies are aware of each other, however, action must be taken. Failure to police the trademark will undermine the trademark owner's obligation to use the mark exclusively, as required by both state and federal law. If the trademark owner allows others to use the trademark without taking any action, the exclusivity is lost and the trademark rights may be destroyed.

7. Junior Users and Other Limitations

The senior user is the first business to adopt the trademark and is therefore the party with priority. A junior user is the business adopting the trademark subsequently. A junior user cannot generally gain the right to use a trademark if it knowingly adopted the trademark of another party. Instead, the law only protects the innocent junior user from losing the investment it has made in its name and the public's interest in identifying the sources of goods. This limited junior protection provides another strong incentive for the senior user to "police" the mark, being careful to let potential junior users know that the trademark is used by a senior user and that the junior use is not permitted.

> [J]unior users, parties who use a mark subsequent to another's use, may retain rights. If the use predates the senior user's [federal] registration, then the [Federal Trademark] Act provides a defense if the mark "was adopted without knowledge of the registrant's prior use and has been continuously used by such party ... from a date prior to ... registration of the mark...."[9]

The geographic scope of the junior user's trademark is typically determined by the nature of the business practices that existed prior to the trademark dispute. In the case of Peaches Records, for example, the Louisiana record store was permitted to operate in the seven-parish region where it sold its records, while the owner of the federally registered trademark in Peaches could sell its records in stores everywhere in the United States other than those seven parishes in Louisiana. A similar dispute between New York's Patsy's Pizzeria and Patsy's Italian Restaurant suggests that the

---

9. Peaches Entm't Corp. v. Entm't Repertoire Assocs., 62 F.3d 690, 692 (5th Cir. 1995) (quoting 15 U.S.C. §1115(b)(5)).

boroughs of New York are sufficiently geographically distinct as to be separated for trademark purposes.

In addition, the failure of the senior trademark holder to police the trademark can sometimes result in a claim of "laches," meaning that the court may choose not to allow the trademark owner to bring a claim if the claim should have been brought in a timely fashion years earlier. If the passage of time has prejudiced the junior user, and the senior user was at fault for not taking action, then the court will not allow the senior user to exercise its rights. Such a determination is at the discretion of the court, but it is a risk that the senior trademark owner should not take.

8. Use of Surnames

Although the use of surnames in business has been common throughout history, the use of a person's name is not a strong trademark strategy. The law provides that trademark registration may be denied if the mark is primarily considered merely a surname. The right to use one's surname as a trademark would preclude many others with the same name from conducting business using their own names. This restraint on a person's livelihood is highly intrusive and should occur only if the public would be greatly confused or misled by the use of a junior surname. McDonald's may be the best example of a surname that should not be used by a second individual to operate a fast-food restaurant. Few other restaurant names, however, should be owned by an individual to the exclusion of others bearing the same name.

Surnames can develop into trademarks. Names have the benefit of being arbitrary as applied to most goods. Retailers with names such as Macy's, JCPenney, Bloomingdale's, and Woolworths all bear little relation between the name and the service. To develop into trademarks, however, the demonstration of longstanding use and acquired secondary meaning must be strong enough to overcome the burden exclusivity would create for others with a similar surname.

Words that double as surnames require additional analysis. Since there are many individuals whose surnames are common words, whether spelled the same or not, the law requires that the limitation on surnames focus on those which are "primarily" surnames. King, Queen, Cotton, Wolf, Fox, Powers and Lane are examples of relatively common surnames that have obvious English language usage. For this category, the trademark office will look at whether the selection is used as a surname or as its English language meaning in determining the eligibility to receive the trademark registration. Names such as Jones, Smith, Rodriguez, Garcia, Liu, Patel, and Eng are all very common names that have no English language usage, so they are always treated as surnames.

Because marks are looked at as a whole, a hyphenated surname such as Hewlett-Packard will be less likely to be treated as a surname. While the question remains whether the public will perceive the name as a surname, as a general statement, the public is less likely to do so. In contrast, if the person seeking to register the trademark goes by a hyphenated name, then the examiner is more likely to treat the name as merely a surname and deny registration.

9. Unfair Competition as a Broader Alternative

It is important for the trademark owner to remember that the goal of federal trademark law is primarily to protect the public from confusion and to stop fraudulent or unfair competition. Section 43(a) of the trademark law creates broad protection for registered and unregistered trademark owners alike to stop competitors from misleading the public by "palming off" one's own products as the products of another party.

> (a) (1) Any person who, on or in connection with any goods or services, or any container for goods, uses in commerce any word, term, name, symbol, or device, or any combination thereof, or any false designation of origin, false or misleading description of fact, or false or misleading representation of fact, which—
>
> > (A) is likely to cause confusion, or to cause mistake, or to deceive as to the affiliation, connection, or association of such person with another person, or as to the origin, sponsorship, or approval of his or her goods, services, or commercial activities by another person, or
> >
> > (B) in commercial advertising or promotion, misrepresents the nature, characteristics, qualities, or geographic origin of his or her or another person's goods, services, or commercial activities,
>
> shall be liable in a civil action by any person who believes that he or she is or is likely to be damaged by such act.[10]

The law does not restrict itself to federally registered trademarks, so legal protection can extend to surnames, nicknames, and phrases. Similarly, it extends to the goods and services themselves, as well as to the packaging and advertising of those goods and services. To maintain a legal action under § 43(a), the trademark use must be false or misleading, and it must be likely to confuse or deceive the public. If these two elements can be established, then the court is likely to protect the senior user of the mark, regardless of the status of registration.

10. Service Marks, Collective Marks, and Certification Marks

In addition to trademarks, marks are used in a number of other situations. A service mark is a mark used for services rather than for goods, or more specifically, "to identify and distinguish the services of one person, including a unique service, from the services of others and to indicate the source of the services, even if that

---

10. U.S. Patent & Trademark Office, U.S. Trademark Law: Rules of Practice & Federal Statutes 232 (2019), https://www.uspto.gov/sites/default/files/documents/tmlaw.pdf; 15 U.S.C. § 1125 (2018) (referred to as § 43(a) of the Lanham Trademark Act).

source is unknown."[11] Service marks have essentially the same relation to services that trademarks have to goods, and the rules are the same for both.

Certification marks range from the "union label" to approvals by Underwriters Laboratory, Better Business Bureau, or other voluntary quality assurance systems. A "certification mark" represents any mark used "to certify regional or other origin, material, mode of manufacture, quality, accuracy, or other characteristics of such person's goods or services or that the work or labor on the goods or services was performed by members of a union or other organization."[12] The owner of the certification mark is typically a union, trade association, or certifying agency. Those owners must manage the certification mark like most trademark owners. Other certification marks are assertions of fact. "Idaho Potatoes" may be used by any potato farmer in Idaho, but not by a potato farmer outside the state.

For those parties acting under the auspices of the certification mark, the mark owner will likely have contractual obligations regarding the conduct of the business and the use of the mark. Those contractual obligations or rules are controlled by the agreement between the certification mark owner and the business being certified.

A collective mark is somewhat different than the certification. A collective mark is "used by the members of a cooperative, an association, or other collective group or organization" such as fraternities, trade associations, and Indian tribes.[13] For example, North-Eastern Band of Cherokee Indians is a collective mark designating membership, as is United Way. The collective mark shows affiliation rather than approval. Chapters of loosely affiliated national organizations are the most common example of collective marks. Of course, some marks may serve both roles, acknowledging the membership in an organization that also sets high minimum competency standards.

Collective marks are a form of service mark, while certification marks may be applied to either goods or services. The rules applying to trademarks for goods apply in the same way for service marks for services.

B. Dilution and Disparagement

Although traditional trademark law has focused on protecting the consumer rather than the property interests of the trademark owner, the doctrines of dilution and disparagement recognize that there are property interests at issue for certain trademarks, particularly highly prominent and publicly recognized marks. As the Supreme Court has explained, "[u]nlike traditional infringement law, the prohibitions against trademark dilution are not the product of common-law development, and are not motivated by an interest in protecting consumers."[14]

---

11. U.S. Patent & Trademark Office, *supra* at 240.
12. 15 U.S.C. § 1127 (2018).
13. *Id.*
14. Moseley v. V Secret Catalogue, Inc., 537 U.S. 418, 429 (2003).

1. Dilution

Certain highly renowned trademarks are so well known that the use of those trademarks in unrelated fields would tend to associate those fields with the senior user's trademark. Failure to provide legal redress in this situation could result in the "dilution" of that mark; it would become associated with a broader range of goods or services. Tiffany lamps, Rolls-Royce cars, and similar elite trademarks are the most obvious examples where this concern exists.

The consequence of protecting trademarks from dilution is to greatly expand the power of the trademark owner. Various states have protected trademarks from dilution since 1925, but only in recent times has the federal statute added dilution to the range of rights protected.

The Federal Trademark Dilution Revision Act provides:

> Subject to the principles of equity, the owner of a famous mark that is distinctive, inherently or through acquired distinctiveness, shall be entitled to an injunction against another person who, at any time after the owner's mark has become famous, commences use of a mark or trade name in commerce that is likely to cause dilution by blurring or dilution by tarnishment of the famous mark, regardless of the presence or absence of actual or likely confusion, of competition, or of actual economic injury.[15]

Federal law places a few limitations on dilution protection. First, the language of the statute itself provides three situations where the use of another company's famous trademark does not interfere with that company's rights. Those three exclusions are "[a]ny fair use, including a nominative or descriptive fair use," "news reporting and news commentary," and "noncommercial use" of the famous mark.[16] These limitations are of a fair use and free speech nature, so they will generally be read into the law of most states as well, though the precise scope of the law's application may still vary from state to state.

In this context, fair use is further expanded to be a use "other than as a designation of source for the person's own goods or services"[17] and to permit uses "in connection with—(i) advertising or promotion that permits consumers to compare goods or services; or (ii) identifying and parodying, criticizing, or commenting upon the famous mark owner or the goods or services of the famous mark owner."[18]

Unlike situations in which a famous trademark is parodied or referenced, the Supreme Court suggests that a direct use of a famous mark in a commercial context may be stopped on far less evidence. The Court referenced statements in the hearings on the new law that "the use of DUPONT shoes, BUICK aspirin, and KODAK pianos

---

15. 15 U.S.C. § 1125(c)(1).
16. 15 U.S.C. § 1125(c)(3).
17. *Id.*
18. *Id.*

would be actionable under this legislation."[19] These congressional statements suggest little evidence is needed when famous marks are duplicated by unauthorized junior users. Entrepreneurs must therefore exercise caution in developing and adopting trademarks if they utilize the famous marks of other companies, even if those companies do not conduct business involving the goods or services of the entrepreneur's new business.

2. Disparagement or Tarnishment

Disparagement or tarnishment represents another property-like interest in the trademark. Disparagement protection provides the trademark owner tools to stop misuse of a company's trademark in a manner that may bring the trademark into disrepute. A popular t-shirt which showed the word "Cocaine" written in the trademarked Coca-Cola script illustrates the nature of tarnishment that companies try to stop. Toy manufactures and children's media often face unauthorized use by adult-oriented businesses trying to use the association for attention and the juxtaposition for humor, but at the expense of the family-oriented business. The law is generally quite supportive of the efforts to stop these adult-only tarnishing uses. Courts are somewhat more respectful of parody and free speech concerns when the tarnishment is less salacious or the trademarks protect less wholesome goods.

Tarnishment, in turn, is defined as "association arising from the similarity between a mark or trade name and a famous mark that harms the reputation of the famous mark,"[20] which allows for a legal cause of action even in the absence of "confusion, of competition, or of actual economic injury."[21]

Despite some limitations on dilution, the 2006 statute has continued to expand the power of trademark anti-tarnishment laws. Courts are highly protective of the trademark holders under the tarnishment law, much more than with general dilution actions or likelihood of confusion claims for non-famous marks. As the court in *V Secret Catalogue, Inc. v. Moseley* explained, "the new Act creates a kind of rebuttable presumption, or at least a very strong inference, that a new mark used to sell sex related products is likely to tarnish a famous mark if there is a clear semantic association between the two."[22]

Blurring is a more complex analysis, much more typical of a trademark infringement action. The statute provides the following:

In determining whether a mark or trade name is likely to cause dilution by blurring, the court may consider all relevant factors, including the following:

(i) The degree of similarity between the mark or trade name and the famous mark.

(ii) The degree of inherent or acquired distinctiveness of the famous mark.

---

19. *Moseley*, 537 U.S. at 431 (2003) (citing H.R. Rep. No. 104-374, at 3 (1995) (Conf. Rep.)).
20. 15 U.S.C. § 1125(c)(2)(C).
21. 15 U.S.C. § 1125(c)(1).
22. V Secret Catalogue, Inc. v. Moseley, 605 F.3d 382, 388 (6th Cir. 2010).

(iii) The extent to which the owner of the famous mark is engaging in substantially exclusive use of the mark.

(iv) The degree of recognition of the famous mark.

(v) Whether the user of the mark or trade name intended to create an association with the famous mark.

(vi) Any actual association between the mark or trade name and the famous mark.[23]

State laws are similar, but they vary considerably from state to state. Although state laws used to have stronger anti-dilution laws than the federal statute, recent changes have made the federal law very protective of famous marks.

Disparagement claims tend to provide a greater scope of protection for trademark owners, allowing them to stop not only the direct use of their trademarks, but also clever puns or indirect references to their marks that the federal courts would not recognize under a dilution claim. For the entrepreneur hoping to develop economic value in his own marks, the temptation to use the literary reference to another party's trademark must be carefully weighed against the cost of fighting a trademark battle, particularly if the likely outcome of such a battle will be a loss of the entrepreneur's trademark and goodwill.

C. Acquiring, Licensing, and Maintaining Trademarks

Because many trademarks are created through usage over time, the nature and formality of trademark acquisition is somewhat different than other forms of intellectual property. In addition, because trademarks have a dual function as a property interest and a consumer protection mechanism, the rules governing their ownership and transfer are unlike most types of property.

1. Use in Commerce

The primary method of acquiring a trademark is through using it in commerce. For federal law, this requires that the use be in interstate commerce, meaning that the goods or services are sold across state lines or marketed to the public from out of state. Mail order and Internet sales serve this purpose well. For a restaurant seeking a service mark in its name, evidence of marketing to customers in neighboring states and the patronage by those customers is strong evidence of interstate commerce.

The nature of the evidence required to establish usage of the trademarks and service marks differs somewhat because trademark owners use the marks differently for goods than services. Evidence of use of a mark for goods in interstate commerce

---

23. 15 U.S.C. § 1125(c)(2)(B).

must appear directly on the goods, on labels, on shipping containers and packages, or on displays. When filing the trademark application, a photograph of the products bearing the trademark is acceptable rather than sending the actual product. Leaflets, brochures, publicity releases, and similar items do not provide evidence of the use of a mark with goods because they are too indirect.

Services must display the service mark in their advertising or sales literature. Signs, brochures about the service, advertisements, and even business cards and stationery may be acceptable evidence of a service mark. These items would not be accepted for evidence of a trademark for goods, but given the lack of a tangible item with which to attach the service mark, they are sufficient.

2. Intent to Use

The United States has modified federal law to permit the filing of trademark applications for trademarks that are not yet used in commerce. The policy change was made in response to growing recognition of this common practice in other countries. Because this is a significant change from prior U.S. practice, it has many limitations. The trademark applicant hoping to protect a trademark not yet in use must proceed with a great deal of care.

The intent to use application allows a company to provide a declaration that it has a bona fide intention to use the mark in commerce. This simple form, along with evidence similar to the type required for trademark use in commerce, will allow a company six months in which to begin using the trademark. This six-month period can be further extended up to three years with extension applications and filing fees.

The actual registration will not take place until after the mark has been used in commerce and the company has filed a form entitled "Allegation of Use," which documents the use of the mark. The intent to use application has a significant advantage for the launch of a new product or service because it allows the entrepreneur to pre-clear the name of the product and avoid the expense of selecting a mark that will be opposed.

3. Elements of an Application — Specimens and Drawings

Although the definition of a trademark includes the broadly inclusive statement that a mark may be "any word, name, symbol, or device," most trademarks are textual—typically common or proper nouns. The second largest category would be comprised of images in the form of designs, pictures, or logos. The text trademark is known as a "standard character" (formerly "typed") drawing, while a drawing including a logo or image is a "stylized or special form" drawing.

One point of confusion between the two categories is the protection of typeface or font. If the trademark owner claims the specific typeface or font is part of the trademark, then that trademark requires a stylized or special form drawing. The special form drawings can also protect the specific choice of color in the trademark, but unless this is specially applied for, the application is based on black and white trademarks only. "The application includes a statement that the mark is in standard characters and no claim is made to any particular font style, size, or color."[24] If the trademark owner wishes to make color, font, size, or image part of the trademark, then it must file the special form application.

To file the federal trademark application, the trademark owner must file an actual example of the trademark as it is actually used in commerce or intended to be used in commerce. The example is known as a "specimen" of the trademark. The specimen shows how the drawing relates to the goods or services for which the application is sought.

The specimens that may be used for the trademark application tie directly to the examples of the trademark that establish that the mark is properly used in interstate commerce. As a result, for goods, the trademark submitted should be on tags, labels, containers, or displays. Given the size and dimensions of products, photographs that capture the specimen and the product are sufficient. The actual products should not be provided to the PTO. The PTO uses the specimen to determine that the trademark is actively used in commerce in conjunction with the product. Thus, invoices, announcements, order forms, bills of lading, leaflets, brochures, publicity releases, letterhead, and business cards are rejected because they fail to show this connection.

Similarly, the specimens that may be used for a service mark application tie directly to the examples of the service mark that establish the mark is properly used in interstate commerce in conjunction with the service promoted. Unlike specimens for trademarks, service marks allow a more general category of specimens, including signs, brochures about the business, advertisements, business cards, and stationary which shows the services provided. The specimen must show the relationship between the mark and the service. As the PTO explains, there must be:

> some reference to the services, that is, it is not just a display of the mark itself.... For example, if the mark sought to be registered is "T.MARKEY" for retail stores featuring men's sportswear, a specimen that only shows the wording "T.MARKEY" and no other matter would not be acceptable, but a specimen that shows the wording "T.MARKEY" on a clothing store sign would be acceptable.[25]

4. Acquisition through Purchase or Licensing

The nature of the property interest in a trademark has a somewhat schizophrenic relationship to traditional notions of property. Trademarks are least like personal property in that they cannot merely be purchased and sold. Because marks must always relate directly to the goods or services used in commerce, they can only be transferred as part of transactions involving those goods or services.

---

24. 37 C.F.R. §2.52(a)(1) (2018).
25. U.S. Patent & Trademark Office, *supra* note 206, at 21.

Instead of wishing to acquire a brand name from a company, it is more likely that another company would like to associate the name with its own goods. This commonly occurs with the sale of t-shirts bearing company brands, but it also occurs commonly with the extension of one brand into another, corporate joint ventures, and similar transactions.

The senior trademark owner can accomplish this by licensing the mark to the goods or services of a third party if certain conditions are met regarding scope and quality control. The most important of these conditions is that the senior trademark owner continues to have a significant involvement in the control of its trademark. Among the key provisions:

- *Control of the mark itself*—so that the licensee cannot change the wording or artwork of the trademark without permission.

- *Control of the goods and services marked*—so that each product or service using the mark is approved by the senior trademark owner.

- *Quality control of the goods and services*—the right and actual practice of reviewing the goods and services on which the trademarks are used to assure that they meet the standards of the senior user.

- *Obligations to police the trademark*—so the junior trademark user and the senior trademark user each have duties to be sure no infringement or unauthorized junior use is occurring.

With a properly drafted license agreement, the licensee becomes a junior user of the senior trademark. This allows great expansion of a trademark's reach into new fields.

5. Benefits of Co-Branding and Licensing

Co-branding is a version of licensing in which the owners of each trademark enter into a cross-license agreement, so that each company is the licensee of the other company's mark for the purpose of promoting a particular good or service.

Cross licensing allows for the co-branding of cellular phones by the manufacturers and the wireless carriers, the expansion of cartoon characters into virtually every conceivable product line, the ability of diet book authors and restaurants to launch food lines, and automobile companies to sell toy versions of their vehicles.

Trademark licensing and co-branding create opportunities for entrepreneurs to jump-start into new lines of business and expand the opportunities of other companies' products. These relationships have the benefit of extending the brand reach of the senior user without distracting that company from its core competency. It provides a strategy for companies who have the potential to diversify but understand that diversification may lead to lack of focus and poor integration of business models across competing sectors. If, instead of adding new divisions, an established company can simply employ a few trademark experts to focus on brand management, new revenue can be found with far less risk.

6. Maintaining Trademarks

Trademarks are highly valuable for a corporation. For commodity products, the premium price differential demanded by brand name goods is a quantitative reflection of the market value of the trademark. A less quantifiable aspect of that value is the shelf space made available to retailers. The market presence that results in greater market share for brand name goods also reflects the economic value of the trademark.

Valuable assets must be carefully maintained. If a trademark no longer reflects the particular source of the goods, the trademark can become the generic word for that class of goods. Professor Charles McManis has written a simple seven-step process to protect trademarks from becoming generic and losing their market value.

(1) Select as fanciful or arbitrary a mark or name as possible.

(2) Register it as a federal trademark at the earliest possible time.

(3) Distinguish it in advertising that the public will recognize it as a trademark (i.e., use distinctive type face, quotation marks, etc., [etc.,] use the term in association with some other term which will function as a generic term and, where registered, use the symbol ®).

(4) Avoid using corruptions of the term.

(5) Use the mark on several different but related products.

(6) Engage in continuous advertising.

(7) Aggressively police the mark by challenging misuse of the mark, not only by competitors and other commercial parties, but by the public at large. To police a mark, one may institute a media monitoring program with follow-up letters of varying degrees of forcefulness reminding editors, publishers, broadcasters and other businesses and public figures who have misused a mark or name, that it is a protected trademark....[26]

Through this seven-step process, the trademark that is carefully selected, registered, thoughtfully used, and actively protected from misuse has the potential to return value to the trademark owner for decades and perhaps even centuries.

D. Enforcement of Trademark Rights

1. Enforcing Trademark Rights before Litigation

Most trademark enforcement does not start or end on the courthouse steps. Trademark enforcement begins with internal policing to assure that the mark is not being altered or modified by company employees, vendors, manufacturers, retailers, or others in the product distribution process. A trademark which feels stale to the em-

---

26. Charles R. McManis & David J. Friedman, Intellectual Property and Unfair Competition in a Nutshell 174–75 (2013).

ployees who see it every day may be just gaining recognition by the public which has only occasional exposure to the mark. Companies must actively police themselves to avoid clever but unregistered modifications to their trademarks since material changes to the trademark will destroy the federal trademark registration.

Trademark owners must also work with newspapers, magazines, and other publishers to assure that a trademarked term is not regularly used as a generic name for the category of goods or turned into a verb regarding the use of such goods. "Xeroxing a copy" is a phrase that risks diluting the Xerox trademark for photocopiers. The trademark owner has the obligation to educate the public on this misuse. Similar, terms such as "googling" risk genericizing the Google trademark for its search engine.

For companies that believe competitors are using their trademarks improperly, the trademark owner generally begins with a "cease and desist" letter. The letter typically explains the ownership of the trademark, the misuse of the trademark and a request that the misuse stop. Before this letter is sent, however, the trademark owner should invest time and resources to investigate the competitor. A trademark search should be conducted to better understand the trademark use by that company. Copies of the infringing trademark, specimens of the trademark on a range of the competitor's goods or services, advertising, and a comprehensive collection of the competitor's trademark use should be collected. The more a trademark owner knows about the activities and use by an alleged infringer, the more effectively it can craft the cease and desist letter, and the more likely it can find a reasonable compromise to the dispute. The research helps the company explore the strength and weakness of its claim before the first shot is fired. As a result, the research may better arm the company for a future fight, or it may keep the company from entering a fight it should not fight or cannot win.

If the company's trademark covers a broad range of uses and the alleged misuse is not directly competitive, the reasonable compromise is for the two not-quite-competitors to enter into a written agreement regarding each company's use. This converts the potential infringement into a licensed activity, sets limits on the changes and results in a stronger, rather than weaker, trademark. If the parties cannot reach such an arrangement, or if the parties are actual competitors, then one of the parties must agree to stop using the infringing trademark. The owner of a trademark cannot back down once it learns of an infringement, because the knowing of the infringement and failing to take action is tantamount to granting permission for the activity, greatly weakening the trademark's scope and value. If both parties believe that they have priority to use the mark, then litigation may be the only solution to settle the priority of the trademark interests.

2. Elements of the Trademark Infringement Claim

To win a trademark action against an infringer of one's trademark, the plaintiff trademark owner must be able to establish that (1) plaintiff has a valid trademark, (2) plaintiff has priority in the use of the trademark, (3) defendant has used an identical or similar trademark, and (4) defendant's use of the mark results in a likelihood of confusion on the part of the public.[27]

The first two elements were discussed in the previous section. Federal registration of the trademark, though not essential, makes the evidence of the first element much easier to establish. Priority requires that the plaintiff be the senior user of the trademark—the party who used it first. As described above, there is a risk that two users were both using the same mark in different geographic regions at the same time. In this case, the junior user can establish priority in its geographic reason.

The third element is a factual question regarding whether the right defendant is in the lawsuit. If the defendant never used an identical or similar mark, it should not be sued. The plaintiff must prove that the defendant used the marks in commerce.

There is usually little evidentiary doubt of this element in cases involving established businesses, but it is the critical element in the case of intellectual property counterfeiters. Counterfeiters will make goods with fake trademarks that are quite close to that of the legitimate trademark owners. They will stay one step ahead of the law and the lawful trademark owners with false names and dummy corporations, making it harder to establish who is actually responsible for the piracy.

3. Likelihood of Confusion

For lawsuits involving legitimate competitors, the likelihood of confusion element is the most complex and heavily disputed. Different courts use different formulas for their analysis of likelihood of confusion, but the formulations tend to summarize the same test:

> [T]he court is required to consider several factors when assessing whether or not there is a likelihood of confusion by the general public: the degree of similarity between the marks in appearance and suggestion; the similarity of the products for which the name is used; the area and manner of concurrent use; the degree of care likely to be exercised by consumers; the strength of the complainant's mark; actual confusion; and an intent on the part of the alleged infringer to palm off his products as those of another.[28]

No one of these factors will determine whether the court will find that it is likely the public will be confused by the defendant's mark. Actual confusion is evidence of likelihood of confusion, but is neither required nor sufficient to answer the test. Instead, the courts use these factors to make a much more subjective determination. The court will find infringement if the two marks are too close to each other when used in the manner before the court.

The factors the court weighs are interrelated. A highly fanciful or arbitrary trademark is stronger whereas a descriptive mark that relies heavily on the attributes of

---

27. Nike, Inc. v. "Just Did It" Enters., 6 F.3d 1225, 1227 (7th Cir. 1993). *See also* A.J. Canfield Co. v. Vess Beverages, Inc., 796 F.2d 903, 906 (7th Cir. 1986).
28. *Nike, Inc.*, 6 F.3d at 1228.

the goods is weaker. So the strength of the trademark will actually vary depending on the particular goods in question. For example, 3M's Post-it brand for notes is not quite as strong for small notepads as it is for removable CD labels or wall charts, because the trademark is increasingly arbitrary for those goods. In a lawsuit, the nature of the goods in dispute may strengthen or weaken the mark.

The similarity of the marks is a critical feature. "Marks may be confusingly similar based on physical design, sounds, psychological, commercial, or social connotations and significance, color scheme, or linguistic characteristics."[29] If a court determines that the marks are not sufficiently similar, the plaintiff will not be able to prove its case. If the words, artwork and colors are all similar, the court is much more likely to find confusion than if only the words have some similarity.

In trademarks, spelling does not count, so "Light" and "Lite" are the same potential trademark. DreamWorks and Dreamwerks are identical for trademark purposes. Trademarks are reviewed in their totality rather than dissected when comparing them for similarity.

The comparison of products or services is also critical. As discussed earlier, identical marks are often used in unrelated fields. The closer the products are to each other, the more reasonable it is to expect the public to be confused by similar trademarks.

Similarly, the nature of the intended consumers of the goods will affect the comparison. The more sophisticated the audience, the greater the trademark owner's burden of establishing the likelihood of confusion. The general public is not as attuned to details in products and services as are more specialized markets. The broad general public, therefore, is not expected to pay too much attention to the trademarks or the goods. In contrast, a more discerning clientele is more likely to understand the nuance in the products and be able to avoid confusion more readily than casual purchasers.

Famous or well-recognized trademarks also cast a larger shadow than marks that are less well-recognized by the public. If the public does not know about a trademark, it cannot be confused by seeing something similar. Put another way, the more famous the trademark, the broader an array of goods and services it can cover.

As a consequence, the strength of the mark may extend from the individual marks to the family of trademarks. Perhaps the best known example of a family of marks comes from the extension by Apple of the iPod to the iPad, iPhone, iTunes, and iOS. Similarly, McDonald's was successful in stopping the use of McBagel by a competitor because the McDonald trademark family included the well-known McMuffin, Mc-Chicken, Big Mac and the lesser known McPizza, McFeast, and McDonuts. Ken Mc-Shea's attempt to launch McBagel was barred because of the fame of McDonald's trademarks and its active policing of those marks.[30]

---

29. Arthur R. Miller & Michael H. Davis, Intellectual Property, Patents, Trademarks, and Copyright in a Nutshell § 17.2, at 291 (6th ed. 2018).

30. McDonald's Corp. v. McBagel's, Inc., 649 F. Supp. 1268 (S.D.N.Y. 1986).

Finally, the intent of the alleged infringer goes to both the culpability of the defendant and the measure of damages. "Most circuits find that where a defendant adopted its mark intending to copy the plaintiff's mark and benefit from the plaintiff's reputation, the court may infer that there is in fact confusing similarity between the marks."[31] If the discovery process or the nature of the trademarks demonstrates a willful intent to model the defendant's trademark on the plaintiff, the courts often find that the defendant's actions were purposefully seeking confusion, which satisfies the likelihood of confusion standard. Intentional misconduct is much more likely to result in the defendant being enjoined from continuing the misuse of the mark and may result in an award of attorneys' fees against the defendant.

4. Nominative Fair Use and Collateral Use

When the defendant uses the plaintiff's trademark to describe the plaintiff's product rather than its own product, the courts will provide it some latitude. This is important under both free speech principles and commercial competitiveness principles. The defendant must be careful to use the mark only to the extent necessary to identify the trademark owner's products and do nothing that suggests sponsorship or endorsement of the defendant's product by the trademark holder.

Fair use allows comparative advertising, identification of the products reviewed in each issue of a consumer products magazine, and allows a certain amount of parody commercial conduct—so that the trademark owners remember not to take themselves too seriously.

Collateral use allows third parties to use a trademark to represent the accurate information about components used within the underlying products. A computer manufacturer has a legal right to identify the trademarked software sold as part of the bundled package of hardware and software shipped to the consumer. The software company cannot stop the manufacturer from including its product if the product is lawfully purchased, and it cannot object to the use of the trademark on the software itself. Collateral use is limited, however. It cannot be used to create a false impression of endorsement or mislead the public as to the association between the companies.

Collateral use also allows repair shops and reprocessors to accurately depict their business without running afoul of the trademarks owned by the companies—often companies who would prefer that no reprocessing of their products takes place. If a product is refurbished and put back into commerce, the reprocessor is not obligated to remove the trademark. Again, as with the product bundler, it cannot use the first manufacturer's trademark to mislead the public as to endorsement or association, but it can use the trademark to show the source of the original goods.

---

31. Anne Gilson Lalonde, 5 Gilson on Trademarks § 5.09 (2018).

5. Other Defenses to Trademark Infringement

There are always defenses to trademark litigation, and these defenses serve as warnings to the trademark owner regarding the diligence necessary to police their trademarks. Professor McManis lists the defenses as "abandonment, loss of distinctiveness (i.e., genericide), functionality, and collateral or fair use ... and the equitable defenses of laches, estoppel, acquiescence, and unclean hands (including misuse)."[32]

If a trademark becomes generic because the term is used for a category of goods rather than for a particular manufacturer's goods, then anyone is free to use that trademark. Similarly, if the trademark owner stops using the trademark in commerce, then it may have been deemed to have abandoned the trademark, giving up its rights to stop others from using the trademark.

The equitable defenses focus on the conduct of the trademark owner and whether justice is served by enforcing the rights of that trademark owner. If the trademark owner was not diligent in pursuing the claim, then the junior user may have invested considerable time and effort in pursuing the uncontested trademark use. Courts may refuse to grant relief to a company that has failed to police its trademarks vigorously and let other competitors use the trademark to grow in the marketplace.

E. Intersection with Copyright

Dastar Corp. v. Twentieth Century Fox Film Corp.
539 U.S. 23 (2003)

JUSTICE SCALIA delivered the opinion of the Court.

In this case, we are asked to decide whether §43(a) of the Lanham Act, 15 U.S.C. §1125(a), prevents the unaccredited copying of a work, and if so, whether a court may double a profit award under §1117(a), in order to deter future infringing conduct.

In 1948, three and a half years after the German surrender at Reims, General Dwight D. Eisenhower completed Crusade in Europe, his written account of the allied campaign in Europe during World War II. Doubleday published the book, registered it with the Copyright Office in 1948, and granted exclusive television rights to an affiliate of respondent Twentieth Century Fox Film Corporation (Fox). Fox, in turn, arranged for Time, Inc., to produce a television series, also called Crusade in Europe, based on the book, and Time assigned its copyright in the series to Fox. The television series, consisting of 26 episodes, was first broadcast in 1949. It combined a soundtrack based on a narration of the book with film footage from the United States Army, Navy, and Coast Guard, the British Ministry of Information and War Office, the National Film Board of Canada, and unidentified "Newsreel Pool Cam-

---

32. MCMANIS & FRIEDMAN, *supra*, at 202.

eramen." In 1975, Doubleday renewed the copyright on the book as the "'proprietor of copyright in a work made for hire.'" Fox, however, did not renew the copyright on the Crusade television series, which expired in 1977, leaving the television series in the public domain.

In 1988, Fox reacquired the television rights in General Eisenhower's book, including the exclusive right to distribute the Crusade television series on video and to sub-license others to do so. Respondents SFM Entertainment and New Line Home Video, Inc., in turn, acquired from Fox the exclusive rights to distribute Crusade on video. SFM obtained the negatives of the original television series, restored them, and repackaged the series on videotape; New Line distributed the videotapes.

Enter petitioner Dastar. In 1995, Dastar decided to expand its product line from music compact discs to videos. Anticipating renewed interest in World War II on the 50th anniversary of the war's end, Dastar released a video set entitled World War II Campaigns in Europe. To make Campaigns, Dastar purchased eight beta cam tapes of the *original* version of the Crusade television series, which is in the public domain, copied them, and then edited the series. Dastar's Campaigns series is slightly more than half as long as the original Crusade television series. Dastar substituted a new opening sequence, credit page, and final closing for those of the Crusade television series; inserted new chapter-title sequences and narrated chapter introductions; moved the "recap" in the Crusade television series to the beginning and retitled it as a "preview"; and removed references to and images of the book. Dastar created new packaging for its Campaigns series and (as already noted) a new title.

Dastar manufactured and sold the Campaigns video set as its own product. The advertising states: "Produced and Distributed by: *Entertainment Distributing*" (which is owned by Dastar), and makes no reference to the Crusade television series. Similarly, the screen credits state "DASTAR CORP presents" and "an ENTERTAINMENT DISTRIBUTING Production," and list as executive producer, producer, and associate producer, employees of Dastar. The Campaigns videos themselves also make no reference to the Crusade television series, New Line's Crusade videotapes, or the book. Dastar sells its Campaigns videos to Sam's Club, Costco, Best Buy, and other retailers and mail-order companies for $25 per set, substantially less than New Line's video set.

In 1998, respondents Fox, SFM, and New Line brought this action alleging that Dastar's sale of its Campaigns video set infringes Doubleday's copyright in General Eisenhower's book and, thus, their exclusive television rights in the book. Respondents later amended their complaint to add claims that Dastar's sale of Campaigns "without proper credit" to the Crusade television series constitutes "reverse passing off"[33] in violation of § 43(a) of the Lanham Act, and in violation of state unfair-competition law. On cross-motions for summary judgment, the District Court found for respondents on all three counts, treating its resolution of the Lanham Act claim as controlling

---

33. Passing off (or palming off, as it is sometimes called) occurs when a producer misrepresents his own goods or services as someone else's. "Reverse passing off," as its name implies, is the opposite: The producer misrepresents someone else's goods or services as his own.

on the state-law unfair-competition claim because "the ultimate test under both is whether the public is likely to be deceived or confused." The court awarded Dastar's profits to respondents and doubled them pursuant to § 35 of the Lanham Act to deter future infringing conduct by petitioner.

The Court of Appeals for the Ninth Circuit affirmed the judgment for respondents on the Lanham Act claim, but reversed as to the copyright claim and remanded. (It said nothing with regard to the state-law claim.) With respect to the Lanham Act claim, the Court of Appeals reasoned that "Dastar copied substantially the entire *Crusade in Europe* series created by Twentieth Century Fox, labeled the resulting product with a different name and marketed it without attribution to Fox[, and] therefore committed a 'bodily appropriation' of Fox's series." It concluded that "Dastar's 'bodily appropriation' of Fox's original [television] series is sufficient to establish the reverse passing off." The court also affirmed the District Court's award under the Lanham Act of twice Dastar's profits. We granted certiorari.

The Lanham Act was intended to make "actionable the deceptive and misleading use of marks," and "to protect persons engaged in ... commerce against unfair competition." While much of the Lanham Act addresses the registration, use, and infringement of trademarks and related marks, § 43(a), is one of the few provisions that goes beyond trademark protection. As originally enacted, § 43(a) created a federal remedy against a person who used in commerce either "a false designation of origin, or any false description or representation" in connection with "any goods or services." As the Second Circuit accurately observed with regard to the original enactment, however— and as remains true after the 1988 revision— § 43(a) "does not have boundless application as a remedy for unfair trade practices." "Because of its inherently limited wording, § 43(a) can never be a federal 'codification' of the overall law of 'unfair competition,'" but can apply only to certain unfair trade practices prohibited by its text.

Although a case can be made that a proper reading of § 43(a), as originally enacted, would treat the word "origin" as referring only "to the geographic location in which the goods originated," the Courts of Appeals considering the issue, beginning with the Sixth Circuit, unanimously concluded that it "does not merely refer to geographical origin, but also to origin of source or manufacture," thereby creating a federal cause of action for traditional trademark infringement of unregistered marks. Moreover, every Circuit to consider the issue found § 43(a) broad enough to encompass reverse passing off. The Trademark Law Revision Act of 1988 made clear that § 43(a) covers origin of production as well as geographic origin.[34] Its language is amply inclusive,

34. Section 43(a) of the Lanham Act now provides:
"Any person who, on or in connection with any goods or services, or any container for goods, uses in commerce any word, term, name, symbol, or device, or any combination thereof, or any false designation of origin, false or misleading description of fact, or false or misleading representation of fact, which—
"(A) is likely to cause confusion, or to cause mistake, or to deceive as to the affiliation, connection, or association of such person with another person, or as to the origin, sponsorship, or approval of his or her goods, services, or commercial activities by another person, or

moreover, of reverse passing off—if indeed it does not implicitly adopt the unanimous court-of-appeals jurisprudence on that subject.

Thus, as it comes to us, the gravamen of respondents' claim is that, in marketing and selling Campaigns as its own product without acknowledging its nearly wholesale reliance on the Crusade television series, Dastar has made a "false designation of origin, false or misleading description of fact, or false or misleading representation of fact, which ... is likely to cause confusion ... as to the origin ... of his or her goods."

That claim would undoubtedly be sustained if Dastar had bought some of New Line's Crusade videotapes and merely repackaged them as its own. Dastar's alleged wrongdoing, however, is vastly different: it took a creative work in the public domain—the Crusade television series—copied it, made modifications (arguably minor), and produced its very own series of videotapes. If "origin" refers only to the manufacturer or producer of the physical "goods" that are made available to the public (in this case the videotapes), Dastar was the origin. If, however, "origin" includes the creator of the underlying work that Dastar copied, then someone else (perhaps Fox) was the origin of Dastar's product. At bottom, we must decide what §43(a)(1)(A) of the Lanham Act means by the "origin" of "goods."

The dictionary definition of "origin" is "the fact or process of coming into being from a source," and "that from which anything primarily proceeds; source." Webster's New International Dictionary 1720–1721 (2d ed. 1949). And the dictionary definition of "goods" (as relevant here) is "[w]ares; merchandise." We think the most natural understanding of the "origin" of "goods"—the source of wares—is the producer of the tangible product sold in the marketplace, in this case the physical Campaigns videotape sold by Dastar. The concept might be stretched (as it was under the original version of §43(a)) to include not only the actual producer, but also the trademark owner who commissioned or assumed responsibility for ("stood behind") production of the physical product. But as used in the Lanham Act, the phrase "origin of goods" is in our view incapable of connoting the person or entity that originated the ideas or communications that "goods" embody or contain. Such an extension would not only stretch the text, but it would be out of accord with the history and purpose of the Lanham Act and inconsistent with precedent.

Section 43(a) of the Lanham Act prohibits actions like trademark infringement that deceive consumers and impair a producer's goodwill. It forbids, for example, the Coca-Cola Company's passing off its product as Pepsi-Cola or reverse passing off Pepsi-Cola as its product. But the brand-loyal consumer who prefers the drink that the Coca-Cola Company or PepsiCo sells, while he believes that that company pro-

---

"(B) in commercial advertising or promotion, misrepresents the nature, characteristics, qualities, or geographic origin of his or her or another person's goods, services, or commercial activities, shall be liable in a civil action by any person who believes that he or she is or is likely to be damaged by such act." 15 U.S.C. §1125(a)(1).

duced (or at least stands behind the production of) that product, surely does not necessarily believe that that company was the "origin" of the drink in the sense that it was the very first to devise the formula. The consumer who buys a branded product does not automatically assume that the brand-name company is the same entity that came up with the idea for the product, or designed the product—and typically does not care whether it is. The words of the Lanham Act should not be stretched to cover matters that are typically of no consequence to purchasers.

It could be argued, perhaps, that the reality of purchaser concern is different for what might be called a communicative product—one that is valued not primarily for its physical qualities, such as a hammer, but for the intellectual content that it conveys, such as a book or, as here, a video. The purchaser of a novel is interested not merely, if at all, in the identity of the producer of the physical tome (the publisher), but also, and indeed primarily, in the identity of the creator of the story it conveys (the author). And the author, of course, has at least as much interest in avoiding passing-off (or reverse passing-off) of his creation as does the publisher. For such a communicative product (the argument goes) "origin of goods" in § 43(a) must be deemed to include not merely the producer of the physical item (the publishing house Farrar, Straus and Giroux, or the video producer Dastar) but also the creator of the content that the physical item conveys (the author Tom Wolfe, or— assertedly—respondents).

The problem with this argument according special treatment to communicative products is that it causes the Lanham Act to conflict with the law of copyright, which addresses that subject specifically. The right to copy, and to copy without attribution, once a copyright has expired, like "the right to make [an article whose patent has expired]—including the right to make it in precisely the shape it carried when patented—passes to the public." "In general, unless an intellectual property right such as a patent or copyright protects an item, it will be subject to copying." The rights of a patentee or copyright holder are part of a "carefully crafted bargain," under which, once the patent or copyright monopoly has expired, the public may use the invention or work at will and without attribution. Thus, in construing the Lanham Act, we have been "careful to caution against misuse or over-extension" of trademark and related protections into areas traditionally occupied by patent or copyright. "The Lanham Act," we have said, "does not exist to reward manufacturers for their innovation in creating a particular device; that is the purpose of the patent law and its period of exclusivity."

Federal trademark law "has no necessary relation to invention or discovery," but rather, by preventing competitors from copying "a source-identifying mark," "reduce[s] the customer's costs of shopping and making purchasing decisions," and "helps assure a producer that it (and not an imitating competitor) will reap the financial, reputation-related rewards associated with a desirable product." Assuming for the sake of argument that Dastar's representation of itself as the "Producer" of its videos amounted to a representation that it originated the creative work conveyed by the videos, allowing a cause of action under § 43(a) for that representation would create a species of mutant copyright law that limits the public's "federal right to 'copy and to use,'" expired copyrights.

When Congress has wished to create such an addition to the law of copyright, it has done so with much more specificity than the Lanham Act's ambiguous use of "origin." The Visual Artists Rights Act of 1990, §603(a), provides that the author of an artistic work "shall have the right ... to claim authorship of that work." That express right of attribution is carefully limited and focused: It attaches only to specified "works of visual art," §101, is personal to the artist, §§106A(b) and (e), and endures only for "the life of the author," at §106A(d)(1). Recognizing in §43(a) a cause of action for misrepresentation of authorship of noncopyrighted works (visual or otherwise) would render these limitations superfluous. A statutory interpretation that renders another statute superfluous is of course to be avoided.

Reading "origin" in §43(a) to require attribution of uncopyrighted materials would pose serious practical problems. Without a copyrighted work as the basepoint, the word "origin" has no discernable limits. A video of the MGM film Carmen Jones, after its copyright has expired, would presumably require attribution not just to MGM, but to Oscar Hammerstein II (who wrote the musical on which the film was based), to Georges Bizet (who wrote the opera on which the musical was based), and to Prosper Merimee (who wrote the novel on which the opera was based). In many cases, figuring out who is in the line of "origin" would be no simple task. Indeed, in the present case it is far from clear that respondents have that status. Neither SFM nor New Line had anything to do with the production of the Crusade television series—they merely were licensed to distribute the video version.

While Fox might have a claim to being in the line of origin, its involvement with the creation of the television series was limited at best. Time, Inc., was the principal if not the exclusive creator, albeit under arrangement with Fox. And of course it was neither Fox nor Time, Inc. that shot the film used in the Crusade television series. Rather, that footage came from the United States Army, Navy, and Coast Guard, the British Ministry of Information and War Office, the National Film Board of Canada, and unidentified "Newsreel Pool Cameramen." If anyone has a claim to being the *original* creator of the material used in both the Crusade television series and the Campaigns videotapes, it would be those groups, rather than Fox. We do not think the Lanham Act requires this search for the source of the Nile and all its tributaries.

Another practical difficulty of adopting a special definition of "origin" for communicative products is that it places the manufacturers of those products in a difficult position. On the one hand, they would face Lanham Act liability for *failing* to credit the creator of a work on which their lawful copies are based; and on the other hand they could face Lanham Act liability for *crediting* the creator if that should be regarded as implying the creator's "sponsorship or approval" of the copy. In this case, for example, if Dastar had simply "copied [the television series] as Crusade in Europe and sold it as Crusade in Europe," without changing the title or packaging (including the original credits to Fox), it is hard to have confidence in respondents' assurance that they "would not be here on a Lanham Act cause of action."

Finally, reading § 43(a) of the Lanham Act as creating a cause of action for, in effect, plagiarism—the use of otherwise unprotected works and inventions without attribution—would be hard to reconcile with our previous decisions. For example, in *Wal-Mart Stores, Inc. v. Samara Brothers, Inc.*, 529 U.S. 205 (2000), we considered whether product-design trade dress can ever be inherently distinctive. Wal-Mart produced "knockoffs" of children's clothes designed and manufactured by Samara Brothers, containing only "minor modifications" of the original designs. We concluded that the designs could not be protected under § 43(a) without a showing that they had acquired "secondary meaning," so that they " 'identify the source of the product rather than the product itself.' " This carefully considered limitation would be entirely pointless if the "original" producer could turn around and pursue a reverse-passing-off claim under exactly the same provision of the Lanham Act. Samara would merely have had to argue that it was the "origin" of the designs that Wal-Mart was selling as its own line. It was not, because "origin of goods" in the Lanham Act referred to the producer of the clothes, and not the producer of the (potentially) copyrightable or patentable designs that the clothes embodied.

Similarly under respondents' theory, the "origin of goods" provision of § 43(a) would have supported the suit that we rejected in *Bonito Boats,* [*Inc. v. Thunder Craft Boats, Inc.*, 489 U.S. 141 971 (1989),] where the defendants had used molds to duplicate the plaintiff's unpatented boat hulls (apparently without crediting the plaintiff). And it would have supported the suit we rejected in *TrafFix* [*Devices, Inc. v. Marketing Displays, Inc.*, 532 U.S. 23 (2001)]: The plaintiff, whose patents on flexible road signs had expired, and who could not prevail on a trade-dress claim under § 43(a) because the features of the signs were functional, would have had a reverse-passing-off claim for unattributed copying of his design.

In sum, reading the phrase "origin of goods" in the Lanham Act in accordance with the Act's common-law foundations (which were *not* designed to protect originality or creativity), and in light of the copyright and patent laws (which *were*), we conclude that the phrase refers to the producer of the tangible goods that are offered for sale, and not to the author of any idea, concept, or communication embodied in those goods. To hold otherwise would be akin to finding that § 43(a) created a species of perpetual patent and copyright, which Congress may not do.

The creative talent of the sort that lay behind the Campaigns videos is not left without protection. The original film footage used in the Crusade television series could have been copyrighted, as was copyrighted (as a compilation) the Crusade television series, even though it included material from the public domain. Had Fox renewed the copyright in the Crusade television series, it would have had an easy claim of copyright infringement. And respondents' contention that Campaigns infringes Doubleday's copyright in General Eisenhower's book is still a live question on remand. If, moreover, the producer of a video that substantially copied the Crusade series were, in advertising or promotion, to give purchasers the impression that the video was quite different from that series, then one or more of the respondents might have a cause of action—not for reverse passing off under the "confusion …

as to the origin" provision of § 43(a)(1)(A), but for misrepresentation under the "misrepresents the nature, characteristics [or] qualities" provision of § 43(a)(1)(B). For merely saying it is the producer of the video, however, no Lanham Act liability attaches to Dastar.

Because we conclude that Dastar was the "origin" of the products it sold as its own, respondents cannot prevail on their Lanham Act claim. We thus have no occasion to consider whether the Lanham Act permitted an award of double petitioner's profits. The judgment of the Court of Appeals for the Ninth Circuit is reversed, and the case is remanded for further proceedings consistent with this opinion. It is so ordered.

Notes and Questions

a. Trademarks provide important property rights for business, but they can also be used to extend exclusive rights that have lapsed in well-known patented products or when rights of publicity have lapsed. In a dispute against parties controlling the trademarks associated with Marilyn Monroe, there has been an ongoing battle to rein in the trademark portfolio of the iconic actress' estate, since her rights of publicity terminated upon her death under New York law. To what extent has Monroe's estate been able to extend her brand through trademark rather than post-mortem rights of publicity? *See A.V.E.L.A., Inc. v. Estate of Marilyn Monroe, L.L.C.*, 241 F. Supp. 3d 461 (S.D.N.Y. 2017).

b. *Dastar* has been interpreted to change the non-contractual rights to credit. *See Williams v. UMG Recordings, Inc.*, 281 F. Supp. 2d 1177 (C.D. Cal. 2003).

c. The distinction between copyrighted works and public domain works was not made by the Supreme Court, and therefore lower courts have not opted to make the distinction. Does a distinction remain regarding the corporate publisher of a work, rather than the author of the work? *See Hustlers, Inc. v. Thomasson*, 73 U.S.P.Q. 2d 1923 (N.D. Ga. 2004).

d. How far does a trademark extend? Ishmael Butler and Maryann Vieira wrote the jazz/hip-hop song "Rebirth of Slick (Cool like Dat)." They performed in commercials for Target Stores using the song, for which they gave permission, but they claim that the song title and lyrics were used in slogans and signage without permission in violation of the Lanham Act, a claim the court did not dismiss. *Butler v. Target Corp.*, 323 F. Supp. 2d 1052 (C.D. Cal. 2004).

e. In *Herb Reed Enters, L.L.C. v. Florida Entm't Mgmt., Inc.*, 736 F.3d 1239 (9th Cir. 2013), the Ninth Circuit extended a limitation on injunctive relief to trademark. In *eBay Inc. v. MercExchange, L.L.C.*, 547 U.S. 388 (2006), the Supreme Court rejected a tradition that allowed intellectual property plaintiffs to rely on a presumption of irreparable injury when seeking preliminary and permanent injunctions. The Supreme Court rejected the presumption for patent litigants and lower courts have extended *eBay* to copyright and trademark as well. The result requires the owner of the trademark for the musical group, The Platters, to establish irreparable harm before enjoining former band members from using the mark. *See Salinger v. Colting*, 607 F.3d

68, 77 (2d Cir. 2010) (applying *eBay* to copyright actions in both preliminary and permanent injunctions).

Problem 6-E

Bryce has recently become interested in the opportunities that are available through capturing public domain material. Tyrell Jones has approached Bryce about creating a new project for a local school, called the "New Masters" series, which is intended to teach music and literary history. Under Bryce's supervision, selected students from the school will rewrite Gilbert & Sullivan operettas using well-recognized modern stories. The students will create new arrangements, adding jazz, rock, hip-hop, and pop sensibilities to the music. The students plan to write original stories based on such literary characters as Peter Pan, Sherlock Holmes, Frankenstein, Dracula, and the Phantom of the Opera, as well as those narratives traditionally associated with them. Only a few plan to use the original Gilbert & Sullivan plots.

Bryce has researched the material and correctly identified that all the written materials are in the public domain. Each work's copyright has expired in the United States. Nonetheless, Bryce has read that there are estates and companies which claim ownership of some trademarks in some of these works. Bryce seeks your advice on whether there are any limitations on the public domain materials. Since some of these works have also been used in more modern works which continue to be protected by copyright, you should also explain the scope of the public domain and the impact of trademark interests on Bryce's upcoming project.

F. Constitutionality

Matal v. Tam

___ U.S. ___, 137 S. Ct. 1744 (2017)

Justice Alito delivered the opinion of the Court with respect to Parts I, II, and III-A; and an opinion with respect to Parts III-B, III-C, and IV, in which The Chief Justice, Justice Thomas, and Justice Breyer join.

This case concerns a dance-rock band's application for federal trademark registration of the band's name, "The Slants." "Slants" is a derogatory term for persons of Asian descent, and members of the band are Asian-Americans. But the band members believe that by taking that slur as the name of their group, they will help to "reclaim" the term and drain its denigrating force.

The Patent and Trademark Office (PTO) denied the application based on a provision of federal law prohibiting the registration of trademarks that may "disparage ... or bring ... into contemp[t] or disrepute" any "persons, living or dead." 15 U.S.C. § 1052(a). We now hold that this provision violates the Free Speech Clause of the First Amendment. It offends a bedrock First Amendment principle: Speech may not be banned on the ground that it expresses ideas that offend.

I

A

The principle underlying trademark protection is that distinctive marks—words, names, symbols, and the like—can help distinguish a particular artisan's goods from those of others. A trademark designates the goods as the product of a particular trader" and "protect[s] his good will against the sale of another's product as his." It helps consumers identify goods and services that they wish to purchase, as well as those they want to avoid.

Federal law does not create trademarks. Trademarks and their precursors have ancient origins, and trademarks were protected at common law and in equity at the time of the founding of our country. Eventually, Congress stepped in to provide a degree of national uniformity, passing the first federal legislation protecting trademarks in 1870. The foundation of current federal trademark law is the Lanham Act, enacted in 1946. By that time, trademark had expanded far beyond phrases that do no more than identify a good or service. Then, as now, trademarks often consisted of catchy phrases that convey a message.

Under the Lanham Act, trademarks that are "used in commerce" may be placed on the "principal register," that is, they may be federally registered. And some marks "capable of distinguishing [an] applicant's goods or services and not registrable on the principal register ... which are in lawful use in commerce by the owner thereof" may instead be placed on a different federal register: the supplemental register. There are now more than two million marks that have active federal certificates of registration. This system of federal registration helps to ensure that trademarks are fully protected and supports the free flow of commerce. National protection of trademarks is desirable, we have explained, because trademarks foster competition and the maintenance of quality by securing to the producer the benefits of good reputation....

C

The Lanham Act contains provisions that bar certain trademarks from the principal register. For example, a trademark cannot be registered if it is "merely descriptive or deceptively misdescriptive" of goods, or if it is so similar to an already registered trademark or trade name that it is "likely ... to cause confusion, or to cause mistake, or to deceive."

At issue in this case is one such provision, which we will call "the disparagement clause." This provision prohibits the registration of a trademark "which may disparage ... persons, living or dead, institutions, beliefs, or national symbols, or bring them into contempt, or disrepute." ...

When deciding whether a trademark is disparaging, an examiner at the PTO generally applies a "two-part test." The examiner first considers the likely meaning of the matter in question, taking into account not only dictionary definitions, but also the relationship of the matter to the other elements in the mark, the nature of the goods or services, and the manner in which the mark is used in the marketplace in connection with the goods or services. If that meaning is found to refer to identifiable persons, institutions, beliefs or national symbols, the examiner moves to the second step, asking whether that meaning may be disparaging to a substantial composite3 of the referenced group. If the examiner finds that a "substantial composite, although not necessarily a majority, of the referenced group would find the proposed mark ... to be disparaging in the context of contemporary attitudes," a prima facie case of disparagement is made out, and the burden shifts to the applicant to prove that the trademark is not disparaging. What is more, the PTO has specified that "[t]he fact that an applicant may be a member of that group or has good intentions underlying its use of a term does not obviate the fact that a substantial composite of the referenced group would find the term objectionable."

D

Simon Tam is the lead singer of "The Slants." He chose this moniker in order to "reclaim" and "take ownership" of stereotypes about people of Asian ethnicity. The group "draws inspiration for its lyrics from childhood slurs and mocking nursery rhymes" and has given its albums names such as "The Yellow Album" and "Slanted Eyes, Slanted Hearts."

Tam sought federal registration of "THE SLANTS," on the principal register, but an examining attorney at the PTO rejected the request, applying the PTO's two-part framework and finding that "there is ... a substantial composite of persons who find the term in the applied-for mark offensive." The examining attorney relied in part on the fact that "numerous dictionaries define 'slants' or 'slant-eyes' as a derogatory or offensive term." The examining attorney also relied on a finding that "the band's name has been found offensive numerous times" — citing a performance that was canceled because of the band's moniker and the fact that "several bloggers and commenters to articles on the band have indicated that they find the term and the applied-for mark offensive."

Tam contested the denial of registration before the examining attorney and before the PTO's Trademark Trial and Appeal Board (TTAB) but to no avail. Eventually, he took the case to federal court, where the *en banc* Federal Circuit ultimately found the disparagement clause facially unconstitutional under the First Amendment's Free Speech Clause. The majority found that the clause engages in viewpoint-based discrimination, that the clause regulates the expressive component of trademarks and consequently cannot be treated as commercial speech, and that the clause is subject to and cannot satisfy strict scrutiny. The majority also rejected the Government's argument that registered trademarks constitute government speech, as well as the Government's contention that federal registration is a form of government subsidy. And the majority opined that even if the disparagement clause were analyzed under this Court's commercial speech cases, the clause would fail the "intermediate scrutiny" that those cases prescribe....

III

Because the disparagement clause applies to marks that disparage the members of a racial or ethnic group, we must decide whether the clause violates the Free Speech Clause of the First Amendment. And at the outset, we must consider three arguments that would either eliminate any First Amendment protection or result in highly permissive rational-basis review. Specifically, the Government contends (1) that trademarks are government speech, not private speech, (2) that trademarks are a form of government subsidy, and (3) that the constitutionality of the disparagement clause should be tested under a new "government-program" doctrine. We address each of these arguments below.

A

The First Amendment prohibits Congress and other government entities and actors from abridging the freedom of speech; the First Amendment does not say that Congress and other government entities must abridge their own ability to speak freely. And our cases recognize that "[t]he Free Speech Clause ... does not regulate government speech."

As we have said, it is not easy to imagine how government could function if it were subject to the restrictions that the First Amendment imposes on private speech. The First Amendment forbids the government to regulate speech in ways that favor some viewpoints or ideas at the expense of others, but imposing a requirement of viewpoint-neutrality on government speech would be paralyzing. When a government entity embarks on a course of action, it necessarily takes a particular viewpoint and rejects others. The Free Speech Clause does not require government to maintain viewpoint neutrality when its officers and employees speak about that venture....

At issue here is the content of trademarks that are registered by the PTO, an arm of the Federal Government. The Federal Government does not dream up these marks, and it does not edit marks submitted for registration. Except as required by the statute involved here, an examiner may not reject a mark based on the viewpoint that it appears to express. Thus, unless that section is thought to apply, an examiner does not inquire whether any viewpoint conveyed by a mark is consistent with Government policy or whether any such viewpoint is consistent with that expressed by other marks already on the principal register. Instead, if the mark meets the Lanham Act's viewpoint-neutral requirements, registration is mandatory (requiring that "[n]o trademark ... shall be refused registration on the principal register on account of its nature unless" it falls within an enumerated statutory exception). And if an examiner finds that a mark is eligible for placement on the principal register, that decision is not reviewed by any higher official unless the registration is challenged. Moreover, once a mark is registered, the PTO is not authorized to remove it from the register unless a party moves for cancellation, the registration expires, or the Federal Trade Commission initiates proceedings based on certain grounds.

In light of all this, it is far-fetched to suggest that the content of a registered mark is government speech. If the federal registration of a trademark makes the mark government speech, the Federal Government is babbling prodigiously and incoherently. It is saying many unseemly things. It is expressing contradictory views. It is unashamedly endorsing a vast array of commercial products and services. And it is providing Delphic advice to the consuming public.

For example, if trademarks represent government speech, what does the Government have in mind when it advises Americans to "make.believe" (Sony), "Think different" (Apple), "Just do it" (Nike), or "Have it your way" (Burger King)? Was the Government warning about a coming disaster when it registered the mark "EndTime Ministries"? ...

This brings us to the case on which the Government relies most heavily, *Walker* [*v. Texas Div., Sons of Confederate Veterans, Inc.*, 576 U.S. ___, ___ 135 S. Ct. 2239, 2245–2247 (2015)], which likely marks the outer bounds of the government-speech doctrine. Holding that the messages on Texas specialty license plates are government speech, the *Walker* Court cited three factors distilled from [*Pleasant Grove City v. Summum*, 555 U.S. 460, 468 (2009)].

First, license plates have long been used by the States to convey state messages. Second, license plates "are often closely identified in the public mind" with the State, since they are manufactured and owned by the State, generally designed by the State, and serve as a form of "government ID." Third, Texas "maintain[ed] direct control over the messages conveyed on its specialty plates." As explained above, none of these factors are present in this case.

In sum, the federal registration of trademarks is vastly different from the beef ads in *Johanns* [*v. Livestock Marketing Assn.*, 544 U.S. 550 (2005)], the monuments in *Summum,* and even the specialty license plates in *Walker.* Holding that the registration of a trademark converts the mark into government speech would constitute a huge and dangerous extension of the government-speech doctrine. For if the registration of trademarks constituted government speech, other systems of government registration could easily be characterized in the same way.... Trademarks are private, not government, speech.

B

We next address the Government's argument that this case is governed by cases in which this Court has upheld the constitutionality of government programs that subsidized speech expressing a particular viewpoint. These cases implicate a notoriously tricky question of constitutional law. We have held that the Government "may not deny a benefit to a person on a basis that infringes his constitutionally protected ... freedom of speech even if he has no entitlement to that benefit." But at the same time, government is not required to subsidize activities that it does not wish to promote. Determining which of these principles applies in a particular case is not always self-evident, but no difficult question is presented here.

Unlike the present case, the decisions on which the Government relies all involved cash subsidies or their equivalent. In *Rust v. Sullivan*, 500 U.S. 173 (1991), a federal law provided funds to private parties for family planning services. In *National Endowment for Arts v. Finley*, 524 U.S. 569 (1998), cash grants were awarded to artists. And federal funding for public libraries was at issue in *United States v. American Library Assn., Inc.*, 539 U.S. 194 (2003). In other cases, we have regarded tax benefits as comparable to cash subsidies.... Cases like *Rust* and *Finley* are not instructive in analyzing the constitutionality of restrictions on speech imposed in connection with such services.

C

Finally, the Government urges us to sustain the disparagement clause under a new doctrine that would apply to "government-program" cases. For the most part, this argument simply merges our government-speech cases and the previously discussed subsidy cases in an attempt to construct a broader doctrine that can be applied to the registration of trademarks. The only new element in this construct consists of two cases involving a public employer's collection of union dues from its employees. But those cases occupy a special area of First Amendment case law, and they are far removed from the registration of trademarks....

Potentially more analogous are cases in which a unit of government creates a limited public forum for private speech. When government creates such a forum, in either a literal or "metaphysical" sense, some content- and speaker-based restrictions may be allowed. However, even in such cases, what we have termed "viewpoint discrimination" is forbidden.

Our cases use the term "viewpoint" discrimination in a broad sense, and in that sense, the disparagement clause discriminates on the bases of "viewpoint." To be sure, the clause evenhandedly prohibits disparagement of all groups. It applies equally to marks that damn Democrats and Republicans, capitalists and socialists, and those arrayed on both sides of every possible issue. It denies registration to any mark that is offensive to a substantial percentage of the members of any group. But in the sense relevant here, that is viewpoint discrimination: Giving offense is a viewpoint.

We have said time and again that "the public expression of ideas may not be prohibited merely because the ideas are themselves offensive to some of their hearers." *Street v. New York*, 394 U.S. 576, 592 (1969). For this reason, the disparagement clause cannot be saved by analyzing it as a type of government program in which some content- and speaker-based restrictions are permitted.

IV

Having concluded that the disparagement clause cannot be sustained under our government-speech or subsidy cases or under the Government's proposed "government-program" doctrine, we must confront a dispute between the parties on the question whether trademarks are commercial speech and are thus subject to the relaxed scrutiny outlined in *Central Hudson Gas & Elec. Corp. v. Public Serv. Comm'n of N.Y.*, 447 U.S. 557 (1980). The Government and *amici* supporting its position argue that all trademarks are commercial speech. They note that the central purposes of trademarks are commercial and that federal law regulates trademarks to promote fair and orderly interstate commerce. Tam and his *amici*, on the other hand, contend that many, if not all, trademarks have an expressive component. In other words, these trademarks do not simply identify the source of a product or service but go on to say something more, either about the product or service or some broader issue. The trademark in this case illustrates this point. The name "The Slants" not only identifies the band but expresses a view about social issues.

We need not resolve this debate between the parties because the disparagement clause cannot withstand even *Central Hudson* review.[35] Under *Central Hudson,* a restriction of speech must serve "a substantial interest," and it must be "narrowly drawn." This means, among other things, that "[t]he regulatory technique may extend only as far as the interest it serves." The disparagement clause fails this requirement.

It is claimed that the disparagement clause serves two interests. The first is phrased in a variety of ways in the briefs. Echoing language in one of the opinions below, the Government asserts an interest in preventing "'underrepresented groups'" from being "'bombarded with demeaning messages in commercial advertising.'" But no matter how the point is phrased, its unmistakable thrust is this: The Government has an interest in preventing speech expressing ideas that offend. And, as we have explained, that idea strikes at the heart of the First Amendment. Speech that demeans on the basis of race, ethnicity, gender, religion, age, disability, or any other similar ground is hateful; but the proudest boast of our free speech jurisprudence is that we protect the freedom to express "the thought that we hate." *United States v. Schwimmer,* 279 U.S. 644, 655 (1929) (Holmes, J., dissenting).

The second interest asserted is protecting the orderly flow of commerce. Commerce, we are told, is disrupted by trademarks that "involv[e] disparagement of race, gender, ethnicity, national origin, religion, sexual orientation, and similar demographic classification." Such trademarks are analogized to discriminatory conduct, which has been recognized to have an adverse effect on commerce.

A simple answer to this argument is that the disparagement clause is not "narrowly drawn" to drive out trademarks that support invidious discrimination. The clause reaches any trademark that disparages *any person, group, or institution.* It applies to trademarks like the following: "Down with racists," "Down with sexists," "Down with homophobes." It is not an anti-discrimination clause; it is a happy-talk clause. In this way, it goes much further than is necessary to serve the interest asserted.

The clause is far too broad in other ways as well. The clause protects every person living or dead as well as every institution. Is it conceivable that commerce would be disrupted by a trademark saying: "James Buchanan was a disastrous president" or "Slavery is an evil institution"?

There is also a deeper problem with the argument that commercial speech may be cleansed of any expression likely to cause offense. The commercial market is well stocked with merchandise that disparages prominent figures and groups, and the line between commercial and non-commercial speech is not always clear, as this case illustrates. If affixing the commercial label permits the suppression of any speech that may lead to political or social "volatility," free speech would be endangered.

---

35. As with the framework discussed in Part III-C of this opinion, we leave open the question whether *Central Hudson* provides the appropriate test for deciding free speech challenges to provisions of the Lanham Act. And nothing in our decision should be read to speak to the validity of state unfair competition provisions or product libel laws that are not before us and differ from § 1052(d)'s disparagement clause.

For these reasons, we hold that the disparagement clause violates the Free Speech Clause of the First Amendment. The judgment of the Federal Circuit is affirmed.

Iancu v. Brunetti

___ U.S. ___, 139 S. Ct. 2294 (2019)

JUSTICE KAGAN delivered the opinion of the Court.

Two Terms ago, in *Matal v. Tam*, 582 U.S. ___, 137 S. Ct. 1744 (2017), this Court invalidated the Lanham Act's bar on the registration of "disparag[ing]" trademarks. 15 U.S.C. § 1052(a). Although split between two non-majority opinions, all Members of the Court agreed that the provision violated the First Amendment because it discriminated on the basis of viewpoint. Today we consider a First Amendment challenge to a neighboring provision of the Act, prohibiting the registration of "immoral[] or scandalous" trademarks. We hold that this provision infringes the First Amendment for the same reason: It too disfavors certain ideas.

I

Respondent Erik Brunetti is an artist and entrepreneur who founded a clothing line that uses the trademark FUCT. According to Brunetti, the mark (which functions as the clothing's brand name) is pronounced as four letters, one after the other: F-U-C-T. But you might read it differently and, if so, you would hardly be alone. That common perception caused difficulties for Brunetti when he tried to register his mark with the U.S. Patent and Trademark Office (PTO).

Under the Lanham Act, the PTO administers a federal registration system for trademarks. *See* 15 U.S.C. §§ 1051, 1052. Registration of a mark is not mandatory. The owner of an unregistered mark may still use it in commerce and enforce it against infringers. But registration gives trademark owners valuable benefits. For example, registration constitutes "prima facie evidence" of the mark's validity. § 1115(a). And registration serves as "constructive notice of the registrant's claim of ownership," which forecloses some defenses in infringement actions. Generally, a trademark is eligible for registration, and receipt of such benefits, if it is "used in commerce." § 1051(a)(1). But the Act directs the PTO to "refuse[] registration" of certain marks. § 1052. For instance, the PTO cannot register a mark that "so resembles" another mark as to create a likelihood of confusion. § 1052(d). It cannot register a mark that is "merely descriptive" of the goods on which it is used. § 1052(e). It cannot register a mark containing the flag or insignia of any nation or State. *See* § 1052(b). There are five or ten more (depending on how you count). And until we invalidated the criterion two years ago, the PTO could not register a mark that "disparage[d]" a "person[], living or dead." § 1052(a); see *Tam*, 582 U.S. ___, 137 S. Ct. 1744, 198 L.Ed.2d 366.

This case involves another of the Lanham Act's prohibitions on registration—one applying to marks that "[c]onsist[] of or comprise[] immoral[] or scandalous matter." § 1052(a). The PTO applies that bar as a "unitary provision," rather than treating the two adjectives in it separately. *In re Brunetti*, 877 F.3d 1330, 1336 (C.A. Fed. 2017). To determine whether a mark fits in the category, the PTO asks whether a "substantial composite of the general public" would find the mark "shocking to the sense of truth, decency, or propriety"; "giving offense to the conscience or moral feelings"; "calling out for condemnation"; "disgraceful"; "offensive"; "disreputable"; or "vulgar."

Both a PTO examining attorney and the PTO's Trademark Trial and Appeal Board decided that Brunetti's mark flunked that test. The attorney determined that FUCT was "a total vulgar" and "therefore[] unregistrable." On review, the Board stated that the mark was "highly offensive" and "vulgar," and that it had "decidedly negative sexual connotations." As part of its review, the Board also considered evidence of how Brunetti used the mark. It found that Brunetti's website and products contained imagery, near the mark, of "extreme nihilism" and "anti-social" behavior. In that context, the Board thought, the mark communicated "misogyny, depravity, [and] violence." The Board concluded: "Whether one considers [the mark] as a sexual term, or finds that [Brunetti] has used [the mark] in the context of extreme misogyny, nihilism or violence, we have no question but that [the term is] extremely offensive."

Brunetti then brought a facial challenge to the "immoral or scandalous" bar in the Court of Appeals for the Federal Circuit. That court found the prohibition to violate the First Amendment. As usual when a lower court has invalidated a federal statute, we granted certiorari.

II

This Court first considered a First Amendment challenge to a trademark registration restriction in *Tam*, just two Terms ago. There, the Court declared unconstitutional the Lanham Act's ban on registering marks that "disparage" any "person[], living or dead." § 1052(a). The eight-Justice Court divided evenly between two opinions and could not agree on the overall framework for deciding the case. (In particular, no majority emerged to resolve whether a Lanham Act bar is a condition on a government benefit or a simple restriction on speech.) But all the Justices agreed on two propositions. First, if a trademark registration bar is viewpoint-based, it is unconstitutional. And second, the disparagement bar was viewpoint-based.

The Justices thus found common ground in a core postulate of free speech law: The government may not discriminate against speech based on the ideas or opinions it conveys. In Justice Kennedy's explanation, the disparagement bar allowed a trademark owner to register a mark if it was "positive" about a person, but not if it was "derogatory." That was the "essence of viewpoint discrimination," he continued, because "[t]he law thus reflects the Government's disapproval of a subset of messages it finds offensive." Justice Alito emphasized that the statute "denie[d] registration to any mark" whose disparaging message was "offensive to a substantial percentage of the members of any group." The bar thus violated the "bedrock First Amendment principle" that the government cannot discriminate against "ideas that offend." Slightly different explanations, then, but a shared conclusion: Viewpoint discrimination doomed the disparagement bar.

If the "immoral or scandalous" bar similarly discriminates on the basis of viewpoint, it must also collide with our First Amendment doctrine. The Government does not argue otherwise. In briefs and oral argument, the Government offers a theory for upholding the bar if it is viewpoint-neutral (essentially, that the bar would then be a reasonable condition on a government benefit). But the Government agrees that under *Tam* it may not "deny registration based on the views expressed" by a mark. "As the Court's *Tam* decision establishes," the Government says, "the criteria for federal trademark registration" must be "viewpoint-neutral to survive Free Speech Clause review." So the key question becomes: Is the "immoral or scandalous" criterion in the Lanham Act viewpoint-neutral or viewpoint-based?

It is viewpoint-based. The meanings of "immoral" and "scandalous" are not mysterious, but resort to some dictionaries still helps to lay bare the problem. When is expressive material "immoral"? According to a standard definition, when it is "inconsistent with rectitude, purity, or good morals"; "wicked"; or "vicious." Webster's New International Dictionary 1246 (2d ed. 1949). Or again, when it is "opposed to or violating morality"; or "morally evil." Shorter Oxford English Dictionary 961 (3d ed. 1947). So the Lanham Act permits registration of marks that champion society's sense of rectitude and morality, but not marks that denigrate those concepts. And when is such material "scandalous"? Says a typical definition, when it "giv[es] offense to the conscience or moral feelings"; "excite[s] reprobation"; or "call[s] out condemnation." Webster's New International Dictionary, at 2229. Or again, when it is "shocking to the sense of truth, decency, or propriety"; "disgraceful"; "offensive"; or "disreputable." Funk & Wagnalls New Standard Dictionary 2186 (1944). So the Lanham Act allows registration of marks when their messages accord with, but not when their messages defy, society's sense of decency or propriety. Put the pair of overlapping terms together and the statute, on its face, distinguishes between two opposed sets of ideas: those aligned with conventional moral standards and those hostile to them; those inducing societal nods of approval and those provoking offense and condemnation. The statute favors the former, and disfavors the latter. "Love rules"? "Always be good"? Registration follows. "Hate rules"? "Always be cruel"? Not according to the Lanham Act's "immoral or scandalous" bar.

The facial viewpoint bias in the law results in viewpoint-discriminatory application. Recall that the PTO itself describes the "immoral or scandalous" criterion using much the same language as in the dictionary definitions recited above. The PTO, for example, asks whether the public would view the mark as "shocking to the sense of truth, decency, or propriety"; "calling out for condemnation"; "offensive"; or "disreputable." Brief for Petitioner 6 (internal quotation marks omitted). Using those guideposts, the PTO has refused to register marks communicating "immoral" or "scandalous" views about (among other things) drug use, religion, and terrorism. But all the while, it has approved registration of marks expressing more accepted views on the same topics.

Here are some samples. The PTO rejected marks conveying approval of drug use (YOU CAN'T SPELL HEALTHCARE WITHOUT THC for pain-relief medication, MARIJUANA COLA and KO KANE for beverages) because it is scandalous to "inappropriately glamoriz[e] drug abuse." But at the same time, the PTO registered marks with such sayings as D.A.R.E. TO RESIST DRUGS AND VIOLENCE and SAY NO TO DRUGS — REALITY IS THE BEST TRIP IN LIFE. Similarly, the PTO disapproved registration for the mark BONG HITS 4 JESUS because it "suggests that people should engage in an illegal activity [in connection with] worship" and because "Christians would be morally outraged by a statement that connects Jesus Christ with illegal drug use." And the PTO refused to register trademarks associating religious references with products (AGNUS DEI for safes and MADONNA for wine) because they would be "offensive to most individuals of the Christian faith" and "shocking to the sense of propriety." *Ex parte Summit Brass & Bronze Works*, 59 U.S.P.Q. 22, 23 (Dec. Com. Pat. 1943); *In re Riverbank Canning Co.*, 95 F.2d 327, 329 (CCPA 1938). But once again, the PTO approved marks—PRAISE THE LORD for a game and JESUS DIED FOR YOU on clothing—whose message suggested religious faith rather than blasphemy or irreverence. Finally, the PTO rejected marks reflecting support for al-Qaeda (BABY AL QAEDA and AL-QAEDA on t-shirts) "because the bombing of civilians and other terrorist acts are shocking to the sense of decency and call out for condemnation." Yet it approved registration of a mark with the words WAR ON TERROR MEMORIAL. Of course, all these decisions are understandable. The rejected marks express opinions that are, at the least, offensive to many Americans. But as the Court made clear in *Tam*, a law disfavoring "ideas that offend" discriminates based on viewpoint, in violation of the First Amendment.

How, then, can the Government claim that the "immoral or scandalous" bar is viewpoint-neutral? The Government basically asks us to treat decisions like those described above as PTO examiners' mistakes. Still more, the Government tells us to ignore how the Lanham Act's language, on its face, disfavors some ideas. In urging that course, the Government does not dispute that the statutory language—and words used to define it—have just that effect. At oral argument, the Government conceded: "[I]f you just looked at the words like 'shocking' and 'offensive' on their face and gave them their ordinary meanings[,] they could easily encompass material that was shocking [or offensive] because it expressed an outrageous point of view or a point of view that most members" of society reject. But no matter, says the Government, because the statute is "susceptible of" a limiting construction that would remove this viewpoint bias. The Government's idea, abstractly phrased, is to narrow the statutory bar to "marks that are offensive [or] shocking to a substantial segment of the public because of their mode of expression, independent of any views that they may express." More concretely, the Government explains that this reinterpretation would mostly restrict the PTO to refusing marks that are "vulgar"—meaning "lewd," "sexually explicit or profane." Such a reconfigured bar, the Government says, would not turn on viewpoint, and so we could uphold it.

But we cannot accept the Government's proposal, because the statute says something markedly different. This Court, of course, may interpret "ambiguous statutory language" to "avoid serious constitutional doubts." *FCC v. Fox Television Stations, Inc.*, 556 U.S. 502, 516 (2009). But that canon of construction applies only when ambiguity exists. "We will not rewrite a law to conform it to constitutional requirements." *United States v. Stevens*, 559 U.S. 460, 481 (2010) (internal quotation marks and alteration omitted). So even assuming the Government's reading would eliminate First Amendment problems, we may adopt it only if we can see it in the statutory language. And we cannot. The "immoral or scandalous" bar stretches far beyond the Government's proposed construction. The statute as written does not draw the line at lewd, sexually explicit, or profane marks. Nor does it refer only to marks whose "mode of expression," independent of viewpoint, is particularly offensive. It covers the universe of immoral or scandalous—or (to use some PTO synonyms) offensive or disreputable—material. Whether or not lewd or profane. Whether the scandal and immorality comes from mode or instead from viewpoint. To cut the statute off where the Government urges is not to interpret the statute Congress enacted, but to fashion a new one.

And once the "immoral or scandalous" bar is interpreted fairly, it must be invalidated. The Government just barely argues otherwise. In the last paragraph of its brief, the Government gestures toward the idea that the provision is salvageable by virtue of its constitutionally permissible applications (in the Government's view, its applications to lewd, sexually explicit, or profane marks). In other words, the Government invokes our First Amendment overbreadth doctrine, and asks us to uphold the statute against facial attack because its unconstitutional applications are not "substantial" relative to "the statute's plainly legitimate sweep." *Stevens*, 559 U.S. at 473 (internal quotation marks omitted). But to begin with, this Court has never applied that kind of analysis to a viewpoint-discriminatory law. In *Tam*, for example, we did not pause to consider whether the disparagement clause might admit some permissible applications (say, to certain libelous speech) before striking it down. The Court's finding of viewpoint bias ended the matter. And similarly, it seems unlikely we would compare permissible and impermissible applications if Congress outright banned "offensive" (or to use some other examples, "divisive" or "subversive") speech. Once we have found that a law "aim[s] at the suppression of" views, why would it matter that Congress could have captured some of the same speech through a viewpoint-neutral statute? *Tam*, 582 U.S., at ___, 137 S. Ct., at 1761 (opinion of Kennedy, J.). But in any event, the "immoral or scandalous" bar is substantially overbroad. There are a great many immoral and scandalous ideas in the world (even more than there are swearwords), and the Lanham Act covers them all. It therefore violates the First Amendment.

We accordingly affirm the judgment of the Court of Appeals.

JUSTICE ALITO, concurring.

… Our decision does not prevent Congress from adopting a more carefully focused statute that precludes the registration of marks containing vulgar terms that play no real part in the expression of ideas. The particular mark in question in this case could be denied registration under such a statute. The term suggested by that mark is not needed to express any idea and, in fact, as commonly used today, generally signifies nothing except emotion and a severely limited vocabulary. The registration of such marks serves only to further coarsen our popular culture. But we are not legislators and cannot substitute a new statute for the one now in force.

CHIEF JUSTICE ROBERTS, concurring in part and dissenting in part.

… [T]he "scandalous" portion of the provision is susceptible of such a narrowing construction. Standing alone, the term "scandalous" need not be understood to reach marks that offend because of the ideas they convey; it can be read more narrowly to bar only marks that offend because of their mode of expression — marks that are obscene, vulgar, or profane....

JUSTICE BREYER, concurring in part and dissenting in part.

Our precedents warn us against interpreting statutes in ways that would likely render them unconstitutional. Following these precedents, I agree with Justice Sotomayor that, for the reasons she gives, we should interpret the word "scandalous" in the present statute to refer only to certain highly "vulgar" or "obscene" modes of expression.

The question, then, is whether the First Amendment permits the Government to rely on this statute, as narrowly construed, to deny the benefits of federal trademark registration to marks like the one at issue here, which involves the use of the term "FUCT" in connection with a clothing line that includes apparel for children and infants....

This case illustrates the limits of relying on rigid First Amendment categories, for the statute at issue does not fit easily into any of these categories.

The Court has not decided whether the trademark statute is simply a method of regulating pure "commercial speech." There may be reasons for doubt on that score. Trademarks, after all, have an expressive component in addition to a commercial one, and the statute does not bar anyone from speaking. To be sure, the statute does regulate the commercial function of trademarks. But it does so in a limited way designed primarily to ensure that a mark identifies the product's source.... Rather than puzzling over categorization, I believe we should focus on the interests the First Amendment protects and ask a more basic proportionality question: Does "the regulation at issue wor[k] harm to First Amendment interests that is disproportionate in light of the relevant regulatory objectives"? *Reed v. Town of Gilbert*, 576 U.S. ___, ___, 135 S. Ct. 2218, 2235–36 (2015).

Based on this proportionality analysis, I would conclude that the statute at issue here, as interpreted by Justice Sotomayor, does not violate the First Amendment.

How much harm to First Amendment interests does a bar on registering highly vulgar or obscene trademarks work? Not much. The statute leaves businesses free to use highly vulgar or obscene words on their products, and even to use such words directly next to other registered marks. Indeed, a business owner might even use a vulgar word as a trademark, provided that he or she is willing to forgo the benefits of registration.

JUSTICE SOTOMAYOR, with whom JUSTICE BREYER joins, concurring in part and dissenting in part.

The Court's decision today will beget unfortunate results. With the Lanham Act's scandalous-marks provision, 15 U.S.C. § 1052(a), struck down as unconstitutional viewpoint discrimination, the Government will have no statutory basis to refuse (and thus no choice but to begin) registering marks containing the most vulgar, profane, or obscene words and images imaginable.

The coming rush to register such trademarks—and the Government's immediate powerlessness to say no—is eminently avoidable. Rather than read the relevant text as the majority does, it is equally possible to read that provision's bar on the registration of "scandalous" marks to address only obscenity, vulgarity, and profanity. Such a narrowing construction would save that duly enacted legislative text by rendering it a reasonable, viewpoint-neutral restriction on speech that is permissible in the context of a beneficial governmental initiative like the trademark-registration system. I would apply that narrowing construction to the term "scandalous" and accordingly reject petitioner Erik Brunetti's facial challenge....

Notes and Questions

a. In the field of titles, trademarks play an important but difficult role. When a word or short phrase is being used as the title of a single creative work, the Lanham Act will not allow that title to be registered as a trademark. It will, however, permit the use of the mark if the title is part of a series of works, such as Harry Potter, Goosebumps, or Nancy Drew.

b. The PTO has a unique definition of a single creative work. It excludes from the prohibition musical bands, television and radio series, and educational seminars because "they are presumed to change with each presentation." The same approach applies to computer software, computer games, coloring books, and activity books. Lanham Act, 15 U.S.C. §§ 1051–1052, 1127; *Herbko Int'l, Inc. v. Kappa Books, Inc.*, 308 F.3d 1156, 1162–63 (Fed. Cir. 2002); https://www.uspto.gov/trademark/laws-regulations/title-single-work-refusal-and-how-overcome-refusal.

c. The battle over titles and trademarks has been fought in professional sports, music, and publishing. In the area of self-published romance novels, a battle erupted over the attempt to trademark the word "cocky" in a series of books using the cocky appellation. Faleena Hopkins authored The Cocky Series featuring the Cocker Brothers. The books included *Cocky Heart Surgeon, Cocky Cowboy, Cocky Biker, Cocky Roomie, Cocky Cop*, and even *Cocky Senator*. After Hopkins began asserting her trademark with cease and desist letters to competitors and the retailer Amazon, the Romance Writers of America (RWA) trade association contacted the Authors Guild and Amazon. Preliminary litigation over the marks began, but ultimately, faced with a strong backlash in the romance community, Hopkins surrendered the trademark and withdrew her claim to the exclusive use of the word Cocky in book titles. The situation highlights the potential power that trademark can provide, but also illustrates the costs and social implications of trying to raise an intellectual property fence around commonly used words and symbols.

d. Justice Roberts asks an important question that has been ignored by the majority in the line of Supreme Court cases including *Dastar, Steven, Tam*, and *Brunetti*: "does the regulation at issue work harm to First Amendment interests that is disproportionate in light of the relevant regulatory objectives?" quoting *Reed v. Town of Gilbert*, 135 S. Ct. 2218, 2235–36 (2015). What will be the consequence to other constitutional rights and societal needs if this question is not returned to the structure of First Amendment analysis?

Problem 6-F

To market an album, Bryce explored various public domain image resources and found an image of a late nineteenth century advertising poster. The ad is considered by Bryce and the band members to be in very bad taste. The product sold using the ad is no longer on the market, though the company that created the product continues to operate, selling food products, kitchen products, cleaners, and other goods. Bryce wishes to use the public domain image as part of the album cover and recapture the once iconic and now offensive image into an ironic statement to promote inclusion and diversity. Bryce comes to you for legal advice as to whether the former owner of the trademark or the trademark office will be able to stop the band's use of the mark as well as any other concerns that you might raise if the album art were to feature this historically accurate but offensive imagery.

G. Exploitation of Fictional Marks

Viacom Int'l, Inc. v. IJR Capital Invs., L.L.C.

891 F.3d 178 (5th Cir. 2018)

Viacom International, Inc. (Viacom) sued IJR Capital Investments, L.L.C. (IJR) for infringing on its common law trademark of The Krusty Krab—a fictional restaurant in the popular "SpongeBob SquarePants" animated television series—after IJR took steps to open seafood restaurants using the same name. The district court granted summary judgment to Viacom on its trademark infringement and unfair competition claims. IJR appeals, asserting that Viacom does not have a valid trademark for The Krusty Krab and that its seafood restaurants would not create a likelihood of confusion between the two marks. We affirm the judgment of the district court.

In 1999, Viacom launched the animated television series "SpongeBob SquarePants" on its Nickelodeon network. The show revolves around SpongeBob SquarePants, a sea sponge that wears square shorts, lives in an underwater pineapple, and works at the fictional The Krusty Krab restaurant as a fry cook with an array of characters including a cranky co-worker and the owner of The Krusty Krab. The show has become the most-watched animated television series for 15 consecutive years, with over 73 million viewers in the second quarter of 2016 alone. While the audience is predominately comprised of children, one-third of all viewers are 18 or older.

The fast food restaurant The Krusty Krab played a prominent role in the pilot episode of the series and has appeared in 166 of 203 episodes. The Krusty Krab was featured in two "SpongeBob SquarePants" feature films that grossed $470 million (and incurred $197 million in promotional expenses). The Krusty Krab Restaurant is also an element of Viacom's mobile app "SpongeBob Moves In" (seven million global downloads), appears in a play called *The SpongeBob Musical*, and is frequently mentioned in the franchise's advertisements and online outreach (approximately seven million page views across platforms per week). The press has referenced The Krusty Krab many times when discussing the show.

The Krusty Krab is also licensed to third parties for a variety of products. These licensed products include: licensed Krusty Krab playsets from Just Play, Mattel, The LEGO Company, and Mega Brands, Inc. ($1.4 million in royalties since 2009), the video game "SpongeBob SquarePants Creature from The Krusty Krab" (over one million units), The Krusty Krab aquarium accessories (187,000 units), reusable franchise-themed stickers of The Krusty Krab, The Krusty Krab shirts sold at The SpongeBob Store at Universal Studios, Florida, and more. Viacom has never attempted to license The Krusty Krab mark to a restaurant. However, Viacom's subsidiary company Paramount Pictures Corporation did license Bubba Gump Shrimp Co. for seafood restaurants based on the fictional business from the 1994 movie "Forrest Gump."

In 2014, IJR's owner, Javier Ramos, decided to open seafood restaurants in California and Texas. Ramos asserts that he was describing the crusted glaze applied to cooked seafood when his friend Ivan Murillo suggested naming the restaurant Crusted Crab, which quickly became The Krusty Krab. Both Murillo and Ramos deny having considered SpongeBob during this conversation, however Murillo has since stated that those who see the name may think of the restaurant from "SpongeBob SquarePants." Also, an IJR investor mentioned SpongeBob "out of the blue" while discussing the restaurant. Ramos said that he first became aware of the fictional restaurant from "SpongeBob SquarePants" when he performed a search using Google to determine if there were restaurants with a name similar to The Krusty Krab.

Because Ramos's search did not find an actual restaurant that used the mark, IJR filed a trademark application with the United States Patent and Trademark Office (USPTO) for THE KRUSTY KRAB. Viacom had not previously registered The Krusty Krab mark. The USPTO approved IJR's mark and published the application for opposition. Viacom did not oppose at this time, and the USPTO issued a notice of allowance for the mark authorizing issuance once IJR filed a statement of use.

Beyond filing an intent-to-use trademark application, IJR also developed a business plan for potential investors in The Krusty Krab. The business plan included a logo for the restaurant and described the eatery as a "Cajun seafood restaurant" that would sell shrimp, crawfish, and po-boys. IJR intended to target families, singles, and students through print, radio, and online advertisements. The business plan makes no reference to the SpongeBob franchise or the fictional restaurant The Krusty Krab. IJR also purchased four domain names for the restaurant concept, leased property in California, and procured restaurant equipment.

In November 2015, Viacom sent a cease-and-desist letter that demanded the withdrawal of IJR's trademark application and alleged infringement of The Krusty Krab mark. IJR promptly responded, declining to cease use and asserting that Viacom does not actually use The Krusty Krab as a trademark and that there was no likelihood of consumer confusion. However, IJR postponed opening any restaurants. Viacom then filed suit in January 2016.

Viacom asserted nine claims against IJR including unfair competition under the Lanham Act and trademark infringement under Texas common law. The complaint included allegations that IJR's use of the mark in connection with restaurant services was likely to cause, or to have caused, confusion or mistake and to have deceived potential customers, causing them to believe that the services offered by IJR were affiliated with, sponsored by, or connected with Viacom; use of the mark would materially influence customers' purchasing decisions for restaurant services; and as a result, Viacom suffered and would continue to suffer damages to its goodwill and reputation.

The district court then granted, in part, Viacom's summary judgment motion on its common law trademark infringement and Lanham Act unfair competition claims. The district court held that: Viacom established ownership of the mark through sales and licensing; Viacom demonstrated that The Krusty Krab has acquired distinctiveness; and every likelihood-of-confusion factor indicated IJR's proposed use would probably cause confusion. Viacom then requested that the district court dismiss its other seven claims with prejudice and enter final judgment. The district court did so, and IJR appealed.

A trademark infringement action under Texas common law is analyzed in the same manner as a Lanham Act claim. For Viacom to prevail on these claims, it must show (1) that it owns a legally protectable mark in The Krusty Krab and (2) that IJR's use of the mark creates a likelihood of confusion as to source, affiliation, or sponsorship.

IJR contends that the district court erred in granting summary judgment for Viacom. We review *de novo* a district court's grant of summary judgment. IJR specifically asserts that there are genuine issues of material fact as to whether Viacom owns a legally protectable mark and whether there is a likelihood of confusion between the two The Krusty Krab marks.

A trademark infringement action cannot be sustained unless the mark is legally protectable. While Viacom has never registered The Krusty Krab mark, the Supreme Court has held that the Lanham Act protects qualifying unregistered marks. The Lanham Act provides that the term "trademark" includes "any word, name, symbol, or device, or any combination thereof" that is used or intended to be used "to identify and distinguish" one's goods "from those manufactured or sold by others." Viacom's mark is legally protectable if it establishes ownership by demonstrating that it uses The Krusty Krab as a source identifier. Often this court has bypassed the use inquiry and conducted only a distinctiveness analysis. However, the two issues are separate questions, and because the use-as-a-source-indicator requirement is at issue in this case Viacom must establish both use and distinctiveness. We first consider the use of The Krusty Krab mark. Whether Viacom actually uses The Krusty Krab as a source identifier is a question of fact.

While registration of a mark is "prima facie evidence of ... the registrant's ownership of the mark," ownership "is established by use, not by registration." An ownership right "accrues when goods bearing the mark are placed on the market." Viacom's mark clearly appears on goods in the market, such as The Krusty Krab playsets and aquarium ornaments. The question in this case, however, is whether Viacom uses

The Krusty Krab to indicate origin because the purpose of trademark law is to prevent competitors from copying a source-identifying mark.

Before we assess whether Viacom uses The Krusty Krab as a source identifier, we address a threshold question: Can specific elements from within a television show—as opposed to the title of the show itself—receive trademark protection? We conclude that they can. While this court has never explored this precise issue, we have affirmed a judgment against the junior use of Conan the Barbarian—the title character of a comic book series—in a restaurant concept. [*See Conan Props., Inc. v. Conans Pizza, Inc.*, 752 F.2d 145, 148, 150 (5th Cir. 1985).] This holding suggests that trademark protection may be granted to certain characters, places, and elements of a broader entertainment entity. Additionally, other courts have unequivocally extended this protection to fictional elements of entertainment franchises. In *Warner Bros., Inc. v. Gay Toys, Inc.*, 658 F.2d 76, 78 (2d Cir. 1981), the Second Circuit held that trademark protection may extend "to the specific ingredients of a successful T.V. series." The Second Circuit held in that case that the General Lee—an orange muscle car with a Confederate flag emblem that was "prominently featured" on the successful television series "The Dukes of Hazzard"—fell within the ambit of Section 43(a) of the Lanham Act. Subsequently, the Seventh Circuit also affirmed an injunction barring the junior user from making a model of the "General Lee." The underlying purposes of trademark are to protect goodwill and "to protect consumers against confusion and monopoly," and "to protect the investment of producers in their trade names to which goodwill may have accrued and which goodwill free-riders may attempt to appropriate by using the first producer's mark, or one that is deceptively similar." Extending trademark protection to elements of television shows that serve as source identifiers can serve those purposes.

The success of "SpongeBob Square Pants" is not in dispute, but use within a popular television series does not necessarily mean that the mark is used as a source identifier. "The salient question" is whether The Krusty Krab mark, as used, will be recognized *in itself* as an indication of origin for the particular product or service. If the mark creates a separate and distinct commercial impression it performs the trademark function of identifying the source. In evaluating whether elements of a television series are trademarks, the focus is on the role that the element plays within the show and not the overall success or recognition of the show itself. When an element only occasionally appears in a successful television series, the indication-of-origin requirement may not be met.

For instance, in *Paramount Pictures Corp. v. Romulan Invasions*, [7 U.S.P.Q.2d 1897 (T.T.A.B. 1988),] Paramount (a subsidiary of Viacom) sought trademark protection on the Romulan mark, a fictional alien race in the "Star Trek" series. The Romulan mark was featured in television episodes, movies, books, licensed plastic spaceship models and dolls, puzzles, games, and more. The Trademark Trial and Appeal Board (T.T.A.B.) concluded that the mark was "only" used "from time to time" and held that Paramount "failed to establish any use of the term Romulan ... as a mark to distinguish its services." Star Trek fans may vehemently disagree with this analysis as a factual matter. However, we cite this decision to illustrate the conceptual aspects of the law in this area.

When an element plays a more central role in a franchise, trademark protection is ordinarily granted. For example, the Southern District of New York held that the Daily Planet, the employer of Clark Kent in "Superman," was a common law trademark because "[t]he totality of evidence demonstrates that the Daily Planet has over the years become inextricably woven into the fabric of the Superman story." Twenty-five years later, the Southern District of New York also held that Kryptonite—a registered trademark—was a protectable ingredient of the broader "Superman" franchise because it is a staple of the Superman character and story, the mark is immediately recognized or associated with the character Superman, and it identifies the entertainment and other goods and services created, distributed and/or licensed by or on behalf of DC Comics. Likewise, the Second and Seventh Circuits granted trademark protection to the General Lee from "The Dukes of Hazzard" because of its critical role in the television series. The Fifth Circuit has upheld trademark protection for a cartoon character that was central to the comic strip.

The Krusty Krab is analogous to protected marks like the Daily Planet, General Lee, and Conan the Barbarian. The mark is integral to "SpongeBob SquarePants," as it appears in over 80% of episodes, plays a prominent role in the SpongeBob films and musical, and is featured online, in video games, and on licensed merchandise. The Krusty Krab's central role in the multi-billion dollar SpongeBob franchise is strong evidence that it is recognized in itself as an indication of origin for Viacom's licensed goods and television services.

Viacom has extensively licensed The Krusty Krab mark. A trade or service mark may be acquired through its use by controlled licensees. Even if only the licensee uses the mark, ownership rights in a trademark or service mark can be acquired and maintained through the use of the mark by a controlled licensee. The record verifies that The Krusty Krab appears on many consumer products including: reusable SpongeBob-themed stickers; multiple Krusty Krab playsets from brands like Lego; an aquarium ornament; a video game; and shirts, among other products. On most of those products, The Krusty Krab is featured prominently and contributes in identifying the good. This licensing regime has generated millions of dollars for Viacom and provides further evidence that Viacom uses The Krusty Krab as a source identifier and therefore owns the mark.

The Krusty Krab's key role in "SpongeBob SquarePants" coupled with the consistent use of the mark on licensed products establishes ownership of the mark because of its immediate recognition as an identifier of the source for goods and services.

While Viacom has established ownership of the mark through its use as a source identifier, Viacom must also prove that The Krusty Krab mark is distinctive in order to establish that it is legally protectable.

A mark can be distinctive in one of two ways. A mark is inherently distinctive if its intrinsic nature serves to identify a particular source. Even if a mark is not inherently distinctive, it can acquire distinctiveness if it has developed secondary meaning. The district court held that Viacom failed to demonstrate that its mark is inherently distinctive, but that The Krusty Krab had acquired distinctiveness through secondary meaning. Because we agree that the mark has acquired distinctiveness through secondary meaning, we pretermit consideration of whether the mark is inherently distinctive.

A mark develops secondary meaning when, in the minds of the public, the primary significance of a mark is to identify the source of the product rather than the product itself. One commentator has explained that "[i]n determining what can qualify as a trademark, it is crucial that the designation in question perform the job of identifying and distinguishing the goods or services with which the symbol appears."[36] To determine whether a mark has acquired secondary meaning, courts consider the following seven factors:

> (1) length and manner of use of the mark or trade dress, (2) volume of sales, (3) amount and manner of advertising, (4) nature of use of the mark or trade dress in newspapers and magazines, (5) consumer-survey evidence, (6) direct consumer testimony, and (7) the defendant's intent in copying the [mark].[37]

Several factors in combination may show that a mark has developed secondary meaning even if each factor alone would not.

Whether a mark has acquired secondary meaning is a question of fact. At summary judgment, this court considers whether IJR raised a fact question as to secondary meaning—i.e. whether consumers associate The Krusty Krab only with Viacom. Viacom's burden of demonstrating secondary meaning is substantial and requires a high degree of proof. Nonetheless, summary judgment may be granted if the record compels the conclusion that the movant is entitled to judgment as a matter of law.

The first factor—length and manner of use—supports Viacom. The Krusty Krab appeared in the pilot episode of "SpongeBob SquarePants" eighteen years ago. Over 80% of the episodes aired from 1999 through today have included The Krusty Krab, and it is a central element of the SpongeBob universe. The recurrent use of The Krusty Krab over the past eighteen years in a widely viewed television program is undisputed, as is the manner of use.

As for volume of sales, Viacom has earned millions on licensed products that display The Krusty Krab mark, and two feature films in the SpongeBob franchise—which prominently featured The Krusty Krab—grossed a combined $470 million. This court has considered the sale of items grossing $30,500 to be low volume, but

---

36. 1 J. THOMAS McCARTHY, TRADEMARKS & UNFAIR COMPETITION § 3.1 (5th ed. 2017).
37. Test Masters Educ. Servs., Inc. v. Robin Singh Educ. Servs., Inc., 799 F.3d 437, 445 (5th Cir. 2015) (quoting [Bd. of Supervisors for La. State Univ. Agric. & Mech. Coll. v.] Smack Apparel Co., 550 F.3d at 476) (alteration in original).

has affirmed a finding of secondary meaning on review of a summary judgment when sales totaled $93 million.

The relevant question with regard to factor three—the amount and manner of advertising—is not the *extent* of the promotional efforts, but their *effectiveness* in altering the meaning of the mark to the consuming public. There have been numerous print and Internet advertisements for The Krusty Krab-licensed products, and $197 million was spent in promotional expenditures for the two "SpongeBob SquarePants" feature films. The effectiveness of this advertising is evident from the success of product sales and the films. Though the effectiveness of the advertising as to The Krusty Krab mark, specifically, has not been directly proven, its depiction in advertisements is such that the public would recognize the mark as more than an artistic backdrop.

With respect to the nature and use of the mark in media—factor four—The Krusty Krab is often referenced by the press. The mark frequently appears on the "SpongeBob SquarePants" social media platforms and is integrated into the SpongeBob website and mobile app. This evidence supports Viacom's assertion that its word mark has acquired secondary meaning.

The record does not contain consumer-survey evidence as to whether The Krusty Krab has acquired secondary meaning, but survey evidence is not required to establish secondary meaning. There is no direct consumer testimony nor any consideration of IJR's intent in the distinctiveness inquiry. Therefore, there is no evidence pertaining to factors five and six. The evidence regarding IJR's intent in copying the mark is discussed in more detail below. That evidence is inconclusive.

IJR does not dispute the underlying facts but asserts that they merely establish that the public recognizes "SpongeBob SquarePants" as a distinct source of products; according to IJR, The Krusty Krab is just a cartoon restaurant. This is not a reasonable inference from the undisputed evidence. The record clearly shows that The Krusty Krab is a focal point in the "SpongeBob SquarePants" television series and films, The Krusty Krab has continually been depicted in the advertising and promotion of the franchise over the past eighteen years, and it is used in the sale of products. The factors lead inescapably to the conclusion that in the minds of consumers, The Krusty Krab identifies the source of products, which is Viacom, the creator of the "SpongeBob SquarePants" fictional universe and its inhabitants. Viacom's mark has acquired distinctiveness through secondary meaning as a matter of law.

Viacom must also prove that IJR's use of The Krusty Krab creates a likelihood of confusion as to source, affiliation, or sponsorship. It has met that burden.

To establish a likelihood of confusion, Viacom must show "a probability of confusion, which is more than a mere possibility of confusion." Word association with Viacom's The Krusty Krab is insufficient to establish a probable likelihood of confusion, and the court "must 'consider the marks in the context that a customer perceives them in the marketplace.'" To assess whether use of a mark creates a likelihood of confusion as to affiliation, sponsorship, or source, this court considers the so-called "digits of confusion." The digits form a "flexible and nonexhaustive list" that includes the following seven factors:

> (1) the type of mark allegedly infringed; (2) the similarity between the two marks; (3) the similarity of the products or services; (4) the identity of retail outlets and purchasers; (5) the identity of the advertising media used; (6) the defendant's intent; and (7) any evidence of actual confusion.[38]

At times, our court has listed eight factors, the additional one being the degree of care exercised by potential purchasers. However, neither of the parties in the present case, nor the district court, has discussed that factor. In any event, no single factor is dispositive, and a finding of a likelihood of confusion need not be supported by a majority of the factors.

Likelihood of confusion is a question of fact. However, summary judgment is proper if the record compels the conclusion that the movant is entitled to judgment as a matter of law. The district court held that all of the factors support a likelihood of confusion and ruled in Viacom's favor. Because all inferences must be made in the non-movant's favor at summary judgment, the district court erred in finding that *every* digit of confusion weighs in Viacom's favor. Nonetheless, Viacom has established that as a matter of law there is a likelihood of confusion between the two marks.

Context is critical to a likelihood-of-confusion analysis, and we must consider the application of each digit in light of the specific circumstances of the case; otherwise, we risk inadvertently lowering the standard of confusion. Because of the posture of this case, context is limited as IJR has not yet opened its restaurant. However, IJR has filed an intent-to-use trademark application for the name "The Krusty Krab" in restaurant services. It has also taken steps towards opening the restaurant such as leasing property, procuring equipment, purchasing domain names, and developing a comprehensive business plan. This court must not divine the theme and details of the restaurant, but the record contains sufficient context to conduct a likelihood-of-confusion analysis.

The first digit, the type of mark, refers to the strength of the mark. In evaluating the strength of The Krusty Krab mark, the focus is on Viacom's mark. The more distinctive a mark, the stronger the mark. Strong marks are entitled to more protection because there is a greater likelihood that consumers will confuse the junior user's use with that of the senior user. Viacom's mark is strong because it has acquired distinctiveness through secondary meaning. Therefore the first digit weighs in favor of a likelihood of confusion.

The second digit is the similarity of the marks. Assessing the similarity of the marks requires consideration of the marks' appearance, sound, and meaning. Even if two marks are distinguishable, we ask whether, under the circumstances of use, the marks are similar enough that a reasonable person could believe the two products

---

38. Scott Fetzer Co. v. House of Vacuums Inc., 381 F.3d 477, 485 (5th Cir. 2004) (quoting Elvis Presley Enters., Inc. v. Capece, 141 F.3d 188, 197 (5th Cir. 1998).

have a common origin or association. Viacom's The Krusty Krab is a word mark, and IJR's mark has identical spelling and pronunciation, including the unconventional use of K's instead of C's. While marks can share a key word and still be stylistically and typographically distinguishable so as to produce different commercial impressions, IJR's mark is verbatim the same and there is no genuine issue of material fact with respect to this digit of confusion. Logos for the two marks may differ, but the words themselves are indistinguishable and would likely confuse consumers as to the source, affiliation or sponsorship of IJR's The Krusty Krab restaurant.

The third digit in the likelihood of confusion analysis is the similarity of the products or services. The more similar the products and services, the greater the likelihood of confusion. Viacom's The Krusty Krab has a distinct theme as a fictional hamburger restaurant, whereas IJR has not fully developed a theme for its planned seafood restaurant. Existing context suggests that the restaurants will have little thematic overlap. For example, IJR's business plan never references SpongeBob, and IJR's sample menu serves po-boys and boiled seafood, not fast food hamburgers. While there is little evidence of thematic overlap between the restaurants, IJR nevertheless plans to open a restaurant, and given the success of SpongeBob, that indicates a likelihood of confusion.

Furthermore, the danger of affiliation or sponsorship confusion increases when the junior user's services are in a market that is one into which the senior user would naturally expand. In *Conan Properties, Inc. v. Conans Pizza, Inc.*, this court recognized the logical extension of fictional characters to restaurants, explaining that today's consumers expect cartoon character endorsements and act favorably toward them in the restaurant setting. Here, both marks already identify restaurants. Furthermore, Viacom could naturally develop a real The Krusty Krab restaurant based on the fictional eatery, as its subsidiary did when it licensed Bubba Gump Shrimp Co., a fictional business in the movie "Forrest Gump," to create a chain of real seafood restaurants. A reasonable jury would find that factor three favors a likelihood of confusion.

The fourth digit is the identity of retail outlets and purchasers. The greater the overlap between retail outlets and purchasers, the greater the likelihood of confusion. IJR does not yet have a retail outlet or customers, but its business plan and Ramos's testimony provide context. IJR plans to open restaurants in California and Texas, and it intends to target the general public, particularly families, singles, and students ... as well as the area's work force. At this general level of abstraction, Viacom also targets the general public, including residents of California and Texas. Based on this broad overlap, the district court found that factor four weighed in Viacom's favor. However, there are substantial differences in the retail outlets and the predominant purchasers that mitigate the possibility of confusion.

The retail outlets have little overlap, as Viacom presumably targets television viewers, toy stores, and online retailers, whereas IJR's services will only be available in brick-and-mortar restaurants. This court previously held that when a senior user distributes primarily through grocery stores and a junior user distributes exclusively through fast food outlets, there are basic differences in modes of distribution even if the senior user also distributes some of its product through fast food outlets. Likewise, Viacom and IJR would have different retail outlets even if there were marginal overlap.

There is some overlap in purchasers—IJR targets families, two-thirds of SpongeBob viewers are children, and one-third of viewers are technically adults—but the core consumers of each mark are dissimilar. Purchaser identity is similar, for example, when the competing marks both target trained cosmetologists or drillers of natural gas. By contrast, substantial dissimilarities existed when the junior user's fast-food pizza patrons were "primarily young (85.6% under 35 years of age), single (61%) males (63.3%)," while the senior user's purchasers of sugar in grocery stores were "predominately middle-aged housewives." There is no empirical data in the present case, and it is not clear how much the identity of consumers and purchasers would overlap. SpongeBob predominately targets children and young adults through mostly digital channels, whereas IJR's retail outlets would be physical restaurants. However, it is reasonable to infer that some children who are SpongeBob fans would influence their parents' or caretakers' decision to eat at a Krusty Krab restaurant, and that adult SpongeBob fans might well dine at a Krusty Krab restaurant, at least once, due to the name. But the extent of the overlap between purchasers cannot be gauged adequately on the record before us.

The fifth digit of confusion is the identity of advertising media. The greater the similarity in the advertising campaigns, the greater the likelihood of confusion. Ramos has testified, and IJR's business plan confirms, that IJR will advertise through traditional media such as television and print, as well as online media including social networks and "Google ads." Viacom advertises "SpongeBob SquarePants" on television—and through it The Krusty Krab mark—and it also promotes the mark online.

This court has held that when both companies use print advertisements, direct mailings, and Internet promotion" it "supports an inference that the parties use similar advertising and marketing channels. On the other hand, when one mark advertises nationally and the other mark advertises locally in a specialized manner, there are significant differences between the advertising media used. Absent any existing advertising by IJR, it is difficult to assess the similarity between the campaigns. We have held that this digit was "minimally probative" when a defendant did not advertise and the record "was unable to provide much information about these ads." Likewise, while there is substantial overlap in the abstract, without specific advertising content, digit five does not weigh in favor of a likelihood of confusion.

The sixth digit is the defendant's intent. Although not necessary to a finding of likelihood of confusion, a defendant's intent to confuse may alone be sufficient to justify an inference that there is a likelihood of confusion. If there is no evidence of intent to confuse, then this factor is neutral. The relevant inquiry is whether IJR intended to derive benefits from Viacom's reputation by using The Krusty Krab mark. Evidence that a defendant intends to "pass off" its product as that of another can be found through imitation of packaging, similar distribution methods, and more.

The district court acknowledged that it was "not clear" whether Ramos intended to derive benefits from Viacom's reputation. Nonetheless, it held that IJR acted in bad faith because Murillo associated the phrase The Krusty Krab with "SpongeBob SquarePants" and Ramos was aware of Viacom's use of the mark before he submitted his trademark application. Murillo's word association, without more, does not establish bad faith at summary judgment. Furthermore, while some courts would infer that Ramos's selection of a mark with knowledge of another's use is a signal of intent, this court has held that, mere awareness of the senior user's mark does not establish bad intent. Also, Murillo averred that he never mentioned SpongeBob during his discussions with Ramos, and IJR asserted that the original Crusted Crab name was created to reference seafood with a crust on it and that the spelling modification was a stylistic decision.

While a jury may disbelieve IJR, at the summary judgment stage there is a genuine issue of material fact as to whether IJR intended to derive benefits from Viacom's The Krusty Krab. IJR asserts that it spontaneously developed its name, and this court has held that organic creation of a mark shows lack of intent and does not support a likelihood of confusion. IJR utilized only one element of the show—The Krusty Krab name—a name that Viacom did not register. These facts are more favorable to IJR than to the *Conans Pizza* junior user, but even when there was a "pervasive, inescapable aura of CONAN THE BARBARIAN," this court held that "sufficient doubt exists regarding whether that use was designed to capitalize on [plaintiff's] goodwill." At summary judgment, this court must "disregard all evidence favorable to the moving party that the jury is not required to believe," and "construe all the evidence and reasonable inferences deduced therefrom in a light most favorable to [IJR]." The district court erred in inferring bad intent, as evidence of IJR's malevolence is circumstantial. Accordingly, this digit does not support a finding of a likelihood of confusion.

The seventh digit is evidence of actual confusion. This is the best evidence of a likelihood of confusion. Even if initial consumer confusion is quickly dispelled, this initial misunderstanding is evidence of confusion. To show actual confusion, a plaintiff may rely on anecdotal instances of consumer confusion or consumer surveys. Viacom commissioned Dr. Blair to perform a consumer survey, and it found that 30% of respondents indicated that a restaurant named The Krusty Krab was "operated by, affiliated or connected with, or approved or sponsored by Viacom" and that 35% of respondents associated such a restaurant with Viacom. There is also anecdotal evidence of confusion: Ivan Murillo admitted that The Krusty Krab calls to mind "SpongeBob SquarePants," and an IJR investor mentioned SpongeBob "out of the blue" while discussing the restaurant.

The district court admitted Dr. Blair's report over IJR's objections—which this court reviews for abuse of discretion—and held that the survey results were "sufficient" to weigh in favor of a likelihood of confusion. Consumer surveys may evidence confusion at levels less than 30%. This court has "set a low bar ... stating that a plaintiff need provide 'very little proof of actual confusion ... to prove likelihood of confusion.'" Construing all evidence in IJR's favor, Blair's survey has probative value and there is anecdotal evidence of actual confusion. We therefore conclude that this digit weighs in favor of a likelihood of confusion.

The record shows that there is no genuine issue of material fact as to likelihood of confusion. The digits of confusion — particularly the strength of Viacom's mark, the identical spelling and pronunciation of the marks, both marks' identification of restaurants, and evidence of actual confusion — dictate that IJR's use of the mark infringes on Viacom's trademark. By creating a connection in the consumer's mind between IJR's restaurant-in-development and The Krusty Krab from "SpongeBob SquarePants," there is an impermissible likelihood of confusion as to source, affiliation, or sponsorship.

While this holding does not grant trademark protection to Viacom in every context, third parties cannot appropriate the goodwill and reputation of The Krusty Krab by naming a restaurant The Krusty Krab absent a showing that the restaurant was developed in a context sufficient to avoid any likelihood of consumer confusion. This case squarely falls within the protection of the Lanham Act and consumers would affiliate Viacom's legally protectable The Krusty Krab mark with IJR's seafood restaurant by the same name.

For the foregoing reasons, we AFFIRM the judgment of the district court.

Notes and Questions

a. Although a lengthy summary judgment opinion, the *Viacom* analysis provides an excellent illustration of how courts apply the factors (or "digits") that go to establish secondary meaning and to establish likelihood of infringement. The opinion provides a model analysis for addressing likelihood of confusion for an unregistered mark, a very common occurrence.

b. One of the longer running battles over the commercialization of fictional brands has involved Homer Simpson's favorite beverage of choice, Duff Beer. Matt Groening and the television producers were reluctant to allow the licensing of Duff Beer, given the demographic age of the animated show's audience, but limited licenses have been used outside the United States and in a few studio-controlled restaurants. That has not, however, stopped a competition in the E.U. and other jurisdictions over the control of the trademark.

c. Fictional terms also show up with regularity in science fiction and fantasy. For an interesting exploration of the card game Sabbac, featured with increasing frequency in the Star Wars universe, see *Lucasfilm Ltd. v. Ren Ventures L.L.C.*, No. 17-cv-07249-RS (N.D. Cal. April 24, 2018).

d. Just as with many of the important milestones in comic book history, Superman led the way in development of trademarks from within the fictional world. *See DC Comics, Inc. v. Powers*, 465 F. Supp. 843 (S.D.N.Y. 1978) (protecting the Daily Planet from unauthorized use as the name of a third party's publication).

e. In the context of videogames, the in-game experience may use third party trademarks. In *E.S.S. Entm't 2000, Inc. v. Rock Star Videos, Inc.*, 547 F.3d 1095 (9th Cir.

2008), the Ninth Circuit permitted the use of real trademarks in a parody of the Los Angeles cityscape to determine "whether the Game would confuse its players into thinking that the Play Pen is somehow behind the Pig Pen or that it sponsors [defendant's] product." *Id.* at 1100. Had a third party's trademark and trade dress been featured in the game, called out in advertisements, and been identical rather than parodies, there might be a greater challenge to their use in the game. *See Elec. Arts, Inc. v. Textron Inc.*, No. C 12-00118 WHA, 2012 WL 3042668 (N.D. Cal. July 25, 2012). Trademarks and trade dress utilized as sets and props for film and television do not face this risk. So, to what extent does this different outcome change because videogames are treated as commercial products rather than communicative works?

Problem 6-G

Bryce calls you to explore an idea. A family member has taken over a local diner, and Bryce has suggested renaming the restaurant Lou's Café and adopting the décor featured in the Back to the Future franchise. Bryce did some research and has not identified any trademark registrations by Universal, the producer of the film, for the trademark or trade dress. Bryce believes that decorating the interior with Back to the Future posters and memorabilia would make the location pop. Advise Bryce of the potential liability if the local diner's owners were to adopt the name and trade dress from the movie.

H. Bibliography

Barton Beebe & Jeanne Fromer, *Are We Running Out of Trademarks? An Empirical Study of Trademark Depletion and Congestion*, 131 HARV. L. REV. 945 (2018).

Sheldon W. Halpern, *Trafficking in Trademarks: Setting Boundaries for the Uneasy Relationship Between "Property Rights" and Trademark and Publicity Rights*, 58 DEPAUL L. REV. 1013 (2009).

Rita Heimes, *Trademarks, Identity, and Justice*, 11 J. MARSHALL REV. INTELL. PROP. L. 133, 134 (2011).

Laura A. Heymann, *Naming, Identity, and Trademark Law*, 86 IND. L.J. 381 (2011).

Anne Gilson LaLonde & Jerome Gilson, *Trademarks Laid Bare: Marks That May Be Scandalous or Immoral*, 101 TRADEMARK REP. 1476 (2011).

Viva R. Moffat, *Mutant Copyrights and Backdoor Patents: The Problem of Overlapping Intellectual Property Protection*, 19 BERKELEY TECH. L.J. 1473 (2004).

Richard A. Posner, *Misappropriation: A Dirge*, 40 HOUS. L. REV. 621 (2003).

Chapter 7

Rights of Publicity and Identity

A. Introduction[1]

The law on publicity rights owes its origins to a theory first identified by Samuel Warren and Louis Brandeis in 1890.[2] In their seminal article, they explained that an individual's protection of person and property "is a principle as old as the common law; but it has been found necessary from time to time to define anew the exact nature and extent of such protection. Political, social, and economic changes entail the recognition of new rights, and the common law, in its eternal youth, grows to meet the new demands of society."[3]

1. Subject Matter of Publicity Rights

The rights of publicity apply only to the commercial exploitation of a person's identity. Under the protection of publicity rights, a person has no legal protection to stop the non-commercial representation or refence to that person. The concept of identity includes name, voice, signature, photograph, or likeness. It typically extends to nicknames and associated catch phrases. For example, Johnny Carson was protected from another company using "Here's Johnny" to sell its products (portable toilets).

The most common types of commercial use involve companies using the name or image of a celebrity in advertisements endorsing a product or shown using the product. Celebrities driving cars, drinking soda, or featuring their names on sporting goods are all examples of commercial use.

The items which should be exempt from the commercial products category are those which are editorial or communicative in nature. Newspapers, televisions shows, movies, music, books, games, and theater are in a very broad category of editorial or communicative services. It should be noted that a newspaper such as the *New York Times* is still sold in a tangible form for a profit. Neither the tangible nature of the newspaper nor the for-profit motive of the business eliminates its communicative

---

1. Adapted from Jon M. Garon, The Entrepreneur's Intellectual Property and Business Handbook (2017).
2. Samuel D. Warren & Louis D. Brandeis, *The Right to Privacy*, 4 Harv. L. Rev. 193 (1890).
3. *Id.*

role. A newspaper is free to print photographs of individuals without their permission because a free press is of much higher societal value than the property rights associated with publicity rights, and this societal value is incorporated into the First Amendment of the U.S. Constitution.

Generally speaking, newspapers, television news, television comedy shows, original paintings (as well as limited edition lithographs), and broadcasts of sporting events will not be considered commercial. Posters, coffee mugs, lunch boxes, and similar memorabilia will generally fall into the commercial category. The difference between these categories can be very subjective, however, resulting in a great deal of ambiguity and hand-wringing.

2. Unfair Competition under the Lanham Act for Rights of Publicity

Section 43(a) is a provision under the trademark statutes regulating unregistered trademarks, and it can be very useful for the protection of names and other attributes of publicity rights. The largest distinction between §43(a) and publicity rights is that a state law publicity claim does not require proof of any misleading conduct or likelihood of confusion. In this way, the federal test is somewhat more demanding than the evidence of impact required in most states.

Lanham Act claims are so common for celebrity cases that courts have adopted a set of factors to determine the likelihood of confusion specifically for these types of claims. The eight factors are as follows:

(1) The level of recognition that the plaintiff has among the segment of the society for whom the defendant's product is intended;

(2) The relatedness of the fame or success of the plaintiff to the defendant's product;

(3) The similarity of the likeness used by the defendant to the actual plaintiff;

(4) Evidence of actual confusion;

(5) Marketing channels used;

(6) Likely degree of purchaser care;

(7) Defendant's intent on selecting the plaintiff; and

(8) Likelihood of expansion of the product lines.

Although these are all factors that are appropriate for consideration in determining the likelihood of confusion, they are not necessarily of equal importance, nor do they necessarily apply to every case.[4]

These factors parallel the likelihood of confusion factors for trademark claims, but they focus on the fame of the plaintiff and the relationship of the fame to the

---

4. Downing v. Abercrombie & Fitch, 265 F.3d 994, 1007–08 (9th Cir. 2001).

defendant's product. At least with regard to the famous plaintiff's complaint about the misuse of her identity for the false endorsement of products, federal protection remains available under this law.

3. Matters Not Protected by Publicity Rights

Because news reporting and other editorial activities are typically outside of the definition of commerce, publicity rights do not affect news, commentary, criticism, or other editorial uses of one's identity. The limitation is not restricted to news reporting. Films, novels, and books based on true stories do not require permission of their subjects, meaning that publicity rights need not be licensed. Having said that, there are many sound business reasons to seek a license, and the lack of publicity rights does not eliminate the need for the producers of these films and authors of these books to be mindful of defamation laws.

Finally, there remains an inherent limitation because names are not unique, even among celebrities. Michael Jackson refers to both the internationally famous youngest brother of the family music group and a nationally famous radio host. Janet Jackson refers to both Michael's equally famous sister and a highly respected professor at Washburn University School of Law. Just as with the trademark laws of surnames, the laws involving publicity rights do not give a celebrity an exclusive right to his or her name to the exclusion of others with the same name.

4. Relationship between Publicity and Copyright

Publicity rights also have a very strange relationship with copyright, particularly in the context of motion picture and television production. Actors become famous for portraying characters, but the actors have no direct ownership interest in those characters. The actors begin to develop a publicity interest not just in their own identity, but in the identity of the copyrighted character owned by the motion picture or television studio.

If the film company wants to use the actual likeness of an actor to sell action figures, then the actor must agree to enter into a new agreement with the producer—often with significant compensation for the actor. Often, the film producer will forego the actor's consent by giving the toys different faces than the actors in the movies. When Paramount Television, the producer of the hit television show *Cheers*, decided to open a series of bars modeled after the set of the show, it could not agree to terms with the actors playing Cliff and Norm. The bars were opened with animatronic mannequins that looked only vaguely like the actors playing the roles. But in the minds of the public, the actors were so closely linked with the roles of the characters that the court found there could still be a likelihood of confusion, despite the attempts to make the dolls look different than the actors.[5]

---

5. Wendt v. Host Int'l, Inc., 125 F.3d 806 (9th Cir. 1997).

If the copyright holder of a television show selects a photograph of the show's cast for the advertising posters and cover of the television series DVDs, only the copyright holder has a property interest in those photographs because the communicative nature of the television show extends to the marketing of that content. The actors depicted in the photograph generally will not have a claim under state rights of publicity. To reinforce this result, however, contracts are used to reinforce this understanding between the parties.

5. Other Limitations on Publicity Rights— First Amendment and Quasi Fair Use

For example, when Cardtoons, L.C. began selling parody major league baseball trading cards, the players objected. Like the Wacky Packages from a generation earlier, these cards served to poke fun and parody the increasingly commercial national pastime. Trading cards are a commercial product, so the only basis for denying the Major League Baseball Players Association's requested injunction to stop the sale of the cards was fair use or First Amendment limitations on their claim.[6]

The *Cardtoons* court found that because the Oklahoma statute did not allow for a fair use exception, it could not infer one from other laws such as copyright or trademark. Without a fair use exception to state publicity law, the court instead limited the application of the state publicity laws so that the laws were consistent with First Amendment protections of speech. By limiting the law, it provided Cardtoons with legal protection to continue selling its parody baseball cards.

In another sports example, the Court of Appeals for the Sixth Circuit attempted to balance the tension between free speech and publicity rights involving a series of lithographs entitled "*Masters of Augusta*" depicting Tiger Woods and other Masters champions. The court explained "[t]here is an inherent tension between the right of publicity and the right of freedom of expression under the First Amendment. This tension becomes particularly acute when the person seeking to enforce the right is a famous actor, athlete, politician, or otherwise famous person whose exploits, activities, accomplishments, and personal life are subject to constant scrutiny and comment in the public media."[7] The court looked to both First Amendment and copyright fair use analysis to shape its opinion. It relied on a California Supreme Court opinion which suggested the fair use test could be synthesized into whether the "celebrity likeness is one of the 'raw materials' from which an original work is synthesized, or whether the depiction or imitation of the celebrity is the very sum and substance of the work in question."[8] After reviewing the First Amendment and

6. Cardtoons, L.C. v. Major League Baseball Players Ass'n, 95 F.3d 959 (10th Cir. 1996).
7. ETW Corp. v. Jireh Publ'g, Inc., 332 F.3d 915, 931 (6th Cir. 2003).
8. *Id.* at 936 (quoting Comedy III Prod., Inc. v. Gary Saderup, Inc., 25 Cal. 4th 387, 406, 21 P.3d 797, 809 (2001)).

fair use issues, it determined that the artist's use of Tiger Woods and the other famous golfers in the limited edition painting and lithographs was a fair use of their publicity rights.

Other cases emphasize the copyright aspects of fair use. The California Supreme Court, in particular, has struggled to use the copyright fair use test. It emphasized the importance of the first factor of copyright's four-prong analysis, focusing on "whether the new work merely 'supersede[s] the objects' of the original creation, or instead adds something new, with a further purpose or different character, altering the first with new expression, meaning, or message; it asks, in other words, whether and to what extent the new work is 'transformative.'"[9] The court also looked to the effect on the marketplace—"does the marketability and economic value of the challenged work derive primarily from the fame of the celebrity depicted? If this question is answered in the negative, then there would generally be no actionable right of publicity."[10]

6. Relation of Protection for State-Law Right

With the growth of the Internet and a new blurring of the distinctions between privacy, publicity and unfair competition, it is likely that the number of states recognizing some type of protection for their citizens will only increase. When added to the federal unfair competition protection of §43(a) and the corresponding state unfair competition law, business owners would be wise to assume that there is some identity ownership in every state.

7. Term of Publicity Rights

Twenty-three states currently recognize a postmortem right either by statute or common law. These states include, among others, California, Florida, and Nevada. The duration of the right after the death of a celebrity varies, ranging from 10 years from the date of death in Washington if there was no commercial value at death, to 100 years from the date of death in Indiana and Oklahoma. California provides for the right to survive 70 years after the death of a celebrity.[11]

The states that have adopted publicity rights through the courts provide even less guidance regarding the existence of postmortem rights or their duration. Because it is clear that some states reject postmortem rights while others extend these rights for an entire century, business decisions will either be very local in nature or they will

---

9. *Comedy III Prod., Inc.*, 21 P.3d at 808 (*quoting* Folsom v. Marsh, 9 F. Cas. 342, 348 (CCD Mass. 1841) (No. 4,901), *in* Campbell v. Acuff-Rose Music, Inc. 510 U.S. 569, 579 (1994)). Although the court may be misguided in rejecting the entirety of the fair use analysis in favor of only two prongs, the explanation of that analysis will be better placed in another publication.

10. *Comedy III Prod., Inc.*, 21 P.3d at 810.

11. Erik W. Kahn & Pou-I "Bonnie" Lee, *"Delebs" and Postmortem Right of Publicity*, Landslide, Jan.–Feb. 2016, at 10, 10–11 (internal footnotes omitted).

focus on the economic value of rights for living parties with the knowledge that the rights will lose some protection after the death of the celebrity.

8. Taxonomy of Publicity Rights Usage

First, there are products focusing on the identity itself. Autobiographies, biographies, personal websites, fan websites, and infomercials typically fall into this category. Docudramas and true-life stories can fall into this category for the persons highlighted by the work. Each of these has content primarily about the celebrity or person featured.

Second, there are products where the particular identity is reproduced in a manner incidental to the product: background photographs that viewers can recognize, names used in song lyrics, personally identifiable data that can be culled from databases, and actors' images when those actors are portraying characters other than themselves (as actors rather than in their role as celebrities). These reflect the most common uses of identity interests, and for these common commercial uses, simple releases are sufficient. In practice, implied consent often suffices, though written documentation always provides greater certainty.

B. Publicity
Zacchini v. Scripps-Howard Broadcasting Co.
433 U.S. 562, 573 (1977)

[The case of the "Human Cannonball" is presented in Chapter I. One particular passage restates the importance of the right of publicity:] [T]he State's interest in permitting a "right of publicity" is in protecting the proprietary interest of the individual in his act in part to encourage such entertainment. As we later note, the State's interest is closely analogous to the goals of patent and copyright law, focusing on the right of the individual to reap the reward of his endeavors and having little to do with protecting feelings or reputation. Second, the two torts differ in the degree to which they intrude on dissemination of information to the public. In "false light" cases the only way to protect the interests involved is to attempt to minimize publication of the damaging matter, while in "right of publicity" cases the only question is who gets to do the publishing. An entertainer such as petitioner usually has no objection to the widespread publication of his act as long as he gets the commercial benefit of such publication.

[New York] Civil Rights Law
§§ 50, 51 McKinney (2019)

§ 50. A person, firm or corporation that uses for advertising purposes, or for the purposes of trade, the name, portrait or picture of any living person without having first obtained the written consent of such person, or if a minor of his or her parent or guardian, is guilty of a misdemeanor.

§ 51. Any person whose name, portrait, picture or voice is used within this state for advertising purposes or for the purposes of trade without the written consent first obtained as above provided may maintain an equitable action in the supreme court of this state against the person, firm or corporation so using his name, portrait, picture or voice, to prevent and restrain the use thereof; and may also sue and recover damages for any injuries sustained by reason of such use and if the defendant shall have knowingly used such person's name, portrait, picture or voice in such manner as is forbidden or declared to be unlawful by section fifty of this article, the jury, in its discretion, may award exemplary damages. But nothing contained in this article shall be so construed as to prevent any person, firm or corporation from selling or otherwise transferring any material containing such name, portrait, picture or voice in whatever medium to any user of such name, portrait, picture or voice, or to any third party for sale or transfer directly or indirectly to such a user, for use in a manner lawful under this article; nothing contained in this article shall be so construed as to prevent any person, firm or corporation, practicing the profession of photography, from exhibiting in or about his or its establishment specimens of the work of such establishment, unless the same is continued by such person, firm or corporation after written notice objecting thereto has been given by the person portrayed; and nothing contained in this article shall be so construed as to prevent any person, firm or corporation from using the name, portrait, picture or voice of any manufacturer or dealer in connection with the goods, wares and merchandise manufactured, produced or dealt in by him which he has sold or disposed of with such name, portrait, picture or voice used in connection therewith; or from using the name, portrait, picture or voice of any author, composer or artist in connection with his literary, musical or artistic productions which he has sold or disposed of with such name, portrait, picture or voice used in connection therewith. Nothing contained in this section shall be construed to prohibit the copyright owner of a sound recording from disposing of, dealing in, licensing or selling that sound recording to any party, if the right to dispose of, deal in, license or sell such sound recording has been conferred by contract or other written document by such living person or the holder of such right. Nothing contained in the foregoing sentence shall be deemed to abrogate or otherwise limit any rights or remedies otherwise conferred by federal law or state law.

California Civil Code

§ 3344 Deering (2012)

(a) Any person who knowingly uses another's name, voice, signature, photograph, or likeness, in any manner, on or in products, merchandise, or goods, or for purposes of advertising or selling, or soliciting purchases of, products, merchandise, goods or services, without such person's prior consent, or, in the case of a minor, the prior consent of his parent or legal guardian, shall be liable for any damages sustained by the person or persons injured as a result thereof. In addition, in any action brought under this section, the person who violated the section shall be liable to the injured party or parties in an amount equal to the greater of seven hundred fifty dollars ($750) or the actual damages suffered by him or her as a result of the unauthorized use, and any profits from the unauthorized use that are attributable to the use and are not taken into account in computing the actual damages. In establishing such profits, the injured party or parties are required to present proof only of the gross revenue attributable to such use, and the person who violated this section is required to prove his or her deductible expenses. Punitive damages may also be awarded to the injured party or parties. The prevailing party in any action under this section shall also be entitled to attorney's fees and costs.

(b) As used in this section, "photograph" means any photograph or photographic reproduction, still or moving, or any videotape or live television transmission, of any person, such that the person is readily identifiable.

(1) A person shall be deemed to be readily identifiable from a photograph when one who views the photograph with the naked eye can reasonably determine that the person depicted in the photograph is the same person who is complaining of its unauthorized use.

(2) If the photograph includes more than one person so identifiable, then the person or persons complaining of the use shall be represented as individuals rather than solely as members of a definable group represented in the photograph. A definable group includes, but is not limited to, the following examples: a crowd at any sporting event, a crowd in any street or public building, the audience at any theatrical or stage production, a glee club, or a baseball team.

(3) A person or persons shall be considered to be represented as members of a definable group if they are represented in the photograph solely as a result of being present at the time the photograph was taken and have not been singled out as individuals in any manner.

(c) Where a photograph or likeness of an employee of the person using the photograph or likeness appearing in the advertisement or other publication prepared by or in behalf of the user is only incidental, and not essential, to the purpose of the publication in which it appears, there shall arise a rebuttable presumption affecting the burden of producing evidence that the failure to obtain the consent of the employee was not a knowing use of the employee's photograph or likeness.

(d) For purposes of this section, a use of a name, voice, signature, photograph, or likeness in connection with any news, public affairs, or sports broadcast or account, or any political campaign, shall not constitute a use for which consent is required under subdivision (a).

(e) The use of a name, voice, signature, photograph, or likeness in a commercial medium shall not constitute a use for which consent is required under subdivision (a) solely because the material containing such use is commercially sponsored or contains paid advertising. Rather it shall be a question of fact whether or not the use of the person's name, voice, signature, photograph, or likeness was so directly connected with the commercial sponsorship or with the paid advertising as to constitute a use for which consent is required under subdivision (a).

(f) Nothing in this section shall apply to the owners or employees of any medium used for advertising, including, but not limited to, newspapers, magazines, radio and television networks and stations, cable television systems, billboards, and transit ads, by whom any advertisement or solicitation in violation of this section is published or disseminated, unless it is established that such owners or employees had knowledge of the unauthorized use of the person's name, voice, signature, photograph, or likeness as prohibited by this section.

(g) The remedies provided for in this section are cumulative and shall be in addition to any others provided for by law.[12]

Downing v. Abercrombie & Fitch

265 F.3d 994 (9th Cir. 2001)

Appellants brought this diversity action against Abercrombie and Fitch ("Abercrombie") for publishing a photograph of them, with identification of their names, for Abercrombie's commercial benefit without the Appellants' authorization. They allege a violation of California's common law and statutory prohibition against misappropriation of a person's name and likeness for commercial purposes, a violation of the Lanham Act for confusion and deception indicating sponsorship of Abercrombie goods, and a claim for negligence and defamation. The district court entered summary judgment for Abercrombie, holding that their California state claims were foreclosed because Abercrombie's use of the photograph was protected by the First Amendment, and those claims were also preempted by the federal Copyright Act; that Hawaii law was the proper choice of law for some of these claims; that the Lanham Act claim was precluded by the First Amendment and it was also precluded by the nominative fair use doctrine; and that there was insufficient evidence to sustain the negligence or defamation claims. The district court had jurisdiction under 28 U.S.C. § 1332, and we have appellate jurisdiction under 28 U.S.C. § 1291. We reverse the grant of summary judgment and remand for trial.

I. Factual Background

Abercrombie is an outfitter catering to young people. The upscale retailer sells casual apparel for men and women, including shirts, khakis, jeans, and outerwear. In addition to sales in approximately 200 stores nationwide, Abercrombie also sells merchandise through its subscription catalog, the "Abercrombie and Fitch Quarterly" ("Quarterly").

The Quarterly is Abercrombie's largest advertising vehicle. It accounts for approximately 80% of Abercrombie's overall advertising budget. The primary purpose

---

12. *See also* CAL CIV. CODE 3344.1 (Deerings 2012) (extending these rights to decedents' estates).

of the Quarterly is to build brand awareness and increase sales. Each issue is over 250 pages in length and embraces a theme such as collegiate lifestyle, back to school, or winter wear. The Quarterly contains photographs of models wearing Abercrombie's garments as well as pictures of the clothing displayed for sale. In addition, approximately one-quarter of each issue is devoted to stories, news and other editorial pieces.

In 1998, Michael Jeffries, Abercrombie's CEO, developed a surfing theme for the upcoming Quarterly. Abercrombie held the photo shoot for the upcoming issue at San Onofre Beach, California. While at the photo shoot, Abercrombie employees Sam Shahid and Savas Abadsidis looked through a compilation of surfing photographs by surf photographer LeRoy Grannis. The photo book contained a picture of Appellants which Grannis had taken at the 1965 Makaha International Surf Championship in Hawaii. Sam Shahid purchased the photograph, along with three other photographs from the book, for $100 each. LeRoy Grannis then handwrote the names of Appellants at the bottom of the photograph.

Subsequently, Sam Shahid showed Appellants' photograph to Jeffries who decided to use the photograph in the upcoming Quarterly. Abercrombie did not obtain Appellants' permission. Jeffries also decided to create t-shirts, exactly like those worn by the Appellants in the photograph, for sale in the upcoming issue. Abercrombie labeled the t-shirts "Final Heat Tees." The t-shirts were advertised for sale in the Quarterly.

The Spring 1999 Quarterly, "Spring Fever," contains a section entitled "Surf Nekkid." The "Surf Nekkid" section includes an article recounting the history of surfing. Abercrombie also included a 700-word story, entitled "Your Beach Should Be This Cool," describing the history of Old Man's Beach at San Onofre, California. The following page exhibits the photograph of Appellants. The two pages immediately thereafter feature the "Final Heat Tees."

The "Spring Fever" issue contains other articles about the surfing lifestyle. An article entitled "Beachcombing" documents the efforts of the Surfrider Foundation, an ecological group founded by surfers. Still another article entitled "Where the Wild Things Are," written by the editor of Surfer Magazine, describes various surfer "types." Also contained in the issue is an interview of Nat Young, former world surfing champion and the first professional surfer. The interview is accompanied by photographs of Young and his son wearing Abercrombie clothing....

On appeal, Appellants contend: (1) Abercrombie's use of the photograph is not protected under the First Amendment; (2) the state law publicity claims are not preempted by the Copyright Act; (3) California law is the proper choice of law for the claim under California Civil Code §3344; (4) triable issues of fact exist with regard to the Lanham Act claims....

The district court's grant of summary judgment is reviewed de novo. We must determine, viewing the evidence in the light most favorable to the nonmoving party, whether there are any genuine issues of material fact and whether the district court correctly applied the relevant substantive law.

ANALYSIS

I. First Amendment and Right of Publicity Claims

The district court concluded that Abercrombie's use of the photograph containing Appellants' names and likenesses was proper because it constituted expression protected under the First Amendment. We disagree.

California has long recognized a common law right of privacy for protection of a person's name and likeness against appropriation by others for their advantage. To sustain a common law cause of action for commercial misappropriation, a plaintiff must prove: "(1) the defendant's use of the plaintiff's identity; (2) the appropriation of plaintiff's name or likeness to defendant's advantage, commercially or otherwise; (3) lack of consent; and (4) resulting injury."

In addition to the common law cause of action, California has provided a statutory remedy for commercial misappropriation under California Civil Code § 3344. The remedies provided for under California Civil Code § 3344 complement the common law cause of action; they do not replace or codify the common law. Section 3344 provides in relevant part, "any person who knowingly uses another's name, voice, signature, photograph, or likeness, in any manner ... for purposes of advertising ... without such person's prior consent ... shall be liable for any damages sustained by the person." Under section 3344, a plaintiff must prove all the elements of the common law cause of action. In addition, the plaintiff must allege a knowing use by the defendant as well as a direct connection between the alleged use and the commercial purpose.

Under both the common law cause of action and the statutory cause of action "no cause of action will lie for the publication of matters in the public interest, which rests on the right of the public to know and the freedom of the press to tell it." This First Amendment defense extends "to almost all reporting of recent events," as well as to publications about "people who, by their accomplishments, mode of living, professional standing or calling, create a legitimate and widespread attention to their activities. However, the defense is not absolute; we must find "a proper accommodation between [the] competing concerns" of freedom of speech and the right of publicity.

In the instant case, Abercrombie defends on the basis of the First Amendment arguing that the photograph illustrates an article about surfing, a matter in the public interest. To support its defense, Abercrombie relies on *Dora v. Frontline Video, Inc.*, 15 Cal. App. 4th 536 (Ct. App. 1993). In *Dora*, the court held that a surfing documentary was in the public interest because it was "about a certain time and place in California history and, indeed, in American legend." *Dora* involved a surfing legend, Mickey Dora, who sued the producer of a video documentary on surfing claiming common law and statutory appropriation of his name and likeness. The trial court entered summary judgment for the film's producer and the California Court of Appeal affirmed. In addressing the First Amendment issue, the court found that the documentary was about a matter of public interest, specifically surfing, and, therefore, the producer was protected by the defense. In so concluding the court stated:

surfing is of more than passing interest to some. It has created a life-style that influences speech, behavior, dress, and entertainment, among other things. A phenomenon of such scope has an economic impact, because it affects purchases, travel, and the housing market. Surfing has also had a significant influence on the popular culture, and in that way touches many people. It would be difficult to conclude that a surfing documentary does not fall within the category of public affairs.

Although the theme of Abercrombie's catalog was surfing and surf culture, a matter of public interest, the use of Appellants' names and pictures is quite different from that involved in the *Dora* case. In *Dora*, Mickey Dora's contribution to the development of the surf life-style and his influence on the sport was "the point of the program." Dora was depicted in the documentary because his identity directly contributed to the story about surfing which came within the protected public interest.

In the current action, there is a tenuous relationship between Appellants' photograph and the theme presented. Abercrombie used Appellants' photograph essentially as window-dressing to advance the catalog's surf-theme. The catalog did not explain that Appellants were legends of the sport and did not in any way connect Appellants with the story preceding it. In fact, the catalog incorrectly identifies where and when the photograph was taken. We conclude that the illustrative use of Appellants' photograph does not contribute significantly to a matter of the public interest and that Abercrombie cannot avail itself of the First Amendment defense.

This case is also distinguishable from *Hoffman v. L.A. Magazine*, 255 F.3d 1180, slip op. at 8591 (9th Cir. 2001), in which the defendant magazine successfully asserted a First Amendment defense to Dustin Hoffman's claim of misappropriation. In that case, L.A. Magazine used a digitally-altered picture of Hoffman, as "Tootsie," in a current designer dress to illustrate its "Grand Illusions" article. We concluded that such use was noncommercial speech entitled to full First Amendment protection. In contrast to the present case, where Abercrombie, itself, used Appellants' images in its catalog to promote its clothing, L.A. Magazine was unconnected to and received no consideration from the designer for the gown depicted in the article. Further, while L.A. Magazine merely referenced a shopping guide buried in the back of the magazine that provided stores and prices for the gown, Abercrombie placed the Appellants' photograph on the page immediately preceding the "Final Heat Tees" for sale. Based on these factors, we conclude that Abercrombie's use was much more commercial in nature and, therefore, not entitled to the full First Amendment protection accorded to L.A. Magazine's use of Hoffman's image.

Accordingly, we reverse the district court's grant of summary judgment in favor of Abercrombie.

II. Federal Copyright Preemption

Abercrombie contends that its right to reproduce and publish the photograph of the Appellants is governed by the federal Copyright Act, and that Appellants' state law claims are preempted by federal copyright law....

The photograph itself, as a pictorial work of authorship, is subject matter protected by the Copyright Act. However, it is not the publication of the photograph itself, as a creative work of authorship, that is the basis for Appellants' claims, but rather, it is the use of the Appellants' likenesses and their names pictured in the published photograph.... [The] point is made in McCarthy's Treatise on Right of Publicity and Privacy:

> The "subject matter" of a Right of Publicity claim is not a particular picture or photograph of plaintiff. Rather, what is protected by the Right of Publicity is the very identity or persona of the plaintiff as a human being ... While copyright in a given photograph may be owned by the person depicted in it, the exact image in that photograph is not the underlying "right" asserted in a Right of Publicity case. To argue that the photograph is identical with the person is to confuse illusion and illustration with reality. Thus, assertion of infringement of the Right of Publicity because of defendant's unpermitted commercial use of a picture of plaintiff is not assertion of infringement of copyrightable "subject matter" in one photograph of plaintiff.

McCarthy, Rights of Publicity and Privacy § 11.13[C] at 11-72–73 (1997).

A recent case in the Fifth Circuit [(*Brown v. Ames,* 201 F.3d 654, 661 (5th Cir. 2000))] held that the Texas tort of misappropriation, which provides protection from the unauthorized appropriation of one's name, image, or likeness was not preempted by the Copyright Act. The case involved a record company's misappropriation of the names and likenesses of individual musicians, song writers, and music producers on the company's CD's, tapes, catalogs, and posters. The court stated that "the tort of misappropriation of a name or likeness protects a person's *persona.* A persona does not fall within the subject matter of copyright." Thus, the court held that § 301 preemption does not apply.

A similar result was reached in a case decided by a California Court of Appeal, *KNB Enterprises v. Matthews,* 78 Cal. App. 4th 362 (2000). The California Court of Appeals held that the state law right of publicity claims were not pre-empted by the Copyright Act. The copyright owner of erotic photographs, which had been displayed without authorization and for profit on an Internet website, brought suit against the website's operator asserting a misappropriation claim under California Civil Code § 3344. The court applied the two-part test for determining preemption and found that neither condition had been met. The court found that "because a human likeness is not copyrightable, even if captured in a copyrighted photograph, the models' section 3344 claims against the unauthorized publisher of their photographs are not the equivalent of a copyright infringement claim and are not preempted by federal copyright law."

We agree with the approach taken by the Fifth Circuit and the reasoning employed in KNB Enterprises. The subject matter of Appellants' statutory and common law right of publicity claims is their names and likenesses. A person's name or likeness is not a work of authorship within the meaning of 17 U.S.C. § 102. This is true notwithstanding the fact that Appellants' names and likenesses are embodied in a copyrightable photograph. The same concept is specifically embodied in 17 U.S.C. § 103, which provides that the copyright in derivative works extends only to the material contributed by the author as distinguished from preexisting material employed in the work.

Abercrombie relies on the California case of *Fleet v. CBS*, 50 Cal. App. 4th 1911 (Ct. App. 1996). This case was distinguished by both the Fifth Circuit in Brown, and the California Court of Appeals in KNB Enterprises. In *Fleet*, the plaintiffs were actors in a copyrighted film. The claims of the plaintiffs were based on their dramatic performance in a film CBS sought to distribute. The court stated:

> We agree that as a general proposition Civil Code section 3344 is intended to protect rights which cannot be copyrighted and that claims made under its provisions are usually not preempted. But appellants' analysis crumbles in the face of one obvious fact: their individual performances in the film White Dragon were copyrightable. Since their section 3344 claims seeks only to prevent CBS from reproducing and distributing their performances in the film, their claims must be preempted by federal copyright law.

This is clearly distinguishable from this case where the Appellants' claim is based on the use of their names and likenesses, which are not copyrightable....

IV. Lanham Act

Appellants contend that the district court erred in denying their claim under section 43(a) of the Lanham Act.... It is perhaps clearer to restate the eight factors as applicable to the celebrity case, which can be stated as:

1. the level of recognition that the plaintiff has among the segment of the society for whom the defendant's product is intended;
2. the relatedness of the fame or success of the plaintiff to the defendant's product;
3. the similarity of the likeness used by the defendant to the actual plaintiff;
4. evidence of actual confusion;
5. marketing channels used;
6. likely degree of purchaser care;
7. defendant's intent on selecting the plaintiff; and
8. likelihood of expansion of the product lines.

Although these are all factors that are appropriate for consideration in determining the likelihood of confusion, they are not necessarily of equal importance, nor do they necessarily apply to every case.

"The Lanham Act's likelihood of confusion standard is predominantly factual in nature." Thus, summary judgment is inappropriate when a jury could reasonably conclude that there is a likelihood of confusion. Application of the eight factors to the current action leads us to conclude that the district court erred in rejecting Appellants' Lanham Act claim at the summary judgment stage.

In applying the factors to this case we reach the following conclusions. First, in considering the recognition that the Appellants have among those persons toward whom the Abercrombie catalog is directed, Appellants cite to a declaration submitted by surf historian Steve Pezman. In the declaration, Pezman asserts that Appellants "are considered legends in the surf community and are still highly well-known and regarded." This declaration from a surf historian provides some evidence that Appellants' names and images enjoy a high level of recognition among average members of society as a whole. In addition, it is undisputed that Appellants are legendary surfers, and thus there is a reasonable inference that Appellants would be known to the young people to whom the Quarterly is directed and who would be purchasing Abercrombie's surf wear.

The second factor is the relatedness of the Appellants' fame and success to the Defendant's product. Appellants' fame is due to their surfing success. Appellants' surfing success could be seen as closely-related to the Abercrombie's surf-related clothing.

Applying the third factor, the similarity of the likeness, to the Appellants is clear because it is an actual photograph of the Appellants with their names designated.

The fourth factor, evidence of actual confusion, also supports Appellants' position. Appellants provided declarations demonstrating that several individuals actually believed that Appellants were endorsing Abercrombie merchandise.

Under the fifth factor, marketing channels used, the catalog was the only marketing channel. It is therefore the likelihood of confusion in that marketing channel that is at issue.

In applying the sixth factor, the inquiry is whether consumers are likely to be particularly careful in determining who endorses the Abercrombie surf apparel, making confusion as to Appellants' endorsement more likely. A jury could reasonably find that young consumers are not likely to be particularly careful when purchasing surf-related clothing.

As to the seventh factor, the relevant question is whether the Defendants intended to profit by confusing consumers concerning the endorsement of the Abercrombie apparel. A jury could reasonably find that Abercrombie intended to indicate to consumers that these legendary surfers were endorsing Abercrombie's merchandise.

The eighth factor is the likelihood of expansion of the product lines. Neither party discusses this factor, however, no evidence has been produced that Abercrombie intends to utilize these photographs in additional product lines.

Application of these factors, leads us to conclude that the district court erred in rejecting Appellants' Lanham Act claim at the summary judgment stage. Viewing the evidence in the light most favorable to Appellants, we conclude that Appellants have raised a genuine issue of material fact concerning a likelihood of confusion as to their endorsement.

V. Doctrine of Nominative Fair Use

The district court concluded that Appellants' Lanham Act claim was barred by the doctrine of nominative fair use. In support of its position that the district court was correct in concluding that Appellants' Lanham Act claim was barred, Abercrombie relies upon *New Kids on the Block v. News America Publishing, Inc.,* 971 F.2d 302 (9th Cir. 1992). In *New Kids,* two newspapers conducted "900" number telephone polls concerning their readers' reactions to the musical group "New Kids on the Block." The newspapers charged their readers 95 cents per minute to respond to the poll. The band, which had its own competing "900" numbers for its fans, filed Lanham Act claims against the two newspapers. The district court granted summary judgment for the defendant newspapers on First Amendment grounds. On appeal, we affirmed on a non-constitutional ground, as appropriate when the constitutional issue can be avoided. We concluded that the newspapers' use of the band name constituted a nominative fair use.

We found that where the defendant uses a trademark to describe the plaintiff's product rather than its own product, a commercial user is entitled to a nominative fair use defense provided the defendant meets three requirements:

1. the product or service in question must be one not readily identifiable without use of the trademark;

2. only so much of the mark or marks may be used as is reasonably necessary to identify the product or service; and

3. the user must do nothing that would, in conjunction with the mark, suggest sponsorship or endorsement by the trademark holder.

Applying the three-part test, we concluded that the newspaper was entitled to the nominative fair use defense.

Abercrombie argues that its use of the photograph was nominative fair use in the same manner as the defendants' purported infringement in New Kids. We disagree. In New Kids, we stated that the test applies only "where the defendant uses a trademark to describe the plaintiff's product, rather than its own." Here, Abercrombie used the photograph in its catalog that was intended to sell its goods. As we have noted in this case involving a celebrity endorsement claim, the mark being protected is the Appellants' names and pictures. There is a genuine issue of material fact as to whether the third criterion is met, whether Abercrombie did nothing that would in conjunction with the Appellants' names and pictures suggest sponsorship or endorsement by the Appellants....

Neither the California state law claims or the Lanham Act claim are precluded by the First Amendment; [and] the California state claims are not preempted by the federal Copyright Act.... REVERSE AND REMAND FOR TRIAL.

Notes and Questions

a. The *Abercrombie* decision provides a roadmap for the entire chapter, by putting the claims of California's common law publicity, statutory publicity, and Lanham

Act side-by-side, as well as thoughtfully discussing the First Amendment defense and the defense of nominative trademark fair use. Each of these claims will be briefly noted, in turn.

b. Common law publicity. Although the New York Court of Appeals quickly rejected the common law discovery of privacy and publicity rights, many other states began to recognize these common law claims. The first was Georgia, in *Pavesich v. New England Life Ins. Co.,* 50 S.E. 68 (Ga. 1905). The Court adopted the right of publicity as described by Warren and Brandeis, recognizing the formulation provided by their law review article. As a common law rule, the range of potential for identification may be broader than that provided by statute. *See Midler v. Ford Motor Co.,* 849 F.2d 460 (9th Cir. 1988) (unique voice); *Motschenbacher v. R.J. Reynolds Tobacco Co.,* 498 F.2d 821 (9th Cir. 1974) (combination of race car and driver).

c. Statutory publicity issues. New York provides only a statutory right of publicity whereas California recognizes both. One of the difficulties of publicity law is that it continues to be a matter of first impression for many states. As a result, states may have an established rule recognizing publicity rights, but no interpretation as to the descendibility or the interest. New York provides statutory law which appears very clear and narrow in scope, but subsequent court interpretation suggests that it embraces all the privacy and publicity rights enumerated by Warren and Brandeis. *See Spahn v. Julian Messner, Inc.,* 221 N.E.2d 543 (N.Y. 1966).

d. Section 43(a) of the Lanham Act. Decisions following *Dastar* have not focused on the facts of the decision but rather the sweeping rhetoric which suggests trademark rights are unavailable to authors. Decisions following *Dastar* have embraced its broad, sweeping effect. *See Williams v. UMG Recordings, Inc.,* 281 F. Supp. 2d 1177, 1185 (C.D. Cal. 2003) ("[T]he Supreme Court's holding did not depend on whether the works were copyrighted or not.... Rather ... the Court noted that protection for communicative products was available through copyright claims."); *Romero v. Buhimschi,* 396 Fed. Appx. 224, 233 (6th Cir. 2010) (unpublished) ("Assuming that a portion of Romero's pleadings could fall under §43(a)(1)(B)'s advertising prong, the misconduct alleged in the pleadings would have to relate to the "nature, characteristics, qualities, or geographic origin" of the manuscript."); *Sybersound Records, Inc. v. UAV Corp.,* 517 F.3d 1137, 1144 (9th Cir. 2008).

e. Nominative Trademark Fair Use. The use of another party's trademark is not always actionable. One common defense is the correct usage of a competitor's or third party's trademark even when done without its permission. For example, a consumer products magazine can identify the products reviewed in each issue by the products' trademarks. This nominative use—identifying the product by its correct name—is permitted even over the objection of the trademark holder. This defense also allows for comparative advertising. This is particularly important in the context of commercial speech which may have less First Amendment protection than other forms of speech. *See Mattel, Inc. v. Walking Mt. Productions,* 353 F.3d 792, 809 (9th Cir. 2003) ("a defendant's use of a plaintiff's mark is nominative where he or she used the plaintiff's mark to describe the plaintiff's product, even if the defendant's ultimate goal is to describe his own product.") (internal citation and quotation omitted).

f. First Amendment concerns. The leading cases in this area are developed in detail, below. Procedurally, these cases allow the defendant to raise the First Amendment as a shield, an affirmative defense which essentially informs the court that it may not interpret the law in a manner that would force the trademark law to become a law abridging the freedom of speech or press. The courts strive to interpret the laws in a manner that does not suggest content regulation. As this area of law continues to be developed, courts might begin to treat trademark law as a form of content-neutral, time, place, or manner restriction. Would this provide greater guidance to courts and parties?

g. There are many examples of publicity and trademark infringement litigation. The following list of cases may not be long, but it is illustrious. A brief chronology sampled from among the leading cases provides an interesting timeline:

- *Motschenbacher v. R.J. Reynolds Tobacco Co.*, 498 F.2d 821 (9th Cir. 1974) (recognizing right of publicity for a sports car driver, identified in part based on his car rather than his name or likeness).

- *Groucho Marx Productions, Inc. v. Day & Night Co.*, 523 F. Supp. 485 (S.D.N.Y. 1981), *rev'd* on other grounds, 689 F.2d 317 (2d Cir. 1982) (addressing right to use real persons in a fictional stage play) (reversed because the Second Circuit determined that New York law should be applied and New York's publicity law is not descendible).

- *Estate of Presley v. Russen*, 513 F. Supp. 1339 (D.N.J. 1981) (contrasting publicity and trademark rights in Elvis Presley and those trademarks used by him, but refusing to prohibit the continued look-alike performances).

- *Carson v. Here's Johnny Portable Toilets, Inc.*, 698 F.2d 831 (6th Cir. 1983) (affirming § 43(a) and other claims for use of a pun on Carson's "Here's Johnny" introduction).

- *Stephano v. News Group Publications*, 64 N.Y.2d 174 (N.Y. 1984) (photograph of professional model not used as advertising or in trade where it accompanied a news article on fashion rather than a paid advertisement).

- *Allen v. National Video, Inc.*, 610 F. Supp. 612 (S.D.N.Y. 1985) (addressing use of look-alikes in advertisements).

- *White v. Samsung Electronics America, Inc.*, 971 F.2d 1395 (9th Cir. 1992) (permitting identity claim to be presented to the jury where the likeness was based on the pearls and hand gesture of a vaguely female robot).

- *Wendt v. Host Int'l, Inc.*, 125 F.3d 806, 812 (9th Cir. 1997) (actors from *Cheers* may have publicity interests in robotic dolls).

- *Seale v. Gramercy Pictures*, 949 F. Supp. 331 (E.D. Pa. 1996) (although no publicity rights claim was recognized for a docudrama of the Black Panther Party founded by plaintiff Bobby Seale and Huey P. Newton, court allowed trial to proceed on whether the soundtrack album using Seale's name and likeness was similarly protected).

- *Comedy III Productions, Inc. v. Gary Saderup, Inc.*, 25 Cal. 4th 387 (2001) (establishing California's transformative test for assessing the commercial or speech aspects of the publicity use).

- *Kirby v. Sega of America, Inc.*, 144 Cal. App. 4th (2006) (use of image in game highly transformative and protected speech).

- *No Doubt v. Activision Publishing, Inc.*, 192 Cal. App. 4th 1018 (2011) ("use of likenesses of members of the real-life rock band No Doubt was not transformative because the images were 'literal recreations of the band members' doing 'the same activity by which the band achieved and maintains its fame.'").

- *In re NCAA Student-Athlete Name & Likeness Licensing Litig.*, 724 F.3d 1268, 1271 (9th Cir. 2013) ("Samuel Keller was the starting quarterback for Arizona State University in 2005 before he transferred to the University of Nebraska, where he played during the 2007 season.").

- *Sivero v. Twentieth Century Fox Film Corp.*, No. B266469, 2018 WL 833696, at *10 (Cal. Ct. App. Feb. 13, 2018) (actors character allegedly lifted from Good Fellas to be used in Simpsons had been "Simpsonized," meaning to be "transformed by the creative and artistic expressions distinctive to The Simpsons").

h. Drawing fine distinctions in publicity rights and the First Amendment continues to baffle courts and commentators. For example, in *Doe v. TCI Cablevision*, 110 S.W.3d 363 (Mo. 2003), professional hockey player "enforcer" Tony Twist argued that his name had been co-opted by the Spawn comic for the character "Anthony 'Tony Twist' Twistelli," a mafia don and enforcer. Although the defamation claim was denied on First Amendment grounds, the right of publicity claim survived. On substantially the same facts, the Missouri Supreme Court rejected the California decision finding First Amendment protection for the comic book. The Missouri Supreme Court explained:

> Right to publicity cases, both before and after *Zacchini*, focus instead on the threshold legal question of whether the use of a person's name and identity is "expressive," in which case it is fully protected, or "commercial," in which case it is generally not protected. For instance, the use of a person's identity in news, entertainment, and creative works for the purpose of communicating information or expressive ideas about that person is protected "expressive" speech. On the other hand, the use of a person's identity for purely commercial purposes, like advertising goods or services or the use of a person's name or likeness on merchandise is rarely protected.

> Several approaches have been offered to distinguish between expressive speech and commercial speech. The Restatement, for example, employs a "relatedness" test that protects the use of another person's name or identity in a work that is "related to" that person. The catalogue of "related" uses includes "the use of a person's name or likeness in news reporting, whether in newspapers, magazines, or broadcast news ... use in entertainment and other

creative works, including both fiction and nonfiction ... use as part of an article published in a fan magazine or in a feature story broadcast on an entertainment program ... dissemination of an unauthorized print or broadcast biography, [and use] of another's identity in a novel, play, or motion picture...." Restatement (Third) of Unfair Competition sec. 47 cmt. c at 549. The proviso to that list, however, is that "if the name or likeness is used solely to attract attention to a work that is *not related* to the identified person, the user may be subject to liability for a use of the other's identity in advertising...." *Id.* (emphasis added).

California courts use a different approach, called the "transformative test," ... "'what is essentially a balancing test between the First Amendment and the right of publicity based on whether the work in question adds significant creative elements so as to be transformed into something more than a mere celebrity likeness or imitation.'" ...

The weakness of the Restatement's "relatedness" test and California's "transformative" test is that they give too little consideration to the fact that many uses of a person's name and identity have both expressive and commercial components. These tests operate to preclude a cause of action whenever the use of the name and identity is in any way expressive, regardless of its commercial exploitation. Under the relatedness test, use of a person's name and identity is actionable only when the use is solely commercial and is otherwise unrelated to that person. Under the transformative test, the transformation or fictionalized characterization of a person's celebrity status is not actionable even if its sole purpose is the commercial use of that person's name and identity. Though these tests purport to balance the prospective interests involved, there is no balancing at all—once the use is determined to be expressive, it is protected. At least one commentator, however, has advocated the use of a more balanced balancing test—a sort of predominant use test—that better addresses the cases where speech is both expressive and commercial:

> If a product is being sold that predominantly exploits the commercial value of an individual's identity, that product should be held to violate the right of publicity and not be protected by the First Amendment, even if there is some "expressive" content in it that might qualify as "speech" in other circumstances. If, on the other hand, the predominant purpose of the product is to make an expressive comment on or about a celebrity, the expressive values could be given greater weight.

Id. at 373–74 (quoting Mark S. Lee, *Agents of Chaos: Judicial Confusion in Defining the Right of Publicity-Free Speech Interface*, 23 Loy. L.A. Ent. L. Rev. 471, 488–98 (2003)). *See also Winter v. D.C. Comics*, 30 Cal. 4th 881, 69 P.3d 473 (2003). On remand in *Doe v. TCI Cablevision*, a St. Louis jury again found for Twist. In January

2005, the $15,000,000 verdict for Twist's publicity rights against Todd McFarlane Productions Inc. drew the Spawn publisher into bankruptcy protection.

Problem 7-B

In posters and flyers for Bryce's "New Masters" series, the name for the reconceived Gilbert & Sullivan series, some of the students used a mock-up of Universal Pictures *Frankenstein* poster and a photograph of Boris Karloff's image as Frankenstein to promote the new play. Redrawn in pen and ink, the poster shows a recognizable Karloff-like monster sporting a Mohawk and nose ring. It does not use Universal's name or logo. Instead the students copied the poster style of the early 1930s. (Copies of the poster art may be viewed or purchased on eBay.)

Tyrell Jones, the faculty member in charge of the project, has called Bryce. The school has been subject to a number of copyright and trademark infringement complaints in recent years, so the central administration is quite sensitive to activity that may invite more complaints. Tyrell has been hearing of objections regarding the mocked-up artwork. Bryce asks your advice and counsel. Explain to Bryce the grounds for objection to the artwork and the extent to which such grounds are supported by law.

C. Sound Alikes

Midler v. Ford Motor Co.

849 F.2d 460 (9th Cir. 1988)

This case centers on the protectibility of the voice of a celebrated chanteuse from commercial exploitation without her consent. Ford Motor Company and its advertising agency, Young & Rubicam, Inc., in 1985 advertised the Ford Lincoln Mercury with a series of nineteen 30 or 60 second television commercials in what the agency called "The Yuppie Campaign." The aim was to make an emotional connection with Yuppies, bringing back memories of when they were in college. Different popular songs of the seventies were sung on each commercial. The agency tried to get "the original people," that is, the singers who had popularized the songs, to sing them. Failing in that endeavor in ten cases the agency had the songs sung by "sound alikes." Bette Midler, the plaintiff and appellant here, was done by a sound alike.

Midler is a nationally known actress and singer. She won a Grammy as early as 1973 as the Best New Artist of that year. Records made by her since then have gone Platinum and Gold. She was nominated in 1979 for an Academy award for Best Female Actress in The Rose, in which she portrayed a pop singer. Newsweek in its June 30, 1986 issue described her as an "outrageously original singer/comedian." Time hailed her in its March 2, 1987 issue as "a legend" and "the most dynamic and poignant singer-actress of her time."

When Young & Rubicam was preparing the Yuppie Campaign it presented the commercial to its client by playing an edited version of Midler singing "Do You Want

To Dance," taken from the 1973 Midler album, "The Divine Miss M." After the client accepted the idea and form of the commercial, the agency contacted Midler's manager, Jerry Edelstein. The conversation went as follows: "Hello, I am Craig Hazen from Young and Rubicam. I am calling you to find out if Bette Midler would be interested in doing … ?" Edelstein: "Is it a commercial?" "Yes." "We are not interested."

Undeterred, Young & Rubicam sought out Ula Hedwig whom it knew to have been one of "the Harlettes" a backup singer for Midler for ten years. Hedwig was told by Young & Rubicam that "they wanted someone who could sound like Bette Midler's recording of [Do You Want To Dance]." … At the direction of Young & Rubicam, Hedwig made a record for the commercial. The Midler record of "Do You Want To Dance" was first played to her. She was told to "sound as much as possible like the Bette Midler record," leaving out only a few "aahs" unsuitable for the commercial. Hedwig imitated Midler to the best of her ability. …

Neither the name nor the picture of Midler was used in the commercial; Young & Rubicam had a license from the copyright holder to use the song. At issue in this case is only the protection of Midler's voice. The district court described the defendants' conduct as that "of the average thief." They decided, "If we can't buy it, we'll take it." The court nonetheless believed there was no legal principle preventing imitation of Midler's voice and so gave summary judgment for the defendants. Midler appeals.

The First Amendment protects much of what the media do in the reproduction of likenesses or sounds. A primary value is freedom of speech and press. The purpose of the media's use of a person's identity is central. … Moreover, federal copyright law pre-empts much of the area. "Mere imitation of a recorded performance would not constitute a copyright infringement even where one performer deliberately sets out to simulate another's performance as exactly as possible." It is in the context of these First Amendment and federal copyright distinctions that we address the present appeal.

Nancy Sinatra once sued Goodyear Tire and Rubber Company on the basis of an advertising campaign by Young & Rubicam featuring "These Boots Are Made For Walkin'," a song closely identified with her; the female singers of the commercial were alleged to have imitated her voice and style and to have dressed and looked like her. The basis of Nancy Sinatra's complaint was unfair competition; she claimed that the song and the arrangement had acquired "a secondary meaning" which, under California law, was protectible. This court noted that the defendants "had paid a very substantial sum to the copyright proprietor to obtain the license for the use of the song and all of its arrangements." To give Sinatra damages for their use of the song would clash with federal copyright law. Summary judgment for the defendants was affirmed.

If Midler were claiming a secondary meaning to "Do You Want To Dance" or seeking to prevent the defendants from using that song, she would fail like Sinatra. But that is not this case. Midler does not seek damages for Ford's use of "Do You Want To Dance," and thus her claim is not preempted by federal copyright law. Copyright protects "original works of authorship fixed in any tangible medium of expression." A voice is not copyrightable. The sounds are not "fixed." What is put forward as protectible here is more personal than any work of authorship.

Bert Lahr once sued Adell Chemical Co. for selling Lestoil by means of a commercial in which an imitation of Lahr's voice accompanied a cartoon of a duck. Lahr alleged that his style of vocal delivery was distinctive in pitch, accent, inflection, and sounds. The First Circuit held that Lahr had stated a cause of action for unfair competition, that it could be found "that defendant's conduct saturated plaintiff's audience, curtailing his market." That case is more like this one. But we do not find unfair competition here. One-minute commercials of the sort the defendants put on would not have saturated Midler's audience and curtailed her market. Midler did not do television commercials. The defendants were not in competition with her.

California Civil Code section 3344 is also of no aid to Midler. The statute affords damages to a person injured by another who uses the person's "name, voice, signature, photograph or likeness, in any manner." The defendants did not use Midler's name or anything else whose use is prohibited by the statute. The voice they used was Hedwig's, not hers. The term "likeness" refers to a visual image not a vocal imitation. The statute, however, does not preclude Midler from pursuing any cause of action she may have at common law; the statute itself implies that such common law causes of action do exist because it says its remedies are merely "cumulative." ... Appropriation of such common law rights is a tort in California....

California will recognize an injury from "an appropriation of the attributes of one's identity." ... [D]efendants here used an imitation to convey the impression that Midler was singing for them.

Why did the defendants ask Midler to sing if her voice was not of value to them? Why did they studiously acquire the services of a sound-alike and instruct her to imitate Midler if Midler's voice was not of value to them? What they sought was an attribute of Midler's identity. Its value was what the market would have paid for Midler to have sung the commercial in person.

A voice is more distinctive and more personal than the automobile accouterments protected in *Motschenbacher* [*v. R.J. Reynolds Tobacco Co.*, 498 F.2d 821 (9th Cir. 1974)]. A voice is as distinctive and personal as a face. The human voice is one of the most palpable ways identity is manifested. We are all aware that a friend is at once known by a few words on the phone.... A fortiori, these observations hold true of singing, especially singing by a singer of renown. The singer manifests herself in the song. To impersonate her voice is to pirate her identity.

We need not and do not go so far as to hold that every imitation of a voice to advertise merchandise is actionable. We hold only that when a distinctive voice of a professional singer is widely known and is deliberately imitated in order to sell a product, the sellers have appropriated what is not theirs and have committed a tort in California. Midler has made a showing, sufficient to defeat summary judgment, that the defendants here for their own profit in selling their product did appropriate part of her identity.

Waits v. Frito-Lay, Inc.

978 F.2d 1093 (9th Cir. 1992)

Defendants Frito-Lay, Inc., and Tracy-Locke, Inc., appeal a jury verdict and award of $2.6 million in compensatory damages, punitive damages, and attorney's fees, in favor of singer Tom Waits. Waits sued the snack food manufacturer and its advertising agency for voice misappropriation and false endorsement following the broadcast of a radio commercial for SalsaRio Doritos which featured a vocal performance imitating Waits' raspy singing voice. On appeal, the defendants mount attacks on nearly all aspects of the judgment....

Tom Waits is a professional singer, songwriter, and actor of some renown. Waits has a raspy, gravelly singing voice, described by one fan as "like how you'd sound if you drank a quart of bourbon, smoked a pack of cigarettes and swallowed a pack of razor blades.... Late at night. After not sleeping for three days." Since the early 1970s, when his professional singing career began, Waits has recorded more than seventeen albums and has toured extensively, playing to sold-out audiences throughout the United States, Canada, Europe, Japan, and Australia. Regarded as a "prestige artist" rather than a musical superstar, Waits has achieved both commercial and critical success in his musical career. In 1987, Waits received *Rolling Stone* magazine's Critic's Award for Best Live Performance, chosen over other noted performers such as Bruce Springsteen, U2, David Bowie, and Madonna. *SPIN* magazine listed him in its March 1990 issue as one of the ten most interesting recording artists of the last five years....

Frito-Lay, Inc. is in the business of manufacturing, distributing, and selling prepared and packaged food products, including Doritos brand corn chips. Tracy-Locke, Inc. is an advertising agency which counts Frito-Lay among its clients. In developing an advertising campaign to introduce a new Frito-Lay product, SalsaRio Doritos, Tracy-Locke found inspiration in a 1976 Waits song, "Step Right Up."...

The story of Tracy-Locke's search for a lead singer for the commercial suggests that no one would do but a singer who could not only capture the feeling of "Step Right Up" but also imitate Tom Waits' voice.... Stephen Carter was among those who auditioned.... When Carter auditioned, members of the Tracy-Locke creative team "did a double take" over Carter's near-perfect imitation of Waits, and remarked to him how much he sounded like Waits....

On the day the commercial was due for release to radio stations across the country, Grossman had a ten-minute long-distance telephone consultation with Tracy-Locke's attorney, asking him whether there would be legal problems with a commercial that sought to capture the same feeling as Waits' music. The attorney noted that there was a "high profile" risk of a lawsuit in view of recent case law recognizing the protectability of a distinctive voice. Based on what Grossman had told him, however, the attorney did not think such a suit would have merit, because a singer's style of music is not protected....

Waits' claim, like Bette Midler's, is for infringement of voice, not for infringement of a copyrightable subject such as sound recording or musical composition. Moreover, the legislative history of section 114 indicates the express intent of Congress that "[t]he evolving common law rights of 'privacy,' 'publicity,' and trade secrets ... remain unaffected [by the preemption provision] as long as the causes of action contain elements, such as an invasion of personal rights ... that are different in kind from copyright infringement." Waits' voice misappropriation claim is one for invasion of a personal property right: his right of publicity to control the use of his identity as embodied in his voice. The trial's focus was on the elements of voice misappropriation, as formulated in Midler: whether the defendants had deliberately imitated Waits' voice rather than simply his style and whether Waits' voice was sufficiently distinctive and widely known to give him a protectable right in its use. These elements are "different in kind" from those in a copyright infringement case challenging the unauthorized use of a song or recording. Waits' voice misappropriation claim, therefore, is not preempted by federal copyright law.

The defendants next contend that the district court committed prejudicial error by rejecting their proposed jury instructions on three elements of the Midler tort: the deliberate misappropriation for commercial purposes of (1) a voice, that is (2) distinctive and (3) widely known. We consider jury instructions as a whole to determine if they are misleading or inadequate. We review challenges to the formulation of jury instructions for abuse of discretion. Whether a jury instruction misstates the elements that must be proved at trial, however, is a question of law which we review *de novo*....

[R]ead as a whole, the instructions were not misleading. In charging the jury, the court repeatedly noted that two claims were presented for determination and gave separate instructions on each claim. The court's voice misappropriation instructions limited the jury's consideration to voice, and in no way implied that it could consider style. Indeed, in addressing the jury in closing argument, Waits' attorney agreed with the defendants that style was not protected. Moreover, the court included an additional instruction that effectively narrowed the jury's focus to Waits' voice and indicated that style imitation alone was insufficient for tort liability. For the defendants to be liable for voice misappropriation, the court stated, the imitation had to be so good that "people who were familiar with plaintiff's voice who heard the commercial *believed plaintiff performed it.* In this connection it is not enough that they were reminded of plaintiff or thought the singer sounded like plaintiff...." (emphasis added). This instruction effectively added an additional element to Midler's formulation of voice misappropriation: actual confusion. The validity of this instruction is not before us in this appeal and we express no opinion on this issue. Even if the jury were initially confused about whether the defendants could be liable simply for imitating Waits' style, this instruction would have disabused them of this notion....

The defendants next argue that reputational damages are available only in defamation actions and that since Waits did not allege or prove defamation, they were unavailable here. Further, they argue, there was no evidence to support the award of such damages because Waits did not show that his career had suffered. Again, we reject these contentions.

We have no doubt, in light of general tort liability principles, that where the misappropriation of identity causes injury to reputation, compensation for such injury is appropriate. Reputational damages, moreover, have been awarded in right of publicity cases. The central issue is not whether these damages were available, but whether the evidence was sufficient to establish injury to Waits' reputation. As we noted above, the jury could have inferred from the evidence that the commercial created a public impression that Waits was a hypocrite for endorsing Doritos. Moreover, it also could have inferred damage to his artistic reputation, for Waits had testified that "part of my character and personality and image that I have cultivated is that I do not endorse products." Finally, from the testimony of Waits' expert witness, the jury could have inferred that if Waits ever wanted to do a commercial in the future, the fee he could command would be lowered by $50,000 to $150,000 because of the Doritos commercial. This evidence was sufficient to support the jury's award of $75,000 for injury to Waits' goodwill and future publicity value.

The jury awarded Waits a total of $2 million in punitive damages for voice misappropriation: $1.5 million against Tracy-Locke and $500,000 against Frito-Lay. The defendants ask that we vacate this award, arguing that punitive damages are unavailable as a matter of law, and alternatively, that the evidence was insufficient to support their award.

In California, exemplary or punitive damages are available "where it is proven by clear and convincing evidence that the defendant has been guilty of oppression, fraud, or malice." The statute defines "malice" in pertinent part as "despicable conduct which is carried on by the defendant with a *willful and conscious disregard of the rights* or safety of others." The defendants contend that because Midler was so recently decided and so imprecise in the scope of its holding, they could not have been aware of the rights they were infringing upon in broadcasting the commercial. Thus, they reason, their conduct was not in "conscious disregard" of Waits' property right in his voice.

Where an issue is one of first impression or where a right has not been clearly established, punitive damages are generally unavailable. The right of a well-known professional singer to control the commercial use of a distinctive voice, however, was not an "issue of first impression" in this case. The right had been established clearly by Midler. The evidence was unequivocal that, although Midler was decided just three months before the conduct at issue, Tracy-Locke personnel responsible for making the Doritos commercial were familiar with the Midler decision. Tracy-Locke was concerned enough that the commercial could result in voice misappropriation liability that it cautioned Frito-Lay of the legal risks in choosing the Carter version. At the same time, however, Tracy-Locke stated its readiness to indemnify Frito-Lay against damages. Frito-Lay, reassured by the indemnification, chose to proceed with the Carter version. In going forward with the commercial, the defendants knowingly took a calculated risk, thereby consciously disregarding the effect of these actions on Waits' legally recognized rights.

The defendants argue, however, that although they may have been aware that legal risks were involved, they had a good faith belief that Waits' rights would not be infringed because they read the legal precedents differently. This argument leaves us unpersuaded. Good faith cannot be manufactured by looking to the law of other jurisdictions to define the rights of California residents. Midler could not be more clear that, in California at least, a well-known singer with a distinctive voice has a property right in that voice. Waits is a California resident, a fact of which Tracy-Locke personnel were aware. The defendants made a conscious decision to broadcast a vocal performance imitating Waits in markets across the country, including San Francisco and Los Angeles. This evidence is sufficient to raise at least a prima facie showing that defendants acted in conscious disregard of rights recognized in California.

Even if punitive damages are available, the defendants argue, the award must be vacated because it is not supported by clear and convincing evidence, as required by California law. Clear and convincing evidence means evidence sufficient to support a finding of "high probability." ...

The evidence the jury heard included testimony that Carter, the Waits' impersonator, told Brenner that Waits had a policy against doing commercials and would not like this one. Brenner knew of Waits' policy because he had tried unsuccessfully to hire him for another commercial. In the face of Brenner's warnings that the commercial sounded too much like Waits and presented serious legal concerns, Grossman called a lawyer. Although the lawyer thought the scenario Grossman painted him did not present a colorable legal problem, Grossman had not told the lawyer that the commercial featured a voice that sounded like Waits—only that the "feeling" of the music was the same. Grossman urged Frito-Lay to choose the Carter version over one that did not sound like Waits....

We believe that, viewed most favorably to Waits, this evidence was adequate to support a finding of high probability that Tracy-Locke and Frito-Lay acted with malice. Despicability reflects a moral judgment, "conscious disregard" a state of mind. A rational jury could have found the defendants' conduct despicable because they knowingly impugned Waits' integrity in the public eye. A rational jury also could have found that the defendants, in spite of their awareness of Waits' legal right to control the commercial use of his voice, acted in conscious disregard of that right by broadcasting the commercial. We therefore affirm the award of punitive damages.

II. *Lanham Act Claim*

Section 43(a) of the Lanham Act, prohibits the use of false designations of origin, false descriptions, and false representations in the advertising and sale of goods and services. Waits' claim under section 43(a) is premised on the theory that by using an imitation of his distinctive voice in an admitted parody of a Tom Waits song, the defendants misrepresented his association with and endorsement of SalsaRio Doritos. The jury found in Waits' favor and awarded him $100,000 in damages. The district court also awarded him attorneys' fees under section 35 of the Lanham Act. On appeal, the defendants argue that Waits lacks standing to bring a Lanham Act claim, that Waits' false endorsement claim fails on its merits, that the damage award is duplicative, and that attorneys' fees are improper. Before we address these contentions, however, we turn to the threshold issue of whether false endorsement claims are properly cognizable under section 43(a) of the Lanham Act, a question of first impression in this circuit.... Section 43(a) now expressly prohibits, *inter alia,* the use of any symbol or device which is likely to deceive consumers as to the association, sponsorship, or approval of goods or services by another person. Moreover, the legislative history of the 1988 amendments also makes clear that in retaining the statute's original terms "symbol or device" in the definition of "trademark," Congress approved the broad judicial interpretation of these terms to include distinctive sounds and physical appearance. In light of persuasive judicial authority and the subsequent congressional approval of that authority, we conclude that false endorsement claims, including those premised on the unauthorized imitation of an entertainer's distinctive voice, are cognizable under section 43(a)....

A false endorsement claim based on the unauthorized use of a celebrity's identity is a type of false association claim, for it alleges the misuse of a trademark, *i.e.,* a symbol or device such as a visual likeness, vocal imitation, or other uniquely distinguishing characteristic, which is likely to confuse consumers as to the plaintiff's sponsorship or approval of the product. Standing, therefore, does not require "actual competition" in the traditional sense; it extends to a purported endorser who has an economic interest akin to that of a trademark holder in controlling the commercial exploitation of his or her identity. Moreover, the wrongful appropriator is in a sense a competitor of the celebrity, even when the celebrity has chosen to disassociate himself or herself from advertising products as has Waits. They compete with respect to the use of the celebrity's name or identity. They are both utilizing or marketing that personal property for commercial purposes. Accordingly, we hold that a celebrity whose endorsement of a product is implied through the imitation of a distinctive attribute of the celebrity's identity, has standing to sue for false endorsement under section 43(a) of the Lanham Act. Tom Waits, therefore, need not be a competitor in the traditional sense to sue under the Lanham Act for the imitation of his voice on the theory that its use falsely associated him with Doritos as an endorser. Rather, his standing was sufficiently established by the likelihood that the wrongful use of his professional trademark, his unique voice, would injure him commercially....

This evidence was sufficient to support the jury's finding that consumers were likely to be misled by the commercial into believing that Waits endorsed SalsaRio Doritos....

The defendants urge us to vacate the damage award on Waits' Lanham Act claim as duplicative of those damages awarded for voice misappropriation representing the fair market value of Waits' services. Waits does not contest this point. Standing by the representations he made to the jury at trial that he was not seeking a double recovery, he asserts on appeal that he "does not oppose a reduction of the final judgment in the amount of $100,000 based on the overlapping Lanham Act award."

In instructing the jury on Waits' Lanham Act claim, the court stated that it could award damages for the fair market value of Waits' services. The jury awarded Waits $100,000 on this claim. It also awarded Waits $100,000 for the fair market value of his services on his voice misappropriation claim. The damages awarded under the Lanham Act, therefore, are duplicative. Accordingly, we vacate this portion of the judgment....

Waits' voice misappropriation claim and his Lanham Act claim are legally sufficient. The court did not err in instructing the jury on elements of voice misappropriation. The jury's verdict on each claim is supported by substantial evidence, as are its damage awards. Its award of damages on Waits' Lanham Act claim, however, is duplicative of damages awarded for voice misappropriation; accordingly we vacate it. Finally, the court did not abuse its discretion in awarding attorneys' fees under the Lanham Act....

Notes and Questions

a. Frito-Lay continued to struggle with the sound-alike cases. In *Oliveira v. Frito-Lay, Inc.*, 251 F.3d 56 (2d Cir. N.Y. 2001), Astrud Oliveira (or Astrud Gilberto) did not fare as well as Tom Waits. The Second Circuit rejected her distinctive voice claim. Her second attempt at Lanham Act protection was more inventive, but also rejected. She claimed her song, "The Girl from Ipanema," was her trademark song such that the use by Frito-Lay created an implied endorsement by her. The court shied away from the novel claim. As it explained:

> We cannot say it would be unthinkable for the trademark law to accord to a performing artist a trademark or service mark in her signature performance.... But for a court now to "recognize" the previously unknown existence of such a right would be profoundly disruptive to commerce. Numerous artists who could assert claims similar to Gilberto's would bring suit against entities that had paid bona fide license fees to all known holders of rights. Indeed, artists who had licensed users under their copyrights and had received fees for the copyright license could bring suits claiming additional compensation for infringement of trademark rights. Immense unforeseen liabilities might accrue, upsetting reasonable commercial expectations.

Id. at 62–63.

The Second Circuit pointed to both the lack of prior case law and the potential disruption for the marketplace. Nonetheless, the claim may be less extreme than that. The court recognized that commercial jingles ("You Deserve a Break Today") or public domain songs ("William Tell Overture" for the Lone Ranger and "Sweet Georgia Brown" for the Harlem Globetrotters) are recognized as trademarks. The distinction is that the song relates to the product or service rather than back to the singer.

Perhaps one-hit wonders like Nancy Sinatra or Astrud Gilberto can be marketed using their signature songs as trademarks. Would the result be different if the song in question was used in commercials and registered as a trademark for those advertised services?

b. The *Waits* Court expanded the liability for sound-alikes, moving past the position it had previously held in *Cher v. Forum Int'l, Ltd.*, 692 F.2d 634 (9th Cir. 1982) (finding for Cher for state unfair competition law and refusing to decide the Lanham Act claim). In this case, an interview granted by the singer/actress was subsequently sold to a hard-core adult magazine and not published by the magazine she believed to be publishing the interview.

c. If a movie distributor changes the rating for a motion picture, does that change give rise to any Lanham Act claim for false endorsement of the motion picture? *See Halicki v. United Artists Communications, Inc.*, 812 F.2d 1213 (9th Cir. 1987). What if the anticipated PG-13 film was edited in a manner to receive a rating of X or NC-17?

d. On the topic of endorsements, to what extent does the use of a song serve as an endorsement of a motion picture or its home video version? Can a composer object to the unintended endorsement created by her song when the song is used in a project the composer finds objectionable? *See Storball v. Twentieth Century Fox Film Corp.*, 1993 U.S. Dist. LEXIS 20455, 30 U.S.P.Q.2d (BNA) 1394 (C.D. Cal. 1993).

e. Modern courts continue to struggle with preemption of copyright and the extent to which the performer's voice can be licensed by the sound recording company without first acquiring the performer's publicity rights in the performance. Should such claims to one's vocal performance be assigned to the sound recording company as a matter of copyright law? *See Laws v. Sony Music Entm't, Inc.*, 448 F.3d 1134 (9th Cir. 2006); *E.S.S. Entm't 2000, Inc. v. Rock Star Videos, Inc.*, 547 F.3d 1095 (9th Cir. 2008) (reproduced in Chap. 15, Sec. C, *infra*).

Problem 7-C

Bryce has stopped by your office with a serious problem. Three years ago, Bryce modeled a very flashy outfit. Last month, a friend showed Bryce a photograph that looked almost the same as the original photograph, except that Bryce's flashy outfit appears to have been modified so as to appear nearly transparent (though not quite pornographic) and the backdrop digitally altered to resemble what can best be described as a bordello. The photograph appears in an adult-content magazine.

Bryce tells you that at the time of the photo-shoot, Bryce signed an agreement licensing name, likeness, and identity in association with the marketing and sales of the modeled clothing. Bryce is convinced that the outfit has been digitally altered to seem much more revealing than the outfit as originally worn. Worse, if Tyrell Jones, the faculty member in charge of the New Masters project, learns of the pictures, Bryce is sure to be fired. Advise Bryce regarding the legal ability to enjoin the distribution of the magazine and to stop all future uses of the offending photograph.

D. Tension between Publicity and Free Speech

Comedy III Prods., Inc. v. Gary Saderup, Inc.

25 Cal. 4th 387 (2001)

... I. THE STATUTE

In this state the right of publicity is both a statutory and a common law right.... Section 990 declares broadly that "Any person who uses a deceased personality's name, voice, signature, photograph, or likeness, in any manner, on or in products, merchandise, or goods, or for purposes of advertising or selling, or soliciting purchases of, products, merchandise, goods, or services, without prior consent from the person or persons specified in subdivision (c), shall be liable for any damages sustained by the person or persons injured as a result thereof." The amount recoverable includes "any profits from the unauthorized use," as well as punitive damages, attorney fees, and costs....

The statute provides a number of exemptions from the requirement of consent to use. Thus a use "in connection with any news, public affairs, or sports broadcast or account, or any political campaign" does not require consent. Use in a "commercial medium" does not require consent solely because the material is commercially sponsored or contains paid advertising; "Rather it shall be a question of fact whether or not the use ... was so directly connected with" the sponsorship or advertising that it requires consent. Finally, subdivision (n) provides that "[a] play, book, magazine, newspaper, musical composition, film, radio or television program," work of "political or newsworthy value," "[s]ingle and original works of fine art," or "[a]n advertisement or commercial announcement" for the above works are all exempt from the provisions of the statute.

Plaintiff Comedy III Productions, Inc. (hereafter Comedy III), brought this action against defendants Gary Saderup and Gary Saderup, Inc. (hereafter collectively Saderup), seeking damages and injunctive relief for violation of section 990 and related business torts.... Comedy III is the registered owner of all rights to the former comedy act known as The Three Stooges, who are deceased personalities within the meaning of the statute. Saderup is an artist with over 25 years' experience in making charcoal drawings of celebrities. These drawings are used to create lithographic and silkscreen masters, which in turn are used to produce multiple reproductions in the form, respectively, of lithographic prints and silkscreened images on T-shirts. Saderup creates the original drawings and is actively involved in the ensuing lithographic and silkscreening processes.

Without securing Comedy III's consent, Saderup sold lithographs and T-shirts bearing a likeness of The Three Stooges reproduced from a charcoal drawing he had made. These lithographs and T-shirts did not constitute an advertisement, endorsement, or sponsorship of any product. Saderup's profits from the sale of unlicensed lithographs and T-shirts bearing a likeness of The Three Stooges was $75,000 and Comedy III's reasonable attorney fees were $150,000.

On these stipulated facts the court found for Comedy III and entered judgment against Saderup awarding damages of $75,000 and attorney fees of $150,000 plus costs.... Saderup ... contends that enforcement of the judgment against him violates his right of free speech and expression under the First Amendment. He raises a difficult issue, which we address below.

The right of publicity is often invoked in the context of commercial speech when the appropriation of a celebrity likeness creates a false and misleading impression that the celebrity is endorsing a product. Because the First Amendment does not protect false and misleading commercial speech, and because even nonmisleading commercial speech is generally subject to somewhat lesser First Amendment protection, the right of publicity may often trump the right of advertisers to make use of celebrity figures.

But the present case does not concern commercial speech. As the trial court found, Saderup's portraits of The Three Stooges are expressive works and not an advertisement for or endorsement of a product. Although his work was done for financial gain, "[t]he First Amendment is not limited to those who publish without charge.... [An expressive activity] does not lose its constitutional protection because it is undertaken for profit."

The tension between the right of publicity and the First Amendment is highlighted by recalling the two distinct, commonly acknowledged purposes of the latter. First, "'to preserve an uninhibited marketplace of ideas' and to repel efforts to limit the '"uninhibited, robust and wide-open" debate on public issues.'" Second, to foster a "fundamental respect for individual development and self-realization. The right to self-expression is inherent in any political system which respects individual dignity. Each speaker must be free of government restraint regardless of the nature or manner of the views expressed unless there is a compelling reason to the contrary."

The right of publicity has a potential for frustrating the fulfillment of both these purposes. Because celebrities take on public meaning, the appropriation of their likenesses may have important uses in uninhibited debate on public issues, particularly debates about culture and values. And because celebrities take on personal meanings to many individuals in the society, the creative appropriation of celebrity images can be an important avenue of individual expression. As one commentator has stated:

> Entertainment and sports celebrities are the leading players in our Public Drama. We tell tales, both tall and cautionary, about them. We monitor their comings and goings, their missteps and heartbreaks. We copy their mannerisms, their styles, their modes of conversation and of consumption. Whether or not celebrities are 'the chief agents of moral change in the United States,' they certainly are widely used—far more than are institutionally anchored elites—to symbolize individual aspirations, group identities, and cultural

values. Their images are thus important expressive and communicative resources: the peculiar, yet familiar idiom in which we conduct a fair portion
of our cultural business and everyday conversation.

(Madow, *Private Ownership of Public Image: Popular Culture and Publicity Rights* 81
Cal. L. Rev. 125, 128 (1993) (Madow), italics and fns. omitted.)

As Madow further points out, the very importance of celebrities in society means
that the right of publicity has the potential of censoring significant expression by
suppressing alternative versions of celebrity images that are iconoclastic, irreverent,
or otherwise attempt to redefine the celebrity's meaning. (Madow, *supra*, 81 Cal.
L.Rev. at pp. 143–145.) A majority of this court recognized as much in *Guglielmi* [*v.
Spelling-Goldberg Productions*, 25 Cal. 3d 860, 869 (1979)]: "The right of publicity
derived from public prominence does not confer a shield to ward off caricature,
parody and satire. Rather, prominence invites creative comment."

For similar reasons, speech about public figures is accorded heightened First
Amendment protection in defamation law.... Giving broad scope to the right of publicity has the potential of allowing a celebrity to accomplish through the vigorous exercise of that right the censorship of unflattering commentary that cannot be
constitutionally accomplished through defamation actions.

Nor do Saderup's creations lose their constitutional protections because they are
for purposes of entertaining rather than informing. As Chief Justice Bird stated in
Guglielmi, invoking the dual purpose of the First Amendment: "Our courts have
often observed that entertainment is entitled to the same constitutional protection
as the exposition of ideas. That conclusion rests on two propositions. First, '[t]he
line between informing and entertaining is too elusive for the protection of the basic
right. Everyone is familiar with instances of propaganda through fiction. What is one
man's amusement, teaches another doctrine.'" "Second, entertainment, as a mode
of self-expression, is entitled to constitutional protection irrespective of its contribution
to the marketplace of ideas. 'For expression is an integral part of the development
of ideas, of mental exploration and of the affirmation of self. The power to realize
his potentiality as a human being begins at this point and must extend at least this
far if the whole nature of man is not to be thwarted.'" ...

Nor does the fact that Saderup's art appears in large part on a less conventional
avenue of communications, T-shirts, result in reduced First Amendment protection.
As Judge Posner stated in the case of a defendant who sold T-shirts advocating the
legalization of marijuana, "its T-shirts ... are to [the seller] what the *New York Times*
is to the Sulzbergers and the Ochs — the vehicle of her ideas and opinions." First
Amendment doctrine does not disfavor nontraditional media of expression.

But having recognized the high degree of First Amendment protection for noncommercial speech about celebrities, we need not conclude that all expression that
trenches on the right of publicity receives such protection. The right of publicity,
like copyright, protects a form of intellectual property that society deems to have
some social utility. "Often considerable money, time and energy are needed to develop

one's prominence in a particular field. Years of labor may be required before one's skill, reputation, notoriety or virtues are sufficiently developed to permit an economic return through some medium of commercial promotion. For some, the investment may eventually create considerable commercial value in one's identity."

The present case exemplifies this kind of creative labor. Moe and Jerome (Curly) Howard and Larry Fein fashioned personae collectively known as The Three Stooges, first in vaudeville and later in movie shorts, over a period extending from the 1920s to the 1940s....

Although surprisingly few courts have considered in any depth the means of reconciling the right of publicity and the First Amendment, we follow those that have in concluding that depictions of celebrities amounting to little more than the appropriation of the celebrity's economic value are not protected expression under the First Amendment. We begin with *Zacchini v. Scripps-Howard Broadcasting Co.,* 433 U.S. 562, 576 (1977)....

To be sure, *Zacchini* was not an ordinary right of publicity case: the defendant television station had appropriated the plaintiff's entire act, a species of common law copyright violation. Nonetheless, two principles enunciated in *Zacchini* apply to this case: (1) state law may validly safeguard forms of intellectual property not covered under federal copyright and patent law as a means of protecting the fruits of a performing artist's labor; and (2) the state's interest in preventing the outright misappropriation of such intellectual property by others is not automatically trumped by the interest in free expression or dissemination of information; rather, as in the case of defamation, the state law interest and the interest in free expression must be balanced, according to the relative importance of the interests at stake.

Guglielmi adopted a similar balancing approach. The purported heir of Rudolph Valentino filed suit against the makers of a fictional film based on the latter's life. *Guglielmi* concluded that the First Amendment protection of entertainment superseded any right of publicity. This was in contrast to the companion *Lugosi* case, in which Chief Justice Bird concluded in her dissenting opinion that there may be an enforceable right of publicity that would prevent the merchandising of Count Dracula using the likeness of Bela Lugosi, with whom that role was identified. *Guglielmi* proposed a balancing test to distinguish protected from unprotected appropriation of celebrity likenesses: "an action for infringement of the right of publicity can be maintained only if the proprietary interests at issue clearly outweigh the value of free expression in this context." ...

On the other side of the equation, the court recognized that [in *Estate of Presley v. Russen,* 513 F. Supp. 1339 (D.N.J. 1981) (*Russen*),] the Elvis impersonation, as in *Zacchini,* represented "'what may be the strongest case for a "right of publicity"— involving, not the appropriation of an entertainer's reputation to enhance the attractiveness of a commercial product, but the appropriation of the very activity by which the entertainer acquired his reputation in the first place.'" Thus, in balancing the considerable right of publicity interests with the minimal expressive or informational value of the speech in question, the *Russen* court concluded that the Presley estate's request for injunctive relief would likely prevail on the merits.

In *Groucho Marx Productions, Inc. v. Day & Night Co.* (S.D.N.Y. 1981) 523 F. Supp. 485, reversed on other grounds (2d Cir. 1982) 689 F.2d 317, the court considered a right of publicity challenge to a new play featuring characters resembling the Marx Brothers. The court found in favor of the Marx Brothers' heirs, rejecting a First Amendment defense. In analyzing that defense, the court posed a dichotomy between "works ... designed primarily to promote the dissemination of thoughts, ideas or information through news or fictionalization," which would receive First Amendment protection, and "use of the celebrity's name or likeness ... largely for commercial purposes, such as the sale of merchandise," in which the right of publicity would prevail. In creating this dichotomy, the court did not appear to give due consideration to forms of creative expression protected by the First Amendment that cannot be categorized as ideas or information. Moreover, the court, borrowing from certain copyright cases, seemed to believe that the validity of the First Amendment defense turned on whether the play was a parody, without explaining why other forms of creative appropriation, such as using established characters in new theatrical works to advance various creative objectives, were not protected by the First Amendment. Nonetheless, the case is in line with *Zacchini*, *Guglielmi* and *Russen* in recognizing that certain forms of commercial exploitation of celebrities that violate the state law right of publicity do not receive First Amendment protection.

It is admittedly not a simple matter to develop a test that will unerringly distinguish between forms of artistic expression protected by the First Amendment and those that must give way to the right of publicity. Certainly, any such test must incorporate the principle that the right of publicity cannot, consistent with the First Amendment, be a right to control the celebrity's image by censoring disagreeable portrayals. Once the celebrity thrusts himself or herself forward into the limelight, the First Amendment dictates that the right to comment on, parody, lampoon, and make other expressive uses of the celebrity image must be given broad scope. The necessary implication of this observation is that the right of publicity is essentially an economic right. What the right of publicity holder possesses is not a right of censorship, but a right to prevent others from misappropriating the economic value generated by the celebrity's fame through the merchandising of the "name, voice, signature, photograph, or likeness" of the celebrity.

Beyond this precept, how may courts distinguish between protected and unprotected expression? Some commentators have proposed importing the fair use defense from copyright law, which has the advantage of employing an established doctrine developed from a related area of the law. Others disagree, pointing to the murkiness of the fair use doctrine and arguing that the idea/expression dichotomy, rather than fair use, is the principal means of reconciling copyright protection and First Amendment rights.

We conclude that a wholesale importation of the fair use doctrine into right of publicity law would not be advisable. At least two of the factors employed in the fair use test, "the nature of the copyrighted work" and "the amount and substantiality of the portion used" seem particularly designed to be applied to the partial copying of works of authorship "fixed in [a] tangible medium of expression" it is difficult to understand why these factors would be especially useful for determining whether the depiction of a celebrity likeness is protected by the First Amendment.

Nonetheless, the first fair use factor—"the purpose and character of the use"—does seem particularly pertinent to the task of reconciling the rights of free expression and publicity. As the Supreme Court has stated, the central purpose of the inquiry into this fair use factor "is to see, in Justice Story's words, whether the new work merely 'supersede[s] the objects' of the original creation, or instead adds something new, with a further purpose or different character, altering the first with new expression, meaning, or message; it asks, in other words, whether and to what extent the new work is 'transformative.' Although such transformative use is not absolutely necessary for a finding of fair use, the goal of copyright, to promote science and the arts, is generally furthered by the creation of transformative works." (*Campbell v. Acuff-Rose Music, Inc.*, 510 U.S. 569, 579 (1994)).

This inquiry into whether a work is "transformative" appears to us to be necessarily at the heart of any judicial attempt to square the right of publicity with the First Amendment. As the above quotation suggests, both the First Amendment and copyright law have a common goal of encouragement of free expression and creativity, the former by protecting such expression from government interference, the latter by protecting the creative fruits of intellectual and artistic labor. The right of publicity, at least theoretically, shares this goal with copyright law. When artistic expression takes the form of a literal depiction or imitation of a celebrity for commercial gain, directly trespassing on the right of publicity without adding significant expression beyond that trespass, the state law interest in protecting the fruits of artistic labor outweighs the expressive interests of the imitative artist.

On the other hand, when a work contains significant transformative elements, it is not only especially worthy of First Amendment protection, but it is also less likely to interfere with the economic interest protected by the right of publicity. As has been observed, works of parody or other distortions of the celebrity figure are not, from the celebrity fan's viewpoint, good substitutes for conventional depictions of the celebrity and therefore do not generally threaten markets for celebrity memorabilia that the right of publicity is designed to protect. Accordingly, First Amendment protection of such works outweighs whatever interest the state may have in enforcing the right of publicity. The right-of-publicity holder continues to enforce the right to monopolize the production of conventional, more or less fungible, images of the celebrity.

There is a fourth factor in the fair use test not yet mentioned, "the effect of the use upon the potential market for or value of the copyrighted work," that bears directly on this question. We do not believe, however, that consideration of this factor would usefully supplement the test articulated here. If it is determined that a work is worthy of First Amendment protection because added creative elements significantly transform the celebrity depiction, then independent inquiry into whether or not that work is cutting into the market for the celebrity's images—something that might be particularly difficult to ascertain in the right of publicity context—appears to be irrelevant. Moreover, this "potential market" test has been criticized for circularity: it could be argued that if a defendant has capitalized in any way on a celebrity's image, he or she has found a potential market and therefore could be liable for such work. . . .

Cardtoons, [*L.C. v. Major League Baseball Players Ass'n*, 95 F.3d 959 (10th Cir. 1996) (*Cardtoons*)], cited by Saderup, is consistent with this "transformative" test. There, the court held that the First Amendment protected a company that produced trading cards caricaturing and parodying well-known major league baseball players against a claim brought under the Oklahoma right of publicity statute. The court concluded that "[t]he cards provide social commentary on public figures, major league baseball players, who are involved in a significant commercial enterprise, major league baseball," and that "[t]he cards are no less protected because they provide humorous rather than serious commentary." The *Cardtoons* court weighed these First Amendment rights against what it concluded was the less-than-compelling interests advanced by the right of publicity outside the advertising context—especially in light of the reality that parody would not likely substantially impact the economic interests of celebrities—and found the cards to be a form of protected expression. While *Cardtoons* contained dicta calling into question the social value of the right of publicity, its conclusion that works parodying and caricaturing celebrities are protected by the First Amendment appears unassailable in light of the test articulated above.

We emphasize that the transformative elements or creative contributions that require First Amendment protection are not confined to parody and can take many forms, from factual reporting to fictionalized portrayal, from heavy-handed lampooning to subtle social criticism.

Another way of stating the inquiry is whether the celebrity likeness is one of the "raw materials" from which an original work is synthesized, or whether the depiction or imitation of the celebrity is the very sum and substance of the work in question. We ask, in other words, whether a product containing a celebrity's likeness is so transformed that it has become primarily the defendant's own expression rather than the celebrity's likeness. And when we use the word "expression," we mean expression of something other than the likeness of the celebrity.

We further emphasize that in determining whether the work is transformative, courts are not to be concerned with the quality of the artistic contribution—vulgar forms of expression fully qualify for First Amendment protection. On the other hand, a literal depiction of a celebrity, even if accomplished with great skill, may still be subject to a right of publicity challenge. The inquiry is in a sense more quantitative than qualitative, asking whether the literal and imitative or the creative elements predominate in the work.

Furthermore, in determining whether a work is sufficiently transformative, courts may find useful a subsidiary inquiry, particularly in close cases: does the marketability and economic value of the challenged work derive primarily from the fame of the celebrity depicted? If this question is answered in the negative, then there would generally be no actionable right of publicity. When the value of the work comes principally from some source other than the fame of the celebrity—from the creativity, skill, and reputation of the artist—it may be presumed that sufficient transformative elements are present to warrant First Amendment protection. If the question is answered in the affirmative, however, it does not necessarily follow that the work is without First Amendment protection—it may still be a transformative work.

In sum, when an artist is faced with a right of publicity challenge to his or her work, he or she may raise as affirmative defense that the work is protected by the First Amendment inasmuch as it contains significant transformative elements or that the value of the work does not derive primarily from the celebrity's fame....

[T]he inquiry is into whether Saderup's work is sufficiently transformative. Correctly anticipating this inquiry, he argues that all portraiture involves creative decisions, that therefore no portrait portrays a mere literal likeness, and that accordingly all portraiture, including reproductions, is protected by the First Amendment. We reject any such categorical position. Without denying that all portraiture involves the making of artistic choices, we find it equally undeniable, under the test formulated above, that when an artist's skill and talent is manifestly subordinated to the overall goal of creating a conventional portrait of a celebrity so as to commercially exploit his or her fame, then the artist's right of free expression is outweighed by the right of publicity. As is the case with fair use in the area of copyright law, an artist depicting a celebrity must contribute something more than a "merely trivial" variation, [but must create] something recognizably "his own" in order to qualify for legal protection.

On the other hand, we do not hold that all reproductions of celebrity portraits are unprotected by the First Amendment. The silkscreens of Andy Warhol, for example, have as their subjects the images of such celebrities as Marilyn Monroe, Elizabeth Taylor, and Elvis Presley. Through distortion and the careful manipulation of context, Warhol was able to convey a message that went beyond the commercial exploitation of celebrity images and became a form of ironic social comment on the dehumanization of celebrity itself. Such expression may well be entitled to First Amendment protection. Although the distinction between protected and unprotected expression will sometimes be subtle, it is no more so than other distinctions triers of fact are called on to make in First Amendment jurisprudence.

Turning to Saderup's work, we can discern no significant transformative or creative contribution. His undeniable skill is manifestly subordinated to the overall goal of creating literal, conventional depictions of The Three Stooges so as to exploit their fame. Indeed, were we to decide that Saderup's depictions were protected by the First Amendment, we cannot perceive how the right of publicity would remain a viable right other than in cases of falsified celebrity endorsements.

Moreover, the marketability and economic value of Saderup's work derives primarily from the fame of the celebrities depicted. While that fact alone does not necessarily mean the work receives no First Amendment protection, we can perceive no transformative elements in Saderup's works that would require such protection.

Saderup argues that it would be incongruous and unjust to protect parodies and other distortions of celebrity figures but not wholesome, reverential portraits of such celebrities. The test we articulate today, however, does not express a value judgment or preference for one type of depiction over another. Rather, it reflects a recognition that the Legislature has granted to the heirs and assigns of celebrities the property right to exploit the celebrities' images, and that certain forms of expressive activity protected by the First Amendment fall outside the boundaries of that right. Stated another way, we are concerned not with whether conventional celebrity images should be produced but with who produces them and, more pertinently, who appropriates the value from their production. Thus, under section 990, if Saderup wishes to continue to depict The Three Stooges as he has done, he may do so only with the consent of the right of publicity holder.

The judgment of the Court of Appeal is affirmed.

Winter v. DC Comics

30 Cal. 4th 881 (2003)

Celebrities have a statutory right of publicity by which they can prohibit others from using their likeness. An obvious tension exists between this right of publicity and the First Amendment to the United States Constitution. In *Comedy III*, we considered when constitutional free speech rights may trump the statutory right of publicity. We formulated "what is essentially a balancing test between the First Amendment and the right of publicity based on whether the work in question adds significant creative elements so as to be transformed into something more than a mere celebrity likeness or imitation." In that case, we concluded that lithographs and T-shirts bearing the likeness of The Three Stooges were not sufficiently transformative to receive First Amendment protection.

In this case, we apply the same balancing test to comic books containing characters that evoke musician brothers Johnny and Edgar Winter. We conclude that, in contrast to a drawing of The Three Stooges, the comic books do contain significant creative elements that transform them into something more than mere celebrity likenesses. Accordingly, the comic books are entitled to First Amendment protection.

In the 1990s, DC Comics published a five-volume comic miniseries featuring "Jonah Hex," a fictional comic book "anti-hero." The series contains an outlandish plot, involving giant worm-like creatures, singing cowboys, and the "Wilde West Ranch and Music and Culture Emporium," named for and patterned after the life of Oscar Wilde. The third volume ends with a reference to two new characters, the "Autumn brothers," and the teaser, "Next: The Autumns of Our Discontent." The cover of volume 4 depicts the Autumn brother characters, with pale faces and long white hair.... One brother wears a stovepipe hat and red sunglasses, and holds a rifle. The second has red eyes and holds a pistol. This volume is entitled, Autumns of Our Discontent, and features brothers Johnny and Edgar Autumn, depicted as villainous half-worm, half-human offspring born from the rape of their mother by a supernatural worm creature that had escaped from a hole in the ground. At the end of volume 5, Jonah Hex and his companions shoot and kill the Autumn brothers in an underground gun battle.

Plaintiffs, Johnny and Edgar Winter, well-known performing and recording musicians originally from Texas, sued DC Comics and others alleging several causes of action including, as relevant here, appropriation of their names and likenesses under Civil Code section 3344. They alleged that the defendants selected the names Johnny and Edgar Autumn to signal readers the Winter brothers were being portrayed; that the Autumn brothers were drawn with long white hair and albino features similar to plaintiffs'; that the Johnny Autumn character was depicted as wearing a tall black top hat similar to the one Johnny Winter often wore; and that the title of volume 4, Autumns of Our Discontent, refers to the famous Shakespearian phrase, "the winter of our discontent." They also alleged that the comics falsely portrayed them as "vile, depraved, stupid, cowardly, subhuman individuals who engage in wanton acts of violence, murder and bestiality for pleasure and who should be killed." ...

We granted the defendants' petition for review to decide whether the comic books are protected under the *Comedy III* transformative test.

Civil Code section 3344 provides as relevant: "(a) Any person who knowingly uses another's name, voice, signature, photograph, or likeness, in any manner, on or in products, merchandise, or goods, or for purposes of advertising or selling, or soliciting purchases of, products, merchandise, goods or services, without such person's prior consent ... shall be liable for any damages sustained by the person or persons injured as a result thereof."

In *Comedy III*, ... [w]e developed a test to determine whether a work merely appropriates a celebrity's economic value, and thus is not entitled to First Amendment protection, or has been transformed into a creative product that the First Amendment protects. The "inquiry is whether the celebrity likeness is one of the 'raw materials' from which an original work is synthesized, or whether the depiction or imitation of the celebrity is the very sum and substance of the work in question. We ask, in other words, whether a product containing a celebrity's likeness is so transformed that it has become primarily the defendant's own expression rather than the celebrity's likeness. And when we use the word 'expression,' we mean expression of something other than the likeness of the celebrity." ...

We made two important cautionary observations. First, "the right of publicity cannot, consistent with the First Amendment, be a right to control the celebrity's image by censoring disagreeable portrayals. Once the celebrity thrusts himself or herself forward into the limelight, the First Amendment dictates that the right to comment on, parody, lampoon, and make other expressive uses of the celebrity image must be given broad scope. The necessary implication of this observation is that the right of publicity is essentially an economic right. What the right of publicity holder possesses is not a right of censorship, but a right to prevent others from misappropriating the economic value generated by the celebrity's fame through the merchandising of the 'name, voice, signature, photograph, or likeness' of the celebrity." Second, "in determining whether the work is transformative, courts are not to be concerned with the quality of the artistic contribution—vulgar forms of expression fully qualify for First Amendment protection. On the other hand, a literal depiction of a celebrity, even if accomplished with great skill, may still be subject to a right of publicity challenge. The inquiry is in a sense more quantitative than qualitative, asking whether the literal and imitative or the creative elements predominate in the work." ...

We then summarized the rule. "In sum, when an artist is faced with a right of publicity challenge to his or her work, he or she may raise as [an] affirmative defense that the work is protected by the First Amendment inasmuch as it contains significant transformative elements or that the value of the work does not derive primarily from the celebrity's fame.....

Application of the test to this case is not difficult.... Although the fictional characters Johnny and Edgar Autumn are less-than-subtle evocations of Johnny and Edgar Winter, the books do not depict plaintiffs literally. Instead, plaintiffs are merely part of the raw materials from which the comic books were synthesized. To the extent the drawings of the Autumn brothers resemble plaintiffs at all, they are distorted for purposes of lampoon, parody, or caricature. And the Autumn brothers are but cartoon characters—half-human and half-worm—in a larger story, which is itself quite expressive. The characters and their portrayals do not greatly threaten plaintiffs' right of publicity. Plaintiffs' fans who want to purchase pictures of them would find the drawings of the Autumn brothers unsatisfactory as a substitute for conventional depictions. The comic books are similar to the trading cards caricaturing and parodying prominent baseball players that have received First Amendment protection. Like the trading cards, the comic books "'are no less protected because they provide humorous rather than serious commentary.'" ...

Plaintiffs also argue, and the Court of Appeal found, that the record contains evidence that defendants were trading on plaintiffs' likenesses and reputations to generate interest in the comic book series and increase sales. This, too, is irrelevant to whether the comic books are constitutionally protected. The question is whether the work is transformative, not how it is marketed. If the work is sufficiently transformative to receive legal protection, "it is of no moment that the advertisements may have increased the profitability of the [work]." (*Guglielmi v. Spelling-Goldberg Productions, supra*, 25 Cal.3d at p. 860, 873 (1979) (conc. opn. of Bird, C.J.).) If the challenged work is transformative, the way it is advertised cannot somehow make it nontransformative. Here, as we have explained, the comic books are transformative and entitled to First Amendment protection.

Accordingly, we conclude that the Court of Appeal erred in finding the existence of triable issues of fact.... As in *Comedy III,* courts can often resolve the question as a matter of law simply by viewing the work in question and, if necessary, comparing it to an actual likeness of the person or persons portrayed. Because of these circumstances, an action presenting this issue is often properly resolved on summary judgment or, if the complaint includes the work in question, even demurrer. This is one of those cases.

The artist in *Comedy III* essentially sold, and devoted fans bought, pictures of The Three Stooges, not transformed expressive works by the artist. Here, by contrast, defendants essentially sold, and the buyers purchased, DC Comics depicting fanciful, creative characters, not pictures of the Winter brothers. This makes all the difference. The comic books here are entitled to First Amendment protection.

Parks v. Laface Records
329 F.3d 437 (2003)

This is a dispute over the name of a song. Rosa Parks is a civil rights icon who first gained prominence during the Montgomery, Alabama bus boycott in 1955. She brings suit against LaFace Records, a record producer, and OutKast, a "rap" (or "hip-hop") music duo, as well as several other named affiliates, for using her name as the title of their song, *Rosa Parks*. Parks contends that Defendants' use of her name constitutes false advertising under § 43(a) of the Lanham Act, and intrudes on her common law right of publicity under Michigan state law. Defendants argue that they are entitled to summary judgment because Parks has failed to show any violation of the Lanham Act or her right of publicity. Defendants further argue that, even if she has shown such a violation, their First Amendment freedom of artistic expression should be a defense as a matter of law to each of these claims. Parks also contends that Defendants' conduct renders them liable under Michigan law for defamation and tortious interference with a business relationship; Defendants have also denied liability with respect to these claims....

Rosa Parks is an historical figure who first gained prominence as a symbol of the civil rights movement in the United States during the 1950s and 1960s. In 1955, while riding in the front of a segregated bus in Montgomery, Alabama, she refused to yield her seat to a white passenger and move to the back of the bus as blacks were required to do by the then-existing laws requiring segregation of the races. A 381-day bus boycott in Montgomery flowed from that one event, which eventually became a catalyst for organized boycotts, sit-ins, and demonstrations all across the South. Her single act of defiance has garnered her numerous public accolades and awards, and she has used that celebrity status to promote various civil and human rights causes as well as television programs and books inspired by her life story. She has also approved a collection of gospel recordings by various artists entitled *Verity Records Presents: A Tribute to Mrs. Rosa Parks* (the "*Tribute*" album), released in 1995.

Defendants are OutKast, comprised of recording artists Andre "Dre" Benjamin and Antwan "Big Boi" Patton; their record producers, LaFace, founded by and named after Antonio "L.A." Reid and Kenny "Babyface" Edmonds; and LaFace's record distributors, Arista Records and BMG Entertainment (collectively "Defendants"). In September 1998, Defendants released the album *Aquemini*. The album's first single release was a song titled *Rosa Parks*, described as a "hit single" by a sticker on the album. The same sticker that contained the name *Rosa Parks* also contained a Parental Advisory warning of "explicit content." ...

[A]. The Lanham Act

Section 43(a) of the Lanham Act creates a civil cause of action against any person who identifies his or her product in such a way as to likely cause confusion among consumers or to cause consumers to make a mistake or to deceive consumers as to association of the producer of the product with another person or regarding the origin of the product or the sponsorship or approval of the product by another person. The language of § 43(a) is broad....

[T]he scope of § 43(a) extends beyond disputes between producers of commercial products and their competitors. It also permits celebrities to vindicate property rights in their identities against allegedly misleading commercial use by others. Celebrities have standing to sue under § 43(a) because they possess an economic interest in their identities akin to that of a traditional trademark holder.

In order to prevail on a false advertising claim under § 43(a), a celebrity must show that use of his or her name is likely to cause confusion among consumers as to the "affiliation, connection, or association" between the celebrity and the defendant's goods or services or as to the celebrity's participation in the "origin, sponsorship, or approval" of the defendant's goods or services. Consumer confusion occurs when "consumers ... believe that the products or services offered by the parties are affiliated in some way," or "when consumers make an incorrect mental association between the involved commercial products or their producers." A "likelihood" means a "probability" rather than a "possibility" of confusion.

Parks contends that Defendants have violated the Lanham Act because the *Rosa Parks* title misleads consumers into believing that the song is about her or that she is affiliated with the Defendants, or has sponsored or approved the *Rosa Parks* song and the *Aquemini* album. She argues that the risk of confusion is enhanced by the fact that her authorized *Tribute* album is in the marketplace alongside Defendants' album featuring the *Rosa Parks* single. As additional evidence for her claim, Parks points to Defendants' concession that they have used the *Rosa Parks* title to advertise and promote both the song and the *Aquemini* album. She also supplies twenty-one affidavits from consumers affirming that they either believed Defendants' song was about Parks or was connected to the *Tribute* album authorized by her....

1. Trademark Right in and Trademark Use of Parks' Name

... We find Parks' prior commercial activities and international recognition as a symbol of the civil rights movement endow her with a trademark interest in her name the same as if she were a famous actor or musician. Therefore, even though Rosa Parks' name might not be eligible for registration as a trademark, and even though

Defendants were not selling Rosa Parks-brand CD's, a viable cause of action also exists under § 43(a) if consumers falsely believed that Rosa Parks had sponsored or approved the song, or was somehow affiliated with the song or the album. We turn then to Defendants' second argument, that even if Parks could establish some likelihood of confusion, the First Amendment protects Defendants' choice of title.

2. *The First Amendment Defense — Three Approaches*

Defendants allege that even if Parks' evidence demonstrates some likelihood of consumer confusion regarding their song and album, their First Amendment right of artistic expression trumps that concern. Defendants make an arguable point. From ancient times, music has been a means by which people express ideas. As such, music is firmly ensconced within the protections of the First Amendment. However, the First Amendment cannot permit anyone who cries "artist" to have *carte blanche* when it comes to naming and advertising his or her works, art though it may be. As the Second Circuit sagely observed, "the purchaser of a book, like the purchaser of a can of peas, has a right not to be misled as to the source [or endorsement] of the product." Courts have adopted three approaches to balance First Amendment interests with the protections of the Lanham Act: (a) the "likelihood of confusion" test; (b) the "alternative avenues" test; and (c) the *Rogers v. Grimaldi* test. [875 F.2d 994 (2d Cir. 1989).] We will examine each one in turn.

One approach is to rely solely on the "likelihood of confusion" factors applied in other, more traditional, trademark cases.... Based upon that evidence, we then decide if the plaintiff has raised a genuine issue of material fact as to the likelihood of consumer confusion. Under this approach, we do not pay special solicitude to an asserted First Amendment defense.... A second approach is the "alternative avenues" test. This is the test urged upon us by Parks, and endorsed by a panel of the Eighth Circuit. Under the "alternative avenues" test, a title of an expressive work will not be protected from a false advertising claim if there are sufficient alternative means for an artist to convey his or her idea....

We conclude that neither the first nor the second approach accords adequate weight to the First Amendment interests in this case. The first approach — unmodified application of the likelihood of confusion factors in trademark cases — gives no weight to First Amendment concerns. Instead, it treats the name of an artistic work as if it were no different from the name of an ordinary commercial product. However, this approach ignores the fact that the artistic work is *not* simply a commercial product but is also a means of communication....

The second approach, the "alternative avenues" test ... is premised on the notion that, just as a real property owner may exclude a speaker from a shopping mall so long as other locations exist for the speaker to deliver his message, a celebrity may prohibit use of his or her name so long as alternative ways exist for the artist to communicate his or her idea.... To suggest that other words can be used as well to express an author's or composer's message is not a proper test for weighing First Amendment rights. As Mark Twain observed, "The difference between the almost-right word and the right word is really a large matter — it's the difference between the 'lightning-bug' and the 'lightning.'" J. Bartlett, *Familiar Quotations* 527 (16th ed.1992). Finally, adopting the "alternative avenues" test would needlessly entangle courts in the process of titling works of art; courts would be asked to determine not just whether a title is reasonably "artistic" but whether a title is "necessary" to communicate the idea. We therefore reject the alternative avenues test.

Finally, a third approach is the one developed by the Second Circuit in *Rogers v. Grimaldi* and adopted by the district court in this case. Under *Rogers*, a title will be protected unless it has "no artistic relevance" to the underlying work or, if there is artistic relevance, the title "explicitly misleads as to the source or the content of the work." ...

In *Rogers*, the plaintiff was dancer and film star Ginger Rogers. Italian movie maker Federico Fellini made a fictional movie titled *Ginger and Fred* about the reunion of two erstwhile cabaret dancers who became known to their fans as Fred and Ginger because they imitated Fred Astaire and Ginger Rogers in their act. Rogers' complaint alleged, *inter alia*, that the title misled viewers into thinking that the movie was about her famous collaboration with Fred Astaire, in violation of the Lanham Act, and that the use of her name infringed her right of publicity. The *Rogers* court, finding that overextension of Lanham Act restrictions in the area of titles might intrude on First Amendment values and that the "alternative avenues" test is insufficient to accommodate the public's interest in free expression, adopted a two-pronged test:

> In the context of allegedly misleading titles using a celebrity's name, that balance [between avoiding consumer confusion and protecting free expression] will normally not support application of the Act unless [1] the title has no artistic relevance to the underlying work whatsoever, or, if it has some artistic relevance, unless [2] the title explicitly misleads as to the source or the content of the work.

Courts in the Second Circuit have routinely applied the *Rogers* test to other Lanham Act cases. The Fifth Circuit has followed suit. In addition, a panel of the Ninth Circuit recently adopted the Rogers test in *Mattel, Inc. v. MCA Records, Inc.* [*v. MCA Records, Inc.*, 296 F.3d 894, 901 (9th Cir. 2002)]. In *Mattel*, the manufacturer of the well-known "Barbie" doll, sued a Danish band, Aqua, for their song Barbie Girl, which, among other things, contained lines that portrayed Barbie in a negative light. Mattel alleged that Aqua's use of the name "Barbie" in the title had confused consumers into believing that Mattel was affiliated with the song. Mattel argued that the song was not about "Barbie" and hence could not be protected by the First Amendment. In the district court, as support, Mattel introduced statements by Aqua band members in interviews that "the song isn't about the doll. We're making fun of the glamorous life." Mattel also supplied evidence that purported to show that individuals were misled into believing Mattel and the song were affiliated in some way. Among the evidence was a survey of 556 persons of various ages in six states, 17% of whom believed that Mattel or "Barbie" was the source of, connected with, or gave permission for the Barbie Girl song.

On appeal from a summary judgment in favor of the defendant, the Ninth Circuit, applying *Rogers*, concluded that the First Amendment outweighed any risk of confusion between Mattel and the song title. Specifically it found:

> Under the first prong of *Rogers*, the use of Barbie in the song title clearly is relevant to the underlying work, namely, the song itself.... The song is about Barbie and the values Aqua claims she represents. The song title does not explicitly mislead as to the source of the work; it does not, explicitly or otherwise, suggest that it was produced by Mattel. The only indication that Mattel might be associated with the song is the use of Barbie in the title; if this were enough to satisfy this prong of the *Rogers* test, it would render *Rogers* a nullity.

The application of *Rogers* in *Mattel*, as well as in cases decided in other circuits, persuades us that *Rogers* is the best test for balancing Defendants' and the public's interest in free expression under the First Amendment against Parks' and the public's interest in enforcement of the Lanham Act. We thus apply the *Rogers* test to the facts before us.

3. *Application of the* Rogers *Test*

The first prong of *Rogers* requires a determination of whether there is any artistic relationship between the title and the underlying work. Parks contends that a cursory review of the Rosa Parks title and the lyrics demonstrates that there is no artistic connection between them. Parks also submits two articles in which members of OutKast are purported to have admitted that the song was not about her. As further evidence, she offers a "translation" of the lyrics of the song Rosa Parks, derived from various electronic "dictionaries" of the "rap" vernacular to demonstrate that the song truly has nothing to do with Parks herself. The "translation" of the chorus reads as follows:

> Be quiet and stop the commotion. OutKast is coming back out [with new music] so all other MCs [mic checkers, rappers, Master of Ceremonies] step aside. Do you want to ride and hang out with us? OutKast is the type of group to make the clubs get hyped-up/excited.

Defendants respond that their use of Parks' name is "metaphorical" or "symbolic." They argue that the historical association between Rosa Parks and the phrase "move to the back of the bus" is beyond dispute and that Parks' argument that the song is not "about" her in a biographical sense is simply irrelevant....

Contrary to the opinion of the district court, we believe that the artistic relationship between the title and the content of the song is certainly not obvious and, indeed, is "open to reasonable debate" for the following reasons.

It is true that the phrase "move to the back of the bus" is repeatedly used in the "hook" or chorus of the song. When the phrase is considered *in the context of the lyrics*, however, the phrase has absolutely nothing to do with Rosa Parks. There could be no stronger, no more compelling, evidence of this fact than the admission of "Dre" (Andre "Dre" Benjamin) that, "We (OutKast) never intended for the song to be about Rosa Parks or the civil rights movement. It was just symbolic, meaning that we comin' back out, so all you other MCs move to the back of the bus." The composers did *not* intend it to be about Rosa Parks, and the lyrics are *not* about Rosa Parks. The lyrics' sole message is that OutKast's competitors are of lesser quality and, therefore, must "move to the back of the bus," or in other words, "take a back seat."

We believe that reasonable persons could conclude that there is no relationship of any kind between Rosa Parks' name and the content of the song—a song that is nothing more and nothing less than a paean announcing the triumph of superior people in the entertainment business over inferior people in that business. *Back of the Bus*, for example, would be a title that is obviously relevant to the content of the song, but it also would not have the marketing power of an icon of the civil rights movement. Choosing Rosa Parks' name as the title to the song unquestionably enhanced the song's potential sale to the consuming public.

The *Rogers* court made an important point which clearly applies in this case. The court said, "poetic license is not without limits. The purchaser of a book, like the purchaser of a can of peas, has a right not to be misled as to the source of the product." The same is also true regarding the content of a song. The purchaser of a song titled *Rosa Parks* has a right not to be misled regarding the content of that song....

We do not mean to imply that Rosa Parks must always be displayed in a flattering manner, or that she should have the ability to prevent any other characterization of her. She is a celebrity and, as such, she cannot prevent being portrayed in a manner that may not be pleasing to her.... The present case, however, does not involve any claim of caricature, parody or satire. It involves, instead, the use of a celebrity's name as the title to a song when it reasonably could be found that the celebrity's name has no artistic relevance to the content of the song. It involves, in short, a reasonable dispute whether the use of Rosa Parks' name was a misrepresentation and false advertising or whether it was a legitimate use of a celebrity's name in some recognized form of artistic expression protected by the First Amendment....

There is a genuine issue of material fact whether the use of Rosa Parks' name as a title to the song and on the cover of the album is artistically related to the content of the song or whether the use of the name Rosa Parks is nothing more than a misleading advertisement for the sale of the song....

[B]. Right of Publicity

The right of publicity protects the identity of a celebrity from exploitive commercial use. "The theory of the right is that a celebrity's identity can be valuable in the promotion of products, and the celebrity has an interest that may be protected from the unauthorized commercial exploitation of that identity." As such, the common law right of publicity forms a species of property right. The right of publicity is governed by state law. Michigan has indicated that it would recognize a right of publicity, and the parties have not questioned that Plaintiff has a right of publicity. The dispute is over its application to the facts of this case.

Parks' right of publicity argument tracks that of her Lanham Act claim. She alleges that Defendants have profited from her fame by using her name solely for a commercial purpose. She supplies much the same evidence in support of her right of publicity claim as she did for her Lanham Act claim: the lyrics of *Rosa Parks*, the "translation," and the press clippings quoting OutKast members. Defendants do not deny that they have used the title *Rosa Parks* commercially, but argue that Parks has produced no evidence that their use was *solely* commercial. Instead, they argue that the choice was also artistic, and that they therefore have a complete defense in the First Amendment.

The district court agreed with Defendants. The district court applied *Rogers*, which, in addition to the false advertising claim under § 43(a), also dealt with a right of publicity action arising under Oregon state law. Under *Rogers*, with respect to a right of publicity claim, a title that uses a celebrity's name will be protected by the First Amendment unless the title is "wholly unrelated" to the content of the work or was "simply a disguised commercial advertisement for the sale of goods or services." The district court found that, as a matter of law, there was an artistic relationship between the title and the content of the song, and therefore it could not be considered "simply a disguised commercial advertisement." Defendants' use of the title to promote the album did not change this result.

A right of publicity claim is similar to a false advertising claim in that it grants a celebrity the right to protect an economic interest in his or her name. However, a right of publicity claim does differ from a false advertising claim in one crucial respect; a right of publicity claim does not require any evidence that a consumer is likely to be confused. All that a plaintiff must prove in a right of publicity action is that she has a pecuniary interest in her identity, and that her identity has been commercially exploited by a defendant.

The parties have stipulated that Parks is famous and that she has used her name to promote other goods and services. She has therefore established an economic interest in her name. Furthermore, Defendants admit that they have used Parks' name as the name of their song, and have used that name to sell the song and their album. They argue, however, that, as with the Lanham Act claim, their First Amendment right of artistic expression should prevail over Parks' claim.

Because a plaintiff bears a reduced burden of persuasion to succeed in a right of publicity action, courts and commentators have recognized that publicity rights carry a greater danger of impinging on First Amendment rights than do rights associated with false advertising claims. We have recognized the importance of a First Amendment defense to right of publicity actions in a recent case. In *Ruffin-Steinback v. de-Passe*, [82 F. Supp. 2d 723, 726–27 (E.D. Mich. 2000), *aff'd*, 267 F.3d 457 (6th Cir. 2001),] friends and family members of the Motown group, the "Temptations," sued the makers of a televised mini-series for the manner in which they and the former group members were portrayed in the film. The plaintiffs alleged that their likenesses were appropriated to endorse a product, the film, without their permission. The court found in that case that the plaintiffs could not overcome the defendant's First Amendment defense, even where the portrayal of the plaintiffs was partly fictionalized, and even where the likenesses of the plaintiffs were used to promote a videocassette version of the mini-series. As with the Lanham Act, then, we must conduct another balancing of interests—Parks' property right in her own name versus the freedom of artistic expression.

In *Rogers*, the Second Circuit held that movie titles are protected from right of publicity actions unless the title is "wholly unrelated" to the content of the work or was "simply a disguised commercial advertisement for the sale of goods or services." This test is supported in the context of other expressive works by comment c of § 47 of the Restatement (Third) of Unfair Competition. It states that "use of another's identity in a novel, play, or motion picture is ... not ordinarily an infringement [of the right of publicity, unless] the name or likeness is used solely to attract attention to a work that is not related to the identified person." ...

For the same reasons we have stated earlier and need not repeat, we believe that Parks' right of publicity claim presents a genuine issue of material fact regarding the question of whether the title to the song is or is not "wholly unrelated" to the content of the song. A reasonable finder of fact, in our opinion, upon consideration of all the evidence, could find the title to be a "disguised commercial advertisement" or adopted "solely to attract attention" to the work....

For the reasons stated, as to Rosa Parks' Lanham Act claim and her common law right of publicity claim, the judgment of the District Court is reversed and this case is remanded for future proceedings not inconsistent with this Opinion....

Tyne v. Time Warner Entm't Co. L.P.

901 So. 2d 802 (Fla. 2005)

We have for review a question of Florida law certified by the United States Eleventh Circuit Court of Appeals that is determinative of a cause pending in that court and for which there appears to be no controlling precedent. We have jurisdiction. *See* art. V, § 3(b)(6), Fla. Const.

The pertinent facts of this case, as set forth by the Eleventh Circuit, are as follows:

In October, 1991, a rare confluence of meteorological events led to a "massively powerful" weather system off the New England coast. The fishing vessel known as the Andrea Gail was caught in this storm and lost at sea. All six of the crewmembers on board the *Andrea Gail*, including Billy Tyne and Dale Murphy, Sr., were presumed to have been killed. Newspaper and television reports extensively chronicled the storm and its impact. Based on these reports, and personal interviews with meteorologists, local fisherman, and family members, Sebastian Junger penned a book, entitled *The*

Perfect Storm: A True Story of Men Against the Sea, recounting the storm and the last voyage of the *Andrea Gail* and its crew. The book was published in 1997.

That same year, Warner Bros. purchased from Junger and his publisher the rights to produce a motion picture based on the book. Warner Bros. released the film, entitled *The Perfect Storm*, for public consumption in 2000. The Picture depicted the lives and deaths of Billy Tyne and Dale Murphy, Sr., who were the main characters in the film. It also included brief portrayals of each individual that is a party to this appeal. Nonetheless, Warner Bros. neither sought permission from the individuals depicted in the picture nor compensated them in any manner.

Unlike the book, the Picture presented a concededly dramatized account of both the storm and the crew of the *Andrea Gail*. For example, the main protagonist in the Picture, Billy Tyne, was portrayed as a down-and-out swordboat captain who was obsessed with the next big catch. In one scene, the Picture relates an admittedly fabricated depiction of Tyne berating his crew for wanting to return to port in Gloucester, Massachusetts. Warner Bros. took additional liberties with the land-based interpersonal relationships between the crewmembers and their families.

While the Picture did not hold itself out as factually accurate, it did indicate at the beginning of the film that "THIS FILM IS BASED ON A TRUE STORY." A disclaimer inserted during the closing credits elaborated on this point with the following statement: "This film is based on actual historical events contained in 'The Perfect Storm' by Sebastian Junger. Dialogue and certain events and characters in the film were created for the purpose of fictionalization."

On August 24, 2000, the Tyne and Murphy children, along with Tigue and Kosko, filed suit against Warner Bros. [in the United States District Court for the Middle District of Florida] seeking recompense under Florida's commercial misappropriation law [section 540.08, Florida Statutes (2000)] and for common law false light invasion of privacy.

Tyne v. Time Warner Entertainment Co., L.P., 336 F.3d 1286, 1288–89 (11th Cir. 2003).

[W]e rephrase the certified question to the specific issue that we conclude is presented by this case.

DOES THE PHRASE "FOR PURPOSES OF TRADE OR FOR ANY COMMERCIAL OR ADVERTISING PURPOSE" IN SECTION 540.08(1), FLORIDA STATUTES, INCLUDE PUBLICATIONS WHICH DO NOT DIRECTLY PROMOTE A PRODUCT OR SERVICE?

The question before this Court is a narrow one. As noted by the federal courts, the Fourth District Court of Appeal considered the applicability of section 540.08,

Florida Statutes,[13] to a publication which did not directly promote a product or service, but this Court has not directly addressed this question.

In *Loft* [*v. Fuller*, 408 So. 2d 619 (Fla. Dist. Ct. 1981)], Dorothy Loft and her two children brought an action for, among other things, violation of section 540.08 for the alleged unauthorized publication of the name and likeness of the Lofts' deceased husband and father, Robert Loft. Robert Loft had been the captain of an Eastern Airlines flight that crashed while en route from New York to Miami in 1972. The crash was followed by reports of the appearance of apparitions of the flight's crew members,

---

13. 540.08. Unauthorized publication of name or likeness.

(1) No person shall publish, print, display or otherwise publicly use for purposes of trade or for any commercial or advertising purpose the name, portrait, photograph, or other likeness of any natural person without the express written or oral consent to such use given by:

(a) Such person; or

(b) Any other person, firm or corporation authorized in writing by such person to license the commercial use of her or his name or likeness; or

(c) If such person is deceased, any person, firm or corporation authorized in writing to license the commercial use of her or his name or likeness, or if no person, firm or corporation is so authorized, then by any one from among a class composed of her or his surviving spouse and surviving children.

(2) In the event the consent required in subsection (1) is not obtained, the person whose name, portrait, photograph, or other likeness is so used, or any person, firm, or corporation authorized by such person in writing to license the commercial use of her or his name or likeness, or, if the person whose likeness is used is deceased, any person, firm, or corporation having the right to give such consent, as provided hereinabove, may bring an action to enjoin such unauthorized publication, printing, display or other public use, and to recover damages for any loss or injury sustained by reason thereof, including an amount which would have been a reasonable royalty, and punitive or exemplary damages.

(3) The provisions of this section shall not apply to:

(a) The publication, printing, display, or use of the name or likeness of any person in any newspaper, magazine, book, news broadcast or telecast, or other news medium or publication as part of any bona fide news report or presentation having a current and legitimate public interest and where such name or likeness is not used for advertising purposes;

(b) The use of such name, portrait, photograph, or other likeness in connection with the resale or other distribution of literary, musical, or artistic productions or other articles of merchandise or property where such person has consented to the use of her or his name, portrait, photograph, or likeness on or in connection with the initial sale or distribution thereof; or

(c) Any photograph of a person solely as a member of the public and where such person is not named or otherwise identified in or in connection with the use of such photograph.

(4) No action shall be brought under this section by reason of any publication, printing, display, or other public use of the name or likeness of a person occurring after the expiration of 40 years from and after the death of such person.

(5) As used in this section, a person's "surviving spouse" is the person's surviving spouse under the law of her or his domicile at the time of her or his death, whether or not the spouse has later remarried; and a person's "children" are her or his immediate offspring and any children legally adopted by the person. Any consent provided for in subsection (1) shall be given on behalf of a minor by the guardian of her or his person or by either parent.

(6) The remedies provided for in this section shall be in addition to and not in limitation of the remedies and rights of any person under the common law against the invasion of her or his privacy.

including Robert Loft, on subsequent flights. Subsequent to the press stories, *The Ghost of Flight 401* was published in 1976. The book was a nonfictionalized account by the author of his investigation of the reports. A movie was also made based on this book. *Loft*, 408 So. 2d at 620.

The Fourth District held as follows:

> In our view, section 540.08, by prohibiting the use of one's name or likeness for trade, commercial or advertising purposes, is designed to prevent the unauthorized use of a name *to directly promote the product or service of the publisher.* Thus, the publication is harmful not simply because it is included in a publication that is sold for a profit, but rather because of the way it associates the individual's name or his personality with something else. Such is not the case here.
>
> While we agree that at least one of the purposes of the author and publisher in releasing the publication in question was to make money through sales of copies of the book and that such a publication is commercial in that sense, this in no way distinguishes this book from almost all other books, magazines or newspapers and simply does not amount to the kind of commercial exploitation prohibited by the statute. We simply do not believe that the term "commercial," as employed by Section 540.08, was meant to be construed to bar the use of people's names in such a sweeping fashion. We also believe that acceptance of appellants' view of the statute would result in substantial confrontation between this statute and the first amendment to the United States Constitution guaranteeing freedom of the press and of speech. Having concluded that the publication as alleged is not barred by Section 540.08, we need not decide if, under the allegations of the complaint, the book was of current and legitimate public interest, thus removing it entirely from the scope of the statute.

Loft, 408 So. 2d at 622–23 (emphasis added) (citations omitted).

We approve the Fourth District's logical construction of section 540.08 in *Loft*. This construction has been applied to cases construing the statute for more than thirty years, and the statute has remained unchanged by the Legislature for this period. For example, in *Valentine v. C.B.S., Inc.*, 698 F.2d 430 (11th Cir. 1983), at issue was a song written by Bob Dylan and Jacques Levy depicting the murder trial of prizefighter Rubin "Hurricane" Carter. The plaintiff, a witness in the murder trial, brought an action alleging a violation of section 540.08 because the song falsely implied that she participated in a conspiracy to unjustly convict Carter. The Eleventh Circuit held that the plaintiff's claim was not actionable under section 540.08....

We disagree with appellants' argument that to uphold the construction given to the statute in Loft renders the exceptions contained in section 540.08(3)(a) and (b) superfluous. Applying the statute to only those situations that "directly promote a product or service" does not necessarily mean that the use is in an advertisement. For example, in *Ewing v. A-1 Management, Inc.*, 481 So. 2d 99 (Fla. 1986), the defendants published the names and addresses of the plaintiffs as parents of a fugitive from justice on a wanted poster distributed by the defendant surety company after the plaintiff's son fled while on bail. The Third District Court of Appeal concluded that while this use of the plaintiffs' names fell within the scope of section 540.08(1), the use was exempted under the newsworthiness exemption of section 540.08(3)(a). Thus, as appellees argue, the newsworthiness exemption served an entirely practical, nonredundant function....

Moreover, it should be emphasized that the Legislature enacted section 540.08 in 1967. Since that time, the only amendment to the statute was to rephrase it in gender neutral terms. The Legislature has not amended the statute in response to the decisions that have required that the statute apply to a use that directly promotes a product or service. This inaction may be viewed as legislative acceptance or approval of the judicial construction of the statute. *Goldenberg v. Sawczak*, 791 So. 2d 1078, 1083 (Fla. 2001).

Finally, as recognized by United States District Court Judge Conway in the decision of the United States District Court, we find that defining the term "commercial purpose" in section 540.08 to apply to motion pictures or similar works raises a fundamental constitutional concern.... It is ... clear that the Picture is entitled to First Amendment protection, and would therefore, be excepted from liability under § 540.08. This provides another basis for this Court's conclusion that Defendants are entitled to summary judgment on these claims....

Notes and Questions

a. Many of the most recent cases involving the tension between First Amendment and publicity rights doctrines occur in the context of video games. Those cases are addressed in Chapter 15.

b. One of the more significant recent cases to address the shifting attitude in the relation between publicity rights and First Amendment interests has been *Cardtoons, L.C. v. Major League Baseball Players Ass'n*, 95 F.3d 959, 976 (10th Cir. 1996). The Tenth Circuit upheld the right to sell parody trading cards, recognizing a First Amendment interest notwithstanding the commercial and nontraditional format of the parody. As the court explained:

> The cards use similar names, recognizable caricatures, distinctive team colors, and commentary about individual players. For example, the card parodying San Francisco Giants' outfielder Barry Bonds calls him "Treasury Bonds," and features a recognizable caricature of Bonds, complete with earring, tipping a bat boy for a 24-karat gold "Fort Knoxville Slugger." The back of the card has a team logo (the "Gents"), and the following text:
>
> Redemption qualities and why Treasury Bonds is the league's most valuable player:

1. Having Bonds on your team is like having money in the bank.
2. He plays so hard he gives 110 percent, compounded daily.
3. He turned down the chance to play other sports because he has a high interest rate in baseball.
4. He deposits the ball in the bleachers.
5. He is into male bonding.
6. He is a money player.
7. He has a 24-karat Gold Glove.
8. He always cashes in on the payoff pitch.

In an opinion fairly contemptuous of both publicity rights and major league baseball, the Tenth Circuit found that the First Amendment interests transcended any publicity rights which may have existed under Oklahoma's law, which closely paralleled California statutes.

c. Courts and legislatures struggle to distinguish commercial activity from expressive activity with regard to publicity rights. *Spahn v. Julian Messner, Inc.*, 221 N.E.2d 543 (N.Y. 1966), may reflect the low point for the New York Court of Appeals' attempts to understand the scope of publicity rights. There, the publication of a fictionalized biography of a real person—a famous baseball player—was construed as essentially a commercial appropriation of that person's identity. The implication is that where the mention of a person's name is incidental to the larger work of fiction, no appropriation will be found; but where the name is used to define and call attention to the work, a court may find appropriation. Given that the item in question was a book rather than a commercial product, the lack of appropriate First Amendment consideration was shocking.

d. In contrast to *Spahn*, the Ninth Circuit dealt with an even more outrageous falsification in *Hoffman v. L.A. Magazine*, 255 F.3d 1180 (9th Cir. 2001). There, L.A. Magazine used Dustin Hoffman's cross-dressing image from "Tootsie" in a digitally added new gown, as the photo illustration for an article entitled "Grand Illusions." As noncommercial speech, the Ninth Circuit found there could not be a claim for invasion of publicity rights from the expressive use of Mr. Hoffman's likeness.

e. Another significant decision was *Montana v. San Jose Mercury News, Inc.*, 34 Cal. App. 4th 790, 792 (Cal. App. 1995). The newspaper printed commemorative posters celebrating Joe Montana's four Super Bowl victories. Originally appearing as a pull-out, these were later sold as $5.00 posters. Seventy percent were given away to charity while the remainder was sold. The decision turned on the nature of the posters:

> Although we have been unable to locate any cases directly on point, several cases discuss First Amendment implications of the sale of posters, videotapes or movies of recognizable individuals without their consent. *Paulsen v. Personality Posters, Inc.*, 59 Misc.2d 444 [299 N.Y.S.2d 501] (N.Y. 1968) is illustrative. There, comedian Pat Paulsen sought a preliminary injunction to bar a poster marketer from selling posters of him with the words "For President"

written at the bottom. Paulsen had conducted a mock campaign for the presidency in 1968. In discussing whether Paulsen's statutorily defined "right of privacy" had been abridged, the court observed "that the statute was not intended to limit activities involving the dissemination of news or information concerning matters of public interest.... [S]uch activities are privileged and do not fall within 'the purposes of trade' contemplated by Section 51 [New York's equivalent of California Civil Code section 3344], notwithstanding that they are also carried on for a profit.... Applying those principles to the poster of Paulsen, the court stated: "When a well-known entertainer enters the presidential ring, tongue in cheek or otherwise, it is clearly newsworthy and of public interest. A poster which portrays plaintiff in that role, and reflects the spirit in which he approaches said role, is a form of public interest presentation to which protection must be extended."

The same could be said here. When Joe Montana led his team to four Super Bowl championships in a single decade, it was clearly a newsworthy event. Posters portraying the 49'ers' victories are, like the poster in Paulsen, a "form of public interest presentation to which protection must be extended."

A similar conclusion was reached in *Jackson v. MPI Home Video*, 694 F.Supp. 483 (N.D.Ill. 1988). In that case, the Reverend Jesse Jackson sought an injunction against the unauthorized distribution of videocassettes of a copyrighted speech he gave at the 1988 Democratic National Convention. The court granted the injunction based on Jackson's copyright claims. At the same time, it noted that Jackson's "chances of success on [his] right to publicity claim appear less than negligible" as the "defendants[] claim[ed] that they were engaged in news reporting...." The court explained that the right of publicity "is based upon the plaintiff's right to use his own name and likeness for his own benefit, and this right is violated when one, without leave, uses it for his benefit and not the plaintiff's. Public figures possess this right with respect to commercial use of their names and likeness. But public figures do not retain the right of publicity against the use of name and likeness in the news media." ...

At the hearing on the summary judgment motion in this case, SJMN submitted undisputed evidence that it sold the posters to advertise the quality and content of its newspaper. The posters were effective in this regard: they were exact reproductions of pages from the paper. They contained no additional information not included on the newspaper pages themselves, and they did not state or imply that Montana endorsed the newspaper. SJMN also submitted evidence showing it set the price of the posters with the intent simply to recover its costs. Where, as here, a newspaper page covering newsworthy events is reproduced for the purpose of showing the quality and content of the newspaper, the subsequent reproduction is exempt from the statutory and common law prohibitions.

f. Another example of the fine line between commercial speech and content was decided in *Astaire v. Best Film & Video Corp.*, 116 F.3d 1297 (9th Cir. 1997). The widow of Fred Astaire sued to enjoin the sale of dance instructional videotapes featuring Astaire's performances. The district court found that the use was not a violation of the California right of publicity, and the Ninth Circuit found there was neither a publicity claim nor any other claim. The testamentary right of publicity in California has since been amended in a manner which may reverse this decision. *See* Cal. Civ. Code § 3344.1 (2004).

g. To what extent is the original work of art, as marketed through lithographs, serigraphs, and similar works, still free to be marketed when these works involve the images of well-known sports figures? *See ETW Corp. v. Jireh Publ'g, Inc.*, 332 F.3d 915 (6th Cir. 2003).

h. There are also ongoing questions regarding the intersection of publicity rights and copyright. Because the state law publicity rights and federal trademark requirements both have different elements than copyright, preemption issues should not arise. Nonetheless, they often do. For example, if the NCAA were to license its collection of collegiate photographs—including thousands of student images—for a fee on a non-exclusive basis, do the students have a claim for either copyright infringement or infringement of their rights of publicity, assuming the license granted to the users was for "a single copy of the image for non-commercial art use"? Does the outcome change if the license includes language that licensee do not obtain "any right or license to use the name or likeness of any individual (including any athlete, announcer, or coach) appearing in the Content in connection with or as an express or implied endorsement of any product or service"? *See Maloney v. T3Media, Inc.*, 853 F.3d 1004 (9th Cir. 2017).

Problem 7-D

Bryce calls you with a quick question. One of the students involved with the New Masters series elected to use modern celebrities rather than literary characters. The project included a scene between Al Pacino and Quentin Tarantino where the Tarantino character sings a highly disparaging song, calling Pacino "old, angry, and ugly." The two characters continue to trade insults until the Pacino character picks up a stage prop and beats Tarantino to death—singing all the while. Bryce wants to know if the school, students, or anyone else can be in legal trouble for the scene. Bryce is also interested to know whether the answer will change if a proposed DVD version of the production is actually sold. Advise Bryce of the potential liability for both a live stage version of the scene, as well as a commercial version of the production sold on DVD.

E. Bibliography

Mark Bartholomew, *A Right Is Born: Celebrity, Property, and Postmodern Lawmaking*, 44 CONN. L. REV. 301 (2011).

Joseph J. Beard, *Clones, Bones and Twilight Zones: Protecting the Digital Persona of the Quick, the Dead and the Imaginary*, 16 BERKELEY TECH. L.J. 1165 (2001).

F. Jay Dougherty, *All the World's Not a Stooge: The "Transformativeness" Test for Analyzing a First Amendment Defense to a Right of Publicity Claim against Distribution of a Work of Art*, 27 COLUM. J.L. & ARTS 1 (2003).

Sheldon W. Halpern, *Trafficking in Trademarks: Setting Boundaries for the Uneasy Relationship Between "Property Rights" and Trademark and Publicity Rights*, 58 DEPAUL L. REV. 1013 (2009).

Rita Heimes, *Trademarks, Identity, and Justice*, 11 J. MARSHALL REV. INTELL. PROP. L. 133, 134 (2011).

Laura A. Heymann, *Naming, Identity, and Trademark Law*, 86 IND. L.J. 381 (2011).

Sarah Konsky, *Publicity Dilution: A Proposal for Protecting Publicity Rights*, 21 SANTA CLARA COMPUTER & HIGH TECH. L.J. 347 (2005).

Roberta Rosenthal Kwall, *Symposium: Intellectual Property Challenges in the Next Century: Article Preserving Personality and Reputational Interests of Constructed Personas Through Moral Rights: A Blueprint for the Twenty-First Century*, 2001 U. ILL. L. REV. 151 (2001).

Bela G. Lugosi, *Competing Perspectives and Divergent Analyses California Expands the Statutory Right of Publicity for Deceased Celebrities while its Courts are examining the First Amendment Limitations of that Statute*, 10 DEPAUL-LCA J. ART & ENT. L. 259 (2000).

Viva R. Moffat, *Mutant Copyrights and Backdoor Patents: The Problem of Overlapping Intellectual Property Protection*, 19 BERKELEY TECH. L.J. 1473 (2004).

Richard A. Posner, *Misappropriation: A Dirge*, 40 HOUS. L. REV. 621 (2003).

Michael Suppappola, *Is Tiger Wood's Swing Really a Work of Art? Defining the Line Between the Right of Publicity and the First Amendment*, 28 W. NEW ENG. L. REV. 57 (2005).

Eugene Volokh, *Freedom of Speech and the Right of Publicity*, 40 HOUS. L. REV. 903 (2003).

W. Mack Webner & Leigh Ann Lindquist, *Transformation: The Bright Line Between Commercial Publicity Rights and the First Amendment*, 37 AKRON L. REV. 171 (2004).

Chapter 8

Contracts:
Credit and Control

This chapter reflects the casebook's transition from the purely legal doctrinal focus of the first eight chapters to the industry-specific focus of the remaining chapters. The underlying legal framework remains contract law. While the primary focus is on employment law, certain aspects of these agreements may be focused on partnership agreements, reflecting yet another legal discipline in the practice.

A. The Negotiated Areas for Talent Contracts — Credit, Compensation, & Control

Regardless of the media in question, most talent contracts turn on three fundamental issues — credit, compensation, and control. Given that so many industries are highly unionized, issues such as working conditions, job descriptions, and other more typical negotiable items tend to be handled at the collective bargaining level rather than through private negotiation.

The corollary of the collective nature of this bargaining is that a contract dispute often involves not only the two parties to the transaction, but the rules set out in various collective bargaining and regulatory settings.

In the wake of *Dastar Corp. v. Twentieth Century Fox Film Corp.* (*see supra* Chapter 6), courts have largely restricted claims of credit to focus on contractual obligations only. Nonetheless, because this shift is so recent and the response to it thus far may not fully reflect any long-term trends, the materials contained in the remainder of this casebook explain the analysis of claims for credit prior to and in wake of the *Dastar* decision.

The influence on credit in *Dastar* also fails to address the interpretation of contracts providing the right to credit and the implications for the public regarding the over-stating of credit. The Copyright Office recognized this deficiency in its 2019 Report of the Register of Copyrights,[1] stating that "Congress may want to consider adopting an amendment to section 43(a) of the Lanham Act that would expand the unfair

---

1. Authors, Attribution, and Integrity: Examining Moral Rights in The United States, A Report of the Register of Copyrights, United States Copyright Office, April 2019.

competition protections to include false representations regarding authorship of expressive works."[2] The Copyright Office report could not address the attribution for non-authors, but the same concerns apply to actors and others who could be economically harmed by misinformation about the origin of creative works.

1. Credit

The right to have one's name listed prominently in association with a work is a prized economic and professional benefit. Parties negotiate over the scope and placement of credit both on the work and on advertisements for the work. In film, the results of negotiated billing appear in the opening credits; in theatre, the negotiated credit can be seen on the marquee and in the playbill; in publishing, the negotiations involve the dust jacket; and in sound recordings, the billing disputes focus on the CD cover. Whatever media is in question, the concepts regarding size and placement of billing are fairly universal.

The most heavily negotiated credit is for "above the title" billing, a term that refers to the positioning of a star's name before the name of the work on a film or above the name of the work on a marquee or in print. If there are two top stars involved in a work, the upper left position is considered the first position in terms of billing. The size of type used for the billing is often a source of discussion as well, with the type size often being negotiated as a percentage of the size of the title credits.

As indicated from the cases below, credits are often used as the basis for future contract negotiations. As a result, the content and position of credits can have a significant financial impact on an artist's future revenue opportunities.

2. Compensation

Compensation is obviously the source of most entertainment negotiation. The negotiations for compensation for sound recordings are so unique that they are treated separately in Chapter 11. For the other industries, compensation is generally paid in three increments: A non-refundable advance upon execution of the initial production agreement; a stipend or salary for the completion of the production; and royalties or profit participation for sharing in the success of the project.

Highly successful artists have a wide range of opportunities competing for the artists' attention. As a result, the decision to participate in any one project necessarily precludes the participation in other projects. Because of this, most artists demand an advance of some form to compensate for the opportunity cost, meaning the lost opportunity caused by agreeing to participate in a future project. This may range from a very

---

2. *Id.* at 4.

modest fee to a significant pay-or-play provision that essentially commits the producer to pay the artist the entire fee whether the production goes forward or not.

The salary is the most traditional employment income, typically paid weekly during the course of a film's production, video game's production, or a play's rehearsal and performance run. Publishers do not typically pay salary to authors nor do record producers pay salary to recording artists. Although the rehearsal period is often more work than production, salary is typically lower during the rehearsal period than during film production or a theatrical run.

Royalties and profit participation are based on the income of the project. Publishing royalties typically range from 10% to 20% of the suggested retail price of a book. Theatrical royalties often run 2% to 6% of all box office receipts for the playwright, director, and star cast members. Motion picture profit participation can be based on some formula of the distributor's adjusted gross income or net income. In the motion picture industry, the deductions before profit participation have become the focus of much controversy because so many expenses are deducted. Whether calculated as a royalty or as a form of profit participation, the purpose of these fees is to reward the artists for the success of the project. These have the second benefit of reducing the cost of production by deferring some of the artist overhead until the income is generated.

3. Control

Control is one of the more controversial aspects of negotiations. Some negotiations for control are overt, such as negotiations over approval of other participants in the project. Other areas for control are over scheduling and locations.

The more difficult area for control focuses on artistic control of the overall project. For example, playwrights have virtually absolute control over the text of their plays, based on a non-negotiable, standardized agreement. Film directors vie for final cut, the ability to control the final editing of the motion picture.

Control is negotiated both directly and indirectly. Often times, powerful stars will only agree to participate in a project once certain preconditions have been met. Although the contract never specifies these conditions, the producer's willingness to engage in negotiations over these preconditions is itself evidence of the star's exercise of significant control over the project.

In every industry, the producers or financiers of projects are the source of power and therefore control all projects at the outset. The ability to fund or withhold funding of a project is the ultimate source of power. This power is immediately limited to the extent it has been negotiated away through collective bargaining agreements or standardized contracts. Further, to launch a project, some of the producer's control must be shared with the creative talent that will develop the project.

An attorney negotiating in the entertainment industry must learn both the express control provisions of contracts and the unexpressed realities through which some participants have *de facto* authority throughout the course of a project's development. Marquee stars, who may have no contractual authority over any aspect of the production, still may have the power to have a director or co-star fired because the value of that actor's goodwill is more tangible than any contractual right. Only by understanding both the express and implicit areas of negotiation can an attorney fully appreciate the nuances of each negotiation.

The other aspect of control may come from the terms of the employment's scope. In *Ahn v. Midway Mfg. Co.*, 965 F. Supp. 1134 (N.D. Ill. 1997), the actors involved in the creation of a video game gave their publicity rights for coin-operated machines. The district court determined the scope of the contract included publicity rights to home computer and video games as well. In contrast, former wrestler and governor Jesse Ventura was able to secure the opposite result. In *Ventura v. Titan Sports, Inc.*, 65 F.3d 725 (8th Cir. 1995), the Eighth Circuit found that the performance and television contracts did not extend to home video tape for the performances staged for wrestling.

Perhaps the most interesting of all the talent cases litigated involved Raquel Welch's termination by David Begelman, from *Cannery Row*. In a decision decertified and inconsistent with established California precedent, the court found a conspiracy to improperly terminate the aging star and found the defendants acted with sufficient bad faith to award punitive damages. Enjoy *Welch v. Metro-Goldwyn-Mayer Film Co.*, 254 Cal. Rptr. 645 (Cal. Ct. App. 1988), *decertified*, 769 P.2d 932 (Cal. 1989), *transferred*, 782 P.2d 594 (Cal. 1989).

Sample Associate Producer Agreement[3]

[This simple agreement assumes that a small production company owned by the writer/director of a project is hiring the person to produce the project. Various aspects of the compensation, credit, and control are represented by the excerpt from the contract.]

This Agreement is made and entered into as of the date first ascribed below, by and between [XYZ Film Company, L.L.C., 1234 Main Street, Hollywood, California 90210] ("Company") and [John Doe, an individual, 5678 W. 46th St., New York, NY 10021] ("Producer"), with reference to the following facts:

Company is a wholly owned limited liability company owned by Jane Roe ("Writer/ Director").

Company has or will acquire rights to a screenplay to be written and directed by Writer/Director and desires to make such screenplay into a motion picture (the "Picture"); and

---

3. Jon M. Garon, Independent Filmmaker's Law and Business Guide 380 (2d ed. Chicago Review Press 2009).

Producer has extensive professional experiences as a line producer and producer of feature motion pictures.

Now Therefore, in consideration of the mutual covenants, conditions, and undertakings hereinafter set forth, the parties hereto agree as follows:

1. Services Provided. Company hereby employs the services of Producer, and Producer hereby accepts such employment, for the purpose of serving as associate producer and line producer of the Picture, for the period of [three (3)] weeks of preproduction, [five (5)] weeks of principal photography on an exclusive basis, and such postproduction as is reasonably necessary for completion of the Picture on a nonexclusive but first-priority basis. Each week shall include six working days. The Producer will provide such services as are generally performed by producers, including his service coordinating the creative, financial, technological, and administrative process throughout the term of this agreement, subject to the direction and control of Company and such other contracts as Company shall enter with other parties.

2. Term. The term of this Agreement shall commence on the date hereof and shall continue thereafter until Producer has fully completed all services required hereunder, unless sooner terminated in accordance with the provisions of this Agreement.

3. Credit. Provided Producer completes all services required hereunder and the Picture is completed by Company, then Producer shall receive credit on the screen, in motion picture trailers, and in paid print advertising issued by Company and under Company's control which is at least 10 inches or larger. The credit shall be "John Doe, Associate Producer." On the screen such credit shall be displayed above or before the title of the Picture in a size of type not less than fifty percent (50%) of the size of type used to display the title of the Picture. At its sole discretion, Company may assign "Produced by" and "Associate Producer" credit to one or more additional persons in addition to Producer in the event Company determines such other person or persons provided substantial producer services in addition to Producer. No casual or inadvertent failure to comply with the provisions of this clause shall be deemed to be a breach of this Agreement by Company. Producer shall notify Company of any breach of this paragraph, after which Company shall take reasonable steps to correct all new prints, copies, and advertising on a prospective basis, but Company shall not be required to recall or alter any prints, copies, or advertisements in production or distribution. No monetary damages are available for breach of Company's duties under this paragraph.

4. Consideration. In consideration for Producer's services hereunder and provided Producer is not in default hereunder, Company shall pay Producer as follows:

   (a) Fixed Consideration. Producer shall receive a stipend of [$100.00] per day actually worked during preproduction and principal photography, not to exceed [Forty-Eight Hundred ($4,800.00)] Dollars. The payment shall be paid on a weekly basis.

(b) Net Profits. If Producer fulfills all Producer's obligations pursuant to this agreement and if Company produces the Picture, Producer shall receive an amount equal to [ten percent (10%)] of one hundred percent (100%) of Net Profits in the Gross Receipts of the Company in the Picture or [One Hundred Thousand ($100,000)] Dollars, whichever is lower.

   (i) Gross Receipts means all income, if any, actually received by Company from the sale, exhibition, or distribution of the Picture in theaters, video/DVD or similar format, broadcast television, satellite, cable exhibition, or any other method of exhibition, display, or performance now known or hereafter created. Gross Receipts does not include income from any other source related to the Picture, including, without limitation, income derived from sale of sequel, prequel, or remake rights, publishing interests such as novelizations, comic books, etc., sales of the screenplay, "making of" or other related projects, or any other spin-offs or related Company projects or activities.

   (ii) The term Net Profits shall mean the Gross Receipts, less the deductions of all Company expenses of every kind related to the Picture. Without limiting the foregoing, the deductions shall include all costs, charges, and expenses paid or incurred in connection with the preparation, production, completion, and delivery of the Picture, deferred compensation, charges for any services, union or trade obligations, interest expenses, obligations to any completion guarantor, legal and accounting charges, the cost of all material, services, facilities, labor, insurance, taxes (other than income, franchise, and like taxes), copyright royalties attributable to the Picture for music, artwork, script, or other, judgments, marketing and promotional expenses, distribution fees, recoveries, settlements, losses, costs, and expenses, including reasonable attorneys' fees, sustained or incurred by Company in connection with the Picture or anything used therein and in connection with the production thereof. Company shall pay Producer twice annually all amounts due hereunder for all monies accrued during the preceding six-month period, not later than forty-five (45) days following the end of each such period.

(c) Reimbursements. Producer shall be reimbursed for all reasonable advances or expenses incurred in the production of the Picture, such as for location scouting, equipment rental, and the like, provided such expenses have been approved by Company in advance and Producer provides adequate documentation and receipts of the expense.

5. Authority. Company shall coordinate with Producer throughout the production to the greatest extent practicable throughout production; provided, however,

Company reserves final approval of all essential production elements including, without limitation, script, budget, casting, locations, and film editing. Subject to direction of Company, Producer shall comply with all contractual and union and guild obligations and Company requirements.

6. Termination.

   (a) This Agreement may be terminated by Company at any time, with or without cause. If Company elects to terminate this Agreement and Producer is not in default hereunder, Company shall pay Producer his accrued fixed compensation and a pro rata proportion of the contingent compensation. (By way of example, if Producer is terminated after 12 days, he will receive 12/48 of his contingent compensation, equal to 25% of 10%, meaning 2.5% of the Net Profits.) The costs of additional producer(s) shall be added to the cost of production. In the event Company determines Producer has materially breached his obligations hereunder, no contingent compensation shall be paid.

   (b) This Agreement may be terminated by Producer upon seven days' advanced written notice. Unless otherwise agreed in writing by the parties, in the event Producer terminates this Agreement, he shall receive only his accrued fixed compensation, but shall not be eligible for any contingent compensation.

7. Work Made for Hire. Company shall own the copyright in the Picture without any claim by Producer. Producer is employed as on a work made for hire as a specially commissioned audiovisual or motion picture work and acknowledges that the copyright in the Picture shall vest exclusively in Company as author.

   (a) The Picture shall be registered for copyright in Company's name both in the United States and elsewhere.

   (b) To the extent Producer has created any copyrighted elements incorporated into the Picture and such work made for hire provision is not recognized by the jurisdiction, Producer hereby assigns all rights or the maximum rights allowed under that jurisdiction's laws to Company, including, without limitation, Rental Lending Rights if recognized, rights to enforce any claim of attribution and integrity, or rights to exploit any interest in the Picture in any media now known or hereafter developed.

8. Unique Services. It is hereby agreed and understood that Producer's services to be furnished hereunder are special, extraordinary, unique, and not replaceable, and that there is no adequate remedy at law for breach of this contract by Producer.

   (a) Company shall be entitled to both legal and equitable remedies as may be available, including both injunctive relief and damages. Company may elect not to submit to arbitration for the purpose of seeking emergency, preliminary, or temporary injunctive relief.

(b) Producer's services shall be in such time, place, and manner as Company may reasonably direct in accordance with customary motion picture industry practice. Such services shall be rendered in an artistic, conscientious, efficient, and punctual manner to the best of Producer's ability to adhere to the budget and shooting schedule.

(c) Producer grants to Company the perpetual nonexclusive right to use and license others to use Producer's name, biography, and reproductions of Producer's physical likeness and voice in connection with the production, exhibition, advertising, promotion, or other exploitation of the Picture and all subsidiary and ancillary rights therein and thereto; provided, however, Company shall not use or authorize the use of Producer's name or likeness as a direct endorsement of any product or service without Producer's prior consent.

9. Resolution of Disputes. ANY AND ALL DISPUTES HEREUNDER SHALL BE RESOLVED BY ARBITRATION OR REFERENCE. ANY PARTY HERETO ELECTING TO COMMENCE AN ACTION SHALL GIVE WRITTEN NOTICE TO THE OTHER PARTY HERETO. THEREUPON, IF ARBITRATION IS SELECTED BY THE PARTY COMMENCING THE ACTION, THE CLAIM ("ARBITRATION MATTER") SHALL BE SETTLED BY ARBITRATION IN ACCORDANCE WITH THE THEN RULES OF THE AMERICAN ARBITRATION ASSOCIATION ("AAA"). The arbitrator or the referee shall diligently pursue determination of any Arbitration under consideration and shall render a decision within one hundred twenty (120) days after the arbitrator or referee is selected. The determination of the arbitrator on all matters referred to it hereunder shall be final and binding on the parties hereto. The award of such arbitrator may be confirmed or enforced in any court of competent jurisdiction. The referee, arbitrator, or its designee shall have full access to such records and physical facilities of the parties hereto as may be required. The costs and expenses of the referee or arbitrator, and the attorneys' fees and costs of each of the parties incurred in such, may be apportioned between the parties by such arbitrator, as the case may be, based upon such arbitrator's determination of the merits of their respective positions.

10. Confidentiality; Publicity. Company shall have the exclusive right to issue and to license others to issue advertising and publicity with respect to the Picture, and Producer shall not circulate, publish, or otherwise disseminate any such advertising or publicity without Company's prior written consent.

11. Assignment. Producer agrees that Company shall have the right to assign, license, delegate, lend, or otherwise transfer all or any part of its rights or duties under this Agreement at any time to any person. Producer acknowledges that the personal services to be rendered by Producer hereunder are of the essence of this Agreement and agrees that he shall not assign this Agreement, in whole or in part, to any person, and that any purported assignment or delegation of duties by Producer shall be null and void and of no force and effect whatsoever.

This Agreement shall inure to the benefit of Company's successors, assigns, licensees, grantees, and associated, affiliated, and subsidiary companies.

12. No Obligation. Company agrees to uses all reasonable efforts to cause the Picture to be produced, however, the parties recognize that the production of an independent motion picture is an inherently difficult undertaking. Company is under no obligation to produce the Picture hereunder. In the event Company abandons production of the Picture hereunder, Producer is entitled to such fixed compensation as had previously accrued and is not entitled to any additional compensation, damage, or loss as a result of such failure to undertake or complete the Picture.

13. Assurances. Each party shall execute all documents and certificates and perform all acts deemed appropriate by the Company or required by this Agreement in connection with this Agreement and the production of the Picture.

Lee v. Marvel Enterprises, Inc.
386 F. Supp. 2d 235 (S.D.N.Y. 2005), *aff'd*,
471 Fed. Appx. 14 (2d Cir. 2012) (unpublished)

The defendant Marvel Enterprises, Inc. ("Marvel") has moved for partial summary judgment in accordance with Rule 56(a), Fed. R. Civ. P., dismissing the claims in the complaint seeking a profit participation from licensing of its characters for merchandising. The plaintiff Stan Lee ("Lee") has cross-moved for partial summary judgment declaring that he is entitled to 10% participation in profits derived by Marvel from television or movie productions, not limited by so-called "Hollywood Accounting," including film/television merchandising when the profits do not result from a fee for licensing. For the reasons set forth below, Marvel's motion is denied, and Lee's cross-motion is granted in part and denied in part.

As of the time these motions were filed, Lee continued to serve as Marvel's chairman emeritus. As discussed below, Lee has contributed significantly to Marvel's growth since his initial employment in 1940. Initially, Marvel's predominant business was publishing comic books, many of which featured characters created by Lee—*e.g.* Spider-Man, the Incredible Hulk, the X-Men, and the Fantastic Four. Marvel has subsequently expanded the use of its characters into movies, television, and merchandising. Lee had a contract with Marvel that permitted him to share in certain of these endeavors. Marvel then suffered the vicissitudes of a control contest and bankruptcy. When it emerged from bankruptcy with new leadership, it entered into a new contract with Lee (the "Agreement"). It is paragraph 4(f) of the Agreement, executed on November 17, 1998, that is the central focus of the present action. Paragraph 4(f) states:

> [Lee] shall be paid a participation equal to 10% of the profits derived during [his] life by Marvel (including subsidiaries and affiliates) from the profits of any live action or animation television or movie (including ancillary rights) productions utilizing Marvel Characters. This participation is not to be de-

rived from the fee charged by Marvel for the licensing of the product or of the characters for merchandise or otherwise ...

This deceptively simple language, drafted by a company and an executive both skilled and experienced in the industry, has given rise to a multimillion dollar controversy because of changes in the way Marvel has conducted business since the execution of the Agreement in November, 1998.

According to Marvel, paragraph 4(f) entitles Lee to 10% participation in only those television and motion picture production deals where Marvel has been afforded rights of net profit participation. (Such net profit participation arrangements are commonly referred to as "Hollywood Accounting" deals.[4]) Lee argues that paragraph 4(f) entitles him to 10% of all profits—including gross profits or gross proceeds—derived from contingent payments to Marvel in connection with the use of Marvel characters in film or television productions.

According to Marvel, pursuant to the second sentence of paragraph 4(f), Lee is barred from any profits from merchandising. According to Lee, he is entitled to participate in all revenue from film/television merchandising with the exception of profits resulting from fees from licensing for merchandise.

Skilled counsel for both sides praise the clarity of the language of paragraph 4(f) to reach directly contrary results. What follows is an effort to clarify and determine the terms of the contractual language under the applicable principles of procedure and construction. This determination has the potential to affect substantially the financial fortunes of the parties....

Prior to the 1994 bankruptcy, the parties entered into an agreement granting Lee a share of Marvel's profits. In 1995, pursuant to this agreement, Marvel paid Lee a 10% participation, which was based on revenue received by Marvel under an arrangement with Danchuk Productions. Under this arrangement, Lee received a percentage of gross receipts. The payments to Marvel were characterized as "profit participation." Marvel remitted 10% ($4,994) to Lee without any deduction for costs. Marvel stated to Lee that this sum "represented your 10% of the profits." The executory portion of this prior agreement was rejected by Marvel during the bankruptcy.

---

4. One commentator has provided the following description of the typical provisions of a "Hollywood accounting" deal:

> The basic net profits formula subtracts from the studio's (distributor's) adjusted gross receipts the production costs, distribution expenses, and distribution fees.... Production costs are all costs directly attributed to the particular film (plus overhead). Production costs include the payments to all other participants in a film including the contingent compensation of gross participants. So, for example, [if a given actor] had fifteen gross points for [a given movie] (that is, he received 15[%] of the gross receipts), every dollar of revenue that the film generated pushed the net profits breakeven point back fifteen cents. Thus, if a film has significant gross participants, the breakeven point quickly recedes. Almost all the box office smashes that failed to produce net profits had significant gross participants.

Victor P. Goldberg, *The Net Profits Puzzle*, 97 Colum. L. Rev. 524, 528–529 (1997).

After Marvel emerged from bankruptcy, the parties on November 17, 1998 executed the Agreement. In addition to paragraph 4(f), the Agreement contains other relevant provisions. Under paragraph 2, Lee is required to devote ten to fifteen hours per week to Marvel's affairs. As consideration for his services, Lee is entitled to receive an annual base salary of $810,000 for the years beginning November 1, 1998 and 1999, $850,000 for the year beginning November 1, 2000, $900,000 for the year beginning November 1, 2001, and $1,000,000 for the year beginning November 1, 2002 and each year thereafter until his death. Upon Lee's death, the Agreement provides for Lee's wife to receive survivor payments in an amount equal to 50% of Lee's base salary as of the time of his death through the time of her death, and for Lee's daughter thereafter to receive survivor payments of $100,000 per year for five years. Under paragraph 4(c) of the Agreement, Lee received 150,000 valuable stock options which Lee has already exercised for a net gain of approximately $1.4 million.

Between November 17, 1998 and today, Marvel has entered into over a thousand merchandising agreements pursuant to which it has licensed to third parties the right to use its characters in connection with various toys, games, collectibles, apparel, interactive games, arcade games and electronics, stationery and school products, health and beauty products, snack foods and beverages, sporting goods, party supplies, and amusement destinations. Merchandising has generated hundreds of millions of dollars in revenue to Marvel during this period.

In August 1998, the film *Blade*, which was based on a Marvel character, was released. Despite the fact that *Blade* apparently generated considerable profits, Marvel was not entitled to participate in these profits based on the terms of the profit-participation provision of the production agreement. This profit-participation provision, which Marvel has characterized as a "Hollywood accounting" provision, entitled Marvel to a share of *Blade*'s "net profits," as that term was defined by the language of the production agreement. Marvel's Rule 30(b)(6) witness stated that "Hollywood accounting" can be interpreted "to mean that you will never see anything — you will never see — the company would not see any revenues from the studio...." Marvel's chief creative officer, Avi Arad, testified that "Hollywood accounting is — is the term used to — studio's deduct everything possible out of film revenues, from cost of the movie to getting a star flowers to — you name it and its in there. And it's expensive and it's hard to monitor, and therefore I'm allergic to it."

Coincident with *Blade*'s box-office success, a determination was made by Marvel to avoid "Hollywood accounting" treatment for the use of the Marvel characters. In its 2001 annual report, Marvel advised that its new movie venture agreements were either "gross profit participation 'dollar one,'" "real profit participation," or "equity (ownership) interests in the films themselves." As stated by Marvel, these new agreements "represent an exciting new source of high margin revenue and are a major departure from the past when [Marvel] made little or no money for such projects."

Marvel's contract with Sony for use of the character Spider-Man (generally regarded as Marvel's most valuable asset) contained a gross-profit participation provision. *Spider-Man: The Movie*, which was released in May, 2002, proved to be a huge box-office hit, earning $114.8 million in its opening weekend (at the time, the largest domestic opening of all time) and more than $800 million in worldwide box-office gross. Based on these receipts, the profit participation provision that Marvel negotiated with Sony has yielded more than $50,000,000 to Marvel.

In its October 30, 2002 press release announcing Marvel's quarterly financial results, Marvel's then president and CEO, Peter Cuneo ("Cuneo"), stated that "Marvel's resurgence throughout 2002 has been supported by the overwhelming popularity and success of *Spider-Man: The Movie*, which has spurred licensing and toy revenues; the expanding scope of our publishing efforts; and our strong and growing line-up of entertainment projects scheduled for release in 2003 and beyond." As set forth in its 2002 annual report, Marvel's toy division alone reported over $100 million in sales of *Spider-Man: The Movie* toys. Marvel's 2003 results were similarly strong, driven by the popularity of the films *X-Men 2*, *Daredevil*, and *Hulk*, all of which featured Marvel characters....

[A.] Profit Participation Pursuant to the First Sentence of Paragraph 4(f) Is Not Limited to Net Profit Participation.

According to Lipson, Marvel's 30(b)(6) witness, Marvel's construction of the first sentence of paragraph 4(f) is based on the plain meaning of the text. According to Lipson, Lee is entitled to participation pursuant to paragraph 4(f) only when a payment by a studio (or producer) to Marvel is the result of a calculation of profit based on "Hollywood Accounting." Marvel argues that Lee is not entitled to share in profits arising from the contingent compensation provision in the Spider-Man agreement (and others like it) because such provisions entail participation in gross receipts and not profits.

However, the first sentence of paragraph 4(f) does not state that Lee's participation is limited to net profits earned by the producer or studio. Nor is the word "profits" defined in the Agreement. Moreover, the first, and therefore preferred, dictionary definition for "profit" is "an advantageous gain or return; benefit" (The American Heritage College Dictionary (3d ed. 2000)); or "a valuable return: gain." (Merriam-Webster Online Dictionary). As demonstrated by the evidence proffered by Lee, these dictionary definitions are consistent with Marvel's own consistent practice in treating all forms of contingent compensation as profit participation.In short, the first sentence of paragraph 4(f) is not ambiguous. It provides that Lee is entitled to share in the results of Marvel's arrangements for movie and television productions involving Marvel characters, however those arrangements may have been characterized as between Marvel and the third party, as long as there is a valuable gain or return, a benefit to Marvel.

It is also apparent that a determination of the profits to which Lee is entitled cannot be made on the basis of the present record.

[B.] "Ancillary Rights" Include Merchandising

The parties differ as to whether the term "ancillary rights," as used in the first sentence of paragraph 4(f), includes merchandising rights. According to Marvel, pursuant to the first sentence of paragraph 4(f), "ancillary rights" are properly defined as whatever rights are granted by Marvel to a licensee under a given film/television production agreement. Marvel argues that "ancillary rights" neither necessarily include nor exclude merchandising; rather, the terms of each individual film or television production agreement determines the substance of these rights. In contrast, Lee argues that the phrase "ancillary rights" describes all rights beyond a film/television production's initial intended distribution, and that such rights are understood in the entertainment industry to necessarily include merchandising....

[T]he phrase "ancillary rights" includes rights ancillary to the basic film or television production itself. According to Lee's expert, it is understood in the motion picture and television industries that such "ancillary rights" include soundtrack, music, and merchandising revenues. Although Marvel's expert asserts that "there is no fixed and accepted definition" of the term "ancillary rights" he admits that the term is understood in the entertainment industry to include "all rights beyond the right to produce and distribute the motion picture for theatrical release." Furthermore, Marvel's expert states that "there are instances where merchandising rights are expressly excluded from the grant of ancillary rights[,]" thereby strongly suggesting that, in general, ancillary rights are understood to include merchandising.

Based on this expert testimony proffered by Lee and Marvel concerning common usage in the relevant industries, it is determined that the phrase "ancillary rights," as used in the first sentence of paragraph 4(f), necessarily includes merchandising rights....

Notes and Questions

a. Third party licensing. Hollywood is an oligopoly, dominated by relatively few major corporations. The commonly owned companies will often enter into contracts, shifting revenue from one subsidiary to another and shifting expenses from one part of the enterprise to another. Revenue participants may be financially harmed by these insider deals. One such example was triggered by the reversion of part of the copyright in Superman.

> In March, 2008, the widow, and the daughter of Jerome Siegel, the co-creator of the iconic comic book superhero Superman, successfully terminated the 1938 grant Jerome Siegel and his creative partner Joseph Shuster had conveyed to DC Comics' predecessor-in-interest, Detective Comics, to the copyright in the Superman material published in the comic book Action Comics No.1. Left unanswered for trial was, inter alia, the question of "whether the license fees paid" by Warner Bros Entertainment Inc. ("Warner Bros") to its corporate sibling, DC Comics, for the audiovisual rights to the Superman copyright pursuant to various licensing agreements entered into during the 1999 to 2002 period "represents the fair market value therefor, or whether the license for the works between the related entities was a 'sweetheart deal.'"

Following a ten-day bench trial, the court ruled in favor of Warner Bros. and DC Comics. *See Siegel v. Warner Bros. Entm't Inc.*, No. CV04-08400-SGLRZX, 2009 WL 2014164, at *1 (C.D. Cal. July 8, 2009).

b. The factual determinations of *Siegel v. Warner Bros.* and *Lee v. Marvel Enterprises, Inc.* shed some light on the types of deals available to the publishers for their film rights. A footnote in *Siegal* offers some details for high-end transactions:

> [T]he film license to the Clive Cussler work Sahara provides for the rights holder to receive 10% of producer's gross and a purchase price of $20 million; the film license to Thomas Harris' work Hannibal contains a 10% of first dollar gross and a $10 million purchase price, the film license to the musical Annie contains a participation of 10% of first dollar gross escalating to 12.5% and a purchase price of $9.5 million; the film license to the Michael Crichton work Timeline has a participation of 10% of "adjusted gross" (which appears to be less than distributor gross) escalating to 20%; and the film licenses to the Tom Clancy works Rainbow Six and Red Rabbit have a participation of 10% in "adjusted gross" with a purchase price of $6 million and $7 million, respectively.

Siegel, 2009 WL 2014164, at note 4 (C.D. Cal. July 8, 2009).

c. There are many complaints that individual employment contracts tied to net profits, to subsidiary licensing techniques, and other strategies all result in a systemic underpayment of profit participants. Nearly all employment agreements, however, require an arbitration proceeding rather than permitting the litigation of these claims, making the documentation of these accounting issues difficult. *See* Neal Robin, *Hit Losers: The Good (Faith) Fight for Net-Profits Payments from Blockbuster Hollywood Productions*, 4 J.L. Tech. & Internet 445 (2013); Marc Simon, *Vertical Integration and Self-Dealing in the Television Industry: Should Profit Participants Be Owed a Fiduciary Duty?*, 19 Cardozo Arts & Ent. L.J. 433 (2001).

Problem 8-A

Bryce wishes to provide profit participation to members of the theatrical company Bryce has established. The company is using the back-end participation to reduce the amount it must pay talent during production, since the company has few financial resources. Provide a draft profit participation provision that is reasonable and can be verified by the parties, while allowing the company to meet its financial obligations to its investors and creditors before paying the profit participants.

B. Performer's Rights to Credit

Williams v. UMG Recordings, Inc.

281 F. Supp. 2d 1177 (C.D. Cal. 2003)

This action is brought by Plaintiff Kelvin Williams d/b/a Uprise Productions ("Plaintiff") against Defendants UMG Recordings, Inc., Universal Music & Video Distribution, Inc., Cash Money Records, Inc., Jeffrey Panzer, Ronald Williams, Bryan Williams, Gary Huckaby and Elston Howard....

Plaintiff styles himself as "a talented young film director/writer/editor." Defendant Cash Money is a record label whose principals are Defendants Ronald and Bryan

Williams. Cash Money has a contract with non-party Universal Records, Inc. ("Universal"), pursuant to which Cash Money pays Defendant UMG Recordings, Inc. ("UMG") (of which Universal is a division) to manufacture and distribute its products. Defendant Panzer is a Senior Vice President of Music Video Production for Universal who also does free-lance work for the Cash Money Defendants. Defendant Universal Music & Video Distribution, Corp. ("UMVD"), an affiliate of UMG, actually distributed the film that is the subject of this suit.

In February of 2000, Plaintiff, Panzer and the Cash Money Defendants collaborated on the production of a documentary. A dispute over Plaintiff's compensation subsequently developed, apparently resulting in bad blood between Plaintiff and Panzer. In the meantime, around March 2000, Plaintiff got involved in another project with Panzer and the Cash Money Defendants involving post-production work on a film entitled "Baller Blockin."

The parties disagree as to the nature and extent of Plaintiff's involvement in the Baller Blockin' project. Plaintiff claims that Defendants contracted with him to restructure the entire film. Plaintiff contends that he re-edited and re-scored the entire film and that it incorporates his copyrighted narration script ("Narration Script"). After Baller Blockin' was released [only on DVD and home video (not in theaters)], Plaintiff discovered his name was not listed in the film's credits and initiated this lawsuit....

Defendants seek reconsideration in part of the July Order dismissing in part Plaintiff's Second Claim for Relief for violation of the Lanham Act.... Specifically, after the issuance of July Order, the United States Supreme Court issued its opinion in *Dastar v. Twentieth Century Fox,* 539 U.S. 23 (2003), and Defendants claim that *Dastar* bars Plaintiff's Lanham Act claim as a matter of law.

Under the Lanham Act, Plaintiff alleges that Defendants engaged in unfair trade practices and unfair competition for appropriating his "copyrighted Narration Script, re-sequencing of scenes and re-scoring of musical content[.]" Specifically, Plaintiff alleges "reverse passing off" based on Defendants' misattribution of film credits for authorship and direction of Baller Blockin' solely to Robert and Bryan Williams.

In the July Order, the Court explained that Section 43(a) of the Lanham Act reaches "'reverse passing off,' which occurs when a person removes or obliterates the original trademark, without authorization, before reselling goods produced by someone else." It further explained that "'mere omission'" of credit, "which obscures the contribution of another to the final product," is actionable under this theory. The Court, acknowledging that the Lanham Act does not create a right of express attribution, held that to recover on his Lanham Act claim, Plaintiff must demonstrate that his alleged contributions in writing the Narration Script and re-editing and re-scoring the film were partially or wholly attributed to others. In other words, Plaintiff cannot seek a remedy under the Lanham Act for credit for contributions not attributed to others. The Court concluded as follows: "The only potentially relevant credit given in the film and on its packaging is that given for 'story/screenplay' and 'editing.'... A triable issue of fact exists as to whether Plaintiff's alleged contributions fall within the categories of 'story/

screenplay' and 'editing' such that failure to include Plaintiff's name in the credits constitutes misattribution under the Lanham Act." ...

In *Dastar*, plaintiff Twentieth Century Fox ("Fox") produced a 26-episode television series called "Crusade in Europe," which initially aired in 1949, featuring military film footage. The copyright on the series expired in 1977, leaving the series in the public domain. Fox later granted to co-plaintiffs SFM Entertainment ("SFM") and New Line Home Video ("New Line") the exclusive right to sell the "Crusade" series on video.

Defendant Dastar sought to compete directly with the SFM and New Line videos by purchasing tapes of the original "Crusade" series and copying and editing them—retaining much of the original series by adding new opening and closing sequences, credits, chapter-title sequences, and narrated introductions, and making a few other cosmetic changes. Dastar also created new packaging and a new title, selling its version as "World War II Campaigns in Europe." ...

The Supreme Court ... acknowledged that the plaintiffs' claim would undoubtedly be sustained if Dastar had bought some of New Line's Crusade videotapes and merely repackaged them as its own. This is because "origin" would refer to the manufacturer or producer of the physical goods that are made available to the public—the videotapes. However, it stated that Dastar's alleged wrongdoing is "vastly different" in that it took a creative work in the public domain—the Crusade television series—copied it, made minor modifications and produced its very own series of videotapes. Under this scenario, if "origin" includes the creator of the underlying work that Dastar copied, then someone else was the origin of Dastar's product. The Supreme Court then determined that the most natural understanding of the "origin" of "goods" is the producer of the tangible product sold in the marketplace (i.e., the videotapes sold by Dastar). It stated that the phrase "origin of goods" in the Lanham Act is "incapable of connoting the person or entity that originated the ideas or communications that 'goods' embody or contain."

The Court then examined the argument that communicative products—products that are valued not primarily for its physical qualities but for the intellectual content that it conveys such as a book or video—should be accorded special treatment. In other words, for a communicative product, "origin of goods" must be deemed to include not merely the producer of the physical item (the video producer Dastar) but also the creator of the content that the physical item conveys (assertedly, the plaintiffs). The Supreme Court rejected this and found that the "problem with this argument ... is that it causes the Lanham Act to conflict with the law of copyright, which addresses that subject specifically." ...

The Court noted the serious practical problems of defining "origin" to require attribution of uncopyrighted materials. It "did not think the Lanham Act requires this search for the source of the Nile and all its tributaries."

The Supreme Court then concluded as follows:

> "In sum, reading the phrase 'origin of goods' in the Lanham Act in accordance
> with the Act's common-law foundations (which were *not* designed to protect

originality or creativity), and in light of the copyright and patent laws (which *were*), we conclude that the phrase refers to the producer of the tangible goods that are offered for sale, and not to the author of any idea, concept, or communication embodied in those goods.... To hold otherwise would be akin to finding that §43(a) created a species of perpetual patent and copyright, which Congress may not do."

Defendants argue that *Dastar* invalidates Plaintiff's Lanham Act claim. This Court agrees with Defendants.... Plaintiff's Lanham Act claim is based on the misattribution of credits for "story/screenplay" and "editing" on the Baller Blockin' film. Plaintiff alleges that he should be given credit for "the authoring of the 'Narration Script'..., editing film sequences and re-scoring the music." Under *Dastar*, however, the Supreme Court specifically held that the phrase "origin of goods" "refers to the producer of tangible goods that are offered for sale, and not to the author of any idea, concept, or communication embodied in those goods." As such, Plaintiff would have a claim if Defendants purchased copies of Plaintiff's goods (i.e. the film) and repackaged them as their own. By contrast, Plaintiff does not have a claim for his authorship and direction embodied in that film. His claim, therefore, is barred as a matter of law.

In his Opposition, Plaintiff argues that *Dastar* is not a broad sweeping dismissal of reverse passing off claims but rather is limited to defining "origin of goods," not the origin of services. He claims that the Supreme Court's sole focus was on the term "origin of goods," and that it did not address the origin of services, which is at issue here. This Court disagrees with Plaintiff. As Defendants assert, the Supreme Court in *Dastar* was concerned with a claim materially identical to Plaintiff's claim here. The claim was that Dastar had made false or misleading representations on its own goods (Dastar's Campaigns videotapes) — just as Plaintiff here claims that Defendants made false or misleading representations on Defendants' own goods (the Baller Blockin' video and DVD). The "goods" are the defendants', not the plaintiff's. *Dastar* makes clear that a claim that a defendant's failure to credit the plaintiff on the defendant's goods is actionable only where the defendant literally repackages the plaintiff's goods and sells them as the defendant's own — not where, as here, Defendants are accused only of failing to identify someone who contributed not goods, but ideas or communications (or, for that matter, "services") to Defendants' product.

Contrary to Plaintiff's argument, based on the *Dastar* Court's holding, the Ninth Circuit cases cited by Plaintiff would be overruled to the extent they find a reverse passing off claim based on the failure to credit the author of any idea, concept or communication embodied in the tangible goods.

Plaintiff contends that his claim survives *Dastar* because he provided "services" as opposed to "goods." However, to the contrary, his claim fails for this reason. All he allegedly provided was "services," rather than goods which Defendants repackaged and resold as their own. Indeed, in *Dastar*, the defendant did exactly what Plaintiff accuses Defendants of doing here — attributing to itself and its employees various "services" that the plaintiffs claimed they, in fact, provided on the defendant's videotapes. The Supreme Court held that the plaintiffs' claim that these credits were misleading because the plaintiffs really provided those services was non-actionable. As Defendants state, Plaintiff's attempt to differentiate the "services" of an "executive producer" or "producer" at issue in Dastar from his alleged "services" as an "editor" and "writer" is a distinction without a difference.

Plaintiff then asserts that "if defendants [sic] argument were accepted, a talented director who directs a Summer blockbuster for example can be deprived of the immense value of such a credit in the entertainment industry, simply because the producer decides to name himself as the director.... A reading that the Lanham Act does not protect those people who provide services on films permits a form of anarchy in the entertainment industry, where anybody could be credited for anyone else's work and have their credit obliterated." However, the Supreme Court directly addressed Plaintiff's assertion. "The problem with this argument according special treatment to communicative products is that it causes the Lanham Act to conflict with the law of copyright, which addresses that subject specifically." In Plaintiff's hypothetical, the director has options to protect his interest—obtaining a contractual right to a credit, relying on the regulation of credits in union collective bargaining agreements (e.g., the Directors Guild) or maintaining the copyright in the film. In light of Dastar, this hypothetical director cannot bring a claim under the Lanham Act.

Finally, Plaintiff attempts to distinguish Dastar by claiming that "the Court focused its analysis of the case on the concept that the involved works were uncopyrighted and the difficulties associated with the origin of the product." To the contrary, the Supreme Court's holding did not depend on whether the works were copyrighted or not. While the film footage at issue in Dastar was not copyrighted at the time of distribution by Dastar, the Court's holding is in no way limited to uncopyrighted material. Rather, in being careful not to extend trademark protections, the Court noted that protection for communicative products was available through copyright claims. In fact, this protection would only be available if a valid copyright existed. Indeed, the Court stated:

> The creative talent of the sort that lay behind the Campaigns videos is not left without protection. The original film footage used in the Crusade television series could have been copyrighted, ..., as was copyrighted (as a compilation) the Crusade television series, even though it included material from the public domain,.... Had Fox renewed the copyright in the Crusade television series, it would have had an easy claim of copyright infringement.

Here, Plaintiff does have a copyright claim. As was set forth in the July Order, "a triable issue of fact exists as to whether Defendants are liable for copyright infringement since the filing of this law suit [sic] in April 2001." As Dastar makes clear, Plaintiff's claim is more appropriately addressed under copyright law rather than under the Lanham Act. Therefore, this Court concludes that Defendants are the "origin" of the Baller Blockin' film insofar as that term is used to define the manufacturer or producer of the physical goods that were made available to the public, and no Lanham Act liability attaches to them. Plaintiff's claim under the Lanham Act fails as a matter of law, and Defendants are entitled to summary judgment with respect to the claim.

Plaintiff argues that in pleading a cause of action for Lanham Act violation, he properly relied on existing law. He states that rather than plead duplicative claims for relief, he opted for the federal Lanham Act claim rather than the statutory unfair business practice and deceptive advertising claims.... Plaintiff's desired statutory unfair business practice claim would be futile. The Ninth Circuit has consistently held that state law unfair competition claims are "congruent" with Lanham Act claims; Plaintiff's putative unfair competition claim would fail for the same reasons his Lanham Act claim fails....

Accordingly, this Court grants Defendants ... Motion for Reconsideration and dismisses Plaintiff's Second Claim for Relief for violation of the Lanham Act.

Notes and Questions

a. Marybeth Peters, when Register of Copyright, commented on the difficulty created by *Dastar*. "[T]he longstanding understanding prior to *Dastar* [was] that section 43(a) is an important means for protecting the moral rights of attribution and integrity."[5] The importance of the §43(a) claim is the pressure it puts on the producers of a project to provide contractual credit.

b. Courts do not allow independent passing off claims by authors who wish to extend their claims of copyright infringement to their screenplays. In *Griffin v. Peele*, a self-published author sued for both copyright and trademark infringement, claiming her book was used for part of the story in Peele's movie, *Get Out*. The court refused to allow the trademark claim. *See Griffin v. Peele*, No. EDCV1701153JGBKKX, 2017 WL 8231241, at *7 (C.D. Cal. Oct. 18, 2017).

c. In *Teter v. Glass Onion, Inc.*, 723 F. Supp. 2d 1138 (W.D. Mo. 2010), the district court applied traditional trademark law for a living artist who objected to a gallery's creation of online thumbnails of the artist's works for promotion. The court recognized that LEE TETER was a trademark which had acquired secondary meaning. Reluctantly, the plaintiff was allowed to survive the motion for summary judgment as to whether the use of the trademark created confusion as to an affiliation between the artist and the gallery which sold the artist's work without authorization.

d. The *Dastar* and *Williams* decisions specifically eliminate claims for reverse passing off. A similar, but slightly distinct claim can be made for false advertising. To what extent does this claim survive? *See Lamothe v. Atlantic Recording Corp.*, 847 F.2d 1403 (9th Cir. 1988), *vacated*, 760 F. Supp. 45 (1991).

e. The right of attribution extends far beyond copyright. Indeed, it may very well be that performers have a much greater stake in the right to credit than do the authors of projects. The law provides little other protection to performers, so stripping them of attribution rights when the question was not before the court seems unkind as well as unnecessary. Unfortunately, the facts in the case provided a poor basis for

5. Statement of Marybeth Peters, Register of Copyrights before the Subcommittee on Courts, The Internet and Intellectual Property of the House Committee on the Judiciary, June 17, 2004, available at http://www.copyright.gov/docs/regstat061704.html.

making these determinations. The footage in *Dastar* was predominantly government war footage or anonymous stock footage. Presumably, copyright in the footage had never existed because the film was public domain governmental works, because the newsreels were never copyrighted (at a time when such formalities had to be followed), or because there had been no renewals of copyright in the stock footage incorporated into the film.

f. Do states have the ability to enforce or amend their unfair competition laws to reach the "false designation of author" or to make the intentional falsification of a credit a civil tort? What would such a statute include?

Problem 8-B

Bryce is concerned about some rumors floating around the local dance club scene. One of Bryce's friends, Alan, has been provided a recording contract at a major studio. Bryce had served as producer for Alan's demo. At the time, Bryce had offered to do the producer work without compensation to assist the friend. Bryce had not asked Alan for any payment, nor had anything been said about the copyright in the sound recording. Bryce had correctly assumed that the record company would professionally rerecord the demo, so that Bryce's work would not be widely marketed.

A problem has arisen, however. Alan has represented that he produced the album himself. Worse, Alan said that Bryce assisted on an earlier demo CD that Bryce considers to be of very inferior quality. Bryce does not want credit on the earlier album and is angered that Alan has taken credit on the second album. Because of the potential that significant money will eventually be involved, Bryce wants to know all of the available options with regard to Alan and the record company. Advise Bryce.

C. Loss of Credit Despite Express Contract

Fleet v. CBS, Inc.

50 Cal. App. 4th 1911 (Cal. Ct. App. 1996)

In this case we are asked to decide a very narrow issue: whether an actor may bring an action for misappropriation of his or her name, image, likeness, or identity under section 3344 of the Civil Code when the only alleged exploitation occurred through the distribution of the actor's performance in a motion picture. The trial court concluded that to the extent California law would permit such claim, it was preempted by federal copyright law. We agree with the trial court and affirm.

The crucial facts are not disputed. In 1985, Legend Productions (Legend), a partnership comprised of Robert Fleet and his wife, Alina Szpak-Fleet (Szpak), entered into a co-production agreement with certain Polish film entities to co-produce two motion pictures, one of which is the subject of this lawsuit.... CBS paid $1,250,000 for these rights. The film commenced shooting on location in Poland in September 1985. Appellant Stephan Fleet is the son of Robert Fleet and Szpak. He and appellant Archie Lee Simpson appeared as actors in the film.

White Dragon Productions entered into separate agreements with one Tadeusz Bugaj to provide financing and with a company known as Performance Guarantees, Inc., to ensure that the film would be completed on time and on budget. In March of 1986, Performance Guarantees stepped in to complete the film and refused to pay the salaries owed to appellants.... CBS went ahead and released the film on videotape under the title "Legend of the White Horse" and, according to the complaint, included a picture of Stephan Fleet on the box.

Appellants brought a complaint against CBS, two of its divisions, and CBS/Fox Video, Inc. (collectively referred to hereafter as CBS) in November of 1993. Insofar as appellants' claims are concerned, the complaint alleges that CBS was notified in March of 1990 that it was not authorized to use the performances of actors Stephan Fleet or Archie Simpson; that Performance Guarantees had breached the terms of the completion bond; that CBS had breached the terms of the distribution agreement; and that "CBS was not authorized to exploit or utilize the Motion Picture in any fashion until the problems and breaches were corrected." The complaint specifically stated that the reason CBS was not authorized to utilize the name, voice, photograph, likeness or performance of appellants in the motion picture was because they were not fully paid. Stephan Fleet further alleged that CBS failed to accord him the credit to which he was contractually entitled on videotape releases of the motion picture; that CBS made unauthorized use of his photograph and likeness on the packaging and advertising materials for the motion picture; and that CBS acquiesced in the re-dubbing of all his speaking parts without his permission.

Based on these allegations, the complaint contended that CBS violated section 3344 of the Civil Code. Section 3344 makes it unlawful to "knowingly use[] another's name, voice, signature, photograph, or likeness, in any manner, on or in products, merchandise, or goods, or for purposes of advertising or selling, or soliciting purchases of, products, merchandise, goods or services, without such person's prior consent, or, in the case of a minor, the prior consent of his parent or legal guardian...." The complaint also contained a claim for unfair business practices based on the asserted violation of Civil Code section 3344. Appellants, along with the other plaintiffs, sought an accounting and a constructive trust.

CBS filed a cross-complaint against Robert Fleet, Szpak, Legend, White Dragon Productions, Krakowski, Eisenhower, Performance Guarantees, and Lawrence Vanger alleging that to the extent CBS did not have the right to distribute the film, it was owed indemnification under its distribution agreement or was entitled to rescind the distribution agreement and obtain refund of the moneys paid thereunder, including interest.

CBS moved for summary judgment. In its separate statement of undisputed facts, CBS set forth the following fact which went undisputed by appellants: "CBS owns the copyright in the Motion Picture pursuant to federal copyright law." The court granted the motion for summary adjudication as to the causes of action for violation of Civil Code section 3344 on the ground that appellants' performances were within the scope of copyright protection in that they were "fixed in a tangible medium of expression" and further found that the rights asserted were equivalent to the exclusive rights of copyright. Thus, the court believed, appellants' claims met the two-pronged test for preemption by the federal copyright law. Because the grant of summary adjudication resolved all of the claims between appellants and CBS, they brought an appeal from the order entered.

Before we begin our analysis, we must emphasize that we are resolving at appellants' insistence only the very narrow issue outlined above. Appellants have repeatedly stressed that "[t]his is not a copyright infringement case" and that their claims are solely a matter of violation of Civil Code section 3344, California's "right to publicity" statute. They assert no interest in the copyright for the motion picture or in any copyright which may cover the individual performances therein....

Under California law, an individual's right to publicity is invaded if another appropriates for his advantage the individual's name, image, identity or likeness. This is an actionable tort under both common law and Civil Code section 3344.

"A common law cause of action for appropriation of name or likeness may be pleaded by alleging (1) the defendant's use of the plaintiff's identity; (2) the appropriation of plaintiff's name or likeness to defendant's advantage, commercially or otherwise; (3) lack of consent; and (4) resulting injury. In addition, to plead the statutory remedy provided in Civil Code section 3344, there must also be an allegation of a knowing use of the plaintiff's name, photograph or likeness for purposes of advertising or solicitation or purchases. Furthermore, recent judicial construction of section 3344 has imposed an additional requirement. A 'direct' connection must be alleged between the use and the commercial purpose."

California law concerning right to publicity, as any state statute or law, is subject to preemption under the supremacy clause of the United States Constitution if it "actually conflicts with a valid federal statute" or " " "stands as an obstacle to the accomplishment and execution of the full purposes and objectives of Congress." ' " In addition, "when acting within constitutional limits, Congress is empowered to preempt state law by so stating in express terms." 17 United States Code section 301, part of the 1976 Copyright Act (hereafter referred to as the Act) expressly prohibits states from legislating in the area of copyright law. It provides: "On and after January 1, 1978, all legal or equitable rights that are equivalent to any of the exclusive rights within the general scope of copyright as specified by section 106 in works of authorship that are fixed in a tangible medium of expression and come within the subject matter of copyright as specified by sections 102 and 103, whether created before or after that date and whether published or unpublished, are governed exclusively by this title. Thereafter, no person is entitled to any such right or equivalent right in any such work under the common law or statutes of any State."

Thus, for preemption to occur under the Act, two conditions must be met: first, the subject of the claim must be a work fixed in a tangible medium of expression and come within the subject matter or scope of copyright protection as described in sections 102 and 103 of 17 United States Code, and second, the right asserted under state law must be equivalent to the exclusive rights contained in section 106.

Appellants insist that neither of these conditions is met and that their claims pose no threat to the federal scheme because a person's name, voice, likeness, and overall persona are not copyrightable and assertion of these rights cannot be equivalent to those that fall under the Act's protection. We agree that as a general proposition Civil Code section 3344 is intended to protect rights which cannot be copyrighted and that claims made under its provisions are usually not preempted. But appellants' analysis crumbles in the face of one obvious fact: their individual performances in the film White Dragon were copyrightable. Since their section 3344 claims seeks only to prevent CBS from reproducing and distributing their performances in the film, their claims must be preempted by federal copyright law.

Section 102 of the Act, by its express terms, protects "original works of authorship fixed in any tangible medium of expression … from which they can be perceived, reproduced, or otherwise communicated, either directly or with the aid of a machine or device." A "work of authorship" is specifically defined to include "dramatic works[.]" A work is fixed in tangible medium of expression "when its embodiment in a copy or phonorecord, by or under the authority of the author, is sufficiently permanent or stable to permit it to be perceived, reproduced, or otherwise communicated for a period of more than transitory duration."

There can be no question that, once appellants' performances were put on film, they became "dramatic work[s]" "fixed in [a] tangible medium of expression" that could be "perceived, reproduced, or otherwise communicated" through "the aid of a machine or device." At that point, the performances came within the scope or subject matter of copyright law protection.

The case of *Zacchini v. Scripps-Howard Broadcasting Co.* 433 U.S. 562 (1977), relied on by appellants, does not point to a different conclusion. There, a performer sued a television station for violating his right of publicity by taping and broadcasting the entirety of his human cannonball act, and the Supreme Court upheld his right to do so. The important distinction between Zacchini's situation and appellants' is that Zacchini had not consented to the taping. A work is fixed in a tangible of expression for purposes of the Act, only if recorded "by or under the authority of the author." Here, appellants' performances in the film were recorded with their active participation and consent.

Appellants deny that the rights which they are asserting under Civil Code section 3344 are equivalent to the rights available under copyright law, but their denial rings hollow. Appellants seek to protect the physical images of their performances captured on film in the subject motion picture and no others. CBS seeks to display or reproduce those images and no others. The owner of a copyright — either the "author" (actor) or his employer (the producer) — is vested with the exclusive rights to, among other things, "reproduce the copyrighted work" and "display the copyrighted work publicly." Appellants may choose to call their claims misappropriation of right to publicity, but if all they are seeking is to prevent a party from exhibiting a copyrighted work they are making a claim "equivalent to an exclusive right within the general scope of copyright."

To support their contention that their right to sue for appropriation of their name, voice, likeness, or persona survives the fixing of their performance in a tangible medium, appellants quote Professor Nimmer's treatise in which it is said that a "name and likeness does not become a work of authorship simply because it is embodied in a copyrightable work such as a photograph." (1 Nimmer on Copyright (1996) § 1.01[B][1][c], pp. 1–22 to 1–23, fn. omitted.) Again, we have no quarrel with this general proposition, but see no basis for its application here. The celebrity who has merely had his picture taken has not engaged in a "dramatic work" or other "work of authorship," and, as Professor Nimmer said, would be afforded no protection under federal copyright law. Thus, if not for state law, he would have no remedy against those who would misappropriate his image for their own gain. Here, in contrast, it was not merely appellants' likenesses which were captured on film — it was their dramatic performances which are, as we have seen, copyrightable. An actor who wishes to protect the use of the image contained in a single, fixed dramatic performance need simply retain the copyright.

The authorities cited by appellants support our understanding. In *Eastwood v. Superior Court*, 149 Cal. App. 3d 409 [(Cal. Ct. App. 1983)], defendant used a photograph of the well-known actor Clint Eastwood, along with his name and likeness, to sell their newspaper. Since neither his name nor his likeness and image as portrayed in the photograph were copyrightable, no issue of preemption arose. The same was true in *Abdul-Jabbar v. General Motors Corp.* 85 F.3d 407 (9th Cir. 1996), wherein defendants used the name "Lew Alcindor" in a television commercial without consent; *Cher v. Forum International, Ltd.* 692 F.2d 634 (9th Cir. 1982), wherein the actress/singer's photograph was used to solicit subscribers to a magazine in such a way as to convey the misimpression that she endorsed the magazine; and *Clark v. Celeb Publishing, Inc.*, 530 F. Supp. 979 (S.D.N.Y. 1981), wherein the photograph of a model was used without her permission to solicit subscribers to a hard core pornographic magazine. Numerous other cases hold that where the defendant uses a lookalike or soundalike, the person whose voice or image is being imitated may state a claim for misappropriation of publicity rights. The state law claims in these cases were not preempted because it was plaintiffs' image or likeness — and not his or her copyrightable dramatic or musical performance — which had been appropriated.

Appellants cite these cases for the proposition that where "the plaintiff neither owns, nor claims to own, the copyright, there is no preemption and the plaintiff is entitled to pursue his or her claim for wrongful appropriation of the rights of privacy and/or publicity even though the medium in which the offending misappropriation has occurred is itself, copyrightable or even copyrighted." Appellants misapprehend the lesson to be drawn from the cases. In each of the cited cases, the right sought to be protected was not copyrightable — Clint Eastwood's likeness captured in a photograph; Kareem Abdul-Jabbar's former name; Bette Midler's distinctive vocal style; Vanna White's distinctive visual image, etc. The plaintiffs in those cases asserted no copyright claims *because they had none to assert*. Here, by contrast, appellants seek to prevent CBS from using performances captured on film. These performances were copyrightable and appellants could have claimed a copyright in them as have the numerous performers whom we discuss in the following section.

We turn to a discussion of the Seventh Circuit's landmark decision in *Baltimore Orioles v. Major League Baseball Players,* 805 F.2d 663 (7th Cir. 1986).... The court in *Baltimore Orioles* concluded that since the games were copyrightable and since the clubs owned the copyrights under the works made for hire doctrine, the players could not prevent the clubs from exploiting the works by asserting a state law claim for violation of the right to publicity. Contrary to what appellants would have us believe, there is nothing controversial about that aspect of the opinion. It follows inescapably from the Act and the conclusions that the players' performances in the baseball games were works of authorship fixed in a tangible medium of expression and that the clubs held the copyright. "By virtue of being videotaped ... the players' performances are fixed in tangible form, and any rights of publicity in their performances that are equivalent to the rights contained in the copyright of the telecast are preempted."

Nor is the Seventh Circuit the only court to have come to the obvious conclusion that a party who does not hold the copyright in a performance captured on film cannot prevent the one who does from exploiting it by resort to state law. In *Brown v. Twentieth Century Fox Film Corp.,* 799 F. Supp. 166 (D.D.C. 1992), James Brown (the Godfather of Soul) brought suit when a clip of his performance of the song *Please, Please, Please*, originally performed in a '60s television show appeared, without his consent, in the 1991 movie The Commitments about a fictional rock and roll band. The court first analyzed his copyright claims and concluded the producer of the television show held the rights to the performance pursuant to the parties' 1964 agreement. Brown alternatively argued that use of his name, likeness, and persona violated his "right of publicity" under a New York law similar to California's. The court concluded that "[b]ecause defendants lawfully acquired the right to use the [television] Show performance ... the alleged violation of the right of publicity cannot be based on their use of that performance."

In *Rooney v. Columbia Pictures Industries, Inc.,* 538 F. Supp. 211 (S.D.N.Y. 1982), actor Mickey Rooney accused several studios of wrongly refusing to deal with him regarding his "publicity rights" in pre-1960 films, and contended they had wrongfully shown the films on commercial and cable television and distributed them on videocassette. The court concluded that the contracts signed by Rooney were broad enough to include transfer of rights covering television and videocassette display of his performances. Turning to the cause of action alleging misappropriation of Rooney's common law "right of publicity," THE COURT HELD: "[A]ny such rights were assigned or waived by the contracts granting defendants all rights in the pre-1960 films." ...

Although they did not all say so expressly, we believe that all these courts would agree with the Seventh Circuit that "[b]ecause a performance is fixed in tangible form when it is recorded, a right of publicity in [such] performance ... is subject to preemption." We concur with these authorities, and also with Professor Nimmer

(1 Nimmer on Copyright, *supra*, § 1.01[B][1], p. 1–14), in holding that a right is equivalent to rights within the exclusive province of copyright when it is infringed by the mere act of reproducing, performing, distributing, or displaying the work at issue. A claim asserted to prevent nothing more than the reproduction, performance, distribution, or display of a dramatic performance captured on film is subsumed by copyright law and preempted. For all the foregoing reasons, the judgment of the trial court is affirmed.

Tamarind Lithography Workshop, Inc. v. Sanders

143 Cal. App. 3d 571 (Cal. Ct. App. 1983)

The essence of this appeal concerns the question of whether an award of damages is an adequate remedy at law in lieu of specific performance for the breach of an agreement to give screen credits. Our saga traces its origin to March of 1969, at which time appellant, and cross-complainant below, Terry Sanders (hereinafter Sanders or appellant), agreed in writing to write, direct and produce a motion picture on the subject of lithography for respondent, Tamarind Lithography Workshop, Inc. (hereinafter referred to as Tamarind or respondent).

Pursuant to the terms of the agreement, the film was shot during the summer of 1969, wherein Sanders directed the film according to an outline/treatment of his authorship, and acted as production manager by personally hiring and supervising personnel comprising the film crew. Additionally, Sanders exercised both artistic control over the mixing of the sound track and overall editing of the picture.

After completion, the film, now titled "Four Stones for Kanemitsu," was screened by Tamarind at its 10th anniversary celebration on April 28, 1970. Thereafter, a dispute arose between the parties concerning their respective rights and obligations under the original 1969 agreement. Litigation ensued and in January 1973 the matter went to trial. Prior to the entry of judgment, the parties entered into a written settlement agreement, which became the premises for the instant action. Specifically, this April 30, 1973, agreement provided that Sanders would be entitled to a screen credit entitled "A Film by Terry Sanders."

Tamarind did not comply with its expressed obligation pursuant to that agreement, in that it failed to include Sanders' screen credits in the prints it distributed. As a result a situation developed wherein Tamarind and codefendant Wayne filed suit for declaratory relief, damages due to breach of contract, emotional distress, defamation and fraud. Sanders cross-complained, seeking damages for Tamarind's breach of contract, declaratory relief, specific performance of the contract to give Sanders screen credits, and defamation. Both causes were consolidated and brought to trial on May 31, 1977. A jury was impaneled for purposes of determining damage issues and decided that Tamarind had breached the agreement and awarded Sanders $25,000 in damages.

The remaining claims for declaratory and injunctive relief were tried by the court. The court made findings that Tamarind had sole ownership rights in the film, that "both June Wayne and Terry Sanders were each creative producers of the film, that

Sanders shall have the right to modify the prints in his personal possession to include his credits." All other prayers for relief were denied. It is the denial of appellant's request for specific performance upon which appellant predicates this appeal....

[T]he issue is whether the jury's damage award adequately compensates Sanders, not only for injuries sustained as a result of the prior exhibitions of the film without Sanders' credits, but also for future injuries which may be incurred as a result of any future exhibitions of the film without his credit. Commensurate with our discussion below, we find that the damages awarded raise an issue that justifies a judgment for specific performance. Accordingly, we reverse the judgment of the lower court and direct it to award appellant the injunctive relief he now seeks.

Our first inquiry deals with the scope of the jury's $25,000 damage award. More specifically, we are concerned with whether or not this award compensates Sanders not only for past or preexisting injuries, but also for future injury (or injuries) as well.

Indeed, it is possible to categorize respondent's breach of promise to provide screen credits as a single failure to act from which all of Sanders' injuries were caused. However, it is also plausible that damages awarded Sanders were for harms already sustained at the date of trial, and did not contemplate injury as a result of future exhibitions of the film by respondent, without appropriate credit to Sanders.

Although this was a jury trial, there are findings of facts and conclusions of law necessitated by certain legal issues that were decided by the court. Finding of fact No. 12 states: "By its verdict the jury concluded that Terry Sanders and the Terry Sanders Company are entitled to the sum of $25,000.00 in damages for all damages suffered by them arising from Tamarind's breach of the April 30th agreement."

The exact wording of this finding was also used in conclusion of law No. 1. Sanders argues that use of the word "suffered" in the past tense is positive evidence that the jury assessed damages only for breach of the contract up to time of trial and did not award possible future damages that might be suffered if the film was subsequently exhibited without the appropriate credit.

Tamarind, on the other hand, contends that the jury was instructed that if a breach occurred the award would be for *all* damages past and future arising from the breach. The jury was instructed: "For the breach of a contract, the measure of damages is the amount which will compensate the party aggrieved, for the economic loss, directly and proximately caused by the breach, or which, in the ordinary course of things, would be likely to result therefrom" and "... economic benefits including enhancement of one's professional reputation resulting in increased earnings as a result of screen credit, if their loss is a direct and natural consequence of the breach, may be recovered for breach of an agreement that provides for screen credit. Economic benefits lost through breach of contract may be estimated, and where the plaintiff [Tamarind], by its breach of the contract, has given rise to the difficulty of proving the amount of loss of such economic benefit, it is proper to require of the defendant [Sanders] only that he show the amount of damages with reasonable certainty and to resolve uncertainty as to the amount of economic benefit against the plaintiff [Tamarind]."

The trial court agreed with Tamarind's position and refused to grant the injunction because it was satisfied that the jury had awarded Sanders all the damages he was entitled to including past and possible future damages. The record does not satisfactorily resolve the issue. However, this fact is not fatal to this appeal because, as we shall explain, specific performance as requested by Sanders will solve the problem.

The availability of the remedy of specific performance is premised upon well established requisites. These requisites include: A showing by plaintiff of (1) the inadequacy of his legal remedy; (2) an underlying contract that is both reasonable and supported by adequate consideration; (3) the existence of a mutuality of remedies; (4) contractual terms which are sufficiently definite to enable the court to know what it is to enforce; and (5) a substantial similarity of the requested performance to that promised in the contract.

It is manifest that the legal remedies available to Sanders for harm resulting from the future exhibition of the film are inadequate as a matter of law. The primary reasons are twofold: (1) that an accurate assessment of damages would be far too difficult and require much speculation, and (2) that any future exhibitions might be deemed to be a continuous breach of contract and thereby create the danger of an untold number of lawsuits.

There is no doubt that the exhibition of a film, which is favorably received by its critics and the public at large, can result in valuable advertising or publicity for the artists responsible for that film's making. Likewise, it is unquestionable that the non-appearance of an artist's name or likeness in the form of screen credit on a successful film can result in a loss of that valuable publicity. However, whether that loss of publicity is measurable dollar wise is quite another matter.

By its very nature, public acclaim is unique and very difficult, if not sometimes impossible, to quantify in monetary terms. Indeed, courts confronted with the dilemma of estimating damages in this area have been less than uniform in their disposition of same. Nevertheless, it is clear that any award of damages for the loss of publicity is contingent upon those damages being reasonably certain, specific, and unspeculative.

The varied disposition of claims for breach of promise to provide screen credits encompasses two schools of thought. On the one hand, there is the view that damages can be ascertained (to within a reasonable degree of certainty) if the trier of fact is given sufficient factual data. On the other hand, there is the equally strong stance that although damages resulting from a loss of screen credits might be identifiable, they are far too imponderable and ethereal to define in terms of a monetary award. If these two views can be reconciled, it would only be by an independent examination of each case on its particular set of facts.

In *Paramount Productions, Inc. v. Smith, supra*, 91 F.2d 863, 866–867, the court was provided with evidence from which the "… jury might easily compute the advertising value of the screen credit." The particular evidence presented included the earnings the plaintiff/writer received for his work on a previous film in which he did not contract for screen credits. This evidence was in turn easily compared with earnings that the writer had received for work in which screen credits were provided as contracted. Moreover, evidence of that artist's salary, prior to his receipt of credit for a play when compared with earnings received subsequent to his actually receiving credit, was "... if believed, likewise sufficient as a gauge for the measure of damages."

In another case dealing with a request for damages for failure to provide contracted-for screen credits, the court in *Zorich v. Petroff*, 152 Cal. App. 2d 806 [313 P.2d 118] (1957) demonstrated an equal awareness of the principle. The court emphasized "... that there was no evidence from which the [trial] court could have placed a value upon the screen credit to be given plaintiff as an associate producer. Incident to this fact, the court went on to surmise that because the motion picture which was at the root of the litigation was an admitted financial failure, screen credit, if given, ... could reasonably have been regarded as a detriment to him."

At the other extreme, it has been held that failure to give an artist screen credit *would* constitute irreparable injury. In *Poe v. Michael Todd Co.*, 151 F. Supp. 801 [(S.D.N.Y. 1957)], the New York district court was similarly faced with an author's claim that his contractual right to screen credit was violated. The court held: "Not only would money damages be difficult to establish, but at best they would hardly compensate for the real injury done. A writer's reputation, which would be greatly enhanced by public credit for authorship of an outstanding picture, is his stock in trade, it is clear that irreparable injury would follow the failure to give screen credit if in fact he is entitled to it."

Notwithstanding the seemingly inflexible observation of that court as to the compensability of a breach of promise to provide screen credits, all three cases equally demonstrate that the awarding of damages must be premised upon calculations, inferences or observations that are logical. Just how logical or reasonable those inferences are regarded serves as the determining factor. Accordingly, where the jury in the matter *sub judice* was fully apprised of the favorable recognition Sanders' film received from the Academy of Motion Picture Arts and Sciences, the Los Angeles International Film Festival, and public television, and further, where they were made privy to an assessment of the value of said exposure by three experts, it is reasonable for the jury to award monetary damages for that ascertainable loss of publicity. However, pecuniary compensation for Sanders' future harm is not a fully adequate remedy.

We return to the remaining requisites for Sanders' entitlement to specific performance. The need for our finding the contract to be reasonable and supported by adequate consideration is obviated by the jury's determination of respondent's breach of that contract. The requisite of mutuality of remedy has been satisfied in that Sanders had fully performed his obligations pursuant to the agreement (i.e., release of all claims of copyright to the film and dismissal of his then pending action against respondents. Similarly, we find the terms of the agreement sufficiently definite to permit enforcement of the respondent's performance as promised.

In the present case it should be obvious that specific performance through injunctive relief can remedy the dilemma posed by the somewhat ambiguous jury verdict. The injunction disposes of the problem of future damages, in that full compliance by Tamarind moots the issue. Of course, violation of the injunction by Tamarind would raise new problems, but the court has numerous options for dealing with the situation and should choose the one best suited to the particular violation.

In conclusion, the record shows that the appellant is entitled to relief consisting of the damages recovered, and an injunction against future injury.... The judgment denying appellants' prayer for injunctive relief is hereby reversed....

Notes and Questions

a. Since most of the disputes arising in the context of this section come from the failure to provide appropriate credit, the primary tools for solving these problems come from well-drafted written agreements. Typically, contracts providing credit also provide that "no inadvertent omission of the credit awarded pursuant to this agreement shall be deemed a breach of this agreement." Inadvertent omission is useful compromise language, because any intentional omission remains actionable while the paragraph should eliminate most litigation over simple mistakes.

b. In cases involving writers' credit for motion pictures, the Writers Guild provides very stringent rules for arbitration of credit claims. In most of these disputes, the producer or distributor of the motion picture has very little interest in which party receives the credit. Instead, the dispute is typically between the various writers who contributed during the life of the project. By resorting to the arbitration process, the producer and distributor can essentially remain out of the dispute and avoid taking sides with any particular writer. In the context of songs and other media, no such third-party procedure is mandated by a collectively bargained agreement.

c. Contract law and copyright law also collide on occasion. To what extent may the author of a work sue the co-author for failure to attribute the work, for copyright infringement, or for breach of contract? Co-authors cannot infringe the copyright of one another. Assuming any such action survives *Dastar*, does omission of one party constitute a form of reverse passing off? *See Cleary v. News Corp.*, 30 F.3d 1255 (9th Cir. 1994) (involving a dispute over the attribution and updated versions of Robert's Rules of Order).

d. The outcome of *Fleet v. CBS* may be fully consistent with both prior case law and industry custom; however, the language of the case suggests some potentially odd results. Would actors from *Legend of White Horse* have a cause of action if their images taken from *Legend of White Horse* were transferred onto t-shirts, mugs, or clocks? Perhaps these uses do not capture the dramatic performance. If so, what would be the result if clips were sold as part of a computer screen-saver program? *See Brown v. Twentieth Century Fox Film Corp.*, 799 F. Supp. 166 (D.D.C. 1992), *aff'd without opinion*, 15 F.3d 1159 (D.C. Cir. 1994).

e. *See* Chapter 3, notes following *Wil-Helm Agency v. Lynn*, for a brief discussion of *KNB Enterprises v. Matthews*, 78 Cal. App. 4th 362 (Cal. Ct. App. 2000), and the different treatment provided to a claim for publicity rights in sexually explicit photographs.

Problem 8-C

Bryce has been asked to compile and edit a series of music videos for a local band named Soundfyre. Bryce has decided to use clips from old black-and-white movies as the visual backdrops for most of the videos, inter-cutting these clips with the footage Bryce filmed of Soundfyre in performance. Bryce is coloring (or colorizing) some of the clips, running some in their original black-and-white configuration, and digitally altering others.

Bryce has confirmed that each of the films selected is in the public domain, but remains concerned that the original filmmakers or actors might object to the use of the clips in the music videos. In addition, Soundfyre has licensed one of the music videos to a local auto dealership to use as the background for its upcoming television commercial.

Advise Bryce on the extent to which additional licenses may be needed to use the public domain film clips as requested.

D. Limiting Credit Exploitation

King v. Innovation Books
976 F.2d 824 (2d Cir. 1992)

Defendants-appellants, Allied Vision, Ltd. and New Line Cinema Corporation, appeal from an order of the United States District Court for the Southern District of New York (Motley, J.) granting a preliminary injunction in favor of plaintiff-appellee Stephen King in connection with King's claims under the Lanham Act and New York law. King, who is the author of such best-selling horror thrillers as "The Shining," "Carrie," and "Salem's Lot," contended that Allied and New Line falsely designated him as the originator of the motion picture "The Lawnmower Man," which was produced by Allied and distributed in North America by New Line. The injunction, which prohibits any use of King's name "on or in connection with" the movie, encompasses two forms of credit to which King objected: (i) a possessory credit, describing the movie as "Stephen King's The Lawnmower Man," and (ii) a "based upon" credit, representing that the movie is "based upon" a short story by King. For the reasons that follow, we affirm the district court's order to the extent that it prohibits use of the possessory credit, but reverse the order to the extent that it prohibits use of the "based upon" credit.

In 1970, King wrote a short story entitled "The Lawnmower Man" (the "Short Story").... In 1978, King assigned to Great Fantastic Picture Corporation the motion picture and television rights for the Short Story. The assignment agreement, which provided that it was to be governed by the laws of England, allowed the assignee the "exclusive right to deal with the [Short Story] as [it] may think fit," including the rights

> (i) to write film treatments [and] scripts and other dialogue versions of all descriptions of the [Short Story] and at all times to add to[,] take from[,] use[,] alter[,] adapt ... and change the [Short Story] and the title[,] characters[,] plot[,] theme[,] dialogue[,] sequences and situations thereof....

> (ii) to make or produce films of all kinds ... incorporating or based upon the [Short Story] or any part or parts thereof or any adaptation thereof.

In return, King received an interest in the profits of "each" film "based upon" the Short Story.

In February 1990, Great Fantastic transferred its rights under the assignment agreement to Allied, a movie production company organized under the laws of the United Kingdom and having offices in London. In May 1990, Allied commissioned a screenplay for a feature-length film entitled "The Lawnmower Man." The screenplay was completed by August 1990, and pre-production work on the movie began in January 1991. By February 1991, Allied began to market the forthcoming movie by placing advertisements in trade magazines and journals. The picture generally was described as "Stephen King's The Lawnmower Man," and as "based upon" a short story by King. Actual filming of the movie began in May 1991....

King initiated the instant suit on May 28, 1992, seeking damages as well as injunctive relief. He claimed that the possessory and "based upon" credits violated section 43(a) of the Lanham Act, *see* 15 U.S.C. §1125(a), as well as the New York common law of unfair competition and contracts, the New York General Business Law, and the New York Civil Rights Law.... The district court agreed with King on all of his claims and granted the injunction on July 2....

We review a district court's issuance of a preliminary injunction for abuse of discretion. Such an abuse of discretion ordinarily consists of either applying an incorrect legal standard or relying on a clearly erroneous finding of fact. As the district court observed, a party such as King seeking an injunction "must demonstrate (1) irreparable harm should the injunction not be granted, and (2) either (a) a likelihood of success on the merits, or (b) sufficiently serious questions going to the merits and a balance of hardships tipping decidedly toward [that] party...."

The district court correctly noted that a false reference to the origin of a work, or a reference which, while not literally false, is misleading or likely to confuse, may form the basis of a claim under section 43(a) of the Lanham Act.

We perceive no error in the district court's conclusion that King is likely to succeed on the merits of his objection to the possessory credit. The district court was entirely entitled to conclude, from the testimony at the preliminary injunction hearing, that a possessory credit ordinarily is given to the producer, director or writer of the film; and that the credit at a minimum refers to an individual who had some involvement in, and/or gave approval to, the screenplay or movie itself. In contrast to other films for which he has been given a possessory credit, King had no involvement in, and gave no approval of, "The Lawnmower Man" screenplay or movie.

Under the circumstances, therefore, the arguments advanced by Allied and New Line as to why the possessory credit is not false—that the other movie credits make clear that King was not the producer, director or writer of the film, and that King has in the past received a possessory credit where he merely approved in advance of the screenplay or movie—do not alter the conclusion that King is likely to succeed on his challenge to the possessory credit. Appellants also contend that King offered no evidence of public confusion in relation to the possessory credit. As will be detailed in our discussion of irreparable harm, however, there was some such evidence offered. In any event, as the district court recognized, no evidence of public confusion is required where, as is the case with the possessory credit, the attribution is false on its face.

As the district court recognized, a "based upon" credit by definition affords more "leeway" than a possessory credit. The district court nevertheless concluded that the "based upon" credit at issue here is misleading and likely to cause confusion to the public, reasoning in essence that the "climactic scene from the Short Story is inserted into the film in a manner wholly unrelated to the Plot of the film," and that the credit "grossly exaggerates" the relationship between the Short Story and the film. While particular findings of fact are subject to the clearly erroneous standard of review, we have said that the weighing of factors in "the ultimate determination of the likelihood of confusion is a legal issue subject to *de novo* appellate review." We believe that in so heavily weighing the proportion of the film attributable to the Short Story in the course of finding the "based upon" credit to be misleading and confusing, the district court applied a standard without sufficient support in the testimony and applicable law.

John Breglio, an attorney of the law firm of Paul, Weiss, Rifkind, Wharton & Garrison specializing in entertainment law, testified as an expert witness for King. Breglio opined that the term "based upon," in the context of royalty obligations under King's assignment agreement, was not identical to the term "based upon" in a movie credit. After speaking of a test of "substantial similarity" between the literary work and movie, and opining that there was not substantial similarity between the Short Story and the film, Breglio went on to state that the industry standard for determining the meaning of a "based upon" movie credit is very similar to that used by copyright lawyers in examining issues of copyright infringement. Breglio further explained that this standard involved looking "at the work as a whole and how much protected material *from the underlying work* appears in the derivative work."

Indeed, in cases of alleged copyright infringement it has long been appropriate to examine the quantitative and qualitative degree to which the allegedly infringed work has been borrowed from, and not simply the proportion of the allegedly infringing work that is made up of the copyrighted material. Accordingly, the propriety of the "based upon" credit should have been evaluated with less emphasis on the proportion of the film attributable to the Short Story, and with more emphasis on the proportion, in quantitative and qualitative terms, of the Short Story appearing in the film. Where a movie draws in material respects from a literary work, both quantitatively and qualitatively, a "based upon" credit should not be viewed as misleading absent persuasive countervailing facts and circumstances. Our concern is the possibility that under the district court's apparent approach, substantially all of a literary work could be taken for use in a film and, if unrelated ideas, themes and scenes are tacked on or around the extracted work, a "based upon" credit would be deemed misleading.

In the case before us, the apparent "core" of the ten page Short Story—a scene in which a character called "the lawnmower man" uses psychokinetic powers to chase another character through his house with a running lawnmower and thereby kill him—is used in the movie. In both the movie and the Short Story, the remains of the murdered man (who is named Harold Parkette in both works) are found in the birdbath by the police; the two police officers in both works have the same names and engage in substantially similar dialogue. As King himself described it, "the core of my story, such as it is, is in the movie." The red lawnmower seen in the movie also appears to be as described in the Short Story. A brief reference to the Pan mythology of the Short Story appears in the movie as well; dialogue between Jobe and another character includes a reference to "Pan pipes of the little people in the grass."

We recognize that several important and entertaining aspects of the Short Story were not used in the film, and that conversely the film contains a number of elements not to be found in the Short Story. However, when the resemblances between the Short Story and the motion picture at issue here are considered together, they establish to our satisfaction that the movie draws in sufficiently material respects on the Short Story in both qualitative and quantitative aspects.

Nor are there any persuasive countervailing facts or circumstances in the record to lead us away from the conclusion that the "based upon" credit is proper in this case. King himself apparently was not bothered much (if at all) by the "based upon" credit, in marked contrast to his sustained and strong objections to the possessory credit, until shortly before he initiated this suit. He has not pointed us to evidence in the record of industry or public perception of, or confusion over, the "based upon" credit beyond the thoughts offered by Breglio. . . .

It is undoubtedly the case that King's assignment agreement does not permit Allied to use King's name fraudulently, and we express no view as to the degree of overlap between the term "based upon" in the King assignment agreement and the term "based upon" in a theatrical credit. However, we do note that the agreement contemplates substantial alterations to the Short Story, and even obligates Allied to give King credit in the case of a film "based wholly or substantially upon" the Short Story. We think that King would have cause to complain if he were *not* afforded the "based upon" credit.

As the district court observed, a presumption of irreparable harm arises in Lanham Act cases once the plaintiff establishes likelihood of success on a claim of literal falseness, as King has established with respect to the possessory credit. Nothing in the record persuades us that the district court erred in concluding that this presumption was not rebutted. . . .

The order of the district court granting a preliminary injunction is affirmed to the extent it prohibits use of the possessory credit, but reversed to the extent it prohibits use of a "based upon" credit.

Notes and Questions

a. In most cases, the individual negotiating the credit strongly desires the maximum recognition possible. For Stephen King, and arguably for Kevin Williamson, the inflated credit became an embarrassment rather than a source of pride. To what extent does the participant in a project have the ability to correct inflation of the credit? *See Follett v. New American Library, Inc.*, 497 F. Supp. 304 (S.D.N.Y. 1980).

b. In the case of Stephen King, and in other situations which arise on occasion, the problem of unwelcome attribution stems from subsequent fame. The arrangement negotiated at the time of the contract was beneficial, but in later years the talent's market worth has increased considerably and the earlier contract rights now take on new meaning. While the contract could limit all changes to the agreed-upon credit so that credit could not be improved, it might prove difficult to negotiate such a contract. Nonetheless, there is probably some compromise language that can be developed considering that the courts interpret credit provisions as assuming that the rights granted are not misleading.

c. In contrast to the normal situation for performers, it is sometimes the vendors that complain. To what extent does an endorsement agreement to promote high fashion or jewelry extend into the performer's personal life? *See Raymond Weil, S.A. v. Theron*, 585 F. Supp. 2d 473 (S.D.N.Y. 2008).

d. The tensions and ambiguity can often come from the choices used in creating the complex agreements surrounding creative properties. These issues become even more difficult when the underlying work is part of a larger series. *See Twentieth Century Fox Film Corp. v. Marvel Enterprises, Inc.*, 155 F. Supp. 2d 1 (S.D.N.Y. 2001), *aff'd in part and remanded*, 277 F.3d 253 (2d Cir. 2002).

Problem 8-D

As Bryce's business has grown, Bryce has come across an opportunity to purchase a very small, local record company (sometimes called a record label). In reviewing the assets of the record label, your office has spent some time reviewing the contracts for each of the records produced or distributed by the company. The due diligence identified one hidden surprise. A back-up singer on one of the lesser known recordings has gone on to become a Grammy-winning recording artist.

Bryce would like to re-release this album with the name of the star prominently featured. The signed recording agreement included a release by the artist to use her name, likeness, voice, and signature in conjunction with the marketing of the album, so Bryce would like to create new artwork for the cover featuring a photograph of this artist.

Advise Bryce on the extent to which the photograph of this Grammy-winning recording artist can be used, as well as what legal limitations might arise.

E. Post-Partnership Ownership: Band Names

Commodores Entertainment Corp. v. McClary
879 F.3d 1114 (11th Cir. 2018)

In this common-law trademark case, Thomas McClary appeals from an order granting judgment as a matter of law to Commodores Entertainment Corporation (CEC) and converting a preliminary injunction into a permanent one against McClary and his corporation, Fifth Avenue Entertainment, L.L.C. The dispute concerned ownership of the mark "The Commodores," the name of a famous Grammy Award-winning rhythm and blues, funk, and soul music band. McClary was an original member of The Commodores, but, by his own admission, he "split from the band" in 1984 to strike out on his own in the world of music. He later formed a musical group that performed as "The 2014 Commodores" and "The Commodores Featuring Thomas McClary." When CEC—a corporation run by two original Commodores who remain active with the group—found out about McClary's group, it filed this lawsuit against McClary and Fifth Avenue claiming trademark infringement, trademark dilution, passing off, false advertising, and unfair competition.

The district court granted CEC a preliminary injunction and enjoined McClary from using the marks; a panel of this Court affirmed. Then, after a two-week trial, the district court granted judgment as a matter of law to CEC and converted the preliminary injunction into a permanent one.

After careful review, we ... conclude that when McClary left the band, he left behind his common-law rights to the marks. Those rights remained with CEC. Moreover, we conclude that the scope of the injunction was not impermissibly broad ... Accordingly, we affirm.

The Commodores was formed in 1968. The group has released over forty albums, has charted seven number-one singles and numerous top-ten hits, and continues to record music and play for audiences around the world. The group's big break came in 1971, when it opened for the Jackson 5 on a world tour. Shortly after the tour, the group signed a recording contract with Motown Record Corporation. The group's first album, "Machine Gun," was released in 1974. Throughout the 1970s, The Commodores became internationally acclaimed with hits including "Easy," "Brick House," "Three Times a Lady," and "Too Hot ta Trot."

Although three other individuals were also involved at the early stages of the group, the "original" members are generally regarded as William King, Ronald LaPread, Thomas McClary, Walter Orange, Lionel Richie, and Milan Williams.1 On March 20, 1978, these six members, along with their manager, Benjamin "Benny" Ashburn, formed a general partnership governed by a General Partnership Agreement. The agreement included a section expressly addressing the use of the name "The Commodores" upon the withdrawal of a partner: "Upon the death or withdrawal of less than a majority of the Partners, the remaining majority of the Partners shall continue to have the right to use the name THE COMMODORES for any purpose." Each partner was permitted to withdraw at any time so long as he provided the group with six months' written notice; notably, one partner's withdrawal would not end the partnership. Two months later, the partners registered CEC as a Nevada corporation.

Around a year later, in 1979, CEC entered into an Exclusive Artist Production Agreement with Motown Record Corporation. This agreement also restricted use of the name: band members could perform as "sidemen" for other artists and groups, but "in no event" could they use the name "Commodores" in connection with that engagement. And the members and the group as a whole were, "joint and not severally, the sole and exclusive owner of all rights in and to the Name." Much like the General Partnership Agreement, this agreement provided that if a member withdrew from the group, neither he nor his heirs would have the right to make individual use of the name. In addition, if "one or more Members [became] a Leaving Member(s), then the Remaining Member(s) [would] automatically and without notice become (jointly and not severally) the sole and exclusive owner of the rights" to the name.

In 1982, Lionel Richie left the group to pursue his solo career; The Commodores continued without him and notified Motown of the change. CEC and Motown entered into a new agreement whereby CEC again "warrant[ed] and represent[ed] that it and [the signee] [were], jointly and not severally, the sole and exclusive owner of all rights in and to the Name" and that "its agreement with the Group provide[d] that no Leaving Member, nor heirs of any member have or will have the right to make any individual use of the Name." This agreement described "Leaving Members" as a member or members who "separate[d] from, and/or ceased to perform with, the remaining Member(s)."

Around the time that Richie left the group, Ashburn passed away. In March 1984, the remaining members of the group (King, LaPread, McClary, Orange, and Williams) executed an "amendment in toto" to the General Partnership Agreement that read this way, in part:

> The principal business activity of the Partnership no longer is to engage in the entertainment business as the Group but is to own, maintain and lease certain motor vehicles and musical and studio equipment to Commodores Entertainment Corporation, a Nevada corporation, (the "Corporation"), which now conducts the business of the Group, and to hold all rights in and to the Group name "THE COMMODORES," the logo thereof, and any service mark, trademark, service name, or tradename associated therewith, and all goodwill inherent therein (collectively referred to as the "Group Name").

Like the other contractual arrangements, this amendment also clarified the use of the group's name: "Upon the death or withdrawal of less than a majority of the Partners, the remaining majority of the Partners shall continue to have the right to use the Group Name for any purpose."

Later in 1984, and by his own admission, McClary "split from the band" to pursue his own solo career. Over time, LaPread and Williams also departed from the group, leaving King and Orange as the only remaining original members. At some point, King and Orange transferred their common-law trademark rights in The Commodores' name and logo to CEC. In 2001, CEC registered four trademarks ("the marks" or "the Commodores marks") with the United States Patent and Trademark Office (PTO). The trademarks were for the word mark "THE COMMODORES" and the word mark "COMMODORES" with a design. They granted CEC exclusive rights to the marks for "[e]ntertainment services, namely live performances by a musical and vocal group," as well as for "[m]usical sound and video recordings, namely, pre-recorded audio cassettes, video tapes, compact discs of live and in-studio musical performances."

The essential question presented in the first phase of the trial was this: What happens to the ownership of a trademark in the name of a performing group when the group's membership has evolved with time? Our analysis starts with the common-law rights to the marks and the original ownership of those rights. While we have created a national system to register marks, common-law rights are not overridden by that registration system. Notably, a plaintiff need not have a registered trademark to use and enforce that mark. Rather, "the use of another's unregistered, i.e., common law, trademark can constitute a violation of § 43(a) where the alleged unregistered trademarks used by the plaintiff are so associated with its goods that the use of the same or similar marks by another company constitutes a false representation that its goods came from the same source." *Tana v. Dantanna's*, 611 F.3d 767, 773 (11th Cir. 2010).

Common-law trademark rights are initially acquired through priority of appropriation. To acquire common-law rights to a trademark, a party must have demonstrated prior use of the mark in commerce. Prior use, in turn, is established with evidence showing, first, adoption, and, second, use in a way sufficiently public to identify or distinguish the marked goods in an appropriate segment of the public mind as those of the adopter of the mark. We have concluded this association was present when "the distribution of the mark was widespread because the mark was accessible to anyone with access to the Internet"; when "the evidence established that members of the targeted public actually associated the mark with the product to which it was affixed"; when "the mark served to identify the source of the product"; and when "other potential users of the mark had notice that the mark was in use in connection with the product."

Common-law trademarks existed in the name "The Commodores," and the original owner of the marks was the group as a whole. In this case, there is no dispute that the marks were used in commerce, beginning with the early days of the group's performances and recordings as "The Commodores." The group was the first to appropriate that term and so acquired the exclusive rights to the trademark. The group began calling itself "The Commodores" sometime around 1969, and the public undoubtedly associated the mark with this famous musical group. The group performed as "The Commodores," released many records (including hits) as "The Commodores," and opened for the Jackson 5 as "The Commodores." Thus, there is no doubt that the group adopted the mark "The Commodores" as its own and that the public associated the mark with the group. Therefore, the original group had, at one point in time, common-law rights to the marks. McClary, as a member of the original group, was one of the holders of those rights.

Ownership of the marks did not stay with McClary when he left the performing group. Rather, ownership of the marks began in, remained in, and could not be divided from the group, as opposed to its individual members.

For starters the uncontroverted record established that McClary left his position in the group known as "The Commodores" more than three decades ago. No reasonable juror could have found that McClary remained with the group in the position he had previously held. Indeed, over time, all of the original group members except for King and Orange left the performing group that continued to release music and to perform as "The Commodores." This included McClary: as he said repeatedly in his own pleadings and testimony and as was confirmed by many trial witnesses, he "split from the band" in 1984 to pursue a solo career.

Between 1985 and 2010, McClary had no interaction with the group as a member. He did not perform with the group, record with the group, or participate in any decisions about performances or recordings. He continued to draw royalties, but these were related to only the songs he wrote or recorded with The Commodores prior to his departure in 1984. The royalties were, in King's words, "money that you receive based upon your past performance as being in the group itself or music that you've written or co-written." Although McClary performed with the group in 2010 and hosted a listening session that King and Orange attended in order to encourage a reunion, these activities in no way suggest continued involvement with the group. Nor do these activities bear any relationship to King's and Orange's continuing involvement with the group since 1968. It is undisputed that King and Orange are the only original members of "The Commodores" who have maintained continuity with the performing group since McClary's departure and that the group continued to perform as "The Commodores" in the years after 1985.

The next question, then, is what became of McClary's rights to the marks after he left the group and undeniably left the band. McClary claims that although the members who left had no involvement with the group, they still maintained common-law rights to use the group's name. We are unpersuaded. Instead, on this record, we determine that the common-law rights to the marks remained with the group members who continued to use and exert control over the group "The Commodores," and no reasonable juror could have found otherwise.

While we are not bound by the determinations of another circuit court, we find the reasoning of the Ninth Circuit to be persuasive, as the district court did. In *Robi v. Reed*, 173 F.3d 736 (9th Cir. 1999), a common-law trademark dispute, defendant Herb Reed founded the band The Platters in 1953 and plaintiff Paul Robi joined the group later; like in this case, the group jointly owned rights to the band name. In 1965, Robi left the group and he never returned; Reed stayed on with The Platters. In 1988, Robi assigned his purported rights in the mark to his wife, Martha, who then began to manage an entirely new musical group also called "The Platters." Martha eventually sued Reed, who was still an active performer, asserting that she had exclusive rights to the name. In holding for Reed, the Ninth Circuit concluded that the rights to the name belonged to the members "who remain[] continuously involved with the group and [are] in a position to control the quality of its services." Reed "ha[d] been in a position to control the quality of its services"; among other things he was "the only surviving member of the five singers who originally began with the group," and was "the only member who ha[d] continuously performed with the group." In contrast, "Paul Robi left the group and never returned to it." The Ninth Circuit adopted the holdings of courts facing similar factual circumstances that determined that a member leaving a music group did not retain a right to use the group's name. Rather, when a member left the group, the "mark remained with the original group."

Likewise, here the mark in "The Commodores" remained with the original group when McClary left. The continuing members of the original group, including King and Orange, are still today in a position to control the group. Given the overwhelming evidence of the control others, including King and Orange, exerted over the performances and business decisions of The Commodores, no reasonable juror could find to the contrary. King and Orange decide how many shows the group will do in a year, and where and when they will perform; they determine the songs, costumes, and production details for their shows; and they are responsible for the group's sounds at those shows. They also make all personnel determinations, such as retaining crew members for performances.

While we are not bound by it, we agree with the panel of our Court that previously considered the facts on appeal of the preliminary injunction and found it significant that the remaining original members controlled the quality and reputation of the band performing as "The Commodores." *Commodores Entm't Corp. v. McClary*, 648 Fed.Appx. 771 (11th Cir. 2016). We agree, given the control sustained by King and Orange, that the original members remaining with the group retained the common-law rights to the marks.

As the district court did, we find that the alternative framework of *Crystal Entertainment & Filmworks, Inc. v. Jurado*, 643 F.3d 1313 (11th Cir. 2011), is not the framework applicable here but nonetheless would yield a similar result. There, a panel of this Court addressed how to determine the ownership of trademark rights where there was no clear prior appropriation by either of the two parties to the case. The district court had determined, and this Court upheld its finding, that an entertainment company had not proven its predecessor in interest had established common-law trademark rights to the name of a musical group as originally constituted. Instead, the courts were tasked with determining the proper rights-holders as between the assignee of the original management company and the three performers who replaced the original members of the group. We followed the district court in adopting a test drawn from *Bell v. Streetwise Records, Ltd.*, 640 F.Supp. 575 (D. Mass. 1986), whereby a court seeking to allocate rights between claimants who could not prove original appropriation of the trademark rights would look to see, first, the "quality or characteristic for which the group is known by the public" and, second, "who controls that quality or characteristic."

McClary's second claim is that the injunction is overbroad because of its extraterritorial reach. The scope of the injunction was first discussed after King and Orange learned that "The Commodores Featuring Thomas McClary" was scheduled to perform in the United Kingdom and in Switzerland. The district court granted their motion for clarification and concluded that the injunction had extraterritorial reach. A panel of this Court affirmed, noting that the parties are citizens of the United States, that McClary's booking agent operates from the United States, that "customer confusion was not limited to the United Kingdom and Switzerland ... but was also present in the United States," that the marks were not registered in a foreign country, and that "use of the marks extraterritorially would have an effect on CEC, a United States corporation." We agree with this determination, even if we are not bound by it, inasmuch as our first opinion addressed only the wisdom and efficacy of a preliminary injunction and today we are called upon to address a permanent injunction.

As the Supreme Court has long said, "Congress in prescribing standards of conduct for American citizens may project the impact of its laws beyond the territorial boundaries of the United States." *Steele v. Bulova Watch Co.*, 344 U.S. 280, 282 (1952). It is also well established that "Congress has the power to prevent unfair trade practices in foreign commerce by citizens of the United States, although some of the acts are done outside the territorial limits of the United States." *Id.* at 286. In *Steele*, Bulova Watch Company sued an American citizen who conducted a business in Mexico City that sold watches with the name "Bulova" stamped on them. Bulova requested injunctive and monetary relief based on asserted violations of United States trademark laws, and the Supreme Court ruled in its favor. We have considered three factors when determining the extraterritorial reach of the Lanham Act: (1) whether the defendant is a United States corporation, (2) whether "the foreign activity had substantial effects in the United States," and (3) whether "exercising jurisdiction would not interfere with the sovereignty of another nation." *Int'l Café, S.A.L. v. Hard Rock Café Int'l (U.S.A.), Inc.*, 252 F.3d 1274, 1278 (11th Cir. 2001).

In this case, it is undisputed that both parties are citizens of the United States. And given the actual confusion that was experienced in the United States in connection with the New York performance, it is likely that McClary's use of the marks abroad would create confusion both abroad and in the United States. McClary's group is also managed in the United States by an American citizen, and his use of the marks affects CEC, an American corporation, both at home and abroad.

As for the final factor, interference with another nation's sovereignty, the question is closer but McClary comes up short. McClary notes that his corporation, Fifth Avenue, filed for a Community Trademark (CTM) in the European Union (EU) — the equivalent of a federally registered trademark in the United States. But McClary has offered no evidence that a CTM has been granted or issued by the Office of Harmonization in the Internal Market (OHIM), the EU's equivalent of the PTO. Rather, he notes that the OHIM denied CEC's opposition to Fifth Avenue's CTM application.

There is no record evidence that Fifth Avenue actually holds a CTM and, correspondingly, no evidence that the extraterritorial reach of the injunction infringes on a foreign nation's sovereignty.

AFFIRMED.

Brother Records, Inc. v. Jardine

318 F.3d 900 (9th Cir. 2003)

Alan Jardine appeals the district court's grant of summary judgment in favor of Brother Records, Inc. ("BRI"), on BRI's Lanham Act, trademark infringement action alleging that Jardine infringed BRI's "The Beach Boys" trademark. Jardine also appeals the district court's grant of summary judgment in favor of BRI on Jardine's counterclaims that BRI breached a lifetime employment agreement and license agreement. Finally, Jardine appeals the district court's denial of his motion to amend his counterclaim to add third-party claims and an additional counterclaim. We have jurisdiction under 28 U.S.C. § 1291, and we affirm.

In 1961, Al Jardine, Mike Love, Brian Wilson, Carl Wilson, and Dennis Wilson formed The Beach Boys. The band shortly thereafter achieved huge commercial success, producing numerous hit songs and touring to huge audiences throughout the country. In 1967, the members of the Beach Boys incorporated BRI to hold and administer the intellectual property rights for The Beach Boys. Currently, BRI is equally owned by four shareholders, who are also its directors: Al Jardine, Mike Love, Brian Wilson, and the estate of Carl Wilson. BRI is the registered owner of "The Beach Boys" trademark.

Over the years, personal difficulties arose between some of the members, and some members of the band decided to not tour full time, or at all. In 1991, the members of the Beach Boys incorporated Brother Tours, Inc., which handled their touring and distributed their touring income. In 1993, the directors of BRI agreed to devote a certain percentage of the touring income to the corporation for use of the trademark and designated a larger percentage of the income to those members who actually toured. By 1998, Carl Wilson had died, Love and Jardine no longer wanted to tour together, and Brian Wilson did not want to tour at all. Love began negotiating with BRI the terms of a license to use "The Beach Boys" trademark in connection with his own band.

BRI's directors met on July 14, 1998, to discuss how the trademark should be used. The representative of Carl Wilson's estate suggested that BRI issue non-exclusive licenses to each shareholder on the same terms and conditions as the license that was being negotiated with Love, thus giving each member an equal right to tour. Three of the four board members, including Jardine, voted to grant each Beach Boy a non-exclusive license. On October 1, 1998, BRI executed a non-exclusive license agreement with Love (the "Love license"). The Love license contained clauses designed to protect the value of the trademark, requiring the licensee to preserve The Beach Boys style and to choose from a list of approved booking agencies and managers.

The parties dispute whether BRI and Jardine entered into a non-exclusive license agreement. After the July 1998 BRI board meeting, Jardine began touring with his own band, using a booking agent and manager that were not included in the list approved by the Love license. On October 25, 1998, Jardine's attorney sent BRI a letter saying that Jardine would be performing as "Beach Boys Family and Friends," and that therefore, "a license from BRI [was] unnecessary." On October 28, 1998, BRI told Jardine that his unlicensed use of the trademark would be an infringement....

Jardine and his band continued to perform using names that included "The Beach Boys" trademark. The performances were promoted under names such as: Al Jardine of the Beach Boys and Family & Friends; The Beach Boys "Family and Friends"; Beach Boys Family & Friends; The Beach Boys, Family & Friends; Beach Boys and Family; as well as, simply, The Beach Boys. Jardine and his band performed in locations and on dates close to Love's "The Beach Boys" shows. With two bands touring as The Beach Boys or as a similar-sounding combination, show organizers sometimes were confused about what exactly they were getting when they booked Jardine's band. A number of show organizers booked Jardine's band thinking they would get The Beach Boys along with special added guests, but subsequently canceled the booking when they discovered that Jardine's band was not what they thought it was. Numerous people who attended one of Jardine's shows said that they had been confused about who was performing. During this time period, BRI sent Jardine cease and desist letters objecting to Jardine's use of the trademark.

On April 9, 1999, BRI filed its complaint in the district court alleging that Jardine was infringing its trademark.... The district court granted summary judgment in favor of BRI and issued a permanent injunction against Jardine's use of the trademark. This timely appeal followed....

Jardine contends that his use of BRI's trademark is protected by either the classic fair use doctrine or the nominative fair use doctrine. In *New Kids on the Block v. News Am. Publ'g Inc.*, 971 F.2d 302 (9th Cir. 1992), we noted that the classic fair use defense could not be applied in that case because "this is not the classic fair use case where the defendant has used the plaintiff's mark to describe the defendant's own product." We then held that, "where the defendant uses a trademark to describe the plaintiff's product, rather than its own ... a commercial user is entitled to a nominative fair use defense." ...

To illustrate this distinction, we cited a number of cases that applied the nominative fair use analysis. For example, in *New Kids*, the defendant newspapers used the New Kids trademark to refer to the music band New Kids itself in order to describe the defendants' own telephone polls about the band. In *Volkswagenwerk AG v. Church*, 411 F.2d 350 (9th Cir. 1969), the defendant car repair shop used the plaintiff's trademarked name "Volkswagen" in a sign that said "Modern Volkswagen Porsche Service." In *Smith v. Chanel, Inc.*, 402 F.2d 562 (9th Cir. 1968), a seller of imitation perfumes advertised its "2d Chance" perfume as indistinguishable from the trademarked "Chanel No. 5" perfume. In *WCVB-TV v. Boston Athletic Ass'n*, 926 F.2d 42 (1st Cir. 1991), a television station referred to and made broadcasts of the trademarked "Boston

Marathon." In all these cases, the defendant used the plaintiff's trademark to refer to the plaintiff's product, and therefore the nominative fair use analysis applied.

Following *New Kids*, we have applied the nominative fair use defense in a number of cases. In most of these cases, the nominative fair use defense, as opposed to the classic fair use defense, clearly applied because the defendant used the plaintiff's mark undeniably to refer to the plaintiff's product, even though the defendant's ultimate goal was to describe his own product. In *Abdul-Jabbar v. Gen. Motors Corp.*, 85 F.3d 407 (9th Cir. 1996), the defendant automobile manufacturer referred to plaintiff, a basketball star who had won an award three years in a row, in a commercial for a car that also had won an award three years in a row. In *Downing v. Abercrombie & Fitch*, 265 F.3d 994 (9th Cir. 2001), the defendant clothing company used the trademarked names and photograph of plaintiffs, surfing champions, to market shirts copied from those worn by plaintiffs in the photograph. These were not cases in which the defendant used the plaintiff's mark only to describe the defendant's own product, and not at all to describe the plaintiff's product. Rather, these were cases in which the defendant used the plaintiff's mark to describe the plaintiff's product — Kareem Abdul-Jabbar himself and the surfing champions themselves — even though the ultimate goal was to describe the defendant's own product....

Here, Jardine argues that either the classic fair use *or* the nominative fair use defense applies. As in *Playboy*, whether the defendant's use of the mark refers to the plaintiff's product at all — and thus whether classic fair use analysis or nominative fair use analysis applies — is not clear. Jardine illustrates this point with his conflicting arguments (1) that his use of "The Beach Boys" mark describes the Beach Boys' product, thus requiring application of the nominative fair use analysis, and (2) that, in the alternative, his use of "The Beach Boys" mark describes only himself — a founding member of the Beach Boys — and not at all to describe the Beach Boys' product, thus requiring application of the classic fair use analysis. Where the defendant uses his or her own title, which happens also to be plaintiff's trademark, defendant can argue convincingly both that the use refers to defendant and that the use refers not at all to defendant. In these situations, the reference-to-trademark-holder distinction often proves more frustrating than helpful.

Rather than contorting ourselves into finding either that Jardine used "The Beach Boys" mark to describe the Beach Boys or that Jardine used "The Beach Boys" mark only to describe himself and not at all to describe the Beach Boys, we analyze each defense separately. We note first that the classic fair use defense, codified in the Lanham Act, 15 U.S.C. § 1115(b)(4), applies only to marks that possess both a primary meaning and a secondary meaning — and only when the mark is used in its primary descriptive sense rather than its secondary trademark sense. Section 1115(b)(4) allows the defense to trademark infringement that

> the use of the name, term or device charged to be an infringement is a use, otherwise than as a mark ... of a term or device which is descriptive of and used fairly and in good faith only to describe the goods or services of such party, or their geographic origin.

We have explained that "the primary cost of recognizing property rights in trademarks is the removal of words ... from our language." We therefore recognized that the classic fair use defense "in essence, forbids a trademark registrant to appropriate a descriptive term for his exclusive use and so prevent others from accurately describing a characteristic of their goods." "If the trademark holder were allowed exclusive rights in such use, the language would be depleted in much the same way as if generic words were protectable." ...

Here, as in Playboy and New Kids, Jardine does not use the trademark in any primary, descriptive sense. That is, Jardine does not use "The Beach Boys" trademark to denote its primary, descriptive meaning of "boys who frequent a stretch of sand beside the sea." Instead, Jardine uses "The Beach Boys" trademark in its secondary, trademark sense, which denotes the music band — and its members — that popularized California surfing culture. This is true regardless of whether Jardine's use of the mark refers to Jardine himself or to the band. Because Jardine does not use the mark in its primary, descriptive sense, the classic fair use defense does not apply.

Where the defendant uses the trademark not in its primary, descriptive sense, but rather in its secondary, trademark sense, the nominative fair use analysis applies.... In *New Kids*, we articulated the three requirements of the nominative fair use defense:

> First, the product or service in question must be one not readily identifiable without use of the trademark; second, only so much of the mark or marks may be used as is reasonably necessary to identify the product or service; and third, the user must do nothing that would, in conjunction with the mark, suggest sponsorship or endorsement by the trademark holder.

Just as it is virtually impossible to refer to the New Kids on the Block, the Chicago Bulls, Volkswagens, or the Boston Marathon without using the trademarked names, so too is it virtually impossible to refer to the Beach Boys without using the trademark, and Jardine therefore meets the first requirement. Also, BRI does not allege that Jardine uses any distinctive logo "or anything else that isn't needed" to identify the Beach Boys, and Jardine therefore satisfies the second requirement.

Jardine fails, however, to meet the third requirement. Jardine's promotional materials display "The Beach Boys" more prominently and boldly than "Family and Friends," suggesting sponsorship by the Beach Boys. Also, there is evidence that Jardine uses "The Beach Boys" trademark to suggest that his band is in fact sponsored by the Beach Boys, as Jardine's management testified that they recommended including the trademark "The Beach Boys" in the name of Jardine's band in order to create or enhance marquee value. Finally, Jardine's use of the trademark caused actual consumer confusion, as both event organizers that booked Jardine's band and people who attended Jardine's shows submitted declarations expressing confusion about who was performing.

Because Jardine's use of the trademark suggested sponsorship or endorsement by the trademark holder, Jardine's nominative fair use argument fails. "The plain language of Rule 56(c) mandates the entry of summary judgment ... against a party who fails to make a showing sufficient to establish the existence of an element essential to that party's case, and on which that party will bear the burden of proof at trial." The district court did not err in concluding that Jardine's use of the Beach Boys' trademark was an infringement. No genuine issue of material fact exists regarding Jardine's suggestion of sponsorship or endorsement by BRI. We therefore affirm the district court's grant of summary judgment in favor of BRI on BRI's trademark infringement claim....

Because no genuine issue of material fact exists regarding the likelihood of confusion, we affirm the district court's grant of summary judgment in favor of BRI on the trademark infringement claim....

Kassbaum v. Steppenwolf Productions, Inc.
236 F.3d 487 (9th Cir. 2000)

This case raises the issue of whether a contract between the parties or section 32(1)(a) of the Lanham Trade-Mark Act, ("Lanham Act"), bars Nicholas Kassbaum ("Kassbaum"), a former member of the rock band "Steppenwolf," from referring to himself in promotional materials for a new band as "formerly of Steppenwolf," an "original member of Steppenwolf," or an "original founding member of Steppenwolf." ... We hold that Kassbaum is not barred by contract or by the Lanham Act from truthfully referring to himself, in promotional materials or otherwise, as a former member of Steppenwolf.

In 1967, John Kay, Jerry Edmonton, Michael Monarch and Goldie McJohn formed a musical band called "Steppenwolf." In 1968, Nicholas Kassbaum, who is professionally known as "Nick St. Nicholas," joined Steppenwolf as a bass player. That year, the band members entered into a partnership agreement whereby the members became co-equal partners and owners in Steppenwolf, and agreed to share equally the band's expenses and income. Also in 1968, the band members signed a recording agreement with Dunhill Records both as partners and as Steppenwolf band members.

From late 1968 until late April 1970, Steppenwolf, with Kassbaum as its bass player, toured the world in concerts and recorded Steppenwolf's well-received music. Kassbaum appeared prominently on Steppenwolf record album covers and authored Steppenwolf compositions. In 1971, John Kay, who had asserted control over Steppenwolf, excluded Kassbaum from the band.

In 1975, after Kassbaum and Michael Monarch had been excluded, and John Kay had stopped performing as Steppenwolf, Kassbaum and Goldie McJohn began to perform as "The New Steppenwolf." This began a series of legal disputes over the different band members' use of the name Steppenwolf.

In 1976, Kassbaum filed a complaint against SI and SPI to obtain an order prohibiting SPI from interfering with Kassbaum's performances as The New Steppenwolf. In 1977, Kassbaum paid $17,500.00 to John Kay and SPI in exchange for their agreement to grant Goldie McJohn and Kassbaum the exclusive right to the use of the name Steppenwolf for the purposes of live performances and recordings.

In 1979, Kassbaum entered into a second agreement whereby SI and SPI granted The New Steppenwolf, Inc. the exclusive right to use the name Steppenwolf until 1981 in connection with recording, production, manufacture, sale and distribution of records and tapes containing performances of a musical group. Kassbaum performed as Steppenwolf from 1977 through 1980.

On May 27, 1980, Kassbaum, The New Steppenwolf, Inc., SI and SPI entered into a third contract ("the 1980 contract") which states, in relevant part:

ACKNOWLEDGEMENT [sic] AND WAIVER.

[KASSBAUM], THE NEW STEPPENWOLF, INC. and GEOFFREY EMORY hereby acknowledge and agree that [SI] and [SPI] own all right, title and interest in the name "STEPPENWOLF". [KASSBAUM], THE NEW STEPPEN-WOLF, INC., and GEOFFREY EMORY hereby acknowledge and agree that [SI] and [SPI] have the sole and exclusive right to use the name "STEPPEN-WOLF" in connection with the production, manufacture and distribution of phonograph records, in live, in-concert performances of a musical group, and all other uses of the name "STEPPENWOLF" in the entertainment industry. [KASSBAUM], THE NEW STEPPENWOLF, INC. and GEOFFREY EMORY now and forever, waive, relinquish and release any and all of their individual or collective rights in the name "STEPPENWOLF" or any other word or phrase incorporating the name "STEPPENWOLF" for any purpose whatsoever. [KASSBAUM], THE NEW STEPPENWOLF, INC. and GEOFFREY EMORY hereby agree to waive, relinquish and release any trademark, trade name, service mark, or service name rights any or all of them may have in the name "STEPPENWOLF." [KASSBAUM], THE NEW STEPPEN-WOLF, INC. and GEOFFREY EMORY further agree to transfer or assign all such trademark, trade name, service mark or service name rights they may have in the name "STEPPENWOLF" to [SI] and [SPI]. Notwithstanding anything to the contrary in the foregoing, nothing contained herein shall be deemed an acknowledgment on the part of [SI] and [SPI] that [KASSBAUM], THE NEW STEPPENWOLF, INC., and/or GEOFFREY EMORY, ever acquired or held any such trademark, trade name, service mark or service name right in the name "STEPPENWOLF."

The contract also provided that, in exchange for this acknowledgment and waiver, "[SI] and [SPI] agree to pay [KASSBAUM], THE NEW STEPPENWOLF, INC. and GEOFFREY EMORY the sum of THREE THOUSAND DOLLARS ($3,000.00)."

From 1980, when the contract was executed, until 1996, Kassbaum performed as "Lone Wolf." During that time, without objection from the parties to the 1980 contract, Kassbaum referred to his historical association with Steppenwolf, describing himself as a "former member of" or "previous member of" Steppenwolf.

From 1996 until the present, Kassbaum has performed in a group called World Classic Rockers. The group is comprised of former members of various musical groups well known to rock music fans including: Randy Meiser, a former member of "Wings;" Spencer Davis, a former member of the "Spencer Davis Group;" Bruce Gary, a former member of "Knack;" and Michael Monarch and Kassbaum, former members of Steppenwolf. While performing as the World Classic Rockers, Kassbaum and the other band members often identified themselves by referring to their former musical associations. For example, one advertisement identifies Kassbaum as "NICK ST. NICHOLAS former member of Steppenwolf." Kassbaum also promoted himself as being a "Former Original Member of Steppenwolf," "Original Founding Member of Steppenwolf," and "Formerly of Steppenwolf."

In response to these promotional claims, SPI and SI sent Kassbaum cease and desist letters asserting that Kassbaum's historical references to Steppenwolf violated federal trademark law and the 1980 contract. Kassbaum then filed a complaint in federal district court seeking a declaration that he is entitled to refer to himself as "Formerly of Steppenwolf," an "Original Member of Steppenwolf," and an "Original Founding Member of Steppenwolf." SPI answered and filed a counterclaim alleging trademark infringement, unfair competition and breach of contract. Thereafter, SPI and SI moved for summary judgment on Kassbaum's complaint for declaratory relief and SPI's counterclaim for breach of contract. SPI and SI also sought permanently to enjoin Kassbaum and his agents from using the name Steppenwolf....

We must decide whether either the 1980 contract or the Lanham Act bars Kassbaum from referring to himself as a former member of Steppenwolf.

As described above, the parties entered into the 1980 contract on May 28, 1980. We must decide whether, by the terms of the contract, Kassbaum agreed that he would not identify himself, for promotional purposes or otherwise, with a true statement that he is a former member of the band Steppenwolf.

We review decisions to grant or deny declaratory relief de novo. Contract interpretation is a question of law we review de novo. We also review grants of summary judgment de novo. "Summary judgment is appropriate when the contract terms are clear and unambiguous, even if the parties disagree as to their meaning." Under California law, we interpret the 1980 contract by examining the contract's language, the parties' clear intentions as expressed in the contract and the circumstances under which the parties contracted.

As Kassbaum concedes, there is no doubt that the 1980 contract "absolutely precludes" Kassbaum from "performing, sponsoring, or endorsing a band entitled Steppenwolf." The question is whether the contracting parties intended that broad language such as "waive, relinquish and release any and all ... rights in the name 'STEPPENWOLF' or any other word or phrase incorporating the name 'STEPPENWOLF' for any purpose whatsoever" would bar Kassbaum from such things as truthfully answering a question about his past (for example) on a talk show, distributing a resume, or truthfully describing his past musical affiliations in promotional materials connected with the World Classic Rockers.

Taken out of context, the language "name 'STEPPENWOLF'" and "for any purposes whatsoever," might be read so broadly as to preclude Kassbaum from writing "Steppenwolf" on the sidewalk in chalk. While SPI and SI do not advocate a restriction that broad, they do appear to contend that the contract language prohibits virtually any reference by Kassbaum to the name Steppenwolf in the context of the "entertainment industry." Thus, SPI and SI contend that Kassbaum contracted away his ability to refer to his past association with Steppenwolf in a resume sent to a recording company, or in a music industry interview touching upon his background, or, at the center of this case, in his promotional references relating to his performance with World Classic Rockers.

We must read the words of the 1980 contract in context. We may not read the contract in a manner that leads to an absurd result. Rather, when we encounter broad language such as "for any purposes whatsoever," we must extend the meaning of such language to cover only those things which it appears the parties intended to contract. When broad language is at issue, we must look to the circumstances under which the parties contracted to determine their intentions at the time of contracting.

Here, those circumstances are a continuing dispute between the parties about ownership and control over the trade name Steppenwolf. Over the years, such ownership and control was transferred from party to party through a series of contracts. First, all of the original band members owned the trade name Steppenwolf. Then, in 1977, after Kassbaum was asked to leave Steppenwolf and began to perform as The New Steppenwolf, the parties resolved a dispute over the right to the trade name Steppenwolf by having Kassbaum pay $17,500.00 to SPI in exchange for the exclusive right to perform as Steppenwolf for the purpose of live performances and recordings. The parties entered into a second agreement in 1979, whereby SI and SPI granted Kassbaum and The New Steppenwolf, Inc. the exclusive right to use the name Steppenwolf in connection with recording, production, manufacture, sale and distribution of records and tapes embodying performance of a musical group until 1981. At the time the parties entered into the 1980 contract, Kassbaum owned the trade name Steppenwolf to the extent specified by the 1979 contract, and had been performing as The New Steppenwolf. The 1980 contract effected the transfer of the trade name Steppenwolf from Kassbaum and The New Steppenwolf to SPI and SI. Thereafter, Kassbaum discontinued his performances as The New Steppenwolf, and began to perform as Lone Wolf and later as a part of the World Classic Rockers.

Under these circumstances, it is clear that the contract's broad language "for any purposes whatsoever," and "all other uses of the name 'STEPPENWOLF' in the entertainment industry" refers to use of the *trade name* Steppenwolf, and not to the simple use of the name to provide accurate historical information that would not lead reasonable people to think Kassbaum's new band was Steppenwolf. The terms of the contract do not bar Kassbaum from referring to his former membership in Steppenwolf in the entertainment industry or otherwise. We therefore hold that the district court erred by granting summary judgment to SPI and SI on the contract counterclaim and by dismissing Kassbaum's complaint for declaratory relief on contract grounds.

Kassbaum's complaint requests, inter alia, a declaratory judgment that section 32(1)(a) of the Lanham Act, does not bar him from stating, particularly in promotional materials, that he was "Formerly of Steppenwolf," an "Original Member of Steppenwolf," or an "Original Founding Member of Steppenwolf." The district court dismissed Kassbaum's complaint and granted SPI and SI's motion for summary judgment. We reverse.

The Lanham Act provides, in pertinent part:

(1) Any person who shall, without the consent of the registrant —

(a) use in commerce any reproduction, counterfeit, copy, or colorable imitation of a registered mark in connection with the sale, offering for sale, distribution, or advertising of any goods or services on or in connection with which such use is likely to cause confusion, or to cause mistake, or to deceive ... shall be liable in a civil action by the registrant....

The purpose of a trademark is to allow customers to identify the manufacturer or sponsor of a good or the provider of a service. Actual consumer confusion is not required for profit recovery; it is sufficient to show a likelihood of confusion combined with willful infringement. For the reasons that follow, we believe that Kassbaum's references to himself in promotional materials as "Formerly of Steppenwolf," an "Original Member of Steppenwolf," and an "Original Founding Member of Steppenwolf," do not cause a likelihood of confusion.[6]

First, we believe the phrases "Formerly of," "Original Member of," and "Original Founding Member of," immediately preceding the name "Steppenwolf" in the promotional materials for World Classic Rockers greatly reduce the likelihood of confusion about the source of the band's music.

Additionally, the context of the historical references to Kassbaum's affiliation with Steppenwolf in World Classic Rockers' promotional materials further reduces any likelihood of confusion between these two bands. In all promotional materials presented to the district court, references to World Classic Rockers are more prominent than are references to Steppenwolf. The materials display the title "World Classic Rockers" on the top or at the center of the page, while references to the band members' former groups, including Steppenwolf, are displayed on the bottom or around the edges of the page. Also, the title "World Classic Rockers" appears in large and bold lettering, while smaller and plainer lettering is used for the titles of the former groups, including Steppenwolf. Finally, while the materials mention multiple former groups, the materials promote only World Classic Rockers, not Steppenwolf, or any other former band.

Our holding is supported by cases in similar contexts. For example, in *Kingsmen v. K-Tel International Ltd.*, 557 F. Supp. 178 (S.D.N.Y. 1983), the district court dis-

---

6. We consider the following factors to test for likelihood of confusion under the Lanham Act: (1) strength of the mark; (2) proximity of the goods; (3) similarity of the marks; (4) evidence of actual confusion; (5) marketing channels used; (6) type of goods and the degree of care likely to be exercised by the purchaser; (7) defendant's intent in selecting the mark; and (8) likelihood of expansion of the product lines.

tinguished the likelihood of confusion that exists when a former member of a band re-records a song under the name of the original band from the likelihood of confusion that exists when the former member re-records a song under his own name with the designation "formerly of" the original band displayed on the recording. The first situation, the court stated, created a likelihood of confusion under the Lanham Act, while the latter, although not then before the court, would not.

In *Playboy Enterprises, Inc. v. Welles*, 7 F. Supp. 2d 1098 (S.D. Cal. 1998), the district court addressed concerns regarding the differences between commercial trademark use and descriptions of individuals that use trade names. In that case, the publisher of Playboy sued a former "Playmate of the Year" for so designating herself on her personal web site, asserting various claims related to trademark. In denying the publisher's motion for preliminary injunction, the court held that defendant was entitled to the "fair use" defense. In holding that the "fair use" defense applied, the court noted that "[i]n the case at bar, Ms. Welles has used the trademark term Playmate of the Year to identify and describe herself.... Ms. Welles earned the title of 'Playboy Playmate of the Year' in 1981 and has used that title ever since, without objection." Because the court applied the "fair use" defense, it found it unnecessary to determine the likelihood of confusion under the Lanham Act. The court, however, went on to state that it did not see any likelihood of confusion under this circuit's eight-factor test.

Finally, we wholeheartedly agree with Justice Holmes's statement about the limits of trademark protection in *Prestonettes, Inc. v. Coty*, 264 U.S. 359, 368, 44 S. Ct. 350, 68 L.Ed. 731 (1924): "When the mark is used in a way that does not deceive the public we see no such sanctity in the word as to prevent its being used to tell the truth. It is not taboo." We reverse the district court's order granting summary judgment to SPI and SI and dismissing Kassbaum's complaint for declaratory judgment as to the Lanham Act issue.

The district court granted SPI and SI's request for a permanent injunction precluding Kassbaum and his agents from using the designations "Formerly of Steppenwolf," "Original Member of Steppenwolf," and "Original Founding Member of Steppenwolf" in promotional materials. Because we hold that Kassbaum is not barred by contract or by the Lanham Act from using these designations, we reverse....

Notes and Questions

a. The variations on the names may clue the audience in as to the relationship between the performer and the band, but these appellations often seem confusing. *See Marshak v. Reed*, 96 CV 2292 (NG) (MLO), 2001 U.S. Dist. LEXIS 880 (E.D.N.Y. Feb. 1, 2001), *reinstated*, 229 F. Supp. 2d 179, (E.D.N.Y. 2002), *aff'd*, 87 Fed. Appx. 208 (2d Cir. N.Y. 2004), for a long discussion of the ongoing battles involving the embattled musicians and their heirs to interests in the band, the Platters.

b. A group of five young men performed under the music group name of Dream Street and Dream Street became a hit. Their album "Dream Street" was listed on Billboard as the Top Independent Album on July 28, 2001; their video was a Most Requested Video on Nickelodeon's internet site and recording opportunities were presented by Disney and Sony. Dream Street was a "concept group" created by a manager-promoter who hires performers to play the roles in the group and directs its performance, much like Menudo, the Monkees and the Spice Girls. Three members of the group wished to leave the manager and the other two members, taking the "Dream Street" name with them. What result? *See In re Applications of Atlantic Recording Corp.*, 747 N.Y.S.2d 889 (N.Y. Sup. Ct. 2002).

c. Nominative fair use may have different meanings in different situations. To what extent does this explanation of nominative fair use distinguish or overrule the explanation provided in *Brother Records, Inc. v. Jardine*? *See Toyota Motor Sales, U.S.A., Inc. v. Tabari*, 610 F.3d 1171, 1182–83 (9th Cir. 2010) ("A finding of nominative fair use is a finding that the plaintiff has failed to show a likelihood of confusion as to sponsorship or endorsement."); *KP Permanent Make-Up, Inc. v. Lasting Impression I, Inc.*, 543 U.S. 111, 118 (2004) (the "burden of proving likelihood of confusion [is] on the party charging infringement.").

d. In some situations the owner of the trademark is no longer related to the musicians themselves. *See Stetson v. Howard D. Wolf & Assocs.*, 955 F.2d 847 (2d Cir. 1992) (the Diamonds); *In re Polar Music International AB*, 714 F.2d 1567 (Fed. Cir. 1983) (ABBA).

e. In the unpublished opinion of *Cash v. Brooks*, 1996 WL 684447 (E.D. Tenn. 1996), the court adjudicated a fight over competing former band members involved with The Temptations and noted the similar claims of other bands. A similar history has occurred with The Platters. *See Herb Reed Enterprises, Inc. v. Monroe Powell's Platters, L.L.C.*, 842 F.Supp.2d 1282 (2012); *Robi v. Five Platters, Inc.*, 918 F.2d 1439 (9th Cir. 1990) (The Platters); *Robi v. Five Platters, Inc.*, 838 F.2d 318 (9th Cir. 1988) (The Platters); *The Five Platters v. Purdie*, 419 F. Supp. 372 (D. Md 1976) (The Platters).

The Beach Boys, The Temptations, and The Platters are not alone. Many groups end up fighting over these assets long after the music has grown old. Among the cases involving litigation similar to that here are *Scholz v. Goudreau*, 901 F.3d 37 (1st Cir. 2018) (Boston); *Marshak v. Treadwell*, No. CV-94-2297 (CPS), 1995 WL 428639 (E.D.N.Y. July 6, 1995) (The Drifters); *Baker v. Parris*, 777 F. Supp. 299 (S.D.N.Y. 1991) (The Five Satins); *Marshak v. Admiral Cruises*, No. 90 Civ. 0317 (PNL), 1991 WL 191233 (S.D.N.Y. Sept. 16, 1991) (The Drifters); *Grondin v. Rossington*, 690 F. Supp. 200 (S.D.N.Y. 1988) (Lynyrd Skynyrd); *Marshak v. Sheppard*, 666 F. Supp. 590 (S.D.N.Y. 1987) (The Drifters); *Marshak v. Sheppard*, 659 F. Supp. 907 (S.D.N.Y. 1987) (the Drifters); *Coasters v. Claridge Hotel*, No. 85-2885, 1986 WL 9783 (D.N.J. Apr. 4, 1986) (The Coasters); *Rick v. Buchansky*, 609 F. Supp. 1522 (S.D.N.Y. 1985) (Vito and The Salutations); *Kingsmen v. K-Tel Intern. Ltd.*, 557 F. Supp. 178 (S.D.N.Y. 1983) (the Kingsmen); *Marshak v. Green*, 505 F. Supp. 1054 (S.D.N.Y. 1981) (The Drifters); *Rare Earth v. Hoorelbeke*, 401 F. Supp. 26 (S.D.N.Y. 1975) (Rare Earth); and *Noone v. Banner*, 398 F. Supp. 260 (S.D.N.Y. 1975) (Herman's Hermits).

f. What structures can be put into band membership agreements to limit the litigation that may affect leaving band members? Assuming that the band is sufficiently sophisticated to negotiate a formal agreement, how does the changing membership over time shape the way in which the agreement should be drafted? For an example of a settlement agreement and its subsequent litigation, see *Scholz v. Goudreau*, 901 F.3d 37 (1st Cir. 2018), regarding the use of the term "original member" for the band Boston.

g. The court involved in the minor agreements for Dream Street had little problem dismissing the notion that the performers had wrested the ownership and control of the trademark away from the producer of the concept band. To what extent, if at all, does the public's perception of a band such as the Monkees attach to the performers rather than the contractual trademark holder? Does such public perception alter a judicial enforcement of a signed trademark agreement?

Problem 8-E

Among the contracts purchased as part of Bryce's record company purchase is a recording agreement for the 1950s band, the "DreamWeavers." Bryce is convinced that the DreamWeavers had a sound and sensibility that was never fully appreciated. Bryce has at least fifteen previously unreleased recordings of the DreamWeavers that Bryce can release contractually. The record label also owns many songs that were released, but could also be re-released. The DreamWeavers last performed together in 1967.

Bryce has noticed, however, that songs recorded during the fifties were generally produced using a rhythm that feels too slow for today's audience. Bryce often comments on the rhythmic differences between the Los Lobos versions of Richie Valens songs and the original recordings as an example of the phenomenon. Rather than merely digitally remastering the songs, Bryce wants to add some new performers and reinvent the DreamWeavers. The contract allows Bryce to control the recording and content of all songs, so the addition or re-recording of the songs is contractually permissible.

Bryce seeks your advice. Bryce would like to re-record the songs and launch a new DreamWeavers touring band. Because the company controls the entire DreamWeavers catalog, the success of the new album could generate potential catalog sales of the other albums as well. DreamWeavers recorded five albums. Only two of the original five DreamWeavers are living, so Bryce will also have to determine how to get permission if necessary. Advise Bryce whether permission is needed from any original members of DreamWeavers, either to record and release the album or to start a touring band using the DreamWeavers name. Also explain the terms such a request for permission might entail if you determine permission is necessary or appropriate.

F. Bibliography and Links

Donald C. Farber, Entertainment Industry Contracts (Looseleaf).

Adam Seth Bialow, *Illusory Profits: Net Profit Agreements in Light of Buchwald v. Paramount*, 10 U. Miami Ent. & Sports L. Rev. 51 (1993).

Barton Beebe & Jeanne C. Fromer, *Are We Running Out of Trademarks? An Empirical Study of Trademark Depletion and Congestion*, 131 Harv. L. Rev. 945 (2018).

Stacey L. Dogan & Mark A. Lemley, *The Merchandising Right: Fragile Theory or Fait Accompli?*, 54 Emory L.J. 461 (2005).

Ellen P. Goodman, *Commercial Speech in an Age of Emerging Technology and Corporate Scandal: Intellectual Property & Cyberlaw*, 58 S.C. L. Rev. 683 (2007).

Alex Kozinski, *Essay: Trademarks Unplugged*, 68 N.Y.U.L. Rev. 960 (1993).

Lisa P. Ramsey, *A Free Speech Right to Trademark Protection?*, 106 Trademark Rep. 797 (2016).

Kelli Shope, *The Final Cut: How SAG's Failed Negotiations with Talent Agents Left the Contractual Rights of Rank-And-File Actors on the Cutting Room Floor*, 26 J. Nat'l Ass'n Admin. L. Judiciary 123 (2006).

Natalie J. Spears & S. Roberts Carter III, *This Brand is my Brand: Litigating Product Image*, 31 Litig. 31 (2005).

Mark Strasser, *Government Speech and Circumvention of the First Amendment*, 44 Hastings Const. L.Q. 37 (2016).

Rebecca Tushnet, *Raising Walls Against Overlapping Rights: Preemption and the Right of Publicity*, 92 Notre Dame L. Rev. 1539 (2017)

Rebecca Tushnet, *Registering Disagreement: Registration in Modern American Trademark Law*, 130 Harv. L. Rev. 867 (2017).

Rebecca Tushnet, *The First Amendment Walks into A Bar: Trademark Registration and Free Speech*, 92 Notre Dame L. Rev. 381 (2016).

L. Lee Wilson, *Music: Naming Names: How Trademarks Go Platinum*, 1 Vand. J. Ent. L. & Prac. 33 (1999).

Websites

Beach Boys, http://thebeachboys.com

Commodores, http://www.commodoreslive.com/

Richie Valens at the Rockabilly Hall of Fame, http://www.rockabillyhall.com/Ritchie Valens.html

Steppenwolf, http://www.steppenwolf.com

Part II

Industry Practice in Entertainment

Chapter 9

Professional Live Theatre

A. Overview

Theatrical performances are the oldest form of organized entertainment, reaching back through the history of western society to the dawn of literate civilization. Originally tied to the religious ceremonies of Greece, theatrical productions lost their former prestige and were eventually reduced to a state of disrepute and penury by, and throughout most of, the Middle Ages. Although heavily regulated, the quality and importance of theatrical productions gradually gained respect beginning in the sixteenth century, and then more so throughout the nineteenth and twentieth.

The rise of the motion picture and television industries dramatically reversed the importance of professional theatre. Nonetheless, stage plays still remain as the primary venue where most aspiring actors first apply their craft, and theatre still serves as a leading cultural and artistic medium. Because of theatre's significant historical role, many of the business conventions incorporated into the music industry, motion picture industry, and television originated with practices started in professional theatre.

U.S. theatre has also had a cultural revival. The success of the musical *Hamilton* by Lin-Manuel Miranda has reinvigorated live theatre as a significant, wide-reaching cultural medium. Disney's *The Lion King* has become the highest grossing entertainment product of all time, earning well over $8 billion since debuting in November 1997. The scale of this success has returned live theatre to the forefront of the entertainment industries.

1. Broadway Theatre

Today, professional theatre is divided into two large and distinct communities— for-profit and nonprofit. Professional theatre continues to be dominated by the New York Broadway theatrical district. Broadway is defined by both its geographic area, covering an area from 42nd Street to 53rd Street and between 6th and 8th Avenues, and by its theatre size, generally requiring a minimum seating capacity of 500 or more seats. In this small section of Manhattan, which is also referred to as the Great White Way, the Shubert Organization dominates the professional theatrical market. The Shubert Organization owns 18 of the 41 Broadway theatres and also owns additional theatres outside New York.

With eight theatres, the Nederlander Organization controls the second largest block of Broadway theatres, while the Jujamcyn Theatres company owns five venues. Roundabout Theatre Co. now owns three of the theatres, including the former dance club Studio 54, which has been converted into a Broadway house. Disney Theatrical Group owns only the New Amsterdam Theatre but often presents additional productions in neighboring houses. This cadre of theatrical real estate owners produces or houses almost all Broadway theatre. Independent producers often co-produce with one of these companies.

In addition to the Broadway theatres, a second class of professional theatres exists throughout New York. Called "Off-Broadway," these are professional theatres which are smaller in size, generally seating between 200–499 patrons. Besides the size of the venues, the other difference between Broadway and Off-Broadway are the terms of the primary collective bargaining agreements. Generally speaking, the salaries paid for Off-Broadway are considerably lower than for Broadway productions. This allows more modest productions to be produced at a profit in the Off-Broadway venues which could not happen on Broadway. Off-Broadway theatres such as the Public Theater also serve as incubators for productions that transfer to Broadway. The Public Theater, for example, helped develop the three transformational musicals *A Chorus Line*, *Rent*, and *Hamilton*.

2. Touring Companies

A third tier of professional theatre exists outside of New York. Generally referred to as touring companies, most of the for-profit professional productions which appear throughout the United States are organized as touring companies. Each company visits a venue for anywhere between a day and a month, setting up shop in a commercial theatre, trucking in the sets, costumes, lights, and actors. When the production is over, the entire show is struck, loaded into trucks, and moved to the next stop on the tour.

Touring companies represent the largest shift in professional for-profit theatre today. Although touring companies historically accounted for only 10% of the industry revenue, they may now account for the majority of theatrical revenue and as much as two-thirds of the professional theatre audience.

3. Nonprofit Professional Theatre

Although for-profit theatre is the part of theatre that is most visible and famous, the most vibrant aspect of American theatre today flows from the nonprofit sector. Nonprofit theatre includes volunteer, community theatres; educational programs, such as college stages; and professional theatres loosely organized through the League of Resident Theatres.

The League of Resident Theatres ("LORT") is nonprofit but highly professional. The actors are members of Equity, and other professionals are typical member of other trade unions. These include the Guthrie Theatre in Minneapolis, the Goodman Theatre in Chicago, the La Jolla Playhouse in San Diego, and Lincoln Center in New York. While not every LORT theatre has a resident company of actors, many do; these represent some of the most innovative and lucrative productions developed in the United States in recent years. The modern production cycle often finds new plays originating at one of the LORT theatres and then transferring to Broadway if the show is believed to have a chance to be a smash hit.

Nonprofit theatres generally rely on season ticket holders and charitable donations to protect themselves from the vagaries of season and taste. A healthy, nonprofit theatre should receive at least half its annual budget from donations. If season ticket sales account for 75% or more of the ticket sales, the theatre can afford to take significant risks in developing new works. Few investors today can match the resources of the LORT theatres.

Interestingly, the notion that each theatre employs a resident company of actors is not an organizational component of the resident theatre's membership requirements, notwithstanding this important traditional distinction between the itinerant New York houses and the stable theatrical companies that operated on the season-production basis. Instead, to be a LORT theatre, the theatre must be a nonprofit, tax exempt organization operating under the LORT—Actor's Equity Association contract. In addition, each season must run at least twelve weeks and each individual production must have at least a three-week rehearsal period. While most LORT theatres greatly exceed these minimums, they provide some consistency for the financial scope and production quality that can be expected from a LORT theatre.

4. The Participants

The character most central to theatre is the playwright. The collective bargaining history of theatre has left the playwright as the undisputed king of the medium. Although the Dramatists Guild is not a union, the Dramatists Guild Approved Production Contract governs all playwright agreements with Broadway producers. Under this contract, no additions, omissions, or alterations may be made to a script without the playwright's consent. The playwright retains ownership of the play or musical, retains control of subsequent productions, and shares approval of the cast, director, and designers with the producer. As a result, the playwright is far more influential for theatre than the screenwriter is for film or the composer is for music.

In a musical, there may be three individuals who collectively become the playwright. The author of the "book" or dialogue; the composer of the musical score; and the lyricist who writes the words put to music. Some musicals continue to have all three participants while others are written by teams of two or by single individuals.

In collaboration with the playwright, the theatrical director integrates the creative elements of set and production design, casting, and character development to create the completed theatrical performance. The stage director supervises all of the creative elements of the project, but unlike the film director, the process under the stage director's supervision is subject to much greater influence by the playwright. The primary voice for the production cannot contractually shift from the writer to the director as it does in film.

For-profit, professional theatre is highly unionized. The League of American Theatres and Producers, Inc., represents the producers and also serves as the parent organization for the annual Tony Awards. Actors' Equity Association ("AEA" or "Equity") represents the actors, and the Dramatists Guild of America, though technically not a union, provides standardization for playwright agreements. The Society of Stage Directors and Choreographers represents directors and choreographers. Additional trade unions represent every other aspect of the theatre experience.

Some of the confusion surrounding the legal agreements in for-profit theatrical production stems from the interlocking collective bargaining agreements used in New York, for-profit theatre. The relatively small number of producers, in tandem with close control of the unions and guilds, in contractual language that is often baffling to the outsider. For example, the Dramatists Guild Approved Production Contract for Plays, which is used by every Broadway production, relies heavily on terms only defined in the collective bargaining agreement between the producers and Equity. For a student interested in the inner workings of Broadway, a careful understanding of each collective bargaining agreement is essential.

Problem 9-A

The success of Bryce's *Juliet Prescott* (*see* Problem 4-A) has served as something of both a blessing and curse for Bryce. The play has caught the attention of New York producers who would like to see it developed for a New York run. Bryce believes that the show is good, but could not survive a New York Times theatrical review in its present condition. Given the pressures of New York, Bryce would like to try to develop the play in a workshop or move it to a small regional or LORT theatre.

Bryce also acknowledges that all the funding for any project would have to come from the theatres or from investors; Bryce has no personal funds to invest. Bryce has asked that you explain the various producing options and how to give the play its best chance of being successful in New York. Also explain how these different choices affect how the play would be financed and how Bryce would be compensated.

B. Employment in the Theatre

This Is Me v. Taylor

157 F.3d 139 (2d Cir. 1998)

Actress Cicely Tyson, through her personal services corporation, plaintiff-appellant This Is Me, Inc., agreed to undertake the lead role in a Broadway production of "The Corn is Green" and in a contemplated taping of the production for television, and sues to recover unpaid fees for her services. Several contracts are arguably in issue;

some are standard Actors' Equity (sometimes "Equity") form contracts, others are not; all are signed by and on behalf of various persons and entities as producers. At issue is the unpaid portion of a so-called "pay or play" guarantee of $750,000 payable if (as happened) the show closed before Tyson earned $750,000 in salary. Among the sufficiency of evidence issues are (i) whether the various contracts are sufficiently interrelated that they may be read together; (ii) whether the contractual phrase "a contract made in relation to the Play" includes a contract governing the videotaping; and (iii) who is bound in respect of the $750,000 pay or play guarantee.

Elizabeth Taylor, the actress, and Zev Bufman, the Broadway producer, formed a theater group to produce live performances of plays on the legitimate stage and video and television versions of the same plays. They chose "The Corn is Green" as their second production, and cast Cicely Tyson in the lead role. The play soon closed, and the video was never made.

This Is Me, the corporation through which Ms. Tyson provides her services, sued Taylor and Bufman (and Zev Bufman Entertainment, Inc.) under the pay or play guarantee. Plaintiff's arguments convinced the jury, which found Taylor and Bufman personally liable. The district court, however, issued judgment as a matter of law in favor of defendants on the grounds that the individual defendants were not signatories to the only contract that contained the guarantee, and that Tyson's arguments linking Taylor and Bufman to that undertaking are barred by the parol evidence rule.

We conclude that there was sufficient evidence from which the jury could find liability, and we therefore reverse. That evidence consists of the underlying and well-disclosed purpose of the enterprise to produce the play on stage as well as on videotape, the drafting history of the contracts, the contemporaneity of the undertakings, the cross-referencing between and among the contracts, and the background undertakings of the Actors' Equity rules, accepted by all the parties, that bind the individual signatories (as producers), as well as any partnership or venture controlled by them, to employment contracts.

Following a prior collaboration as producer and actor, Zev Bufman and Elizabeth Taylor decided to "put a theater group together" to produce plays on Broadway. They agreed generally that Bufman "would take care of the business end of it" and Taylor "would take care of the artistic end of it," specifically by "trying to get people to participate and become involved in the group."

Taylor and Bufman entered into a letter of intent providing that: (i) "all profits and losses will be shared equally between us;" (ii) the primary purpose of the Group was "the production of legitimate stage plays and television/film versions of such plays;" (iii) the Group would "produce three (3) plays each year;" (iv) it would be "of the essence at this time that we do not consider any play unless we are able to acquire or have an option to acquire the rights to televise such productions;" and (v) Taylor and Bufman would "be co-producers of every project" and would "each consult with the other with respect to all major decisions." Taylor testified that upon receiving the letter of intent, she scratched out the word "losses" on her copy before signing; she maintains that therefore she is not responsible for any losses. The letter of intent contemplated a more formal contract and the formation of a "new corporation" to carry out the venture, but neither eventuality came to pass.

For the Group's second project—a live production and videotape of Emlyn Williams's play, "The Corn is Green"—Bufman and Taylor decided to seek Cicely Tyson's services to star in the play. Taylor took the lead in recruiting Tyson, with whom she had worked before. In several phone calls and a lunch meeting, Taylor played a key role in reconciling creative differences between Tyson and the author of the play regarding whether use of the original screenplay would be appropriate. Throughout these discussions, Taylor referred to Bufman as her partner and noted that they were in this "50–50."

Tyson agreed to appear in the live theater production and the videotape production of "The Corn is Green," and exacted the $750,000 "pay or play" guarantee. The guarantee reflected that Tyson, who was at the height of her career, would have to turn down other opportunities in film, television, and stage, and commit nearly a year to "The Corn is Green."

An initial contract—later superseded—addressed all the undertakings concerning the stage and videotape performances of the play. This contract (hereinafter the "superseded contract") was dated December 9, 1982, and was executed by Cicely Tyson on behalf of This Is Me and by Zev Bufman on behalf of Zev Bufman Entertainment, Inc. Ms. Tyson also signed an inducement letter to bind herself personally, which is addressed to "Zev Bufman Entertainment, Inc. d/b/a The Elizabeth Theatre Group." The obligations of the superseded contract were afterward bifurcated and expressed in two new contracts executed contemporaneously in August 1983, which provided that they were to be read together to constitute the entire agreement covering This Is Me's services in "The Corn is Green."

The first of these contracts was a standard Actors' Equity document, a run of the play contract that guaranteed Tyson's weekly salary for the Broadway run, without guaranteeing the length of the run. The producer listed on this contract was an entity called "The Corn Company" and the individual signatory was Zev Bufman.

The second of these contracts related to the video production, and contained the pay or play guarantee in the amount of the difference between $750,000 and salary paid under the run of the play contract (the "video contract"). This contract was between Zev Bufman Entertainment, Inc. and This Is Me.

Two further undertakings are potentially implicated as well, both of which arise from the efforts of Actors' Equity to protect its members from defaulting producers:

> It is conceded that the relationship between the actors and the producers in this production was governed by the Actors' Equity Association Agreement and Rules Governing Employment Under the Production Contract (the "Equity Agreement and Rules"). Bufman testified that "in order to put on a play in an Equity playhouse," he "had to abide by the collective bargaining agreement."

The "Security Agreement" (also an industry standard agreement), signed by Zev Bufman, requires the producer to "promptly pay to the Actors any and all sums due," including sums due under employment agreements "made in relation to the Play," and defines "producer" broadly to "include[] the individual, firm, partnership or corporation or any combination thereof producing or controlling the production of said Play."

After out-of-town tryouts, "The Corn is Green" had a short run on Broadway, and its closing was unlamented by the critics. The video was never made, and Ms. Tyson received only the weekly salary payments made under the run of the play agreement.

Later, Tyson commenced an arbitration against Bufman, Taylor and Zev Bufman Entertainment, Inc. She won an award of $607,078.86 against Zev Bufman Entertainment, Inc., and at the behest of the individual defendants, agreed to permanently stay the arbitration as against Bufman and Taylor (preserving, however, the right of This Is Me to pursue claims against Bufman and Taylor in court).

The present action followed. The jury found that both Taylor and Bufman were liable to Tyson for "the unpaid balance of the $750,000 she was to receive for performing in the Corn is Green," but the district court granted judgment as a matter of law dismissing the complaint on the grounds that (1) only the video agreement contained the pay or play guarantee; (2) that agreement unambiguously bound only Zev Bufman Entertainment, Inc.; and (3) the Security Agreement could not be "reasonably read to require anything more than the payments due under the Run-of-the-Play (sic) Contract that it was designed to secure." This Is Me appealed; for the reasons that follow, we reverse.

Federal Rule of Civil Procedure 50 provides that if a jury returns a verdict for which there is not a legally sufficient evidentiary basis, the district court may either order a new trial or direct the entry of judgment as a matter of law. "The same standard that applies to a pretrial motion for summary judgment pursuant to Fed. R. Civ. P. 56 also applies to motions for judgment as a matter of law during or after trial pursuant to Rule 50." A district court may not grant a motion for a judgment as a matter of law unless "the evidence is such that, without weighing the credibility of the witnesses or otherwise considering the weight of the evidence, there can be but one conclusion as to the verdict that reasonable [persons] could have reached." Weakness of the evidence does not justify judgment as a matter of law; as in the case of a grant of summary judgment, the evidence must be such that "a reasonable juror would have been compelled to accept the view of the moving party." We review a grant of judgment as a matter of law de novo....

Under New York law, all writings forming part of a single transaction are to be read together. The district court properly instructed the jury on this principle:

> New York law requires that all writings which form part of a single transaction and are designed to effectuate the same purpose be read together, even though they were executed on different dates and were not all between the same parties. It is for you to determine whether the Actors' Equity run of the play

contract, the Actors' Equity security agreement and the contractual obligation to pay This Is Me $750,000 were each intended to be binding on all the same parties, and were intended to impose the same obligations on each of the parties, even though they were set forth in different documents.

We conclude that there was sufficient evidence—the drafting history and chronology, the cross-referencing of the agreements, the integral nature of the undertakings for the stage and video performance, the relationships among the producing parties and entities, and the background assumptions furnished by the Equity rules—for the jury, as properly instructed, to find that Taylor and Bufman were personally liable on the pay or play guarantee. That conclusion requires a further look at the terms of the various contracts, and their cross-referencing of each other.

A. The Superseded Contract

The original contract for Tyson's services in the production, a letter agreement dated December 9, 1982 between This Is Me and Zev Bufman Entertainment, Inc., provided that Tyson would perform in the stage production and that a performance of that stage production would be videotaped. Zev Bufman Entertainment, Inc. undertook to pay salary for the run of the play, but not less than $750,000, installments of which would be paid at specified intervals "whether or not the Artist is actually performing":

> We guaranty to "pay or play" to [This Is Me] for the services of [Tyson], the total sum of Seven Hundred Fifty Thousand ($750,000) Dollars plus Actors Equity Minimum Rehearsal Salary during the period of rehearsals....

This document also provided that the parties would enter into a standard Actors' Equity Association run of the play contract, but that the pay or play obligation would supersede the run of the play agreement "notwithstanding any provisions therein to the contrary."

This original agreement was split into two superseding agreements, one concerned with the stage performances and undertaking to pay weekly salary for the run of the play, the other concerned with the video performance and undertaking the pay or play guarantee. Conflicting evidence was offered to explain this drafting history, but the jury was free to credit testimony that the producers wanted to keep the pay or play guarantee out of the run of the play contract that would be filed with Actors' Equity in order to reduce the bond required under the Equity rules.

B. The Run of the Play Contract

The run of the play contract was signed by Tyson on behalf of This Is Me and by Bufman on behalf of The Corn Company as "producer," a word left undefined by the contract, except that in Paragraph 9 the binding effect is said to reach the individual signatory as well as persons for whom the signatory acts:

> Individual signature required. The Producer agrees that execution of this Contract binds not only the producing company, but the individual signator to this Contract as well as any person under whose authority this Contract

is executed. The jury could find that Zev Bufman was personally bound because he affixed his signature, and that Taylor was bound because Bufman acted on her authority.

The run of the play contract incorporates by reference the Actors' Equity agreement and rules, and recites that they are the essence of the contractual relationship between the parties, that they set forth the minimum conditions under which the actor may work for the producer, and that they may not be waived or modified without Equity's written consent. It is therefore significant that Paragraph 7 of the Equity rules extends the binding effect of contracts beyond their signatories:

> All contracts of employment signed pursuant to these Rules are binding not only upon the signers on the face thereof, but upon any and all corporations, co-partnerships, enterprises and/or groups which said signers or each of them directs, controls, or is interested in, and are hereby agreed to be adopted as their contract by each of them.

By virtue of that clause, the run of the play contract is unquestionably binding upon Taylor and Bufman as producers, but that fact is of limited import, because the pay or play guarantee that this suit seeks to enforce does not appear in the run of the play contract. For reasons stated later in this opinion, however, there was sufficient evidence from which the jury could find that the video agreement, which contains the pay or play guarantee, cross-references the run of the play contract, which in turn incorporates the Equity rules. The interlocking nature of the agreements and the Equity rules is further confirmed by the fact that the Equity agreement and rules prohibit the videotaping of any production in which members of Equity are employed without the express permission of Equity and without adhering to the terms and conditions established by Equity.

C. The Video Contract

The video contract, signed on behalf of Zev Bufman Entertainment, Inc., guarantees payment to This Is Me of the difference between $750,000 and the salary paid pursuant to the run of the play contract. The contract recites that it constitutes the parties' "full and binding agreement with respect to ... our proposed film and/or video recording of 'The Corn is Green,'" and that it is "intended to be executed concurrently with a 'Run of the Play' Actors Equity Association contract with respect to the Artist's services in a live stage production of the play." ...

When the contracts are read together in light of the other evidence, there are two entirely sufficient analyses that can support the jury verdict against Taylor and Bufman.

First, the video contract (which contains the $750,000 guarantee) cross-references the run of the play contract, which in turn expressly incorporates the Actors' Equity rules. And the run of the play contract, which does not say that it constitutes the parties' full and binding agreement, can be read to incorporate the video contract without contradicting its own express terms. Paragraph 9 of the run of the play contract provides that an individual who signs it in a representative capacity is also bound, and Paragraph 7 of the Equity rules extends the binding power of any employment agreement still further to any partnership or enterprise directed by the signatory. Thus the jury could have concluded that Zev Bufman's signature on the video contract on behalf of Zev Bufman Entertainment, Inc. also bound: (i) himself and (ii) the Elizabeth Theatre Group, an enterprise in which he was a partner. The jury could then further have assessed individual liability against Taylor as derivative of the Elizabeth Theatre Group's liability, because there was evidence (including Taylor's own statements to Tyson) from which the jury could conclude that Ms. Taylor was a partner in the Elizabeth Theatre Group.

Alternatively, the jury could have relied on the Security Agreement (read in conjunction with the run of the play contract and video contract). The Security Agreement provides that it applies to all "individual employment contracts," and defines such contracts as "any agreement of employment heretofore or hereafter entered into between an Actor and the Guarantor or Producer in relation to the Play." The pertinent inquiry under this theory is whether evidence was presented from which the jury reasonably could conclude: (i) that the video contract, in addition to the run of the play contract, was an agreement "in relation to the Play;" and (ii) that Taylor and Bufman fit the definition of producers....

For these reasons, the jury was free to find that Bufman and Taylor were producers, and that the video contract was an employment agreement made in relation to the play. The district court's view—that only the run of the play contract is a contract "in relation to the Play"—may be fairer, and better supported by evidence; but that is not for us to say. As long as there is some evidence based upon which the jury could have held Zev Bufman and Elizabeth Taylor individually liable, we must reinstate the verdict....

The judgment of the district court is reversed, and the jury's verdict reinstated.

H.A. Artists & Associates, Inc. v. Actors' Equity Ass'n
451 U.S. 704 (1981)

JUSTICE STEWART delivered the opinion of the Court.

The respondent Actors' Equity Association (Equity) is a union representing the vast majority of stage actors and actresses in the United States. It enters into collective-bargaining agreements with theatrical producers that specify minimum wages and other terms and conditions of employment for those whom it represents. The petitioners are independent theatrical agents who place actors and actresses in jobs with producers. The Court of Appeals for the Second Circuit held that the respondents' system of regulation of theatrical agents is immune from antitrust liability by reason of the statutory labor exemption from the antitrust laws. We granted certiorari to consider the availability of that exemption in the circumstances presented by this case.

Equity is a national union that has represented stage actors and actresses since early in this century. Currently representing approximately 23,000 actors and actresses, it has collective-bargaining agreements with virtually all major theatrical producers in New York City, on and off Broadway, and with most other theatrical producers throughout the United States. The terms negotiated with producers are the minimum conditions of employment (called "scale"); an actor or actress is free to negotiate wages or terms more favorable than the collectively bargained minima.

Theatrical agents are independent contractors who negotiate contracts and solicit employment for their clients. The agents do not participate in the negotiation of collective-bargaining agreements between Equity and the theatrical producers. If an agent succeeds in obtaining employment for a client, he receives a commission based on a percentage of the client's earnings. Agents who operate in New York City must be licensed as employment agencies and are regulated by the New York City Department of Consumer Affairs pursuant to New York law, which provides that the maximum commission a theatrical agent may charge his client is 10% of the client's compensation.

In 1928, concerned with the high unemployment rates in the legitimate theater and the vulnerability of actors and actresses to abuses by theatrical agents, including the extraction of high commissions that tended to undermine collectively bargained rates of compensation, Equity unilaterally established a licensing system for the regulation of agents. The regulations permitted Equity members to deal only with those agents who obtained Equity licenses and thereby agreed to meet the conditions of representation prescribed by Equity. Those members who dealt with nonlicensed agents were subject to union discipline.

The system established by the Equity regulations was immediately challenged. In *Edelstein v. Gillmore*, 35 F.2d 723 [(2d. Cir. 1929)], the Court of Appeals for the Second Circuit concluded that the regulations were a lawful effort to improve the employment conditions of Equity members. In an opinion written by Judge Swan and joined by Judge Augustus N. Hand, the court said:

> "The evils of unregulated employment agencies (using this term broadly to include also the personal representative) are set forth in the defendants' affidavits and are corroborated by common knowledge.... Hence the requirement that, as a condition to writing new business with Equity's members, old contracts with its members must be made to conform to the new standards, does not seem to us to justify an inference that the primary purpose of the requirement is infliction of injury upon plaintiff, and other personal representatives in a similar situation, rather than the protection of the supposed interests of Equity's members. *The terms they insist upon are calculated to secure from personal representatives better and more impartial service, at uniform and cheaper rates, and to improve conditions of employment of actors by theater managers.* Undoubtedly the defendants intend to compel the plaintiff to give up rights under existing contracts which do not conform to the new standards set up by Equity, but, as already indicated, *their motive in so doing is to benefit themselves and their fellow actors in the economic struggle.* The financial loss to plaintiff is incidental to this purpose."

The essential elements of Equity's regulation of theatrical agents have remained unchanged since 1928. A member of Equity is prohibited, on pain of union discipline, from using an agent who has not, through the mechanism of obtaining an Equity license (called a "franchise"), agreed to comply with the regulations. The most important of the regulations requires that a licensed agent must renounce any right to take a commission on an employment contract under which an actor or actress receives scale wages.[1] To the extent a contract includes provisions under which an actor or actress will sometimes receive scale pay—for rehearsals or "chorus" employment, for example—and sometimes more, the regulations deny the agent any commission on the scale portions of the contract. Licensed agents are also precluded from taking commissions on out-of-town expense money paid to their clients. Moreover, commissions are limited on wages within 10% of scale pay, and an agent must allow his client to terminate a representation contract if the agent is not successful in procuring employment within a specified period. Finally, agents are required to pay franchise fees to Equity. The fee is $200 for the initial franchise, $60 a year thereafter for each agent, and $40 for any subagent working in the office of another. These fees are deposited by Equity in its general treasury and are not segregated from other union funds.

In 1977, after a dispute between Equity and Theatrical Artists Representatives Associates (TARA)—a trade association representing theatrical agents—a group of agents, including the petitioners, resigned from TARA because of TARA's decision to abide by Equity's regulations. These agents also informed Equity that they would not accept Equity's regulations, or apply for franchises. The petitioners instituted this lawsuit in May 1978, contending that Equity's regulations of theatrical agents violated §§ 1 and 2 of the Sherman Act, 26 Stat. 209, as amended, 15 U.S.C. §§ 1 and 2....

Labor unions are lawful combinations that serve the collective interests of workers, but they also possess the power to control the character of competition in an industry. Accordingly, there is an inherent tension between national antitrust policy, which seeks to maximize competition, and national labor policy, which encourages cooperation among workers to improve the conditions of employment. In the years immediately following passage of the Sherman Act, courts enjoined strikes as unlawful restraints of trade when a union's conduct or objectives were deemed "socially or economically harmful." In response to these practices, Congress acted, first in the Clayton Act, and later in the Norris-LaGuardia Act, to immunize labor unions and labor disputes from challenge under the Sherman Act.

---

1. The minimum, or "scale," wage varies. In August 1977, for example, the minimum weekly salary was $335 for Broadway performances, and $175 for performances off Broadway. Scale wages are set by a collective-bargaining agreement between Equity and the producers, to which the agents are not parties. When an agent represents an actor or actress whose professional reputation is not sufficient to demand a salary higher than scale, the agent hopes to develop a relationship that will become continually more remunerative as the performer's professional reputation grows, and with it the power to demand an ever higher salary. No agent is required to represent an actor or actress whom he does not wish to represent.

Section 6 of the Clayton Act, 15 U.S.C. § 17, declares that human labor "is not a commodity or article of commerce," and immunizes from antitrust liability labor organizations and their members "lawfully carrying out" their "legitimate [objectives]." Section 20 of the Act prohibits injunctions against specified employee activities, such as strikes and boycotts, that are undertaken in the employees' self-interest and that occur in the course of disputes "concerning terms or conditions of employment," and states that none of the specified acts can be "held to be [a] [violation] of any law of the United States." This protection is re-emphasized and expanded in the Norris-La-Guardia Act, which prohibits federal-court injunctions against single or organized employees engaged in enumerated activities, and specifically forbids such injunctions notwithstanding the claim of an unlawful combination or conspiracy. While the Norris-LaGuardia Act's bar of federal-court labor injunctions is not explicitly phrased as an exemption from the antitrust laws, it has been interpreted broadly as a statement of congressional policy that the courts must not use the antitrust laws as a vehicle to interfere in labor disputes.

In *United States v. Hutcheson,* 312 U.S. 219, the Court held that labor unions acting in their self-interest and not in combination with nonlabor groups enjoy a statutory exemption from Sherman Act liability.... The Court explained that this exemption derives not only from the Clayton Act, but also from the Norris-LaGuardia Act, particularly its definition of a "labor dispute," in which Congress "reasserted the original purpose of the Clayton Act by infusing into it the immunized trade union activities as redefined by the later Act." Thus under *Hutcheson,* no federal injunction may issue over a "labor dispute," and "§ 20 [of the Clayton Act] removes all such allowable conduct from the taint of being a 'violation of any law of the United States,' including the Sherman [Act]."

The statutory exemption does not apply when a union combines with a "non-labor group." Accordingly, antitrust immunity is forfeited when a union combines with one or more employers in an effort to restrain trade. In *Allen Bradley Co. v. Electrical Workers,* 325 U.S. 797, for example, the Court held that a union had violated the Sherman Act when it combined with manufacturers and contractors to erect a sheltered local business market in order "to bar all other business men from [the market], and to charge the public prices above a competitive level." The Court indicated that the union efforts would, standing alone, be exempt from antitrust liability, but because the union had not acted unilaterally, the exemption was denied. Congress "intended to outlaw business monopolies. A business monopoly is no less such because a union participates, and such participation is a violation of the Act."

Court of Appeals properly recognized that the threshold issue was to determine whether or not Equity's franchising of agents involved any combination between Equity and any "non-labor groups," or persons who are not "parties to a labor dispute." And the court's conclusion that the trial court had not been clearly erroneous in its finding that there was no combination between Equity and the theatrical producers to create or maintain the franchise system is amply supported by the record.

The more difficult problem is whether the combination between Equity and the agents who agreed to become franchised was a combination with a "nonlabor group."

The answer to this question is best understood in light of *Musicians v. Carroll,* 391 U.S. 99. There, four orchestra leaders, members of the American Federation of Musicians, brought an action based on the Sherman Act challenging the union's unilateral system of regulating "club dates," or one-time musical engagements. These regulations, *inter alia,* enforced a closed shop; required orchestra leaders to engage a minimum number of "sidemen," or instrumentalists; prescribed minimum prices for local engagements;[2] prescribed higher minimum prices for traveling orchestras; and permitted leaders to deal only with booking agents licensed by the union.

Without disturbing the finding of the Court of Appeals that the orchestra leaders were employers and independent contractors, the Court concluded that they were nonetheless a "labor group" and parties to a "labor dispute" within the meaning of the Norris-LaGuardia Act, and thus that their involvement in the union regulatory scheme was not an unlawful combination between "labor" and "nonlabor" groups. The Court agreed with the trial court that the applicable test was whether there was "job or wage competition or some other economic interrelationship affecting legitimate union interests between the union members and the independent contractors."

The Court also upheld the restrictions on booking agents, who were *not* involved in job or wage competition with union members. Accordingly, these restrictions had to meet the "other economic interrelationship" branch of the disjunctive test quoted above. And the test was met because those restrictions were " 'at least as intimately bound up with the subject of wages'... as the price floors." The Court noted that the booking agent restrictions had been adopted, in part, because agents had "charged exorbitant fees, and booked engagements for musicians at wages ... below union scale."

The restrictions challenged by the petitioners in this case are very similar to the agent restrictions upheld in the *Carroll* case. The essential features of the regulatory scheme are identical: members are permitted to deal only with agents who have agreed (1) to honor their fiduciary obligations by avoiding conflicts of interest, (2) not to charge excessive commissions, and (3) not to book members for jobs paying less than the union minimum. And as in *Carroll,* Equity's regulation of agents developed in response to abuses by employment agents who occupy a critical role in the relevant labor market. The agent stands directly between union members and jobs, and is in a powerful position to evade the union's negotiated wage structure.

The peculiar structure of the legitimate theater industry, where work is intermittent, where it is customary if not essential for union members to secure employment

---

2. These consisted of a minimum scale for sidemen, a "leader's fee," which was twice the sidemen's scale in orchestras of at least four, and an additional 8% for social security, unemployment insurance, and other expenses. In addition, if a leader did not appear but designated a subleader, and four or more musicians performed, the leader was required to pay from his leader's fee 1.5 times the sidemen's scale to the subleader.

through agents, and where agents' fees are calculated as a percentage of a member's wage, makes it impossible for the union to defend even the integrity of the minimum wages it has negotiated without regulation of agency fees.

The Court of Appeals found that "the union *cannot* eliminate wage competition among its members without regulation of the fees of the agents." Wage competition is prevented not only by the rule precluding commissions on scale jobs. Actors and actresses could also compete over the percentage of their wages they were willing to cede to an agent, subject only to the restrictions imposed by state law.

The regulations are "brought within the labor exemption [because they are] necessary to assure that scale wages will be paid...." They "embody ... a direct frontal attack upon a problem thought to threaten the maintenance of the basic wage structure." Agents must, therefore, be considered a "labor group," and their controversy with Equity is plainly a "labor dispute" as defined in the Norris-LaGuardia Act: "representation of persons in negotiating, fixing, maintaining, changing, or seeking to arrange terms or conditions of employment, regardless of whether or not the disputants stand in the proximate relation of employer and employee."

Agents perform a function—the representation of union members in the sale of their labor—that in most nonentertainment industries is performed exclusively by unions. In effect, Equity's franchise system operates as a substitute for maintaining a hiring hall as the representative of its members seeking employment.

Finally, Equity's regulations are clearly designed to promote the union's legitimate self-interest. In a case such as this, where there is no direct wage or job competition between the union and the group it regulates, the *Carroll* formulation to determine the presence of a nonlabor group—whether there is " 'some ... economic interrelationship affecting legitimate union interests ...' "

The question remains whether the fees that Equity levies upon the agents who apply for franchises are a permissible component of the exempt regulatory system. We have concluded that Equity's justification for these fees is inadequate. Conceding that *Carroll* did not sanction union extraction of franchise fees from agents, Equity suggests, only in the most general terms, that the fees are somehow related to the basic purposes of its regulations: elimination of wage competition, upholding of the union wage scale, and promotion of fair access to jobs. But even assuming that the fees no more than cover the costs of administering the regulatory system, this is simply another way of saying that without the fees, the union's regulatory efforts would not be subsidized—and that the dues of Equity's members would perhaps have to be increased to offset the loss of a general revenue source. If Equity did not impose these franchise fees upon the agents, there is no reason to believe that any of its legitimate interests would be affected....

For the reasons stated, the judgment of the Court of Appeals is affirmed in part and reversed in part, and the case is remanded for proceedings consistent with this opinion.

It is so ordered.

Makarova v. United States

201 F.3d 110 (2d Cir. 2000)

In 1982, Natalia Makarova was injured when a piece of scenery fell on her shoulder at the Kennedy Center for the Performing Arts in Washington, D.C. At the time of the injury, Makarova was performing in a production of the musical "On Your Toes," and a witness for Makarova asserts that she was widely regarded as the world's best prima ballerina.

The Kennedy Center was the producer of "On Your Toes." As producer, it: (1) contracted with the estates of the musical's authors for the right to "produce and present" the show; (2) contracted directly with the director and stage manager; (3) arranged a letter of credit for bond coverage for the show; (4) paid performers throughout the Washington, D.C. run of the show; and (5) maintained workers' compensation coverage for the show's performers and workers.

The contract for Makarova's services was between the Kennedy Center, as producer, and "NMK Productions, Inc. f/s/o Natalia Makarova." NMK Productions, Inc. was Makarova's "personal services corporation," and the term "f/s/o" means "for the services of."

Makarova personally signed a rider to the contract, certifying "that she [had] read and approved all the terms and conditions of said contract, and agreed to perform her services, as performing actress in 'On Your Toes', in accordance with said contract and the Rules of the Actors' Equity Association ... *as though the undersigned had entered into this contract*" (emphasis added). The rider further provided that Makarova would "perform services hereunder in accordance with the terms and conditions of Actors' Equity Association's Standard Run-of-the-Play Contract," which incorporated by reference a standardized set of protocols called the "Agreement and Rules Governing Employment" ("Agreement and Rules").

The incorporated Agreement and Rules provided that the "producer agrees to obtain and maintain Workmen's Compensation Insurance Coverage for all Actors ... in his employ." The Agreement and Rules also included a choice of law provision for employment contracts stating that "all contracts of employment shall be subject to, be construed by, and all the rights of the parties thereto shall be determined by the laws of the State of New York."

Her contract required Makarova to: (1) play a specific part in the musical; (2) maintain a contractually specified rehearsal and performance schedule; (3) have her hair styled in accord with the time period of the show; (4) wear shoes and make-up provided by the Kennedy Center; and (5) provide her exclusive services to the Kennedy Center during the term of the contract.

The Kennedy Center ("United States") is part of the Smithsonian Institution, which is owned and operated by the federal government. In 1984, Makarova filed a federal administrative claim against the Kennedy Center for her injuries. In 1997, thirteen years later, Makarova filed a civil suit against the United States pursuant to the Federal Tort Claims Act, 28 U.S.C. § 1346 (1994) ("FTCA"), in the United States District Court for the Southern District of New York (Preska, J.). Makarova claimed that the United States government was responsible for the injuries that she sustained during her fateful performance....

It is undisputed that the Kennedy Center is an entity of the United States government. However, "the United States, as sovereign, is immune from suit save as it consents to be sued..., and the terms of its consent to be sued in any court define that court's jurisdiction to entertain the suit." The doctrine of sovereign immunity is jurisdictional in nature, and therefore to prevail, the plaintiff bears the burden of establishing that her claims fall within an applicable waiver. The FTCA waives the government's sovereign immunity only for:

> claims against the United States, for money damages ... for injury or loss of property, or personal injury or death caused by the negligent or wrongful act or omission of any employee of the Government while acting within the scope of his office or employment, under circumstances where the United States, if a private person, would be liable to the claimant in accordance with the law of the place where the act or omission occurred.

Both parties concede that the FTCA governs Makarova's complaint, and that, accordingly, subject matter jurisdiction exists only if a private defendant could have been sued by Makarova in Washington, D.C. — "the place where the act or omission occurred."

Under the FTCA, courts are bound to apply the law of the state (or here, the district) where the accident occurred. Under District of Columbia law, the exclusive remedy for an "employee" seeking damages from her employer for a work-related injury is the District Workers' Compensation Act. If Makarova was an "employee" of the Kennedy Center, then her remedy lay with the District of Columbia Workers' Compensation Act and not the FTCA.

Pointing to the choice of law provision in the contract, the United States argues, and the district court found, that the question of whether Makarova was an "employee" is governed by New York law.

For her part, Makarova contends that the contract's choice of law provision should not be triggered until we first determine under District of Columbia law whether she was a party to an "employment contract." She also maintains, that in any event, she was not an "employee" of the Kennedy Center under either New York or District of Columbia law....

Under New York law, "there is no absolute rule for determining whether one is an independent contractor or an employee." However, the typical test of whether one is an independent contractor lies in the control exercised by the employer, and in who has the right to direct what will be done and when and how it will be done.

Applying these principles, Makarova was an "employee" rather than an independent contractor. She was: (1) required to play a specific part in a specific musical; (2) required to meet a contractually specified rehearsal and performance schedule; (3) contractually obligated to have her hair styled in accord with the time period of the show; (4) required to wear shoes and make-up provided by the Kennedy Center; and (5) obligated to provide her exclusive services to the Kennedy Center during the term of her contract. Although Makarova had a significant say over her own dancing and acting, the director and the Kennedy Center maintained artistic control over the show, including Makarova's performance.

Indeed, New York courts have repeatedly found performance artists to be "employees." A performer who has entered into a written contract with a producer for a stipulated sum and a time certain, with the time and place of work to be determined by the producer, has been held to be the producer's "employee." As long as the employer exercises control over such aspects of the workers' employment as the dates and times of performances and the work to be performed, New York law would appear to treat him or her as an employee. The Kennedy Center exercised sufficient control over Makarova to render her an employee as a matter of New York law.

Under District of Columbia law, an "employee" is "every person ... in the service of another under any contract of hire or apprenticeship, written or implied, in the District of Columbia."

Makarova satisfied this definition. She is a person, who was "in the service of another," performing for the Kennedy Center in the District of Columbia. Makarova was also "under a contract of hire," having agreed to play a specific role in "On Your Toes" for a specific amount of time.

The Kennedy Center also qualified as Makarova's "employer" under the District of Columbia Workers' Compensation Act, because it was an "individual, firm, association, or corporation ... using the service of another for pay." The Kennedy Center was the producer of "On Your Toes," and paid Makarova to perform in it....

Moreover, there are equitable considerations compelling the conclusion that Makarova was an "employee" of the Kennedy Center—she had earlier accepted the benefits of being one. On that occasion, Makarova hurt her chin during a rehearsal. Part of the medical treatment that she received for that injury was paid for by the Kennedy Center's workers' compensation insurer, which covered the Kennedy Center's "Players, Entertainers or Musicians" and "all other employees." Having accepted the workers' compensation benefits of being a Kennedy Center employee, Makarova cannot now argue that she should be free of the strictures of that same workers' compensation regime.

Makarova maintains that she was paid by the Kennedy Center as an independent contractor. The evidence of this, however, is equivocal. It is unclear whether Makarova was paid as an independent contractor, an employee, or both, because the Kennedy Center's payroll records prior to 1983 are not in the record. In 1983, after she had rejoined the cast of "On Your Toes" while it was touring, Makarova was listed haphazardly as both an "independent contractor" and a "regular employee" by the Kennedy Center. Makarova did receive an IRS form 1099 in 1982, listing $1275.00 in "nonemployee compensation." However, that amount represented less than her salary from the Kennedy Center for a single two-week pay period. Such a modest sum of "nonemployee compensation" does not establish whether Makarova was classified by the Kennedy Center as an employee or an independent contractor for its payroll purposes. In any event, the occasional characterization of Makarova as an independent contractor in the Kennedy Center's records would be insufficient to classify her under either New York or District of Columbia law as an independent contractor rather than an employee.

Makarova tenders other considerations which she believes make her an independent contractor, including the argument that she was a "star," which somehow apparently makes her something less of an employee. None of these arguments are persuasive. We conclude that Makarova was an employee of the Kennedy Center and, as such, was covered by its workers' compensation insurance. She could not have brought suit against a private employer in Washington, D.C., and therefore, under the FTCA, she could not have done so against the government.

For the foregoing reasons, the district court did not err when it granted the government's motion to dismiss Makarova's complaint.... Accordingly, we AFFIRM the grant of appellee's motion for dismissal for lack of subject matter jurisdiction.

Gennaro v. Rosenfield

600 F. Supp. 485 (S.D.N.Y 1984)

In the eyes of many, Hollywood's heyday was the era of the musical, often based on the Broadway show. One of the preeminent films of that era, "Singin' In The Rain," starred Gene Kelly, Debbie Reynolds, and Donald O'Connor. This litigation concerns an apparently new phenomenon—the proposed stage adaptation of that now legendary film.

The plaintiffs, Peter Gennaro, and his company, Geannie Productions, Inc., allege that Mr. Gennaro has contracted to choreograph the proposed Broadway production of "Singin' In The Rain" for the defendant, Maurice Rosenfield. The plaintiffs claim that the defendant has breached this contract and, therefore, seek damages for breach of contract and defamation. Presently before the Court is the plaintiffs' motion for a preliminary injunction which, in essence, would prevent the defendant from engaging any other choreographer pending the outcome of the litigation. The Court must deny this motion for the reasons stated below.

The individual plaintiff, Peter Gennaro, is a choreographer and dancer. He has choreographed a number of well-known Broadway musicals, including "Fiorello," "The Unsinkable Molly Brown," and "Annie" (for which he won a Tony Award). Mr. Gennaro is also the president of the corporate plaintiff, Geannie Productions, Inc. The defendants, Maurice and Lois Rosenfield, are husband and wife. Mr. Rosenfield is a Broadway producer. Among his credits are the 1980 Broadway musical "Barnum" and the 1983 revival of Tennessee Williams's "The Glass Menagerie." In 1980, Mr. Rosenfield acquired the right to adapt "Singin' In The Rain" for stage presentation from Metro-Goldwyn-Mayer and Robbins Music Company. Rosenfield subsequently granted a license to Harold Fielding for the London production of "Singin' In The Rain."

The events giving rise to the instant controversy commenced in November 1980, when Ian Bevan, a British theatrical agent and manager, contacted Mr. Gennaro's agent and attorney, Robert M. Cavallo. According to Mr. Cavallo, Mr. Bevan said that Mr. Fielding wanted Peter Gennaro to choreograph the London production. Mr. Cavallo relayed this offer to Mr. Gennaro, who allegedly said that he would agree to choreograph the London production only on the condition that he also receive the option to choreograph any first-class stage production of "Singin' In The Rain" in the United States, including any Broadway production. Mr. Gennaro alleges that Mr. Bevan proceeded to negotiate with Mr. Cavallo for Mr. Gennaro's services and with Mr. Rosenfield to obtain the desired option. The plaintiff further alleges that an agreement was reached on both counts and that the option agreement was embodied in a January 20, 1983, letter signed by both Bevan and Rosenfield.

On February 2, 1983, Mr. Fielding forwarded a copy of the January 20 letter to Mr. Gennaro along with his own letter confirming an agreement between himself and Mr. Gennaro. According to this letter, Mr. Bevan had "negotiated conditions for [Mr. Gennaro to choreograph] the American and other first-class productions of "Singin' In The Rain" which [would] be separately confirmed to [Mr. Gennaro] by the American producer, Mr. Maurice Rosenfield." On April 5, 1983, Ronald Taft, Mr. Rosenfield's attorney, forwarded a draft contract to Mr. Cavallo and requested Mr. Cavallo's comments. According to Mr. Rosenfield, this contract concerned both the London and American productions. Mr. Gennaro maintains that the April 5 draft only concerned the London production. For unknown reasons, Mr. Cavallo informed Mr. Taft that he would not comment on the draft. At the same time, Mr. Cavallo was negotiating with Mr. Fielding. On April 14, 1984, Harold Fielding, Ltd. and Geannie Productions, Inc. entered into a written agreement with regard to Mr. Gennaro's role in the London production. Mr. Gennaro alleges that this agreement formalized the January 20 letter with respect to the American production.

In early June, Mr. Rosenfield visited Mr. Cavallo in his New York office. Precisely what transpired at that meeting is unclear. Soon thereafter, Mr. Cavallo sent Mr. Taft a letter commenting on the April 5 draft. There were no further discussions about that document.

The London production opened on June 30, 1983, and is still running. Mr. Gennaro has met twice with Mr. and Mrs. Rosenfield since the opening, once in June 1983, and again in December 1983. Precisely what was said at those meetings is also in dispute.

During the summer of 1984, Mr. Cavallo heard that the American production of "Singin' In The Rain" was being planned and that the plans did not involve Peter Gennaro. On September 17, 1984, Mr. Cavallo sent a mailgram to Mr. Rosenfield advising him that Mr. Gennaro had elected to exercise the option to choreograph the American production. On September 20, 1984, Mr. Taft responded for Mr. Rosenfield in a letter that stated, "Mr. Rosenfield has not asked Mr. Gennaro whether he would like to choreograph the production of "Singin' In The Rain" which Mr. Rosenfield plans to produce in New York." The plaintiffs then brought the instant action by order to show cause seeking, *inter alia*, a preliminary negative injunction enjoining the defendants and their agents from

(a) producing any American first-class stage production of the musical "Singin' In The Rain" (the "American production") with choreography by any choreographer other than Peter Gennaro;

(b) entering into any contract for choreography of the American production with any choreographer other than Peter Gennaro;

(c) advertising, promoting or otherwise publicizing the American production, in print or any other media, whereby the actual or prospective choreography is represented as by any choreographer other than Peter Gennaro....

A court will grant preliminary injunctive relief if a plaintiff can show (a) irreparable harm and (b) either (1) likelihood of success on the merits or (2) sufficiently serious questions going to the merits to make them a fair ground for litigation and a balance of hardships tipping decidedly toward the party requesting the preliminary relief. Even if the plaintiffs have established irreparable harm, they have shown neither a likelihood of success on the merits, nor a balance of hardships tipping decidedly in their favor.

A. Irreparable Harm

An inadequate remedy at law is a necessary prerequisite to a showing of irreparable harm. Mr. Gennaro argues that he will continue to suffer two wrongs for which money damages will not compensate: harm to his reputation and erosion of his professional skills. While it may be that the harm to the plaintiff's reputation constitutes irreparable harm, we do not believe that erosion of his skills constitutes such harm.

Although courts recognize that atrophy of professional skills could constitute irreparable harm, we are aware of only one case finding that, under the facts established, such atrophy constitutes irreparable harm. In that case, *Neeld v. American Hockey League*, 439 F. Supp. 459 (W.D.N.Y. 1977), the court found that a young hockey player would suffer irreparable harm were he denied the right to play professional hockey during the pendency of his lawsuit challenging certain league restrictions that would have prevented him from playing.... Mr. Gennaro argues that the alleged breach of contract will limit his opportunities for work, thereby denying him the chance to develop and refine his skills. The plaintiff's situation, however, differs markedly from the young hockey player's in *Neeld*. The plaintiff, an established choreographer with a first class reputation, will not be denied the opportunity to embark on a promising artistic career. Nor are his skills likely to diminish or atrophy. Since he has already choreographed the London production, the Broadway production represents less than a unique opportunity to develop his skills. In addition, as a top flight choreographer, he is likely to gain other work during the time he would be choreographing "Singin' In The Rain." Thus, we decline to follow *Neeld*. The plaintiff has not established that his skills will diminish so as to cause him irreparable harm.

Mr. Gennaro also asserts that his reputation has been irreparably harmed. In his words,

> The world of theatre is small, and its every event is illuminated by the bright spotlight of public curiosity. Reputations which have been built up over many years can be torn apart overnight when it appears that other artists are more desirable. Colleagues have been asking me why I was "replaced" as choreographer for the American production. The situation is painfully embarrassing to me and is severely damaging the first-class reputation and professional credibility I have worked so hard to establish over so many years. I have no traditional monetary remedy, since no amount of money can fully compensate me for this injury; indeed, its subtle effects can never be fully known.

Several cases from this circuit establish that damage to reputation often constitutes irreparable injury and justifies injunctive relief.... Peter Gennaro has worked for many years to establish a reputation as a first class choreographer. His reputation is of great commercial value to him. The apparent replacement of the plaintiff could damage his reputation in the theatre community. Those who had thought Mr. Gennaro would choreograph the production may now hold him in lower esteem. As the plaintiffs correctly point out, such damage to reputation is difficult if not impossible to measure in money terms.

On the other hand, show business arrangements often take into account considerations other than artistic merit. One bad review cannot tarnish the image of an established artist such as Peter Gennaro. Theatre people may well find fault with Mr. Rosenfield in this situation — particularly in light of the success of the London production. This situation resembles that where a baseball manager replaces the starting pitcher in the late innings despite the fact that he is pitching a shut out and has a comfortable lead. If the relief pitcher fails, the manager looks terrible.

B. The Likelihood of Success on the Merits

Setting aside the question of irreparable harm, we next consider whether the plaintiffs have demonstrated a likelihood of success on the merits. We conclude that they have not.

The nub of this case is a dispute over whether Mr. Rosenfield ever contracted with Mr. Gennaro. In determining whether a contract exists, the objective intent of the parties as manifested by their expressed words and deeds at the time of the alleged contract controls. If the parties' expressions and conduct would lead a reasonable person to determine that they intended to reach a binding agreement, their agreement will be enforced.

Mr. Gennaro asserts that the January 20 letter from Ian Bevan to Maurice Rosenfield countersigned by Mr. Rosenfield, standing alone, constitutes a binding contract. That letter states, in part:

> I write to record the heads of agreement I have reached on your behalf in negotiations with Mr. Robert M. Cavallo ... for the services of Mr. Peter Gennaro as choreographer for the above production [("Singin' In The Rain")].

His services have been engaged by Harold Fielding Ltd. for the London production.... Subject to that production running not less than 100 consecutive performances, you undertake to offer Mr. Gennaro a contract to choreograph the first American and/or Broadway production....

This letter is to record in "heads of agreement" style the basic terms agreed between you and Mr. Gennaro, which terms will now be converted into a formal document or documents in such form as shall be to the approval of your respective legal advisers. By our respective signatures to this letter we confirm to each other and to Mr. Gennaro that the basic terms to be incorporated into the formal documentation are those outlined in this letter.

The letter further specified Gennaro's fee and his share of the royalties. No other terms were detailed.

Acknowledging that this letter contemplated more formal documentation, the plaintiffs nevertheless contend that it constitutes a binding agreement. They rely on authority to the effect that a letter containing the essential terms of a contract may create a binding obligation although the parties may have contemplated executing a more formal agreement at a later date. The plaintiffs argue that the evidence conclusively establishes that the parties intended the January 20 letter to be a contract. The plaintiffs point out that the letter contained the material financial terms of the deal and that Mr. Gennaro's agent made it known to Mr. Fielding that Mr. Gennaro would not choreograph the London production unless he had an option to choreograph the Broadway production. To buttress this position, Mr. Cavallo and Mr. Gennaro also offer their recollection of several conversations with Mr. Rosenfield allegedly confirming the agreement. The plaintiffs also submit a letter from Mr. Bevan that purports to support their position. Standing alone, their evidence might establish the likelihood of success on the merits.

However, the defendants make a number of points in rebuttal. They thus make clear that whether the January 20 letter is a contract is, at most, a serious question going to the merits and a fair ground for litigation.

The defendants first argue that the behavior of the parties subsequent to January 20, 1983, indicated their intention *not* to be bound by the January 20 letter. They also take issue with the plaintiffs' characterization of the January 20 letter. According to the defendants, "the January 20 letter is not a contract because it expressly provides that it is to be followed by a detailed agreement to be crafted and approved by counsel and to contain additional terms." "[Such] an agreement ... does not bind the parties until such documentation and approval are accomplished." ... Whether the parties intended to contract is a serious question for the factfinder.

The defendants also claim that the January 20 letter is not sufficiently definite to constitute a binding agreement. Under the general principles of contract law, there can be no contract if the parties fail to agree on all the essential terms. The January 20, 1983, letter specifies only the fee and royalty terms. Mr. Cavallo asserts that this accords with industry practice, an assertion that the defendants vigorously dispute.

We are not sure who has the better of this dispute, but we are certain that the plaintiffs have not demonstrated that they are likely to prevail.

The plaintiffs also argue that, even if the January 20 letter is too indefinite to constitute a contract, the April 14 long form agreement between Geannie Productions, Inc. and Harold Fielding Ltd. is sufficiently definite. This detailed agreement contains the essential terms necessary for a binding contract. However, the defendants argue that Fielding lacked actual or apparent authority to bind Rosenfield. In rebuttal, the plaintiffs argue that, even if Fielding lacked actual authority, he had apparent authority. The *Restatement (Second) of the Law of Agency* § 8 defines apparent authority as "the power to affect the legal relations of another person by transactions with third persons, professedly as agent for the other, arising from and in accordance with the other's manifestations to such third persons." According to Mr. Gennaro, Mr. Rosenfield manifested Mr. Fielding's authority in his January 20 letter. The defendants, of course, reject this contention. They claim that the plaintiffs have alleged no act by Mr. Rosenfield whereby he conferred authority upon Mr. Fielding to act as his agent or whereby he communicated that authority to Mr. Gennaro or Mr. Cavallo. Again, the facts are so vague that to draw any conclusion with regard to the likelihood of either side prevailing on the authority issue is impossible....

The foregoing discussion leaves no doubt that the plaintiffs have not established the likelihood of success on the merits. There exist too many unresolved factual questions to justify any such conclusion.

C. The Balance of Hardships

Given our conclusion regarding the likelihood of success on the merits, we may grant the requested relief only if the plaintiff can "show that the harm which he would suffer from the denial of his motion is 'decidedly' greater than the harm which [the defendants] would suffer if the motion was granted." In this case, the balance of hardships does not tip decidedly in favor of the plaintiffs. We therefore decline to grant the requested relief.

If the motion is denied, the plaintiffs may suffer some additional irreparable harm. However, even if we accept Mr. Gennaro's assertion of irreparable harm, most of the damage to his reputation has already been done. No doubt, if we grant the requested relief, a group of individuals who would otherwise learn of Mr. Gennaro's alleged dismissal will remain uninformed (assuming the defendants choose to go ahead with the production). A denial of injunctive relief will harm the plaintiff's reputation among this group. However, the plaintiff's primary concern is his reputation among those in the theatre industry. That group is well informed, and has by now learned of this controversy. Thus, the denial of injunctive relief will do little to mitigate the total harm the plaintiff will suffer as a result of his alleged replacement.

On the other hand, should we grant the requested relief, the defendants will have two choices. They may hire Mr. Gennaro, or abandon the production. Abandonment, while not unrealistic—given the assertions to this effect in Mr. Rosenfield's papers— would constitute self-inflicted harm. We do not believe such harm is cognizable or relevant to our determination. Assuming Mr. Rosenfield opts to have Mr. Gennaro choreograph his production, Mr. Rosenfield would find himself in the uncomfortable position of working closely with someone whom he allegedly had replaced, had litigated against, and had no desire to work with. In addition, Mr. Rosenfield would be forced to abandon any discussions or contract into which he might have already entered with another choreographer. He would then suffer the obvious consequences of such an action. In our view, the defendants will suffer at least as much if not more harm from a grant of injunctive relief than the plaintiffs will suffer from a denial.

Although our judgment about the relative harms each party would suffer is subjective, we think it clear that the plaintiff has failed to show that the balance of hardships tips decidedly in his favor. Therefore, we decline to grant the requested prohibitive injunctive relief.

The plaintiffs' motion for preliminary injunctive relief is denied. We will endeavor to schedule a trial of the factual issues as soon as the parties indicate that they have completed discovery and are ready. SO ORDERED.

Notes and Questions

a. The life of the stage actor remains a difficult one, with extremely high unemployment, long hours during rehearsal, and a high risk that a play may be closed within days of opening. The Equity agreements interpreted in *This is Me v. Taylor* remain standard for the industry. Central to these are the provisions that minimum weekly pay cannot be waived and that there is personal rather than merely corporate liability.

b. Productions such as *Phantom of the Opera* and *Cirque Du Soleil* are modern examples of the classic stage extravaganza. Flying actors and death-defying stunts are part of the allure. Nonetheless, the activities of actors are that of any other workers and therefore covered by worker's compensation insurance and limits on liability. *See Eckis v. Sea World Corp.*, 64 Cal. App. 3d 1 (Cal. App. 4th Dist. 1976) (injury "sustained while riding Shamu the Whale" limited to worker's compensation system, despite evidence that Sea World knew the whale would attack divers who did not wear wet suits and still asked Ms. Eckis to ride the whale wearing a bikini for publicity pictures).

c. Consider *Bailey v. Disney Worldwide Shared Services*, 950 N.Y.S.2d 607 (N.Y. Sup. Ct. 2012). The Court summarizes the accident and resulting litigation as follows:

> On May 20, 2008, plaintiff, Adrian Bailey, an actor performing in The Little Mermaid, a Broadway musical, walked out onto a bridge suspended 35-feet over the stage in order to get ready for his role in a matinee performance of the play. Trap doors on the bridge, known as the "Eric trap," after a character in the play who descends through the trap doors, had been left open after a pre-show test. Plaintiff fell through the open trap doors and suffered serious injuries. A backstage automation operator controlled the trap doors. The automation operator failed to look at the display monitors showing that the trap doors had not been closed after the pre-show check,

as he was playing a video game on his personal computer instead of checking the monitors.

Showman, pursuant to a purchasing agreement with Disney, built the bridge along with its trap doors. Niscon, which did not have a direct contractual relationship with Disney, provided the automation system, known as Raynok, that allowed the trap doors on the bridge to be remotely operated. Disney then sold the bridge to Buena Vista Theatrical Group, LTD (Buena Vista), another Disney entity which produced the Little Mermaid; Buena Vista was the employer of both plaintiff and the automation operator who failed to check his monitor. The Nederlander entities leased the theater used in The Little Mermaid and provided some union labor to the production, including a stage hand who was supposed to check the bridge before allowing actors on to it.

Plaintiff's allegations in the amended complaint and bill of particulars are made generally against all defendants. Plaintiff alleges that defendants are liable in negligence (first cause of action), as well as for breach of the warranties of fitness for a particular use (the second cause of action) and merchantability (the third cause of action); finally, plaintiff alleges that defendants are liable under a theory of strict products liability (fourth cause of action).

Which parties will be liable for the injuries, if any, sustained by the performer Adrian Bailey?

d. Because of the strength of the theatrical unions, this industry is generally better than most others in having its agreements in writing. A second aspect of this structure is that only a few of the many possible terms involving theatrical production are actually negotiable. Despite the express language of such contracts that they must be signed to be binding, does an oral promise to enter into an approved collective bargaining agreement serve to bind the parties? *See Elvin Associates v. Franklin,* 735 F. Supp. 1177 (S.D.N.Y. 1990) (Aretha Franklin agreed to appear in *Sing Mahalia Sing,* based on the life of Mahalia Jackson. The producer relied on oral promises and arranged the production. Franklin ultimately dropped out of the production as a result of her fear of flying and inability to travel.).

e. The hiring process for theatre is complicated by the very particular needs for each part, more general employment law, and the competing interests of directors, playwrights, and producers. Producers may be seeking marquee value; playwrights see the images of the actors who were in their imagination while writing; and directors need a cast which blends together and meets the director's vision. Noted director Harold Clurman wrote that "the writer, who contractually has the last word in the matter, must sometimes be persuaded that the actor the director wants is the right choice for a particular role." HAROLD CLURMAN, ON DIRECTING 66 (Fireside ed., 1997).

f. Federal employment antidiscrimination law under Title VII of the Civil Rights Act of 1964, generally prohibits all forms of discrimination in hiring. An exception exists, however, so that "[i]t shall not be an unlawful employment practice for an employer to hire and employ employees … on the basis of his religion, sex, or national origin in those certain instances where religion, sex, or national origin is a bona fide occupational qualification reasonably necessary to the normal operation of that particular business or enterprise.…" 42 U.S.C. § 2000e-2(e) (1994). Race is not included in the exception. To what extent would the courts be compelled to read race into the statute under First Amendment principles, or on a similar basis? Would the decision change based on whether the part was for a principal part rather than merely a chorus member?

g. Sometimes performers themselves become controversial. *See Redgrave v. Boston Symphony Orchestra, Inc.*, 855 F.2d 888, 904 (1988) (*en banc*). The Boston Symphony Orchestra found grudging legal support after it cancelled Vanessa Redgrave's performance in response to her support of the Palestine Liberation Organization.

h. Like every art form, some performances are only about the reward. Does an actor in a one-person show have any legitimate grounds to demand his right to be considered for a Tony Award? *See Mason v. American Theatre Wing*, 165 Misc. 2d 432, 627 N.Y.S.2d 539 (N.Y. Sup. Ct. 1995).

Problem 9-B

Based on the suggestions you provided to Bryce, *Juliet Prescott* has been added to the upcoming theatrical season of the Kernochan Theatre, a premiere LORT theatre in upper Manhattan. Bryce is serving as director for the production. Bryce has been paid $2,500 for three weeks of rehearsal, as well as the LORT minimums in the dual capacity of director and playwright.

Bryce was having a great time working with accomplished professional talent during the rehearsal. The creativity of the cast has resulted in Bryce's changing a good deal of the stage direction and even some of the script to capture the thoughts and suggestions of the cast.

Unfortunately, at the end of the second week of rehearsal, Bryce fell off a platform that had been constructed but not yet secured on the set. The theatre engineer has acknowledged that the platform should not have been available for use until it had been secured and has sent an apology to Bryce and Bryce's family.

From the hospital, you have received a telephone call. Bryce's mother wants Bryce to sue the theatre for the accident. Bryce is primarily concerned about keeping control of the production as director and playwright. Bryce wants the production to be postponed. While Bryce is hopeful the hospital stay will only last a few days, Bryce wants to know what will happen if the injury is much worse. Advise Bryce regarding (i) the potential to sue the theatre for negligence and (ii) the theatre's ability to continue to stage the play without Bryce, including the theatre's ability to modify the script. (You may find it helpful to preview the discussion involving the Approved Production Contract, below, on the question of modification of the script.)

C. Playwrights

1. The Approved Production Contract

In explaining the central tenets of the Approved Production Contract to potential member playwrights, the Dramatists Guild explains the agreements as follows:

The Guild maintains standard or model contracts for all levels of productions: First-Class/Broadway, regional, and smaller houses nationwide; plus other important model contracts such as commission agreements and collaboration agreements—the most comprehensive contracts in the world. Under these contracts:

- No additions, omissions, or alterations to your script may be made without your consent.
- You and the producer have the approval of the cast, director, and designers, and will confer on many elements of the production.
- The rights granted to the producer cease if you are not paid your royalties.
- You own the copyright and all other rights to the play.
- You reserve the right to control the play for all other performances and uses.

The influence provided to playwrights pursuant to these agreements cannot be understated. No other media allows the creative writer such authority and autonomy.

Perhaps the most striking aspect of the Approved Production Contract is that the provisions granting approval have no requirements of reasonability, while ensuring that no changes can be made without the author's approval.

Sections 8.01(b) and 8.01(c) provide that a dissatisfied producer can object to the playwright's position to the Dramatists Guild. While the Dramatists Guild can confer with the playwright, it "shall have no power to compel Author to agree to such change." Powerful contract language, indeed.

Childress v. Taylor
945 F.2d 500 (2d Cir. 1991)

This appeal requires consideration of the standards for determining when a contributor to a copyrighted work is entitled to be regarded as a joint author. The work in question is a play about the legendary Black comedienne Jackie "Moms" Mabley. The plaintiff-appellee Alice Childress claims to be the sole author of the play. Her claim is disputed by defendant-appellant Clarice Taylor, who asserts that she is a joint author of the play. Taylor, Paul B. Berkowsky, Ben Caldwell, and the "Moms" Company appeal from the February 21, 1991, judgment of the District Court for the Southern District of New York (Charles S. Haight, Jr., Judge) determining, on motion for summary judgment, that Childress is the sole author. We affirm.

Defendant Clarice Taylor has been an actress for over forty years, performing on stage, radio, television, and in film. After portraying "Moms" Mabley in a skit in an off-off-Broadway production ten years ago, Taylor became interested in developing a play based on Mabley's life. Taylor began to assemble material about "Moms" Mabley, interviewing her friends and family, collecting her jokes, and reviewing library resources.

In 1985, Taylor contacted the plaintiff, playwright Alice Childress, about writing a play based on "Moms" Mabley. Childress had written many plays, for one of which she won an "Obie" award. Taylor had known Childress since the 1940s when they were both associated with the American Negro Theatre in Harlem and had previously acted in a number of Childress's plays....

Taylor turned over all of her research material to Childress, and later did further research at Childress's request. It is undisputed that Childress wrote the play, entitled "Moms: A Praise Play for a Black Comedienne." However, Taylor, in addition to providing the research material, which according to her involved a process of sifting through facts and selecting pivotal and key elements to include in a play on "Moms" Mabley's life, also discussed with Childress the inclusion of certain general scenes and characters in the play. Additionally, Childress and Taylor spoke on a regular basis about the progress of the play....

Childress filed for and received a copyright for the play in her name. Taylor produced the play at the Green Plays Theatre in Lexington, New York, during the 1986 summer season and played the title role. After the play's run at the Green Plays Theatre, Taylor planned a second production of the play at the Hudson Guild Theatre in New York City.

At the time Childress agreed to the project, she did not have any firm arrangements with Taylor, although Taylor had paid her $2,500 before the play was produced. On May 9, 1986, Taylor's agent, Scott Yoselow, wrote to Childress's agent, Flora Roberts, stating:

> Per our telephone conversation, this letter will bring us up-to-date on the current status of our negotiation for the above mentioned project:
>
> 1. CLARICE TAYLOR will pay ALICE CHILDRESS for her playwriting services on the MOMS MABLEY PROJECT the sum of $5,000.00, which will also serve as an advance against any future royalties.
>
> 2. The finished play shall be equally owned and be the property of both CLARICE TAYLOR and ALICE CHILDRESS.
>
> It is my understanding that Alice has commenced writing the project. I am awaiting a response from you regarding any additional points we have yet to discuss.

Flora Roberts responded to Yoselow in a letter dated June 16, 1986:

> As per our recent telephone conversation, I have told Alice Childress that we are using your letter to me of May 9, 1986 as a partial memo preparatory to our future good faith negotiations for a contract. There are two points which I include herewith to complete your two points in the May 9th letter, i.e.:
>
> 1) The $5,000 advance against any future royalties being paid by Clarice Taylor to Alice Childress shall be paid as follows. Since $1,000 has already

been paid, $1,500 upon your receipt of this letter and the final $2,500 to be paid upon submission of the First Draft, but in no event later than July 7, 1986.

2) It is to be understood that pending the proper warranty clauses to be included in the contract, Miss Childress is claiming originality for her words only in said script....

In March 1987, Childress rejected the draft agreement proposed by Taylor, and the parties' relationship deteriorated. Taylor decided to mount another production of the play without Childress. Taylor hired Ben Caldwell to write another play featuring "Moms" Mabley; Taylor gave Caldwell a copy of the Childress script and advised him of elements that should be changed....

Taylor contended that she was a joint author with Childress, and therefore shared the rights to the play....

Co-authorship was well known to the common law. An early formulation, thought by Learned Hand to be the first definition of "joint authorship," [as] "a joint laboring in furtherance of a common design." Judge Hand endorsed that formulation in the District Court, concluding that the book for the comic opera "Sweethearts" was a work of joint authorship.... The [1976] Copyright Act defines a "joint work" as

> a work prepared by two or more authors with the intention that their contributions be merged into inseparable or interdependent parts of a unitary whole....

In common with many issues arising in the domain of copyrights, the determination of whether to recognize joint authorship in a particular case requires a sensitive accommodation of competing demands advanced by at least two persons, both of whom have normally contributed in some way to the creation of a work of value. Care must be taken to ensure that true collaborators in the creative process are accorded the perquisites of co-authorship and to guard against the risk that a sole author is denied exclusive authorship status simply because another person rendered some form of assistance. Copyright law best serves the interests of creativity when it carefully draws the bounds of "joint authorship" so as to protect the legitimate claims of both sole authors and co-authors.

Some aspects of the statutory definition of joint authorship are fairly straightforward. Parts of a unitary whole are "inseparable" when they have little or no independent meaning standing alone. That would often be true of a work of written text, such as the play that is the subject of the pending litigation. By contrast, parts of a unitary whole are "interdependent" when they have some meaning standing alone but achieve their primary significance because of their combined effect, as in the case of the words and music of a song....

The legislative history also clarifies other aspects of the statutory definition, but leaves some matters in doubt. Endeavoring to flesh out the definition, the committee reports state:

[A] work is "joint" if the authors collaborated with each other, or if *each* of the authors prepared his or her contribution with the knowledge and *intention* that it would be merged with the contributions of other authors as "inseparable or interdependent parts of a unitary whole." The touchstone here is the *intention, at the time the writing is done,* that the parts be absorbed or combined into an integrated unit....

This passage appears to state two alternative criteria—one focusing on the act of collaboration and the other on the parties' intent. However, it is hard to imagine activity that would constitute meaningful "collaboration" unaccompanied by the requisite intent on the part of both participants that their contributions be merged into a unitary whole, and the case law has read the statutory language literally so that the intent requirement applies to all works of joint authorship.

A more substantial issue arising under the statutory definition of "joint work" is whether the contribution of each joint author must be copyrightable or only the combined result of their joint efforts must be copyrightable....

The insistence on copyrightable contributions by all putative joint authors might serve to prevent some spurious claims by those who might otherwise try to share the fruits of the efforts of a sole author of a copyrightable work, even though a claim of having contributed copyrightable material could be asserted by those so inclined. More important, the prevailing view strikes an appropriate balance in the domains of both copyright and contract law. In the absence of contract, the copyright remains with the one or more persons who created copyrightable material. Contract law enables a person to hire another to create a copyrightable work, and the copyright law will recognize the employer as "author." Similarly, the person with non-copyrightable material who proposes to join forces with a skilled writer to produce a copyrightable work is free to make a contract to disclose his or her material in return for assignment of part ownership of the resulting copyright. And, as with all contract matters, the parties may minimize subsequent disputes by formalizing their agreement in a written contract.

It seems more consistent with the spirit of copyright law to oblige all joint authors to make copyrightable contributions, leaving those with non-copyrightable contributions to protect their rights through contract.

There remains for consideration the crucial aspect of joint authorship—the nature of the intent that must be entertained by each putative joint author at the time the contribution of each was created. The wording of the statutory definition appears to make relevant only the state of mind regarding the unitary nature of the finished work—an intention "that their contributions be merged into inseparable or interdependent parts of a unitary whole." However, an inquiry so limited would extend joint author status to many persons who are not likely to have been within the contemplation of Congress. For example, a writer frequently works with an editor who makes numerous useful revisions to the first draft, some of which will consist of additions of copyrightable expression. Both intend their contributions to be merged into inseparable parts of a unitary whole, yet very few editors and even fewer writers would expect the editor to be accorded the status of joint author, enjoying an undivided half interest in the copyright in the published work.

Similarly, research assistants may on occasion contribute to an author some protectable expression or merely a sufficiently original selection of factual material as would be entitled to a copyright, yet not be entitled to be regarded as a joint author of the work in which the contributed material appears. What distinguishes the writer-editor relationship and the writer-researcher relationship from the true joint author relationship is the lack of intent of both participants in the venture to regard themselves as joint authors.

Focusing on whether the putative joint authors regarded themselves as joint authors is especially important in circumstances, such as the instant case, where one person (Childress) is indisputably the dominant author of the work and the only issue is whether that person is the sole author or she and another (Taylor) are joint authors. This concern requires less exacting consideration in the context of traditional forms of collaboration, such as between the creators of the words and music of a song....

Though joint authorship does not require an understanding by the co-authors of the legal consequences of their relationship, obviously some distinguishing characteristic of the relationship must be understood in order for it to be the subject of their intent. In many instances, a useful test will be whether, in the absence of contractual agreements concerning listed authorship, each participant intended that all would be identified as co-authors. Though "billing" or "credit" is not decisive in all cases and joint authorship can exist without any explicit discussion of this topic by the parties, consideration of the topic helpfully serves to focus the fact-finder's attention on how the parties implicitly regarded their undertaking....

Examination of whether the putative co-authors ever shared an intent to be co-authors serves the valuable purpose of appropriately confining the bounds of joint authorship arising by operation of copyright law, while leaving those not in a true joint authorship relationship with an author free to bargain for an arrangement that will be recognized as a matter of both copyright and contract law. Joint authorship entitles the co-authors to equal undivided interests in the work. That equal sharing of rights should be reserved for relationships in which all participants fully intend to be joint authors. The sharing of benefits in other relationships involving assistance in the creation of a copyrightable work can be more precisely calibrated by the participants in their contract negotiations regarding division of royalties or assignment of shares of ownership of the copyright....

Childress was asked to write a play about "Moms" Mabley and did so. To facilitate her writing task, she accepted the assistance that Taylor provided, which consisted largely of furnishing the results of research concerning the life of "Moms" Mabley. As the actress expected to portray the leading role, Taylor also made some incidental suggestions, contributing ideas about the presentation of the play's subject and possibly some minor bits of expression. But there is no evidence that these aspects of Taylor's role ever evolved into more than the helpful advice that might come from the cast, the directors, or the producers of any play. A playwright does not so easily acquire a co-author.

Judge Haight was fully entitled to bolster his decision by reliance on the contract negotiations that followed completion of the script. Though his primary basis for summary judgment was the absence of any evidence supporting an inference that Childress shared "Taylor's notion that they were co-authors," he properly pointed to the emphatic rejection by Childress of the attempts by Taylor's agent to negotiate a co-ownership agreement and Taylor's acquiescence in that rejection. Intent "at the time the writing is done" remains the "touchstone," but subsequent conduct is normally probative of a prior state of mind.

Taylor's claim of co-authorship was properly rejected, and with the rejection of that claim, summary judgment for Childress was properly entered on her copyright and unfair competition claims, and on defendants' counterclaim. The judgment of the District Court is affirmed.

Thomson v. Larson

147 F.3d 195 (2d Cir. 1998)

Rent, the Pulitzer Prize and Tony Award-winning Broadway modern musical based on Puccini's opera *La Boheme*, began in 1989 as the joint project of Billy Aronson and composer Jonathan Larson. Aronson and Larson collaborated on the work until their amicable separation in 1991. At that time, Larson obtained Aronson's permission to develop the play on his own. By written agreement, Larson promised that the title would always be "RENT a rock opera by Jonathan Larson. Original concept and additional lyrics by Billy Aronson." In return, Aronson agreed that he would "not ... be considered [an] active collaborator or co-author of RENT."

In the summer of 1992, Larson's *Rent* script was favorably received by James Nicola, Artistic Director of the New York Theatre Workshop ("NYTW"), a nonprofit theater company in the East Village. Larson continued to develop and revise the "workshop version" of his *Rent* script. In the spring of 1993, Nicola urged Larson to allow the NYTW to hire a playwright or a bookwriter to help revamp the storyline and narrative structure of the play. But Larson "absolutely, vehemently and totally rejected [Nicola's] suggestion of hiring a bookwriter" and "was insistent on making RENT entirely his own project." Larson received a grant in the spring of 1994 to pay for a workshop production of *Rent*, which was presented to the public in the fall of 1994 in a series of ten staged performances produced by the NYTW and directed by Michael Greif. "The professional consensus concerning the show, after the studio production, was that it was, at a minimum, very promising and that it needed a great deal of work." Artistic Director Nicola once again suggested to Larson that he consider working with a bookwriter, which Larson "adamantly and steadfastly refused, consistently emphasizing his intention to be the only author of RENT."

In May 1995, in preparation for *Rent*'s off-Broadway opening scheduled for early 1996, Larson agreed to the NYTW's hiring of Lynn Thomson, a professor of advanced playwrighting at New York University, as a dramaturg[3] to assist him in clarifying the storyline of the musical. Thomson signed a contract with the NYTW, in which she agreed to provide her services with the workshop production from May 1, 1995, through the press opening, scheduled for early February of 1996. The agreement stated that Thomson's "responsibilities shall include, but not be limited to: Providing dramaturgical assistance and research to the playwright and director." In exchange, the NYTW agreed to pay "a fee" of $2000, "in full consideration of the services to be rendered" and to provide for billing credit for Thomson as "Dramaturg." The Thomson/NYTW agreement was silent as to any copyright interests or any issue of ownership with respect to the final work.

In the summer and fall of 1995, Thomson and Larson worked extremely intensively together on the show. For the most part, the two worked on the script alone in Larson's apartment. Thomson testified that revisions to the text of *Rent* didn't begin until early August 1995. Larson himself entered all changes directly onto his computer, where he kept the script, and Thomson made no contemporaneous notes of her specific contributions of language or other structural or thematic suggestions. Thomson alludes to the "October Version" of *Rent* as the culmination of her collaborative efforts with Larson. That new version was characterized by experts as "a radical transformation of the show."

A "sing-through" of the "October Version" of *Rent* took place in early November 1995. And on November 3, 1995, Larson signed a contract with the NYTW for ongoing revisions to *Rent*. This agreement identified Larson as the "Author" of *Rent* and made no reference to Thomson. The contract incorporated by reference an earlier draft author's agreement that set forth the terms that would apply if the NYTW opted to produce *Rent*. The earlier draft author's agreement gave Larson approval rights over all changes in text, provided that any changes in text would become his property, and assured him billing as "sole author."

The final dress rehearsal was held on January 24, 1996. Just hours after it ended, Larson died suddenly of an aortic aneurysm. Over the next few weeks, Nicola, Greif, Thomson, and musical director Tim Weil worked together to fine-tune the script.[4] The play opened off-Broadway on February 13, 1996, to rave reviews. On February 23, *Rent*'s move to Broadway was announced. Since its opening on Broadway on April 29, 1996, the show has been "an astounding critical, artistic, and commercial success."

---

3. Dramaturgs provide a range of services to playwrights and directors in connection with the production and development of theater pieces. According to Thomson's testimony, the role of the dramaturg "can include any number of the elements that go into the crafting of a play," such as "actual plot elements, dramatic structure, character details, themes, and even specific language."

4. All four agreed that they would not claim authorship in any of the material created during this time. Accordingly, before *Rent* opened off-Broadway, Nancy Dickmann, Managing Director of the NYTW, asked each of them to sign waivers disclaiming any copyright interest in the material they contributed. Thomson alone refused.

Before the Broadway opening, Thomson, in view of her contributions to *Rent*, sought compensation and title page dramaturgical credit from the Broadway producers. And on April 2, 1996, she signed a contract in which the producers agreed to pay her $10,000 plus a nominal $50/week for her dramaturgical services. Around the same time, upon the producers' advice, Thomson approached Allan S. Larson, Nanette Larson, and Julie Larson McCollum ("Larson Heirs"), the surviving members of Jonathan Larson's family, to request a percentage of the royalties derived from the play. In a letter to the Larson family, dated April 8, 1996, Thomson stated that she believed Larson, had he lived, would have offered her a "small percentage of his royalties to acknowledge the contribution I made." In reply, the Larson Heirs offered Thomson a gift of 1% of the author's royalties. Negotiations between Thomson and the Larson Heirs, however, broke down.

After the parties failed to reach a settlement, Thomson brought suit against the Larson Heirs, claiming that she was a co-author of *Rent* and that she had never assigned, licensed, or otherwise transferred her rights. Thomson sought declaratory relief and a retroactive and on-going accounting under the Copyright Act. Specifically, she asked that the court declare her a "co-author" of *Rent* and grant her 16% of the author's share of the royalties....

The district court properly defined the principal question in this case as: "not whether Lynn Thomson made a great contribution to the show. It is not whether she has been or ought to be compensated differently than she has been compensated. It is about whether what happened between Lynn Thomson and Jon Larson met the statutory definition as it has been construed by the higher courts of a joint work." In analyzing this issue, the district court made numerous findings of fact and then applied the *Childress* test to these facts.

... [The Court first reviews the standard provided in *Childress v. Taylor*.]

The potential danger of allowing anyone who makes even a minimal contribution to the writing of a work to be deemed a statutory co-author—as long as the two parties intended the contributions to merge—motivated the court to set forth a two-pronged test. A co-authorship claimant bears the burden of establishing that each of the putative co-authors (1) made independently copyrightable contributions to the work; and (2) fully intended to be co-authors. The court attempted to strike a balance between "ensuring that true collaborators in the creative process are accorded the perquisites of co-authorship," while at the same time, "guarding against the risk that a sole author is denied exclusive authorship status simply because another person renders some form of assistance."

1. Independently Copyrightable Contributions

Childress held that collaboration alone is not sufficient to establish joint authorship. Rather, the contribution of each joint author must be independently copyrightable. Without making specific findings as to any of Thomson's claims regarding lyrics or other contributions, the district court concluded that Thomson "made at least some non-*de minimis* copyrightable contribution," and that Thomson's contributions to the *Rent* libretto were "certainly not zero." Once having said that, the court decided the case on the second *Childress* prong—mutual intent of co-authorship. It hence did not reach the issue of the individual copyrightability of Thomson's varied alleged contributions (plot developments, thematic elements, character details, and structural components).

2. Intent of the Parties

a. Mutual Intent Requirement

Childress mandates that the parties "entertain in their minds the concept of joint authorship." This requirement of mutual intent recognizes that, since co-authors are afforded equal rights in the co-authored work, the "equal sharing of rights should be reserved for relationships in which all participants fully intend to be joint authors." ...

The [*Childress*] court stated that "in many instances, a useful test will be whether, in the absence of contractual arrangements concerning listed authorship, each participant intended that all would be identified as co-authors." But it is also clear that the intention standard is not strictly subjective. In other words, co-authorship intent does not turn solely on the parties' own words or professed state of mind. Rather, the *Childress* court suggested a more nuanced inquiry into factual indicia of ownership and authorship, such as how a collaborator regarded herself in relation to the work in terms of billing and credit, decision making, and the right to enter into contracts....

b. Evidence of Larson's Intent

i. Decision making Authority

An important indicator of authorship is a contributor's decision making authority over what changes are made and what is included in a work. The district court determined that Larson "retained and intended to retain at all times sole decision-making authority as to what went into [*Rent*]." In support of its conclusion, the court relied upon Thomson's statement that she was "flattered that [Larson] was asking [her] to contribute actual language to the text" and found that this statement demonstrated that even Thomson understood "that the question whether any contribution she might make would go into the script was within Mr. Larson's sole and complete discretion."[5] Moreover, as the court recognized, the November agreement between Larson and the NYTW expressly stated that Larson had final approval over all changes to *Rent* and that all such changes would become Larson's property.

In this respect, the district court also credited a telephone interview Larson gave in October 1995 to a high school student, in which Larson "said, in substance, that

---

5. There was also documentary evidence before the district court that confirmed the advisory nature of Thomson's role. Thus, a set of notes Thomson wrote to Larson began, "Please know that everything is intended as a question but might sound differently in the shorthand of the writing." And other notes, addressed to Nicola and Grief, read: "Usual disclaimer; the following is meant to generate discussion. Even when I offer 'solutions' what I mean is only to communicate a response by example...."

he wrote everything in *Rent* and distinguished writers in the theater from writers in the other media by saying that in the theater the writer is the king." ("In theater, as opposed to film and television, dramatists retain copyright to their work, [and] are independent contractors....") The district court found this statement significant because it "evidences Mr. Larson's view that *Rent* in all respects was his, he was the king."

ii. Billing

... The district court found ... that the billing was unequivocal: "Every script brought to [the court's] attention says "*Rent*, by Jonathan Larson." In addition, Larson "described himself in the biography he submitted for the playbill in January 1996, nine days before he died, as the author/composer, and listed Ms. Thomson on the same document as dramaturg." And while, as Ms. Thomson argues, it may indeed have been highly unusual for an author/composer to credit his dramaturg with a by-line, we fail to see how Larson's decision to style her as "dramaturg" on the final page in *Rent* scripts reflects a co-authorship intent on the part of Larson. The district court properly concluded that "the manner in which [Larson] listed credits on the scripts strongly supports the view that he regarded himself as the sole author."

iii. Written Agreements with Third Parties

Just as the parties' written agreements with each other can constitute evidence of whether the parties considered themselves to be co-authors, so the parties' agreements with outsiders also can provide insight into co-authorship intent, albeit to a somewhat more attenuated degree.

The district court found that Larson "listed himself or treated himself as the author in the November 1995 revisions contract that he entered into with the NYTW, which in turn incorporated the earlier draft author's agreement that had not been signed." That agreement identifies Larson as *Rent*'s "Author" and does not mention Thomson....

c. Conclusion

Based on all of the evidence, the district court concluded that "Mr. Larson never regarded himself as a joint author with Ms. Thomson." We believe that the district court correctly applied the *Childress* standards to the evidence before it and hold that its finding that Larson never intended co-authorship was not clearly erroneous....

[Thomson also asserted rights to her portions of Rent used in the production. The court dismissed these claims because they had not been brought out at trial, but suggesting that Thomson may have exclusive rights to some portions of Rent that can be asserted.]

Notes and Questions

a. Perhaps one of the greatest changes from the Minimum Basic Production Contract to the Approved Production Contract was the formulation for a producer's rights to subsidiary income. As the financial risk for producing Broadway plays has increased dramatically in the past few decades, producers need the potential windfall that a play might have if adapted as a movie or television series. Nonetheless, questions remain as to the scope of these provisions. *See Houlihan v. McCourt*, 2002 U.S. Dist.

LEXIS 13850 (N.D. Ill. July 23, 2002) (involving the rights to receive book and motion picture income where the book and film were based on the life story of the author but not his autobiographical play).

b. Although issues of joint authorship occur from time to time in every industry, it has been theatrical productions that have generated the most significant legal issues. This is likely caused by the fact that film, television, and recording industries are large business enterprises which contractually assign copyright to the corporate entity, aggregating the copyright interests acquired from the various participants. If every potential joint author has signed an assignment of copyright for the benefit of the corporate producer, it is far less relevant what the technical copyright status had been for each of the assignees.

Nonetheless, there have been a few instances of litigation involving joint authorship in media other than theatre. *See Corwin v. Quinonez*, 858 F. Supp. 2d 903 (N.D. Ohio 2012) (after band's demise, plaintiff band member sought declaratory judgment that he was joint author of compositions recorded by band); *Gaiman v. McFarlane*, 360 F.3d 644 (7th Cir. 2004) (author Neil Gaiman sought declaratory judgment that he was joint author of certain comic book characters used by Todd McFarlane); *Aalmuhammed v. Lee*, 202 F.3d 1227 (9th Cir. 1999) (participant in production of *Malcolm X* claimed joint authorship with filmmaker Spike Lee).

c. *Aalmuhammed v. Lee* provides some insights into the difference between theatrical and motion picture production.

In 1991, Warner Brothers contracted with Spike Lee and his production companies to make the movie *Malcolm X*, to be based on the book, *The Autobiography of Malcolm X*. Lee co-wrote the screenplay, directed, and co-produced the movie, which starred Denzel Washington as Malcolm X. Washington asked Jefri Aalmuhammed to assist him in his preparation for the starring role because Aalmuhammed knew a great deal about Malcolm X and Islam. Aalmuhammed, a devout Muslim, was particularly knowledgeable about the life of Malcolm X, having previously written, directed, and produced a documentary film about Malcolm X.

Aalmuhammed joined Washington on the movie set. The movie was filmed in the New York metropolitan area and Egypt. Aalmuhammed presented evidence that his involvement in making the movie was very extensive. He reviewed the shooting script for Spike Lee and Denzel Washington and suggested extensive script revisions. Some of his script revisions were included in the released version of the film; others were filmed but not included in the released version. Most of the revisions Aalmuhammed made were to ensure the religious and historical accuracy and authenticity of scenes depicting Malcolm X's religious conversion and pilgrimage to Mecca.

Aalmuhammed submitted evidence that he directed Denzel Washington and other actors while on the set, created at least two entire scenes with new characters, translated Arabic into English for subtitles, supplied his own voice for voice-overs, selected the proper prayers and religious practices for the characters, and edited parts of the movie during post production. Washington testified in his deposition that Aalmuhammed's contribution to the movie was "great" because he "helped to rewrite, to make more authentic." Once production ended, Aalmuhammed met with numerous Islamic organizations to persuade them that the movie was an accurate depiction of Malcolm X's life.

Aalmuhammed never had a written contract with Warner Brothers, Lee, or Lee's production companies, but he expected Lee to compensate him for his work. He did not intend to work and bear his expenses in New York and Egypt gratuitously. Aalmuhammed ultimately received a check for $25,000 from Lee, which he cashed, and a check for $100,000 from Washington, which he did not cash....

Aalmuhammed claimed that the movie *Malcolm X* was a "joint work" of which he was an author, thus making him a co-owner of the copyright. He sought a declaratory judgment to that effect, and an accounting for profits. He is not claiming copyright merely in what he wrote or contributed, but rather in the whole work, as a co-author of a "joint work." The district court granted defendants summary judgment against Mr. Aalmuhammed's copyright claims....

A "joint work" in this circuit "requires each author to make an independently copyrightable contribution" to the disputed work. *Malcolm X* is a copyrightable work, and it is undisputed that the movie was intended by everyone involved with it to be a unitary whole. It is also undisputed that Aalmuhammed made substantial and valuable contributions to the movie, including technical help, such as speaking Arabic to the persons in charge of the mosque in Egypt, scholarly and creative help, such as teaching the actors how to pray properly as Muslims, and script changes to add verisimilitude to the religious aspects of the movie.... The best objective manifestation of a shared intent, of course, is a contract saying that the parties intend to be or not to be co-authors. In the absence of a contract, the inquiry must of necessity focus on the facts.... Aalmuhammed was not the person who has actually formed the picture by putting the persons in position, and arranging the place.... Spike Lee was, so far as we can tell from the record. Aalmuhammed, like Larson's dramaturg, could make extremely helpful recommendations, but Spike Lee was not bound to accept any of them, and the work would not benefit in the slightest unless Spike Lee chose to accept them. Aalmuhammed lacked control over the work, and absence of control is strong evidence of the absence of co-authorship....

Warner Brothers required Spike Lee to sign a "work for hire" agreement, so that even Lee would not be a co-author and co-owner with Warner Brothers. It would be illogical to conclude that Warner Brothers, while not wanting to permit Lee to own the copyright, intended to share ownership with individuals like Aalmuhammed who worked under Lee's control, especially ones who at the time had made known no claim to the role of co-author. No one, including Aalmuhammed, made any indication to anyone prior to litigation that Aalmuhammed was intended to be a co-author and co-owner....

The broader construction that Aalmuhammed proposes would extend joint authorship to many "overreaching contributors," like the dramaturg in *Thomson*, and deny sole authors "exclusive authorship status simply because another person rendered some form of assistance." Claim jumping by research assistants, editors, and former spouses, lovers and friends would endanger authors who talked with people about what they were doing, if creative copyrightable contribution were all that authorship required.

Id. at 1229–36.

d. In both *Childress* and *Thomson*, the actual cases turned much more on intent than on questions of independent copyrightability. Perhaps the position advanced by Professor Nimmer then is more appropriate: that the combined work need be copyrightable, but that each contribution need not be. In the event one party provides a highly abstract outline of characters, plots, and settings to the second author, who creates the copyrighted expression based on that work, and what is the legal status of each author?

Assuming that the intent of the parties to create a joint work was manifest, should the court enforce that understanding or strip the first partner of her efforts? Assuming there is a written agreement between the parties to be treated as joint authors, does the Second Circuit approach require that the court deny the terms of the agreement if it cannot find independent creation of authorship from each party?

e. Because the Dramatists Guild is not a union, it does not operate under an exemption from the anti-trust laws. To address this decades-old problem, legislation entitled "The Playwrights' Licensing Relief Act of 2002" was drafted to allow collective bargaining by the Dramatists Guild notwithstanding its non-union status. The legislation has yet to be enacted, and the Dramatists Guild remains in its precarious position.

f. In contrast to *Aalmuhammed*, the role of a band or musical performer as joint author may raise additional interests in the filming of that performance. Does an actor have a copyright interest in her filmed performance? What if the actor is also a performing musician? *See Morrill v. Smashing Pumpkins,* 157 F. Supp. 2d 1120, 2001 U.S. Dist. LEXIS 16720 (C.D. Cal. 2001).

g. Like *Childress v. Taylor*, the problem of joint authorship seems exacerbated in the highly collaborative environment of smaller, non-union theatres. Does the hiring of a playwright to create a script specifically for the theatre add to the suggestion of joint authorship or provide a justification of a work for hire relationship? *See Cabrera v. Teatro del Sesenta, Inc.,* 914 F. Supp. 743 (D.P.R. 1995).

Problem 9-C

Fortunately for Bryce, the injury sustained from the fall during rehearsal was less problematic than initially feared. Bryce recovered quickly enough for *Juliet Prescott* to be delayed only one week. Good reviews and an enthusiastic producer have kept the show running for an additional three weeks.

While the New York producers were impressed with the current, LORT version of *Juliet Prescott*, they would like it to be expanded into a full-blown Broadway musical. They introduced Bryce to a few possible composers to assist Bryce in punching up the musical numbers, perhaps add an additional opening number to the second act, and "improve the sophistication of a few refrains."

Bryce is unsure of what this would mean in terms of control of the production. Bryce is also unsure what financial and control interest this new composer would have in the musical if they did decide to work together. Bryce would like you to explain the status of the ownership of the show, both under the Approved Production Contract and under any contractual proposal you would suggest. All the suggested composers are themselves members of the Dramatists Guild, so the agreement would need to be consistent with the terms of the Approved Production Contract for both Bryce and the composer. Finally, Bryce is open to any advice you might wish to give on whether working with one of these composers would make sense for the project.

D. Bibliography and Links

Donald C. Farber, Producing Theatre: A Comprehensive Legal and Business Guide (1997).

Donald C. Farber, From Option to Opening: A Guide to Producing Plays Off-Broadway (1989).

Charles Grippo, The Stage Producer's Business & Legal Guide (2002).

Shelley Attadgie, *Combating the Actor's Sacrifice: How to Amend Federal Labor Law to Influence the Labor Practices of Theaters and Incentivize Actors to Fight for Their Rights*, 40 Cardozo L. Rev. 1045 (2018).

Matthew T. Bodie, *Lessons from the Dramatists Guild for the Platform Economy*, 2017 U. Chi. Legal F. 17 (2017).

Michael W. Carroll, *Copyright's Creative Hierarchy in the Performing Arts*, 14 Vand. J. Ent. & Tech. L. 797 (2012).

Carolyn Casselman, *Staffing the 21st Century Theater: Technological Evolution and Collective Bargaining*, 25 Colum. J.L. & Arts 401 (2003).

Mollie Galchus, *"The Song Is Ended but the Melody Lingers on": Protecting the Cultural History of the Great American Songbook in the Face of the Public Domain*, 92 St. John's L. Rev. 661 (2018).

Kara Krakower, *Finding the Barre: Fitting the Untried Territory of Choreography Claims into Existing Copyright Law*, 28 Fordham Intell. Prop. Media & Ent. L.J. 671 (2018).

Mary LaFrance, *Authorship, Dominance, and the Captive Collaborator: Preserving the Rights of Joint Authors,* 50 Emory L.J. 193 (2001).

Susan P. Liemer, *Understanding Artists' Moral Rights: A Primer,* 7 B.U. Pub. Int. L.J. 41 (1998).

David Manella, *"Anything Goes": Regulating the Conduct of Money-Bundling Broadway Co-Producers,* 41 Colum. J.L. & Arts 641 (2018).

Carter Anne McGowan, Twittergate: *Rethinking the Casting Director Contract,* 21 Fordham Intell. Prop. Media & Ent. L.J. 365 (2011).

Laura Temme, *To Be, or Not to Be: The Potential Consequences of Granting Copyright Protection for Stage Directions,* 9 Cybaris An Intell. Prop. L. Rev. 1 (2018).

Talia Yellin, *New Directions for Copyright: The Property Rights of Stage Directors,* 24 Colum.-VLA J.L. & Arts 317 (2001).

Websites

The Dramatists Guild, www.dramatistsguild.org ("the only professional association for playwrights, composers, and lyricists. Membership is open to all dramatic writers, regardless of their production history.")

Live Broadway Online, www.livebroadway.com (sponsored by the League of American Theatres and Producers, Inc.)

Off Broadway Online, www.offbroadwayonline.com/home.php ("the official website of Off Broadway, presented by the Alliance of Resident Theatres/New York")

League of Resident Theatres, www.Lort.org

BackStage, www.backstage.com

Playbill, www.Playbill.com

Business Committee for the Arts, Inc., http://www.bcainc.org

Chapter 10

Music Publishing

A. Overview of the Music Industries

1. The Industry at a Glance

Music is generally divided into two discrete industries: the music publishing business and the record business. Music publishing includes printed music, the income generated from the public performance of music, and more generally the business activities of composers and lyricists. The record business or sound recording business includes the manufacture and distribution of CDs, DVDs, and more generally the business activities related to bands and performing artists. Changes in digital music, however, have increasingly integrated these two aspects of the music industries. Changes in federal law and industry practice have created new overlaps between the two areas.

The music industries are the most complex and rapidly changing in the entertainment industries, and arguably in the entire economy. Universal Music Group has approximately 22.5% of the global music publishing market; Sony/ATV Music Publishing has 13.7%; Warner Music Group has 13.2% and BMG Rights Management is at 12%. The remaining 40% of the market is held by regional publishers around the globe and much smaller entities.

The music industries have contracted substantially since 1999 when peer-to-peer file sharing was first introduced. 2013 was the first year since 1999 that the international revenue for music saw an increase in income. The transition to streaming and growth of Pandora, Apple Music, Spotify, and various other services, as well as a resurgence in live performance and the expansion of video gaming and its use of music, have all helped to reinvigorate the music industry, returning it to a growth industry after decades of decline. Although CD sales have dropped 34% from their highest levels in 1988, 75% of the music revenue has shifted to paid music streaming services. The change in revenue streams also shifts the income towards composers and publishers and away from record labels.

The technology of the music business has become a morass of acronyms for compositions, compact disks, digital files, downloads, and many others. The earlier terms may no longer be literally correct, but they reflect what musicians create. An album is a collection of recorded songs; each song is a cut on the album; and when only one song is released, it is a single. These terms apply whether created on vinyl to be placed on a record player with a stylus, to be burned or pressed onto a compact disk, to be downloaded by the purchaser of the song, to be broadcast, or to be streamed. Since each of these modalities has a slightly different set of parameters, musical production and distribution agreements have become exceptionally complex documents.

2. Limited Rights of the Composer

A recorded song begins with a composition. The authors of the composition are the owners of their copyrighted work, but unlike most other areas of copyright law, they will lose some of the exclusive rights to their work once the song is recorded and made available to the public. Once a composition has been recorded and publicly distributed, the law allows any additional party who wishes to make his or her own sound recording of the composition the right to do so without asking the composition copyright owner for permission. This is very different from the rights granted to other authors. Book authors control whether other publishers can republish their books or adapt them into films. But the composer must let all recording artists make records, granting the composer only the right to control the first recording of the work.

For a sound recording company (the "record company" or "label") to record a song that has previously been recorded, it follows the obligations of notice and payment provided in § 115 of the Copyright Act. The payment to the composer for the rights to create the new recording are known as mechanical rights fees. In practice, the publisher typically manages the mechanical rights licensing on behalf of the composer. The statute explains the limitation:

Copyrights § 115. Scope of exclusive rights in nondramatic musical works: Compulsory license for making and distributing phonorecords:

In the case of nondramatic musical works, the exclusive rights provided by clauses (1) and (3) of section 106, to make and to distribute phonorecords of such works, are subject to compulsory licensing under the conditions specified by this section.

(a) Availability and Scope of Compulsory License.

(1) When phonorecords of a nondramatic musical work have been distributed to the public in the United States under the authority of the copyright owner, any other person, including those who make phonorecords or digital phonorecord deliveries, may, by complying with the provisions of this section, obtain a compulsory license to make and distribute phonorecords of the work. A person may obtain a compulsory license only if his or her primary purpose in making phonorecords is to distribute them to the public for private use, including by means of a digital phonorecord delivery. A person may not obtain a compulsory license for use of the work in the making of phonorecords duplicating a sound recording fixed by another, unless: (i) such sound recording was fixed lawfully; and (ii) the making of the phonorecords was authorized by the owner of copyright in the sound recording or, if the sound recording was fixed be-

fore February 15, 1972, by any person who fixed the sound recording pursuant to an express license from the owner of the copyright in the musical work or pursuant to a valid compulsory license for use of such work in a sound recording.

(2) A compulsory license includes the privilege of making a musical arrangement of the work to the extent necessary to conform it to the style or manner of interpretation of the performance involved, but the arrangement shall not change the basic melody or fundamental character of the work, and shall not be subject to protection as a derivative work under this title, except with the express consent of the copyright owner.

3. Ownership of a Record

A single actually contains a number of different rights. The breakdown of these interests will help students and lawyers understand both the complexity of negotiating transactions and of reformulating the industry's current structure.

A single begins with written musical compositions. Many songs have two writers, a composer who writes the music and a lyricist who writes the words for the song. These two components of each song are typically written together with the intention that a single copyrighted work is created, so the composer and lyricist are joint authors of the song. Often, one person serves as both composer and lyricist. (This person is referred to as composer or songwriter throughout the text.)

Once a song is written, it must be arranged for performance by multiple musical instruments. In some situations, this is little more than adding chord structure to the melody, but in other situations it entails having an arranger write a complex series of orchestrations and additional parts for various instruments to play. If the arrangement and orchestrations embody original works of authorship, these may also be subject to copyright protection. Because the arrangements are dependent on the original song, commonly the arranger is hired as an employee in a work-made-for-hire capacity so that no additional copyright owner is added.

With the arrangement completed, the song is now ready for recording. A producer is hired (sometimes for the entire album, but increasingly for each particular song). The producer then helps shape the arrangement, directs the recording artist, selects takes, and serves as the controlling authority over the sound of the final master tape. Given the creative input, the producer is typically the copyright holder for the master tape of the finished song. On occasion, however, the performing artist undertakes the editorial and authorial functions of the producer and may therefore share the producer's copyright.

If the producer copied portions of the music, rhythm or other component from a different recording, then this digital sample must be licensed from its copyright holder. In some situations, the sample's copyright holder can earn as much as 50% of the recording copyright, although payments ranging from 10% to 33% are more typical.

Background singers and musicians are not likely to have any copyright interest in the work, but they will be entitled to royalties for sales and public performances based on collective bargaining agreements negotiated by the American Federation of Musicians, or other unions. They will also have a modest royalty due for the digital public performance rights.

Assuming that an album has ten songs or cuts collected for a single performing artist, the masters may have ten different producers and ten different composer/lyricist teams. The record label is the company that aggregates these rights, arranges for the manufacturing of the album, pays for its marketing, provides for its distribution, and collects income for the use of the recording in other media. The record label will also acquire the necessary copyrights or licenses, hire the musicians, and control the selection and order of the songs.

Finally, the record label will hire writers to create liner notes and artists to design the album cover and will attach its trademarks to indicate the source of the record manufacture and distribution.

On the publishing side, the composer and lyricist typically retain the copyright in their songs and enter into a publishing agreement. In the most typical arrangement, they assign the copyright in the song to the publisher in exchange for 50% of the royalties. The publisher exploits the written song in at least four markets: (1) print sheet-music sales; (2) blanket licenses through the performing rights societies for television, radio, and public performances; (3) direct licenses for films, DVDs, home video, and theatrical productions (grand rights); and (4) mechanical licenses for the right to include the song on each physical and digital medium. In this example, the composer and lyricist are entitled to a payment for each copy of the song embodied in a CD, vinyl album, MP3 file, or other format.

The recording industry, however, is governed by the record labels rather than the publishers. The label must license the song from the publisher, paying a mechanical royalty for the right to embody the song in each recording.

The performing artist enters into a contract with the label, assigning any copyright interest for an interest in the royalties generated through the sale of the copies of the recording and through direct licensing of the recording in any other medium. The label also acquires the copyright interest of each producer, each musician, the arranger, and all others who contributed to the recording of each rendition of the song.

Finally, in many modern recording agreements, the performing artist is also the composer and lyricist for some or all of the compositions. As a result, the line between publishing rights and recording rights sometimes blurs.

Although most attention has been paid to the recording industry, changes in technology have also affected the music publishing industry as well. Composers and lyricists have not been compensated when songs are distributed as unauthorized MP3 files, resulting in a loss of income as dramatic as that recently experienced in the recording industry. The Internet's competition with television and radio may erode these income sources as well.

In 2018, Title III of the Music Modernization Act, entitled the Allocation for Music Producers Act, extended the digital performance rights for sound recording copyright holders and for performing artists that were first added in 1995. Under the revised law, the copyright owner of the sound recording, the featured performer on the sound recording and the other artists are now all allotted a share of the streaming licensing fee revenues. The sound recording copyright owner shall earn 50% of the statutory royalties, 45% will go to the featured artists on the recording, 2.5% to the nonfeatured musicians, and 2.5% to the nonfeatured vocalists. In addition, a modification to the regulations governing SoundExchange—the rights organization that collects the funds for distribution—provides an expectation to distribute 2% of the covered royalties to the producer, mixer, or sound engineer of the sound recording, unless there is an objection by the sound recording copyright owner.

4. Monetization of a Song

Another way of understanding the rights embodied in the record is to follow the royalty payment that must be made for the use of the song. There are five or more music royalties, relating to the different copyrights held by the authors of the composition and the creators of the sound recording. This list of licenses illustrates the relationships of the parties described in the section above.

Print Music Publishing Rights: The composer/publisher is entitled to payment for all use of the sheet music from the composition, whether created to sell as sheet music, in music books, or on lyric websites.

Mechanical Royalties: A mechanical royalty is paid to the composer/publisher for each copy of the composition embodied in a physical or digital work. The synchronization license gives the creator of the work the right to record its own version of the song, but it does not give the creator of the work any right to use the master sound recording created by any other record label or producer.

Synchronization Royalties: The composer/publisher is entitled to a negotiated license fee for each use of a composition in an audiovisual work. All films, videogames, and other audiovisual works must pay for the right to synchronize the composition with the work.

Master Use License: The owner of the sound recording copyright is entitled to be paid for the right to reproduce the actual sound recording in the audiovisual work.

Both a synchronization license and a master use license are required to make a music video, motion picture, audio greeting card, or commercial.

Public Performance Royalties (Non-Digital): The composer/publisher is entitled to a royalty for each use of a composition in a public performance. Public performances occur when a song is performed live in a bar, performed in concert, broadcast on radio, used as background music in a large store, when a radio station is played in a large venue, and in similar situations. For many public performance environments, a performance rights organization (PRO) such as BMI, ASCAP, or SESAC serves to provide a license to the venue at which the musical performance takes place and collects the royalties on behalf of all of its members.

Digital Performance Rights: Separately from the public performance rights of the composers/publishers, copyright law recognizes a public performance right in the digital performance of sound recordings. These rights are owned by the producer/record label that holds the copyright in the master sound recordings. As described above, the Copyright Act specifies how these royalties are set and distributed to the record label, the featured performing artist, the non-featured artists, the musicians, and the engineers and producers.

5. Exclusive Writing Agreements

From the 1920s to the 1940s, the height of Tin Pan Alley, musicians would sell the copyright in their songs outright for a few dollars, never to see another payment or royalty. The anomalous two-term copyright protection provided by the 1909 Copyright Act helped to limit the negative consequences to a small degree. The transfer of copyright could not bind the composer unless the transfer of the second term was in writing. In addition, the writing bound only the transferor, so if the composer died prior to the beginning of the second copyright term, then the right to renew passed to the composer's spouse or as otherwise provided under the statute. This had only a modest impact on the law, but it provided some minimal relief.

To avoid any possible loss of copyright, the music publishing companies turned to the work for hire doctrine. By employing composers full-time, in their music writing capacity, these writers were employees in every legal sense, and as a result, the copyright vested in the publisher as employer. The employee never was an owner of the copyright and no renewal rights were created in these employees.

While this practice is largely gone, some issues of exclusivity remain. The most important is the scope of the music publishing agreement. The agreement may provide that every song written during the term of the contract is subject to the terms of the agreement. If the music publisher is providing comprehensive service by promoting all of the composer's songs, managing the mechanical royalties, and generally aiding the songwriting career, then this may be a reasonable provision. If the publisher is really working to administrate the songs from a single album or particular albums, then this exclusivity may become a form of overreaching that musicians should seek to avoid.

As each song is created, the copyright holders should execute a publishing split sheet that specifies the percentage each of the writers receive for the song. The split sheet should also include the percentage for each of the producers, if there is more than one producer. Having these percentages specified at the time each work is created will eliminate many of the conflicts that can emerge once the work begins to be exploited.

6. Relations between Publishers and Record Companies

The music publishing industry is sufficiently independent of the sound recording industry that most agreements to record a band's albums are not tied to owning the publishing rights as well. Oddly, this may be the only area in which some form of tying is not the presumptive model. Nonetheless, these functions are discrete, and a musician is generally better served by licensing publishing rights separately from recording rights. As consolidation in the music publishing and sound recording industries continues, however, the independence between these two functions has also waned. As the recording contract deals have changed, the "360 Deal" gives the recording company an ownership stake in all the revenue from the signed artist, including all the revenue that was originally kept out of the recording contract agreement. The 360 Deal merges the roles of record producer and publisher, potentially giving the artist more support by the record label, but always giving the record label more control and leverage.

B. Publisher Agreements

Folkways Music Publishers, Inc. v. Weiss

989 F.2d 108 (2d Cir. 1993)

Plaintiff, Folkways Music Publishers, Inc. ("Folkways") appeals from an order of the Southern District of New York, John F. Keenan, Judge, confirming an arbitration award and granting summary judgment to defendants, George David Weiss, June Peretti, Luigi Creatore (the "Songwriters"), and Abilene Music Corporation. The district court found that the arbitrators, who had granted renewal rights in the song "The Lion Sleeps Tonight" to the Songwriters, had not exceeded their authority or manifestly disregarded the law. We affirm.

This appeal involves a song entitled "The Lion Sleeps Tonight" (the "Lion version") written by the Songwriters which Folkways claims infringes its copyright in the songs "Mbube" and "Wimoweh." According to Folkways, the underlying music for the latter two songs was composed by Solomon Linda who assigned all rights, title, and interest in his song, called "Mbube," to Gallo Africa, Ltd. ("Gallo") in 1952. On May 7, 1952, Gallo registered a claim to copyright "Mbube" in the United States. After the expiration of the original term on December 31, 1980, the renewal rights in the song vested in Linda's widow. Allegedly, she thereafter assigned Folkways all of her rights in "Mbube."

In 1951, Pete Seeger and the Weavers, under the pseudonym Paul Campbell ("Campbell") wrote a new arrangement of "Mbube" entitled "Wimoweh." Campbell assigned all rights and copyright interests in "Wimoweh" to Folkways which subsequently registered a claim to copyright the song on January 17, 1952. On November 30, 1979, the original term of the copyright was renewed in Campbell's name and thereafter assigned to Folkways.

In 1961, the Songwriters wrote another version of "Wimoweh," the Lion version, which was published by Token Music Publishing Company ("Token"). Token registered a claim to copyright on October 17, 1961, and licensed the use of the Lion version for phonograph records and public performance. On October 31, 1961, Folkways alerted Token of its claim that the Lion version infringed its copyright in "Wimoweh."

In response, Token ceded its rights as publisher of the Lion version to Folkways and the Songwriters entered into the agreement which is the subject of this suit. The Songwriters allegedly executed five documents, including acknowledgments of the infringement and assignments of rights in the Lion version to Folkways. Two of these documents are central to the disposition of this case. On November 6, 1961, Folkways drafted a letter which was signed by the Songwriters, providing for a distribution of public performance royalties payable by Broadcast Music, Inc., Folkways' performing rights society, for uses of the Lion version. In addition, the parties entered into a "Standard Popular Songwriter Contract" ("the Agreement") also dated November 6, 1961. This contract transferred and assigned all rights in the Lion version to Folkways, including "the right to secure copyright therein throughout the entire world and to have and to hold the said copyright and all rights of whatsoever nature thereunder existing, subject to the terms of this agreement." On December 18, 1961, Folkways registered a claim to copyright in the Lion version. This original term expired on December 31, 1989.

Folkways alleges that in October 1989, Weiss on behalf of the Songwriters notified it that he believed Folkways' rights to be limited to the original term of the copyright. He stated that, subsequent to the expiration of the initial copyright term, the Songwriters would exercise their rights in the Lion version absent payment from Folkways for rights in the renewal term. Folkways refused and the Songwriters filed a demand for arbitration on September 13, 1990 pursuant to the 1961 Agreement.

In their demand, the Songwriters sought a declaration that they were "the sole and exclusive owners of all rights in and to the [Lion version], including worldwide copyright, since the composition entered its United States renewal term of copyright." They also sought to compel Folkways to notify its licensees that it no longer had any interest in the copyright in the Lion version. Lastly, the Songwriters requested they be awarded all revenue Folkways had received since the beginning of the renewal term stemming from use of the Lion version. Folkways then filed a copyright infringement action in the district court. Folkways argued that the Songwriters' use of the Lion version since the beginning of the renewal term infringed on its rights not only in the Lion version but also in "Mbube," "Wimoweh," and one other version of the song owned by Folkways ("the underlying works"). Folkways also asked the district court to stay the arbitration or limit its scope to renewal rights in the Lion version. The district court granted the Songwriters' demand for arbitration and denied Folkway's motion.

The arbitration panel ruled that rights to the Lion version had reverted to the Songwriters at the end of the initial copyright term and that the Songwriters "shall have the right to exploit the Composition free of any and all claims from Folkways...." The award, however, did not explicitly discuss whether the Songwriters' use of the

Lion version would infringe on Folkways' copyrights in the underlying works. Nonetheless, the arbitrators did say quite plainly that Folkways would have no claims against the Songwriters' use of the Lion version....

Folkways appeals from the affirmance [of the arbitration by the district court] on alternative grounds: first, it argues that the district court misinterpreted the award in finding that it resolved rights to the underlying music; second, it contends that if the district court was correct in its finding that the award determined the rights to the underlying music, then the arbitrators exceeded their powers; third, it claims that if the district court's interpretation was correct then the award is irrational and in manifest disregard of the law

Initially, Folkways contends that the district court misunderstood the import of the arbitration award. The award stated that "all rights in and to the composition 'The Lion Sleeps Tonight' (the 'Composition') shall revert to [the Songwriters].... CLAIMANTS shall have the right to exploit the Composition free of any and all claims from Folkways...." The district court found that this language clearly barred any infringement claims by Folkways against the Songwriters based on rights to the underlying music. In opposition, Folkways argues that the district court misread the words "composition" and "revert," ignoring the "obvious" meaning they have in the award. According to Folkways, "composition" can only refer to the original material added by the songwriters to the Lion version and not to the aspects of the Lion version which stem from the underlying works. Moreover, they argue that material never owned by the Songwriters cannot "revert" to them. As the district court noted, however, the arbitrators determined that the Songwriters had the right to exploit the composition "free of *'any* and *all'* claims" from *Folkways.* In finding that the award encompassed rights to the underlying works, the district court properly interpreted the award.

In effect, Folkways argues that this is an improper understanding of the law of copyright, that the arbitrators could not have been mistaken as to the law, and thus that the district court incorrectly interpreted the award. As the district court's reading of the award is proper, this argument is really a challenge to the validity of the arbitrators' award and not to the district court's review. We deal with this challenge below.

Folkways' second argument focuses on the arbitration award itself, attacking the breadth of the arbitrators' determination ...

Folkways, as the party challenging the award, bears a heavy burden of proof. In the order to proceed with arbitration, the district court stated that the arbitrators may pass on the issue of rights to the underlying music. The district court found that the broad language of the Agreement, which required arbitration as to "'any and all differences, disputes or controversies arising out of this contract' ..." permitted such a determination. We agree that this language granted the arbitrators the scope to determine rights in the underlying works. As such, we cannot say that the arbitrators exceeded their authority in reaching this issue.

Lastly, Folkways contends that the arbitrators' decision was in "manifest disregard" of the law. In order to advance the goals of arbitration, courts may vacate awards only for an overt disregard of the law and not merely for an erroneous interpretation. As we noted in *Merrill Lynch, Pierce, Fenner & Smith, Inc. v. Bobker*, 808 F.2d 930 (2d Cir. 1986), "'manifest disregard of the law' by arbitrators is a judicially-created ground for vacating their arbitration award.... [I]t clearly means more than error or misunderstanding with respect to the law. The error must have been obvious and capable of being readily and instantly perceived by the average person qualified to serve as an arbitrator."

In order to vacate for "manifest disregard," a court must find that the arbitrators knew of a governing legal principle yet refused to apply it or ignored it altogether. Moreover, the law ignored by the arbitrators must be "well defined, explicit, and clearly applicable" if the award is to be vacated....

The district court did not misconstrue the arbitration award and that award was not in manifest disregard of the law of copyright. In light of the above discussion, we uphold the district court's confirmation of the arbitration award and grant of summary judgment to the Songwriters.

In re Isbell Records, Inc.

774 F.3d 859 (5th Cir. 2014)

The popular song Whoomp! (There It Is) was released in 1993. For more than half of the song's existence — since 2002 — the parties to this action have been litigating the question of who owns the composition copyright to the song. After an eleven-day trial, the district court ruled that, as a matter of law, Plaintiff-Appellee Alvertis Isbell owned the copyright and Defendant-Appellant DM Records, Inc. was liable for copyright infringement. The jury awarded over $2 million in damages. DM Records appeals these and several other district court decisions. We AFFIRM the district court in all respects.

In 1993, Cecil Glenn and Steven James (collectively, "Tag Team") wrote and produced the song Whoomp! (There It Is) ("Whoomp!"). Tag Team entered into an Exclusive Producers Agreement ("Recording Agreement") with Bellmark Records ("Bellmark") that governed the relationship between Tag Team and Bellmark. The Recording Agreement discussed, *inter alia,* the ownership of the sound recordings and the payment of royalties. Exhibit B to the Recording Agreement, titled "Assignment of Compositions and Rights to Copyright" addressed Whoomp!'s composition copyright. The first paragraph stated:

> [F]or good and valuable consideration, receipt of which is hereby acknowledged, the undersigned Assignors do hereby sell, assign, transfer and set over unto *Bellmark's affiliated designee publisher,* its successors and assigns, fifty percent (50%) of the entire rights, title and interests throughout the world and universe, including, without limitation, the copyrights and any registration and copyright applications relating thereto....

(emphasis added). The second paragraph stated:

> and fifty percent (50%) of the right, title and interest of the undersigned Assignors, vested and contingent therein and thereto, subject to the terms and

conditions of the Memorandum Agreement between Assignors and Assignee dated effective March 30, 1993 and for the term of the copyrights and all renewals and extensions thereof.

The third paragraph stated:

Assignors agrees that the Assignee(s) has the sole, exclusive worldwide and universal right to administer and exploit the copyrights and musical composition, to print, sell, dramatize, use and license any and all uses of the copyrights and compositions, to execute in Assignee(s) own name any and all licenses and agreements whatsoever affecting or respecting the compositions and copyrights.... This statement of exclusive rights is only in clarification and amplification of the rights of Assignee(s) and not in limitation thereof.

Alvertis Isbell ("Bell") was the president of Bellmark, which was in the business of owning sound recordings. In 1977, Bell formed his own music publishing company, Alvert Music. In 1997, Bellmark filed for bankruptcy in the Eastern District of Texas. In 1999, following bankruptcy court approval, DM Records, Inc. ("DM") purchased Bellmark's assets for $166,000. The assets subject to the sale were not defined, but rather included "all property of the company." The order approving the sale provided: "the sale of purchased assets is made as is, where is, without any representations or warranties concerning the estate's right, title or interest, if any, in such assets." Bellmark's bankruptcy case was closed in 2001. After purchasing Bellmark's assets, DM exploited the composition copyright of Whoomp!.

In 2002, Bell (doing business as Alvert Music) filed this copyright infringement action against DM in the Northern District of Texas seeking a declaratory judgment that Alvert Music—not DM, as purchaser of Bellmark's assets—is the rightful owner of the composition copyright for Whoomp!. Bell also sought damages for the alleged infringement.

At trial, the parties each elicited testimony about the Recording Agreement and the parties' subsequent actions that they claimed proved that either Bellmark or Alvert Music was assigned the composition copyright. The district court granted Bell's motion and denied DM's motion. Specifically, the court found that: 1) the interpretation of the Recording Agreement was a question of law under California law; 2) Bellmark is a separate entity from its affiliated designee publisher; and 3) Bellmark's affiliated designee publisher was Alvert Music. Thus, Alvert Music was the owner of Whoomp! and DM was liable for copyright infringement.

After ruling on the ownership of the composition copyright as a matter of law, the district court submitted the question of damages to the jury. The jury found actual damages of $2,131,482.28 and statutory damages of $132,500 for DM's willful infringement of the Whoomp! composition copyright. Bell elected to recover actual damages for DM's infringement of Whoomp!, and the district court entered a judgment to that effect.

DM argues that the jury's damages award is rendered erroneous by the district court's ruling on ownership and its jury instructions. The jury awarded Bell $2,131,482.28 in actual damages for the infringement in the Whoomp! composition copyright, a figure that is essentially 100 percent of the royalties DM collected from licensing Whoomp!. DM contends that, since the court ruled that Bell owned only fifty percent of the copyright, he should have only been awarded, at most, fifty percent of the royalties. Specifically, DM claims that the following instruction was erroneous because it misled the jury into believing that all royalties must go to Bell: that DM "does not now have, and it has never had, an ownership interest in the musical composition copyright for Whoomp!".

DM's argument essentially seems to be that Bell, as fifty percent owner of the copyright, may not, as a matter of law, recover damages for Tag Team's share. The jury's award of over $2 million in damages is, in fact, the full amount of all royalties received by DM without a reduction for Tag Team's fifty percent share. It appears to be an issue of first impression in our court whether a partial owner of a copyright can ever be awarded infringement damages for his co-owner's share. In *Edward B. Marks Music Corp. v. Jerry Vogel Music Co.*, 140 F.2d 268 (2d Cir. 1944), the Second Circuit held that "the recovery shall be confined to the plaintiff's own part; that is to say, to its own actual damages, to its proper share of any statutory damages, and to its proper share of the profits." *Edward B. Marks* is distinguishable because it dealt with the non-joinder of a copyright co-owner and did not involve a situation where there was evidence from which the jury could find that the plaintiff was administrator for all of the royalties. Here, there was evidence in the record from which the jury could have determined, as it did, that Bell is entitled to 100 percent of the royalties in the first instance. There was testimony that Bell is the administrator of 100 percent of the royalties and is responsible for accounting to Tag Team. As such, the jury could have determined that Bell was properly awarded 100 percent of the royalties, from which it could pay Tag Team its share.

For the foregoing reasons, we AFFIRM the various district court rulings that DM challenges on appeal.

Notes and Questions

a. The publishing industry has not had nearly the litigation tradition as that of the recording industry. As a result, the few courts that have had to deal with publishing issues have struggled to understand the context of the issue, as these excerpts illustrate. In a footnote, the Second Circuit explained the situation as follows:

> The parties and the District Court called the first category "Performance Royalties" and the second category "Publishing Royalties." The Court's opinion defined "Performance Royalties" as "monies directly generated by record sales and other sound recordings" and "Publishing Royalties" as "monies generated by the exploitation of the musical compositions themselves—that is, the words and the music of the songs." The Court explained that "in the music industry, Publishing Royalties are typically created through

the efforts of a musical publishing company or administrator who licenses use of the work to third parties. Such licenses include: (a) mechanical licenses that allow other record companies to use the work ('cover' songs), (b) public performance fees when a song is played on the radio or in a concert, (c) sampling rights that permit other artists to use pieces of the song, and (d) synchronization rights when a musical work is used in a movie, commercial or television show." We do not think clarity is promoted by using the phrase "Performance Royalties" to mean income from record sales and at the same time using the phrase "Publishing Royalties" to include "public performance fees."

We note that although the terms "performance royalties" and "publishing royalties" have been used in a few reported appellate opinions, these terms are not terms of art with precise meanings. Indeed, they have not been given consistent meanings. We have said that "performance royalties" are "paid by the performer to performing rights societies such as [ASCAP], of which the songwriter and publisher are members.... ASCAP's practice is to distribute half of the performance royalties to the songwriter ('writer distributions'), and the remaining half to the publisher ('publisher distributions').... The songwriter and publisher may by contract alter the allocation of performance royalties." *Larry Spier, Inc. v. Bourne Co.*, 953 F.2d 774, 776 (2d Cir. 1992). By "performer" we refer not only to the person who sings the song but also to "radio stations, television stations, restaurants, stores and other entities that 'perform' music publicly." *Woods v. Bourne Co.*, 60 F.3d 978, 984 (2d Cir. 1995). The Ninth Circuit has used "performance royalties" to refer to the income due a song composer for licensing the synchronization right that permits a song to be recorded on the soundtrack of a movie.

Appellate courts have used the phrase "publishing royalties" in the context of music to have various meanings. The Nimmer treatise categorizes the primary sources of revenue for the owner of a copyright in a musical composition as "public performance income, mechanical licenses, synchronization licenses, ... and print publishing revenues." 6 Nimmer on Copyright § 30.02[F], at 30–102 (2002).

Jasper v. Bovina Music, Inc., 314 F.3d 42, 44 n.1 (2d Cir. 2002).

b. Compare this description with that in *Larry Spier, Inc. v. Bourne Co.*, 953 F.2d 774, 775 (2d Cir. 1992):

Plaintiff-appellant Larry Spier, Inc. appeals from a summary judgment entered in the United States District Court for the Southern District of New York (Haight, J.) in favor of defendant-appellee Bourne Company. Both parties are music publishers, and the district court concluded that Bourne was entitled to judgment as a matter of law because the Copyright Act of 1976, prohibits recognition of the assignment under which Spier claims ownership of certain disputed copyrights....

This case recalls the bygone era of Tin Pan Alley and the popular music of another day. Between 1925 and 1931, successful songwriter Dave Dreyer joined with some famous co-authors in assigning to Irving Berlin, Inc., as publisher, copyrights for five songs still popular enough to generate royalties worth fighting over: "Cecelia," written with Herman Ruby; "Me and My Shadow," "Back in Your Own Back Yard," and "There's a Rainbow 'Round My Shoulder," written with Billy Rose and Al Jolson; and "Wabash Moon," written with Morton Downey and Billy McKenney. Irving Berlin, Inc. is the predecessor in interest of defendant-appellee Bourne Company. The initial term of each copyright was 28 years, and the five copyrights therefore were scheduled to expire between 1953 and 1959. In 1951, prior to the expiration of the initial term of the copyrights, Dreyer assigned to Bourne the right to renew the copyrights. Like the original assignment agreements, the 1951 agreements allocated the various types of royalties to be earned from the songs between Dreyer, as co-author, and Bourne, as publisher. The royalties earned from the manufacture and sale of records of the songs (known as "mechanical royalties") were split evenly between Dreyer and Bourne, as were royalties from licenses for use of the songs in broadcasts and movies. Dreyer was paid a royalty for each copy of the sheet music sold as well.

The Dreyer songs also generated royalties from public performances of the songs (known as "performance royalties"). In the music business, performance royalties are paid by the performer to performing rights societies such as the American Society of Composers, Authors, and Publishers ("ASCAP"), of which the songwriter and publisher are members. Dreyer and Bourne were members of ASCAP. ASCAP's practice is to distribute half of the performance royalties to the songwriter ("writer distributions"), and the remaining half to the publisher ("publisher distributions"). While the songwriter and publisher may by contract alter the allocation of the performance royalties, Dreyer and Bourne did not do so. Under the assignment agreement, Bourne was entitled to retain all of the publisher distributions made by ASCAP. The agreement further provided that its terms were subject to any existing arrangements between Dreyer or Bourne and ASCAP, apparently meaning that Dreyer was entitled to retain all writer distributions made by ASCAP. In any event, Dreyer and Bourne interpreted the agreement over the years in this manner, with writer distributions being paid to Dreyer and publisher distributions to Bourne.

It appears that Bourne duly renewed the copyrights prior to expiration. Under the copyright laws then in effect, the so-called "renewal term" of the copyrights would have continued until 1981–87. The most recent Copyright Act further extends the life of the Dreyer copyrights until 2000–2006.

[The remainder of the dispute involved which party had the right to license the music in the renewal term of the agreement. The Second Circuit interpreted §304(c) of the Copyright Act to allow the children of the copyright holder to terminate the earlier grants of publishing rights and transfer them to a different publishing company.]

Id.

c. Mechanical Royalties to the Original Songwriters: The Controlled Composition Clause. The controlled composition clause is actually a provision of the sound recording agreement rather than the publishing agreement; however, its importance to the revenue structure for a recording artist makes the discussion of this provision and its application clearer in the context of the publishing industry.

As noted in the introduction, under Copyright Act § 115, a record label must pay either a negotiated price or a statutory royalty for each copy of a song sold. If a band writes its own music, then the record label would be paying the band (and its publisher) for rights in addition to the payment for the recording of the album. As a result, record labels will generally limit the amount of money they will pay for the mechanical royalties, or the number of songs on which they will pay royalties, or both. For example, a contract may provide that the label will pay for 85% of the total mechanical license fee for the first ten songs, and no mechanical fees for additional songs. If the songs are written by the recording artist, then this provision results in a reduction of mechanical royalties.

If the band does write all its own music, then the controlled composition clause of the recording agreement will serve to reduce the revenue available to the band. The situation becomes much more complicated if the compositions are written by only a few of the band members. Then the costs of the controlled composition revenue reduction will fall on the composers in the group rather than the entire group as a whole.

If the band records songs written by third parties, the situation can become very expensive for the recording artists. The mechanical license fees required under § 115 are required to be paid. If the controlled composition clause shifts this cost from the record label to the recording artists, then the band itself will be responsible for this fee.

If an album includes ten cuts, the current royalty owed to the composers is $0.91 per album (i.e., 10 x $0.091). On a gold album of 500,000 copies manufactured and sold, that equals a payment of $455,000 from the label to the publisher. The amount would increase to $591,500 if there were thirteen songs on the album. The publisher typically retains fifty percent of the income and the composer retains the other fifty percent.

Under the worst circumstances, assume thirteen songs are on an album which is subject to both the percentage and song limitation. In that case, the royalties owed for thirteen songs on a gold album are $591,500. From that, the label will pay for only 85% of ten songs and therefore cover only $386,750 of the total amount due. The remaining $204,750 will be deducted from the recording artist's royalties.

This example illustrates how the interplay between the publishing agreements and the recording agreements is essential to fully understanding the implications of most music contracts.

d. It is common for bands to form companies to hold the rights of their members' copyrights and distribute the income from those companies. What techniques are available to protect a songwriter who is also a member of a band from loss of control when the copyrights are assigned to the band? *See Cusano v. Klein*, 280 F. Supp. 2d 1035 (C.D. Cal. 2003) (dismissing former KISS guitarist and songwriter's claims for improper assignment of song copyrights and failure to properly account for royalties).

e. Is the publisher's fee worth 50% of the royalties? The costs associated with collection and licensing are significant, but so are the benefits of having a publisher actively market a composition for recording by other bands or for use in commercials, films, and in other formats. Nonetheless, for successful composers, an alternative is to form a wholly-owned publishing company.

The composer can then choose to do without a third-party publisher, or the composer can have his or her publishing company enter into a co-publishing agreement with a third-party publisher. In this manner, the composer keeps the 50% of the royalties earned as the composer and splits the remaining 50% earned by the two publishing companies, retaining 75% of the total available royalties. A similar agreement, known as an administration agreement, provides for a limited term (typically 3–5 years) during which the commercial publisher assists the wholly owned publishing house.

f. In addition to the more traditional troubles confronting a performing artist, a few musicians have been sued over the content of their lyrics on copyright and trademark grounds. *See Mattel, Inc. v. MCA Records, Inc.*, 296 F.3d 894 (9th Cir. 2002) (allowing the use of Barbie name in song); *Parks v. LaFace Records*, 329 F.3d 437 (6th Cir. 2003) (reviewing use of the name of Civil Rights icon Rosa Parks in song lyrics).

g. The Lion Never Sleeps—In 2006, after years of litigation in the United States and South Africa, the estate of Solomon Linda settled its claims regarding the music composition rights that had reverted to the family in *Wimoweh* and *Mbube,* the underlying composition popularized as *The Lion Sleeps Tonight.* As shown in *Folkways Music Publishers, Inc. v. Weiss*, 989 F.2d 108 (2d Cir. 1993), this has been a musical legacy fraught with intrigue. Over 150 artists are reported to have covered the various versions of the song. The author, Zulu composer Solomon Linda, died in 1962. He had named the song *Mbube* from the Zulu word for lion. Pete Seeger transcribed the song for his folk band, The Weavers, who corrupted the word to *Wimoweh.* Although Disney chose not to reproduce the song on the *Lion King* soundtrack album, it used the song in both the film and the live stage version of the production.

h. Renewal and termination rights continue to vex publishers and authors alike. The rules are complex, confusingly drafted, and intended to force renegotiations more than to allow authors to reclaim their works. Renewal rights under the 1909 Copyright Act were assignable whereas termination rights under the 1976 Copyright Act are not. But the transfer of the renewal right requires the transferring artist to be living. In *Roger Miller Music, Inc. v. Sony/ATV Pub., L.L.C.,* 672 F.3d 434 (6th Cir. 2012), a court addresses what happens when the artist dies after the renewal is filed but before that renewal takes effect:

This case presents an interstitial issue of copyright law. Miller's assignment of the renewal copyright would indisputably have been made effective if he had still been living at the commencement of the renewal term on January 1, 1993. Equally indisputable is that the assignment would have been rendered ineffective if Miller had died before 1992. This case is before us because Miller was still living at the time in 1992 that his assignee applied to register the copyright, but Miller died before the start of the renewal term. RMMI contends that Miller must have been living at the start of the renewal term to effectuate his assignment to Sony, but Sony counters that Miller needed to survive only until the time at which the application was filed. Sony is correct that the Copyright Act supports the effectiveness of assignments in such circumstances.

Id. at 437.

Problem 10-B

Bryce is interested in cutting a demo CD featuring six songs that Bryce wrote: two hip-hop versions of 1890s Gilbert & Sullivan songs and four songs written by various popular folk writers from the 1960s. Bryce expects to sell a few thousand copies of the CD, if lucky, and to give away an additional 500. Advise Bryce how to obtain the necessary rights to license the songs for Bryce's demo CD, explaining how many of the copies would have to be paid for under the license.

C. Performing Rights Societies & Copyright Enforcement

Introduction

As defined by the Copyright Act, "[a] 'performing rights society' is an association, corporation, or other entity that licenses the public performance of nondramatic musical works on behalf of copyright owners of such works, such as the American Society of Composers, Authors and Publishers (ASCAP), Broadcast Music, Inc. (BMI), and SESAC, Inc." (17 U.S.C. § 101). ASCAP was the first of these societies in the United States, formed through the leadership of Victor Herbert in 1914. By joining the songwriters (both composers and lyricists) together in one collective organization, it enabled this organization to use its negotiating leverage against restaurants, theatres, movie-houses, and other venues in which music was performed either for an admission fee or as part of the value provided in the cost of the food or drink.

Part of ASCAP's troubles stemmed from its own success. To create a competitor to ASCAP, BMI was founded in 1939. By 1941, however, some of ASCAP's practices had gained the attention of the U.S. Justice Department. The 1941 consent decree created ongoing federal jurisdiction over many of the activities of the organization. Through a myriad of court cases and amendments to the consent decree in 1950, 1960, and 2001 the federal government and the industry set out the structural rules under which

ASCAP and BMI operate. Continuing jurisdiction is vested in the Southern District of New York, which serves as the rate-setting court for disputes involving the royalties paid for licenses. Increasingly, these rate determination proceedings struggle to keep up with the changing demands of technology as music is now delivered via digital radio, on cable systems, and through online streaming on the Internet in addition to the traditional venues of radio, television, and retail shops such as restaurants and retailers. The summary of the consent decrees can be seen in any of the ASCAP or BMI license agreements (available online at www.ASCAP.com or www.BMI.com). The most important aspects of the antitrust limitations are as follows:

1. No exclusivity;

2. No discriminatory pricing—similar license for similar licensee;

3. Broadcasters must have choice of per program or blanket license;

4. Membership requirements must be open and subject to court control;

5. Performing rights societies are prohibited from licensing to motion pictures or theatrical productions. Dramatic rights (grand rights) are prohibited and instead must be source licensed;

6. A licensee can complain that fees are unreasonable to the District Court, and the performing rights society has the burden to establish fairness of fees; and

7. Royalties must be fairly and objectively distributed.

Broadcast Music, Inc. v. Weigel Broadcasting Co.

488 F. Supp. 2d 411 (S.D.N.Y. 2007)

Broadcast Music Inc.'s petition seeks an order exercising the Court's rate-setting authority under article XIV of the BMI Consent Decree,[1] setting reasonable music license terms and fees for Weigel Broadcasting Company's two local commercial television stations for the time period of April 1, 1999 to December 31, 2004 and, on an interim basis, from January 1, 2005 on....

BMI is a non-profit music licensing organization that, on behalf of approximately 300,000 composers, songwriters and music publishers, licenses non-exclusive rights to publicly perform approximately 4.5 million musical works to a variety of music users, including local commercial television stations. BMI offers a blanket license and a per program license to local commercial television stations for monthly fees. Stations that choose the blanket license may, for a pre-determined flat fee, perform all of the music in BMI's repertoire as often as they like during the license period. Those that choose a per program license can also perform all of BMI's music as often as they like, but their fees are based on the percentage of their total revenues that de-

---

1. United States v. Broadcast Music, Inc., 1966 Trade Cas. (CCH) ¶ 71,941 (S.D.N.Y. 1966), as amended by, 1996-1 Trade Cas. (CCH) ¶ 71,378 (S.D.N.Y. 1994).

rived from programs with performances of BMI music (other than music for which they held a license from another source, such as the composer).

Weigel is a television broadcasting company that operates two full-power television stations, WCIU-TV in Chicago, Illinois and WDJT-TV in Milwaukee, Wisconsin. WCIU is not affiliated with a television network, such as NBC, ABC or CBS. It airs primarily syndicated programming, which it obtains from television producers, studios or other third parties. That programming, like most commercial television programming, contains copyrighted music in BMI's repertoire, for which WCIU obtains a blanket license from BMI.

BMI's ability to license the public performance rights in its music is governed by a consent decree that settled an antitrust suit brought by the United States ("BMI Consent Decree" or "Decree"). Under the Decree, BMI is required to make licenses available for public performances of its music and to provide applicants with proposed license fees upon request. BMI Consent Decree Arts. VIII(B), XIV(A). If BMI and an applicant cannot agree on a license fee, either party may apply to this court for the determination of reasonable or interim license terms and fees. *Id.* at Art. XIV(A).

Because television programming often contains copyrighted music, the television industry formed a non-profit volunteer association to negotiate music license terms and fees with performing rights organizations such as BMI and its chief competitor, the American Society of Composers, Authors and Publishers ("ASCAP"). That association has existed in one form or another since before the BMI Consent Decree was entered, and is now known as the Television Music Licensing Committee ("TMLC"). The majority of the approximately 1,300 full-power local commercial television stations[2] in the United States now authorize the TMLC to negotiate on their behalf, and virtually all others agree to be bound by the outcome of the TMLC's negotiations with BMI or a rate-court proceeding between the TMLC and BMI.

Historically, local television stations represented by the TMLC or its predecessors paid music license fees to BMI and ASCAP equal to a percentage of each station's revenues. In 1993, however, the ASCAP rate court rejected the percentage of revenue fee and set a flat license fee for the entire local commercial television industry. Following that decision, the TMLC told BMI that it would no longer negotiate music license fees on a percentage of revenue basis, and instead demanded a single, overall industry-wide fee, which the TMLC would then allocate among the individual stations.

In April 2002, BMI and the TMLC concluded three years of negotiations and reached an agreement for an annual industry-wide blanket-license fee of $85 million, which the industry would yield to BMI for its aggregate annual use of BMI-licensed music if all stations chose the blanket license. Under that agreement, in 2002 through 2004 a portion of that $85 million base fee would be allocated to every station in the industry.

---

2. The ABC, NBC and CBS television networks have separate licenses to perform BMI music.

The negotiation and agreement upon the industry-wide fee terminated BMI's contribution to the process: the allocation among the members of their respective contributions toward that amount was devised by, and carried out by, the Television Music License Committee.

The TMLC devised an allocation formula based primarily on television "ratings," which measure the size of a television audience. Taking ratings data compiled by Nielsen, each of the roughly 210 markets in the country as measured by Nielsen was placed in one of nine categories, each of which was arithmetically weighted "to reflect, within a broad parameter, that a household in the 150th market does not represent the same value as a household in the New York market." (The word "value," of course, refers to the desirability to advertisers, and the amount they will pay, for air time.) Within each market a series of computations apportioned the total blanket license fee assigned to that market among the stations in it, according to each station's share of the viewing audience at different times during the average day.

Oversimplifying the process, it resulted in allocating each market's portion of the total $85 million among the stations in that market, according to the portion they enjoyed of that market's television audience.

From 1995 to April 1, 1999, Weigel agreed to be bound by the outcome of the TMLC's negotiations with BMI, and executed a blanket BMI license agreement for WCIU. The terms of the license and allocation formula for the 1995–1999 period were essentially the same as those for the 1999–2004 period, except for increases in BMI's industry-wide blanket base fee.

In May 1998, WCIU's monthly blanket fees under its 1995–1999 BMI license increased from $5,882 to $9,002. Weigel rejected the increase.... Despite subsequent communications and meetings, the parties have been unable to agree on music license fees for the period of April 1, 1999 to the present. On November 19, 2004, BMI filed its petition for an order setting reasonable license fees for Weigel's stations.

The relationship between BMI and Weigel is governed by, and BMI has limited flexibility under, the Decree. The general method of setting a reasonable fee is well-recognized in case law. Essentially, it proceeds from prices paid in other transactions between willing sellers and buyers more or less similarly situated to the particular case. Those transactions (called "benchmarks") are evaluated, their differences from the present case are weighed, and a process of triangulation and adjustment develops the proper figure for the case at hand.

As described in *United States v. Broadcast Music, Inc. (Music Choice)*, 316 F.3d 189, 194 (2d Cir.2003):

> In making a determination of reasonableness (or of a reasonable fee), the court attempts to make a determination of the fair market value — "the price that a willing buyer and a willing seller would agree to in an arm's length transaction." [*ASCAP v. Showtime/The Movie Channel*, 912 F.2d 563, 569 (2d Cir.1990)]. This determination is often facilitated by the use of a benchmark — that is, reasoning by analogy to an agreement reached after arms'

length negotiation between similarly situated parties. Indeed, the benchmark methodology is suggested by the BMI consent decree itself, of which article VIII(A) enjoins disparate treatment of similarly situated licensees.

That is the usual, and approved, method. As the court continued:

> While in some instances there may be reason to approximate fair market value on the basis of something other than the prices paid by consumers, in the absence of factors suggesting a different measure the price willing buyers and sellers agree upon in arm's-length transactions appears to be the best measure.

Music Choice, 316 F.3d at 195 (citing authority).

Since the most appropriate benchmarks may not exactly fit the case at hand, they may need adjustment to produce a proper figure. Examples of such adjustments are given in a later opinion of the Court of Appeals in the same *Music Choice* case, 426 F.3d 91, 97 (2d Cir.2005), elaborating on the rate court's duty:

> In choosing a benchmark and determining how it should be adjusted, a rate court must determine "the degree of comparability of the negotiating parties to the parties contending in the rate proceeding, the comparability of the rights in question, and the similarity of the economic circumstances affecting the earlier negotiators and the current litigants[.]"

Id. at 95, quoting [*United States v. ASCAP (Application of Buffalo Broadcasting Co., Inc.)*, Civ. No. 13-95 (WCC), 1993 U.S. Dist. LEXIS 2566 (S.D.N.Y. Feb. 26, 1993)], at *61.

These principles are encapsulated in article VIII(A) of the Decree, which forbids BMI from making or honoring any agreement resulting in different fees between similar licensees. That is not a matter of discretion or business preference, but a prohibition BMI must follow, on pain of contempt:

> Defendant shall not enter into, recognize as valid or perform any performing rights license agreement which shall result in discriminating in rates or terms between licensees similarly situated ...

BMI Consent Decree Art. VIII(A).

But the prohibition does not stop there. It recognizes that within the same principle there is the corollary that different fees must be allowed for licensees whose situations are different. The proviso allows for adjustments based upon business factors which justify them:

> ... provided, however, that differentials based upon applicable business factors which justify different rates or terms shall not be considered discrimination within the meaning of this section[.]

Id.

Accordingly, BMI must give Weigel the same rate it gives all others who are similarly situated; but equally, its rate to Weigel must recognize any business factors affecting Weigel which justify treating Weigel differently.

In this case there is only one available "benchmark." It consists of the uniform process to which each of the 1,300 members of the industry have agreed, and which operates neutrally as to each of them. The dollar figure to be paid by each station is calculated once for the following year and billed monthly.

Thus, the only "benchmark" in the industry lies in the acceptance by all its members (save Weigel) of their respective portions of the overall fee obligation. Of course that does not mean that the process produced a reasonable rate with respect to Weigel. If it did not, a reasonable rate must be set for Weigel, regardless whether that results in the other members of the industry bearing a greater or lesser proportion of the $85 million.

However, the virtual unanimity (even Weigel, up to a point) of the industry's acceptance of the negotiation-and-allocation method and its results, when each member had the ability to opt-out and make a rate court challenge as Weigel ultimately did, has two consequences. It provides hundreds of "benchmark" transactions in support of that method, and it leaves an absence of competing benchmarks.

Thus the question in this case is simple: whether, under article VIII(A) of the Decree there are "differentials based upon applicable business factors which justify different rates or terms" in Weigel's case. If there are, Weigel should pay a different, reasonable rate. If there are not, BMI is prohibited from offering different terms to Weigel.

The differences which Weigel perceives between its business and that of the other stations in the industry are not apparent when viewing the evidence as a whole. Nor are they shown, even when aggregated, to present "differentials based upon applicable business factors which justify different rates or terms" in the words of article VIII(A) of the Decree.

Like many other stations, WCIU has no local news program, which requires a large initial and continuing investment. Similarly, its sports programming contracts are not unique, and they allow WCIU to avoid substantial costs while attracting a large audience. Some of its advertisers choose (or not) to advertise on those of WCIU's programs which primarily target African-Americans, as "other stations around the country do as well." Its programming "has been, and had been, shown on numerous other stations across the country." Many other stations in the country are family-owned and privately held. Its programming generates less than average revenue at certain times of day, but is "exceptionally competitive" at others.

Even though each factor Weigel mentions is unexceptional in the industry, their individual or cumulative effect upon Weigel might justify an adjustment to the benchmark for Weigel. Whether that is the case is best determined by comparing WCIU's license fees, as a percentage of its revenues, to the percentages of their revenues that are paid as fees by the other stations in the industry. All parties agree that the percentages-of-revenues comparisons are the most meaningful, because the firms' revenues capture the net effect of all their business variations.

As a percentage of WCIU's revenues, its BMI license fees are equal to or less than the license fees paid by many other stations in the industry. Of all blanket-license stations in the top 50 markets in the country, 104 paid a higher percentage of their program revenues in BMI fees in at least one year during the years 1999–2004 than the highest percentage of WCIU's revenues billed to it by BMI during any of those years. . . .

Weigel asks the court to set a rate for WCIU based on the total BMI fees paid by the entire local television industry over the 1999–2004 time period as a percentage (approximately 0.33% to 0.41% by different calculations) of the industry's estimated program revenues during that period, instead of what WCIU was billed: 0.59% of its revenues in 1999, 0.54% in 2000, 0.49% in 2001, 0.69% in 2002, 0.63% in 2003, and 0.68% in 2004.

The concept is unrealistic. That percentage represents an amalgam of those stations who paid more and those who paid less than the average, and there is no support for the assumption that a reasonable fee for Weigel would fall at the middle. The more refined and ramified process employed by the TMLC in allocating the portions of the overall fee treated Weigel more rationally than merely arbitrarily selecting an average. . . .

For the foregoing reasons, the petition is granted and weigel is directed to pay BMI at the rates established by the BMI/TMLC license agreement and allocation from April 1, 1999 to date, with interest at the legal rate, but with credit for the payments already made. So ordered.

MOB Music Pub. v. Zanzibar on the Waterfront, L.L.C.

698 F. Supp. 2d 197 (D.D.C. 2010)

This is an action for copyright infringement arising under the United States Copyright Act, 17 U.S.C. § 101. Plaintiffs allege that defendants infringed their copyrights by giving unauthorized public performances of six musical compositions at defendants' establishment, Zanzibar on the Waterfront Restaurant. Pending before the Court is Plaintiffs' Motion for Summary Judgment. Upon consideration of the motion, the response and reply thereto, the applicable law, and the entire record, the Court hereby **GRANTS** Plaintiff's Motion for Summary Judgment.

Plaintiffs are the purported owners of six musical compositions at issue in this action. . . . Defendant Zanzibar on the Waterfront, L.L.C. is the owner and operator of Zanzibar on the Waterfront Restaurant—a nightclub and restaurant located in the District of Columbia, where live music is routinely performed. Defendant Michel L. Daley is the managing member of Zanzibar on the Waterfront. In his capacity as managing member, Defendant Daley performs a variety of functions for Zanzibar on the Waterfront Restaurant, including obtaining insurance, making bank deposits, signing checks, hiring and firing employees, marketing and promoting the restaurant, entering into licensing agreements for the restaurant, and handling all legal matters—including lawsuits.

Each plaintiff in this action is a member of the American Society of Composers, Authors and Publishers ("ASCAP"), to which they have granted a nonexclusive right to license non-dramatic public performances of their copyrighted musical compositions. On behalf of plaintiffs and its more than 360,000 members, ASCAP issues licenses to thousands of television networks, radio stations, nightclubs, restaurants, and other establishments whose owners desire to have public performances of copyrighted musical compositions in the ASCAP repertory.

Defendants were licensed to have live performances of any of the hundreds of thousands of works in the ASCAP repertory for periods prior to August 15, 2006. Effective August 15, 2006, however, ASCAP terminated defendants' license for failure to pay license fees. Although ASCAP representatives made repeated offers to reinstate the license of Zanzibar on the Waterfront, defendants have failed to renew their ASCAP license. Accordingly, defendants have been without a license to have live performances of musical compositions in the ASCAP repertory since August 15, 2006.

On the evening of November 16, 2007, an investigator for ASCAP visited Zanzibar on the Waterfront Restaurant for the purpose of "making a contemporaneous list of the titles of all musical compositions performed during [his] visit which [he] was able to recognize." During his visit, the ASCAP investigator heard performances of five songs in the ASCAP repertory.... Plaintiffs filed suit against defendants on September 19, 2008, alleging that these musical compositions were performed in violation of the Copyright Act....

On August 24, 2009, plaintiffs filed a motion for summary judgment. Plaintiffs seek (i) statutory damages in the amount of $10,000 for each cause of action, for a total of $60,000; (ii) an injunction prohibiting further infringing performances of any copyrighted musical compositions in the ASCAP repertory; and (iii) reasonable attorney's fees and costs.... Plaintiffs' motion for summary judgment is now ripe for determination by the Court....

"A plaintiff seeking to establish copyright infringement must prove '(1) ownership of a valid copyright, and (2) copying of constituent elements of the work that are original.'" *Stenograph L.L.C. v. Bossard Assoc., Inc.*, 144 F.3d 96, 99 (D.C.Cir.1998) (quoting *Feist Publ'ns, Inc. v. Rural Tel. Serv. Co.*, 499 U.S. 340, 361, (1991)). In the music performance context, these requirements have been alternatively stated as: (1) originality and authorship of the compositions involved; (2) compliance with the formalities required to secure a copyright; (3) plaintiff's ownership of the copyright; and (4) defendant's public performance of the compositions.

To establish ownership of valid copyrights to the musical compositions at issue in this case, plaintiffs have filed copies of the copyright registration certificates for each musical composition as well as other pertinent documents demonstrating chain of title. Because these copyright registration certificates constitute prima facie evidence of plaintiffs' valid copyrights, defendants have the burden of establishing the invalidity of plaintiffs' titles....

Because plaintiffs are listed as the copyright claimants on the certificates of registration, they have satisfied their initial burden of demonstrating copyright ownership. As the leading treatise on this issue explains:

If the plaintiff was the author of the work in issue, he has no problem of proof beyond proving such authorship in establishing his ownership of the copyright. Where, however, the plaintiff claims not as author but as a direct or mesne assignee of the author, the question arises as to where the burden of proof lies in establishing the chain of title. Here, a distinction must be observed between a plaintiff who, as assignee of the copyright, (either common law or statutory), first registered a claim of statutory copyright in his name, and a plaintiff who was merely an assignee of a previously registered copyright. As the former has obtained a certificate of registration that constitutes *prima facie* evidence of the validity of his copyright, and of the facts stated therein, the defendant has the burden of controverting the plaintiff's chain of title. However, an assignee of a previously registered statutory copyright has the burden of proving his chain of title because nothing in the registration certificate evidences his right to claim through the original copyright claimant. Once such evidence is offered by the plaintiff, the burden shifts to the defendant to establish the invalidity of plaintiff's title.

3–12 Nimmer on Copyright § 12.11[C]. As defendants have produced no evidence to controvert plaintiffs' chain of title to the songs "Cha Cha Slide," "Around the Way Girl," "In Da Club," and "Big Poppa," the Court concludes that plaintiffs have established their ownership of valid copyrights for these musical compositions. [The Court also rejects defendant's claim that plaintiffs did not have proper chain of title for Bob Marley works "Jamming" and "Is This Love."] Accordingly, the Court finds that plaintiffs have established proof of ownership of all musical compositions at issue in this case.

In order to establish copyright infringement, plaintiffs must also establish that the six copyrighted musical compositions owned by plaintiffs were performed at the Zanzibar on the Waterfront Restaurant without plaintiffs' permission. The affidavits of Kevin McDonough and Mark Eanes—the [ASCAP] investigators—establish proof of the infringing behavior. Although defendants have generally denied that the musical compositions were performed at the restaurant on the dates alleged, they have offered no affirmative proof that the compositions were not performed. Nor have defendants offered any evidence that they received permission from the individual plaintiffs to perform the disputed musical compositions. Defendants, therefore, have failed to raise a genuine issue of fact necessary to defeat plaintiffs' motion for summary judgment.

In sum, the Court concludes that plaintiffs' have established that defendants unlawfully infringed upon their copyrights for "Cha Cha Slide," "Around the Way Girl," "In Da Club," "Big Poppa," "Jamming," and "Is This Love" through the unauthorized performance of these musical compositions at Zanzibar on the Waterfront Restaurant on November 17, 2007 and February 1, 2009. Accordingly, the Court hereby **GRANTS** plaintiffs' motion for summary judgment....

With respect to Defendant Daley, plaintiffs argue that he may be held vicariously liable for the copyright infringements because, *inter alia,* (i) he is the managing member of Zanzibar on the Waterfront, L.L.C. and is held out to the public as such; (ii) he has a supervisory role with respect to the operations of Zanzibar on the Waterfront

Restaurant; (iii) he has the right and ability to supervise the decision of which music is performed at Zanzibar on the Waterfront Restaurant; and (iv) he derives a direct financial benefit from the operation of Zanzibar on the Waterfront in the form of a salary and dividends. Defendants do not dispute these facts, nor do they respond to plaintiffs' arguments in their opposition brief. The Court will nevertheless, however, briefly review the law of vicarious liability.

It is well established that an individual may be held vicariously liable for copyright infringement if he (i) has the "right and ability" to supervise the infringing activity and (ii) has a "direct financial interest" in such activities. The imposition of liability on a controlling individual is based upon the belief that the individual is in a position to control the conduct of the entity which is the primary infringer. Lack of knowledge of the infringing activity, however, is not a defense; nor is the fact that independent contractors hired by defendants performed the infringing musical compositions. Indeed, "[e]ven when a restaurant proprietor instructs band members not to perform copyrighted music at his establishment, or inserts a provision to that effect in the band's contract, such proprietor cannot escape vicarious liability when he has a right to supervise and a financial interest in such performance." [*EMI April Music, Inc. v. White*, 618 F. Supp. 2d 497, 507 (E.D. Va. 2009)] (citing cases). Accordingly, the fact that "[t]he selection of songs played at the Defendants' club is determined by non-employee, independent contractors who are hired to play music at the club," does not absolve Defendant Daley of liability. Therefore, because it is undisputed that Defendant Daley had the right and ability to supervise the infringing activity, and because Defendant Daley had a financial interest in the infringing activity through his operation of the profit-making establishment, the Court concludes that Defendant Daley is jointly and severally liable, along with his co-defendant Zanzibar on the Waterfront, L.L.C., for the copyright infringements that are the subject of this action.

Having found defendants jointly and severally liable for the infringing behavior, the Court will now address the question of damages and relief.

Plaintiffs seek statutory damages pursuant to 17 U.S.C. §504(c)(1). Section 504(c)(1) directs the Court to award a copyright owner an amount "not less than $750 or more than $30,000" for each piece of work infringed. 17 U.S.C. §504(c)(1). In a case where a defendant has willfully violated a copyright, the Court "may increase the award of statutory damages to a sum of not more than $150,000" for each piece of work infringed.

It is important to note that statutory damages "are intended not merely for the restitution of reparation of injury, but to deter wrongful conduct." *EMI April Music*, 618 F.Supp.2d at 508 (internal quotation marks omitted). As the Supreme Court has long recognized:

> [A] rule of liability which merely takes away the profits from an infringement would offer little discouragement to infringers. It would fall short of an effective sanction for enforcement of the copyright policy. The statutory rule, formu-

lated after long experience, not merely compels restitution of profit and reparation for injury but also is designed to discourage wrongful conduct.

F.W. Woolworth Co. v. Contemporary Arts, 344 U.S. 228, 233 (1952). Indeed, in cases
such as this, courts have routinely awarded statutory damages in amounts between
two and three times the license fees.

Plaintiffs represent that had defendants been properly licensed by ASCAP to date,
defendants would owe approximately $26,395.15 in license fees and finance charges.
Plaintiffs argue that an award of damages equivalent to the ASCAP license fees, however, is insufficient to deter defendants from continued infringement of copyrighted
music, and urge the Court to award damages of $10,000 per infringement—for a
total of $60,000.

The Court agrees that damages in the amount of the ASCAP license fee, alone,
are insufficient to deter defendants from additional copyright infringements. Indeed,
after this lawsuit was filed, plaintiffs had to amend their complaint to add an additional
claim of copyright infringement which occurred on February 1, 2009—five months
after plaintiffs had instituted this action. Accordingly, the Court concludes that damages in the amount of $6,000 per infringement are warranted for the unlawful per-
formances of "Cha Cha Slide," "Around the Way Girl," "In Da Club," "Jamming," and
"Is This Love," which occurred on November 16, 2007, for a total of $30,000 (which
is slightly more than the total ASCAP license fee "saved"). The Court concludes that
damages in the amount of $10,000 are warranted for the unlawful performance of
"Big Poppa," which occurred several months after this lawsuit was filed and therefore
after defendants were put on notice of their infringing activity. Defendants are therefore jointly and severally liable in the amount of $40,000 in statutory damages.

Plaintiffs also seek a permanent injunction prohibiting defendants from publicly
performing any of the copyrighted musical compositions in the ASCAP repertory.
Pursuant to 17 U.S.C. §502(a), the Court may grant "temporary and final injunctions
on such terms as it may deem reasonable to prevent or restrain infringement of a
copyright." 17 U.S.C. §502(a). Because plaintiffs have established that defendants
have repeatedly infringed upon their copyrights by unlawfully performing their
musical compositions, and in view of defendants' unwillingness to renew their ASCAP
license despite ASCAP's repeated efforts, the Court concludes that a permanent injunction is warranted. Accordingly, the Court hereby **ORDERS** that defendants and
all persons acting under the direction, control, permission, or authority of defendants
are permanently **ENJOINED AND RESTRAINED** from publicly performing, or causing to be performed, or aiding and abetting the public performance of, any and all
music in the ASCAP repertory without proper authorization.

Finally, plaintiffs seek reasonable costs and attorney's fees in the amount of
$74,712.22. 17 U.S.C. §505 permits "the court in its discretion" to award "the recovery
of full costs by or against any party" as well as "reasonable attorney's fees to the prevailing party." 17 U.S.C. §505. Considering all the facts in this case, including plaintiffs'
interest in vindicating the rights provided to them by Congress in the Copyright Act,

plaintiffs' need to amend its complaint to add an additional infringement, and the protracted nature of this litigation, the Court concludes that an award of costs and attorney's fees is warranted. Having carefully reviewed the Declaration of Mr. Zelenko, the Court concludes that an award of attorney's fees in the amount of $69,145.00 and costs of $5,567.22 is reasonable. Defendants are therefore jointly and severally liable in the amount of $74,712.22 for attorney's fees and costs.

For the foregoing reasons, plaintiffs' motion for summary judgment is **GRANTED.**

Notes and Questions

a. Under the 1909 Copyright Act, one of the threshold issues for enforcement of a copyrighted work was whether the use of the work was for profit. Section 110 of the current Copyright Act provides similar limitations on the copyright holder by making certain rights unenforceable against nonprofit use. The seminal start of ASCAP's licensing power began when the Supreme Court recognized that an orchestra playing music in nightclubs constituted a for-profit use of the copyrighted works:

> These two cases present the same question: whether the performance of a copyrighted musical composition in a restaurant or hotel without charge for admission to hear it infringes the exclusive right of the owner of the copyright to perform the work publicly for profit.... The plaintiff owns the copyright of a lyric comedy in which is a march called "From Maine to Oregon." It took out a separate copyright for the march and published it separately. The defendant hotel company caused this march to be performed in the dining room of the Vanderbilt Hotel for the entertainment of guests during meal times, in the way now common, by an orchestra employed and paid by the company. It was held by the Circuit Court of Appeals, reversing the decision of the District Court, that this was not a performance for profit within the meaning of the act. The other case is similar so far as the present discussion is concerned. The plaintiffs were the composers and owners of a comic opera entitled "Sweethearts," containing a song of the same title as a leading feature in the performance. There is a copyright for the opera and also one for the song which is published and sold separately. This the Shanley Company caused to be sung by professional singers, upon a stage in its restaurant on Broadway, accompanied by an orchestra....
>
> If the rights under the copyright are infringed only by a performance where money is taken at the door they are very imperfectly protected. Performances not different in kind from those of the defendants could be given that might compete with and even destroy the success of the monopoly that the law intends the plaintiffs to have. It is enough to say that there is no need to construe the statute so narrowly. The defendants' performances are not eleemosynary. They are part of a total for which the public pays, and the fact that the price of the whole is attributed to a particular item which those present are expected to order, is not important. It is true that the music is

not the sole object, but neither is the food, which probably could be got cheaper elsewhere. The object is a repast in surroundings that to people having limited powers of conversation or disliking the rival noise give a luxurious pleasure not to be had from eating a silent meal. If music did not pay it would be given up. If it pays it pays out of the public's pocket. Whether it pays or not the purpose of employing it is profit and that is enough. Decrees reversed.

Herbert v. Shanley Co., 242 U.S. 591 (1917).

b. The first battle was waged between the musicians and the restaurateurs, and battles between the two have continued since *Shanley* was decided. In 1998, as part of the statutory package that increased the length of the copyright term by twenty years, Congress changed the statutory balance back in favor of the restaurants and shops. The Fairness in Music Licensing Act of 1998 created a music licensing exception for restaurants and other establishments meeting either size specifications or equipment limitations. Section 110(5) provides as follows:

(5)(A) except as provided in subparagraph (B), communication of a transmission embodying a performance or display of a work by the public reception of the transmission on a single receiving apparatus of a kind commonly used in private homes, unless—

(i) a direct charge is made to see or hear the transmission; or

(ii) the transmission thus received is further transmitted to the public;

(B) communication by an establishment of a transmission or retransmission embodying a performance or display of a nondramatic musical work intended to be received by the general public, originated by a radio or television broadcast station licensed as such by the Federal Communications Commission, or, if an audiovisual transmission, by a cable system or satellite carrier, if—

(i) in the case of an establishment other than a food service or drinking establishment, either the establishment in which the communication occurs has less than 2,000 gross square feet of space (excluding space used for customer parking and for no other purpose), or the establishment in which the communication occurs has 2,000 or more gross square feet of space (excluding space used for customer parking and for no other purpose) and—

(I) if the performance is by audio means only, the performance is communicated by means of a total of not more than 6 loudspeakers, of which not more than 4 loudspeakers are located in any 1 room or adjoining outdoor space; or

(II) if the performance or display is by audiovisual means, any visual portion of the performance or display is communicated by means of a total of not more than 4 audiovisual devices, of which not more than 1 audiovisual device is located in any 1 room, and no such audiovisual device has a diagonal screen size greater than 55 inches, and any audio portion of the performance or display is communicated by means of a total of not more than 6 loudspeakers, of which not more than 4 loudspeakers are located in any 1 room or adjoining outdoor space;

(ii) in the case of a food service or drinking establishment, either the establishment in which the communication occurs has less than 3,750 gross square feet of space (excluding space used for customer parking and for no other purpose), or the establishment in which the communication occurs has 3,750 gross square feet of space or more (excluding space used for customer parking and for no other purpose) and—

(I) if the performance is by audio means only, the performance is communicated by means of a total of not more than 6 loudspeakers, of which not more than 4 loudspeakers are located in any 1 room or adjoining outdoor space; or

(II) if the performance or display is by audiovisual means, any visual portion of the performance or display is communicated by means of a total of not more than 4 audiovisual devices, of which not more than 1 audiovisual device is located in any 1 room, and no such audiovisual device has a diagonal screen size greater than 55 inches, and any audio portion of the performance or display is communicated by means of a total of not more than 6 loudspeakers, of which not more than 4 loudspeakers are located in any 1 room or adjoining outdoor space;

(iii) no direct charge is made to see or hear the transmission or retransmission;

(iv) the transmission or retransmission is not further transmitted beyond the establishment where it is received; and

(v) the transmission or retransmission is licensed by the copyright owner of the work so publicly performed or displayed;

17 U.S.C. § 110(5). In addition, Congress added § 513 to assist these companies in their rate hearings. It allows the restaurant owner to sue in his home district rather than in New York and guarantees that the restaurant can continue to perform the music:

Pending the completion of such proceeding, the individual proprietor shall have the right to perform publicly the copyrighted musical compositions in the repertoire of the performing rights society by paying an interim license rate or fee into an interest bearing escrow account with the clerk of the court, subject to retroactive adjustment when a final rate or fee has been determined, in an amount equal to the industry rate, or, in the absence of an industry rate, the amount of the most recent license rate or fee agreed to by the parties.

17 U.S.C. § 513(5).

c. What does ASCAP or BMI have to prove to show that the defendant is willfully liable? *See Jobete Music Co. v. Johnson Commc'ns., Inc.*, 285 F. Supp. 2d 1077 (S.D. Ohio 2003).

d. Wait staff at commercial restaurants (or the guests themselves) will frequently sing the copyrighted tune "Happy Birthday." For decades, the copyright owner claimed that the work was registered in 1935, so if the restaurant did not have an ASCAP or BMI license, is the restaurant liable? *See Bonneville Intern. Corp. v. Peters*, 347 F.3d 485, 487 (3d Cir. 2003) ("every time you hear the ubiquitous refrain from "Happy Birthday" in a public performance, a subsidiary of AOL/TimeWarner cashes a royalty check."). In 2016, however, a lawsuit established that the song was first published as the "Good Morning and Birthday Song" in 1893. The provenance of the song was explained in Robert Brauneis, *Copyright and the World's Most Popular Song*, 56 J. COPYRIGHT SOCIETY U.S.A. 335, 338–40 (2009).

e. The history behind the Fairness in Music Licensing Act may provide some insight to the current law. The Supreme Court addressed the scope of the performance license in *Twentieth Century Music Corp. v. Aiken*, 422 U.S. 151 (1975).

> George Aiken owns and operates a small fast-service food shop in downtown Pittsburgh, Pa., known as "George Aiken's Chicken." Some customers carry out the food they purchase, while others remain and eat at counters or booths. Usually the "carry-out" customers are in the restaurant for less than five minutes, and those who eat there seldom remain longer than 10 or 15 minutes.
>
> A radio with outlets to four speakers in the ceiling receives broadcasts of music and other normal radio programming at the restaurant. Aiken usually turns on the radio each morning at the start of business. Music, news, entertainment, and commercial advertising broadcast by radio stations are thus heard by Aiken, his employees, and his customers during the hours that the establishment is open for business.
>
> On March 11, 1972, broadcasts of two copyrighted musical compositions were received on the radio from a local station while several customers were in Aiken's establishment. Petitioner Twentieth Century Music Corp. owns the copyright on one of these songs, "The More I See You"; petitioner Mary Bourne the copyright on the other, "Me and My Shadow." Petitioners are members of the American Society of Composers, Authors and Publishers (ASCAP), an association that licenses the performing rights of its members to their copyrighted works. The station that broadcast the petitioners' songs was licensed by ASCAP to broadcast them. Aiken, however, did not hold a license from ASCAP.
>
> The precise statutory issue in the present case is whether Aiken infringed upon the petitioners' exclusive right, under the Copyright Act of 1909, 17 U.S.C. § 1(e), "[t]o perform the copyrighted work publicly for profit." We may assume that the radio reception of the musical compositions in Aiken's

restaurant occurred "publicly for profit." When this statutory provision was enacted in 1909, its purpose was to prohibit unauthorized performances of copyrighted musical compositions in such public places as concert halls, theaters, restaurants, and cabarets. An orchestra or individual instrumentalist or singer who performs a copyrighted musical composition in such a public place without a license is thus clearly an infringer under the statute.

The entrepreneur who sponsors such a public performance for profit is also an infringer—direct or contributory. With the advent of commercial radio, a broadcast musical composition could be heard instantaneously by an enormous audience of distant and separate persons operating their radio receiving sets to reconvert the broadcast to audible form. It was soon established in the federal courts that the broadcast of a copyrighted musical composition by a commercial radio station was a public performance of that composition for profit—and thus an infringement of the copyright if not licensed.

To hold in this case that the respondent Aiken "performed" the petitioners' copyrighted works would result in a regime of copyright law that would be both wholly unenforceable and highly inequitable.

The practical unenforceability of a ruling that all of those in Aiken's position are copyright infringers is self-evident. One has only to consider the countless business establishments in this country with radio or television sets on their premises—bars, beauty shops, cafeterias, car washes, dentists' offices, and drive-ins—to realize the total futility of any evenhanded effort on the part of copyright holders to license even a substantial percentage of them.

The Court of Appeals observed that ASCAP now has license agreements with some 5,150 business establishments in the whole country, noting that these include "firms which employ on premises sources for music such as tape recorders and live entertainment." As a matter of so-called "policy" or "practice," we are told, ASCAP has not even tried to exact licensing agreements from commercial establishments whose radios have only a single speaker.

Id.

As a result of the Supreme Court ruling, the practice arose that ASCAP and BMI limited the licensing of radios to those stores and restaurants which had more than four speakers or otherwise exceeded the usage made by Mr. Aiken.

f. In *Pandora Media, Inc. v. ASCAP*, 785 F.3d 73, 77 (2d Cir. 2015), the Second Circuit explained that the ASCAP consent decree unambiguously prohibits a publisher's "partial withdrawal" of the right to license the songs in its catalog to some of ASCAP's licensees but not to others. Instead, ASCAP is required "to license its entire repertory to all eligible users; publishers may not license works to ASCAP for licensing to some eligible users but not others."

g. In *United States v. Broad. Music, Inc.*, 720 F. App'x 14 (2d Cir. 2017) a very different question emerged about partial licensing. Here, BMI challenged a ruling that it could not offer "fractional licenses," meaning licenses for which it had some of the copyright holder's rights but not all of the rights. For example, if two people co-author a song and one of them is a member of ASCAP and one of them is a member of BMI, then the licensee would need the rights from both ASCAP and BMI to properly license the work. This is actually a very common occurrence, and given the market dominance of those two PROs, must licensing issues are resolved by having licenses from both organizations. As the opinion explained, "[e]ach individual co-owner has a right to public performance, and such a right is not associated specifically with "full-work" licensing or with an indivisibility principle." The court did not find the fractional licenses to violate the consent decree.

h. New technologies continue to create challenges to the licensing from the performing rights societies. These include Internet streaming (*United States v. ASCAP in re AOL, RealNetworks and Yahoo! Inc.*, 559 F. Supp. 2d 332 (S.D.N.Y. 2008), *vacated*, 627 F.3d 64 (2d Cir. 2010) (AOL, Yahoo!)) and online videos (*United States v. ASCAP* by United States v. Am. Soc'y of Composers, 2010 U.S. App. LEXIS 19983 (2d Cir. Sept. 28, 2010) (YouTube)). As streaming grows in economic importance, the legal issues in these licenses will take on increased importance as well.

i. A critical question for the performance rights societies has been the characterization of digital downloads. While online streaming of content is undoubtedly a public performance of the content, what about the ephemeral performance of music content as it is made available to a consumer's computer or mobile device?

> In answering the question of whether a download is a public performance, we turn to Section 101 of the Copyright Act, which states that "[t]o 'perform' a work means to recite, render, play, dance, or act it, either directly or by means of any device or process." 17 U.S.C. § 101. A download plainly is neither a "dance" nor an "act." Thus, we must determine whether a download of a musical work falls within the meaning of the terms "recite," "render," or "play."

> The ordinary sense of the words "recite," "render," and "play" refer to actions that can be perceived contemporaneously. To "recite" is "to repeat from memory or read aloud esp[ecially] before an audience," Webster's Third New International Dictionary 1895 (1981); to "render" is to "say over: recite, repeat,"; and to "play" is to "perform on a musical instrument," "sound in performance," "reproduce sound of recorded material," or "act on a stage or in some other dramatic medium,". All three actions entail contemporaneous perceptibility.

> Because the electronic download itself involves no recitation, rendering, or playing of the musical work encoded in the digital transmission, we hold that such a download is not a performance of that work, as defined by § 101.

United States v. Am. Soc'y of Composers, 627 F.3d 64, 71–73 (2d Cir. 2010).

j. New forms of performance rights societies for sound recordings are being developed under the Music Modernization Act of 2018. These societies, however, cover the rights of the sound recording copyright holder rather than the publisher. Because they are creatures of statute, they do not fall within the consent decrees that enable the government to manage ASCAP and BMI. In time, however, there will also be First Amendment challenges regarding the obligation to pay and distribute funds in the manner set out by Congress. To what extent does the historical consent decree control over ASCAP and BMI thwart the First Amendment rights of the music publishers?

k. Rate setting for the independent television stations. The Television Music License Committee (TVMLC) provides this summary of its role:

> The Television Music License Committee (TVMLC) is a non-profit trade association, that represents all full-power, commercial television stations in the United States and its territories in negotiations for music performing rights licenses that stations sign with the two largest Performing Rights Organizations (PRO's), ASCAP and BMI. Through a settlement of a lawsuit filed by some broadcasters and funded by the TVMLC, SESAC has agreed to negotiate industry-wide licenses with the Committee through 2035.

> We also designed the method of allocating industry-wide fees among all of the stations licensed by ASCAP, BMI and SESAC (the vast majority of local television stations), subject to agreement of the PRO or court approval and then we calculate the fees billed to each individual station. After stations sign their individual agreements, we try to help resolve problems between stations and all of the PRO's. We are the station's advocate.

From Revenue Base to Reduced Fixed Fee and Per Program, TELEVISION MUSIC LICENSE COMMITTEE, LLC, https://tvmlc.com (last visited Sept. 12, 2019).

In the earliest versions of these licenses, stations paid fees as a percentage of their revenues. In the early 1990s, after decades of negotiation and litigation, the TVMLC was able to get ASCAP and BMI to provide stations with an industry-wide fixed fee license accompanied by a meaningful per program license. This per program license allows some stations to achieve significant reductions in fees paid to ASCAP and to BMI by direct or source licensing the music used in local and syndicated programming. Over the last 15 years, these two changes taken together have accounted for over a billion dollars of savings when compared to what stations would have paid under the previous revenue-based industry licenses.

Problem 10-C

For the past two months, Bryce has been earning extra money by managing a local bar several nights each week. To keep the customers amused, Bryce occasionally brings in an electric guitar and plays songs. In fact, as Bryce explains to you over the telephone, it worked so well that Bryce invited some local bands to liven the place up. Bryce swears that the only songs played were songs written by Bryce or others in the bands. Bryce was amazed that letters from both ASCAP and BMI arrived at the bar.

The bar owner and manager are both quite upset. While Bryce does not remember singing the songs listed in the cease and desist letters, Bryce does remember talking with the college kids who had notepads and were listening to the songs very intently. The bar has stopped Bryce and all other bands from appearing. The owner wants to know what is likely to happen if he ignores the letters or how he can go about correcting Bryce's mistake. Bryce is fairly confident that the owner will go after Bryce for any costs, so Bryce wants you to provide advice which Bryce can use to negotiate with ASCAP, BMI, and the bar owner.

D. Antitrust Regulation of the Performing Rights Societies

United States v. ASCAP

No. 41-1395 (WCC), 2001 U.S. Dist. LEXIS 23707,
2001-1 Trade Cas. (CCH) P73474, 2001-2 Trade Cas.
(CCH) P73474 (S.D.N.Y. June 11, 2001)

Plaintiff having filed its complaint herein on February 26, 1941, the original defendants having appeared and filed their answer to the complaint denying the substantive allegations thereof, all parties having consented, without trial or adjudication of any issue of fact or law therein, to the entry of a Civil Decree and Judgment, filed March 4, 1941, to the entry of an Amended Final Judgment on March 14, 1950, as subsequently amended and modified and to the entry of an Order thereunder issued on January 7, 1960, as subsequently amended and modified;

The parties having moved the Court to amend the Amended Final Judgment,

NOW, THEREFORE, before the taking of any testimony, and without trial or adjudication of any issue of fact or law herein, without admission by the defendant American Society of Composers, Authors and Publishers with respect to any such issue, and upon consent of all remaining parties hereto, it is hereby

ORDERED, ADJUDGED, AND DECREED that the Amended final Judgment be amended as follows:

I. Jurisdiction. This Court has jurisdiction of the subject matter hereof and of all parties hereto. The complaint states a claim upon which relief may be granted against ASCAP under Section 1 of the Sherman Act, 15 U.S.C. §1.

II. Definitions. As used in this Second Amended Final Judgment:

(A) "ASCAP" means the American Society of Composers, Authors and Publishers;

(B) "ASCAP music" means any work in the ASCAP repertory;

(C) "ASCAP repertory" means those works the right of public performance of which ASCAP has or hereafter shall have the right to license at the relevant point in time;

(D) "Background/foreground music service" means a person that transmits performances of music to subscribers and that furnishes to those subscribers equipment not otherwise available to the general public that enables subscribers to make the transmitted performances on their premises. A background/foreground music service does not include radio or television stations or networks, cable television networks or systems, persons that transmit renditions of music to private homes, apartments, or hotel or motel guest rooms, or persons that transmit renditions of music to subscribers that charge admission;

(E) "Blanket License" means a non-exclusive license that authorizes a music user to perform ASCAP music, the fee for which does not vary depending on the extent to which the music user in fact performs ASCAP music;

(F) "Broadcaster" means any person who transmits audio or audio-visual content substantially similar to content that is transmitted by over-the-air or cable radio or television stations or networks as they existed on the date of entry of this Second Amended Final Judgment or that transmits the signal of another broadcaster: (1) over the air, (2) via cable television or direct broadcast satellite, or (3) via other existing or yet-to-be-developed transmission technologies, to audiences using radios, television sets, computers, or other receiving or playing devices;

(G) "Music user" means any person that (1) owns or operates an establishment or enterprise where copyrighted musical compositions are performed publicly, or (2) is otherwise directly engaged in giving public performances of copyrighted musical compositions;

(H) "On-line music user" means a person that publicly performs works in the ASCAP repertory via the Internet or similar transmission facility including any succeeding transmission technologies developed after entry of this Second Amended Final Judgment;

(I) "Performing rights organization" means an association or corporation, such as ASCAP, Broadcast Music, Inc., or SESAC, Inc., that collectively licenses rights of public performance on behalf of numerous copyright owners;

(J) "Per-program license" means a non-exclusive license that authorizes a broadcaster to perform ASCAP music in all of the broadcaster's programs, the fee for which varies depending upon which programs contain ASCAP music not otherwise licensed for public performance;

(K) "Per-segment license" means a non-exclusive license that authorizes a music user to perform any or all works in the ASCAP repertory in all segments of the music users's activities in a single industry, the fee for which varies depending upon which segments contain ASCAP music not otherwise licensed for public performance;

(L) "Person" means an individual, partnership, firm, association, corporation or other business or legal entity;

(M) "Program" means either a discrete program exhibited by a broadcaster or on-line music user or, if such broadcaster or on-line music user does exhibit discrete programs, such other portion of the transmissions made by the broadcaster or on-line music user as shall be agreed to by ASCAP and the broadcaster or on-line music user or as shall be determined by the Court in a proceeding conducted under Section IX of this Second Amended Final Judgment;

(N) "Public list" means such records that indicate the title, date of U.S. copyright registration, if any, writer and current publisher or other copyright owner of all works in the ASCAP repertory, including, but not limited to, the public electronic list;

(O) "Public electronic list" means separate databases of: (1) works in the ASCAP repertory that have been registered with ASCAP since January 1, 1991, or identified in ASCAP's surveys of performed works since January 1, 1978, identifying the title, writer, and current publisher or other copyright owner of each work; and (2) current ASCAP members;

(P) "Representative music user" means a music user whose frequency, intensity and type of music usage is typical of a group of similarly situated music users;

(Q) "Right of public performance" means, and "perform" refers to, the right to perform a work publicly in a nondramatic manner, sometimes referred to as the "small performing right," and any equivalent rights under foreign copyright law, including, but not limited to, rights known as the rights of transmission, retransmission, communication, diffusion and rediffusion;

(R) "Similarly situated" means music users or licenses in the same industry that perform ASCAP music and that operate similar businesses and use music in similar ways and with similar frequency; factors relevant to determining whether music users or licensees are similarly situated include, but are not limited to, the nature and frequency of musical performances, ASCAP's cost of administering licenses, whether the music users or licensees complete with one another, and the amount and source of the music users' revenue;

(S) "Through-to-the-Audience License" means a license that authorizes the simultaneous or so-called "delayed" performances of ASCAP music that are contained in content transmitted or delivered by a music user to another music user with whom the licensee has an economic relationship relating to that content;

(T) "Total license fee" means the sum of all fees paid by the music user in connection with the license, including any fee for ambient or incidental uses but excluding the administrative charges authorized by Section VII(B) of this Second Amended Final Judgment;

(U) "Work" means any copyrighted musical composition; and

(V) "Writer" means a person who has written the music or lyrics of a work.

III. Applicability. The provisions of this Second Amended Final Judgment shall apply to ASCAP, its successors and assigns, and to each of its officers, directors, agents, employees, and to all other persons in active concert or participation with any of them who shall have received actual notice of this Second Amended Final Judgment by personal service or otherwise. Except as provided an Sections IV (A) and (B) of this Second Amended Final Judgment, none of the injunctions or requirements herein imposed upon ASCAP shall apply to the acquisition or licensing of the right to perform musical compositions publicly solely outside the United States of America, its territories or possessions.

IV. Prohibited Conduct. ASCAP is hereby enjoined and restrained from:

(A) Holding, acquiring, licensing, enforcing, or negotiating concerning any foreign or domestic rights in copyrighted musical compositions other than rights of public performance on a non-exclusive basis; provided; however, that ASCAP may collect and distribute royalties for home recording devices and media to the extent such royalty collection is required or authorized by statute;

(B) Limiting, restricting, or interfering with the right of any member to issue, directly or through an agent other than a performing rights organization, non-exclusive licenses to music users for rights of public performance;

(C) Entering into, recognizing, enforcing or claiming any rights under any license for rights of public performance which discriminates in license fees or other terms and conditions between licensees similarly situated;

(D) Granting any license to any music user for rights of public performance in excess of five years' duration;

(E) Granting to, enforcing against, collecting any monies from, or negotiating with any motion picture theater exhibitor concerning the right of public performance for music synchronized with motion pictures;

(F) Asserting or exercising any right or power to restrict from public performance by any licensee of ASCAP any work in order to exact additional consideration for the performance thereof, or for the purpose of permitting the fixing or regulating of fees for the recording or transcribing of such work; nothing in this Section IV(F) shall be construed to prevent ASCAP, when so directed by the member in interest in respect of a work, from restricting performances of a work in order reasonably to protect the work against indiscriminate performances, or the value of the public performance rights therein, or the dramatic or "grand" performing rights therein or to prevent ASCAP from restricting performances of a work so far as may be reasonably necessary in connection with any claim or litigation involving the performing rights in any such work;

(G) Instituting, threatening to institute, maintaining, continuing, sponsoring, funding or providing any legal services for any suit or proceeding against any motion picture theater exhibitor for copyright infringement relating to the nondramatic public performance of any work contained in a motion picture, provided, however, that nothing this Section IV(G) shall preclude

ASCAP from pursuing its own *bona fide* independent interest in any such suit or proceeding; and

(H) Issuing to any broadcaster any license the fee for which is based upon a percentage of the income received by the licensee from programs that include no ASCAP music unless the broadcaster to whom such license shall be issued shall desire a license on such a basis; provided, however, that this Section IV(H) shall not limit the discretion the Court in a proceeding conducted under Section IX of this Second Amended Final Judgment to determine a license fee on any appropriate basis.

V. Through-to-the-Audience Licenses. ASCAP is hereby ordered and directed to issue upon request, a through-to-the-audience license to a broadcaster, an on-line user, a background/foreground music service, and an operator of any yet-to-be-developed technology that transmits content to other music users with whom it has an economic relationship relating to that content; provided, however, that, in accordance with Section III of this Second Amended Final Judgment, ASCAP shall not be required to issue a through-to-the-audience license to perform ASCAP music outside the United States. The fee for a through-to-the-audience license shall take into account the value of all performances made pursuant to the license.

VI. Licensing. ASCAP is hereby ordered and directed to grant to any music user making a written request therefor a non-exclusive license to perform all of the works in the ASCAP repertory; provided, however, that ASCAP shall not be required to issue a license to any music user that is in material breach or default of any license agreement by failing to pay to ASCAP any license fee that is indisputably owed to ASCAP. ASCAP shall not grant to any music user a license to perform one or more specified works in the ASCAP repertory, unless both the music user and member or members in interest shall have requested ASCAP in writing to do so, or unless ASCAP, at the written request of the prospective music user shall have sent a written notice of the prospective music user's request for a license to each such member at the member's last known address, and such member shall have failed to reply within thirty (30) days thereafter.

VII. Per-Program and Per-Segment Licenses.

(A) ASCAP is ordered and directed to offer, upon written request:

(1) To a broadcaster, a per-program license that shall, in addition, cover ambient and incidental uses and shall not require any record-keeping or monitoring of ambient and incidental uses; and

(2) To a background/foreground music service or to an on-line music user, a per-segment license if (a) the music user's performances of music can be tracked and monitored to determine with reasonable accuracy which segments of the music user's activity are subject to an ASCAP license fee; (b) the music user's performances of music can be attributed to segments commonly recognized within the music user's industry for which a license fee can be assessed; and (c) administration of the license will not

impose an unreasonable burden on ASCAP, the per-segment license shall, in addition, cover ambient and incidental uses without any record-keeping or monitoring of those uses if that is reasonably necessary to afford a genuine choice among the types of licenses offered, or of the benefits of any of those types of licenses, if a portion of any on-line music user's transmissions consists of programs substantially similar to those transmitted by over-the-air or cable radio or television stations or networks as they existed on the date of entry of this Second Amended Final Judgment, or is a retransmission of any broadcaster's programs, it shall be presumed that each individual program shall constitute a segment and for those segments the on-line music user need not meet the requirements of subsections (a), (b) and (c) of this section.

(B) ASCAP may charge any music user that selects a per-program license or a per-segment license a fee to recover its reasonable cost of administering the license.

(C) Nothing in this Second Amended Final Judgment shall prevent ASCAP and any music user from agreeing on any other form of license.

(D) The fee for a per-program license and for any per-segment license issued to an on-line user shall be at the option of ASCAP either:

(1) Expressed in terms of dollars, requiring the payment of a specified amount for each program or segment that contains works in the ASCAP repertory not otherwise licensed for public performance; or

(2) Expressed as a percentage of the music user's revenue attributable to each program or segment that contains works in the ASCAP repertory not otherwise licensed for public performance.

VIII. Genuine Choice.

(A) ASCAP shall use its best efforts to avoid any discrimination among the various types of licenses offered to any group of similarly situated music users that would deprive those music users of a genuine choice among the various types of licenses offered, or of the benefits of any of those types of licenses.

(B) For a representative music user, the total license fee for a per-program or per-segment license shall, at the time the license fee is established, approximate the fee for a blanket license; for the purpose of making that approximation, it shall be assumed for the purposes of this Section VIII(B) that all of the music user's programs or segments that contain performances of ASCAP music are subject to an ASCAP fee.

(C) ASCAP shall maintain an up-to-date system for tracking music use by per-program and per-segment licenses; ASCAP shall not be required to incur any unreasonable costs in maintaining such system; ASCAP may require its members and such licensees to provide ASCAP with all information reasonably necessary to administer the per-program or per-segment license including, but not limited to:

(1) cue sheets or music logs;

(2) the date of performance of a work and identification of the program or other segment of the music user's activities that contained the performance;

(3) the title of the work performed; and

(4) the writer, publisher or performing artist;

such requirements shall be designed to avoid unreasonable burdens on ASCAP, ASCAP members and licenses.

(D) The terms and requirements of any license shall be designed to avoid imposing any unreasonable burdens or costs on licensees or ASCAP.

IX. Determination of Reasonable Fees.

(A) ASCAP shall, upon receipt of a written request for a license for the right of public performance of any, some or all of the works in the ASCAP repertory, advise the music user in writing of the fee that it deems reasonable for the license requested or the information that it reasonably requires in order to quote a reasonable fee. In the event ASCAP requires such additional information, it shall so advise the music user in writing, and shall advise the music user in writing of the fee that it deems reasonable within sixty (60) days of receiving such information. If the parties are unable to reach agreement within sixty (60) days from the date when the request for a license is received by ASCAP, or within sixty (60) days of ASCAP's request for information, whichever is later, the music user may apply to the Court for a determination of a reasonable fee retroactive to the date of the written request for a license, and ASCAP shall, upon receipt of notice of the filing of such request, promptly give notice of the filing to the Assistant Attorney General in charge of the Antitrust Division. If the parties are unable to agree upon a reasonable fee within ninety (90) days from the date when ASCAP advises the music user of the fee that it deems reasonable or requests additional information from the music user, and if the music user has not applied to the Court for a determination of a reasonable fee, ASCAP may apply to the Court for the determination of a reasonable fee retroactive to the date of a written request for a license and ASCAP shall upon filing such application promptly give notice of the filing to the Assistant Attorney General in charge of the Antitrust Division.

(B) In any such proceeding, the burden of proof shall be on ASCAP to establish the reasonableness of the fee it seeks except that, where a music user seeks a per-segment license, the music user shall have the burden of demonstrating that is performances of music can be tracked and monitored to determine with reasonable accuracy which segments of the music user's activity are subject to an ASCAP fee and of demonstrating that the music user's performances of music can be attributed to segments commonly recognized within the music user's industry for which a license fee can be assessed.

(C) The fees negotiated by ASCAP and any music user during the first five years that ASCAP licenses music users in that industry shall not be evidence of the reasonableness of any fees (other than an interim fee as provided in Section IX(F) of this Second Amended Final Judgment) for any license in any proceeding under this Section IX.

(D) Should ASCAP not establish that the fee it requested is reasonable, then the Court shall determine a reasonable fee based upon all the evidence.

(E) The parties shall have the matter ready for trial by the Court within one year of the filing of the application unless ASCAP and at least one music user request that the Court delay the trial for an additional period not to exceed one year. No other delay shall be granted unless good cause is shown for extending such schedule. Pending the completion of any such negotiations or proceedings, the music user shall have the right to perform any, some or all of the works in the ASCAP repertory to which its application pertains, without payment of any fee or other compensation, but subject to the provisions of Section IX(F) of this Second Amended Final Judgment, and to the final order or judgment entered by the Court in such proceeding.

(F) When a music user has the right to perform works in the ASCAP repertory pending the completion of any negotiations or pending proceeding provided for in Section IX(A) of this Second Amended Final Judgment, either the music user or ASCAP may apply to the Court to fix an interim fee pending final determination or negotiation of a reasonable fee. The Court shall then fix an interim fee within ninety (90) days of such application for an interim fee retroactive to the date of the written request for a license, allowing only such limited discovery, if any, that the Court deems necessary to the fixing of such interim fee. In fixing such interim fee, there shall be a presumption that the last existing license (if any) between the music user and ASCAP, or between licensees similarly situated to the music user and ASCAP, sets forth the appropriate interim fee. If the Court fixes such interim fee, ASCAP shall then issue and the music user shall accept a license providing for the payment of a fee at such interim rate from the date of the request by such music user for a license pursuant to Section IX(A) of this Second Amended Final Judgment. If the music user fails to accept such a license or fails to pay the interim fee in accordance therewith, such failure shall be ground for the dismissal of its application for a reasonable fee, if any.

(G) When a reasonable fee has been determined by the Court, ASCAP shall be required to offer a license at a comparable fee to all other similarly situated music users who shall thereafter request a license of ASCAP; provided, however, that any license agreement that has been executed between ASCAP and another similarly situated music user prior to such determination by the

Court shall not be deemed to be in any way affected or altered by such determination for the term of such license agreement.

(H) Nothing in this Section IX shall prevent any applicant or licensee from attacking in the aforesaid proceedings or in any other controversy the validity of the copyright of any of the compositions in the ASCAP repertory, nor shall this Second Amended Final Judgment be construed as importing any validity or value to any of said copyrights.

(I) Pursuant to its responsibility to monitor and ensure compliance with this Second Amended Final Judgment, the United States may participate fully in any proceeding brought under this Section IX. Any order or agreement governing the confidentiality of documents or other products of discovery in any such proceeding shall contain the following provisions:

(1) The Department of Justice (the "Department") may make a written request for copies of any documents, deposition transcripts or other products of discovery ("products of discovery") produced in the proceeding. If the Department makes such a request to a party other than the party who produced the materials in the proceeding or to a deponent ("the producing party"), the Department and the party to whom it directed the request shall provide a copy of the request to the producing party. The producing party must file any objection to the request with the Court within thirty days of receiving the request; if the producing party does not file such an objection, the person to whom the Department directed its request shall provide the materials to the Department promptly;

(2) Any party to the proceeding may provide the Department with copies of any products of discovery produced in the proceeding. Any party who provides the Department with copies of any product of discovery shall inform the other parties to the proceeding within fifteen days of providing such materials to the Department. The producing party must file any objection to the production within fifteen days of receiving such notice; and

(3) The Department shall not disclose any products of discovery that it obtains under this order that have been designated as "confidential" in good faith or as otherwise protectable under Fed. R. Civ. P. 26(c)(7) to any third party without the consent of the producing party, except as provided in the Antitrust Civil Process Act, *15 U.S.C. §1313*(c), (d), or as otherwise required by law.

X. Public Lists.

(A) Within 90 days of entry of this Second Amended Final Judgment, ASCAP shall, upon written request from any music user or prospective music user:

(1) Inform that person whether any work identified by title and writer is in the ASCAP repertory; or

(2) Make a good faith effort to do so if identifying information other than title and writer is provided.

(B) Within 90 days of entry of this Second Amended Final Judgment, ASCAP shall:

(1) Make the public list available for inspection at ASCAP's offices during regular business hours, maintain it thereafter, and update it annually; and

(2) Make the public electronic list available through on-line computer access (*e.g.*, the Internet), update it weekly, make copies of it available in a machine-readable format (*e.g.*, CD-ROM) for the cost of reproduction, and update the machine-readable copies semi-annually.

(C) Beginning 90 days after entry of this Second Amended Final Judgment, the first written offer of a license that ASCAP makes to a music user or prospective music user shall describe how to gain access to the public list and public electronic list and describe the variety of works in the ASCAP repertory, including, but not limited to, a list of writers, genres of music and works that illustrates that variety.

(D) After the date on which ASCAP makes the public electronic list available pursuant to Section X(B)(2) of this Second Amended Final Judgment, ASCAP shall not institute or threaten to institute, maintain, continue, sponsor, fund (wholly or partially, directly or indirectly) or provide any legal services for, any suit or proceeding against any music user for copyright infringement relating to the right of nondramatic public performance of any work in the ASCAP repertory that is not, at the time of the alleged infringement, identified on the public electronic list; provided, however, that nothing in this Section X shall preclude ASCAP from pursuing its own *bona fide* independent interest in any such suit or proceeding. This Section X(D) shall not apply to any such suit or proceeding pending on the date of entry of this Second Amended Final Judgment.

XI. Membership.

A. ASCAP is hereby ordered and directed to admit to membership, non-participating or otherwise:

(1) Any writer who shall have had at least one work regularly published, whether or not performance of the work has been recorded in an ASCAP survey; or

(2) Any person actively engaged in the music publishing business, whose musical publications have been used or distributed on a commercial scale for at least one year, and who assumes the financial risk involved in the normal publication of musical works.

B. (1) ASCAP shall distribute to its members the monies received by licensing rights of public performance, less its costs, primarily on the basis of performances of its members' works (excluding those works licensed by the member directly) as indicated by objective surveys of performances periodically made by or for ASCAP, provided, however, that ASCAP may make special awards of its distributable revenues to writers and publishers whose works have a unique prestige value, or which make a significant contribution to the ASCAP repertory. Distribution of ASCAP's distributable revenue based on such objective surveys shall reflect the value to ASCAP of performances in the various media, and the method or formula for such distribution shall be fully and clearly disclosed to all members. Upon written request of any member, ASCAP shall disclose information sufficient for that member to determine exactly how that member's payment was calculated by ASCAP.

(2) Where feasible, ASCAP shall conduct, or cause to have conducted, a census or a scientific, randomly selected sample of the performances of the works of its members. Such census or sample shall be designed to reflect accurately the number and identification of performances and the revenue attributable to those performances, made in accordance with a design made and periodically reviewed by an independent and qualified person.

(3) ASCAP shall not restrict the right of any member to withdraw from membership in ASCAP at the end of any calendar year upon giving three months' advance written notice to ASCAP; provided, however, that any writer or publisher member who resigns from ASCAP and whose works continue to be licensed by ASCAP by reason of the continued membership of a co-writer, writer or publisher of any such works, may elect to continue receiving distribution for such works on the same basis and with the same elections as a member would have, so long as the resigning member does not license the works to any other performing rights licensing organization for performance in the United States. ASCAP may require a written acknowledgment from such resigning member that the works have not been so licensed.

(a) A resigning member shall receive distribution from ASCAP for performances occurring through the last day of the member's membership in ASCAP, regardless of the date the revenue are received.

(b) ASCAP shall not, in connection with any member's resignation, change the valuation of that member's works or the basis on which distribution is made to that member, unless such changes are part of similar changes applicable to all members in the resigning member's classification.

(c) Notwithstanding the foregoing, for any member who resigns from ASCAP, ASCAP is enjoined and restrained from requiring that member to agree that the withdrawal of such works be subject to any rights or obligations existing between ASCAP and its licensees, provided, however, that ASCAP may make withdrawal of any works from the ASCAP repertory subject to any license agreement between ASCAP and any licensee that is in effect on the date that this provision becomes effective.

C. Each provision of Section XI(B) of this Second Amended Final Judgment shall only be effective upon entry of an order in *United States v. Broadcast Music, Inc.,* 2001 U.S. Dist. LEXIS 10368, No. 64 Civ. 3787 (S.D.N.Y.), that contains a substantially identical provision. Until the provisions of Section XI(B)(3) of this Second Amended Final Judgment become effective, ASCAP shall not enter into any contract with a writer or publisher requiring such writer or publisher to grant to ASCAP performing rights for a period in excess of five years.

D. Notwithstanding the provisions of Section XI (B)(3) and (C) of this Second Amended Final Judgment, a member who requests and receives an advance from ASCAP shall remain a member of ASCAP and shall be entitled to exercise any right to resign until the advance has been fully recouped or repaid....

XIV. Retention of Jurisdiction. Jurisdiction of this cause is retained for the purpose of enabling any of the parties to this Second Amended Final Judgment to make application to the Court for such further orders and directions as may be necessary or appropriate in relation to the construction of or carrying out of this Second Amended Final Judgment, for the modification thereof, for the enforcement of compliance therewith and for the punishment of violations thereof. It is expressly understood, in addition to the foregoing, that:

(A) The plaintiff may at any time after entry of this Second Amended Final Judgment, upon reasonable notice, apply to the Court for the vacation of said Judgment, or its modification in any respect, including the dissolution of ASCAP; and

(B) If, at any time after the entry of this Second Amended Final Judgment, a stipulated amended final judgment is entered in United States v. Broadcast Music, Inc., 2001 U.S. Dist. LEXIS 10368, No. 64 Civ. 3787 (S.D.N.Y.), ASCAP may move the Court, and the Court shall grant such motion, to substitute the relevant terms of that stipulated amended final judgment for those of this Second Amended Final Judgment.

XV. Effective Date. This Second Amended Final Judgment shall become effective three months from the date of entry hereof whereupon the Amended Final Judgment entered on March 14, 1950, all modifications or amendments thereto, the Order entered thereunder on January 7, 1960, and all modifications and amendments thereto (collectively the "Amended Final Judgment") and the Final Judgment in *United States v. The American Society of Composers, Authors and Publishers*, (formerly Civ. No. 42-245 (S.D.N.Y.)) entered on March 14, 1950 and all modifications and amendments thereto (the "Foreign Decree") shall be vacated. This Second Amended Final Judgment shall not be construed to make proper or lawful or sanction any acts which occurred prior to the date hereof which were enjoined, restrained or prohibited by the Amended Final Judgment or the Foreign Decree.

Notes and Questions

a. The 1941 ASCAP consent decree set forth the basic structure of the performing rights societies which still governs today. At its heart, the original consent decree provided:

> [ASCAP] shall not, with respect to any musical composition, acquire or assert any exclusive performing right as agent, trustee or otherwise on behalf of any copyright owner ... to pay for such right a share of, or an amount measured by, the receipts or revenues of said defendants.... [ASCAP] shall not enter into, recognize as valid or perform any performing license agreement which shall result in discriminating in price or terms between licensees similarly situated; provided, however, that differentials based upon applicable business factors which justify different prices or terms shall not be considered discriminations within the meaning of this subparagraph; and provided further that nothing contained in this subparagraph shall prevent price changes from time to time by reason of changing conditions affecting the market for or marketability of performing rights.

United States v. ASCAP, No. 13-95, 1941 U.S. Dist. LEXIS 3944, 1941 Trade Cas. (CCH) P56104 (S.D.N.Y. Mar. 4, 1941). The 1941 decree introduced the blanket license, per program license, and per segment or per-use licensing structure, although the terms for these practices have varied over the years.

b. BMI has a similar but unique history. Although founded to be a better partner for radio than ASCAP, that distinction did not last long.

> BMI, founded in 1939, is a not-for-profit organization, which functions as the representative of the owners of copyrighted music to license performances of the recordings. BMI issues non-exclusive licenses to music users and distributes its revenues as royalties to its affiliated composers and music publishers, who are the owners of the copyrights. BMI typically issues blanket licenses, that is, licenses to broadcast, for a finite period of time, any and all of the approximately 4.5 million musical works in its portfolio. Because of unique conditions recognized as potentially anti-competitive, BMI's business operations, like those of its chief competitor, the American Society of Composers, Authors and Publishers (ASCAP), are regulated by a court-approved consent decree....

United States v. Broad. Music, Inc., 316 F.3d 189, 190 (2d Cir. 2003).

The 1966 action against BMI illustrates both the similarities and the original differences between the two organizations. The 1966 consent decree focused primarily on radio licensing structures with only passing references to public performances and exclusive licenses. Instead, the additional prohibitions concern BMI's activities as a record producer or music publisher. *See United States v. Broadcast Music, Inc.*, 1966 Trade Cas. (CCH) P 71,941 (S.D.N.Y. 1966):

IV. Defendant [BMI] is enjoined and restrained from:

(A) Failing to grant permission, on the written request of all writers and publishers of a musical composition including the copyright proprietor thereof, allowing such persons to issue to a music user making direct performances to the public a non-exclusive license permitting the making of specified performances of such musical composition by such music user directly to the public, provided that the defendant shall not be required to make payment with respect to performances so licensed.

(B) Engaging in the commercial publication or recording of music or in the commercial distribution of sheet music or recordings.

V. (A) Defendant shall not refuse to enter into a contract providing for the licensing by defendant of performance rights with any writer who shall have had at least one copyrighted musical composition of his writing commercially published or recorded, or with any publisher of music actively engaged in the music publishing business whose musical publications have been commercially published or recorded and publicly promoted and distributed for at least one year, and who assumes the financial risk involved in the normal publication of musical works; provided, however, that defendant shall have the right to refuse to enter into any such contract with any writer or publisher who does not satisfy reasonable standards of literacy and integrity if the defendant is willing to submit to arbitration in the County, City and State of New York the reasonableness and applicability of such standards, under the rules then prevailing of the American Arbitration Association, with any writer or publisher with who defendant has refused so to contract....

VI. (A) Defendant shall not acquire rights of public performance in any musical compositions from any publisher under a contract which requires the officers, directors, owners or employees of such publisher to refrain from publishing or promoting musical works licensed through another performing rights organization, provided that nothing contained in this paragraph shall prevent defendant from entering into a contract with a publishing entity which requires such entity not to license any performance rights through any other performing rights organization during the terms of the contract, and requiring that any works licensed by such officers, directors, owners or employees through another performing rights organization be licensed by a separate publishing entity which does not have a name identical with or similar to the name of any publishing entity with which defendant has contracted.

(B) Defendant shall not enter into any agreement for the acquisition or the licensing of performing rights which requires the recording or public performance of any stated amount or percentage of music, the performing rights in which are licensed or are to be licensed by defendant.

VII. (A) Defendant shall make available at reasonable intervals, to all writers and publishers who have granted performance rights to it, a complete statement of the performance rates (to writers, those applicable to writers, and to publishers, those applicable to publishers), currently utilized by it for all classifications of performance and musical compositions.

(B) Defendant will not offer or agree to make payments in advance for a stated period for future performing rights which are not either repayable or to be earned by means of future performance to any writer or publisher who, at the time of such offer or agreement, is a member of or under direct contract for the licensing of such performing rights with any other United States performing rights licensing organization, provided that this restriction shall not apply (1) in the case of any such writer or publisher who at any time prior to said offer or agreement had licensed performing rights through defendant or (2) in the case of any such writer or publisher who is a member of or directly affiliated with any other United States performing rights licensing organization which makes offers or makes payments similar to those forbidden in this subparagraph to writers or publishers then under contract to defendant.

(C) Defendant shall include in all contracts which it tenders to writers, publishers and music users relating to the licensing of performance rights a clause requiring the parties to submit to arbitration in the City, County and State of New York under the then prevailing rules of the American Arbitration Association, all disputes of any kind, nature or description in connection with the terms and conditions of such contracts or arising out of the performance thereof or based upon an alleged breach thereof.

VIII. (A) Defendant shall not enter into, recognize as valid or perform any performing rights license agreement which shall result in discriminating in rates or terms between licensees similarly situated; provided, however, that differentials based upon applicable business factors which justify different rates or terms shall not be considered discrimination within the meaning of this section; and provided further that nothing contained in this section shall prevent changes in rates or terms from time to time by reason of changing conditions affecting the market for or marketability of performing rights.

(B) Defendant shall, upon the request of any unlicensed broadcaster, license the rights publicly to perform its repertory by broadcasting on either a per program or per programming period basis, at defendant's option. The fee for this license shall relate only to programs (including announcements), or to programming periods, during which a licensed composition is performed. The fee shall be expressed, at defendant's option, either (1) in dollars, (2) as a percentage of the revenue which the broadcaster received for the use of its broadcasting facilities or (3), in the case of sustaining programs or programming periods, as a percentage of the applicable card rate had the program or programming period been commercially sponsored. In the event defendant offers to license broadcasters on bases in addition to a per program or per programming period basis, defendant shall act in good faith so that there shall be a relationship between such per program or such per programming period basis and such other bases, justifiable by applicable business factors including availability, so that there will be no frustration of the purpose of this section to afford broadcasters alternative bases of license compensation.

IX. (A) Defendant shall not license the public performance of any musical composition or compositions except on a basis whereby, insofar as network broadcasting by a regularly constituted network is concerned, the issuance of a single license, authorizing and fixing a single license fee for such performance by network broadcasting, shall permit the simultaneous broadcasting of such performance by all stations on the network which shall broadcast such performance, without requiring separate licenses for such several stations for such performance.

(B) With respect to any musical composition in defendant's catalogue of musical compositions licensed for broadcasting and which is or shall be lawfully recorded for performance on specified commercially sponsored programs on an electrical transcription or on other specially prepared recordation intended for broadcasting purposes, defendant shall not refuse to offer to license the public performance by designated broadcasting stations of such compositions by a single license to any manufacturer, producer or distributor of such transcription or recordation or to any advertiser or advertising agency on whose behalf such transcription or recordation shall have been made who may request such license, which single license shall authorize the broadcasting of the recorded composition by means of such transcription or recordation by all stations enumerated by the licensee, on terms and conditions fixed by defendant, without requiring separate licenses for such enumerated stations.

(C) Defendant shall not, in connection with any offer to license by it the public performance of musical compositions by music users other than broadcasters, refuse to offer a license at a price or prices to be fixed by defendant with the consent of the copyright proprietor for the performance of such specific (i.e., per piece) musical compositions, the use of which shall be requested by the prospective licensee.

X.(A) Defendant shall not assert or exercise any right or power to restrict from public performance by any licensee of defendant any copyrighted musical composition in order to exact additional consideration for the performance thereof, or for the purpose of permitting the fixing or regulating of fees for the recording or transcribing of such composition; provided, however, that nothing in this paragraph shall prevent defendant from restricting performances of a musical composition in order reasonably to protect the work against indiscriminate performance or the value of the public performance rights therein or to protect the dramatic performing rights therein, or, as may by reasonably necessary in connection with any claim or litigation involving the performance rights in any such composition.

> (B) Defendant, during the term of any license agreements with any class of licensees, shall not make any voluntary reductions in the fees payable under any such agreements, provided, however, that nothing herein shall prevent defendant from lowering any fees or rates to any or all classes of licensees in response to changing conditions affecting the value or marketability of its catalogue to such class or classes, or where necessary to meet competition....

c. The Southern District of New York continues to have jurisdiction as the so-called rate court, setting the fees for the use of the various ASCAP and BMI licenses. To what extent does the rapid change in technologies modify the rate setting of the court? *Compare United States v. Broad. Music, Inc.*, 316 F.3d at 190, *with ASCAP v. Showtime/The Movie Channel, Inc.*, 912 F.2d 563 (2d Cir. 1990).

d. Do the changes caused by the Internet to music distribution change the antitrust posture of ASCAP and BMI, or should they continue to be governed by the consent decrees first enforced in 1941 and 1966? If either organization were formed today, would such formation and operation violate the Sherman Antitrust Act?

Problem 10-D

Having recorded a demo CD, Bryce now wishes to begin making income from the performing rights of the compositions. Even though no one is presently broadcasting or performing Bryce's compositions, Bryce is both hopeful and eager. Advise Bryce on how to join a performing rights society, and which society might be the best fit.

E. Grand Performing Rights v. Small Performing Rights

Introduction

The distinction between grand performing rights and small performing rights becomes significant, because the source from which to license the music may change depending on the nature of the rights. The Copyright Act does not use these terms. Instead, it uses the undefined term "nondramatic rights" but makes no effort to interpret this term.

The ASCAP consent decree references the copyright concept of nondramatic rights under the industry term "small performing rights" without explaining either term. Nonetheless, the antitrust prohibitions which limit the scope of the performing rights societies' licensing eliminate their ability to provide any licenses to cover grand performing rights. As a result, this distinction sometimes results in significant confusion and occasional litigation.

Frank Music Corp. v. Metro-Goldwyn-Mayer, Inc.
772 F.2d 505 (9th Cir. 1985)

This copyright infringement suit arises out of defendants' use of five songs from plaintiffs' dramatico-musical play *Kismet* in a musical revue staged at defendant MGM Grand Hotel in 1974–76. After a bench trial, the district court found infringement and awarded the plaintiffs $22,000 as a share of defendants' profits. Plaintiffs appeal and defendants cross-appeal. We affirm in part, reverse in part, and remand.

The original version of *Kismet* was a dramatic play, written by Edward Knoblock in 1911. Knoblock copyrighted the play as an unpublished work in that year and again as a published work in 1912. Knoblock's copyright expired in 1967, and the dramatic play *Kismet* entered the public domain.

In 1952, plaintiff Edwin Lester acquired the right to produce a musical stage production of the dramatic play *Kismet*. Lester hired plaintiffs Luther Davis and Charles Lederer to write the libretto and plaintiffs Robert Wright and George Forrest to write the music and lyrics for the musical adaptation. In 1953 and 1954, Lederer and Davis copyrighted their dramatico-musical play *Kismet*, and in 1953, Wright and Forrest assigned to plaintiff Frank Music Corporation the right to copyright all portions of the musical score written for *Kismet*. Frank Music subsequently obtained copyrights for the entire musical score and for each of the songs in the score.

In 1954, Lederer, Wright, and Forrest entered into a license agreement with Loew's, Inc., a predecessor of Metro-Goldwyn-Mayer, Inc., ("MGM, Inc.") granting to it the right to produce a musical motion picture based on plaintiffs' play. MGM released its motion picture version of *Kismet*, starring Howard Keel and Ann Blyth, in 1955.

The story presented in the MGM film and in plaintiffs' dramatico-musical play is essentially the same as that told in Knoblock's dramatic play. It is the tale of a day in the life of a poetic beggar named Hajj and his daughter, Marsinah. The story is set in ancient Baghdad, with major scenes in the streets of Baghdad, the Wazir's palace, an enchanted garden, and the Wazir's harem.

On April 26, 1974, defendant MGM Grand Hotel premiered a musical revue entitled *Hallelujah Hollywood* in the hotel's Ziegfeld Theatre. The show was staged, produced, and directed by defendant Donn Arden. It featured ten acts of singing, dancing, and variety performances. Of the ten acts, four were labeled as "tributes" to MGM motion pictures of the past, and one was a tribute to the "Ziegfeld Follies." The remaining acts were variety numbers, which included performances by a live tiger, a juggler, and the magicians, Siegfried and Roy.

The Ziegfeld Theatre, where *Hallelujah Hollywood* was performed, is a lavish showplace. Its special features, including huge elevators used to raise or lower portions of the stage and ceiling lifts capable of lowering performers down into the audience during the shows, reportedly provide impressive special effects.

Act IV of *Hallelujah Hollywood*, the subject of this lawsuit, was entitled "Kismet," and was billed as a tribute to the MGM movie of that name. Comprised of four scenes, it was approximately eleven and one-half minutes in length. It was set in ancient Baghdad, as was plaintiffs' play, and the characters were called by the same or similar names to those used in plaintiffs' play. Five songs were taken in whole or in part from plaintiffs' play. No dialogue was spoken during the act, and, in all, it contained approximately six minutes of music taken directly from plaintiffs' play.

The total running time of *Hallelujah Hollywood* was approximately 100 minutes, except on Saturday nights when two acts were deleted, shortening the show to 75 minutes. The show was performed three times on Saturday evenings, twice on the other evenings of the week.

On November 1, 1974, plaintiffs informed MGM Grand that they considered *Hallelujah Hollywood* to infringe their rights in *Kismet*. MGM Grand responded that it believed its use of plaintiffs' music was covered by its blanket license agreement with the American Society of Composers, Authors and Publishers ("ASCAP"). In 1965, plaintiffs had granted to ASCAP the right to license certain rights in the musical score of their play *Kismet*.

Plaintiffs filed this action, alleging copyright infringement, unfair competition, and breach of contract. MGM Grand continued to present *Hallelujah Hollywood*, including Act IV "Kismet," until July 16, 1976, when the hotel substituted new music in Act IV. In all, the "Kismet" sequence was used in approximately 1700 performances of the show.

A. *Scope of the ASCAP License*

Paragraph one of the ASCAP license gives MGM Grand the right to perform publicly "non-dramatic renditions of the separate musical compositions" in the ASCAP repertory.

> Society grants and Licensee accepts for a period commencing as of January 1, 1974 and ending December 31, 1978 a license to perform publicly by means of live entertainment or mechanical music (as defined in paragraph 2), and by no other means, at or in any part of section of the hotel or motel known as MGM Grand Hotel, 3645 Las Vegas Blvd. So., Las Vegas, Nv. 29109 non-dramatic renditions of the separate musical compositions copyrighted or composed by members of Society and of which Society shall have the right to license the performing rights.

Paragraph three excludes from the license "dramatico-musical works, or songs [accompanied by] visual representation of the work from which the music is taken...."

> This license shall not extend to or be deemed to include: (a) Oratorios, choral, operatic or dramatico-musical works (including plays with music, revues and ballets) in their entirety, or songs or other excerpts from operas or musical plays accompanied either by words, pantomime, dance, or visual representation of the work from which the music is taken; but fragments of instrumental selections from such works may be instrumentally rendered without words, dialogue, costume, accompanying dramatic action or scenic accessory, and unaccompanied by any stage action or visual representation (by motion

picture or otherwise) of the work of which such music forms a part. (b) Any work (or part thereof) whereof the stage presentation and singing rights are reserved.

…

Act IV "Kismet" was accompanied by "visual representation" of plaintiffs' play. Accordingly, defendants' use was excluded from the ASCAP license by the express terms of paragraph three. We conclude, however, that there is no reason to consider, as the district court did, whether Act IV was "non-dramatic."

The district court found the following "visual representations": plaintiffs' songs were performed in *Hallelujah Hollywood* by singers identified as characters from plaintiffs' *Kismet*, dressed in costumes designed to recreate *Kismet*, and the performance made use of locale, settings, scenery, props, and dance style music of the type used in plaintiffs' work.

The defendants do not challenge the finding that their production contained these visual representations. They argue, instead, that the district court failed to give sufficient consideration to whether the visual representations in Act IV were "of the work from which the music is taken," i.e., plaintiffs' *Kismet*. Defendants suggest that this distinction is important because plaintiffs' *Kismet* is a derivative work. They argue that many of the visual representations, (e.g., street scenes in ancient Baghdad, swarming bazaars, and an oriental palace), could be said to be derived from Edward Knoblock's 1911 dramatic version of *Kismet* rather than from plaintiffs' *Kismet*. Since Knoblock's play is in the public domain, defendants contend these visual representations are not protectable by plaintiffs' copyright. Defendants further argue that other elements of the "visual representations," such as choreography style and character names, also are not protectable by copyright.

… [D]efendants' argument is unpersuasive because it is simply irrelevant. The question we face is not whether the "visual representations" are copyrightable, but whether the use of a copyrighted work exceeds the scope of an ASCAP license because visual representations accompanied the songs. The license agreement does not refer to "copyrightable" visual representations. The district court was not clearly erroneous in finding that Act IV "Kismet" was accompanied by sufficient[3] visual representations derived from plaintiffs' play to place the songs' use beyond the scope of the ASCAP license.

The district court properly concluded that defendants infringed plaintiffs' copyrights in *Kismet*.

[On remand the district court recalculated the damages only to have that decision again overturned as the Circuit Court increased the portion of the revenue earned

---

3. Whether some visual representations, less significant than those presented here (*e.g.*, performance of the same five songs as those performed here by a single character dressed in ancient Arabian costume), would be enough to take a performance out of the ASCAP license is a more difficult question, which we need not resolve.

by the hotel to the portion of the musical improperly performed. *See Frank Music Corp. v. Metro-Goldwyn-Mayer, Inc.*, 886 F.2d 1545, 1557 (9th Cir. Cal. 1989), *cert. denied Metro-Goldwyn-Mayer, Inc. v. Frank Music Corp.*, 494 U.S. 1017, (1990) ("We vacate the damages award. We conclude that the proper apportionment entitles plaintiffs to 9% of the direct profits from *Hallelujah Hollywood*.... Accordingly, plaintiffs are entitled to $551,844.54 as their share of direct profits and $699,963.10 as their share of indirect profits.").]

Robert Stigwood Group, Ltd. v. Sperber
457 F.2d 50 (2d Cir. 1972)

The rock opera *Jesus Christ Superstar* and several of its individual musical compositions have enjoyed large commercial success as well as substantial critical acclaim. More than two million records and tape cartridges of the full opera have been sold, the authorized touring production grossed over one million dollars in its first four weeks, and tickets to the Broadway version have been among the more difficult to acquire. We can understand, therefore, the desire of promoters and producers throughout the country to capitalize on the success of *Jesus Christ Superstar*, and it is not surprising that one consequence of its explosive yet impermanent popularity is litigation. The role of the courts must be to prevent exploitation of the opera in a manner that infringes the rights of the creators of the work and their assignees.

Timothy Rice wrote the libretto for *Jesus Christ Superstar* and Andrew Lloyd Webber composed the score of the opera's overture and 22 songs which depict the last seven days in the life of Christ. Rice and Webber assigned the rights in the work (except "King Herod's Song") to Leeds Music Limited which duly obtained United States copyrights for the opera as a "dramatico-musical composition" pursuant to 17 U.S.C. §5(d) and for several of the individual songs as "musical compositions" pursuant to 17 U.S.C. §5(e). Leeds Music Limited assigned the United States copyrights to Leeds Music Corporation. The Robert Stigwood Group Limited ("Stigwood") acquired the rights for stage productions and dramatic presentations of the opera, and its rights are those allegedly infringed. Defendant Betty Sperber is a booking agent doing business as "The Original American Touring Company" ("OATC") and concerts presented by it are represented as being performed by The Original American Touring Company. The business details of the concerts are handled by Betty Sperber Management of which Sperber is President. Each OATC so-called concert consists of 20 of the 23 songs from *Jesus Christ Superstar*, sung sequentially with one exception, and three additional religious works. Sperber avers that other programs not involving *Jesus Christ Superstar* are planned by OATC.

Stigwood brought this suit, *inter alia*, to enjoin: one, OATC's performance of *Jesus Christ Superstar* or portions thereof; two, any references to *Jesus Christ Superstar* in advertisements for OATC performances; and three, use of the name The Original American Touring Company. The district court's preliminary injunction, issued pursuant to 17 U.S.C. §112, barred only the references to *Jesus Christ Superstar* in OATC advertisements, and both parties appealed.

OATC's claim that its productions do not infringe Stigwood's rights is based upon the usual and customary agreement between the American Society of Composers, Authors and Publishers ("ASCAP") and Leeds Music Corporation, an ASCAP member. Although a complete description of the purpose of ASCAP and its methodology are unnecessary to our decision, some understanding of its function is vital to an examination of the agreements it makes with its members. The Copyright Act of 1909 granted several rights to the holders of copyrights in works including the exclusive right "to perform the copyrighted work publicly for profit if it be a musical composition."

Composers and publishers soon realized it was impractical for each copyright holder to attempt to enforce this right since he could not possibly police all public performances for profit of every musical composition throughout the United States. ASCAP was formed to meet this need. By obtaining licenses from its members, this organization, staffed for the purpose, could enforce the performing rights of its members. It was believed, however, that each copyright owner could appropriately police and license performances of musical comedies or operas because of the relative infrequency of such productions and the lengthy preparation and publicity which must precede these productions. *See*, Nimmer, "Copyright 1955," 43 Cal. L. Rev. 791, 798 (1955).

In any event, ASCAP is authorized by its members to license only nondramatic performing rights of compositions in its repertory. Consequently, pursuant to the standard ASCAP agreement utilized here, ASCAP was authorized by Leeds to give:

> 1. (b) The non-exclusive right of public performance of the separate numbers, songs, fragments or arrangements, melodies or selections forming part or parts of musical plays and dramatico-musical compositions, the Owner reserving and excepting from this grant the right of performance of musical plays and dramatico-musical compositions in their entirety, or any part of such plays or dramatico-musical compositions on the legitimate stage.

Thus, while ASCAP licensees can perform the individual songs from *Jesus Christ Superstar*, whether copyrighted individually or merely as part of the opera as a whole, paragraph 3 of the standard license indicates that it does not extend to presentations of:

> (a) Oratorios, choral, operatic, or dramatico-musical works ... in their entirety or songs or other excerpts from operas or musical plays accompanied either by word, pantomime, dance or visual representation of the work from which the music is taken; but fragments or instrumental selections from such works may be instrumentally rendered without words, dialogue, costume, accompanying dramatic action or scenic accessory and unaccompanied by any stage action or visual representation (by motion picture or otherwise) of the work of which such music forms a part.

Both parties and the court agree, therefore, that selections from *Jesus Christ Superstar* can be properly presented by ASCAP licensees if they are presented in "nondramatic" performances. Accordingly, we must decide if OATC's performances fall into the "dramatic" or "nondramatic" category.

The Copyright Act distinguishes between "musical" and "dramatico-musical" works. Dramatico-musical works are considered dramas for the purpose of 17 U.S.C. § 1(d). ["Musical" works] are infringed only by public performances for profit whereas ["dramatico-musical" works] are infringed by any public performance.

In our effort to find some guidance in distinguishing between musical and dramatico-musical productions, we were soon to learn of the dearth of cases on the subject. We received some aid, however, from Judge Learned Hand's statement that a performance in "words and music alone may constitute a dramatic performance, and it did not matter that the performance was only of a scene or part of a scene." *Herbert v. Shanley*, 222 F. 344, 345 (S.D.N.Y. 1915) (citations omitted), affirmed, 229 F. 340 (2d Cir. 1916), reversed on other grounds, 242 U.S. 591 (1917). The Supreme Court's reversal of *Herbert*, however, nipped this line of cases in the bud by construing the "for profit" language so liberally that it obviated the need for further litigation over what was "dramatic" or "nondramatic."

The only case cited to us which discusses the scope of the ASCAP license is *April Productions, Inc. v. Strand Enterprises, Inc.*, 221 F.2d 292 (2d Cir. 1955). In *April* the copyright owner of *The Student Prince* sued the proprietor of a cabaret, "The Harem," for infringement based upon performances there of a medley of songs from *The Student Prince*. The medley was a small part of one of ten scenes of the nightclub's show, and was not connected by a story line or otherwise. The Court stated:

> Even if The Harem put on a dramatic performance, [the entire show of ten scenes], the selections ... were not part of it. The worst that could be said would be that they were sung in an intermission between the acts of a dramatic performance. Such a rendition is "nondramatic" within the meaning of the license.

In the opinion, Judge Dimock (District Judge, sitting by designation), laboring without guidance or precedent, of course, was unable to cite us to a single authority.

In any event, Strand's use of several songs from *The Student Prince* pales by comparison with Sperber's use of almost the entire score from *Jesus Christ Superstar*. The twenty musical compositions from *Superstar* were almost the entire OATC performance rather than less than one-tenth as in "The Harem" club's show. Moreover, *April* has been severely criticized as inadequately protective of and virtually extinguishing dramatic performing rights with respect to musical compositions. As Professor Nimmer puts it:

> Under the rule of this case one could by simply obtaining an ASCAP license perform in a new musical play all of the music from "South Pacific" providing the "book" for the new production is not borrowed from "South Pacific." The ASCAP membership could hardly have intended to permit the performance of their musical compositions in Broadway musicals or similar productions in return for mere payment of the ASCAP fee.

M. Nimmer, Copyright § 125.6 (1971).

Where the defendant has not even supplied a *new* "book" in its performances, a determination that dramatic rights have been infringed would seem simple. But, OATC asserts that plaintiff's "book" is not used either and insists that there is no story line whatever to defendant's performances. Recently, in *Rice v. American Program Bureau*, 446 F.2d 685 (2d Cir. 1971) a panel of this court in a 2–1 decision, favored this contention of defendants. *Rice* also dealt with performances of *Jesus Christ Superstar* allegedly executed pursuant to the ASCAP license. Because of the sparse record before it, the majority was unable to conclude that the performance was "dramatic." It did however, make clear that "presentation of all of the songs from the opera *Jesus Christ Superstar* without costumes, words, or scenery, but in sequence could arguably develop the overall plot of the opera, and ... might possibly be 'dramatic.'" We have come to the conclusion that the fuller record before us establishes that a dramatic story is developed by defendant's productions, as Judge Smith in his dissenting opinion in *Rice* would have found and District Judge Motley did find even on the skimpier record there.

... [Twenty] of 23 *Superstar* selections are performed in defendant's concert, all but one in identical sequence as in the copyrighted opera. The conclusion is inescapable that the story of the last seven days in the life of Christ is portrayed in the OATC performances substantially as in *Superstar*. One might appropriately ask why, if OATC did not intend that the same story be told, would it insist on preserving the sequence of the songs presented in *Jesus Christ Superstar*, which when performed in that fashion, tell the story even in the absence of intervening dialogue? As *Rice* instructed, the lack of scenery or costumes in the OATC production does not *ipso facto* prevent it from being dramatic. Indeed, radio performances of operas are considered dramatic, because the story is told by the music and lyrics. There can be no question that the OATC concerts, in which singers enter and exit, maintain specific roles and occasionally make gestures, and in which the story line of the original play is preserved by the songs which are sung in almost perfect sequence using 78 of the 87 minutes of the original copyrighted score, is dramatic. And, the admitted desire of defendants to make reference to the opera in its advertisement provides further evidence that the performance is intended to come as close as possible to the original dramatico-musical....

In view of our disposition of the primary issue in this case and the accompanying discussion, our resolution of the remaining issues may be of only academic interest. Nevertheless, we feel obliged to affirm the conclusion reached below and in *Rice* that defendants cannot make reference to *Jesus Christ Superstar* in its advertisements. Sperber argues that there can be no copyright in titles, and, for the first time on appeal, claims that no protection can be afforded on any other theory because of Supreme Court decisions in *Sears, Roebuck & Co. v. Stiffel Co.*, 376 U.S. 225 (1964) and *Compco Corp. v. Day-Brite Lighting, Inc.*, 376 U.S. 234 (1964). We disagree. *Sears* and *Compco* prevent protection outside of the copyright laws, of works which Congress could have protected but chose not to. It may be that titles are not "writings" in the constitutional sense and thus cannot be protected by copyright but can be protected under unfair competition doctrine. In any event, *Sears* and *Compco* carved out a specific exemption for trademarks and labels of products which can be protected to prevent deception of the public. That is precisely the situation we have here. Thus, while Sears could manufacture a pole lamp identical to Stiffel's, it could not call it a Stiffel pole lamp. Similarly, OATC may perform songs under the ASCAP license but may not indicate that they are from the opera. The Senate Judiciary Committee, in its proposed general revision of the Copyright Law, preserves the right to regulate deceptive trade practices outside of the copyright laws. Since the title *Jesus Christ Superstar* may well be associated with the opera as a whole and thus a "secondary meaning" has developed, we agree with the district court that defendants must be enjoined from directly or indirectly advertising or in any way representing any presentation as being from *Jesus Christ Superstar* or any song, instrumental selection or excerpt as taken therefrom in whole or in part. We also agree, however, that subject to the conditions we have set forth in Part I, the individual song titles can be listed.

Finally, although we do not doubt that the defendants chose the name "The Original American Touring Company" with the hope of misleading the public, we agree with the district court that there is insufficient evidence in the record to support an inference of likelihood of confusion strong enough to underpin a preliminary injunction to restrain the use of that name, provided the restrictions we have set forth are observed.... The preliminary injunction is modified as we have indicated. The mandate shall issue forthwith.

Notes and Questions

a. In *Gershwin v. Whole Thing Co.*, 208 U.S.P.Q. 557 (C.D. Cal. 1980), the Whole Thing Company created a forty-song musical tribute to George and Ira Gershwin entitled *Let's Call the Whole Thing Gershwin* (the "Play"), which was produced at the Westwood Playhouse. On behalf of the Gershwin interests, George Gershwin originally objected, but relented sufficiently to allow a limited run at the Westwood Playhouse. When Broadway backers contacted the play's producers, the relationship broke down and the producers sought to rely upon the small performing rights ASCAP license to continue to produce the show. In granting a preliminary injunction, the court rejected this approach:

> To show that serious questions are raised sufficient to require litigation (and to show probable success on the merits), Mr. Gershwin makes three principal arguments. First, Mr. Gershwin argues that performances of the Play after January 31, 1980 infringe his copyrights. Mr. Gershwin argues that Whole Thing is required to have a license from Mr. Gershwin even though Whole Thing has a license from music publishers. The copyright laws permit an owner of a copyright to transfer some or all of the rights comprised in a copyright, and Mr. Gershwin had previously transferred some rights to certain music publishers. In general, the publishers have been granted small performing rights (or non-dramatic rights) to certain Gershwin songs. Mr.

Gershwin contends that he generally retains grand performing rights (also known as grand rights or dramatic rights).

There are two basic tests to determine whether grand rights are required. Grand rights are required if: (1) a song is used to tell a story, M. Nimmer, Nimmer on Copyrights § 10.10(G), at 10–92 (1979); or (2) a song is performed with dialogue, scenery, or costumes, Finkelstein [ASCAP's former general attorney], The Composer and the Public Interest — Regulation or Performing, 19 L. & Contemp. Prob. 275, 283 n.32 (1954). In response, Whole Thing argues that the music publishers have granted it grand rights.

Id.

b. Courts are often forced to make subjective decisions. *See April Productions, Inc. v. Strand Enterprises, Inc.*, 221 F.2d 292 (2d Cir. 1955) (night club performance of medley from *The Student Prince* as one scene in a ten scene show not a dramatic use, so ASCAP license sufficient). *See also Rice v. American Program Bur.*, 446 F.2d 685 (2d Cir. 1971) (modifying an injunction against the performance of a concert version of *Jesus Christ Superstar*, but allowing multiple songs to be performed in sequence, without costume or staging).

c. The Riverview Dinner Club, a licensee of both ASCAP and BMI, is trying to increase business by changing the floor shows and musical entertainment. The first proposal is to have so-called theme nights, where a particular artist's music is featured all evening. Beatles nights, Cole Porter nights, and Beach Boys nights are planned under this proposal. Are the ASCAP and BMI licenses sufficient? Would there be any change if the evening features the life story of any of the featured artists?

d. A second proposal recommends that the evenings be themed with "love," "new romance," "old friends," or similar motifs. The performers would create characters that would relate to each other through the lyrics of the selected songs. All the songs would come from the ASCAP and BMI repertories. Are the existing ASCAP and BMI licenses sufficient? Would there be any difference if a cover charge were required?

e. In 1888, in *Kennedy v. McTammany*, 33 F. 584 (C.C.D. Mass. 1888), the Circuit Court for the District of Massachusetts reviewed the copyright protection for piano rolls. "The sole question in issue is whether these perforated sheets of paper are an infringement of copyrighted sheet music. To the ordinary mind it is certainly a difficult thing to consider these strips of paper as sheet music. There is no clef, or bars, or lines, or spaces, or other marks which are found in common printed music, but only plain strips of paper with rows of holes or perforations." As a result, no copyright protection was found.

Twenty years later, in 1908, the Supreme Court endorsed the *Kennedy v. McTammany* result in *White-Smith Music Publishing Co. v. Apollo Co.*, 209 U.S. 1, 9 (1908). According to the White-Smith Court, in "1902 from seventy to seventy-five thousand [player pianos] were in use in the United States, and that from one million to one million and a half of such perforated musical rolls ... were made in this country in that year." Given the widespread use of these piano rolls and the public's reliance on this free source of entertainment, the Court felt incapable of reversing the practice. The decision anticipates much of the *Sony v. Universal* discussion which was to follow seven decades later.

The 1909 Copyright Act reversed *White-Smith Music Publishing*. Section 1(e) of the 1909 Act provided copyright protection to musical works embodied in "any system of notation or any form of record in which the thought of an author may be recorded and from which it may be read or reproduced." This covered both piano rolls and the newly developed wax cylinders that were the first step in the creation of sound recordings, phonograms, and albums.

Congress wished to grant copyright holders the exclusive right to record their work on piano rolls or phonograph records, but feared that the large musical publishers would then be able to dominate the marketplace for popular music. As a compromise, the exclusive right to record the musical composition was initially vested in the copyright holder. Once exercised, however, any other recording company willing to pay the fee set by Congress could also exercise the right to record the composition. This mandatory permission became the first compulsory license under the Copyright Act. This rule is embodied in the current Copyright Act as §114, providing a statutory royalty rate and structure for making cover recordings.

Immediately, companies began paying the two-cent per copy fee. Some companies chose to physically copy the piano rolls manufactured by others, particularly those owned by the Aeolian Co., the largest owner of piano roll copyrights. In *Aeolian Co. v. Royal Music Roll Co.*, 196 F. 926 (W.D.N.Y. 1912), the court interpreted the Copyright Act compulsory mechanical license to cover only the copyrighted work embodied in the piano roll. The payment did not give permission to physically copy the piano roll itself. To create a physical copy of the piano roll required a license that could only be purchased through direct negotiation with the piano roll manufacturer. The piano roll was protected by this interpretation of the Copyright Act and by state unfair competition law. In 1971, Congress extended copyright protection directly to the phonograph album.

f. Producers of a play based on the life of Sam Cooke wanted Cooke's music as part of the show, but they did not wish to obtain grand performing rights for the production. Was the strategy to perform a musical medley onstage prior to the opening of the play a reasonable solution? *See ABKCO Music, Inc. v. Washington*, 2011 U.S. Dist. LEXIS 120081, 100 U.S.P.Q.2d (BNA) 1669 (E.D. Mich. Oct. 18, 2011).

Problem 10-E

With the success of Bryce's *Juliet Prescott*, Bryce has been approached to write and direct a musical for the Prometheus Theatre. Candi, the executive director, is planning an entire season of George Gershwin, including both piano concerts and musicals. As the kick-off for the season, she wants to create a review, tentatively entitled *From Ira to George*, celebrating the brother composer's early life and George's transformation from a song plugger to Broadway star and classical composer.

Candi has asked Bryce to write the book for the musical, incorporating all or some of the many songs written by the composing duo. The Prometheus Theatre is licensed by both ASCAP and BMI, so Candi told Bryce no additional rights are needed. Bryce seeks your advice. To what extent can Bryce write such a production under the ASCAP or BMI licenses? What else must Bryce do?

F. Bibliography and Links

Bob Kohn, Kohn on Music Licensing (5th ed. 2018).

Donald S. Passman, All You Need to Know About the Music Business (10th ed. 2019).

Mark Halloran, The Musician's Business & Legal Guide (5th ed. 2017).

Ken Abdo & Jason Abdo, *What You Need to Know About the Music Modernization Act*, 35 Ent. & Sports Law. 5 (2019).

Todd Brabec & Jeffrey Brabec, *The New and Complex World of Television Music Licensing*, 27 Ent. & Sports Law. 1 (2009).

Todd Brabec, *The Performance Right—A World in Transition*, 42 Mitchell Hamline L. Rev. 16 (2016).

Daniel Cantor, *How Many Guests May Attend a Wedding Reception Before ASCAP Shows Up? Or, What Are the Limits of the Definition of Perform "Publicly" Under 17 U.S.C. § 101?*, 27 Colum. J.L. & Arts 79 (2003).

Peter DiCola, *Money from Music: Survey Evidence on Musicians' Revenue and Lessons About Copyright Incentives*, 55 Ariz. L. Rev. 301 (2013).

Joseph P. Fishman, *Music as a Matter of Law*, 131 Harv. L. Rev. 1861 (2018).

Jon M. Garon, *Normative Copyright: A Conceptual Framework for Copyright Philosophy and Ethics*, 88 Cornell L. Rev. 1278 (2003).

Ari Herstand, *How To Make It in the New Music Business: Practical Tips on Building a Loyal Following and Making a Living as a Musician* (2d. Ed. 2019).

Jay Mason All, *Again, from the Top! The Continuing Pursuit of a General Public Performance Right in Sound Recordings*, 22 Alb. L.J. Sci. & Tech. 1 (2012).

Lateef Mtima, *Digital Tools and Copyright Clay: Restoring the Artist/audience Symbiosis*, 38 Whittier L. Rev. 104 (2018).

Douglas Okorocha, *A Full 360: How the 360 Deal Challenges the Historical Resistance to Establishing a Fiduciary Duty Between Artist and Label*, 18 UCLA Ent. L. Rev. 1 (2011).

Dotan Oliar & Nicholas Matich, *Copyright Preregistration: Evidence and Lessons from the First Seven Years, 2005–2012*, 55 Ariz. L. Rev. 1073 (2013).

Sepehr Shahshahani, *The Role of Courts in Technology Policy*, 61 J.L. & Econ. 37 (2018).

Don E. Tomlinson, *Everything That Glitters Is Not Gold: Songwriter-Music Publisher Agreements and Disagreements*, 18 Hastings Comm. & Ent L.J. 85 (1995).

Cydney A. Tune, *Music Licensing—From the Basics to the Outer Limits, Part 1: Music Licensing Basics*, 21 ENT. & SPORTS LAW., no. 3, 2003, at 1.

Cydney A. Tune, *Music Licensing—From the Basics to the Outer Limits, Part 2: Key Considerations for Potential Licensees and Licensors of Music*, 21 ENT. & SPORTS LAW., no. 4, 2004, at 3.

Cydney A. Tune, *Music Licensing—From the Basics to the Outer Limits, Part 3: The Myriad World of Music Licenses*, 22 ENT. & SPORTS LAW., no. 1, 2004, at 5.

Websites

AMERICAN FEDERATION OF MUSICIANS, https://www.afm.org

ASCAP, https://www.ascap.com

BMI, https://www.bmi.com

NATIONAL MUSIC PUBLISHERS' ASSOCIATION, http://www.nmpa.org

HARRY FOX AGENCY, https://www.harryfox.com/#/

BILLBOARD, https://www.billboard.com

ROLLING STONE MAGAZINE, https://www.rollingstone.com

SESAC, https://www.sesac.com

Chapter 11

Music Distribution and the Sound Recording Industry

As discussed in Chapter 10 on Music Publishing, the recording industry and the music publishing industry are closely entwined but historically distinct in revenue and structure. With the growth of Apple Music, YouTube, Pandora, Spotify, SiriusXM and other streaming services, the revenue of the sound recording industry has also shifted from the sale of records (including tapes, CDs, and downloads) to the public performance rights embodied in digital Copyright Act § 106(6) "in the case of sound recordings, to perform the copyrighted work publicly by means of a digital audio transmission."

A. Finances in the Recording Industry

1. Mechanical Rights Licensing under the 2018 Orrin G. Hatch-Bob Goodlatte Music Modernization Act and the Mechanical Licensing Collective

The right of performance for music was first included in the United States copyright laws in 1897. The largest of the player piano roll companies was considered to be threatening monopoly power over the mechanical recordings of music as embodied in the player piano rolls. *See White-Smith Music Publishing Co. v. Apollo Co.*, 209 U.S. 1 (1908). As a result, the 1909 Copyright Act included a compulsory license that any other party wishing to use the mechanical right to make its own recording could do so upon paying the compulsory licensing fee. Today, that rule is embodied in § 114 of the Copyright Act.

114. Scope of exclusive rights in sound recordings

(a) The exclusive rights of the owner of copyright in a sound recording are limited to the rights specified by clauses (1), (2), (3) and (6) of section 106, and do not include any right of performance under section 106(4).

(b) The exclusive right of the owner of copyright in a sound recording under clause (1) of section 106 is limited to the right to duplicate the sound recording in the form of phonorecords or copies that directly or indirectly recapture the actual sounds fixed in the recording. The exclusive right of the owner of copyright in a sound recording under clause (2) of section 106 is limited to the right to prepare a derivative work in which the actual sounds fixed in the sound recording are rearranged, remixed, or otherwise altered in sequence or quality. The exclusive rights of the owner of copyright in a sound recording under clauses (1) and (2) of section 106 do not extend to the making or duplication of another sound recording that consists entirely of an independent fixation of other sounds, even though such sounds imitate or simulate those in the copyrighted sound recording. The exclusive rights of the owner of copyright in a sound recording under clauses (1), (2), and (3) of section 106 do not apply to sound recordings included in educational television and radio programs (as defined in section 397 of title 47) distributed or transmitted by or through public broadcasting entities (as defined by section 118(f)): Provided, That copies or phonorecords of said programs are not commercially distributed by or through public broadcasting entities to the general public.

(c) This section does not limit or impair the exclusive right to perform publicly, by means of a phonorecord, any of the works specified by section 106(4).

The 2018 amendments to the Copyright Act substantially change the manner in which a party would seek to notify the Copyright Office of its intent to pay the statutory royalty to make a new sound recording embodying the previously published composition. Although non-digital uses will remain unchanged, the Copyright Office will no longer accept "notices to obtain licenses." Instead, under the amendments, users will be able to obtain a blanket license that will cover all musical works available for compulsory licensing for digital downloads (or digital phonorecord deliveries). A new Mechanical Licensing Collective (MLC) will be created pursuant to regulations of the Copyright Office which will operate in a manner quite similar to a performing rights organization (PRO). The MLC will receive notices from downloading service companies and charge fees as established through proceedings before the Copyright Royalty Judges to establish the administrative assessment.

The new process will greatly increase the likelihood that the publishers and record labels will be paid for the use of their songs when licensed downloads occur.

The Copyright Office has also explained that "[p]rior to the license availability date (January 1, 2021), liability may be limited to royalties due under the compulsory license if the digital music provider complies with certain requirements, including engaging in good-faith, commercially reasonable efforts to identify and locate each copyright owner of a musical work they use on their service."

2. Performance Rights Organizations for the Sound Recording Industry

SoundExchange serves as the performing rights organization (PRO) that collects royalties for the digital public performance royalties owed to the record labels (as owners of the copyrights of the sound recordings) pursuant to the rights provided in § 106(6) as provided in the Digital Performance Right in Sound Recording Act of 1995 and Digital Millennium Copyright Act of 1998.

The scope of the digital public performance right is narrow. Section 114 provides the categories and exemptions for the public performance right. Because the right did not extend to all public performance of sound recordings, the statute also exempts digital rebroadcast of what was historically an analog or over-the-air broadcast. As such, a broadcast transmission and, in many cases, its digital rebroadcast are not covered.

SoundExchange instead collects the statutory fees that are paid to lawfully license non-interactive streaming services. The rules that distinguish interactive and non-interactive focus on the customer's ability to control precisely which songs are being played. The music service provider is free to negotiate directly rather than to use SoundExchange, and as a result, some of the largest music services have negotiated directly with the record labels.

The statutory license excludes all on-demand services and other interactive series. If a service falls into the interactive category, then the service provider cannot rely on the statutory license and must instead license the content directly, a complex and detailed process.

The fees collected by SoundExchange are divided under the statute, with the copyright owner of the sound recording masters (typically the record label) receiving 50%, the featured artist on the recording receiving 45%, the non-featured vocalists receiving 2.5%, and the session musicians receiving 2.5%.

3. Production Agreements: General Structures

a. Producer Agreement

The producer agreement is the contract between the record producer (who may hold the copyright to the master tape or master recording) and either the recording artist or the record company (label). Typically, the producer is selected by mutual agreement between the label and the recording artist. This is often a function of influence; such that junior artists are more typically assigned producers based on the label's needs while senior artists have the ability to command particular producers to help create or maintain their sound.

In recent years, it has become increasingly common for the producer to work on a particular song or group of songs, leaving the recording artist and the label more control over the totality of the CD. As packaging has created multiple editions of the CDs (including videos, bonus songs, and other material), the CD no longer has the integrity as a cohesive product that the LP once had.

The goal of the label is to acquire the copyrights to all aspects of the CD, so it will typically require the producer to assign the copyright to the label in exchange for payment. Similarly, the recording artist agreement assigns all copyright interest of the recording artist to the label (see below). Because the performing artist may also share in the joint copyright ownership of the master tape with the producer, this arrangement provides significant efficiency. Assignments of both joint authors' copyrights are necessary to fully exploit the work.

b. Pressing and Distribution Agreement

Smaller labels will sometimes enter into Pressing and Distribution Agreements with the larger distributors. These arrangements serve as upstream sub-licensing agreements, allowing the smaller label to specialize in particular talent, while relying on the larger distributor's infrastructure for distribution and advertising. The small label will assign the right to the mechanical license for advertising and distribution by the distributor.

c. Master Purchase Agreement

This arrangement allows the owner of a particular master tape to assign the copyright, including the mechanical rights and all other uses of the artist's performance, in exchange for the royalties along with an advance or fee. Such agreements can be used to assign master tapes from the performing artists to labels (particularly when the master was created as a demo). Similar deals can be used to move master tapes from one label to another.

d. Recording Artist Agreement

The recording artist agreement is the most significant contract in the life of the performing and recording artist. The terms of this agreement are responsible for the financial future of the artist and generally represent the most troubling aspects of the recording industry. Typically, these exclusive agreements provide for the production of a single CD with the option of the label to order additional CDs to be created by the artist. Although the contract covers a band as a group, it is structured to control each of the individual members of the group — even if members leave or join.

The recording artist is typically given a lump-sum budget (not necessarily the cash) as an advance. This large advance payment is used to pay for the production expenses of creating the CD. The actual payment budgeted for the recording artist may be quite modest, particularly if the production costs, studio musicians, studio recording time, producer fees, and incidental expenses start to exceed the original budgets. A $150,000 advance can quickly begin to disappear. At $3,000–$5,000 per song, the producer may earn $30,000–$65,000 of the advance depending on the rate and number of songs on the CD. Studio time, musicians, studio rentals, and engineering fees can easily cost at least $100,000, resulting in little or no payments to the recording artist. Further, since this payment is an advance against future royalties, the entire amount must be recouped before the recording artist will begin to earn royalties from the sale of the CD.

4. Recording Artist Contracts: Budgets and Income to the Recording Artist

The details of the recording artist agreement reflect some of the most Byzantine contracting practices of the entertainment industries. Recording artists suffer from royalty deductions for items such as breakage fees that date back to the lacquer records of the 1920s but continue to be included in poorly negotiated form agreements.

The law review article by Lynn Morrow, *The Recording Artist Agreement: Does it Empower or Enslave?*, 3 Vand. J. Ent. L. & Prac. 40 (2001) [hereinafter Morrow], provides an excellent summary of the costs and practices of the field. As Morrow points out, the label pays all production expenses for a CD only as an advance. The label recoups (or collects) these costs before the recording artist receives any income from the sales of the CD. In contrast, the marketing expenses for the CD are label overhead, not charged back to the recording artist. Music videos, which serve as both marketing and product, are the subject of much negotiation.

There are a number of key provisions over which the entertainment attorney needs to be particularly watchful. Donald Passman, Lynn Morrow, and other analysts focus on these provisions because they are likely to be the areas where negotiations are most likely to reduce the costs expected to be borne by the recording artist and because they seem the least reasonable. At the end of the day, however, real financial success for the artist can be measured by the size of the cash advance actually received and the limitation on the length of the contract.

(i) The Advance. As discussed earlier, the advance is more accurately described as a budget for the production of the CD from which all other expenses must be paid, including studio musicians, song producers, arrangers, engineers, and studio rental expenses. A large advance can quickly disappear if the recording process goes slowly. Teaching a client that time wasted in a studio comes directly out of the client's pocket may change some of the recording artist's behavior. This is where good management is critical.

(ii) Royalties and Deductions. The recording artist typically receives a royalty rate based on either the suggested retail price of the album or the wholesale price of the album to retailers. Against this royalty, a number of deductions are made, so that the actual royalty is often a small fraction of the theoretical percentage of retail sales.

First, since the royalty is typically "all in," other royalty participants are deducted. If the record producer receives a 3% royalty, then the 12% "all in" royalty of the artist has a 9% effective rate. Morrow, *supra*, at 45.

Second, the total income against which the royalty is calculated is reduced for free goods (2 of 10 given free for promotion), packaging expenses (10%–15% reduction), and breakage expenses (10%–20% reduction). No royalties are paid on copies of a work sold through record clubs or in discounted mid-price sales (*i.e.*, discount racks). These charges can reduce the potential income from a CD by half.

Third, since the mechanical fees are charged for the number of times each composition is recorded and produced, not the number sold, the reductions for free goods, breakage, and record clubs do not reduce the mechanical royalty rate owed to the publisher.

Finally, the label will reserve significant income against the prospect of returned CDs so that money actually due to be paid to the artist may be delayed as long as two years. The cumulative effect of all these charges and deductions is that it far too common for a recording artist to never receive a royalty check. Only the most popular and best managed of recording artists earn significant income from their recording contracts.

(iii) Cross-collateralization. Instead of receiving actual royalties, the recording artist earns money from other sources, such as from the mechanical license fees for writing the songs, the performance fees from touring, product license fees from tee-shirts and souvenirs, and through advances on future albums. The recording budget generally increases with each successful prior album. Both Morrow and Passman provide useful charts and typical contract language.

Morrow provides an excellent explanation of how these fees are cross-collateralized, so that the expense for each album is charged against royalty income for future albums:

> [A]ny unrecouped sums payable to a record company in connection with one album may be recouped from royalties earned by any of the artist's other albums. Record companies use cross-collateralization so that an artist's success helps to cover any previous or future losses.

Morrow, *supra*, at 44. The result of cross-collateralization is that even one unsuccessful album will generally absorb the royalty income for the artist.

The lesson for the entertainment attorney is to recognize that some of these reductions against royalties can be eliminated and that the recording artist's production management can greatly affect the financial success or failure of the artist's career.

5. Deal Structures and the Rise of the 360 Deal

In defense of the record company business model, in 2010, IFPI published a booklet, Investing in Music, to explain the business model of the sound recording industry. IFPI tries to make the economic case that recording companies' success involves significant investment and a good deal of risk. IFPI reports that few artists are ultimately successful, with a success ratio among successful acts hovering somewhere between one-in-five to one-in-ten.

Artists are paid royalties based on the sale of their music. In addition, the record company will invest its own funds on marketing and promotion for the sale of the artist. These investments include direct advertising, investing in public relations and media events, financial relationships with broadcasters, and merchandising. The record company will also advance additional funds — loans that will be deducted from the artist's royalties as advance payments to the artist, payment for the recording costs, and payment for the production videos. (Production videos can be negotiated to be treated as marketing costs and therefore not deductible from royalties.)

In recent years, as the revenue from sales of CDs has declined and cassettes tapes disappeared, record companies have sought to gain a portion of the artist's revenue from additional sources, specifically tour income and public performance income. Tour income had historically been reserved exclusively for the artist, while public performance revenue was historically collected through the performing rights societies and managed by the music publishing companies.

These new arrangements go by a number of different labels, including Multiple Rights Agreements, Broad Rights Agreements, or 360 Deals. In essence, the record company promises broader economic support and a one-stop-shop for the artist's services in exchange for a percentage of revenue from all of the artist's revenue streams.

> Broad rights or "360 degree" deals are increasingly widespread. The terms of these agreements commit music companies to greater investment across a range of artists' activities in return for a proportion of the revenue stream from all of them. This diverse investment benefits an artist's longevity and means there is not the same pressure on an artist to go into the recording studio in order to recoup their heavy investment costs.

> This form of non-traditional licensing income is becoming an increasingly important revenue channel for music companies.[1]

Potentially any company can enter into a full-service agreement with any musical artist. The broadcasting and touring giant Live Nation demonstrated this with very aggressive deals for Madonna and Jay-Z. Most of such deals, however, are coming from the record companies as they seek to maintain control over the changing musical landscape.

For artists without the market clout of a superstar, the value of a 360 Deal must be carefully scrutinized. The risks of cross-collateralization are magnified when all revenue streams are combined. Similarly, the artist bears a much greater risk of failure if the record company underperforms, fails to adequately invest, adopts a strategy that does not fully fit with the artist's vision, or simply misses its target. At the same time, if the artist receives a substantially larger advance and a binding commitment to invest in marketing, promotion, and tour support that is measurably larger than competing offers without the 360 Deal components (and subject to rigorous audit rights to assure compliance), then such an offer may be worth considering.

The 360 Deal and the expansion of record label control of the artist comes at a time when artists have much greater access to equipment, self-promotion, and direct

---

1. JOHN KENNEDY & ALISON WENHAM, INVESTING IN MUSIC 19 (Mar. 2010), https://ifpi.at/website 2018/wp-content/uploads/2018/12/investing-in-music.pdf.

marketing than ever before. Today, the vast majority of musicians record their own music, book their own tours, and use guerilla marketing to promote their professional activities. As such, the recording industry of today is becoming more highly stratified between the artists signed to labels and those who are truly independent. This trend is likely to continue as the ramifications to changes in technology and music consumption continue to transform the industries built on music.

Notes and Questions

a. From the label's perspective, it is better if the producer is an employee of the record company for copyright purposes, so that the copyright in the master is created as a work for hire, because copyright law does not support the practice of merely declaring an independent producer a provider of a specially commissioned work. Section 101 provides two separate definitions of work for hire. The first situation covers "a work prepared by an employee within the scope of his or her employment" which vests copyright authorship in the employer for employees engaged in their professional activities.

The second situation is the one which is more controversial. It provides nine special categories[2] under which the parties can agree in writing in advance. The nine categories do not include sound recording. In 1999, an attempt was made to insert this tenth category as a technical amendment to the Satellite Home Viewer Improvement Act of 1999. The response to this addition was fierce, resulting in The Work Made for Hire and Copyright Corrections Act of 2000, which not only deleted "as a sound recording" from the definition, but explicitly applied the deletion retroactively to negate any introduction of the term.

b. What legal rights might a label have if it entered into a work-for-hire agreement in December 1999 when the "as a sound recording" category existed in the definition of work-for-hire, but which was subsequently and retroactively deleted? Does the December 1999 agreement constitute an assignment, or does the copyright remain with the producer?

---

2. [A] work specially ordered or commissioned for use as a contribution to a collective work, as a part of a motion picture or other audiovisual work, as a translation, as a supplementary work, as a compilation, as an instructional text, as a test, as answer material for a test, or as an atlas, if the parties expressly agree in a written instrument signed by them that the work shall be considered a work made for hire. For the purpose of the foregoing sentence, a "supplementary work" is a work prepared for publication as a secondary adjunct to a work by another author for the purpose of introducing, concluding, illustrating, explaining, revising, commenting upon, or assisting in the use of the other work, such as forewords, afterwords, pictorial illustrations, maps, charts, tables, editorial notes, musical arrangements, answer material for tests, bibliographies, appendixes, and indexes, and an "instructional text" is a literary, pictorial, or graphic work prepared for publication and with the purpose of use in systematic instructional activities.
17 U.S.C. § 101.

c. IFPI reports that digital delivery of music has become the cause for optimism in the record industry with a number of positive economic trends. "In 2018, the global recorded music market grew by 9.7%. It is the fourth consecutive year of global growth and the highest rate of growth since IFPI began tracking the market in 1997." Globally, recorded music has exceeded $19.1 billion in revenue, the highest since 2006. In comparison, however, in 2001, the revenue was nearly $24 billion, so the changes to the industry have not entirely been made up through streaming. *See* IFPI, Global Music Report 2019: State of the Industry (2019).[3]

d. The RIAA provides U.S. statistics. "In 2018, revenues from recorded music in the United States grew 12% to $9.8 billion at estimated retail value. For the third year in a row, double-digit growth was driven primarily by increased revenues from paid subscription services including Spotify, Apple Music, Tidal, Amazon and others, which reached more than 50 million subscriptions in the United States for the first time. Revenues measured at wholesale value also grew 12% to $6.6 billion." In the U.S., streaming now accounts for 75% of the revenue while digital download and physical copies in the form of CDs and vinyl each make up roughly the remaining revenue. Vinyl has grown to nearly 38% of the physical sales revenues, as CD usage collapses and physical collections are becoming the pastime of music lovers and hobbyists. Synch licensing represents a mere 3% of the total.[4]

e. At the 2004 Midwest Art, Entertainment & Sports Law Institute — Signing and Developing Artists in a Download Economy, attorney Peter Strand commented that a $300,000 production budget "shrinks in the dryer," so that a $30,000 production budget for an independent label would be "a good deal."[5] In addition to the budget for an album, a major label typically spends several hundred thousand dollars on marketing, promotion, and publicity (e.g., print, TV, and radio advertising, videos, independent radio promotion services, etc.), distribution and tour support for the artist. He noted that less than 1% of albums actually recoup costs and provide a "clean profit."

Problem 11-A

A local band has begun covering some of Bryce's songs. Bryce is thrilled. The band, Soundfyre, is a five-member rock and blues band. On occasion Bryce would join the band, playing bass, sax, and keyboards. To Bryce's surprise, Soundfyre has invited Bryce to join the band on a permanent basis. Bryce needs advice.

The band has a recording contract and has already produced one album. The album sold only about 75,000 units but the label is willing to give Soundfyre a chance

3. https://www.ifpi.org/news/IFPI-GLOBAL-MUSIC-REPORT-2019.

4. *RIAA 2018 Year-End Music Industry Revenue Report*, RIAA fig. 2 (Feb. 28, 2019), https://www.riaa.com/riaa-releases-2018-year-end-music-industry-revenue-report/.

5. Peter Strand, Address at the *Midwest Art, Entertainment & Sports Law Institute*: *Signing and Developing Artists in a Download Economy* (July 9, 2004).

with a second album. Bryce really wants Soundfyre to use Bryce's songs but is not sure if joining the band is the best plan. Advise Bryce regarding the financial and business implications of joining the band and what options might be available.

B. Producers and Copyright Ownership

Systems XIX, Inc. v. Parker

30 F. Supp. 2d 1225 (N.D. Cal. 1998)

Plaintiff Maritime Hall Productions (Maritime) owns Maritime Hall, a combined amphitheater and recording studio in San Francisco, California. Defendants are Lawrence Parker (Parker), a performer of rap music who performs under the name "KRS-ONE", and Zomba Recording Corporation (Zomba), the record company responsible for the marketing and distribution of Parker's songs. Zomba is the copyright owner of Parker's musical compositions and recordings.

In mid-January 1997, Albert Cook, a concert promoter, contacted Maritime's president, Boots Hughston, to arrange a concert involving Parker at the Maritime Hall. Over the course of the next four weeks, Cook, Hughston, and Wesley Powell, Parker's road manager, negotiated the terms of the performance contract.

According to Hughston, Cook explained to Hughston during the negotiations that Parker was creating a new album and that if Maritime were to record Parker's performance, those recordings might be used on the new album. Hughston informed Cook that Maritime would require compensation and producer credits if Parker included a Maritime Hall recording on an album. Although the parties' negotiations were reduced to an Artist Engagement Contract, neither party signed the agreement due, in part, to an inability to agree on terms relating to the production and recording of Parker's live performance.

Parker states that he customarily records his performances for purposes of self-evaluation. On March 15, 1997, the day of the concert, Parker claims that since Parker's own sound engineer was absent, Powell requested Maritime to record the concert. Maritime proceeded to set up its recording equipment, including stage and audience microphones, audio lines and video cameras. Powell and Hughston then discussed the recording process for the concert. According to Hughston, Powell observed the pre-concert recording set-up, asked some questions about the video cameras, but appeared primarily concerned with receiving "the master" of the performance. A "master" tape refers to a professional sound quality digital audio tape that has been mixed and equalized.

Maritime recorded the concert and provided Powell with a master tape of the concert after the show. In the summer of 1997, Parker released an album "I Got Next" (the album). Two tracks on the album were taken from the sound recording of the concert on March 15, 1997. Although each of the remaining sixteen tracks on the album listed producer credits, the two tracks from the Maritime Hall concert sound recording contained no reference to producer credits or venue. Following the release of the album, Maritime requested compensation and producer credit listing from Zomba for its use of the sound recording on the album. Zomba did not reply to Maritime's request.

Maritime filed this action for declaratory relief and damages against Parker and Zomba on October 30, 1997. Maritime seeks a judicial determination of its rights under the Copyright Act with respect to the sound recording. In the alternative, Maritime seeks recovery in *quantum meruit* for Zomba's allegedly unauthorized use of the sound recording. Defendants filed the instant motion for summary judgment on August 7, 1998....

1. Maritime's rights under the Copyright Act

Maritime claims joint copyright ownership of the sound recordings. Defendants respond that Maritime is not a joint author of the sound recordings because Zomba and Parker lacked the requisite intent to create a joint work and never authorized Maritime to use the underlying musical compositions to make the sound recording.

Section 101 of the Copyright Act of 1976 (Act) defines a 'joint work' as: "a work prepared by two or more authors with the intention that their contributions be merged into inseparable or interdependent parts of a unitary whole." A party claiming joint authorship must establish that the authors 1) intended to merge their contributions into a unitary whole and 2) contributed copyrightable subject matter to the joint work.

A. Intention of the parties

i. The applicable standard

For a joint work to exist, the putative authors must have intended to merge their respective contributions into a unitary whole. Defendants first argue that under *Childress v. Taylor*, 945 F.2d 500 (2nd Cir. 1991), the parties' intent turns on their subjective expectations. Maritime responds that the courts scrutinize the subjective intent of the parties under the heightened *Childress* test only where the copyright claimant does not occupy a traditional authorship role as contemplated by Congress. In the case of sound recordings, Maritime argues that since Congress explicitly recognized the potential joint authorship roles of producer and artist, the *Childress* test is inapplicable to the instant facts. Rather than a subjective standard, Maritime contends that the parties' intent should be measured against an objective, factual standard as contemplated by the Act.

The Court agrees with Maritime that the subjective standard under *Childress* does not apply to the instant facts. *Childress* involved an actress/ research assistant who claimed joint authorship of a play. The *Childress* court evaluated the intention of the parties based on a subjective standard to prevent the extension of "joint authorship status to many persons who are not likely to have been within the contemplation of Congress."

In contrast to the playwright/ research assistant relationship in *Childress*, the producer/ performer relationship here was under the specific contemplation of Congress as joint authors of a sound recording under the Act. Congress discussed in the Act's legislative history that "the copyrightable elements of a sound recording will usually, though not always, involve 'authorship' both on the part of the performers whose performance is captured and on the part of the record producer responsible for setting up the session, capturing and electronically processing the sounds, and compiling and editing them to make a final sound recording." H.R. Rep. No. 94-1476, 94th Cong., 2nd Sess. 56 (1976).

The standard by which the intent of the parties is measured is not strictly subjective as urged by Defendants. Rather, the requisite intent will be found if, based on an objective, factual standard, the parties prepared the sound recording "with the intention that their contributions be merged into inseparable or interdependent *parts of a unitary whole.*"

ii. Did Zomba possess the requisite intent to create a joint work?

Defendants contend that they did not share a mutual intent with Maritime to create a joint work in the sound recordings. Defendants argue that since neither Zomba nor Parker ever had any direct communication with Maritime, much less asked Maritime to professionally record the concert, defendants could not have intended the creation of a joint work with Maritime.

Maritime responds that defendants did share an intention with Maritime to co-author the sound recording, as demonstrated by copyright practice, industry custom, and the factual circumstances in which the sound recording was produced.

Maritime first argues that sound recordings by their nature are usually joint works. For example, according to the United States Copyright Office, "[s]ound recording authorship may be contributed by the performer or the record producer. Usually, authorship is contributed by both performer and producer." Compendium of Copyright Office Practices, United States Copyright Office, § 495.01 at 400–37 (1984).

Maritime next argues that as an experienced artist, Parker understood the inherently collaborative nature of producing a live performance. Parker was aware of both the technical and creative efforts that are customarily required of producers, as well as the acknowledgment of those efforts through the industry practice of 1) crediting producers on an album for their contribution in recording a particular track and 2) requesting third party producers to transfer their rights in the track in exchange for royalty payments.

Finally, Maritime contends that when Parker requested, through his road manager, that Maritime record his performance, Parker intended to create a collaborative joint work with Maritime, in accordance with copyright practice and industry custom. Powell, the road manager, claims that he did not request a professional recording, but merely asked Maritime to activate a tape recorder. Maritime points out, however, that both Parker and Powell knew prior to the concert that Parker was going to be professionally recorded because the recording equipment, including large microphones and video cameras, was plainly visible from the stage.

After the concert, Parker's road manager left with the "master" tape. Parker and Zomba ultimately used the sound recording on the album. Maritime concludes that by requesting a recording of the concert, which was later commercially released, defendants intended that the parties merge their creative efforts in the production of a sound recording.

The Court finds that Maritime has demonstrated the existence of triable issues of fact with respect to the intention of the parties. Contrary to defendants' contentions, whether Zomba or Parker ever directly asked Maritime to record the concert is not dispositive of the question of the parties' intent.

Maritime has submitted evidence that Parker requested Maritime to record him. Parker knew Maritime was employing professional equipment while he was being recorded. Parker, through his road manager, sought out the tape after the concert, and ultimately used the tape on his album. From these circumstances a jury could reasonably conclude that Parker/ Zomba and Maritime shared an implied agreement to jointly create a sound recording of the concert through the interdependent contributions of Parker's performance and Maritime's recordation and production thereof.

B. Copyrightable contribution

Copyright protection applies only to those claimants that have made an original contribution. Maritime argues that it contributed copyrightable subject matter to the sound recordings through the arrangement and administration of recording equipment, the electronic processing of sounds, and the balancing, equalization, and integration of vocal, instrumental and audience components into a blended whole.

Defendants contend, however, that as a matter of law, Maritime is precluded from making copyrightable contributions to the sound recording because Maritime did not have Zomba's consent to make those contributions. Zomba owns the exclusive copyright to the musical compositions that form the basis of the sound recording. Defendants correctly maintain that to assert a claim of joint authorship over the sound recordings, Maritime must have obtained Zomba's permission to use Parker's musical compositions in the sound recordings. Defendants conclude that since Zomba did not authorize Maritime to use the underlying compositions in the sound recording, Maritime had no legal right to make copyrightable contributions in the production of the sound recording.

Permission to employ pre-existing copyrighted material in a sound recording need not be in writing, but can be granted orally or implied from conduct in the form of a non-exclusive license. Maritime argues that it received a non-exclusive license from defendants to use Parker's underlying musical compositions in the sound recording. Maritime contends that its license was implied from the following conduct: 1) Parker's road manager asked Maritime to record the performance; 2) Parker performed in front of two highly conspicuous audience microphones; and 3) Parker and Zomba accepted and released the sound recordings.

Defendants argue that since Zomba owned the copyrights to Parker's musical compositions, only Zomba could grant Maritime a license to use the compositions. Defendants contend that Maritime has presented evidence of an implied license based only on the conduct of Powell and Parker, and not of Zomba.

The Court finds that whether Maritime had an implied license to use Parker's musical compositions based on the conduct of Zomba or its agents is a question of fact that cannot be resolved on summary judgment. It is true that Zomba owns the copyright to Parker's musical compositions. Zomba, however, also vested Parker with the authority to perform those compositions at Maritime's venue. At the venue, Parker requested that Maritime record his musical compositions. Since Parker states that he "customarily" records his own performances, it should have come as no surprise to Zomba that Parker asked Maritime to record the concert.

From these facts, a jury could reasonably conclude that Parker, vested with Zomba's authority to perform the copyrighted compositions, acted as Zomba's agent when he requested Maritime to record the concert. In light of Zomba's later acceptance and commercial exploitation of the sound recordings, it is a question of fact whether Parker's request to record the performance constituted an implied license for Maritime to use the underlying compositions to produce the sound recording.

2. Maritime's unjust enrichment claim

Defendants contend that Maritime's equitable claim for unjust enrichment is preempted by the Copyright Act under 17 U.S.C. § 301. Maritime responds that preemption does not apply because the subject matter of its state law claim falls outside the scope of the Act....

The Court finds that the rights which Maritime seeks to enforce in its claim for unjust enrichment is equivalent to the rights of a copyright owner under §§ 106(1) and 106(3) of the Act. Section 106(1) ensures a copyright owner the right "to reproduce the copyrighted work in copies or phonorecords." Section 106(3) protects the right of copyright owners to distribute those copies to the public for sale.

In its state law claim, Maritime seeks recovery from defendants for their wrongful profits from Maritime's interest in the sound recording. Under the Act, Maritime, as putative joint author, possesses the right under §§ 106(1) and 106(3) to share in the profits of Zomba's reproduction and distribution of the sound recordings. Under federal copyright law or in *quantum meruit*, Maritime is seeking the same thing: compensation for the reproduction and distribution of the sound recordings. Under the third prong, therefore, the rights Maritime asserts under its state law claim are equivalent to rights within the general scope of copyright as specified in § 106.

The sound recording is a work of authorship fixed in a tangible medium of expression and the work comes within the subject matter of copyright under § 102(a)(7). Further, the rights sought to be vindicated in Maritime's unjust enrichment claim are rights involving reproduction and distribution that are clearly equivalent to the rights prescribed by §§ 106(1) and 106(3). Consequently, § 301(a) preempts Maritime's unjust enrichment claim....

Forward v. Thorogood

985 F.2d 604 (1st Cir. 1993)

This is an appeal from a final judgment determining the copyright ownership of certain unpublished tape recordings of the musical group George Thorogood and the Destroyers (the "Band"). The district court ruled that the Band held the copyright to the tapes and enjoined appellant John Forward from making commercial use of the recordings. We affirm.

The basic facts can be briefly stated. Forward is a music aficionado and record collector with a special interest in blues and country music. In 1975, Forward was working as a bus driver when he first met Thorogood at a Boston nightclub where the Band was performing. Forward was immediately taken with the Band's act and struck up a friendship with Thorogood. Thorogood and his fellow band members, a drummer and a guitar player, had been playing together at East Coast colleges and clubs since 1973.

Upon learning that the Band had yet to release its first album, Forward began a campaign to persuade his friends at Rounder Records to sign the Band to a recording contract. Rounder Records is a small, Boston-based record company specializing in blues and folk music. As part of this effort, Forward arranged and paid for two recording sessions for the Band in 1976. The purpose of the sessions was to create a "demo" tape that would capture Rounder Records' interest. At Forward's invitation, one of the principals of Rounder Records attended the Band's second recording session. Other than requesting specific songs to be recorded, Forward's contribution to the sessions was limited to arranging and paying for them.

Rounder Records was impressed by what it heard; the day after the second session, it arranged to sign the Band to a contract. The Band agreed that Forward could keep the tapes for his own enjoyment, and they have remained in his possession ever since. In 1977, the Band's first album was released under the Rounder Records label. Forward was singled out for "special thanks" in the album's acknowledgements. Since then, Thorogood and the Destroyers have released a number of records and gone on to achieve success as a blues/rock band.

The dispute between the parties arose in early 1988, when Forward told the Band that he intended to sell the 1976 tapes to a record company for commercial release. The Band objected, fearing that release of the tapes would harm its reputation; they were, the district court found, of "relatively primitive quality" compared to the Band's published work. On July 5, 1988, Forward filed suit in the district court, seeking a declaratory judgment that he held the common law copyright to the tapes. Determination of copyright ownership is governed by the common law of copyright because the tapes are unpublished and were recorded in 1976, prior to the January 1, 1978, effective date of the Copyright Act of 1976. The Band responded with a counterclaim for declaratory and injunctive relief....

On this appeal, Forward's first theory in support of his claim of copyright ownership is based on his ownership and possession of the tapes. According to Forward, ownership of a copyrightable work carries with it ownership of the copyright. Alternatively, he argues that the evidence mandated a finding that the copyright was implicitly transferred to him along with the demo tapes. We find no merit in either claim.

The creator of a work is, at least presumptively, its author and the owner of the copyright. The performer of a musical work is the author, as it were, of the performance. The courts, in applying the common law of copyright, did in a number of cases infer from an unconditional sale of a manuscript or painting an intent to transfer the copyright. This doctrine, often criticized and subject to various judicial and statutory exclusions is the source of Forward's principal claim. The difficulty for Forward is that even under the doctrine this physical transfer merely created a presumption and the ultimate question was one of intent.

In this case, the district court found that "[n]either the band nor any of its members ever conveyed, or agreed to convey, their copyright interest in the tapes to Forward." Rather the Band allowed Forward to keep the tapes solely for his personal enjoyment. Forward's disregard of this central finding is premised on a highly artificial attempt to claim "constructive possession" of the tapes from the outset and then to argue that any reservation by the Band at the end of the sessions was an invalid attempt to reconvey or qualify his copyright. The reality is that the Band never surrendered the copyright in the first place and the transfer of the tapes' ownership to Forward was not a sharply defined event distinct from the reservation of the Band's rights....

Forward's second theory of copyright ownership involves the "works for hire" doctrine. Under this doctrine, a judicially developed notion later codified in the Copyright Act of 1909, an employer is deemed the "author" and copyright holder of a work created by an employee acting within the scope of employment. Although initially confined to the traditional employer-employee relationship, the doctrine has been expanded to include commissioned works created by independent contractors, with courts treating the contractor as an employee and creating a presumption of copyright ownership in the commissioning party at whose "instance and expense" the work was done.[6] Forward maintains that the tapes, created at his "instance and expense," are commissioned works to which he holds the copyright.

The district court rejected this claim, finding that the evidence did not support it. The court said that, although Forward booked and paid for the studio time, he neither employed nor commissioned the band members nor did he compensate or agree to compensate them. While the lack of compensation may not be decisive, see, e.g., [*Community for Creative Non-Violence v. Reid*, 490 U.S. 730, 734 (1989)] (donated commissioned work), the evidence as a whole amply supports the trial judge's con-

---

6. The Copyright Act of 1976 altered the works for hire doctrine so that only certain types of commissioned works qualify as works for hire, and then only if the parties have agreed in writing to treat it as such. *See Community for Creative Non-Violence*, 490 U.S. at 738. The Act's provisions on works for hire operate prospectively and do not govern this case.

clusion. Nothing suggests that the tapes were prepared for the use and benefit of Forward. Rather, the purpose was to provide demo tapes to entice a recording company. Forward was a fan and friend who fostered this effort, not the Archbishop of Saltzburg commissioning works by Mozart.

Finally, Forward argues that he is at least a co-owner of the copyright as a "joint author" of the tape recordings.... In appraising this claim, our concern is with Forward's musical or artistic contribution rather than his encouragement to the Band or his logistical support.

The district court found that "Forward made no musical or artistic contribution" to the tapes, explaining that Forward did not serve as the engineer at the sessions or direct the manner in which the songs were played or sung. The trial judge noted that Forward did request that certain songs be played but "the band then played those songs in precisely the same manner that it always played them." The district court's concise and unqualified findings are fully supported by the evidence.

Forward has only one legal prop for his contrary claim and it is a weak one. In the House Report on the Copyright Act of 1976, the committee observed that the copyright in sound recordings "will usually, though not always, involve 'authorship' both ... [by the artist and by] the record producer responsible for setting up the recording session, capturing and electronically processing the sounds, and compiling and editing them to make the final sound recording." H. Rep. No. 94-1476, 94th Cong., 2d Sess. 56 (1976). It is apparent from this passage that the "producer" envisaged by the committee is one who engages in artistically supervising and editing the production. That is exactly what Forward did not do in this case....

In 1995, a legislative compromise amended §§ 106 and 114 to provide a limited copyright. Under § 106, a copyright interest now exists for performers "in the case of sound recordings, to perform the copyrighted work publicly by means of a digital audio transmission." Congress amended the law in 1998 to incorporate the dramatic changes caused by Internet broadcasting to the original regulations. Under § 114 of the Copyright Act, digital performances are regulated in three general categories.

Notes and Questions

a. Under traditional copyright law, a musical performing artist holds no copyright in his or her performance. As a result, the performers do not receive any income from radio play or other public performances of their recordings except as negotiated under union recording agreements. Nonetheless, as copyright interests have continued to expand since 1972 when federal law first recognized copyright in sound recordings, an increasing number of possible ownership claims have arisen. State laws often protect sound recording made prior to February 15, 1972.

b. Jenny Smith, a musician, engineer, and record producer, serves as producer for three cuts on a CD. Part of the Producer's Agreement states that the three song masters were created as a work-for-hire as a specially commissioned work. Both Ms. Smith and the label duly sign the agreement. If there is no additional assignment provision in the contract, who is the author of the three song masters? *See Staggers v. Real Authentic Sound,* 77 F. Supp. 2d 57 (D.D.C. 1999).

c. Industry custom generally places the copyright ownership of a master tape in the record label to assure all copyright interests are collected into a single entity so the final work may be exploited through reproductions, sales, and licenses. To what extent does this custom govern the interpretation of copyright law?

d. Does the composer of a song have a claim to compensation or control over the sampling of another sound recording embodying some portion of the composer's work? *See Newton v. Diamond,* 349 F.3d 591 (9th Cir. 2003).

e. Does the mechanical license cover any composer's interest in a song sample? Compare the results under 17 U.S.C. § 115 (compulsory license for making and distributing phonorecords) with the type license generally used by the industry as provided by the Harry Fox Agency.

f. The international management of copyrights only compounds the problems for the copyright owners. The copyrights in the underlying compositions must be maintained in each country where the sound recording is sold. These rights are often held by local entities, and the local recording distributor must secure those rights. For an example where Sony was deemed to overreact to the failure to maintain these underlying rights, *see Point Prods. A.G. v. Sony Music Entm't, Inc.,* 215 F. Supp. 2d 336 (S.D.N.Y. 2002).

g. In 2009, legislation was introduced to extend a public performance right for radio or "audio transmissions." The effect would be to extend the mandatory statutory licensing to AM and FM radio.

h. Can a person sell a sound recording and still exploit the underlying composition? Not through litigation. The distinction between these two aspects of a song tested the differing standards for sound recordings and the underlying musical compositions. To the extent that these standards can be compared, *see Newton v. Diamond,* 388 F.3d 1189 (9th Cir. 2004).

i. When does a producer's claim of copyright ownership in the master recordings accrue? *See Diamond v. Gillis,* 357 F. Supp. 2d 1003 (E.D. Mich. 2005).

j. In seeking statutory damages for the unauthorized sale of digital albums, what is the work—the individual songs or the compilation as a whole? *See Bryant v. Media Rights Prods.,* 603 F.3d 135 (2d Cir. 2010).

k. Record companies actively support the marketing of recording artists by distributing many copies of the recordings for free on CD, sending the discs to record stores, broadcasters, and others. To what extent can they restrict the resale of these free copies to avoid flooding the used-CD market? *See UMG Recordings, Inc. v. Augusto,* 628 F.3d 1175 (9th Cir. 2011).

Problem 11-B

Bryce is a bit upset. Two of Bryce's songs were rewritten by the drummer in Soundfyre. Bryce acknowledges that late one night after one of the performances, Bryce had said "do whatever you want" regarding the songs, but Bryce did not think it was anything other than bar talk, and Bryce did not consider that the statement was intended to waive fees or rights.

The forthcoming album by Soundfyre includes the two songs in question. The CD lists Bryce and Jeri Thundar as authors of the songs. Bryce is not receiving mechanical royalties. Advise Bryce what options are available to collect on the income from the songs and correct the credits provided on the album.

C. Scope of Prior Licenses

Thomas v. Gusto Records, Inc.

939 F.2d 395 (6th Cir. 1991)

The musicians in this suit have achieved a high degree of success in "popular music." B.J. Thomas is most famous for his recording of the theme song for the movie "Butch Cassidy and the Sundance Kid," "Rain Drops Keep Fallin' on My Head." Burt Bacharach and Hal Davis wrote the song originally for Bob Dylan to record. Thomas also had a number one hit with "Another Somebody Done Somebody Wrong Song." Among his accolades are eleven gold records, two platinum albums, and five Grammy awards.

Thomas and the Shirelles entered into contracts with Scepter Records, Inc. in 1968 and 1961, respectively. The provisions of the two contracts in question are identical, except as to the royalty rate, and provide the following:

> 4. For the rights herein granted and the service to be rendered by you we shall pay you as royalty a sum equal to [4% for the Shirelles] [5% for Thomas] of the net retail list price in the United States of America based on 90% of all double-faced records manufactured and sold by us and paid for, on both faces of which are embodied only the selections recorded hereunder; and one-half of the respective amounts of such royalties of 90% of all records manufactured and sold by us and paid for on only one face of which are embodied only the selections recorded hereunder. In the case of phonograph records and other copies manufactured and sold in foreign countries by any subsidiary, affiliate, licensee or nominees to whom we have supplied a copy or duplicate of a master or matrix or tape of any such recordings, we will pay you one-half of the United States of America royalty rate out of all net license fees paid and received by us for phonograph records and other copies so manufactured and sold....

Gusto and G.M.L. assert that paragraph four is unambiguous with regard to royalties from domestic licensing, arguing that the "obvious implication" of silence on the issue is that the parties agreed there would be no such royalties. We do not find that implication so obvious.

Both parties agree that New York law should be applied to resolve this issue. The resolution of any ambiguity in a written contract is to be determined by the court as a matter of law. Not only are these contracts silent on many issues, e.g. domestic licensing royalties, many of the provisions which the contracts do set forth are perfectly obscure. Paragraph eight of both contracts, for example, if read independently, could be interpreted as a provision in which Thomas and the Shirelles signed away any and all rights. Indeed, the defendants assert this is what the paragraph means with respect to royalties from domestic licensing. Without an integration clause or more evidence in the documents supporting this harsh interpretation, we cannot accept this reading of the contracts. Because of the ambiguities in these contracts, we believe the district court properly looked beyond the written contract to determine the true intentions of the parties.

New York cases have consistently held that custom may be used to clarify ambiguities or to "fill gaps" in an agreement. Gusto asserts these cases are inapposite because custom and practice cannot be used to contradict the express terms of the contracts. The problem with this argument is that the contracts in question are silent with respect to royalties from domestic licensing; there are no express terms in the contracts explaining the parties' intentions on this issue. Paragraph 4 sets forth the royalty rate on the record company's own sales and on *foreign* sales by "any subsidiary, affiliate, licensee or nominee[]." ... Because no provision in the contracts of B.J. Thomas or the Shirelles pertains to royalties from domestic licensing income which could be contradicted by incorporating into the contracts the custom in the music industry with respect to that issue, the district court properly accepted the fifty percent royalty rate as the rate intended by the parties.

Greenfield v. Philles Records

98 N.Y.2d 562 (N.Y. 2002)

In this contract dispute between a singing group and their record producer, we must determine whether the artists' transfer of full ownership rights to the master recordings of musical performances carried with it the unconditional right of the producer to redistribute those performances in any technological format. In the absence of an explicit contractual reservation of rights by the artists, we conclude that it did.

In the early 1960s, Veronica Bennett (now known as Ronnie Greenfield), her sister Estelle Bennett and their cousin Nedra Talley, formed a singing group known as "The Ronettes." They met defendant Phil Spector, a music producer and composer, in 1963 and signed a five-year "personal services" music recording contract (the Ronettes agreement) with Spector's production company, defendant Philles Records, Inc. The plaintiffs agreed to perform exclusively for Philles Records and in exchange, Philles Records acquired an ownership right to the recordings of the Ronettes' musical performances. The agreement also set forth a royalty schedule to compensate plaintiffs for their services. After signing with Philles Records, plaintiffs received a single collective cash advance of approximately $15,000.

The Ronettes recorded several dozen songs for Philles Records, including "Be My Baby," which sold over a million copies and topped the music charts. Despite their popularity, the group disbanded in 1967 and Philles Records eventually went out of business. Other than their initial advance, plaintiffs received no royalty payments from Philles Records.

Beyond their professional relationship, however, was the story of the personal relationship between Spector and plaintiff Ronnie Greenfield. They married in 1968 but separated after a few years. Greenfield initiated a divorce proceeding against Spector in California and a settlement was reached in 1974. As part of that agreement, Spector and Greenfield executed mutual general releases that purported to resolve all past and future claims and obligations that existed between them, as well as between Greenfield and Spector's companies.

Defendants subsequently began to capitalize on a resurgence of public interest in 1960s music by making use of new recording technologies and licensing master recordings of the Ronettes' vocal performances for use in movie and television productions, a process known in entertainment industry parlance as "synchronization." The most notable example was defendants' licensing of "Be My Baby" in 1987 for use in the motion picture "Dirty Dancing." Defendants also licensed master recordings to third parties for production and distribution in the United States (referred to as domestic redistribution), and sold compilation albums containing performances by the Ronettes. While defendants earned considerable compensation from such licensing and sales, no royalties were paid to any of the plaintiffs.

As a result, plaintiffs commenced this breach of contract action in 1987, alleging that the 1963 agreement did not provide Philles Records with the right to license the master recordings for synchronization and domestic redistribution, and demanded royalties from the sales of compilation albums. Although defendants initially denied the existence of a contract, in 1992 they stipulated that an unexecuted copy of the contract would determine the parties' rights. Defendants thereafter argued that the agreement granted them absolute ownership rights to the master recordings and permitted the use of the recordings in any format, subject only to royalty rights. Following extensive pretrial proceedings, Supreme Court ruled in plaintiffs' favor and awarded approximately $3 million in damages and interest.

The Appellate Division affirmed, concluding that defendants' actions were not authorized by the agreement with plaintiffs because the contract did not specifically transfer the right to issue synchronization and third-party domestic distribution licenses. Permitting plaintiffs to assert a claim for unjust enrichment, the Court found that plaintiffs were entitled to the music recording industry's standard 50% royalty rate for income derived from synchronization and third-party licensing. We granted leave to appeal.

We are asked on this appeal to determine whether defendants, as the owners of the master recordings of plaintiffs' vocal performances, acquired the contractual right to issue licenses to third parties to use the recordings in connection with television, movies and domestic audio distribution. The agreement between the parties consists of a two-page document, which apparently was widely used in the 1960s by music producers signing new artists. Plaintiffs executed the contract without the benefit of counsel. The parties' immediate objective was to record and market the Ronettes' vocal performances and "[m]ake therefrom phonograph records and/ or tape recordings and other similar devices (excluding transcriptions)."[7] The ownership rights provision of the contract provides:

> "All recordings made hereunder and all records and reproductions made therefrom together with the performances embodied therein, shall be entirely [Philles'] property, free of any claims whatsoever by you or any person deriving any rights of interest from you. Without limitation of the foregoing, [Philles] shall have the right to make phonograph records, tape recordings or other reproductions of the performances embodied in such recordings by any method now or hereafter known, and to sell and deal in the same under any trade mark or trade names or labels designated by us, or we may at our election refrain therefrom."

Plaintiffs concede that the contract unambiguously gives defendants unconditional ownership rights to the master recordings, but contend that the agreement does not bestow the right to exploit those recordings in new markets or mediums since the document is silent on those topics. Defendants counter that the absence of specific references to synchronization and domestic licensing is irrelevant. They argue that where a contract grants full ownership rights to a musical performance or composition, the only restrictions upon the owner's right to use that property are those explicitly enumerated by the grantor/ artist.

Despite the technological innovations that continue to revolutionize the recording industry, long-settled common-law contract rules still govern the interpretation of agreements between artists and their record producers. The fundamental, neutral precept of contract interpretation is that agreements are construed in accord with the parties' intent....

The pivotal issue in this case is whether defendants are prohibited from using the master recordings for synchronization, and whatever future formats evolve from new technologies, in the absence of explicit contract language authorizing such uses. Stated another way, does the contract's silence on synchronization and domestic licensing create an ambiguity which opens the door to the admissibility of extrinsic evidence to determine the intent of the parties? We conclude that it does not and, because there is no ambiguity in the terms of the Ronettes agreement, defendants are entitled to exercise complete ownership rights, subject to payment of applicable royalties due plaintiffs.

New York has well-established precedent on the issue of whether a grantor retains any rights to artistic property once it is unconditionally transferred.... A broad grant of ownership rights, coupled with the absence of a reservation clause, was similarly dispositive in *Burnett v Warner Bros. Pictures* (67 N.Y.2d 912, 501 N.Y.S.2d 815, 492 N.E.2d 1231 [1986], affg 113 AD2d 710, 493 N.Y.S.2d 326). In that case, the plaintiffs had assigned all of their rights in a play that was later adapted into a movie,

---

7. "Transcriptions" were large discs used for reproducing musical performances for radio broadcasts.

"Casablanca," and subsequently led to the defendant's spinoff television series. We affirmed the Appellate Division's conclusion that if "the plaintiff intended to retain certain rights, specific clauses to that effect should have been included in the agreement" because the parties' contract assigned "all imaginable rights" to *Warner Brothers* (113 A.D.2d at 712–713).

In analogous contexts, other courts have recognized that broad contractual provisions, similar to those in the Ronettes agreement, convey virtually unfettered reproduction rights to license holders in the absence of specific exceptions to the contrary. In *Boosey & Hawkes Music Publs. Ltd. v Walt Disney Co.* (145 F.3d 481 [2d Cir 1998]), the plaintiff granted distribution rights in foreign countries to Igor Stravinsky's musical composition "The Rite of Spring," including the "right, license, privilege and authority to record [the composition] in any manner, medium or form" for use in the motion picture "Fantasia" to the Walt Disney Company. After Disney reproduced the song in videocassette and laser disc versions for foreign distribution, the plaintiff sought breach of contract damages on the basis that the agreement did not explicitly provide for distribution in new technological mediums.

The United States Court of Appeals for the Second Circuit reiterated its precedent that "'licensee[s] may properly pursue any uses which may reasonably be said to fall within the medium as described in the license.'" As applied to the facts of *Boosey*, the Second Circuit concluded that the broad language employed in the contract granted Disney the authority to use the musical composition in the videocassette version of the movie in the absence of any contractual indication otherwise. Thus, the language of the contract was the controlling factor in interpreting the agreement:

> "If the contract is more reasonably read to convey one meaning, the party benefited by that reading should be able to rely on it; the party seeking exception or deviation from the meaning reasonably conveyed by the words of the contract should bear the burden of negotiating for language that would express the limitation or deviation"

We agree with these prevalent rules of contract construction — the unconditional transfer of ownership rights to a work of art includes the right to use the work in any manner unless those rights are specifically limited by the terms of the contract. However, if a contract grants less than full ownership or specifies only certain rights to use the property, then other, unenumerated rights may be retained by the grantor.

In this case, plaintiffs concede that defendants own the master recordings. Notably, the agreement explicitly refers to defendants' "right to make phonograph records, tape recordings or *other reproductions* of the performances embodied in such recordings by *any method now or hereafter known,* and to sell and deal in the same." Plaintiffs contend that the breadth of the ownership provision is limited by the agreement's introductory paragraph, which states that defendants' purpose for purchasing plaintiffs' performances was to make "phonograph records and/ or tape recordings and other similar devices." However, when read in conjunction with the ownership provision, a reasonable meaning emerges — the phrase "other similar devices" refers to defendants' right to reproduce the performances by any current or future technological methods. We also reject plaintiffs' assertion that the royalty schedule restricts the scope of defendants' ownership rights. That section of the agreement provides compensation rights to plaintiffs; it does not inhibit defendants' ability to use the master recordings. We therefore hold that the Ronettes agreement, "read as a whole to determine its purpose and intent" is susceptible to only one reasonable interpretation— defendants are authorized to license the performances for use in visual media, such as movies and television commercials or broadcasts, and for domestic release by third parties in audio formats.

Plaintiffs' reliance upon *B.J. Thomas v Gusto Records* (939 F.2d 395 [6th Cir. 1991]) is misplaced. In *Thomas,* the United States Court of Appeals for the Sixth Circuit purportedly applied New York law and held that the parties' agreements were ambiguous regarding the artists' right to royalties from domestic licensing because the contracts were silent on the issue. The dispute in *Thomas*—whether the contract's compensation clause entitled the plaintiffs to royalties from the issuance of domestic licenses—is not the same as the question posed in this case, which concerns the scope of owners' rights to use their property. Furthermore, *Thomas'* suggestion that the failure of a contract to address certain categories of royalties allows a court to look beyond the four corners of the document to discern the parties' true intent conflicts with our established precedent that silence does not equate to contractual ambiguity....

Defendants acknowledge that the royalty schedule for domestic sales encompasses the sale of records, compact discs and other audio reproductions by entities holding domestic third-party distribution licenses from Philles Records. In light of that concession, we remit this case to Supreme Court to recalculate plaintiffs' damages for royalties due on all such sales. Damages should be determined pursuant to the applicable schedule incorporated in the agreement rather than based on industry standards....

Malmsteen v. Universal Music Group, Inc.

940 F. Supp. 2d 123 (S.D.N.Y. 2013)

This case arises out of a recording contract between plaintiff Yngwie J. Malmsteen, a musician, and defendant UMG Recordings, Inc. ("UMG"). Malmsteen is a professional musician. Defendant UMG, a record company, is a wholly owned subsidiary of PolyGram Holdings, Inc., which in turn is a wholly owned subsidiary of defendant Universal Music Group, Inc. UMG was formerly known as PolyGram Records, Inc. ("PolyGram"), having changed its name in 1999.

On November 1, 1985, PolyGram and DeNovo Productions ("DeNovo"), a division of DeNovo Music Group, Inc., entered into the recording contract at issue in this case. Malmsteen is DeNovo's successor-in-interest under the Agreement.

Under its Agreement with DeNovo, PolyGram was given the exclusive right to record "Master Recordings" by Malmsteen during the term of the Agreement, and to reproduce and sell those recordings. A "Master Recording" is defined as "[a]ny recording of sound, whether or not coupled with a visual image, by any method and on any substance or material, whether now or hereafter known, intended for reproduction in the form of Phonograph Records, or otherwise, including Audio-Visual Recordings." Agreement § 13.01. The Agreement provides that such Master Recordings are "entirely the property of [UMG]" and that UMG "and its subsidiaries, affiliates, and licensees shall have the sole, exclusive and unlimited right ... to manufacture Records ... embodying ... the performances embodied on Master Recordings." Agreement § 5.01. The Agreement also gives UMG the "exclusive right to publicly perform and otherwise utilize [Malmsteen's] performances in connection with Audio-Visual Recordings for promotional and commercial purposes." *Id.* § 5.02(a)(i). Under the Agreement, UMG is obliged to pay Malmsteen royalties on income derived from its exploitation of Master Recordings; the means of calculating these royalties are set forth in Article 7.

UMG is required to provide Malmsteen with semiannual royalty accountings "on or before September 30th for the period ending the preceding June 30th, and on or before March 31st for the period ending the preceding December 31st." Agreement § 8.01.

The "Term" of the Agreement expired in the early 1990s, after Malmsteen had delivered four Master Recordings to UMG. Some of UMG's obligations under the Agreement were explicitly tied to the duration of the Agreement's Term, and therefore expired at this point. However, UMG's obligation to account to Malmsteen for royalties remains ongoing.

Malmsteen argues that UMG breached the Agreement in three distinct ways, each related to the calculation and payment of royalties owed to him. The Court reviews the facts relevant to each of these theories, in turn.

The Royalty Rate on Sales of Digital Downloads

UMG sells Records in a variety of formats, including digital downloads sold through non-affiliated third-party retailers such as Apple's iTunes Music Store. In 1985, however, when the Agreement was executed, these modern means of distribution did not exist. The Agreement accordingly contains no express provision regarding sales of digital downloads.

UMG has been crediting Malmsteen for royalties on sales of digital downloads at the rates applicable, under the Agreement, to the sale of "Records" and "Phonograph Records" through "Normal Retail Channels." "Records" and "Phonograph Records" are defined as:

> Any device now or hereafter known, on or by which sound may be recorded and reproduced, which is manufactured or distributed primarily for home and/or consumer and/or juke box use and/or use on or in means of transportation including "sight and sound" devices or Audio-Visual Devices.

"Normal Retail Channels," in turn, are defined as "[n]ormal retail distribution channels, excluding sales of Records described in [§§ 7.05–7.08], herein." The royalty rate applicable to such sales ranges from 8% to 15%, depending on the location of the sale, the total number of albums sold, and whether the Record sold is an "Album" or a "Single." Different royalty rates apply to the sale of Records through certain specified methods of distribution outside of the "Normal Retail Channels." Relevant here, under § 7.06, Malmsteen is entitled to a 50% royalty on Records sold by such methods, which include:

> licenses of Master Recordings to Non-Affiliated Third Parties for sales of Records by such licenses through direct mail, mail order, or in conjunction with TV advertising, including through methods of distribution such as "key outlet marketing" (distribution through retail fulfillment centers in conjunction with special advertisements on radio or television), or by any combination of the methods set forth above or other methods.

In this lawsuit, Malmsteen argues that § 7.06(a)(ii), and not the provisions governing the sale of "Records" and "Phonograph Records" through "Normal Retail Channels," governs the sale of digital downloads, and therefore that UMG has breached the Agreement by calculating royalties at the lower rates provided for under §§ 7.01–7.03.

Recoupment of Video Production Costs

UMG maintains two separate accounts for Malmsteen's royalties, one for income derived from exploitation of his audio recordings ("Audio Account") and one for income derived from exploitation of his video recordings ("Video Account"). The royalties from these accounts are not payable to Malmsteen, however, "until such time as all Advances ... have been repaid to [UMG]." An "Advance" is defined as "a prepayment of royalties and shall be charged against and shall be recoupable from all royalties accruing hereunder." Included among these Advances are 50% of UMG's video production costs for a defined number of Audio-Visual Recordings. UMG is similarly entitled to recoup 50% of the production costs of the Concert Video. Accordingly, UMG is entitled to recoup from Malmsteen's audio royalties 50% of the expenses it incurred in producing Malmsteen's video recordings, including the Concert Video, in the late 1980s and early 1990s. The parties do not dispute UMG's entitlement to recoup such expenses. Rather, they dispute whether UMG has in fact limited its calculation of recoupment to 50% of video production costs. Malmsteen claims that UMG has applied a higher percentage of its expenses against his royalties. [In a portion of the opinion not reprinted, the court notes that there is no evidence that UMG was assigning more than 50% of the video costs to Malmsteen.]

Breach of Contract

"Under New York law, a breach of contract claim requires proof of (1) an agreement, (2) adequate performance by the plaintiff, (3) breach by the defendant, and (4) damages." *Fischer & Mandell, LLP v. Citibank, N.A.*, 632 F.3d 793, 799 (2d Cir.2011). Here, there is no dispute about the existence of an agreement. Rather, the parties' disputes turn on (1) the interpretation of provisions of the Agreement and (2) factual questions whether defendants have breached its terms.

Generally, summary judgment is appropriate in a contract dispute only where the contract's terms are unambiguous, whereas "interpretation of ambiguous contract language is a question of fact to be resolved by the factfinder." However, summary judgment is also appropriate "when the [contract] language is ambiguous and there is relevant extrinsic evidence, but the extrinsic evidence creates no genuine issue of material fact and permits interpretation of the agreement as a matter of law." *Nycal Corp. v. Inoco PLC,* 988 F.Supp. 296, 299 (S.D.N.Y.1997)

Malmsteen argues that defendants breached the Agreement by: (1) failing to pay the proper royalty rate for sales of digital downloads [and] (2) deducting improper video production costs from audio royalties.

The Royalty Rate on Sales of Digital Downloads

The parties' first dispute involves a pure question of contract interpretation: which royalty provision applies to sales of digital downloads? As a threshold matter, digital downloads are clearly Records, as defined in § 13.02 of the Agreement. The phrase "[a]ny device now or hereafter known on or by which sound may be recorded and re-produced" manifests the clear intent of the contracting parties that the definition of Record encompass as-yet-undeveloped technologies. This broad definition evinces a practical recognition of the constantly evolving nature of music recording technology.

This leaves the question whether digital downloads are Records sold through "Normal Retail Channels," or rather by one of the specific means of distribution enumerated in § 7.06(a)(ii). UMG persuasively argues that the royalty rates set forth in §§ 7.01–7.03 apply here. In today's market, the phrase "Normal Retail Channels" comfortably encompasses digital downloads sold through Apple's iTunes store and similar platforms—brick-and-mortar record shops have gone the way of the 8-track, the phonograph, and the mastodon.

Applying the 8–15% royalty rate contained in §§ 7.01–7.03 to retail sales of digital downloads, rather than the 50% rate contained in § 7.06(a)(ii), also accords with the structure of the Agreement: For sales to consumers through normal retail channels that are reliably and readily measured, the contract provides for a lower rate; by contrast, as to the unique and, at least potentially, less traceable methods of distribution to consumers listed in § 7.06(a)(ii), the artist, Malmsteen, is assigned a higher rate of compensation. Because "Records" are defined broadly enough to include digital downloads, and because the sales of these downloads through media like the iTunes store are the normal retail channels in today's music industry, §§ 7.01–7.03 unambiguously govern the applicable royalty rates here.

Malmsteen argues that the 50% royalty rate set forth in § 7.06(a)(ii) applies. That provision, however, does not fit. Section 7.06(a)(ii) covers "licenses of Master Recordings to Non-Affiliated Third Parties for sales of Records" by the following specifically enumerated means of distribution: "direct mail, mail order, or in conjunction with TV advertising, including through methods of distribution such as 'key outlet marketing' (distribution through retail fulfillment centers in conjunction with special advertisements on radio or television)." Agreement § 7.06(a)(ii). The sale of digital downloads does not resemble any of these methods. Recognizing this, Malmsteen argues that digital downloads are nonetheless picked up by the residual clause following this list: "or by any combination of the methods set forth above *or other methods*." *Id.* (emphasis added). In Malmsteen's view, the phrase "or other methods" has essentially no limit.

Malmsteen's reading of the Agreement is undermined by two basic principles of contractual interpretation. First, under the principle of *ejusdem generis*, when a general phrase, such as "or other methods," follows a list of specific terms, the general phrase must be interpreted to refer to items of the same ilk as those specifically listed. Here, however, digital downloads are unlike the specific means of distribution enumerated in §7.06(a)(ii). Second, as Malmsteen notes, an interpretation rendering contractual provisions redundant or superfluous is disfavored. Here, interpreting "or other methods" as Malmsteen does—to be essentially limitless—would render superfluous both the specifically enumerated list in that section and the separate subsection addressing the sale of Records through record clubs. *See* Agreement §7.06(a)(iii).

For these reasons, Malmsteen's reading of the Agreement is unpersuasive: Section 7.06(a)(ii) cannot reasonably be interpreted to cover sales of digital downloads. Accordingly, UMG was correct to apply the royalty rates set forth in §§7.01–7.03 to the sale of digital downloads, and summary judgment is merited in UMG's favor on this claim.

For the foregoing reasons, defendants' motion for summary judgment is granted, and plaintiffs motion for summary judgment is denied.

F.B.T. Productions, L.L.C. v. Aftermath Records

621 F.3d 958 (9th Cir. 2010)

This dispute concerns the percentage of royalties due to Plaintiffs F.B.T. Productions, L.L.C., and Em2M, L.L.C., under their contracts with Defendant Aftermath in connection with the recordings of Marshal B. Mathers, III, professionally known as the rap artist Eminem. Specifically, F.B.T. and Aftermath disagree on whether the contracts' "Records Sold" provision or "Masters Licensed" provision sets the royalty rate for sales of Eminem's records in the form of permanent downloads and mastertones. Before trial, F.B.T. moved for summary judgment that the Masters Licensed provision unambiguously applied to permanent downloads and mastertones. The district court denied the motion. At the close of evidence, F.B.T. did not move for judgment as a matter of law, and the jury returned a verdict in favor of Aftermath. On appeal, F.B.T. reasserts that the Masters Licensed provision unambiguously applies to permanent downloads and mastertones. We agree that the contracts are unambiguous and that the district court should have granted summary judgment to F.B.T. We therefore reverse the judgment and vacate the district court's order awarding Aftermath its attorneys' fees.

F.B.T. signed Eminem in 1995, gaining exclusive rights to his recordings. In 1998, F.B.T. signed an agreement transferring Eminem's exclusive recording services to Aftermath. The "Records Sold" provision of that agreement provides that F.B.T. is to receive between 12% and 20% of the adjusted retail price of all "full price records sold in the United States ... through normal retail channels." The agreement further provides that "[n]otwithstanding the foregoing," F.B.T. is to receive 50% of Aftermath's net receipts "[o]n masters licensed by us ... to others for their manufacture and sale of records or for any other uses." The parties refer to this provision as the "Masters Licensed" provision. The contract defines "master" as a "recording of sound, without or with visual images, which is used or useful in the recording, production or manufacture of records." The agreement does not contain a definition of the terms "licensed" or "normal retail channels."

In 2002, Aftermath's parent company, Defendant UMG Recordings, Inc., concluded an agreement with Apple Computer, Inc., that enabled UMG's sound recordings, including the Eminem masters, to be sold through Apple's iTunes store as permanent downloads. Permanent downloads are digital copies of recordings that, once downloaded over the Internet, remain on an end-user's computer or other device until deleted. The contract between UMG and Apple is but one example of the many agreements that Aftermath has concluded to sell sound recordings in digital formats since approximately 2001. Since 2003, Aftermath has also concluded contracts with major cellular telephone network carriers to sell sound recordings as mastertones, which are short clips of songs that can be purchased by users to signal incoming calls, popularly known as ringtones.

In 2003, F.B.T. and Aftermath entered into a new agreement that terminated the 1998 agreement. The 2003 agreement increased some royalty rates, but incorporated the wording of the Records Sold and Masters Licensed provisions from the 1998 agreement. In 2004, the parties amended the agreement to provide that "Sales of Albums by way of permanent download shall be treated as [U.S. Normal Retail Channel] Net Sales for the purposes of escalations." Escalations are increases in the royalty rate when total album sales surpass certain targets. The amendment further provides, "Except as specifically modified herein, the Agreement shall be unaffected and remain in full force and effect."

F.B.T. brought suit after a 2006 audit showed that Aftermath had been applying the Records Sold provision to calculate the royalties due to F.B.T. for sales of Eminem's recordings in the form of permanent downloads and mastertones. Before trial, F.B.T. moved for summary judgment that the Masters Licensed provision unambiguously applied to those sales. Aftermath cross-moved for summary judgment. It argued, in part, that the 2004 amendment showed that the parties intended the Records Sold provision to apply to permanent downloads.

After provisionally reviewing the undisputed extrinsic evidence, the district court concluded that the agreements were reasonably susceptible to either party's interpretation and denied both motions for summary judgment. At trial, only Aftermath moved for judgment as a matter of law at the close of the evidence. The court denied the motion. The jury returned a verdict in favor of Aftermath, and the district court awarded Aftermath its attorneys' fees of over $ 2.4 million. F.B.T. timely appealed the district court's final judgment and award of attorneys' fees. We have jurisdiction pursuant to 28 U.S.C. § 1291 and we reverse....

Turning to the agreements in question, the Records Sold provision contains the royalty rate for "full price records sold in the United States ... through normal retail channels." On summary judgment, Aftermath argued that the Records Sold provision applied because permanent downloads and mastertones are records, and because iTunes and other digital music providers are normal retail channels in the United States.

However, the agreements also provide that "notwithstanding" the Records Sold provision, F.B.T. is to receive a 50% royalty on "masters licensed by [Aftermath] ... to others for their manufacture and sale of records or for any other uses." The parties' use of the word "notwithstanding" plainly indicates that even if a transaction arguably falls within the scope of the Records Sold provision, F.B.T. is to receive a 50% royalty if Aftermath licenses an Eminem master to a third party for "any" use. A contractual term is not ambiguous just because it is broad. Here, the Masters Licensed provision explicitly applies to (1) masters (2) that are licensed to third parties for the manufacture of records "or for any other uses," (3) "notwithstanding" the Record Sold provision. This provision is admittedly broad, but it is not unclear or ambiguous.

Accordingly, to determine whether the Masters Licensed provision applies, we must decide whether Aftermath licensed the Eminem masters to third parties. Aftermath argues that there was no evidence that it or F.B.T. used the term "licensed" in a technical sense. In the ordinary sense of the word, a license is simply "permission to act." WEBSTER'S THIRD NEW INTERNATIONAL DICTIONARY OF THE ENGLISH LANGUAGE 1304 (2002). Aftermath did not dispute that it entered into agreements that permitted iTunes, cellular phone carriers, and other third parties to use its sound recordings to produce and sell permanent downloads and mastertones. Those agreements therefore qualify as licenses under Aftermath's own proposed construction of the term.

The conclusion that Aftermath licensed the Eminem masters to third parties also comports well with and finds additional support in federal copyright law. When one looks to the Copyright Act, the terms "license" and "sale" have well differentiated meanings, and the differences between the two play an important role in the overall structures and policies that govern artistic rights. For example, under the language of the Act and the Supreme Court's interpretations, a "sale" of a work may either be a transfer in title of an individual copy of a work, or a sale of all exclusive intellectual property rights in a work.

There is no dispute that Aftermath was at all relevant times the owner of the copyrights to the Eminem recordings at issue in this case, having obtained those rights through the recording contracts in exchange for specified royalty payments. Pursuant to its agreements with Apple and other third parties, however, Aftermath did not "sell" anything to the download distributors. The download distributors did not obtain title to the digital files. The ownership of those files remained with Aftermath, Aftermath reserved the right to regain possession of the files at any time, and Aftermath obtained recurring benefits in the form of payments based on the volume of downloads.

Much as Section 109 describes a "sale" under the "first sale" doctrine, various other sections of the Copyright Act illuminate the meaning of the term "license." For example, section 114(f), titled "Licenses for Certain Nonexempt Transmissions," describes the statutory authorization for a third party to exercise public performance rights that otherwise remain the exclusive rights of a copyright holder and defines this authorization as a "license." Section 115, titled "Scope of Exclusive Rights in Non-dramatic Musical Works: Compulsory License for Making and Distributing Phonorecords," refers directly to the statutory authorization for artists to exercise the copyright owner's right to make and distribute phonorecord "covers" as a license, but again makes it clear that title remains with the copyright owner.

Under our case law interpreting and applying the Copyright Act, too, it is well settled that where a copyright owner transfers a copy of copyrighted material, retains title, limits the uses to which the material may be put, and is compensated periodically based on the transferee's exploitation of the material, the transaction is a license.

It is easily gleaned from these sources of federal copyright law that a license is an authorization by the copyright owner to enable another party to engage in behavior that would otherwise be the exclusive right of the copyright owner, but without transferring title in those rights. This permission can be granted for the copyright itself, for the physical media containing the copyrighted work, or for both the copyright and the physical media.

When the facts of this case are viewed through the lens of federal copyright law, it is all the more clear that Aftermath's agreements with the third-party download vendors are "licenses" to use the Eminem master recordings for specific purposes authorized thereby—i.e., to create and distribute permanent downloads and master-tones—in exchange for periodic payments based on the volume of downloads, without any transfer in title of Aftermath's copyrights to the recordings. Thus, federal copyright law supports and reinforces our conclusion that Aftermath's agreements permitting third parties to use its sound recordings to produce and sell permanent downloads and mastertones are licenses.

Furthermore, the sound recordings that Aftermath provided to third parties qualify as masters. The contracts define a "master" as a "recording of sound ... which is used or useful in the recording, production or manufacture of records." Aftermath admitted that permanent downloads and mastertones are records. The sound recordings that Aftermath supplied to third parties were "used or useful" in the production of permanent downloads and mastertones, so those sound recordings were masters. Because Aftermath permitted third parties to use the Eminem masters to produce and sell records, in the form of permanent downloads and mastertones, F.B.T. is entitled to a 50% royalty under the plain terms of the agreements.

Aftermath argues that the 2004 amendment to the agreements clarified that the Records Sold provision sets the royalty for permanent downloads. However, the 2004 amendment states only that albums sold as permanent downloads are to be counted "for purposes of escalations" under the Records Sold provision, and that "[e]xcept as specifically modified herein, the Agreement shall be unaffected and remain in full force and effect." Read in context, the plain language of the amendment provides that sales of permanent downloads by third parties count towards escalations on the royalty owed when Aftermath itself sells records through normal retail channels. It does not state, and in no way implies, that the royalty rate for the sale of the permanent downloads by third parties is set by the Records Sold provision.

Nor did any of the evidence regarding industry custom or the parties' course of performance support Aftermath's interpretation that the Records Sold provision applies. Aftermath's expert explained that the Masters Licensed provision had in the past been applied "only to compilation records and incorporation into movies, TV shows, and commercials." It was, however, undisputed that permanent downloads and mastertones only came into existence from 2001 to 2003. Consequently, the fact that the Masters Licensed provision had never previously been applied to those forms of licensing is immaterial. There is no indication that the parties intended to confine the contract to the state of the industry in 1998. To the contrary, the contract contemplated advances in technology. It provided that Aftermath had the right to exploit the "masters in any and all forms of media now known and hereinafter developed." Aftermath's evidence of how the Masters Licensed provision had been applied in the past therefore did not cast doubt on its application to permanent downloads and mastertones.

Furthermore, Aftermath renewed its agreement with F.B.T. in 2003, by which time permanent downloads and mastertones were coming into existence. Aftermath argued that subsequent to renewal, F.B.T. had "never objected to Defendants' payment of royalties under the Records Sold provision until the auditor raised the issue in 2006." However, Aftermath provided no evidence that F.B.T. knowingly acquiesced to payment under the Records Sold provision between 2003 and 2006. It showed that F.B.T. had received statements that included royalties for permanent downloads and mastertones, but it was uncontroverted that F.B.T. did not audit those royalty statements until 2006. F.B.T. had no obligation to audit the statements any earlier than it did, and it immediately raised the issue with Aftermath after the audit. Accordingly, Aftermath cannot use F.B.T.'s lack of objection to payments made before 2006 to prove how it interpreted the agreements. The undisputed extrinsic evidence provisionally reviewed by the district court therefore did not support Aftermath's interpretation that the Records Sold provision applies.

In sum, the agreements unambiguously provide that "notwithstanding" the Records Sold provision, Aftermath owed F.B.T. a 50% royalty under the Masters Licensed provision for licensing the Eminem masters to third parties for any use. It was undisputed that Aftermath permitted third parties to use the Eminem masters to produce and sell permanent downloads and mastertones. Neither the 2004 amendment nor any of the parole evidence provisionally reviewed by the district court supported Aftermath's interpretation that the Records Sold provision applied. Because the agreements were unambiguous and were not reasonably susceptible to Aftermath's interpretation, the district court erred in denying F.B.T. summary judgment.

The judgment in favor of Aftermath is REVERSED, the district court's order granting Aftermath its attorneys' fees is VACATED, and the case is REMANDED for further proceedings consistent with this opinion.

[The parties continued to litigate the interpretation of the agreements and the implications for damage calculations. The District Court's opinion on the interpretation of net receipts is illuminating.]

F.B.T. Productions, L.L.C. v. Aftermath Records

827 F. Supp. 2d 1092 (C.D. Cal. 2011)

. . .

Net Receipts

The Masters Licensed provision states that FBT and Eminem's "royalty shall be an amount equal to [50%] of our net receipts." The parties dispute what comprises "our net receipts." Defendants argue that net receipts means the revenue Aftermath receives from licensing downloads and mastertones less Aftermath's direct costs from that licensing. These direct costs include mechanical royalties and distribution fees. Plaintiffs argue that neither mechanical royalties nor distribution fees should be deducted from the gross revenue that Aftermath receives from licensing.

First, it is clear that the term "our" refers to Aftermath. Aftermath is the only entity responsible for licensing that signed the agreements. It is also clear that "net receipts" contemplates some type of deduction. The definition of "net" is "free from, or not subject to, any deduction; remaining after all necessary deductions have been made." Oxford English Dictionary at 340 (2d ed. 1989). Moreover, the term "net" was used elsewhere by the parties to denote a subtraction. In the provision dealing with the licensing of videos, the parties defined "net receipts" as "gross receipts solely attributable to Videos hereunder less (1) any and all direct costs and/or third party payments in connection with the creation, manufacture, exploitation or use of said Videos; and (2) an additional fee in lieu of any overhead or distribution fee of twelve percent (12%) of the gross receipts in connection therewith." Similarly, section 16(a) defines "Net Sales" as "gross sales, less returns, credits and reserves against anticipated returns and credits." And section 12(b) defines "net" as "the amount otherwise payable to Artist after deducting all third party reductions." In accord with these definitions, net receipts is reasonably read to mean Aftermath's gross revenue from licensing less Aftermath's direct costs associated with licensing.

Plaintiffs urge a different interpretation of "our net receipts" based on extrinsic evidence. Plaintiffs argue that testimony and exhibits introduced at trial show that Aftermath does not deduct mechanical royalties or distribution fees from the licensing income received from conditional downloads and streams. Thus, Plaintiffs conclude, mechanical royalties and distribution fees should not be deducted when it comes to permanent downloads and mastertones. Plaintiffs' conclusion does not follow from the evidence. The reason Aftermath does not deduct mechanical royalties or distribution fees from income received from licensing conditional downloads and streams is because Aftermath does not pay those costs for licensing conditional downloads and streams. In contrast, it is undisputed Aftermath does have to pay mechanical royalties and distribution fees for permanent downloads and mastertones. Aftermath's practice with regard to costs that do not exist for conditional downloads and streams cannot be relevant to whether Aftermath may deduct costs that indisputably do exist for permanent downloads and mastertones. Accordingly, Aftermath's "net receipts" are its gross revenues from the licensing of masters, less the direct costs of mechanical royalties and distribution fees....

New Medium and Container Charge Deductions

Defendants also argue that other provisions in the agreements should be read to apply to the Masters Licensed royalty rate. Section 5(f) of the 2003 Agreement states "[t]he royalty payable to you for New Mediums will be seventy five percent (75%) of the otherwise applicable royalty rate." New Mediums are "records ... in any software medium (including, without limitation, 'digital audio tape,' 'digital compact disc,' 'and mini-disc' and transmission directly into the home) in which recorded music is not in general commercial distribution in the United States as of January 1, 1997."

Defendants further argue they are entitled to take a deduction known as a "Container Charge." The agreements provide that "[f]or purposes of computing royalties, there will be deducted from the [applicable price] ... twenty-five percent (25%) thereof for records in the form of digital records (including, without limitation, Compact Discs), and for all records in any other form now known or hereafter devised."

The meaning of the New Medium and Container Charge deductions in relation to the Masters Licensed provision is unclear from the plain language of the agreements. In the New Medium definition, the phrase "transmission directly into the home" could be reasonably read to apply to permanent downloads. On the other hand, the types of "records" specifically contemplated by the New Medium provision are audio tapes, compact discs, and mini-discs. These physical mediums suggest the parties contemplated the application of the New Medium deduction to the Records Sold provision and not the Masters Licensed provision. Likewise, the Container Charge provision specifically contemplates compact discs. And even the term "Container Charge," which Defendants themselves use to refer to this charge, suggests a product sold in a "container," not the mere licensing of container-less downloads and mastertones.

Due to the ambiguous language of these clauses, the Court will turn to extrinsic evidence to shed light on their meaning. It is undisputed that the licensing of conditional downloads and streams is covered by and paid under the Masters Licensed provision. It is also undisputed that conditional downloads and streams utilize the same technology as permanent downloads. At trial, Defendants agreed that they pay for conditional downloads and streams "according to the terms of the contract." Lastly, Defendants concede they have never taken a New Medium or Container Charge deduction from royalties for licensing of conditional downloads and streams. Defendants have, therefore, admitted they do not read the agreements to allow for a New Medium or Container Charge deduction from Masters Licensed royalties derived from the licensing of conditional downloads and streams. Defendants do not offer any reason, and the terms of the agreements do not admit of any reason, why these deductions would apply to permanent downloads and mastertones under the Masters Licensed provision, but not to products utilizing the same technology under the same Masters Licensed provision. The Court concludes that Defendants' course of performance demonstrates that, before this litigation arose, Defendants did not understand the agreements to allow for these deductions under the Masters Licensed provision. The parties' pre-dispute understanding of the terms of the agreements controls over the post-dispute interpretation offered by Defendants.

Defendants contend that the Ninth Circuit's *F.B.T.* opinion found that the parties' course of performance could not change the language of a contract and therefore Defendants' past practice in regards to the New Medium and Container Charge deductions is irrelevant. The Ninth Circuit held that none of the evidence offered by the parties "regarding industry custom or the parties' course of performance support[ed] Aftermath's interpretation." As this sentence plainly indicates, the Ninth Circuit did not hold that a parties' course of performance cannot be used to inform the meaning of contractual terms. Rather, the Ninth Circuit only held that the course of performance evidence proffered by Defendants on appeal did not support the contract interpretation urged by Defendants. In contrast, here the course of performance evidence directly supports the interpretation, proffered by Plaintiffs, that the New Medium and Container Charge deductions do not apply to the Masters Licensed provision. Consequently, Defendants may not argue that the New Medium and Container Charge deductions apply, when the parties' performance shows these deductions do not apply to the Masters Licensed provision....

[T]he phrase "our net receipts" in the Masters Licensed provision means Aftermath's gross revenue from licensing, less the direct costs of mechanical royalties and distribution fees; and the New Medium and Container Charge deductions do not apply to the Masters Licensed provision.

IT IS SO ORDERED.

Notes and Questions

a. Since *Boosey-Hawkes*, New York courts have been reluctant to upset large grants of rights on the basis that the contracts were silent or that new technologies were not in existence at the time. *See Maljack Prods. v. GoodTimes Home Video Corp.*, 81 F.3d 881, 885 (9th Cir 1996) (music rights granted for synchronization of film included right to synchronize music in videocassette format); *Chambers v. Time Warner, Inc.*, 123 F. Supp. 2d 198, 200–201 (S.D.N.Y. 2000), *vacated on other grounds, and remanded by* 282 F3d 147 (2d Cir 2002) (transfer of master recording to digital format not precluded). The trend has remained true even when the change has been the subsequent recognition of a legal interest in the sound recording that had not existed at the time of contract.

b. In the case of a performer's interest in a digital transmission, this right is relatively recent in origin and has not been interpreted, so all recording artists presumably have this interest. The ability of some artists to retain this interest has yet to be litigated.

c. If the band dismisses a member during its recording sessions, should it re-record the songs without the former band member? Does the band or the record label have any duty to the former band member, either before or after delivery of the completed master has occurred? *See Poley v. Sony Music Entm't, Inc.*, 163 Misc. 2d 127, 619 N.Y.S.2d 923 (N.Y. Sup. Ct. 1994), *aff'd*, 222 A.D.2d 308, 636 N.Y.S.2d 10 (App. Div. 1995).

Problem 11-C

Bryce is interested in creating a more successful and more equitable record distribution system. Bryce is convinced that bands such as Soundfyre would do better avoiding the larger distributors in favor of a greater return from independent companies, even though it would mean a significantly lower marketing budget. As a result, Bryce is willing to earn "far less than the big distributors" if the musicians are willing to join in a collective or collaborative venture whereby everyone helps promote the sales of the albums through a common catalog, website, compilations CDs, and tour promotions.

Bryce is trying to create a local label. Bryce has interested some local investors in the idea. Bryce wants to structure the compensation and promotional terms for the bands that might be interested in the project. Prepare an outline of the key features such a contract might contain that would be attractive to both the bands and the potential investors. If you have other ideas that might be of assistance to Bryce in structuring such a promotion and distribution company, provide those suggestions as well.

D. Promotion and Exploitation of the Recording Artist

Contemporary Mission, Inc. v. Famous Music Corp.
557 F.2d 918 (2d Cir. 1977)

This is an appeal by Famous Music Corporation ("Famous") from a verdict rendered against it in favor of Contemporary Mission, Inc. ("Contemporary"), in the United States District Court for the Southern District of New York, after a jury trial before Judge Richard Owen. Contemporary cross-appeals from a ruling which excluded testimony concerning its prospective damages. The dispute between the parties relates to Famous' alleged breach of two contracts.

Contemporary is a nonprofit charitable corporation organized under the laws of the State of Missouri with its principal place of business in Connecticut. It is composed of a small group of Roman Catholic priests who write, produce and publish musical compositions and recordings. In 1972 the group owned all of the rights to a rock opera entitled VIRGIN, which was composed by Father John T. O'Reilly, a vice-president and member of the group. Contemporary first became involved with Famous in 1972 as a result of O'Reilly's efforts to market VIRGIN.

Famous is ... a wholly-owned subsidiary of the Gulf+Western Corporation, and, until July 31, 1974, it was engaged in the business of producing musical recordings for distribution throughout the United States. Famous' president, Tony Martell, is generally regarded in the recording industry as the individual primarily responsible for the successful distribution of the well-known rock operas TOMMY and JESUS CHRIST SUPERSTAR.... On August 16, 1972, [the parties] executed the so-called "VIRGIN Recording Agreement" ("VIRGIN agreement") on behalf of their respective organizations.

The terms of the VIRGIN agreement were relatively simple. Famous agreed to pay a royalty to Contemporary in return for the master tape recording of VIRGIN and the exclusive right to manufacture and sell records made from the master. The agreement also created certain "Additional Obligations of Famous" which included, inter alia: the obligation to select and appoint, within the first year of the agreement, at least one person to personally oversee the nationwide promotion of the sale of records, to maintain contact with Contemporary and to submit weekly reports to Contemporary; the obligation to spend, within the first year of the agreement, no less than $50,000 on the promotion of records; and the obligation to release, within the first two years of the agreement, at least four separate single records from VIRGIN....

On May 8, 1973, the parties entered into a distribution contract which dealt with musical compositions other than VIRGIN. This, the so-called "Crunch agreement," granted to Famous the exclusive right to distribute Contemporary's records in the United States. Famous agreed to institute a new record label named "Crunch," and a number of records were to be released under it annually. Contemporary agreed to deliver ten long-playing records and fifteen single records during the first year of the contract. Famous undertook to use its "reasonable efforts" to promote and distribute the records. Paragraph 15 of the Crunch agreement stated that a breach by either party would not be deemed material unless the non-breaching party first gave written notice to the defaulting party and the defaulting party failed to cure the breach within thirty days. The notice was to specify the nature of the alleged material breach. The contract prohibited assignment by Contemporary, but it contained no provision relating to Famous' right to assign.

Although neither VIRGIN nor its progeny was ever as successful as the parties had originally hoped, the business relationship continued on an amicable basis until July 31, 1974. On that date, Famous' record division was sold to ABC Records, Inc. (ABC). When O'Reilly complained to Martell that Famous was breaking its promises, he was told that he would have to look to ABC for performance. O'Reilly met with one of ABC's lawyers and was told that ABC was not going to have any relationship with Contemporary. On August 21, 1974, Contemporary sent a letter to Famous pursuant to paragraph 15 of the Crunch agreement notifying Famous that it had "materially breached Paragraph 12, among others, of (the Crunch) Agreement in that (it had) attempted to make a contract or other agreement with ABC-Dunhill Record Corporation (ABC Records) creating an obligation or responsibility in behalf of or in the name of the Contemporary Mission." Paragraph 12 of the Crunch agreement provides, in full, as follows:

> This agreement shall not be construed as one of partnership or joint venture, nor shall it constitute either party as the agent or legal representative of the other. Neither party shall have the right, power or authority to make any contract or other agreement, or to assume or create any obligation or responsibility, express or implied, in behalf of or in the name of the other party or to bind the other party in any manner for anything whatsoever.

This lawsuit followed....

Famous vigorously contends ... that the jury's conclusion, that it had failed to adequately promote VIRGIN prior to the sale to ABC, is at war with the undisputed facts and cannot be permitted to stand. In particular they argue that they spent the required $50,000 and appointed the required overseer for the project. The flaw in this argument is that its focus is too narrow. The obligations to which it refers are but two of many created by the VIRGIN agreement.

Under the doctrine of *Wood v. Lucy, Lady Duff-Gordon*, 222 N.Y. 88, 118 N.E. 214 (1917), Famous had an obligation to use its reasonable efforts to promote VIRGIN on a nationwide basis. That obligation could not be satisfied merely by technical compliance with the spending and appointment requirements of paragraph 14 of the agreement. Even assuming that Famous complied fully with those requirements, there was evidence from which the jury could find that Famous failed to adequately promote VIRGIN. The question is a close one, particularly in light of Martell's obvious commitment to the success of VIRGIN and in light of the efforts that were in fact exerted and the lack of any serious dispute between the parties prior to the sale to ABC. However, there was evidence that Famous prematurely terminated the promotion of the first single record, "Got To Know," shortly after its release, and that Famous limited its promotion of the second record, "Kyrie," to a single city, rather than promoting it nationwide. Moreover, there was evidence that, prior to the sale to ABC, Famous underwent a budget reduction and cut back its promotional staff. From this, the jury could infer that the promotional effort was reduced to a level that was less than adequate. On the whole, therefore, we are not persuaded that the jury's verdict should be disturbed.

There is no dispute that the sale of Famous' record division to ABC constituted an assignment of the Crunch agreement to ABC. The assignment of a bilateral contract includes both an assignment of rights and a delegation of duties. The distinctions between the two are important.

> Perhaps more frequently than is the case with other terms of art, lawyers seem prone to use the word "assignment" inartfully, frequently intending to encompass within the term the distinct (concept) of delegation.... An assignment involves the transfer of rights. A delegation involves the appointment of another to perform one's duties.

J. Calamari & J. Perillo, Contracts § 254 (1970) (footnote omitted). Famous' arguments with respect to the Crunch agreement ignore this basic distinction, and the result is a distortion of several fundamental principles of contract law.

It is true, of course, as a general rule, that when rights are assigned, the assignor's interest in the rights assigned comes to an end. When duties are delegated, however, the delegant's obligation does not end.

> One who owes money or is bound to any performance whatever, cannot by any act of his own, or by any act in agreement with any other person, except his creditor, divest himself of the duty and substitute the duty of another. "No one can assign his liabilities under a contract without the consent of the party to whom he is liable."
>
> This is sufficiently obvious when attention is called to it, for otherwise obligors would find an easy practical way of escaping their obligations....

3 Williston on Contracts § 411 (3d ed. 1960) (footnote omitted). This is not to say that one may not delegate his obligations. In fact, most obligations can be delegated as long as performance by the delegate will not vary materially from performance by the delegant. The act of delegation, however, does not relieve the delegant of the ultimate responsibility to see that the obligation is performed. If the delegate fails to perform, the delegant remains liable.

Judge Owen correctly charged the jury that "after the assignment of the contract by Famous to ABC, Famous remained liable for any obligation that was not fulfilled by ABC." This was a correct statement of the law, and Famous' assault upon it, while valiant, is without merit....

The problem for Famous, of course, was that, having sold its entire record division to ABC, it had stripped itself of its ability to cure the breach....

During the trial, Contemporary sought to introduce a statistical analysis, together with expert testimony, in order to prove how successful the most successful of its single recordings, "Fear No Evil," would have become if the VIRGIN agreement had not been breached as a result of the sale to ABC. Based upon its projection of the success of that recording, Contemporary hoped to prove what revenues that success would have produced. Judge Owen excluded this evidence on the ground that it was speculative.

There can no dispute that Contemporary "is entitled to the reasonable damage flowing from the breach of" the VIRGIN agreement by Famous, and that "the measure of the damage is the amount necessary to put (Contemporary) in (the) exact position as (it) would have been if the contract had not been breached." ... [U]nder the longstanding New York rule, when the existence of damage is certain, and the only uncertainty is as to its amount, the plaintiff will not be denied a recovery of substantial damages. Moreover, the burden of uncertainty as to the amount of damage is upon the wrongdoer, and the test for admissibility of evidence concerning prospective damages is whether the evidence has any tendency to show their probable amount. The plaintiff need only show a "stable foundation for a reasonable estimate of royalties he would have earned had defendant not breached." ...

We are confident that under the principles enunciated above the exclusion of the evidence proffered by Contemporary was error. This is not a case in which the plaintiff sought to prove hypothetical profits from the sale of a hypothetical record at a hypothetical price in a hypothetical market. At the time of the sale to ABC, the record was real, the price was fixed, the market was buying and the record's success, while modest, was increasing. Even after the promotional efforts ended, the record was withdrawn from the marketplace, it was carried, as a result of its own momentum, to an additional 10,000 sales and to a rise from approximately number 80 on the "Hot Soul Singles" chart of Billboard magazine to number 61. It cannot be gainsaid that if someone had continued to promote it, and if it had not been withdrawn from the market, it would have sold more records than it actually did. Thus, it is certain that Contemporary suffered some damage in the form of lost royalties. The same is not true, however, of the existence of damage in the form of lost opportunities for concert tours, theatrical tours or similar benefits....

The judgment of the district court is affirmed in all respects except as to its ruling with regard to lost royalties, and the case is remanded to the district court for further proceedings in accordance with this opinion....

Notes and Questions

a. The label's duty to promote a work is often framed in the most general of terms, while the label's ability to exploit a work is retained against every conceivable eventuality. As the power and influence of a recording artist increases, these contractual provisions are often the point for new negotiation.

b. The contractual relations between the parties is often quite complex, sometimes involving many participants. In some instances, this may lead to individuals or entities that are not parties to a particular transaction having an influence on its signing or enforcement, which raises the potential for the additional tort, tortious interference with contractual relations. *See TVT Records v. Island Def Jam Music Group*, 279 F. Supp. 2d 366 (S.D.N.Y. 2003).

c. To what extent do parties who are not signatories to these contracts have standing? Depending on the nature of the contract and the conflict, there may be intended third party beneficiaries who have standing to enforce claims or to object to breaches of the contracts.

d. The contract provisions at issue above reflect that a significant portion of an album's marketing occurs when it is first released. However, an album creates an income stream that can potentially last for many years. Approximately half the income generated by sound recordings is derived from back catalog sales. The back catalog is a label's backlist of songs previously produced and distributed but not currently being marketed and promoted. Compilation albums, such as The Beatles 1 CD, constitute yet another important economic source of revenue from the catalog. Given these economics, is it helpful or appropriate for a recording artist to put some limitations or time constraints on the publicity rights granted to the record labels?

e. In many cases, the recording artists deliver more songs than the number of cuts that are included on the album or CD. What happens to those previously unreleased songs? Can the record label create new albums out of unreleased songs, or should unpublished sound recordings expire after a reasonable period of time? *See Levert v. Phila. Int'l Records*, No. 04-1489, 2004 U.S. Dist. LEXIS 11825 (E.D. Pa. Apr. 9, 2004) ("Plaintiffs Edward Levert and Walter Williams are singers and performers who form the musical group known as The O'Jays. The O'Jays have been recording music for more than forty years and ... recorded more than fifty records, including nine 'platinum records' and ten 'gold records.'").

f. Despite the impression that contracts in the music business are rarely enforced, there can be tremendous costs for failing to abide by a contract or failing to renegotiate a new arrangement. In *Smith v. Positive Prods.*, 419 F. Supp. 2d 437 (S.D.N.Y. 2005), the district court allowed the enforcement of an arbitration provision against Jonathan "Lil Jon" Smith for twice failing to participate in a concert tour in Japan. Positive Productions, the Japanese concert promotion company, received $379,874 in an arbitration held under the American Arbitration Association rules. Lil Jon ignored the arbitration proceeding, but he was unsuccessful in vacating the judgment.

Problem 11-D

As a result of the dispute between Bryce and Soundfyre, Soundfyre's label has elected not to exercise the option for the band's third album. Although Bryce never joined the band, Bryce is concerned not only because Soundfyre's success was generating Bryce income (thanks to your expert advice settling the dispute) but also because Bryce was hoping to build on the association with the band. Soundfyre is particularly upset because the label has stopped the advertising campaign for the band's second album.

Bryce is learning a lesson. In talking to potential labels, Bryce wants to ensure that any album is fully under Bryce's control and heavily promoted. Explain to Bryce what provisions can be added to a standard contract to provide the protections Bryce needs, as well as the likely response by most labels.

E. Term, Renewals, and Extensions of Recording Contracts

MCA Records, Inc. v. Newton-John

90 Cal. App. 3d 18 (1979)

Defendant Olivia Newton-John, a singer, appeals a preliminary injunction restraining her from recording for anyone other than plaintiff MCA Records while MCA's action is pending "or until April 1, 1982, if that date shall occur during the pendency of this action." ...

On April 1, 1975, the parties entered the following agreement: Defendant Newton-John would record and deliver to plaintiff master recordings for two albums per year for an initial period of two years, and, at plaintiff's option, further similar recordings for three additional periods of one year each. If defendant failed to deliver a recording when due, plaintiff would become entitled to extend the term of the agreement. In return, plaintiff would pay defendant royalties and a nonreturnable advance of $250,000 for each recording received during the initial two years, and an advance of $100,000 for each recording received during the option years. The cost of producing the recordings would be borne by defendant.

The first three recordings were delivered on schedule; the fourth was delivered late. Plaintiff exercised its first option to renew, but never received another recording. Under the terms of the contract plaintiff paid defendant approximately $2,500,000 in royalties and nonreturnable advances.

On May 31, 1978, the parties filed breach-of-contract actions against one another. Both parties sought damages and injunctive relief, and defendant additionally sought declaratory relief. Plaintiff obtained a preliminary injunction, and defendant has appealed.

Defendant asserts the preliminary injunction was improperly granted because: (1) the agreement failed to guarantee payment of minimum compensation of $6,000 a year; (2) she had already been suspended by the plaintiff and could not be further restrained from engaging in her occupation; and (3) there was no showing or finding that irreparable injury would be imminent if the injunction were not granted.

A. A party to a personal service contract may not be enjoined from rendering personal services to others unless, under the terms of the contract, she is guaranteed minimum annual compensation of $6,000. Defendant argues that the agreement at bench fails to meet the statutory minimum because the cost of producing two recordings a year exceeds $194,000, and when this expense is deducted from the guaranteed $200,000 annual advance, her net compensation becomes less than $6,000 annually.

The trial court found: (1) the "minimum compensation" referred to in the statutes does not mean "net profits"; (2) even if it did, suitable recordings could be made at costs that would net the defendant minimum compensation of $6,000 a year. It is decisive here that under the terms of the agreement exclusive control of production costs remained in defendant's hands at all times. Defendant was free to record in as tight-fisted or as open-handed a manner, costwise, as she chose. Defendant's interpretation of the minimum compensation statutes would allow her to nullify her contract at any time merely by increasing her production expenses, which at all times remained under her exclusive control. We do not believe the Legislature intended to sanction such a one-sided bargain, and we agree with the trial court's ruling in both its aspects....

B. Defendant next contends she cannot be suspended by plaintiff and at the same time enjoined from rendering personal services for others. But defendant has not been suspended. She is still free to record for plaintiff, and, in the event she chooses to record, nothing in the agreement relieves plaintiff from its obligation to compensate her.

C. Defendant maintains the grant of the preliminary injunction was improper because plaintiff failed to show, and the trial court failed to explicitly find, that such relief was necessary to prevent irreparable injury. The grant of a preliminary injunction lies within the discretion of the trial court, and an explicit finding of irreparable harm is not required to sustain the trial court's exercise of that discretion. In requesting injunctive relief plaintiff alleged that if defendant were permitted to record for a competitor, it would suffer irreparable injury, both in loss of profits and loss of goodwill. This allegation was supported by substantial evidence that defendant's services are unique. Absent any indication to the contrary, we can presume from the trial court's order granting the preliminary injunction that the court did in fact find that irreparable injury would be imminent unless the injunction were granted.

Defendant contends that even if the court did not err in granting a preliminary injunction, it erred in authorizing the preliminary injunction to extend beyond the five-year term of the agreement. Plaintiff responds, in effect, that so long as defendant fails to perform her obligations under the contract, the term of the agreement, and thus of the preliminary injunction, may be extended until the seven-year statutory maximum has elapsed.

Because a period of five years has not yet passed since defendant began her employment on April 1, 1975, the issue of the availability to plaintiff of injunctive relief after April 1, 1980, is technically premature. Nevertheless, we consider the language in the preliminary injunction extending its possible duration to April 1, 1982, inappropriate for two reasons:

First, if defendant had performed under the contract, plaintiff would not be entitled to prevent her from recording for competitors at the end of the five-year term of the agreement. We have grave doubts that defendant's failure to perform her obligations under the contract can extend the term of the contract beyond its specified five-year maximum.

Second, the injunction appealed here is merely a preliminary injunction, whose sole function is to preserve the status quo pending a final judgment in the action. Plaintiff's general duty to exercise due diligence in the prosecution of its action and to bring it to conclusion within a reasonable time is particularly strong when, as here, the cause involves injunctive and declaratory relief. To the extent the phrase "until April 1, 1982" suggests that plaintiff, without taking further action, may prevent defendant from recording for competitors until 1982, the phrase is misleading.

The order for preliminary injunction is modified by deleting the phrase, "or until April 1, 1982, if that date shall occur during the pendency of this action," and as so modified, the order is affirmed.

California Labor Code § 2855

§ 2855. Enforcement of contract to render personal service; Personal service in production of phonorecords

(a) Except as otherwise provided in subdivision (b), a contract to render personal service, other than a contract of apprenticeship as provided in Chapter 4 (commencing with Section 3070), may not be enforced against the employee beyond seven years from the commencement of service under it. Any contract, otherwise valid, to perform or render service of a special, unique, unusual, extraordinary, or intellectual character, which gives it peculiar value and the loss of which can not be reasonably or adequately compensated in damages in an action at law, may nevertheless be enforced against the person contracting to render the service, for a term not to exceed seven years from the commencement of service under it. If the employee voluntarily continues to serve under it beyond that time, the contract may be referred to as affording a presumptive measure of the compensation.

(b) Notwithstanding subdivision (a):

(1) Any employee who is a party to a contract to render personal service in the production of phonorecords in which sounds are first fixed, as defined in Section 101 of Title 17 of the United States Code, may not invoke the provisions of subdivision (a) without first giving written notice to the employer in accordance with Section 1020 of the Code of Civil Procedure, specifying that the employee from and after a future date certain specified in the notice will no longer render service under the contract by reason of subdivision (a).

(2) Any party to such a contract shall have the right to recover damages for a breach of the contract occurring during its term in an action commenced during or after its term, but within the applicable period prescribed by law.

(3) In the event a party to such a contract is, or could contractually be, required to render personal service in the production of a specified quantity of the phonorecords and fails to render all of the required service prior to the date specified in the notice provided in paragraph (1), the party damaged by the failure shall have the right to recover damages for each phonorecord as to which that party has failed to render service in an action which, notwithstanding paragraph (2), shall be commenced within 45 days after the date specified in the notice.

Notes and Questions

a. Record labels often exert influence on the composition of the bands under contract. The structure of the Recording Agreement and Band Member Agreements typically bind all band members, whether such a band member tries to leave the label voluntarily or is fired by the band. The most obvious concern for recording artists is the limitation this may have on the rights to produce new work after leaving a band. A label can elect to offer a solo recording contract to the leaving band member on terms very favorable to the label because that label already owns the rights to record that performer. While most deals seem to eventually work out, the agreements put the recording artists in a particularly weak bargaining position.

b. In addition to the lack of leverage, the Band Member Agreements also create a substantial financial risk for the departing band member. If the recording of subsequent CDs goes over budget, then those expenses are treated as advances that the label can recoup from royalties. The Band Member Agreement does not typically put any limits on this liability. A band member such as Bautista who records a solo album for the same label (or another label under common ownership) will see the royalties used to offset that recording artist's share of any unrecouped advances on the former band's albums. This is an example of a cross-collateralization that incorporates the practice of charging all unrecouped expenses from one album to all others produced by the recording artist. Cross-collateralization can quickly make a recording artist a debt-slave to a label. This practice can be truly pernicious when the debts derive from solo activities attributed to the rest of the band.

c. The Recording Agreement and Band Member Agreement are drafted to create a single relationship. Despite the technical reading by the Southern District of New York in *EMI Latin v. Bautista*, No. 03 Civ. 0947(WHP), 2003 WL 470333 (S.D.N.Y. Feb. 24, 2003), Band Member Agreements often provide that they incorporate the terms of the Recording Agreement by reference and any modification of the Recording Agreement serves as an amendment to the Band Member Agreement. Alternatively, at the time of drafting any modification of the Recording Agreement, a rider to the Band Member Agreement can be executed.

These amendments often extend the life of these contracts well beyond their initial terms. Some specifically provide that the modifications of the Band Member Agreements are to be made by a majority vote, or that the band has authorized its manager to negotiate and amend the agreement on behalf of the band. In each case, the general delegation means that the band is more likely to come to terms with the label, but also more likely that individual band members may be bound to terms he or she would consider unacceptable.

d. New York and many other states do not have the same employment statutes as California. As a result, the choice of law provisions of recording agreements may play a significant role. Nonetheless, the California courts tend to see these provisions as significant to public welfare, so that a mere recitation of jurisdiction may not carry weight if the performer resides in California during the term of the agreement.

e. The second provision of § 2855 makes the recording artist liable for damages to the label in the event of non-performance. While the idea that a party to a contract is liable for damages as a result of non-performance is generally not controversial, the provision takes on a different context in the recording business. Typically, poor employment performance results in termination rather than expectation damages. California has singled out recording artists for § 2855 in a rather odd, if not constitutionally suspect manner. Further, as many commentators suggest, the issue of damages is particularly controversial. The risk of receiving expectation damages from the performing artist, rather than merely being reimbursed for any advances or other *quantum meruit* award, has a significant chilling effect which strengthens the negotiation position of the label and undermines the benefits of § 2855(a). *See* Note, *California Labor Code Section 2855 and Recording Artists' Contracts*, 116 HARV. L. REV. 2632, 2643–45 (2003).

f. California historically required a $6,000 minimum annual income to claim specific performance. Despite this relatively low amount (which once had been a bit more significant before inflation), labels often tried to avoid the direct expense.

In *Foxx v. Williams*, 244 Cal. App. 2d 223, 52 Cal. Rptr. 896 (1966), the court addressed the impact of an agreement for royalties only. It found that the right to receive royalties does not meet the statutory requirement for actually receiving specific minimum compensation. In *MCA Records, Inc. v. Newton-John* (above), the court distinguished the situation:

> [C]omedian Redd Foxx agreed to record comedy routines for Williams, a record manufacturer and distributor. In return, Foxx was to receive royalties from the sale of the records. Foxx sued Williams and Williams' recording company for an accounting, and the company cross-complained for damages and injunctive relief. The lower court enjoined Foxx from recording for anyone other than cross-complainant, but the appellate court reversed for the reason that Foxx' royalty contract did not guarantee him annual compensation of $6,000. Unlike the defendant at bench, who is guaranteed minimum annual compensation of $200,000 in the form of nonreturnable advances in addition to any royalties she may receive, Foxx' sole compensation was in the form of royalties contingent upon prospective sales which could amount to nothing.

MCA Records, Inc. v Newton-John, 90 Cal. App. at 22–23 (1979).

In *Motown Record Corp. v. Brockert*, 160 Cal. App. 3d 123, 132–33 (1984) (often known as the Teena Marie case), the record company attempted to meet the payment minimum by providing itself an option to pay the $6,000 statutory minimum. The court found that this was not the same as the guaranteed minimum payment, so specific performance was ruled unavailable.

g. In 1993, California recognized that the $6,000 requirement had lost much of its market value and amended the statutory threshold of Cal Civ. Code § 3423 for specific performance. It briefly increased the amount to $50,000, but then withdrew that amount in favor of the current statute:

> § 3423. When injunction may not be granted. An injunction may not be granted:
>
> … (e) To prevent the breach of a contract the performance of which would not be specifically enforced, other than a contract in writing for the rendition of personal services from one to another where the promised service is of a special, unique, unusual, extraordinary, or intellectual character, which gives it peculiar value, the loss of which cannot be reasonably or adequately compensated in damages in an action at law, and where the compensation for the personal services is as follows:
>
> (1) As to contracts entered into on or before December 31, 1993, the minimum compensation provided in the contract for the personal services shall be at the rate of six thousand dollars ($6,000) per annum.

(2) As to contracts entered into on or after January 1, 1994, the criteria of subparagraph (A) or (B), as follows, are satisfied:

(A) The compensation is as follows:

(i) The minimum compensation provided in the contract shall be at the rate of nine thousand dollars ($9,000) per annum for the first year of the contract, twelve thousand dollars ($12,000) per annum for the second year of the contract, and fifteen thousand dollars ($15,000) per annum for the third to seventh years, inclusive, of the contract.

(ii) In addition, after the third year of the contract, there shall actually have been paid for the services through and including the contract year during which the injunctive relief is sought, over and above the minimum contractual compensation specified in clause (i), the amount of fifteen thousand dollars ($15,000) per annum during the fourth and fifth years of the contract, and thirty thousand dollars ($30,000) per annum during the sixth and seventh years of the contract. As a condition to petitioning for an injunction, amounts payable under this clause may be paid at any time prior to seeking injunctive relief.

(B) The aggregate compensation actually received for the services provided under a contract that does not meet the criteria of subparagraph (A), is at least 10 times the applicable aggregate minimum amount specified in clauses (i) and (ii) of subparagraph (A) through and including the contract year during which the injunctive relief is sought. As a condition to petitioning for an injunction, amounts payable under this subparagraph may be paid at any time prior to seeking injunctive relief.

(3) Compensation paid in any contract year in excess of the minimums specified in subparagraphs (A) and (B) of paragraph (2) shall apply to reduce the compensation otherwise required to be paid under those provisions in any subsequent contract years....

h. The seven-year limitation was enacted into California law in 1931, extending the term from two years to seven. (It harkens back to the biblical proscription on bonded slavery; the slave owner was required to free the slave and provide financial support to give the former slave meaningful economic support. Anyone desiring to remain a slave after the seven-year period had to agree to be marked as a permanent slave by having his ear pierced with an awl.) The law was quickly associated with Hollywood because Olivia de Havilland fought to terminate her studio contract with Warner Bros. Her original contract was for one year, with six additional options, but Warner Bros. added time periods when Ms. de Havilland was unavailable or under suspension. The court found that the law was for seven calendar years and terminated the contract.

The time limitation does not mean seven years of actual service regardless of the time over which such service extends, but means seven calendar years from the commencement of service. *See De Haviland v Warner Bros. Pictures, Inc.*, 67 Cal. App. 2d 225, 153 P.2d 983 (1944).

i. Because of the harsh results imposed by the recording contracts, courts do not give the record labels leeway in exercising the options to continue an artist. Essentially, the courts tend to treat these renewal periods as if there were a time-of-the-essence approach. The difficulty of this approach is that the exact date for renewal is often conditioned on an event rather than a date. In *Polygram Records, Inc. v. Buddy Buie Productions,* 520 F. Supp. 248 (S.D.N.Y. 1981), the court was required to interpret the series of events that occurred when the master recording and the "reference lacquer"—a copy of the master tape (essentially a pre-production album) was offered to Polygram as delivery. The renewal period for the contract was based on the date of acceptance, and the Southern District found that receipt of the reference lacquer and payment constituted acceptance. The court rejected the contention that the reference lacquer was at first considered subject to additional editing and therefore not accepted. Polygram's week-late renewal of the contract was not timely and all obligations to Polygram terminated.

Problem 11-E

Bryce is again considering joining Soundfyre. Bryce remains very concerned about inheriting the costs each band member must still recoup from the band's previous recordings. Bryce is also concerned that the association will only last a year or two and does not want to be captive to Soundfyre's record label. Bryce asks you to draft proposed language to provide Soundfyre and its record label that would allow Bryce to join the band but not be bound by the typical band membership agreement with regard to debt and future recording obligations.

F. Accountability under Recording Contracts

In many instances, the combination of advances, low royalty rates, and bookkeeping irregularities resulted in the recording artist never receiving any income after the advance. Renewed popularity of these recordings decades after the initial contract has resulted in significant income that was never distributed to the recording artists. For example, in *Greenfield v. Philles Records,* 98 N.Y.2d 562 (N.Y. 2002), the Ronettes never received any royalties from Phil Spector's Philles Records, Inc., despite a surge in popularity during the 1980s and the marriage of Ronettes' Ronnie Greenfield to Spector. Courts apply different approaches to these cases of failure to account or to pay royalties.

Peterson v. Highland Music, Inc.

140 F.3d 1313 (9th Cir. 1998)

This case involves an attempt by the Kingsmen, a musical group, to secure a rescission of the contract by which they assigned to others the rights to their popular recording of the hit song, "Louie, Louie." We review three actions consolidated on appeal. In the first, the parties litigated the right to rescind. In the second, the defendants sought a declaratory judgment to limit the effect of the judgment of rescission. In the third, the district court imposed contempt sanctions upon the defendants for their refusal to comply with the judgment of rescission. We affirm the district court in all respects.

The facts of this procedurally convoluted case are relatively simple. The members of the Kingsmen seek to secure their rights to the master recordings (the "Masters") of their hit song, "Louie, Louie." The group made the recording over thirty years ago. They then sold the Masters to one Specter Records ... in return for nine per cent of any profits or licensing fees that the recording might generate. The Kingsmen and Specter entered into their contract in 1968. Specter's interest in the Masters was eventually transferred to Gusto Records and GML, who were the named defendants in the rescission action. The parties do not dispute that the Kingsmen have never received a single penny of the considerable royalties that "Louie, Louie" has produced over the past thirty years.

In 1993, the Kingsmen brought suit in federal district court in California for rescission of the contract, basing their claim entirely on actions (or inactions) by the defendants that fell within the four-year statutory limitations period. After a full trial, the district court ruled in plaintiffs' favor and granted the rescission, restoring possession of the Masters to the Kingsmen....

Defendants [] contend that the district court erred in holding that the statute of limitations does not bar a remedy of rescission in this case. In California, the statute of limitations for an action seeking rescission of a contract is four years. *See* Cal. Code Civ. Proc. § 337. Specifically, the statute provides that an aggrieved party must commence such an action within four years "from the date upon which the facts that entitled the aggrieved party to rescind occurred." Both parties agree that the period of limitations has long since run with respect to the first occasions on which defendants breached their agreement. Both parties also agree that defendants have breached their agreement repeatedly over the course of the past thirty years, and did so, repeatedly, within four years of the time that plaintiffs commenced this action. Defendants' claim is that, even in the face of multiple and continuing breaches of the agreement, the California statute should be read to bar any action that is not commenced within four years of the *first* occasion on which an aggrieved party could have requested rescission. Defendants cite no authority for this proposition, and we reject it.

In analyzing requests for rescission where there have been multiple breaches under an installment contract, California courts have held that each breach starts the clock afresh for statute of limitations purposes. In *Conway v. Bughouse, Inc.*, 105 Cal. App. 3d 194, 164 Cal. Rptr. 585 (1980), for example, a California appeals court looked to the manner in which money would be paid under a pension contract in determining how a party's failure to make any given payment should affect the tolling of the statute of limitations.

The total amount of money to be paid to [the pensioner] is not a fixed sum which is to be paid out over a period of time. To the contrary, the total amount owed is unascertainable until the date of [the pensioner's] death because each payment is separate and contingent upon [the survival of the pensioner and his adherence to the terms of the contract]. As each payment is separable from the others and is not a part of a total payment, the agreement should logically be considered an installment contract for purposes of determination of the application of the statute of limitations.

The same holds true in the present case: There is no fixed amount to be paid out over time under the Kingsmen's contract, but rather a continuing obligation to pay a portion of the profits and royalties on "Louie, Louie" as the recording gets used over time.

The district court in this case made it clear that, in determining whether rescission was warranted and appropriate, it was relying upon breaches that had occurred within the limitations period. To find for defendant under these circumstances would be to hold that California law forever bars a party from seeking a remedy of rescission after it has once passed up the opportunity to do so, regardless of the nature of any future breaches of the other party's obligations. We have found no authority that would support such a reading of California law. We therefore affirm the district court's conclusion that the statute of limitations does not bar rescission of the contract in this case....

On the merits, the district court found that the rescission of the Kingsmen's contract was effective as of the date of the filing of the Kingsmen's complaint. We agree. Under California law, "a party to a contract [can] rescind it and ... such rescission [can] be accomplished by the rescinding party by giving notice of the rescission and offering to restore everything of value which [the rescinding party has] received." When a party gives notice of rescission, it has effected the rescission, and any subsequent judicial proceedings are for the purpose of confirming and enforcing that rescission. Thus, when the Kingsmen filed suit in 1993, they rescinded the contract and became owners of the Masters. The lawsuit that followed confirmed that their rescission was a proper one and resulted in an order enforcing that rescission. The district court correctly ruled that, as the owners of the Masters, the Kingsmen are entitled to all income derived from the exploitation of the recordings following September 29, 1993, the date of the notice of rescission.

[The court also upholds findings of contempt related to the failure to abide by the district court decision.] The district court's rulings in these consolidated actions are well-reasoned and supported by ample evidence in the record. We affirm in all respects.

Cabot v. Jamie Record Co.

No. 96-4672, 1999 U.S. Dist. LEXIS 5549 (E.D. Pa. Apr. 22,1999),
aff'd, 248 F.3d 1129 (3d Cir. 2000) (without opinion)

This court has subject matter jurisdiction over this action by reason of diversity of citizenship and amount pursuant to 28 U.S.C. § 1332. Plaintiff, Gilbert A. Cabot, is a resident and citizen of California. Defendants, Jamie Record Co. and Jamie Music Publishing Co. t/a Dandelion Music Co., are corporations organized and existing under Pennsylvania law with their principal places of business in Philadelphia, Pennsylvania. As pled, the amount in controversy exceeds $50,000, the statutory minimum at the time the complaint was filed. The parties agree and this court finds that the substantive law for Pennsylvania controls. In the late 1960s, Cabot produced a number of phonograph records including "Fireball" and "Love Can Make You Happy" (together "the compositions"). The song, "Love Can Make You Happy," was recorded by the group "The Mercy" pursuant to an agreement between Cabot and the group's manager and songwriter, Jack Sigler, Jr.... In 1969, Cabot, relinquished his copyrights and all other rights in the compositions to Dandelion and Jamie Record in exchange for advances and promises of future royalties. On February 26, 1969, Cabot, under the unregistered trade name, Gil Cabot Enterprises, Inc. (hereinafter "Gil Cabot Enterprises"), entered into a "Master Purchase Agreement" by which he sold the master recordings of the compositions and all rights attendant thereto to Jamie Record [and Cabot's company]. Rendezvous/Tobac entered into a "Participation Agreement" by which it sold to Dandelion the copyrights and rights to copyright, print, publish, sell, use, or license the use of the compositions....

As a successor-in-interest to Gil Cabot Enterprises and Rendezvous/Tobac, Cabot now sues for rescission of the Master Purchase and Participation Agreements (together "the agreements").... Cabot's principle contention is that the agreements should be rescinded and he should be allowed to recapture his copyrights and all other rights in the compositions because of failure of consideration by the defendants at the time the agreements were made. Cabot further contends that an extended period of nonpayment and failure to account by defendants, equivalent to Pennsylvania's four-year statute of limitations period for breaches of contract, specifically from 1991 to 1995, constituted a material breach going to the essence of the contract. Cabot also asserts that royalties that were paid prior to this time were not the total of the sums due and owing to him under the agreements....

Under the Master Purchase Agreement ownership of the master recordings of the compositions was transferred from Cabot to Jamie Record. The Master Purchase Agreement provided in relevant part:

> (1.) This letter sets forth the agreement between you [Gil Cabot Enterprises, Inc.] and ourselves [Jamie Record], your and our heirs and distributees, successors and assigns, for the sale to us of two phonograph masters recorded by Mercy
>
> (2.) You hereby warrant and represent that you are the sole and exclusive owner of the following master recordings of: Love "Can Make You Happy" b/w Fireball [sic]....
>
> Such masters and all records and reproductions made therefrom together with the performances embodied therein, shall be entirely our property, free of any claims whatsoever by you or any person deriving any rights or interests

from you. Without limitation of the foregoing, we shall have the right to make records or other reproductions of the performances embodied in such recordings ... and to sell and deal in the same under any trademarks or trade names or labels designated by us, and perform the same publicly and permit public performance by any method now or hereafter known throughout the world.

... The consideration paid to Gil Cabot Enterprises under the Master Purchase Agreement was a one thousand dollar ($1000) cash advance and royalties derived from the sale and/ or licensing of the recordings of the compositions. Generally, Cabot was to receive a seventeen percent (17%) royalty, payable upon the wholesale price, exclusive of taxes, on ninety percent (90%) of all records sold. For sales outside of the United States, Cabot was to receive one-half of the seventeen percent (17%) otherwise payable.... Jamie Record was to provide Gil Cabot Enterprises bi-annually with an accounting and payment of net income due: "Accounts shall be made to you within sixty days after the first day of January and July of each year for the preceding six months period and shall be accompanied by payment of accrued royalties less any then unrecouped advances...." However, Jamie Record did not send out financial statements every six months as required. For earnings from 1972 to 1976, there were no statements issued by it until February 22, 1977. Nonetheless, some payments were received, though not regularly, [b]etween the period 1969 and 1986, ... amounting to approximately $52,000....

Pursuant to the Participation Agreement, Dandelion acquired exclusive ownership of the copyrights and the right to copyright, print, publish, sell, use, or license the use of the compositions anywhere in the world. The Participation Agreement stated, in relevant part:

> (1.) [Rendezvous/ Tobac] agrees and acknowledges that [Dandelion] is the sole and exclusive owner of the copyright Title: (1) "LOVE 'CAN MAKE YOU HAPPY'" (2) "FIREBALL" ... hereinafter called the "Musical Compositions," for the territory of the World subject only to limitations thereon and the rights of the authors and/ or composers set forth in an agreement between [Dandelion] and Authors & Composers....

> (2.) [Dandelion] shall have the sole and exclusive right to print, publish, sell, use and license the use of the Musical Composition in the aforementioned territory, and to execute in its own name any and all licenses and agreements whatsoever affecting or respecting the Musical Composition, including but not limited to licenses for mechanical reproduction, public performance, synchronization uses and sub-publication. This statement of exclusive rights being in clarification and amplification of its rights as copyright owner and not in limitation thereof.

The consideration paid to Rendezvous/Tobac under the Participation Agreement was a one thousand dollar ($1000) cash advance and royalties derived from the compositions. Generally, Dandelion received a fee of ten percent (10%) of the total revenues. The remaining ninety percent (90%) was to be divided equally between Rendezvous/Tobac and Dandelion.

Under that agreement, Rendezvous/Tobac was also to receive direct payments from Broadcast Music, Inc. ("BMI") which was licensed to collect royalties for public performances of the compositions. BMI was to pay a fifty percent (50%) share of any performance income to Dandelion and a fifty percent (50%) share to Rendezvous/Tobac. The Participation Agreement stated that Dandelion was to provide Rendezvous/Tobac bi-annually with an accounting and payment of net income: "All sums payable to [Rendezvous/Tobac] pursuant hereto by [Dandelion], shall be accounted for, in writing and paid at the time of accounting, at the same time as [Dandelion] customarily accounts to authors and composers, but in no event less than twice a year."

Dandelion did not send out statements every six months as required by the Participation Agreement. As with the Master Purchase Agreement, there were no statements issued to Rendezvous/Tobac from 1972 to 1976. One cumulative statement was issued in 1997. Between the period 1969 and 1986, Rendezvous/Tobac received payments amounting to approximately $9,200 from Dandelion under the Participation Agreement. From 1970 to the present, Cabot received payments from BMI under the Participation Agreement. From 1991 to 1995, Cabot received more that $10,500 under the Participation Agreement from BMI directly.

In October 1986, Dandelion decided to suspend payments due to Rendezvous/Tobac under the Participation Agreement, after it suspended the payments to Sundi Records under the Master Purchase Agreement. Accountings were also not issued during that time. On July 10, 1998, this court ordered Dandelion to pay to Rendezvous/Tobac all sums withheld since 1986. Dandelion has tendered payment of those amounts but these sums have not been accepted.

Legal Conclusions

Rescission, an equitable rather than a legal remedy, "amounts to the unmaking of a contract, and is not merely a termination of the rights and obligations of the parties towards each other, but is an abrogation of all rights and responsibilities of the parties towards each other from the inception of the contract." *Metropolitan Property and Liability Insurance Co. v. Commonwealth of Pennsylvania*, 97 Pa. Commw. 219, 509 A.2d 1346, 1348 (Pa. Commw. Ct. 1986), *aff'd*, 517 Pa. 218, 535 A.2d 588 (Pa. 1987). Through equitable powers, a court may intervene to grant rescission when there are allegations of failure of consideration, fraud, and mistake. Cabot has based his claim of rescission on all of these grounds.

This court finds that the defendants' failure to make timely and accurate payments and regular accountings does not justify rescission of the Master Purchase and Participation Agreements. Not every breach of a contract justifies rescission. Under Pennsylvania law, rescission "is appropriate only under extraordinary circumstances when the complaining party has suffered a breach of such a fundamental and material nature that it affects the very essence of the contract and serves to defeat the object of the parties." It is well settled that an executed agreement should not be rescinded on the basis of inadequate consideration in the absence of fraud or mistake. Rescission has been allowed in cases in which a publisher has made none of the royalty payments. The rationale behind such a rescission is that "an essential objective of a contract between a composer and publisher is the payment of royalties, and a complete failure to pay means this objective has not been achieved."

Cabot cannot assert that there has been no payment whatsoever under the contract. Rather, he argues that rescission is warranted because defendants paid nothing between 1991 and 1995, the applicable statute of limitations period. Cabot argues that several other circuits have limited themselves to the statute of limitations period in evaluating whether a defendants' failure to pay and to make regular accounts warrants rescission. Cabot has cited no cases in this circuit that stand for such proposition. Nevertheless, this court finds that defendant's breaches of agreement both over the life of the agreements and during the applicable statute of limitations period, are not sufficient to warrant rescission here.

Between 1969 and 1986, Cabot received approximately $52,000 from defendants under the Master Purchase Agreements and $9,200 under the Participation Agreement. Further, BMI has made payments to Cabot since 1970 under the Participation Agreement. Jamie Record also paid additional consideration to Sigler pursuant to the Master Purchase Agreement. Payments to Sigler from Jamie Record under the Master Purchase Agreement and to Cabot from BMI under the Participation Agreement, continued during the statute of limitations period. In fact, from 1991 to 1995 Cabot received $10,574 from BMI directly.

While the defendants have breached the Master Purchase and Participation Agreements by failing to make timely payments and regular accountings to Cabot, and perhaps have not fully compensated Cabot under the agreements, these breaches only amount to inadequate consideration and failure to comply fully with the contractual provisions. It is well settled that a party may not avail itself of the equity powers of the court if there exists or existed an adequate remedy at law. Here, Cabot could have been, or can be, made whole by an award of damages. In fact, the tender of payments withheld by the defendants since 1986, may have fully compensated Cabot....

Further, rescission is inappropriate in this case because the parties cannot be placed in their pre-contractual positions at this time, as that would mean restoring the 1969 status quo in 1997. Rescission is ordinarily granted only where the parties to the contract can be restored to substantially the same position they occupied when the contract was made. The songs were popular primarily in 1969 and 1970. This success was due in some significant part to the efforts of the defendants. Thus, if rescission was granted, Cabot would necessarily benefit from any value that the defendants have added to the compositions, and the defendants would lose the benefit of those efforts.

Cabot asserts that the defendants had an obligation to exploit or actively solicit and promote interest in the compositions and the Sundi label by maximizing on the past popularity of the compositions.... The only terms for distribution of the compositions and the label are stated briefly in the Master Purchase Agreement at paragraph 15:

It is understood and agreed that the above recording will be released by Jamie Record Co. on the Sundi label, with the logo 'Nationally distributed by Jamie/Guyden D. Corp.,' and you agree that we shall be exclusive distributors of all recordings on the Sundi label so long as this Agreement is in effect.

No duties were imposed in the agreements regarding exploitation, or active promotion, of the compositions and label. Thus, under the plain language of the Master Purchase Agreement, Jamie Record was bound only to release the compositions on the Sundi label with the described logo, and was given the exclusive right to distribute on the Sundi label. Likewise, the Participation Agreement only provided Dandelion with the "exclusive right to print, publish, sell, use and license the use of the compositions and to execute in its own name any and all licenses and agreements affecting or respecting the Musical Compositions...."

Where the language of a contract is clear and unambiguous, the intent is to be discovered only from the express language of the agreement and the plain meaning of the agreement will be enforced. While Cabot may have expected a subsequent, more formal agreement to be reached regarding distribution under the Master Purchase Agreements, such an agreement would not have altered the Master Purchase Agreements' original terms.

Cabot asserts that even absent an explicit contractual duty, the nature of the relationship of the parties and the transfer of all title and control over the copyrights and master recordings to Jamie Record and Dandelion, created an implied duty for them to exploit. Cabot cites second circuit cases, applying New York law, in an attempt to support his assertion that even in the absence of specific contractual language, the defendants had an implied duty to exploit the compositions and actively to promote distribution of the Sundi label.... At best, the second circuit cases hold that a publisher, holding exclusive rights in a work, has an implied duty to exercise good faith and sound business judgment in working a copyright. Those cases do not stand for the proposition that there is an implied duty to exploit a copyright in the manner that Cabot urged, and that a publisher is obligated to promote the work regardless of circumstances, costs, or other conditions that might erode popularity, such as the passage of time and change in consumer taste....

Cabot's claim for rescission of the Master Purchase Agreement and Participation Agreement is denied....

Notes and Questions

a. Ambiguity in the scope of the license transfers remains a common problem. In *Greenfield v. Philles Records*, the New York Court of Appeals reversed the Appellate Division because it found that the comprehensive assignment left no ambiguity regarding the scope of the rights transfer. Although not discussed in the opinion, the silence on synchronization rights could have been particularly instructive since this was not a new technology, but rather the right to use the sound recordings as part of a motion picture. Producer Phil Spector was certainly aware of the possibility, and undoubtedly, Ms. Greenfield and the other Ronettes also knew of the possibility that the sound recording could be sold for use in movies.

b. Another important aspect of *Greenfield* was the drafting of the agreement. The agreement provided for a transfer of all rights, but provided compensation to the recording artist only in selected income streams. The silence of the contract resulted in all income from the synchronization being kept by Philles Records and no royalties being paid. In this age of rapidly changing technologies, it is appropriate to provide an "other revenue" royalty provision that provides a blended royalty rate for all income streams not otherwise identified in the agreement. This will protect today's recording artists from income opportunities that will develop during the many decades covered by the transfer of the exploitation rights.

c. As in most areas of the law, most cases ultimately settle. In a high-profile dispute between Lil Wayne with his former mentor Birdman and the labels Cash Money Records and Universal Music Group, the dispute lasted over three years and delayed Wayne's *Tha Carter V* release. Ultimately the claim for $51 million in unpaid fees and royalties was settled for an unacknowledged amount reputed to be more than $10 million. Shortly after the settlement, in October 2018, Wayne released the album. The album earned 480,000 equivalent album units, placing it number 1 in the Billboard 200 Albums chart and a top Metacritic score, making it a financial, critical, and fan victory.

d. Despite the importance of the contracts used by the major record labels and the sophistication of the parties, key terms remain vague, ambiguous, and shrouded in mystery. In *Pettibone v. WB Music Corp.*, 767 F. App'x. 145 (2d Cir. 2019), the court was asked to interpret an indemnification clause regarding the author's obligation to indemnify the label in the case of a copyright infringement case over the song "Vogue." Tom Pettibone and Warner Music won the infringement action, but the label's legal fees approached $1 million. As the court explained:

> Warner withheld in excess of $500,000 in royalties due Pettibone to offset the attorneys' fees it had incurred in defending the suit. When Pettibone demanded payment of the royalties, Warner refused to comply, contending that under Section 8.1 of the Agreement — the indemnification provision — Warner was entitled to withhold the royalties. Section 8.1 provides in relevant part:

> > Each party will indemnify the other against any loss or damage (including court costs and reasonable attorneys' fees) due to a breach of this agreement by that party which results in a judgment against the other party or which is settled with the other party's prior written consent (not to be unreasonably withheld). In addition, [Pettibone's] indemnity shall extend to the "deductible" under [Warner's] errors-and-omissions policy without regard to judgment or settlement. Each party is entitled to be notified of any action against the other brought with respect to [the song "Vogue"], and to participate in the defense thereof by counsel of its choice, at its sole cost and expense.

We conclude that Section 8.1 is pock-marked with ambiguity and, in fact, more readily evinces an understanding between the parties that, in the absence of a breach, each party will shoulder its own attorneys' fees and costs. First, section 8.1 contains language that explicitly cabins the indemnification obligation to attorneys' fees and costs arising from a breach of the Agreement. In contrast, there is no explicit mention of whether an indemnification obligation exists absent such a breach. Second, section 8.1 states that "each party is entitled to be notified of any action against the other brought with respect to [the song 'Vogue'], and to participate in the defense thereof by counsel of its choice, at its *sole cost and expense.*" Third, section 8.1, read as a whole, can be reasonably interpreted to limit Pettibone's indemnification obligation, *in the event of Pettibone's breach,* to the retention amount set forth in Warner's Insurance Policy, regardless of the amount of any judgment or settlement against Warner resulting from that breach. This reading gives effect to every word of section 8.1. It also makes economic sense, as Warner's Insurance Policy likely covers it for breach-related damages in excess of the retention amount. Warner's argument to the contrary relies heavily on the second sentence of section 8.1, which provides that Pettibone's "indemnity shall extend to the 'deductible' under [Warner's] errors-and-omissions policy without regard to judgment or settlement." Warner argues that the only reasonable reading of "without regard to judgment or settlement" is "without regard to *breach.*" As previously discussed, to the extent Warner urges that it intended to bury, in section 8.1, a highly unorthodox fee-shifting provision that is astonishing in its breadth, the contractual language undoubtedly "fails to disclose its purpose."

The effort to shift the litigation fees to Pettibone serve as a useful reminder that the sharp practices of the music industry do not end with the drafting of the contracts. Every interaction must be monitored to assure fair and accurate accounting.

e. Despite contract language limiting the audit of books to one year, misleading royalty statements may trigger the delayed discovery doctrine and toll the time provided under the contract. *See Weatherly v. Universal Music Publ'g Grp.*, 125 Cal. App. 4th 913, 23 Cal. Rptr. 3d 157 (2004).

f. To what extent is the presumptive relationship between a band and record company exclusive? In *Bucciarelli-Tieger v. Victory Records, Inc.*, 488 F. Supp. 2d 702 (N.D. Ill. 2007), the court refused to go beyond the text of the agreement. "The agreement contains no exclusivity provision, nor does any of its language appear to prevent plaintiffs from recording elsewhere during the life of the agreement." At the same time, the decision included some practical limitations — not written into the agreement. "Our interpretation does not mean plaintiffs can market the same albums to another record company, or even re-record the same tracks, and plaintiff clarified that this was not their argument. It simply means plaintiffs are free to record other albums or tracks for another record company during the life of the agreement with defendants. Defendants even admit in their motion that within the industry standard there are exceptions to the rule of exclusivity."

g. Sometimes the problem with the accountability exists on both sides of the recording agreement. Such is the saga of the Bay City Rollers, who have been litigating a royalty dispute with Arista Records — at least through 2011 — that stemmed from non-payments in 1981. *See Faulkner v. Arista Records L.L.C.*, 797 F. Supp. 2d 299 (S.D.N.Y. 2011).

Problem 11-F

Despite the somewhat contentious relationship between Bryce and Soundfyre, Bryce has agreed to appear as a principal musician on the band's next album and participate in limited appearances. Based on your advice and Bryce's personal career aspirations, Bryce does not wish to join the band or become subject to the exclusive recording agreement.

Prepare a deal memo that can serve as an outline for an agreement that Bryce and Soundfyre can offer to the label so that Bryce can participate on the album without joining the band.

G. Bibliography and Links

AL KOHN & BOB KOHN, KOHN ON MUSIC LICENSING (5th ed. 2018).

MARK HALLORAN, THE MUSICIAN'S BUSINESS & LEGAL GUIDE (5th ed. 2017).

DONALD S. PASSMAN, ALL YOU NEED TO KNOW ABOUT THE MUSIC BUSINESS (10th ed. 2019).

Howard B. Abrams, *Copyright's First Compulsory License*, 26 SANTA CLARA HIGH TECH. L.J. 215 (2010).

Brian C. Drobnik, *Art & Industry Forum: Truckin' In Style Along the Avenue: How the Grateful Dead Turned Alternative Business and Legal Strategies Into a Great American Success Story*, 2 VAND. J. ENT. L. & PRAC. 242 (2000).

Antonia Eliason, *Lillian McMurry and the Blues Contracts of Trumpet Records*, 87 MISS. L.J. 279 (2018).

Patryk Galuszka, *Undisclosed Payments to Promote Records on the Radio: An Economic Analysis of Anti-Payola Legislation*, 11 VA. SPORTS & ENT. L.J. 38 (2011).

Thomas W. Joo, *Remix Without Romance*, 44 CONN. L. REV. 415 (2011).

Glynn S. Lunney, Jr., *Copyright Lost*, 59 IDEA: L. REV. FRANKLIN PIERCE CENTER FOR INTELL. PROP. 193 (2018).

Nora Miles, *Pop Goes the Commercial: The Evolution of the Relationship Between Popular Music and Television Commercials*, 5 VAND. J. ENT. L. & PRAC. 121 (2003).

Lynn Morrow, *The Recording Artist Agreement: Does It Empower or Enslave?*, 3 VAND. J. ENT. L. & PRAC. 40 (2001).

Kayla Mullen, *Applying the De Minimus Exception to Sound Recordings: Digital Samplers Are Neither Thieves nor Infringers*, 99 J. PAT. & TRADEMARK OFF. SOC'Y 731 (2017).

Henry H. Perritt, Jr., *New Business Models for Music*, 18 Vill. Sports & Ent. L.J. 63 (2011).

Shannon Price, *Remembering the Classics: Impact of the Classics Act on Memory Institutions, Orphan Works, and Mass Digitization*, 26 UCLA Ent. L. Rev. 79 (2019)

Kathryn Rosenberg, *Restoring the Seven Year Rule in the Music Industry*, 26 Fordham Intell. Prop. Media & Ent. L.J. 275 (2015).

Websites

Recording Industry of America, https://www.RIAA.com

American Association for Independent Music, https://www.a2im.org

IFPI, International Federation of the Phonographic Industry, https://www.ifpi.org

Chapter 12

Film Production Rights, Financing and Distribution

A. Overview

Although the impact of technology convulsed through the music industry before taking root in the film industry, the activities that make up the film and television industries are now in the midst of a rapid and profound restructuring. Film itself has been replaced by digital recording for many years, but the more significant changes are the venues and modes in which the audience consumes its film and television content.

Motion picture theaters and multiplexes continue to prosper. For 2018, the global box office earned $41.1 billion, with $11.9 being earned in the U.S. China is the second largest market at $9 billion.[1] These earnings are essentially the same as the prior year, and the forecast for the domestic box office continues to look like it will stay approximately the same in the coming years, unable to grow at the rate of inflation.

In comparison, however, the global home entertainment market increased 16% over the past year to a record $55.7 billion. In the U.S., the increase in digital spending was 24%.[2] Cable continues to decline slightly, with approximately 50 million subscriptions as compared to the 180 online video subscriptions, but cable earned $55.4 billion in subscription revenue for 2018, making it the highest revenue generator in the marketplace.[3]

The rapid growth of online video subscriptions is reflected in other shifts in the industry. Netflix, a disruptive technology company, has transformed itself into one of the largest motion picture studios and has become a member of the Motion Picture Association of America (MPAA). The MPAA's current membership is now Disney, Netflix, Paramount, Universal, and Warner Bros. Twentieth Century Fox had been a member until its acquisition by Disney in 2019.

The increasing takeover of the formerly separate film and television industries will continue to change the distribution of filmed content and reshape the nature of the

---

1. MPAA, Theatrical and Home Entertainment Market Environment Report 2018, at 5 (2018), https://www.mpaa.org/research-docs/2018-theatrical-home-entertainment-market-environment-theme-report/.

2. *Id.* at 30.

3. *Id.* at 37.

content. Historically, films were individual projects ranging in running time of 73 minutes to three or more hours. U.S. television created series that typically included 13 or 22 episodes per year and were renewed annually. Broadcasters and premium cable companies also toyed with the miniseries format of 4 to 8 episodes for a project that could last one year or have multiple years. The online video subscription services run many feature films, but they also run series that can include any number of episodes per season, any number of seasons per year, and any number of years in length. The lack of standardization has created a bit of confusion for the consumer and a great deal more confusion for the production companies.

The remainder of this chapter will focus on the production aspects of the content. The caselaw and general outlines included apply to all modes of distributing the content. Particular contracts will vary to set the expected delivery of the initial work, but since most rights acquisition agreements allow the producers to change from feature film to television series, the addition of online video formats do not substantially change the nature of producing the content nearly as much as they change the manner of distributing and consuming the content.

1. Production at a Glance[4]

The billions of dollars funneled into local economies by the film industry are spent in modest increments through on-location productions and the rare, but spectacular, creation of production studios. Such studios consist of permanent production offices, production shops for creating sets and costumes, and sound stages where filming can take place in a controlled environment.

a. The Studio Production

Studios may also have outdoor back lots where semi-permanent sets are left standing for use in various productions on a regular basis. The term "studio" represents both the dominant corporations in the motion picture industry as well as the physical structures those companies utilize in creating their film product. Studios may mean "the larger, fully integrated production, distribution and marketing companies," as well as the soundstages, back lots, offices, and editing rooms such companies control.

The positive economic impact of a studio can be attributed to direct employment by the studio as well as the indirect impact of employment from service providers to the studio's activities. Such service providers include film laboratories, construction houses, prop rentals, and other related industries, as well as those support services that are the same for any large employer, including construction, housing, restaurants, catering, and retail.

---

4. Adapted from Jon M. Garon, *Star Wars: Film Permitting, Prior Restraint & Government's Role in the Entertainment Industry*, 17 Loy. L.A. Ent. L.J. 1 (1996) (most footnotes omitted, others renumbered) (reprinted with author's permission).

Unfortunately, the high cost of constructing a new studio is only the first obstacle to creating a significant local production facility. The industrial infrastructure is necessary to make the studio operate productively. This infrastructure includes trained production staff with expertise in the skill crafts — carpenters, artists, electricians — and access to communities where professional acting talent lives or will purchase second homes. Industrial support services must also be located within a convenient distance, including film laboratories, equipment rental houses for lighting and other equipment, and other ancillary companies.

b. The Location Production

To film "on location" simply means that the filming takes place somewhere other than a soundstage. Unlike a soundstage, the production company does not own the location; thus, the property owner must approve any necessary modifications to the property. Locations often need to be painted, redecorated, or distressed to match the desired look for the film. High voltage electric cables need to be used during the filming and larger productions often require additional bathroom facilities to accommodate the needs of a large cast and crew. For cities, counties, and states vying to get a toehold in location productions, the primary selling tool is the scenic nature of the landscape. The success of Astoria, Oregon illustrates the point.

When New Line Cinema chose Astoria, Ore. over Wilmington, N.C. for principal location shooting for *Teenage Mutant Ninja Turtles III*, it was because the studio needed something different. Wilmington, the site of the first two Turtles movies, could not offer proximity to both ocean and mountains. Oregon's rugged Coastal Range and powerful coastline gave the location scouts exactly what they were looking for.

Similarly, the Maine Film Office highlights the features of its region. "Natural assets including mountains, coastline, forests, farms, rivers, lakes, villages, cities and people provide a stunning backdrop for work or play." Nevada's brochure and production guide carries a similar theme, as reflected in the "message from the Governor" printed in the Nevada Production Directory: "We take pride in offering a variety of unique locations, dazzling neon, isolated ghost towns, majestic mountain ranges and desolate dry lake beds. You'll find it all!" For locations in areas that have studios and significant resident production, convenience becomes more critical than scenery. Virtually anything filmed can be shot on-location rather than in the studio; thus, many of the mundane areas become film locations for those production companies already in the area. Every project has specific needs, most of which are not particularly exotic.

c. The Various Media

Like locations, the types of projects also differ greatly from medium to medium. The location requirements and the economic impact of filming will vary greatly depending on the type of production and the purpose of the filming. The various media that comprise the entertainment industry can be categorized into a number of distinct production types. While they all share many of the same characteristics, each has a distinct economic impact.

i. Feature Motion Pictures

Feature motion pictures are movies most commonly thought of as the product of Hollywood. Budgets for feature films range from a few hundred thousand dollars when made by small, independent film companies to more than $400 million for the largest spectaculars. Feature films typically use dozens, if not hundreds, of different locations.

Historically, a feature motion picture had six release windows: "domestic and international theatrical release" through first-run motion picture theaters; "pay-per-view," which allows for films to be seen in the home via cable television; "video kiosk rental and direct sale," which provides copies of the film for sale or rental through retail outlets; "cable television premieres" on premium movie stations such as HBO or Showtime; "network television release" broadcast over the air on television paid for through commercial sponsorship rather than by the viewers; and "syndicated television release" broadcast on local television stations unaffiliated with networks or at times in the television schedule not controlled by the networks.

Netflix has disrupted this model substantially. To make its premium feature films eligible for Oscar contention, Netflix will run those films for the minimum time required to submit the film for the Academy Award, which is typically a week. The Academy of Motion Picture Arts and Sciences is adjusting the eligibility to make it harder for Netflix to make its online video distribution features eligible as theatrical films, but the Academy is fighting a losing battle. Amazon Prime has increased its production and will likely follow Netflix practices. Apple may do the same. Since Hulu is now owned by Disney, Hulu will be less disruptive of the distribution windows. The disruption will also likely cause a continued shrinkage in the length of each window. Historically, the exclusive windows tended to each run six months, but the pressure from the online streamers has eliminated the windows for some movies and reduced their length for others.

ii. Industrial Films

A significant segment of production in areas like New York City, Chicago, and the periphery of Hollywood (such as Orange County) is industrial films (or industrials) that traditionally include projects produced as training programs, educational films, and similar non-broadcast markets. The area has expanded tremendously with the advent of home videotape, but has become increasingly nonprofessional because of the ability to upload a YouTube video or a video to one of dozens of video hosting platforms.

Nonetheless, from a production side, semi-professional industrials for corporate image pieces shown to a broad general public, traditional training films, motivational and sales projects, point-of-purchase videos, product demos, employee benefits programs, interactive videos, tape cut-ins for live teleconferences and other projects still provide significant production work for union and non-union talent behind the camera.

While budgets for industrials are significantly lower than for most feature films, the technical requirements and "below the line budget" (which excludes star, director, and producer salaries) are often very similar to that of feature films. In these projects, the improvement in home recording equipment and editing equipment has dramatically reduced the cost of production and increased the technical quality.

iii. Television Production

Television production includes a wide variety of different projects, including specials, one-hour series, half-hour comedies, talk shows, and music videos. Television productions have significantly lower budgets than motion pictures and work on a much tighter time schedule. Unlike feature films and industrials, however, many television productions require weekly or even daily projects. As a result, a regular location for a long-running television show will generate significant local revenue.

iv. Commercials

As a distinct type of television production, television commercials are actually the most expensive medium as judged on a cost-per-minute basis. The top commercials may have as many locations as a television episode or industrial film with crew sizes and expenditures comparable to that of a feature film. Commercials are the most frequently shot motion picture form. Television commercials for local retailers are created in virtually every television market in the country. National advertising campaigns tend to be created in the major markets such as Los Angeles, New York City, Miami, and Chicago because of the access to talent and production companies.

2. The Film Industry: Key Participants[5]

1. Producers. The producer provides the key leadership, management, and supervision for the entire film project. This includes the "creative, financial, technological and administrative process throughout all phases of production from inception to completion, including coordination, supervision and control of all other talents and crafts, subject to the provisions of their collective bargaining agreements and personal service contracts."[6] Like the CEO or president of a corporation, the producer is responsible for all final executive decisions and personally participates in many of the choices made in every aspect of the project.

A good producer must have a solid grasp of the financial, artistic, and technical aspects of filmmaking. Often the task requires that the producer bring strong-willed

---

5. Adapted from Jon Garon, The Independent Filmmaker's Law & Business Guide To Financing, Shooting, & Distributing Independent & Digital Films (2d ed. 2009) (reprinted with author's permission).
6. Frequently Asked Questions, Producers Guild of America, https://www.producersguild.org/page/faq (last visited October 5, 2019).

professionals together to make hard decisions that balance the filmmaker's vision against the financial resources and technical limitations of the project. Experience, problem-solving skills, and strong management techniques are the essential qualities of a good producer.

Executive producers, on the other hand, are generally involved in the project only indirectly, helping raise funds or coordinating multiple films at the conceptual level. Few independent films have executive producers, except as a way of securing additional capital by providing the credit to inactive but essential financial participants. Occasionally, executive producer credit is provided to important cast members who use their influence to sign the remaining members of the cast and crew. By taking an extra hand in the production, these actors empower the film to go forward.

Associate producer is a title that is often liberally distributed to production participants who undertake many of the producer's duties, whether in coordination with the producer or by their own initiative. Although this credit is sometimes used in bargaining, independent filmmakers may wish to grant associate producer status to the individual who stands out throughout the production process, the unsung hero who went well beyond the job description or who paid to ensure that the project was completed.

The Producers Guild of America distinguishes between entrepreneurial producers and employee producers. In the independent filmmaking context, the entrepreneurial producer is the filmmaker — the person who takes it upon herself to initiate the project. An employee producer is a person hired by the financier of the project to manage the film's production.

If the filmmaker is not an entrepreneurial producer, then she must entrust the producing responsibilities to an employee producer, and take pains to ensure that he is under her direction and employ, rather than under the authority of the distributor or other financier of the project. The producer's control of the budget gives him primary authority over the film, so the filmmaker can retain control only to the extent that the producer answers to her and no one else.

This is not to suggest that the filmmaker should not employ a producer at all. If she (like most artists) lacks the experience, problem-solving skills, or management strength to do the job herself, an independent professional will add perspective to the project, enabling the filmmaker to make prudent, responsible choices. Even if the producer can be overruled, his advice and alternative viewpoints will prove invaluable.

2. Writers. If a writer is a member of the Writers Guild, then union rules prohibit her from working with a nonunion company. Whether the individual writer chooses to follow this rule, however, is her choice rather than the concern of the production company. The only danger in working with a union writer on a nonunion production is that she could change her mind and refuse to deliver a script unless the film company signs the WGA Theatrical and Television Basic Agreement (commonly called the Writers Guild Minimum Basic Agreement, or WGA-MBA). A film company may be-

come a signatory to the WGA-MBA simply by contacting the Writers Guild. The WGA-MBA provides an excellent structure for negotiations whether or not the writer is actually a member of the union.

The motion picture writer may be the loneliest person in Hollywood. Although the job may include the development of the story, the preparation of the treatment, or the writing of the shooting script, each of these tasks is done in relative isolation. To protect its members from loss of credit and status, the Writers Guild insists that the writer's work be highly restricted and noncollaborative. While this does not stop collaboration from occurring, it does illustrate the solitary nature of the writer's role in the process. The job for the writer will depend significantly on the relationship of the story to the screenplay. The writer of an original screenplay will typically play a much more central role than a person adapting a novel or dramatizing a true story.

3. Directors. According to the Directors Guild of America, the job of the director is "to contribute to all of the creative elements of a film and to participate in molding and integrating them into one cohesive dramatic and aesthetic whole."[7] This somewhat vague description nonetheless captures the essence of the director's role. The director (typically the filmmaker but not always, as described previously), supervises all the creative elements of the production, imprinting his vision of the story, sound, design, and essence of the film onto the project. Technically, the director need only be responsible for the actions of the cast and the camera; in reality, the director remains integral to the entire production.

Unlike with screenwriters, the use of multiple directors occurs rarely and results in significant confusion in those unfortunate situations where it is required. The director is usually attached to the project early and thereafter participates in all the other employment arrangements for the production. The director should know about, or help decide, virtually all issues involved with the production, including the casting, employment of other creative personnel, and creative decisions involving script, locations, set design, scheduling, and postproduction editing. The producer generally has authority over the director, but throughout most of preproduction and principal photography, the director has practical control over much of the project.

Since its inception in 1939, the role of the Directors Guild has traditionally been to provide representation on issues of credit, control, and finances. The DGA represents directors, assistant directors, and unit production managers. Because the motion picture has evolved into a director's medium more than the medium of any other artist, the union focuses primarily on its relationship with the studios. Within the independent filmmaking arena, the filmmakers are typically the directors, so the union has little to do in that respect. Nonetheless, the DGA Minimum Basic Agree-

---

7. BASIC AGREEMENT OF 2017, §7-101 (Directors Guild of America), https://www.dga.org/Contracts/Creative-Rights/Basic-Agreement-Article-7.aspx (last visited October 5, 2019).

ment can serve as a useful guide even in the context of low-budget nonunion film-making, and is mandatory for any union production. The DGA-MBA provides for compensation minimums, mandatory credit, and rules on the relationship between the director and the production company.

The DGA also offers a side letter that serves as a rider to the DGA-MBA, providing reduced director minimums. The side letter has changed in recent years to improve the opportunities for union directors to participate in low-budget productions. The side letter provides various minimum fees depending on the budget of the production. It also allows for the deferral of some of the director's payments.

4. Assistants. The team of unit production manager (UPM) and first assistant director (AD) fill out the senior management of the film production. The UPM implements the decisions of the producer, and the first AD implements those of the director.

The UPM oversees the logistical details of the production, working through the budget, scheduling, finance, travel, and myriad additional issues that affect the film. She will negotiate many of the agreements for the production and arrange (and re-arrange) the production schedule. On union productions, despite their budgetary role, UPM positions are governed by the Directors Guild.

A related position to the UPM is that of line producer. On an independent film, there is likely to be only a line producer or a UPM, but not both. In a larger production, the UPM may be a standing employee of the producer who moves from one film project to the next, serving each project exclusively while the producer provides nonexclusive services to a number of films at various stages of development. In this situation, the film company may also hire a line producer who has on-set operational responsibility for the film's expenses.

The first assistant director runs the set, ensuring that each day's schedule is ready for the director — that the call times for shooting, costuming, and makeup are co-ordinated so each cast member can be costumed and ready in time for his scheduled appearance. The first AD works with the cast and serves as an intermediary between cast and crew whenever necessary.

5. Actors. The actors portray the characters in the film. More formally, acting may be defined as "the performing art in which movement, gesture, and intonation are used to realize a fictional character for the stage, for motion pictures, or for television."[8] The task is as simple as that, but it remains perhaps the most difficult role in the creative arts. Some film roles may be portrayed by experienced professionals with years of training to project their emotions on film. Others are portrayed by untrained individuals who simply appear onscreen in the manner sought by the di-

---

8. *Acting, Encyclopedia Britannica Online*, www.britannica.com/EBchecked/topic/4329/acting (last visited October 5, 2019).

rector of the film. Casting choices are often the most fundamental to the success of the entire project.

3. The Antitrust Experience in Hollywood

For all its glamour, Hollywood has always been a small town, with everyone knowing each other's business. This aphorism was historically too accurate, with the industry being the subject of repeated antitrust actions. The most significant of these was *United States v. Paramount Pictures, Inc.*, 334 U.S. 131 (1948). Although the Supreme Court noted in passing that the motion picture was entitled to First Amendment protection, the Court quickly moved past this issue to ban the horizontal and vertical price fixing by the motion picture companies. As the Court explained, "The District Court found that two price-fixing conspiracies existed—a horizontal one between all the [the major motion picture distributors]; a vertical one between each distributor-defendant and its licensees." The Court, therefore, banned the practice of setting the minimum price for theatre tickets charged by the exhibitors. Similarly, it required the distributors divest themselves of their major ownership of the exhibitors to eliminate the vertical price fixing.

Another of the practices banned was block-booking. The Court explained that "[b]lock-booking is the practice of licensing, or offering for license, one feature or group of features on condition that the exhibitor will also license another feature or group of features released by the distributors during a given period. The films are licensed in blocks before they are actually produced." A corollary practice was blind-selling, described as "a practice whereby a distributor licenses a feature before the exhibitor is afforded an opportunity to view it." The practice was also barred:

> Where a high quality film greatly desired is licensed only if an inferior one is taken, the latter borrows quality from the former and strengthens its monopoly by drawing on the other. The practice tends to equalize rather than differentiate the reward for the individual copyrights. Even where all the films included in the package are of equal quality, the requirement that all be taken if one is desired increases the market for some. Each stands not on its own footing but in whole or in part on the appeal which another film may have. As the District Court said, the result is to add to the monopoly of the copyright in violation of the principle of the patent cases involving tying clauses.

Finally, the Court banned all practices that discriminated against the smaller, independent theatre chains, requiring the studios to engage in open, competitive bidding for the films once they were completed and available for viewing. The results of *United States v. Paramount* swept through Hollywood, fundamentally altering the financial structure of the old studios and paving the way for the rise of independent producers.

The continuing antitrust activities remained the focus of significant court action. In *United States v. Loew's, Inc.*, 371 U.S. 38 (1962), the Supreme Court barred the practice of block-booking to television stations. The Court summed up the antitrust violation simply: "To use the trial court's apt example, forcing a television station which wants 'Gone With The Wind' to take 'Getting Gertie's Garter' as well is taking undue advantage of the fact that to television as well as motion picture viewers there is but one 'Gone With The Wind.'" The Court allowed motion pictures to be sold in blocks or groups, but only if "there is no requirement, express or implied, for the purchase of more than one film." This caveat allowed the film studios to copy the copyright licensing approach of the performing rights societies such as ASCAP and BMI—licensing each work individually or in groups to maximize efficiency.

Notes and Questions

a. With Disney's acquisition of Fox, there are very few motion picture studios left—Disney, Paramount, Warner Bros., and Universal. But the question of monopoly power may be misplaced, since the market for competition may not really be among the four remaining studios but the competition between film and its rival entertainment media, such as videogames.

b. The motion picture industry remains one of the most unionized sectors of the U.S. economy. These collective bargaining agreements are essential to retain the high quality of employment opportunities within the industry. Each job is hotly contested by the unions. *See Am. Fed'n of Musicians of U.S. & Can. v. Paramount Pictures Corp.*, 903 F.3d 968, 971 (9th Cir. 2018).

> Since at least 1946, major motion picture studios and the musicians, conductors, and orchestras who score motion pictures have agreed to a series of collective bargaining agreements governing the musicians' hiring, wages, and work conditions when they score a motion picture for a signatory studio. This case concerns whether Paramount Pictures breached a recent vintage of those agreements, the Basic Theatrical Motion Picture Agreement of 2010 ("Basic Agreement"). The musicians' bargaining representative, the American Federation of Musicians of the United States and Canada ("AFM"), sued Paramount—a signatory to the Basic Agreement—after the motion picture Same Kind of Different as Me ("SKODAM") was scored in Slovakia. AFM alleged that Paramount breached its obligation under Article 3 of the Basic Agreement to score domestically, with AFM musicians, any motion picture that it produces domestically....

> The Basic Agreement is a labor agreement involving scoring musicians, and Article 3 functions as a work preservation provision that dictates when a signatory has to hire those musicians. Therefore, Article 3 applies when a signatory studio produces a motion picture and has authority over the hiring and employment of scoring musicians.

The Ninth Circuit remanded to determine whether Paramount had produced the film. It rejected the district court's interpretation "that a studio produces a motion picture when the studio 'makes' or 'shoots' the principal photography," explaining that "[w]hether a studio also employs the cast and crew is not relevant to Article 3."

c. Although many of these cases seem to be part of Hollywood's ancient lore, the battles and antitrust accusations continue. *See Six West Retail Acquisition, Inc. v. Sony Theatre Mgmt. Corp.*, 203 F.R.D. 98, 51 Fed. R. Serv. 3d (West) (S.D.N.Y. 2001) (Sony, which now owns some of the Loews theaters, was accused of block-booking and refusing to deal with a small, exhibitor chain).

d. Many states also regulated the practices of exclusive theatrical runs, blind-bidding, block-booking, and other anticompetitive activities. These statutes have generally been upheld as constitutional. *See Associated Film Distribution Corp. v. Thornburgh*, 614 F. Supp. 1100 (E.D. Pa. 1985); *Allied Artists Pictures Corp. v. Rhodes*, 496 F. Supp. 408 (S.D. Ohio 1980). Nonetheless, recent changes to copyright jurisprudence have brought some of these decisions into question. *See Orson, Inc. v. Miramax Film Corp.*, 189 F.3d 377 (3d Cir. 1999) (determining that the exhibition regulations were preempted by federal copyright law).

e. Given the requirements that distributors no longer engage in blind-selling, the studios regularly screen movies prior to their sale. Nonetheless, the distributors often try to promote these films to the greatest extent possible. At what point does the promise of the next big blockbuster move from hype to guarantee? *See Presidio Enters., Inc. v. Warner Bros. Distrib. Corp.*, 784 F.2d 674 (5th Cir. 1986).

B. Production Agreements and Budgets

1. Film Finance and Control

Despite comments that film is primarily a filmmaker's medium, production expenses and marketing expenses can sometimes exceed $250 million, making each major film a huge financial commitment. As a result, the motion picture studios/distributors wield tremendous influence on every aspect of the film.

A small percentage of films are created directly by the motion picture studio itself. The more typical arrangement, however, is the negative pick-up agreement, whereby an independent film company is formed for purpose of creating a film. This is the type of agreement litigated in *Filmline (Cross-Country) Productions, Inc. v. United Artists*, below. In this arrangement, the distributor agrees to purchase the final film (at the completed negative stage) in exchange for a set price. This assures the distributor that any overruns are paid by the producer rather than the distributor. At each stage in the process, the distributor must verify and approve of compliance with the budget and the agreed-upon script. Payments are made in increments, which are timed to the production schedule.

Smaller films are often financed independently of the distributors and sold to distributors after they are completed. While a few independent films reap both critical acclaim and financial windfalls for their creators and financial backers, the vast majority of these films are never exhibited to the general public and result in complete financial losses for their investors.

2. Final Cut

Depending on the contractual arrangement, the director's influence over the final project will vary. For a director, the most important aspect of control stems from the concept of final cut. The most successful or most influential of directors negotiate the final approval rights over the content of their films. Even these rights are not absolute. The directors must meet all the contractual preconditions to exercise such control. Typically, this means that the film must be edited to an agreed length (typically somewhere between 93–120 minutes), conform to an agreed MPAA rating (most likely PG-13), come within budget (including all pre-approved overages), and substantially contain the same scenes and dialogue as provided in the final shooting script.

Steven Spielberg exercised such a degree of final cut over *Schindler's List* that he retained the right to personally supervise the film's adaptation into every foreign language and every foreign censorship edit. Because disputes over final cut are covered by the Directors Guild collective bargaining agreement, these cases are not typically reported. The few reported cases involve editing for television. Chapter 13 details the leading cases involving final cut and the editing for television that regularly occur.

The most significant benefit to directing an independently financed film is the autonomy it affords. Because there is no distributor financing, there rarely is the type of editorial pressure on the filmmaker that occurs with studio pictures. Nonetheless, distributors will sometimes insist on changes to films as a condition of purchasing them for distribution. In this vein, the director is never completely free from outside influences.

3. Motion Picture Budgets

The motion picture budget can range from a few thousand dollars for digital equipment rental and pizza to hundreds of millions of dollars. Whatever the budget, the primary structure and approach remain the same.

The budgets are divided into halves—above the line and below the line. Above the line expenses are those marquee components of the motion picture, such as the fees for the stars, director, writer, and producer. Everything else is below the line. Typical Hollywood budgeting sets the above the line and below the line costs in an informal equilibrium. As the budget for stars and director grow more lavish, so do the expenses below the line for locations, designs, travel, costumes and other elements of the production.

The rise of the special effects movie, exemplified by trilogies such as *The Matrix* and *Lord of the Rings*, suggests a new model for budgeting, with special effects constituting such a large starring role and percentage of the budget that the above the line expenses must be reduced to afford production. Steven Spielberg's *Jurassic Park* established this new approach by casting dinosaurs as the stars and forgoing the costs of hiring a bankable cast.

At the other end of the spectrum, a 35mm independent film can still be made for $5–$10 million with the production values and professional cast and crew comparable to that of the blockbuster. Films shot using digital technology can be made with less equipment and simpler lighting and power requirements, so these films can be shot at an even lower budget. As a result, the costs that determine the budget of a motion picture may emphasize the cost for the cast members, the cost for the locations, the cost for the special effects, or a combination of all those attributes.

Filmline (Cross-Country) Productions, Inc. v. United Artists Corp.

865 F.2d 513 (2d Cir. 1989)

This is an action for damages resulting from an alleged breach of contract. Defendants appeal from a judgment awarding plaintiffs damages in the amount of $2,189,889 plus $869,900 in prejudgment interest after a trial without a jury.

The subject matter of this suit is a letter agreement dated as of February 11, 1982 [for a "negative pick-up agreement] (the "Agreement"), as amended, between defendant United Artists Corp. ("UA") and plaintiffs Filmline (Cross-Country) Productions, Inc. ("Filmline") and Yellowbill Finance Limited ("Yellowbill") for the production of a film entitled "Cross Country" (the "Picture"). The Agreement called for Filmline to produce the Picture, with interim financing to be provided by Yellowbill, and obliged UA to purchase the Picture if Filmline produced it in accordance with the terms of the Agreement. Provision for the interim financing was made in a separate contract between Filmline and Yellowbill.

The Picture was produced, but UA acted to terminate the Agreement as production drew to a conclusion, asserting unacceptable variation from "an approved screenplay." The district court found that UA's stated reason for repudiating the contract was a pretext, the real reason being that UA sought to avoid a financial commitment to the picture. The district court held that while UA had a right to terminate prior to filming, it waived that right by failing to exercise it in a timely fashion and by participating in the actual filming of the picture. Thus, UA's later repudiation of its obligation to purchase and distribute the picture was deemed to constitute a breach of the contract. We affirm.

The basic events underlying this dispute are the formation of the Agreement between Filmline, UA and Yellowbill for the production of the Picture, an ensuing period during which the screenplay was revised, the actual filming of the Picture which began on May 11, 1982, and UA's repudiation of the Agreement on June 24, 1982 when the filming of the Picture was two days from completion. The Agreement provided that Yellowbill would finance the film, that Filmline would produce it, and that UA would purchase the Picture upon completion. Central to the case is UA's right of approval of the screenplay for the Picture under the Agreement.

Section 5 of the Agreement states that "UA shall have the following approvals with respect to the production of the Picture," specifying the director of the Picture, the screenplay writer, lead actors and actresses, the director of photography, the production designer and the film editor, but not the screenplay itself. Section 2 of the Agreement, which deals with development of the screenplay, provides:

> UA shall read and submit to [Filmline] such comments, if any, as it may have with respect to each draft of the screenplay. [Filmline] shall cause each draft of the screenplay to be rewritten in accordance with UA's suggested changes. The foregoing procedure shall be repeated until such time as UA and [Filmline] are satisfied with the final screenplay to be utilized for the production of the picture. UA and [Filmline] agree to accomplish the foregoing as promptly as reasonably possible so as not to frustrate the timely production of the Picture.

Section 15 of the Agreement states Filmline's obligation to produce the picture in conformity with the approved screenplay, and UA's resulting obligation to purchase, in the following terms:

> Provided that the Picture shall be produced in strict conformity with the approved screenplay and story board (except only for such minor changes as may be required by the exigencies of production), and provided further that [Filmline] has performed all of its obligations hereunder and is not in breach of any representation, warranty, covenants or agreements hereunder, UA agrees to pay to [Filmline] upon full delivery of the Picture ... a sum ... in an amount equal to the final certified negative cost of the Picture ... up to the sum of Two Million Five Hundred Thousand Dollars ($2,500,000)....

Similarly, Section 3(b) of the financing agreement between Filmline and Yellowbill provides that "the Film shall be based on the Script, as approved pursuant to the UA Agreement, except for minor deviations of the kind usual in the course of production of a film."

Section 4.01 of UA's "Standard Terms and Conditions" (the "Terms") provides in part:

> In the event [Filmline] shall breach or become in default of performance of any material term, condition or covenant contained in this Agreement, or shall breach any representation or warranty contained in this Agreement, and shall fail to cure, correct or remedy such breach or default *within thirty (30) days after service of written notice specifying same*, ... United may:
>
> > (1) terminate this Agreement in its entirety and be relieved of any obligations to advance or cause to be advanced any further monies or to pay the Purchase Price for the Picture or any part thereof....

All rights and remedies to United under this agreement are cumulative and the exercise of one shall not limit or affect its right concurrently or subsequently to exercise any other rights or remedies as it may have at law, in equity, under this Agreement or otherwise (emphasis added).

Section 8.04 of the Terms states that "this Agreement shall be construed and interpreted under the laws of the State of New York governing agreements which are wholly executed and performed therein."

UA entered into the Agreement based upon its evaluation of an initial draft of the screenplay. UA's agent in these activities was Charles Lippincott, vice president of acquisitions, who reviewed the initial screenplay and subsequent alterations. After reviewing the initial draft of the screenplay, Lippincott requested a number of alterations. On April 17, 1982, Lippincott met with Pieter Kroonenberg, one of the principals of Filmline, to discuss a revised draft of the screenplay dated April 13, 1982. Lippincott expressed his dissatisfaction with the April 13th screenplay and repeated requests for certain modifications. On April 19, 1982, UA (for whom Lippincott acted), Filmline and Yellowbill entered into an amendment (the "April Amendment") to the Agreement which provides in part:

> This will confirm the approval by UA of the following elements:
>
> > (a) The April 13, 1982 revised screenplay, as further revised in accordance with the changes agreed to by UA and Filmline on April 17, 1982, provided that it is acknowledged that UA reserves the right to request minor changes to said screenplay prior to the confirmed May 11, 1982 start date of principal photography. . . .

The April Amendment also included approvals of the casting as to four characters, the "story board as to Scenes 1B through 35C," the director of photography, the production designer and the film editor (subject to the later enlistment of a supervisory film editor "at UA's request and subject to UA's approval").

Some revisions were made to the April 13 screenplay, resulting in a final screenplay, to be used for filming, dated May 7, 1982. Lippincott reviewed this final screenplay on May 11, 1982, which was also the date for commencement of filming. The district court determined that the May 7th screenplay did not make the orally agreed changes required by the April Amendment. Thus, after Lippincott's May 11th review, UA had the right to terminate the contract, subject to a thirty day right of cure by Filmline. Lippincott chose, however, not to give notice of termination. Instead, Lippincott actively participated in the filming, reviewing further revisions of the screenplay and appearing on the scene of shooting from May 11 to May 16 and June 1 to June 4. On several occasions, Lippincott assured plaintiffs that production was proceeding acceptably. Only on June 20, 1982, did Lippincott complain to plaintiffs that he did not believe that the picture was working out as he had hoped.

On June 24, 1982, independent developments within UA precipitated the termination. UA's senior management had evidently been misinformed as to the existence of a UA commitment to purchase the Picture. Discovery of the commitment by Lippincott's superiors was followed by a telephone conversation with Lippincott in which he apprised senior management of his growing pessimism about the commercial prospects for the film. Immediately thereafter, UA transmitted a termination notice to Filmline which stated in part:

> It has come to our attention that (A) the Picture is not being produced *in strict conformity with the approved screenplay* and storyboard, (B) you have failed to perform certain of your obligations under the Agreement (including,

without limitation, your obligation to obtain UA's approval as to certain production and creative elements and to fully and in good faith consult with UA as to certain other creative elements), and (C) you have breached certain of your representations, warranties, covenants and agreements contained in the Agreement (including, without limitation, the covenants relating to (A) and (B) above).

Based on the foregoing, this is to advise you that UA's obligations under the Agreement are hereby terminated and that US [sic] will not accept delivery of the Picture if and when completed. Nor will UA pay you the Cash Purchase Price (as defined in paragraph 15 of the Agreement) for the Picture in the event you attempt to tender delivery of the completed Picture to UA.

UA's purported notice of termination included no provision for Filmline to cure, correct or remedy its asserted defaults. Filmline's counsel responded promptly in writing, denying any breach on Filmline's part and contending that UA's purported notice of termination was itself an anticipatory breach of the Agreement.

Filmline and Yellowbill subsequently arranged for alternate distribution, but the Picture was a commercial failure. On January 26, 1983, Filmline and Yellowbill commenced the instant litigation. Prior to the trial of the case, the district court denied a motion by UA to dismiss or stay the action in favor of a California state court action initiated by UA, or alternatively for a transfer of the action to the United States District Court for the Central District of California pursuant to 28 U.S.C. § 1404(a) (1982). After trial, the district court ruled that UA had waived its right to terminate for failure of the screenplay to conform with the provisions of the April Amendment, determined the various damages issues tendered by the parties, and concluded that UA was liable to Filmline and Yellowbill in the amount of $2,189,889, plus pre-judgment interest on that amount from January 26, 1983. This appeal followed.

It is undisputed that this diversity action is governed by New York law. Indeed, as noted earlier, Section 8.04 of the Terms explicitly so provides.

UA's purported notice of termination specified that the Picture was "not being produced in strict conformity with the approved screenplay and storyboard...." Both at trial, and on appeal, however, UA contended that there was never an approved screenplay, because the requirement stated in the April Amendment that the screenplay be "further revised in accordance with the changes agreed to by UA and Filmline on April 17, 1982" had never been fulfilled. UA contends that it allowed Filmline to go forward with screening of the Picture and attempt to bring it into conformity with "the changes agreed to by UA and Filmline on April 17, 1982," and legitimately terminated the Agreement and UA's responsibilities thereunder when Filmline failed in that attempt. The district court rejected that position, concluding that New York law required an election by UA either to terminate on May 11, 1982, prior to the inception of filming, or to waive the breach that had by then become manifest and continue performance under the contract.

We concur in the district court's general view of New York law. UA, however, cites to us New York authorities which mitigate the rigor of this rule. *Lenkay Sani Products Corp. v. Benitez*, 47 A.D.2d 524, 362 N.Y.S.2d 572 (2d Dep't 1975), is typical. In *Lenkay*, machines were delivered which did not function properly, and the buyer offered the manufacturer an opportunity to remedy the defects. When this effort failed, the buyer sued to recover the partial payments it had made for the machinery, and the manufacturer counterclaimed for the balance of the purchase price, claiming acceptance by the buyer and waiver of the defects. The Appellate Division rejected this contention, stating:

> Where a buyer has knowledge that the goods do not conform to the contract specifications, but nevertheless accepts them, he may revoke his acceptance and rescind the contract if the acceptance was on the reasonable assumption that the nonconformity would be seasonably cured, but cure was not effected.

Although this decision was premised upon a specific provision of the Uniform Commercial Code, other New York cases apply the principle more broadly. We applied this rule in *S.D. Hicks & Son Co. v. J.T. Baker Chemical Co.*, 307 F.2d 750 (2d Cir. 1962), a diversity case governed by New York law. In that case, defendant undertook to construct a chemical processing plant and guaranteed its performance. Defendant then sought additional compensation for bringing the finished plant into compliance with the guarantee, contending that the buyer's initial acceptance of the plant constituted a waiver of the guarantee. We rejected that contention, stating:

> [T]here is no warrant for the position that a party to a contract waives his rights under the contract by failing to insist upon performance at the due date and by urging and encouraging the other party to perform thereafter.

We would have some difficulty in applying the rule for which UA contends to the facts of this case, given the equivocal conduct of the parties at the inception of the shooting of the Picture, and the foreknowledge of all parties that Filmline would incur the bulk of its expense in performing the Agreement by shooting the Picture. We deem the inquiry mooted, however, because even on the assumption that Filmline was in breach and UA was entitled to terminate when it purported to do so on June 24, 1982, it is clear that UA's notice of termination did not conform to the Agreement and was therefore ineffective under New York law.

Specifically, UA's purported notice of termination made no effort to comply with the explicit requirement, stated in section 4.01 of the Terms, that Filmline was to be accorded an opportunity "to cure, correct or remedy such breach or default within thirty days of written notice specifying same...." Under New York law, that defect is fatal to UA's position.

In *General Supply and Constr. Co. v. Goelet*, 241 N.Y. 28, 148 N.E. 778 (1925), remittitur amended, 241 N.Y. 507, 150 N.E. 532 (1925), the defendant purported to terminate a contract for the construction of a building. As the court described it, the contract provided "that the owner might terminate the contract at any time upon certificate of the architect that the work was being unreasonably delayed and that such delay was sufficient ground for termination of the contract." 241 N.Y. at 34, 148 N.E. at 779. Rejecting the owner's purported termination of the contract without obtaining the contractually required certificate, the Court of Appeals stated:

> Though [the owner] may have been justified ... in his belief that the contractor would not thereafter mend his ways and finish the work within a reasonable time, yet where such delay did not amount to abandonment [the owner] could not rescind the contract for that reason, *except according to its terms.*... Having indicated purpose to keep the contract alive in spite of delays on the part of the contractor, the owner could not suddenly abandon the purpose and treat as essential an element of the contract which he had previously waived, as ground for termination. The termination of the contract in this case without the required previous notice and without a certificate from the architect *in accordance with the terms of the contract* was wrongful....

We conclude that on this record, New York courts would apply the clear New York rule requiring termination of a contract in accordance with its terms.... Accordingly, since UA's purported termination was in violation of the terms of the Agreement, it was inoperative and plaintiffs are entitled to recover for breach of contract.

The district court reached this result by a different route, concluding that by allowing the filming of the Picture to proceed on May 11, 1982, UA waived Filmline's failure to conform the Picture to the requirements of the April Amendment.[9] As indicated earlier, we do not deem it necessary to resolve the waiver issue. That is, we conclude that whether or not UA waived Filmline's failure to conform the screenplay to the requirements of the April Amendment, UA's purported notice of termination dated June 24, 1982 was in any event ineffective under New York law because it did not comply with the Agreement. It is settled that we may affirm on any basis that is supported by the record, regardless of the ground upon which the trial court relied.

UA contends that the district court vastly overstated the damages properly recoverable, assuming a breach of contract. Specifically, UA argues that the district court erroneously rejected UA's contention that "the plaintiffs' damages must be reduced by the amount it would cost plaintiffs to reshoot the entire Picture in strict conformity

---

9. The district court also found that UA's purported notice of termination was pretextual, although not relying upon that finding for its conclusion as to liability. This finding was amply supported by the record, especially by testimony from an arbitration to which UA was a party, introduced into evidence at the trial below, which demonstrated that UA's notice of termination was motivated by a desire to extricate UA from its obligations under the Agreement when UA's senior management belatedly learned its provisions on or about June 24, 1982. Again, in view of the failure of UA's purported notice of termination to comply with the requirements of the Agreement, we need not reach the question whether a pretextual motivation might in some circumstances invalidate an otherwise effective termination.

with the May 7 screenplay." The district court concluded that "had UA not wrongfully terminated the contract, UA would have and in good faith could have only required Filmline to conform to the May 7 screenplay the eleven scenes which [UA] actually preferred in the May 7 version," at a cost of $20,901. These determinations are not clearly erroneous, and are accordingly affirmed.... The judgment of the district court is affirmed.

Buchwald v. Paramount Pictures, Corp.

1990 Cal. App. LEXIS 634, 13 U.S.P.Q.2d (BNA)
1497 (Cal. Super. Ct. Jan. 31,1990)

At the outset the Court desires to indicate what this case is and is not about. It is not about whether Art Buchwald or Eddie Murphy is more creative. It is clear to the Court that each of these men is a creative genius in his own field and each is an uniquely American institution. This case is also not about whether Eddie Murphy made substantial contributions to the film "Coming to America." The Court is convinced he did. Finally, this case is not about whether Eddie Murphy "stole" Art Buchwald's concept "King for a Day." Rather, this case is primarily a breach of contract case between Buchwald and Paramount (not Murphy) which must be decided by reference to the agreement between the parties and the rules of contract construction, as well as the principals of law enunciated in the applicable legal authorities.

As indicated, the starting point for the analysis of this case is the contract between Buchwald and Paramount. Pursuant to this agreement Buchwald transferred to Paramount "the sole and exclusive motion picture and other rights" to the "original story and concept written by Art Buchwald ... tentatively entitled 'KING FOR A DAY', also known as 'It's a Crude, Crude World' (which material, as defined in said Standard Terms is hereinafter called the 'Work')." In the agreement Buchwald warranted "[t]hat the Work is original with Author; that neither the Work nor any part thereof are taken from or based upon any other material or any motion picture...." As is pertinent to the present case, the agreement provided that:

> "'Work' means the aforementioned Material and includes all prior, present and future versions, adaptations and translations thereof (whether written by Author or by others), its theme, story, plot, characters and their names, its title or titles and subtitles, if any,..., and each and every part of all thereof. 'Work' does not include the material referred to in paragraph 2(f) above, written or prepared by Purchaser or under Purchaser's Authority."

Finally, the agreement entitled Buchwald to certain "contingent consideration" "[f]or the first theatrical motion picture (the 'Picture'): If, but only if, a feature length theatrical motion picture shall be produced based upon Author's Work."

Since the agreement provided Buchwald was entitled to payment only if Paramount produced "a feature length theatrical motion picture" "based upon Author's Work," the threshold inquiry in this case is what is meant by the term "based upon." Because the term is not defined in the contract, it was the Court's hope that the term had a specific meaning in the entertainment industry and that the experts who testified would so indicate. Unfortunately, there was as little agreement among the experts concerning the meaning of this term as there was between plaintiffs and Paramount concerning whether "Coming to America" is based upon Buchwald's treatment. For example, David Kirkpatrick testified that his understanding of "based upon," as used in the entertainment industry, is that "there exists some underlying antecedents that triggered the realization of the story in a screenplay." ...

Since the Court found the testimony of the entertainment experts, both individually and collectively, to be of little value with respect to the "based upon" issue, the Court turned to the appellate decisions of this State for guidance. Fortunately, that guidance existed. Indeed, as will be discussed more fully below, the Court believes these decisions provide a road map through the "based upon" mine field.

In cases involving infringement, which this case is not, it has been held that an inference of copying may arise where there is proof of access to the material with a showing of similarity.... These same rules have been applied in a case involving a cause of action alleging breach of an express contract.

In the present case, there is no real issue concerning Eddie Murphy's access to Buchwald's concept. Indeed, the evidence is that Murphy knew about Buchwald's concept. Specifically, it is undisputed that in the spring of 1983, Paramount creative executives Kirkpatrick and Katzenberg met with Murphy and his manager, Robert Wachs, at the Ma Maison Restaurant and discussed Buchwald's concept with them. In fact, it was reported that Murphy was positively responsive to the "King for a Day" presentation and indicated that he liked playing the African character in the movie "Trading Places." Murphy himself testified (by way of deposition) that he had "a very vague recollection, maybe of Jeff [Katzenberg] going into the 'King for a Day' thing. 'You'd be great in it.'" Murphy further testified that Katzenberg "liked the idea of it, I guess, 'cause I remember."

There is other, persuasive evidence on the issue of access. For example, on June 6, 1983, Kirkpatrick sent Wachs a short outline of Buchwald's "King for a Day." Wachs admitted that he read at least part of the Buchwald's treatment. Finally, there is evidence that Kirkpatrick discussed "King for a Day" with Eddie Murphy on at least three occasions subsequent to the meeting at the Ma Maison Restaurant in the spring of 1983.

Since there is no real issue concerning access, the focus must then be on the question of similarity. Similarity is, of course, a question of fact for the trier of fact to determine. The parties have directed a substantial amount of their attention to the issue of similarity. Paramount contends that there must be substantial similarity between Buchwald's treatment and "Coming to America" in order for Buchwald to succeed in this case....

Although the Court believes the cases relied upon by Paramount are inapplicable to the issue of the extent of similarity that is required in this case, the Court has concluded the two controlling cases with respect to this issue are *Fink* [*v. Goodson-Todman*

Enterprises, Ltd., 9 Cal. App. 3d 996, 1013 (1970)], and *Weitzenkorn* [*v. Lesser*, 40 Cal. 2d 778 (1953)].

In Fink, as in the present case, the contract between the parties obligated the defendant to compensate the plaintiff if the defendant created a series "based on Plaintiff's Program or any material element contained in [it]." The Court stated that a "'[m]aterial element' could range from a mere basic theme up to an extensively elaborated idea, depending upon what might be proved as the concept of the parties." With respect to the contract cause of action, the Court framed the issue: "[W]hether ... defendants have based their series on a material element of plaintiff's program." The Court noted that its "based on any material element" test was "quite close to the concept of 'inspiration for' which was the key to the upholding of an implied contract count in *Minniear v. Tors,* 266 Cal. App. 2d 495, 505 [(1968)]."

Similarly, in *Weitzenkorn, supra,* the contract obligated the defendants to pay for plaintiffs' composition "if they used it or any portion of it, regardless of its originality."

Based on the decisions in *Fink* and *Weitzenkorn,* and the contract involved in this case, the Court concludes that Paramount's obligation to pay Buchwald arose if "Coming to America" is based upon a material element of or was inspired by Buchwald's treatment. As the Court in Fink noted, this determination is to be made by searching for "points of similarity" both quantitatively and qualitatively. It is to this search that the Court now turns.

Before engaging in a comparison of "King for a Day" and "Coming to America," the Court wishes to state the obvious. Specifically, plaintiff has the burden of proving similarity by a preponderance of the evidence. "'Preponderance of the evidence' means evidence that has more convincing force than that opposed to it."

In Buchwald's treatment, a rich, educated, arrogant, extravagant, despotic African potentate comes to America for a state visit. After being taken on a grand tour of the United States, the potentate arrives at the White House. A gaffe in remarks made by the President infuriates the African leader. His sexual desires are rebuffed by a black woman State Department officer assigned to him. She is requested by the President to continue to serve as the potentate's United States escort. While in the United States, the potentate is deposed, deserted by his entourage and left destitute. He ends up in the Washington ghetto, is stripped of his clothes, and befriended by a black lady. The potentate experiences a number of incidents in the ghetto, and obtains employment as a waiter. In order to avoid extradition, he marries the black lady who befriended him, becomes the emperor of the ghetto and lives happily ever after.

In "Coming to America" the pampered prince of a mythical African kingdom (Zamunda) wakes up on his 21st birthday to find that the day for his prearranged marriage has arrived. Discovering his bride to be very subservient and being unhappy about that fact, he convinces his father to permit him to go to America for the ostensible purpose of sowing his "royal oats." In fact, the prince intends to go to America to find an independent woman to marry. The prince and his friend go to Queens, New

York, where their property is stolen and they begin living in a slum area. The prince discovers his true love, Lisa, whose father—McDowell—operates a fast-food restaurant for whom the prince and his friend begin to work. The prince and Lisa fall in love, but when the King and Queen come to New York and it is disclosed who the prince is, Lisa rejects the prince's marriage invitation. The film ends with Lisa appearing in Zamunda, marrying the prince and apparently living happily ever after.

There are, to be sure, differences between Buchwald's "King for a Day" and "Coming to America." However, as noted above, where, as here, the evidence of access is overwhelming, less similarity is required. Moreover, "'[E]ven if the similar material is quantitatively small, if it is qualitatively important … the trier of fact … may properly find substantial similarity.'"

In his opening statement, counsel for plaintiffs made the following comparison of "King for a Day" and "Coming to America":

> Both are modern day comedies. The protagonist is a young black member of royalty from a mythical African kingdom, pampered and extremely wealthy, well-educated. They both come to a large city on the American East Coast. And they arrive as a fish out of water from this foreign kingdom.
>
> Abruptly, finding themselves without royal trappings of money and power, they end up in the black, urban American ghetto, about as far culturally as they could ever hope to be from their pampered, royal status in their mythical kingdom. Each character abandons his regal attitudes. Both live in the ghetto as poor blacks experiencing the realities of ghetto life.
>
> Each takes a menial job as (sic) a series of harrowing and comedic adventures in the ghetto, is humanized and enriched by his experiences. Love always triumphing over all, each meets and falls in love with a beautiful young American woman whom he will marry and make his Queen and live happily ever after in his mythical African kingdom.

The Court agrees with this comparison. In fact, the Court believes that these similarities alone, given the language of the contract involved in this case and the law that liability in a contract case can arise even if a non-substantial element is copied, might well be sufficient to impose contract liability on Paramount. The fact is, however, that other compelling evidence of similarity exists.

In the original script written by Tab Murphy that was indisputably based upon Buchwald's treatment, the king ends up as an employee of a fast food restaurant where he ultimately foils a robbery attempt by use of a mop. In "Coming to America" the prince is also employed by a fast food restaurant and foils a robbery attempt by use of a mop. These similar "gimmicks" provide compelling evidence that the evolution of plaintiffs' idea provided an inspiration for "Coming to America." …

There are other factors that are present in this case that strongly support plaintiffs' position that Buchwald's original concept and its subsequent development at Paramount was the inspiration for "Coming to America." For example, the evidence is overwhelming that for two years Paramount considered "King for a Day" to be a project that was being developed for Eddie Murphy. In fact, when "Coming to America" was made, its star was Eddie Murphy. Additionally, during the development of "King for a Day" it was contemplated Murphy would portray multiple characters. In "Coming to America" he did.

Moreover, when "King for a Day" was under development, Paramount sought to interest John Landis in directing the movie. On July 1, 1983, David Kirkpatrick of Paramount sent to Landis a description of "King for a Day." In fact, Landis directed "Coming to America." The fact that Landis was aware of Buchwald's concept for "King for a Day" is important. Since the evidence revealed that Landis had creative input into "Coming to America," it is his access and knowledge, in addition to Eddie Murphy's, that it is relevant to the issue of similarity.

It is also important to observe that one of the promotional ideas utilized in connection with "Coming to America" was a "King for a Day" concept where a prize winner was afforded the opportunity to go on a shopping spree.

As indicated above, there are differences between Buchwald's treatment and "Coming to America." One of the principal differences is that the king in Buchwald's original treatment was despotic, while the prince in "Coming to America" is kind and naive. The fact is, however, that early in the development process Paramount desired to make Buchwald's king more likable. Indeed, by the time Francis Veber submitted his second script, which was clearly based upon Buchwald's original treatment, the king had none of his despotic characteristics. As indicated above the Court believes that "Coming to America" must be compared with the Buchwald treatment as it was developed in the Tab Murphy and Veber scripts.

The other significant difference between Buchwald's treatment and "Coming to America" is the motivation that brought the principal character to America. In Buchwald's treatment the motivation was to obtain military weapons from the United States. In "Coming to America" it was to find an independent wife. This dissimilarity does not, however, require a finding that "Coming to America" is not "based upon" Buchwald's work.

In many ways, the decision in *Weitzenkorn, supra,* is similar to the present case. *Weitzenkorn* was a breach of contract case in which the plaintiff sued to recover damages by reason of the defendant's use of her Tarzan/Fountain of Youth idea. Although both plaintiff's idea and the defendant's movie involved Tarzan, there were striking dissimilarities between the two. In plaintiff's story, Tarzan entered the area where the Fountain of Youth was located because he was captured by the evil persons who dwelled in the area. By contrast, in the defendant's version Tarzan voluntarily entered the area which was occupied by a king who was a friend of Tarzan. In plaintiff's version, Tarzan undertook his journey to rescue Boy. In defendant's version, Tarzan was on a mission of mercy to find a missing aviatrix. In plaintiff's version, the evil queen and her subjects disintegrated when Tarzan destroyed the Fountain of Youth. In defendant's version, the ending was totally different.

In *Weitzenkorn* the Court found no similarity as to form and manner of expression between plaintiff's composition and defendant's movie. Although both works included the same characters in Africa being involved with a mythical Fountain of Youth, the moral of each was entirely different. Specifically, the moral of plaintiff's work was that eternal youth was not a blessing. The moral of defendant's work was that eternal youth was a reward for good.

In spite of the significant differences between plaintiff's and defendant's work, the Court concluded that the trial court had erroneously sustained the demurrers of the defendants without leave to amend. Because the defendants had expressly agreed to compensate the plaintiff if they used plaintiff's composition, or any portion of it, the Court concluded that plaintiff's complaint stated a cause of action "no matter how slight or commonplace the portion which" the defendants used.

Finally, *Blaustein v. Burton,* 9 Cal. App. 3d 961 (1970), is also instructive. In this case plaintiff's idea of using Richard Burton and Elizabeth Taylor as the stars of "Taming of the Shrew," together with several ideas with respect to how and where the movie should be made, was held to give rise to contract liability.

Based upon the authorities discussed above and the provisions of the contract involved in this case, the Court concludes that "Coming to America" is a movie that was "based upon" Buchwald's treatment "King for a Day." "Bearing in mind the unlimited access ... [proved] in this case and the rule that the stronger the access the less striking and numerous the similarities need be, ... [the Court concludes that Paramount has] appropriated and used a qualitatively important part of plaintiff's material in such a way that features discernible in ... [Paramount's] work are substantially similar thereto."[10]

Finally, the Court wishes again to emphasize that its decision is in no way intended to disparage the creative talent of Eddie Murphy. It was Paramount and not Murphy who prepared the agreement in question. It is Paramount and not Murphy that obligated itself to compensate Buchwald if any material element of Buchwald's treatment was utilized in or inspired a film produced by Paramount. "Coming to America" is no less the product of Eddie Murphy's creativity because of the Court's decision than it was before this decision was rendered....

The Court understands there will now be an accounting phase of this case. The Court desires to make it clear that, depending on the evidence adduced during the accounting phase, the possibility exists that Paramount's accounting practices may make the imposition of tort damages appropriate.

Notes and Questions

a. Both the *based upon* clause and the *pay or play* clause of production agreements create significant controversy. These terms are traditional entertainment clauses which

---

10. The statement by Judge Learned Hand in *Fred Fisher, Inc. v. Dillingham,* 293 F.145 (1924), is appropriate to quote at this point. Judge Hand stated: "Everything registers somewhere in our memories, and no one can tell what may evoke it." Eddie Murphy, with commendable candor, admitted as much when he testified (by way of deposition) that he did not know "what triggers my subconscious."

have no corollary in copyright law or in any other professions or industries. As a result, courts struggle to interpret them, often with only the vaguest notions of industry trade and custom.

b. Pay or Play agreements reflect the opportunity costs associated with agreeing to participate in a project without knowing whether it will actually take place. Producing a movie is a chicken-or-the-egg proposition. Without the right cast, no one will finance or green-light the project; without the financing and green-light, no top talent will agree to commit to the project. There are two methods available to break this impasse. First, the agreement may be conditional. For example, the financing of a film may be conditioned on the commitment of a particular cast or director. The obligation cannot be invoked unless the condition is satisfied.

The second method is through the pay or play clause in an employment agreement. Here, the star performer or director is guaranteed a salary whether or not the project begins. This compensates the individual for the work which might be given up because the scheduled commitment interferes with other possible projects. (This is the opportunity cost associated with each project.) As reflected in *Locke v. Warner Bros., Inc*, the pay or play clause may result in a sizable payment to the artist, but it still does not reflect the true value that the completed project would have provided — particularly if the project had received widespread acclaim. 57 Cal. App. 4th 354 (Ct. App. 1997). To the extent that some projects flop, the difference between the guaranteed payment and the potential value of the contract is necessarily speculative.

c. As the court identified in *Buchwald*, based upon credit and the compensation which follows is only roughly analogous to the substantial similarity test of copyright. While access is a critical element, similarity is not nearly as important as paternity. Projects can transform significantly from the first treatment to the final cut. Writers, actors, directors, and producers are constantly adding new material. Nonetheless, if the conceptual strands of the original, contractual project still exist at the end of the project, then the based upon credit and contractual obligations should survive.

d. Regarding *Coming to America*, others made claims of infringement. Because these claims were based on copyright infringement rather than contract law, the evidence of substantial similarity required a much higher degree of similarity than Buchwald's claim that there was a contractual relationship between the two works. *See Beal v. Paramount Pictures Corp.*, 20 F.3d 454 (11th Cir. 1994).

e. Alternatives to *based upon* clauses might be appropriate in some contracts. Producers are reluctant to owe money and to have too many claimants on a project. Just as the Writers Guild of America has rules limiting writers' credits, producers might elect to place limits on the eligibility for based upon credit. Such limitations might be based on time, content, or paternity. First, the acquisition agreement could provide that based upon credit will only be available if principle photography for the motion picture begins within a short time period, typically one to two years from the inception of the contract. Time may be a reasonable limiting tool on the assumption that the longer a project takes, the less likely the original submission was the creative spark for the project and the more likely other people have become responsible for the project's success.

Second, contracts could define based upon as requiring substantial similarity between the submission and the final project. While much more limited than the based upon clause in *Buchwald*, the test would be more stringent and more likely to be understood.

Third, *based upon* could be awarded on a good faith chain of paternity. Essentially, such a clause would provide that so long as the producers did not purchase a third party's treatment or script, then based upon credit would be available. Under this test, if a third party's material was also purchased, an arbitration would be held and the material most substantially incorporated into the final project would receive the based upon credit. This last test is closest in concept to the method that the Writers Guild of America employs in its arbitrations. The requirement of the arbitration helps avoid the bad faith purchase of other rights simply to break the chain of paternity.

f. Studios often try very hard to lure the most successful talent. These deals sometimes include transactions for third parties, entered into as favors for the valuable star. If those transactions do not go well, might it raise questions of good faith regarding the studio's commitment to that transaction? *See Locke v. Warner Bros*, 57 Cal. App. 4th 354.

g. To what extent can a motion picture studio ensure good press? What possible legal or ethical issues are raised by this license agreement provision used by The Walt Disney Company in its licensing of movie trailers to website retailers?

> The Website in which the Trailers are used may not be derogatory to or critical of the entertainment industry or of [Disney] (and its officers, directors, agents, employees, affiliates, divisions and subsidiaries) or of any motion picture produced or distributed by [Disney] ... [or] of the materials from which the Trailers were taken or of any person involved with the production of the Underlying Works. Any breach of this paragraph will render this license null and void and Licensee will be liable to all parties concerned for defamation and copyright infringement, as well as breach of contract....

Video Pipeline, Inc. v. Buena Vista Home Entm't, Inc., 342 F.3d 191, 203 (3d Cir. 2003).

Problem 12-B

Based on the reception to *Juliet Prescott* (*see* Problem 4-A), Bryce has been offered the opportunity to modernize, adapt and direct another Shakespearean-based tragedy. This time, Bryce is working on *Leer*, a contemporary retelling of the classic story centered around a somewhat bizarre musical family. Obviously based upon *King Lear*, Bryce has written *Leer* as a modern day parable about society's descent and degeneration into an overly sex-focused pop culture. In the story, a film mogul who was once powerful at the height of the studio era had married a jazz singer who died of a drug overdose shortly after the birth of their third daughter. The eldest daughter, a pop diva, marries her record producer, and cuts her father out of her production deals; the middle daughter buys her father's former studio from a bankruptcy auction, only to cut, remake, and colorize his films; the third daughter, however, refuses not only to buy into the industry, but also to assist her aging father in making his long sought-after comeback.

To attract the cast needed to successfully complete this project, Bryce has tried to structure a contract that can attract the quality actor needed to play Leer. Since the budget will be modest, Bryce asks you to outline the deal points necessary to land the leading player.

In addition, Bryce is worried because the screenplay is not yet completed. Bryce is very concerned that the producer may use the *Leer* structure with another writer/director, so Bryce asks you to outline a deal memo that will protect Bryce even if the *Leer* concept is utilized by the producers with someone other than Bryce. Provide Bryce with a deal memo outlining the star's contract and a deal memo outlining the producer's agreement with Bryce as writer and director.

C. Derivative Interests and Bundling of Motion Picture Interests

Russell v. Price

612 F.2d 1123 (9th Cir. 1979)

Defendants distributed copies of the film "Pygmalion," the copyright for which had expired. They were sued by the owners of the renewal copyright in the George Bernard Shaw play upon which the film was based....

In 1913 Shaw registered a copyright on his stage play "Pygmalion." The renewal copyright on the play, obtained in 1941 and originally scheduled to expire in 1969, was extended by Congressional action to the year 1988. Shaw died in 1950 and the plaintiffs, except for Janus Films, are current proprietors of the copyright. Janus Films is a licensee.

In 1938 a derivative version of the play, a motion picture also entitled "Pygmalion," was produced under a license from Shaw; neither the terms nor the licensee's identity appear in the record. The film was produced by Gabriel Pascal, copyrighted by Loew's, and distributed by Metro-Goldwyn-Mayer ("MGM"). For undisclosed reasons, the film's copyright was allowed to expire in 1966. When and if the original film rights agreement expired is also not disclosed....

Defendants' main contention on the primary issue in this litigation is simply stated: Because the film copyright on "Pygmalion" has expired, that film is in the public domain, and, consequently, prints of that film may be used freely by anyone. Thus, they argue that their renting out of the film does not infringe the statutory copyright on Shaw's play.

Defendants admit that any new motion picture or other derivative work produced without the permission of the proprietors of the copyright on Shaw's play would infringe that underlying copyright. Defendants rely almost entirely on the recent opinion of Judge Friendly in *Rohauer v. Killiam Shows, Inc.*, 551 F.2d 484 (2d Cir.), *cert. denied*, 431 U.S. 949 (1977). However, in so relying, they ignore or fail to appreciate the significant differences between that case and this one.

In *Rohauer* the author of a novel which was statutorily copyrighted in 1925 assigned exclusive movie rights to one Moskowitz, specifically promising in the contract to reassign to him or his successor in interest all film rights for the novel's copyright renewal term. A successful silent film was made under that assignment and separately copyrighted in 1926 by an assignee of Moskowitz. Unfortunately, the novel's author died prior to the end of the novel's first copyright term. The author's daughter, as statutory beneficiary of the right to renew, inherited the renewal term free from the film license granted by her mother. The daughter then granted exclusive movie and television rights for the renewal term to Rohauer. Killiam Shows, Inc., successor in interest to the 1926 film's renewal copyright, allowed the film to be shown on educational television without Rohauer's or the daughter's authorization, whereupon the latter two brought a copyright infringement action against Killiam.

The Second Circuit held on those facts that the derivative film's independent copyright entitled the defendant to continue showing the film without infringing rights under the renewal copyright in the underlying novel. Defendants here understand by this that a derivative copyright covers more than the new matter which the producer of the derivative work added to the underlying work. Thus, they say that when the derivative copyright expires the whole product enters the public domain free of the monopoly protection of any subsisting copyright in the underlying work. The court's opinion in *Rohauer*, however, makes it clear that this is simply not the case.

First, the *Rohauer* court placed heavy emphasis on the nongratuitous intent of the nonsurviving author to convey film rights in the novel's renewal term, a promise which had been bargained for in the initial assignment. The defendants here have never bargained with Shaw or his successors for anything, nor do they enjoy any relationship with anyone who had so bargained.

A second important difference between the favored party in Rohauer and the defendants here is that the defendant Killiam there was the proprietor of the still valid copyright in the film. By virtue of that copyright, Killiam was held to have sufficient rights in the matter derived from the novel to continue showing it as part of the film. A prominent rationale in that case for awarding those limited rights in favor of the owner of the derivative copyright is the protection and encouragement of the "large and independently copyrightable" "literary, musical and economic" contributions of the "person who with the consent of the author has created an opera or a motion picture film" from a copyrighted novel. However, whatever place sympathy for the position of creators of derivative works might properly have under the 1909 Copyright Act, the defendants here can take advantage of none, having contributed nothing to the production of the film "Pygmalion".

Nor is it apparent under *Rohauer* that such sympathy should have any place at all when the independent copyright on the derivative work has been allowed to expire. For then there is no longer a conflict between two copyrights, each apparently granting "their proprietors overlapping "exclusive' rights to use whatever underlying material ... had been incorporated into the derivative film." Comment, *Derivative Copyright and the 1909 Act New Clarity or Confusion?*, 44 Brooklyn L.Rev. 905, 912 (1978) (footnote omitted). Thus, the persons who might have had standing to raise the *Rohauer* claim here could, consistently with that case, be held to have forfeited it by their failure to renew the derivative copyright. Defendants here could never have laid claim to the right recognized in *Rohauer*, and we perceive no reason to award it to them at the expense of the holders of the renewal copyright which still covers the Shaw play.

Thus, we reaffirm, without finding it necessary to repeat the rationale, the well-established doctrine that a derivative copyright protects only the new material contained in the derivative work, not the matter derived from the underlying work. Thus, although the derivative work may enter the public domain, the matter contained therein which derives from a work still covered by statutory copyright is not dedicated to the public. *G. Ricordi & Co. v. Paramount Pictures, Inc.*, 189 F.2d 469 (2d Cir. 1951).... The established doctrine prevents unauthorized copying or other infringing use of the underlying work or any part of that work contained in the derivative product so long as the underlying work itself remains copyrighted. Therefore, since exhibition of the film "Pygmalion" necessarily involves exhibition of parts of Shaw's play, which is still copyrighted, plaintiffs here may prevent defendants from renting the film for exhibition without their authorization.

Defendants seek finally to avoid this result by citing *Classic Film Museum, Inc. v. Warner Bros., Inc.*, 597 F.2d 13 (1st Cir. 1979), *aff'g* 453 F. Supp. 852 (D. Me. 1978). That decision concerned "the legal effect of an expired statutory copyright on work derived from an underlying work in which there exists a common-law copyright." Although defendants would have us ignore the major difference between an underlying common-law copyright and an underlying statutory copyright (the former extending in perpetuity, the latter restricted in length) that difference is the linchpin of the court's holding in Classic Film that a person could exhibit the motion picture "A Star is Born," on which the film copyright had expired, without infringing the common-law copyright in the unpublished screenplay and musical score from which the film was derived. The court found the *Ricordi* doctrine inapplicable for the following reason:

> "... Any protection offered by the *Ricordi* doctrine was limited to the fixed life of the underlying copyright (28 years plus the renewal period). The *Ricordi* doctrine is not equally applicable where there is an underlying common-law copyright which might extend indefinitely. Such unending protection of the derivative work would allow the *Ricordi* exception to swallow the rule of limited monopoly found in the constitution and copyright statutes."

The underlying statutory copyright in the instant case will expire in 1988. After that time Budget may freely distribute its copies of the 1938 film. The result we reach here does not conflict with the limited monopoly policy rooted in the Copyrights Clause of the constitution and advanced in the congressional acts.

For the foregoing reasons, we conclude that defendants' activities here infringed the subsisting copyright in Shaw's play and were properly enjoined....

Affirmed.

Stewart v. Abend
495 U.S. 207 (1990)

JUSTICE O'CONNOR delivered the opinion of the Court.

The author of a pre-existing work may assign to another the right to use it in a derivative work. In this case the author of a pre-existing work agreed to assign the rights in his renewal copyright term to the owner of a derivative work, but died before the commencement of the renewal period. The question presented is whether the owner of the derivative work infringed the rights of the successor owner of the pre-existing work by continued distribution and publication of the derivative work during the renewal term of the pre-existing work.

Cornell Woolrich authored the story "It Had to Be Murder," which was first published in February 1942 in Dime Detective Magazine. The magazine's publisher, Popular Publications, Inc., obtained the rights to magazine publication of the story and Woolrich retained all other rights. Popular Publications obtained a blanket copyright for the issue of Dime Detective Magazine in which "It Had to Be Murder" was published.

The Copyright Act of 1909 (1909 Act) provided authors a 28-year initial term of copyright protection plus a 28-year renewal term. In 1945, Woolrich agreed to assign the rights to make motion picture versions of six of his stories, including "It Had to Be Murder," to B. G. De Sylva Productions for $9,250. He also agreed to renew the copyrights in the stories at the appropriate time and to assign the same motion picture rights to De Sylva Productions for the 28-year renewal term. In 1953, actor Jimmy Stewart and director Alfred Hitchcock formed a production company, Patron, Inc., which obtained the motion picture rights in "It Had to Be Murder" from De Sylva's successors in interest for $10,000.

In 1954, Patron, Inc., along with Paramount Pictures, produced and distributed "Rear Window," the motion picture version of Woolrich's story "It Had to Be Murder." Woolrich died in 1968 before he could obtain the rights in the renewal term for petitioners as promised and without a surviving spouse or child. He left his property to a trust administered by his executor, Chase Manhattan Bank, for the benefit of Columbia University. On December 29, 1969, Chase Manhattan Bank renewed the copyright in the "It Had to Be Murder" story pursuant to 17 U.S.C. § 24. Chase Manhattan assigned the renewal rights to respondent Abend for $650 plus 10% of all proceeds from exploitation of the story.

"Rear Window" was broadcast on the ABC television network in 1971. Respondent then notified petitioners Hitchcock (now represented by co-trustees of his will), Stewart, and MCA Inc., the owners of the "Rear Window" motion picture and renewal rights in the motion picture, that he owned the renewal rights in the copyright and that their distribution of the motion picture without his permission infringed his copyright in the story. Hitchcock, Stewart, and MCA nonetheless entered into a second license with ABC to rebroadcast the motion picture. In 1974, respondent filed suit against these same petitioners, and others, in the United States District Court for the Southern District of New York, alleging copyright infringement. Respondent dismissed his complaint in return for $25,000.

Three years later, the United States Court of Appeals for the Second Circuit decided *Rohauer v. Killiam Shows, Inc.*, 551 F. 2d 484, *cert. denied*, 431 U.S. 949 (1977), in which it held that the owner of the copyright in a derivative work may continue to use the existing derivative work according to the original grant from the author of the pre-existing work even if the grant of rights in the pre-existing work lapsed. Several years later, apparently in reliance on *Rohauer*, petitioners re-released the motion picture in a variety of media, including new 35 and 16 millimeter prints for theatrical exhibition in the United States, videocassettes, and videodiscs. They also publicly exhibited the motion picture in theaters, over cable television, and through videodisc and videocassette rentals and sales.

Respondent then brought the instant suit in the United States District Court for the Central District of California against Hitchcock, Stewart, MCA, and Universal Film Exchanges, a subsidiary of MCA and the distributor of the motion picture. Respondent's complaint alleges that the release of the motion picture infringes his copyright in the story because petitioners' right to use the story during the renewal term lapsed when Woolrich died before he could register for the renewal term and transfer his renewal rights to them.

Respondent also contends that petitioners have interfered with his rights in the renewal term of the story in other ways. He alleges that he sought to contract with Home Box Office (HBO) to produce a play and television version of the story, but that petitioners wrote to him and HBO stating that neither he nor HBO could use either the title, "Rear Window" or "It Had to Be Murder." Respondent also alleges that petitioners further interfered with the renewal copyright in the story by attempting to sell the right to make a television sequel and that the re-release of the original motion picture itself interfered with his ability to produce other derivative works.... The issue before the court, therefore, was whether petitioners were entitled to distribute and exhibit the motion picture without respondent's permission despite respondent's valid copyright in the pre-existing story. Relying on the renewal provision of the 1909 Act, 17 U.S.C. § 24, respondent argued before the Court of Appeals that because he obtained from Chase Manhattan Bank, the statutory successor, the renewal right free and clear of any purported assignments of any interest in the renewal copyright, petitioners' distribution and publication of "Rear Window" without authorization infringed his renewal copyright. Petitioners responded that they had the right to continue to exploit "Rear Window" during the 28-year renewal period because Woolrich had agreed to assign to petitioners' predecessor in interest the motion picture rights in the story for the renewal period....

Petitioners would have us read into the Copyright Act a limitation on the statutorily created rights of the owner of an underlying work. They argue in essence that the rights of the owner of the copyright in the derivative use of the pre-existing work are extinguished once it is incorporated into the derivative work, assuming the author of the pre-existing work has agreed to assign his renewal rights. Because we find no support for such a curtailment of rights in either the 1909 Act or the 1976 Act, or in the legislative history of either, we affirm the judgment of the Court of Appeals....

The right of renewal found in § 24 provides authors a second opportunity to obtain remuneration for their works. Section 24 provides:

> "[T]he author of [a copyrighted] work, if still living, or the widow, widower, or children of the author, if the author be not living, or if such author, widow, widower, or children be not living, then the author's executors, or in the absence of a will, his next of kin shall be entitled to a renewal and extension of the copyright in such work for a further term of twenty-eight years when application for such renewal and extension shall have been made to the copyright office and duly registered therein within one year prior to the expiration of the original term of copyright."

17 U.S.C. § 24 (1976 ed.)

Since the earliest copyright statute in this country, the copyright term of ownership has been split between an original term and a renewal term.... The 1831 renewal provisions created "an entirely new policy, completely dissevering the title, breaking up the continuance ... and vesting an absolutely new title eo nomine in the persons designated." In this way, Congress attempted to give the author a second chance to control and benefit from his work. Congress also intended to secure to the author's family the opportunity to exploit the work if the author died before he could register for the renewal term. "The evident purpose of [the renewal provision] is to provide for the family of the author after his death. Since the author cannot assign his family's renewal rights, [it] takes the form of a compulsory bequest of the copyright to the designated persons."

In its debates leading up to the Copyright Act of 1909, Congress elaborated upon the policy underlying a system comprised of an original term and a completely separate renewal term. See *G. Ricordi & Co. v. Paramount Pictures, Inc.*, 189 F. 2d 469, 471 (CA2) (the renewal right "creates a new estate, and the ... cases which have dealt with the subject assert that the new estate is clear of all rights, interests or licenses granted under the original copyright"), *cert. denied*, 342 U.S. 849 (1951). "It not infrequently happens that the author sells his copyright outright to a publisher for a comparatively small sum." H.R. Rep. No. 2222, 60th Cong., 2d Sess., 14 (1909). The renewal term permits the author, originally in a poor bargaining position, to renegotiate the terms of the grant once the value of the work has been tested. "[U]nlike real property and other forms of personal property, [a copyright] is by its very nature incapable of accurate monetary evaluation prior to its exploitation." 2 M. Nimmer & D. Nimmer, Nimmer on Copyright § 9.02, p. 9–23 (1989) (hereinafter Nimmer). "If the work proves to be a great success and lives beyond the term of twenty-eight years, ... it should be the exclusive right of the author to take the renewal term, and the law should be framed ... so that [the author] could not be deprived of that right." H.R. Rep. No. 2222, *supra*, at 14. With these purposes in mind, Congress enacted the renewal provision of the Copyright Act of 1909. With respect to works in their original or renewal term as of January 1, 1978, Congress retained the two-term system of copyright protection in the 1976 Act.

Applying these principles in *Miller Music Corp. v. Charles N. Daniels, Inc.*, 362 U.S. 373 (1960), this Court held that when an author dies before the renewal period arrives, his executor is entitled to the renewal rights, even though the author previously assigned his renewal rights to another party. "An assignment by an author of his renewal rights made before the original copyright expires is valid against the world, if the author is alive at the commencement of the renewal period. If the author dies before that time, the "next of kin obtain the renewal copyright free of any claim founded upon an assignment made by the author in his lifetime. These results follow not because the author's assignment is invalid but because he had only an expectancy to assign; and his death, prior to the renewal period, terminates his interest in the renewal which by § 24 vests in the named classes." The legislative history of the 1909 Act echoes this view: "The right of renewal is contingent. It does not vest until the end [of the original term]. If [the author] is alive at the time of renewal, then the original contract may pass it, but his widow or children or other persons entitled would not be bound by that contract." Thus, the renewal provisions were intended to give the author a second chance to obtain fair remuneration for his creative efforts and to provide the author's family a "new estate" if the author died before the renewal period arrived.

An author holds a bundle of exclusive rights in the copyrighted work, among them the right to copy and the right to incorporate the work into derivative works. By assigning the renewal copyright in the work without limitation, as in Miller Music, the author assigns all of these rights. After *Miller Music*, if the author dies before the commencement of the renewal period, the assignee holds nothing. If the assignee of all of the renewal rights holds nothing upon the death of the assignor before arrival of the renewal period, then, a fortiori, the assignee of a portion of the renewal rights, e.g., the right to produce a derivative work, must also hold nothing.

Application of this rule to this case should end the inquiry. Woolrich died before the commencement of the renewal period in the story, and, therefore, petitioners hold only an unfulfilled expectancy. Petitioners have been "deprived of nothing. Like all purchasers of contingent interests, [they took] subject to the possibility that the contingency may not occur."

The reason that our inquiry does not end here, and that we granted certiorari, is that the Court of Appeals for the Second Circuit reached a contrary result in *Rohauer v. Killiam Shows, Inc.*, 551 F. 2d 484 (1977). Petitioners' theory is drawn largely from

Rohauer. The Court of Appeals in *Rohauer* attempted to craft a "proper reconciliation" between the owner of the pre-existing work, who held the right to the work pursuant to *Miller Music,* and the owner of the derivative work, who had a great deal to lose if the work could not be published or distributed. Addressing a case factually similar to this case, the court concluded that even if the death of the author caused the renewal rights in the pre-existing work to revert to the statutory successor, the owner of the derivative work could continue to exploit that work. The court reasoned that the 1976 Act and the relevant precedents did not preclude such a result and that it was necessitated by a balancing of the equities:

> "[T]he equities lie preponderantly in favor of the proprietor of the derivative copyright. In contrast to the situation where an assignee or licensee has done nothing more than print, publicize and distribute a copyrighted story or novel, a person who with the consent of the author has created an opera or a motion picture film will often have made contributions literary, musical and economic, as great as or greater than the original author.... [T]he purchaser of derivative rights has no truly effective way to protect himself against the eventuality of the author's death before the renewal period since there is no way of telling who will be the surviving widow, children or next of kin or the executor until that date arrives."

The Court of Appeals for the Second Circuit thereby shifted the focus from the right to use the pre-existing work in a derivative work to a right inhering in the created derivative work itself. By rendering the renewal right to use the original work irrelevant, the court created an exception to our ruling in *Miller Music* and, as petitioners concede, created an "intrusion" on the statutorily created rights of the owner of the pre-existing work in the renewal term.

Though petitioners do not, indeed could not, argue that its language expressly supports the theory they draw from *Rohauer,* they implicitly rely on § 6 of the 1909 Act, 17 U.S.C. § 7 (1976 ed.), which states that "dramatizations ... of copyrighted works when produced with the consent of the proprietor of the copyright in such works ... shall be regarded as new works subject to copyright under the provisions of this title." Petitioners maintain that the creation of the "new," i.e., derivative, work extinguishes any right the owner of rights in the pre-existing work might have had to sue for infringement that occurs during the renewal term.

We think, as stated in Nimmer, that "[t]his conclusion is neither warranted by any express provision of the Copyright Act, nor by the rationale as to the scope of protection achieved in a derivative work. It is moreover contrary to the axiomatic copyright principle that a person may exploit only such copyrighted literary material as he either owns or is licensed to use." 1 Nimmer § 3.07[A], pp. 3–23 to 3–24 (footnotes omitted). The aspects of a derivative work added by the derivative author are that author's property, but the element drawn from the pre-existing work remains on grant from the owner of the pre-existing work. *See Russell v. Price,* 612 F.2d 1123, 1128 (CA9 1979) (reaffirming "well-established doctrine that a derivative copyright protects only the new material contained in the derivative work, not the matter derived from the underlying work"), *cert. denied*, 446 U.S. 952 (1980). So long as the pre-existing work remains out of the public domain, its use is infringing if one who employs the work does not have a valid license or assignment for use of the pre-existing work. It is irrelevant whether the pre-existing work is inseparably intertwined with the derivative work. Indeed, the plain language of § 7 supports the view that the full force of the copyright in the pre-existing work is preserved despite incorporation into the derivative work....

In fact, if the 1976 Act's termination provisions provide any guidance at all in this case, they tilt against petitioners' theory. The plain language of the termination provision itself indicates that Congress assumed that the owner of the pre-existing work possessed the right to sue for infringement even after incorporation of the pre-existing work in the derivative work.

> "A derivative work *prepared* under authority of the grant before its termination may continue to be utilized under the terms of the grant after its termination, but this privilege does not extend to the preparation after the termination of other derivative works based upon the copyrighted work covered by the terminated grant." § 304(c)(6)(A) (emphasis added).

Congress would not have stated explicitly in § 304(c)(6)(A) that, at the end of the renewal term, the owner of the rights in the pre-existing work may not terminate use rights in existing derivative works unless Congress had assumed that the owner continued to hold the right to sue for infringement even after incorporation of the pre-existing work into the derivative work.

Accordingly, we conclude that neither the 1909 Act nor the 1976 Act provides support for the theory set forth in *Rohauer*. And even if the theory found some support in the statute or the legislative history, the approach set forth in *Rohauer* is problematic. Petitioners characterize the result in *Rohauer* as a bright-line "rule." The Court of Appeals in *Rohauer*, however, expressly implemented policy considerations as a means of reconciling what it viewed as the competing interests in that case. While the result in *Rohauer* might make some sense in some contexts, it makes no sense in others. In the case of a condensed book, for example, the contribution by the derivative author may be little, while the contribution by the original author is great. Yet, under the *Rohauer* "rule," publication of the condensed book would not infringe the pre-existing work even though the derivative author has no license or valid grant of rights in the pre-existing work. Thus, even if the *Rohauer* "rule" made sense in terms of policy in that case, it makes little sense when it is applied across the derivative works spectrum. Indeed, in the view of the commentators, *Rohauer* did not announce a "rule," but rather an "interest-balancing approach."

Finally, petitioners urge us to consider the policies underlying the Copyright Act. They argue that the rule announced by the Court of Appeals will undermine one of the policies of the Act—the dissemination of creative works—by leading to many fewer works reaching the public. Amicus Columbia Pictures asserts that "[s]ome owners of underlying work renewal copyrights may refuse to negotiate, preferring instead to retire their copyrighted works, and all derivative works based thereon, from public use. Others may make demands — like respondent's demand for 50% of petitioners' future gross proceeds in excess of advertising expenses … — which are so exorbitant that a negotiated economic accommodation will be impossible." These arguments are better addressed by Congress than the courts.…

For the foregoing reasons, the judgment of the Court of Appeals is affirmed, and the case is remanded for further proceedings consistent with this opinion.

Notes and Questions

a. The Second Circuit had quickly followed *Russel v. Price* with *Filmvideo Releasing Corp. v. Hastings*, 668 F.2d 91 (2d Cir. 1981) (Hopalong Cassidy motion pictures), which set the stage for the Supreme Court decision to clarify the role played by a pre-existing grant of copyright.

b. As noted in *Stewart v. Abend*, Congress eliminated the renewal provision, replacing it with a right to terminate the grant of a copyright. The termination provisions seek to introduce the same Congressional policy of providing copyright holders a second opportunity to benefit from the copyrighted work created. Because no such rights exist for works-made-for-hire, the characterization of a transfer as an assignment or as a work for hire may have tremendous significance. These issues persist. *See Marvel Characters, Inc. v. Simon*, 310 F.3d 280 (2d Cir. 2002) (remanding to trial the issue of work for hire status of the creation of Captain America).

c. The copyright status of unpublished screenplays has been one of the more difficult areas to reconcile with the caselaw, specifically *Russel v. Price* and *Stewart v. Abend*. The Ninth Circuit and Second Circuit have both concluded that the common law copyrights in these screenplays cannot be recognized. As the Second Circuit explained:

> In *Batjac* [*Prods. Inc. v. Goodtimes Home Video Corp.*, 160 F.3d 1223, 1225, 1236 (9th Cir. 1998)], the Ninth Circuit ruled that the publication of a motion picture publishes so much of the underlying screenplay as was disclosed in the motion picture. The court reasoned that a contrary rule would turn on its head the copyright principle of limited monopoly, in that "the copyright in any film that has entered the public domain under the 1909 Act could be resurrected by an unpublished screenplay." We find this reasoning persuasive and consonant with the principles approved in our prior cases, to wit, that when the author consents to the inclusion of his work in a derivative work, the publication of the derivative work, to the extent that it discloses the original work, also constitutes publication of that underlying work. We conclude in the present case, based on the statute and the principles underlying the scope of copyright protection, that if a previously unpublished screenplay is embodied in a motion picture, so much of the screenplay as is disclosed in the motion picture is published when the motion picture is published. This interpretation is also consistent with the longstanding approach apparently taken by the Copyright Office, that the publication of a derivative work constitutes publication of so much of the underlying work as is disclosed in the derivative work.

Shoptalk, Ltd. v. Concorde-New Horizons Corp., 168 F.3d 586, 592 (2d Cir. 1999). A somewhat different analysis may be required if the rights to the screenplay were not fully transferred to the production company. *See Welles v. Turner Entm't Co.*, 503 F.3d 728 (9th Cir. 2007) (reviewing rights reserved to Orson Welles for the screenplay to Citizen Kane).

d. The issues of pre-existing literary works are not the only problems faced by filmmakers incorporating copyrighted images. For example, a documentary filmmaker captured a 75-second performance of a musician's act which was included in the motion picture without the musician's consent. In a subsequent action for violation of her rights of publicity and trademark, what is the expected result? *Compare Man v. Warner Bros., Inc.*, 317 F. Supp. 50 (S.D.N.Y. 1970) (documentary *Woodstock*), *with Zacchini v. Scripps-Howard Broad. Co.*, 433 U.S. 562 (1977) (human cannonball).

e. Like documentary footage, incorporation may sometimes come from prior staged performances. One common problem occurs when a filmmaker desires to use scenes filmed during the shooting of its motion picture as part of an upcoming sequel. None of the actors in the original film have been hired to appear in the sequel, but have signed a contract allowing for the use of their names and likenesses. Does the film company need an additional agreement with each of the actors? *See Donahue v. Artisan Entm't, Inc.*, 2002 U.S. Dist. LEXIS 5930 (S.D.N.Y. Apr. 3, 2002).

f. Still images may create the same concerns. *Compare Brown v. McCormick*, 87 F. Supp. 2d 467 (D. Md. 2000), *aff'd*, 243 F.3d 536 (4th Cir. 2001) (finding infringement for use of copyrighted quilt patterns in film but awarding a surprisingly low award of damages for the various infringing activities stemming from the motion picture entitled *How to Make an American Quilt*), *with Sandoval v. New Line Cinema Corp.*, 147 F.3d 215 (2d Cir. 1998) (brief showing of photographs in background of scene *de minimis* given how indistinguishable the images appeared).

Problem 12-C

Bryce has been diligently working on *Leer*. Bryce has become very concerned that since Shakespeare's original play is in the public domain, the newly drafted screenplay and film will not be protected by copyright. Advise Bryce on the extent to which copyright will protect both the *Leer* screenplay and the finished motion picture.

D. Character Licensing

New Line Cinema Corp. v. Easter Unlimited, Inc.

17 U.S.P.Q.2d (BNA) 1631 (E.D.N.Y. 1989)

The Elm Street Venture and the Fourth New-Line-Heron Venture are joint ventures and registered the series of four motion pictures in the United States Copyright Office of the Library of Congress based on assignments of rights in New Line Cinema Corporation. The plaintiffs collectively own all the copyrights to the four films issued.

The theme of the films is the terror expressed through viewing Freddy and the mystery and confusion between reality and dreams. Freddy is the only means of expressing the idea. The appearance of Freddy that expresses the idea gives copyright protection to the character of Freddy, independent of the films' copyright protection. *Walt Disney Productions v. Air Pirates,* 581 F.2d 751, 755 (9th Cir. 1978), *cert. denied,* 439 U.S. 1132 (1979) (A comic book character which contains "unique elements of expression" is protectible).

Freddy's character is revealed through the expression of his scarred face and glove with protruding razor blades (a copy is appended). Copyright protection is extended to the component part of the character which significantly aids in identifying the character.

Copyright Protection

Copyright infringement may be established by showing access to the protected work and substantial similarity. The wide circulation of the films and the Freddy products distributed in the trade gave Easter access to Freddy and the Freddy glove.

The recorded conversation on May 3, 1989 between Anthony Spiesman, a private investigator employed by New Line, and Mitchell Schiff, an Easter employee, convinced this court that Easter copied the Freddy glove.

In answer to Spiesman's question as to whether Easter designs the items it sells, Schiff replied: "Some of the time. Some items we just see around. You know capturing someone else's ideas and modifying it to what we think is better. The Krueger stuff is gone to the movies.... Yeah and like the Nightmare thing, you know everybody puts this little name on it and you don't have any royalty involved."

Copying may also be established by showing access and substantial similarity. Easter claims the difference in the gloves defeats plaintiff's claim of substantial similarity, i.e., the Freddy glove consists of

> "brown cloth with armor-like articulations and openings on the inner side of the fingers and the palm.... By contrast the HAND is a glove of tightfitting black nylon with no openings. The visual impression of the black nylon is more elegant, with a vampirish ghoulish effect as opposed to the utilitarian look and feel of Freddy's glove.

"The extensions to the black fabric of the HAND are more like thin flat nails. They could be made to flop about and by way of construction, lay flat on a place perpendicular to the 'knives' extending from the Freddy glove. Freddy's knives on the other hand look like rigid steel stilettos."

Easter places undue emphasis on the dissimilarity of the two gloves. "Even if a copied portion be relatively small in proportion to the entire work, if qualitatively important, the finder of fact may find substantial similarity." Since copyright protects the "expression of [an] idea," where the copy is of "the expression of the idea," substantial similarity is established no matter how little is copied.

In *Warner Bros. v. American Broadcasting Companies,* 720 F.2d 231, 241 (2d Cir. 1983) in a claim of infringement, the court, finding a sufficient dissimilarity between the copyrighted character of Superman, and the fictional character of Ralph Hinkley, the principal figure in the television series, "The Greatest American Hero," noted:

> A somewhat paradoxical aspect of infringement disputes, especially pertinent to claims of character infringement, concerns the attention courts give both to similarities and differences in the two works at issue. Professor Nimmer categorically asserts as a proposition, "It is entirely immaterial that in many respects plaintiff's and defendant's works are dissimilar if in other respects similarity as to a substantial element of plaintiff's work can be shown." 3 Nimmer § 13.03(B) at 13–38. In Hand's pithy phrase, "No plagiarist can excuse the wrong by showing how much of his work he did not pirate." *Sheldon v. Metro-Goldwyn Pictures Corp.*, 81 F.2d 49, 56 (2d Cir.), *cert. denied,* 298 U.S. 669, 56 S. Ct. 835, 80 L.Ed. 1391 (1936). Yet Professor Nimmer also recognizes, as a second proposition, that "a defendant may legitimately avoid infringement by intentionally making sufficient changes in a work which would otherwise be regarded as substantially similar to that of the plaintiff's, 3 Nimmer § 13.03(B) at 13-38.1 to -38.2.

We find that Easter attempted to avoid infringement and failed.

Trademark Infringement and Unfair Competition

The Lanham Act claim is based on section 43(a) of the Lanham Act. The section protects unregistered as well as registered marks. Registration gives jurisdictional and procedural advantages to the registrant. The right to trademark protection however arises from use and not from registration.

We find that an appreciable number of ordinarily prudent purchasers of items found in novelty stores during the Halloween season are likely to be mislead or confused as to the source of Easter's glove. This is particularly true when presented with the attachment on which the glove is inserted showing the word NIGHTMARE in a form of print similar to New Line's presentation of Freddy's glove. In examining both gloves presented to the potential market of teenagers and young adults, the likelihood of confusion is apparent.

New Line has a valuable property right in the character Freddy Krueger and the Freddy glove acquired over a period of about five years at great expense. Easter with full knowledge of New Line's right designed a glove with a view to appropriating that right for its own gain and resulting in New Line's loss.

New Line has shown (a) the possibility of irreparable injury and (b) likelihood of success on the merits and is therefore entitled to preliminary injunctive relief. The motion for a preliminary injunction is granted....

Conan Properties International L.L.C. v. Sanchez

2018 WL 3869894 (E.D.N.Y. Aug. 15, 2018)

Conan Properties International L.L.C. ("CPI") and Robert E. Howard Property Inc. ("REH") (collectively, "plaintiffs") sued Ricardo Jové Sanchez for copyright and trademark infringement under 17 U.S.C. § 106 and 15 U.S.C. § 1125(a). Sanchez, who is a resident of Spain, failed to appear, and plaintiffs moved for default judgment.

CPI and REH own copyrights and trademarks in pulp fiction novels, comic books, and graphic novels written by Robert E. Howard in the 1930s. They feature Conan the Barbarian and, as relevant here, six other characters: (1) Kull; (2) Ironhand, also known as Esau Cairn; (3) Bran Mak Morn; (4) Dark Agnes; (5) Solomon Kane; and (6) El Borak (collectively, minus Conan, "REH Characters"). CPI owns the rights to Conan and REH owns the rights to the REH Characters. Plaintiffs allege that Sanchez violated their rights by manufacturing, displaying, and selling (or offering for sale) miniature sculptures of these copyright-protected characters on Facebook and Kickstarter. Sanchez offered the sculptures for prices ranging from €27 (about $31) to €10,000 (about $11,425). Plaintiffs submitted a takedown notice under the Digital Millennium Copyright Act ("DMCA") to compel Kickstarter to remove the sculptures, and Sanchez filed a counter-notice, causing them to remain. Plaintiffs filed this suit, seeking $70,000 in damages and a permanent injunction. When Sanchez failed to appear, the clerk entered default and the plaintiffs moved for a default judgment.

The Court referred the motion to the Magistrate Judge, who found liability as to three of the characters: El Borak, Solomon Kane, and Kull. She reasoned plaintiffs failed to allege that the remaining characters, including Conan, were sufficiently original or distinct to warrant copyright protection. The Magistrate Judge also found liability for trademark infringement. Finally, she recommended an award of $3,000 in statutory damages for each of the three unlawfully copied characters and the denial of injunctive relief.

Plaintiffs object to the recommendations regarding copyright liability for the remaining characters, damages, and injunctive relief. The Court reviews these portions of the R&R de novo.

A party's default "constitute[s] a concession of all well pleaded allegations of liability." To determine whether plaintiff's allegations are well pleaded, the Court applies the same standards that govern a motion to dismiss under Rule 12(b)(6). Thus, the complaint must plead "enough facts to state a claim to relief that is plausible on its face," and "allow the court to draw the reasonable inference that the defendant is liable for the misconduct alleged."

Plaintiffs argue that the Magistrate Judge erroneously departed from these pleading standards. The Court agrees. Courts in this circuit require a copyright complaint to allege: "(1) which specific original works are the subject of the copyright claim, (2) that plaintiff owns the copyrights in those works, (3) that the copyrights have been registered in accordance with the statute, and (4) by what acts and during what time the defendant infringed the copyright."[11] The Complaint meets these requirements.

A. Subject of the Copyright Claims

The Complaint contains an exhaustive list of specific original works that are the subject of the copyright claim. These include seven original literary works in which Conan first appeared, and numerous other works, such as comic books and graphic novels, in which he has been portrayed. The subject works also include about 90 works in which one or more of the REH characters are portrayed. All of these works are listed by name and copyright registration number. The Complaint further alleges which parts of those works are the subject of the claims by specifying the particular infringed characters by name. Plaintiffs plausibly alleged which works are the subject of their claims.

B. Ownership and Registration of Copyright in the Works

Production of a certificate of registration made before or within five years after first publication of the work constitutes prima facie evidence of the validity of the copyright. At the pleading stage, courts have accepted the registration number alone. Here, the Complaint alleges ownership of the copyright in each of the underlying works in which the characters first appeared and lists the registration number for each. In supplemental submissions, plaintiffs include copies of the certificates of registration and a declaration by Fredrik Malmberg, a representative of both plaintiffs, describing transfer of the copyrights in the underlying works from the successors and heirs of Robert E. Howard to the plaintiffs. This is more than enough to satisfy the ownership and registration elements.

For the purpose of demonstrating ownership of a valid copyright covering the *characters*, the Magistrate Judge disregarded the copyright registrations in the underlying works, assuming that only registration of the characters themselves would suffice. Given that the Copyright Office does not separately register characters, the Magistrate Judge reasoned that plaintiffs must instead allege copyright ownership by providing detailed descriptions of the characters' "metes and bounds." The Magistrate Judge therefore held that plaintiffs' copyrights in the characters were invalid because they were not sufficiently delineated to receive copyright protection.

That conclusion erroneously treats characters as separate and distinct copyright subject matter, divorced from the works in which they are embodied. To be sure,

---

11. In Feist Publications, Inc. v. Rural Tel. Serv. Co., 499 U.S. 340, 361 (1991), the Supreme Court stated, on review of a summary judgment decision, that a copyright claim requires proof of "(1) ownership of a valid copyright, and (2) copying of constituent elements of the work that are original." The first three elements listed in the text correspond to the first item in *Feist*, and the fourth element corresponds to the second. At the pleading stage, the plaintiff "need not specify which individual elements within the work are protected" because the certificate of registration is "prima facie evidence of the work's originality." 6 Patry on Copyright § 19:5 (citing 17 U.S.C. § 410).

courts outside this circuit lend some support to that view.[12] However, the Second Circuit recognizes that copyright protection for characters is a result of their embodiment in original works of authorship. *See Warner Bros. Inc. v. Am. Broad. Companies, Inc.*, 720 F.2d 231, 235 (2d Cir. 1983) ("Plaintiffs own the copyrights in various works embodying the character Superman and have thereby acquired copyright protection for the character itself."); *Burroughs v. Metro-Goldwyn-Mayer, Inc.*, 519 F. Supp. 388, 391 (S.D.N.Y. 1981), *aff'd*, 683 F.2d 610 (2d Cir. 1982) ("characters that are well-delineated in the Tarzan works of Edgar Rice Burroughs are protected from infringement by the copyright in the work itself."). Because the characters are elements of the underlying literary and graphic works in which they appear, plaintiffs' copyright registration in the underlying works satisfies the requirement that they plead ownership and registration of valid copyrights.

The Magistrate Judge correctly observed that a character will not receive copyright protection unless it is "distinctively delineated." However, the Court shares Professor Nimmer's view that questions regarding the scope of character delineation and protection "belong not to [a] discussion of copyright's subject matter but, instead, to the inquiry into substantial similarity." 1 Melville B. Nimmer and David Nimmer, *Nimmer on Copyright* § 2.12[A][1] (Rev. ed. 2018). The issue of substantial similarity is "[s]ubsumed within the fourth element—infringing acts," *McDonald v. K-2 Indus., Inc.*, 108 F. Supp. 3d 135, 139 (W.D.N.Y. 2015) and will be discussed further below.

By requiring plaintiffs to plead specific facts showing their entitlement to a separate and distinct copyright in their characters, the Magistrate Judge improperly heightened the pleading requirements under ... Rule 12(b)(6). Plaintiffs plausibly alleged that they owned a valid, registered copyright in the characters by virtue of their copyright in the underlying works.

C. Defendant's Acts of Infringement

Plaintiffs were required to allege how and when Sanchez infringed their copyrights. They alleged that, "during the three-year period preceding the filing of this action," Sanchez (1) manufactured and distributed unauthorized statues of Conan and the REH Characters on Kickstarter (or offered to do so); (2) publicly displayed images

---

12. A widely recognized example is Warner Bros. Pictures v. Columbia Broad. Sys., 216 F.2d 945, 950 (9th Cir. 1954), where the court held that transfer of the copyright in a story did not include exclusive rights to use the story's characters unless they "really constitute[d] the story being told." The Seventh Circuit called that decision "wrong," Gaiman v. McFarlane, 360 F.3d 644, 660 (7th Cir. 2004), and the Second Circuit stated that a broad reading of it would contradict public policy and "effectively permit the unrestrained pilfering of characters," Goodis v. United Artists Television, Inc., 425 F.2d 397, 406 (2d Cir. 1970). Even the Ninth Circuit has abandoned its suggestion that characters are separate and distinct from the underlying work. *See, e.g.*, Walt Disney Prods. v. Air Pirates, 581 F.2d 751, 754 (9th Cir. 1978) ("The fact that [Disney's] characters are not the separate subject of a copyright does not preclude their protection, however, because Section 3 of the then Copyright Act provided that Disney's copyrights included protection for 'all the copyrightable component parts of the work copyrighted.'").

of the unauthorized statues on Kickstarter and Facebook; and (3) publicly displayed other images of Conan and the REH Characters, including a picture of Conan as depicted by Arnold Schwarzenegger in a film poster from the 1980s. Exhibits attached to the Complaint include screen shots of the statue images as they appeared on Kickstarter and Facebook. Although plaintiffs did not allege the precise date of the infringement, the Facebook screen shots include the month and day, and no more is required. It would be impracticable to require plaintiffs to plead the date the statues were manufactured; few people other than Sanchez likely know that information. These allegations are sufficient to plausibly allege how and when the infringement occurred.

The Magistrate Judge found no liability as to four of the characters because plaintiffs did not make detailed allegations regarding which aspects of the characters were original and thus protectable. As explained above, these questions are part the inquiry into "substantial similarity"—that is, whether "the copying is illegal because a substantial similarity exists between the defendant's work and the protectible elements of plaintiff[s']." Substantial similarity and originality are questions of fact. By alleging that Sanchez's sculptures and images were infringing copies of the characters in plaintiffs' works, plaintiffs plausibly alleged that the similarities between the two were substantial. On the present motion, as on a motion to dismiss, the Court accepts those allegations as true.

Courts have inquired further into substantial similarity on a motion to dismiss "when a defendant raises the question of substantial similarity at the pleadings stage...." And courts have required specific allegations regarding substantial similarity when the complaint leaves doubt about what protectable aspects of the plaintiff's work allegedly have been infringed.

Here, by contrast, the issue of substantial similarity has not been raised, and the Complaint leaves no doubt about which parts of plaintiffs' works underlie their infringement claims. The plaintiffs plausibly allege that Sanchez's sculptures and images infringe the seven characters listed by name in their Complaint.

The Court adopts the [magistrate's report] insofar as it found liability for copyright infringement regarding El Borak, Solomon Kane, and Kull. However, it modifies the [magistrate's report] to find liability based on the four remaining characters: Conan, Ironhand (also known as Esau Cairn), Bran Mak Morn, and Dark Agnes. The Court also adopts, without objection, the finding of liability for trademark infringement, which was without error.

[D]. Statutory Damages

Although a defendant's default is generally an admission of liability, "it is not considered an admission of damages." Plaintiffs challenge the Magistrate Judge's recommendation to award only $9,000 in statutory damages and to deny permanent injunctive relief.

The Magistrate Judge recommended a statutory damages award of $3,000 per character, reasoning such an amount would be sufficient to compensate plaintiffs and deter future infringement. Among other things, she considered that Sanchez was an individual artist with a small operation who had nonetheless continued his infringing conduct after he was notified of it.

Plaintiffs object on several grounds, each based on the premise that the Magistrate Judge ignored the willfulness of Sanchez's infringement. Statutory damages normally range from $750 to $30,000 per work, but where a plaintiff proves willfulness, "the court in its discretion may increase the award of statutory damages to a sum of not more than $150,000" per work. However, the enhancement is discretionary — a finding of willfulness does not require an award above the $30,000 range. Here, even if the Court were to find willful infringement, a statutory damages award of $3,000 would be appropriate. The Court therefore adopts the Magistrate Judge's valuation of statutory damages at $3,000 per character. However, given the Court's conclusion that plaintiffs established liability for infringement based on seven separate characters, not three, the total damages shall be $21,000.

[E]. Permanent Injunction

The Magistrate Judge declined to recommend injunctive relief, reasoning primarily that plaintiffs failed to show irreparable harm. Plaintiffs argue that irreparable harm is established where, as here, there is a likelihood of continuing infringement. Under 17 U.S.C. § 502(a), the court may "grant temporary and final injunctions on such terms as it may deem reasonable to prevent or restrain infringement of a copyright." An injunction is appropriate if the plaintiff establishes past or imminent irreparable harm, money damages are inadequate, the balance of hardships tips in his favor, and the public interest would not be disserved. *Salinger v. Colting*, 607 F.3d 68, 79–80 (2d Cir. 2010) (citing *eBay Inc. v. MercExchange, L.L.C.*, 547 U.S. 388, 391 (2006)). Courts routinely address these concerns by awarding injunctive relief in copyright cases where liability is established and there is a threat of continuing infringement. Here, there was a strong threat of continuing infringement. After receiving a DMCA takedown notice, Sanchez filed a counter-notice insisting his sculptures were legal and continued to sell them under thinly veiled, generic names. For example, he changed "Conan the Barbarian" to "The Barbarian" and "Dark Agnes" to "Swordswoman." The Magistrate Judge speculated that he did so for the innocent purpose of avoiding trademark infringement. Even if that were so — and the Court is skeptical — it also suggests Sanchez's belief that he could freely copy plaintiffs' characters so long as he avoided using their exact names. Such a belief increases the likelihood of ongoing infringement.

Plaintiff also submitted a photo of one of Sanchez's sculptures posted to Facebook months after this lawsuit began. The Magistrate Judge disregarded it because the statue appeared to have been supplied by someone other than Sanchez. However, the photo is no less an infringing copy than the characters themselves. It therefore shows that Sanchez's initial conduct has extended beyond his control and caused additional instances of infringement, making it less likely that monetary damages alone will be adequate. Given the threat of continuing infringement and that monetary damages alone are inadequate, injunctive relief is appropriate.

For the foregoing reasons, plaintiff CPI is awarded $3,000 in statutory damages and plaintiff JEH is awarded $18,000 in statutory damages. Sanchez is permanently enjoined from unlawfully manufacturing, selling, or publicly displaying characters that infringe on plaintiffs' copyrights and trademarks.

Notes and Questions

a. Comic book rights have engendered a great deal of litigation. *See Lee v. Marvel Enters., Inc.*, 765 F. Supp. 2d 440, 445 (S.D.N.Y. 2011) *aff'd*, 471 Fed. App'x. 14 (2d Cir. 2012) (unpublished); *Abadin v. Marvel Entm't, Inc.*, No. 09 Civ. 715, 2010 WL 1257519 (S.D.N.Y. Mar. 31, 2010); *Stan Lee v. Marvel Enters., Inc.*, 386 F. Supp. 2d 235 (S.D.N.Y. 2005) (involving various claims related to Stan Lee's ownership of rights to the Marvel universe); *Marvel Characters, Inc. v. Kirby*, 726 F.3d 119 (2d Cir. 2013) (involving work of Jack Kirby on Fantastic Four and other projects for Marvel); *Siegel v. Warner Bros. Entm't, Inc.*, 658 F. Supp. 2d 1036 (C.D. Cal. 2009) (involving origins and ownership of Superman); *Gary Friedrich Enters., L.L.C. v. Marvel Characters, Inc.*, 716 F.3d 302 (2d Cir. 2013) (reflecting the disputed authorship of Ghost Rider).

b. Different film projects may result in very different merchandise. In *Twentieth Century Fox Film Corp. v. Suarez Corp.*, 46 U.S.P.Q.2d (BNA) 1312 (S.D.N.Y. 1998), a mail-order jeweler quickly created a design to mimic that worn by the star of *Titanic*. While the court refused to order a preliminary injunction against the jeweler, that was only because the court found the voluntary steps taken to withdraw from the marketplace made the injunction redundant and overreaching. As a result, Fox suddenly found itself in the jewelry business.

c. One of the most difficult aspects of character licensing is understanding the scope of such licenses. Literary characters are created within their literary world, but they often have the ability to transcend these worlds. In the bitter dispute between Marvel Comics and Twentieth Century Fox, this battle waged on for the supremacy of the *X-Men* characters as these superheroes transcended the confines of the *X-Men* comic books, animated television series and feature films by appearing in a live-action television series called *Mutant X*. Whereas the *X-Men* characters are endowed with superpowers, mere mortal lawyers are ultimately left struggling to determine these superheroes' final fates through the interpretation of licensing agreements contested between warring protagonists. *See Twentieth Century Fox Film Corp. v. Marvel Enters.*, 155 F. Supp. 2d 1 (S.D.N.Y. 2001), *aff'd in part, rev'd in part*, 277 F.3d 253 (2d Cir. 2002).

d. A deeper understanding of the licensing of characters can be gleaned from the ownership dispute involving the Jim Henson characters, Wilkins and Wontkins, created for John H. Wilkins Company coffee advertisements:

> In the late 1950s, when a copyright user wanted to obtain perpetual rights in a character (distinct from rights in a work in which the character appeared) it was the practice of the copyright bar to spell this out in no uncertain terms. One compelling reason for this is that in 1954, the Ninth Circuit had issued

its opinion in *Warner Bros. Pictures, Inc. v. Columbia Broadcasting Pictures, Inc. v. Columbia Broadcasting System, Inc.*, 216 F.2d 945 (9th Cir. 1954), which held that the clearest possible language was needed to divest Dashiell Hammet of his rights in his detective character Sam Spade, the principal character in The Maltese Falcon, and that his grant of motion picture, radio and television rights in The Maltese Falcon to Warner Bros. did not, as asserted by Warner Bros., give it the exclusive right to use Sam Spade in those media. In the wake of this watershed case, the copyright bar was on notice that there was the strongest presumption that even when an author transferred the copyright in a work in which a character was fully delineated, the author retained the right to use the character in sequels or other works. After that decision any copyright lawyer representing a user wishing to buy exclusive rights in a character would make certain that the assignment documents said so unmistakably and unequivocally.

Jim Henson Prods. v. John T. Brady & Assocs., 16 F. Supp. 2d 259, 277 (S.D.N.Y. 1997).

e. Characters also leave themselves open to significant claims of parody. Recent examples include *World Wrestling Fed'n. Entm't, Inc. v. Big Dog Holdings, Inc.*, 280 F. Supp. 2d 413 (W.D. Pa. 2003) (wrestling characters); *Warner Bros. v. American Broad. Cos.*, 720 F.2d 231 (2d Cir. 1983) (Superman parody); *Mattel Inc. v. Walking Mt. Prods.*, 353 F.3d 792 (9th Cir. 2003) (Barbie doll).

f. Another point regarding character licensing is the difficulty of knowing which characters will prove successful and unsuccessful when promoted for marketing. Despite the vagaries of popularity, the contractual obligations to promote characters may not be readily ignored just because of changing market conditions. *See Marsu, B.V. v. Walt Disney Co.*, 185 F.3d 932 (9th Cir. 1999) (obligation to promote European characters through creation of television show).

The opposite problem also occurs from time to time. In *Tom Doherty Associates v. Saban Entertainment*, 60 F.3d 27 (2d Cir. 1995), what had been a reasonable licensing agreement to turn children's television into modestly popular children's books became far less interesting to the licensor when its Mighty Morphin Power Rangers suddenly became the must-have characters among the pre-school set. Nonetheless, Saban's attempt to ignore the preexisting book publishing agreement could not be ignored simply because the characters were suddenly economic superheroes.

Problem 12-D

Bryce has called with an interesting issue that has developed during the creation of *Leer*. In writing material for the screenplay (*e.g.*, the scenes for the three sisters and the character sketches), Bryce believes the basis for a spin-off project has arisen. Entitled *Regan's Revenge*, Bryce outlined a novel based on Leer's second daughter, the villainous movie mogul. Bryce has also completed the first three chapters of the novel. The novel uses the relationship between Regan and Leer (derived from the relationship between Regan and Lear in Shakespeare's stage play) as the background for a dark comic look at Hollywood.

Bryce has received an offer to publish the novel, along with a publishing contract that requires a right of first refusal on motion picture rights to the novel. The production agreement for *Leer* assigns the copyright in the screenplay to the producers, including all sequel and prequel rights. The present screenplay for *Leer* has only three scenes with Regan. Bryce believes the character could be reduced even more, if necessary. Advise Bryce on the extent to which copyright law, trademark law, or customary industry contractual provisions would treat Bryce's development of *Regan's Revenge* as separate from *Leer*, and on Bryce's possible courses of action.

E. Ratings

Maljack Prods. v. Motion Picture Ass'n of America
52 F.3d 373 (D.C. Cir. 1995)

Maljack, an independent movie and video production company, sued the industry's major trade association, the Motion Picture Association of America, for breach of contract. Maljack asserted that the Association's film-rating arm had discriminated against it because it was not a member of the Association. The district court dismissed the complaint under Fed. R. Civ. P. 12(b)(6) for failure to state a claim, holding that Maljack's assertions of discrimination—that its movie had received an "X" rating for violence, while more violent films produced by companies belonging to the Association had been given "R"s—were not adequate to allege a breach of the ratings contract. We reverse....

Maljack is an Illinois corporation primarily engaged in distributing videocassettes to the home market. Its first major venture into the production of general-release films came in the mid-1980s, when it produced Henry: Portrait of a Serial Killer, a movie depicting, in documentary style, the life of a fictional serial murderer loosely based on a person on death row in Texas. Maljack concedes that Henry contains several explicit scenes of physical violence, including depictions of two rapes and several brutal murders.

The Motion Picture Association of America is a New York-incorporated trade association consisting of many of the largest American producers and distributors of television programs and motion pictures. Maljack is not a member. Among its other activities, the Association operates the Code and Rating Administration ("CARA"), located in California, which reviews movies prior to their release and evaluates their suitability for viewing by children. At the time of the events at issue, CARA rated movies either "G," "PG," "PG-13," "R," or "X"—with the exception of the last, all federally registered certification marks owned by the Association. Submission of a film to CARA is wholly voluntary, and producers are free to distribute movies without obtaining an Association rating.

In March 1988 Maljack submitted Henry to CARA for rating and paid a fee calibrated to the film's production costs. CARA gave Henry an "X" on grounds of its violence. That marked it, according to the Association's published general description of the rating, as having an "accumulation of brutal or sexually connected language, or of explicit sex or excessive and sadistic violence" that rendered it "patently an adult film." A representative of CARA explained that four sequences in the movie were particularly offensive and would have to be cut before CARA would even consider giving Henry an "R," the next most restrictive rating. Maljack refused to make the cuts and instead appealed the "X" rating to the Association's Classification and Rating Appeals Board. The Appeals Board affirmed the "X" rating.

In February 1989 Maljack surrendered the ratings certificate for Henry and chose instead to distribute the movie unrated. Maljack alleges that the picture was not as successful as it would have been if the Association had given Henry an "R": a substantial number of movie theaters will not show films that either are "X"-rated or lack a CARA rating altogether. Maljack maintains that the Association denied Henry an "R" rating because it was a small, independent production company that did not belong to the Association.

Maljack filed a two-count complaint against the Association in May 1990. Count I asked the court to cancel the Association's registered certification mark for the "R" rating on the grounds that the defendant applied its ratings in an illegally discriminatory fashion; the trial court dismissed this count on jurisdictional grounds, and Maljack does not appeal that ruling. Count II alleged that the Association's discrimination breached a covenant of good faith and fair dealing implied by law in CARA's agreement to rate Henry for a set fee. The district court also dismissed this count, holding that the complaint was devoid of non-conclusory factual allegations capable of supporting an inference that the Association had acted unfairly or in bad faith. Maljack moved to amend its complaint, but the district court denied leave to amend on the ground that the proposed amended complaint suffered from the same basic flaw.

Maljack now appeals both the dismissal of its original complaint and the denial of leave to amend. We need reach only the first issue....

We review de novo the district court's dismissal of the complaint for failure to state a claim. At this stage of the litigation the plaintiff's burden is relatively light.... At the same time, we are not to accept inferences drawn by Maljack if they are unsupported by the alleged facts, nor will we accept purely legal conclusions masquerading as factual allegations.

The parties and the district court have so far assumed that California law governs the rating agreement, and we will proceed on the same assumption. Under California law, "all contracts contain an implied covenant of good faith and fair dealing [that] "'requires each contracting party to refrain from doing anything to injure the right of the other to receive the benefits of the agreement.'" A complaint alleging breach of this covenant must plead deliberate and conscious bad faith on the part of the defendant:

> [A]llegations which assert such a claim must show that the conduct of the defendant, whether or not it also constitutes a breach of a consensual con-

tract term, demonstrates a failure or refusal to discharge contractual responsibilities, prompted not by an honest mistake, bad judgment or negligence but rather by a conscious and deliberate act, which unfairly frustrates the agreed common purposes and disappoints the reasonable expectations of the other party thereby depriving that party of the benefits of the agreement.

If the Association deliberately gave Henry an "X" rating instead of an "R" because Maljack was not a member, it breached this implied covenant. The Association's assertion that Maljack "bargained to receive CARA's subjective judgment and nothing more" is inaccurate: as it stated in its complaint, Maljack reasonably expected that CARA would rate Henry in good faith based upon the content of the film alone and not the identity of its producer and that producer's links (or lack of links) to the Association. This expectation of fair dealing is protected under California law as if it were an explicit obligation of the contract.

The question, then, is whether the original complaint adequately alleged the sort of discrimination that would violate the implied covenant. Maljack pled the following:

- That it did not belong to the Association,
- That although Henry contained some violent scenes, "the scenes were neither overly explicit or gory as compared to other films produced or released by members of the [Association] and given a "R" rating by the [Association],"
- That because of the small ($1,100) rating fee paid by Maljack under CARA's production-cost-based sliding scale, CARA was aware that Henry was not a major-studio "big budget" film,
- That CARA gave Henry an "X" rating without ever explaining "why other films containing equal or greater violence and released by member companies of the [Association] had received an "R" rating," [and]
- That the Association breached the covenant of good faith and fair dealing implied in the rating agreement "by rating [Henry] in a discriminatory manner when compared to other films it had given an 'R' rating to." The Association objects to the conclusory tone of this last paragraph and faults Maljack for never stating explicitly that it was discriminated against because it did not belong to the Association. This is too stingy a reading of the complaint. The context makes clear the plaintiff's claim that the discrimination mentioned in the last paragraph flowed from Maljack's non-member status.

The Association's more serious objection is that the mere fact that Henry received an "X" while more violent films by member companies were rated "R" cannot logically support an inference that CARA acted with improper motive. It is true, as the Association points out, that the complaint would have been stronger if it had alleged that the rating criteria were biased against independent producers, or that CARA had a pattern of giving unwarranted "X" ratings to similar movies, or that the Association's member companies had a financial interest in sabotaging Henry, or that there was some direct communication from the Association indicating bad faith.

But the absence of such confirming data does not nullify what has been alleged. Disparate treatment is the essence of all discrimination claims: at their core is always the assertion that the defendant has treated like cases differently on the basis of some impermissible criterion. And this is exactly what Maljack's complaint has alleged. The fact, which we must take as true, that the Association routinely assigned "R" ratings to member films more violent than Henry certainly suggests that it may have applied a different standard to Henry because of the identity of its producer. Later on, of course, at the summary judgment or trial phase of this litigation, it will not be easy for Maljack to show so skewed a ratings pattern as to support the inference necessary to meet California's quite demanding requirements for demonstrating bad faith, but federal pleading standards do not require the plaintiff to stuff its complaint with all of the details establishing the discrepancy. This is especially true in a case where, as here, the alleged discriminator is applying rather broad and amorphous criteria (e.g., "excessive ... violence"), so that countless details may be needed to support an inference of discrimination.

The Association effectively conceded at oral argument that this method of proof — comparing treatment in an individual case to the pattern of related decisions — is meaningful in this context. When asked to consider a hypothetical case in which a children's film like Snow White was given an "X" rating, Association counsel acknowledged that an observer could legitimately say something was amiss: Snow White's "X" would be so out of line with CARA's other decisions as to raise a compelling inference of something more than a simple judgment error or difference of opinion. Such logic is no different from that contained in Maljack's complaint. Henry the Serial Killer may be no Snow White (nor even her wicked stepmother), but the degree of difference is a question of fact, and we must now take the facts to be as Maljack alleges.

We therefore reverse the district court's order dismissing the original complaint and remand the case for further proceedings.

So ordered.

Notes and Questions

a. *From Hays Onward.*

Taking their cue from the baseball scandal involving the Chicago White Sox [in which professional baseball hired former federal judge Kenesaw Mountain Landis as the first baseball commissioner to "clean up the game"], the film producers decided that the best antidote for their Jewish, immoral product was a commissioner of film who was beyond reproach. The choice was Will Hays, former postmaster general of the United States. Hays had most recently served as President Harding's campaign manager. As a Republican and a Presbyterian elder, he represented the perfect image for the Jewish film industry. Hays was elected president of the Motion Picture Producers and Distributors of America. The members were the major studios, Columbia (now Sony), Metro-Goldwyn-Mayer, Paramount, RKO (now also owned by

Paramount's parent company Viacom), Twentieth Century-Fox, United Artists, Universal, and Warner Bros. With the addition of Disney and the merger of United Artists into Metro-Goldwyn-Mayer, the list has remained essentially unchanged.

The Hays Office, as the organization was generally known, undertook to clean up the image of the film industry. Initially, this was a rather ad hoc process of reviewing movies and clearing them for distribution, with a healthy dose of public relations thrown in at every step. By 1927, however, the Hays Office began to formalize its practices. In 1927, the Hays Office promulgated the Production Code, an official document outlining the principles of film production for approved films in the United States....

The Hays Office established a comprehensive process of prior review of source material to ensure that plays and novels were acceptable before they were purchased as the subjects for future films. The Production Code banned scenes, such as a man and woman sharing a bed (even if married); topics such as promiscuity, brutality, or pleasant depictions of immorality; and words ranging from "God" and "sex" to "guts," "nuts," "nerts," and "louse." Hays Office members were fined as much as $25,000 for violating the Code. These exacting rules and fines applied to every major studio and distributor in the United States. With detailed constraints and complete participation, there is no doubt that the films produced were more highly scrutinized than any governmental regulation could have created....

The greatest problem of the Production Code was its success. Although it has been significantly modified in response to the concerns that only Will Hays and a few deputies dictated the tastes and morality for the entire company, the reality is that the current Motion Picture Association of America (MPAA) has not significantly modified the effects of this system to this day.... The success of the Production Code existed before the films were granted protection by free speech. It was designed as a fence around a fence, crafted to ensure that Hollywood films were not censored by the governmental review boards out of fear of the negative press that would ensue and of the difficulties a finding of immorality would have on the already negotiated distribution agreements. As such, it resulted in far greater censorship than would have been required by the government, probably more stringent than would have been tolerated by the public of its elected officials. But as a voluntary activity, it was not in the interest of the filmmakers, distributors, exhibitors, or government officials to complain....

For the public, two important imprints were left by the Hays Office legacy. The first deals with voluntary censorship. The notion that voluntary censorship is a benign, unintrusive model designed to promote positive values without sacrificing free expression or democratic values has been sold to us since 1922. In addition to motion pictures, the media has added voluntary ratings to television, music, and video games, often at the urging of Congress....

Following the massacre of high school students in Littleton, Colorado in 1999, President Clinton pressured the National Association of Theater Owners to enforce the so-called voluntary movie-ratings restrictions by requiring photographic identification. Under the policy now enforced by the vast majority of theater exhibitors ... [p]arents who wish to encourage their teenage children to attend appropriate but mature films must accompany them to the theater. While still technically voluntary, the system urged by the President seems much like the governmental ban on alcohol and tobacco from which it is modeled.

The second legacy of the Hays Office was to weaken the impact of state-sponsored censorship. The fence within the fence of the Hays Office effectively marginalized the state and local film boards. Their threat kept the Hays Office humming, but only so no film board could have an opportunity to complain about the content of a Hollywood film. The effect was to desensitize the public and the courts to the real censorship taking place.…

Jon M. Garon, *Entertainment Law*, 76 Tul. L. Rev. 559, 649 (2002).

b. While the decision to allow adult films to be designated by anyone as "X" made sense, the pervasive nature of the ratings made the NC-17 inevitable. At the same time, the very need for the NC-17 rating reinforces how much more significant the ratings actually are than suggested by the MPAA. Rather than merely serving as a voluntary guide for concerned parents, the ratings may take on unintended roles. To what extent do the MPAA rating guidelines provide an unintended seal of approval for theatrical motion pictures? For another example of the problems caused by the X rating for mainstream films, *see Miramax Films Corp. v. Motion Picture Ass'n,* 148 Misc. 2d 1, 560 N.Y.S.2d 730 (N.Y. Sup. Ct. 1990).

c. Why is it critical that the MPAA has trademarked each of the ratings it uses within the rating system? Do these marks actually meet the legal standards for being registered trademarks as either the source of goods or an endorsement thereof?

d. Enterprising businesses might see other opportunities to make use of the ratings designation. Could a clothing manufacturer design a line of children's clothes rated "PG-13" and a lower-cut line rated "R"? *See Motion Picture Ass'n. of Am. v. Rated R Clothing, Inc.,* 646 F. Supp. 22 (S.D.N.Y. 1986).

e. The ratings are used by parents as a guide to let them and their children select appropriate viewing material, as well as by most exhibitors looking to control who is permitted to enter the theatre. Is such a restriction by the theatrical exhibitors free of any First Amendment concerns? Is the failure to enforce the rating restrictions the potential cause for liability? *See Delgado v. Am. Multi-Cinema, Inc.,* 72 Cal. App. 4th 1403, 85 Cal. Rptr. 2d 838 (Ct. App. 1999); *Rosen v. Budco, Inc.,* 10 Phila. Co. Rptr. 112 (Pa. C.P. 1983).

f. Colleges and universities sometimes play the role of *in loco parentis*, serving as surrogate parents for the students on campus. Can a college campus prohibit the showing of X or NC-17 films in school facilities? Does it matter if the school is a private institution or a publicly funded state college? *See Swope v. Lubbers*, 560 F. Supp. 1328 (W.D. Mich. 1983).

g. With the advent of DVDs, a new sub-market has developed for "R" rated films. Distributors now market DVDs that have both exhibition rated and unrated versions in video stores. To what extent will this trend undermine the impact of the MPAA? Will rules be forthcoming to bar the two-rating distribution of DVDs?

h. In addition to the MPAA, ratings systems now exist for music, broadcast television and cable, and video games. Have these additional ratings regimes improved the usefulness of the ratings? Do these guides have the impact intended by their advocates?

i. The MPAA also operates an aggressive anti-piracy division and a title registry service. The MPAA's Title Registration Bureau is voluntary, but all members of the MPAA use it, as do most other theatrical producers and distributors. The system allows any member to object to the use of a registered title or title similar to that of a registered title. Studios tend to use the system aggressively to make naming new films somewhat difficult. In the case of the dispute between The Weinstein Company and Warner Bros., the movie originally entitled *The Butler* received a notice of objection by Warner Bros. because it was the same title as one used in 1916 for a short, silent film. An arbitration hearing determined that The Weinstein Company could use *Lee Daniels' The Butler* because that title had also been registered by The Weinstein Company and Warner Bros. had failed to object to the use of the phrase "the butler" as part of another title. Because The Weinstein Company had marketed the movie under its original title during the pendency of the arbitration, however, it received a $400,000 fine.

Problem 12-E

Bryce received a green light to proceed with the screenplay for *Leer* as a filmed musical in the genre of modern rock opera as popularized by *Chicago*, *American Idiot*, or *Book of Mormon*. Bryce now faces a problem. Bryce's rewrites of the script and extensive character development made certain scenes more graphic and sexual than the initial draft. The producers are objecting to the explicit content of the revisions. They believed the original script served to condemn the immoral lifestyle of the characters while Bryce's most recent changes seem to celebrate that immorality. Because of these new explicit scenes, the producers are concerned that Bryce may not be able to deliver an "R" rated film.

The contract specified that Bryce would use best efforts to deliver a "PG-13" rated film, but required the producers to accept delivery of the finished film with an "R" rating if Bryce could not, in good faith, edit the film in a manner that was consistent with the approved screenplay, if such edit resulted in an "R" rating.

Bryce seeks your advice. To what extent can the production agreement require editing of a film to receive a particular MPAA rating, and what can Bryce do to avoid creating an "NC-17" film or having the production cancelled? Provide Bryce with guidance on how to best address the situation.

F. Bibliography and Links

PAUL A. BAUMGARTEN, DONALD C. FARBER & MARK FLEISCHER, PRODUCING, FINANCING & DISTRIBUTING FILM: A COMPREHENSIVE LEGAL & BUSINESS GUIDE (2d ed. 1992).

JON GARON, THE INDEPENDENT FILMMAKER'S LAW & BUSINESS GUIDE TO FINANCING, SHOOTING, & DISTRIBUTING INDEPENDENT & DIGITAL FILMS (2d ed. 2009).

MARK LITWAK, DEALMAKING IN THE FILM & TELEVISION INDUSTRY (4th ed. 2016).

SCHUYLER M. MOORE, THE BIZ: THE BASIC BUSINESS, LEGAL & FINANCIAL ASPECTS OF THE FILM INDUSTRY (5th ed. 2018).

Peter Decherney, *Auteurism on Trial: Moral Rights and Films on Television*, 2011 WIS. L. REV. 273 (2011).

Catherine L. Fisk, *The Role of Private Intellectual Property Rights in Markets for Labor and Ideas: Screen Credit and the Writers Guild of America, 1938–2000*, 32 BERKELEY J. EMP. & LAB. L. 215 (2011).

Jeanne C. Fromer, *The Unregulated Certification Mark(et)*, 69 STAN. L. REV. 121 (2017).

Michael J. Fucci, *Facing the Future: An Analysis of the Television Ratings System*, 6 UCLA ENT. L. REV. 1 (1998).

Jon M. Garon, *Star Wars: Film Permitting, Prior Restraint & Government's Role in the Entertainment Industry*, 17 LOY. L.A. ENT. L.J. 1 (1996).

Jeremy Geltzer, *Forbidden Films and the First Amendment*, 2016 WIS. L. REV. FORWARD 1 (2016).

Justin Hughes, *Actors as Authors in American Copyright Law*, 51 CONN. L. REV. 1 (2019).

Richard M. Mosk, *Motion Picture Ratings in the United States*, 15 CARDOZO ARTS & ENT. L.J. 135 (1997).

Claire Piepenburg, *Not Yet Rated: Self-Regulation and Censorship Issues in the U.S. Film Industry*, 25 UCLA ENT. L. REV. 97 (2018).

Randle B. Pollard, *"Cut — and That's a Wrap" — the Film Industry's Fleecing of State Tax Incentive Programs*, 50 AKRON L. REV. 425 (2016).

Tracy Reilly, *Copyright and a Synergistic Society*, 18 MINN. J.L. SCI. & TECH. 575 (2017).

Ben Sheffner, *Why Movie Studios Care About Right of Publicity*, 42 COLUM. J.L. & ARTS 341 (2019).

Joel Timmer, *The First Amendment and Content Restrictions in State Film Incentive Programs*, 38 LOY. L.A. ENT. L. REV. 37 (2018).

Websites

CALIFORNIA FILM COMMISSION, http://film.ca.gov/

Directors Guild of America, http://www.dga.org/

IATSE, https://www.iatse.net/

Motion Picture Association of America, http://www.mpaa.org

Parental Advisory Label, Recording Industry Association of America, https://www.riaa.com/resources-learning/parental-advisory-label/

Screen Actors Guild, https://www.sagaftra.org/

Ratings Guide, The Entertainment Software Rating Board (ESRB), https://www.esrb.org/ratings/ratings_guide.aspx

The Producers Guild of America, http://www.producersguild.org

TV Parental Guidelines, http://www.tvguidelines.org/

Writers Guild of America West, http://www.wga.org/

Chapter 13

Television and Cable Production Agreements

A. Structure of the Television and Cable Market

1. Introduction

The home entertainment industry known as "television" includes broadcast television, cable, satellite, sales and rentals of content on DVDs, Blu-Ray Discs, and other physical media, Internet-based distribution by video hosting companies and by commercial content producers. Because of the historical growth of the television business and the ubiquity of the TV as the primary viewing device, all these content forms are usually understood as television.

As this excerpt explains, television grew out of the radio broadcast industry.

The battle to control the television industry was fought through a series of interdependent battles; fights over technology; competition for content; influence over the artists; and finally a race to win over the public. Each of these battles established the framework for the next competition, as the players shifted in their influence and power....

At its origins, the battle to control television was understood merely as a race to establish and patent a new technology. But even this introductory step combined technology with finance and management. RCA, led by David Sarnoff, won the competition because RCA combined these elements at a time when no other competitor had mastery of all three. RCA ... was in a position to invest not only the research needed to perfect and continually improve the broadcast of television but also the manufacture of the home television consoles and the content development in performers, scripts, and events to make the market essential to the new viewers....

Sarnoff built RCA into the dominant leader in radio. [CBS was formed in 1927 but was not a major broadcaster until the post-war television era.] Writing in 1938, the FCC explained that "[t]he largest and oldest national organization is the National Broadcasting Company, Inc., founded in 1926, a subsidiary of the Radio Corporation of America. NBC operates two network systems, known as the "Red" and "Blue" networks." The FCC ultimately passed regulations forcing NBC to divest itself of two networks, resulting in the sale of the Blue network, which was renamed and grew into ABC....

By the end of World War II ... the focus shifted to the three dominant national radio networks, NBC, CBS, and fledgling ABC.... Within a decade, the golden age of television would be nearly over.[1]

The motion picture producers viewed television as a threat to their business. In addition to producing films, the film studios had monopoly control over the theaters across the country. Radio already kept audience members at home. The expansion of broadcast into television would make the competition worse. As a result, most studios ignored or fought the growth of television, allowing it to become an even greater source of competition.

Broadcasting television is expensive and limited to the line-of-sight broadcast of the Very High Frequency band (channels 2–13) and the Ultra High Frequency band (channels 14–51). To protect the integrity of analog signals, the FCC tightly controlled the licenses for stations. In rural areas, access to broadcast television was often sparse, so community antenna television (CATV) filled the gap.

CATV systems receive the signals of television broadcasting stations, amplify them, transmit them by cable or microwave, and ultimately distribute them by wire to the receivers of their subscribers. CATV systems characteristically do not produce their own programming, and do not recompense producers or broadcasters for use of the programming which they receive and redistribute. Unlike ordinary broadcasting stations, CATV systems commonly charge their subscribers installation and other fees.

The CATV industry has grown rapidly since the establishment of the first commercial system in 1950.... By late 1965, it was reported that there were 1,847 operating CATV systems, that 758 others were franchised but not yet in operation, and that there were 938 applications for additional franchises....

CATV systems perform either or both of two functions. First, they may supplement broadcasting by facilitating satisfactory reception of local stations in adjacent areas in which such reception would not otherwise be possible; and second, they may transmit to subscribers the signals of distant stations entirely beyond the range of local antennae. As the number and size of CATV systems have increased, their principal function has more frequently become the importation of distant signals. In 1959, only 50 systems employed microwave relays, and the maximum distance over which signals were transmitted was 300 miles; by 1964, 250 systems used microwave, and the transmission distances sometimes exceeded 665 miles.[2]

---

1. Jon M. Garon, *Hidden Hands that Shaped the Marketplace of Ideas: Television's Early Transformation from Medium to Genre*, 19 U. Denver Sports & Ent. L.J. 30, 31-15 (2016) (internal citations omitted).

2. United States v. Sw. Cable Co., 392 U.S. 157, 161–63 (1968).

The explosive growth of CATV in the 1960s was then accompanied by premium channels like Home Box Office (HBO) and Showtime that were either sent directly to consumers via microwave or carried on the CATV systems. Over time, the technology improved, allowing cable systems to go from a dozen channels to hundreds of channels. As television broadcast transitioned to digital signals, the ability to carry more channels also increased. Viewership patterns shifted from an emphasis on the broadcast stations to the premium channels; from the network news stations to cable news; and eventually to content originating with the cable channels rather than broadcasters.

Satellite systems such as DIRECTV and Dish Network provided a national footprint for the distribution of cable channel content. Though the FCC regulates them separately than the cable systems, they largely serve as another distribution platform.

The digital transformation has added another shift. Known as "over the top" (OTT) content, a new group of content creators and distributors have challenged the dominance of the broadcast networks and the cable systems. These programmers include Netflix, Amazon Prime, Hulu (now owned by Disney), YouTube, Vimeo, Apple TV, and many others. Following the pattern of CATV, Netflix and Amazon initially served as alternative distributors. In 1999, Netflix began as an alternative to Blockbuster, mailing DVDs to consumers' homes on a subscription basis. By 2007, the ability to stream Internet content was more cost effective than mailing DVDs. With "House of Cards" in 2013, it moved into original programming and, in 2019, joined the MPAA as one of the major production studios in the U.S. Amazon's content service, Amazon Prime, has followed suit.

In contrast, YouTube began in 2005 as a video-sharing service that paid little heed to copyright enforcement, becoming the home to a massive collection of pirated and unauthorized content. Google purchased the company the following year, transforming it from a piratical haven to an advertising mecca. The platform mixed consumer uploads of commercially released content with original programming from the public. Video producers have uploaded content of every possible type onto the platform, with millions of how-to videos, original comedy series, music videos, and professional narrative series with high-end production values. YouTube also partners with the major film and television studios to deliver on-demand commercial content and to create its own original programming.

The digital transformation of television has also enabled the content producers to distribute the content on all digital video devices. While television sets remain a fixture in almost every home, an increasingly significant amount of content is viewed on computers, tablets, phones, watches, and other mobile devices. Every traditional television distributor now produces its content for all platforms. Content producers are experimenting with the order in which content is produced for various platforms. CBS, for example, is producing a number of *Star Trek* television series for its online platform before releasing that content on cable and broadcast, reversing the historical distribution patterns and indicating a shift by the content producers away from the cable distributors.

2. Television Networks, Stations, and Studios[3]

Programming is a critical input for broadcast television stations to compete effectively in the industry. Stations combine local programming, either produced in-house or acquired from independent sources, syndicated programming, and/or network programming. The mix of programming varies by station, and depends on whether the station is affiliated with a network or operates as an independent station. Whether or not a station is affiliated with one of the four major networks (ABC, CBS, Fox, or NBC) has a significant impact on the composition of the station's revenues, expenses, and operations.

Most full-power commercial stations (approximately 92 percent) get at least some of their programming from broadcast networks on their primary signals. Commercial broadcast networks generally fall into five main categories: English-language (*e.g.*, ABC, CBS, Fox, NBC, The CW, and MyNetworkTV); Spanish-language (*e.g.*, Univision, Telemundo, and TeleFutura); shopping (*e.g.*, HSN); religious (*e.g.*, TBN and CTN); and regional specialty networks (*e.g.*, Memorable Entertainment Television). Three of the major networks (ABC, CBS, and NBC) generally provide their affiliates with about 22 hours per week of prime time programming. Fox, MyNetworkTV, and The CW supply affiliates with up to 15 hours per week of prime time programming. In addition, these networks may supply affiliates with daytime programming (*e.g.*, morning news programs, game shows, talk shows (including Sunday public affairs), and late night programs). Spanish language and religious networks provide nearly round-the-clock programming for affiliates.

Broadcast stations also acquire programming from television syndicators that distribute original ("first-run syndication") programming, such as *Jeopardy!* and *Judge Judy*, or reruns of network television series ("off-net" syndication), such as reruns of *Seinfeld* and *The Simpsons*, to television stations. In addition, local broadcast stations produce programming in-house, such as local newscasts, public affairs shows, and coverage of regional and local sporting events....

Analyzing the largest group owners in terms of revenue results in a similar list. According to *TVNewsCheck*, the top station groups in 2011 in terms of revenue include Fox, CBS, NBCUniversal, ABC, Tribune, Sinclair, Gannett, Hearst, Belo Corp., and Univision....

Some stations are vertically integrated upstream, with suppliers of programming, as well as downstream, with distributors of programming. For instance, the stations' parent company may have ownership interests in television production studios, movie studios, sports teams, broadcast television networks, cable networks, or syndicators. Similarly, Comcast's acquisition of NBC/Universal resulted in downstream vertical integration of NBC's [owned and operated (O&O)] stations with a cable MVPD [Multi-channel Video Programming Distributor].

---

3. Excerpts from FCC, 15th Annual Assessment of the Status of Competition in the Market for the Delivery of Video Programming, July 19, 2013 (superseded).

[The] parent companies of six of the top seven station groups — ION Media Networks, Univision Communications, Inc., CBS Television Stations, Fox Television Stations, NBC Universal Stations, and ABC Owned Television Stations, representing 188 O&Os, own all or part of at least one broadcast television network. Broadcast networks typically own and operate their own stations in the largest television markets. Spanish-language broadcast networks, *e.g.*, Univision and Telemundo, own and operate television stations in the largest Spanish-speaking markets....

The Walt Disney Company Form 10-K Description of Business Operations

For the year ended December 31, 2018[4]

The Walt Disney Company [(Company, We)], together with its subsidiaries, is a diversified worldwide entertainment company with operations in four business segments: Media Networks, Parks and Resorts, Studio Entertainment, and Consumer Products & Interactive Media....

During fiscal 2018, the Company entered into an Amended and Restated Agreement and Plan of Merger with Twenty-First Century Fox, Inc, (21CF) that includes the acquisition of certain 21CF businesses, the most significant of which are the Twentieth Century Fox film and television studios, certain cable networks (including FX and Nat Geo), 21CF's international television businesses and 21CF's 30% interest in Hulu. The closing of the acquisition is expected to occur in the first half of calendar year 2019.

The Company is developing a new direct-to-consumer (DTC) service, Disney+, that is scheduled to launch in the U.S. in late 2019. Disney+ will offer Disney, Pixar, Marvel and Lucasfilm movies released theatrically after calendar 2018. It will also feature an array of exclusive original series and movies, along with titles/episodes from the Company's film and television libraries.

Media Networks

The Media Networks segment includes cable and broadcast television networks, television production and distribution operations, domestic television stations and radio networks and stations. The Company also has investments in entities that operate programming services, including television networks, which are accounted for under the equity method of accounting.

The businesses in the Media Networks segment principally generate revenue from the following:

- fees charged to cable, satellite and telecommunications service providers (traditional Multi-channel Video Programming Distributors (MVPD)), over-the-top (OTT) digital MVPDs (DMVPD) (both collectively referred to as MVPDs)

---

4. https://www.thewaltdisneycompany.com/wp-content/uploads/2019/01/2018-Annual-Report.pdf.

and television stations affiliated with our domestic broadcast television network for the right to deliver our programs to their customers/subscribers ("affiliate fees");

- the sale to advertisers of time in programs for commercial announcements ("ad sales"); and
- the license to television networks and distributors of the right to use our television programming ("program sales").

Operating expenses primarily consist of programming and production costs, participations and residuals expense, technical support costs, operating labor and distribution costs.

Cable Networks

Our primary cable networks are branded ESPN, Disney and Freeform. These networks produce their own programs or acquire rights from third parties to air their programs on our networks. Cable networks derive the majority of their revenues from affiliate fees and, for certain networks (primarily ESPN and Freeform), ad sales. Generally, the Company's cable networks provide programming under multi-year licensing agreements with MVPDs that include contractually specified rates on a per subscriber basis. The amounts that we can charge to MVPDs for our cable network programming is largely dependent on the quality and quantity of programming that we can provide and the competitive market for programming services. The ability to sell time and the rates received for commercial announcements are primarily dependent on the size and nature of the audience that the network can deliver to the advertiser as well as overall advertiser demand. We also sell programming developed by our cable networks worldwide to television broadcasters, to subscription video-on-demand (SVOD) services (such as Netflix, Hulu and Amazon) and in home entertainment formats (such as DVD, Blu-ray and electronic home video license)....

ESPN is a multimedia sports entertainment company owned 80% by the Company and 20% by Hearst Corporation. ESPN operates eight 24-hour domestic television sports channels.... ABC Television Network, which is branded ESPN on ABC. ESPN owns 19 television channels outside of the United States (primarily in Latin America and Australia) that reach 61 countries and territories in four languages (English, Spanish, Portuguese and French).

Disney. The Company operates over 100 Disney branded television channels, which are broadcast in 34 languages and 164 countries/territories.

Broadcasting

Our broadcasting business includes a domestic broadcast network, television production and distribution operations, and eight owned domestic television stations.

Domestic Broadcast Television Network

The Company operates the ABC Television Network (ABC), which as of September 29, 2018, had affiliation agreements with 244 local television stations reaching almost 100% of U.S. television households. ABC broadcasts programs in the primetime, daytime, late night, news and sports "dayparts." ABC produces its own programs and also acquires programming rights from third parties as well as entities that are owned by or affiliated with the Company. ABC derives the majority of its revenues from ad sales. The ability to sell time for commercial announcements and the rates received are primarily dependent on the size and nature of the audience that the network can deliver to the advertiser as well as overall advertiser demand for time on network broadcasts.

ABC also receives fees from affiliated television stations for the right to broadcast ABC programming. ABC network programming is available digitally on internet-connected devices to authenticated MVPD subscribers. Non-subscribers have more limited access to on-demand episodes. ABC provides online access to certain programming through the ABC App and website. ABC also provides in-depth worldwide news coverage online through websites, the ABC NewsApp, OTT apps and to select distribution partners.

Television Production and Distribution

The Company produces the majority of its scripted television programs under the ABC Studios banner. Program development is carried out in collaboration with independent writers, producers and creative teams, with a focus on one-hour dramas and half-hour comedies, primarily for primetime broadcasts. Primetime programming produced either for our networks or for third-party television networks for the 2018/2019 television season includes nine returning and seven new one-hour dramas, six returning and four new half-hour comedies, and three returning non-scripted series. Additionally, the Company is producing original first run series for SVOD services (including Hulu). The Company also produces *Jimmy Kimmel Live* for late night and a variety of primetime specials, as well as syndicated, news and daytime programming. We distribute the Company's productions worldwide to television broadcasters, SVOD services (including Hulu), and on home entertainment formats.

Competition and Seasonality

The Company's Media Networks businesses compete for viewers primarily with other broadcast and cable networks, independent television stations and other media, such as online video services and video games. With respect to the sale of advertising time, we compete with other television networks and radio stations, independent television stations, MVPDs and other advertising media such as digital content, newspapers, magazines and billboards. Our television and radio stations primarily compete for audiences and advertisers in local market areas.

The Company's Media Networks businesses face competition from other networks for carriage by MVPDs. The Company's contractual agreements with MVPDs are renewed or renegotiated from time to time in the ordinary course of business. Consolidation and other market conditions in the cable, satellite and telecommunication distribution industry and other factors may adversely affect the Company's ability to obtain and maintain contractual terms for the distribution of its various programming services that are as favorable as those currently in place....

CBS Corporation Form 10-K Description of Business Operations

For the year ended December 31, 2018[5]

The Company operates businesses which span the media and entertainment industries, including the CBS Television Network, cable networks, content production and distribution, television stations, direct-to-consumer digital streaming services and other internet-based businesses, and consumer publishing. The Company's principal strategy is to create and acquire premium content that is widely accepted by audiences and generate affiliate and subscription fee, licensing and advertising revenues from the distribution of this content on multiple media platforms and to various geographic locations. The Company plans to increase its investment in premium content to enhance its opportunities for revenue growth, which include exhibiting the Company's content on its direct-to-consumer digital streaming services; expanding the distribution of its content internationally; and securing compensation from multi-channel video programming distributors ("MVPDs"), including cable, direct broadcast satellite ("DBS"), telephone company, and other distributors, as well as third-party live television digital streaming offerings ("virtual MVPDs"), for authorizing the MVPDs' and virtual MVPDs' carriage of the Company's owned television stations (also known as "retransmission fees") and cable networks, and securing compensation from television stations affiliated with the CBS Television Network ("station affiliation fees," also known as "reverse compensation"). The Company also seeks to grow its advertising revenues by monetizing all content viewership as industry measurements evolve to reflect viewers' changing habits.

The Company competes with many different entities and media in various markets worldwide. In addition to competition in each of its businesses, the Company competes for opportunities in the entertainment business with other diversified entertainment companies such as The Walt Disney Company, NBCUniversal Media, L.L.C., Twenty-First Century Fox, Inc. and the WarnerMedia segment of AT&T Inc., formerly Time Warner Inc....

The Entertainment segment consists of the CBS Television Network; CBS Television Studios and CBS Global Distribution Group (composed of CBS Studios International and CBS Television Distribution), the Company's television production and syndication operations; Network 10, the Company's commercial broadcast network in Australia; CBS Interactive, the Company's online content networks for information and entertainment; CBS Sports Network, the Company's cable network focused on college athletics and other sports; CBS Films; and the Company's direct-to-consumer digital streaming services CBS All Access, CBSN, CBS Sports HQ, ET Live and 10 All Access.

Television Network. The CBS Television Network through CBS Entertainment™, CBS News® and CBS Sports® distributes a comprehensive schedule of news and public

---

5. https://www.sec.gov/ix?doc=/Archives/edgar/data/813828/000081382819000006/cbs_10k-123118.htm.

affairs broadcasts, sports and entertainment programming to more than 200 domestic affiliates reaching throughout the U.S., including 15 of the Company's owned and operated television stations, and to affiliated stations in certain U.S. territories.

The CBS Television Network primarily derives revenues from the sale of advertising time for its network broadcasts. A significant portion of the sale of advertising spots for the network's non-sports programming occurs annually generally during May through July in the industry's upfront advertising market for the upcoming television broadcast season, which runs for one year generally commencing in mid-September. Overall advertising revenue for the network is also impacted by audience ratings for its programming and market conditions, including demand in the scatter advertising market, in which advertisers purchase the remaining advertising spots closer to the broadcast of the related programming. The Company offers dynamic advertising insertions for the CBS Television Network's on-demand programming, which allows the Company to change advertisements at any time within such programming and offer advertisers greater audience reach. The Company is focused on developing advanced advertising products that enable advertisers to target specific audience segments. In addition, the CBS Television Network's revenues include station affiliation fees. . . .

Generally, a network will license a specified number of episodes for broadcast on the network in the U.S. during a license period. Remaining distribution rights, including international and/or off network syndication rights, are typically retained by the Company or, in the case of co-productions, distribution rights are shared with the co-producer for U.S. or international markets. The network license fee for a series episode is normally lower than the costs of producing the episode; however, the Company's objective is to recoup its costs and earn a profit through various forms of distribution, including international licensing, domestic syndication and digital streaming of episodes. Generally, international sales of network series are made within one year of the U.S. network run and series must have a network run of at least three or four years to be successfully sold in domestic off-network syndication; however, increasingly, these time frames are being shortened, particularly for sales to digital streaming services. In off-network syndication, the Company distributes series, such as Hawaii Five-O, Criminal Minds, Blue Bloods, Elementary, NCIS, NCIS: Los Angeles and NCIS: New Orleans as well as a library of older television programs. The Company also produces and/or distributes first-run syndicated series such as Wheel of Fortune, Jeopardy!, Entertainment Tonight, Inside Edition, Dr. Phil, The Doctors, Rachael Ray, Hot Bench and Judge Judy and produces The Good Fight, Star Trek: Discovery, No Activity, Strange Angel and Tell Me a Story for streaming on CBS All Access. The Company also distributes syndicated and other programming internationally.

The Company continues to monetize its content through digital media. It enters into and renews numerous multi-year licensing agreements for distribution of certain of its programming to various services reaching countries throughout the world, particularly the U.S., Canada and in Europe. These services include digital streaming on subscription or advertiser-supported video-on-demand services, including services by Amazon, Bell Media, Hotstar, Netflix, Stan Entertainment and Telefonica; virtual MVPDs, including DIRECTV NOW, Hulu with Live TV and YouTube TV; and digital downloading on various electronic sell-through services owned by Amazon, Apple, Google and Microsoft, among others.

Comcast Corporation Form 10-K Description of Business Operations

For the year ended December 31, 2018[6]

Comcast Corporation ("Comcast") and NBCUniversal Media, L.L.C. ("NBCUniversal") [(collectively "we," "us")]. Comcast owns all of the common equity interests in NBCUniversal.... NBCUniversal [operates] in four reportable business segments: Cable Networks, Broadcast Television, Filmed Entertainment and Theme Parks (collectively, the "NBCUniversal segments")....

NBCUniversal is one of the world's leading media and entertainment companies that develops, produces and distributes entertainment, news and information, sports, and other content for global audiences, and owns and operates theme parks worldwide.

Cable Networks

NBCUniversal's Cable Networks segment consists of a diversified portfolio of national cable networks that provide a variety of entertainment, news and information, and sports content, regional sports and news networks, international cable networks, and cable television studio production operations. It also owns various digital properties, which include brand-aligned websites.

The regional sports and news networks together serve more than 27 million households across the United States, including in markets such as Baltimore/Washington, Boston, Chicago, Philadelphia, Portland, Sacramento and San Francisco.

NBCUniversal's Cable Networks segment generates revenue primarily from the distribution and licensing of its programming and from the sale of advertising on its networks and digital properties. It markets and distributes cable network programming in the United States and internationally to multichannel video providers, including both traditional providers of linear programming and virtual providers who provide streaming services for linear programming. It also markets and distributes cable network programming to subscription video on demand services, such as those offered by Amazon, Hulu and Netflix. These distributors may provide its content on television, including via video on demand services, online and through mobile apps.

NBCUniversal's cable networks produce their own programs or acquire the rights to programming from third parties, including sports programming rights that are discussed below under the heading "Broadcast Television." NBCUniversal's cable tel-

---

6. https://www.cmcsa.com/financials/sec-filings-NBCUniversal?field_nir_sec_form_group_target_id%5B%5D=471&field_nir_sec_date_filed_value=&items_per_page=10#views-exposed-form-widget-sec-filings-table.

evision studio production operations identify, develop and produce original content for its own cable networks and third parties. It licenses its owned content, including programming from its cable network production operations, to cable and broadcast networks and subscription video on demand services. It also sells its owned content on standard-definition DVDs and Blu-ray discs (together, "DVDs") and through digital distribution services such as iTunes.

Broadcast Television

NBCUniversal's Broadcast Television segment operates the NBC and Telemundo broadcast networks, which together serve viewers and advertisers in all 50 states. The Broadcast Television segment also includes owned NBC and Telemundo local broadcast television stations, the NBC Universo national cable network, broadcast television studio production operations, and various digital properties, which primarily include brand-aligned websites. The Broadcast Television segment generates revenue primarily from the sale of advertising on its networks and digital properties, from the licensing of its programming, and from the fees received under retransmission consent agreements and associated fees received from NBC-affiliated and Telemundo-affiliated local broadcast television stations.

NBC Network

The NBC network distributes entertainment, news and sports programming that reaches viewers in virtually all U.S. television households through more than 200 affiliated stations across the United States, including NBCUniversal's 11 owned NBC-affiliated local broadcast television stations. The NBC network's programming library consists of rights of varying nature to more than 100,000 episodes of popular television content, including current and classic titles, unscripted programming, sports, news, long-form and short-form programming, and locally produced programming from around the world....

The broadcast television studio production operations develop and produce original content, including scripted and unscripted programming series and talk shows. This original content is licensed to broadcast networks, cable networks and local broadcast television stations owned by NBCUniversal and third parties, as well as to subscription video on demand services, and it is sold on DVDs and through digital distribution services both in the United States and internationally. The broadcast television studio production operations also produce first-run syndicated shows for local markets that are broadcast on local broadcast television stations in the United States on a market-by-market basis. They currently distribute some of their television programs after their initial broadcast, as well as older television programs from their library, to local broadcast television stations and cable networks in the off-network syndication market.

NBC Local Broadcast Television Stations

As of December 31, 2018, NBCUniversal owned and operated 11 NBC-affiliated local broadcast television stations, including stations in 8 of the top 10 general markets, that collectively reached approximately 32 million U.S. television households and represent approximately 29% of U.S. television households. In addition to broadcasting the NBC network's national programming, its local broadcast television stations produce news, sports, public affairs and other programming that addresses local needs and acquire syndicated programming from other sources.

Telemundo

Telemundo is a leading Hispanic media company that produces, acquires and distributes Spanish-language content in the United States and internationally. Telemundo's operations include the Telemundo network, its 28 owned local broadcast television stations and the NBC Universo national cable network.

The Telemundo network is a leading Spanish-language broadcast network featuring original telenovelas, movies, news, specials and sporting events. Telemundo develops original programming primarily through its production studio and also acquires the rights to programming from third parties. It holds the Spanish-language U.S. broadcast rights to FIFA World Cup soccer through 2026.

Telemundo Local Broadcast Television Stations

As of December 31, 2018, Telemundo owned 28 local broadcast television stations affiliated with the Telemundo network, including stations in 18 of the top 20 U.S. Hispanic markets, which collectively reached approximately 70% of U.S. Hispanic television households as of December 31, 2018. Telemundo also owns an independent television station in Puerto Rico....

Twenty-First Century Fox, Inc., Form 10-K Description of Business Operations

For the year ended December 31, 2018[7]

The Company produces and licenses news, business news, sports, general entertainment, factual entertainment and movie programming for distribution primarily through cable television systems, direct broadcast satellite operators, telecommunications companies and online video distributors in the United States and internationally.

Fox News and Fox Business Network. Fox News owns and operates the Fox News Channel, the top rated 24/7 all news national cable channel currently available in approximately 87 million U.S. households according to Nielsen Media Research, as well as the Fox Business Network which is currently available in approximately 84 million U.S. households....

Competition

General. Cable network programming is a highly competitive business. Cable networks compete for content and distribution and, when distribution is obtained, for viewers and advertisers with free-to-air broadcast television, radio, print media, motion picture theaters, DVDs, Blu-ray high definition format discs ("Blu-rays"), Internet delivered free, advertising supported, subscription and rental services, wireless and

---

7. http://investor.21cf.com/sec-filings/sec-filing/10-k/0001564590-18-021493.

portable viewing devices and other sources of information and entertainment. Important competitive factors include the prices charged for programming, the quantity, quality and variety of programming offered, the accessibility of such programming, the ability to adapt to new technologies and distribution platforms, quality of user experience and the effectiveness of marketing efforts.

Fox News and Fox Business Network. Fox News Channel's primary competition comes from the cable networks CNN, HLN (CNN's Headline News) and MSNBC. Fox Business Network's primary competition comes from the cable networks CNBC and Bloomberg Television. Fox News Channel and Fox Business Network also compete for viewers and advertisers within a broad spectrum of television networks, including other non-news cable networks and free-to-air broadcast television networks.

Sports programming operations. A number of basic and pay television programming services, such as ESPN and NBC Sports Network, as well as free-to-air stations and broadcast networks, provide programming that also targets FS1, FS2, BTN and the FSN RSNs' respective audience. On a national level, the primary competitors to FS1, FS2, BTN and FSN are ESPN, ESPN2, NBC Sports Network, Golf Channel and league-owned networks such as NFL Network, NHL Network, NBA TV and MLB Network. In regional markets, the FSN RSNs and BTN compete with other RSNs (including those operated by team owners, collegiate conferences and cable television distributors), local broadcast television stations and other sports programming providers and distributors. FS1, FS2, BTN and FSN also face competition online from ESPN+, Yahoo Sports, Facebook, Twitter, ESPN.com, NBCSports.com and CBSSports.com, among others.

In addition, FS1, FS2, BTN, the FSN RSNs and FSN compete, to varying degrees, for sports programming rights.... Additionally, cable television distributors and online and social media properties such as Amazon, Yahoo Sports, Facebook and Twitter compete with the Company's cable sports networks by acquiring and distributing sports content to their online users.

FX and FXX. FX and FXX face competition from a number of basic cable and pay television programming services, such as USA Network ("USA"), TNT, Spike TV, HBO and Showtime, as well as free-to-air broadcast networks, and Internet subscription and rental services such as Netflix and Amazon, and free-to-consumer video sharing websites such as YouTube, that provide programming that targets the same viewing audience as FX and FXX. FX and FXX also face competition from these programming services in the acquisition of distribution rights to movie and series programming....

Television

The Company is engaged in the operation of broadcast television stations and the acquisition, marketing and distribution of broadcast network programming in the United States.

Fox Television Stations. Fox Television Stations, L.L.C. ("Fox Television Stations") owns and operates 28 full power stations, including stations located in nine of the top ten largest designated market areas ("DMAs"). Fox Television Stations owns and operates duopolies in 11 DMAs, including the three largest DMAs, New York, Los Angeles and Chicago.

Of the 28 full power stations, 17 stations are affiliates of Fox ("Fox Affiliates")....

Fox Broadcasting Company ("Fox")

Fox has 208 Fox Affiliates, including 17 stations owned and operated by the Company, which reach approximately 99.9% of all U.S. television households. In general, each week Fox regularly delivers to its affiliates 15 hours of prime-time programming, 60 minutes of late-night programming on Saturday and 60 minutes of news programming on Sunday.... In addition, a significant component of Fox's programming consists of sports programming, with Fox providing to its affiliates live coverage of the NFC of the NFL (including coverage of the NFC playoffs) and MLB (including post-season and the World Series), as well as live coverage of the Monster Energy NASCAR Cup Series (including the Daytona 500), USGA golf events (including the men's U.S. Open), college football and basketball, UFC and international soccer (including FIFA World Cup events). The Company has acquired rights to the NFL's Thursday Night Football package and will begin airing live coverage of these games in August 2018....

[News Corp.]

On June 28, 2013, the Company completed the separation of its business into two independent publicly traded companies (the "News Corp Separation") by distributing to its stockholders shares of the new News Corporation ("News Corp"). The Company retained its interests in a global portfolio of cable, broadcast, film, pay-TV and satellite assets spanning six continents. News Corp holds the Company's former businesses including newspapers, information services and integrated marketing services, digital real estate services, book publishing, digital education and sports programming and pay-TV distribution in Australia.

3. Production

As television developed, the broadcasters that supplied content to their owned and operated stations and their affiliated local broadcast stations had nearly absolute market power of the studios that created the television content. The FCC promulgated regulations to separate the content ownership from the content distribution. Although those regulations are no longer in place, they shaped the industry norms for the financing and production of broadcast and cable television content. That history never applied to the OTT content companies, so the content created for Netflix, Amazon Prime and the other online content providers does not follow this pattern.

To produce a new television series for network television (ABC, CBS, NBC, or Fox), the writer of a project will first create a script for the television pilot and a series bible, which provides an outline of the episodes that will be created for the first season, the characters, locations, and other major production elements. The combination of the pilot script and production bible will be used to determine the likely budget of the series. Casting can dramatically alter the production costs of a television series, but other major choices involving the use of studio production or location production, the format of the filming, and the scope of special effects needed will help determine the budget and production needs.

To get the project from paper to broadcast requires two agreements. There must be a production studio responsible for making the television series, and there must be a television network responsible for broadcasting the show during a timeslot. Each of the major four broadcasters also serves as a television producer, but television studios often buy from outside studios. Each of the motion picture studios also have television divisions, as do hundreds of other production companies in the U.S. and abroad. Because there are so many more production studios than network distributors, it is typical that the writer who originated a television project will enter into an agreement with the studio before entering into an agreement with the network, but the transaction can occur in either order, depending on the preexisting relationships among the parties.

The writer who originated a project will actually seek out an executive producer to organize and sell the project. The most successful television producers often have preexisting agreements with studios to provide a certain number of series. From this point forward, the producer takes over the development of the project.

The executive producer will hire a showrunner for the project. The showrunner will typically be the originating writer or a seasoned television producer, but the executive producer could identify other talented individuals to take on the role. The showrunner is the person with day-to-day operational control of the series.

The writers working on the developing show are employees of the television studio. The content is owned by the television studio under a work-for-hire agreement. Residuals are contractually arranged, with the basic agreements governed by the Writers Guild of America collective bargaining agreements.

The television studio serves to finance the project and negotiate with the networks to air the series. The negotiation between the studio and the network can substantially restructure the original idea. Because of the dramatic changes that may occur between the initial pitch for the television series and the demands of the network, both the idea and the personnel can change significantly.

The next step is for the network to order a new script or a new script and pilot episode. Even if a pilot episode is ordered, there will be significant give and take with the network over the revised pilot script before the pilot is shot. Occasionally, a project will be so competitive that the networks will go straight to an initial series order of 10 or 13 episodes. Most projects, however, make it to the script step or to the pilot step, but do not receive an episode order. Less than ten percent of the projects that make it to the pilot step receive an initial order. Of those, most will run for only single series. They may renewed for the rest of the year, increasing the order to 22 episodes. Roughly a quarter of the shows that originated in a season will get renewed for the second season.

The economics also reflect the complex relationship between the television studio and the network broadcaster. The network will pay a negotiated price for the episodes in exchanges for the right to air the episodes a limited number of times. The television studio will retain ownership of the copyright. If the series is popular and stays on television for five seasons or longer, the television studio will own more than 100 episodes of the series. A television show with more than 100 episodes is extremely valuable in the syndication market. It will be sold to cable channels, globally, and as reruns on broadcast channels. Shows with fewer than 100 episodes can also be sold, but those are harder to sell and generally are not as valuable.

As a result of the very different financial interests of the television studio and the broadcast network, the costs to produce content, to pay cast members, to renew shows, and to promote projects are very complicated relationships.

In contrast to the traditional broadcast model, the new OTT structure has none of the historical separations. Instead, Netflix buys its original programming outright. The television studio producing the show does not lose money on its episodes, but it sells all control of the content to Netflix. Netflix is interested in being able to provide a deep library of content without needing to renegotiate with its competitors for access to valuable content. The other OTT systems are moving towards this model.

Notes and Questions

a. Television is rapidly changing, and the industry rules are changing even more dramatically than in music. As noted in the next chapter, the FCC's mandate to regulate television is actually to regulate the individual station licenses. As more content moves to the OTT systems and broadcaster apps, the role of the FCC is likely to be reduced significantly.

b. Retransmission consent and must-carry provisions are more fully described in other FCC documents. *See* Federal Communications Commission, 26 FCC Rcd 11919 (15), *In-State Broadcast Programming: Report to Congress Pursuant to Section 304 of the Satellite Television Extension and Localism Act of 2010* (2011); *Retransmission Consent and Exclusivity Rules: Report to Congress Pursuant to Section 208 of the Satellite Home Viewer Extension and Reauthorization Act of 2004*, MB Docket No. 05-28 (Sept. 8, 2005), http://hraunfoss.fcc.gov/edocs_public/attachmatch/DOC-260936A1.doc.

c. The FCC has attempted numerous efforts at maintaining vertical and horizontal market concentration rules, but given the difficulty in proving anti-competitive harm and the First Amendment implications of such ownership restrictions, the Commission has had little success in court. *See Comcast Corp. v. FCC*, 579 F.3d 1, 10 (D.C. Cir. 2009); *Time Warner Entm't Co. v. FCC*, 240 F.3d 1126, 1136, 1139 (D.C. 2001).

d. Entertainment employment jobs are extremely difficult to get, and career success is hard to maintain. Composer Irving Berlin captured its essence with this stanza in "There's No Business Like Show Business":

There's no people like show people

They smile when they are low

Even with a turkey that you know will fold

You may be stranded out in the cold

But still you wouldn't change it for a sack of gold

Let's go on with the show, let's go on with the show.

Given that culture and history, it is not surprising that the use of interns has long been a fixture in the entertainment industries. *Glatt v. Fox Searchlight Pictures, Inc.*, 811 F.3d 528 (2d Cir. 2016), provides a helpful guide to the difference. *See also Wang v. Hearst Corp.*, 877 F.3d 69 (2d Cir. 2017).

Plaintiffs, who were hired as unpaid interns, claim compensation as employees under the Fair Labor Standards Act and New York Labor Law.... [T]he proper question is whether the intern or the employer is the primary beneficiary of the relationship. The primary beneficiary test has three salient features. First, it focuses on what the intern receives in exchange for his work. Second, it also accords courts the flexibility to examine the economic reality as it exists between the intern and the employer. Third, it acknowledges that the intern-employer relationship should not be analyzed in the same manner as the standard employer-employee relationship because the intern enters into the relationship with the expectation of receiving educational or vocational benefits that are not necessarily expected with all forms of employment (though such benefits may be a product of experience on the job)....

In the context of unpaid internships, we think a non-exhaustive set of considerations should include:

1. The extent to which the intern and the employer clearly understand that there is no expectation of compensation. Any promise of compensation, express or implied, suggests that the intern is an employee—and vice versa.

2. The extent to which the internship provides training that would be similar to that which would be given in an educational environment, including the clinical and other hands-on training provided by educational institutions.

3. The extent to which the internship is tied to the intern's formal education program by integrated coursework or the receipt of academic credit.

4. The extent to which the internship accommodates the intern's academic commitments by corresponding to the academic calendar.

5. The extent to which the internship's duration is limited to the period in which the internship provides the intern with beneficial learning.

6. The extent to which the intern's work complements, rather than displaces, the work of paid employees while providing significant educational benefits to the intern.

7. The extent to which the intern and the employer understand that the internship is conducted without entitlement to a paid job at the conclusion of the internship.

Applying these considerations requires weighing and balancing all of the circumstances. No one factor is dispositive and every factor need not point in the same direction for the court to conclude that the intern is not an employee entitled to the minimum wage. In addition, the factors we specify are non-exhaustive — courts may consider relevant evidence beyond the specified factors in appropriate cases. And because the touchstone of this analysis is the "economic reality" of the relationship, a court may elect in certain cases, including cases that can proceed as collective actions, to consider evidence about an internship program as a whole rather than the experience of a specific intern....

Glatt, 811 F.3d at 536–37.

Problem 13-A

Bryce has learned that a local cable channel has been broadcasting an unauthorized video of a live performance recorded of Bryce's band. The channel is either public access or paid access, Bryce is unsure. The program episode that includes Bryce's music also shows audience shots in which questionable and unsavory activity may be taking place. Bryce is unsure what was happening among the patrons but is embarrassed by the use of the band's performance to highlight the lewd, embarrassing conduct.

Bryce has contacted the program's producers, but they are uninterested in removing the content. Bryce does not wish to bring a copyright lawsuit or other legal action, but is hoping the cable company might be of assistance. Advise Bryce regarding the options that might be available.

B. Television Writer Agreements

Writers Guild of America West
Residuals for High-Budget Subscription Video on Demand (HBSVOD) Programs[8]

The 2017 MBA includes increased residuals for HBSVOD programs when they are reused on the original SVOD service. The new residual formulas include, for services with 1 million or more subscribers in the U.S. and Canada, a domestic residual of 35% of an applicable minimum after 90 days of availability.

Residuals will also be due for reuse on foreign affiliated SVOD services. In general, if an HBSVOD program is available worldwide on the SVOD service, the residual payment will be a percent of the domestic residual (35% for each of the first three years, a declining percent thereafter). If the HBSVOD program is available in some foreign markets, but not worldwide, the residual will be 1.2% of the license fee for the foreign markets.

---

8. https://www.wga.org/members/finances/residuals/hbsvod-programs.

The new contract provisions also establish new subscriber tiers, which determine the residual. Provided are examples of residuals for the first three years of availability of episodes made for Netflix, Amazon and Hulu.

- Netflix (45+ million domestic subscribers) will have a new domestic residual of $20,121 for a half-hour episode and $36,571 for a one-hour episode.
- Amazon (20–45 million domestic subscribers) will have a new domestic residual of $13,414 for a half-hour episode and $24,380 for a one-hour episode.
- Hulu (5–20 million domestic subscribers) will have a new domestic residual of $8,718 for a half-hour episode and $15,846 for a one-hour episode.

For these examples, we assume that Netflix and Amazon make the episodes available worldwide. Because Hulu currently operates in the U.S. only, we do not include a foreign SVOD residual payment. After the first three years, writers will continue to receive an annual residual payment for domestic and foreign SVOD reuse if the program remains available on the SVOD service.

Writers Guild of America
Standard Writing Services Contract

… The WGAW has created a standard writing services contract, now available via download (below)—which can be tailored to reflect the negotiated terms of any writing services contract you negotiate. We encourage you to use it in place of deal memos or those quickly jotted notes you write to confirm the terms just negotiated. The standard writing services contract is available in two versions—one for directly employed writers and the other for writers employed through loan-outs.…

WRITER'S THEATRICAL SHORT-FORM CONTRACT

…

6. COMPENSATION:

A. Guaranteed Compensation (see 11, below): $___

B. Contingent Compensation (see 11, below): $___

C. Profit Participation: If sole writing credit, ___% of (Net/Gross) Proceeds; Reducible for shared credit to ___% (see 27, below)

7. Specific material upon which services are to be based, if any ___ (a copy will be sent to Writer under separate cover): ___ …

13. BONUS:

A. For sole writing credit: $___

B. For shared writing credit: $___. Shared credit bonus will be paid on commencement of principal photography if no other writer has been engaged; balance to be paid on determination of writing credit.

C. For "green light" or engagement of an "element": $___. If Writer is writer of record or is most recent writer on the Project at the time the Project is given a "green light" by a studio or an element is attached on a pay-or-play basis, Writer shall be given a bonus of ___ Dollars ($___) which may may not be applied against the bonus in A. or B., above....

24. RESULTS AND PROCEEDS: Work-Made-For-Hire: Writer acknowledges that all results, product and proceeds of Writer's services (including all original ideas in connection therewith) are being specially ordered by Producer for use as part of a Motion Picture and shall be considered a "work made for hire" for Producer as specially commissioned for use as a part of a motion picture in accordance with Sections 101 and 201 of Title 17 of the U.S. Copyright Act. Therefore, Producer shall be the author and copyright owner thereof for all purposes throughout the universe without limitation of any kind or nature. In consideration of the monies paid to Lender hereunder, Producer shall solely and exclusively own throughout the universe in perpetuity all rights of every kind and nature whether now or hereafter known or created in and in connection with such results, product and proceeds, in whatever stage of completion as may exist from time to time, including: (i) the copyright and all rights of copyright; (ii) all neighboring rights, trademarks and any and all other ownership and exploitation rights now or hereafter recognized in any Territory, including all rental, lending, fixation, reproduction, broadcasting (including satellite transmission), distribution and all other rights of communication by any and all means, media, devices, processes and technology; (iii) the rights to adapt, rearrange, and make changes in, deletions from and additions to such results, product and proceeds, and to use all or any part thereof in new versions, adaptations, and other Motion Pictures including Remakes and Sequels; (iv) the right to use the title of the Work in connection therewith or otherwise and to change such title; and (v) all rights generally known as the "moral rights of authors." ...

26. NO INJUNCTIVE RELIEF:

The sole right of Writer as to any breach or alleged breach hereunder by Company shall be the recovery of money damages, if any, and the rights herein granted by Writer shall not terminate by reason of such breach. In no event may Writer terminate this Agreement or obtain injunctive relief or other equitable relief with respect to any breach of Company's obligations hereunder.

27. PROFIT PARTICIPATION: Terms to be negotiated in good faith. If the parties fail to reach agreement ___ months after execution hereof, either party, upon 30 days notice to the other, may submit the matter to what is known as a "baseball arbitration," in which each party presents one profit proposal and the arbitrator is required to adopt one of the two proposals. The arbitrator shall be selected and the arbitration conducted pursuant to the Voluntary Labor Arbitration Rules of the AAA.

Sandy Veith & Vuelta International, Inc. v. MCA Inc.

1997 Cal. App. Unpub. LEXIS 1 (1997)

[Most of the litigation involving television development has to do with ownership of ideas as they evolve into scripts. It is axiomatic that ideas are not protected by copyright whereas written expression has copyright protection. In the collaborative world of television, a great deal of activity and investment occurs around projects that are still in the idea stage of development. Unless the concept's creator is a member of the Writer's Guild of America and protected by a pre-existing contract, the general result is for the idea submission to be unprotected. Copyright cannot protect the ideas, and in most cases, there is no sufficient written agreement to protect the creators of television concepts even when the ideas served as the basis for subsequent television series.

The somewhat convoluted factual history of "Northern Exposure" illustrates a contractual dispute involving the development of a hit television series and the difficulties of ascribing origination. The following is an unpublished opinion.]

The defendants, MCA, Inc. and Universal City Studios, Inc. (collectively, "Universal") appeal a judgment in favor of the plaintiffs, Sandy Veith and Vuelta International Inc., entered following a jury verdict in the total sum of $7.29 million. Veith, a television writer and producer, asserted a claim against Universal based upon a breach of contract which involved Universal's failure to pay certain bonus compensation due under Veith's exclusive term contract.

The Writers Guild of America, West, Inc. (herein, "Writer's Guild") has appeared in this matter as amicus curiae. Veith is a member of the Writer's Guild and as such is a third-party beneficiary of a collective bargaining agreement (CBA) between the Writer's Guild and the Alliance of Motion Picture & Television Producers, Inc. Universal is a signatory to the CBA.

The CBA, which was effective August 8, 1988 through May 1, 1992, determines, among other things, (1) minimum rates of payment, (2) rules relating to credit, and (3) rights to "residual" participation, if any, in future exploitation and the profits therefrom. While the CBA sets minimum standards for pay, "in many cases individuals with notable skills and achievements ('track records'), with special relation to particular projects, with multiple creative roles, with combined creative and entrepeneurial roles, or with other sources of bargaining power, can obtain compensation well above the collectively-bargained minimum contractual rates, as well as varying measures of artistic control."

FACTUAL AND PROCEDURAL BACKGROUND

Sometime in late 1980 or early 1981, Veith was approached by William Sackheim, an experienced producer and writer, who asked Veith to collaborate on "Coletta," Bill's idea for a television series.[9] Bill's idea involved a doctor compelled to serve in a rural area for four or five years in order to pay off the scholarship which enabled him to attend medical school. Bill had prepared a written document which he denominated a "presentation" or "back story" on the "Coletta" project, which is less detailed than a "format" or some other type of creative product. A writer who prepares

---

9. As a matter of convenience and to avoid confusion we will hereafter refer to William Sackheim simply as "Bill" in order to differentiate him from Ray Sackheim, who is Bill's brother and was, at relevant times, Veith's agent.

a "presentation" rather than a "format" is not entitled to the so-called "created by" credit. Bill and Veith agreed that Veith would write the project, and began fleshing out the idea and developing a storyline.

In March 1981, Veith, with Bill's assistance, entered into a written exclusive term contract with Universal (the "Agreement"), effective June 1, 1981, to use his creative talents exclusively for Universal to develop original ideas for television programming. The Agreement provided for a one year term, with two successive annual options, the first for an additional year, and the second for an additional two year term. During the term of the Agreement, Universal could use Veith in all media as a writer and as a producer.

Veith was guaranteed a specified annual salary, which was a nonreturnable advance against certain "per assignment" fees set forth in Exhibit A to the Agreement ("Exhibit A").

In other words, if Veith completed sufficient assignments, Universal would pay Veith additional sums based on the completion of such assignments. Exhibit A showed the fees per assignment for work as a writer and as a producer, and differentiated between such creative products as "story & teleplay," "story only," "teleplay only," "treatment," and "format only." Exhibit A also provided that "If Veith should render any services hereunder in collaboration (or as a team) with another artist or artists, fees, percentages, (pursuant to this EXHIBIT 'A' or in the Agreement to which this EXHIBIT 'A' is attached) etc., will be proportionately reduced."

Of particular relevance to this appeal, in addition to the guaranteed compensation and additional sums based on the completion of such assignments, Veith was entitled to additional payments under the Agreement if certain conditions were met. Specifically, the Agreement provided that if a prime time television series were to be licensed for exhibition as a direct result of a pilot photoplay for which Veith received sole or partial teleplay credit and sole or partial separation of rights[10] Veith would be entitled to various additional sums (the bonus), as, when and to the extent required by the CBA.

With respect to the bonus, the Agreement provided:

> "4. [Veith] shall be entitled to the following additional payments which do
> not apply against salary listed in Paragraph 2 above.

---

10. "For WGA [Writers Guild Association] screen writers, so-called 'separation of rights' (Article 16(A) of the WGA agreement) is a critical concept. A writer's entitlement to 'separation of rights' depends on the originality and substantiality of the writer's contribution to the film and flow from having written the story. For example, minor rewrites do not qualify. A writer who has 'separation of rights' receives the major package of WGA-negotiated benefits, including novelization, remake, sequel (and perhaps turnaround), etc. The requirements to attain 'separation of rights' are spelled out in detail in the WGA agreement. There are somewhat different but also detailed specifications for 'separation of rights' for television writers." ("Ownership and Control of Intellectual Property Rights in Motion Pictures and Audiovisual Works: Contractual and Practical Aspects—Response of the United States to the ALAI Questionnaire, ALAI Congress, Paris, Sept. 20, 1995," 20 Colum.-VLA J.L. & Arts, *supra*, at p. 459, fn. 51).

"a) If a prime time episodic television series is licensed for exhibition as a direct result of a pilot photoplay for which [Veith] receives sole Teleplay credit and additionally receives sole 'separation of rights' on the series, we shall pay [Veith] whichever of the following sequel royalties is applicable: $2,000 for sequels 30 minutes in length, $2,250 for sequels over 30 but not more than 60 minutes in length; $2,500 for sequels over 60 but not more than 90 minutes in length, $2,750 for sequels over 90 minutes in length. One-half of the aforementioned sequel royalty shall be deemed earned for receiving sole 'separation of rights' on the series and one-half shall be deemed earned for receiving sole Teleplay credit on said pilot photoplay. To the extent Veith receives less than sole 'separation of rights' and/or less than sole Teleplay credit on said pilot, the sequel royalty will be proportionately reduced (*e.g.*, if Veith receives sole 'separation of rights' with respect to a series hereunder and one-half Teleplay credit on the pilot photoplay that directly results in a series sale, the 30 minute length sequel royalty would be $1,000 for sole 'separation of rights' and $500 for one-half Teleplay credit, or a total of $1,500). Sequel royalties shall be payable as and when required by the WGA. Any WGA-required sequel royalty or character payment shall be deemed an advance against any contractual sequel royalty hereunder and the converse shall be equally true.

"b) [Veith] shall be entitled to receive residuals on sequel royalties payable as, when and to the extent required by the [CBA].

"c) [Veith] shall be entitled to receive a 'hyphenate bonus' as required by the [CBA] payable as, when and to the extent required by the [CBA].

"d) With respect to all writing assignments hereunder, [Veith] shall receive scale residuals payable as, when and to the extent required by the [CBA]." ...

"6. During the term of this agreement, Veith shall have no right to acquire or dispose of (for his own account or otherwise) whether personally or through a firm or corporation he controls, rights in and to any literary, motion picture, television and/or related material. All writing and other materials on which he is engaged during the term of this agreement (to the extent not based on source material furnished by us) shall be deemed created by him during the term hereof. Veith agrees to give us forthwith a list of properties owned or controlled by him. With respect to such properties, if during the term he desires to sell or license such properties, he must first offer such properties to us and we shall have a 21-day negotiation with respect to the sale or license of such properties; if thereafter, Veith desires to sell or license said properties to others on terms less favorable to himself than last offered to us, Veith shall advise us in writing of the terms and conditions of such proposed licensing or sale and we shall have a 7-day first refusal with respect to such deal. As to properties not contained in the list, they shall be deemed created during the term. ...

"It is understood that Sandy Veith is an employee of Vuelta International, Inc., and that all material to be written hereunder shall be a work for hire for us and we shall be the owner thereof, …"

It is Universal's failure to pay such bonus which is at the heart of this case.

At some point before Veith actually began working for Universal, he and Bill met with Warren Littlefield and Jeff Sagansky of the NBC network and pitched the "Coletta" project to them. Littlefield liked it, and asked what Veith and Bill wanted. They wanted NBC to pay for six scripts; he offered to pay for four, and asked where they thought they would be taking "Coletta," that is, what studio would be producing it. Bill told him that Veith was going to Universal, and they therefore would take it to Universal because Bill wanted Universal to produce it.

NBC ultimately purchased an option from Universal to produce "Coletta." Veith, who was by then working for Universal, wrote the story and screenplay for "Coletta," and Bill, who was with another studio, was to supervise the project. This deal was evidenced by a written agreement between NBC and Universal for a half-hour pilot script to be written by Veith and supervised by Bill, and by a second written agreement between NBC and Universal for three backup scripts. Universal also amended Bill's consulting contract to give him additional compensation if "Coletta" was produced as a series.

Veith wrote a "Coletta" story for NBC, which approved it, apparently the preliminary step to beginning work on a teleplay. In January or February of 1982, Veith delivered a pilot teleplay of "Coletta" to NBC. After a note session with people from NBC and Universal, Universal agreed to pay for three back-up scripts, and hired two other writers to work on them, one of whom was a writer named Bill Dial, whose resulting familiarity with "Coletta" became relevant about 8 years later, in 1990. Veith participated in the writing and rewriting of the back-up scripts.

Sometime in 1982, Universal "extended and suspended" its Agreement with Veith so that he could take a year off to produce "Love, Sidney" with Tony Randall in New York. In consideration for being given leave to produce "Love, Sidney," Veith agreed with Universal that he would continue to render required consultative services in connection with "our project 'Coletta'" during the period of his leave, for no additional compensation, and, in fact, he and Bill continued to work on "Coletta" during the year Veith was in New York. However, sometime in 1982, Jeff Sagansky of NBC decided not to go with "Coletta" as a series. In 1983, Universal exercised an option to extend the Agreement and, on June 6, 1983, signed an amendment to the Agreement which increased the remuneration due to Veith under the Agreement (the "Amendment").

After NBC turned down "Coletta," Veith was working for Warner Bros., and was too busy to make changes to "Coletta." However, Veith knew another writer at Universal, Joel Blasberg, whom he thought might be able to revise "Coletta" using a new locale where Veith had grown up. Blasberg wrote a new "Coletta" story, using the same central characters as before, but set the location of the story in the Florida Keys, and it was presented to ABC as a possible half-hour comedy; however, ABC would not commit to the project. Veith and Bill subsequently decided "Coletta" should be made into an hour-long program, to take advantage of the revised, exotic setting. Veith had to rewrite the characters, and Universal introduced him to a "one hour writer," Steve Brown. Veith, Brown, Bill and Charmiane Balian, Universal's vice-president of drama development, then pitched "Coletta" to Greg Mayday at CBS. Bill also met with Michelle Brustin of NBC's drama department about the possibility of making "Coletta" an hour-long program (dramas are usually an hour in length, while comedies are usually half-hour in length). Bill continued to try to sell "Coletta" to a network. In 1985, he met with an executive of ABC and told her about "Coletta." She suggested that he approach Stu Bloomberg, who was in charge of comedy at ABC, so Bill, Blasberg and Bloomberg all met and talked about "Coletta" as set in the Florida Keys. As a result, Bill told Universal's executives that they had a shot at selling "Coletta" to ABC.

In 1986, ABC entered into an option agreement with Universal for another script of "Coletta" set in the Florida Keys. Veith, whose contract with Universal had by this time expired, was then working at Warner Bros. Blasberg, who was working as a writer under contract to Universal, was selected to write the script. Universal asked Veith to sign a letter agreement, dated June 27, 1986, which would give Universal an extension of time within which to commence exploitation of the television sequel rights to "Coletta" related to the rewrite by Blasberg (the Extension Agreement). Veith did not immediately agree to sign the June 27, 1986 agreement. In late June and early July of 1986, although Veith was working at Warner Bros., and although he had not signed the Extension Agreement, he accompanied Blasberg to the Florida Keys for several days, to work on ideas for the rewrite and to show Blasberg how to mine Veith's boyhood home for characters for the series.

Universal continued to pressure Veith to sign some form of an extension agreement, and ultimately Veith did so, granting to Universal two additional extensions of time within which to continue the pilot and series development of "Coletta" for television production. Universal also tried to get Veith to agree to a less remunerative bonus provision, but Veith insisted that he would not give up his existing deal, and Universal finally acceded on this point. Blasberg prepared "Coletta" scripts which were presented to ABC as a possible half-hour comedy series, but in 1987 ABC passed on "Coletta." Thus, by 1987, both NBC and ABC had taken a look at "Coletta" and had passed; the other network, CBS, had also looked at it but had refused to make a commitment.

Apparently all was quiet on the "Coletta" front until the evening of July 12, 1990, when Veith received a telephone call from Bill Dial, one of the writers hired by Universal to work on the "Coletta" back-up scripts in 1982. Dial had just seen the first episode of "Northern Exposure," and called to tell Veith it sounded "an awful lot" like "Coletta." Veith had not seen the show himself, but soon received more calls from other people about the remarkable similarity between "Northern Exposure" and "Coletta." Veith obtained a copy of a "Northern Exposure" script and determined for himself that it was very similar.

On July 13, 1990, one day after the initial broadcast of "Northern Exposure," Veith called the Writer's Guild and then on July 16, he wrote to Stacy Murphy at the Guild, sent him two scripts to compare, and asked what he should do. He had discovered that not only were the scripts similar, but also the same players, other than the writers, had been involved in both projects (*i.e.* Kerry McCluggage, Richard Lindheim, Charmiane Balian, and Brad Johnson of Universal and Jeff Sagansky, who, while at NBC, had bought an option on "Coletta" and who had then, while President of CBS Television, bought "Northern Exposure" in 1989). He also learned that Lee Gabler, his agent at Creative Artists Agency, Inc., represented Joshua Brand and John Falsey, the creators, writers and producers of "Northern Exposure." However, when he first contacted Gabler about the similarity between "Coletta" and "Northern Exposure," Gabler acted as though he had no idea who the writers and producers of "Northern Exposure" might be, and would have to find out.

In January of 1993, Veith filed suit against Universal and Creative Artists Agency, Inc. for breach of written contract, breach of implied contract, breach of fiduciary duty, and for an accounting.[11] His complaint alleged, in relevant part, that pursuant to paragraph 4 (a)–(e) of the Agreement, he was to receive, in addition to a fixed salary, specific dollar amounts *if a prime time episodic television series was licensed as a result of his creative efforts.* Such compensation included sequel royalties, residuals on sequel royalties, series and teleplay bonuses, a hyphenate bonus, scale residuals on writing assignments, a share of Universal's net profits, writing and producing fees and syndication fees.

At trial, substantial evidence was produced from which the jury reasonably could infer that Universal's executives intentionally supplied material amounts of the "Coletta" story and teleplay to Brand and Falsey without telling them that the material came from "Coletta." There was also evidence that Universal was motivated to do so, because it had a significant financial incentive in the form of a blind commitment from ABC in 1987 and from NBC in 1989 to have Brand and Falsey, rather than some other writer or writers, come up with an acceptable idea for a television series. Finally, there was also evidence that the similarities between "Coletta" and "Northern Exposure" were so significant on many different elements of plot, characterization and detail that they could not be the result of a coincidence, and which indicated that the "Northern Exposure" story and teleplay came about as a direct result of Veith's "Coletta" story and teleplay.

Veith put on evidence of damages he suffered not only as a result of his loss of the bonus, but also as a result of the loss of future earning capacity occasioned by not receiving the creative credit for the very successful prime time television series, "Northern Exposure." On direct examination, one of plaintiff's expert witnesses, Veith's agent, Ray Sackheim testified that in his opinion, the future monetary value of being credited as the creator of a show like "Northern Exposure" was $10 to $25 million.

---

11. By the time of trial, Veith had dismissed Creative Artists Agency, Inc., as a defendant and had dropped all causes of action against Universal except for breach of contract. This, of course, has no effect on his ability to argue that Universal breached the implied covenant of good faith and fair dealing in the Agreement; there is no reason to assert a separate cause of action for breach of the implied covenant of good faith and fair dealing unless the plaintiff wishes to seek a tort recovery.

He also opined that "Coletta" would have been a better series than "Northern Exposure." Defense counsel did not cross-examine Sackheim on his opinion as to the amount of damages, nor move to strike such opinion, nor is there any indication in the record that Universal made a motion in limine to exclude such evidence.

Robert Schiller, another witness for Veith, who had 45 years of experience in writing and producing many well-known television programs, testified that in his opinion, the future value over a writer's career of receiving credit as the creator of a successful series, *i.e.*, one which ran three or four seasons, was a minimum of $5 million, based on the usefulness of such credit in getting offers of other employment and deals.

In addition to this direct testimony on the damages Veith had suffered as a result of the loss of future earning capacity because of his failure to receive created by credit on "Northern Exposure," there was also circumstantial evidence related to this issue, in the form of testimony related to Veith's and Brand and Falsey's respective careers, *i.e.*, to the different programs on which they had worked as writers and producers and on which they had or had not received various creative credits, and the sums they had earned for their work as their careers progressed.

In 1994, after a five-week trial, the jury returned a special verdict against Universal and awarded Veith $7.29 million in damages, and judgment was entered thereon on October 14, 1994. On November 1, 1994, Universal made a timely motion for judgment notwithstanding the verdict, and at the same time filed its notice of intention to move for new trial. Both motions were denied by the trial court on December 8, 1994.

ISSUES PRESENTED

... First, is there substantial evidence that Universal breached the Agreement with Veith, and prevented Veith from fulfilling the condition precedent to Universal's duty to pay Veith the bonus? Second, can Universal avoid the consequences of its breach of the Agreement by relying on the arbitration provisions of the CBA? ...

1. *Substantial Evidence Supports the Jury's Determination that Universal Breached the Agreement and Prevented Veith from Fulfilling the Condition Precedent to Receiving the Bonus Under Paragraph 4 of the Agreement*

" 'Every contract imposes upon each party a duty of good faith and fair dealing in its performance and its enforcement.'... The covenant of good faith finds particular application in situations where one party is invested with a discretionary power affecting the rights of another. Such power must be exercised in good faith." In general, the covenant imposes a duty upon all parties to a contract not to deprive the other parties of the contract's benefits. The covenant " '... not only imposes upon each contracting party the duty to refrain from doing anything which would render performance of the contract impossible by any act of his own, but also the duty to do everything that the contract presupposes that he will do to accomplish its purpose.' " In other words, good faith performance of a contract "emphasizes faithfulness to an agreed common purpose and consistency with the justified expectations of the other party." Thus, "a breach of the implied covenant can result from conduct permitted by the express (or implied-in-fact) terms of the contract."

This rule was developed "in the contract arena and is aimed at making effective the agreement's promises." ... In short, the covenant is an implied-in-law term of the contract. Therefore, its breach will always result in a breach of the contract, although a breach of a consensual (*i.e.*, an express or implied-in-fact) contract term will not necessarily constitute a breach of the covenant. To establish a breach of the covenant, the obligee must demonstrate "conscious and deliberate" conduct on the part of the obligor which was designed to frustrate the obligee's contract rights, *i.e.*, conduct which constitutes " 'unfair dealing rather than mistaken judgment.' " Just what conduct will meet this criteria must be determined on a case by case basis and will depend on the contractual purposes and reasonably justified expectations of the parties.

Here, Universal's promise to pay Veith the bonus was conditioned on (1) the licensing of a prime time television series as a direct result of a pilot photoplay in which Veith was sufficiently involved so as to be entitled to sole or partial teleplay credit and separation of rights, and (2) Veith's actual receipt of sole or partial teleplay and separation of rights credits on such series. Thus, under the implied covenant of good faith and fair dealing, Universal had a duty not only to refrain from doing anything which would render Veith's performance of these conditions impossible, but also the duty to do everything that the contract presupposed would be necessary so that Veith could perform such conditions.

The evidence shows that Universal breached these duties. Specifically, there was substantial evidence that executives from Universal, and possibly Jeff Sagansky from CBS, intentionally "fed" significant aspects of the "Coletta" story and teleplay to Brand and Falsey during the development of the "Northern Exposure" project. There was also substantial evidence that Universal knew that (1) Veith, as the writer of both the "Coletta" story and teleplay, was entitled, at the very least, to be listed in the "Notice of Tentative Writing Credits" (NTWC) and to compete for writing credits and separation of rights on "Northern Exposure" pursuant to the CBA; (2) Brand and Falsey were unaware that they had been given "Coletta" material during the development of the "Northern Exposure" project; (3) Brand and Falsey, as the producers of "Northern Exposure," would fill out the NTWC which would be sent to the Writer's Guild as part of the process of determining final credits; (4) Brand and Falsey, being unaware of the "Coletta/Northern Exposure" connection, had no reason to think that Veith should be listed as a participating writer on the NTWC for "Northern Exposure"; (5) anyone not listed by Brand and Falsey as a participating writer on the NTWC would not be sent a copy of the notice; (6) anyone not sent a copy of the NTWC would not be able to deliver to the Writer's Guild a written protest of the tentative credits and request for arbitration of credits within the extremely short amount of time before the producers' tentative allocation of credits became final; and (7) once the allocation of credits became final, there was no method under the CBA by which the issue of the actual allocation of credits could be reopened.[12]

---

12. The CBA does provide that the allocation of credits can be reopened under circumstances not applicable here, *i.e.*, if material changes have been made in a script after the credits have been determined under the NTWC procedure, then either the company or the participating writer and

Thus, there is substantial evidence that Universal engaged in "conscious and deliberate" conduct which frustrated Veith's justifiable expectations under the Agreement by preventing him from fulfilling the condition precedent to Universal's duty to pay him the bonus, *i.e.*, that he receive teleplay credit and separation of rights for his story and teleplay on which "Northern Exposure" was based. Because Universal prevented or made impossible the performance or happening of the condition precedent, the condition was excused. Because the condition precedent was excused, and because the jury found that but for Universal's prevention, Veith would have obtained teleplay credit and separation of rights, Universal was obligated to pay Veith the bonus, and its failure to do so constituted a breach of the Agreement.

2. *Arbitration Under the CBA Was Not Available to Veith Either as the Exclusive Remedy for His Claim Nor as a Method by Which to Mitigate His Damages.*

Universal contends that the judgment must be reversed and a judgment in its favor entered as a matter of law because Veith's right to writing credits is governed exclusively by the CBA, and lawfully cannot be the subject of an individual contract such as the Agreement, nor can Veith seek a judicial remedy for the breach of such right. We agree that in the case of a *dispute* over entitlement to writing credits, only the Writer's Guild can determine who is entitled to such credits. However, if writers who participated in the authorship of a story and/or teleplay unanimously agree on the allocation of writing credits, the Writer's Guild is *not* involved in making an award of credits. (CBA, Television Schedule A, Television Credits, subparagraph 6.) In any event, only writers, either through unanimous agreement, or through the Writer's Guild's arbitration of credits process, can award writing credits.

This, however, does not mean that the jury here, *for purposes of calculating Veith's contractual damages*, could not conclude that, but for Universal's conduct, Veith *would* have had a right to particular kinds of creative credits, *i.e.*, "created by," and "written by" as to story and/or teleplay, and to the separation of rights which then flowed from his right to the other kinds of credit. *This is entirely different than awarding Veith the actual credits.* As pointed out by Veith's attorney at oral argument, Veith will *never* receive credit as the sole or partial creator or writer of "Northern Exposure." His name will never appear on the screen each time the program is shown in reruns. All he will receive is *damages.*

Universal also contends that, as a matter of law, the CBA *required* Veith to submit this claim to arbitration. Whether Veith was required to arbitrate this claim under the CBA is a question of law. For the following reasons, we conclude that the CBA does *not* provide for, nor require, arbitration of this particular dispute.

a. *Universal Waived Its Right to Demand Arbitration*

If Universal believed that Veith was required to arbitrate this claim rather than bringing an action at law, its remedy was to file a petition to compel arbitration

---

the Writer's Guild jointly may reopen the credit allocation by making a claim to the Writer's Guild or the company within 48 hours after completion of the writing claimed to justify revision of the credits. (*See* CBA, Television Schedule A, Television Credits, subparagraph 19.)

(which, coincidentally, is exactly what it did in *Universal City Studios, Inc.* v. *Writers Guild of America, Inc.*, U.S.D.C. Case No. CV 96-3732-DT (Ex) (C.D. Cal. July 11, 1996) (the *Blasberg* action), a case of which Universal has asked this court to take judicial notice, and which we discuss, *infra*). For whatever reason, Universal did not do so. The contractual right to demand arbitration may be waived by the failure to demand arbitration within a reasonable time. What constitutes a reasonable time is normally a question of fact requiring an examination of all of the circumstances, including any prejudice the opposing party suffered as a result of the delay. In this case, Universal never demanded arbitration and therefore, we hold, as a matter of law, that Universal waived its right to demand arbitration.

b. *The CBA Does Not Provide for nor Require Arbitration of This Particular Dispute.*

Article 8 of the CBA is entitled "Credits for Screen Authorship (General)." It provides, in relevant part: "The Company agrees that credits for screen authorship shall be given only pursuant to the terms of and in the manner prescribed in the applicable Schedule A attached hereto and by this reference incorporated herein, with respect to credits for screen authorship finally determined during the term hereof, and with respect to credits for screen authorship finally determined after the expiration of the term hereof involving material written during the term hereof or during the term of a prior collective bargaining agreement between the Company and the Guild; ..."

Article 12 of the CBA is entitled "Court Proceedings." Subsection A of Article 12 is entitled "Disputes Concerning Credits." Article 12.A provides, in relevant part: "Nothing in this [CBA] shall limit the rights of the Guild or any writer to assert any and all appropriate legal and equitable rights and remedies to which the Guild or such writer is entitled in courts of competent jurisdiction with regard to an alleged breach of Article 8 and Schedule A of this [CBA] with respect to writing credit; subject, however, to the following conditions and limitations:

"...

"2. If the Guild or the writer commences any proceedings in court with respect to any such alleged breach prior to the submission of the dispute to arbitration hereunder, then neither the Guild nor the writer may submit such dispute to arbitration *and no arbitrator shall have jurisdiction to consider the alleged breach of such credit provision.*" (Italics added.)

In other words, Veith had the option to litigate any dispute related to screen credits rather than submitting it to arbitration, and if he filed suit before Universal submitted the matter to arbitration, which it had the right to do under Article 12.A.3., then the arbitrator had no jurisdiction over the matter.

In its amicus curiae brief, the Writer's Guild contends that under Article 12.A., a writer may only pursue his or her legal and equitable remedies for breach of credit privileges and benefits *after* credits have been determined, and that neither the Writer's Guild nor the writer "may pursue in court that determination of *entitlement to credit*" (emphasis added). Nothing we hold here is to the contrary. However, the Writer's

Guild is the sole arbitor of screen credits so long as the writer is either listed on the NTWC or receives notice that he or she has not been listed and the NTWC has not become final. Under the facts of this case where Veith was neither listed on the NTWC nor given notice he was not so listed *and* where the NTWC has become final, there is nothing in the CBA that prevents Veith from pursuing the only other legal remedy available to him, *i.e.*, filing suit. Furthermore, Veith's claim against Universal was for damages for breach of contract, not for a determination awarding him created by or written by credit on "Northern Exposure," and, in fact, Veith pursued his action for breach of contract against Universal only *after* the credit determination for the credits on "Northern Exposure" had become final, and he had no other remedy.

That Veith had no remedy under the CBA once the credit determination became final is clear. Television Schedule A of the CBA, paragraph 13, provides, in relevant part: "If within the time specified [in the NTWC], a written protest of the tentative credits has not been delivered to the Guild, the tentative writing credits shall become final." The only provision for vacating or otherwise attacking a credit determination that has become final which is made in Television Schedule A, or anywhere else in the CBA for that matter, is found at paragraph 19 of Television Schedule A, which provides:

"In the event that after the screen credits are determined as hereinabove provided, material changes are made in the script, either the Company or a participant and the Guild jointly may reopen the credit determination by making a claim to the Guild or Company as the case may be, within forty-eight (48) hours after completion of the writing claimed to justify the revision of credits, in which case the procedure for determining such revised credits will be the same as that provided for the original determination of credits." Thus, the CBA does not provide for arbitration over entitlement to credit *once the credit determination became final*, except in one circumstance clearly not applicable here.

Our conclusion that, as a matter of law, arbitration under the CBA was simply not available as a method for resolving this particular dispute, puts an end to Universal's argument that Veith could and should have mitigated his damages by pursuing arbitration to try to have the allocation of creative credits changed after such credits became final, and resolves Universal's contentions on appeal that the trial court committed various errors in connection with the mitigation issue.

… [The court addresses and upholds the jury award of damages.]

Jacobs v. CBS Broadcasting, Inc.
291 F.3d 1173 (9th Cir. 2002)

Plaintiffs Mike Jacobs, Jr., William Webb, and Westwind Releasing Corporation filed this action against Defendant CBS Broadcasting, Inc., alleging that CBS had breached a contract to give Plaintiffs production credit when it produced a television series called *Early Edition*. The district court granted summary judgment to CBS on the ground that an earlier nonjudicial proceeding precluded Plaintiffs from bringing their claim to court. We reverse because that nonjudicial proceeding was too informal to have preclusive effect.

Michael Givens is a script writer and a member of the Writers' Guild of America (WGA). Givens wrote a script titled *The Fourth Estate a/k/a/Final Edition* (*Final Edition*). Westwind optioned *Final Edition* for the purpose of securing a television broadcast commitment from a network. Under the agreement between Givens and Westwind, any writing credit to be accorded Givens was to be determined pursuant to the WGA's Minimum Basic Agreement (MBA) credit-determination procedures. Givens was entitled to additional compensation under the contract only if the WGA awarded him a "written by" or "screenplay by" credit.

CBS later agreed with Westwind to acquire the broadcast rights to *Final Edition* (First Agreement). In a second contract, CBS bought all rights to *Final Edition* from Westwind *and* Givens (Second Agreement). The Second Agreement provided that, "*if a project is produced based upon the literary property*, CBS agrees ... to provide credit to William Webb and Mike Jacobs, Jr. as Co-Executive Producers (or Executive Producers at CBS' election) on a shared card" (emphasis added). The Second Agreement also incorporated the provision in the original contract between Givens and Westwind stating that any writing credit for Givens would be governed by the WGA's credit-determination procedures.

CBS eventually participated in the production of a series called *Early Edition*, which shared a common premise with Givens' *Final Edition* script. In *Early Edition* and *Final Edition*, a man is able to predict the future when he comes into possession of the next day's newspaper, and he attempts to alter events that are yet to occur. However, when the Notice of Tentative Writing Credits for *Early Edition* was issued, Givens was not listed as a "participating writer" who was entitled to receive credit. Givens complained to the WGA, citing those provisions of the MBA setting forth the circumstances under which WGA members such as Givens are entitled to writing credit. The WGA responded by suspending the credits process and informing Columbia Tristar, one of the producers of *Early Edition*, that if *Early Edition* aired with credits different from those that the WGA ultimately found to be proper, the WGA would pursue damages on behalf of the WGA-credited writers.

The WGA undertook an investigation and concluded that Givens was not a "participating writer" of *Early Edition*. Givens sought review of the participating-writer decision but, after engaging in additional investigation, the WGA reaffirmed its conclusion that Givens was not entitled to writing credit. After this second determination, Givens asked the WGA to reconsider its decision. The WGA again decided that Givens was not entitled to credit. In a letter to Givens, the WGA noted that its determination that Givens was not a participating writer precluded it from representing him in any subsequent writing-credit arbitration against CBS.

While Givens was pursuing his WGA appeals, Givens, Jacobs, Webb, and Westwind filed this action in Los Angeles County Superior Court. They argued that the *Early Edition* project was "based upon" the literary property *Final Edition* and that, accordingly, CBS had breached its contract by not providing them with writing and production credit. CBS removed the action to federal court. Next, CBS filed a Notice of Initiation of Arbitration, which sought a decision pursuant to the WGA's arbitration procedure on two questions: (1) whether Givens had a right to enforce the contractual provisions of the Second Agreement with respect to *Early Edition* independently of the processes and standards for determining writing credit set forth in the MBA, and (2) whether Givens had a right to pursue a writing-credit claim in a judicial forum. The district court stayed proceedings in federal court pending the outcome of the arbitration.

The WGA arbitrator ruled in favor of CBS. The arbitrator held that allowing Givens to litigate his claims would undermine the finality of the MBA's "fast, fair, and effective system for determining credit." Givens stipulated to an order confirming the arbitration award. Accordingly, Givens is not a party to this appeal.

CBS then filed a motion for summary judgment against the remaining Plaintiffs, who seek production credit regardless of who actually wrote the *Early Edition* scripts. Arguing that Plaintiffs' claims for production credit were entirely derivative of Givens' claim for writing credit, CBS asserted that the formal WGA arbitration had a preclusive effect on Plaintiffs' federal action. The district court rejected that argument, but nonetheless granted summary judgment on the alternate ground that the earlier WGA participating-writer determination involving Givens had a nonmutual collateral estoppel effect on Plaintiffs' action.

Under the doctrine of nonmutual collateral estoppel, it is not necessary that the earlier and later proceedings involve the same parties or their privies. To the contrary, a nonparty to the earlier proceeding may invoke the doctrine *against* a party who *is* bound by the proceeding. The district court in this case applied the doctrine of nonmutual collateral estoppel, holding that, because Plaintiffs were in privity with Givens, CBS could invoke the WGA participating-writer determination against them even though CBS had not been a party to that proceeding. Plaintiffs filed a timely notice of appeal.

We review de novo the district court's grant of summary judgment. We also review de novo the district court's determination that a prior decision has preclusive effect.

A. *California Law on Collateral Estoppel (Issue Preclusion) Applies.*

CBS argues that the WGA's determination that Givens was not a participating writer precludes Plaintiffs from litigating whether *Early Edition* is "based upon" *Final Edition*. To prevail, CBS must establish that the WGA participating-writer proceeding satisfies the requirements for application of collateral estoppel. Because this is a diversity action, state law controls whether the WGA participating-writer determination has a preclusive effect on Plaintiffs' claims for production credit.... Accordingly, we look to California law for the governing principles.

B. *The WGA Participating-Writer Proceeding Is Not Entitled to Preclusive Effect.*

Under California law, CBS must demonstrate that the WGA participating-writer determination was adjudicatory in nature before that determination can have collateral estoppel effect. Additionally, CBS must show that: (1) the issue decided in the WGA proceeding is identical to that presented in Plaintiffs' action; (2) the issue was actually litigated in the WGA proceeding; (3) the issue was necessarily decided in the WGA proceeding; (4) there was a final judgment on the merits in the WGA proceeding; and (5) Plaintiffs were a party or in privity with a party to the WGA proceeding. Plaintiffs argue that the first of these factors is dispositive and that the district court erred in giving the WGA participating-writer determination preclusive effect because that determination lacked the procedural safeguards that California courts require. We agree.

In order to have an issue-preclusive effect in a later judicial action in California, an arbitration must have been conducted with certain procedural safeguards. As the California Supreme Court recently explained:

> Whether collateral estoppel is fair and consistent with public policy in a particular case depends in part upon the character of the forum that first decided the issue later sought to be foreclosed. In this regard, courts consider the judicial nature of the prior forum, *i.e.*, its legal formality, the scope of its jurisdiction, and its procedural safeguards, particularly including the opportunity for judicial review of adverse rulings.

Vandenberg [*v. Superior Court*], 982 P.2d at 237 (Cal. 1999). The California Courts of Appeal have similarly noted that it is "appropriate to give collateral estoppel effect to findings made during an arbitration, *so long as the arbitration had the elements of an adjudicatory procedure*." *Kelly v. Vons Cos.*, 67 Cal. App. 4th 1329, 79 Cal. Rptr. 2d 763, 767 (Ct. App. 1998). The need for procedural safeguards and legal formality is especially acute in the circumstances of this case because "collateral estoppel is invoked by a nonparty to the prior litigation. Such cases require close examination to determine whether nonmutual use of the doctrine is fair and appropriate."

When deciding whether an arbitration was sufficiently adjudicatory in nature, courts apply the same standards used to determine whether an administrative proceeding should have collateral estoppel effect. Accordingly, courts must examine such factors as whether

> (1) the [arbitration] was conducted in a judicial-like adversary proceeding; (2) the proceedings required witnesses to testify under oath; (3) the [arbitral] determination involved the adjudicatory application of rules to a single set of facts; (4) the proceedings were conducted before an impartial hearing officer; (5) the parties had the right to subpoena witnesses and present documentary evidence; and (6) the [arbitrator] maintained a verbatim record of the proceedings. Additional factors include whether the hearing officer's decision was adjudicatory and in writing with a statement of reasons. Finally, [whether] that reasoned decision [was] adopted by the director of the agency with the potential for later judicial review.

Imen v. Glassford, 201 Cal. App. 3d 898, 247 Cal. Rptr. 514, 518 (Ct. App. 1988).

The WGA participating-writer determination did not provide the requisite procedural safeguards to give it issue-preclusive effect in California. The determination was made after an informal "investigation" into Givens' claims. The WGA did not take formal testimony from interested parties but, instead, engaged in "discussions" with Givens, his agent, CBS, and Columbia Tristar. Givens had no opportunity to cross-examine witnesses. Neither did Jacobs or Webb. Further, none of them had a right to examine the evidence presented by CBS and others. Givens and CBS simply provided the WGA with relevant information about the development of each project, and the WGA arrived at its conclusions through an examination of those materials. Finally, the WGA's participating-writer determination was subject to only very limited judicial review.

Thus, although undoubtedly conducted with care and in good faith, the WGA participating-writer proceeding was insufficiently formal and provided too few procedural safeguards to constitute an adjudicatory proceeding. Because the remaining Plaintiffs did not agree to litigate their entitlement to production credit in an informal arbitral forum, under California law the WGA's decision on writing credit does not preclude the litigation of Plaintiffs' claims in a judicial proceeding.

Although Givens *did* agree to arbitrate his entitlement to writing credit, he is no longer a plaintiff in this action. REVERSED and REMANDED for further proceedings consistent with this opinion.

Notes and Questions

a. The principal cases demonstrate the structures used for development of television projects. Significant income and value is ascribed to the final writers on the television pilots. Among professional writers who are members of the Writers Guild of America (WGA), this system works relatively well. Each writer is bound by the collective bargaining agreement to arbitrate the dispute, and the WGA focuses on the extent to which each writer's material exists in the final script as filmed. This question ignores the ownership of the original idea, the chain of development, and the obligations to the writers outside of the actual writing credit. For non-writers or writers who are not members of the union, this process may leave them out of the loop.

b. Another benefit the television networks receive from the writer's credit provisions of the agreement stems from the WGA's role in credit determinations. Whatever the network promises as a contingent reward, it will condition the proffered bonuses, benefits, and interests on the writer receiving exclusive writing credit. In this way, the network can essentially offer everyone involved in a project the same agreement, knowing that the WGA arbitration process will eliminate the risk that more than one person will earn the reward.

In drafting agreements, writers should be careful to separate out "based upon" or other forms of credit as distinct from the writer's credit subject to the WGA arbitration process.

c. The process of moving a television script or motion picture screenplay from first draft to completed television series or motion picture is complex, slow, arbitrary, and often disheartening. Nonetheless, movies and television shows are being produced every year. The industry relies heavily on the two work-for-hire categories of the Copyright Act to vest ownership of the screenplays in the production companies that make these projects and later exploit the works through remakes, sequels, and prequels. In *Horror Inc. v. Miller*, 335 F. Supp. 3d 273 (D. Conn. 2018) (appeal pending), Victor Miller, the original screenwriter for *Friday the 13th*, brought a successful declaratory judgment action that he could terminate his transfer of the copyright in the screenplay. Miller wrote the script pursuant to a WGA short-form agreement. There was no provision to assign the script as a specially-commissioned work in a writing signed by both parties as part of an audiovisual work. Instead, the transfer of the copyright was considered a work for hire as an employee authoring the work within the scope of the employee's duties. Applying *Community for Creative Non-Violence v. Reid*, 490 U.S. 730 (1989), the district court found that the factors needed to find an employee relationship were not present. Since the collaboration between Miller and the producer were typical of independent film productions, the case has the potential to have significant ramifications if it is upheld on appeal and extended to the Second and Ninth Circuits.

d. In addition to the contractual problems between networks and competing development teams, networks can run afoul of the scope of the rights received when they purchase pre-existing literary rights. *See Twentieth Century Fox Film Corp. v. Marvel Enters.*, 155 F. Supp. 2d 1 (S.D.N.Y. 2001).

e. A television series has been advertised with the same name and concept as one your client pitched to a television network five years earlier. Many of the elements are similar and various executives have moved from the network at which your client had pitched the story to the network which ultimately produced the television series in question. What is the legal challenge you must bring and what is the likely result? *See Shaw v. Lindheim*, 809 F. Supp. 1393 (C.D. Cal. 1992).

Problem 13-B

Bryce arrives at your office with a box and explains once having tried to write for television. From the box, Bryce shows you a written pilot episode for a television series, a story bible for that series, and a treatment of the series concepts. The story bible is a compendium of characters, settings, and other details that need to take place in each episode to maintain consistency and build story arcs from episode to episode. The treatment contains a three-page summary of the pilot episode's plot and brief introductions to the story's characters.

Unfortunately, Bryce's writing efforts were rejected by Yin/Yang Television. Bryce never had a development contract for this television series. Instead, the entire project had been written "on spec" with the hope that the television show would be picked up.

Bryce is now convinced that a television show about to air this fall is heavily based on—if not outright copied from—the work Bryce submitted to Yin/Yang Television. Bryce does not expect the pilot to be an exact match since so much changes during the development of any show. Nonetheless, Bryce is convinced that between the story bible and treatment, all of the important elements of Bryce's project appear in the new show. Since the producer and show runner have worked with Bryce on projects in the past and both were employed at Yin/Yang, Bryce is convinced that there has been access to the materials and conversations about the project, even though Bryce never formally pitched it to either individual in their official capacity. Explain to Bryce the ability to use the story bible and treatment to prove infringement, as well as what procedural steps are necessary bring any action.

C. TV Substantial Similarity

Willis v. HBO

57 Fed. App'x 902 (2d. Cir. 2003) (unpublished opinion)

Plaintiff-Appellant Patricia Willis appeals from a judgment of the United States District Court for the Southern District of New York (John S. Martin, Jr., Judge) granting summary judgment in favor of Defendant-Appellee Home Box Office ("HBO"). We affirm for substantially the reasons stated by the District Court in its opinion and order of November 5, 2001.

In her complaint, Willis alleges that the HBO television series *Arli$$* infringes on her copyrighted outline for a proposed television series entitled *Schmoozers*. It is true that both works are situation comedies that feature a money-driven talent agent as their primary character, and that satirize the American entertainment industry as being wholly populated by self-absorbed, morally-depraved individuals. It is also true that both works surround the primary character with a supporting cast comprised of a hapless, male sidekick and an intelligent, female assistant. We agree with the District Court, however, that such similarities are based on stereotypical characters and stock themes, and thus any copying by the defendant related to noncopyrightable aspects of Willis' work.

Willis argues that, apart from individual aspects of *Schmoozers*, the "total concept and feel" of the two works are substantially similar. We reject that assertion because we do not think that any reasonable trier of fact could so conclude. As already pointed out, the generalized similarities between *Arli$$* and *Schmoozers* relate to unoriginal elements of Willis' work. More importantly, the distinctive "total concept and feel" of *Arli$$* is shaped primarily by its use of a dramatic device in which each episode of the series is presented as a narrated reading of a chapter from the main character's autobiography. This enables *Arli$$* to take comedic advantage of the sharp contrast between the main character's overblown and self-reverential view of an event in his life—which the audience learns throughout the episode by means of somber voiceover from that character—and the chaotic, immoral manner in which the event actually transpired. In *Schmoozers*, by contrast, the comedic foil to the main character is not the main character himself but a supporting character who occasionally relates direct criticism of her boss's actions to the audience.

Willis also contends that the District Court erred in dismissing her claims under New York law because "[a] state claim based upon an implied-in-fact obligation to compensate a plaintiff for use of an idea is not preempted...." While there is some support for the general principle that an implied-in-fact contract claim is not pre-empted by federal copyright law, Willis' complaint does not actually plead an im-plied-in-fact contract claim, nor does it even set forth facts that would arguably support such a claim. As we observed in *Nadel v. Play-By-Play Toys & Novelties, Inc.*, 208 F.3d 368 (2d Cir. 2000), a recent case involving implied-in-fact contracts under New York law:

> Of course, the mere disclosure of an ... idea to a defendant ... will not au-tomatically entitle a plaintiff to compensation upon the defendant's subse-quent use of the idea. An implied-in-fact contract requires such elements as consideration, mutual assent, legal capacity and legal subject matter.... The element of mutual assent ... must be inferred from the facts and circum-stances of each case, including such factors as the specific conduct of the parties, industry custom, and course of dealing.

Willis' complaint contains nothing from which "a court may justifiably infer that the promise [to pay Willis for subsequent use of her ideas] would have been explicitly made [by HBO], had attention been drawn to it." ...

The judgment of the District Court is hereby affirmed.

Warner Bros., Inc. v. ABC

720 F.2d 231 (2d Cir. 1983)

The primary issue raised by this appeal is whether as a matter of law the fictional character Ralph Hinkley, the principal figure in a television series, "The Greatest American Hero," is not sufficiently similar to the fictional character Superman, the hero of comic books, television, and more recently films, so that claims of copyright infringement and unfair competition may be dismissed without consideration by a jury.... Plaintiffs own the copyrights in various works embodying the character Su-perman and have thereby acquired copyright protection for the character itself. Since the creation of Superman in 1938, plaintiffs have exploited their rights with great success, portraying Superman in several media and licensing the character for a variety of merchandising purposes. Through plaintiffs' efforts, Superman has attained an extremely high degree of exposure and recognition.

In 1978, building on previous Superman works, plaintiff Warner Bros., Inc. released a motion picture entitled "Superman, The Movie" (*Superman I*) and more recently two sequels....

In *Superman I* and in previous Superman works, Superman is portrayed as a brave, fearless hero, endowed with superhuman powers. His strength, speed, vision, and hearing far exceed the physical capabilities of mere mortals. He is impervious to bullets. In early works, Superman displayed extraordinary leaping ability, in later works this skill had become the power of flight, as Superman is regularly seen soaring through the sky, arms stretched ahead, then landing agilely on his feet ready for action. Superman engages in a series of exploits against assorted criminals and villains who pose threats not only to public safety but also to national security and even world peace. Regardless of his adversary, Superman always prevails....

The substantial commercial success of *Superman I* and the attendant publicity prompted many requests for licenses permitting use of the Superman character in connection with the merchandising of toys, greeting cards, apparel, and other products. It also led ABC to seek a license for production of a television series about "Superboy" based on the early adventures of Superman. Plaintiffs, who were planning to make their own sequels and derivative works, refused ABC permission to proceed with its proposed project.

Unable to obtain this license, ABC assigned to Cannell, the principal of the third-party defendant production company, the task of creating a "pilot" program for a TV series involving a superhero. Cannell produced a program, and subsequently a weekly series, entitled "The Greatest American Hero" (*Hero*), which he described as being about "what happens when you [the average person] become Superman." *Hero*'s protagonist, Ralph Hinkley, was given attributes intended to identify him as an "ordinary guy." Hinkley is portrayed as a young high school teacher attempting to cope with a recent divorce, a dispute over the custody of his son, and the strain that his domestic problems place upon his work and his relationship with his girlfriend. Although Hinkley is attractive, his physical appearance is not imposing: he is of medium height with a slight build and curly, somewhat unkempt, blond hair.

In the pilot show, as described on the prior appeal:

> Hinkley's van breaks down en route to a high school field trip in the desert. While walking along a road in search of help, Hinkley is nearly run over by an out-of-control automobile driven by Bill Maxwell, an American undercover agent. Maxwell has been searching the desert for his missing FBI partner who, unbeknownst to Maxwell, has been murdered by a band of extremists. Maxwell and Hinkley are suddenly approached by a brightly glowing spaceship from which descends the image of Maxwell's deceased partner. Hinkley is handed a magical caped costume—a red leotard with a tunic top, no boots, and a black cape—which, when worn, endows him with fantastic powers. Unfortunately, however, Hinkley loses the instruction book that accompanied the intergalactic gift and is left only with the verbal instruction that he should use his powers to save the world from self-destruction. Hinkley grudgingly accepts the mission after being importuned to do so by Maxwell.

Hinkley's magical costume endows him with superhuman speed and strength, the ability to fly, imperviousness to bullets, and what Cannell calls "holographic vision, "the power to perceive sights and sounds occurring out of his line of vision. Partly for lack of the instruction book that accompanied the costume and partly because some of his character traits remain dominant when he is wearing the suit, Hinkley as a superhero is not an unqualified success. He uses his superpowers awkwardly and fearfully. When flying, Hinkley shouts with fright and makes crash-landings, sometimes crumpling in a heap or skidding nearly out of control to a stop. Though protected from bullets by his costume, Hinkley cringes and cowers when shot at by villains.

In the pilot episode of *Hero*, the reaction of the first man who sees Hinkley in his costume, which he has put on in a gas station washroom, is fear that Hinkley is some sort of pervert who may harm the man or his seven-year-old son, Jerry. While the man calls for the police, Jerry notices that Hinkley is trying to fly but does not know how. The youngster patiently explains that Hinkley must take three steps and jump vigorously into the air. Hinkley manages to get airborne, has difficulty steering, barely avoids colliding with a fire escape, and finally crashes into a brick wall, knocking himself out. Police officers arrest him and take him to a hospital, where he protests in vain to a nurse that he is not crazy....

The *Hero* series contains several visual effects and lines that inevitably call Superman to mind, sometimes by way of brief imitation, sometimes by mention of Superman or another character from the Superman works, and sometimes by humorous parodying or ironic twisting of well-known Superman phrases. Hinkley's suit invests him with most of Superman's powers, and the suit, like Superman's, is a tight-fitting leotard with a chest insignia and a cape. Their outfits differ in that Superman wears a blue leotard with red briefs, boots, and cape, while Hinkley's costume is a red leotard with a tunic top, no boots, and a black cape. In one scene, as Hinkley is running at super speed, smoke emerges from his footsteps, and the sound of a locomotive is heard. A similar scene occurs in *Superman I*, though even without seeing the movie it would be difficult not to be reminded by the *Hero* scene of Superman, who is regularly described as "more powerful than a locomotive." When Hinkley first views himself in a mirror holding his costume in front of him, he says, "It's a bird ... it's a plane ... it's Ralph Hinkley." The youngster, Jerry, watching Hinkley's unsuccessful first effort to fly, tells him, "Superman wouldn't do it that way." In a scene with his girlfriend, who is aware of the powers that come with the magic costume, Hinkley says, "Look at it this way ... you're already one step up on Lois Lane. She never found out who Clark Kent really was." ...

The basic issues concerning the copyright infringement claim are whether the *Hero* and *Superman* works are substantially similar so as to support an inference of copying and whether the lack of substantial similarity is so clear as to fall outside the range of reasonably disputed fact questions requiring resolution by a jury. The similarity to be assessed must concern the expression of ideas, not the ideas themselves, a distinction easier to assert than to apply. Though the issue of substantial similarity is frequently a fact issue for jury resolution, we have recognized that a court may determine non-infringement as a matter of law on a motion for summary judgment, either because the similarity between two works concerns only "*non*-copyrightable elements of the plaintiff's work," or because no reasonable jury, properly instructed, could find that the two works are substantially similar. Before assessing the District Court's determination that summary judgment was appropriate in this case, we consider the principles that guide decisions in this area.

It is a fundamental objective of the copyright law to foster creativity. However, that law has the capacity both to augment and diminish the prospects for creativity. By assuring the author of an original work the exclusive benefits of whatever commercial success his or her work enjoys, the law obviously promotes creativity. At the same time, it can deter the creation of new works if authors are fearful that their creations will too readily be found to be substantially similar to preexisting works. The idea-expression dichotomy originated in the case law and is now codified in the statute, in an effort to enable courts to adjust the tension between these competing effects of copyright protection. Though imprecise, it remains a useful analytic tool for separating infringing from non-infringing works, especially when the essence of the work sought to be protected is a story and the allegedly infringing work is accused of what Professor Nimmer calls "comprehensive nonliteral similarity," 3 *Nimmer* § 13.03[A] [1], duplicating the "fundamental essence or structure" of a work. Confronting a claim of that sort, courts have often invoked Learned Hand's "abstractions" test, or Professor Chaffee's "pattern" test.[13]

[Judge Hand's abstractions test, *Nichols v. Universal Pictures Corp.*, *supra*, 45 F.2d at 121, provides that] "[u]pon any work, and especially upon a play, a great number of patterns of increasing generality will fit equally well, as more and more of the incident is left out. The last may perhaps be no more than the most general statement of what the play is about, and at times consist only of its title; but there is a point in this series of abstractions where they are no longer protected, since otherwise the playwright could prevent the use of his 'ideas,' to which, apart from their expression, his property is never extended."

When, as in this case, the claim concerns infringement of a character, rather than a story, the idea-expression distinction has proved to be especially elusive. In *Nichols*, Hand applied his "abstractions" test in determining that neither the plot nor the characters of "Abie's Irish Rose" were infringed by a similar play called "The Cohens and the Kellys." He noted that no case then decided had found infringement of a character described only by written word, although he recognized the possibility that a literary character could be sufficiently delineated to support a claim of infringement by a second comer, copyrightability of a literary character has on occasion been recognized....

In determining whether a character in a second work infringes a cartoon character, courts have generally considered not only the visual resemblance but also the totality of the characters' attributes and traits. A pertinent consideration, formulated in a case concerning greeting cards in which characters were one element of the art work, is the extent to which the allegedly infringing character captures the "total concept and feel" of the copyrighted character.

---

13. "No doubt, the line does lie somewhere between the author's idea and the precise form in which he wrote it down. I like to say that the protection covers the 'pattern' of the work ... the sequence of events, and the development of the interplay of characters." Chafee, *Reflections on the Law of Copyright*, 45 COLUM. L. REV. 503, 513–14 (1945).

A somewhat paradoxical aspect of infringement disputes, especially pertinent to claims of character infringement, concerns the attention courts give both to similarities and differences in the two works at issue. Professor Nimmer categorically asserts as a proposition, "It is entirely immaterial that in many respects plaintiff's and defendant's works are dissimilar if in other respects similarity as to a substantial element of plaintiff's work can be shown." In Hand's pithy phrase, "No plagiarist can excuse the wrong by showing how much of his work he did not pirate." Yet Professor Nimmer also recognizes, as a second proposition, that "a defendant may legitimately avoid infringement by intentionally making sufficient changes in a work which would otherwise be regarded as substantially similar to that of the plaintiff's." The two propositions are not facially inconsistent; the second proposition contemplates a work that *would be* substantially similar if its author had not made changes from the plaintiff's work. Yet in practice the distinction between the two propositions has become somewhat blurred. We have observed that "numerous differences tend to undercut substantial similarity." This observation appears to go beyond Professor Nimmer's second proposition by emphasizing the significance of differences that do not necessarily change features of the plaintiff's work, but may be entirely additional. To that extent, the observation modifies the first proposition.

The tension between these two propositions perhaps results from their formulation in the context of literary works and their subsequent application to graphic and three-dimensional works. A story has a linear dimension: it begins, continues, and ends. If a defendant copies substantial portions of a plaintiff's sequence of events, he does not escape infringement by adding original episodes somewhere along the line. A graphic or three-dimensional work is created to be perceived as an entirety. Significant dissimilarities between two works of this sort inevitably lessen the similarity that would otherwise exist between the total perceptions of the two works. The graphic rendering of a character has aspects of both the linear, literary mode and the multidimensional total perception. What the character thinks, feels, says, and does and the descriptions conveyed by the author through the comments of other characters in the work episodically fill out a viewer's understanding of the character. At the same time, the visual perception of the character tends to create a dominant impression against which the similarity of a defendant's character may be readily compared, and significant differences readily noted.

Ultimately, care must be taken to draw the elusive distinction between a substantially similar character that infringes a copyrighted character despite slight differences in appearance, behavior, or traits, and a somewhat similar though non-infringing character whose appearance, behavior, or traits, and especially their combination, significantly differ from those of a copyrighted character, even though the second character is reminiscent of the first one. Stirring one's memory of a copyrighted character is not the same as appearing to be substantially similar to that character, and only the latter is infringement. An entirely separate issue of infringement, also posed by this case, concerns what Professor Nimmer calls "fragmented literal similarity," duplicating the exact or nearly exact wording of a fragment of the protected work.

With respect to such claims, courts have invoked two distinct doctrines. First, a *de minimis* rule has been applied, allowing the literal copying of a small and usually insignificant portion of the plaintiff's work. Second, under the "fair use" doctrine, codified in 17 U.S.C. § 107, courts have allowed the taking of words or phrases when adapted for use as commentary or parody.

The "parody" branch of the "fair use" doctrine is itself a means of fostering the creativity protected by the copyright law. It also balances the public interest in the free flow of ideas with the copyright holder's interest in the exclusive use of his work. Especially in an era of mass communications, it is to be expected that phrases and other fragments of expression in a highly successful copyrighted work will become part of the language. That does not mean they lose all protection in the manner of a trade name that has become generic. No matter how well known a copyrighted phrase becomes, its author is entitled to guard against its appropriation to promote the sale of commercial products. That doctrine enabled the proprietors of the Superman copyright to prevent a discount chain from using a television commercial that parodied well-known lines associated with Superman. *D.C. Comics, Inc. v. Crazy Eddie, Inc.*, 205 U.S.P.Q. (BNA) 1177 (S.D.N.Y. 1979) ("Look! ... Up in the sky! ... It's a bird! ... It's a plane ... It's ... Crazy Eddie!"). But an original work of authorship with elements of parody, though undoubtedly created in the hope of commercial success, stands on a different footing from the products of a discount chain. Whatever aesthetic appeal such a work may have results from the creativity that the copyright law is designed to promote. It is decidedly in the interests of creativity, not piracy, to permit authors to take well-known phrases and fragments from copyrighted works and add their own contributions of commentary or humor. After all, any work of sufficient notoriety to be the object of parody has already secured for its proprietor considerable financial benefit. According that proprietor further protection against parody does little to promote creativity, but it places a substantial inhibition upon the creativity of authors adept at using parody to entertain, inform, or stir public consciousness.

Applying these principles to this case, we conclude that Chief Judge Motley correctly entered summary judgment for the defendants on the claim of copyright infringement. Plaintiffs make no claim that the *Hero* pilot, subsequent episodes, or "promos" infringed the story of any Superman works. Their contention is that the *Hero* character, Ralph Hinkley, is substantially similar to Superman and that the *Hero* works impermissibly copied what plaintiffs call the "indicia" of Superman, a concept broad enough to include Superman's costume, his abilities, the well-known lines associated with him — in short, anything occurring in the *Hero* works that might remind a viewer of Superman.

The total perception of the Hinkley character is not substantially similar to that of Superman. On the contrary, it is profoundly different. Superman looks and acts like a brave, proud hero, who has dedicated his life to combating the forces of evil. Hinkley looks and acts like a timid, reluctant hero, who accepts his missions grudgingly and prefers to get on with his normal life. Superman performs his superhuman feats with skill, verve, and dash, clearly the master of his own destiny. Hinkley is perplexed by the superhuman powers his costume confers and uses them in a bumbling, comical fashion. In the genre of superheroes, Hinkley follows Superman as, in the genre of detectives, Inspector Clouseau follows Sherlock Holmes....

The unfair competition and trademark dilution claims present slightly different issues, but, as will appear, we agree with Chief Judge Motley that defendants were entitled to summary judgment on these claims as well as on the infringement claims.... [W]e have noted that "the absence of substantial similarity leaves little basis for asserting a likelihood of confusion or palming off" for purposes of a claim under section 43(a) of the Lanham Act. We do not doubt that the image of a cartoon character and some indicia of that character can function as a trademark to identify the source of a work of entertainment. But, as with claims of copyright infringement, courts retain an important authority to monitor the outer limits of substantial similarity within which a jury is permitted to make the factual determination whether there is a likelihood of confusion as to source....

We agree with Chief Judge Motley that a visual comparison of the Superman works with the *Hero* series and "promos" establishes as a matter of law a lack of substantial similarity that would create a likelihood of confusion as to source. Our discussion of the differences in "total concept and feel" of the central characters of Superman and Hinkley applies to the issue of likelihood of confusion as well as to copyright infringement. We do not doubt that there may be some viewers among the television audience who think that the *Hero* series was produced or authorized by those responsible for the Superman movies, television series, or comics. Some may come to that conclusion with respect to every film or television program portraying a character with superhuman abilities. Perhaps some viewers think that every program with a dramatic courtroom lawyer was made by the producers of the Perry Mason series, or that every show featuring a doctor is a spin-off of the Marcus Welby series. The "average lay observer" test, however, must be applied by fact-finders within an outer limit of reasonable fact-finding marked by the courts. Otherwise the scope of protection a competitor is entitled to enjoy would be expanded far beyond what Congress prescribed in the Lanham Act. Thus, as we concluded with respect to the copyright claim, the availability of survey evidence indicating that some viewers associated the *Hero* series with Superman does not create a *reasonably* disputed factual issue of likelihood of confusion as to source when the works are as different as those in this case....

We also recognize that lack of substantial similarity is not a complete answer to a Lanham Act claim, since a second comer can violate section 43(a) by falsely representing his goods as those of the trademark owner. A claim of "passing off" or "palming off" may be established even if the goods are not confusingly similar; the wrong is in the misrepresentation of a common source. However, in this case this aspect of the section 43(a) claim is also defeated as a matter of law by visual comparison of the works in question. Whether a television viewer could be misled into thinking that the *Hero* series was produced or authorized by those responsible for the Superman films depends on the extent to which the *Hero* programs and "promos" convey such a misrepresentation, even if it was not intended. Plainly there is no overt claim in this regard, and we agree with Chief Judge Motley that perceiving the materials through the eyes and ears of the average lay observer does not create a fair jury issue as to whether a misrepresentation of common source or sponsorship has been implied. The works are too fundamentally different, and the references in the *Hero* programs and "promos" to names and fragments of lines associated with Superman are pointedly made for purposes of contrast.

Plaintiffs fare no better to the extent that their claims are based on New York's common law of unfair competition or the state anti-dilution statute. We have recognized the breadth of New York's common law tort of unfair competition and have not hesitated to apply it to pirated audio-visual works, so long as the cause of action was not preempted by the Copyright Act of 1976.... However, to the extent that plaintiffs are relying on state unfair competition law to allege a tort of "passing off," they are not asserting rights equivalent to those protected by copyright and therefore do not encounter preemption. Their claim fails nevertheless on the merits. The lack of a fairly triable issue of fact as to "passing off" defeats this aspect of the state law claim, just as it did the similar theory advanced under the Lanham Act.

Robinson v. Viacom Int'l

93 Civ. 2539 (RPP), 1995 U.S. Dist. LEXIS 9781
(S.D.N.Y. July 13, 1995)

... Plaintiffs Tom Robinson ("Robinson") and Phil Herter ("Herter") charge Defendants Viacom International, Inc. ("Viacom"), MTV Networks ("MTV"), Ripe Productions, Inc. ("Ripe"), American Broadcasting Companies, Inc. ("ABC"), Penny Stallings, and Rick Mitz with copyright infringement and other unauthorized use of a "Treatment" and a Script created by the two Plaintiffs for a proposed television series to be titled variously as "Deja Vu" or "Four Characters in Search of a Sitcom" (collectively, "Four Characters") based on the production and telecast of a series titled "Hi Honey! I'm Home" ("Hi Honey") by ABC and Nickelodeon/Nick at Nite ("Nickelodeon").

[Prior dealings between the parties create access to the treatment and script which is not otherwise discussed by the court.]

A. Four Characters

"Four Characters" presents two sharply contrasting families: the Walldenski family, a contemporary American suburban family, and whose house is haunted by the Johnson family, an idealized television family derived from the sitcom archetype dating back to the 1950s. Plaintiffs' work consists of a four-page Treatment of the "Four Characters" series, and a 25-page Script for a pilot episode....

B. Hi Honey.... Episode One of "Hi Honey" introduces the Duffs as a single-parent contemporary American family living in suburban New Jersey. Elaine Duff is a single mother working for the phone company and raising two sons after her husband Ted "ran away." The Duff's house appears quite messy, and several locks are mounted on the front door. Mike, the older son, is a high school sophomore who apparently spends most of his free time watching television, and he is upset to learn that reruns of his favorite old black and white show, called "Hi Honey! I'm Home," have just been cancelled. Mike's 10-year old brother Sidney, who is usually called Skunk, dresses as a rebel and sports a "punk-style" haircut. A homeless man named Malcolm appears at the Duff's door, and provokes a hostile reaction from Elaine.

After returning home from work one day, Elaine drags her two boys to meet their new next-door neighbors, the Nielsons, and to ask them to sign her petition for a woman's right to choose. Honey Nielson greets the Duffs, and invites them into her immaculate house (Elaine rolls her eyes when Honey apologizes for its condition). The decor in the Nielsons' house is dated, and the Nielsons' clothes also reflect fashions from the 1950s. Honey is exuberant and unsophisticated, and constantly offers her guests various baked goods. Mike's suspicions are immediately raised by the Nielsons' resemblance to the "Hi Honey! I'm Home" family, and each detail he observes confirms his feeling that the Nielsons are somehow connected to the show he watches each afternoon. The Nielson children, Chuckie and Babbs, are also naive and wholesome, and Mike immediately shows a love interest in Babbs, his high school classmate. . . .

Stock Themes. Related to the requirement of originality under copyright law is the exclusion of protection for "stock themes." Copyright protection does not extend to "'stock' themes commonly linked to a particular genre." Such customary themes, or "scenes a faire," are not copyrightable as a matter of law. Examples of scenes a faire include disgruntled police officers, superheroes lifting cars to show strength and the setting of a POW camp in Hitler's Germany. "Stock themes" or "scenes a faire" in Plaintiffs' work are not eligible for copyright protection.

Idea v. Expression. Copyright law protects only a "particular expression of ideas, not [] the ideas themselves, a distinction easier to state than to apply." To determine whether two works are "so substantially similar as to reveal an infringement of one by the other, courts must decide whether the similarities shared by the works are something more than mere generalized ideas or themes."

Comparison of two works for substantial similarity is "a task generally performed after detailed examination of the works themselves. . . ." To make this determination, a court may break down the works into the following components: plot, characters, total concept and feel (mood), setting, format and pace. A comparison of these components in the Plaintiffs' Treatment and Script with the four episodes of "Hi Honey" reveals the following similarities and differences between the two works.

a. Plot. At the outset, it should be noted that the underlying plot devices used in both parties' works exhibit certain similarities. Both works revolve around the interplay between a contemporary family and a 1950s era television family. Plaintiffs argue that no prior television show was identified by Defendants "which features a television family (qua electronic television images) that comes to exist in the real world. . . . [or] that has as one of its central characters a television family that is a composite of idealized television sitcom families of the past." However, juxtaposition of the two families constitutes an idea, not an expression, and Plaintiffs may not be granted a monopoly in this idea, even if the Plaintiffs' formulation is novel. Plaintiffs argue that the plots of the two works are the same since they both involve "a modern family in a suburban neighborhood [which] discovers that they are living in proximity to the incarnations of a television sitcom family." Plaintiffs' capsule description abstracts their own plot which involves ghosts haunting the house of a modern family, and which is quite different from Defendants' work where the Nielson family appears to be almost normal to outsiders.

Plaintiffs also attempt to provide specific examples of plot similarities between the two works. Plaintiffs point out that both works begin with one family moving into a new neighborhood, Rips but in "Hi Honey" the newcomers are the television family, while "Four Characters" involves a contemporary family moving into a new home. Plaintiffs contend that in both works the elder contemporary child discovers the identity of the television family, but Plaintiffs do not mention that in "Hi Honey" the older Duff son is the only person who recognizes the Nielsons. Plaintiffs also argue that the plot suggestion in their Treatment for an episode based on shoplifting is similar to Episode Eight of "Hi Honey" in which three boys steal money from a neighbor's house to buy shoes, however this effort to protect a minimally developed plot suggestion would encompass virtually any sitcom plot involving a theft by a young person—an unoriginal storyline common to numerous family-based sitcoms. Other such comparisons by the Plaintiffs are similarly faulty (*i.e.* the use of brownies as a motif in both works, humorous cooking escapades). Furthermore, this highlighting of similarities chosen from a number of episodes "would seem as a general matter to allow a plaintiff to cast too wide a net." Plot ideas outlined in Plaintiffs' Treatment are not developed sufficiently to merit protection, especially in light of their derivative nature (most actually constitute cliches gleaned from a long line of family-based sitcoms). Plaintiffs' attempts to note specific similarities between the plots of the two works fail as either too general or because they concern unoriginal components which are not protectible under copyright law.

Plaintiffs only produced one script, and its plot is significantly different from that used to introduce the characters in Episode One of "Hi Honey." Plaintiffs' plot concerns the Walldenski's perception of the Johnsons and their unique view of 1950s values brought into their home by what Herter described as "ghost[s]." Defendants' series involves a 1950s family interacting with all of modern society, and visible to everyone. This is a significant difference in plot between the two works, and prevents a finding of substantial similarity.

b. Characters. Plaintiffs claim that substantial similarity exists between the characters in the two works. In comparing the characters of two works, a court must consider the "totality of their attributes and traits." "No character infringement claim can succeed unless plaintiff's original conception sufficiently developed the character, and defendants have copied this development and not merely the broader outlines."

Robinson testified that the Johnson family was developed "based [] on our joint memory of things that we had seen as reruns." The "Four Characters" Script presents essentially no character development beyond introducing characters clearly derived from a long line of family-based sitcoms. The Treatment similarly compiles attributes which are not original and relies only on the device of the Johnsons haunting the

Walldenskis' house for originality. Plaintiffs may not claim copyright protection for the characters in their work because they lack originality.

Similarities between characters in the two works relate only to non-protectible stock themes. "Copyright law will not protect characters where 'it is virtually impossible to write about a particular fictional theme without employing certain stock or standard literary devices.'" Furthermore, the similarities identified by Plaintiffs between characters in the two works exist only at the abstract level of unprotectible ideas. For example, although Plaintiffs assert that the contemporary fathers in the two works are identical, the contemporary father in "Hi Honey" has run away and never appears on-screen. Plaintiffs argue that the two characters are nevertheless "identical" since they are both undergoing mid-life crises, but at this level of identity all middle-aged father characters are potentially similar. Plaintiffs also contend that the contemporary younger son, Skunk, in "Hi Honey" "matches precisely" Defendants' description of the contemporary daughter in "Four Characters," Shelia, since Skunk was involved in a theft as was Shelia. The identity perceived here by Plaintiff exists at a level too general to support substantial similarity: the "Four Characters" incident revolved around a shoplifting by the daughter to obtain clothes, whereas the theft in "Hi Honey" was of money in a neighbor's house so that Skunk and his friends could buy sneakers. Plaintiffs argue that the 1950s son in "Hi Honey," Chuckie Nielson, is similar to the athletic 1950s son in "Four Characters" since Chuckie, although overweight and generally portrayed as an outcast, is seen returning home from a baseball game in uniform. This similarity is also at too abstract a level to merit copyright protection.

c. Total Concept and Feel. Plaintiffs claim that Defendants' work is substantially similar in its "total concept and feel." As Judge Haight recently noted, "Courts must pay particular attention to summary judgment motions in cases where a plaintiff claims that defendant's work copies the "total concept and feel" of plaintiff's work. Accepting an overly broad scope for protectable "total concept and feel" threatens the basic principal of copyright law: that concepts and ideas may not be copyrighted, and that only a particular expression of an idea may be copyrighted."

The broad theme of a 1950s era sitcom family interacting with a contemporary family is an unprotectible idea. Furthermore, the device of characters appearing in color or black and white to emphasize a temporal contrast has been used in numerous television and motion picture settings.

d. Setting. Plaintiffs claim that the settings in both works are identical: "a middle-class suburb." However, this is not a protectible element since settings such as an opening "with a frontal shot of … a solid two story house with a well-maintained lawn shaded by stately trees[,]" have been commonly found in sitcoms for over 30 years. Similarly, the type and arrangement of furniture in the living rooms of the two families and the appliances in the kitchen are not ideas original with plaintiffs, and are unprotectible under copyright law.

e. Format. Plaintiffs argue that "the choice of a comedy … [to] treat the social issues at the heart of the shows in a light manner" renders the two works identical, as does the use of a five-minute prologue to introduce the central conflict for the episode. This format is common to many sitcoms, and is not a protectible element of Plaintiff's work.

f. Pace. The "up-tempo" pace of the two works is common to virtually all sitcoms, and is not a protectible element of Plaintiffs' work.

Conclusion. Defendants have shown that any similarities between "Hi Honey" and "Four Characters" relate only to unprotectible elements, and that no reasonable jury, properly instructed, could find that the works are substantially similar.... [All remaining state court and Lanham Act claims dismissed.]

Notes and Questions

a. A few additional comments from the district court in *Willis v. HBO*, 2001 U.S. Dist. LEXIS 17887 (S.D.N.Y. 2001) may also be of interest:

> Many people would consider the phrase "sleazy talent agent" to be redundant. While this is no doubt as unfair a stereotype as is the "sleazy lawyer," no one could reasonably claim a copyright in the concept of a sleazy talent agent. The question presented here is what degree of detail must an author add to such a well-recognized stock character in order to obtain copyright protection.

> Defendant now moves for summary judgment contending that the only similarity between Arli$$ and Schmoozers is that both employ well-known concepts which no one may copyright. Plaintiff contends, however, that there are such significant similarities in the details of her Treatment for Schmoozers and the series Arli$$ that a trier of fact could conclude that Arli$$ violates her Schmoozers copyright. To support her claim she relies upon the report of an "expert" in television studies who details what he considers to be the significant similarities between Schmoozers and Arli$$ and concludes that the two series are "uniquely alike." ... The problem with Plaintiff's claim and her "expert's" report is that, to the extent that there are similarities, they are found either in stock characters, or themes that are common to the talent agency business, or to situation comedies in general or in trivial detail that are not essential to either series. Plaintiff's arguments also ignore the significant differences between the two series and strain to find similarities where none exist.

Id.

b. Some ideas seem more similar than others. Steve Fischer, creator of the characters Steve and Bluey, and the comic strip "There's a Dog Under my Bed," lost in a claim dispute regarding "Blue's Clues" despite documentation that Fischer had been in correspondence with Nickelodeon U.K. for the production of a children's animated television series. Nickelodeon U.S. is the producer of "Blue's Clues," a children's animated television series originally featuring the human Steve and his dog, Blue. *See Fischer v. Viacom Int'l Inc.*, 115 F. Supp. 2d 535 (D. Md. 2000).

c. When does a character become a sufficiently protected element that the use of a similar character will infringe the copyright? *Compare Rice v. Fox Broad. Co.*, 330 F.3d 1170 (9th Cir. 2003) (competing video and television products for The Mystery Magician), *with Metro-Goldwyn-Mayer, Inc. v. Am. Honda Motor Corp.*, 900 F. Supp. 1287 (C.D. Cal. 1995) (use of secret agent like James Bond), *and Anderson v. Stallone*, 1989 U.S. Dist. LEXIS 11109 (C.D. Cal. 1989) (use of Rocky character in an unauthorized sequel "spec" script).

d. To what extent is the Fox reality show, *Trading Spouses*, a copy of the British-made and ABC-acquired *Wife Swap*? The world may never know. Trademark, trade dress, and bad etiquette claims were dismissed, though the copyright claim was allowed. *See RDF Media Ltd. v. Fox Broad. Co.*, 372 F. Supp. 2d 556 (C.D. Cal. 2005).

e. Who wants to share in being a millionaire? On the issue of fair dealing when negotiating syndication and related rights for sale to the same conglomerate, see *Celador International Ltd. v. The Walt Disney Co.*, 347 F. Supp. 2d 846 (C.D. Cal. 2004). Owners of *Who Wants to Be a Millionaire* can bring claims for an alleged breach of the covenant of good faith and fair dealing when selling rights to other entities or divisions commonly owned by a party to the agreement.

f. Occasionally the similarity between two broadcast television shows will be so overwhelming that the producer does have a copyright action:

> Infringement can occur where—without copying a single line—the later author borrows wholesale the entire backdrop, characters, inter-relationships, genre, and plot design of an earlier work. Imagine, for example, that the first Sherlock Holmes stories had been penned and copyrighted last year by Sir Arthur Conan Doyle, and Logroño had then written his own sequels carrying everything forward into a new plot. Here, ..."El Condominio" is ..."an unauthorized derivative work. In effect ... both programs are the same with only a difference in name and transmitted via a different channel. Specifically, the setting, character names, costumes, character interactions, comedy line, mood, [and] camera angles are almost identical in both sitcoms."

TMTV, Corp. v. Mass Prods., 645 F.3d 464, 470–471 (1st Cir. 2011) (quoting the District Court).

g. Television programming elicits a great deal of copyright litigation by parties claiming that their unsolicited material has been copied. The courts, therefore, often make a preliminary determination of substantial similarity on motions to dismiss and summary judgment.

> The analysis of [Plaintiff's] copyright infringement claim is straightforward. Whether the "ordinary observer" or "more discerning observer" test is employed, the appropriate inquiry is whether the copying of protectable elements "is quantitatively and qualitatively sufficient to support a finding of infringement." *Nihon Keizai Shimbun, Inc. v. Comline Bus. Data, Inc.*, 166 F.3d 65, 70 (2d Cir.1999) (internal quotation marks omitted). In applying this test, "we examine the similarities in such aspects as the total concept and feel,

theme, characters, plot, sequence, pace and setting." *Williams v. Crichton*, 84 F.3d 581, 588 (2d Cir.1996).

Alexander v. Murdoch, 502 Fed. Appx. 107, 109 (2d Cir. 2012) (unpublished).

Problem 13-C

Inspired by a cable television marathon, Bryce comes to you for advice. Bryce wants to rewrite the James Bond character to reinvigorate the franchise. Bryce recognizes that the copyright is owned by United Artists, but believes that a fresh and innovative approach to the character will reenergize it in a way that it has lost since the end of the Cold War and the fall of the Berlin Wall.

Bryce says the idea is not another hackneyed return to the Middle East, but instead marries the adventure and gadgetry of Bond's best films with the intrigue and complexity of John LeCarre's Smiley character. Advise Bryce on how best to proceed.

D. Editing for Television

Preminger v. Columbia Pictures Corp.

267 N.Y.S.2d 594 (Sup. Ct. 1966), *aff'd*, 269 N.Y.S.2d 913 (App. Div.), *aff'd*, 18 N.Y.2d 659 (1966)

The interesting question presented for decision is the right of a producer, in the absence of specific contractual provision, to prevent, by injunction, minor cuts in his motion picture, when shown on television, and the usual breaks for commercials. The litigation involves the production of the motion picture "Anatomy of a Murder."

The complaint alleges that plaintiff Preminger is a producer and director of motion pictures, including the motion picture involved; and plaintiff Carlyle Productions, Inc., a California corporation, was the owner of all rights to the picture, and Carlyle Productions, a limited New York partnership, its assignee; that Carlyle Productions, Inc., entered into a series of agreements with Columbia Pictures Corporation between 1956 and 1959, which are collectively referred to as the contract, copies of which are annexed to the complaint.

Defendant Columbia and defendant Screen Gems, Inc., its subsidiary, the complaint continues, have licensed over 100 television stations to exhibit the motion picture on television, and those license agreements purport to give the licensees the right to cut, to eliminate portions of the picture, and to interrupt the remainder of the picture for commercials and other extraneous matter.

Unless enjoined, the complaint asserts, defendants will (a) detract from the artistic merit of "Anatomy of a Murder"; (b) damage Preminger's reputation; (c) cheapen and tend to destroy Anatomy's commercial value; (d) injure plaintiffs in the conduct of their business; and (e) falsely represent to the public that the film shown is Preminger's film.

It is then alleged, and not denied, that "Anatomy" is one of a very few motion pictures with a rating of AA-1; that it has been licensed in blocks of 60 to 300 pictures; and that the others are artistically and commercially inferior to "Anatomy".

Finally it is alleged that defendants have allocated an unfairly and unreasonably low share of license fees to "Anatomy". This allegation is denied.

All these acts are described as willful and wanton breaches of the contract with Carlyle as owner and Preminger as producer.

Injunctive relief and accounting, for plaintiffs' damages, are prayed for.

Specifically, it is demanded that judgment be granted: (a) enjoining defendants from performing their obligations under the licensing agreements; (b) enjoining defendants from entering into further agreements violative of plaintiffs' rights; (c) enjoining defendants to withdraw all prints previously distributed; (d) directing defendants to account to plaintiffs, for what are presumably plaintiffs' damages; profits are not requested; and (e) other and further relief....

Thus, the only question before the court in this proceeding is the plaintiffs' right to a permanent injunction.

The plaintiffs plant themselves upon article VIII of the contract, which provides: "You [Carlyle] shall have the right to make the final cutting and editing of the Picture, but you shall in good faith consider recommendations and suggestions with respect thereto made by us [Columbia]; nevertheless, you shall have final approval thereof, provided however that notwithstanding the foregoing, in the event that cutting or re-editing is required in order to meet censorship requirements and you shall fail or refuse to comply therewith, then we shall have the right to cut and edit the Picture in order to meet censorship requirements without obligation on our part to challenge the validity of any rule, order, regulation or requirement of any national, state or local censorship authority." The import of the paragraph is that plaintiffs have the right to make the final "cutting and editing" of the picture; giving the defendants the right to make suggestions, only.

This article must be read, however, in juxtaposition with article X of the contract, which provides as follows: "The rights herein granted, without limiting the generality of the foregoing, shall include and embrace all so-called 'theatrical' as well as 'non-theatrical' rights in the Picture (as those terms are commonly understood in the motion picture industry); and shall include the right to use film of any and all gauges. You hereby give and grant to us throughout the entire world the exclusive and irrevocable right during the term herein specified to project, exhibit, reproduce, transmit and perform, and authorize and license others to project, exhibit, reproduce, transmit and perform, the picture and prints thereof by television, and in any other manner, and by any other means, method or device whatsoever, whether mechanical, electrical or otherwise, and whether now known or hereafter conceived or created."

This article, it will be noted, which contains the specific grant of television rights, makes no reference to "cutting and editing".

In these circumstances the court is inclined to the view that the right to the "final" cutting and editing, reserved to the plaintiffs, is limited to the original or theatrical production of the picture, and not to showings on television; and that as to such showings, in the absence of specific contractual provision, the parties will be deemed to have adopted the custom prevailing in the trade or industry.

This view is confirmed by the authorities and fortified by the evidence.

We begin with the proposition that the law is not so rigid, even in the absence of contract, as to leave a party without protection against publication of a garbled version of his work. This, as pointed out by Frank, J., concurring in *Granz v. Harris*, 198 F. 2d 585, 589 [(2d Cir. 1952)] is not novel doctrine.

The court "appreciates that the failure of the community ... to protect its gifted men of letters led to tragedies which comprise scars in the history of civilization." And in Granz the United States Court of Appeals for the Second Circuit held that publication of a truncated version of plaintiffs' phonograph recording should be enjoined. In the case at bar, however, the contract must serve as a guide to the intention of the parties.

Thus, where the parties have particularized the terms of a contract, an apparently inconsistent general statement to a different effect must yield. Therefore, the clause in this contract, general in its terms, giving plaintiffs the right to "finally" cut and edit as to the original production of the motion picture, must yield to the specific clause with respect to television showing, which contained no such right. So it is, too, that in the construction of a contract, weight will be given to the custom prevailing in the trade to which it refers. This brings us to a review of the evidence, on which, of course, the burden of proof rests on the plaintiffs.

At the trial, extensive testimony was presented by both sides with respect to the normal customs prevailing in the television and motion picture industries as to the significance of the right to "final cut."

A review of the testimony demonstrates that, at least for the past 15 years, the right to interrupt the exhibition of a motion picture on television for commercial announcements and to make minor deletions to accommodate time segment requirements or to excise those portions which might be deemed, for various reasons, objectionable, has consistently been considered a normal and essential part of the exhibition of motion pictures on television. Implicit in the grant of television rights is the privilege to cut and edit.

No proof has been adduced that this cutting and editing would be done in such a manner as to interfere with the picture's story line.

The licensing agreements provide:

> Licensee shall telecast each print, as delivered by Distributor, in its entirety. However, Licensee may make such minor cuts or elimination as are necessary to conform to time segment requirements or to the orders of any duly authorized public censorship authority and may add commercial material at the places and of the lengths indicated by Distributor, but under no circum-

> stances shall Licensee delete the copyright notice or the credits incorporated in the pictures as delivered by the Distributor, provided, however, in no event may the insertion of any commercial material adversely affect the artistic or pictorial quality of the picture or materially interfere with its continuity.

Defendants' witnesses, Lacey of WCBS, Howard of WNBC and Gilbert of WABC, testified with respect to the practices customarily prevailing throughout the television industry. Plaintiffs' witnesses did not controvert the testimony concerning the customary practices in the trade with regard to interruptions for commercials, and minor cuts. As a matter of fact, Sherwin, one of plaintiffs' witnesses, the program director of KHJ, Los Angeles, testified, as had defendants' witnesses, that his station had never purchased any motion picture without the right to make interruptions as well as minor cuts. Whether or not, in an isolated instance, a picture was exhibited with less than the customary number of commercials is not determinative of the issue. We are concerned not with what might have happened in some rare instance but instead with what was the common practice and custom at the time the parties herein signed their contract....

With respect to the expression "final cut", sufficient testimony was adduced to indicate that this phrase, as used in article VIII of the contract, relates only to a phase in the production of the picture for theatrical showing and has no relation to the interruptions and minor cuts here under discussion. Even plaintiffs' own witnesses identified the "final cutting and editing" of a picture as the last stage in its production for theatrical exhibition.

Although plaintiffs consistently refer to the practice of interrupting and making minor cuts as "mutilation", their own witnesses have conceded that the minor cuts customarily made in a television exhibition of a picture have such a minimal impact upon its over-all effect that these are rarely even noticed.

Undisputed is the fact that not a single television station has ever failed to insist upon the right to interrupt for commercials. Similarly unrefuted is defendants' proof to the effect that no station ever purchased a motion picture without reserving to itself the right to interrupt for commercials and to make minor cuts.

Plaintiff Preminger admitted that when he signed the agreement for "Anatomy of a Murder", he was aware that the practice of the television industry was to interrupt motion pictures for commercials and to make minor cuts. Aware of this practice, plaintiffs at the time the instant contract was signed nevertheless did not specifically provide for conditions other than those known to them to be prevalent in the industry.

Two contracts between Preminger and United Artists Corporation were received in evidence. These were contracts pertaining to "Man With The Golden Arm" and "The Moon Is Blue", the last two pictures produced by Preminger prior to "Anatomy of a Murder", which he made for Columbia. In both the contract for "The Moon Is Blue" and the contract for "Man With The Golden Arm", clauses appeared which demonstrate that Preminger was aware of the prevailing practice in the television industry with respect to interrupting motion pictures for commercials and making minor cuts therein for normal television purposes. These contracts further show that when Preminger desired to prevent television distribution in the normal manner, he so provided.

In the contract between the Carlyle corporation and United Artists Corporation, dated December 20, 1954, for "Man With The Golden Arm," it was expressly provided that United Artists' right "to make such changes, additions, alterations, cuts, interpolations and eliminations as may be required for the distribution of the picture in television" should be subject to the approval of producer.... Both Preminger and United Artists were aware that granting the producer this right of approval was tantamount to giving him a veto power over ultimate television distribution of the film, for in other provisions of both of the above contracts it was expressly recognized that television distribution was not to take place without the producer's prior approval. Plaintiffs' entry into the instant contract which failed to contain such a clause may be considered by the court as evidence of the parties' intention....

So standardized has the practice of interrupting films for commercials become, that guidelines have been established in the television industry as to the maximum number of commercials regarded as acceptable in a given time period.

The television industry serves a great public need and its services have ofttimes, and perhaps at some financial sacrifice, been offered in the public interest. Despite such apparent unselfish public service, it should not be overlooked that the industry, like every other business, has as its primary objective the accumulation of profits. Sponsorship of programs, by advertisers, provides a station with its only source of revenue and though it ofttimes interrupts its programs with what some viewers feel to be an inordinate amount of advertising, since its primary purpose is to advertise the products of its sponsors, such interruptions in the absence of governmental or industry regulation can only be controlled by contractual arrangement.

It is of no import that some viewers may not approve of the advertising practices prevalent in the industry—that is, the number and types of commercials. However, the parties to this distribution agreement signed it knowing of the existence of such practices. The plaintiffs, as well as any independent producer or director, could have obviated this problem by specifically prohibiting such cuts or interruptions by contract. This, of course, might have had an adverse effect on the extent of television distribution—an eventuality which most producers would not welcome. Accordingly, in the absence of any contractual provision to the contrary, they must be deemed to have contemplated that what was permissible, under the existing practice, would continue in effect.

The criterion for the determination of what the defendants were likely to do with respect to interrupting and cutting the subject film, in the absence of a specific contractual arrangement, was not what plaintiffs might disapprove of or dislike but, rather, what was the normal custom and practice in the industry.

The issues in the case, in the court's view, are therefore issues of law: *i.e.,* (1) whether plaintiffs may thwart the making of minor cuts or interpolations in the absence of specific contractual provision; the court finds the answer to this question to be in the negative; and (2) whether, under this contract, in the light of the custom in the trade, plaintiffs left to the station masters the right to use their judgment and exercise their discretion, instead of plaintiffs', as to which minor cuts, eliminations, and interpolations are appropriate. In view of the variety of stations, localities, audiences, and commercials, the court answers this question in the affirmative.

The running time of the full motion picture is 161 minutes. The brochure for WABC-TV advertised the picture to potential sponsors as a 100-minute feature. The station master, however, testified, and the court credits his testimony, that this was a mistake; that it was never intended to permit any such extensive cutting. This applies as well to the asserted cutting of the picture to 53 minutes. Obviously such cuts would not be minor and indeed could well be described as mutilation. Should such "mutilation" occur in the future, plaintiffs may make application to this court for injunctive or other relief against such violation as they may be advised....

Gilliam v. ABC
538 F.2d 14 (2d Cir. 1976)

Plaintiffs, a group of British writers and performers known as "Monty Python," appeal from a denial by Judge Lasker in the Southern District of a preliminary injunction to restrain the American Broadcasting Company (ABC) from broadcasting edited versions of three separate programs originally written and performed by Monty Python for broadcast by the British Broadcasting Corporation (BBC). We agree with Judge Lasker that the appellants have demonstrated that the excising done for ABC impairs the integrity of the original work. We further find that the countervailing injuries that Judge Lasker found might have accrued to ABC as a result of an injunction at a prior date no longer exist. We therefore direct the issuance of a preliminary injunction by the district court.

Since its formation in 1969, the Monty Python group has gained popularity primarily through its thirty-minute television programs created for BBC as part of a comedy series entitled "Monty Python's Flying Circus." In accordance with an agreement between Monty Python and BBC, the group writes and delivers to BBC scripts for use in the television series. This scriptwriters' agreement recites in great detail the procedure to be followed when any alterations are to be made in the script prior to recording of the program.[14] The essence of this section of the agreement is that,

---

14. The Agreement provides:

V. When script alterations are necessary it is the intention of the BBC to make every effort to inform and to reach agreement with the Writer. Whenever practicable any necessary alterations (other than minor alterations) shall be made by the Writer. Nevertheless the BBC shall at all times have the right to make (a) minor alterations and (b) such other alterations as in its opinion are necessary in order to avoid involving the BBC in legal action or bringing the BBC into disrepute. Any decision under (b) shall be made at a level not below that of Head of Department. It is however agreed that after a script has been accepted by the BBC alterations will not be made by the BBC under (b) above unless (i) the Writer, if available when the BBC requires the alterations to be made, has been asked to agree to them but is not willing to do so and (ii) the Writer has had, if he so requests and if the BBC agrees that while BBC retains final authority to make changes, appellants or their representatives exercise optimum control over the scripts consistent with BBC's authority and only minor changes may be made without prior consultation with the writers. Nothing in the scriptwriters' agreement entitles BBC to alter a program once it has been recorded. The agreement further provides that, subject to the terms therein, the group retains all rights in the script.

Under the agreement, BBC may license the transmission of recordings of the television programs in any overseas territory. The series has been broadcast in this country primarily on non-commercial public broadcasting television stations, although several of the programs have been broadcast on commercial stations in Texas and Nevada. In each instance, the thirty-minute programs have been broadcast as originally recorded and broadcast in England in their entirety and without commercial interruption.

In October 1973, Time-Life Films acquired the right to distribute in the United States certain BBC television programs, including the Monty Python series. Time-Life was permitted to edit the programs only "for insertion of commercials, applicable censorship or governmental ... rules and regulations, and National Association of Broadcasters and time segment requirements." No similar clause was included in the scriptwriters' agreement between appellants and BBC. Prior to this time, ABC had sought to acquire the right to broadcast excerpts from various Monty Python programs in the spring of 1975, but the group rejected the proposal for such a disjoined format. Thereafter, in July 1975, ABC agreed with Time-Life to broadcast two ninety-minute specials each comprising three thirty-minute Monty Python programs that had not previously been shown in this country.

Correspondence between representatives of BBC and Monty Python reveals that these parties assumed that ABC would broadcast each of the Monty Python programs "in its entirety." On September 5, 1975, however, the group's British representative inquired of BBC how ABC planned to show the programs in their entirety if approximately 24 minutes of each 90 minute program were to be devoted to commercials. BBC replied on September 12, "we can only reassure you that ABC have decided to run the programmes 'back to back,' and that there is a firm undertaking not to segment them."

ABC broadcast the first of the specials on October 3, 1975. Appellants did not see a tape of the program until late November and were allegedly "appalled" at the discontinuity and "mutilation" that had resulted from the editing done by Time-Life for

---

time permits if rehearsals and recording are to proceed as planned, an opportunity to be represented by the Writers' Guild of Great Britain (or if he is not a member of the Guild by his agent) at a meeting with the BBC to be held within at most 48 hours of the request (excluding weekends). If in such circumstances there is no agreement about the alterations then the final decision shall rest with the BBC. Apart from the right to make alterations under (a) and (b) above the BBC shall not without the consent of the Writer or his agent (which consent shall not be unreasonably withheld) make any structural alterations as opposed to minor alterations to the script, provided that such consent shall not be necessary in any case where the Writer is for any reason not immediately available for consultation at the time which in the BBC's opinion is the deadline from the production point of view for such alterations to be made if rehearsals and recording are to proceed as planned.

ABC. Twenty-four minutes of the original 90 minutes of recording had been omitted. Some of the editing had been done in order to make time for commercials; other material had been edited, according to ABC, because the original programs contained offensive or obscene matter....

We ... reach the question whether there is a likelihood that appellants will succeed on the merits. In concluding that there is a likelihood of infringement here, we rely especially on the fact that the editing was substantial, *i.e.*, approximately 27 per cent of the original program was omitted, and the editing contravened contractual provisions that limited the right to edit Monty Python material. It should be emphasized that our discussion of these matters refers only to such facts as have been developed upon the hearing for a preliminary injunction. Modified or contrary findings may become appropriate after a plenary trial....

Appellants first contend that the question of ownership is irrelevant because the recorded program was merely a derivative work taken from the script in which they hold the uncontested copyright. Thus, even if BBC owned the copyright in the recorded program, its use of that work would be limited by the license granted to BBC by Monty Python for use of the underlying script. We agree.

Section 7 of the [1909] Copyright Law, provides in part that "adaptations, arrangements, dramatizations ... or other versions of ... copyrighted works when produced with the consent of the proprietor of the copyright in such works ... shall be regarded as new works subject to copyright...." Manifestly, the recorded program falls into this category as a dramatization of the script, and thus the program was itself entitled to copyright protection. However, section 7 limits the copyright protection of the derivative work, as works adapted from previously existing scripts have become known, to the novel additions made to the underlying work. Thus, any ownership by BBC of the copyright in the recorded program would not affect the scope or ownership of the copyright in the underlying script.

Since the copyright in the underlying script survives intact despite the incorporation of that work into a derivative work, one who uses the script, even with the permission of the proprietor of the derivative work, may infringe the underlying copyright. If the proprietor of the derivative work is licensed by the proprietor of the copyright in the underlying work to vend or distribute the derivative work to third parties, those parties will, of course, suffer no liability for their use of the underlying work consistent with the license to the proprietor of the derivative work. Obviously, it was just this type of arrangement that was contemplated in this instance. The scriptwriters' agreement between Monty Python and BBC specifically permitted the latter to license the transmission of the recordings made by BBC to distributors such as Time-Life for broadcast in overseas territories.

One who obtains permission to use a copyrighted script in the production of a derivative work, however, may not exceed the specific purpose for which permission was granted.... Appellants herein ... claim that revisions in the script, and ultimately in the program, could be made only after consultation with Monty Python, and that

ABC's broadcast of a program edited after recording and without consultation with Monty Python exceeded the scope of any license that BBC was entitled to grant.

The rationale for finding infringement when a licensee exceeds time or media restrictions on his license—the need to allow the proprietor of the underlying copyright to control the method in which his work is presented to the public—applies equally to the situation in which a licensee makes an unauthorized use of the underlying work by publishing it in a truncated version. Whether intended to allow greater economic exploitation of the work, as in the media and time cases, or to ensure that the copyright proprietor retains a veto power over revisions desired for the derivative work, the ability of the copyright holder to control his work remains paramount in our copyright law. We find, therefore, that unauthorized editing of the underlying work, if proven, would constitute an infringement of the copyright in that work similar to any other use of a work that exceeded the license granted by the proprietor of the copyright.

If the broadcast of an edited version of the Monty Python program infringed the group's copyright in the script, ABC may obtain no solace from the fact that editing was permitted in the agreements between BBC and Time-Life or Time-Life and ABC. BBC was not entitled to make unilateral changes in the script and was not specifically empowered to alter the recordings once made; Monty Python, moreover, had reserved to itself any rights not granted to BBC. Since a grantor may not convey greater rights than it owns, BBC's permission to allow Time-Life, and hence ABC, to edit appears to have been a nullity....

ABC next argues that under the "joint work" theory adopted in *Shapiro, Bernstein & Co. v. Jerry Vogel Music, Inc.*, 221 F.2d 569 (2d Cir. 1955), the script produced by Monty Python and the program recorded by BBC are symbiotic elements of a single production. Therefore, according to ABC, each contributor possesses an undivided ownership of all copyrightable elements in the final work and BBC could thus have licensed use of the script, including editing, written by appellants.

The joint work theory as extended in *Shapiro* has been criticized as inequitable unless "at the time of creation by the first author, the second author's contribution [is envisaged] as an integrated part of a single work," and the first author intends that the final product be a joint work. Furthermore, this court appears to have receded from a broad application of the joint work doctrine where the contract which leads to collaboration between authors indicates that one will retain a superior interest. In the present case, the screenwriters' agreement between Monty Python and BBC provides that the group is to retain all rights in the script not granted in the agreement and that at some future point the group may license the scripts for use on television to parties other than BBC. These provisions suggest that the parties did not consider themselves joint authors of a single work. This matter is subject to further exploration at the trial, but in the present state of the record, it presents no bar to issuance of a preliminary injunction.

Aside from the question of who owns the relevant copyrights, ABC asserts that the contracts between appellants and BBC permit editing of the programs for commercial television in the United States. ABC argues that the scriptwriters' agreement allows appellants the right to participate in revisions of the script only *prior* to the recording of the programs, and thus infers that BBC had unrestricted authority to revise after that point. This argument, however, proves too much. A reading of the contract seems to indicate that Monty Python obtained control over editing the script only to ensure control over the program recorded from that script. Since the scriptwriters' agreement explicitly retains for the group all rights not granted by the contract, omission of any terms concerning alterations in the program after recording must be read as reserving to appellants exclusive authority for such revisions.

Finally, ABC contends that appellants must have expected that deletions would be made in the recordings to conform them for use on commercial television in the United States. ABC argues that licensing in the United States implicitly grants a license to insert commercials in a program and to remove offensive or obscene material prior to broadcast. According to the network, appellants should have anticipated that most of the excised material contained scatological references inappropriate for American television and that these scenes would be replaced with commercials, which presumably are more palatable to the American public....

Several of the deletions made for ABC, such as elimination of the words "hell" and "damn," seem inexplicable given today's standard television fare. If, however, ABC honestly determined that the programs were obscene in substantial part, it could have decided not to broadcast the specials at all, or it could have attempted to reconcile its differences with appellants. The network could not, however, free from a claim of infringement, broadcast in a substantially altered form a program incorporating the script over which the group had retained control.

Our resolution of these technical arguments serves to reinforce our initial inclination that the copyright law should be used to recognize the important role of the artist in our society and the need to encourage production and dissemination of artistic works by providing adequate legal protection for one who submits his work to the public. We therefore conclude that there is a substantial likelihood that, after a full trial, appellants will succeed in proving infringement of their copyright by ABC's broadcast of edited versions of Monty Python programs. In reaching this conclusion, however, we need not accept appellants' assertion that any editing whatsoever would constitute infringement. Courts have recognized that licensees are entitled to some small degree of latitude in arranging the licensed work for presentation to the public in a manner consistent with the licensee's style or standards. That privilege, however, does not extend to the degree of editing that occurred here especially in light of contractual provisions that limited the right to edit Monty Python material.

It also seems likely that appellants will succeed on the theory that, regardless of the right ABC had to broadcast an edited program, the cuts made constituted an actionable mutilation of Monty Python's work. This cause of action, which seeks redress for deformation of an artist's work, finds its roots in the continental concept of droit moral, or moral right, which may generally be summarized as including the right of the artist to have his work attributed to him in the form in which he created it.

American copyright law, as presently written, does not recognize moral rights or provide a cause of action for their violation, since the law seeks to vindicate the economic, rather than the personal, rights of authors. Nevertheless, the economic incentive for artistic and intellectual creation that serves as the foundation for American copyright law, cannot be reconciled with the inability of artists to obtain relief for mutilation or misrepresentation of their work to the public on which the artists are financially dependent. Thus courts have long granted relief for misrepresentation of an artist's work by relying on theories outside the statutory law of copyright, such as contract law, or the tort of unfair competition. Although such decisions are clothed in terms of proprietary right in one's creation, they also properly vindicate the author's personal right to prevent the presentation of his work to the public in a distorted form.

Here, the appellants claim that the editing done for ABC mutilated the original work and that consequently the broadcast of those programs as the creation of Monty Python violated the Lanham Act §43(a), 15 U.S.C. §1125(a). This statute, the federal counterpart to state unfair competition laws, has been invoked to prevent misrepresentations that may injure plaintiff's business or personal reputation, even where no registered trademark is concerned. It is sufficient to violate the Act that a representation of a product, although technically true, creates a false impression of the product's origin.

These cases cannot be distinguished from the situation in which a television network broadcasts a program properly designated as having been written and performed by a group, but which has been edited, without the writer's consent, into a form that departs substantially from the original work.... In such a case, it is the writer or performer, rather than the network, who suffers the consequences of the mutilation, for the public will have only the final product by which to evaluate the work. Thus, an allegation that a defendant has presented to the public a "garbled," distorted version of plaintiff's work seeks to redress the very rights sought to be protected by the Lanham Act, 15 U.S.C. §1125(a), and should be recognized as stating a cause of action under that statute....

After hearing argument of this appeal, this panel also viewed and compared the two versions. We find that the truncated version at times omitted the climax of the skits to which appellants' rare brand of humor was leading and at other times deleted essential elements in the schematic development of a story line. We therefore agree with Judge Lasker's conclusion that the edited version broadcast by ABC impaired the integrity of appellants' work and represented to the public as the product of appellants what was actually a mere caricature of their talents.

We believe that a valid cause of action for such distortion exists and that therefore a preliminary injunction may issue to prevent repetition of the broadcast prior to final determination of the issues....

Tristar Pictures v. Director's Guild of America
160 F.3d 537 (9th Cir. 1998)

Director Michael Apted was unhappy with the way Tristar Pictures edited his film, *Thunderheart,* for television. With the help of the Directors Guild of America (DGA), Apted sought a pseudonym for the director's credit, for as his name is so is he.

Cinephiles believe the director is the true author of a film: It's Coppola's *Godfather,* Spielberg's *Schindler's List* and Verhoeven's *Robocop.* So too when things go badly: It's Coppola's *One from the Heart,* Spielberg's *Lost World* and Verhoeven's *Showgirls.* With his reputation on the line, Apted was concerned when he learned that Tristar would shorten *Thunderheart* by nearly half an hour in order to show it on commercial television.[15] Tristar asked Apted to help trim the movie from 118 minutes, its running time in theatres, down to 90 minutes (a two-hour slot minus commercials). Apted refused and insisted that *Thunderheart* be shown in its entirety. Tristar decided to proceed over Apted's objection and hired an editor who made 270 separate cuts totaling 22 minutes, sped up the credits to steal two more minutes, and compressed the rest of the film electronically to gain another four. Apted then asked that his name be taken off the edited picture, but Tristar refused. After an arbitrator ruled in favor of Apted, Tristar brought a petition in state court claiming that the arbitrator had overstepped his authority. The DGA then removed the case to federal court, and the district court upheld the award. Tristar appeals.

Apted's relationship with Tristar is governed by a collective bargaining agreement (the Basic Agreement) negotiated between the studios and the DGA. Two clauses of the agreement are relevant to this appeal. One of them, section 8-211, governs claims by a director that he is entitled to a pseudonym. In order to avail himself of this remedy, a director must first persuade the Director's Council of the DGA that he is entitled to a pseudonym. If the Council assents, the pseudonym question is presented to a joint panel composed of two representatives from the studio and two from the DGA. If a majority of the joint panel sides with the director, the film's directing credit goes to a fictitious director, typically "Alan Smithee." If not, the studio may continue to use the director's name.

The second relevant provision is the Basic Agreement's arbitration clause. Section 2-101 sets forth the arbitrator's jurisdiction, which embraces the capacious range of "all grievances, disputes or controversies over the interpretation or application" of the Basic Agreement. The arbitrator's authority can be invoked under a normal ar-

---

15. *Thunderheart* tells the story of a young FBI agent (Val Kilmer) sent to the Pine Ridge Sioux reservation in the 1970s to investigate the violence between traditionalist and progressive factions. The film was shot on location in South Dakota with an indigenous supporting cast. Apted explains that he made a moral commitment to the Sioux about the type of film *Thunderheart* would be, and the cut version wasn't it. For example, Tristar cut a multi-minute pow-wow scene, which Apted says infringed on his creative role as director and violated his moral obligation to present a well-rounded picture of the Sioux tradition.

bitration procedure, set forth in section 2-300 of the Basic Agreement, or under an expedited arbitration procedure, found in section 2-400.

In this case, the Director's Council agreed with Apted and on July 7th called for the convocation of a joint panel to consider whether Apted was entitled to a pseudonym. As of July 12, 1995, however, just six days before *Thunderheart* was scheduled to air, the joint panel had not yet met. The DGA therefore called for expedited arbitration of the dispute under section 2-400. The arbitration took place two days later.

The arbitrator did not rule on Apted's pseudonym claim, explaining that this was a dispute "most appropriately" resolved by the joint panel. But he agreed that Tristar's cuts were so severe as to breach Tristar's duty of good faith and fair dealing set forth in section 7-1502 of the Basic Agreement. As a result, the arbitrator made a conditional award: If the joint panel did not grant Apted a pseudonym, Tristar would have to show a disclaimer that reflected Apted's view of the edited version.[16] The awarded disclaimer read:

> This film is not the version originally released. 22 minutes have been cut out. The director, Michael Apted, believes this alteration changes the narrative and characterization and is not associated with it. The film has also been electronically speeded up. The director believes that this alteration changes the pace of the performance and is not associated with it.

This put Tristar in a box. If it used Apted's name, it would be forced to air the disclaimer, which would make it look as if the film had been butchered. If it used a pseudonym, it would lose the attraction of a respected director. Tristar chose what it saw as the lesser of the two evils, and when *Thunderheart* aired on Fox, sans disclaimer, it carried the label "An Adam Smithy Film."

Tristar argues that the arbitrator lacked jurisdiction over the dispute. Under Tristar's reading of the Basic Agreement, all disputes concerning the editing of a film are governed by the pseudonym clause, and the only remedy available to a director unhappy with the studio's editing decision is to seek a pseudonym. While the language of the arbitration clause is very broad, Tristar argues, it should not be read so as to render superfluous the more specific procedure in the pseudonym clause, which is calibrated to resolve disputes about whether edits made to a movie so change its character as to render it no longer the director's work.

Tristar's argument is not without force. The pseudonym procedure does contain a carefully negotiated mechanism for dealing with precisely the type of dispute that arose between Apted and Tristar. Notably, the procedure gives the studio considerable leverage in resisting a claim by the director. Because the joint panel is made up of an equal number of members nominated by the studio and the DGA, a director can only obtain a pseudonym by persuading at least one member nominated by the studio;

---

16. Tristar had already indicated that it planned to run a standard disclaimer, reading: "This film has been modified from its original version. It has been formatted to fit this screen and edited to run in the time allotted and for content."

a tie vote denies the director the pseudonym. By contrast, the studio has no particular leverage for resisting a ruling by the arbitrator—other than the inertial force of being the non-moving party. The pseudonym clause also gives the director only one possible remedy—a pseudonym—while (as we see in this case) the arbitrator can grant other types of relief. Finally, the contract provides no standard for obtaining relief from the joint council, while the arbitrator is limited to any ground available under the terms of the contract and applicable principles of contract law, such as breach of the covenant of good faith and fair dealing. Given these differences, it would seem almost foolish for a director to avail himself of the pseudonym procedure rather than seeking relief under the arbitration clause. Indeed, a director might proceed under the pseudonym procedure and, if unhappy with the result, then seek a separate remedy under the arbitration clause over the same issue.

Tristar also notes that the arbitrator himself saw a tension between the broad sweep of the arbitration clause and the pseudonym procedure. He therefore found that arbitration was not the "most appropriate way" to resolve a dispute over a pseudonym, noting that the parties had established the pseudonym clause as the method for resolving disputes of that sort. Seizing upon this concession by the arbitrator as to the scope of his authority, Tristar argues that the pseudonym provision carves out an area where even the expansive arbitration clause does not reach. By making the arbitration award provisional upon whether a pseudonym is granted, Tristar claims, the arbitrator impermissibly tread upon ground he admitted he had no right to occupy.

Were we interpreting the Basic Agreement in the first instance, this would be a difficult case, but we are not. We are reviewing the award of an arbitrator who ruled on this issue and held that Tristar had violated the implied promise of good faith and fair dealing contained in Article 7 of the Basic Agreement. Tristar's challenge to the arbitrator's jurisdiction fails, not only because of the broad language of the arbitration clause, but also because of Tristar's prior actions. Although Tristar did suggest at the arbitration hearing that the arbitrator had no authority to decide certain issues, it chose to argue that the arbitrator lacked authority rather than simply refusing to come to the table. In this manner, Tristar "by [its] conduct evinced clearly its intent to allow the arbitrator to decide not only the merits of the dispute but also the question of arbitrability." Instead of resting on its present contention that the arbitrator could not grant Apted the relief he sought, Tristar put on evidence of its good faith in editing the film, tacitly admitting that it was plausible for the arbitrator to assume jurisdiction over the dispute.

Tristar's complaint that the arbitrator effectively forced it to grant Apted a pseudonym, thereby circumventing section 8-211 of the Basic Agreement and impermissibly extending the limits of his jurisdiction, also fails. Our review of the scope of an arbitrator's award is extremely narrow: We may ask only "whether the arbitrator's solution can be rationally derived from some plausible theory of the general framework or intent of the agreement." The Basic Agreement gives the arbitrator ample leeway in fashioning remedies: Section 2-501 empowers the arbitrator "to require [the studio] to change or re-do any film titles … or to order any other reasonable relief the Arbitrator deems appropriate in the circumstances, whether relating to credit on the screen or in advertising or any other arbitrable matter...." This clause invokes the rule that "where it is contemplated that the arbitrator will determine remedies for contract violations that he finds, courts have no authority to disagree with his honest judgment in that respect." The arbitrator's ruling that the covenant of good faith and fair dealing gives an aggrieved director more remedies than just seeking a Smithee is not completely implausible....

Tristar finally argues that affirming this award will create a per se rule prohibiting studios from editing movies for television. We are unconvinced that a single award will have any such effect. Although section 2-309 says that awards interpreting a term of the Basic Agreement are binding on the DGA and the studio, it also instructs that "in any subsequent arbitration ... involving an interpretation of the same term or terms of the [Basic Agreement], the Arbitrator may determine whether or not, as a result of the different combination of facts, the prior arbitration award is relevant or determinative of the issue in such subsequent arbitration." Furthermore, if the arbitrator's decision was indeed so far removed from the spirit of the agreement, the parties are free to renegotiate the governing rules to preclude such awards in the future.

We are bound by the very deferential standard of review that we must give arbitral decisions. "Courts ... do not sit to hear claims of factual or legal error by an arbitrator as an appellate court does in reviewing decisions of lower courts.... That a court is convinced [an arbitrator] committed serious error does not suffice to overturn his decision." Regardless of whether this is the solution that we would come up with through our own independent interpretation of the Basic Agreement, we must abide by the arbitrator's plausible interpretation of the agreement. *AFFIRMED*.

Notes and Questions

a. The transition from a theatrically dominated entertainment experience to one dominated by television was not an easy one. Originally, the motion picture studios attempted to boycott television, refusing to provide the new medium with even their older movies. This allowed the radio industry and talent agencies to take primary control of the new medium. Whether a similar transition has begun again with regard to cable — or perhaps even the Internet — remains to be seen.

b. An early example of the problems inherent in editing for television occurred in *Autry v. Republic Productions, Inc.*, 213 F.2d 667 (9th Cir. 1954). Gene Autry sued to stop having seven of his feature length movies edited down to 53 minutes in length. Seven minutes were dedicated to commercials in each hour of television programming. The court recognized that the studios had the right to edit the films (including the right to edit them down to 53 minutes), but it also recognized that "some such cutting and editing could result in emasculating the motion pictures so that they would no longer contain substantially the same motion and dynamic and dramatic qualities which it was the purpose of the artist's employment to produce." *See also Jaeger v. Am. Int'l Pictures, Inc.*, 330 F. Supp. 274 (S.D.N.Y. 1971).

c. The Second Circuit also addressed the contractual control once held by television writers. *See McGuire v. United Artists Television Prods., Inc.*, 254 F. Supp. 270 (S.D. Cal. 1966), for another example of the courts struggling to frame the reservation of rights clause, this time in television contracts.

d. In addition to the implications *Dastar Corp. v. Twentieth Century Fox Film Corp.*, 539 U.S. 23 (2003), has towards copyright and trademark, it also opens the door to potentially renewed interest in mining old films or television episodes for public domain materials.

e. The triggering of the copyright term for television and motion pictures is a bit difficult to track. Prior to the 1976 Copyright Act, works could retain a perpetual, common law copyright. Publication divested this interest. At the point of publication, a work had to be properly registered. Failure to meet the statutory formalities of registration, notice, and deposit would result in the work falling into the public domain. Despite this, a public performance did not constitute publication, so neither a live performance of a play nor a public exhibition of a motion picture constituted a publication.

On the other hand, to reach statutory copyright, the courts and Congress determined that the production and distribution of copies of a work to television broadcasters was a sufficient publication to constitute an act of publication. *See ABC, Inc. v. PrimeTime 24, Joint Venture*, 67 F. Supp. 2d 558, 561 (M.D.N.C. 1999) ("Just as it is clear that mere broadcast does not constitute publication, it is also clear that 'the distribution of copies of a motion picture to television stations for broadcast purposes constitutes an act of publication.'" (quoting Nimmer on Copyright § 4.11[B] at 4–57)). If the work is presented to a single broadcaster, however, that did not automatically constitute a publication under the 1909 Copyright Act or the current statute. *See Burke v. Nat'l Broad. Co.*, 598 F.2d 688 (1st Cir. 1979); 17 U.S.C. § 101 (publication requires an offer "to distribute copies [of the work] to a group of persons for purposes of ... public performance....").

Problem 13-D

Bryce is hoping someday to be in a position to retain final cut. Given Bryce's current professional status, it generally is not an issue. However, Bryce is both confident and hopeful. To this end, Bryce has asked that you review the film production agreement for Bryce's *Juliet Prescott* (*see* Problem 4-A). Bryce would like to assign all the copyright distribution rights of this film and all of Bryce's other works into a newly formed publishing and distribution company.

Bryce has asked that you provide contracts to that new company. At the moment, Bryce is the sole member and manager of this new Limited Liability Company. Bryce expects to bring on other investors eventually and to use the company to distribute the works. Bryce does not wish to transfer the rights to edit the works, hoping this will create a form of final cut control in the works.

Explain to Bryce the efficacy of this strategy and provide a deal memorandum outlining the terms of the transaction between Bryce and the company. You may wish to consult with your corporate or business associates as well to discuss what fiduciary or other obligations Bryce may have towards the company and future members. Finally, you may wish to review whether any professional conflict of interest exists when representing a client and the client's wholly-owned business when you know that additional owners are going to be invited to join the entity.

E. Bibliography and Links

Howard J. Blumenthal and Oliver R. Goodenough, This Business of Television (4th ed. 2006).

Mark Litwak, Dealmaking in the Film & Television Industry (4th ed. 2016).

Anthony J. Casey & Andres Sawicki, *The Problem of Creative Collaboration*, 58 Wm. & Mary L. Rev. 1793 (2017).

James L. Baughman, *Minow's Viewers: Understanding the Response to the "Vast Wasteland" Address*, 55 Fed. Comm. L.J. 449 (2003).

Anna R. Buono & Alonzo Wickers IV, *Montz v. Pilgrim Films & Television, Inc.: Copyright Preemption and Idea Submission Cases*, 28 Comm. Lawyer 4 (2011).

Jesse Haskins, *Commercial Skipping Technology and the New Market Dynamic: The Relevance of Antitrust Law to an Emerging Technology*, 8 Duke L. & Tech. Rev. 1 (2009).

Peter M. Hoffman & Lindsee Gendron, *Judicial Review of Arbitration Awards after Cable Connection: Towards a Due Process Model*, 17 UCLA Ent. L. Rev. 1 (2010).

Sarah Howes, *Creative Equity: A Practical Approach to the Actor's Copyright*, 42 Mitchell Hamline L. Rev. 70 (2016).

Justin Hughes, *Actors as Authors in American Copyright Law*, 51 Conn. L. Rev. 1 (2019).

Nicholas Johnson, *Forty Years of Wandering in the Wasteland*, 55 Fed. Comm. L.J. 521 (2003).

William Lehr & Douglas Sicker, *Would You Like Your Internet with or Without Video?*, 2017 U. Ill. J.L. Tech. & Pol'y 73 (2017).

Daniel A. Lyons, *Technology Convergence and Federalism: Who Should Decide the Future of Telecommunications Regulation?*, 43 U. Mich. J.L. Reform 383 (2010).

Newton N. Minow, *Television and the Public Interest*, 55 Fed. Comm. L.J. 395 (2003).

Henry H. Perritt, Jr., *Keeping the Internet Invisible: Television Takes Over*, 21 J. Tech. L. & Pol'y 121 (2017).

Zahr Said, *Embedded Advertising and the Venture Consumer*, 89 N.C.L. Rev. 99 (2010).

David W. Sussman, *Are our Pastimes Past their Time? How Will the Media Industry Disruption and Changes to the Legal Environment Affect the Sports Industry?*, 67 Syracuse L. Rev. 449 (2017).

Jon Tanaka, *Promoting Asian American Representation Through Copyright: Moral Rights in the Last Airbender and Fair Use in Ms. Marvel*, 25 Asian Am. L.J. 88 (2018).

John Tehranian, *Sex, Drones & Videotape: Rethinking Copyright's Authorship-Fixation Conflation in the Age of Performance*, 68 Hastings L.J. 1319 (2017).

Websites

Alliance of Motion Picture and Television Producers, https://www.amptp.org/

Canadian Media Producers Association, https://cmpa.ca/

Chapter 14

Television and Cable Regulation

Television was once a very discrete method of watching content broadcast over the air by local stations. Some of those stations were owned or affiliated with network systems such as ABC, CBS, NBC and Fox, while other stations were independent. The independent stations played reruns—syndicated television content previously broadcast by the networks or originally syndicated content such as game shows and talk shows. Cable systems expanded the content on television, adding access to content provided by stations in distant markets, adding premium channels, including HBO and Showtime, and expanding cable-only channels such as Nickelodeon, MTV, ESPN, CNN, and hundreds of others. Satellite television systems DirecTV and Dish Network created a competitor to cable that provided much the same service while avoiding the need for municipal licensing of the cable lines and optic cables. Telephone service providers have also introduced competition to the cable systems.

In recent years, however, this model has been challenged by new technologies and modes of viewership. Most of the television networks and cable/satellite systems offer delivery through the Internet to phones, tablets, and computers, as do some of the individual television stations. Additional content providers are native only to the Internet through web browser or app services. Leading market disruptors Netflix, Amazon Prime, YouTube, Vimeo and other services provide content on a streaming or downloading platform that permits the viewer to select a particular program rather than watch a streaming channel. Cable systems provide digital video recorders and on-demand services to provide viewers the ability to select programs rather than watch streamed channels. The result is that television today is no longer based on the television itself or the TV stations that once defined the industry.

Despite the rapid change in the source and structure of television content, the regulation by the Federal Communications Commission (FCC or Commission) remains largely based on the ability to license television broadcast stations and to regulate cable franchises. The station licenses remain extremely valuable, and many of the corporations that own commercial broadcast stations are the leaders in non-broadcast television content. For Disney (owner of ABC and ESPN), National Amusements, Inc. (controlling shareholder of CBS and Viacom), and Comcast (owner of NBCUniversal, which in turn owns NBC and Telemundo), the FCC has influence on its operations outside of the directly-owned broadcast stations and cable system franchises through the leverage it provides on the conglomerate. With the sale of 21st Century Fox to Disney, Fox Television is the only major television network that does not share ownership with a motion picture production studio.

A. Overview

Communications Marketplace Report, Excerpts[1]
FCC 18-181

In the United States, consumers can access video programming content from multiple sources, only some of which are licensed or regulated by the Commission. Some video providers, like broadcast television stations, have been in the marketplace for over 70 years, whereas other providers, like online video providers, are much more recent additions to the marketplace. Below we examine the current state of the marketplace and provide data regarding competition among and between the different types of providers.

The major participants in the marketplace for the delivery of video programming can be divided into three categories:

- **Television Broadcasters:** These entities broadcast video content over the air, and consumers can receive this content via a television set connected to an antenna. Participants in this category include local television stations affiliated with broadcast networks (e.g., ABC, CBS, FOX, and NBC), independent commercial television stations, and noncommercial educational television stations. Television stations offer a set schedule of programs through the day, as well as live sporting events, news coverage, and other real-time broadcasts of events.

- **Multichannel video programming distributors (MVPDs):** These providers use wireline or satellite technologies to deliver video programming to consumers. MVPD packages typically include linear channels—both cable channels and retransmitted broadcast channels—and video on demand (VOD) content.[2] Traditional cable providers (e.g., Comcast, Charter, and smaller cable operators), telephone company providers (e.g., Verizon Fios), and direct broadcast satellite (DBS) providers (e.g., DISH Network and DIRECTV) are all MVPDs.

---

1. The 185-page Communications Marketplace Report consolidates various FCC reports pursuant to Section 401 of the Repack Airwaves Yielding Better Access for Users of Modern Services Act of 2018 (RAY BAUM'S Act), Pub. L. No. 115-141, 132 Stat. 1087 (codified at 47 U.S.C. § 163) (RAY BAUM'S Act). The excerpts are reordered, highly edited, and omit most numbering and footnotes.

2. Linear channels offer specific video programs at a specific time of day in a manner akin to broadcast television. VOD programs are stored electronically by the provider and can be viewed by the consumer at any time, i.e., on demand.

- **Online video distributors (OVDs):** These participants use the Internet to deliver video content to consumers.[3] In addition to providing linear video channels and VOD content, OVDs often rent and sell video content to their customers. OVDs include large companies like Netflix, Hulu, Amazon, and DISH Sling TV, as well as numerous other providers, some of which focus on small or niche audiences.

Broadcast Television Stations

The Commission licenses broadcast television stations consistent with the Communications Act. While licenses were formerly granted pursuant to comparative hearings among interested applicants, presently broadcast licenses are awarded by auction; however, the Commission has not auctioned a license for any new full power commercial television stations since 2011. While the majority of broadcast television station licensees are part of larger companies that are involved in other industries, some large owners, such as Sinclair Broadcast Group, Inc., Tribune Media Co., TEGNA, Inc., Media General/Nexstar Broadcasting Group, Inc., and Gray Television, Inc., focus almost exclusively on the broadcast industry.

Commercial television broadcast stations essentially serve two distinct sets of customers: consumer audiences and advertisers. While fees received from MVPDs for the right to retransmit the signals of the broadcast stations have increased in recent years, broadcasters continue to derive revenues primarily by selling time to advertisers during their broadcasts. The amount of revenue generated depends largely on the size and demographic characteristics of the audiences that broadcasters reach. Accordingly, broadcasters seek to provide content that will attract viewers and maximize their audiences.

Individual commercial stations compete primarily with other commercial broadcast stations within their local markets (Designated Market Areas or DMAs) for audiences and advertising revenue. Other media, including competing video providers; local, regional, and national cable networks; and Internet sites, also earn advertising revenues by attracting audiences within the geographic areas they serve. A broadcast station's advertising revenues depends on viewership of its television programs, regardless of whether consumers receive the station's signal over the air or via an MVPD.

The number of broadcast television stations has remained relatively stable in recent years. The over-the-air reach of a broadcast television station is determined largely by the height of the transmission tower and the power of the transmitter. Buildings, hills, and other objects, however, may interfere with over-the-air signals. As discussed

---

3. For purposes of this section, we define OVD as "an entity that distributes video programming (1) by means of the Internet or other Internet Protocol (IP)-based transmission path; (2) not as a component of an MVPD subscription or other managed video service; and (3) not solely to customers of a broadband Internet access service owned or operated by the entity or its affiliates." *See Annual Assessment of the Status of Competition in the Market for the Delivery of Video Programming*, Eighteenth Report, 32 FCC Rcd 568, 570 n. 4 (MB 2017) (18th Report).

in more detail below, many television broadcasters use digital transmission technologies to offer multiple program streams (multicast channels) to consumers in an effort to provide more programming and features to consumers.

MVPDs offering service within a DMA typically carry the local broadcast television stations assigned to the DMA, rebroadcasting the stations' signals to all the MVPDs' subscribers. In part this is because broadcast stations typically hold exclusive rights to broadcast the programming of their affiliated network in a market. Thus, unlike cable networks that are available nationwide, most broadcast television stations are retransmitted by MVPDs only within the station's assigned DMA. Rebroadcast of television stations by online virtual MVPDs follows a similar pattern — subscribers located in a DMA receive local broadcast television stations from the same DMA.

Television Broadcaster Business Models and Competitive Strategies

Distribution and Delivery. Broadcast television stations reach consumers by broadcasting signals directly over the air to homes, as well as through carriage agreement with MVPDs and OVDs, which retransmit the signals of stations to households subscribing to their services. As such, broadcasters are in the business of both content distribution and content delivery. When broadcasters negotiate with MVPDs and OVDs for carriage of their programming, they are in the business of content distribution — similar to cable networks. When broadcasters deliver programming using their free over-the-air service, they are in the business of content delivery — similar to facilities-based MVPDs.

Additionally, most commercial broadcast stations also produce some of their own programming content, typically news or local sports and events, in addition to acquiring programming from affiliated broadcast networks or from syndicators.

Advertising. A broadcast station sells advertising time based on the number or percentage of households in a market viewing the broadcast station's programming. Revenue from advertising accounts for the largest share of television broadcasters' revenue. In 2016 and 2017, respectively, broadcasters earned about 67% of total revenue ($20.7 billion) and 62% of total revenue ($19.1 billion) from advertising sales. Fees obtained from MVPDs and virtual MVPDs for the retransmission of the station's signal make up the second largest category of broadcast stations revenue.

Retransmission Consent Fees. Many television broadcast stations generate revenue by granting MVPDs the right to carry their signal. Pursuant to Section 325 of the [Telecommunications] Act, MVPDs may not retransmit a local television broadcaster's signal without the station's express permission.[4] If a station elects re-

---

4. 47 U.S.C. § 325(b). Every three years, commercial television stations must elect either the right to grant consent for the MVPDs in their DMA to retransmit their station's signal or the right to receive mandatory carriage by those MVPDs. *Id.* § 325(b)(3)(B); 47 CFR §§ 76.56(b), 76.64.

transmission consent, the broadcaster and MVPD negotiate a carriage agreement, which often includes monetary or other types of compensation to the television broadcaster. In 2016 and 2017, respectively, broadcasters earned about 25% of their revenue ($7.9 billion) and 30% of their revenue ($9.3 billion) from retransmission consent fees.

Many broadcast television stations differentiate themselves from both other stations and cable channels by offering local news, exclusive news stories, investigative reporting, regional and local sports, and coverage of community events. In 2017, the average television station aired 5.6 hours of local news per weekday, down slightly from 2016. Although local news is becoming more available from other sources, local broadcast television stations remain the most viewed source and the most preferred source for emergency news.

In addition to broadcast network and local news programming, broadcast television stations negotiate with national program distributors and syndicators to be exclusive providers of first-run and rerun content in their DMAs. Syndicated programming often represents a long-term financial commitment. Stations usually purchase syndicated programming two to three years in advance and sometimes must make multi-year commitments. An average broadcast television station spends an estimated 26.8% of its expenses on acquiring syndicated programming.

Ownership of Content. Some large broadcast television station groups have ownership interests in content. For example, Disney, which owns ABC, also owns the Disney cable channels, television and movie studios, and a majority interest in ESPN. In 2018, Disney entered into an agreement to acquire assets from Fox, including the FX Networks, National Geographic Partners, Fox's interests in Hulu, Fox's film production business (Twentieth Century Fox, Fox Searchlight Pictures, and Fox 2000 Pictures) and Fox's television creative units (Twentieth Century Fox Television, FX Productions, and Fox21).

Similarly, CBS Corporation's ownership interests include CBS Television Network, The CW (a joint venture between CBS Corporation and Warner Bros. Entertainment), Network Ten Australia, CBS Television Studios, CBS Studios International, CBS Television Distribution, CBS Consumer Products, CBS Home Entertainment, CBS Interactive, CBS Films, Showtime Networks, CBS Sports Network, Pop (a joint venture between CBS Corporation and Lionsgate), Smithsonian Networks, Simon & Schuster, CBS Television Stations, CBS EcoMedia, and CBS Experiences.

Multichannel video programming distributors (MVPDs)

An MVPD is an entity that sells packages of cable and broadcast channels to consumers. MVPDs include traditional cable providers (e.g., Comcast, Charter), DBS providers (e.g., DISH Network, DIRECTV), and telco providers (e.g., AT&T U-verse, Verizon Fios). MVPDs typically offer both linear cable and broadcast channels, as well as video-on-demand programs. Because households typically subscribe to only one MVPD, video competition between MVPDs generally can be viewed as "winner-take-all"—an MVPD either wins the household or loses out to a rival MVPD.

Availability to Consumers. Cable MVPDs generally exist in non-overlapping franchise areas and, as a result, do not compete directly with one another for the same subscriber, so most consumers have access to only one cable MVPD. Where cable overbuilders exist (for example, RCN or Wide Open West) consumers have access to more than one cable MVPD. Ordinarily, there is not more than one such overbuilder in a particular geographic area. Telephone company MVPDs rarely compete with one another for the same subscribers; however, they almost always overbuild areas already served by at least one cable company. DIRECTV and DISH Network have national footprints and almost all consumers nationwide have access to both DBS MVPDs.

Subscribership. At the end of 2017, seven MVPDs each had over one million video subscribers. These include four cable companies (Comcast, Charter, Cox, and Altice), DISH Network (a DBS MVPD), Verizon Fios (a telephone company MVPD), and AT&T (a combined telephone company MVPD and DBS MVPD). MVPDs as a group have been losing subscribers since 2013. MVPDs lost about 3.6 million video subscribers over the period. Cable MVPDs lost 986,000 subscribers; DBS MVPDs lost 1,693,000 subscribers; and telephone company MVPDs lost 903,000 subscribers.

Ownership of Content. Some MVPDs have ownership interests in cable, broadcast, and regional sports networks that allow them to vertically integrate their ownership of a distribution network with ownership of video programming. For example, Comcast owns a dozen cable channels, including the NBC Sports Network, USA, E!, Syfy, MSNBC, CNBC, Bravo, Oxygen, and the Golf Channel; regional sports networks in Baltimore/Washington, Boston, Chicago, Philadelphia, Portland (Oregon), Sacramento, and San Francisco; the NBC and Telemundo broadcast networks; 11 NBC-affiliated broadcast stations, 17 Telemundo-affiliated broadcast stations; and Universal Pictures. When acquiring NBC Universal, Comcast explained that, in part, its acquisition of programming assets was designed to facilitate offering expanded VOD and TV Everywhere services. More recently, AT&T acquired Time Warner, which included the Warner Bros Studios, as well as the HBO, Turner, and CNN channels. When announcing plans to merge, AT&T explained that ownership of Time Warner content would accelerate innovation in the mobile environment and improve targeted advertising.

Online video distributors (OVDs)

An OVD is an entity that distributes video programming to consumers over the Internet, not as a component of an MVPD subscription, and not solely to customers of an ISP owned or operated by the entity or its affiliates. OVDs employ a wide variety of strategies and business models to attract and retain viewers, as reflected in the different approaches that OVDs take regarding the size and variety of their video libraries and the decisions they make regarding ownership of content. Other differences may include whether the OVD offers a linear programming service that includes cable and broadcast channels, whether it sells or rents movies and TV shows, its pricing and geographic availability, and what devices the service supports.

Video Libraries and Ownership of Content. In contrast to MVPDs, which rarely compete in terms of exclusive content, many OVDs differentiate themselves by offering original and exclusive content. Some OVDs offer large libraries with thousands of movies and TV shows from many media companies covering many genres. Others offer smaller libraries focusing on content from specific media companies, networks, or genres. Although most OVD content is not original — it first appeared in theaters or on broadcast or cable networks — some OVDs negotiate exclusive streaming rights to attract consumers seeking specific movies and TV shows.

Some OVDs had ownership interests in content when they launched. For example, Hulu is a joint venture of Walt Disney, Comcast, and AT&T, and Sony owns Crackle. Other OVDs, like Netflix and Amazon Prime, launched without ownership interests in content but subsequently included original content in their offerings. Although final numbers are not yet available, analysts expect that in 2018, Netflix will spend $6 billion on content acquisition, an increase of more than $1 billion over the $4.7 billion it spent in 2017. Analysts also indicate that of the $8 billion Netflix is expected to spend on content in 2018, approximately $2.1 billion will be spent on developing original programming, with the remainder invested in content acquisition and licensing costs.

According to the Chief Content Officer for Netflix, the company's shift to original content "is driven by more favorable economics — as opposed to licensing TV shows and films owned by Hollywood studios — and the expectation that big media companies would eventually put more weight into their own streaming-subscription services." Netflix also has explained that its decision to own content was driven by the belief that content owners like Disney would raise prices or pull licensing deals and start their own online video services.

Similarly, after spending $3.7 billion on content in 2017, Amazon is expected to increase content spending to $5.1 billion in 2018, with $1 billion directed toward original programming. Amazon has explained that its investment in original content is designed to lure consumers to Amazon Prime and drive merchandise sales. Hulu spent $2.5 billion in 2017 and plans to spend approximately $3.1 billion in 2018. Of that total, Hulu's spending on original content is expected to total $219 million.

OVDs focusing on offering original or exclusive VOD content may view themselves as supplements to MVPD services with every consumer a potential customer. Many consumers appear to view these OVDs as supplements and subscribe to more than one. In the summer of 2018, Leichtman Research Group estimated that among households that subscribe to an OVD offering VOD content, 63% subscribe to more than one.

Cable and Broadcast Channels. Apart from OVDs specializing in live sports, most OVDs traditionally offered libraries of video content available on-demand for consumer viewing. A significant recent development in the Internet delivery of video services has been the increasing number of entities offering online packages of linear cable and broadcast channels. S&P Global now refers to these entities as "virtual multichannel" providers because they offer linear content similar to traditional MVPDs.

Leichtman Research Group refers to these entities as "online pay TV providers" and discusses them alongside MVPDs. Leichtman considers the Internet as simply another delivery technology akin to coaxial cable, DBS, and fiber. Entities providing online packages of cable and broadcast channels have also been referred to as "virtual MVPDs" and this is the term we will use.

Virtual MVPDs like Sling TV, DIRECTV NOW, Hulu Live TV, YouTube TV, and PlayStation Vue offer packages of broadcast and cable channels similar to the small and medium-sized channel packages offered by MVPDs. Layer3 TV offers a large channel package similar to the full channel lineups that MVPDs offer. Virtual MVPDs offering similar packages of cable and broadcast channels may see themselves as potential substitutes to traditional cable, telco, or satellite delivered MVPDs, and thus may view competition as winner-take-all with most consumers subscribing to only one provider. On the other hand, no two virtual MVPDs offer exactly the same channels, and consumers with strong preferences for specific channels may not view all virtual MVPDs as good substitutes for one another. In particular, some virtual MVPDs do not offer access to all local broadcast stations or regional sports networks. In addition to channel offerings, consumers comparing virtual MVPDs also take account of prices and features like access to a digital video recorder (DVR) in the cloud.

Sale and Rental. While some OVDs offer access to a library of video programming for a set monthly subscription, others offer video content for sale and rental. Online video sales allow consumers to purchase a digital copy of a video program for a one-time fee. The program is then downloaded and stored either locally (e.g., on a hard drive) or remotely via a cloud storage service. Purchased and downloaded videos can be viewed repeatedly and whenever the consumer chooses. Online video rentals allow consumers to download a digital copy but require the consumer to start watching within a set period (e.g., 30 days) and finish watching within a set period (e.g., 24 hours). Once the program has been watched or the rental period has expired, the consumer can no longer view the program.

Pricing. Some OVDs offering VOD content are fully supported by advertisements and provide unlimited viewing of a catalog of video programs for free. Others require users to pay a monthly subscription fee to access their content. The fees for such services range from $4.99 per month to $14.99 per month. Subscription prices for virtual MVPDs offering packages of cable and broadcast channels range from $15 per month to $80 per month depending on the package selected. Our review of some OVDs specializing in sports showed season prices ranging from a low of $4.99/month for Major League Soccer to a high of $199.99/season for the National Basketball Association.

In contrast to MVPDs, which offer new customers multi-month discounts, OVDs rarely offer lower prices to new customers as an inducement to subscribe. Many OVDs, however, offer a free trial period that gives consumers an opportunity to explore the provider's content library and test the service on various devices. When the free trial period is over, OVDs typically offer service on a month-to-month basis, charging both new and old customers the same price for service that can be cancelled at any time.

Geographic Availability. Although traditional OVDs offering video content are available nationwide to anyone with an Internet connection, OVDs offering linear packages of cable and broadcast channels may differ in their geographic reach. Availability may be based on contractual arrangements with cable networks, broadcast stations, and other content owners. Availability may also require building, or contracting with, content distribution networks (CDNs) to enhance the speed and quality of video content delivered to consumers. Layer3 TV delivers its video service over existing wireline facilities, leasing the necessary capacity from local broadband providers.

Supported Devices. OVDs further differentiate their services by the number of devices that can be connected to the service at the same time. Moreover, not all devices work with all online services. For example, the Apple TV streaming device did not include an app for Amazon Prime until the end of 2017, and the Google Chromecast streaming device currently does not have an app for Amazon Prime. Notably, Amazon, Google, Apple, and Sony are each both OVDs and manufacturers of Internet-connected devices, and each has its own business plan for whether and how to make its OVD content accessible on devices manufactured by rival entities. S&P Global maintains that entities that provide both video services and devices "can give a service an edge in terms of search, discovery and app placement."

FCC, The Public and Broadcasting[5]
Introduction

This Manual is published by the Federal Communications Commission (FCC), the federal agency directed by Congress to regulate broadcasting. It provides a brief overview of the regulation of broadcast radio and television licensees, describing how the FCC authorizes broadcast stations, the various rules relating to broadcast programming and operations that stations must comply with, and the essential obligation of licensees that their stations serve their local communities.

In exchange for obtaining a valuable license to operate a broadcast station using the public airwaves, each radio and television licensee is required by law to operate its station in the "public interest, convenience and necessity." Generally, this means it must air programming that is responsive to the needs and problems of its local community of license. To do this, each non-exempt station licensee must identify the needs and problems and then specifically treat these local matters in the news, public affairs, political and other programming that it airs....

The FCC and Its Regulatory Authority

The Communications Act. The FCC was created by Congress in the Communications Act for the purpose of "regulating interstate and foreign commerce in communication by wire and radio so as to make available, so far as possible, to all the people of the United States, without discrimination on the basis of race, color, religion,

---

5. The Public and Broadcasting, Federal Communications Commission, http://www.fcc.gov/media/radio/public-and-broadcasting (revised Aug. 2019).

national origin, or sex, a rapid, efficient, Nation-wide, and world-wide wire and radio communications service...." (In this context, the word "radio" covers both broadcast radio and television.) The Communications Act authorizes the Commission to "make such regulations not inconsistent with law as it may deem necessary to prevent interference between stations and to carry out the provisions of the Act." It directs us to base our broadcast licensing decisions on whether those actions will serve the public interest, convenience, and necessity.

How the FCC Adopts Rules. As is the case with most other federal agencies, the FCC generally cannot adopt or change rules without first describing or publishing the proposed rules and asking the public for comment....

FCC Regulation of Broadcast Radio and Television. The FCC allocates a portion of the broadcast spectrum to new broadcast stations based upon both the relative needs of various communities for additional broadcast outlets, and specified engineering standards designed to prevent interference among stations and other communications users. Whenever we review an application—whether to build a new station, modify or renew the license of an existing station or sell a station—we must determine if granting the application would serve the public interest. As mentioned earlier, we expect station licensees to be aware of the important problems and issues facing their local communities and to foster public understanding by presenting programming that relates to those local issues.

Broadcasters—not the FCC or any other government agency—are responsible for selecting the material they air. The First Amendment and the Communications Act expressly prohibit the Commission from censoring broadcast matter. Our role in overseeing program content is very limited. We license only individual broadcast stations. We do not license TV or radio networks (such as CBS, NBC, ABC or Fox) or other organizations that stations have relationships with, such as PBS or NPR, except if those entities are also station licensees. In general, we also do not regulate information provided over the Internet, nor do we intervene in private disputes involving broadcast stations or their licensees. Instead, we usually defer to the parties, courts, or other agencies to resolve these disputes.

The Licensing of TV and Radio Stations

Commercial and Noncommercial Educational Stations. The FCC licenses FM radio and full power TV stations as either commercial or noncommercial educational (NCE). (Most AM radio stations are licensed as commercial facilities.) Class A television, low power television and television translator stations are neither designated commercial or NCE. Commercial stations usually support themselves through the sale of advertising. In contrast, NCE stations generally meet their operating expenses with contributions received from listeners and viewers, and also may receive government funding. In addition, NCE stations may receive contributions from for-profit entities and are permitted to acknowledge these contributions or underwriting donations with announcements naming and generally describing the contributing party or donor. However, NCE stations cannot broadcast commercials or other promotional announcements on behalf of for-profit entities. The limitations on NCE stations are discussed further in this Manual....

Applications for License Renewal. Stations must renew their licenses before they expire. Renewal applications are due on a staggered basis depending upon the state in which the station is licensed. Before we can renew a station's license, we must first determine whether, during the preceding license term, the licensee has served the public interest, has not committed any serious violations of the Communications Act or the FCC's rules, and has not committed other violations which, taken together, would constitute a pattern of abuse....

Digital Television. All full-power television stations have operated in digital mode since 2009. All Class A television stations began operating digitally in 2015. Low power television and television translator stations must complete their transition to digital by July 31, 2021.

Digital Radio. The FCC also approved digital operation for AM and FM radio broadcast stations (HD radio). As with DTV, digital radio substantially improves the quality of the radio signal and allows a station to offer multicasting over several programming streams, as well as certain enhanced services. Unlike the mandatory digital transition deadline for television stations, radio stations can continue to operate in analog and have discretion whether also to transmit in digital and, if so, when to begin operating digitally. To receive the digital signals of stations that choose to operate in digital, consumers will have to purchase new receivers.

Because digital radio technology allows a radio station to transmit simultaneously in both analog and digital, listeners can use their current radios to receive the analog signals of radio stations that transmit both analog and digital signals. Receivers are being marketed that incorporate both modes of reception, with the ability to automatically switch to the analog signal if the digital signal cannot be detected or is lost by the receiver....

Broadcast Programming: Basic Law and Policy

The FCC and Freedom of Speech. The First Amendment, as well as Section 326 of the Communications Act, prohibits the Commission from censoring broadcast material and from interfering with freedom of expression in broadcasting. The Constitution's protection of free speech includes programming that may be objectionable to many viewers or listeners. Therefore, the FCC cannot prevent the broadcast of any particular point of view. In this regard, the Commission has observed that "the public interest is best served by permitting free expression of views." However, the right to broadcast material is not absolute. There are some restrictions on the material that a licensee can broadcast. These restrictions are discussed below.

Licensee Discretion. Because the Commission cannot dictate to licensees what programming they air, each individual radio and TV station licensee generally has discretion to select what its station broadcasts and to otherwise determine how it can best serve its community of license. Licensees are responsible for selecting their entertainment programming, as well as programs concerning local issues, news, public affairs, religion, sports events, and other subjects. As discussed further in this Manual, broadcast licensees must periodically make available detailed information about the programming they air to meet the needs and problems of their communities, which can be found in each station's public file. They also decide how their programs will be structured and whether to edit or reschedule material for broadcasting. In light of the First Amendment and Section 326 of the Communications Act, we do not substitute our judgment for that of the licensee, nor do we advise stations on artistic standards, format, grammar, or the quality of their programming. Licensees also have broad discretion regarding commercials, with the exception of those for political candidates during an election, and the limitations on advertisements aired during children's programming.

Criticism, Ridicule, and Humor Concerning Individuals, Groups, and Institutions. The First Amendment's guarantee of freedom of speech similarly protects programming that stereotypes or may otherwise offend people with regard to their religion, race, national background, gender, or other characteristics. It also protects broadcasts that criticize or ridicule established customs and institutions, including the government and its officials. The Commission recognizes that, under our Constitution, people must be free to say things that the majority may abhor, not only what most people may find tolerable or congenial. However, if you are offended by a station's programming, we urge you to make your concerns known in writing to the station licensee.

Programming Access. In light of their discretion to formulate their programming, station licensees are not required to broadcast everything that is offered or otherwise suggested to them. Except as required by the Communications Act, including the use of stations by candidates for public office, licensees have no obligation to allow any particular person or group to participate in a broadcast or to present that person or group's remarks.

Broadcast Programming: Law and Policy on
Specific Kinds of Programming

Broadcast Journalism

Introduction. As noted above, in light of the fundamental importance of the free flow of information to our democracy, the First Amendment and the Communications Act bar the FCC from telling station licensees how to select material for news programs or prohibiting the broadcast of an opinion on any subject. We also do not review anyone's qualifications to gather, edit, announce, or comment on the news. These decisions are the station licensee's responsibility. Nevertheless, there are two issues related to broadcast journalism that are subject to Commission regulation: hoaxes and news distortion.

Hoaxes. The broadcast by a station of false information concerning a crime or catastrophe violates the FCC's rules if:

• The station licensee knew that the information was false;

• Broadcasting the false information directly causes substantial public harm; and

• It was foreseeable that broadcasting the false information would cause such harm.

In this context, a "crime" is an act or omission that makes the offender subject to criminal punishment by law, and a "catastrophe" is a disaster or an imminent disaster involving violent or sudden events affecting the public. The broadcast must cause direct and actual damage to property or to the health or safety of the general public, or diversion of law enforcement or other public health and safety authorities from their duties, and the public harm must begin immediately. If a station airs a disclaimer before the broadcast that clearly characterizes the program as fiction and the disclaimer is presented in a reasonable manner under the circumstances, the program is presumed not to pose foreseeable public harm.

News Distortion. The Commission often receives complaints concerning broadcast journalism, such as allegations that stations have aired inaccurate or one-sided news reports or comments, covered stories inadequately, or overly dramatized the events that they cover. For the reasons noted previously, the Commission generally will not intervene in these cases because it would be inconsistent with the First Amendment to replace the journalistic judgment of licensees with our own. However, as public trustees, broadcast licensees may not intentionally distort the news. The FCC has stated that "rigging or slanting the news is a most heinous act against the public interest." The Commission will investigate a station for news distortion if it receives documented evidence of rigging or slanting, such as testimony or other documentation, from individuals with direct personal knowledge that a licensee or its management engaged in the intentional falsification of the news. Of particular concern would be evidence of the direction to employees from station management to falsify the news. However, absent such a compelling showing, the Commission will not intervene.

Political Broadcasting: Candidates for Public Office. In recognition of the vital role that broadcasting plays in the electoral process, the Communications Act and the Commission's rules impose specific obligations on broadcasters regarding political advertising

- **Reasonable Access.** Section 312(a)(7) of the Communications Act and Section 73.1943 of the Commission's rules require commercial broadcast stations to provide reasonable access to candidates for federal elective office. This means that commercial television and radio stations must allow legally qualified federal candidates to purchase reasonable amounts of broadcast time throughout their campaigns in all dayparts (i.e., in all parts of the broadcast day), including television prime time and radio drive time. The right bestowed upon federal candidates to purchase broadcast time is not absolute. Stations may take into account certain factors in determining whether a request to purchase broadcast time is reasonable. Reasonable access does not extend to state and local candidates, and stations have discretion whether to accept or refuse requests for the purchase of broadcast time by candidates running in state and local elections.

- **Equal Opportunities.** Section 315(a) of the Communications Act and Section 73.1941 of the Commission's rules require that if a station allows a legally qualified candidate for any public office to use its facilities (i.e., make a positive identifiable appearance on the air for at least four seconds), it must give equal opportunities to all other candidates for that office to also use the station. Equal opportunities apply to all commercial and non-commercial stations, as well as all legally qualified candidates for public office (federal, state, and local) throughout their campaigns. Stations are prohibited from censoring ads that are paid for or sponsored by legally qualified candidates and their authorized organizations. As a consequence, stations are protected from liability if these ads contain defamatory material. Certain news-related programs are exempt from equal opportunities. Therefore, an appearance by a legally qualified candidate on a bona fide newscast, regularly scheduled bona fide news interview program, certain documentaries, and on-the-spot coverage of a bona fide news event (including debates and political conventions) does not trigger equal opportunities for opposing candidates.

- **Lowest Unit Charge.** Section 315(b) of the Communications Act and Section 73.1942 of the Commission's rules require that during the 45-days preceding a primary or primary runoff election and during the 60-days preceding a general or special election, stations cannot charge legally qualified candidates or their authorized organizations more than the lowest unit charge for the same class, same amount of time, and same daypart as they charge their most favored commercial customers. Therefore, during these narrow windows, candidates are entitled to the benefit of all volume discounts even if they purchase a single advertisement. At all other times during political campaigns (i.e., outside of the windows), stations can charge candidates no more than they charge commercial advertisers for comparable use of their facilities.

- **Online Political Files.** Section 315(e) of the Communications Act and Section 73.1943 of the Commission's rules require all stations to maintain online political files. Information must be uploaded to https://publicfiles.fcc.gov as soon as possible when a station receives a request for the purchase of airtime that is made by—or on behalf of—any legally qualified candidate (federal, state or local) or is made by an issue advertiser and the ad communicates a message relating to any political matter of national importance. In addition, records of all free time must be placed in the political file. The information that must be uploaded about requests for the purchase of broadcast time include whether the request is accepted or rejected, the rate charged, the date/time the ad ran or will run, the class of time purchased, the name of the candidate, the office being sought, the issues that are referenced, the name of the person or entity purchasing the time, and a list of executives of the sponsoring entity.

- **Sponsorship Identification.** Section 317 of the Communications Act and Section 73.1212 of the Commission's rules require stations to ensure that political ads have appropriate sponsorship identification. Therefore, all ads must identify the entity that is paying for or sponsoring the advertisement.

Objectionable Programming

Programming Inciting "Imminent Lawless Action." The Supreme Court has ruled that the government can curtail speech if it is both: (1) intended to incite or produce "imminent lawless action;" and (2) likely to "incite or produce such action." Even when this legal test is met, any review that might lead to a curtailment of speech is generally performed by the appropriate criminal law enforcement authorities, not by the FCC.

Obscene, Indecent, or Profane Programming. Although, for the reasons discussed earlier, the Commission is generally prohibited from regulating broadcast content, the courts have held that the FCC's regulation of obscene and indecent programming is constitutional because of society's interest in protecting children from potentially harmful programming and supporting parents' ability to determine the programming their children will be exposed to at home.

Obscene Material. Obscene material is not protected by the First Amendment and cannot be broadcast at any time. To be obscene, the material must have all of the following three characteristics:

- An average person, applying contemporary community standards, must find that the material, as a whole, appeals to the prurient interest;

- The material must depict or describe, in a patently offensive way, sexual conduct specifically defined by applicable law; and

- The material, taken as a whole, must lack serious literary, artistic, political, or scientific value.

Indecent Material. Indecent material is protected by the First Amendment, so its broadcast cannot constitutionally be prohibited at all times. However, the courts have upheld Congress' prohibition of the broadcast of indecent material during times of the day when there is a reasonable risk that children may be in the audience, which the Commission has determined to be between the hours of 6 a.m. and 10 p.m. Indecent programming is defined as "language or material that, in context, depicts or describes, in terms patently offensive as measured by contemporary community standards for the broadcast medium, sexual or excretory organs or activities." Broadcasts that fall within this definition and are aired between 6 a.m. and 10 p.m. may be subject to enforcement action by the FCC.

Profane Material. Profane material also is protected by the First Amendment so its broadcast cannot be outlawed entirely. The Commission has defined this program matter to include language that is both "so grossly offensive to members of the public who actually hear it as to amount to a nuisance" and is sexual or excretory in nature or derived from such terms. This material may be the subject of possible Commission enforcement action if it is broadcast within the same time period applicable to indecent programming: between 6 a.m. and 10 p.m....

Violent Programming. An issue of concern to the public over the years has been violent television programming and the negative impact this broadcast material may have on children. At the request of 39 members of the U.S. House of Representatives, the FCC conducted a proceeding asking the public's comment on violent programming. In April 2007, the Commission delivered a Report to Congress recommending that the industry voluntarily commit to reducing the amount of this programming viewed by children.

The V-Chip and TV Program Ratings. In light of the widespread concern about obscene, indecent, profane, violent, or otherwise objectionable programming, in 1996 Congress passed a law to require TV sets with screens 13 inches or larger to be equipped with a "V-Chip"—a device that allows parents to program their sets to block TV programming that carries a certain rating. Since 2000, all sets manufactured with screens 13 inches or larger must contain the V-Chip technology. This technology, which must be activated by parents, works in conjunction with a voluntary television rating system created and administered by the television industry and others. It enables parents to identify programming containing sexual, violent, or other content that they believe may be harmful to their children. All the major broadcast networks and most of the major cable networks encode their programming with this ratings information to work with the V-Chip. However, some programming, such as news and sporting events, and unedited movies aired on premium cable channels, are not rated. In 2004, the FCC expanded the V-Chip requirement to apply also to devices that do not have a display screen but are used with a TV set, such as a VCR.

Other Broadcasting Content Regulation

Station Identification. Stations must air identification announcements when they sign on and off for the day. They also must broadcast these announcements every hour, as close to the start of the hour as possible, at a natural programming break.

Children's Television Programming. The Children's Television Act of 1990 (CTA) imposes two requirements on television broadcasters relating to children's video programming:

- Commercial television broadcast licensees must limit the amount of commercial matter that may be aired during children's programs to not more than 10.5 minutes per hour on weekends and not more than 12 minutes per hour on weekdays. The Commission has determined that these children's programming commercial limits apply to programs originally produced and broadcast for an audience of children 12 years old and under; and).

- Through its review of television broadcast license renewal applications, the Commission must consider whether television licensees have served "the educational and informational needs of children through the licensee's overall programming, including programming specifically designed to serve such needs."

Commercial Limits. As mentioned above, the Commission's rules implementing the CTA's limits on commercial matter in children's programming require commercial TV broadcasters to limit the amount of commercial matter in children's programs to no more than 10.5 minutes/hour on weekends and 12 minutes/hour on weekdays. The Commission applies these limits to all video programming, free or pay, directed to children 12 and under. For purposes of the commercial limits, commercial matter is airtime sold for purposes of selling a product or service and promotions of television programs or video programming services other than children's or other age-appropriate programming appearing on the same channel, or promotions for children's educational and informational programming appearing on any channel....

Host Selling. Separate from the commercial limits, since 1974 the Commission has also required that advertising in children's programs be clearly separated from program content. The goal of this policy is to help children distinguish between commercials and program content. There are three applications of this separation principle: 1) bumpers between program and advertising content (e.g., "and now for a commercial break"); 2) the host selling policy, which prohibits the use of program talent to deliver commercials; and 3) program-length commercials (PLC), which the Commission defines as "a program associated with a product in which commercials for that product are aired" (when a PLC occurs, then the entire program is considered a commercial)....

Educational and Informational Programming. To implement the CTA's educational and informational programming mandate, the Commission has adopted a "core programming" processing guideline that applies to commercial and noncommercial educational television licensees. Pursuant to the guideline, television licensees are eligible for routine staff-level approval of the CTA portion of their renewal applications if they air at least three hours of "core" children's television programming, per week. Digital stations that choose to air more than one stream of free, over-the-air video programming must air proportionally more children's educational programming than stations that air only one stream of free, over-the-air video programming. Core programming is defined as follows:

- Educational and Informational. The programming must further the educational and informational needs of children 16 years old and under (this includes their intellectual/cognitive or social/emotional needs).

- Specifically Designed to Serve These Needs. A program is considered "specifically designed to serve the educational and information needs of children" if: 1) that is its significant purpose; 2) it is aired between the hours of 7 a.m. and 10 p.m.; 3) it is a regularly scheduled weekly program; and 4) it is at least 30 minutes in duration.

...

Sponsorship Identification. The sponsorship identification requirements contained in the Communications Act and the Commission's rules generally require that, when money or other consideration for the airing of program material has been received by or promised to a station, its employees or others, the station must broadcast full disclosure of that fact at the time of the airing of the material, and identify who provided or promised to provide the consideration. This requirement is grounded in the principle that members of the public should know who is trying to persuade them with the programming being aired. This disclosure requirement also applies to the broadcast of musical selections for consideration (so-called "payola") and the airing of certain video news releases....

Loud Commercials. Television commercials must have the same average volume as the programs they accompany. In the Commercial Advertisement Loudness Mitigation (CALM) Act, Congress directed the FCC to establish rules that require broadcasters and pay TV providers ensure the commercials they transmit to viewers comply with an industry-developed technical standard, the Advanced Television Systems Committee's A/85 Recommended Practice. Broadcasters and pay TV providers that demonstrate a pattern or trend of failing to comply can be subject to Commission enforcement action. The FCC does not regulate the volume of radio programming, including commercials....

False or Misleading Advertising. The Federal Trade Commission has primary responsibility for determining whether an advertisement is false or deceptive and for taking action against the sponsor. The Food and Drug Administration has primary responsibility for the safety of food and drug products. Depending on the nature of the advertisement, you should contact these agencies regarding those you believe may be false or misleading.

Offensive Advertising. Unless a broadcast advertisement is found to be in violation of a specific law or rule, the government cannot take action against it. However, if you believe that an advertisement is offensive because of the nature of the item advertised, the scheduling of the announcement, or the way the message is presented, you should consider addressing your complaint directly to the station or network involved, providing the date and time of the broadcast and the product or advertiser in question. This will help those involved in the selection of advertising material to become better informed about audience opinion.

Tobacco and Alcohol Advertising. Federal law prohibits the airing of advertising for cigarettes, little cigars, smokeless tobacco, and chewing tobacco on radio, TV, or any other medium of electronic communication under the FCC's jurisdiction. However, the advertising of smoking accessories, cigars, pipes, pipe tobacco, or cigarette-making machines is not prohibited. Congress has not enacted any law prohibiting broadcast advertising of any kind of alcoholic beverage, and the FCC does not have a rule or policy regulating these advertisements.

Subliminal Programming. The Commission sometimes receives complaints regarding the alleged use of subliminal perception techniques in broadcast programming. Subliminal programming is designed to be perceived on a subconscious level only. Regardless of whether it is effective, the broadcast of subliminal material is inconsistent with a station's obligation to serve the public interest because it is designed to be deceptive....

Must-Carry or Retransmission Consent Election. Elections (for commercial television stations) or must-carry requests (noncommercial television stations) 73.3526(e)(15), 73.3527(e)(12) (retain for duration of election or request period). These are statements of a station's election to be carried on multichannel video program distributor (MVPD) systems, such as cable systems or direct broadcast satellite services, either by negotiated retransmission consent agreements or by mandatory carriage under the Commission's rules. There are two ways that a broadcast TV station can choose to be carried over a cable or satellite system: "must-carry" or "retransmission consent." Each is discussed below.

Must carry. TV stations are generally entitled to be carried on cable television systems in their local markets. A station that chooses to exercise this right receives no compensation from the cable system. Satellite carriers may decide to offer local stations in a designated market area. If they choose to offer one station, then they must carry all the stations in that market that request carriage.

Retransmission Consent. Instead of exercising their "must-carry" rights, commercial TV stations may choose to receive compensation from a cable system or satellite carrier in return for granting permission to the cable system or satellite carrier to carry the station. This option is available only to commercial TV stations. Because it is possible a station that elects this option may not reach an agreement with the cable system, it may ultimately not be carried by the system.

Every three years, commercial TV stations must decide whether their relationship with each local cable system and satellite carrier that offers local service will be governed by must-carry or by retransmission consent agreements. Each commercial station must keep a copy of its decision in the public file for the three-year period to which it pertains.

Noncommercial stations are not entitled to compensation in return for carriage on a cable or satellite system, but they may request mandatory carriage on the system. If an NCE asks for carriage, then a copy of the request must be kept in the public file for the duration of time the request covers.

FCC, Cable Television[6]
Introduction

The Federal Communications Commission first established rules in 1965 for cable systems which received signals by microwave antennas. In 1966, the Commission established rules for all cable systems (whether or not served by microwave). The Supreme Court affirmed the Commission's jurisdiction over cable in *United States v. Southwestern Cable Co.*, 392 U.S. 157 (1968). The Court ruled that "the Commission has reasonably concluded that regulatory authority over CATV is imperative if it is to perform with appropriate effectiveness certain of its responsibilities." The Court found the Commission needed authority over cable systems to assure the preservation of local broadcast service and to effect an equitable distribution of broadcast services among the various regions of the country.

In 1972, new rules regarding cable television became effective. These rules required cable television operators to obtain a certificate of compliance from the Commission prior to operating a cable television system or adding a television broadcast signal. The rules applicable to cable operators fell into several broad subject areas—franchise

6. Cable Television, Federal Communications Commission, https://www.fcc.gov/media/engineering/cable-television.

standards, signal carriage, network program nonduplication and syndicated program exclusivity, nonbroadcast or cablecasting services, cross-ownership, equal employment opportunity, and technical standards. Cable television operators who originated programming were subject to equal time, sponsorship identification and other provisions similar to rules applicable to broadcasters. Cable operators were also required to maintain certain records and to file annual reports with the Commission concerning general statistics, employment, and finances.

In succeeding years, the Commission modified or eliminated many of the rules. Among the more significant actions, the Commission deleted most of the franchise standards in 1977, substituted a registration process for the certificate of compliance application process in 1978, and eliminated the distant signal carriage restrictions and syndicated program exclusivity rules in 1980. In 1983, the Commission deleted its requirement that cable operators file financial information. In addition, court actions led to the deletion of pay cable programming rules in 1977.

1984 Congressional Policy and Rules. In October 1984, the U.S. Congress amended the Communications Act of 1934 by adopting the Cable Communications Policy Act of 1984. The 1984 Cable Act established policies in the areas of ownership, channel usage, franchise provisions and renewals, subscriber rates and privacy, obscenity and lockboxes, unauthorized reception of services, equal employment opportunity, and pole attachments. The new law also defined jurisdictional boundaries among federal, state and local authorities for regulating cable television systems.

1992 Congressional Policy and Rules. Following the 1984 Cable Act, the number of households subscribing to cable television systems increased, as did the channel capacity of many cable systems. However, competition among distributors of cable services did not increase, and, in many communities, the rates for cable services far outpaced inflation. Responding to these problems, Congress enacted the Cable Television Consumer Protection and Competition Act of 1992. The 1992 Cable Act mandated a number of changes in the manner in which cable television is regulated.

In adopting the 1992 Cable Act, Congress stated that it wanted to promote the availability of diverse views and information, to rely on the marketplace to the maximum extent possible to achieve that availability, to ensure cable operators continue to expand their capacity and program offerings, to ensure cable operators do not have undue market power, and to ensure consumer interests are protected in the receipt of cable service. The Commission has adopted regulations to implement these goals.

1996 Congressional Policy and Rules. In adopting the Telecommunications Act of 1996, Congress noted that it wanted to provide a pro-competitive, de-regulatory national policy framework designed to accelerate rapidly private sector deployment of advanced telecommunications and information technologies and services to all Americans by opening all telecommunications markets to competition. The Commission has adopted regulations to implement the requirements of the 1996 Act and the intent of Congress.

What is Cable Television?

Cable television is a video delivery service provided by a cable operator to subscribers via a coaxial cable or fiber optics. Programming delivered without a wire via satellite or other facilities is not "cable television" under the Commission's definitions.

A **cable television system operator** is any person or group of persons who provides cable service over a cable system and directly or through one or more affiliates owns a significant interest in such cable system, or who otherwise controls or is responsible for, through any arrangement, the management and operation of such a cable system.

Cable service is the transmission to subscribers of video programming, or other programming service. This definition includes any subscriber selection required in choosing video programming or other programming service.

A **cable system** is a facility, consisting of a set of closed transmission paths and associated signal generation, reception, and control equipment that is designed to provide cable service which includes video programming and which is provided to multiple subscribers within a community. This term does not include:

(1) a facility that serves only to retransmit the television signals of one or more television broadcast stations;

(2) a facility that serves subscribers without using any public right-of-way;

(3) a facility of a common carrier which is subject in whole or in part, to the provisions of Title II of the Communications Act, except that such facility shall be considered a cable system to the extent such facility is used in the transmission of video programming directly to subscribers, unless the extent of such use is solely to provide interactive on demand services;

(4) an open video system; or

(5) any facilities of any electric utility used solely for operating its electric utility system.

Cable services are often provided in **tiers**. A tier is a category of cable service or services provided by a cable operator for which a separate rate is charged by the cable operator. There are three types of cable service: basic service, cable programming service, and per-channel or per-program (sometimes called pay-per-view) service.

Basic service is the lowest level of cable service a subscriber can buy. It includes, at a minimum, all over-the-air television broadcast signals carried pursuant to the must-carry requirements of the Communications Act, and any public, educational, or government access channels required by the system's franchise agreement. It may include additional signals chosen by the operator. Basic service is generally regulated by the local franchising authority (the local or state entity empowered by Federal, State, or local law to grant a franchise to a cable company to operate in a given area).

Cable programming service includes all program channels on the cable system that are not included in basic service, but are not separately offered as per-channel or per-program services. Pursuant to a 1996 federal law, the rates charged for cable programming services tiers provided after March 31, 1999 are not regulated. There may be one or more tiers of cable programming service.

Per-channel or per-program service includes those cable services that are provided as single-channel tiers by the cable operator, and individual programs for which the cable operator charges a separate rate Neither of these services is regulated by the local franchising authorities or the Commission.

A **local exchange carrier (LEC)** is a telephone company which provides local telephone service.

A **multichannel video programming distributor (MVPD)** is any person such as, but not limited to, a cable operator, a multichannel multipoint distribution service, a direct broadcast satellite service, or a television receive-only satellite program distributor, who makes available for purchase, by subscribers or customers, multiple channels of video programming....

State and Local Regulation of Cable Systems

A variety of laws and regulations for cable television exist at the state and local level. Some states, such as Massachusetts, regulate cable television on a comprehensive basis through a state commission or advisory board established for the sole purpose of cable television regulation. In Alaska, Connecticut, Delaware, New Jersey, Rhode Island, and Vermont, the agencies are state public utility commissions. In Hawaii, regulation of cable television is the responsibility of the Department of Commerce and Consumer Affairs. In other areas of the country, cable is regulated by local governments such as a city cable commission, city council, town council, or a board of supervisors. These regulatory entities are called "local franchising authorities." In addition, most states have one or more state laws specifically applicable to cable television, dealing most commonly with such subjects as franchising, theft of service, pole attachments, rate regulation and taxation.

The 1992 Cable Act codified, and the Commission has adopted, a regulatory plan allowing local and/or state authorities to select a cable franchisee and to regulate in any areas that the Commission did not preempt. Local franchising authorities have adopted laws and/or regulations in areas such as subscriber service requirements, public access requirements and franchise renewal standards. Under the 1992 Cable Act, local franchising authorities have specific responsibility for regulating the rates for basic cable service and equipment.

The Communications Act requires that no new cable operator may provide service without a franchise and establishes several policies relating to franchising requirements and franchise fees. The Communications Act authorizes local franchising authorities to grant one or more franchises within their jurisdiction. However, a local franchising authority may not grant an exclusive franchise, and may not unreasonably withhold its consent for new service. Included in the grant of a franchise to a cable system are rights relating to the construction of the system, including the local franchising authority's authorization to use public rights-of-way, easements, and to establish the areas to be served. In addition, the law requires just compensation to property owners who have suffered damages as a result of a cable operator's construction, operation, installation, or removal of its cable television facilities. Moreover, franchising authorities are required to ensure that access to cable service is not denied to any group of potential residential cable subscribers on the basis of income class....

Signal Carriage Requirements

The 1992 Cable Act established new standards for television broadcast station signal carriage on cable systems. Under these rules, each local commercial television broadcast station was given the option of selecting mandatory carriage ("must-carry") or retransmission consent ("may carry") for each cable system serving the same market as the commercial television station. The market of a television station is currently established by its Designated Market Area (DMA) as defined by Nielsen and/or modified by the Commission. Every county in the country is assigned to a DMA, and those cable systems and television stations in the same DMA are considered to be in the same market. Upon the request of a television station or a cable system, the Commission has the authority to modify the DMA to which a station is assigned.

Must-Carry/Retransmission Consent Election.

Every three years, every local commercial television station has the right to elect either must-carry or retransmission consent....

Election of Must-Carry Status. Generally, if a local commercial television station elects must-carry status, it is entitled to insist on cable carriage in its local market. Each cable system with more than 12 channels must set aside up to one-third of its channel capacity for must-carry stations. For example, if a cable system has 60 channels, it must set aside 20 of those channels for must-carry stations. If there are 25 stations in the market which elected must-carry, the cable operator may choose 20 to carry. On the other hand, if only 15 stations elected must-carry in the market, the cable system would have to carry all 15 of these stations. A must-carry station has a statutory right to a channel position, usually its over-the-air channel number, or another channel number on which it has historically been carried.

Retransmission Consent Election. A cable system is not permitted to carry a commercial station without the station's consent. Stations electing must carry status are considered to have given their consent. Therefore, if the local commercial television station elects retransmission consent, the cable system must obtain that station's consent prior to carrying or transmitting its signal. Except for "superstations," a cable system may not carry the signal of any television broadcast station that is not located in the same market as the cable system without that broadcaster's consent. Superstations are transmitted via satellite, usually nationwide, and the cable system may carry such stations outside their local market without their consent. The negotiations between a television station and a cable system are private agreements which may, but need not, include some form of compensation to the television station such as money, advertising time, or additional channel access....

Manner of Carriage

Subject to the Commission's network nonduplication, syndicated exclusivity and sports broadcasting rules, cable systems must carry the entirety of the program schedule of every local television station carried pursuant to the mandatory carriage provisions or the retransmission consent provisions of the 1992 Cable Act. A broadcaster and a cable operator may negotiate for partial carriage of the signal where the station is not eligible for must carry rights, either because of the station's failure to meet the requisite definitions or because the cable system is outside the station's market. In those situations where the carriage in the entirety rule applies, the primary video and accompanying audio of all television broadcast stations must be carried in full, without alteration or deletion of their content. Ancillary services such as closed captioning and program-related material in the vertical blanking interval must be carried. However, other information contained in the vertical blanking interval need not be carried.

Syndicated Program Exclusivity Protection. With respect to non-network programming, cable systems that serve at least 1,000 subscribers may be required, upon proper notification, to provide syndicated protection to broadcasters who have contracted with program suppliers for exclusive exhibition rights to certain programs within specific geographic areas, whether or not the cable system affected is carrying the station requesting this protection. However, no cable system is required to delete a program broadcast by a station which is either significantly viewed or which places a NLSCor better contour over the community of the cable system.

Network Program Nonduplication. Commercial television station licensees are entitled to protect the network programming they have contracted for by exercising nonduplication rights against more distant television broadcast stations carried on a local cable television system that serves more than 1,000 subscribers. Commercial broadcast stations may assert these nonduplication rights regardless of whether or not their signals are being transmitted by the local cable system and regardless of when, or if, the network programming is scheduled to be broadcast. Generally, the zone of protection for such programming cannot exceed thirty-five miles for stations licensed to a community in the Commission's list of top 100 television markets or fifty-five miles for stations licensed to communities in smaller television markets. In addition, a cable operator does not have to delete the network programming of any station which the Commission has previously recognized as significantly viewed in the cable community.

Sports Programming Blackouts. A cable system located within 35 miles of the city of license of a broadcast station where a sporting event is taking place may not carry the live television broadcast of the sporting event on its system if the event is not available live on a local television broadcast station, if the holder of the broadcast rights to the event, or its agent, requests such a blackout. The holder of the rights is responsible for notifying the cable operator of its request for program deletion at least the Monday preceding the calendar week during which the deletion is desired.

If no television broadcast station is licensed to the community in which the sports event is taking place, the 35-mile blackout zone extends from the broadcast station's licensed community with which the sports event or team is identified. If the event or local team is not identified with any particular community (for instance, the New England Patriots), the 35-mile blackout zone extends from the community nearest the sports event which has a licensed broadcast station. The sports blackout rule does not apply to cable television systems serving less than 1,000 subscribers, nor does it require deletion of a sports event on a broadcast station's signal that was carried by a cable system prior to March 31, 1972. The rule does not apply to sports programming carried on nonbroadcast program distribution services such as ESPN. These services, however, may be subject to private contractual blackout restrictions.

For example, if the Boston Celtics are playing the Atlanta Hawks at home in a National Basketball Association ("NBA") game, and the game is not broadcast live on a Boston television station, and the NBA sends a blackout notice to cable systems within 35 miles of Boston, those systems will have to delete the game which is carried on their systems by "superstation" WTBS from Atlanta. If a sports event were carried, for example, on ESPN or a regional subscription sports network, any blackout would be the result of a private contractual agreement between the holder of the rights to the event and the sports network.

Copyright

The Copyright Act requires cable operators to obtain a compulsory license for the carriage of programming. The cable operator pays the fee to the copyright office, for distribution to the copyright holders of the program material. The fee for each cable system is based on the system's "gross receipts" from the carriage of broadcast signals and the number of "distant signal equivalents" a term identifying non-network programming from distant television stations carried by the system.

Under the Commission's must-carry rules, a cable operator is not required to carry a signal of a television broadcast station if that station would be considered a distant signal under the Copyright Act, unless the station agrees to indemnify the cable operator for any increased copyright liability resulting from carriage of the signal....

Program Content Regulations

Cable television system operators generally make their own selection of channels and programs to be distributed to subscribers in response to consumer demands. The Commission does, however, have rules in some areas that are applicable to programming—called "origination cablecasting" that is subject to the editorial control of the system operator. The rules generally do not apply to the contents of broadcast signals or access channels over which the system operator has no editorial control.

Cable subscribers may request a "lockbox" from cable operators to prevent viewing of any channel on which objectional programming may appear. Cable operators are required to make lockboxes available for sale or lease to customers who request them. Lockboxes can also be purchased from other commercial distributors.

The 1996 Act included several provisions that were designed to increase the subscriber's ability to control the programming coming into the home. Section 551 of the 1996 Act required representatives of the broadcast and cable television industries to develop, within one year after enactment of the 1996 Act, voluntary rules to rate programming that contains violence and sexual or other indecent material. The industry proposed the *TV Parental Guidelines* and the proposal was approved by the Commission in March 1998. The *TV Parental Guidelines* (labels and content indicators and respective meanings) are:

> **TV-Y**—This program is designed to be appropriate for all children.
>
> **TV-Y7**—This program is designed for children age 7 and above. Note: For those programs where fantasy violence may be more intense or more combative than other programs in this category, such programs will be designated TV-Y7-FV.
>
> **TV-G**—Most parents would find this program suitable for all ages.
>
> **TV-PG**—This program contains some material that parents may find unsuitable for younger children. The program contains one or more of the following: moderate violence (V), some sexual situations (S), infrequent coarse language (L), or some suggestive dialogue (D).
>
> **TV-14**—This program contains some material that many parents would find unsuitable for children under 14 years of age. This program contains one or more of the following: intense violence (V), intense sexual situations (S), strong coarse language (L), or intensely suggestive dialogue (D).
>
> **TV-MA**—This program is specifically designed to be viewed by adults and therefore may be unsuitable for children under 17. This program contains one or more of the following: graphic violence (V), explicit sexual activity (S), or crude indecent language (L).

The ratings icons and associated symbols appear for 15 seconds at the beginning of all rated programming. Sports, news, commercials, promotions and unedited movies with a Motion Picture Association of America (MPAA) rating that are aired on premium cable channels are exempt from these ratings.

The 1996 Act also required that television receivers manufactured or imported for use in the United States be equipped with circuitry that is capable of identifying all programs with a common rating and blocking individual channels during selected time periods. This is the circuitry commonly referred to as the "V-chip." This requirement applies to all television sets with a least a 13 inch screen. Manufacturers of such equipment were required to include a v-chip on at least 50% of their products by July 1, 1999 and on the remaining 50% by January 1, 2000. The Commission also required that personal computers that include a television tuner and a 13 inch or larger monitor must also include the v-chip. However, the requirement to rate programming applies only to video transmissions that are delivered to the computer by using the television tuner. Video transmissions delivered over the Internet or via computer networks are not required to be rated.

The parental control devices that MVPDs provide to their subscribers offer additional options to filter television viewing. Both analog and digital cable boxes allow parents to block channels and lock the settings with passwords. Newer digital boxes offer more extensive filtering capabilities that allow programs to be blocked by rating, channel, or program title. Movies can be blocked according to MPAA ratings. Some boxes also allow subscribers to block access to an entire service, such as VOD, and allow subscribers to block content based on time and day.

Section 504 of the 1996 Act required a cable operator to fully scramble or block the audio and video portions of programming services not specifically subscribed to by a household. The cable operator must fully scramble or block the programming in question upon the request of the subscriber and at no charge to the subscriber. In addition, Section 505 states that cable operators or other multichannel video programming distributors who offer sexually explicit programming or other programming that is indecent on any channel(s) primarily dedicated to sexually-oriented programming must fully scramble or block both the audio and video portions of the channels so that someone who does not subscribe to the channel does not receive it. Until a multichannel video distributor complies with this provision, the distributor cannot provide the programming during hours when a significant number of children are likely to view it.

In 1996, the Commission adopted interim rules to implement Section 505 of the 1996 Act. The interim rules established the hours of 6:00 a.m. to 10:00 p.m. as those hours when a significant number of children are likely to have access to and view the programming. However, before the rules could take effect, Section 505 was challenged in the courts and a federal court in Delaware issued a decision (*Playboy Entertainment Group v. U.S.*, [529 U.S. 803 (2000)]) which determined that Section 505 is unconstitutional. An appeal of this decision was filed with the U.S. Supreme Court. In May 2000, the U.S. Supreme Court also determined that Section 505 is unconstitutional. Thus, the Commission's rules implementing Section 505 cannot be enforced. However, persons who wish to prevent the viewing of such programming may do so by obtaining a "lockbox" or by exercising the options provided in Section 504 of the 1996 Act.

Finally, Section 506 of the 1996 Cable Act allows cable operators to refuse to transmit any public access or leased access program which contains obscenity, indecency, or nudity. In June 1996, the U.S. Supreme Court narrowed application of Section 506 in a decision (*Denver Area Educational Telecommunications Consortium, Inc. v. FCC*, [518 US 727 (1996)]) which held that cable operators may decline to carry indecent programming on leased access channels, but cannot exercise the same control over programming on public access channels.

Political Cablecasting

Once a cable system allows a legally qualified candidate for public office to use its facilities, it must afford "equal opportunities" to all other candidates for that office to use its facilities. The cable system may not censor the content of a candidate's material in any way, and may not discriminate between candidates in practices, regulations, facilities or services rendered while making time available to such candidates. Candidate appearances which are exempt from the "equal opportunities" rules include appearances on a bona fide newscast, bona fide news interview, bona fide news documentary, or during on-the-spot coverage of a bona fide news event.

Cable television systems may charge political candidates only the "lowest unit charge" of the system for the same class and amount of time for the same time period, during the 45 days preceding a primary or runoff election and the 60 days preceding a general or special election. Candidates should be charged no more per unit than the system charges its most favored commercial advertisers for the same classes and amounts of time for the same time periods. Information concerning the rates, terms, conditions and all discounts and privileges offered to commercial advertisers should be disclosed and made available to candidates....

Commercial Limits in Children's Programs

Regulations implemented pursuant to the Children's Television Act of 1990 restrict the amount of commercial matter that cable operators may cablecast on programs originally produced and broadcast primarily for children 12 years old and younger. Cable operators may transmit no more than 10.5 minutes of commercial matter per hour during children's programming on weekends and no more than 12 minutes of commercial matter per hour on weekdays. Cable systems must maintain records available for public inspection which document compliance with the rule.

Cigarette Advertising

Advertisements for cigarettes, little cigars and smokeless tobacco are prohibited on any medium of electronic communication subject to the jurisdiction of the Federal Communications Commission. Laws against these types of advertising have criminal penalties and are administered by the U.S. Department of Justice rather than by the Commission....

Cable System Ownership

The Commission rules restrict the ownership interest of cable operators and their ability to own or control video programming services. These rules also restrict the ability of Broadcast Radio Service ("BRS") (formerly known as Multichannel Multipoint Distribution Service ("MMDS")) and SMATV systems to own or control interests in cable systems. While there are no prohibitions on foreign ownership of cable television systems, foreign governments or their representatives may not own CARS stations.

National Subscriber (Horizontal) Limits

Section 613 of the Communications Act requires the Commission to prescribe rules establishing reasonable limits on the number of cable subscribers served by an individual cable operator through its ownership or control of local cable systems.... By limiting the horizontal concentration of the cable industry, the Commission seeks to prevent the concentration of local cable systems into the hands of only a few large operators and to limit the ability of multiple system operators to exercise undue influence in the program acquisition market.

The Commission's 30% ownership limit has been reviewed in the courts several times. In 2001, in *Time Warner Entertainment Co. v. FCC*, 240 F.3d 1126 (D.C. Cir. 2001) ("*Time Warner II*") the court did not vacate the 30% horizontal limit, but found that the record did not adequately support that limit, and reversed and remanded to the Commission. In 2008, the Commission released an Order re-establishing the 30% limit using more recent, empirical data to reach this result. In 2009, in *Comcast Corp. v. FCC*, 579 F.3d 1 (D.C. Cir. 2009), the court vacated the horizontal ownership limit without remand. In that decision, the court found that the Commission failed to demonstrate that allowing a cable operator to serve more than 30% of all cable subscribers would threaten competition or diversity in programming.

Vertical Ownership Restrictions

To prevent vertically integrated cable systems from unduly favoring their affiliated programmers over non-affiliated program providers, the Commission, in 1993, imposed a 40% limit on the number of channels that can be occupied by video programmers affiliated with the particular cable system. In this context, vertical integration refers to common ownership of both cable systems and program networks, channels, services or production companies. For purposes of determining common ownership, all interests of 5% or greater are recognized unless there is no possibility of such interests exerting control or influence over the cable system. In 2001, the decision in *Time Warner II* reversed and remanded the 40% channel occupancy limit, finding that the Commission had failed to justify its vertical limit with record evidence, and had failed adequately to consider the benefits and harms of vertical integration or current MVPD market conditions in its analysis. In 2008, the Commission issued a Further Notice of Proposed Rulemaking seeking comment on issues relating to the appropriate vertical ownership limit, including the appropriate methodology for determining the limit and how to define the relevant programming and distribution markets....

Protection of Subscriber Privacy

Cable operators generally are prohibited from using their cable systems to collect personally identifiable information concerning any subscriber without the prior written or electronic consent of the subscriber. However, cable operators may collect this information if necessary to render cable television or other service to the subscriber or to detect unauthorized reception of cable communications.

Cable operators generally are also prohibited from disclosing personally identifiable information without the prior written or electronic consent of the subscriber. However, there are certain circumstances where the cable operator may do so. A cable operator may disclose this information if such disclosure is necessary to render, or conduct a legitimate business activity related to, cable television or other service provided to the subscriber. The operator may also disclose such information pursuant to a court order authorizing the disclosure, however, the subscriber must be notified of such an order by the person to whom the order is directed (such as a government agency or the cable operator). Finally, the cable operator may disclose the names and addresses of subscribers, but the cable operator must provide the subscriber the opportunity to prohibit or limit such disclosure. Moreover, the cable operator must ensure the disclosure does not reveal, directly or indirectly, the extent of any viewing or other use by the subscriber or the nature of any transaction made by the subscriber over the cable system.

At the time of entering into an agreement to provide cable service or any other service to a subscriber, cable operators must notify the subscriber of the following: the nature of any personally identifiable information collected, or that will be collected, regarding the subscriber; the nature of the use of such information; the nature, frequency, and purpose of any possible disclosure of such information; including an identification of the types of persons to whom the disclosure may be made, the period during which such information will be maintained by the cable operator, the times and place at which the subscriber may gain access to such information, and the limitations with respect to collection and disclosure of information by a cable operator and the right of subscribers to enforce these limitations. Notice to the subscriber must be in the form of a separate, written statement and must be clear and conspicuous. Notice must also be given at least once every year that the agreed upon service is provided. "Personally identifiable information" does not include any record of aggregate data which does not identify particular persons....

Notes and Questions

a. The overview provided above serves as a roadmap of regular FCC concerns. The FCC is actively involved in promoting localism and diversity of viewpoint, but the net effect may be of questionable value. The FCC has prohibited the networks from programming in the hour prior to prime time. While some of the local stations created original news or other programming, this FCC rule created the opportunity to market game shows and "Entertainment Tonight."

b. The public good premise behind the regulation of the airwaves exists, at least in part, because the extremely valuable broadcast spectrum is provided free of charge to the licensed stations. In exchange, the broadcasts must be in the public interest. Because of First Amendment concerns, however, this has not historically been treated as a public privilege that could be conditioned on the limitations of the broadcaster's free speech interests. Does the recent Supreme Court First Amendment jurisprudence create a new regulatory paradigm for television? Does the advent of cable, satellite, Internet, and mobile television allow regulators to treat broadcast television as only a portion of the television marketplace, or does broadcaster free speech still have a protected place for the courts?

c. Much of the regulation for television and cable stems from an understanding of the demographic market area (DMA). "A DMA is a specific media research area that is used by Nielsen Media Research to identify television stations whose broadcast signals reach a specific area and attract the most viewers. DMA boundaries are widely accepted and used by all types of companies to target and keep track of advertising." *Steak N Shake Co. v. Burger King Corp.*, 323 F. Supp. 2d 983, 986 n.2 (E.D. Mo. 2004).

d. What is the appropriate antitrust marketplace for television and cable: should over-the-air, cable, and satellite be considered a single market or should each be a discrete market for antitrust analysis? If it is one market, then what about the potential competition from Internet content providers and from the telephone companies (known as incumbent local exchange carriers, "LECs" or "ILECs")?

e. Challenges to broadcast television come from cable, telephone, Internet providers and satellite companies. In *Dish Network Corp. v. FCC*, 653 F.3d 771 (9th Cir. 2011), the court summarized the regulation of satellite television:

> There are only two major Direct Broadcast Satellite providers in the United States: [DirecTV], which has about 18.5 million subscribers, and DISH, which has about 14.1 million subscribers. They rely on assigned radio frequency bands to transmit signals to consumers from satellites located at designated orbital locations in space. The transmissions are governed by the Federal Communications Commission (FCC) and international regulations.

> The United States has been assigned eight orbital locations for providing satellite service. Each location is divided into 32 satellite channels. Transmissions from satellites in the same orbital location may cause signal interference, so Congress has authorized the FCC to grant licenses to satellite service providers assigning them the use of specified channels at particular orbital locations. The licenses are limited in duration and the FCC may grant or renew them only if doing so will serve the public interest, convenience, or necessity.

> In 1999, Congress created an exception to copyright law to better enable competition between satellite TV and cable TV. The Satellite Home Viewer Improvement Act of 1999 (SHVIA) amended the Copyright Act to create statutory copyright licenses for satellite carriers that allow them to retransmit a local broadcast station's signal without first getting permission from the individual copyright holders. The copyright license is also subject to statutory and regulatory conditions.

> As a condition of their licenses, carriers have certain public obligations. For example, they must also carry, on request, the signals of all other television broadcast stations in the same local market. 47 U.S.C. §338(a)(1). Additionally, all satellite providers must set aside four to seven percent of their channel capacity for "noncommercial programming of an educational or informational nature." 47 U.S.C. §335(b). Finally, and particularly relevant to the case at hand, satellite service providers are required to treat all local television stations the same regarding picture quality.

B. Content Regulation

Red Lion Broadcasting Co. v. FCC

395 U.S. 367 (1969)

The Federal Communications Commission has for many years imposed on radio and television broadcasters the requirement that discussion of public issues be presented on broadcast stations, and that each side of those issues must be given fair coverage. This is known as the fairness doctrine, which originated very early in the history of broadcasting and has maintained its present outlines for some time. It is an obligation whose content has been defined in a long series of FCC rulings in particular cases, and which is distinct from the statutory requirement of § 315 of the Communications Act[7] that equal time be allotted all qualified candidates for public office. Two aspects of the fairness doctrine, relating to personal attacks in the context of controversial public issues and to political editorializing, were codified more precisely in the form of FCC regulations in 1967. The two cases before us now, which were decided separately below, challenge the constitutional and statutory bases of the doctrine and component rules. Red Lion involves the application of the fairness doctrine to a particular broadcast, and RTNDA arises as an action to review the FCC's 1967 promulgation of the personal attack and political editorializing regulations, which were laid down after the Red Lion litigation had begun.

---

7. Communications Act of 1934, Tit. III, 48 Stat. 1081, as amended, 47 U.S.C. § 301 *et seq.* Section 315 now reads:

"315. Candidates for public office; facilities; rules.

"(a) If any licensee shall permit any person who is a legally qualified candidate for any public office to use a broadcasting station, he shall afford equal opportunities to all other such candidates for that office in the use of such broadcasting station: *Provided,* That such licensee shall have no power of censorship over the material broadcast under the provisions of this section. No obligation is imposed upon any licensee to allow the use of its station by any such candidate. Appearance by a legally qualified candidate on any—

"(1) bona fide newscast,

"(2) bona fide news interview,

"(3) bona fide news documentary (if the appearance of the candidate is incidental to the presentation of the subject or subjects covered by the news documentary), or

"(4) on-the-spot coverage of bona fide news events (including but not limited to political conventions and activities incidental thereto), shall not be deemed to be use of a broadcasting station within the meaning of this subsection. Nothing in the foregoing sentence shall be construed as relieving broadcasters, in connection with the presentation of newscasts, news interviews, news documentaries, and on-the-spot coverage of news events, from the obligation imposed upon them under this chapter to operate in the public interest and to afford reasonable opportunity for the discussion of conflicting views on issues of public importance.

"(b) The charges made for the use of any broadcasting station for any of the purposes set forth in this section shall not exceed the charges made for comparable use of such station for other purposes.

"(c) The Commission shall prescribe appropriate rules and regulations to carry out the provisions of this section."

The Red Lion Broadcasting Company is licensed to operate a Pennsylvania radio station, WGCB. On November 27, 1964, WGCB carried a 15-minute broadcast by the Reverend Billy James Hargis as part of a "Christian Crusade" series. A book by Fred J. Cook entitled "Goldwater—Extremist on the Right" was discussed by Hargis, who said that Cook had been fired by a newspaper for making false charges against city officials; that Cook had then worked for a Communist-affiliated publication; that he had defended Alger Hiss and attacked J. Edgar Hoover and the Central Intelligence Agency; and that he had now written a "book to smear and destroy Barry Goldwater." When Cook heard of the broadcast he concluded that he had been personally attacked and demanded free reply time, which the station refused. After an exchange of letters among Cook, Red Lion, and the FCC, the FCC declared that the Hargis broadcast constituted a personal attack on Cook; that Red Lion had failed to meet its obligation under the fairness doctrine, to send a tape, transcript, or summary of the broadcast to Cook and offer him reply time; and that the station must provide reply time whether or not Cook would pay for it. On review in the Court of Appeals for the District of Columbia Circuit, the FCC's position was upheld as constitutional and otherwise proper.

Not long after the Red Lion litigation was begun, the FCC issued a Notice of Proposed Rule Making, 31 Fed. Reg. 5710, with an eye to making the personal attack aspect of the fairness doctrine more precise and more readily enforceable, and to specifying its rules relating to political editorials. After considering written comments supporting and opposing the rules, the FCC adopted them substantially as proposed. Twice amended, the rules were held unconstitutional in the RTNDA litigation by the Court of Appeals for the Seventh Circuit, on review of the rule-making proceeding, as abridging the freedoms of speech and press.

As they now stand amended, the regulations read as follows:

"Personal attacks; political editorials.

"(a) When, during the presentation of views on a controversial issue of public importance, an attack is made upon the honesty, character, integrity or like personal qualities of an identified person or group, the licensee shall, within a reasonable time and in no event later than 1 week after the attack, transmit to the person or group attacked (1) notification of the date, time and identification of the broadcast; (2) a script or tape (or an accurate summary if a script or tape is not available) of the attack; and (3) an offer of a reasonable opportunity to respond over the licensee's facilities.

"(b) The provisions of paragraph (a) of this section shall not be applicable (1) to attacks on foreign groups or foreign public figures; (2) to personal attacks which are made by legally qualified candidates, their authorized spokesmen, or those associated with them in the campaign, on other such candidates, their authorized spokesmen, or persons associated with the candidates in the campaign; and (3) to bona fide newscasts, bona fide news interviews, and on-the-spot coverage of a bona fide news event (including commentary or analysis contained in the foregoing programs, but the provisions of paragraph (a) of this section shall be applicable to editorials of the licensee).

"NOTE: The fairness doctrine is applicable to situations coming within [(3)], above, and, in a specific factual situation, may be applicable in the general area of political broadcasts [(2)], above. See, section 315(a) of the Act, 47 U.S.C. 315 (a); Public Notice: Applicability of the Fairness Doctrine in the Handling of Controversial Issues of Public Importance. 29 F.R. 10415. The categories listed in [(3)] are the same as those specified in section 315(a) of the Act.

"(c) Where a licensee, in an editorial, (i) endorses or (ii) opposes a legally qualified candidate or candidates, the licensee shall, within 24 hours after the editorial, transmit to respectively (i) the other qualified candidate or candidates for the same office or (ii) the candidate opposed in the editorial (1) notification of the date and the time of the editorial; (2) a script or tape of the editorial; and (3) an offer of a reasonable opportunity for a candidate or a spokesman of the candidate to respond over the licensee's facilities: Provided, however, that where such editorials are broadcast within 72 hours prior to the day of the election, the licensee shall comply with the provisions of this paragraph sufficiently far in advance of the broadcast to enable the candidate or candidates to have a reasonable opportunity to prepare a response and to present it in a timely fashion."

47 CFR §§ 73.123, 73.300, 73.598, 73.679 (all identical).

Believing that the specific application of the fairness doctrine in Red Lion, and the promulgation of the regulations in RTNDA, are both authorized by Congress and enhance rather than abridge the freedoms of speech and press protected by the First Amendment, we hold them valid and constitutional, reversing the judgment below in RTNDA and affirming the judgment below in Red Lion.

The history of the emergence of the fairness doctrine and of the related legislation shows that the Commission's action in the Red Lion case did not exceed its authority, and that in adopting the new regulations the Commission was implementing congressional policy rather than embarking on a frolic of its own.

Before 1927, the allocation of frequencies was left entirely to the private sector, and the result was chaos. It quickly became apparent that broadcast frequencies constituted a scarce resource whose use could be regulated and rationalized only by the Government. Without government control, the medium would be of little use because of the cacophony of competing voices, none of which could be clearly and predictably heard. Consequently, the Federal Radio Commission was established to allocate frequencies among competing applicants in a manner responsive to the public "convenience, interest, or necessity."

... There is a twofold duty laid down by the FCC's decisions and described by the 1949 Report on Editorializing by Broadcast Licensees. The broadcaster must give adequate coverage to public issues, and coverage must be fair in that it accurately reflects the opposing views. This must be done at the broadcaster's own expense if sponsorship is unavailable. Moreover, the duty must be met by programming obtained at the licensee's own initiative if available from no other source. The Federal Radio Commission had imposed these two basic duties on broadcasters since the outset, and in particular respects the personal attack rules and regulations at issue here have spelled them out in greater detail.

When a personal attack has been made on a figure involved in a public issue, both the doctrine of cases such as Red Lion, and also the 1967 regulations at issue in RTNDA require that the individual attacked himself be offered an opportunity to respond. Likewise, where one candidate is endorsed in a political editorial, the other candidates must themselves be offered reply time to use personally or through a spokesman.

These obligations differ from the general fairness requirement that issues be presented, and presented with coverage of competing views, in that the broadcaster does not have the option of presenting the attacked party's side himself or choosing a third party to represent that side. But insofar as there is an obligation of the broadcaster to see that both sides are presented, and insofar as that is an affirmative obligation, the personal attack doctrine and regulations do not differ from the preceding fairness doctrine....

In light of the fact that the "public interest" in broadcasting clearly encompasses the presentation of vigorous debate of controversial issues of importance and concern to the public; the fact that the FCC has rested upon that language from its very inception a doctrine that these issues must be discussed, and fairly; and the fact that Congress has acknowledged that the analogous provisions of §315 are not preclusive in this area, and knowingly preserved the FCC's complementary efforts, we think the fairness doctrine and its component personal attack and political editorializing regulations are a legitimate exercise of congressionally delegated authority. The Communications Act is not notable for the precision of its substantive standards and in this respect the explicit provisions of §315, and the doctrine and rules at issue here which are closely modeled upon that section, are far more explicit than the generalized "public interest" standard in which the Commission ordinarily finds its sole guidance, and which we have held a broad but adequate standard before. We cannot say that the FCC's declaratory ruling in Red Lion, or the regulations at issue in RTNDA, are beyond the scope of the congressionally conferred power to assure that stations are operated by those whose possession of a license serves "the public interest."

The broadcasters challenge the fairness doctrine and its specific manifestations in the personal attack and political editorial rules on conventional First Amendment grounds, alleging that the rules abridge their freedom of speech and press. Their contention is that the First Amendment protects their desire to use their allotted frequencies continuously to broadcast whatever they choose, and to exclude whomever they choose from ever using that frequency. No man may be prevented from saying or publishing what he thinks, or from refusing in his speech or other utterances to give equal weight to the views of his opponents. This right, they say, applies equally to broadcasters.

Although broadcasting is clearly a medium affected by a First Amendment interest, differences in the characteristics of new media justify differences in the First Amendment standards applied to them. For example, the ability of new technology to produce sounds more raucous than those of the human voice justifies restrictions on the sound level, and on the hours and places of use, of sound trucks so long as the restrictions are reasonable and applied without discrimination. . . .

Just as the Government may limit the use of sound-amplifying equipment potentially so noisy that it drowns out civilized private speech, so may the Government limit the use of broadcast equipment. The right of free speech of a broadcaster, the user of a sound truck, or any other individual does not embrace a right to snuff out the free speech of others. . . .

This is not to say that the First Amendment is irrelevant to public broadcasting. On the contrary, it has a major role to play as the Congress itself recognized in § 326, which forbids FCC interference with "the right of free speech by means of radio communication." Because of the scarcity of radio frequencies, the Government is permitted to put restraints on licensees in favor of others whose views should be expressed on this unique medium. But the people as a whole retain their interest in free speech by radio and their collective right to have the medium function consistently with the ends and purposes of the First Amendment. It is the right of the viewers and listeners, not the right of the broadcasters, which is paramount. It is the purpose of the First Amendment to preserve an uninhibited marketplace of ideas in which truth will ultimately prevail, rather than to countenance monopolization of that market, whether it be by the Government itself or a private licensee. . . . It is the right of the public to receive suitable access to social, political, esthetic, moral, and other ideas and experiences which is crucial here. That right may not constitutionally be abridged either by Congress or by the FCC.

Rather than confer frequency monopolies on a relatively small number of licensees, in a Nation of 200,000,000, the Government could surely have decreed that each frequency should be shared among all or some of those who wish to use it, each being assigned a portion of the broadcast day or the broadcast week. The ruling and regulations at issue here do not go quite so far. They assert that under specified circumstances, a licensee must offer to make available a reasonable amount of broadcast time to those who have a view different from that which has already been expressed on his station. The expression of a political endorsement, or of a personal attack while dealing with a controversial public issue, simply triggers this time sharing. As we have said, the First Amendment confers no right on licensees to prevent others from broadcasting on "their" frequencies and no right to an unconditional monopoly of a scarce resource which the Government has denied others the right to use. . . .

It is strenuously argued, however, that if political editorials or personal attacks will trigger an obligation in broadcasters to afford the opportunity for expression to speakers who need not pay for time and whose views are unpalatable to the licensees, then broadcasters will be irresistibly forced to self-censorship and their coverage of controversial public issues will be eliminated or at least rendered wholly ineffective. Such a result would indeed be a serious matter, for should licensees actually eliminate their coverage of controversial issues, the purposes of the doctrine would be stifled.

At this point, however, as the Federal Communications Commission has indicated, that possibility is at best speculative. The communications industry, and in particular the networks, have taken pains to present controversial issues in the past, and even now they do not assert that they intend to abandon their efforts in this regard.[8] It would be better if the FCC's encouragement were never necessary to induce the broadcasters to meet their responsibility. And if experience with the administration of these doctrines indicates that they have the net effect of reducing rather than enhancing the volume and quality of coverage, there will be time enough to reconsider the constitutional implications. The fairness doctrine in the past has had no such overall effect....

Licenses to broadcast do not confer ownership of designated frequencies, but only the temporary privilege of using them. Unless renewed, they expire within three years. The statute mandates the issuance of licenses if the "public convenience, interest, or necessity will be served thereby." In applying this standard the Commission for 40 years has been choosing licensees based in part on their program proposals....

In view of the scarcity of broadcast frequencies, the Government's role in allocating those frequencies, and the legitimate claims of those unable without governmental assistance to gain access to those frequencies for expression of their views, we hold the regulations and ruling at issue here are both authorized by statute and constitutional.[9] The judgment of the Court of Appeals in Red Lion is affirmed and that in RTNDA reversed and the causes remanded for proceedings consistent with this opinion.

---

8. The President of the Columbia Broadcasting System has recently declared that despite the Government, "we are determined to continue covering controversial issues as a public service, and exercising our own independent news judgment and enterprise. I, for one, refuse to allow that judgment and enterprise to be affected by official intimidation." F. Stanton, Keynote Address, Sigma Delta Chi National Convention, Atlanta, Georgia, November 21, 1968. Problems of news coverage from the broadcaster's viewpoint are surveyed in W. Wood, Electronic Journalism (1967).

9. We need not deal with the argument that even if there is no longer a technological scarcity of frequencies limiting the number of broadcasters, there nevertheless is an economic scarcity in the sense that the Commission could or does limit entry to the broadcasting market on economic grounds and license no more stations than the market will support. Hence, it is said, the fairness doctrine or its equivalent is essential to satisfy the claims of those excluded and of the public generally. A related argument, which we also put aside, is that quite apart from scarcity of frequencies, technological or economic, Congress does not abridge freedom of speech or press by legislation directly or indirectly multiplying the voices and views presented to the public through time sharing, fairness doctrines, or other devices which limit or dissipate the power of those who sit astride the channels of communication with the general public. Cf. Citizen Publishing Co. v. United States, 394 U.S. 131 (1969).

FCC v. Pacifica Foundation

438 U.S. 726 (1978)

Mr. Justice Stevens delivered the opinion of the Court.

This case requires that we decide whether the Federal Communications Commission has any power to regulate a radio broadcast that is indecent but not obscene.

A satiric humorist named George Carlin recorded a 12-minute monologue entitled "Filthy Words" before a live audience in a California theater. He began by referring to his thoughts about "the words you couldn't say on the public, ah, airwaves, um, the ones you definitely wouldn't say, ever." He proceeded to list those words and repeat them over and over again in a variety of colloquialisms. The transcript of the recording, which is appended to this opinion, indicates frequent laughter from the audience.

At about 2 o'clock in the afternoon on Tuesday, October 30, 1973, a New York radio station, owned by respondent Pacifica Foundation, broadcast the "Filthy Words" monologue. A few weeks later a man, who stated that he had heard the broadcast while driving with his young son, wrote a letter complaining to the Commission. He stated that, although he could perhaps understand the "record's being sold for private use, I certainly cannot understand the broadcast of same over the air that, supposedly, you control."

The complaint was forwarded to the station for comment. In its response, Pacifica explained that the monologue had been played during a program about contemporary society's attitude toward language and that, immediately before its broadcast, listeners had been advised that it included "sensitive language which might be regarded as offensive to some." Pacifica characterized George Carlin as "a significant social satirist" who "like Twain and Sahl before him, examines the language of ordinary people.... Carlin is not mouthing obscenities, he is merely using words to satirize as harmless and essentially silly our attitudes towards those words." Pacifica stated that it was not aware of any other complaints about the broadcast.

Pacifica makes two constitutional attacks on the Commission's order. First, it argues that the Commission's construction of the statutory language broadly encompasses so much constitutionally protected speech that reversal is required even if Pacifica's broadcast of the "Filthy Words" monologue is not itself protected by the First Amendment. Second, Pacifica argues that inasmuch as the recording is not obscene, the Constitution forbids any abridgment of the right to broadcast it on the radio.

The first argument fails because our review is limited to the question whether the Commission has the authority to proscribe this particular broadcast. As the Commission itself emphasized, its order was "issued in a specific factual context." That approach is appropriate for courts as well as the Commission when regulation of indecency is at stake, for indecency is largely a function of context—it cannot be adequately judged in the abstract.

The approach is also consistent with *Red Lion Broadcasting Co. v. FCC*, 395 U.S. 367 (1969). In that case the Court rejected an argument that the Commission's regulations defining the fairness doctrine were so vague that they would inevitably abridge the broadcasters' freedom of speech. The Court of Appeals had invalidated the regulations because their vagueness might lead to self-censorship of controversial program content. This Court reversed.

It is true that the Commission's order may lead some broadcasters to censor themselves. At most, however, the Commission's definition of indecency will deter only the broadcasting of patently offensive references to excretory and sexual organs and activities. While some of these references may be protected, they surely lie at the periphery of First Amendment concern. The danger dismissed so summarily in *Red Lion*, in contrast, was that broadcasters would respond to the vagueness of the regulations by refusing to present programs dealing with important social and political controversies. Invalidating any rule on the basis of its hypothetical application to situations not before the Court is "strong medicine" to be applied "sparingly and only as a last resort." We decline to administer that medicine to preserve the vigor of patently offensive sexual and excretory speech.

When the issue is narrowed to the facts of this case, the question is whether the First Amendment denies government any power to restrict the public broadcast of indecent language in any circumstances. For if the government has any such power, this was an appropriate occasion for its exercise.

The words of the Carlin monologue are unquestionably "speech" within the meaning of the First Amendment. It is equally clear that the Commission's objections to the broadcast were based in part on its content. The order must therefore fall if, as Pacifica argues, the First Amendment prohibits all governmental regulation that depends on the content of speech. Our past cases demonstrate, however, that no such absolute rule is mandated by the Constitution.

The classic exposition of the proposition that both the content and the context of speech are critical elements of First Amendment analysis is Mr. Justice Holmes' statement for the Court in *Schenck v. United States*, 249 U.S. 47, 52 (1919):

> We admit that in many places and in ordinary times the defendants in saying all that was said in the circular would have been within their constitutional rights. But the character of every act depends upon the circumstances in which it is done.... The most stringent protection of free speech would not protect a man in falsely shouting fire in a theatre and causing a panic. It does not even protect a man from an injunction against uttering words that may have all the effect of force.... The question in every case is whether the words used are used in such circumstances and are of such a nature as to create a clear and present danger that they will bring about the substantive evils that Congress has a right to prevent.

Other distinctions based on content have been approved in the years since *Schenck*. The government may forbid speech calculated to provoke a fight. See *Chaplinsky v. New Hampshire*, 315 U.S. 568 (1942). It may pay heed to the " 'commonsense differences' between commercial speech and other varieties." *Bates v. State Bar of Arizona*,

433 U.S. 350, 381 (1977). It may treat libels against private citizens more severely than libels against public officials. See *Gertz v. Robert Welch, Inc.*, 418 U.S. 323 (1974). Obscenity may be wholly prohibited. *Miller v. California*, 413 U.S. 15, 93 (1973). And only two Terms ago we refused to hold that a "statutory classification is unconstitutional because it is based on the content of communication protected by the First Amendment." *Young v. American Mini Theatres*, 427 U.S. 50, 52 (1976).

The question in this case is whether a broadcast of patently offensive words dealing with sex and excretion may be regulated because of its content. Obscene materials have been denied the protection of the First Amendment because their content is so offensive to contemporary moral standards. *Roth v. United States*, 354 U.S. 476 (1957). But the fact that society may find speech offensive is not a sufficient reason for suppressing it. Indeed, if it is the speaker's opinion that gives offense, that consequence is a reason for according it constitutional protection. For it is a central tenet of the First Amendment that the government must remain neutral in the marketplace of ideas. If there were any reason to believe that the Commission's characterization of the Carlin monologue as offensive could be traced to its political content—or even to the fact that it satirized contemporary attitudes about four-letter words—First Amendment protection might be required. But that is simply not this case. These words offend for the same reasons that obscenity offends. Their place in the hierarchy of First Amendment values was aptly sketched by Mr. Justice Murphy when he said: "Such utterances are no essential part of any exposition of ideas, and are of such slight social value as a step to truth that any benefit that may be derived from them is clearly outweighed by the social interest in order and morality." *Chaplinsky v. New Hampshire*, 315 U.S., at 572.

Although these words ordinarily lack literary, political, or scientific value, they are not entirely outside the protection of the First Amendment. Some uses of even the most offensive words are unquestionably protected. Indeed, we may assume, *arguendo*, that this monologue would be protected in other contexts. Nonetheless, the constitutional protection accorded to a communication containing such patently offensive sexual and excretory language need not be the same in every context. It is a characteristic of speech such as this that both its capacity to offend and its "social value," to use Mr. Justice Murphy's term, vary with the circumstances. Words that are commonplace in one setting are shocking in another. To paraphrase Mr. Justice Harlan, one occasion's lyric is another's vulgarity.

In this case it is undisputed that the content of Pacifica's broadcast was "vulgar," "offensive," and "shocking." Because content of that character is not entitled to absolute constitutional protection under all circumstances, we must consider its context in order to determine whether the Commission's action was constitutionally permissible.

We have long recognized that each medium of expression presents special First Amendment problems. *Joseph Burstyn, Inc. v. Wilson*, 343 U.S. 495, 502–503 (1952). And of all forms of communication, it is broadcasting that has received the most limited First Amendment protection. Thus, although other speakers cannot be licensed except under laws that carefully define and narrow official discretion, a broadcaster may be deprived of his license and his forum if the Commission decides that such an action would serve "the public interest, convenience, and necessity." Similarly, although the First Amendment protects newspaper publishers from being required to print the replies of those whom they criticize, it affords no such protection to broadcasters; on the contrary, they must give free time to the victims of their criticism.

The reasons for these distinctions are complex, but two have relevance to the present case. First, the broadcast media have established a uniquely pervasive presence in the lives of all Americans. Patently offensive, indecent material presented over the airwaves confronts the citizen, not only in public, but also in the privacy of the home, where the individual's right to be left alone plainly outweighs the First Amendment rights of an intruder. Because the broadcast audience is constantly tuning in and out, prior warnings cannot completely protect the listener or viewer from unexpected program content. To say that one may avoid further offense by turning off the radio when he hears indecent language is like saying that the remedy for an assault is to run away after the first blow. One may hang up on an indecent phone call, but that option does not give the caller a constitutional immunity or avoid a harm that has already taken place.

Second, broadcasting is uniquely accessible to children, even those too young to read. Although Cohen's written message might have been incomprehensible to a first grader, Pacifica's broadcast could have enlarged a child's vocabulary in an instant. Other forms of offensive expression may be withheld from the young without restricting the expression at its source. Bookstores and motion picture theaters, for example, may be prohibited from making indecent material available to children. We held in *Ginsberg v. New York*, 390 U.S. 629 (1968), that the government's interest in the "well-being of its youth" and in supporting "parents' claim to authority in their own household" justified the regulation of otherwise protected expression. The ease with which children may obtain access to broadcast material, coupled with the concerns recognized in *Ginsberg*, amply justify special treatment of indecent broadcasting.

It is appropriate, in conclusion, to emphasize the narrowness of our holding. This case does not involve a two-way radio conversation between a cab driver and a dispatcher, or a telecast of an Elizabethan comedy. We have not decided that an occasional expletive in either setting would justify any sanction or, indeed, that this broadcast would justify a criminal prosecution. The Commission's decision rested entirely on a nuisance rationale under which context is all-important. The concept requires consideration of a host of variables. The time of day was emphasized by the Commission. The content of the program in which the language is used will also affect the composition of the audience, and differences between radio, television, and perhaps closed-circuit transmissions, may also be relevant. As Mr. Justice Sutherland wrote a "nuisance may be merely a right thing in the wrong place,—like a pig in the parlor instead of the barnyard." We simply hold that when the Commission finds that a pig has entered the parlor, the exercise of its regulatory power does not depend on proof that the pig is obscene.

The judgment of the Court of Appeals is reversed.

Reno v. American Civil Liberties Union

521 U.S. 844 (1997)

JUSTICE STEVENS delivered the opinion of the Court.

At issue is the constitutionality of two statutory provisions enacted to protect minors from "indecent" and "patently offensive" communications on the Internet. Notwithstanding the legitimacy and importance of the congressional goal of protecting children from harmful materials, we agree with the three-judge District Court that the statute abridges "the freedom of speech" protected by the First Amendment.

Sexually Explicit Material

Sexually explicit material on the Internet includes text, pictures, and chat and "extends from the modestly titillating to the hardest-core." Systems have been developed to help parents control the material that may be available on a home computer with Internet access. A system may either limit a computer's access to an approved list of sources that have been identified as containing no adult material, it may block designated inappropriate sites, or it may attempt to block messages containing identifiable objectionable features. "Although parental control software currently can screen for certain suggestive words or for known sexually explicit sites, it cannot now screen for sexually explicit images." Nevertheless, the evidence indicates that "a reasonably effective method by which parents can prevent their children from accessing sexually explicit and other material which parents may believe is inappropriate for their children will soon be widely available."

The Telecommunications Act of 1996, was an unusually important legislative enactment. As stated on the first of its 103 pages, its primary purpose was to reduce regulation and encourage "the rapid deployment of new telecommunications technologies." The major components of the statute have nothing to do with the Internet; they were designed to promote competition in the local telephone service market, the multichannel video market, and the market for over-the-air broadcasting. The Act includes seven Titles, six of which are the product of extensive committee hearings and the subject of discussion in Reports prepared by Committees of the Senate and the House of Representatives. By contrast, Title V—known as the "Communications Decency Act of 1996" (CDA)—contains provisions that were either added in executive committee after the hearings were concluded or as amendments offered during floor debate on the legislation. An amendment offered in the Senate was the source of the two statutory provisions challenged in this case. They are informally described as the "indecent transmission" provision and the "patently offensive display" provision.

The first, 47 U.S.C. §223(a) (1994 ed., Supp. II), prohibits the knowing transmission of obscene or indecent messages to any recipient under 18 years of age. It provides in pertinent part:

(a) Whoever—

(1) in interstate or foreign communications—

....

(B) by means of a telecommunications device knowingly—

(i) makes, creates, or solicits, and

(ii) initiates the transmission of,

any comment, request, suggestion, proposal, image, or other communication which is obscene or indecent, knowing that the recipient of the communication is under 18 years of age, regardless of whether the maker of such communication placed the call or initiated the communication;

....

(2) knowingly permits any telecommunications facility under his control to be used for any activity prohibited by paragraph (1) with the intent that it be used for such activity,

shall be fined under Title 18, or imprisoned not more than two years, or both."

The second provision, §223(d), prohibits the knowing sending or displaying of patently offensive messages in a manner that is available to a person under 18 years of age. It provides:

(d) Whoever—

(1) in interstate or foreign communications knowingly—

(A) uses an interactive computer service to send to a specific person or persons under 18 years of age, or

(B) uses any interactive computer service to display in a manner available to a person under 18 years of age,

any comment, request, suggestion, proposal, image, or other communication that, in context, depicts or describes, in terms patently offensive as measured by contemporary community standards, sexual or excretory activities or organs, regardless of whether the user of such service placed the call or initiated the communication; or

(2) knowingly permits any telecommunications facility under such person's control to be used for an activity prohibited by paragraph (1) with the intent that it be used for such activity,

shall be fined under Title 18, or imprisoned not more than two years, or both.

The breadth of these prohibitions is qualified by two affirmative defenses. See §223(e)(5). One covers those who take "good faith, reasonable, effective, and appropriate actions" to restrict access by minors to the prohibited communications. §223(e)(5)(A). The other covers those who restrict access to covered material by requiring certain designated forms of age proof, such as a verified credit card or an adult identification number or code. §223(e)(5)(B).

In arguing for reversal, the Government contends that the CDA is plainly constitutional under three of our prior decisions: (1) *Ginsberg v. New York,* 390 U.S. 629

(1968); (2) *FCC v. Pacifica Foundation*, 438 U.S. 726 (1978); and (3) *Renton v. Playtime Theatres, Inc.*, 475 U.S. 41 (1986). A close look at these cases, however, raises—rather than relieves—doubts concerning the constitutionality of the CDA.

In *Ginsberg*, we upheld the constitutionality of a New York statute that prohibited selling to minors under 17 years of age material that was considered obscene as to them even if not obscene as to adults. We rejected the defendant's broad submission that "the scope of the constitutional freedom of expression secured to a citizen to read or see material concerned with sex cannot be made to depend on whether the citizen is an adult or a minor." In rejecting that contention, we relied not only on the State's independent interest in the well-being of its youth, but also on our consistent recognition of the principle that "the parents' claim to authority in their own household to direct the rearing of their children is basic in the structure of our society."

In four important respects, the statute upheld in *Ginsberg* was narrower than the CDA. First, we noted in *Ginsberg* that "the prohibition against sales to minors does not bar parents who so desire from purchasing the magazines for their children." Under the CDA, by contrast, neither the parents' consent—nor even their participation—in the communication would avoid the application of the statute. Second, the New York statute applied only to commercial transactions, whereas the CDA contains no such limitation. Third, the New York statute cabined its definition of material that is harmful to minors with the requirement that it be "utterly without redeeming social importance for minors." The CDA fails to provide us with any definition of the term "indecent" as used in § 223(a)(1) and, importantly, omits any requirement that the "patently offensive" material covered by § 223(d) lack serious literary, artistic, political, or scientific value. Fourth, the New York statute defined a minor as a person under the age of 17, whereas the CDA, in applying to all those under 18 years, includes an additional year of those nearest majority.

In *Pacifica*, we upheld a declaratory order of the Federal Communications Commission, holding that the broadcast of a recording of a 12-minute monologue entitled "Filthy Words" that had previously been delivered to a live audience "could have been the subject of administrative sanctions." The Commission had found that the repetitive use of certain words referring to excretory or sexual activities or organs "in an afternoon broadcast when children are in the audience was patently offensive" and concluded that the monologue was indecent "as broadcast." The respondent did not quarrel with the finding that the afternoon broadcast was patently offensive, but contended that it was not "indecent" within the meaning of the relevant statutes because it contained no prurient appeal. After rejecting respondent's statutory arguments, we confronted its two constitutional arguments: (1) that the Commission's construction of its authority to ban indecent speech was so broad that its order had to be set aside even if the broadcast at issue was unprotected; and (2) that since the recording was not obscene, the First Amendment forbade any abridgment of the right to broadcast it on the radio.

In the portion of the lead opinion not joined by Justices Powell and Blackmun, the plurality stated that the First Amendment does not prohibit all governmental regulation that depends on the content of speech. Accordingly, the availability of constitutional protection for a vulgar and offensive monologue that was not obscene depended on the context of the broadcast. Relying on the premise that "of all forms of communication" broadcasting had received the most limited First Amendment protection, the Court concluded that the ease with which children may obtain access to broadcasts, "coupled with the concerns recognized in *Ginsberg*," justified special treatment of indecent broadcasting.

As with the New York statute at issue in *Ginsberg*, there are significant differences between the order upheld in *Pacifica* and the CDA. First, the order in *Pacifica*, issued by an agency that had been regulating radio stations for decades, targeted a specific broadcast that represented a rather dramatic departure from traditional program content in order to designate when — rather than whether — it would be permissible to air such a program in that particular medium. The CDA's broad categorical prohibitions are not limited to particular times and are not dependent on any evaluation by an agency familiar with the unique characteristics of the Internet. Second, unlike the CDA, the Commission's declaratory order was not punitive; we expressly refused to decide whether the indecent broadcast "would justify a criminal prosecution." Finally, the Commission's order applied to a medium which as a matter of history had "received the most limited First Amendment protection," in large part because warnings could not adequately protect the listener from unexpected program content. The Internet, however, has no comparable history. Moreover, the District Court found that the risk of encountering indecent material by accident is remote because a series of affirmative steps is required to access specific material.

In *Renton*, we upheld a zoning ordinance that kept adult movie theaters out of residential neighborhoods. The ordinance was aimed, not at the content of the films shown in the theaters, but rather at the "secondary effects" — such as crime and deteriorating property values — that these theaters fostered: "'It is th[e] secondary effect which these zoning ordinances attempt to avoid, not the dissemination of "offensive" speech.'" According to the Government, the CDA is constitutional because it constitutes a sort of "cyberzoning" on the Internet. But the CDA applies broadly to the entire universe of cyberspace. And the purpose of the CDA is to protect children from the primary effects of "indecent" and "patently offensive" speech, rather than any "secondary" effect of such speech. Thus, the CDA is a content-based blanket restriction on speech, and, as such, cannot be "properly analyzed as a form of time, place, and manner regulation."

These precedents, then, surely do not require us to uphold the CDA and are fully consistent with the application of the most stringent review of its provisions.

In *Southeastern Promotions, Ltd. v. Conrad*, 420 U.S. 546, 557 (1975), we observed that "[e]ach medium of expression ... may present its own problems." Thus, some of our cases have recognized special justifications for regulation of the broadcast media that are not applicable to other speakers. In these cases, the Court relied on the history of extensive Government regulation of the broadcast medium, see, *e.g.*, *Turner Broadcasting System, Inc. v. FCC*, 512 U.S. 622, 637–638 (1994); and its "invasive" nature, see *Sable Communications of Cal., Inc. v. FCC*, 492 U.S. 115, 128 (1989).

Those factors are not present in cyberspace. Neither before nor after the enactment of the CDA have the vast democratic forums of the Internet been subject to the type of government supervision and regulation that has attended the broadcast industry. Moreover, the Internet is not as "invasive" as radio or television. The District Court specifically found that "[c]ommunications over the Internet do not 'invade' an individual's home or appear on one's computer screen unbidden. Users seldom encounter content 'by accident.'" It also found that "[a]lmost all sexually explicit images are preceded by warnings as to the content," and cited testimony that "'odds are slim' that a user would come across a sexually explicit sight by accident."

We distinguished *Pacifica* in *Sable* on just this basis. In *Sable*, a company engaged in the business of offering sexually oriented prerecorded telephone messages (popularly known as "dial-a-porn") challenged the constitutionality of an amendment to the Communications Act of 1934 that imposed a blanket prohibition on indecent as well as obscene interstate commercial telephone messages. We held that the statute was constitutional insofar as it applied to obscene messages but invalid as applied to indecent messages. In attempting to justify the complete ban and criminalization of indecent commercial telephone messages, the Government relied on *Pacifica*, arguing that the ban was necessary to prevent children from gaining access to such messages. We agreed that "there is a compelling interest in protecting the physical and psychological well-being of minors" which extended to shielding them from indecent messages that are not obscene by adult standards, but distinguished our "emphatically narrow holding" in *Pacifica* because it did not involve a complete ban and because it involved a different medium of communication. We explained that "the dial-it medium requires the listener to take affirmative steps to receive the communication" "Placing a telephone call," we continued, "is not the same as turning on a radio and being taken by surprise by an indecent message."

The vagueness of the CDA is a matter of special concern for two reasons. First, the CDA is a content-based regulation of speech. The vagueness of such a regulation raises special First Amendment concerns because of its obvious chilling effect on free speech. Second, the CDA is a criminal statute. In addition to the opprobrium and stigma of a criminal conviction, the CDA threatens violators with penalties including up to two years in prison for each act of violation. The severity of criminal sanctions may well cause speakers to remain silent rather than communicate even arguably unlawful words, ideas, and images. As a practical matter, this increased deterrent effect, coupled with the "risk of discriminatory enforcement" of vague regulations, poses greater First Amendment concerns than those implicated by the civil regulation reviewed in *Denver Area Ed. Telecommunications Consortium, Inc. v. FCC*, 518 U.S. 727 (1996).

The Government argues that the statute is no more vague than the obscenity standard this Court established in *Miller v. California*, 413 U.S. 15 (1973). But that is not so. In *Miller*, this Court reviewed a criminal conviction against a commercial vendor who mailed brochures containing pictures of sexually explicit activities to individuals who had not requested such materials. Having struggled for some time to establish a definition of obscenity, we set forth in *Miller* the test for obscenity that controls to this day:

(a) whether the average person, applying contemporary community standards would find that the work, taken as a whole, appeals to the prurient interest; (b) whether the work depicts or describes, in a patently offensive way, sexual conduct specifically defined by the applicable state law; and (c) whether the work, taken as a whole, lacks serious literary, artistic, political, or scientific value.

Because the CDA's "patently offensive" standard (and, we assume, arguendo, its synonymous "indecent" standard) is one part of the three-prong *Miller* test, the Government reasons, it cannot be unconstitutionally vague.

The Government's assertion is incorrect as a matter of fact. The second prong of the *Miller* test—the purportedly analogous standard—contains a critical requirement that is omitted from the CDA: that the proscribed material be "specifically defined by the applicable state law." This requirement reduces the vagueness inherent in the open-ended term "patently offensive" as used in the CDA. Moreover, the *Miller* definition is limited to "sexual conduct," whereas the CDA extends also to include (1) "excretory activities" as well as (2) "organs" of both a sexual and excretory nature.

The Government's reasoning is also flawed. Just because a definition including three limitations is not vague, it does not follow that one of those limitations, standing by itself, is not vague. Each of *Miller*'s additional two prongs—(1) that, taken as a whole, the material appeal to the "prurient" interest, and (2) that it "lac[k] serious literary, artistic, political, or scientific value"—critically limits the uncertain sweep of the obscenity definition. The second requirement is particularly important because, unlike the "patently offensive" and "prurient interest" criteria, it is not judged by contemporary community standards. This "societal value" requirement, absent in the CDA, allows appellate courts to impose some limitations and regularity on the definition by setting, as a matter of law, a national floor for socially redeeming value. The Government's contention that courts will be able to give such legal limitations to the CDA's standards is belied by *Miller*'s own rationale for having juries determine whether material is "patently offensive" according to community standards: that such questions are essentially ones of fact.

We are persuaded that the CDA lacks the precision that the First Amendment requires when a statute regulates the content of speech. In order to deny minors access to potentially harmful speech, the CDA effectively suppresses a large amount of speech that adults have a constitutional right to receive and to address to one another. That burden on adult speech is unacceptable if less restrictive alternatives would be at least as effective in achieving the legitimate purpose that the statute was enacted to serve.

Notes and Questions

a. In *FCC v. Fox Television Stations, Inc.*, 567 U.S. 239 (2012) (*Fox II*), the Supreme Court invalidated a series of indecency fines for "fleeting expletives." That case, in turn, was based on *FCC v. Fox Television Stations, Inc.*, 556 U.S. 502, 529 (2009) (*Fox I*). In *Fox I*, the Court held that the Federal Communication Commission's decision to modify its indecency enforcement regime to regulate so-called fleeting expletives was neither arbitrary nor capricious, but it declined to determine whether it was constitutional. On remand, the Second Circuit found the policy was unconstitutionally vague, but the Supreme Court instead determined the FCC had failed to provide adequate notice under a Fifth Amendment Due Process Clause analysis to the broadcasters. The fine against ABC was vacated.

In the concurring opinion for *Fox II*, Justice Ginsburg stated "[i]n my view, the Court's decision in [*Pacifica*] was wrong when it issued. Time, technological advances, and the Commission's untenable rulings in the cases now before the Court show why *Pacifica* bears reconsideration."

b. In *Iancu v. Brunetti*, ___ U.S. ___, 139 S. Ct. 2294 (2019), the Supreme Court struck down a longstanding provision of the Lanham Trademark act restricting immoral or scandalous matter. Although the circuit court distinguished *Pacifica*, the majority opinion provides no reference to this line of cases. Justice Breyer raised the issue, but only in a concurrence. Most of the medium-based distinctions made in *Pacifica* have since been overruled by the Court, further eroding its continuing application.

c. Cable is only one of many speech areas purportedly regulated by Congress or otherwise subject to First Amendment limitations. The list includes: radio, *National Broadcasting Co. v. United States*, 319 U.S. 190 (1943) (successfully regulated); newspapers, *Miami Herald Publishing Co. v. Tornillo*, 418 U.S. 241 (1974) (not subject to regulation); personal solicitation, *Riley v. National Federation of Blind of N.C., Inc.*, 487 U.S. 781 (1988) (not subject to much regulation); cable, *Turner Broad. Sys. v. FCC*, 520 U.S. 180 (1997) (successfully regulated); Internet, *Reno v. ACLU*, 521 U.S. 844 (1997) (not subject to regulation); and satellite, *Satellite Broad. & Communs. Ass'n v. FCC*, 275 F.3d 337 (4th Cir. Va. 2001) (subject to regulation).

d. Given the changes in technology, what is the continuing validity of the scarcity doctrine raised by the *Red Lion* Court? Should the Court look only to television or should media, such as the Internet, be balanced against the risks of scarcity?

e. Clear Channel Communications has become the largest owner of radio stations and networks in the United States. It provides this description on LinkedIn:

> With 243 million monthly listeners in the U.S., Clear Channel Media and Entertainment has the largest reach of any radio or television outlet in America. The company owns and operates 850 broadcast radio stations, serving more than 150 markets throughout the U.S., and more than 140 radio stations in Australia and New Zealand. Plus, iHeartRadio—a free, industry-leading, digital music service—gives users instant access to more than 1,500 live radio stations and allows them to create custom stations inspired by favorite artists or songs, anywhere they are.

On June 4, 2004, it entered into a consent decree with the FCC regarding a large number of ongoing complaints against its personalities and DJs. The consent decree provides in part:

> 1. The Commission has been investigating whether Clear Channel Communications, Inc. and its direct and indirect subsidiaries that hold FCC au-

thorizations ("Clear Channel") may have violated restrictions on the broadcast of obscene, indecent or profane material.[10] ...

4. Based on the record before us, in particular Clear Channel's admission that some of the material it broadcast was indecent in violation of 47 C.F.R. § 73.3999, the significant remedial efforts that Clear Channel has already taken and the additional remedial efforts to which Clear Channel has agreed, we conclude that there are no substantial and material questions of fact in regard to these matters as to whether Clear Channel possesses the basic qualifications, including its character qualifications, to hold or obtain any FCC licenses or authorizations....

Consent Decree

1. The Federal Communications Commission and Clear Channel Communications, Inc., for itself and on behalf of its direct and indirect subsidiaries that hold FCC authorizations, hereby enter into this Consent Decree for the purpose of resolving and terminating certain forfeiture proceedings, investigations and complaints currently being conducted by, or pending before, the Commission relating to possible violations of the Indecency Laws by Clear Channel Stations....

9. Clear Channel represents that it has adopted, and is currently in the process of implementing, a company-wide compliance plan for the purpose of preventing the broadcast of material violative of the Indecency Laws. A summary of that plan is set forth in the Attachment. Clear Channel agrees, to the extent it has not already done so, to implement this compliance plan within thirty (30) days of the Effective Date and to keep such compliance plan in effect for three (3) years after the Effective Date. Clear Channel reserves the right to revise the plan from time to time, provided that the Commission shall be given not less than thirty (30) days advance written notice of any revisions to the plan....

11. Clear Channel waives any and all rights it may have to seek administrative or judicial reconsideration, review, appeal or stay, or to otherwise challenge or contest the validity of this Consent Decree and the Adopting Order, provided no modifications are made to the Consent Decree adverse to Clear Channel or any Clear Channel Station. If the Commission, or the United States acting on its behalf, brings a judicial action to enforce the terms of the Adopting Order or this Consent Decree, or both, Clear Channel will not contest the validity of this Consent Decree or of the Adopting Order and will waive any statutory right to a trial *de novo*. If Clear Channel brings a judicial action to enforce the terms of the Adopting Order or this Consent Decree, or both, the Commission will not contest the validity of this Consent Decree or of the Adopting Order....

10. 18 U.S.C. § 1464; 47 C.F.R. § 73.3999 (2004).

Federal Communications Commission, *In the Matter of Clear Channel Communications, Inc.*, FCC 04-128, adopted June 4, 2004.[11]

The concern raised by the Clear Channel consent decree flows from the risks associated with the strategic attempt to chill this marketplace. Company-wide compliance encouraged against the threat of substantial punishment for past and future practices creates the ideal governmental control over the broadcaster. As the largest company in the field, its compliance with the FCC will certainly impact all programming. The consent decree also removes a major source of financial support for other stations which are unwilling to enter into agreements with the government.

f. The Supreme Court struck down the FCC regulations related to fleeting expletives as a violation of the Due Process Clause of the Fifth Amendment. See *FCC v. Fox TV Stations, Inc.*, 132 U.S. 2307 (2012) (finding inadequate notice was provided to broadcasters for regulations relating to the federal law prohibiting the broadcasting of "any ... indecent ... language," 18 U.S.C. § 1464, which includes expletives referring to sexual or excretory activity or organs).

C. Cable Systems

Turner Broad. System v.
Federal Communications Commission
512 U.S. 622 (1994) (*Turner I*)

Sections 4 and 5 of the Cable Television Consumer Protection and Competition Act of 1992 require cable television systems to devote a portion of their channels to the transmission of local broadcast television stations. This case presents the question whether these provisions abridge the freedom of speech or of the press, in violation of the First Amendment.

The role of cable television in the Nation's communications system has undergone dramatic change over the past 45 years. Given the pace of technological advancement and the increasing convergence between cable and other electronic media, the cable industry today stands at the center of an ongoing telecommunications revolution with still undefined potential to affect the way we communicate and develop our intellectual resources.

Broadcast and cable television are distinguished by the different technologies through which they reach viewers. Broadcast stations radiate electromagnetic signals from a central transmitting antenna. These signals can be captured, in turn, by any television set within the antenna's range. Cable systems, by contrast, rely upon a physical, point-to-point connection between a transmission facility and the television

---

11. Available at http://hraunfoss.fcc.gov/edocs_public/attachmatch/FCC-04-128A1.pdf.

sets of individual subscribers. Cable systems make this connection much like telephone companies, using cable or optical fibers strung aboveground or buried in ducts to reach the homes or businesses of subscribers. The construction of this physical infrastructure entails the use of public rights-of-way and easements and often results in the disruption of traffic on streets and other public property. As a result, the cable medium may depend for its very existence upon express permission from local governing authorities.

In contrast to commercial broadcast stations, which transmit signals at no charge to viewers and generate revenues by selling time to advertisers, cable systems charge subscribers a monthly fee for the right to receive cable programming and rely to a lesser extent on advertising. In most instances, cable subscribers choose the stations they will receive by selecting among various plans, or "tiers," of cable service. In a typical offering, the basic tier consists of local broadcast stations plus a number of cable programming networks selected by the cable operator. For an additional cost, subscribers can obtain channels devoted to particular subjects or interests, such as recent-release feature movies, sports, children's programming, sexually explicit programming, and the like. Many cable systems also offer pay-per-view service, which allows an individual subscriber to order and pay a one-time fee to see a single movie or program at a set time of the day.

On October 5, 1992, Congress overrode a Presidential veto to enact the Cable Television Consumer Protection and Competition Act of 1992, (1992 Cable Act or Act). Among other things, the Act subjects the cable industry to rate regulation by the Federal Communications Commission (FCC) and by municipal franchising authorities; prohibits municipalities from awarding exclusive franchises to cable operators; imposes various restrictions on cable programmers that are affiliated with cable operators; and directs the FCC to develop and promulgate regulations imposing minimum technical standards for cable operators. At issue in this case is the constitutionality of the so-called must-carry provisions, contained in §§ 4 and 5 of the Act, which require cable operators to carry the signals of a specified number of local broadcast television stations.

Section 4 requires carriage of "local commercial television stations," defined to include all full power television broadcasters, other than those qualifying as "noncommercial educational" stations under § 5, that operate within the same television market as the cable system. § 4, 47 U.S.C. §§ 534(b)(1)(B), (h)(1)(A) (1988 ed., Supp. IV). Cable systems with more than 12 active channels, and more than 300 subscribers, are required to set aside up to one-third of their channels for commercial broadcast stations that request carriage. § 534(b)(1)(B). Cable systems with more than 300 subscribers, but only 12 or fewer active channels, must carry the signals of three commercial broadcast stations. § 534(b)(1)(A).

If there are fewer broadcasters requesting carriage than slots made available under the Act, the cable operator is obligated to carry only those broadcasters who make the request. If, however, there are more requesting broadcast stations than slots available, the cable operator is permitted to choose which of these stations it will carry.

§ 534(b)(2). The broadcast signals carried under this provision must be transmitted on a continuous, uninterrupted basis, § 534(b)(3), and must be placed in the same numerical channel position as when broadcast over the air. § 534(b)(6). Further, subject to a few exceptions, a cable operator may not charge a fee for carrying broadcast signals in fulfillment of its must-carry obligations. § 534(b)(10).

Section 5 of the Act imposes similar requirements regarding the carriage of local public broadcast television stations, referred to in the Act as local "noncommercial educational television stations." 47 U.S.C. § 535(a) (1988 ed., Supp. IV).[12]

Taken together, therefore, §§ 4 and 5 subject all but the smallest cable systems nationwide to must-carry obligations, and confer must-carry privileges on all full power broadcasters operating within the same television market as a qualified cable system.

Congress enacted the 1992 Cable Act after conducting three years of hearings on the structure and operation of the cable television industry. The conclusions Congress drew from its factfinding process are recited in the text of the Act itself. In brief, Congress found that the physical characteristics of cable transmission, compounded by the increasing concentration of economic power in the cable industry, are endangering the ability of over-the-air broadcast television stations to compete for a viewing audience and thus for necessary operating revenues. Congress determined that regulation of the market for video programming was necessary to correct this competitive imbalance.

In particular, Congress found that over 60 percent of the households with television sets subscribe to cable, and for these households cable has replaced over-the-air broadcast television as the primary provider of video programming. § 2(a)(17). This is so, Congress found, because "most subscribers to cable television systems do not or cannot maintain antennas to receive broadcast television services, do not have input selector switches to convert from a cable to antenna reception system, or cannot otherwise receive broadcast television services." In addition, Congress concluded that due to "local franchising requirements and the extraordinary expense of constructing more than one cable television system to serve a particular geographic area," the overwhelming majority of cable operators exercise a monopoly over cable service. § 2(a)(2). "The result," Congress determined, "is undue market power for the cable operator as compared to that of consumers and video programmers."

According to Congress, this market position gives cable operators the power and the incentive to harm broadcast competitors. The power derives from the cable op-

---

12. "Noncommercial educational television stations" are defined to include broadcast stations that are either (1) licensed by the FCC as a "noncommercial educational television broadcast station" and have, as licensees, entities which are eligible to receive grants from the Corporation for Public Broadcasting; or (2) owned and operated by a municipality and transmit "predominantly noncommercial programs for educational purposes." §§ 535(l)(1)(A)–(B).

erator's ability, as owner of the transmission facility, to "terminate the retransmission of the broadcast signal, refuse to carry new signals, or reposition a broadcast signal to a disadvantageous channel position." § 2(a)(15). The incentive derives from the economic reality that "cable television systems and broadcast television stations increasingly compete for television advertising revenues." By refusing carriage of broadcasters' signals, cable operators, as a practical matter, can reduce the number of households that have access to the broadcasters' programming, and thereby capture advertising dollars that would otherwise go to broadcast stations.

Congress found, in addition, that increased vertical integration in the cable industry is making it even harder for broadcasters to secure carriage on cable systems, because cable operators have a financial incentive to favor their affiliated programmers. Congress also determined that the cable industry is characterized by horizontal concentration, with many cable operators sharing common ownership. This has resulted in greater "barriers to entry for new programmers and a reduction in the number of media voices available to consumers."   In light of these technological and economic conditions, Congress concluded that unless cable operators are required to carry local broadcast stations, "there is a substantial likelihood that ... additional local broadcast signals will be deleted, repositioned, or not carried,"; the "marked shift in market share" from broadcast to cable will continue to erode the advertising revenue base which sustains free local broadcast television; and that, as a consequence, "the economic viability of free local broadcast television and its ability to originate quality local programming will be seriously jeopardized."

Soon after the Act became law, appellants filed these five consolidated actions in the United States District Court for the District of Columbia against the United States and the Federal Communications Commission (hereinafter referred to collectively as the Government), challenging the constitutionality of the must-carry provisions. Appellants, plaintiffs below, are numerous cable programmers and cable operators. After additional parties intervened, a three-judge District Court convened under 28 U.S.C. § 2284 to hear the actions....

There can be no disagreement on an initial premise: Cable programmers and cable operators engage in and transmit speech, and they are entitled to the protection of the speech and press provisions of the First Amendment.

Through "original programming or by exercising editorial discretion over which stations or programs to include in its repertoire," cable programmers and operators "seek to communicate messages on a wide variety of topics and in a wide variety of formats." By requiring cable systems to set aside a portion of their channels for local broadcasters, the must-carry rules regulate cable speech in two respects: The rules reduce the number of channels over which cable operators exercise unfettered control, and they render it more difficult for cable programmers to compete for carriage on the limited channels remaining. Nevertheless, because not every interference with speech triggers the same degree of scrutiny under the First Amendment, we must decide at the outset the level of scrutiny applicable to the must-carry provisions....

But the rationale for applying a less rigorous standard of First Amendment scrutiny to broadcast regulation, whatever its validity in the cases elaborating it, does not apply in the context of cable regulation. The justification for our distinct approach to broadcast regulation rests upon the unique physical limitations of the broadcast medium.

As a general matter, there are more would-be broadcasters than frequencies available in the electromagnetic spectrum. And if two broadcasters were to attempt to transmit over the same frequency in the same locale, they would interfere with one another's signals, so that neither could be heard at all....

Although courts and commentators have criticized the scarcity rationale since its inception, we have declined to question its continuing validity as support for our broadcast jurisprudence, and see no reason to do so here. The broadcast cases are inapposite in the present context because cable television does not suffer from the inherent limitations that characterize the broadcast medium. Indeed, given the rapid advances in fiber optics and digital compression technology, soon there may be no practical limitation on the number of speakers who may use the cable medium. Nor is there any danger of physical interference between two cable speakers attempting to share the same channel. In light of these fundamental technological differences between broadcast and cable transmission, application of the more relaxed standard of scrutiny adopted in *Red Lion* and the other broadcast cases is inapt when determining the First Amendment validity of cable regulation.

This is not to say that the unique physical characteristics of cable transmission should be ignored when determining the constitutionality of regulations affecting cable speech. They should not. But whatever relevance these physical characteristics may have in the evaluation of particular cable regulations, they do not require the alteration of settled principles of our First Amendment jurisprudence.

Although the Government acknowledges the substantial technological differences between broadcast and cable, it advances a second argument for application of the *Red Lion* framework to cable regulation. It asserts that the foundation of our broadcast jurisprudence is not the physical limitations of the electromagnetic spectrum, but rather the "market dysfunction" that characterizes the broadcast market. Because the cable market is beset by a similar dysfunction, the Government maintains, the *Red Lion* standard of review should also apply to cable. While we agree that the cable market suffers certain structural impediments, the Government's argument is flawed in two respects. First, as discussed above, the special physical characteristics of broadcast transmission, not the economic characteristics of the broadcast market, are what underlies our broadcast jurisprudence. Second, the mere assertion of dysfunction or failure in a speech market, without more, is not sufficient to shield a speech regulation from the First Amendment standards applicable to nonbroadcast media.

By a related course of reasoning, the Government and some appellees maintain that the must-carry provisions are nothing more than industry-specific antitrust legislation, and thus warrant rational basis scrutiny under this Court's "precedents governing legislative efforts to correct market failure in a market whose commodity is speech," such as *Associated Press v. United States,* 326 U.S. 1 (1945), and *Lorain Journal Co. v. United States,* 342 U.S. 143 (1951). This contention is unavailing. *Associated Press* and *Lorain Journal* both involved actions against members of the press brought under the Sherman Antitrust Act, a law of general application. But while the enforcement of a generally applicable law may or may not be subject to heightened scrutiny under the First Amendment, that single out the press, or certain elements thereof, for special treatment "pose a particular danger of abuse by the State," *Arkansas Writers' Project, Inc. v. Ragland,* 481 U.S. 221, 228 (1987), and so are always subject to at least some degree of heightened First Amendment scrutiny. Because the must-carry provisions impose special obligations upon cable operators and special burdens upon cable programmers, some measure of heightened First Amendment scrutiny is demanded.

The First Amendment, subject only to narrow and well-understood exceptions, does not countenance governmental control over the content of messages expressed by private individuals. Our precedents thus apply the most exacting scrutiny to regulations that suppress, disadvantage, or impose differential burdens upon speech because of its content. Laws that compel speakers to utter or distribute speech bearing a particular message are subject to the same rigorous scrutiny. In contrast, regulations that are unrelated to the content of speech are subject to an intermediate level of scrutiny, because in most cases they pose a less substantial risk of excising certain ideas or viewpoints from the public dialogue.

Deciding whether a particular regulation is content-based or content-neutral is not always a simple task. We have said that the "principal inquiry in determining content-neutrality ... is whether the government has adopted a regulation of speech because of [agreement or] disagreement with the message it conveys." See *R.A.V. v. St. Paul,* 505 U.S. 377, 386 (1992) ("The government may not regulate [speech] based on hostility—or favoritism—towards the underlying message expressed"). The purpose, or justification, of a regulation will often be evident on its face. But while a content-based purpose may be sufficient in certain circumstances to show that a regulation is content-based, it is not necessary to such a showing in all cases. Nor will the mere assertion of a content-neutral purpose be enough to save a law which, on its face, discriminates based on content.

As a general rule, laws that by their terms distinguish favored speech from disfavored speech on the basis of the ideas or views expressed are content-based. By contrast, laws that confer benefits or impose burdens on speech without reference to the ideas or views expressed are in most instances content-neutral.

Insofar as they pertain to the carriage of full power broadcasters, the must-carry rules, on their face, impose burdens and confer benefits without reference to the content of speech. Although the provisions interfere with cable operators' editorial discretion by compelling them to offer carriage to a certain minimum number of broadcast stations, the extent of the interference does not depend upon the content of the cable operators' programming. The rules impose obligations upon all operators, save those with fewer than 300 subscribers, regardless of the programs or stations they now offer or have offered in the past. Nothing in the Act imposes a restriction, penalty, or burden by reason of the views, programs, or stations the cable operator has selected or will select. The number of channels a cable operator must set aside depends only on the operator's channel capacity, hence, an operator cannot avoid or mitigate its obligations under the Act by altering the programming it offers to subscribers. *Cf. Miami Herald Publishing Co. v. Tornillo*, 418 U.S. at 256–257 (newspaper may avoid access obligations by refraining from speech critical of political candidates).

The must-carry provisions also burden cable programmers by reducing the number of channels for which they can compete. But, again, this burden is unrelated to content, for it extends to all cable programmers irrespective of the programming they choose to offer viewers. And finally, the privileges conferred by the must-carry provisions are also unrelated to content. The rules benefit all full power broadcasters who request carriage—be they commercial or noncommercial, independent or network-affiliated, English or Spanish language, religious or secular.

The aggregate effect of the rules is thus to make every full power commercial and noncommercial broadcaster eligible for must-carry, provided only that the broadcaster operates within the same television market as a cable system.

It is true that the must-carry provisions distinguish between speakers in the television programming market. But they do so based only upon the manner in which speakers transmit their messages to viewers, and not upon the messages they carry: Broadcasters, which transmit over the airwaves, are favored, while cable programmers, which do not, are disfavored. Cable operators, too, are burdened by the carriage obligations, but only because they control access to the cable conduit. So long as they are not a subtle means of exercising a content preference, speaker distinctions of this nature are not presumed invalid under the First Amendment.

The must-carry provisions, on their face, do not burden or benefit speech of a particular content does not end the inquiry. Our cases have recognized that even a regulation neutral on its face may be content-based if its manifest purpose is to regulate speech because of the message it conveys....

Appellants maintain that the must-carry provisions trigger strict scrutiny because they compel cable operators to transmit speech not of their choosing. Relying principally on *Miami Herald Publishing Co. v. Tornillo*, 418 U.S. 241 (1974), appellants say this intrusion on the editorial control of cable operators amounts to forced speech which, if not per se invalid, can be justified only if narrowly tailored to a compelling government interest.

Tornillo affirmed an essential proposition: The First Amendment protects the editorial independence of the press. The right-of-reply statute at issue in *Tornillo* required any newspaper that assailed a political candidate's character to print, upon request by the candidate and without cost, the candidate's reply in equal space and prominence. Although the statute did not censor speech in the traditional sense—it only required newspapers to grant access to the messages of others—we found that it imposed an impermissible content-based burden on newspaper speech. Because the right of access at issue in *Tornillo* was triggered only when a newspaper elected to print matter critical of political candidates, it "exacted a penalty on the basis of ... content." We found, and continue to recognize, that right-of-reply statutes of this sort are an impermissible intrusion on newspapers' "editorial control and judgment."

Tornillo and *Pacific Gas & Electric* [*Co. v. Public Utilities Comm'n of Cal.*, 475 U.S. 1 (1986),] do not control this case for the following reasons. First, unlike the access rules struck down in those cases, the must-carry rules are content-neutral in application. They are not activated by any particular message spoken by cable operators and thus exact no content-based penalty. Likewise, they do not grant access to broadcasters on the ground that the content of broadcast programming will counterbalance the messages of cable operators. Instead, they confer benefits upon all full power, local broadcasters, whatever the content of their programming.

Second, appellants do not suggest, nor do we think it the case, that must-carry will force cable operators to alter their own messages to respond to the broadcast programming they are required to carry. Given cable's long history of serving as a conduit for broadcast signals, there appears little risk that cable viewers would assume that the broadcast stations carried on a cable system convey ideas or messages endorsed by the cable operator.

Finally, the asserted analogy to *Tornillo* ignores an important technological difference between newspapers and cable television. Although a daily newspaper and a cable operator both may enjoy monopoly status in a given locale, the cable operator exercises far greater control over access to the relevant medium. A daily newspaper, no matter how secure its local monopoly, does not possess the power to obstruct readers' access to other competing publications—whether they be weekly local newspapers, or daily newspapers published in other cities. Thus, when a newspaper asserts exclusive control over its own news copy, it does not thereby prevent other newspapers from being distributed to willing recipients in the same locale.

The same is not true of cable. When an individual subscribes to cable, the physical connection between the television set and the cable network gives the cable operator bottleneck, or gatekeeper, control over most (if not all) of the television programming that is channeled into the subscriber's home. Hence, simply by virtue of its ownership of the essential pathway for cable speech, a cable operator can prevent its subscribers from obtaining access to programming it chooses to exclude. A cable operator, unlike speakers in other media, can thus silence the voice of competing speakers with a mere flick of the switch.

Turner Broadcasting System v. Federal Communications Commission

520 U.S. 180 (1997) (*Turner II*)

On appeal, we agreed with the District Court that must-carry does not "distinguish favored speech from disfavored speech on the basis of the ideas or views expressed," but is a content-neutral regulation designed "to prevent cable operators from exploiting their economic power to the detriment of broadcasters," and "to ensure that all Americans, especially those unable to subscribe to cable, have access to free television programming — whatever its content." We held that, under the intermediate level of scrutiny applicable to content-neutral regulations, must-carry would be sustained if it were shown to further an important or substantial governmental interest unrelated to the suppression of free speech, provided the incidental restrictions did not "burden substantially more speech than is necessary to further" those interests. Although we "had no difficulty concluding" the interests must-carry was designed to serve were important in the abstract, a four-Justice plurality concluded genuine issues of material fact remained regarding whether "the economic health of local broadcasting is in genuine jeopardy and need of the protections afforded by must-carry," and whether must-carry "'burdens substantially more speech than is necessary to further the government's legitimate interests.'" ...

The District Court oversaw another 18 months of factual development on remand "yielding a record of tens of thousands of pages" of evidence, comprised of materials acquired during Congress' three years of pre-enactment hearings, as well as additional expert submissions, sworn declarations and testimony, and industry documents obtained on remand. Upon consideration of the expanded record, a divided panel of the District Court again granted summary judgment to appellees.

The court held must-carry to be narrowly tailored to promote the Government's legitimate interests. It found the effects of must-carry on cable operators to be minimal, noting evidence that: most cable systems had not been required to add any broadcast stations since the rules were adopted; only 1.2 percent of all cable channels had been devoted to broadcast stations added because of must-carry; and the burden was likely to diminish as channel capacity expanded in the future. The court proceeded to consider a number of alternatives to must-carry that appellants had proposed, including: a leased-access regime, under which cable operators would be required to set aside channels for both broadcasters and cable programmers to use at a regulated price; use of so-called A/B switches, giving consumers a choice of both cable and broadcast signals; a more limited set of must-carry obligations modeled on those earlier used by the FCC; and subsidies for broadcasters. The court rejected each in turn, concluding that "even assuming that [the alternatives] would be less burdensome" on cable operators' First Amendment interests, they "are not in any respect as effective in achieving the government's [interests]." Judge Jackson would have preferred a trial to summary judgment, but concurred in the judgment of the court.

This direct appeal followed. We noted probable jurisdiction, and we now affirm.

We begin where the plurality ended in *Turner*, applying the standards for intermediate scrutiny enunciated in [*United States v.*] *O'Brien*, [391 U.S. 367 (1968)]. A content-neutral regulation will be sustained under the First Amendment if it advances important governmental interests unrelated to the suppression of free speech and does not burden substantially more speech than necessary to further those interests. As noted in Turner, must-carry was designed to serve "three interrelated interests:

(1) preserving the benefits of free, over-the-air local broadcast television, (2) promoting the widespread dissemination of information from a multiplicity of sources, and (3) promoting fair competition in the market for television programming." We decided then, and now reaffirm, that each of those is an important governmental interest. We have been most explicit in holding that "'protecting noncable households from loss of regular television broadcasting service due to competition from cable systems' is an important federal interest." Forty percent of American households continue to rely on over-the-air signals for television programming. Despite the growing importance of cable television and alternative technologies, "'broadcasting is demonstrably a principal source of information and entertainment for a great part of the Nation's population.'" We have identified a corresponding "governmental purpose of the highest order" in ensuring public access to "a multiplicity of information sources." And it is undisputed the Government has an interest in "eliminating restraints on fair competition..., even when the individuals or entities subject to particular regulations are engaged in expressive activity protected by the First Amendment."

On remand, and again before this Court, both sides have advanced new interpretations of these interests in an attempt to recast them in forms "more readily proven." The Government downplays the importance of showing a risk to the broadcast industry as a whole and suggests the loss of even a few broadcast stations "is a matter of critical importance."

Taking the opposite approach, appellants argue Congress' interest in preserving broadcasting is not implicated unless it is shown the industry as a whole would fail without must-carry, and suggest Congress' legitimate interest in "assuring that the public has access to a multiplicity of information sources," extends only as far as preserving "a minimum amount of television broadcast service."

These alternative formulations are inconsistent with Congress' stated interests in enacting must-carry. The congressional findings do not reflect concern that, absent must-carry, "a few voices," would be lost from the television marketplace. In explicit factual findings, Congress expressed clear concern that the "marked shift in market share from broadcast television to cable television services," resulting from increasing market penetration by cable services, as well as the expanding horizontal concentration and vertical integration of cable operators, combined to give cable systems the incentive and ability to delete, reposition, or decline carriage to local broadcasters in an attempt to favor affiliated cable programmers. Congress predicted that "absent the reimposition of [must-carry], additional local broadcast signals will be deleted, repositioned, or not carried" with the end result that "the economic viability of free local broadcast television and its ability to originate quality local programming will be seriously jeopardized."

At the same time, Congress was under no illusion that there would be a complete disappearance of broadcast television nationwide in the absence of must-carry. Congress recognized broadcast programming (and network programming in particular) "remains the most popular programming on cable systems." Indeed, reflecting the popularity and strength of some broadcasters, Congress included in the Cable Act a provision permitting broadcasters to charge cable systems for carriage of the broadcasters' signals.

Congress was concerned not that broadcast television would disappear in its entirety without must-carry, but that without it, "significant numbers of broadcast stations will be refused carriage on cable systems," and those "broadcast stations denied carriage will either deteriorate to a substantial degree or fail altogether."

Nor do the congressional findings support appellants' suggestion that legitimate legislative goals would be satisfied by the preservation of a rump broadcasting industry providing a minimum of broadcast service to Americans without cable. We have noted that " 'it has long been a basic tenet of national communications policy that "the widest possible dissemination of information from diverse and antagonistic sources is essential to the welfare of the public.' " " 'Increasing the number of outlets for community self-expression' " represents a " 'long-established regulatory goal in the field of television broadcasting.' " Consistent with this objective, the Cable Act's findings reflect a concern that congressional action was necessary to prevent "a reduction in the number of media voices available to consumers." Congress identified a specific interest in "ensuring [the] continuation" of "the local origination of [broadcast] programming," an interest consistent with its larger purpose of promoting multiple types of media, and found must-carry necessary "to serve the goals" of the original Communications Act of 1934 of "providing a fair, efficient, and equitable distribution of broadcast services." In short, Congress enacted must-carry to "preserve the existing structure of the Nation's broadcast television medium while permitting the concomitant expansion and development of cable television."

Although Congress set no definite number of broadcast stations sufficient for these purposes, the Cable Act's requirement that all cable operators with more than 12 channels set aside one-third of their channel capacity for local broadcasters, refutes the notion that Congress contemplated preserving only a bare minimum of stations. Congress' evident interest in "preserving the existing structure," of the broadcast industry discloses a purpose to prevent any significant reduction in the multiplicity of broadcast programming sources available to noncable households. . . .

The dissent proceeds on the assumption that must-carry is designed solely to be (and can only be justified as) a measure to protect broadcasters from cable operators' anticompetitive behavior. Federal policy, however, has long favored preserving a multiplicity of broadcast outlets regardless of whether the conduct that threatens it is motivated by anticompetitive animus or rises to the level of an antitrust violation. . . .

We have no difficulty in finding a substantial basis to support Congress' conclusion that a real threat justified enactment of the must-carry provisions. We examine first the evidence before Congress and then the further evidence presented to the District Court on remand to supplement the congressional determination.

Cable systems also have more systemic reasons for seeking to disadvantage broadcast stations: Simply stated, cable has little interest in assisting, through carriage, a competing medium of communication. As one cable-industry executive put it, " 'our job is to promote cable television, not broadcast television.'" The incentive to subscribe to cable is lower in markets with many over-the-air viewing options. Evidence adduced on remand indicated cable systems have little incentive to carry, and a significant incentive to drop, broadcast stations that will only be strengthened by access to the 60% of the television market that cable typically controls.

Congress could therefore reasonably conclude that cable systems would drop broadcasters in favor of programmers — even unaffiliated ones — less likely to compete with them for audience and advertisers....

It was more than a theoretical possibility in 1992 that cable operators would take actions adverse to local broadcasters; indeed, significant numbers of broadcasters had already been dropped. The record before Congress contained extensive anecdotal evidence about scores of adverse carriage decisions against broadcast stations. Congress considered an FCC-sponsored study detailing cable system carriage practices in the wake of decisions by the United States Court of Appeals for the District of Columbia Circuit striking down prior must-carry regulations. Substantial evidence demonstrated that absent must-carry the already "serious," problem of noncarriage would grow worse because "additional local broadcast signals will be deleted, repositioned, or not carried." The record included anecdotal evidence showing the cable industry was acting with restraint in dropping broadcast stations in an effort to discourage reregulation.

We think it apparent must-carry serves the Government's interests "in a direct and effective way." Must-carry ensures that a number of local broadcasters retain cable carriage, with the concomitant audience access and advertising revenues needed to support a multiplicity of stations. Appellants contend that even were this so, must-carry is broader than necessary to accomplish its goals. We turn to this question.

The second portion of the *O'Brien* inquiry concerns the fit between the asserted interests and the means chosen to advance them. Content-neutral regulations do not pose the same "inherent dangers to free expression," that content-based regulations do, and thus are subject to a less rigorous analysis, which affords the Government latitude in designing a regulatory solution. Under intermediate scrutiny, the Government may employ the means of its choosing "'so long as the ... regulation promotes a substantial governmental interest that would be achieved less effectively absent the regulation,'" and does not "'burden substantially more speech than is necessary to further'" that interest.

The must-carry provisions have the potential to interfere with protected speech in two ways. First, the provisions restrain cable operators' editorial discretion in creating programming packages by "reducing the number of channels over which [they] exercise unfettered control." Second, the rules "render it more difficult for cable programmers to compete for carriage on the limited channels remaining."

Appellants say the burden of must-carry is great, but the evidence adduced on remand indicates the actual effects are modest. Significant evidence indicates the vast majority of cable operators have not been affected in a significant manner by must-carry. Cable operators have been able to satisfy their must-carry obligations 87 percent of the time using previously unused channel capacity; 94.5 percent of the 11,628 cable systems nationwide have not had to drop any programming in order to fulfill their must-carry obligations; the remaining 5.5 percent have had to drop an average of only 1.22 services from their programming; and cable operators nationwide carry 99.8 percent of the programming they carried before enactment of must-carry. Appellees note that only 1.18 percent of the approximately 500,000 cable channels nationwide is devoted to channels added because of must-carry; weighted for subscribership, the figure is 2.4 percent. Appellees contend the burdens of must-carry will soon diminish as cable channel capacity increases, as is occurring nationwide....

We cannot displace Congress' judgment respecting content-neutral regulations with our own, so long as its policy is grounded on reasonable factual findings supported by evidence that is substantial for a legislative determination. Those requirements were met in this case, and in these circumstances the First Amendment requires nothing more. The judgment of the District Court is affirmed.

American Broadcasting Companies, Inc. v. Aereo, Inc.

573 U.S. 431 (2014)

JUSTICE BREYER delivered the opinion of the Court.

The Copyright Act of 1976 gives a copyright owner the "exclusive righ[t]" to "perform the copyrighted work publicly." 17 U.S.C. § 106(4). The Act's Transmit Clause defines that exclusive right as including the right to "transmit or otherwise communicate a performance ... of the [copyrighted] work ... to the public, by means of any device or process, whether the members of the public capable of receiving the performance ... receive it in the same place or in separate places and at the same time or at different times." § 101.

We must decide whether respondent Aereo, Inc., infringes this exclusive right by selling its subscribers a technologically complex service that allows them to watch television programs over the Internet at about the same time as the programs are broadcast over the air. We conclude that it does.

For a monthly fee, Aereo offers subscribers broadcast television programming over the Internet, virtually as the programming is being broadcast. Much of this programming is made up of copyrighted works. Aereo neither owns the copyright in those works nor holds a license from the copyright owners to perform those works publicly.

Aereo's system is made up of servers, transcoders, and thousands of dime-sized antennas housed in a central warehouse. It works roughly as follows: First, when a subscriber wants to watch a show that is currently being broadcast, he visits Aereo's website and selects, from a list of the local programming, the show he wishes to see.

Second, one of Aereo's servers selects an antenna, which it dedicates to the use of that subscriber (and that subscriber alone) for the duration of the selected show. A server then tunes the antenna to the over-the-air broadcast carrying the show. The antenna begins to receive the broadcast, and an Aereo transcoder translates the signals received into data that can be transmitted over the Internet.

Third, rather than directly send the data to the subscriber, a server saves the data in a subscriber-specific folder on Aereo's hard drive. In other words, Aereo's system creates a subscriber-specific copy—that is, a "personal" copy—of the subscriber's program of choice.

Fourth, once several seconds of programming have been saved, Aereo's server begins to stream the saved copy of the show to the subscriber over the Internet. (The subscriber may instead direct Aereo to stream the program at a later time, but that aspect of Aereo's service is not before us.) The subscriber can watch the streamed program on the screen of his personal computer, tablet, smart phone, Internet-connected television, or other Internet-connected device. The streaming continues, a mere few seconds behind the over-the-air broadcast, until the subscriber has received the entire show.

Aereo emphasizes that the data that its system streams to each subscriber are the data from his own personal copy, made from the broadcast signals received by the particular antenna allotted to him. Its system does not transmit data saved in one subscriber's folder to any other subscriber. When two subscribers wish to watch the same program, Aereo's system activates two separate antennas and saves two separate copies of the program in two separate folders. It then streams the show to the subscribers through two separate transmissions—each from the subscriber's personal copy.

This case requires us to answer two questions: First, in operating in the manner described above, does Aereo "perform" at all? And second, if so, does Aereo do so "publicly"? We address these distinct questions in turn.

Does Aereo "perform"? See § 106(4) ("[T]he owner of [a] copyright ... has the exclusive righ[t] ... to *perform* the copyrighted work publicly" (emphasis added)); § 101 ("To *perform* ... a work 'publicly' means [among other things] to transmit ... a performance ... of the work ... to the public ..." (emphasis added)). Phrased another way, does Aereo "transmit ... a performance" when a subscriber watches a show using Aereo's system, or is it only the subscriber who transmits? In Aereo's view, it does not perform. It does no more than supply equipment that "emulate[s] the operation of a home antenna and [digital video recorder (DVR)]." Like a home antenna and DVR, Aereo's equipment simply responds to its subscribers' directives. So it is only the subscribers who "perform" when they use Aereo's equipment to stream television programs to themselves.

Considered alone, the language of the Act does not clearly indicate when an entity "perform[s]" (or "transmit[s]") and when it merely supplies equipment that allows others to do so. But when read in light of its purpose, the Act is unmistakable: An entity that engages in activities like Aereo's performs.

History makes plain that one of Congress' primary purposes in amending the Copyright Act in 1976 was to overturn this Court's determination that community antenna television (CATV) systems (the precursors of modern cable systems) fell outside the Act's scope. In *Fortnightly Corp. v. United Artists Television, Inc.*, 392 U.S. 390 (1968), the Court considered a CATV system that carried local television broadcasting, much of which was copyrighted, to its subscribers in two cities. The CATV provider placed antennas on hills above the cities and used coaxial cables to carry the signals received by the antennas to the home television sets of its subscribers. The system amplified and modulated the signals in order to improve their strength and efficiently transmit them to subscribers. A subscriber "could choose any of the ... programs he wished to view by simply turning the knob on his own television set." The CATV provider "neither edited the programs received nor originated any programs of its own."

Asked to decide whether the CATV provider infringed copyright holders' exclusive right to perform their works publicly, the Court held that the provider did not "perform" at all. And a CATV provider "falls on the viewer's side of the line."

The Court reasoned that CATV providers were unlike broadcasters:

> Broadcasters select the programs to be viewed; CATV systems simply carry, without editing, whatever programs they receive. Broadcasters procure programs and propagate them to the public; CATV systems receive programs that have been released to the public and carry them by private channels to additional viewers.

Instead, CATV providers were more like viewers, for "the basic function [their] equipment serves is little different from that served by the equipment generally furnished by" viewers. "Essentially," the Court said, "a CATV system no more than enhances the viewer's capacity to receive the broadcaster's signals [by] provid[ing] a well-located antenna with an efficient connection to the viewer's television set." Viewers do not become performers by using "amplifying equipment," and a CATV provider should not be treated differently for providing viewers the same equipment.

In *Teleprompter Corp. v. Columbia Broadcasting System, Inc.*, 415 U.S. 394 (1974), the Court considered the copyright liability of a CATV provider that carried broadcast television programming into subscribers' homes from hundreds of miles away. Although the Court recognized that a viewer might not be able to afford amplifying equipment that would provide access to those distant signals, it nonetheless found that the CATV provider was more like a viewer than a broadcaster. It explained: "The reception and rechanneling of [broadcast television signals] for simultaneous viewing is essentially a viewer function, irrespective of the distance between the broadcasting station and the ultimate viewer."

The Court also recognized that the CATV system exercised some measure of choice over what to transmit. But that fact did not transform the CATV system into a broadcaster. A broadcaster exercises significant creativity in choosing what to air, the Court reasoned. In contrast, the CATV provider makes an initial choice about which broadcast stations to retransmit, but then "'simply carr[ies], without editing, whatever programs [it] receive[s].'"

In 1976 Congress amended the Copyright Act in large part to reject the Court's holdings in *Fortnightly* and *Teleprompter*. Congress enacted new language that erased the Court's line between broadcaster and viewer, in respect to "perform[ing]" a work. The amended statute clarifies that to "perform" an audiovisual work means "to show its images in any sequence or to make the sounds accompanying it audible." Under this new language, *both* the broadcaster *and* the viewer of a television program "perform," because they both show the program's images and make audible the program's sounds.

Congress also enacted the Transmit Clause, which specifies that an entity performs publicly when it "transmit[s] ... a performance ... to the public." Cable system activities, like those of the CATV systems in *Fortnightly* and *Teleprompter,* lie at the heart of the activities that Congress intended this language to cover. The Clause thus makes clear that an entity that acts like a CATV system itself performs, even if when doing so, it simply enhances viewers' ability to receive broadcast television signals.

Congress further created a new section of the Act to regulate cable companies' public performances of copyrighted works. Section 111 creates a complex, highly detailed compulsory licensing scheme that sets out the conditions, including the payment of compulsory fees, under which cable systems may retransmit broadcasts.

Congress made these three changes to achieve a similar end: to bring the activities of cable systems within the scope of the Copyright Act.

This history makes clear that Aereo is not simply an equipment provider. Rather, Aereo, and not just its subscribers, "perform[s]" (or "transmit[s]"). Aereo's activities are substantially similar to those of the CATV companies that Congress amended the Act to reach.

Aereo's equipment may serve a "viewer function"; it may enhance the viewer's ability to receive a broadcaster's programs. It may even emulate equipment a viewer could use at home. But the same was true of the equipment that was before the Court, and ultimately before Congress, in *Fortnightly* and *Teleprompter.*

We recognize, and Aereo and the dissent emphasize, one particular difference between Aereo's system and the cable systems at issue in *Fortnightly* and *Teleprompter*. The systems in those cases transmitted constantly; they sent continuous programming to each subscriber's television set. In contrast, Aereo's system remains inert until a subscriber indicates that she wants to watch a program. Only at that moment, in automatic response to the subscriber's request, does Aereo's system activate an antenna and begin to transmit the requested program.

Next, we must consider whether Aereo performs petitioners' works "publicly," within the meaning of the Transmit Clause. Under the Clause, an entity performs a work publicly when it "transmit[s] ... a performance ... of the work ... to the public." Aereo denies that it satisfies this definition. It reasons as follows: because each of these performances is capable of being received by one and only one subscriber, Aereo transmits privately, not publicly. Even assuming Aereo's first argument is correct, its second does not follow.

But what about the Clause's further requirement that Aereo transmit a performance "to the public"? As we have said, an Aereo subscriber receives broadcast television signals with an antenna dedicated to him alone. Aereo's system makes from those signals a personal copy of the selected program. It streams the content of the copy to the same subscriber and to no one else. One and only one subscriber has the ability to see and hear each Aereo transmission. The fact that each transmission is to only one subscriber, in Aereo's view, means that it does not transmit a performance "to the public."

In terms of the Act's purposes, these differences do not distinguish Aereo's system from cable systems, which do perform "publicly." Viewed in terms of Congress' regulatory objectives, why should any of these technological differences matter? They concern the behind-the-scenes way in which Aereo delivers television programming to its viewers' screens. They do not render Aereo's commercial objective any different from that of cable companies. Nor do they significantly alter the viewing experience of Aereo's subscribers. Why would a subscriber who wishes to watch a television show care much whether images and sounds are delivered to his screen via a large multi-subscriber antenna or one small dedicated antenna, whether they arrive instantaneously or after a few seconds' delay, or whether they are transmitted directly or after a personal copy is made? And why, if Aereo is right, could not modern CATV systems simply continue the same commercial and consumer-oriented activities, free of copyright restrictions, provided they substitute such new technologies for old? Congress would as much have intended to protect a copyright holder from the unlicensed activities of Aereo as from those of cable companies.

The text of the Clause effectuates Congress' intent. Aereo's argument to the contrary relies on the premise that "to transmit ... a performance" means to make a single transmission. But the Clause suggests that an entity may transmit a performance through multiple, discrete transmissions. That is because one can "transmit" or "communicate" something through a *set* of actions. Thus one can transmit a message to one's friends, irrespective of whether one sends separate identical e-mails to each friend or a single e-mail to all at once. So can an elected official communicate an idea, slogan, or speech to her constituents, regardless of whether she communicates that idea, slogan, or speech during individual phone calls to each constituent or in a public square.

The fact that a singular noun ("a performance") follows the words "to transmit" does not suggest the contrary. One can sing a song to his family, whether he sings the same song one-on-one or in front of all together. Similarly, one's colleagues may watch a performance of a particular play—say, this season's modern-dress version of "Measure for Measure"—whether they do so at separate or at the same showings. By the same principle, an entity may transmit a performance through one or several transmissions, where the performance is of the same work.

The Transmit Clause must permit this interpretation, for it provides that one may transmit a performance to the public "whether the members of the public capable of receiving the performance ... receive it ... at the same time or at different times."

§ 101. Were the words "to transmit ... a performance" limited to a single act of communication, members of the public could not receive the performance communicated "at different times." Therefore, in light of the purpose and text of the Clause, we conclude that when an entity communicates the same contemporaneously perceptible images and sounds to multiple people, it transmits a performance to them regardless of the number of discrete communications it makes.

We do not see how the fact that Aereo transmits via personal copies of programs could make a difference. The Act applies to transmissions "by means of any device or process." *Ibid.* And retransmitting a television program using user-specific copies is a "process" of transmitting a performance. A "cop[y]" of a work is simply a "material objec[t] ... in which a work is fixed ... and from which the work can be perceived, reproduced, or otherwise communicated." So whether Aereo transmits from the same or separate copies, it performs the same work; it shows the same images and makes audible the same sounds. Therefore, when Aereo streams the same television program to multiple subscribers, it "transmit[s] ... a performance" to all of them.

Moreover, the subscribers to whom Aereo transmits television programs constitute "the public." Aereo communicates the same contemporaneously perceptible images and sounds to a large number of people who are unrelated and unknown to each other. This matters because, although the Act does not define "the public," it specifies that an entity performs publicly when it performs at "any place where a substantial number of persons outside of a normal circle of a family and its social acquaintances is gathered." The Act thereby suggests that "the public" consists of a large group of people outside of a family and friends.

Neither the record nor Aereo suggests that Aereo's subscribers receive performances in their capacities as owners or possessors of the underlying works. This is relevant because when an entity performs to a set of people, whether they constitute "the public" often depends upon their relationship to the underlying work. When, for example, a valet parking attendant returns cars to their drivers, we would not say that the parking service provides cars "to the public." We would say that it provides the cars to their owners. We would say that a car dealership, on the other hand, does provide cars to the public, for it sells cars to individuals who lack a pre-existing relationship to the cars. Similarly, an entity that transmits a performance to individuals in their capacities as owners or possessors does not perform to "the public," whereas an entity like Aereo that transmits to large numbers of paying subscribers who lack any prior relationship to the works does so perform.

Finally, we note that Aereo's subscribers may receive the same programs at different times and locations. This fact does not help Aereo, however, for the Transmit Clause expressly provides that an entity may perform publicly "whether the members of the public capable of receiving the performance ... receive it in the same place or in separate places and at the same time or at different times." In other words, "the public" need not be situated together, spatially or temporally. For these reasons, we conclude that Aereo transmits a performance of petitioners' copyrighted works to the public, within the meaning of the Transmit Clause.

For these reasons, we conclude that Aereo "perform[s]" petitioners' copyrighted works "publicly," as those terms are defined by the Transmit Clause. We therefore reverse the contrary judgment of the Court of Appeals, and we remand the case for further proceedings consistent with this opinion.

It is so ordered.

Fox Television Stations, Inc v. Aereokiller, L.L.C.

851 F.3d 1002 (2017)

We must decide whether a service that captures copyrighted works broadcast over the air, and then retransmits them to paying subscribers over the Internet without the consent of the copyright holders, is a "cable system" eligible for a compulsory license under the Copyright Act.

The Copyright Act of 1976 gives copyright holders six "exclusive rights," including the exclusive right "to perform" copyrighted works "publicly." 17 U.S.C. § 106(4). The Act provides that "[a]nyone who violates any of the exclusive rights of the copyright owner … is an infringer." This case concerns an important limitation on the Act's provision for exclusive rights.[13]

Under § 111 of the Act, a "cable system" is eligible for a so-called compulsory license that allows it to retransmit "a performance or display of a work" that had originally been broadcast by someone else — even if such material is copyrighted — without having to secure the consent of the copyright holder. So long as the cable system pays a statutory fee to the Copyright Office and complies with certain other regulations, it is protected from infringement liability. Compulsory licenses are highly coveted, in no small part because, according to the Copyright Office, the royalty payments the Act requires cable companies to pay are "*de minimis*" when compared to the gross receipts and revenues the cable industry collects, a gap suggesting that the government-set rates fall well below market levels. U.S. Copyright Office, *Satellite Home Viewer Extension and Reauthorization Act § 109 Report* 43 (2008) ("SHVERA Report").

This lawsuit pits a group of broadcast stations and copyright holders (collectively, "Fox") against an entity now known as FilmOn X ("FilmOn"). FilmOn operates a service that uses antennas to capture over-the-air broadcast programming, much of it copyrighted, and then uses the Internet to retransmit such programming to paying subscribers, all without the consent or authorization of the copyright holders. The

---

13. As of this writing, at least seven federal courts have weighed in on whether Internet-based retransmission services count as "cable systems" under § 111. The district court here is the only one to conclude that they do. A panel of the Second Circuit unanimously said no. WPIX, Inc. v. ivi, Inc., 691 F.3d 275, 276 (2d Cir. 2012) (*ivi II*). So have five district courts: three in the Southern District of New York, one in the District for the District of Columbia, and one in the Northern District of Illinois. WPIX, Inc. v. ivi, Inc., 765 F.Supp.2d 594, 600 (S.D.N.Y. 2011) (*ivi I*); Fox Television Stations, Inc. v. FilmOn X L.L.C., 150 F.Supp.3d 1, 7 (D.D.C. 2015); Filmon X, L.L.C. v. Window to the World Commc'ns, Inc., No. 13 C 8451, 2016 WL 1161276, at *7 (N.D. Ill. Mar. 23, 2016); CBS Broad. Inc. v. FilmOn.com, Inc., No. 10 CIV. 7532 NRB, 2014 WL 3702568, at *4 (S.D.N.Y. July 24, 2014); Am. Broad. Cos., Inc. v. Aereo, Inc., No. 12-CV-1540, 2014 WL 5393867, at *3 (S.D.N.Y. Oct. 23, 2014).

Supreme Court recently held that such a service does "perform" the retransmitted works "publicly," and hence infringes the copyright holders' exclusive performance rights. *American Broad. Cos. v. Aereo, Inc.*, 573 U.S. 431 (2014). Fox sued FilmOn for copyright infringement in 2012; in its most recent defense, FilmOn claims that it is a "cable system" eligible for a compulsory license under § 111.

The relevant provision of the Copyright Act defines "cable system" as follows:

> A "cable system" is a facility, located in any State, territory, trust territory, or possession of the United States, that in whole or in part receives signals transmitted or programs broadcast by one or more television broadcast stations licensed by the Federal Communications Commission, and makes secondary transmissions of such signals or programs by wires, cables, microwave, or other communications channels to subscribing members of the public who pay for such service. For purposes of determining the royalty fee under subsection (d)(1), two or more cable systems in contiguous communities under common ownership or control or operating from one headend shall be considered as one system.

17 U.S.C. § 111(f)(3). The parties offer dueling interpretations § 111, each grounded in various aspects of its text, its perceived purposes, and slices of its legislative history.

Fox and FilmOn each claim that the plain meaning of § 111 resolves this case in its favor. We will first discuss Fox's interpretation, then FilmOn's, and only then — if we conclude that the meaning of § 111 is ambiguous on the question presented — will we consider the views of the Copyright Office.

Fox maintains that § 111's "plain text makes clear that the relevant 'facility' comprises the *entire* retransmission service — both the service's means of receiving broadcast signals *and* its means of making secondary transmissions to the paying subscribers." The Copyright Office has not endorsed this interpretation. Nevertheless, under Fox's reading, FilmOn would necessarily be excluded from § 111's definition of "cable system" because FilmOn retransmits broadcast signals over the Internet, and yet the Internet "is in no sense under [its] ownership or control." Indeed, FilmOn concedes that it "uses a communications channel beyond its facility" to make secondary transmissions. "That concession," says Fox, "should decide this case."

Fox's theory is not implausible. As Fox points out, and as FilmOn does not dispute, "[a] traditional cable system is a 'facility' in this sense: It … retransmits [broadcast] signals directly to its subscribers over a transmission path fully within its control." Nevertheless, we cannot conclude that the statute *compels* the conclusion that to qualify as a "cable system," a retransmission service must encompass or have control over the means it uses to transmit material to paying subscribers.

The most important difficulty with Fox's interpretation is that it finds insufficient support in the text of the statute. Recall the relevant language: to be a "cable system," a facility must "make[] secondary transmissions of [broadcast] signals or programs *by* wires, cables, microwave, or other communications channels." 17 U.S.C. § 111(f)(3) (emphasis added). Nothing in that language on its face compels the conclusion that the facility must *control* the retransmission medium—the wires, cables, microwaves, or other communications channels—that it relies on to deliver its retransmissions. Fox does not cite any specialized or technical meaning, and as a matter of ordinary interpretation, the text could certainly be read the other way.

In addition, § 111(a)(3) specifically discusses a scenario in which one entity selects the content or recipients of a secondary transmission, while a different entity supplies the communications channel. According to that provision, a "carrier" who "provid[es] wires, cables, or other communications channels for the use of others" is not liable for copyright infringement, while the upstream entity who exercises "control over the content or selection of the primary transmission or over the particular recipients of the secondary transmission" may be liable. 17 U.S.C. § 111(a)(3). Section 111(a)(3), therefore, suggests that a facility may be said to make secondary transmissions even if it does not exercise ownership or control over the communications channel it uses. If that is true, then FilmOn's lack of ownership or control over the Internet does not necessarily exclude it from the class of facilities that "make[] secondary transmissions ... by wires, cables, microwave, or other communications channels."

Although Fox's plain-meaning construction has not convinced us, Fox can prevail if we defer to the views of the Copyright Office. FilmOn urges us not to do so because, FilmOn insists, the plain meaning of § 111 supports *its* position. FilmOn strives mightily to demonstrate that the plain meaning of § 111 unambiguously entitles it to a compulsory license.

FilmOn first argues that § 111 "should be interpreted in a technology agnostic manner." FilmOn would have us read § 111 as making compulsory licenses available to *any* facility that retransmits broadcast signals or programming, no matter its technological features or characteristics. That position is a poor fit with § 111's text and structure. First of all, if Congress had intended § 111 to service the entire secondary transmission community, doling out statutory licenses without regard to the technological makeup of its members, it would have been easy enough for Congress to say so (and in fact, Congress came very close to doing just that in the Transmit Clause, as we discuss in the next paragraph). Instead, Congress specified that § 111 applies only to "cable systems," and it defined "cable system" in a detailed, if arguably ambiguous, way. Second, and relatedly, if Congress meant § 111 to sweep in secondary transmission services with indifference to their technological profile, then it was strange for Congress to have provided separate compulsory license provisions—§§ 119 and 122—for broadcast retransmissions by satellite carriers. The way to prevent discrimination on the basis of technology, one might say, is to stop discriminating on the basis of technology. Congress chose a different course.

Undeterred, FilmOn relies on the Supreme Court's recent decision in *Aereo*, which, FilmOn insists, "recognized section 111's technology agnosticism." But *Aereo* did nothing of the sort. *Aereo* dealt with an altogether different provision of the Copyright Act, the Transmit Clause, which defines the scope of a copyright holder's exclusive right by delineating the class of activities that count as public performances and hence infringe such right. Significantly, the Transmit Clause refers in sweeping terms to transmissions or communications made "by means of *any* device or process," and broadly defined "device" and "process" to mean "one now known *or later developed*." The glaring textual differences between § 101 and § 111 render the *Aereo* decision of very little help to FilmOn's plain-meaning argument. Moreover, it would be perfectly coherent to pair a broad reading of the Transmit Clause with a narrow reading of the compulsory license provision, insofar as both such readings would work in tandem to bolster the property interests of copyright holders. Nothing in § 111 or *Aereo* makes such a reading unreasonable.

Nor can we conclude that the Copyright Act's broad purposes compel the conclusion that Internet-based retransmission services are eligible for compulsory licenses under § 111. Rather, we see powerful arguments that such a reading could very well undermine the balance of interests Congress attempted to strike when it designed § 111. That is especially so when § 111 is viewed in the context of its enactment.

In brief, when Congress passed the Copyright Act of 1976, it overturned two earlier Supreme Court decisions which had held that cable systems were not liable for copyright infringement on the theory that they did not actually "perform" the works they retransmitted at all. *Teleprompter Corp. v. Columbia Broad. Sys., Inc.*, 415 U.S. 394, 408 (1974); *Fortnightly Corp. v. United Artists Television*, 392 U.S. 390, 399 (1968). Congress therefore acted to restore a measure of protection to copyright owners. At the same time, however, Congress recognized that cable systems served an important public good, by enabling geographically distant and isolated communities to receive over-the-air broadcasts that would otherwise not reach them. But in 1976 the cable industry was a fledgling one; cable systems had little market power and little ability to overcome the considerable transaction costs they would incur if they had to negotiate individual licenses directly with copyright owners. Congress responded to these economic conditions by enacting § 111, which relieved cable systems of the need to sit down with every copyright holder before retransmitting their copyrighted broadcast works. Section 111 also helped protect the infrastructure investments cable systems have undertaken in the years prior to the Act. And the broadcast companies and copyright owners benefitted to some extent as well, insofar as they could now reach viewers they would not otherwise have been able to access. Fundamentally, however, § 111 was Congress's attempt to balance the socially useful role cable systems had come to play, on the one hand, against the property interests and creative incentives of copyright holders, on the other.

One could reasonably conclude that extending § 111 to Internet-based retransmission services would not further, and might in fact jeopardize, the values just described. For one, cable systems serve limited geographic communities, but an Internet-based service has no geographic boundary—it can retransmit works across the globe instantaneously—meaning that Internet-based retransmission poses a more serious threat to the value and integrity of copyrighted works. Such threat is exacerbated insofar as Internet retransmissions are more vulnerable than traditional cable to unauthorized copying and other acts of piracy. For another, many copyright owners are capable of transmitting their works over the Internet on their own; they do not need to rely on third parties to do so, as they had to rely on cable companies if they wanted to reach the isolated, distant communities cable systems traditionally served. Relatedly, compared to cable systems and satellite carriers, Internet-based retransmission services have not needed to make the same sort of investments in a delivery platform infrastructure. Finally, there is no evidence that Internet-based services lack market power or face prohibitive transaction costs of the sort that justified the compulsory license for cable systems.

To be sure, we agree with FilmOn that there are important values on its side of the equation as well. Still, our conclusion from this discussion is a predictable one: the array of competing interests at stake does not unambiguously counsel for or against a broad reading of § 111.

Finally, we note two additional reasons to reject FilmOn's argument that § 111 must be read to encompass Internet-based retransmission services.

As courts have explained in the past, compulsory licenses represent a "limited exception to the copyright holder's exclusive right to decide who shall make use of his [work]," and courts should not "expand the scope of the compulsory license provision beyond what Congress intended ... nor interpret it in such a way as to frustrate that purpose." *Fame Publishing Co. v. Ala. Custom Tape, Inc.*, 507 F.2d 667, 670 (5th Cir. 1975). Such canon supports a narrow construction of § 111.

Additionally, as Fox points out, interpreting § 111 so as to include Internet-based retransmission services would risk putting the United States in violation of certain of its treaty obligations. An age-old canon of construction instructs that "an act of Congress ought never to be construed to violate the law of nations if any other possible construction remains." *Murray v. Schooner Charming Betsy*, 6 U.S. 64, 118, (1804). FilmOn does not have a satisfactory answer to this argument.

For the foregoing reasons, we cannot accept FilmOn's argument that § 111 *must* be read in such a way as to make Internet-based retransmission services eligible for compulsory licenses. All of that being said, however, we would not go so far as to conclude that it would be clearly *impermissible* to say that FilmOn qualifies for a compulsory license under § 111. The text of § 111 is written in broad terms, and both sides can make plausible arguments about the statute's purposes and legislative history. Hence, although we do not believe the interpretive scales are in equipoise, we do not foreclose the possibility that the statute could reasonably be read to include Internet-based retransmission services.

Because the statute does not speak clearly to the precise question before us, we must decide how much weight to give the views of the Copyright Office. The Copyright Office has published its views on the meaning of § 111 through a few different channels. We group them into two broad categories.

First, in 1992 and again in 1997 the Office engaged in notice-and-comment rulemaking in order to decide whether burgeoning retransmission technologies—specifically, satellite and microwave retransmission systems—could be classified as "cable systems" under § 111. The 1992 and 1997 rulemakings did not purport to consider

Internet-based retransmission services. In the final rules' preambles, however, the Office stated broadly "that a provider of broadcast signals [must] be an inherently localized transmission media of limited availability to qualify as a cable system." Cable Compulsory Licenses: Definition of Cable Systems, 62 Fed. Reg. 18,705-02, 18,707 (April 17, 1997) (codified at 37 C.F.R. pt. 201); *see also* Cable Compulsory License; Definition of Cable System, 57 Fed. Reg. 3284-01, 3292 (Jan. 29, 1992) (codified at 37 C.F.R. pt. 201) ("Examination of the overall operation of section 111 proves that the compulsory license applies only to localized retransmission services."). Everyone acknowledges that the foregoing interpretation of "cable system" would rule out Internet-based retransmission services like FilmOn. But the parties disagree sharply about whether such interpretation should have any bearing on our analysis.

Since 1997, the Office has on at least four occasions specifically and unequivocally said that, in its view, Internet-based retransmission services are not "cable systems" under § 111, but it has not done so in connection with any rulemaking. Instead, the Office has communicated its position largely through official reports and testimony before Congress.

Under *Skidmore*,[14] and having already determined that the meaning of § 111 is ambiguous on the precise question before us, we must now ask whether the Copyright Office's interpretation is persuasive and reasonable.

First, the Office's decision to reject Internet-based retransmission services because they do not use a localized retransmission medium finds sufficient support in the text, structure, and basic purposes of the Copyright Act. Such interpretation aligns with § 111's many instances of location-sensitive language, including "headends," 17 U.S.C. § 111(f)(3), "contiguous communities," and "distant signal equivalent." As the Office points out — and as FilmOn does not dispute — such references "would have no meaning when applied to … nationwide retransmission facilities." Nor does FilmOn dispute the Office's claim that "at the time Congress created the cable compulsory license, the FCC regulated the cable industry as a highly localized medium of limited availability, suggesting that Congress, cognizant of the FCC's regulations and the market realities, fashioned a compulsory license with a local rather than a national scope."

Furthermore, confining "cable systems" to localized retransmission media is a sensible way to construe the phrase "other communications channels" so that it does not sweep in every possible retransmission technology. The Office's position is not rigidly originalist, as its ability to accommodate Satellite Master Antenna Television systems demonstrates. Rather, it is a plausible attempt to maintain the balance Congress struck between the public's interest in ever-improved access to broadcast television and the property rights of copyright holders.

---

14. Under *Skidmore*, the weight we give to an agency interpretation "will depend upon the thoroughness evident in its consideration, the validity of its reasoning, its consistency with earlier and later pronouncements, and all those factors which give it power to persuade, if lacking power to control." Skidmore v. Swift & Co., 323 U.S. 134, 140 (1944).

Lest there be any doubt, we note that for years Congress has indisputably been aware of the Office's position that Internet-based services are ineligible under § 111, and yet "Congress has frequently amended or reenacted the relevant provisions without change."

The Office's position is longstanding, consistently held, and was arrived at after careful consideration; and it addresses a complex question important to the administration of the Copyright Act. Not only that, but Congress has effectively acquiesced in it. We are persuaded that all of this more than suffices under *Skidmore*.

FilmOn and other Internet-based retransmission services are neither clearly eligible nor clearly ineligible for the compulsory license § 111 makes available to "cable systems." The Copyright Office says they are not eligible. Because the Office's views are persuasive, and because they are reasonable, we defer to them. The judgment of the district court is therefore

REVERSED.

Notes and Questions

a. What is the purpose of the must carry rules? Why has the issue been so heavily litigated by the cable industry? Does the expansion of the cable capacity change understanding of the analysis?

b. Was Turner's claim of First Amendment compelled speech a credible argument, or was this simply a legal box into which the cable operator wished to frame a tug-of-war over valuable cable licenses?

c. In 1999, Congress extended some of the rules of the cable industry to the burgeoning satellite industry. The Satellite Home Viewer Improvement Act of 1999 (SHVIA) was immediately challenged by industry on grounds similar to that of *Turner*. In *Satellite Broad. & Communs. Ass'n v. FCC*, 275 F.3d 337 (4th Cir. 2001), the court explained that

> By enacting SHVIA, Congress sought to promote competition between the satellite and cable industries by creating a statutory copyright license that allows satellite carriers to carry the signals of local broadcast television stations without obtaining authorization from the holders of copyrights in the individual programs aired by those stations. The Act also imposes a "carry one, carry all" rule, which was designed to "preserve free television for those not served by satellite or cable and to promote widespread dissemination of information from a multiplicity of sources."

The "carry one, carry all" rule is arguably less intrusive than the must carry provisions for cable regulation because satellite companies have a choice. If they elect to utilize the statutory copyright for any local broadcast, the satellite provider must carry all local stations which request carriage in the local market. The Fourth Circuit found this a content neutral regulation that was narrowly tailored to the continuing mission of maintaining free over-the-air television.

d. Systems such as Netflix and Amazon Prime rely on licensed, original programming for their content. YouTube relies heavily on user content rather than purchasing content for sale. Other models have developed or are developing. Where does FCC regulation fit in this environment?

e. The definitions of local markets impact the must carry regulations and the 'carry one, carry all' rule. In addition, these definitions impact the calculations for advertising revenue and sales coverage for syndicated television programming. A television station on the fringe of a market may benefit from lower costs to obtain programming, but it then risks being omitted from the increasingly critical must carry rules.

f. Regulating Internet Service Providers as Common Carriers. In 2015, the FCC adopted rules to move ISPs under the jurisdiction of Title II of the Communications Act of 1934 and Section 706 of the Telecommunications Act of 1996, classifying the services as common carriers and providing a basis for instituting net neutrality regulations. The reclassification was necessary because The D.C. Circuit Court of Appeals had previously determined that similar regulations were not supported by the statute for ISPs under Title I. *See Verizon Communications Inc. v. FCC*, 740 F.3d 623 (D.C. Cir. 2014). The net neutrality rules were short-lived, however, because of the change in political administrations. The net neutrality rules were withdrawn. In response, California has enacted its own net neutrality statute while other states are suing to challenge the withdrawal of the rule. The California legislation is also being challenged in court on preemption and other grounds.

D. Bibliography and Links

Mark R. Arbuckle, *How the FCC Killed the Fairness Doctrine: A Critical Evaluation of the 1985 Fairness Report Thirty Years After Syracuse Peace Council*, 15 First Amend. L. Rev. 331 (2017).

Ashutosh Bhagwat, *When Speech Is Not "Speech,"* 78 Ohio St. L.J. 839 (2017).

John Blevins, *The New Scarcity: A First Amendment Framework for Regulating Access to Digital Media Platforms*, 79 Tenn. L. Rev. 353 (2012).

Kevin W. Delaney, *Aereo, the Public Performance Right, and the Future of Broadcasting*, 42 Rutgers Computer & Tech. L.J. 19 (2016).

Nick Gamse, *The Indecency of Indecency: How Technology Affects the Constitutionality of Content-Based Broadcast Regulation*, 22 Fordham Intell. Prop. Media & Ent. L.J. 287 (2012).

W. Mike Jayne, *Fairness Doctrine 2.0: The Ever-Expanding Definition of Neutrality Under the First Amendment*, 16 First Amend. L. Rev. 466 (2018).

Michael Kaneb, *Neither Realistic nor Constitutionally Sound: The Problem of the FCC's Community Standard for Broadcast Indecency Determinations*, 49 B.C. L. Rev. 1081 (2008).

R. Randall Kelso, *The Structure of Modern Free Speech Doctrine: Strict Scrutiny, Intermediate Review, and "Reasonableness" Balancing*, 8 Elon L. Rev. 291 (2016).

Leslie Kendrick, *Content Discrimination Revisited*, 98 Va. L. Rev. 231 (2012).

William Lehr & Douglas Sicker, *Would You Like Your Internet with or Without Video?*, 2017 U. Ill. J.L. Tech. & Pol'y, 73 (2017).

Henry H. Perritt, Jr., *Keeping the Internet Invisible: Television Takes Over*, 21 J. Tech. L. & Pol'y 121 (2017).

Joel Timmer, *Promoting and Infringing Free Speech? Net Neutrality and the First Amendment*, 71 Fed. Comm. L.J. 1 (2018).

Millicent Usoro, *A Medium-Specific First Amendment Analysis on Compelled Campaign Finance Disclosure on the Internet*, 71 Fed. Comm. L.J. 299, 301 (2019).

Websites

Federal Communications Commission, www.FCC.gov

The European Institute for the Media (EIM), http://www.eim.org/ ("a think tank for research and strategy concerning developments in European media and communications, based in Düsseldorf and Paris")

Columbia Institute for Tele-Information, New York (www.citi.columbia.edu)

Chapter 15

Video Games, eSports, and Social Media

A. Overview of the Industry

Origins — Video Games, Role Playing Games and Virtual Worlds[1]

Since the advent of Pong,[2] computer gamers having been searching for increasingly realistic — or at least photorealistic — experiences with their computer-generated content. As the technology has allowed for ever more realistic images, sound, and even tactile response, the game experience has grown far beyond hi-score lists to become immersive, interactive environments. The "virtual environment is an interactive computer simulation which lets its participants see, hear, use, and even modify the simulated objects in the computer-generated environment."[3]

Attributes of the genre include the ability to involve a very large number of simultaneous participants online through the Internet or other networking systems, and the ability for the participant to take on a character or role in the game. As some of these gaming environments involve millions of players, they are now coined "massively multi-player online role-playing games (MMORPG)."[4] The user-created characters in these worlds are referred to as "avatars," virtual representations of the players.

The online role-playing games trace their lineage to *Dungeons and Dragons* and the genre of role-playing games in which participants would create characters who would navigate in the fictional worlds created and managed by dungeon masters. In

---

1. Adapted from Jon M. Garon, *Playing in the Virtual Arena: Avatars, Publicity and Identity Reconceptualized through Virtual Worlds and Computer Games*, 11 Chap. L. Rev. 465 (2008) (some text and footnotes omitted, other footnotes re-numbered).

2. "*Pong*, while not the first videogame, was the first coin-op arcade game and the first mainstream videogame that was available throughout the U.S. *Pong* was the impetus for the development of the videogaming industry, almost single-handedly creating both the home and the arcade videogame markets." *Atari Pong*, IGN, http://www.ign.com/wikis/history-of-video-game-consoles/Pong (last updated July 10, 2013, 7:02 PM).

3. Woodrow Barfield, *Intellectual Property Rights in Virtual Environments: Considering the Rights of Owners, Programmers and Virtual Avatars*, 39 Akron L. Rev. 649 (2006) (citation omitted).

4. *See id.* at 650.

Dungeons and Dragons, the players would give themselves the attributes of wizards, warriors, trolls, elves, and similar mythic characters. The interaction of the players and their characters would last in story arcs that could run for indefinite periods, and there may even be some characters still in use from 1974 when the rules were first published. Character attributes were kept on note cards and interactions mediated through polyhedral dice.

The *Dungeons and Dragons* genre moved to the online environment with games such as *World of Warcraft*, *The Lord of the Rings Online: Shadows of Angmar*, *Warhammer Online*, *EVE Online*, *Anarchy Online*, *RuneScape*, *Rappelz*, and *Shadow of Legend*. The genre also includes science fiction worlds such as the *Matrix Online* and *Star Wars Galaxies*.

Professor Erez Reuveni suggests two attributes that define the MMORPG and virtual worlds, separating them from classic computer or their Dungeons and Dragons' predecessors.[5] "Unlike traditional computer games ... virtual worlds are persistent and exist independently of any individual's presence. Virtual worlds exist in real time even after a specific player logs off, and a person's actions can permanently shape the virtual world."[6] While this is a literary distinction, the persistence and literary independence may also provide a framework for treating certain aspects of these works as distinct from novels, computer games, or motion pictures.

The persistence and literary independence of online role-playing games have spawned an entirely new genre from the fantasy worlds. In environments such as *Second Life*, *Moove*, *Active Worlds*, or *There*, the environment is a fantasy alternative to modern reality, with businesses, lounges, universities, and other brick-and-mortar equivalents. These environments are "near worlds," alternate realities set in the present with only modest changes from the world around us.

The attraction of virtual worlds comes from the technological opportunities to animate and enhance the interactions on a borderless, international landscape; the billions of dollars in revenue to be earned by the publishers and purveyors of these environments; and a growing cultural and commercial environment within each of the virtual worlds. Corporations, for example, are exploring the use of *Second Life* as a methodology and platform for employee training.[7] As communications educator Montse Anderson noted, "programs such as *Second Life* have the potential to enhance learning because they allow people to interact with each other, rather than reading a manual."[8]

In the ensuing decade, virtual worlds failed to significantly dominate as a platform for commerce, education or social interaction. Virtual reality technology has not ad-

5. Erez Reuveni, *On Virtual Worlds: Copyright and Contract Law at the Dawn of the Virtual Age*, 82 Ind. L.J. 261 (2007).
6. *Id.* at 265.
7. Andrew Johnson, *Virtual Training: Phoenix Couple Launch Venture to Help Companies Use Virtual World to Educate, Orient New Employees*, Ariz. Republic, Nov. 5, 2007, at Business 6.
8. *Id.*

vanced at a pace that makes immersive experiences simple and ubiquitous. In contrast, as mobile has become increasingly important as a gaming platform, augmented reality games have become a far more important platform.

Perhaps the most widely adopted augmented reality game is Niantic's 2016 mobile game "Pokémon GO," which was based on the trading card game and animated television show. Niantic was formed at Google, which originally funded the developer to create a mobile-based augmented reality game. The first such game, Ingress, required users to leave their homes and explore the real world. Ingress integrated Google Maps, GPS, and other phone features to create real-world competitive games that used the mobile phone as a gaming interface. Pokémon GO took that a step further by introducing Pokémon in real-world locations. In the first three years since the game's launch, it has racked up more than one billion installations and $2 billion in revenue. More importantly, it has established an entire genre that other companies are now moving to satisfy.

The other significant change has been the growth of "eSports." eSports is the term used for the transformation of videogames into a competitive, organized gaming platform, with large live events, massive viewership of videogame play, recognized superstar players, high-value prize money, and commercial underwriting. The content involves many multiplayer games and is not limited to videogame versions of traditional sports competitions.

Streaming services such as Twitch allow players to stream their games to be watched live online, and global events combine broadcast game play with live crowds that can, at times, fill the largest stadiums in the world. This market has also grown from nothing to a $1 billion industry in five years. As the trends of increased augmented reality gaming, expanded eSports marketing, and improved augmented and virtual reality technology each speed up in the ensuing decade, the videogaming market is likely going to evolve significantly yet again.

Wikis, Blogs, Social Media — The Content of the Curatorial Audience[9]

"User-generated content can be found on wikis, blogs, Twitter feeds, YouTube, Facebook, and pirate websites, as well as in virtual worlds, reactions to news stories, reactions to others' reproductions of news stories, and ratings for products...."[10] In most media, however, content is generated in a range of forms, not merely the dichotomous choices of commercial publisher or open source community. Journalism today, for example, reflects a range of modalities which — at one extreme — only publish the edited content created by their full-time professional staff and — at the

---

9. Excerpt from Jon M. Garon, *Wiki Authorship, Social Media and the Curatorial Audience*, 1 HARV. J. SPORTS & ENT. L. 95 (2010) (some text and footnotes omitted, other footnotes re-numbered).

10. Debora Halbert, *Mass Culture and the Culture of the Masses: A Manifesto for User-Generated Rights*, 11 VAND. J. ENT. & TECH. L. 921, 924 (2009).

other extreme—utilize citizen journalism with unmediated content generated from unpaid, volunteer investigators and community authors.[11]

Freelance journalists, stringers, wire copy, letters to the editor, reader comments, viewer photos, storm-watchers, Twitter reports, live-from-the-scene unverified video, and similar news sources illustrate the many ways in which even so-called traditional journalism blends the content provided by full-time professionals with a wide range of other content creators. The label "user-generated content," therefore, creates an artificial dichotomy of publisher/nonpublisher content or one-to-many versus many-to-many content consumption which does not exist in practice. The authorship of distributed content reflects a continuum from the individual to the collective, from a sole scribe to a republic. If wikis represent the paradigmatic example of many-to-many collaborative authorship, the essence of individual, user-generated authorship would likely be Internet weblogs or blogs.

For this modern *audience*—an increasingly archaic characterization—sharing knowledge among friends is an important form of user-generated information. Like wikis and blogs, social media networks rely on the participation of the users to create timely, relevant content.[12] By 2007, the top three social media sites attracted over 153 million unique visitors.

Broadly speaking, Internet users value the participation in the community as more important than the content of the contribution they are making to that community. As a result, the participatory culture has a decidedly curatorial nature. A great deal of the content is not original material but postings, re-postings, commentary and conversation, making the participant a curator of the content with which he or she interacts. The curatorial audience has become an engaged participant in the creation and dissemination of content. In many ways, however, the traditional functions usurped by the curatorial audience have been the functions of the publisher and distributor more than the author. The relatively modest participation in the wikis and other forms of content creation is dwarfed by the massive participation in the social networks, video-sharing sites, and other media that modulate how content is distributed.

Nevertheless, social media's new content modalities reflect a paradigmatic shift. "The shift from a one-to-many entertainment and information infrastructure to a many-to-many infrastructure has deep consequences on many levels. It has made possible on a massive scale content such as fan fiction, mashups, music remixes, cloud computing, and collages; blogs have transformed access to, and arguably the nature

---

11. *See* Marcy Wheeler, *How Noninstitutionalized Media Change the Relationship Between the Public and Media Coverage of Trials*, 71 Law & Contemp. Probs. 135 (2008).

12. *See* Cindy Royal, Ass'n Educ. Journalism and Mass Commc'n User-Generated Content: How Social Networking Translates to Social Capital (2008), http://citation.allacademic.com/meta/p_mla_apa_research_citation/2/7/1/1/9/pages271193/p271193-1.php.

of, information."[13] But the nature of the traffic strongly suggests that while all new media transformation is possible, it is content distribution where the greatest transformation is taking place. The curatorial audience has wrested control out of the distributors' hands. Wikis, blogs, and video posts now share the same characteristics of television, music, journalism, and academic publishing. All content distribution models incorporate some level of the many-to-many modality. The curatorial audience is a participant in every aspect of content: creation, distribution, and consumption.

In addition to casual gaming, the handheld smart phones and tablet expansion of the gaming environment has come as the traditional video console manufacturers— Nintendo, Sony, and Microsoft—are increasingly relying on online interactivity for their game play and product distribution. Companies such as Gamefly, GottaPlay, and Gamerang are now facing direct competition from the media giants Google and Facebook, while Verizon provides a robust digital subscription service for PC-based gaming. In addition, the virtual reality headset manufacturers are evolving into direct competitors of the console providers. For mobile, the Apple App Store and the Google Play Store provide digital distribution for the smartphone and tablet marketplace.

The impact of the social media on the gaming experience is further interconnectivity between these various aspects of interactive behavior and play. Companies will increasingly be seeking economic and legal mechanisms to use customer information to enhance their social networks, game subscriptions, and advertising revenues using the community aspects of social media and the interactive aspects of gaming to create a pervasive consumer experience. The separation between video games, virtual worlds, and social media may become less helpful than distinctions among social networks based on the demographic targets and financial models adopted by these interactive media conglomerates.

Notes and Questions

a. Video games are protected under copyright law, which afford protection of original works fixed in a tangible medium. The visual and auditory elements of video games are the proper subject matter of copyright under its protection of audiovisual works. The statute also affords video games protection as literary works under the statute, because the copyright statute recognizes the underlying computer code constituting a video game program as a literary work. Therefore, copyright protection extends to video games as expressive works, and the exclusive rights under copyright relevant to audiovisual or literary works all apply to video games. As with any work seeking copyright protection, the protection is limited to expression contained in the audiovisual or literary work, and does not encompass those elements within the video game that are essentially functional, or essentially constitute an idea. The unauthorized sale of identical or substantially similar video games will almost always warrant a

---

13. Daniel Gervais, *The Tangled Web of UGC: Making Copyright Sense of User-Generated Content,* 11 Vand. J. Ent. & Tech. L. 841, 842–43 (2009).

finding of copyright infringement. Examples of video game infringements include *Tetris Holding, L.L.C. v. Xio Interactive, Inc.*, 863 F. Supp. 2d 394, 415 (D.N.J. 2012) (finding both copyright and trade dress infringement despite the geometric nature of the game); *Nintendo of America, Inc. v. Brown*, 94 F.3d 652 (9th Cir. 1996) (holding the sale of identical unauthorized copies of plaintiff's video games by the defendant constituted copyright infringement); *United States v. O'Reilly*, 794 F.2d 613 (11th Cir. 1986) (stating that copyright infringement was sufficiently shown when even a portion of a defendant's video game was identical to another copyrighted video game); *Midway Mfg. Co. v. Dirkschneider*, 571 F. Supp. 282 (D. Neb. 1983) (finding that where three allegedly infringing video games were identical in virtually every detail to a another's video games, a *prima facie* case of copyright infringement was established by the plaintiff); *Midway Mfg. Co. v. Bandai-America, Inc.*, 546 F. Supp. 125 (D.N.J. 1982) (holding the elements of the defendant's "Packri Monster" video game were so similar to plaintiff's "Pac Man" game as to approach being identical); *Atari, Inc. v. Armenia, Ltd.*, 1981 U.S. Dist. LEXIS 16561 (N. D. Ill. Nov. 3, 1981) (holding defendant's *War of the Bugs* game was virtually identical in display, control, and arrangement to plaintiff's *Centipede* game as to constitute copyright infringement).

b. The Copyright Office has not always been friendly to registration for the simplest of games. For the plight of the video game *Breakout, see Atari Games Corp. v. Oman*, 979 F.2d 242 (D.C. Cir. 1992). After rejecting the copyright registration of the claim in prior district and federal courts, Judge Ruth Bader Ginsburg rejected the prior jurisprudence holding "the rejection of Breakout was unreasonable when measured against the Supreme Court's instruction that the requisite level of creativity [for copyrightability] is extremely low." *Feist Publ'n v. Rural Tel. Serv. Co.*, 499 U.S. 340, 344 (1991) (internal quotation omitted). *See also Atari, Inc. v. Amusement World, Inc.*, 547 F. Supp. 222, 224–25 (D. Md. 1981) (similarities between copyrighted elements of Asteroid and Meteors insufficient to find infringement.)

c. The tremendous growth of video games and interactivity has been fueled, at least in part, by technological growth of the game device controllers. Many of these disputes include patented innovation. *See Anascape, Ltd. v. Nintendo of Am., Inc.*, 601 F.3d 1333, 1334 (Fed. Cir. 2010), regarding the invalidity of extending a 1996 wand patent to later innovations. As is clear from *Anascape, Ltd. v. Nintendo of Am., Inc.*, years of innovation preceded Nintendo's commercial breakthrough in 2006.

Nintendo integrated the right mix of technology, style, and content to reinvigorate the console industry in 2006 with the Wii and its wireless motion-sensing wand controller. Apple achieved similar impact in the smartphone market with its touchscreen controls and gyroscope and accelerometers movement sensors in the 2007 iPhone. Activision expanded consumer options and experience with its guitar-shaped controller for the popular *Guitar Hero* franchise. The popularity and importance of controller design has led to a variety of patent claims and infringement actions. For example, Gibson Guitar sparred with Activision over the Gibson's patented guitar controller. Activision had licensed Gibson's trademarks for *Guitar Hero*, but Gibson claimed the guitar-shaped game controller also infringed Gibson's patent for the controller which allowed an interactive demo mode of the company's electric guitars. *See Activision Publ'g., Inc. v. Gibson Guitar Corp.*, 2009 U.S. Dist. LEXIS 21931 (C.D. Cal. Feb. 26, 2009).

d. Does the sale of modified devices create trademark liability? A finding of infringement depends on whether the use of the trademark would produce a likelihood of confusion as to the source of the modification device. *Compare Midway Mfg. Co. v. Strohon*, 564 F. Supp. 741 (N.D. Ill. 1983), *with Sony Comput. Entm't Am., Inc. v. Gamemasters*, 87 F. Supp. 2d 976 (N.D. Cal. 1999).

e. The sale of emulator devices does not raise the same trademark or copyright issues as modified devices. Emulator devices have been held to not infringe trademarks because there is no likelihood of confusion as to the source of the emulator. *Sony Comput. Entm't, Inc. v. Connectix Corp.*, 203 F.3d 596 (9th Cir. 2000).

B. Advertising and Endorsements

FTC Publishes Final Guides Governing Endorsements, Testimonials

(10/05/2009)

Changes Affect Testimonial Advertisements, Bloggers, Celebrity Endorsements

The Federal Trade Commission ... approved final revisions to the guidance it gives to advertisers on how to keep their endorsement and testimonial ads in line with the FTC Act.

The notice incorporates several changes to the FTC's Guides Concerning the Use of Endorsements and Testimonials in Advertising, which address endorsements by consumers, experts, organizations, and celebrities, as well as the disclosure of important connections between advertisers and endorsers. The Guides were last updated in 1980.

Under the revised Guides, advertisements that feature a consumer and convey his or her experience with a product or service as typical when that is not the case will be required to clearly disclose the results that consumers can generally expect. In contrast to the 1980 version of the Guides — which allowed advertisers to describe unusual results in a testimonial as long as they included a disclaimer such as "results not typical" — the revised Guides no longer contain this safe harbor.

The revised Guides also add new examples to illustrate the long standing principle that "material connections" (sometimes payments or free products) between advertisers and endorsers — connections that consumers would not expect — must be disclosed. These examples address what constitutes an endorsement when the message is conveyed by bloggers or other "word-of-mouth" marketers. The revised Guides specify that while decisions will be reached on a case-by-case basis, the post of a blogger who receives cash or in-kind payment to review a product is considered an endorsement. Thus, bloggers who make an endorsement must disclose the material connections they share with the seller of the product or service. Likewise, if a company refers in an advertisement to the findings of a research organization that conducted research sponsored by the company, the advertisement must disclose the connection between the advertiser and the research organization. And a paid endorsement — like any other advertisement — is deceptive if it makes false or misleading claims.

Celebrity endorsers also are addressed in the revised Guides. While the 1980 Guides did not explicitly state that endorsers as well as advertisers could be liable under the FTC Act for statements they make in an endorsement, the revised Guides reflect Commission case law and clearly state that both advertisers and endorsers may be liable for false or unsubstantiated claims made in an endorsement — or for failure to disclose material connections between the advertiser and endorsers. The revised Guides also make it clear that celebrities have a duty to disclose their relationships with advertisers when making endorsements outside the context of traditional ads, such as on talk shows or in social media.

The Guides are administrative interpretations of the law intended to help advertisers comply with the Federal Trade Commission Act; they are not binding law themselves. In any law enforcement action challenging the allegedly deceptive use of testimonials or endorsements, the Commission would have the burden of proving that the challenged conduct violates the FTC Act. . . .

Title 16: PART 255 — Guides Concerning Use of Endorsements and Testimonials in Advertising

Authority: 38 Stat. 717, as amended; 15 U.S.C. 41–58
Source: 74 FR 53138, Oct. 15, 2009, unless otherwise noted

§ 255.0 Purpose and definitions.

(a) The Guides in this part represent administrative interpretations of laws enforced by the Federal Trade Commission for the guidance of the public in conducting its affairs in conformity with legal requirements. Specifically, the Guides address the application of Section 5 of the FTC Act (15 U.S.C. 45) to the use of endorsements and testimonials in advertising. The Guides provide the basis for voluntary compliance with the law by advertisers and endorsers. Practices inconsistent with these Guides may result in corrective action by the Commission under Section 5 if, after investigation, the Commission has reason to believe that the practices fall within the scope of conduct declared unlawful by the statute.

The Guides set forth the general principles that the Commission will use in evaluating endorsements and testimonials, together with examples illustrating the application of those principles. The Guides do not purport to cover every possible use of endorsements in advertising. Whether a particular endorsement or testimonial is deceptive will depend on the specific factual circumstances of the advertisement at issue.

(b) For purposes of this part, an endorsement means any advertising message (including verbal statements, demonstrations, or depictions of the name, signature, likeness or other identifying personal characteristics of an individual or the name or seal of an organization) that consumers are likely to believe reflects the opinions, beliefs, findings, or experiences of a party other than the sponsoring advertiser, even if the views expressed by that party are identical to those of the sponsoring advertiser. The party whose opinions, beliefs, findings, or experience the message appears to reflect will be called the endorser and may be an individual, group, or institution.

(c) The Commission intends to treat endorsements and testimonials identically in the context of its enforcement of the Federal Trade Commission Act and for purposes of this part. The term endorsements is therefore generally used hereinafter to cover both terms and situations.

(d) For purposes of this part, the term product includes any product, service, company or industry.

(e) For purposes of this part, an expert is an individual, group, or institution possessing, as a result of experience, study, or training, knowledge of a particular subject, which knowledge is superior to what ordinary individuals generally acquire.

Example 1: A film critic's review of a movie is excerpted in an advertisement. When so used, the review meets the definition of an endorsement because it is viewed by readers as a statement of the critic's own opinions and not those of the film producer, distributor, or exhibitor. Any alteration in or quotation from the text of the review that does not fairly reflect its substance would be a violation of the standards set by this part because it would distort the endorser's opinion. [*See* § 255.1(b).]

Example 2: A TV commercial depicts two women in a supermarket buying a laundry detergent. The women are not identified outside the context of the advertisement. One comments to the other how clean her brand makes her family's clothes, and the other then comments that she will try it because she has not been fully satisfied with her own brand. This obvious fictional dramatization of a real life situation would not be an endorsement.

Example 3: In an advertisement for a pain remedy, an announcer who is not familiar to consumers except as a spokesman for the advertising drug company praises the drug's ability to deliver fast and lasting pain relief. He purports to speak, not on the basis of his own opinions, but rather in the place of and on behalf of the drug company. The announcer's statements would not be considered an endorsement.

Example 4: A manufacturer of automobile tires hires a well-known professional automobile racing driver to deliver its advertising message in television commercials. In these commercials, the driver speaks of the smooth ride, strength, and long life of the tires. Even though the message is not expressly declared to be the personal opinion of the driver, it may nevertheless constitute an endorsement of the tires. Many consumers will recognize this individual as being primarily a racing driver and not merely a spokesperson or announcer for the advertiser. Accordingly, they may well believe the driver would not speak for an automotive product unless he actually believed in what he was saying and had personal knowledge sufficient to form that belief. Hence, they would think the advertising message reflects the driver's personal views. This attribution of the underlying views to the driver brings the advertisement within the definition of an endorsement for purposes of this part.

Example 5: A television advertisement for a particular brand of golf balls shows a prominent and well-recognized professional golfer practicing numerous drives off the tee. This would be an endorsement by the golfer even though she makes no verbal statement in the advertisement.

Example 6: An infomercial for a home fitness system is hosted by a well-known entertainer. During the infomercial, the entertainer demonstrates the machine and states it is the most effective and easy-to-use home exercise machine that she has ever tried. Even if she is reading from a script, this statement would be an endorsement, because consumers are likely to believe it reflects the entertainer's views.

Example 7: A television advertisement for a houseware store features a well-known female comedian and a well-known male baseball player engaging in light-hearted banter about products each one intends to purchase for the other. The comedian says she will buy him a Brand X, portable, high-definition television so he can finally see the strike zone. He says he will get her a Brand Y juicer so she can make juice with all the fruit and vegetables thrown at her during her performances. The comedian and baseball player are not likely to be deemed endorsers because consumers will likely realize the individuals are not expressing their own views.

Example 8: A consumer who regularly purchases a particular brand of dog food decides one day to purchase a new, more expensive brand made by the same manufacturer. She writes in her personal blog that the change in diet has made her dog's fur noticeably softer and shinier, and that in her opinion, the new food definitely is worth the extra money. This posting would not be deemed an endorsement under the Guides.

Assume that rather than purchase the dog food with her own money, the consumer gets it for free because the store routinely tracks her purchases and its computer has generated a coupon for a free trial bag of this new brand. Again, her posting would not be deemed an endorsement under the Guides.

Assume now that the consumer joins a network marketing program under which she periodically receives various products about which she can write reviews if she wants to do so. If she receives a free bag of the new dog food through this program, her positive review would be considered an endorsement under the Guides.

§ 255.1 General considerations.

(a) Endorsements must reflect the honest opinions, findings, beliefs, or experience of the endorser. Furthermore, an endorsement may not convey any express or implied representation that would be deceptive if made directly by the advertiser. [*See* § 255.2(a) and (b) regarding substantiation of representations conveyed by consumer endorsements.

(b) The endorsement message need not be phrased in the exact words of the endorser, unless the advertisement affirmatively so represents. However, the endorsement may not be presented out of context or reworded so as to distort in any way the endorser's opinion or experience with the product. An advertiser may use an endorsement of an expert or celebrity only so long as it has good reason to believe that the endorser continues to subscribe to the views presented. An advertiser may satisfy this obligation by securing the endorser's views at reasonable intervals where reasonableness will be determined by such factors as new information on the performance or effectiveness of the product, a material alteration in the product, changes in the performance of competitors' products, and the advertiser's contract commitments.

(c) When the advertisement represents that the endorser uses the endorsed product, the endorser must have been a bona fide user of it at the time the endorsement was given. Additionally, the advertiser may continue to run the advertisement only so long as it has good reason to believe that the endorser remains a bona fide user of the product. [*See* § 255.1(b) regarding the "good reason to believe" requirement.]

(d)Advertisers are subject to liability for false or unsubstantiated statements made through endorsements, or for failing to disclose material connections between themselves and their endorsers [*see* § 255.5]. Endorsers also may be liable for statements made in the course of their endorsements.

. . . .

Example 5: A skin care products advertiser participates in a blog advertising service. The service matches up advertisers with bloggers who will promote the advertiser's products on their personal blogs. The advertiser requests that a blogger try a new body lotion and write a review of the product on her blog. Although the advertiser does not make any specific claims about the lotion's ability to cure skin conditions and the blogger does not ask the advertiser whether there is substantiation for the claim, in her review the blogger writes that the lotion cures eczema and recommends the product to her blog readers who suffer from this condition. The advertiser is subject to liability for misleading or unsubstantiated representations made through the blogger's endorsement. The blogger also is subject to liability for misleading or unsubstantiated representations made in the course of her endorsement. The blogger is also liable if she fails to disclose clearly and conspicuously that she is being paid for her services. [*See* § 255.5.]

In order to limit its potential liability, the advertiser should ensure that the advertising service provides guidance and training to its bloggers concerning the need to ensure that statements they make are truthful and substantiated. The advertiser should also monitor bloggers who are being paid to promote its products and take steps necessary to halt the continued publication of deceptive representations when they are discovered.

§ 255.2 Consumer endorsements.

(a) An advertisement employing endorsements by one or more consumers about the performance of an advertised product or service will be interpreted as representing that the product or service is effective for the purpose depicted in the advertisement. Therefore, the advertiser must possess and rely upon adequate substantiation, including, when appropriate, competent and reliable scientific evidence, to support such claims made through endorsements in the same manner the advertiser would be required to do if it had made the representation directly, *i.e.*, without using endorsements. Consumer endorsements themselves are not competent and reliable scientific evidence.

(b) An advertisement containing an endorsement relating the experience of one or more consumers on a central or key attribute of the product or service also will likely be interpreted as representing that the endorser's experience is representative of what consumers will generally achieve with the advertised product or service in actual, albeit variable, conditions of use. Therefore, an advertiser should possess and rely upon adequate substantiation for this representation. If the advertiser does not have substantiation that the endorser's experience is representative of what consumers will generally achieve, the advertisement should clearly and conspicuously disclose the generally expected performance in the depicted circumstances, and the advertiser must possess and rely on adequate substantiation for that representation.[14]

Nonetheless, the Commission cannot rule out the possibility that a strong disclaimer of typicality could be effective in the context of a particular advertisement. Although the Commission would have the burden of proof in a law enforcement action, the Commission notes that an advertiser possessing reliable empirical testing demonstrating that the net impression of its advertisement with such a disclaimer is non-deceptive will avoid the risk of the initiation of such an action in the first instance.

(c) Advertisements presenting endorsements by what are represented, directly or by implication, to be "actual consumers" should utilize actual consumers in both the audio and video, or clearly and conspicuously disclose that the persons in such advertisements are not actual consumers of the advertised product.

. . .

§ 255.5 Disclosure of material connections.

When there exists a connection between the endorser and the seller of the advertised product that might materially affect the weight or credibility of the endorsement (*i.e.*, the connection is not reasonably expected by the audience), such connection must be fully disclosed. For example, when an endorser who appears in a television commercial is neither represented in the advertisement as an expert nor is known to a significant portion of the viewing public, then the advertiser should clearly and conspicuously disclose either the payment or promise of compensation prior to and in exchange for the endorsement or the fact that the endorser knew or had reason to know or to believe that if the endorsement favored the advertised product some ben-

---

14. The Commission tested the communication of advertisements containing testimonials that clearly and prominently disclosed either "Results not typical" or the stronger "These testimonials are based on the experiences of a few people and you are not likely to have similar results." Neither disclosure adequately reduced the communication that the experiences depicted are generally representative. Based upon this research, the Commission believes that similar disclaimers regarding the limited applicability of an endorser's experience to what consumers may generally expect to achieve are unlikely to be effective.

efit, such as an appearance on television, would be extended to the endorser. Additional guidance, including guidance concerning endorsements made through other media, is provided by the examples below.

...

Example 2: A film star endorses a particular food product. The endorsement regards only points of taste and individual preference. This endorsement must, of course, comply with § 255.1; but regardless of whether the star's compensation for the commercial is a $1 million cash payment or a royalty for each product sold by the advertiser during the next year, no disclosure is required because such payments likely are ordinarily expected by viewers.

...

Example 7: A college student who has earned a reputation as a video game expert maintains a personal weblog or "blog" where he posts entries about his gaming experiences. Readers of his blog frequently seek his opinions about video game hardware and software. As it has done in the past, the manufacturer of a newly released video game system sends the student a free copy of the system and asks him to write about it on his blog. He tests the new gaming system and writes a favorable review. Because his review is disseminated via a form of consumer-generated media in which his relationship to the advertiser is not inherently obvious, readers are unlikely to know that he has received the video game system free of charge in exchange for his review of the product, and given the value of the video game system, this fact likely would materially affect the credibility they attach to his endorsement. Accordingly, the blogger should clearly and conspicuously disclose that he received the gaming system free of charge. The manufacturer should advise him at the time it provides the gaming system that this connection should be disclosed, and it should have procedures in place to try to monitor his postings for compliance.

Example 8: An online message board designated for discussions of new music download technology is frequented by MP3 player enthusiasts. They exchange information about new products, utilities, and the functionality of numerous playback devices. Unbeknownst to the message board community, an employee of a leading playback device manufacturer has been posting messages on the discussion board promoting the manufacturer's product. Knowledge of this poster's employment likely would affect the weight or credibility of her endorsement. Therefore, the poster should clearly and conspicuously disclose her relationship to the manufacturer to members and readers of the message board.

Example 9: A young man signs up to be part of a "street team" program in which points are awarded each time a team member talks to his or her friends about a particular advertiser's products. Team members can then exchange their points for prizes, such as concert tickets or electronics. These incentives would materially affect the weight or credibility of the team member's endorsements. They should be clearly and conspicuously disclosed, and the advertiser should take steps to ensure that these disclosures are being provided.

Notes and Questions

a. As highlighted in the new guidelines for endorsements and testimonials, the guides provide a form of safe harbor from a finding by the FTC that a party has committed "unfair or deceptive acts or practices" in violation of 15 U.S.C. § 45. To what extent do the new guidelines shift the standards for material or deceptive practices?

b. The FTC continues to bring actions and to send letters to social media influencers and others who promote brands online as well as to bring stronger actions for large schemes to defraud the public. A campaign comprised of ninety cease-and-desist letters illustrates their efforts:

FTC Staff Reminds Influencers and Brands to Clearly Disclose Relationship

Commission aims to improve disclosures in social media endorsements
April 19, 2017
http://www.ftc.gov/news-events/press-releases/2017/04/
ftc-staff-reminds-influencers-brands-clearly-disclose

After reviewing numerous Instagram posts by celebrities, athletes, and other influencers, Federal Trade Commission staff recently sent out more than 90 letters reminding influencers and marketers that influencers should clearly and conspicuously disclose their relationships to brands when promoting or endorsing products through social media.

The letters were informed by petitions filed by Public Citizen and affiliated organizations regarding influencer advertising on Instagram, and Instagram posts reviewed by FTC staff. They mark the first time that FTC staff has reached out directly to educate social media influencers themselves.

The FTC's Endorsement Guides provide that if there is a "material connection" between an endorser and an advertiser—in other words, a connection that might affect the weight or credibility that consumers give the endorsement—that connection should be clearly and conspicuously disclosed, unless it is already clear from the context of the communication. A material connection could be a business or family relationship, monetary payment, or the gift of a free product. Importantly, the Endorsement Guides apply to both marketers and endorsers.

In addition to providing background information on when and how marketers and influencers should disclose a material connection in an advertisement, the letters each addressed one point specific to Instagram posts—consumers viewing Instagram posts on mobile devices typically see only the first three lines of a longer post unless they click "more," which many may not do. The staff's letters informed recipients that when making endorsements on Instagram, they should disclose any material connection above the "more" button.

The letters also noted that when multiple tags, hashtags, or links are used, readers may just skip over them, especially when they appear at the end of a long post—meaning that a disclosure placed in such a string is not likely to be conspicuous.

Some of the letters addressed particular disclosures that are not sufficiently clear, pointing out that many consumers will not understand a disclosure like "#sp," "Thanks [Brand]," or "#partner" in an Instagram post to mean that the post is sponsored.

The staff's letters were sent in response to a sample of Instagram posts making endorsements or referencing brands. In sending the letters, the staff did not predetermine in every instance whether the brand mention was in fact sponsored, as opposed to an organic mention.

In addition to the Endorsement Guides, the FTC has previously addressed the need for endorsers to adequately disclose connections to brands through law enforcement actions and the staff's business education efforts. The staff also issued FTC's Endorsement Guides: What People are Asking, an informal business guidance document that answers frequently asked questions. The staff's letters to endorsers and brands enclosed copies of both guidance documents. The FTC is not publicly releasing the letters or the names of the recipients at this time.

United States of America

FEDERAL TRADE COMMISSION

Washington, D.C. 20580

Mary K. Engle
Associate Director

{*Date*}
{*Address*}

Dear {*Influencer*}:

The Federal Trade Commission is the nation's consumer protection agency. As part of our consumer protection mission, we work to educate marketers about their responsibilities under truth-in-advertising laws and standards, including the FTC's Endorsement Guides.

1. The Endorsement Guides are published in 16 C.F.R. Part 255.

2. The post is available at {*URL*}.

I am writing regarding your attached Instagram post endorsing {*product or service*}. You posted a picture of {*description of picture*}. You wrote, "{*quotation from Instagram post**}."

The FTC's Endorsement Guides state that if there is a "material connection" between an endorser and the marketer of a product—in other words, a connection that might affect the weight or credibility that consumers give the endorsement—that connection should be clearly and conspicuously disclosed, unless the connection is already clear from the context of the communication containing the endorsement. Material connections could consist of a business or family relationship, monetary payment, or the provision of free products to the endorser.

The Endorsement Guides apply to marketers and endorsers.

- [If there is a material connection between you and {*Marketer*}, that connection should be clearly and conspicuously disclosed in your endorsements.] *or*

- [It appears that you have a business relationship with {*Marketer*}. Your material connection to that company should be clearly and conspicuously disclosed in your endorsements.]

To make a disclosure both "clear" and "conspicuous," you should use unambiguous language and make the disclosure stand out. Consumers should be able to notice the disclosure easily, and not have to look for it. For example, consumers viewing posts in their Instagram streams on mobile devices typically see only the first three lines of a longer post unless they click "more," and many consumers may not click "more." Therefore, you should disclose any material connection above the "more" button. In addition, where there are multiple tags, hashtags, or links, readers may just skip over them, especially where they appear at the end of a long post.

If you are endorsing the products or services of any marketers with whom you have a material connection, you may want to review the enclosed FTC staff publication, *The FTC Endorsement Guides: What People are Asking*. I'm also enclosing a copy of the *Endorsement Guides* themselves. (Both documents are available online at business.ftc.gov.)

If you have any questions, please contact Mamie Kresses at (202) 326-2070 or mkresses@ftc.gov. Thank you.

Very truly yours,

Mary K. Engle
Associate Director
Division of Advertising Practices

Problem 15-B

Bryce has been writing a series of "new media" reviews, including music, films, and video games. As Bryce's following has grown, Bryce has begun receiving free access to subscription media websites which allows access to material on a preview basis and to avoid the sometimes substantial fees for the games, downloads, and streams. In light of the new guidelines, advise Bryce whether disclosure of the free content is required, and if so, what method of disclosure meets the FTC guidelines.

C. Scope of First Amendment Protections

Regulation of the video game industry takes two major forms. The first is government regulations. These regulations take the form of restrictions on the sale, use, or licensing of establishments that deal in video games. Over the years, as home video game systems have become more prevalent, the focus of such government regulatory efforts have moved from arcade establishments to video game retailers. Most government regulations pertaining to video games fail due to First Amendment issues, as courts have been more willing to recognize video games as a type of expression that is to be afforded the full protection of the First Amendment, and must survive a strict scrutiny constitutional analysis to be upheld.

Second, under pressure from consumer groups, the video game industry has adopted a voluntary ratings system, where games are categorized based on their content and their appropriateness for certain consumers. Many retailers have bowed to public pressure and have adopted private regulations as to the sale of such games to minors based on this ratings scheme. Again, this system is voluntary, and does not invoke any of the constitutional issues that direct government content-based regulation present. However, state efforts to regulate video games through adoption of this voluntary regulatory scheme have failed based on due process grounds.

Brown v. Entertainment Merchants Association

564 U.S. 786 (U.S. 2011)

JUSTICE SCALIA delivered the opinion of the Court.

We consider whether a California law imposing restrictions on violent video games comports with the First Amendment.

California Assembly Bill 1179 (2005), Cal. Civ. Code Ann. §§ 1746–1746.5 (West 2009) (Act), prohibits the sale or rental of "violent video games" to minors, and requires their packaging to be labeled "18." The Act covers games "in which the range of options available to a player includes killing, maiming, dismembering, or sexually assaulting an image of a human being, if those acts are depicted" in a manner that "[a] reasonable person, considering the game as a whole, would find appeals to a deviant or morbid interest of minors," that is "patently offensive to prevailing standards in the community as to what is suitable for minors," and that "causes the game, as a whole, to lack serious literary, artistic, political, or scientific value for minors." § 1746(d)(1)(A). Violation of the Act is punishable by a civil fine of up to $1,000. § 1746.3....

California correctly acknowledges that video games qualify for First Amendment protection. The Free Speech Clause exists principally to protect discourse on public matters, but we have long recognized that it is difficult to distinguish politics from entertainment, and dangerous to try. "Everyone is familiar with instances of propaganda through fiction. What is one man's amusement, teaches another's doctrine." *Winters v. New York*, 333 U.S. 507, 510 (1948). Like the protected books, plays, and movies that preceded them, video games communicate ideas—and even social messages—through many familiar literary devices (such as characters, dialogue, plot, and music) and through features distinctive to the medium (such as the player's interaction with the virtual world). That suffices to confer First Amendment protection. Under our Constitution, "esthetic and moral judgments about art and literature ... are for the individual to make, not for the Government to decree, even with the mandate or approval of a majority." *United States v. Playboy Entertainment Group, Inc.,* 529 U.S. 803, 818 (2000). And whatever the challenges of applying the Constitution to ever-advancing technology, "the basic principles of freedom of speech and the press, like the First Amendment's command, do not vary" when a new and different medium for communication appears. *Joseph Burstyn, Inc. v. Wilson,* 343 U.S. 495, 503 (1952).

The most basic of those principles is this: "[A]s a general matter, ... government has no power to restrict expression because of its message, its ideas, its subject matter, or its content." *Ashcroft v. American Civil Liberties Union,* 535 U.S. 564, 573 (2002) (internal quotation marks omitted). There are of course exceptions. "'From 1791 to the present,' ... the First Amendment has 'permitted restrictions upon the content of speech in a few limited areas,' and has never 'include[d] a freedom to disregard these traditional limitations.' *United States v. Stevens,* 559 U.S. ___, ___, 130 S. Ct. 1577 (2010) (quoting *R.A.V. v. St. Paul,* 505 U.S. 377, 382–383 (1992)). These limited areas — such as obscenity, *Roth v. United States,* 354 U.S. 476, 483 (1957), incitement, *Brandenburg v. Ohio,* 395 U.S. 444, 447–449 (1969) *(per curiam)*, and fighting words, *Chaplinsky v. New Hampshire,* 315 U.S. 568, 572 (1942) — represent "well-defined and narrowly limited classes of speech, the prevention and punishment of which have never been thought to raise any Constitutional problem," *id.,* at 571–572.

Last Term, in *Stevens,* we held that new categories of unprotected speech may not be added to the list by a legislature that concludes certain speech is too harmful to be tolerated. *Stevens* concerned a federal statute purporting to criminalize the creation, sale, or possession of certain depictions of animal cruelty. *See* 18 U.S.C. §48 (amended 2010). The statute covered depictions "in which a living animal is intentionally maimed, mutilated, tortured, wounded, or killed" if that harm to the animal was illegal where the "the creation, sale, or possession t[ook] place," §48(c)(1). A saving clause largely borrowed from our obscenity jurisprudence, exempted depictions with "serious religious, political, scientific, educational, journalistic, historical, or artistic value," §48(b). We held that statute to be an impermissible content-based restriction on speech. There was no American tradition of forbidding the *depiction of* animal cruelty — though States have long had laws against *committing* it.

The Government argued in *Stevens* that lack of a historical warrant did not matter; that it could create new categories of unprotected speech by applying a "simple balancing test" that weighs the value of a particular category of speech against its social costs and then punishes that category of speech if it fails the test. We emphatically rejected that "startling and dangerous" proposition. "Maybe there are some categories of speech that have been historically unprotected, but have not yet been specifically identified or discussed as such in our case law." *Id.,* at ___, 130 S. Ct. 1577, 176. But without persuasive evidence that a novel restriction on content is part of a long (if heretofore unrecognized) tradition of proscription, a legislature may not revise the "judgment [of] the American people," embodied in the First Amendment, "that the benefits of its restrictions on the Government outweigh the costs." *Id.,* at ___, 130 S. Ct. 1577, 176.

That holding controls this case. As in *Stevens*, California has tried to make violent-speech regulation look like obscenity regulation by appending a saving clause required for the latter. That does not suffice. Our cases have been clear that the obscenity exception to the First Amendment does not cover whatever a legislature finds shocking, but only depictions of "sexual conduct," *Miller* [*v. California*, 413 U.S. 15 (1973)], *supra*, at 24.

Stevens was not the first time we have encountered and rejected a State's attempt to shoehorn speech about violence into obscenity. In *Winters*, we considered a New York criminal statute "forbid[ding] the massing of stories of bloodshed and lust in such a way as to incite to crime against the person," 333 U.S., at 514. The New York Court of Appeals upheld the provision as a law against obscenity. "[T]here can be no more precise test of written indecency or obscenity," it said, "than the continuing and changeable experience of the community as to what types of books are likely to bring about the corruption of public morals or other analogous injury to the public order." *Id.*, at 514. That is of course the same expansive view of governmental power to abridge the freedom of speech based on interest-balancing that we rejected in *Stevens*. Our opinion in *Winters*, which concluded that the New York statute failed a heightened vagueness standard applicable to restrictions upon speech entitled to First Amendment protection, made clear that violence is not part of the obscenity that the Constitution permits to be regulated. The speech reached by the statute contained "no indecency or obscenity in any sense heretofore known to the law." *Id.*, at 519.

Because speech about violence is not obscene, it is of no consequence that California's statute mimics the New York statute regulating obscenity-for-minors that we upheld in *Ginsberg v. New York*, 390 U.S. 629 (1968). That case approved a prohibition on the sale to minors of *sexual* material that would be obscene from the perspective of a child. We held that the legislature could "adjus[t] the definition of obscenity 'to social realities by permitting the appeal of this type of material to be assessed in terms of the sexual interests ...' of ... minors." *Id.*, at 638. And because "obscenity is not protected expression," the New York statute could be sustained so long as the legislature's judgment that the proscribed materials were harmful to children "was not irrational." 390 U.S., at 641.

The California Act is something else entirely. It does not adjust the boundaries of an existing category of unprotected speech to ensure that a definition designed for adults is not uncritically applied to children. California does not argue that it is empowered to prohibit selling offensively violent works *to adults*—and it is wise not to, since that is but a hair's breadth from the argument rejected in *Stevens*. Instead, it wishes to create a wholly new category of content-based regulation that is permissible only for speech directed at children.

That is unprecedented and mistaken. "[M]inors are entitled to a significant measure of First Amendment protection, and only in relatively narrow and well-defined circumstances may government bar public dissemination of protected materials to them." *Erznoznik v. Jacksonville*, 422 U.S. 205, 212–213 (1975). No doubt a State possesses legitimate power to protect children from harm, but that does not include a free-floating power to restrict the ideas to which children may be exposed. "Speech that is neither obscene as to youths nor subject to some other legitimate proscription cannot be suppressed solely to protect the young from ideas or images that a legislative body thinks unsuitable for them." *Erznoznik, supra,* at 213–214.

California's argument would fare better if there were a longstanding tradition in this country of specially restricting children's access to depictions of violence, but there is none. Certainly the *books* we give children to read—or read to them when they are younger—contain no shortage of gore. Grimm's Fairy Tales, for example, are grim indeed. As her just deserts for trying to poison Snow White, the wicked queen is made to dance in red hot slippers "till she fell dead on the floor, a sad example of envy and jealousy." THE COMPLETE BROTHERS GRIMM FAIRY TALES 198 (2006 ed.). Cinderella's evil stepsisters have their eyes pecked out by doves. And Hansel and Gretel (children!) kill their captor by baking her in an oven.

High-school reading lists are full of similar fare. Homer's Odysseus blinds Polyphemus the Cyclops by grinding out his eye with a heated stake. In the Inferno, Dante and Virgil watch corrupt politicians struggle to stay submerged beneath a lake of boiling pitch, lest they be skewered by devils above the surface. And Golding's Lord of the Flies recounts how a schoolboy called Piggy is savagely murdered *by other children* while marooned on an island. W. GOLDING, LORD OF THE FLIES 208–209 (1997 ed.).[15]

This is not to say that minors' consumption of violent entertainment has never encountered resistance. In the 1800s, dime novels depicting crime and "penny dreadfuls" (named for their price and content) were blamed in some quarters for juvenile delinquency. When motion pictures came along, they became the villains instead.

---

15. Justice Alito accuses us of pronouncing that playing violent video games "is not different in 'kind'" from reading violent literature. Well of course it is different in kind, but not in a way that causes the provision and viewing of violent video games, unlike the provision and reading of books, not to be expressive activity and hence not to enjoy First Amendment protection. Reading Dante is unquestionably more cultured and intellectually edifying than playing Mortal Kombat. But these cultural and intellectual differences are not constitutional ones. Crudely violent video games, tawdry TV shows, and cheap novels and magazines are no less forms of speech than The Divine Comedy, and restrictions upon them must survive strict scrutiny—a question to which we devote our attention in Part III, *infra.* Even if we can see in them "nothing of any possible value to society..., they are as much entitled to the protection of free speech as the best of literature." Winters v. New York, 333 U.S. 507, 510 (1948).

[Justice Alito, Dissenting, stated the following:

In the view of the Court, all those concerned about the effects of violent video games—federal and state legislators, educators, social scientists, and parents—are unduly fearful, for violent video games really present no serious problem. Spending hour upon hour controlling the actions of a character who guns down scores of innocent victims is not different in "kind" from reading a description of violence in a work of literature.

The Court is sure of this; I am not. There are reasons to suspect that the experience of playing violent video games just might be very different from reading a book, listening to the radio, or watching a movie or a television show.

Id. at 180 L. Ed. 2d 708, 724 (U.S. 2011).]

"The days when the police looked upon dime novels as the most dangerous of text-books in the school for crime are drawing to a close.... They say that the moving picture machine ... tends even more than did the dime novel to turn the thoughts of the easily influenced to paths which sometimes lead to prison." Moving Pictures as Helps to Crime, N.Y. Times, Feb. 21, 1909, quoted in Brief for Cato Institute, at 8. For a time, our Court did permit broad censorship of movies because of their capacity to be "used for evil," *see Mutual Film Corp. v. Industrial Comm'n of Ohio*, 236 U.S. 230, 242 (1915), but we eventually reversed course, *Joseph Burstyn, Inc.*, 343 U.S., at 502. Radio dramas were next, and then came comic books. Many in the late 1940s and early 1950s blamed comic books for fostering a "preoccupation with violence and horror" among the young, leading to a rising juvenile crime rate. But efforts to convince Congress to restrict comic books failed. And, of course, after comic books came television and music lyrics.

California claims that video games present special problems because they are "interactive," in that the player participates in the violent action on screen and determines its outcome. The latter feature is nothing new: Since at least the publication of THE ADVENTURES OF YOU: SUGARCANE ISLAND in 1969, young readers of choose-your-own-adventure stories have been able to make decisions that determine the plot by following instructions about which page to turn to. As for the argument that video games enable participation in the violent action, that seems to us more a matter of degree than of kind. As Judge Posner has observed, all literature is interactive. "[T]he better it is, the more interactive. Literature when it is successful draws the reader into the story, makes him identify with the characters, invites him to judge them and quarrel with them, to experience their joys and sufferings as the reader's own." *American Amusement Machine Assn. v. Kendrick*, 244 F.3d 572, 577 (7th Cir. 2001) (striking down a similar restriction on violent video games).

Justice Alito has done considerable independent research to identify video games in which "the violence is astounding." "Victims are dismembered, decapitated, disemboweled, set on fire, and chopped into little pieces.... Blood gushes, splatters, and pools." Justice Alito recounts all these disgusting video games in order to disgust us—but disgust is not a valid basis for restricting expression. And the same is true of Justice Alito's description of those video games he has discovered that have a racial or ethnic motive for their violence—" 'ethnic cleansing' [of] ... African Americans, Latinos, or Jews." To what end does he relate this? Does it somehow increase the "aggressiveness" that California wishes to suppress? Who knows? But it does arouse the reader's ire, and the reader's desire to put an end to this horrible message. Thus, ironically, Justice Alito's argument highlights the precise danger posed by the California Act: that the *ideas* expressed by speech—whether it be violence, or gore, or racism—and not its objective effects, may be the real reason for governmental proscription.

Because the Act imposes a restriction on the content of protected speech, it is invalid unless California can demonstrate that it passes strict scrutiny—that is, unless it is justified by a compelling government interest and is narrowly drawn to serve that interest. *R.A.V.*, 505 U.S., at 395. The State must specifically identify an "actual problem" in need of solving, *Playboy*, 529 U.S., at 822–823, and the curtailment of free speech must be actually necessary to the solution, *see R.A.V., supra*, at 395. That is a demanding standard. "It is rare that a regulation restricting speech because of its content will ever be permissible." *Playboy, supra*, at 818.

California cannot meet that standard. At the outset, it acknowledges that it cannot show a direct causal link between violent video games and harm to minors. Rather, relying upon our decision in *Turner Broadcasting System, Inc. v. FCC*, 512 U.S. 622 (1994), the State claims that it need not produce such proof because the legislature can make a predictive judgment that such a link exists, based on competing psychological studies. But reliance on *Turner Broadcasting* is misplaced. That decision applied *intermediate scrutiny* to a content-neutral regulation. California's burden is much higher, and because it bears the risk of uncertainty, ambiguous proof will not suffice.

The State's evidence is not compelling. California relies primarily on the research of Dr. Craig Anderson and a few other research psychologists whose studies purport to show a connection between exposure to violent video games and harmful effects on children. These studies have been rejected by every court to consider them, and with good reason: They do not prove that violent video games *cause* minors to *act* aggressively (which would at least be a beginning). Instead, "[n]early all of the research is based on correlation, not evidence of causation, and most of the studies suffer from significant, admitted flaws in methodology." *Video Software Dealers Assn.* [*v. St. Louis County*], 556 F.3d at 964 [8th Cir. 2003]). They show at best some correlation between exposure to violent entertainment and minuscule real-world effects, such as children's feeling more aggressive or making louder noises in the few minutes after playing a violent game than after playing a nonviolent game.

Even taking for granted Dr. Anderson's conclusions that violent video games produce some effect on children's feelings of aggression, those effects are both small and indistinguishable from effects produced by other media. In his testimony in a similar lawsuit, Dr. Anderson admitted that the "effect sizes" of children's exposure to violent video games are "about the same" as that produced by their exposure to violence on television. And he admits that the *same* effects have been found when children watch cartoons starring Bugs Bunny or the Road Runner, or when they play video games like Sonic the Hedgehog that are rated "E" (appropriate for all ages), or even when they "vie[w] a picture of a gun."

Of course, California has (wisely) declined to restrict Saturday morning cartoons, the sale of games rated for young children, or the distribution of pictures of guns. The consequence is that its regulation is wildly underinclusive when judged against its asserted justification, which in our view is alone enough to defeat it. Underinclusiveness raises serious doubts about whether the government is in fact pursuing the interest it invokes, rather than disfavoring a particular speaker or viewpoint. Here, California has singled out the purveyors of video games for disfavored treatment—at least when compared to booksellers, cartoonists, and movie producers—and has given no persuasive reason why.

The Act is also seriously underinclusive in another respect—and a respect that renders irrelevant the contentions of the concurrence and the dissents that video games are qualitatively different from other portrayals of violence. The California Legislature is perfectly willing to leave this dangerous, mind-altering material in the hands of children so long as one parent (or even an aunt or uncle) says it's OK. And there are not even any requirements as to how this parental or avuncular relationship is to be verified; apparently the child's or putative parent's, aunt's, or uncle's say-so suffices. That is not how one addresses a serious social problem.

California claims that the Act is justified in aid of parental authority: By requiring that the purchase of violent video games can be made only by adults, the Act ensures that parents can decide what games are appropriate. At the outset, we note our doubts that punishing third parties for conveying protected speech to children *just in case* their parents disapprove of that speech is a proper governmental means of aiding parental authority. Accepting that position would largely vitiate the rule that "only in relatively narrow and well-defined circumstances may government bar public dissemination of protected materials to [minors]." *Erznoznik*, 422 U.S., at 212–213.

But leaving that aside, California cannot show that the Act's restrictions meet a substantial need of parents who wish to restrict their children's access to violent video games but cannot do so. The video-game industry has in place a voluntary rating system designed to inform consumers about the content of games. The system, implemented by the Entertainment Software Rating Board (ESRB), assigns age-specific ratings to each video game submitted: EC (Early Childhood); E (Everyone); E10+ (Everyone 10 and older); T (Teens); M (17 and older); and AO (Adults Only—18 and older). The Video Software Dealers Association encourages retailers to prominently display information about the ESRB system in their stores; to refrain from renting or selling adults-only games to minors; and to rent or sell "M" rated games to minors only with parental consent. In 2009, the Federal Trade Commission (FTC) found that, as a result of this system, "the video game industry outpaces the movie and music industries" in "(1) restricting target-marketing of mature-rated products to children; (2) clearly and prominently disclosing rating information; and (3) restricting children's access to mature-rated products at retail." FTC, Report to Congress, Marketing Violent Entertainment to Children 30 (Dec. 2009). This system does much to ensure that minors cannot purchase seriously violent games on their own, and that parents who care about the matter can readily evaluate the games their children bring home. Filling the remaining modest gap in concerned-parents' control can hardly be a compelling state interest.

And finally, the Act's purported aid to parental authority is vastly overinclusive. Not all of the children who are forbidden to purchase violent video games on their own have parents who *care* whether they purchase violent video games. While some of the legislation's effect may indeed be in support of what some parents of the restricted children actually want, its entire effect is only in support of what the State thinks parents *ought* to want. This is not the narrow tailoring to "assisting parents" that restriction of First Amendment rights requires.

...

California's effort to regulate violent video games is the latest episode in a long series of failed attempts to censor violent entertainment for minors. While we have pointed out above that some of the evidence brought forward to support the harmfulness of video games is unpersuasive, we do not mean to demean or disparage the concerns that underlie the attempt to regulate them—concerns that may and doubtless do prompt a good deal of parental oversight. We have no business passing judgment on the view of the California Legislature that violent video games (or, for that matter, any other forms of speech) corrupt the young or harm their moral development. Our task is only to say whether or not such works constitute a "well-defined and narrowly limited clas[s] of speech, the prevention and punishment of which have never been thought to raise any Constitutional problem," *Chaplinsky*, 315 U.S., at 571–572, (the answer plainly is no); and if not, whether the regulation of such works is justified by that high degree of necessity we have described as a compelling state interest (it is not). Even where the protection of children is the object, the constitutional limits on governmental action apply.

California's legislation straddles the fence between (1) addressing a serious social problem and (2) helping concerned parents control their children. Both ends are legitimate, but when they affect First Amendment rights they must be pursued by means that are neither seriously underinclusive nor seriously overinclusive. As a means of protecting children from portrayals of violence, the legislation is seriously underinclusive, not only because it excludes portrayals other than video games, but also because it permits a parental or avuncular veto. And as a means of assisting concerned parents it is seriously over inclusive because it abridges the First Amendment rights of young people whose parents (and aunts and uncles) think violent video games are a harmless pastime. And the overbreadth in achieving one goal is not cured by the underbreadth in achieving the other. Legislation such as this, which is neither fish nor fowl, cannot survive strict scrutiny.

We affirm the judgment below.

Twitch Interactive, Inc., v. John and Jane Does 1 Through 100
2019 WL 3718582 (N.D. Cal. 08/07/2019)

ORDER GRANTING PLAINTIFF'S EX PARTE APPLICATION FOR LEAVE TO SERVE THIRD-PARTY SUBPOENAS

Plaintiff Twitch Interactive, Inc. brings claims against numerous Doe defendants who allegedly coordinated to post racist, misogynistic, and violent content on its online video platform. Twitch has determined certain addresses associated with this activity, but it has been unable to identify the actors through its own efforts. Twitch now applies ex parte for limited expedited discovery and leave to serve subpoenas on Twitter, Google, Microsoft/Hotmail, Discord, Verizon, Comcast Cable Communications L.L.C., Contina, Charter Communications Inc., Optimum Online, Suddenlink

Communications, and OVH Hosting to learn the Doe the identities of the Doe defendants. For reasons stated below, I will grant the application.

BACKGROUND

Twitch is an online streaming video platform that operates www.twitch.tv. Its members can stream videos in real time and share content that predominantly features video games, sports, and creative arts. While users do not have to register to watch videos on Twitch, they must register an account if they wish to stream. To register an account on Twitch, the user must agree to be bound by Twitch's Terms of Service, Community Guidelines, Developer Services Agreement, and Trademark Guidelines. Twitch has been an Amazon subsidiary since 2014.

On June 14, 2019, Twitch filed a complaint alleging that a group of unnamed defendants "flooded the Twitch.tv directory for the game Artifact with dozens of videos that violated Twitch's policies and terms." These videos included a video of the March 2019 Christchurch mosque attack, pornography, copyrighted movies and televisions shows, and racist and misogynistic videos. Though Twitch took down the prohibited content and permanently suspended the accounts that posted it, "the offensive videos quickly reappeared using new accounts." Twitch contends that the defendants used "bots" to manipulate the viewer counts of the offensive videos, driving traffic to this material. The defendants used websites such as Google, Discord, and Weebly to communicate about and coordinate their efforts. After these platforms banned the defendants, they set up additional Discord groups and used a website, www.artifact streams.com, which features Twitch's registered "GLITCH" mark prominently. The defendants also created the Twitter account @TwitchToS, which uses Twitch's registered "TWITCH" mark.

In response to these activities, Twitch suspended streaming for all new Twitch accounts, modified its systems to require two-factor authentication for all streaming accounts, and spent time and money researching and taking action against the defendants. In doing so, it "expended significant resources."

On June 27, 2019, Twitch applied ex parte for leave to serve Internet Service Providers (ISPs) and social media companies associated with the defendants. Application for Leave to Serve a Third-Party Subpoena. Twitch seeks the identities of the Doe defendants, which it will use to effectuate service.

LEGAL STANDARD

Although Federal Rule of Civil Procedure 26(d)(1) generally prohibits discovery prior to a Rule 26(f) conference, parties may conduct early discovery with a court order. Fed. R. Civ. P. 26(d)(1). Courts in the Ninth Circuit apply the "good cause" standard to determine whether such an order is appropriate. "Good cause exists where the need for expedited discovery, in consideration of the administration of justice, outweighs the prejudice to the responding party." *UMG Recordings, Inc. v. Doe*, No. C 08-1193 SBA, 2008 WL 4104214, at *5 (N.D. Cal. Sept. 3, 2008) (compiling cases).

In applying this standard, courts consider whether the plaintiff has (i) "identif[ied] the missing party with sufficient specificity such that the Court can determine that defendant is a real person or entity who could be sued in federal court"; (ii) "identif[ied] all previous steps taken to locate the elusive defendant"; (iii) "establish[ed] to the Court's satisfaction that [the suit] could withstand a motion to dismiss"; and (iv) filed a request showing "a reasonable likelihood that the discovery process will lead to identifying information about defendant that would make service of process possible." *Columbia Ins. Co. v. Seescandy.com*, 185 F.R.D. 573, 578–80 (N.D. Cal. 1999). Courts have granted early discovery where the plaintiff seeks facts that would make service on the defendant possible.

DISCUSSION

I. GOOD CAUSE FOR EARLY DISCOVERY

There is good cause for early discovery here because (i) Twitch has identified the defendants with sufficient particularity, (ii) Twitch has taken steps to locate the individuals, (iii) the complaint is likely to survive a motion to dismiss, and (iv) early discovery will likely lead to the defendants' identities.

A. Identifying Defendant with Sufficient Specificity

Under the first factor, a plaintiff must identify the unknown party with sufficient specificity such that the court can determine that the defendant is a real person or entity that could be sued in federal court.

Twitch has sufficiently established that the Doe defendants are real persons or entities. Twitch claims that the defendants posted prohibit content on Twitch's platform, violated Twitch's terms by creating new accounts after a permanent suspension, used bots to manipulate their viewer counts and drive traffic to their channels, infringed on Twitch's registered trademarks, and used third-party websites to coordinate posting prohibited content. Carl Hester, a Senior Incident Response Engineer at Twitch, conducted an investigation into the accounts that streamed the prohibited material. In the course of this investigation, Hester identified Twitch user "Skel," a Gmail and Hotmail address linked to Skel's Twitch accounts, and the IP addresses associated with the accounts. Additionally, Twitch has identified "thousands" of IP addresses connected with the accounts streaming prohibited content. Several of these IP addresses were searched using "a reverse WhoIs tool," which provides ISP and geolocation information for IP addresses. This search identified the IP addresses geolocated in the United States and found they were associated with the following internet service providers: Verizon, Comcast, Contina, Charter, Optimum, and Suddenlink. The search additionally identified several IP addresses associated with a Canadian cloud computing company named OVH.

Twitch has also made a sufficient showing that the Doe defendants are subject to specific personal jurisdiction in California.

B. Previous Steps Taken to Identify Defendants

To be entitled to early discovery, a plaintiff must have taken sufficient steps to locate the defendant prior to petitioning the court.

Twitch took numerous steps to identify the defendants as part of its internal investigation into the May 2019 attack. It identified a Twitch user "Skel," and located two email addresses and two IP addresses connected with Skel's accounts. Twitch identified the IP addresses associated with accounts that streamed prohibited content, conducted a reverse IP address lookup using WhoIs, and identified the following ISPs: Verizon, Comcast, Contina, Charter, Optimum, Suddenlink, and OVH (a Canadian cloud computing company). Twitch identified the website that the defendants allegedly used to coordinate their attacks and found an email address associated with the website. Twitch also located the Discord groups the defendants used. Finally, Twitch's counsel sent a copy of the complaint to the email addresses associated with Skel's accounts and the website, asking defendants to identify themselves.

These efforts are sufficient to satisfy this factor.

C. Ability to Withstand Motion to Dismiss

Next, a plaintiff must demonstrate that the claims could likely withstand a motion to dismiss by "mak[ing] some showing that an act giving rise to civil liability actually occurred and that the discovery is aimed at revealing specific identifying features of the person or entity who committed that act." Seescandy, 185 F.R.D. at 580. I assess each cause of action in turn.

1. Federal Trademark Infringement

To state a claim for trademark infringement, a plaintiff must allege "(1) ownership of a valid mark (i.e., a protectable interest), and (2) that the alleged infringer's use of the mark is likely to cause confusion, or to cause mistake, or to deceive consumers." *Rise Basketball Skill Development, L.L.C. v. K Mart Corp.*, No. 16-cv-04895-WHO, 2017 WL 2775030, at *3 (N.D. Cal. June 27, 2017) (citing *Reno Air Racing Ass'n, Inc. v. McCord*, 452 F.3d 1126, 1134 (9th Cir. 2006).

Twitch has submitted copies of its U.S. Patent and Trademark Office registrations for the "GLITCH" and "TWITCH" marks. Twitch contends that it "has attained substantial goodwill and strong recognition in the GLITCH and TWITCH marks and the marks have come to be exclusively associated with Twitch." Twitch has also alleged that the defendants use the GLITCH mark on www.artifactstreams.com and use the TWITCH mark on Twitter account @TwitchTOS. These allegations are likely sufficient to survive a motion to dismiss.

2. Breach of Contract

To state a claim for breach of contract, a plaintiff must plead: "(1) the contract, (2) plaintiff's performance or excuse for nonperformance, (3) defendant's breach, and (4) damage to plaintiff therefrom." *Kaar v. Wells Fargo Bank, N.A.*, No. C 16-01290 WHA, 2016 WL 3068396, at *1 (N.D. Cal. June 1, 2016) (citation omitted).

Twitch's breach of contract claim is based on its terms of service agreement. Twitch alleges that it has "dutifully performed its obligations pursuant to the Terms." To register for a Twitch account, users "must affirmatively accept the Terms." Twitch alleges that the defendants violated the terms by streaming prohibited content, manipulating their identifying information, impairing other users' enjoyment of Twitch, and using bots to manipulate their statistics on Twitch. Twitch asserts that defendants' breach caused it lost profits and led it to expend resources to combat the attack. These allegations are likely sufficient to survive a motion to dismiss.

3. Trespass to Chattels

To state a claim for trespass to chattels, a plaintiff stating a claim must allege that "(1) the defendant intentionally and without authorization interfered with the plaintiff's possessory interest in the computer system and (2) the defendant's unauthorized [use] proximately caused damage to the plaintiff." *In re Facebook Internet Tracking Litig.*, 263 F. Supp. 3d 836, 842 (N.D. Cal. 2017) (citation omitted). "California case law has long recognized that consent to enter may be limited and that a trespass claim may lie when the scope of consent is exceeded." *In re Apple Inc. Device Performance Litig.*, 347 F. Supp. 3d 434, 455 (N.D. Cal. 2018).

Twitch alleges that the Doe defendants streamed pornography, copyrighted movies and television shows, racist and misogynistic videos, and a video of the March 2019 Christchurch mosque attack. Twitch contends its terms of service "expressly prohibit anyone who access or uses the Twitch Services from posting obscene, pornographic, violent, or otherwise harmful content." Defendants' unauthorized use allegedly caused Twitch to suffer the damages referenced above. These allegations are likely sufficient to survive a motion to dismiss.

4. Fraud

"To state a fraud claim under California law, a plaintiff must allege with particularity: (1) false representations as to material fact; (2) knowledge of its falsity; (3) intent to defraud; (4) actual and justifiable reliance; and (5) resulting damage." *Bonete v. World Savings Bank, FSB*, No. 15-01219 JSW, 2015 WL 12990148, at *6 (N.D. Cal. Aug. 11, 2015) (citation omitted). To comply with Federal Rule of Civil Procedure 9(b), a party alleging fraud "must state with particularity" the circumstances constituting fraud. Fed. R. Civ. P. 9(b). "Averments of fraud must be accompanied by 'the who, what, when, where, and how' of the misconduct charged." *Vess v. Ciba-Geigy Corp. USA*, 317 F.3d 1097, 1106 (9th Cir. 2003).

Twitch alleges that the defendants committed fraud when they agreed to abide by Twitch's terms of service with no intention of doing so. After Twitch banned the defendants from its platform, they "misrepresented and concealed their identities and other personally identifying information (such as IP addresses)" to create new Twitch accounts and repost the offending material. Twitch justifiably relied on these representations when it allowed the defendants to access its services. These allegations are likely sufficient to survive a motion to dismiss.

D. Likelihood that Discovery Will Lead to Identifying Information

Last, Twitch must show "a reasonable likelihood that the discovery process will lead to identifying information about defendant that would make service of process possible." Twitch has submitted copies of the subpoenas it intends to send, which request "physical address, email address, secondary or recovery email address, records of session times and duration including logs of IP addresses, length of service including account [start] date, any other subscriber number or identity including any temporarily assigned network address; and means and source of payment, including any credit card or bank account numbers." There is a reasonable likelihood that in response to these subpoenas, Verizon, Comcast, Contina, Charter, Optimum, Suddenlink, and OVH will provide the names and addresses of the individuals involved in the May 2019 attack. It is also reasonably likely that Google, Discord, Microsoft, and Twitter will provide information identifying the individuals associated with @Twitch-TOS, the Discord groups, Skel's email addresses, and the email address associated with www.artifactstreams.com. That said, Twitch should be able to obtain information sufficient to identify and serve process on the Doe defendants without subpoenaing credit card or bank account numbers. It has not shown the need for this information at this stage; Twitch shall amend the subpoenas to omit these requests.

II. PROTECTIVE ORDER

"[U]nder Rule 26(c), the Court may sua sponte grant a protective order for good cause shown." *McCoy v. Southwest Airlines Co. Inc.*, 211 F.R.D. 381, 385 (C.D. Cal. 2002). Courts in this district have granted protective orders where the plaintiff sought early discovery to identify an IP address subscriber. This case does not involve pornographic content, but it does involve allegations of inflammatory conduct. In addition, the mere fact that an individual is the ISP subscriber does not necessarily mean he or she is the infringing party.

Given the nature of the alleged conduct, I will grant a protective order to the limited extent that any information regarding the defendants by Twitch from the ISPs and social media companies will be treated as confidential for a limited duration. Specifically, Twitch may not publicly disclose this information until the Doe defendants have the opportunity to file an application in this Court to be allowed to proceed in this litigation anonymously and I have ruled on that application. If the Doe defendants fail to file an application for leave to proceed anonymously within 30 days after their information is disclosed to Twitch's counsel, this limited protective order will expire. If the Doe defendants include identifying information within their requests to proceed anonymously, I find good cause to order the papers filed under seal until I have the opportunity to rule on the request. If the Doe defendants include identifying information with their requests to proceed anonymously and the request is placed under seal, I will direct Doe defendants to submit a copy of the under-seal request to Twitch and ensure that Twitch has time to respond.

CONCLUSION

For good cause shown, Twitch's ex parte application for leave to file third-party subpoenas is GRANTED.

Mil-Spec Monkey, Inc. v. Activision Blizzard, Inc.

74 F. Supp. 3d 1134 (N.D. Cal. 2014)

I. INTRODUCTION

In this action arising from claims of copyright and trademark infringement, plaintiff Mil-Spec Monkey, Inc. ("MSM") avers that the video game *Call of Duty: Ghosts,* created and published by defendant Activision Publishing, Inc. and Activision Blizzard, Inc. (collectively, "Activision") makes illicit use of MSM's "angry monkey" trademark, among the most popular morale patch designs the company promotes and sells online and through third parties. Activision, which bears no relationship to MSM, includes in *Ghosts* an image visually similar to MSM's "angry monkey" mark as a patch players may select to place on their avatars' uniforms in its multi-player game mode. When selected by players, the *Ghosts* "angry monkey" patch appears at various points during game play. It moreover appears in Activision's pre-release promotional trailer for *Ghosts'* multi-player edition. Because *Ghosts* is an expressive work, and its disputed design bears some level of artistic relevance to the game and is not explicitly misleading—meeting both prongs of the test set forth originally in *Rogers v. Grimaldi*, 875 F.2d 994 (2d Cir.1989), and adopted by the Ninth Circuit—Activision's motion must be granted [dismissing all trademark and unfair competition claims].

II. BACKGROUND

A. *MSM and the "Angry Monkey" Morale Patch Design.*

MSM is a military supply and outfitting company that specializes in the design and creation of unofficial military morale patches. A morale patch, as MSM defines it, is any wearable patch that military personnel are not authorized to wear or are strictly prohibited from wearing. According to MSM, members of the military frequently wear morale patches in unofficial contexts to express a sense of personal identity. Its morale patch bearing the disputed "angry monkey" mark is one of MSM's most well-known and popular patch designs.

MSM has since at least 2007 been selling a variety of "angry monkey" patches through its website and online store, in addition to promoting it online, at tradeshows, and via broad distribution of printed and electronic promotional materials. From MSM's "extensive use and promotion of its Angry Monkey Mark," the company avers, "such mark enjoys considerable goodwill, widespread recognition, and secondary meaning in commerce, and has become associated with MSM as its single source of origin."

B. *Activision and Call of Duty: Ghosts.*

Activision designs, publishes, and distributes video games, including the highly successful *Call of Duty* series. *Call of Duty's* military action fantasy games allow each player to assume the role of a military soldier and battle other players or a computer-controlled opponent to complete different missions on the game's digital battlefields.

Ghosts, released in November 2013, is Activision's tenth installment in the series. Like its predecessors, Ghosts depicts highly realistic combat in a near-future, war-torn setting, featuring numerous characters, complex narratives, and advanced graphics. *Ghosts* features several game modes, including a single-player campaign with a predetermined plot, and various online multi-player modes in which participants can both collaborate as "squads" and compete against one another.

C. *The "Angry Monkey" Morale Patch in Ghosts.*

Players using the customization menus in multi-player mode may select from a total of over six hundred patches to place on their avatars' uniforms. Thirty-two "standard-issue" patches are available at the start of the game; more become "un-locked" as rewards for players who complete objectives and missions. The *Ghosts* "angry monkey" patch appears to players in the in-game menu of avatar-customizing options as one of the "standard-issue" thirty-two patches available to all players in multi-player mode at the start of the game; it does not appear at all in the game's single-player mode.

MSM alleges that Activision "willfully" makes use of the "angry monkey" mark "so as to cause confusion or mistake or to deceive consumers" "as to the source, af-filiation, or sponsorship of the … design" and thereby take advantage of MSM's brand and relationship with consumers. Activision now moves for partial summary judgment against MSM on its four claims grounded in trademark protection, solely on the theory that *Ghosts'* avail of the disputed "angry monkey" design is protected by the First Amendment.

III. LEGAL STANDARD

Summary judgment is proper where the pleadings, discovery and affidavits show that there is "no genuine issue as to any material fact and [that] the moving party is entitled to judgment as a matter of law."

IV. DISCUSSION

A. *Ghosts Is an Expressive Work Entitled to First Amendment Protection.*

As explained in *Brown v. Entertainment Merchants Association*, ___ U.S. ___, 131 S. Ct. 2729, 2733, 180 L.Ed.2d 708 (2011), video games are core speech entitled to First Amendment safeguards:

Like the protected books, plays, and movies that preceded them, video games communicate ideas—and even social messages—through many familiar literary de-vices (such as characters, dialogue, plot, and music) and through features distinctive to the medium (such as the player's interaction with the virtual world). That suffices to confer First Amendment protection.… [W]hatever the challenges of applying the Constitution to ever-advancing technology, "the basic principles of freedom of speech and the press, like the First Amendment's command, do not vary" when a new and different medium for communication appears.

Review of the filed copy of *Ghosts* and videos of game play reflects that the game's multi-player mode—in which the "angry monkey" patch appears—exhibits all of the characteristics *Novalogic* recognized in *Modern Warfare 3* and deserves safe haven under the mantle of First Amendment protection for video games set forth in *Brown*. Its highly realistic visual graphics, complex narratives, distinctive use of music and sound, and multitude of dimensions on which players may interact with the game and one another, earn *Ghosts* the same status. That multi-player mode allows gamers to customize characters, select "maps" for play, and drive the outcome—rather than follow the predetermined plot available in single-player mode—does little to under-mine this point. *See Brown*, 131 S. Ct. at 2738 (Video games do not present "special problems" merely because they are "interactive"; such a "feature is nothing new: Since at least the publication of The Adventures of You: Sugarcane Island in 1969, young readers of choose-your-own-adventure stories have been able to make decisions that determine the plot by following instructions about which page to turn to.").

MSM, however, contends that this step of the Ninth Circuit's framework includes a threshold requirement that a mark must be a "cultural icon" in order for the *Rogers* two-pronged test, discussed further below, even to apply to its use in the underlying work. It bases this argument on a misreading of *Mattel, Inc. v. MCA Records, Inc.*, 296 F.3d 894, 900–02 (9th Cir.2002) (finding against the "Barbie" trademark holder in favor of the creators of the song "Barbie Girl" to deem the song, which pokes fun at the values its creators felt were represented by the Barbie brand, an expressive work), and cites for support an outlier decision from this district, *Rebelution, L.L.C. v. Perez*, 732 F.Supp.2d 883 (N.D.Cal.2010). While *Mattel* indeed opined that "with fame comes unwanted attention," and that a trademark owner certainly may not prohibit all reference to his or her mark once it "becomes an integral part of our vocabulary," — as Barbie has — the fact that Barbie made its way into the global lexicon does not mean every mark must do so in order for its use to be protected by the First Amendment.

Mattel, rather, stands for the proposition that a trademark owner may not control public discourse whenever the public "imbues his mark with a meaning beyond its source-identifying function" — a far more inclusive standard than the "cultural icon" one MSM advocates. Moreover, *Mattel* applies this rule not as a threshold limitation to reaching *Rogers*, but rather as part of the analysis under *Rogers'* first prong. Subsequent Ninth Circuit authority affirms this reading. MSM points out that *E.S.S. Entertainment 2000, Inc. v. Rock Star Videos, Inc.*, [547 F.3d 1095 (9th Cir. 2008),] does not contain a discussion of the threshold to applying *Rogers* because in that case, the plaintiff E.S.S. conceded that the video game at issue was entitled to First Amendment protection. E.S.S. did so, however, *not* on the premise that the mark at issue was a "cultural icon," but rather because the game was an expressive work. The court clearly states as much: "E.S.S. concedes that the game is artistic and that therefore the *Rogers* test applies."

As addressed further below, because of its popularity among military personnel and the significance of patches in the military world, MSM's "angry monkey" mark has taken on a meaning beyond purely denoting a link to MSM. *Ghosts'* multi-player mode makes protectable use of this meaning under the *Rogers* test.

B. *Ghosts' Use of the "Angry Monkey" Design Is Protected by the First Amendment.*

Trademark law is concerned with protecting the symbols, elements and devices used to identify a particular product in the marketplace, and to prevent confusion as to its source. *New Kids on the Block v. News America Publishing, Inc.*, 971 F.2d 302, 305 (9th Cir.1992); *Whitehead v. CBS/Viacom, Inc.*, 315 F.Supp.2d 1, 13 (D.D.C.2004). It offers mark owners a means to prevent others from duping consumers into buying a product they mistakenly believe is sponsored by or affiliated with the trademark owner. Accordingly, "[t]rademark rights do not entitle the owner to quash an unauthorized use of the mark by another who is communicating ideas or expressing points of view." *Mattel*, 296 F.3d at 900 (internal quotation marks and citations omitted).

As *Ghosts* constitutes an expressive work, the question becomes whether Activision's particular use of MSM's "angry monkey" mark within the game merits First Amendment protection. To decide whether the First Amendment precludes Lanham Act and related claims, the Ninth Circuit has adopted the test developed by the Second Circuit in *Rogers v. Grimaldi*, 875 F.2d 994 (2d Cir.1989). As *Rogers* declared, "in general, the [Lanham] Act should be construed to apply to artistic works only where the public interest in avoiding consumer confusion outweighs the public interest in free expression. The Ninth Circuit expressly adopted this test in *Mattel*, as discussed above, and later extended it to apply not only to titles of works, but furthermore to registered marks used in the bodies of other works.

The Ninth Circuit's two-pronged analysis based on *Rogers* finds an artistic work's use of a trademark that would otherwise violate the Lanham Act not actionable unless (1) the use of the mark has "no artistic relevance to the underlying work whatsoever," or (2) it has some artistic relevance, but "explicitly misleads as to the source or the content of the work." *E.S.S.*, 547 F.3d at 1100.

1. "Artistic Relevance"

Mattel and its Ninth Circuit progeny are highly protective of speech. "[O]nly the use of a trademark with 'no artistic relevance to the underlying work whatsoever' would not merit First Amendment protection. In other words, the level of relevance merely must be above zero." While E.S.S. readily acknowledged that Los Angeles's Play Pen strip club was by no means a "cultural icon," the court held that a reasonable way for the video game creators to achieve their artistic vision—a "cartoon-style parody of East Los Angeles"—was to recreate a "critical mass" of the buildings and businesses that constitute it. It was, therefore, of "some artistic relevance" to include a strip club "similar in look and feel to the Play Pen," even if the club had little to do with the premise of the game.

The creators of *Ghosts'* multi-player mode likewise aimed to design a realistic combat experience, the intensity of which is heightened by sophisticated features permitting players to customize their avatars' identities and engage with other players in the virtual environment. The incorporation of combat force names, military gear, geographic locations, and myriad other real-world references coalesce into a "critical mass," not unlike that in *E.S.S.*, to achieve a "look and feel" consistent with the game creators' vision. One small part of this vision is the "angry monkey" patch, which when placed alongside many other patches used in *Ghosts*, represents part of an authentic universe of morale patches, like those available in the real world. The parties agree that "morale patches are popular among military personnel and are often worn in unofficial contexts to allow the wearer to express a sense of personal of identity," and that the "angry monkey" is "among MSM's most well-known designs." Its inclusion in the game therefore bears "some artistic relevance" to the creators' goal of offering players a feeling of personal identity and authenticity during game play.

MSM offers no support for its conclusory allegation that Activision's use of MSM's mark has no expressive purpose, and only incorporates the "angry monkey" design into *Ghosts'* menu of available patches to gain a misleading endorsement from MSM. It argues that Activision's use of the "angry monkey" design bears no artistic relevance to *Ghosts* because the armed forces prohibit soldiers from choosing to wear unofficial morale patches on their uniforms out in the field. But MSM invokes no authority, nor is there any, for the proposition that use of a mark must sufficiently mimic reality to fall within the First Amendment's safe haven. Nor does the fact that the "angry monkey" design only appears in multi-player mode, may not be selected by any player, and may not appear for many hours or sessions of game play, diminish that its artistic relevance to *Ghosts* is "above zero."

MSM's allegation that *Ghosts'* use of the "angry monkey" mark constitutes purely commercial speech, precluding it from broad First Amendment protection, is similarly without merit. MSM itself defines commercial speech as that which "does no more than propose a commercial transaction." That the *Ghosts* "angry monkey" design briefly appears in the pre-release trailer for the game's multi-player mode and (for free to all players) in a menu that also allows players to access additional patches for purchase, does not diminish its artistic relevance within the game. MSM, therefore, puts forward no genuine issue of material fact as to whether the use of the "angry monkey" design in *Ghosts* meets this prong of the *Rogers* test.

2. *"Explicitly Misleading"*

"Explicitly misleading" use of a mark requires that the defendant make an affirmative and overt statement that indicates a relationship with or endorsement by the plaintiff. *Rogers,* 875 F.2d at 999 (offering the phrases "an authorized biography" and "Jane Fonda's Workout Book" as examples). An instance where the sole indication that the plaintiff might be affiliated with the defendant's work is the use of the mark itself is not "explicitly misleading." *Mattel,* 296 F.3d at 902; *see also Brown,* 724 F.3d at 1245–46 (mere use of the player's likeness was insufficient to meet this standard).

MSM fails to demonstrate a genuine issue of material fact as to whether Activision has behaved in an "explicitly misleading" manner. Indeed, MSM has not put forth a single argument that Activision has affirmatively purported in any way to share a relationship with MSM. Activision's *Ghosts* packaging is very clear as to its origin and source, prominently bearing the title *Call of Duty,* identifying its creator as Activision, and boasting to be "the best selling first person action franchise of all time." MSM's sole contention to address this prong of *Rogers*—that Activision has included its version of the "angry monkey" design in promotional materials and thereby "actually mis[led] consumers"—therefore falls short.

V. CONCLUSION

For all of the foregoing reasons, MSM has failed to present a genuine issue of triable fact to overcome Activision's contention that its use of the "angry monkey" mark in *Ghosts* is protected by the First Amendment. Accordingly, Activision's motion for partial summary judgment on MSM's claims for trademark infringement under the Lanham Act; false designation of origin; unfair competition under California statute; and common law trademark infringement, is granted.

IT IS SO ORDERED.

Voluntary Regulations—The Entertainment Software Rating Board (ESRB)

In response to consumer pressures to restrict certain video game sales and usage by minors, and in response to court rulings restricting the ability of governments to directly regulate such video game content, the video game industry itself developed and adopted a voluntary system of game ratings. The Entertainment Software Rating Board (ESRB) is the body responsible for the ratings system in use in the United States and Canada. The ESRB was established in 1994 by the Entertainment Software Association (ESA), and assigns content ratings to video and computer games, enforcing industry-adopted advertising guidelines as to rated games. The current ratings system consists of six ratings categories, assigned by trained ratings personnel, on the basis of sexual, violent, and other potentially objectionable content within the game.

EARLY CHILDHOOD: Titles rated EC (Early Childhood) have content that may be suitable for ages 3 and older. Contains no material that parents would find inappropriate.

EVERYONE: Titles rated E (Everyone) have content that may be suitable for ages 6 and older. Titles in this category may contain minimal cartoon, fantasy or mild violence and/or infrequent use of mild language.

EVERYONE 10+: Titles rated E10+ (Everyone 10 and older) have content that may be suitable for ages 10 and older. Titles in this category may contain more cartoon, fantasy or mild violence, mild language and/or minimal suggestive themes.

TEEN: Titles rated T (Teen) have content that may be suitable for ages 13 and older. Titles in this category may contain violence, suggestive themes, crude humor, minimal blood, simulated gambling, and/or infrequent use of strong language.

MATURE: Titles rated M (Mature) have content that may be suitable for persons ages 17 and older. Titles in this category may contain intense violence, blood and gore, sexual content and/or strong language.

ADULTS ONLY: Titles rated AO (Adults Only) have content that should only be played by persons 18 years and older. Titles in this category may include prolonged scenes of intense violence and/or graphic sexual content and nudity.

While this six-tier rating system is voluntary, the submission guidelines of the ESBA, the comprehensive membership of the ESA, and private store policies that only allow sales of rated games within their stores effectively means that virtually all games sold in the United States and Canada are rated by the ESRB.[16] The ESRB also provides advertising guidelines for publishers to adhere to, and retailers often use the ESRB ratings to implement their own voluntary policies as to sales to minors. In this way, ESRB ratings are a private matter, and do not implicate the same First Amendment issues that direct government regulations do.

Notes and Questions

a. A very significant case decided just before *Brown v. EMA* was *E.S.S. Entm't 2000, Inc. v. Rock Star Videos, Inc.*, 547 F.3d 1095 (9th Cir. 2008). Rockstar Games, Inc. distributes the very popular Grand Theft Auto series of games. ESS Entertainment 2000, Inc., operates a strip club, which features females dancing nude, on the eastern edge of downtown Los Angeles under the name Play Pen Gentlemen's Club ("Play Pen"), which was depicted within the game as an East Los Santos strip club called the Pig Pen. After applying the *Rogers* analysis, the court found that the use of the Pig Pen trademark did not infringe similar trademarks used by Play Pen. *E.S.S.* has helped redefine and expand the *Rogers* Test:

> To qualify for First Amendment Protection under *Rogers v. Grimaldi* on sum-mary judgment, EA must establish as a matter of law that its use of Dillinger was "related" in some way to the "content of the expressive work." The *Rogers* "relatedness" test bars trademark claims unless the use of the plaintiff's likeness is "wholly unrelated to the [work] or [is] simply a disguised com-mercial advertisement for the sale of goods or services." To properly analyze this issue, the Court must therefore consider a two-part test: First, the Court must determine whether the use of the mark has any artistic relevance to the underlying work whatsoever; second, if the use of the trademark has some relevance, the Court must determine whether it explicitly misleads the public as to the source or content of the work.

E.S.S. Entertainment 2000, Inc. v. Rock Star Videos, 547 F.3d 1095, 1099 (9th Cir. 2008) (citing *Rogers v. Grimaldi*, 875 F.2d 994, 999, 1004 (2d Cir. 1989)).

A similar result was reached in *Dillinger, L.L.C. v. Elec. Arts, Inc.*, 2011 U.S. Dist. LEXIS 64006, at *4 (S.D. Ind. June 16, 2011), where Dillinger, L.L.C. tried to assert its trademark rights in the name "Dillinger" regarding a gun utilized in the Godfather group of organized crime games. The court found the name Dillinger related to the organized crime game and was not misleading, providing First Amendment rights protection to defendants.

b. To what extent does the determination of whether video game content is pro-tected speech determine the rigor of the constitutional tests applied? Courts have taken three major approaches to the question over the years:

> *Video games* per se *contain expressive or informative content:* When courts determine that video games contain expressive or informative content *per*

---

16. Entertainment Software Rating Board, Frequently Asked Questions, http://www. esrb.org/ratings/faq.jsp (last visited Oct. 4, 2019).

se, courts generally apply strict scrutiny to regulations that attempt to restrict video game sales or usage. Compare *Interactive Dig. Software Ass'n v. St. Louis Cty.*, 329 F.3d 954 (8th Cir. 2003) (determining that elements of a video games are expressive speech in the same way as other media, are to be given full First Amendment protection, and statutes that prohibit use, sale, or exposure to minor of certain violent or explicit video games are to be subjected to strict scrutiny analysis); *Am. Amusement Mach. Ass'n v. Kendrick*, 244 F.3d 572 (7th Cir. 2001) (holding that a preliminary injunction against a municipality seeking to enforce an ordinance requiring parental content for minor to play certain classes of video games should be granted, because the ordinance would likely be struck down on free expression grounds); *Entm't Software Ass'n v. Granholm*, 404 F. Supp. 2d 978 (E.D. Mich. 2005) (striking down a state statute prohibiting minors from buying or playing violent video games, maintaining that violent depictions in such games are to be accorded full constitutional protection as expression).

Video games may contain expressive or informative content in certain circumstances: When courts take this approach to video games as protected speech, courts examine the particular content of the game in question on a case-by-case basis, sometimes finding the game to contain such speech, and sometimes finding certain games to be devoid of expression or information and more analogous to sports or board games. In *Wilson v. Midway Games, Inc.*, 198 F. Supp. 2d 167 (D. Conn. 2002), the court held that a particular work being labeled a "video game" did not necessarily mean the work has or lacks protectable expression. Instead the question is whether the particular game in question is essentially pure mechanical entertainment or whether the game does actually contain protectable expression of ideas that would afford it protection under the First Amendment.

Video games per se *do not contain expressive or informative content:* In the earlier round of cases, courts often determined that video games had no expressive or informative content and thereby applied the rational relation test to determine whether regulations are constitutionally permissible that restrict video game use or sales. Such cases include *Malden Amusement Co., Inc. v. City of Malden*, 582 F. Supp. 297 (D. Mass. 1983) (ruling that a city ordinance restricting the placement and amount of amusement machines was permissible because the activity being regulated contained no protectable expression, but was essentially mechanical entertainment); *America's Best Family Showplace Corp. v. City of New York, Dept. of Bldgs.*, 536 F. Supp. 170 (E.D.N.Y. 1982) (holding that city zoning and licensing laws related to coin-operated video games implicated no First Amendment concerns, because the activity did not consist of protectable speech); *People v. Walker*, 354 N.W.2d 312 (Mich. Ct. App. 1984) (rejecting a challenge to a local ordinance prohibiting minor presence at arcades by stating that video games were not entitled to any particular First Amendment protection as a class of entertainment); *Kaye v. Planning & Zoning Com.*, 472 A.2d 809 (Conn. Super. Ct. 1983) (finding local regulation of video games through special permit restrictions did not violate the First Amendment, because the games did not communicate or contain any particular ideas).

c. Is there tort liability to video game producers for contributing to third party actions producing wrongful death or injury? Generally, courts have been unsympathetic to plaintiffs in cases where injured parties attempt to hold video game producers liable for third party actions, maintaining that video games enjoy protection as expression under the First Amendment. In *James v. Meow Media, Inc.*, 300 F.3d 683 (6th Cir. 2002), the court dismissed a wrongful death suit against a video game producer accused of tort liability because the plaintiff's specific complaints regarding the features of the game which allegedly contributed to the tort alleged were the expressive aspects of the game that are protected as expression under the First Amendment). *See also Wilson v. Midway Games, Inc.*, 198 F. Supp. 2d 167 (D. Conn. 2002) (holding that a video game producer could not be held liable in a wrongful death tort action for allegedly contributing to violent behavior that lead to death, because the allegations in the particular case went directly to the game's violence and interactivity, aspects of the game protected as expression under the First Amendment).

d. Some state statutes have attempted to utilize the voluntary private ratings system as a basis for government regulation of video game sales and usage. The adoption of the video game industry's own voluntary ratings system as a basis by which to classify video games and restrict use or sales to minors has been deemed unconstitutional. In *Entm't Software Ass'n v. Hatch*, 443 F. Supp. 2d 1065 (D. Minn. 2006), the court struck down a state statute criminalizing the sale of video games classified by the video game retailers' own rating system, because games are rated by a non-government body, without any supervision by the public and without any recourse for ratings decisions through official channels, effectively restricting speech by means of the government through private action. To what extent has the motion picture and music industries utilized these same voluntary standards that are incorporated into laws or ordinances?

e. Can the producer of anti-spam or other content control software block access to video games based on content or pop-up advertising? *See Zango, Inc. v. Kaspersky Lab, Inc.*, 568 F.3d 1169 (9th Cir. 2009).

f. To what extent can a public official "block" a person from his Twitter account in response to the political views that person has expressed, or does such access discrimination violate the First Amendment? *See Knight First Amendment Inst. at Columbia Univ. v. Trump*, 928 F.3d 226 (2d Cir. 2019).

Problem 15-C

Bryce has been collaborating with a video game publisher to produce a new interactive game for use in virtual worlds or as a stand-alone networked computer game. Based on the social life of a rock star, the game includes features for creating bands, touring, performing, and initiating bar fights. Bryce's partners also created an "adult" version that featured the sex and drugs of rock-and-roll lore. Bryce found the adult version to be highly graphic and extreme.

Bryce is concerned about the project. The parties have not specified any rating for the software prior to its creation, but Bryce is uncomfortable being associated with a graphic, adult game. Bryce is also nervous that the game can be banned from virtual world communities by the operators or lead to criminal liability. Please advise Bryce regarding the legal and business risks associated with Bryce's role on the project.

D. Publicity Rights in Video Games

Hart v. Electronic Arts, Inc.

717 F.3d 141 (2013)

In 2009, Appellant Ryan Hart ("Appellant" or "Hart") brought suit against Appellee Electronic Arts, Inc. ("Appellee" or "EA") for allegedly violating his right of publicity as recognized under New Jersey law. Specifically, Appellant's claims stemmed from Appellee's alleged use of his likeness and biographical information in its *NCAA Football* series of videogames. The District Court granted summary judgment in favor of Appellee on the ground that its use of Appellant's likeness was protected by the First Amendment. For the reasons set forth below, we will reverse the grant of summary judgment and remand the case back to the District Court for further proceedings....

Hart was a quarterback, player number 13, with the Rutgers University NCAA Men's Division I Football team for the 2002 through 2005 seasons. As a condition of participating in college-level sports, Hart was required to adhere to the National Collegiate Athletic Association's ("NCAA") amateurism rules as set out in Article 12 of the NCAA bylaws. *See, e.g.,* NCAA, *2011–12 NCAA Division I Manual* § 12.01.1 (2011) ("Only an amateur student-athlete is eligible for inter-collegiate athletics participation in a particular sport."). In relevant part, these rules state that a collegiate athlete loses his or her "amateur" status if (1) the athlete "[u]ses his or her athletics skill (directly or indirectly) for pay in any form in that sport," *id.* § 12.1.2, or (2) the athlete "[a]ccepts any remuneration or permits the use of his or her name or picture to advertise, recommend or promote directly the sale or use of a commercial product or service of any kind," *id.* § 12.5.2.1.[17] In comporting with these bylaws, Hart purportedly refrained from seizing on various commercial opportunities. On the field, Hart excelled. At 6'2", weighing 197 pounds, and typically wearing a visor and armband on his left

---

17. The NCAA Manual also states that where a collegiate athlete's
    name or picture appears on commercial items ... or is used to promote a commercial
    product sold by an individual or agency without the student-athlete's knowledge or permission, the student athlete (or the institution acting on behalf of the student-athlete) is
    required to take steps to stop such an activity in order to retain his or her eligibility for intercollegiate athletics.

NCAA, *2011–12 NCAA Division I Manual* § 12.5.2.2 (2011).

wrist, Hart amassed an impressive list of achievements as the Scarlet Knights' starting quarterback....

Hart's participation in college football also ensured his inclusion in EA's successful *NCAA Football* videogame franchise. EA, founded in 1982, is "one of the world's leading interactive entertainment software companies," and "develops, publishes, and distributes interactive software worldwide" for consoles, cell phones, and PCs. EA's catalogue includes *NCAA Football,* the videogame series at issue in the instant case. The first edition of the game was released in 1993 as *Bill Walsh College Football.* EA subsequently changed the name first to *College Football USA* (in 1995), and then to the current *NCAA Football* (in 1997). New editions in the series are released annually, and "allow[] users to experience the excitement and challenge of college football" by interacting with "over 100 virtual teams and thousands of virtual players." ...

In no small part, the *NCAA Football* franchise's success owes to its focus on realism and detail—from realistic sounds, to game mechanics, to team mascots. This focus on realism also ensures that the "over 100 virtual teams" in the game are populated by digital avatars that resemble their real-life counterparts and share their vital and biographical information. Thus, for example, in *NCAA Football 2006,* Rutgers' quarterback, player number 13, is 6'2" tall, weighs 197 pounds and resembles Hart. Moreover, while users can change the digital avatar's appearance and most of the vital statistics (height, weight, throwing distance, etc.), certain details remain immutable: the player's home state, home town, team, and class year.

Appellant filed suit against EA in state court for, among other things, violation of his right of publicity.... The District Court ruled in favor of Appellee, holding that *NCAA Football* was entitled to protection under the First Amendment.... The matter is now before us for review.

Discussion

We begin our analysis by noting the self-evident: video games are protected as expressive speech under the First Amendment. *Brown v. Entm't Merchs. Ass'n,* ___ U.S. ___, 131 S. Ct. 2729, 2733, 180 L.Ed.2d 708 (2011). As the Supreme Court has noted, "video games communicate ideas—and even social messages—through many familiar literary devices (such as characters, dialogue, plot, and music) and through features distinctive to the medium (such as the player's interaction with the virtual world)." *Id.* As a result, games enjoy the full force of First Amendment protections. As with other types of expressive conduct, the protection afforded to games can be limited in situations where the right of free expression necessarily conflicts with other protected rights.

The instant case presents one such situation. Here, Appellee concedes, for purposes of the motion and appeal, that it violated Appellant's right of publicity; in essence, misappropriating his identity for commercial exploitation. However, Appellee contends that the First Amendment shields it from liability for this violation because *NCAA Football* is a protected work. To resolve the tension between the First Amendment and the right of publicity, we must balance the interests underlying the right to free expression against the interests in protecting the right of publicity. *See Zacchini v. Scripps-Howard Broad. Co.*, 433 U.S. 562, 574–75 (1977).[18]

Courts have taken varying approaches in attempting to strike a balance between the competing interests in right of publicity cases, some more appealing than others. In our discussion below, we first consider the nature of the interests we must balance and then analyze the different approaches courts have taken to resolving the tension between the First Amendment and the right of publicity.

A. The Relevant Interests at Issue

Before engaging with the different analytical schemes, we first examine the relevant interests underlying the rights of free expression and publicity.

1. Freedom of Expression

Freedom of expression is paramount in a democratic society, for "[i]t is the function of speech to free men from the bondage of irrational fears." *Whitney v. California*, 274 U.S. 357, 376 (1927) (Brandeis, J., concurring). As Justice Louis Brandeis wrote nearly a century ago:

> Those who won our independence believed that the final end of the state was to make men free to develop their faculties.... They valued liberty both as an end and as a means. They believed liberty to [be] the secret of happiness and courage to be the secret of liberty. They believed that freedom to think as you will and to speak as you think are means indispensable to the discovery and spread of political truth; that without free speech and assembly discussion would be futile; that with them, discussion affords ordinarily adequate protection against the dissemination of noxious doctrine; that the greatest menace to freedom is an inert people; that public discussion is a political duty; and that this should be a fundamental principle of the American government.

Id. at 375.

In keeping with Justice Brandeis' eloquent analysis, the great legal minds of generations past and present have recognized that free speech benefits both the individual and society....

The interest in safeguarding the integrity of these protections therefore weighs heavily in any balancing inquiry. Still, instances can and do arise where First Amendment protections yield in the face of competing interests. Ultimately, we must determine whether the interest in safeguarding the right of publicity overpowers the interest in safeguarding free expression.

2. The Right of Publicity

The right of publicity grew out of the right to privacy torts, specifically, from the tort of "invasion of privacy by appropriation." J. Thomas Mccarthy, The Rights of

---

18. While it is true that the right of publicity is a creature of state law and precedent, its intersection with the First Amendment presents a federal issue, and, thus, permits us to engage in the sort of balancing inquiry at issue here. *See, e.g., Zacchini*, 433 U.S. at 566–68.

Publicity and Privacy § 1:23 (2d ed. 2012).... However, this early conceptualization had limitations, particularly when it came to protecting the property interests of celebrities and people already in the public eye.... The first case to describe this protection as a "right of publicity" was *Haelan Labs., Inc. v. Topps Chewing Gum, Inc.*, 202 F.2d 866 (2d Cir.1953) (concerning baseball cards in gum packages). There, the Second Circuit held that "in addition to and independent of that right of privacy..., a man has a right in the publicity value of his photo graph.... This right might be called a 'right of publicity.'" *Id.* at 868. New Jersey courts, which had long recognized a "right of privacy [and] a right of property," were not far behind in voicing their support for this concept. *Ettore v. Philco Television Broad. Corp.*, 229 F.2d 481, 491 (3d Cir.1956).

In the seminal case of *Palmer v. Schonhorn Enters., Inc.*, the Superior Court of New Jersey noted that

> [p]erhaps the basic and underlying theory is that a person has the right to enjoy the fruits of his own industry free from unjustified interference. It is unfair that one should be permitted to commercialize or exploit or capitalize upon another's name, reputation or accomplishments merely because the owner's accomplishments have been highly publicized.

96 N.J.Super. 72, 232 A.2d 458, 462 (Ch.Div.1967) (citations omitted) (finding an infringement of property rights where a golfer's name was used in connection with a golf game)....

New Jersey law therefore recognizes that "[t]he right to exploit the value of [an individual's] notoriety or fame belongs to the individual with whom it is associated," for an individual's "name, likeness, and endorsement carry value and an unauthorized use harms the person both by diluting the value of the name and depriving that individual of compensation." *McFarland v. Miller*, 14 F.3d 912, 919, 923 (3d Cir.1994). As such, the goal of maintaining a right of publicity is to protect the property interest that an individual gains and enjoys in his identity through his labor and effort. Additionally, as with protections for intellectual property, the right of publicity is designed to encourage further development of this property interest.

Since neither the New Jersey courts nor our own circuit have set out a definitive methodology for balancing the tension between the First Amendment and the right of publicity, we are presented with a case of first impression. We must therefore consult the approaches of other courts in the first instance.

B. How Courts Balance the Interests

We begin our inquiry by looking at *Zacchini v. Scripps-Howard Broadcasting Co.*, the only Supreme Court case addressing the First Amendment in a right of publicity context. In this case, the Court called for a balancing test to weigh the interest underlying the First Amendment against those underpinning the right of publicity. 433 U.S. at 574–75. This decision sets the stage for our analysis of three systematized analytical frameworks that have emerged as courts struggle with finding a standardized way for performing this balancing inquiry.

1. *Zacchini* and the Need for Balance

... In setting out the interests at issue in the case, the Supreme Court noted (as we did above) that "the State's interest in permitting a 'right of publicity' is in protecting the proprietary interest of the individual in his act in part to encourage such entertainment." This aspect of the right, the Court noted, was "analogous to the goals of patent and copyright law," given that they too serve to protect the individual's ability to "reap the reward of his endeavors." In *Zacchini,* the performance was the "product of [Zacchini's] own talents and energy, the end result of much time, effort and expense." Thus much of its economic value lay "in the right of exclusive control over the publicity given to his performance." Indeed, while the Court noted that "[a]n entertainer such as petitioner usually has no objection to the widespread publication of his act as long as [he] gets the commercial benefit of such publication," the claim at issue in the *Zacchini* concerned "the strongest case for a 'right of publicity,'" because it did not involve the "appropriation of an entertainer's reputation to enhance the attractiveness of a commercial product," but instead involved "the appropriation of the very activity by which the entertainer acquired his reputation in the first place." ...

In the wake of *Zacchini,* courts began applying a balancing inquiry to resolve cases where a right of publicity claim collided with First Amendment protections. While early cases approached the analysis from an ad hoc perspective, *see, e.g., Guglielmi v. Spelling-Goldberg Prods.,* 25 Cal.3d 860, 160 Cal.Rptr. 352, 603 P.2d 454 (1979) (en banc), courts eventually began developing standardized balancing frameworks. Consequently, we now turn our attention to more standardized balancing tests to see whether any of them offer a particularly compelling methodology for resolving the case at hand and similar disputes.[19]

2. The Modern Balancing Tests

Following *Zacchini,* courts began developing more systematized balancing tests for resolving conflicts between the right of publicity and the First Amendment. Of these, three tests are of particular note: the commercial-interest-based Predominant

---

19. We reject as inapplicable in this case the suggestion that those who play organized sports are not significantly damaged by appropriation of their likeness because "players are rewarded, and handsomely, too, for their participation in games and can earn additional large sums from endorsement and sponsorship arrangements." *C.B.C. Distrib. & Mktg., Inc. v. Major League Baseball Advanced Media, L.P.,* 505 F.3d 818, 824 (8th Cir.2007) (discussing Major League Baseball players); *see also, e.g., Cardtoons, L.C. v. Major League Baseball Players Ass'n,* 95 F.3d 959, 974 (10th Cir.1996) ("[T]he additional inducement for achievement produced by publicity rights are often inconsequential because most celebrities with valuable commercial identities are already handsomely compensated."). If anything, the policy considerations in this case weigh in *favor* of Appellant. As we have already noted, intercollegiate athletes are forbidden from capitalizing on their fame while in school. Moreover, the NCAA most recently estimated that "[l]ess than one in 100, or 1.6 percent, of NCAA senior football players will get drafted by a National Football League (NFL) team." NCAA, Estimated Probability of Competing in Athletics Beyond the High School Interscholastic Level, available at http://www.ncaa.org/wps/wcm/connect/public/ncaa/pdfs/2012/estimated+probability+of+competing+in +athletics+beyond+the+high+school+interscholastic+level. Despite all of his achievements, it should be noted that Ryan Hart was among the roughly ninety-nine percent who were not drafted after graduation.

Use Test, the trademark-based *Rogers* Test, and the copyright-based Transformative Use Test. The *Rogers* and Transformative Use tests are the most well-established, while the Predominant Use Test is addressed below only because Appellant argues in favor of its adoption. We consider each test in turn, looking at its origins, scope of application, and possible limitations. For the reasons discussed below, we adopt the Transformative Use Test as being the most appropriate balancing test to be applied here.

a. Predominant Use Test

Appellant urges us to adopt the Predominant Use Test, which first appeared in *Doe v. TCI Cablevision,* 110 S.W.3d 363 (Mo.2003) (en banc), a case that considered a hockey player's right of publicity claim against a comic book publishing company. In *TCI,* Anthony "Tony" Twist, a hockey player, brought suit against a number of individuals and entities involved in producing and publishing the *Spawn* comic book series after the introduction of a villainous character named Anthony "Tony Twist" Twistelli.

In balancing Twist's property interests in his own name and identity against the First Amendment interests of the comic book creators, the *TCI* court rejected both the Transformative Use and *Rogers* tests, noting that they gave "too little consideration to the fact that many uses of a person's name and identity have both expressive and commercial components." The Supreme Court of Missouri considered both tests to be too rigid, noting that they operated "to preclude a cause of action whenever the use of the name and identity is in any way expressive, regardless of its commercial exploitation." The court instead applied what it called a "sort of predominant use test":

> If a product is being sold that predominantly exploits the commercial value of an individual's identity, that product should be held to violate the right of publicity and not be protected by the First Amendment, even if there is some 'expressive' content in it that might qualify as 'speech' in other circumstances. If, on the other hand, the predominant purpose of the product is to make an expressive comment on or about a celebrity, the expressive values could be given greater weight.

Id. (quoting Mark S. Lee, *Agents of Chaos: Judicial Confusion in Defining the Right of Publicity-Free Speech Interface,* 23 Loy. L.A. Ent. L. Rev. 471, 500 (2003)). The *TCI* court considered this to be a "more balanced balancing test [particularly for] cases where speech is both expressive and commercial." After applying the test, the court ruled for Twist, holding that "the metaphorical reference to Twist, though a literary device, has very little literary value compared to its commercial value."

We decline Appellant's invitation to adopt this test. By our reading, the Predominant Use Test is subjective at best, arbitrary at worst, and in either case calls upon judges to act as both impartial jurists and discerning art critics. These two roles cannot coexist. Indeed, Appellant suggests that pursuant to this test we must evaluate "what value [Appellee is] adding to the First Amendment expressiveness [of *NCAA Football*] by appropriating the commercially valuable likeness?" Since "[t]he game would have the exact same level of First Amendment expressiveness if [Appellee] didn't appropriate Mr. Hart's likeness," Appellant urges us to find that *NCAA Football* fails the Predominant Use Test and therefore is not shielded by the First Amendment. Such reasoning, however, leads down a dangerous and rightly-shunned road: adopting Appellant's suggested analysis would be tantamount to admitting that it is proper for courts to analyze select elements of a work to determine how much they contribute to the entire work's expressiveness. Moreover, as a necessary (and insidious) consequence, the Appellant's approach would suppose that there exists a broad range of seemingly expressive speech that has no First Amendment value.

Appellee rightly argues that the Predominant Use Test is antithetical to our First Amendment precedent, and we likewise reject the Test. We instead turn our attention to the *Rogers* Test, which was proposed by Appellee and which draws its inspiration from trademark law.

b. The *Rogers* Test

The *Rogers* Test looks to the relationship between the celebrity image and the work as a whole.[20] As the following discussion demonstrates, however, adopting this test would potentially immunize a broad swath of tortious activity. We therefore reject the *Rogers* Test as inapposite in the instant case.

Various commentators have noted that right of publicity claims—at least those that address the use of a person's name or image in an advertisement—are akin to trademark claims because in both instances courts must balance the interests in protecting the relevant property right against the interest in free expression. It is little wonder, then, that the inquiry championed by Appellee originated in a case that also focused upon alleged violations of the trademark-specific Lanham Act. *Rogers v. Grimaldi*, 875 F.2d 994 (2d Cir. 1989).

In that case, Ginger Rogers brought suit against the producers and distributors of *Ginger and Fred*, a film that was alleged to infringe on Rogers' right of publicity and confuse consumers in violation of the Act. (Despite its title, the film was not about either Ginger Rogers or Fred Astaire.) In analyzing the right of publicity claim under Oregon law, the Second Circuit noted Oregon's "concern for the protection of free expression," and held that Oregon would not "permit the right of publicity to bar the use of a celebrity's name in a movie title unless the title was wholly unrelated to the movie or was simply a disguised commercial advertisement for the sale of goods or services." *Id.* at 1004 (internal quotation marks omitted). After applying this test, the *Rogers* court concluded that the right of publicity claim merited dismissal because "the title 'Ginger and Fred' is clearly related to the content of the movie and is not a disguised advertisement for the sale of goods and services or a collateral commercial product."

---

20. The various cases and scholarly sources refer to this test in three different ways: the Relatedness Test, the Restatement Test, and the *Rogers* Test. The "Relatedness" moniker should be self-explanatory even at this early point in our discussion; the propriety of the other two names will become clear shortly. For our purposes, we will refer to the test as the *Rogers* Test.

But while the test, as articulated in *Rogers,* arguably applied only to the use of celebrity identity in a work's title, Appellee suggests that the test can — and should — be applied more broadly.

Ultimately, we find that the *Rogers* Test does not present the proper analytical approach for cases such as the one at bar. While the Test may have a use in trademark-like right of publicity cases, it is inapposite here. We are concerned that this test is a blunt instrument, unfit for widespread application in cases that require a carefully calibrated balancing of two fundamental protections: the right of free expression and the right to control, manage, and profit from one's own identity.... [T]he right of publicity is broader and, by extension, protects a greater swath of property interests. Thus, it would be unwise for us to adopt a test that hews so closely to traditional trademark principles. Instead, we need a broader, more nuanced test, which helps balance the interests at issue in cases such as the one at bar. The final test — the Transformative Use Test — provides just such an approach.

c. The Transformative Use Test

Looking to intellectual property law for guidance on how to balance property interests against the First Amendment has merit. We need only shift our gaze away from trademark, to the broader vista of copyright law. Thus, we come to the case of *Comedy III Prods., Inc. v. Gary Saderup, Inc.,* which imported the concept of "transformative" use from copyright law into the right of publicity context. 25 Cal.4th 387 (2001). This concept lies at the core of a test that both Appellant and Appellee agree is applicable to this case: the Transformative Use Test.

i. Genesis of the Transformative Use Test

The Transformative Use Test was first articulated by the Supreme Court of California in *Comedy III.* That case concerned an artist's production and sale of t-shirts and prints bearing a charcoal drawing of the Three Stooges. The California court determined that while "[t]he right of publicity is often invoked in the context of commercial speech," it could also apply in instances where the speech is merely expressive. *Id.,* 106 Cal.Rptr.2d 126. The court also noted, however, that when addressing expressive speech, "the very importance of celebrities in society means that the right of publicity has the potential of censoring significant expression by suppressing alternative versions of celebrity images that are iconoclastic, irreverent or otherwise attempt to redefine the celebrity's meaning." Thus, while the "the right of publicity cannot, consistent with the First Amendment, be a right to control the celebrity's image by censoring disagreeable portrayals," *id.,* the right, like copyright, nonetheless offers protection to a form of intellectual property that society deems to have social utility.

After briefly considering whether to import the "fair use" analysis from copyright, the *Comedy III* court decided that only the first fair use factor, "the purpose and character of the use," was appropriate. *Id.,* 106 Cal.Rptr.2d 126, 21 P.3d at 808. Specifically, the *Comedy III* court found persuasive the Supreme Court's holding in *Campbell v. Acuff-Rose Music, Inc.* that the central purpose of the inquiry into this fair use factor 'is to see ... whether the new work merely "supercede[s] the objects" of the original creation, or instead adds something new, with a further purpose or different character, altering the first with new expression, meaning, or message; it asks, in other words, whether and to what extent the new work is "*transformative.*"

Id. (emphasis added) (citing *Campbell v. Acuff-Rose Music, Inc.*, 510 U.S. 569, 579 (1994)).

Going further, the court explained that works containing "significant transformative elements" are less likely to interfere with the economic interests implicated by the right of publicity. For example, "works of parody or other distortions of the celebrity figure are not, from the celebrity fan's viewpoint, good substitutes for conventional depictions of the celebrity and therefore do not generally threaten markets for celebrity memorabilia that the right of publicity is designed to protect." *Id.* The court was also careful to emphasize that "the transformative elements or creative contributions" in a work may include — under the right circumstances — factual reporting, fictionalized portrayal, heavy-handed lampooning, and subtle social criticism. *Id.* ("The inquiry is in a sense more quantitative than qualitative, asking whether the literal and imitative or the creative elements predominate in the work.").

Restating its newly-articulated test, the Supreme Court of California held that the balance between the right of publicity and First Amendment interests turns on

[w]hether the celebrity likeness is one of the "raw materials" from which an original work is synthesized, or whether the depiction or imitation of the celebrity is the very sum and substance of the work in question. We ask, in other words, *whether the product containing a celebrity's likeness is so transformed that it has become primarily the defendant's own expression rather than the celebrity's likeness.* And when we use the word "expression," we mean expression of something other than the likeness of the celebrity.

Id. (emphasis added).

Applying this test, the court concluded that charcoal portraits of the Three Stooges did violate the Stooges' rights of publicity, holding that the court could "discern no significant transformative or creative contribution" and that "the marketability and economic value of [the work] derives primarily from the fame of the celebrities depicted."

ii. Application of the Transformative Use Test

Given its relative recency, few courts have applied the Transformative Use Test, and consequently there is not a significant body of case law related to its application. Nonetheless, a handful of cases bear mention as they help frame our inquiry.

In 2003, the Supreme Court of California revisited the Transformative Use Test when two musicians, Johnny and Edgar Winter, who both possessed long white hair and albino features, brought suit against a comic book company over images of two villainous half-man, half-worm creatures, both with long white hair and albino features, named Johnny and Edgar Autumn. *Winter v. DC Comics*, 30 Cal.4th 881 (2003).

As the brothers' right of publicity claims necessarily implicated DC Comics' First Amendment rights, the *Winter* court looked to the Transformative Use Test. In summarizing the test, the court explained that "[a]n artist depicting a celebrity must contribute something more than a 'merely trivial' variation, [but must create] something recognizably 'his own,' in order to qualify for legal protection." *Id.*, 69 P.3d at 478 (alteration in original) (quoting *Comedy III*, 21 P.3d at 810–11). Thus, in applying the test, the *Winter* court held that

> [a]lthough the fictional characters Johnny and Edgar Autumn are less-than-subtle evocations of Johnny and Edgar Winter, the books do not depict plaintiffs literally. Instead, plaintiffs are merely part of the raw materials from which the comic books were synthesized. To the extent the drawings of the Autumn brothers resemble plaintiffs at all, they are distorted for purposes of lampoon, parody, or caricature. And the Autumn brothers are but cartoon characters — half-human and half-worm — in a larger story, which is itself quite expressive.

Id., 69 P.3d at 479. The court therefore found that "fans who want to purchase pictures of [the Winter brothers] would find the drawing of the Autumn brothers unsatisfactory as a substitute for conventional depictions." Consequently, the court rejected the brothers' claims for a right of publicity violation.

Also in 2003, the Sixth Circuit decided *ETW*, a case focusing on a photograph of Tiger Woods set among a collage of other, golf-related photographs. As we previously noted, while *ETW* mentioned both the *Rogers* case and the Restatement (Third) of Unfair Competition, the test it ultimately applied was a combination of an ad-hoc approach and the Transformative Use Test. *See ETW*, 332 F.3d at 937–38. In holding that the collage "contain[ed] significant transformative elements," *id.* at 938, the court compared it to the Three Stooges portraits from *Comedy III*, and noted that the collage "does not capitalize solely on a literal depiction of Woods." *Id.* Instead, the "work consists of a collage of images in addition to Woods's image which are combined to describe, in artistic form, a historic event in sports history and to convey a message about the significance of Woods's achievement in that event."...

iii. The Transformative Use Test and Video Games

In mid-2006, the California Court of Appeal decided *Kirby v. Sega of America, Inc.*, 144 Cal.App.4th 47 (2006), which addressed a musician's right of publicity claim against a video game company. Specifically, the musician (Kierin Kirby) had claimed that Sega misappropriated her likeness and signature phrases for purposes of creating the character of Ulala, a reporter in the far flung future. In applying the Transformative Use Test, the court noted that not only did Kirby's signature phrases included "ooh la la" but that both she and the videogame character would often use phrases like "groove," "meow," "dee-lish," and "I won't give up." *Id.* at 613. The court also found similarities in appearance between Kirby and Ulala, based on hair style and clothing choice. *Id.* At the same time, the court held that differences between the two did exist — both in appearance and movement — and that Ulala was not a mere digital recreation of Kirby. *Id.* Thus, the court concluded that Ulala passed the Transformative

Use Test, rejecting Kirby's argument that the differences between her and the character added no additional meaning or message to the work. *Id.* at 616–17 ("A work is transformative if it adds 'new expression.' That expression alone is sufficient; it need not convey any 'meaning or message.'"); *see also id.* at 617 ("[A]ny imitation of Kirby's likeness or identity in Ulala is not the sum and substance of that character.").

Several years later, in early 2011, the California courts again confronted the right of publicity as it related to video games in *No Doubt v. Activision Publishing, Inc.*, 192 Cal.App.4th 1018, 122 Cal.Rptr.3d 397 (2011). The case centered on *Band Hero,* a game that allows player to "simulate performing in a rock band in time with popular songs" by selecting digital avatars to represent them in an in-game band. *Id.* at 401. Some of the avatars were digital recreations of real-life musicians, including members of the band No Doubt. After a contract dispute broke off relations between the band and the company, No Doubt sued, claiming a violation of their rights of publicity. The California Court of Appeal applied the Transformative Use Test.

The *No Doubt* court began by noting that "in stark contrast to the 'fanciful creative characters' in *Winter* and *Kirby,*" the No Doubt avatars could not be altered by players and thus remained "at all times immutable images of the real celebrity musicians." *Id.* at 410. But this fact, by itself, did not end the court's inquiry since "even literal reproductions of celebrities can be 'transformed' into expressive works based on the context into which the celebrity image is placed." *Id.* (citing *Comedy III,* 106 Cal.Rptr.2d 126, 21 P.3d at 811). Looking to the context of the *Band Hero* game, the court found that "no matter what else occurs in the game *during the depiction of the No Doubt avatars,* the avatars perform rock songs, the same activity by which the band achieved and maintains its fame." *Id.* at 410–11 (emphasis added). The court explained:

> [T]he avatars perform [rock] songs as literal recreations of the band members. That the avatars can be manipulated to perform at fanciful venues including outer space or to sing songs the real band would object to singing, or that the avatars appear in the context of a videogame *that contains many other creative elements,* does not transform the avatars into anything other than the exact depictions of No Doubt's members doing exactly what they do as celebrities.

Id. at 411 (emphasis added). As a final step in its analysis, the court noted that Activision's use of highly realistic digital depictions of No Doubt was motivated by a desire to capitalize on the band's fan-base, "because it encourages [fans] to purchase the game so as *to perform as, or alongside, the members of No Doubt.*" *Id.* (emphasis added). Given all this, the court concluded that Activision's use of No Doubt's likenesses did infringe on the band's rights of publicity. *Id.* at 411–12.

iv. Analysis of the Transformative Use Test

Like the Predominant Use and *Rogers* tests, the Transformative Use Test aims to balance the interest protected by the right of publicity against those interests preserved by the First Amendment. In our view, the Transformative Use Test appears to strike the best balance because it provides courts with a flexible — yet uniformly applicable—analytical framework. Specifically, the Transformative Use Test seems to excel precisely where the other two tests falter. Unlike the *Rogers* Test, the Transformative Use Test maintains a singular focus on whether the work sufficiently transforms the celebrity's identity or likeness, thereby allowing courts to account for the fact that misappropriation can occur in any market segment, including those related to the celebrity.

On the other hand, unlike the Predominant Use Test, applying the Transformative Use Test requires a more circumscribed inquiry, focusing on the specific aspects of a work that speak to whether it was merely created to exploit a celebrity's likeness. This test therefore recognizes that if First Amendment protections are to mean anything in right of publicity claims, courts must *begin* by considering the extent to which a work is the creator's own expression.

Additionally, the Transformative Use Test best comports with the cautionary language present in various right of publicity cases. Specifically, we believe that an initial focus on the creative aspects of a work helps address our own concern from *Facenda,* where we noted that "courts must circumscribe the right of publicity." *Facenda* [*v. N.F.L. Films, Inc.*], 542 F.3d at 1032 [(3d Cir. 2008)]. As our discussion below demonstrates, the Transformative Use Test effectively restricts right of publicity claims to a very narrow universe of expressive works. Moreover, we believe that the Transformative Use Test best exemplifies the methodology suggested by Justice Powell's dissent in *Zacchini:*

> Rather than begin with a quantitative analysis of the performer's behavior—is this or is this not his entire act?—we should direct initial attention to the actions of the news media: what use did the station make of the film footage? When a film is used, as here, for a routine portion of a regular news program, I would hold that the First Amendment protects the station from a "right of publicity" or "appropriation" suit, absent a strong showing by the plaintiff that the news broadcast was a subterfuge or cover for private or commercial exploitation.

Zacchini, 433 U.S. at 581 (Powell, J., dissenting). Consistent with Justice Powell's argument, the Transformative Use Test begins by asking "what use did the [defendant] make of the [celebrity identity]?" ...

C. Application

In applying the Transformative Use Test to the instant case, we must determine whether Appellant's identity is sufficiently transformed in *NCAA Football.* As we mentioned earlier, we use the term "identity" to encompass not only Appellant's likeness, but also his biographical information. It is the combination of these two parts—which, when combined, identify the digital avatar as an in-game recreation of Appellant—that must be sufficiently transformed.

Having thus cabined our inquiry to the appropriate form of Appellant's identity, we note that—based on the combination of both the digital avatar's appearance and the biographical and identifying information—the digital avatar does closely resemble the genuine article. Not only does the digital avatar match Appellant in terms of hair color, hair style and skin tone, but the avatar's accessories mimic those worn by Appellant during his time as a Rutgers player. The information, as has already been noted, also accurately tracks Appellant's vital and biographical details. And while the inexorable march of technological progress may make some of the graphics in earlier editions of *NCAA Football* look dated or overly-computerized, we do not believe that video game graphics must reach (let alone cross) the uncanny valley to support a right of publicity claim. If we are to find some transformative element, we must look somewhere other than just the in-game digital recreation of Appellant. Cases such as *ETW* and *No Doubt*, both of which address realistic digital depictions of celebrities, point to the next step in our analysis: context.

Considering the context within which the digital avatar exists—effectively, looking at how Appellant's identity is "incorporated into and transformed by" *NCAA Football*—provides little support for Appellee's arguments. The digital Ryan Hart does what the actual Ryan Hart did while at Rutgers: he plays college football, in digital recreations of college football stadiums, filled with all the trappings of a college football game. This is not transformative; the various digitized sights and sounds in the video game do not alter or transform the Appellant's identity in a significant way. *See No Doubt*, 122 Cal.Rptr.3d at 410–11 ("[N]o matter what else occurs in the game during the depiction of the No Doubt avatars, the avatars perform rock songs, the same activity by which the band achieved and maintains its fame."). Indeed, the lack of transformative context is even more pronounced here than in *No Doubt*, where members of the band could perform and sing in outer space.

Even here, however, our inquiry is not at an end. For as much as the digital representation and context evince no meaningful transformative element in *NCAA Football*, a third avatar-specific element is also present: the users' ability to alter the avatar's appearance. This distinguishing factor ensures that we cannot dispose of this case as simply as the court in *No Doubt*. Indeed, the ability for users to change the avatar accounted, in large part, for the District Court's deciding that *NCAA Football* satisfied the Transformative Use Test. We must therefore consider to what extent the ability to alter a digital avatar represents a transformative use of Appellant's identity.

At the outset, we note that the mere presence of this feature, without more, cannot satisfy the Transformative Use Test. True, interactivity is the basis upon which First Amendment protection is granted to video games in the first instance. However, the balancing test in right of publicity cases does not look to whether a particular work *loses* First Amendment protection. Rather, the balancing inquiry looks to see whether the interests protected by the right of publicity are sufficient to *surmount* the already-existing First Amendment protections. As *Zacchini* demonstrated, the right of publicity can triumph even when an essential element for First Amendment protection is present. In that case, the human cannonball act was broadcast *as part of the newscast*. To hold, therefore, that a video game should satisfy the Transformative Use Test simply because it includes a particular interactive feature would lead to improper results. Interactivity cannot be an end onto itself.

Moreover, we are wary of converting the ability to alter a digital avatar from mere feature to talisman, thereby opening the door to cynical abuse. If the mere presence of the feature were enough, video game companies could commit the most blatant acts of misappropriation only to absolve themselves by including a feature that allows users to modify the digital likenesses. We cannot accept that such an outcome would adequately balance the interests in right of publicity cases. As one amicus brief noted:

> [U]nder [Appellee's] application of the transformative test [sic], presumably no infringement would be found if individuals such as the Dalai Lama and the Pope were placed within a violent "shoot-em-up" game, so long as the game include[d] a "mechanism" by which the user could manipulate their characteristics.

With this concern in mind, therefore, we consider whether the type and extent of interactivity permitted is sufficient to transform the Appellant's likeness into the Appellee's own expression. We hold that it does not.

In *NCAA Football,* Appellee seeks to create a realistic depiction of college football for the users. Part of this realism involves generating realistic representations of the various college teams—which includes the realistic representations of the players. Like Activision in *No Doubt,* therefore, Appellee seeks to capitalize on the respective fan bases for the various teams and players. Indeed, as the District Court recognized, "it seems ludicrous to question whether video game consumers enjoy and, as a result, purchase more EA-produced video games as a result of the heightened realism associated with actual players." *Hart,* 808 F.Supp.2d at 783 (quoting James J.S. Holmes & Kanika D. Corley, *Defining Liability for Likeness of Athlete Avatars in Video Games,* L.A. Law., May 2011, at 17, 20). Moreover, the realism of the games—including the depictions and recreations of the players—appeals not just to home-team fans, but to bitter rivals as well. Games such as *NCAA Football* permit users to recreate the setting of a bitter defeat and, in effect, achieve some cathartic readjustment of history; realistic depictions of the players are a necessary element to this. That Appellant's likeness is the *default* position only serves to support our conclusion that realistic depictions of the players are the "sum and substance" of these digital facsimiles. Given that Appellant's unaltered likeness is central to the core of the game experience, we are disinclined to credit users' ability to alter the digital avatars in our application of the Transformative Use Test to this case....

In an attempt to salvage its argument, Appellee suggests that *other* creative elements of *NCAA Football,* which do not affect Appellant's digital avatar, are so numerous that the videogames should be considered transformative. We believe this to be an improper inquiry.... [W]hile we recognize the creative energies necessary for crafting the various elements of *NCAA Football* that are not tied directly to reality, we hold that they have no legal significance in our instant decision.

To hold otherwise could have deleterious consequences for the state of the law. Acts of blatant misappropriation would count for nothing so long as the larger work, on balance, contained highly creative elements in great abundance. This concern is particularly acute in the case of media that lend themselves to easy partition such as video games. It cannot be that content creators escape liability for a work that uses a celebrity's unaltered identity in one section but that contains a wholly fanciful creation in the other, larger section.

For these reasons, we hold that the broad application of the Transformative Use Test represents an inappropriate application of the standard. Consequently, we shall not credit elements of *NCAA Football* that do not, in some way, affect the use or meaning of Appellant's identity....

IV. Conclusion

We therefore hold that the *NCAA Football 2004, 2005* and *2006* games at issue in this case do not sufficiently transform Appellant's identity to escape the right of publicity claim and hold that the District Court erred in granted summary judgment in favor of Appellee.

AMBRO, Circuit Judge, dissenting.

... The Transformative Use Test gives First Amendment immunity where, in an expressive work, an individual's likeness has been creatively adapted in some way. Correctly applied, this test strikes an appropriate balance between countervailing rights—the publicity interest in protecting an individual's right to benefit financially when others use his identifiable persona for their own commercial benefit versus the First Amendment interest in insulating from liability a creator's decision to interweave real-life figures into its expressive work.

My colleagues limit effectively their transformative inquiry to Hart's identity alone, disregarding other features of the work. This approach, I believe, does not find support in the cases on which they rely. Further, my colleagues penalize EA for the realism and financial success of *NCAA Football,* a position I find difficult to reconcile with First Amendment protections traditionally afforded to true-to-life depictions of real figures and works produced for profit. Because I conclude that the Transformative Use Test protects EA's use of Hart's likeness in *NCAA Football,* I respectfully dissent....

The Transformative Use Test I support would prevent commercial exploitation of an individual's likeness where the work at issue lacks creative contribution that transforms that likeness in a meaningful way. I sympathize with the position of Hart and other similarly situated college football players, and understand why they feel it is fair to share in the significant profits produced by including their avatar likenesses into EA's commercially successful video game franchise. I nonetheless remain convinced that the creative components of *NCAA Football* contain sufficient expressive transformation to merit First Amendment protection. Thus I respectfully dissent, and would affirm the District Court's grant of summary judgment in favor of EA.

In re NCAA Student-Athlete Name & Likeness Licensing Litigation

724 F.3d 1268 (2013)

Video games are entitled to the full protections of the First Amendment, because "[l]ike the protected books, plays, and movies that preceded them, video games communicate ideas—and even social messages—through many familiar literary devices (such as characters, dialogue, plot, and music) and through features distinctive to the medium (such as the player's interaction with the virtual world)." *Brown v. Entm't Merchs. Ass'n,* ___ U.S. ___, 131 S. Ct. 2729, 2733, 180 L.Ed.2d 708 (2011). Such rights are not absolute, and states may recognize the right of publicity to a degree consistent with the First Amendment. *Zacchini v. Scripps-Howard Broad. Co.,* 433 U.S. 562, 574–75, 97 S. Ct. 2849, 53 L.Ed.2d 965 (1977). In this case, we must balance the right of publicity of a former college football player against the asserted First Amendment right of a video game developer to use his likeness in its expressive works.

The district court concluded that the game developer, Electronic Arts ("EA"), had no First Amendment defense against the right-of-publicity claims of the football player, Samuel Keller. We affirm. Under the "transformative use" test developed by the California Supreme Court, EA's use does not qualify for First Amendment protection as a matter of law because it literally recreates Keller in the very setting in which he has achieved renown. The other First Amendment defenses asserted by EA do not defeat Keller's claims either.

Samuel Keller was the starting quarterback for Arizona State University in 2005 before he transferred to the University of Nebraska, where he played during the 2007 season. EA is the producer of the *NCAA Football* series of video games, which allow users to control avatars representing college football players as those avatars participate in simulated games. In *NCAA Football,* EA seeks to replicate each school's entire team as accurately as possible.

EA's game differs from reality in that EA omits the players' names on their jerseys and assigns each player a home town that is different from the actual player's home town. However, users of the video game may upload rosters of names obtained from third parties so that the names do appear on the jerseys....

[Keller's Right of Publicity Claim]

The California Supreme Court formulated the transformative use defense in *Comedy III Productions, Inc. v. Gary Saderup, Inc.,* 25 Cal.4th 387 (2001). The defense is "a balancing test between the First Amendment and the right of publicity based on whether the work in question adds significant creative elements so as to be transformed into something more than a mere celebrity likeness or imitation." The California Supreme Court explained that "when a work contains significant transformative elements, it is not only especially worthy of First Amendment protection, but it is also less likely to interfere with the economic interest protected by the right of publicity." The court rejected the wholesale importation of the copyright "fair use" defense into right-of-publicity claims, but recognized that some aspects of that defense are "particularly pertinent."

Comedy III gives us at least five factors to consider in determining whether a work is sufficiently transformative to obtain First Amendment protection. First, if "the celebrity likeness is one of the 'raw materials' from which an original work is synthesized," it is more likely to be transformative than if "the depiction or imitation of the celebrity is the very sum and substance of the work in question." Second, the work is protected if it is "primarily the defendant's own expression"—as long as that expression is "something other than the likeness of the celebrity." This factor requires an examination of whether a likely purchaser's primary motivation is to buy a reproduction of the celebrity, or to buy the expressive work of that artist. Third, to avoid making judgments concerning "the quality of the artistic contribution," a court should conduct an inquiry "more quantitative than qualitative" and ask "whether the literal and imitative or the creative elements predominate in the work." Fourth, the California Supreme Court indicated that "a subsidiary inquiry" would be useful in close cases: whether "the marketability and economic value of the challenged work derive primarily from the fame of the celebrity depicted." Lastly, the court indicated that "when an artist's skill and talent is manifestly subordinated to the overall goal of creating a conventional portrait of a celebrity so as to commercially exploit his or her fame," the work is not transformative.

We have explained that "[o]nly if [a defendant] is entitled to the [transformative] defense *as a matter of law* can it prevail on its motion to strike," because the California Supreme Court "envisioned the application of the defense as a question of fact." *Hilton* [*v. Hallmark Cards*, 599 F.3d 894,910 (9th Cir.2009)]. As a result, EA "is only entitled to the defense as a matter of law if no trier of fact could reasonably conclude that the [game] [i]s not transformative."

California courts have applied the transformative use test in relevant situations in four cases. First, in *Comedy III* itself, the California Supreme Court applied the test to T-shirts and lithographs bearing a likeness of The Three Stooges and concluded that it could "discern no significant transformative or creative contribution." The court reasoned that the artist's "undeniable skill is manifestly subordinated to the overall goal of creating literal, conventional depictions of The Three Stooges so as to exploit their fame." "[W]ere we to decide that [the artist's] depictions were protected by the First Amendment," the court continued, "we cannot perceive how the right of publicity would remain a viable right other than in cases of falsified celebrity endorsements."

Second, in *Winter v. DC Comics*, the California Supreme Court applied the test to comic books containing characters Johnny and Edgar Autumn, "depicted as villainous half-worm, half-human offspring" but evoking two famous brothers, rockers Johnny and Edgar Winter. 30 Cal.4th 881, 134 Cal.Rptr.2d 634, 69 P.3d 473, 476 (2003). The court held that "the comic books are transformative and entitled to First Amendment protection." It reasoned that the comic books "are not just conventional depictions of plaintiffs but contain significant expressive content other than plaintiffs' mere likenesses." "To the extent the drawings of the Autumn brothers resemble plaintiffs at all, they are distorted for purposes of lampoon, parody, or caricature." Importantly, the court relied on the fact that the brothers "are but cartoon characters ... in a larger story, which is itself quite expressive."

Third, in *Kirby v. Sega of America, Inc.*, the California Court of Appeal applied the transformative use test to a video game in which the user controls the dancing of "Ulala," a reporter from outer space allegedly based on singer Kierin Kirby, whose "'signature' lyrical expression ... is 'ooh la la.'" 144 Cal.App.4th 47, 50 Cal.Rptr.3d 607, 609–10 (2006). The court held that "Ulala is more than a mere likeness or literal depiction of Kirby," pointing to Ulala's "extremely tall, slender computer-generated physique," her "hairstyle and primary costume," her dance moves, and her role as "a space-age reporter in the 25th century," all of which were "unlike any public depiction of Kirby." "As in *Winter*, Ulala is a 'fanciful, creative character' who exists in the context of a unique and expressive video game."

Finally, in *No Doubt v. Activision Publishing, Inc.*, the California Court of Appeal addressed Activision's *Band Hero* video game. 192 Cal.App.4th 1018, 122 Cal.Rptr.3d 397, 400 (2011), *petition for review denied*, 2011 Cal. LEXIS 6100 (Cal. June 8, 2011) (No. B223996). In *Band Hero*, users simulate performing in a rock band in time with popular songs. Users choose from a number of avatars, some of which represent actual rock stars, including the members of the rock band No Doubt. Activision licensed No Doubt's likeness, but allegedly exceeded the scope of the license by permitting users to manipulate the No Doubt avatars to play any song in the game, solo or with members of other bands, and even to alter the avatars' voices. The court held that No Doubt's right of publicity prevailed despite Activision's First Amendment defense because the game was not "transformative" under the *Comedy III* test. It reasoned that the video game characters were "literal recreations of the band members," doing "the same activity by which the band achieved and maintains its fame." According to the court, the fact "that the avatars appear in the context of a videogame that contains many other creative elements[ ] does not transform the avatars into anything other than exact depictions of No Doubt's members doing exactly what they do as celebrities." The court concluded that "the expressive elements of the game remain manifestly subordinated to the overall goal of creating a conventional portrait of No Doubt so as to commercially exploit its fame."

We have also had occasion to apply the transformative use test. In *Hilton v. Hallmark Cards*, we applied the test to a birthday card depicting Paris Hilton in a manner reminiscent of an episode of Hilton's reality show *The Simple Life*. 599 F.3d at 899. We observed some differences between the episode and the card, but noted that "the basic setting is the same: we see Paris Hilton, born to privilege, working as a waitress." We reasoned that "[w]hen we compare Hallmark's card to the video game in *Kirby*, which transported a 1990s singer (catchphrases and all) into the 25th century and transmogrified her into a space-age reporter, ... the card falls far short of the level of new expression added in the video game." As a result, we concluded that "there is enough doubt as to whether Hallmark's card is transformative under our case law that we cannot say Hallmark is entitled to the defense as a matter of law."

With these cases in mind as guidance, we conclude that EA's use of Keller's likeness does not contain significant transformative elements such that EA is entitled to the defense as a matter of law. The facts of *No Doubt* are very similar to those here. EA is alleged to have replicated Keller's physical characteristics in *NCAA Football,* just as the members of No Doubt are realistically portrayed in *Band Hero.* Here, as in *Band Hero,* users manipulate the characters in the performance of the same activity for which they are known in real life — playing football in this case, and performing in a rock band in *Band Hero.* The context in which the activity occurs is also similarly realistic — real venues in *Band Hero* and realistic depictions of actual football stadiums in *NCAA Football.* As the district court found, Keller is represented as "what he was: the starting quarterback for Arizona State" and Nebraska, and "the game's setting is identical to where the public found [Keller] during his collegiate career: on the football field."

EA argues that the district court erred in focusing primarily on Keller's likeness and ignoring the transformative elements of the game as a whole. Judge Thomas, our dissenting colleague, suggests the same. We are unable to say that there was any error, particularly in light of *No Doubt,* which reasoned much the same as the district court in this case: "that the avatars appear in the context of a videogame that contains many other creative elements[] does not transform the avatars into anything other than exact depictions of No Doubt's members doing exactly what they do as celebrities." *No Doubt,* 122 Cal.Rptr.3d at 411. EA suggests that the fact that *NCAA Football* users can alter the characteristics of the avatars in the game is significant. Again, our dissenting colleague agrees. *See* Dissent at 1286–87. In *No Doubt,* the California Court of Appeal noted that *Band Hero* "d[id] not permit players to alter the No Doubt avatars in any respect." The court went on to say that the No Doubt avatars "remain at all times immutable images of the real celebrity musicians, in stark contrast to the 'fanciful, creative characters' in *Winter* and *Kirby.*" *Id.* The court explained further:

> [I]t is the differences between *Kirby* and the instant case ... which are de-terminative. In *Kirby,* the pop singer was portrayed as an entirely new char-acter — the space-age news reporter Ulala. In *Band Hero,* by contrast, no matter what else occurs in the game during the depiction of the No Doubt avatars, the avatars perform rock songs, the same activity by which the band achieved and maintains its fame. Moreover, the avatars perform those songs as literal recreations of the band members. That the avatars can be manip-ulated to perform at fanciful venues including outer space or to sing songs the real band would object to singing, or that the avatars appear in the context of a videogame that contains many other creative elements, does not trans-form the avatars into anything other than exact depictions of No Doubt's members doing exactly what they do as celebrities.

Id. at 410–11.

Judge Thomas says that "[t]he Court of Appeal cited character immutability as a chief factor distinguishing [*No Doubt*] from *Winter* and *Kirby.*" Dissent at 1287. Though No Doubt certainly mentioned the immutability of the avatars, we do not read the California Court of Appeal's decision as turning on the inability of users to alter the avatars. The key contrast with *Winter* and *Kirby* was that in those games the public figures were transformed into "fanciful, creative characters" or "portrayed as ... entirely new character[s]." *No Doubt*, 122 Cal.Rptr.3d at 410. On this front, our case is clearly aligned with *No Doubt*, not with *Winter* and *Kirby*. We believe No Doubt offers a persuasive precedent that cannot be materially distinguished from Keller's case.

The Third Circuit came to the same conclusion in *Hart v. Electronic Arts, Inc.*, 717 F.3d 141 (3d Cir.2013). In *Hart*, EA faced a materially identical challenge under New Jersey right-of-publicity law, brought by former Rutgers quarterback Ryan Hart. Though the Third Circuit was tasked with interpreting New Jersey law, the court looked to the transformative use test developed in California. Applying the test, the court held that "the *NCAA Football* ... games at issue ... do not sufficiently transform [Hart]'s identity to escape the right of publicity claim," reversing the district court's grant of summary judgment to EA.

As we have, the Third Circuit considered the potentially transformative nature of the game as a whole, and the user's ability to alter avatar characteristics. Asserting that "the lack of transformative context is even more pronounced here than in *No Doubt*," and that "the ability to modify the avatar counts for little where the appeal of the game lies in users' ability to play as, or alongside[,] their preferred players or team," the Third Circuit agreed with us that these changes do not render the *NCAA Football* games sufficiently transformative to defeat a right-of-publicity claim.

Judge Ambro dissented in *Hart*, concluding that "the creative components of *NCAA Football* contain sufficient expressive transformation to merit First Amendment protection." But in critiquing the majority opinion, Judge Ambro disregarded *No Doubt* and *Kirby* because "they were not decided by the architect of the Transformative Use Test, the Supreme Court of California." He thus "d[id] not attempt to explain or distinguish the[se cases'] holdings except to note that [he] believe[s] *No Doubt*, which focused on individual depictions rather than the work in its entirety, was wrongly decided in light of the prior precedent in *Comedy III* and *Winter*." ... Like the majority in *Hart*, we rely substantially on *No Doubt*, and believe we are correct to do so.

Given that *NCAA Football* realistically portrays college football players in the context of college football games, the district court was correct in concluding that EA cannot prevail as a matter of law based on the transformative use defense at the anti-SLAPP stage. *Cf. Hilton*, 599 F.3d at 910–11.

EA urges us to adopt for right-of-publicity claims the broader First Amendment defense that we have previously adopted in the context of false endorsement claims under the Lanham Act: the *Rogers* test.

Rogers v. Grimaldi is a landmark Second Circuit case balancing First Amendment rights against claims under the Lanham Act. 875 F.2d 994 (2d Cir.1989). The case involved a suit brought by the famous performer Ginger Rogers against the producers and distributors of *Ginger and Fred,* a movie about two fictional Italian cabaret performers who imitated Rogers and her frequent performing partner Fred Astaire. Rogers alleged both a violation of the Lanham Act for creating the false impression that she endorsed the film and infringement of her common law right of publicity....

We first endorsed the *Rogers* test for Lanham Act claims involving artistic or expressive works in *Mattel, Inc. v. MCA Records, Inc.*, 296 F.3d 894, 902 (9th Cir.2002). We agreed that, in the context of artistic and literary titles, "[c]onsumers expect a title to communicate a message about the book or movie, but they do not expect it to identify the publisher or producer," and "adopt[ed] the *Rogers* standard as our own." *Id.* Then, in *E.S.S. Entertainment 2000, Inc. v. Rock Star Videos, Inc.*, we considered a claim by a strip club owner that video game maker Rock Star incorporated its club logo into the game's virtual depiction of East Los Angeles, violating the club's trademark right to that logo. We held that Rock Star's use of the logo and trade dress was protected by the First Amendment and that it therefore could not be held liable under the Lanham Act. *Id.* at 1099–1101. In so doing, we extended the Rogers test slightly, noting that "[a]lthough this test traditionally applies to uses of a trademark in the title of an artistic work, there is no principled reason why it ought not also apply to the use of a trademark in the body of the work."

In this case, EA argues that we should extend this test, created to evaluate Lanham Act claims, to apply to right-of-publicity claims because it is "less prone to misinterpretation" and "more protective of free expression" than the transformative use defense. Although we acknowledge that there is some overlap between the transformative use test formulated by the California Supreme Court and the *Rogers* test, we disagree that the *Rogers* test should be imported wholesale for right-of-publicity claims. Our conclusion on this point is consistent with the Third Circuit's rejection of EA's identical argument in *Hart*. As the history and development of the *Rogers* test makes clear, it was designed to protect consumers from the risk of consumer confusion — the hallmark element of a Lanham Act claim. The right of publicity, on the other hand, does not primarily seek to prevent consumer confusion. Rather, it primarily "protects a form of intellectual property [in one's person] that society deems to have some social utility." ...

California has developed two additional defenses aimed at protecting the reporting of factual information under state law. One of these defenses only applies to common law right-of-publicity claims while the other only applies to statutory right-of-publicity claims. *Montana v. San Jose Mercury News, Inc.*, 34 Cal.App.4th 790 (1995). Liability will not lie for common law right-of-publicity claims for the "publication of matters in the public interest." Similarly, liability will not lie for statutory right-of-publicity claims for the "use of a name, voice, signature, photograph, or likeness in connection with any news, public affairs, or sports broadcast or account, or any political campaign." Cal. Civ.Code § 3344(d). Although these defenses are based on First Amendment concerns, *Gill v. Hearst Publ'g Co.*, 40 Cal.2d 224, 253 P.2d 441, 443–44 (1953), they are not coextensive with the Federal Constitution, *New Kids on the Block v. News Am. Publ'g, Inc.*, 971 F.2d 302, 310 n. 10 (9th Cir.1992), and their application is thus a matter of state law.

EA argues that these defenses give it the right to "incorporate athletes' names, statistics, and other biographical information" into its expressive works, as the defenses were "designed to create 'extra breathing space' for the use of a person's name in connection with matters of public interest." Keller responds that the right of publicity yields to free use of a public figure's likeness only to the extent reasonably required to report information to the public or publish factual data, and that the defenses apply only to broadcasts or accounts of public affairs, not to EA's *NCAA Football* games, which do not contain or constitute such reporting about Keller.

California courts have generally analyzed the common law defense and the statutory defense separately, but it is clear that both defenses protect only the act of publishing or reporting.... EA is not publishing or reporting factual data. EA's video game is a means by which users can play their own virtual football games, not a means for obtaining information about real-world football games. Although EA has incorporated certain actual player information into the game (height, weight, etc.), its case is considerably weakened by its decision not to include the athletes' names along with their likenesses and statistical data. EA can hardly be considered to be "reporting" on Keller's career at Arizona State and Nebraska when it is not even using Keller's name in connection with his avatar in the game. Put simply, EA's interactive game is not a publication of facts about college football; it is a game, not a reference source. These state law defenses, therefore, do not apply.

Under California's transformative use defense, EA's use of the likenesses of college athletes like Samuel Keller in its video games is not, as a matter of law, protected by the First Amendment. We reject EA's suggestion to import the *Rogers* test into the right-of-publicity arena, and conclude that statelaw defenses for the reporting of information do not protect EA's use. AFFIRMED.

THOMAS, Circuit Judge, dissenting:

Because the creative and transformative elements of Electronic Arts' *NCAA Football* video game series predominate over the commercial use of the athletes' likenesses, the First Amendment protects EA from liability. Therefore, I respectfully dissent....

The five considerations articulated in *Comedy III*, and cited by the majority, are whether: (1) the celebrity likeness is one of the raw materials from which an original work is synthesized; (2) the work is primarily the defendant's own expression if the expression is something other than the likeness of the celebrity; (3) the literal and imitative or creative elements predominate in the work; (4) the marketability and economic value of the challenged work derives primarily from the fame of the celebrity depicted; and (5) an artist's skill and talent has been manifestly subordinated to the overall goal of creating a conventional portrait of a celebrity so as to commercially exploit the celebrity's fame....

Although these considerations are often distilled as analytical factors, Justice Mosk was careful in *Comedy III* not to label them as such. Indeed, the focus of *Comedy III* is a more holistic examination of whether the transformative and creative elements of a particular work predominate over commercially based literal or imitative depictions. The distinction is critical, because excessive deconstruction of *Comedy III* can lead to misapplication of the test. And it is at this juncture that I must respectfully part ways with my colleagues in the majority.

The majority confines its inquiry to how a single athlete's likeness is represented in the video game, rather than examining the transformative and creative elements in the video game as a whole. In my view, this approach contradicts the holistic analysis required by the transformative use test. *See Hart v. Elec. Arts, Inc.*, 717 F.3d 141, 170–76 (3d Cir.2013) (Ambro, J., dissenting). The salient question is whether the entire work is transformative, and whether the transformative elements predominate, rather than whether an individual persona or image has been altered.

When EA's *NCAA Football* video game series is examined carefully, and put in proper context, I conclude that the creative and transformative elements of the games predominate over the commercial use of the likenesses of the athletes within the games.

Notes and Questions

a. The saga of the NCAA litigation involving amateur players' rights of publicity continues as a class action. *See In re NCAA Student-Athlete Name & Likeness Licensing Litig.*, C 09-1967 CW, 2013 WL 5979327 (N.D. Cal. 2013) (order granting in part and denying in part, motion for class certification). Another consequence of the litigation is pressure on the NCAA to amend rules related to student athlete reimbursements and the ability of student athletes to earn income while maintaining athletic eligibility.

b. Would the *Keller* decision have the same outcome for use of players' name and likeness in television content? *See Accord Facenda v. N.F.L. Films, Inc.*, 542 F.3d 1007, 1031–32 (3d Cir. 2008) (sportscaster's breach of contract and right of publicity claims not preempted by copyright where sportscaster's contract allowed defendant to use sportscaster's voice recordings in context of sports broadcasts, not in context of television advertisements for video game). In *Dryer v. NFL*, 2010 U.S. Dist. LEXIS 24817 (D. Minn. Jan. 26, 2010), the district court has taken a much more sympathetic approach for the former players:

> Plaintiffs in this putative class action are former professional football players. They contend that Defendant National Football League ("NFL") is violating their common-law and statutory rights of publicity by using video footage from games in which they played as part of the NFL Films' promotional videos, such as the "History" series, which includes videos called "The Fabulous Fifties" and "Sensational 60s." There is no dispute that these videos are used to promote the NFL. In the course of that promotion, the NFL uses both the Plaintiffs' names and images of Plaintiffs from their playing days.... [F]or the purposes of this Motion ... the films at issue are commercial speech. Moreover, Plaintiffs have sufficiently established that the constitutional protection to be afforded the films may not outweigh Plaintiffs' interests in their own identities.

c. In contrast with *Dryer v. NFL*, earlier California decisions treated the somewhat promotional television content as non-commercial speech.

Defendant Major League Baseball Properties, Inc. (MLBP), is a limited agent for each of the Clubs for certain purposes involving the use of the Clubs' trademarks. MLBP licenses the use of each Club's right to the game-related images of its current and former players. MLBP produces certain print and video publications including All-Star and World Series programs of its own.... Defendant The PHoenix Communications Group, Inc. (PHoenix), was authorized by MLBP to produce and distribute audiovisual programs containing game performances and related activities. For 13 years between 1985 and 1998, PHoenix produced certain television shows including: This Week in Baseball, Pennant Chase, and Major League Baseball Magazine, containing footage of earlier games. It also satisfied video footage requests made by third parties....

The challenged uses involve statements of historical fact, descriptions of these facts or video depictions of them. Plaintiffs never suggest how Baseball's actions impair their economic interests. It appears equally likely that plaintiffs' marketability is enhanced by Baseball's conduct challenged here. Balancing plaintiffs' negligible economic interests against the public's enduring fascination with baseball's past, we conclude that the public interest favoring the free dissemination of information regarding baseball's history far outweighs any proprietary interests at stake. Therefore, the trial court was correct to grant summary adjudication on this cause of action.

Gionfriddo v. Major League Baseball, 94 Cal. App. 4th 400 (Cal. Dist. Ct. App. 2001)

d. The Romantics recorded "What I Like About You" in 1979. The song was used in *Guitar Hero Encore: Rocks the 80's*. Although the song was licensed for the video game, no trademark of the Romantics or publicity rights in its members were obtained. To what extent does the performance of an individual create a sufficient identity that one's publicity rights have been exploited? *See Romantics v. Activision Publ'g, Inc.*, 574 F. Supp. 2d 758 (E.D. Mich. 2008).

e. The *Hart* Court quotes from *No Doubt v. Activision, Inc.*, 192 Cal. App. 4th 1018, 122 Cal. Rptr. 3d 397 (Cal. App. 2011), regarding a finding of violation of publicity rights. To what extent would this result have changed were the case not primarily for a breach of contract?

Problem 15-D

As described in Problem 15-C, Bryce has been collaborating with a video game publisher to produce a new interactive game based on the social life of a rock star. The game includes features for creating bands, touring, performing, and initiating bar fights. In both the *Teen* and *Mature* versions of the game, it uses fictional bands and music created and recorded by Bryce.

Bryce and the other producers would like to incorporate music written by additional artists and incorporate famous bands into the game play. In particular, one of the producers believes that bands that have famously split up would be particular fun to incorporate into the game play and suggests that fair use would allow the game to use the Beach Boys, the Beatles, and other famously disbanded groups. Please identify the elements of the game that require licenses and advise Bryce the extent to which the game producers may rely on fair use for the game play.

E. Contract Issues for Consumers

Clickwrap, Shrinkwrap, TOS, and EULA

Clickwrap and shrinkwrap agreements are a method of securing an agreement with the end-user of a particular piece of software, including video games, requiring the user to comply with certain terms in using the software. Shrinkwrap agreements often take the form of a notice on the packaging of a particular software title, which puts a purchaser on notice that there are additional terms that must be complied with to use the software, terms which are usually included inside the product packaging. Browsewrap is the term used to describe such provisions when they are posted as links on a website. Typically, a website's privacy policy or copyright infringement policy are made accessible by use of a footer on the bottom of the website page. Shrinkwrap and browsewrap do not have any physical manifestation of assent.

Clickwrap agreements provide all the material terms of the contract in a page that requires the consumer to check a box or click on an "I agree" button as a condition to accessing the content of the game or website. In this way, the transaction guarantees the consumer has had access to the terms of the agreement and has manifested consent through some physical conduct. These contracts are generally referred to as "Terms of Service Agreements" (TOS) or "End User License Agreements" (EULA). Issues arising as to the enforceability of such agreements are essentially matters of contract law; therefore, the application of law and enforceability questions can vary considerably from jurisdiction to jurisdiction applying the applicable state law.

Courts have held clickwrap and shrinkwrap agreements enforceable on varied grounds. Some have found that the clickwrap or shrinkwrap agreement provided sufficient notice of additional terms that were required to use that particular piece of software. The leading case upholding clickwrap and shrinkwrap agreements is *ProCD, Inc. v. Zeidenberg*, 86 F.3d 1447 (7th. Cir. 1997), where the court found that the shrinkwrap notice on the packaging provided sufficient notice of additional terms within the package and software that required compliance for usage. In *Davidson & Assocs. v. Jung*, 422 F.3d 630 (8th Cir. 2005), the Eight Circuit upheld a TOS and EULA to stop unauthorized game reproduction as well as reverse engineering of *World of Warcraft*.

Beyond recognizing the existence of a contract, however, courts will also look to the substance of the transaction, as discussed in the following opinion.

Bragg v. Linden Research, Inc.

487 F. Supp. 2d 593 (E.D. Pa. 2007)

This case is about virtual property maintained on a virtual world on the Internet. Plaintiff, March Bragg, Esq., claims an ownership interest in such virtual property. Bragg contends that Defendants, the operators of the virtual world, unlawfully confiscated his virtual property and denied him access to their virtual world. Ultimately at issue in this case are the novel questions of what rights and obligations grow out of the relationship between the owner and creator of a virtual world and its resident-customers. While the property and the world where it is found are "virtual," the dispute is real....

I. Background

A. Second Life

The defendants in this case, Linden Research Inc. ("Linden") and its Chief Executive Officer, Philip Rosedale, operate a multiplayer role-playing game set in the virtual world[21] known as "Second Life." Participants create avatars[22] to represent themselves, and Second Life is populated by hundreds of thousands of avatars, whose interactions with one another are limited only by the human imagination. According to Plaintiff, many people "are now living large portions of their lives, forming friendships with others, building and acquiring virtual property, forming contracts, substantial business relationships and forming social organizations" in virtual worlds such as Second Life. Owning property in and having access to this virtual world is, moreover, apparently important to the plaintiff in this case.

B. Recognition of Property Rights

In November 2003, Linden announced that it would recognize participants' full intellectual property protection for the digital content they created or otherwise owned in Second Life. As a result, Second Life avatars may now buy, own, and sell virtual goods ranging "from cars to homes to slot machines."[23] Most significantly for this case, avatars may purchase "virtual land," make improvements to that land, exclude other avatars from entering onto the land, rent the land, or sell the land to

---

21. The virtual world at issue is an interactive computer simulation which lets its participants see, hear, use, and even modify the simulated objects in the computer-generated environment. *See* Woodrow Barfield, *Intellectual Property Rights in Virtual Environments: Considering the Rights of Owners, Programmers and Virtual Avatars*, 39 Akron L. Rev. 649, 649 (2006) (defining virtual world).

22. The term "avatar" derives etymologically from the Sanskrit word for crossing down or descent and was used originally to refer to the earthly incarnation of a Hindu deity. Webster's II New Riverside University Dictionary 141 (1998). Since the advent of computers, however, "avatar" is also used to refer to an Internet user's virtual representation of herself in a computer game, in an Internet chat room, or in other Internet fora. *See* Wikipedia, Definition of Avatar, *available at* http://en.wikipedia.org.

23. Although participants purchase virtual property using the virtual currency of "lindens," lindens themselves are bought and sold for real U.S. dollars. Linden maintains a currency exchange that sets an exchange rate between lindens and U.S. dollars. Third parties, including ebay.com, also provide additional currency exchanges.

other avatars for a profit. Assertedly, by recognizing virtual property rights, Linden would distinguish itself from other virtual worlds available on the Internet and thus increase participation in Second Life.

Defendant Rosedale personally joined in efforts to publicize Linden's recognition of rights to virtual property. For example, in 2003, Rosedale stated in a press release made available on Second Life's website that:

> Until now, any content created by users for persistent state worlds, such as Everquest® or Star Wars Galaxies™, has essentially become the property of the company developing and hosting the world.... We believe our new policy recognizes the fact that persistent world users are making significant contributions to building these worlds and should be able to both own the content they create and share in the value that is created. The preservation of users' property rights is a necessary step toward the emergence of genuinely real online worlds.

Press Release, Linden Lab, Linden Lab Preserves Real World Intellectual Property Rights of Users of its Second Life Online Services (Nov. 14, 2003). After this initial announcement, Rosedale continued to personally hype the ownership of virtual property on Second Life.... Rosedale even created his own avatar and held virtual town hall meetings on Second Life where he made representations about the purchase of virtual land. Bragg "attended" such meetings and relied on the representations that Rosedale made therein.

C. Plaintiffs' Participation in Second Life

In 2005, Plaintiff Marc Bragg, Esq., signed up and paid Linden to participate in Second Life. Bragg claims that he was induced into "investing" in virtual land by representations made by Linden and Rosedale in press releases, interviews, and through the Second Life website. Bragg also paid Linden real money as "tax" on his land. By April 2006, Bragg had not only purchased numerous parcels of land in his Second Life, he had also digitally crafted "fireworks" that he was able to sell to other avatars for a profit. Bragg also acquired other virtual items from other avatars.

The dispute ultimately at issue in this case arose on April 30, 2006, when Bragg acquired a parcel of virtual land named "Taessot" for $ 300. Linden sent Bragg an email advising him that [Taesot] had been improperly purchased through an "exploit." Linden took Taesot away. It then froze Bragg's account, effectively confiscating all of the virtual property and currency that he maintained on his account with Second Life.

Bragg brought suit against Linden and Rosedale in the Court of Common Pleas of Chester County, Pennsylvania, on October 3, 2006.[24] Linden and Rosedale removed the case to this Court and then, within a week, moved to compel arbitration....

---

24. Bragg's complaint contains counts under the Pennsylvania Unfair Trade Practices and Consumer Protection Law, 73 P.S. § 201-1, *et seq.* (Count I), the California Unfair and Deceptive Practices Act, Cal. Bus. & Prof. Code § 17200 (Count II), California Consumer Legal Remedies Act, Ca. Civ. Code § 1750, *et seq.* (Count III), fraud (Count IV), the California Civil Code § 1812.600, *et seq.* (Count V), conversion (Count VI), intentional interference with a contractual relations (Count VII), breach of contract (Count VIII), unjust enrichment (Count IX), and tortious breach of the covenant of good faith and fair dealing (Count X).

Defendants ... filed a motion to compel arbitration that seeks to dismiss this action and compel Bragg to submit his claims to arbitration according to the Rules of the International Chamber of Commerce ("ICC") in San Francisco.

III. Motion to Compel Arbitration

A. Relevant Facts

Before a person is permitted to participate in Second Life, she must accept the Terms of Service of Second Life (the "TOS") by clicking a button indicating acceptance of the TOS. Bragg concedes that he clicked the "accept" button before accessing Second Life. Included in the TOS are a California choice of law provision, an arbitration provision, and forum selection clause. Specifically, located in the fourteenth line of the thirteenth paragraph under the heading "GENERAL PROVISIONS," and following provisions regarding the applicability of export and import laws to Second Life, the following language appears:

> Any dispute or claim arising out of or in connection with this Agreement or the performance, breach or termination thereof, shall be finally settled by binding arbitration in San Francisco, California under the Rules of Arbitration of the International Chamber of Commerce by three arbitrators appointed in accordance with said rules.... Notwithstanding the foregoing, either party may apply to any court of competent jurisdiction for injunctive relief or enforcement of this arbitration provision without breach of this arbitration provision.

...

C. Application

1. Unconscionability of the Arbitration Agreement

Bragg resists enforcement of the TOS's arbitration provision on the basis that it is "both procedurally and substantively unconscionable and is itself evidence of defendants' scheme to deprive Plaintiff (and others) of both their money and their day in court."

Section 2 of the [Federal Arbitration Act] provides that written arbitration agreements "shall be valid, irrevocable, and enforceable, save upon such grounds as exist at law or in equity for the revocation of any contract." 9 U.S.C. § 2. Thus, "generally applicable contract defenses, such as fraud, duress, or unconscionability, may be applied to invalidate arbitration agreements without contravening § 2." *Doctor's Assocs. v. Casarotto*, 517 U.S. 681, 687, 116 S. Ct. 1652, 134 L. Ed. 2d 902 (1996) (citations omitted). When determining whether such defenses might apply to any purported agreement to arbitrate the dispute in question, "courts generally ... should apply ordinary state-law principles that govern the formation of contracts." *First Options of Chicago, Inc. v. Kaplan*, 514 U.S. 938, 944 (1995). Thus, the Court will apply California state law to determine whether the arbitration provision is unconscionable.

Under California law, unconscionability has both procedural and substantive components. The procedural component can be satisfied by showing (1) oppression through the existence of unequal bargaining positions or (2) surprise through hidden terms common in the context of adhesion contracts. The substantive component can be satisfied by showing overly harsh or one-sided results that "shock the conscience." The two elements operate on a sliding scale such that the more significant one is, the less significant the other need be. However, a claim of unconscionability cannot be determined merely by examining the face of the contract; there must be an inquiry into the circumstances under which the contract was executed, and the contract's purpose, and effect.

(a) Procedural Unconscionability

A contract or clause is procedurally unconscionable if it is a contract of adhesion. A contract of adhesion, in turn, is a "standardized contract, which, imposed and drafted by the party of superior bargaining strength, relegates to the subscribing party only the opportunity to adhere to the contract or reject it." *Comb v. PayPal, Inc.*, 218 F. Supp. 2d 1165, 1172 (N.D. Cal. 2002). Under California law, "the critical factor in procedural unconscionability analysis is the manner in which the contract or the disputed clause was presented and negotiated." *Nagrampa v. MailCoups, Inc.*, 469 F.3d 1257, 1282 (9th Cir. 2006). "When the weaker party is presented the clause and told to 'take it or leave it' without the opportunity for meaningful negotiation, oppression, and therefore procedural unconscionability, are present." *Id.* (internal quotation and citation omitted).

The TOS are a contract of adhesion. Linden presents the TOS on a take-it-or-leave-it basis. A potential participant can either click "assent" to the TOS, and then gain entrance to Second Life's virtual world, or refuse assent and be denied access. Linden also clearly has superior bargaining strength over Bragg. Although Bragg is an experienced attorney, who believes he is expert enough to comment on numerous industry standards and the "rights" or participants in virtual worlds, he was never presented with an opportunity to use his experience and lawyering skills to negotiate terms different from the TOS that Linden offered.

Moreover, there was no "reasonably available market alternatives [to defeat] a claim of adhesiveness." ... The procedural element of unconscionability also "focuses on ... surprise." *Gutierrez v. Autowest, Inc.*, 114 Cal. App. 4th 77 (Ct. App. 2003) (citations omitted). In determining whether surprise exists, California courts focus not on the plaintiff's subjective reading of the contract, but rather, more objectively, on "the extent to which the supposedly agreed-upon terms of the bargain are hidden in the prolix printed form drafted by the party seeking to enforce the disputed terms." *Id.* In *Gutierrez*, the court found such surprise where an arbitration clause was "particularly inconspicuous, printed in eight-point typeface on the opposite side of the signature page of the lease." *Id.*

Here, although the TOS are ubiquitous throughout Second Life, Linden buried the TOS's arbitration provision in a lengthy paragraph under the benign heading "GENERAL PROVISIONS."

Comb is most instructive. In that case, the plaintiffs challenged an arbitration provision that was part of an agreement to which they had assented, in circumstances similar to this case, by clicking their assent on an online application page. The defendant, PayPal, was a large company with millions of individual online customers. The plaintiffs, with one exception, were all individual customers of PayPal. Given the small amount of the average transaction with PayPal, the fact that most PayPal customers were private individuals, and that there was a "dispute as to whether PayPal's competitors offer their services without requiring customers to enter into arbitration agreements," the court concluded that the user agreement at issue "satisfie[d] the criteria for procedural unconscionability under California law." *Id.* at 1172–73. Here, as in *Comb*, procedural unconscionability is satisfied.

(b) Substantive Unconscionability

Even if an agreement is procedurally unconscionable, "it may nonetheless be enforceable if the substantive terms are reasonable." Substantive unconscionability focuses on the one-sidedness of the contract terms. Here, a number of the TOS's elements lead the Court to conclude that Bragg has demonstrated that the TOS are substantively unconscionable.

(i) Mutuality

Under California law, substantive unconscionability has been found where an arbitration provision forces the weaker party to arbitrate claims but permits a choice of forums for the stronger party. In other words, the arbitration remedy must contain a "modicum of bilaterality." This principle has been extended to arbitration provisions that allow the stronger party a range of remedies before arbitrating a dispute, such as self-help, while relegating to the weaker party the sole remedy of arbitration.

In *Comb*, for example, the court found a lack of mutuality where the user agreement allowed PayPal "at its sole discretion" to restrict accounts, withhold funds, undertake its own investigation of a customer's financial records, close accounts, and procure ownership of all funds in dispute unless and until the customer is "later determined to be entitled to the funds in dispute." 218 F. Supp. 2d at 1173–74. Also significant was the fact that the user agreement was "subject to change by PayPal without prior notice (unless prior notice is required by law), by posting of the revised Agreement on the PayPal website." *Id.*

Here, the TOS contain many of the same elements that made the PayPal user agreement substantively unconscionable for lack of mutuality. The TOS proclaim that "Linden has the right at any time for any reason or no reason to suspend or terminate your Account, terminate this Agreement, and/or refuse any and all current or future use of the Service without notice or liability to you." TOS P 7.1. Whether or not a customer has breached the Agreement is "determined in Linden's sole discretion." *Id.* Linden also reserves the right to return no money at all based on mere "suspicions of fraud" or other violations of law. *Id.* Finally, the TOS state that "Linden may amend this Agreement … at any time in its sole discretion by posting the amended Agreement [on its website]." TOS P 1.2.

In effect, the TOS provide Linden with a variety of one-sided remedies to resolve disputes, while forcing its customers to arbitrate any disputes with Linden. This is precisely what occurred here. When a dispute arose, Linden exercised its option to use self-help by freezing Bragg's account, retaining funds that Linden alone determined were subject to dispute, and then telling Bragg that he could resolve the dispute by initiating a costly arbitration process. The TOS expressly authorized Linden to engage in such unilateral conduct. As in *Comb*, "[f]or all practical purposes, a customer may resolve disputes only after [Linden] has had control of the disputed funds for an indefinite period of time," and may only resolve those disputes by initiating arbitration. 218 F. Supp. 2d at 1175.

Linden's right to modify the arbitration clause is also significant. "The effect of [Linden's] unilateral right to modify the arbitration clause is that it could ... craft precisely the sort of asymmetrical arbitration agreement that is prohibited under California law as unconscionable. This lack of mutuality supports a finding of substantive unconscionability.

[The court then reviewed the costs and fee-splitting provisions, determining that Bragg would have to advance $3,750 to $8,625 at the outset, but the expenses could reach as high as $13,687.50. The high cost, in relation to the claim support the finding of unconscionability. Similarly, the court found the forum selection clause requiring travel to San Francisco "appears to be yet one more means by which the arbitration clause serves to shield [Linden] from liability instead of providing a neutral forum in which to arbitrate disputes." Quoting *Comb*.]

Arbitration before the ICC, pursuant to the TOS, must be kept confidential pursuant to the ICC rules. Applying California law to an arbitration provision, the Ninth Circuit held that such confidentiality supports a finding that an arbitration clause was substantively unconscionable. The Ninth Circuit reasoned that if the company succeeds in imposing a gag order on arbitration proceedings, it places itself in a far superior legal posture by ensuring that none of its potential opponents have access to precedent while, at the same time, the company accumulates a wealth of knowledge on how to negotiate the terms of its own unilaterally crafted contract. The unavailability of arbitral decisions could also prevent potential plaintiffs from obtaining the information needed to build a case of intentional misconduct against a company....

This does not mean that confidentiality provisions in an arbitration scheme or agreement are, in every instance, per se unconscionable under California law. Here, however, taken together with other provisions of the TOS, the confidentiality provision gives rise for concern of the consciousability of the arbitration clause. Thus, the confidentiality of the arbitration scheme that Linden imposed also supports a finding that the arbitration clause is unconscionable....

(c) Conclusion

When a dispute arises in Second Life, Linden is not obligated to initiate arbitration. Rather, the TOS expressly allow Linden, at its "sole discretion" and based on mere "suspicion," to unilaterally freeze a participant's account, refuse access to the virtual and real currency contained within that account, and then confiscate the participant's virtual property and real estate. A participant wishing to resolve any dispute, on the other hand, after having forfeited its interest in Second Life, must then initiate arbitration in Linden's place of business. To initiate arbitration involves advancing fees to pay for no less than three arbitrators at a cost far greater than would be involved in litigating in the state or federal court system. Moreover, under these circumstances, the confidentiality of the proceedings helps ensure that arbitration itself is fought on an uneven field by ensuring that, through the accumulation of experience, Linden becomes an expert in litigating the terms of the TOS, while plaintiffs remain novices without the benefit of learning from past precedent.

Taken together, the lack of mutuality, the costs of arbitration, the forum selection clause, and the confidentiality provision that Linden unilaterally imposes through the TOS demonstrate that the arbitration clause is not designed to provide Second Life participants an effective means of resolving disputes with Linden. Rather, it is a one-sided means which tilts unfairly, in almost all situations, in Linden's favor. As in *Comb,* through the use of an arbitration clause, Linden "appears to be attempting to insulate itself contractually from any meaningful challenge to its alleged practices." 218 F. Supp. 2d at 1176.

The Court notes that the concerns with procedural unconscionability are somewhat mitigated by Bragg's being an experienced attorney. However, "because the unilateral modification clause renders the arbitration provision severely one-sided in the substantive dimension, even moderate procedural unconscionability renders the arbitration agreement unenforceable." *Net Global Mktg.* [*v. Dialtone, Inc.*], 217 Fed. Appx. 598, 2007 U.S. App. LEXIS 674, at *9 (9th Cir. Jan. 9, 2007) (internal citations omitted).

Finding that the arbitration clause is procedurally and substantively unconscionable, the Court will refuse to enforce it.

Notes and Questions

a. In *Lewis v. YouTube, L.L.C.,* 244 Cal. App. 4th 118, 197 Cal. Rptr. 3d 219 (2015), and in *Darnaa, L.L.C. v. Google Inc.,* 236 F. Supp. 3d 1116, 1125–26 (N.D. Cal. 2017), *aff'd sub nom. Darnaa, L.L.C. v. Google L.L.C.,* 756 F. App'x 674 (9th Cir. 2018), the California state and federal courts have addressed the applicability of a clickwrap agreement in the context of a limitation-of-liability clause. Section 10 of the YouTube terms of service agreement, which agreement is appended to the complaint, provided:

> IN NO EVENT SHALL YOUTUBE … BE LIABLE TO YOU FOR ANY DIRECT, INDIRECT, INCIDENTAL, SPECIAL, PUNITIVE, OR CONSEQUENTIAL DAMAGES WHATSOEVER RESULTING FROM … (IV) ANY INTERRUPTION OR CESSATION OF TRANSMISSION TO OR FROM OUR SERVICES … [OR] (V) ANY ERRORS OR OMISSIONS IN ANY CONTENT OR FOR ANY LOSS OR DAMAGE OF ANY KIND INCURRED AS A RESULT OF YOUR USE OF ANY CONTENT … WHETHER BASED ON WARRANTY, CONTRACT, TORT, OR ANY OTHER LEGAL THEORY.…

Plaintiffs argued that this exculpatory language as applied to the removal of music videos without the consent of the video owners could not waive the fundamental state contractual rights to an implied covenant of good faith and fair dealing. In both cases, however, the courts gave broad enforcement to the exculpatory language, barring attacks on the agreement under the theory of a breach of the implied covenant of good faith and fair dealing.

b. State court interpretations of clickwrap agreements vary. Not all have enforced the provisions, particularly of browsewrap or shrinkwrap agreements which do not include some manifestation of assent by the consumer. *Compare Snap-On Bus. Sols. Inc. v. O'Neil & Assocs.*, 708 F. Supp. 2d 669, 672 (N.D. Ohio 2010), *with Specht v. Netscape Communs. Corp.*, 306 F.3d 17 (2d Cir. 2002). *See also Nguyen v. Barnes & Noble Inc.*, 763 F.3d 1171, 1175–76 (9th Cir. 2014) ("the validity of [a] browsewrap contract depends on whether the user has actual or constructive knowledge of a website's terms and conditions.").

c. The highly popular *World of Warcraft* computer game has had difficulty protecting the game play from automated player enhancements that allow users to gain unfair advantage in the game and distort the internal gaming economies. MDY Industries, Inc. created a "bot" software program, Glider, that automated play for gamers away from their computers. Is the software client on the player's computer sufficient to constitute a technological measure that is protected by copyright? If so, then automated game programs can be barred as infringing the DMCA anti-circumvention provisions of the Copyright Act. *See MDY Indus., L.L.C. v. Blizzard Entm't, Inc.*, 616 F. Supp. 2d 958 (D. Ariz. 2009).

d. The Copyright Act provides the exclusive source of protection for "all legal and equitable rights that are equivalent to any of the exclusive rights within the general scope of copyright...." *See* 17 U.S.C. § 301(a). To what extent does copyright law preempt the enforceability of clickwrap agreements? *Compare Davidson & Assocs. v. Jung*, 422 F.3d 630 (8th Cir. 2005), *with Vault v. Quaid Software Ltd.*, 847 F.2d 255, 268–70 (5th Cir. 1988).

Problem 15-E

As described in Problem 15-C, Bryce has been collaborating with a video game publisher to produce a new interactive game based on the social life of a rock star. The game includes features for creating bands, touring, performing, and initiating bar fights. In both the *Teen* and *Mature* versions of the game, it uses fictional bands and music created and recorded by Bryce. To deal with the issues involved with the use of the game, draft an appropriate Terms of Service or End User License Agreement to protect the producers and users of the game, as well as to set forth sufficient limits on the users to allow the licensing of content necessary to create the game.

F. Bibliography and Links

Greg Lastowka, Virtual Justice—The New Laws of Online Worlds 10 (2010).

Kyle Coogan, *Let's Play: A Walkthrough of Quarter-Century-Old Copyright Precedent as Applied to Modern Video Games*, 28 Fordham Intell. Prop. Media & Ent. L.J. 381 (2018).

Thomas F. Cotter & Irina Y. Dmitrieva, *Integrating the Right of Publicity with First Amendment and Copyright Preemption Analysis*, 33 Colum. J.L. & Arts 165 (2010).

Marc Edelman, *Closing the "Free Speech" Loophole: The Case for Protecting College Athletes' Publicity Rights in Commercial Video Games*, 65 Fla. L. Rev. 553, 554 (2013).

Joshua A.T. Fairfield, *The God Paradox*, 89 B.U.L. Rev. 1017 (2009).

Christopher J. Ferguson, *Violent Video Games, Sexist Video Games, and the Law: Why Can't We Find Effects?*, 14 Ann. Rev. L. & Soc. Sci. 411 (2018).

Jon M. Garon, *Publicity Rights in Entertainment: From Second-Life to the Afterlife: Playing in the Virtual Arena: Avatars, Publicity, and Identity Reconceptualized through Virtual Worlds and Computer Games*, 11 Chap. L. Rev. 465 (2008).

James Grimmelmann, *Saving Facebook*, 94 Iowa L. Rev. 1137 (2009).

Salil K. Mehra, *Paradise Is a Walled Garden? Trust, Antitrust, and User Dynamism*, 18 Geo. Mason L. Rev. 889 (2011).

Raymond T. Nimmer, *Information Wars and the Challenges of Content Protection in Digital Contexts*, 13 Vand. J. Ent. & Tech. L. 825 (2011).

Crystal Nwaneri, *Ready Lawyer One: Legal Issues in the Innovation of Virtual Reality*, 30 Harv. J.L. & Tech. 601 (2017)

Suzanne E. Rogers, *Transforming with Avatars: Video Game Developer Licensing Considerations*, 65 J. Copyright Soc'y U.S.A. 57 (2018).

Sok Min Yun, *A Comparative Overview of Esports Against Traditional Sports Focused in the Legal Realm of Monetary Exploitation, Cheating, and Gambling*, 37 Cardozo Arts & Ent. L.J. 513 (2019).

Websites

Berkman Center for Internet and Society, http://cyber.law.harvard.edu/

Electronic Frontier Foundation, http://www.eff.org/

Engadget, http://www.engadget.com/

G4, http://g4tv.com/

Game Zone, http://www.gamezone.com

Pew Research Center's Internet & American Life Project, http://www.pewinternet.org/

Twitch, https://www.twitch.tv/

Wired, http://www.wired.com/

Chapter 16

Digital Distribution, Piracy, and Technology

A. Why Many-to-Many Matters[1]

In the pre-Internet marketplace, radio and television were dominated by national broadcasters that commanded the substantial majority of the audience's attention. Major markets were dominated by a small number of newspapers, supplemented by national magazines. These media outlets provided a highly stable structure for the purchase of advertising. The cost for visibility in these outlets was high, leading to a powerful position for large national advertisers over new entrants and upstart competitors.

The non-paid media was managed by this small oligarchy of media outlets, and the critics, business columnists, and analysts commanded tremendous influence over the industry. The Broadway theatre market was perhaps the most extreme version of this concentration, with a single bad review able to close an otherwise promising show. *New York Times* critic Frank Rich was disparagingly nicknamed "the Butcher of Broadway," and playwright Christopher Durang once wrote that Rich "represents this Great Deaf Ear I must somehow get through to in order to reach a theater-going public."[2] In the fashion industry, that honor may have been held by American *Vogue*'s Anna Wintour. Her former assistant, Lauren Weisberger, wrote *The Devil Wears Prada*, which became a *New York Times* bestseller and top grossing motion picture.

While other industries did not always have the *New York Times* or *Vogue* as the platform for the all-powerful opinion makers, most industries were shaped by powerful insiders. This structure and hierarchy added stability for entrenched businesses and created significant barriers for those storming the walls.

The Internet changed everything.

---

1. Jon M. Garon, The Entrepreneur's Intellectual Property and Business Handbook 63–64, 89–91, (2018).
2. Chip Brown, *How Frank Rich Became the Butcher of Broadway*, Deadspin: The Stacks (July 13, 2017, 3:12 PM) (originally Chip Brown, *The Most Powerful Man on Broadway*, GQ, June 1990, at 172), http://thestacks.deadspin.com/how-frank-rich-became-the-butcher-of-broadway-1796376 800.

The emergence of online media companies like Mark Cuban's Broadcast.com, up-start YouTube, illegal media distributors Napster and Grokster, and open platform blogs on Blogger.com and Wordpress.com, enabled the public to have free access to content coming from a virtually unlimited number of sources.

The piracy played an important role in spreading the sources of content, encouraging the public to seek more remote corners of the Internet for free, if unauthorized, broadcasts, and economically harming the incumbent media companies. The oligarchy faced direct losses from piracy and direct competition from anyone at home with a computer and an interest in uploading content.

The result was a fundamental restructuring of how the world receives its content. Although traditional media, particularly sports, continues to be created by the large film and television companies, radio struggled, and newspapers radically reduced their journalistic staffs, if they did not close entirely.

For advertising, Google, Yahoo!, and Bing delivered advertisements to increasingly segmented groups among the site users. Instead of having to spend millions of dollars to sell an ad to everyone who watches a particular television episode, an advertiser could select to spend a few dollars for each consumer who actually clicked on an advertisement. Suddenly, the interactivity of the Internet provided a mechanism for every advertiser of every size to pay for advertising on a more even playing field.

The consequence for established companies was the democratization of content, which at its best means that content on the Internet gets attention because of its popularity rather than the speaker's or seller's market share. The lack of structure means that Internet content is not necessarily so much democratized as anarchistic and chaotic. Nonetheless, the many-to-many model has eliminated the command-and-control structure that had benefited the content creators and major marketing companies in the prior century.

Technological Changes Impacting Fair Use

Classic copyright fair use allows copying for such purposes as comment, criticism, research, news reporting, or education. Rather than requiring that a book critique receive permission for quoting brief passages from a book, fair use allows the critic to copy without permission. Similarly, parody sketches on *Saturday Night Live* and other shows are allowed to use copyrighted films or television shows because such parodies are a form of criticism. Fair use primarily applies to copyright, but it has also found its way into trademark law and may occasionally apply to publicity rights.

With the advent of the modern entertainment age, new forms of fair use have been recognized by the courts. The most famous was identified by the Supreme Court in *Sony v. Universal*,[3] the lawsuit that defined Sony's right to make the Betamax video-

---

3. *Sony Corp. of Am. v. Universal City Studios, Inc.*, 464 U.S. 417 (1984).

tape recorder. The Supreme Court recognized that there may be a fair use in copying broadcast television shows for later viewing—known as time-shifting. This was found to be a new form of fair use.

Beginning with the Betamax, time-shifting technology revolutionized modern consumer entertainment. Courts have since acknowledged "space shifting," which made the ripping of music CDs into MP3s a legal form of fair use, so long as the person doing the ripping owns the CD being ripped.[4] This added to the public's perception that downloading content from Internet was a fair use of that content, when copied for the purpose of time shifting and space shifting. Despite feeble efforts by YouTube and others to limit unauthorized downloading, the practice has become ubiquitous and accepted. In much the same way, expanded fair use recognition has led to an assumption (again without explicit court action) that making multiple backup copies of software and digital media is also fair use.

Fair use allows people to make unauthorized copies and performances of copyrighted works. The key to fair use is that it cannot replace the economic opportunity of the copyright owner. If the unauthorized use replaces the business of the copyright owner, then it will not be considered fair use. Similarly, if the business is based on encouraging copyright infringement by others or providing all the tools for copyright infringement, then that business can be liable for inducing copyright infringement by others.[5]

An elegant summary of the effect of publishing piracy was written by Harlan Ellison, noted futurist and novelist. On February 22, 2001, in response to the ongoing litigation, *Ellison v. Robertson*, Ellison issued the following statement as part of his plea to finance his lawsuit through Kick Internet Piracy "to protect writers' creative properties."[6]

> [With my lawyer, I] filed a lawsuit against the above parties to stop them from posting my works on the Internet without permission. This is copyright infringement. Rampant. Out of control. Pandemic.

---

4. *Recording Indus. Ass'n of Am. v. Diamond Multimedia Sys., Inc.*, 180 F.3d 1072 (9th Cir. 1999).

5. *MGM Studios Inc. v. Grokster, Ltd.*, 545 U.S. 913 (2005).

6. Reprinted with permission of the author. Harlan Ellison (1934–2018) was an iconic writer of the twentieth century. The *New York Times* included the following in his obituary:

> Mr. Ellison looked at storytelling as a "holy chore," which he pursued zealously for more than 60 years. His output includes more than 1,700 short stories and articles, at least 100 books and dozens of screenplays and television scripts. And although he was ranked with eminent science fiction writers like Ray Bradbury and Isaac Asimov, he insisted that he wrote speculative fiction, or simply fiction.

> "Call me a science fiction writer," Mr. Ellison said on the Sci-Fi Channel (now SyFy) in the 1990s. "I'll come to your house and I'll nail your pet's head to a coffee table. I'll hit you so hard your ancestors will die."

http://www.nytimes.com/2018/06/29/obituaries/harlan-ellison-intensely-prolific-science-fiction-writer-dies-at-84.html.

AOL, RemarQ/Critical Path and a host of self-serving individuals seem to think that they can allow the dissemination of writers' work on the internet without authorization, and without payment, under the banner of "fair use" or the idiot slogan "information must be free." A writer's work is not information: it is our creative property, our livelihood and our families' annuity. Why should any artist, of any kind, continue creating new work, eking out an existence in pursuit of a career, following the muse, when little internet thieves, rodents without ethic or understanding, steal and steal and steal, conveniencing themselves and "screw the author"? What we're looking at is the death of the professional writer!

This is not only *my* fight, I'm not the only one whose work is being pirated. Hundreds of writers' stories, entire books, and the work of a lifetime, everyone from Isaac Asimov to Roger Zelazny: Their work has been thrown onto the web by these smartass vandals who find it an imposition to have to pay for the goods. (But gawd forbid you try to appropriate something of *theirs* ... listen to 'em squeal!)

The outcome of this case will affect every writer, editor, photographer, artist, musician, poet, sculptor, actor, book designer, publisher and reader. What we're looking at is the anarchy of ignorant thieves ripping off those who labor for an honest payday, because they conveniently honor the lie that everything should be theirs for the taking....

Do not, for an instant, buy into the cultural mythology that all artists are rich. A few are, but most have a hard row to hoe just subsisting, holding down second jobs. Most creators practice their art because they love it. If it were only for the bucks, they'd fare better as dentists, plumbers, or steam fitters. I'm fighting for myself, of course, but I'm also doing this for Avram Davidson, who died broke; for Roger Zelazny, who had to work like a dog till the day he pitched over; and for Gerald Kersh, whose work was reprinted and pirated in sixty-five countries, while he had to borrow money from friends to fight off the cancer. This is your fight, too, gang ... and now we need your help!

Mr. Ellison's personalization of the impact of piracy does more than economic models to articulate that the corrosive effect of piracy has already begun to erode the creative markets. The cases and materials below illustrate how far this jurisprudence has come — and how far it has to go.

Other authors and artists take a very different approach. For musicians and performers who can make their artistic living through performance income rather than publication rights, there have been many who embrace free internet content and others who rely on the audience's voluntary payments as sufficient.

The battles over illegal piracy, the potential for secondary liability for companies involved in digital content distribution, and the unpredictable scope of fair use have led content producers, distributors, and consumers to seek out a new model of content access. The new model is increasingly a subscription model that provides a large library of content always available for a monthly subscription fee. With the rise of Spotify and Pandora in music; Netflix, Hulu, and Amazon Prime in video; Twitch, Xbox, and Nintendo for gaming; Amazon Unlimited and Audible for books; and Apple seeking to create subscriptions for magazines, newspapers, and books, this model will significantly reduce the tensions surrounding piracy enforcement issues. Even in the fields of academic publishing, there are myriad efforts to move from expensive course materials being sold or rented to students and instead licensed to the student or the institution.

B. Unauthorized Recording & Distribution

As part of the 1994 Uruguay Round Agreements enacted pursuant to the General Agreement on Tariffs and Trade ("GATT") annexed to the WTO Agreement, additional criminal and civil protections were added to create liability for the unauthorized copying of live musical performances:

1. 18 U.S.C.S. § 2319A (2003)

Unauthorized fixation of and trafficking in sound recordings and music videos of live musical performances:

(a) Offense. Whoever, without the consent of the performer or performers involved, knowingly and for purposes of commercial advantage or private financial gain—(1) fixes the sounds or sounds and images of a live musical performance in a copy or phonorecord, or reproduces copies or phonorecords of such a performance from an unauthorized fixation; (2) transmits or otherwise communicates to the public the sounds or sounds and images of a live musical performance; or (3) distributes or offers to distribute, sells or offers to sell, rents or offers to rent, or traffics in any copy or phonorecord fixed as described in paragraph (1), regardless of whether the fixations occurred in the United States; shall be imprisoned for not more than 5 years or fined in the amount set forth in this title, or both, or if the offense is a second or subsequent offense, shall be imprisoned for not more than 10 years or fined in the amount set forth in this title, or both....

2. 17 U.S.C. § 1101. Unauthorized Fixation and Trafficking in Sound Recordings and Music Videos

(a) Unauthorized Acts.—Anyone who, without the consent of the performer or performers involved—

(1) fixes the sounds or sounds and images of a live musical performance in a copy or phonorecord, or reproduces copies or phonorecords of such a performance from an unauthorized fixation,

(2) transmits or otherwise communicates to the public the sounds or sounds and images of a live musical performance, or

(3) distributes or offers to distribute, sells or offers to sell, rents or offers to rent, or traffics in any copy or phonorecord fixed as described in paragraph (1), regardless of whether the fixations occurred in the United States,

shall be subject to the remedies provided in sections 502 through 505, to the same extent as an infringer of copyright.

United States v. Moghadam
175 F.3d 1269 (11th Cir. 1999)

In 1994, Congress passed a statute criminalizing the unauthorized recording, the transmission to the public, and the sale or distribution of or traffic in unauthorized recordings of live musical performances. *See* 18 U.S.C. § 2319A. [Similar civil liability was enacted as well and codified in 17 U.S.C. § 1101.] Appellant Ali Moghadam was convicted of violating that law (herein sometimes referred to as the "anti-bootlegging statute") after he pleaded guilty to knowingly distributing, selling, and trafficking in bootleg (unauthorized) compact discs featuring live musical performances by recording artists including Tori Amos and the Beastie Boys. The present appeal challenges the constitutional power of Congress to enact this legislation. In the district court, Moghadam moved to dismiss the indictment, arguing that the statute was unconstitutional because it did not fall within any of the federal legislative powers enumerated in Article I, § 8 of the Constitution....

[F]or most of the nation's history, sound recordings were not protected. In 1971, Congress extended copyright protection to sound recordings. Sound Recording Act of 1971, 17 U.S.C. § 102(a)(7) (including "sound recordings" in the list of copyrightable "works of authorship"). This meant that persons who made unauthorized reproductions of records or tapes, which is known as "piracy," could be prosecuted or face civil liability for copyright infringement. The copyright law, especially as amended by further statutes, went far toward securing the rights of musicians and recording artists to receive fair benefit from their creative efforts....

[I]n contrast to the six exclusive rights of a copyright owner spelled out in 17 U.S.C. § 106, it appears that the only exclusive right created by the anti-bootlegging statute is to record and/or re-communicate one's performance.... [T]he protections that the anti-bootlegging statutes confer on musicians are best described as "quasi-copyright" or *sui generis* protections.

[Although the court discusses the reach of the Copyright Clause to the type of legal protection afforded under the statute, it chooses not to decide whether the statute is a constitutional exercise of authority. Instead, it allows the legislation to be deemed constitutional under the Commerce Clause.]

Section 2319A clearly prohibits conduct that has a substantial effect on both commerce between the several states and commerce with foreign nations. The link between bootleg compact discs and interstate commerce and commerce with foreign nations is self-evident. For example, one of the elements of the offense is that the activity must have been done "for purposes of commercial advantage or private financial gain." 18 U.S.C. §2319A(a). If bootlegging is done for financial gain, it necessarily is intertwined with commerce. Bootleggers depress the legitimate markets because demand is satisfied through unauthorized channels. Generally speaking, performing artists who attract bootleggers are those who are sufficiently popular that their appeal crosses state or national lines. The very reason Congress prohibited this conduct is because of the deleterious economic effect on the recording industry. The specific context in which §2319A was enacted involved a treaty with foreign nations, called for by the World Trade Organization, whose purpose was to ensure uniform recognition and treatment of intellectual property in international commerce. The context reveals that the focus of Congress was on interstate and international commerce....

Summarizing our narrow holding in this case, we assume *arguendo*, without deciding, that the anti-bootlegging statute cannot satisfy the fixation requirement of the Copyright Clause; we hold that the statute satisfies the "substantial effects" test of the post-*Lopez* Commerce Clause jurisprudence [*United States v. Lopez*, 514 U.S. 549 (1995)]; we hold that the Commerce Clause can provide the source of Congressional power in this case because the extension of copyright-like protection here is not fundamentally inconsistent with the fixation requirement of the Copyright Clause; and thus under the circumstances of this case, we reject Moghadam's constitutional challenge to his conviction....

Notes and Questions

a. In addition to the bar on unauthorized fixation, other provisions criminalize the counterfeiting of a copyrighted work, 18 U.S.C. §2318 (2010), and create RICO predicate jurisdiction. *See* 18 U.S.C. §1960(b) (2006).

b. As the *Moghadam* court explains, "The anti-bootlegging statute grew out of the Agreement on Trade Related Aspects of Intellectual Property ('TRIPs').... TRIPs became law by operation of the Uruguay Round Agreements Act ('URAA'), Pub.L. No. 103-465, 108 Stat. 4809 (1994), a comprehensive act dealing with matters of international trade." In essence, then, the extension of copyright or Commerce Clause protection to the act of fixation, fills the final gap in the creative process and keeps the United States consistent with the other content-producing nations.

c. The discomfort shown by the *Moghadam* court at extending copyright protection raises interesting issues. One view is that since a derivative work cannot be copyrighted without the express permission of the copyright holder, such a derivative work is an infringement of the source work. Given that precedent, no work can be copyrighted without the express permission of the copyright owner, and the unauthorized work is an infringement of the copyright owner's rights. The other view, however, posits that an author does not exist until the work exists. Therefore, there can be no injury since there is no copyright owner with standing.

The Copyright Clause of the United States Constitution provides Congress the power "to promote the Progress of Science and the useful Arts, by securing for limited Times to Authors and Inventors the exclusive Right to their respective Writings and

Discoveries." U.S. Const. art. I, §8, cl. 8. The question of whether an author cannot exist until the writing is fixed tends to take on a rather theosophical patina, which tends to belie the actual creative process for many authors.

d. Other than the need to conform United States law to the TRIPS treaty, what practical consequence does the statute's extension of protection provide to copyright holders and law enforcement?

e. The FBI has unveiled a new labeling system to reinforce its anti-piracy efforts. Like the copyright warning on videotapes and DVDs, the new logo will be featured on music CDs, software, and other intellectual property products. *See* http://www. fbi.gov/page2/feb04/pirates021904.html.

f. Courts have struggled to reconcile the Copyright Clause with the Commerce Clause regarding the constitutionality of the anti-trafficking statutes. Courts continue to uphold the legislation. *See United States v. Martignon*, 492 F.3d 140 (2d Cir. 2007) (upholding 18 U.S.C. §2319A); *Kiss Catalog, Ltd. v. Passport Int'l Prods.*, 405 F. Supp. 2d 1169 (C.D. Cal. 2005) (upholding 17 U.S.C. §1101).

> [T]he analysis of The *Trade-Mark Cases* [100 U.S. 82 (1879),] is more to the point. There, the Supreme Court noted that legislation that could not be permitted under the Copyright Clause could nevertheless pass muster under the Commerce Clause—if the independent requirements of that clause were met. Under the more restrictive view of the Commerce Clause that prevailed at the time, those requirements were not met. As noted above, modern case law has expanded the interpretation of the Commerce Clause and modem cases upholding trademark protection are based on the Commerce Clause. Therefore, once the Court concludes that the Statute does not fall within the purview of the Copyright Clause, it need no longer consider whether it complies with the limitations of the Copyright Clause. To do so imports into the Commerce Clause limits that clause does not have. That the Statute might provide "copyright-like" or "copyright-related" protection to matters clearly not covered by the Copyright Clause is not important. One need only find an alternative source of constitutional authority. This Court finds such authority in the Commerce Clause.

Kiss Catalog, Ltd. v. Passport Int'l Prods., 405 F. Supp. 2d 1169, 1174–75 (C.D. Cal. 2005).

Problem 16-B

Bryce and some other members of Soundfyre stop by your office. While surfing the Internet, Bryce came across a multimedia file of Soundfyre's live concert from the previous week. The clip featured Bryce performing duets with Freddi, the bass player. Bryce explained that they know the material had been audiotaped and video-taped the previous week at a private club because they recognized the songs being played and the logo displayed on the back of the stage. Bryce is particularly upset because they had been testing out some new songs that were not even completely finished.

Advise Bryce as to which laws may have been broken, what civil remedies might be available, and how best to proceed.

C. Traditional Bootlegging of Branded Merchandise

Plant v. Does

19 F. Supp. 2d 1316 (S.D. Fla. 1998)

THIS CAUSE comes before the Court upon Plaintiffs' *Ex Parte* Emergency Motion for Order to Show Cause on Motion for Preliminary Injunction with Temporary Restraining Order ("TRO") and Order of Seizure, filed May 21, 1998. Defendants, as they are unknown and have not been served, were unable to file a response. The Court entertained oral argument from Plaintiffs' counsel on May 21, 1998. At the conclusion of the TRO hearing, the Court announced its decision denying Plaintiff's motion and dismissing the case in open court. The day following the Court's announcement of its ruling, Plaintiff sought and obtained a TRO from the U.S. District Court for the Middle District of Florida, prohibiting unnamed parties from selling souvenir merchandise in Florida, South Carolina, and North Carolina.

Plaintiffs are rock musicians and the companies licensed to sell their souvenir merchandise. Plaintiffs Plant and Page, former members of the rock and roll band Led Zeppelin, are currently on a nationwide music tour. As well as owning the intellectual property rights to their own names and likenesses, Plant and Page are co-owners of the Led Zeppelin trademark. Plaintiffs seek a nationwide injunction directed at as yet unknown "bootleggers" who sell t-shirts and souvenir items bearing Plant and Page likenesses or the Led Zeppelin logo. Plaintiffs ask this Court to authorize the U.S. Marshal or other law enforcement authorities to seize and impound any apparently infringing merchandise sold within a twenty-five mile radius of Page/Plant concerts.... [The court first upbraided the plaintiffs for filing for the TRO on the eve of the concert and for failing to properly identify the rulings that were adverse to the relief sought.]

That being said, the Court will turn to whether the law permits Plaintiffs to obtain ex parte equitable relief to prevent unknown parties from engaging in what might be illegal behavior in the future. Although other courts have granted such relief, this Court is convinced that doing so would neither comport with federal procedural rules nor the dictates of justice. First, Plaintiffs have not made a sufficient showing that the Court has personal jurisdiction over the unknown Defendants. Plaintiffs have not served Defendants with process, and have elected not to do so until Defendants' property has already been seized. The Court initially notes that although plaintiffs are permitted to use fictitious names in their complaints. "Federal courts do not favor the naming of 'John Doe' defendants." In addition, "a district court does not have jurisdiction over unnamed defendants unless they have been served with a summons and a copy of the complaint." Courts generally permit the use of fictitious names when the only way a plaintiff can obtain the name of a defendant who has harmed him is through the discovery process in a case filed against that defendant as an unnamed party. The use of a fictitious name is not generally permitted as a tool by which a private plaintiff may obtain a broad-based order preventing any and all members of society from engaging in future behavior that might or might not later be found to have violated the plaintiff's rights.

Moreover, in order to survive dismissal for lack of jurisdiction, Plaintiffs must "demonstrate[] that they have engaged in a reasonably diligent search to identify the unknown defendants [and] ... inform[] the Court of any efforts they have taken to provide these individuals with constructive notice." Furthermore, the requirement that "unknown parties have at least constructive notice is no dispensable formality; rather, it is an essential element of due process without which a court has no jurisdiction to bind the absent parties."

Plaintiffs simply assert that the use of a fictitious name is proper because "said parties cannot be identified until they actually appear at said concerts." In the very same paragraph, however, Plaintiffs state that, unless enjoined, these individuals will "travel[] on to the next concert" and sell their merchandise. This clearly indicates that the same individuals follow the band from concert to concert, selling their wares. Plaintiffs give no explanation as to why they are unable to obtain the identities of these individuals. Indeed, Plaintiffs do not indicate that they have even ever attempted to ascertain the identity of these individuals. This Court declines to suspend time-honored procedural rules simply because Plaintiffs did not wish to expend a modest amount of their ample resources to do a routine preliminary factual investigation before bringing suit in this federal Court. Given the considerations discussed above, courts have concluded that they lack personal jurisdiction over these unknown bootleggers. In addition, Plaintiffs' case must fail for lack of justiciability. As the Second Circuit observed in *Heldman v. Sobol*, 962 F.2d 148, 153–54 (2d Cir. 1992):

> Federal courts may decide only actual cases and controversies. *See* U.S. Const. art. III, § 2. The parameters of the case or controversy limitation emerge from the cluster of justiciability doctrines — doctrines that incorporate concerns about the proper role of the judiciary in a democratic society and the need to assure an adversarial presentation of the issues.

Serious justiciability problems arise from the facts that Defendants cannot possibly be here to defend their position, Defendants at this time have not committed any injurious act, and Defendants, for all the Court knows, may never have committed any similar injurious acts in the past. As Judge Clemon observed in his well-reasoned opinion in *Rock Tours*, [*Ltd. v. Does*, 507 F. Supp. 63, 66 (N.D. Ala. 1981)]:

> At this point, plaintiffs have no adversaries in this Court. This proceeding has been wholly ex parte. Although the lack of actual defendants has apparently not posed an insurmountable barrier to preliminary injunctive relief in at least sixteen similar federal district court cases, this Court is not so sanguine in an ex parte proceeding. While plaintiffs take comfort in the fact that in those cases there is usually no challenge

to the ex parte relief granted by the Courts; in this Court's view, the absence of challenges may simply beg the question of whether the proceedings are truly adversary proceedings....

> Under these circumstances, this Court doubts "... the existence of a sufficient adversary interest to stimulate the parties to a full presentation of the facts and arguments, which in our adversary system is available from the parties." At this time, the instant action is not a justiciable one for purposes of ex parte injunctive relief.

In our uniquely American governmental system of checks and balances, courts play a necessarily limited role. They do not create the law, and they do not execute the law. Rather, courts exist solely to resolve disputes between actual parties involved in actual controversies. They may not issue advisory opinions, and they may not address contingencies or hypothetical situations. The doctrine of justiciability grows out of this recognition that the role of courts is limited.... The relief sought by Plaintiffs extends far beyond the powers of this one federal district Court. Plaintiffs ask this Court first to create a law authorizing the U.S. Marshal to seize on sight any merchandise that reasonably appears to the Marshal to infringe on a trademark and second to execute the law by ordering the Marshal to seize the merchandise. For this reason, Judge Clemon concluded:

> Basically, plaintiffs seek through this Court a mechanism under which to seize and impound the allegedly bootleg merchandise to be sold by the unnamed defendants ... It would appear, therefore, that this controversy is one which may be more appropriately addressed to the legislative or executive branches.

Rock Tours, Inc., 507 F. Supp. at 66.

Finally, policy consideration militate against granting injunctive relief. The public interest can hardly be served by this Court ordering armed police personnel to forcibly confiscate the merchandise of unsuspecting vendors at a rock concert where people are probably already in a rowdy mood. In sum, the hornets' nest of procedural problems and policy implications posed by this case simply prevents the Court from granting the extreme and broad based injective relief requested by Plaintiffs. If district courts are not rigorous in their application of Constitutional standards and enforcement of venerable procedural mandates, it is the individual citizen that bears risk of getting stung. This Court agrees with the poignant opinion in *National Football League Props., Inc. v. Coniglio*, 554 F. Supp. 1224, 1225 (D.D.C. 1983):

> Plaintiff seeks a [seizure] order without notice to any defendant, and before it has even effected service of its complaint on all defendants. Indeed, plaintiff has not even identified all of the potentially numerous defendants to whom this sweeping order would apply other than by the designation "Various John Does and Jane Does, and ABC Companies." Even on the surface, the order requested by plaintiff would appear to invite catastrophe. It promises a nightmare of jurisdictional flaws, deprivations of due process, and windfall litigation that could ensue for years to come. This is not even to mention the

physical spectacle of the United States Marshall Service, which is already greatly overburdened in its work, in the company of paid thugs (euphemistically styled "security representatives") roaming the streets of Washington to confiscate the merchandise of small businessmen and other licensed vendors who sell their wares in the open air. In short, the relief plaintiff seeks would open a veritable Pandora's box of problems that this court cannot even begin to imagine now.

The law should reward reason over haste and adherence to fair procedure over sweeping judicial power. The Court recognizes that bootlegging is a social problem; however, federal litigation is not a cure-all, and judicial authority may not be invoked every time a private litigant wishes to obtain a quick fix to what he perceives to be society's ailments. Federal procedural rules, incorporating the principles of jurisdiction and justiciability, are not mere technicalities, and they cannot be abandoned even in the most compelling of cases. They must not be abandoned in this case. Justice will never be served in the long run by submerging the procedural doctrines which protect all litigants in all cases to one individual's wanton quest to achieve success in his particular case....

SKS Merch, L.L.C. v. Barry

233 F. Supp. 2d 841 (E.D. Ky. 2002)

This matter is before the Court on the Plaintiffs' Motions for a nationwide Preliminary Injunction and a Permanent Injunction. Having reviewed the pleadings in this matter, and having considered the arguments of counsel, the Court will grant both Motions for the reasons set forth below.

Plaintiff Toby Keith Covel, d/b/a Toby Keith ("Keith"), is a country music recording artist and performer. Plaintiff SKS is a Tennessee limited liability company. Authorized by Keith, SKS manufactures, markets and sells t-shirts, hats, and other merchandise bearing Keith's name, photograph, logo, likeness, tour information, and/or image, or which is otherwise associated with Keith's music career. SKS sells the merchandise at Keith's concerts throughout the country; SKS's primary focus is the sale of this concert merchandise, which is unique from other authorized Toby Keith merchandise. SKS remits taxes in each venue in which the merchandise is sold. In many venues, a license is required (and properly obtained) in order for SKS to lawfully sell its merchandise.

As explained by the Affidavit and testimony of Billy Ray Eden ("Eden"), an SKS representative, "bootleggers" have sold and continue to sell unauthorized, unlicensed versions of t-shirts, hats, and other merchandise bearing Keith's name, photograph, logo, likeness, tour information, and/or image. This "bootlegged" merchandise is sold without any authorization or license from SKS or Keith. The bootleggers appear at successive concerts, essentially following Keith on his nationwide concert tour and to other performances. Mr. Eden's Affidavit and testimony explains that bootlegging activities have occurred during concerts in seven (7) different states. The Affidavit details multiple instances of bootlegging at eleven (11) separate Keith concerts, while Mr. Eden's testimony also addressed bootlegging activity at a recent Keith performance in Greenville, South Carolina. Mr. Eden also testified that, at Keith's concert in Ypsilanti, Michigan, on October 17, 2002, Robert P. Conderato ("Conderato") was charged with bootlegging activity. Conderato was observed by a law enforcement officer selling t-shirts featuring Keith's logo. Conderato conceded that he did not have a license or any authorization from SKS to sell the t-shirts. Moreover, the bootleg t-shirts have also appeared on eBay, an internet auction site.

Mr. Eden's testimony also established the difficulty confronted by SKS in obtaining the names and addresses of the bootleg vendors who appear at Keith's concerts and performances. Typically, the bootleg vendors disappear before SKS employees can find them, confiscate their goods, or question them regarding their names and addresses. SKS employees have managed to identify at least some of the bootleggers: named Defendants Mike Barry, Lou Black, and Louie Cutone. At a hearing on the pending Motions, the Plaintiffs produced photographs depicting various persons allegedly engaged in selling bootleg merchandise at and around Keith's concerts. The photographs evidence the Plaintiffs' ongoing but ultimately futile efforts to identify and stop the bootleg vendors.

Mr. Eden also testified that he and other members of the SKS staff have been subjected to threats of violence by the bootleg vendors. Local law enforcement officers in the areas in which Keith performs routinely advise SKS that they will make no effort to identify the bootleg vendors, seize the bootleg merchandise, or charge the vendors with any offense or violation unless the Plaintiffs have an injunction issued by a federal court prohibiting the sale of the bootleg merchandise. Having lacked such an injunction, the Plaintiffs have been unable to consistently persuade local law enforcement to aid them in any predictable way in their attempt to prevent the bootlegging activity at and around Keith's concerts.

Because of its inability to thwart the bootleggers without intervention by a federal court, the Plaintiffs filed a Complaint on November 19, 2002, alleging violations of the Lanham Act by the named and unnamed Defendants. The Plaintiffs also sought a Temporary Restraining Order and a Preliminary Injunction. After a hearing on November 19, 2002, the Court granted the Plaintiffs' request for a Temporary Restraining Order. The Order enjoined the named and unnamed Defendants from selling or offering to sell t-shirts, hats, and other merchandise bearing the photograph, likeness, image, and/or logo of Keith without the Plaintiffs' authorization within a 25-mile radius of Keith's November 23, 2002, performance in Lexington, Kentucky. The Order further authorized law enforcement officers to seize any such merchandise. The Order provided that it, as well as related pleadings, would be served upon the Defendants when and if law enforcement or the Plaintiffs observed the sale of bootleg merchandise. The Temporary Restraining Order was secured by a $500 bond by the Plaintiffs and was set to expire within ten (10) days of its issuance. The Temporary Restraining Order also scheduled a hearing on the Plaintiffs' Motion for a Preliminary Injunction for November 27, 2002.

The Plaintiffs then filed a renewed Motion for a nationwide Preliminary Injunction, as well as a Motion for a Permanent Injunction pertaining to the Eastern District of Kentucky.

Although no bootleg vendors were identified during Keith's November 23, 2002, performance in Lexington, Kentucky, the ongoing and pervasive nature of the bootlegging activity at and around Keith's performances was established by Mr. Eden's Affidavit and his testimony at the November 27, 2002, hearing. At that hearing, the Plaintiffs produced numerous examples of authorized and unauthorized Toby Keith merchandise. The unauthorized merchandise, sold by bootleg vendors, apparently includes t-shirts with torn tags, an indication of poor quality. Some bootleg t-shirts bear erroneous concert dates. Although the bootleg versions are of poorer quality and contain minor inaccuracies, the images and logos printed on the unauthorized merchandise are essentially identical, or at least substantially similar, to those printed on the authorized merchandise.

At the hearing, Mr. Eden explained the difficulty in quantifying and recovering the profits lost by SKS due to the bootleg activity. Because the bootleg vendors flee when approached by the Plaintiffs, the exact number and price of the unauthorized, unlicensed t-shirts, hats, and other merchandise cannot be calculated. Even if such a calculation were possible, the bootleg vendors' refusal to identify themselves or provide addresses make any recovery by the Plaintiffs almost impossible.

I. THE PLAINTIFFS ARE ENTITLED TO A NATIONWIDE PRELIMINARY INJUNCTION RESTRAINING THE SALE OF UNAUTHORIZED, UNLICENSED MERCHANDISE BEARING KEITH'S NAME, LIKENESS, PHOTOGRAPH, TOUR INFORMATION, AND/OR IMAGE

A. The Plaintiffs Satisfy Each Prerequisite for the Issuance of a Preliminary Injunction

A motion for a preliminary injunction requires this Court to consider and balance four factors:

> (1) whether the movant has a strong likelihood of success on the merits; (2) whether the movant would suffer irreparable injury without the injunction; (3) whether issuance of the injunction would cause substantial harm to others [and balancing the harm to the moving party if the injunction is denied against the harm to others if the injunction is granted]; and (4) whether the public interest would be served by the issuance of the injunction.

Although the factors are to be balanced against each other, each factor need not be satisfied to issue a preliminary injunction. As explained below, the Court finds that the Plaintiffs have satisfied each factor relevant to the issuance of a preliminary injunction. The Court also notes, however, that irreparable harm is often presumed when a preliminary injunction is requested to enjoin a violation of the Lanham Act. "Simply fulfilling the requirements of the statute or, in other words, fulfilling the first factor for an injunction to issue—showing a strong likelihood of success on the merits—is all that is needed for the Court to issue an injunction."

Thus, in the context of a Lanham Act claim, a showing of likelihood of confusion as to sponsorship, approval, or association will itself establish the requisite likelihood of success on the merits and a risk of irreparable harm. The Court finds that the Plaintiffs satisfy each prerequisite for the issuance of a nationwide Preliminary Injunction enjoining the unauthorized sale of merchandise bearing Keith's name, photograph, logo, likeness, tour information, and/or image.

1. *The Plaintiffs are likely to succeed on the merits of their Lanham Act claim*

The Plaintiffs have demonstrated a strong likelihood that they will succeed on the merits of their Lanham Act claim against the named and unnamed Defendants. The Lanham Act generally prohibits the unauthorized sale of merchandise bearing Keith's photograph, image, name, likeness, and/or logo....

The testimony and evidence offered by the Plaintiffs establishes that the sale of bootleg merchandise associated with Keith is a consistent and pervasive problem throughout the nation. A strong likelihood exists that the Defendants have sold and will continue to sell merchandise bearing Keith's name, photograph, image, likeness, tour information, and/or logo which has not been authorized or licensed by the Plaintiffs. For example, Mr. Eden testified that SKS obtained forty-eight (48) t-shirts from bootleg vendors at Keith's November 22, 2002, performance in Greenville, South Carolina. The bootleggers who routinely appear at and around Keith's performances often sell their unauthorized merchandise from parking lots and exit ramps. The Defendants, both named and unnamed, scatter when questioned by SKS employees. Such conduct is hardly consistent with vendors of authorized, licensed merchandise. The Defendants' pattern of conduct establishes a strong likelihood that the bootleg activities will continue throughout Keith's 2003 performance tour.

The Defendants have misappropriated Keith's name, photograph, likeness, and image without authorization or license from the Plaintiffs. Because it appears to be nearly identical to the licensed, authorized merchandise, the bootleg merchandise clearly causes a likelihood of confusion as to Keith's association with and sponsorship and approval of that merchandise. Although the Defendants' outright misappropriation of the Plaintiffs' merchandise designs may make such an analysis unnecessary, the Plaintiffs have satisfied the test set forth in *Frisch's Restaurants, Inc. v. Elby's Big Boy of Steubenville, Inc.*, 670 F.2d 642 (6th Cir. 1982), for determining whether a defendant's goods cause a likelihood of confusion under the Lanham Act.... The Plaintiffs' mark is obviously strong: the t-shirts and other merchandise legitimately sold by the Plaintiffs feature distinctive photographs and images of Keith and his logos and tour information. The goods sold by both parties are clearly related: both the Plaintiffs and the Defendants sell t-shirts, hats and other merchandise bearing Keith's name, photograph, likeness, tour information, and/or image, as evidenced by the t-shirts produced at the hearing. The Defendants' bootleg merchandise is unmistakably similar to the Plaintiffs legitimate merchandise. Mr. Eden's testimony established that actual confusion has resulted from the sale of the bootleg merchandise. Many of Keith's fans reported to SKS that they believed the bootleg merchandise to be "official" Keith merchandise. Both parties almost exclusively use the marketing channels made available at and around Keith's performances. Finally, the merchandise sold by both parties will expand at a concurrent rate, as Keith's career and performances continue.

The most critical *Frisch's* factor is the defendant's intent. If the defendant's mark "was adopted with the intent of deriving benefit from the reputation of [the plaintiff], that fact alone may be sufficient to justify the inference that there is confusing similarity." In other words,

> [A] defendant who purposely chooses a particular mark because it is similar to that of a senior user [the plaintiff] is saying, in effect, that he thinks that there is at least a possibility that he can divert some business from the senior user—and the defendant ought to know at least as much about the likelihood of confusion as the trier of fact.

Little Caesar Enterprises, Inc. v. Pizza Caesar, Inc., 834 F.2d 568, 572 (6th Cir. 1987). Direct testimony is not necessary to establish wrongful intent; instead, the defendant's intent may be inferred from the defendant's acts.

Here, the Defendants' intent is obvious: the Defendants intend to derive a benefit from Keith's reputation and performances. Otherwise, the Defendants would not sell t-shirts and other merchandise which so closely resemble the merchandise sold by the Plaintiffs or which makes use of Keith's likeness, image, photograph, logos, and/or tour information. This fact alone establishes a likelihood of confusion and, correspondingly, the Plaintiffs' likelihood of success on the merits of their Lanham Act claim.

2. The Plaintiffs will suffer irreparable harm absent the issuance of a nationwide preliminary injunction

As explained above, irreparable harm may be presumed from a finding of a likelihood of confusion as to the Plaintiffs' sponsorship and approval of and association with the merchandise sold by the Defendants. However, the Plaintiffs have independently established that they will be irreparably harmed absent a Preliminary Injunction enjoining the sale of bootleg merchandise related to Keith throughout the nation. Absent such relief, the Defendants' bootleg activity will be permitted to continue unabated, in blatant violation of the Lanham Act. Mr. Eden's testimony established that, in several jurisdictions, law enforcement officers expressly stated that no action would be taken against the bootleg vendors absent an injunctive order from a federal court. Even if SKS could identify all of the bootleg vendors, the Plaintiffs could not recover the damages caused by the bootleg activity. Because the Plaintiffs have no way to ascertain the number of t-shirts or hats sold by the bootleg vendors, they cannot calculate the number of legitimate sales to performance attendees which they lost due to the bootleg vendors' activities. Even if such a calculation could be made, the Defendants' nomadic nature and refusal to identify themselves would make any collection of damages by the Plaintiffs exceedingly improbable. The Plaintiffs have also been subjected to threats of violence from the unnamed Defendants, hampering their ability to learn the identity and addresses of the bootleg vendors.

No adequate remedy at law exists. The Plaintiffs' rights under the Lanham Act may be protected only by the issuance of a preliminary injunction against the sale of unauthorized merchandise bearing Keith's name, likeness, photograph, logo, tour information, and/or image throughout the country.

3. *The issuance of a nationwide Preliminary Injunction will not cause substantial harm to others*

The named and unnamed Defendants who appear at Keith's performances with bootleg merchandise for sale can hardly argue that they will be harmed by an order preventing them from violating the Lanham Act. The bootleg vendors have no conceivable right to continue violating the law. In the event that the Defendants are somehow harmed by the presence of the Preliminary Injunction, the Plaintiffs' bond will compensate them. As further set forth below, this Court is authorized to condition its injunction as equitably appropriate. For example, a preliminary injunction is not binding upon any defendant until and unless it is served with this Court's Order granting the injunction. Additionally, the defendants may be supplied with the Plaintiff's pleadings to date and/or notify the Defendants how to contest any seizure of goods or the existence of the Preliminary Injunction.

4. *The issuance of a Preliminary Injunction will serve the public interest*

The issuance of a nationwide Preliminary Injunction will serve the public interest. The public is obviously not served by ongoing violations of the Lanham Act. Further, as established by Mr. Eden's testimony and the t-shirts produced at the November 27, 2002, hearing, the bootleg vendors typically sell inferior and misleading merchandise to often unsuspecting concert attendees who believe they are buying "official" Toby Keith merchandise.

The public interest will also be served by an injunction which ensures the proper licensing and taxation of legitimate vendors of Keith merchandise. Legal vendors of concert merchandise are properly licensed and remit taxes on their sales, while the bootleg vendors are unlicensed and, presumably, remit no taxes.

B. The Preliminary Injunction Issued to the Plaintiffs Must be Nationwide

This Court is authorized to grant a nationwide preliminary injunction against violations of the Lanham Act. Nationwide injunctions have been issued in connection with performance tours in at least three (3) unreported, unpublished district court cases. Some district courts have held that nationwide preliminary injunctions are inappropriate in cases involving nationally touring performers. *See Plant v. Does,* 19 F. Supp.2d 1316 (S.D. Fla. 1998); *Brockum Co. v. Various John Does,* 685 F. Supp. 476 (E.D. Penn. 1988). However, this Court considers *Plant* to be distinguishable from this case. As for *Brockum,* this Court rejects the analysis upon which that opinion was based....

Certainly, Rule 65(d) requires actual notice, by service or otherwise, for an unnamed person acting in concert or participation with a named defendant to be bound by an injunction. Actual notice can and will be given when the nationwide injunction is served upon bootleg vendors throughout the country.

II. THE PLAINTIFFS ARE ENTITLED TO A PERMANENT INJUNCTION AGAINST THE SALE OF UNAUTHORIZED TOBY KEITH MERCHANDISE WITHIN THIS JURISDICTION

In addition to a nationwide Preliminary Injunction against the sale of unauthorized merchandise throughout the United States, the Plaintiffs are also entitled to a Permanent Injunction against such sales within the Eastern District of Kentucky.

To obtain a permanent injunction, an applicant must establish the following: (1) that it has prevailed on the merits; (2) that it will suffer continuing irreparable harm; (3) that it has no adequate remedy at law.

World Wrestling Entertainment, Inc. v. Unidentified Parties

770 F.3d 1143 (5th Cir. 2014)

World Wrestling Entertainment, Inc. ("WWE"), seeks *ex parte* seizure and temporary restraining orders against unnamed Defendants under the *ex parte* seizure provision of the Trademark Counterfeiting Act (the "Act").1 The district court denied relief and certified its order for interlocutory appeal pursuant to 28 U.S.C. § 1292(b). We allowed appeal and now VACATE the order of the district court and REMAND for further proceedings consistent with this opinion.

WWE presented evidence establishing that it owns many valuable trademarks and earns significant revenues from the sale of merchandise bearing those marks at live WWE events across the country. The evidence further established that WWE can readily identify the unauthorized designs of counterfeit merchandise and that WWE makes its own merchandise sales directly—it does not license third parties to sell merchandise at live events. WWE alleges that Defendants work as "fly-by-night" counterfeiters, setting up shop near WWE events and cannibalizing WWE's merchandise sales by purveying unauthorized products. As the district court acknowledged, WWE faces a real threat from such counterfeiters who, upon detection and notice of suit, disappear without a trace and hide or destroy evidence, only to reappear later at the next WWE event down the road. This is the very nature of the "fly-by-night" bootlegging industry.

WWE brought suit in the district court seeking *ex parte* seizure and temporary restraining orders under the *ex parte* seizure provision of the Act. The district court denied relief, concluding that WWE had not proved "specific facts" about the identities of "person[s] against whom seizure would be ordered."

Section 1116(d)(4) provides:

The court shall not grant [a seizure application] unless ... the court finds that it clearly appears from specific facts that—

(i) an order other than an *ex parte* seizure order is not adequate to achieve the purposes of section 1114 of this title;

(ii) the applicant has not publicized the requested seizure;

(iii) the applicant is likely to succeed in showing that the person against whom seizure would be ordered used a counterfeit mark in connection with the sale, offering for sale, or distribution of goods or services;

(iv) an immediate and irreparable injury will occur if such seizure is not ordered;

(v) the matter to be seized will be located at the place identified in the application;

(vi) the harm to the applicant of denying the application outweighs the harm to the legitimate interests of the person against whom seizure would be ordered of granting the application; and

(vii) the person against whom seizure would be ordered, or persons acting in concert with such person, would destroy ... or otherwise make such matter inaccessible to the court, if the applicant were to proceed on notice to such person.

Without knowing the identities of persons against whom seizure would be ordered, the district court thought it was unable to evaluate WWE's likelihood of success in showing such persons had used a counterfeit mark, whether the harm to WWE outweighed the harm to such persons, or whether such persons would destroy or make inaccessible the infringing goods upon notice. The district court applied similar reasoning in denying WWE's request for a temporary restraining order.

The district court's granular focus on the "identity" of unnamed Defendants misinterpreted the statutory requirement and its application here. The district court is correct that *ex parte* seizure orders should not be granted at will, and it commendably gave the requirements careful attention. It is the case that the Act constrains the issuance of such orders with certain procedural protections for the persons against whom they are issued. The district court concluded that it could not, ex ante, identify the persons against whom orders would issue as required by section 1116(d), an appropriate concern but one not present on the specific facts here.

The district court's concern overlooks a predicate established in this case: WWE does not license third parties to sell merchandise at live events. Rather, it makes its own merchandise sales directly. The resulting confined universe of authorized sellers of WWE merchandise necessarily "identifies" any non-WWE seller as a counterfeiter. WWE cannot know in advance the specific identities of counterfeiters who will present themselves at any given event, but it does know that any non-affiliated seller at or near an event is almost certainly a counterfeiter. In this case, therefore, the "person[s] against whom seizure would be ordered" are readily identifiable as any non-affiliated person purporting to sell WWE merchandise at or near a live WWE event. Provided that observation of unauthorized sales themselves is sufficient to identify a counterfeiter, as in this case, we see no reason why the district court cannot evaluate the requirements for *ex parte* seizure and temporary restraining orders to issue. We conclude from the record that WWE has met its burden under section 1116(d), and that the orders sought here should issue.

Accordingly, the order of the district court is VACATED, and this case REMANDED for further proceedings consistent with this opinion.

Notes and Questions

a. For many bands, the products sold as part of their concerts and tours are the most important revenue available to them. Unlike the record sales where the band receives a fraction of the total retail and is charged for most of the production costs, the licensee fees for t-shirts, cups, posters, and other memorabilia is essentially cost-free net revenue to the bands. The licensors assume the risks associated with the sales and returns of the goods. As such, this income may make the difference between a successful and failed career.

b. Courts continue to struggle with the appropriateness of ex parte orders and the breadth of enforcement powers. In some situations, the courts focus on the case or controversy requirement under Article III. *See Live Nation Merch., Inc. v. Does*, No. 18CV2703-GPB(JLB), 2018 WL 6326321, at *3 (S.D. Cal. Dec. 4, 2018):

> Plaintiff has failed to make a "clear showing" of each element of standing. It simply relies on numerous instances of bootlegging of other popular musical groups where courts have granted TRO applications with unknown defendants. However, those instances demonstrate a history of bootlegging in the music concert industry but does not satisfy the injury-in-fact for purposes of Plaintiff's standing to sue. Merely relying on other district courts' summary rulings based on facts distinct from the current case are not supportive.

c. The debate between the district courts reflects a growing dissatisfaction with the tools available to stop intellectual property theft. To some, these tools are too limited, while to others, the tools are unreasonably broad. *See also Recording Indus. Ass'n of Am. v. Verizon Internet Servs.*, 351 F.3d 1229 (D.C. Cir. 2003) (vacating and quashing subpoenas against Verizon pursuant to 17 U.S.C.S. §512(h), that were used to identify ISP customers who were allegedly involved in illegal downloading).

d. What steps might a band or a venue take to reduce the bootlegging of non-licensed products?

e. Even with a default judgment, there remain significant difficulties in proving actual damages, calculating statutory damages, tracing assets, and identifying the various works being infringed. *See Bravado Int'l Group Merch. Servs. v. Ninna, Inc.*, 655 F. Supp. 2d 177 (E.D.N.Y. 2009) (entering a default judgment against some but not all of the individual defendants and web companies Cmegamall.com, Rocktshirts punk.com, and Mosh-pitt.com for $300,000 in statutory damages for use of a counterfeit mark on an Iron Maiden t-shirt and ordering a permanent injunction prohibiting the defendants from "selling, manufacturing, and/or distributing any items bearing the names, trademarks, logos, or likenesses of Morrissey, Metallica, Slayer, Korn, Guns N' Roses, Led Zeppelin, The Clash, Iron Maiden, Motorhead, or Depeche Mode.").

Problem 16-C

Bryce was approached by a friend with an offer to make some extra money at an upcoming concert of a national mega-tour. Tickets to the show sold out almost immediately, so the chance to attend the concert was nearly as enticing as the chance to make some money working at it.

Bryce was employed by a seller of music paraphernalia. The seller gave Bryce $300.00 to go shopping for souvenirs, in what Bryce originally thought was an attempt by the seller to determine "what were the hottest items going." Having completed the shopping, Bryce now suspects that the goods to be sold at the upcoming concert may be knock-offs of the items Bryce purchased. It is not uncommon today to find knock-offs or pirated goods that include authentic-looking copyright notices, trademark notices, and in some cases, fictitious labels.

After making a few inquiries with the so-called "friend," Bryce felt the earlier suspicions to be confirmed that none of the goods to be sold at the concert have been approved by the bands in the mega-tour, meaning that all the goods are unlicensed bootleg products.

Bryce seeks your advice on how to handle the situation and how to report the suspicious activity. Bryce is unsure whether this constitutes state or federal crimes, or both. Assist Bryce in reporting the criminal activity. In addition, identify the legal or corporate authorities to whom reports of the suspicious conduct should be submitted.

D. Unauthorized Distribution Using Peer-to-Peer File Sharing

Introduction

The rapid rise of digital technology has stripped both courts and Congress of the ability to keep up with the changes. The seminal modern case, *A&M Records v. Napster, Inc.*, no longer reflects the state of the art for peer-to-peer file sharing, but it best captures the doctrinal, technological, and social trends critical to understanding the revolution taking place in music distribution.

Sony Corp. of America v. Universal City Studios, Inc., 464 U.S. 417 (1984), framed the modern debate. There, the Court addressed the introduction of the video tape recorder. In what was drafted to be a very narrow ruling, the Court excused Sony of secondary liability because its machine had substantial noninfringing uses—a concept adapted without authority or precedent from patent law. The Ninth Circuit's discussion of the scope of injunction, below, harkens back to this concept in *Sony* and guides both the design of the Grokster software and the Court's determination of liability. In essence, the *Napster* decision created a structural template for software designers to meet. If the program can eliminate central control and direct benefit to the distributor, then the substantial noninfringing use will preclude liability. The case of *In re Aimster Copyright Litigation*, 334 F.3d 643, 653 (7th Cir. 2003), affirmed a preliminary injunction against a peer-to-peer file sharing company using an economic harms approach to analyzing contributory infringement and vicarious liability. Taken together, the line of *Sony-Napster-Aimster-Grokster* represents a developmental chain in peer-to-peer software jurisprudence.

The last of these Supreme Court cases is *ABC, Inc. v. Aereo, Inc.*, 573 U.S. 431 (2014), a case that focuses more on the technology and federal regulation of broadcast, cable, and satellite retransmissions than piracy and secondary liability. *Aereo* is reproduced in Chapter 14.

Napster also represents an important decision in terms of the impact of the software on the music industry. The Ninth Circuit's recognition of market harm and changes to music distribution came well before the impact was truly being felt. Unlike the *Sony* Court, which vastly underestimated the changes to be brought by the video cassette, the Ninth Circuit was much quicker to anticipate the transformative impact of the technology.

In this way, the *Napster* litigation anticipated the changes to the legal doctrines of fair use, the technological innovations which would result from these legal standards, and the social impact or normative effect that the availability of peer-to-peer technology would bring. Although the decision is already dated in terms of subsequent case law, it remains the central, transformative decision in this body of jurisprudence.

A&M Records v. Napster, Inc.
239 F.3d 1004 (9th Cir. 2001)

Plaintiffs are engaged in the commercial recording, distribution and sale of copyrighted musical compositions and sound recordings. The complaint alleges that Napster, Inc. ("Napster") is a contributory and vicarious copyright infringer. On July 26, 2000, the district court granted plaintiffs' motion for a preliminary injunction. The injunction was slightly modified by written opinion on August 10, 2000. The district court preliminarily enjoined Napster "from engaging in, or facilitating others in copying, downloading, uploading, transmitting, or distributing plaintiffs' copyrighted musical compositions and sound recordings, protected by either federal or state law, without express permission of the rights owner." We affirm in part, reverse in part and remand....

In 1987, the Moving Picture Experts Group set a standard file format for the storage of audio recordings in a digital format called MPEG-3, abbreviated as "MP3." Digital MP3 files are created through a process colloquially called "ripping." Ripping software allows a computer owner to copy an audio compact disk ("audio CD") directly onto a computer's hard drive by compressing the audio information on the CD into the MP3 format. The MP3's compressed format allows for rapid transmission of digital audio files from one computer to another by electronic mail or any other file transfer protocol.

Napster facilitates the transmission of MP3 files between and among its users. Through a process commonly called "peer-to-peer" file sharing, Napster allows its users to: (1) make MP3 music files stored on individual computer hard drives available for copying by other Napster users; (2) search for MP3 music files stored on other users' computers; and (3) transfer exact copies of the contents of other users' MP3 files from one computer to another via the Internet. These functions are made possible by Napster's MusicShare software, available free of charge from Napster's Internet site, and Napster's network servers and server-side software. Napster provides technical support for the indexing and searching of MP3 files, as well as for its other functions, including a "chat room," where users can meet to discuss music, and a directory where participating artists can provide information about their music.

In order to copy MP3 files through the Napster system, a user must first access Napster's Internet site and download the MusicShare software to his individual computer. Once the software is installed, the user can access the Napster system. A first-time user is required to register with the Napster system by creating a "user name" and password.

If a registered user wants to list available files stored in his computer's hard drive on Napster for others to access, he must first create a "user library" directory on his computer's hard drive. The user then saves his MP3 files in the library directory, using self-designated file names. He next must log into the Napster system using his user name and password. His MusicShare software then searches his user library and verifies that the available files are properly formatted. If in the correct MP3 format, the names of the MP3 files will be uploaded from the user's computer to the Napster servers. The content of the MP3 files remains stored in the user's computer.

Once uploaded to the Napster servers, the user's MP3 file names are stored in a server-side "library" under the user's name and become part of a "collective directory" of files available for transfer during the time the user is logged onto the Napster system. The collective directory is fluid; it tracks users who are connected in real time, displaying only file names that are immediately accessible. . . .

Plaintiffs claim Napster users are engaged in the wholesale reproduction and distribution of copyrighted works, all constituting direct infringement. Secondary liability for copyright infringement does not exist in the absence of direct infringement by a third party. It follows that Napster does not facilitate infringement of the copyright laws in the absence of direct infringement by its users. The district court agreed. We note that the district court's conclusion that plaintiffs have presented a prima facie case of direct infringement by Napster users is not presently appealed by Napster. We only need briefly address the threshold requirements.

A. Infringement

Plaintiffs must satisfy two requirements to present a prima facie case of direct infringement: (1) they must show ownership of the allegedly infringed material and (2) they must demonstrate that the alleged infringers violate at least one exclusive right granted to copyright holders under 17 U.S.C. § 106. Plaintiffs have sufficiently demonstrated ownership. The record supports the district court's determination that "as much as eighty-seven percent of the files available on Napster may be copyrighted and more than seventy percent may be owned or administered by plaintiffs."

The district court further determined that plaintiffs' exclusive rights under § 106 were violated: "here the evidence establishes that a majority of Napster users use the service to download and upload copyrighted music. And by doing that, it constitutes — the uses constitute direct infringement of plaintiffs' musical compositions, recordings." Napster users who upload file names to the search index for others to copy violate plaintiffs' distribution rights. Napster users who download files containing copyrighted music violate plaintiffs' reproduction rights. Napster asserts an affirmative defense to the charge that its users directly infringe plaintiffs' copyrighted musical compositions and sound recordings.

B. Fair Use

Napster contends that its users do not directly infringe plaintiffs' copyrights because the users are engaged in fair use of the material. Napster identifies three specific alleged fair uses: sampling, where users make temporary copies of a work before purchasing; space-shifting, where users access a sound recording through the Napster system that they already own in audio CD format; and permissive distribution of recordings by both new and established artists.

The district court considered factors listed in 17 U.S.C. § 107, which guide a court's fair use determination. These factors are: (1) the purpose and character of the use; (2) the nature of the copyrighted work; (3) the "amount and substantiality of the portion used" in relation to the work as a whole; and (4) the effect of the use upon the potential market for the work or the value of the work. The district court first conducted a general analysis of Napster system uses under § 107, and then applied its reasoning to the alleged fair uses identified by Napster. The district court concluded that Napster users are not fair users. We agree. We first address the court's overall fair use analysis.

1. Purpose and Character of the Use. This factor focuses on whether the new work merely replaces the object of the original creation or instead adds a further purpose or different character. In other words, this factor asks "whether and to what extent the new work is 'transformative.'" The district court first concluded that downloading MP3 files does not transform the copyrighted work. This conclusion is supportable. Courts have been reluctant to find fair use when an original work is merely retransmitted in a different medium. This "purpose and character" element also requires the district court to determine whether the allegedly infringing use is commercial or noncommercial. A commercial use weighs against a finding of fair use but is not conclusive on the issue....

We also note that the definition of a financially motivated transaction for the purposes of criminal copyright actions includes trading infringing copies of a work for other items, "including the receipt of other copyrighted works." *See* No Electronic Theft Act ("NET Act") (defining "Financial Gain").

2. The Nature of the Use. Works that are creative in nature are "closer to the core of intended copyright protection" than are more fact-based works. The district court determined that plaintiffs' "copyrighted musical compositions and sound recordings are creative in nature … which cuts against a finding of fair use under the second factor." We find no error in the district court's conclusion.

3. The Portion Used. "While 'wholesale copying does not preclude fair use per se,' copying an entire work 'militates against a finding of fair use.'" The district court determined that Napster users engage in "wholesale copying" of copyrighted work because file transfer necessarily "involves copying the entirety of the copyrighted work." We agree. We note, however, that under certain circumstances, a court will conclude that a use is fair even when the protected work is copied in its entirety.

4. Effect of Use on Market. "Fair use, when properly applied, is limited to copying by others which does not materially impair the marketability of the work which is copied." "[T]he importance of this [fourth] factor will vary, not only with the amount of harm, but also with the relative strength of the showing on the other factors." The proof required to demonstrate present or future market harm varies with the purpose and character of the use:

> A challenge to a noncommercial use of a copy-righted work requires proof either that the particular use is harmful, or that if it should become widespread, it would adversely affect the potential market for the copyrighted work.… *If the intended use is for commercial gain, that likelihood [of market harm] may be presumed. But if it is for a noncommercial purpose, the likelihood must be demonstrated.*

Sony, 464 U.S. at 451 (emphases added).

Addressing this factor, the district court concluded that Napster harms the market in "at least" two ways: it reduces audio CD sales among college students and it "raises barriers to plaintiffs' entry into the market for the digital downloading of music." The district court relied on evidence plaintiffs submitted to show that Napster use harms the market for their copyrighted musical compositions and sound recordings.…

[T]he district court made sound findings related to Napster's deleterious effect on the present and future digital download market. Moreover, lack of harm to an established market cannot deprive the copyright holder of the right to develop alternative markets for the works. Here, … the record supports the district court's finding that the "record company plaintiffs have already expended considerable funds and effort to commence Internet sales and licensing for digital downloads." Having digital downloads available for free on the Napster system necessarily harms the copyright holders' attempts to charge for the same downloads.…

Accordingly, we next address whether Napster is secondarily liable for the direct infringement under two doctrines of copyright law: contributory copyright infringement and vicarious copyright infringement.

IV.

We first address plaintiffs' claim that Napster is liable for contributory copyright infringement. Traditionally, "one who, with knowledge of the infringing activity, induces, causes or materially contributes to the infringing conduct of another, may be held liable as a 'contributory' infringer." Put differently, liability exists if the defendant engages in "personal conduct that encourages or assists the infringement."

The district court determined that plaintiffs in all likelihood would establish Napster's liability as a contributory infringer. The district court did not err; Napster, by its conduct, knowingly encourages and assists the infringement of plaintiffs' copyrights.

A. Knowledge.

Contributory liability requires that the secondary infringer "know or have reason to know" of direct infringement. The district court found that Napster had both actual and constructive knowledge that its users exchanged copyrighted music. The district court also concluded that the law does not require knowledge of "specific acts of infringement" and rejected Napster's contention that because the company cannot distinguish infringing from noninfringing files, it does not "know" of the direct infringement.

It is apparent from the record that Napster has knowledge, both actual and constructive, of direct infringement.

The district court found actual knowledge because: (1) a document authored by Napster co-founder Sean Parker mentioned "the need to remain ignorant of users' real names and IP addresses 'since they are exchanging pirated music'"; and (2) the Recording Industry Association of America ("RIAA") informed Napster of more than 12,000 infringing files, some of which are still available. The district court found constructive knowledge because: (a) Napster executives have recording industry experience; (b) they have enforced intellectual property rights in other instances; (c) Napster executives have downloaded copy-righted songs from the system; and (d) they have promoted the site with "screen shots listing infringing files."

Napster claims that it is nevertheless protected from contributory liability by the teaching of *Sony Corp. v. Universal City Studios, Inc.*, 464 U.S. 417 (1984). We disagree. We observe that Napster's actual, specific knowledge of direct infringement renders *Sony*'s holding of limited assistance to Napster. We are compelled to make a clear distinction between the architecture of the Napster system and Napster's conduct in relation to the operational capacity of the system.

The *Sony* Court refused to hold the manufacturer and retailers of video tape recorders liable for contributory infringement despite evidence that such machines could be and were used to infringe plaintiffs' copyrighted television shows. *Sony* stated that if liability "is to be imposed on petitioners in this case, it must rest on the fact that they have sold equipment with constructive knowledge of the fact that their customers may use that equipment to make unauthorized copies of copy-righted material." The *Sony* Court declined to impute the requisite level of knowledge where the defendants made and sold equipment capable of both infringing and "substantial noninfringing uses" (adopting a modified "staple article of commerce" doctrine from patent law).

We are bound to follow *Sony*, and will not impute the requisite level of knowledge to Napster merely because peer-to-peer file sharing technology may be used to infringe plaintiffs' copyrights. We depart from the reasoning of the district court that Napster failed to demonstrate that its system is capable of commercially significant noninfringing uses. The district court improperly confined the use analysis to current uses, ignoring the system's capabilities. Consequently, the district court placed undue weight on the proportion of current infringing use as compared to current and future noninfringing use.... Regardless of the number of Napster's infringing versus noninfringing uses, the evidentiary record here supported the district court's finding that plaintiffs would likely prevail in establishing that Napster knew or had reason to know of its users' infringement of plaintiffs' copyrights.

... [I]f a computer system operator learns of specific infringing material available on his system and fails to purge such material from the system, the operator knows of and contributes to direct infringement. Conversely, absent any specific information which identifies infringing activity, a computer system operator cannot be liable for contributory infringement merely because the structure of the system allows for the exchange of copyrighted material. To enjoin simply because a computer network allows for infringing use would, in our opinion, violate Sony and potentially restrict activity unrelated to infringing use.

We nevertheless conclude that sufficient knowledge exists to impose contributory liability when linked to demonstrated infringing use of the Napster system. The record supports the district court's finding that Napster has actual knowledge that specific infringing material is available using its system, that it could block access to the system by suppliers of the infringing material, and that it failed to remove the material.

B. Material Contribution.

Under the facts as found by the district court, Napster materially contributes to the infringing activity. Relying on *Fonovisa*, [*Inc. v. Cherry Auction, Inc.*, 76 F.3d 259 (9th Cir. 1996),] the district court concluded that "without the support services defendant provides, Napster users could not find and download the music they want with the ease of which defendant boasts." We agree that Napster provides "the site and facilities" for direct infringement. The district court correctly applied the reasoning in *Fonovisa*, and properly found that Napster materially contributes to direct infringement.

We affirm the district court's conclusion that plaintiffs have demonstrated a likelihood of success on the merits of the contributory copyright infringement claim. We will address the scope of the injunction in part VIII of this opinion.

We turn to the question whether Napster engages in vicarious copyright infringement. Vicarious copyright liability is an "outgrowth" of respondeat superior. In the context of copyright law, vicarious liability extends beyond an employer/employee relationship to cases in which a defendant "has the right and ability to supervise the infringing activity and also has a direct financial interest in such activities." ...

A. Financial Benefit.

The district court determined that plaintiffs had demonstrated they would likely succeed in establishing that Napster has a direct financial interest in the infringing activity. We agree. Financial benefit exists where the availability of infringing material "acts as a 'draw' for customers." Ample evidence supports the district court's finding that Napster's future revenue is directly dependent upon "increases in user-base." More users register with the Napster system as the "quality and quantity of available music increases." We conclude that the district court did not err in determining that Napster financially benefits from the availability of protected works on its system.

B. Supervision.

The district court determined that Napster has the right and ability to supervise its users' conduct. We agree in part. The ability to block infringers' access to a particular environment for any reason whatsoever is evidence of the right and ability to supervise. Here, plaintiffs have demonstrated that Napster retains the right to control access to its system. Napster has an express reservation of rights policy, stating on its website that it expressly reserves the "right to refuse service and terminate accounts in [its] discretion, including, but not limited to, if Napster believes that user conduct violates applicable law ... or for any reason in Napster's sole discretion, with or without cause."

To escape imposition of vicarious liability, the reserved right to police must be exercised to its fullest extent. Turning a blind eye to detectable acts of infringement for the sake of profit gives rise to liability. The district court correctly determined that Napster had the right and ability to police its system and failed to exercise that right to prevent the exchange of copyrighted material. The district court, however, failed to recognize that the boundaries of the premises that Napster "controls and patrols" are limited. Put differently, Napster's reserved "right and ability" to police is cabined by the system's current architecture. As shown by the record, the Napster system does not "read" the content of indexed files, other than to check that they are in the proper MP3 format.

Napster, however, has the ability to locate infringing material listed on its search indices, and the right to terminate users' access to the system. The file name indices, therefore, are within the "premises" that Napster has the ability to police. We recognize that the files are user-named and may not match copyrighted material exactly (for example, the artist or song could be spelled wrong). For Napster to function effectively, however, file names must reasonably or roughly correspond to the material contained in the files, otherwise no user could ever locate any desired music. As a practical matter, Napster, its users and the record company plaintiffs have equal access to infringing material by employing Napster's "search function."

Our review of the record requires us to accept the district court's conclusion that plaintiffs have demonstrated a likelihood of success on the merits of the vicarious copyright infringement claim. Napster's failure to police the system's "premises," combined with a showing that Napster financially benefits from the continuing availability of infringing files on its system, leads to the imposition of vicarious liability. We address the scope of the injunction in part VIII of this opinion. [The court next addressed and rejected protection for Napster under § 1008 of the Audio Home Recording Act of 1992 and § 512 of the Digital Millennium Copyright Act as well as affirmative defenses of waiver, implied license and copyright misuse.]

The district court correctly recognized that a preliminary injunction against Napster's participation in copyright infringement is not only warranted but required. We believe, however, that the scope of the injunction needs modification in light of our opinion. Specifically, we reiterate that contributory liability may potentially be imposed only to the extent that Napster: (1) receives reasonable knowledge of specific infringing files with copyrighted musical compositions and sound recordings; (2) knows or should know that such files are available on the Napster system; and (3) fails to act to prevent viral distribution of the works. The mere existence of the Napster system, absent actual notice and Napster's demonstrated failure to remove the offending material, is insufficient to impose contributory liability.

Conversely, Napster may be vicariously liable when it fails to affirmatively use its ability to patrol its system and preclude access to potentially infringing files listed in its search index. Napster has both the ability to use its search function to identify infringing musical recordings and the right to bar participation of users who engage in the transmission of infringing files.

The preliminary injunction which we stayed is overbroad because it places on Napster the entire burden of ensuring that no "copying, downloading, uploading, transmitting, or distributing" of plaintiffs' works occur on the system. As stated, we place the burden on plaintiffs to provide notice to Napster of copyrighted works and files containing such works available on the Napster system before Napster has the duty to disable access to the offending content. Napster, however, also bears the burden of policing the system within the limits of the system. Here, we recognize that this is not an exact science in that the files are user named. In crafting the injunction on remand, the district court should recognize that Napster's system does not currently appear to allow Napster access to users' MP3 files.

Based on our decision to remand, Napster's additional arguments on appeal going to the scope of the injunction need not be addressed. We, however, briefly address Napster's First Amendment argument so that it is not reasserted on remand. Napster contends that the present injunction violates the First Amendment because it is broader than necessary. The company asserts two distinct free speech rights: (1) its right to publish a "directory" (here, the search index) and (2) its users' right to exchange information. We note that First Amendment concerns in copyright are allayed by the presence of the fair use doctrine. There was a preliminary determination here that Napster users are not fair users. Uses of copyrighted material that are not fair uses are rightfully enjoined....

Napster contends that the district court should have imposed a monetary penalty by way of a compulsory royalty in place of an injunction.... Imposing a compulsory royalty payment schedule would give Napster an "easy out" of this case. If such royalties were imposed, Napster would avoid penalties for any future violation of an injunction, statutory copyright damages and any possible criminal penalties for continuing infringement. The royalty structure would also grant Napster the luxury of either choosing to continue and pay royalties or shut down. On the other hand, the wronged parties would be forced to do business with a company that profits from the wrongful use of intellectual properties. Plaintiffs would lose the power to control their intellectual property: they could not make a business decision *not* to license their property to Napster, and, in the event they planned to do business with Napster, compulsory royalties would take away the copyright holders' ability to negotiate the terms of any contractual arrangement.

We affirm in part, reverse in part and remand.

MGM Studios, Inc. v. Grokster Ltd.

545 U.S. 913 (2005)

JUSTICE SOUTER delivered the opinion of the Court.

The question is under what circumstances the distributor of a product capable of both lawful and unlawful use is liable for acts of copyright infringement by third parties using the product. We hold that one who distributes a device with the object of promoting its use to infringe copyright, as shown by clear expression or other affirmative steps taken to foster infringement, is liable for the resulting acts of infringement by third parties.

Respondents, Grokster, Ltd., and StreamCast Networks, Inc., defendants in the trial court, distribute free software products that allow computer users to share electronic files through peer-to-peer networks, so called because users' computers communicate directly with each other, not through central servers. The advantage of peer-to-peer networks over information networks of other types shows up in their substantial and growing popularity. Because they need no central computer server to mediate the exchange of information or files among users, the high-bandwidth communications capacity for a server may be dispensed with, and the need for costly server storage space is eliminated. Since copies of a file (particularly a popular one) are available on many users' computers, file requests and retrievals may be faster than on other types of networks, and since file exchanges do not travel through a server, communications can take place between any computers that remain connected to the network without risk that a glitch in the server will disable the network in its entirety. Given these benefits in security, cost, and efficiency, peer-to-peer networks are employed to store and distribute electronic files by universities, government agencies, corporations, and libraries, among others.[7]

Other users of peer-to-peer networks include individual recipients of Grokster's and StreamCast's software, and although the networks that they enjoy through using the software can be used to share any type of digital file, they have prominently employed those networks in sharing copyrighted music and video files without authorization. A group of copyright holders (MGM for short, but including motion picture studios, recording companies, songwriters, and music publishers) sued Grokster and StreamCast for their users' copyright infringements, alleging that they knowingly and intentionally distributed their software to enable users to reproduce and distribute the copyrighted works in violation of the Copyright Act, 17 U.S.C. § 101 et seq. (2000 ed. and Supp. II). MGM sought damages and an injunction.

Discovery during the litigation revealed the way the software worked, the business aims of each defendant company, and the predilections of the users. Grokster's eponymous software employs what is known as FastTrack technology, a protocol developed by others and licensed to Grokster. StreamCast distributes a very similar product except that its software, called Morpheus, relies on what is known as Gnutella technology. A user who downloads and installs either software possesses the protocol to send requests for files directly to the computers of others using software compatible with FastTrack or Gnutella. On the FastTrack network opened by the Grokster software, the user's request goes to a computer given an indexing capacity by the software and designated a supernode, or to some other computer with comparable power and capacity to collect temporary indexes of the files available on the computers of users connected to it. The supernode (or indexing computer) searches its own index and may communicate the search request to other supernodes. If the file is found, the supernode discloses its location to the computer requesting it, and the requesting user can download the file directly from the computer located. The copied file is placed in a designated sharing folder on the requesting user's computer, where it is available for other users to download in turn, along with any other file in that folder.

In the Gnutella network made available by Morpheus, the process is mostly the same, except that in some versions of the Gnutella protocol there are no supernodes....

Although Grokster and StreamCast do not therefore know when particular files are copied, a few searches using their software would show what is available on the networks the software reaches. MGM commissioned a statistician to conduct a systematic search, and his study showed that nearly 90% of the files available for down-

---

7. Peer-to-peer networks have disadvantages as well. Searches on peer-to-peer networks may not reach and uncover all available files because search requests may not be transmitted to every computer on the network. There may be redundant copies of popular files. The creator of the software has no incentive to minimize storage or bandwidth consumption, the costs of which are borne by every user of the network. Most relevant here, it is more difficult to control the content of files available for retrieval and the behavior of users.

load on the FastTrack system were copyrighted works.[8] Grokster and StreamCast dispute this figure, raising methodological problems and arguing that free copying even of copyrighted works may be authorized by the rightholders. They also argue that potential noninfringing uses of their software are significant in kind, even if infrequent in practice. Some musical performers, for example, have gained new audiences by distributing their copyrighted works for free across peer-to-peer networks, and some distributors of unprotected content have used peer-to-peer networks to disseminate files, Shakespeare being an example. Indeed, StreamCast has given Morpheus users the opportunity to download the briefs in this very case, though their popularity has not been quantified.

As for quantification, the parties' anecdotal and statistical evidence entered thus far to show the content available on the FastTrack and Gnutella networks does not say much about which files are actually downloaded by users, and no one can say how often the software is used to obtain copies of unprotected material. But MGM's evidence gives reason to think that the vast majority of users' downloads are acts of infringement, and because well over 100 million copies of the software in question are known to have been downloaded, and billions of files are shared across the FastTrack and Gnutella networks each month, the probable scope of copyright infringement is staggering.

Grokster and StreamCast concede the infringement in most downloads, and it is uncontested that they are aware that users employ their software primarily to download copyrighted files, even if the decentralized FastTrack and Gnutella networks fail to reveal which files are being copied, and when. From time to time, moreover, the companies have learned about their users' infringement directly, as from users who have sent e-mail to each company with questions about playing copyrighted movies they had downloaded, to whom the companies have responded with guidance. And MGM notified the companies of 8 million copyrighted files that could be obtained using their software.

Grokster and StreamCast are not, however, merely passive recipients of information about infringing use. The record is replete with evidence that from the moment Grokster and StreamCast began to distribute their free software, each one clearly voiced the objective that recipients use it to download copyrighted works, and each took active steps to encourage infringement.

After the notorious file-sharing service, Napster, was sued by copyright holders for facilitation of copyright infringement, StreamCast gave away a software program of a kind known as OpenNap, designed as compatible with the Napster program and open to Napster users for downloading files from other Napster and OpenNap users' computers. Evidence indicates that "it was always [StreamCast's] intent to use [its OpenNap network] to be able to capture email addresses of [its] initial target market so that [it] could promote [its] StreamCast Morpheus interface to them," indeed, the OpenNap program was engineered "'to leverage Napster's 50 million user base.'"

---

8. By comparison, evidence introduced by the plaintiffs in A & M Records, Inc. v. Napster, Inc., 239 F.3d 1004 (9th Cir. 2001), showed that 87% of files available on the Napster filesharing network were copyrighted. *Id.* at 1013.

StreamCast monitored both the number of users downloading its OpenNap program and the number of music files they downloaded. It also used the resulting Open-Nap network to distribute copies of the Morpheus software and to encourage users to adopt it. Internal company documents indicate that StreamCast hoped to attract large numbers of former Napster users if that company was shut down by court order or otherwise, and that StreamCast planned to be the next Napster. A kit developed by StreamCast to be delivered to advertisers, for example, contained press articles about StreamCast's potential to capture former Napster users, and it introduced itself to some potential advertisers as a company "which is similar to what Napster was." It broadcast banner advertisements to users of other Napster-compatible software, urging them to adopt its OpenNap. An internal e-mail from a company executive stated: "'We have put this network in place so that when Napster pulls the plug on their free service … or if the Court orders them shut down prior to that … we will be positioned to capture the flood of their 32 million users that will be actively looking for an alternative.'"

Thus, StreamCast developed promotional materials to market its service as the best Napster alternative. One proposed advertisement read: "Napster Inc. has announced that it will soon begin charging you a fee. That's if the courts don't order it shut down first. What will you do to get around it?" Another proposed ad touted StreamCast's software as the "# 1 alternative to Napster" and asked "when the lights went off at Napster … where did the users go?" StreamCast even planned to flaunt the illegal uses of its software; when it launched the OpenNap network, the chief technology officer of the company averred that "the goal is to get in trouble with the law and get sued. It's the best way to get in the news."

The evidence that Grokster sought to capture the market of former Napster users is sparser but revealing, for Grokster launched its own OpenNap system called Swaptor and inserted digital codes into its Web site so that computer users using Web search engines to look for "Napster" or "free filesharing" would be directed to the Grokster Web site, where they could download the Grokster software. And Grokster's name is an apparent derivative of Napster.

StreamCast's executives monitored the number of songs by certain commercial artists available on their networks, and an internal communication indicates they aimed to have a larger number of copyrighted songs available on their networks than other file-sharing networks. The point, of course, would be to attract users of a mind to infringe, just as it would be with their promotional materials developed showing copyrighted songs as examples of the kinds of files available through Morpheus. Morpheus in fact allowed users to search specifically for "Top 40" songs, which were inevitably copyrighted. Similarly, Grokster sent users a newsletter promoting its ability to provide particular, popular copyrighted materials.

In addition to this evidence of express promotion, marketing, and intent to promote further, the business models employed by Grokster and StreamCast confirm that their principal object was use of their software to download copyrighted works. Grokster and StreamCast receive no revenue from users, who obtain the software itself for nothing. Instead, both companies generate income by selling advertising space, and they stream the advertising to Grokster and Morpheus users while they are employing the programs. As the number of users of each program increases, advertising opportunities become worth more. While there is doubtless some demand for free Shakespeare, the evidence shows that substantive volume is a function of free access to copyrighted work. Users seeking Top 40 songs, for example, or the latest release by Modest Mouse, are certain to be far more numerous than those seeking a free Decameron, and Grokster and StreamCast translated that demand into dollars.

Finally, there is no evidence that either company made an effort to filter copyrighted material from users' downloads or otherwise impede the sharing of copyrighted files. Although Grokster appears to have sent e-mails warning users about infringing content when it received threatening notice from the copyright holders, it never blocked anyone from continuing to use its software to share copyrighted files. StreamCast not only rejected another company's offer of help to monitor infringement, but blocked the Internet Protocol addresses of entities it believed were trying to engage in such monitoring on its networks....

The District Court held that those who used the Grokster and Morpheus software to download copyrighted media files directly infringed MGM's copyrights, a conclusion not contested on appeal, but the court nonetheless granted summary judgment in favor of Grokster and StreamCast as to any liability arising from distribution of the then current versions of their software. Distributing that software gave rise to no liability in the court's view, because its use did not provide the distributors with actual knowledge of specific acts of infringement.

The Court of Appeals affirmed. In the court's analysis, a defendant was liable as a contributory infringer when it had knowledge of direct infringement and materially contributed to the infringement. But the court read *Sony Corp. of America v. Universal City Studios, Inc.*, 464 U.S. 417 (1984), as holding that distribution of a commercial product capable of substantial noninfringing uses could not give rise to contributory liability for infringement unless the distributor had actual knowledge of specific instances of infringement and failed to act on that knowledge. The fact that the software was capable of substantial noninfringing uses in the Ninth Circuit's view meant that Grokster and StreamCast were not liable, because they had no such actual knowledge, owing to the decentralized architecture of their software. The court also held that Grokster and StreamCast did not materially contribute to their users' infringement because it was the users themselves who searched for, retrieved, and stored the infringing files, with no involvement by the defendants beyond providing the software in the first place.

The Ninth Circuit also considered whether Grokster and StreamCast could be liable under a theory of vicarious infringement. The court held against liability because the defendants did not monitor or control the use of the software, had no agreed-upon right or current ability to supervise its use, and had no independent duty to police infringement....

MGM and many of the *amici* fault the Court of Appeals' holding for upsetting a sound balance between the respective values of supporting creative pursuits through copyright protection and promoting innovation in new communication technologies by limiting the incidence of liability for copyright infringement. The more artistic protection is favored, the more technological innovation may be discouraged; the administration of copyright law is an exercise in managing the trade-off.

The tension between the two values is the subject of this case, with its claim that digital distribution of copyrighted material threatens copyright holders as never before, because every copy is identical to the original, copying is easy, and many people (especially the young) use file-sharing software to download copyrighted works. This very breadth of the software's use may well draw the public directly into the debate over copyright policy ... As the case has been presented to us, these fears are said to be offset by the different concern that imposing liability, not only on infringers but on distributors of software based on its potential for unlawful use, could limit further development of beneficial technologies.

The argument for imposing indirect liability in this case is, however, a powerful one, given the number of infringing downloads that occur every day using Stream-Cast's and Grokster's software. When a widely shared service or product is used to commit infringement, it may be impossible to enforce rights in the protected work effectively against all direct infringers, the only practical alternative being to go against the distributor of the copying device for secondary liability on a theory of contributory or vicarious infringement.

One infringes contributorily by intentionally inducing or encouraging direct infringement, and infringes vicariously by profiting from direct infringement while declining to exercise a right to stop or limit it.[9] Although "the Copyright Act does not expressly render anyone liable for infringement committed by another," *Sony Corp. v. Universal City Studios*, 464 U.S. at 434....

[W]here an article is "good for nothing else" but infringement, there is no legitimate public interest in its unlicensed availability, and there is no injustice in presuming or imputing an intent to infringe. Conversely, the doctrine absolves the equivocal conduct of selling an item with substantial lawful as well as unlawful uses, and limits liability to instances of more acute fault than the mere understanding that some of

---

9. We stated in *Sony Corp. of America v. Universal City Studios, Inc.*, 464 U.S. 417 (1984), that "'the lines between direct infringement, contributory infringement and vicarious liability are not clearly drawn'.... Reasoned analysis of [the *Sony* plaintiffs' contributory infringement claim] necessarily entails consideration of arguments and case law which may also be forwarded under the other labels, and indeed the parties ... rely upon such arguments and authority in support of their respective positions on the issue of contributory infringement," *id.* at 435, n.17 (quoting *Universal City Studios, Inc. v. Sony Corp.*, 480 F. Supp. 429, 457–458 (C.D. Cal. 1979)). In the present case MGM has argued a vicarious liability theory, which allows imposition of liability when the defendant profits directly from the infringement and has a right and ability to supervise the direct infringer, even if the defendant initially lacks knowledge of the infringement. Because we resolve the case based on an inducement theory, there is no need to analyze separately MGM's vicarious liability theory.

one's products will be misused. It leaves breathing room for innovation and a vigorous commerce.

The parties and many of the *amici* in this case think the key to resolving it is the *Sony* rule and, in particular, what it means for a product to be "capable of commercially significant noninfringing uses." MGM advances the argument that granting summary judgment to Grokster and StreamCast as to their current activities gave too much weight to the value of innovative technology, and too little to the copyrights infringed by users of their software, given that 90% of works available on one of the networks was shown to be copyrighted. Assuming the remaining 10% to be its noninfringing use, MGM says this should not qualify as "substantial," and the Court should quantify Sony to the extent of holding that a product used "principally" for infringement does not qualify. As mentioned before, Grokster and StreamCast reply by citing evidence that their software can be used to reproduce public domain works, and they point to copyright holders who actually encourage copying. Even if infringement is the principal practice with their software today, they argue, the noninfringing uses are significant and will grow.

We agree with MGM that the Court of Appeals misapplied *Sony*, which it read as limiting secondary liability quite beyond the circumstances to which the case applied. *Sony* barred secondary liability based on presuming or imputing intent to cause infringement solely from the design or distribution of a product capable of substantial lawful use, which the distributor knows is in fact used for infringement. The Ninth Circuit has read *Sony*'s limitation to mean that whenever a product is capable of substantial lawful use, the producer can never be held contributorily liable for third parties' infringing use of it; it read the rule as being this broad, even when an actual purpose to cause infringing use is shown by evidence independent of design and distribution of the product, unless the distributors had "specific knowledge of infringement at a time at which they contributed to the infringement, and failed to act upon that information." Because the Circuit found the StreamCast and Grokster software capable of substantial lawful use, it concluded on the basis of its reading of *Sony* that neither company could be held liable, since there was no showing that their software, being without any central server, afforded them knowledge of specific unlawful uses.

This view of *Sony*, however, was error, converting the case from one about liability resting on imputed intent to one about liability on any theory. Because *Sony* did not displace other theories of secondary liability, and because we find below that it was error to grant summary judgment to the companies on MGM's inducement claim, we do not revisit *Sony* further, as MGM requests, to add a more quantified description of the point of balance between protection and commerce when liability rests solely on distribution with knowledge that unlawful use will occur. It is enough to note that the Ninth Circuit's judgment rested on an erroneous understanding of *Sony* and to leave further consideration of the *Sony* rule for a day when that may be required.

Sony's rule limits imputing culpable intent as a matter of law from the characteristics or uses of a distributed product. But nothing in *Sony* requires courts to ignore evidence of intent if there is such evidence, and the case was never meant to foreclose rules of fault-based liability derived from the common law. Thus, where evidence goes beyond a product's characteristics or the knowledge that it may be put to infringing uses, and shows statements or actions directed to promoting infringement, *Sony*'s staple-article rule will not preclude liability.

The classic case of direct evidence of unlawful purpose occurs when one induces commission of infringement by another, or "entices or persuades another" to infringe, Black's Law Dictionary 790 (8th ed. 2004), as by advertising. Thus at common law a copyright or patent defendant who "not only expected but invoked [infringing use] by advertisement" was liable for infringement "on principles recognized in every part of the law."

The rule on inducement of infringement as developed in the early cases is no different today.[10] Evidence of "active steps ... taken to encourage direct infringement," such as advertising an infringing use or instructing how to engage in an infringing use, show an affirmative intent that the product be used to infringe, and a showing that infringement was encouraged overcomes the law's reluctance to find liability when a defendant merely sells a commercial product suitable for some lawful use.

For the same reasons that *Sony* took the staple-article doctrine of patent law as a model for its copyright safe-harbor rule, the inducement rule, too, is a sensible one for copyright. We adopt it here, holding that one who distributes a device with the object of promoting its use to infringe copyright, as shown by clear expression or other affirmative steps taken to foster infringement, is liable for the resulting acts of infringement by third parties. We are, of course, mindful of the need to keep from trenching on regular commerce or discouraging the development of technologies with lawful and unlawful potential. Accordingly, just as *Sony* did not find intentional inducement despite the knowledge of the VCR manufacturer that its device could be used to infringe, mere knowledge of infringing potential or of actual infringing uses would not be enough here to subject a distributor to liability. Nor would ordinary acts incident to product distribution, such as offering customers technical support or product updates, support liability in themselves. The inducement rule, instead, premises liability on purposeful, culpable expression and conduct, and thus does nothing to compromise legitimate commerce or discourage innovation having a lawful promise.

The only apparent question about treating MGM's evidence as sufficient to withstand summary judgment under the theory of inducement goes to the need on MGM's part to adduce evidence that StreamCast and Grokster communicated an inducing message to their software users. The classic instance of inducement is by advertisement or solicitation that broadcasts a message designed to stimulate others to commit violations....

---

10. Inducement has been codified in patent law.

In StreamCast's case, of course, the evidence just described was supplemented by other unequivocal indications of unlawful purpose in the internal communications and advertising designs aimed at Napster users ("When the lights went off at Napster ... where did the users go?") Whether the messages were communicated is not to the point on this record. The function of the message in the theory of inducement is to prove by a defendant's own statements that his unlawful purpose disqualifies him from claiming protection (and incidentally to point to actual violators likely to be found among those who hear or read the message). Proving that a message was sent out, then, is the preeminent but not exclusive way of showing that active steps were taken with the purpose of bringing about infringing acts, and of showing that infringing acts took place by using the device distributed. Here, the summary judgment record is replete with other evidence that Grokster and StreamCast, unlike the manufacturer and distributor in *Sony*, acted with a purpose to cause copyright violations by use of software suitable for illegal use.

Three features of this evidence of intent are particularly notable. First, each company showed itself to be aiming to satisfy a known source of demand for copyright infringement, the market comprising former Napster users. StreamCast's internal documents made constant reference to Napster, it initially distributed its Morpheus software through an OpenNap program compatible with Napster, it advertised its OpenNap program to Napster users, and its Morpheus software functions as Napster did except that it could be used to distribute more kinds of files, including copyrighted movies and software programs. Grokster's name is apparently derived from Napster, it too initially offered an OpenNap program, its software's function is likewise comparable to Napster's, and it attempted to divert queries for Napster onto its own Web site. Grokster and StreamCast's efforts to supply services to former Napster users, deprived of a mechanism to copy and distribute what were overwhelmingly infringing files, indicate a principal, if not exclusive, intent on the part of each to bring about infringement.

Second, this evidence of unlawful objective is given added significance by MGM's showing that neither company attempted to develop filtering tools or other mechanisms to diminish the infringing activity using their software. While the Ninth Circuit treated the defendants' failure to develop such tools as irrelevant because they lacked an independent duty to monitor their users' activity, we think this evidence underscores Grokster's and StreamCast's intentional facilitation of their users' infringement.[11]

Third, there is a further complement to the direct evidence of unlawful objective. It is useful to recall that StreamCast and Grokster make money by selling advertising

---

11. Of course, in the absence of other evidence of intent, a court would be unable to find contributory infringement liability merely based on a failure to take affirmative steps to prevent infringement, if the device otherwise was capable of substantial noninfringing uses. Such a holding would tread too close to the Sony safe harbor.

space, by directing ads to the screens of computers employing their software. As the record shows, the more the software is used, the more ads are sent out and the greater the advertising revenue becomes. Since the extent of the software's use determines the gain to the distributors, the commercial sense of their enterprise turns on high-volume use, which the record shows is infringing. This evidence alone would not justify an inference of unlawful intent, but viewed in the context of the entire record its import is clear.

The unlawful objective is unmistakable....

In sum, this case is significantly different from *Sony* and reliance on that case to rule in favor of StreamCast and Grokster was error. *Sony* dealt with a claim of liability based solely on distributing a product with alternative lawful and unlawful uses, with knowledge that some users would follow the unlawful course. The case struck a balance between the interests of protection and innovation by holding that the product's capability of substantial lawful employment should bar the imputation of fault and consequent secondary liability for the unlawful acts of others....

There is substantial evidence in MGM's favor on all elements of inducement, and summary judgment in favor of Grokster and StreamCast was error. On remand, reconsideration of MGM's motion for summary judgment will be in order. The judgment of the Court of Appeals is vacated, and the case is remanded for further proceedings consistent with this opinion.

[The precise role of *Sony* continues to be debated. The Court split between concurrences by Justices Ginsburg and Breyer on whether Grokster's product is "capable of 'substantial' or 'commercially significant' noninfringing uses." Each concurrence had three votes.]

Notes and Questions

a. The court decisions quote *Sony* extensively as the framework for the various interpretations of fair use in the context of a new technology which is being used extensively for copyright piracy, but which also has great potential for substantial noninfringing uses.

b. Two excellent but very different works provide the history and context of the *Sony* decision. *Compare* PAUL GOLDSTEIN, COPYRIGHT'S HIGHWAY: FROM GUTENBURG TO THE CELESTIAL JUKEBOX 41–44 (1994), *with* JAMES LARDNER, FAST FORWARD, A MACHINE AND THE COMMOTION IT CAUSED (Revised ed. Pierce Law 2002).

c. These three cases, *Napster*, *Aimster*, and *Grokster*, suggest very different attitudes towards both the plaintiffs and defendants. Was the *Grokster* Court correct in ignoring the choices made by the software designers to create software intentionally to thwart the secondary liability standards of contributory infringement and vicarious liability? In the alternative, did the *Napster* Court overstate the secondary liability standards to stop the direct infringement being conducted?

d. The *Napster* Court discussed the impact that peer-to-peer file sharing may have had on the sale of CDs, but what about the creation of new opportunities, such as live concerts broadcast over the Internet? Did the sudden rise in popularity of these services affect either the value or enforceability of these agreements? *See Profile Publ'g & Mgmt. Corp. APS v. Musicmaker.com, Inc.,* 242 F. Supp. 2d 363, 364 (S.D.N.Y. 2003).

e. The dissent in *ABC, Inc. v. Aereo, Inc.,* 573 U.S. 431 (2014) (the majority opinion is reproduced in Chapter 14), focuses on the regulations of cable and satellite to restrict a company from getting out of those regulatory schemes through clever technology. But the dissent has a different view.

JUSTICE SCALIA, with whom JUSTICE THOMAS and JUSTICE ALITO join, dissenting.

This case is the latest skirmish in the long-running copyright battle over the delivery of television programming. Petitioners, a collection of television networks and affiliates (Networks), broadcast copyrighted programs on the public airwaves for all to see. Aereo, respondent, operates an automated system that allows subscribers to receive, on Internet-connected devices, programs that they select, including the Networks' copyrighted programs. The Networks sued Aereo for several forms of copyright infringement, but we are here concerned with a single claim: that Aereo violates the Networks' "exclusive righ[t]" to "perform" their programs "publicly." 17 U.S.C. § 106(4). That claim fails at the very outset because Aereo does not "perform" at all. The Court manages to reach the opposite conclusion only by disregarding widely accepted rules for service-provider liability and adopting in their place an improvised standard ("looks-like-cable-TV") that will sow confusion for years to come.

The Networks' claim is governed by a simple but profoundly important rule: A defendant may be held directly liable only if it has engaged in volitional conduct that violates the Act. This requirement is firmly grounded in the Act's text, which defines "perform" in active, affirmative terms: One "perform[s]" a copyrighted "audiovisual work," such as a movie or news broadcast, by "show[ing] its images in any sequence" or "mak[ing] the sounds accompanying it audible." And since the Act makes it unlawful to copy or perform copyrighted works, not to copy or perform in general, the volitional-act requirement demands conduct directed to the plaintiff's copyrighted material. Every Court of Appeals to have considered an automated-service provider's direct liability for copyright infringement has adopted that rule.

The volitional-conduct requirement is not at issue in most direct-infringement cases; the usual point of dispute is whether the defendant's conduct is infringing (e.g., Does the defendant's design copy the plaintiff's?), rather than whether the defendant has acted at all (e.g., Did this defendant create the infringing design?). But it comes right to the fore when a direct-infringement claim is lodged against a defendant who does nothing more than operate an automated, user-controlled system. Internet-service providers are a prime example. When one user sends data to another, the provider's equipment facilitates the transfer automatically. Does that mean that the provider is directly liable when the transmission happens to result in the "reproduc[tion]," § 106(1), of a copyrighted work? It does not. The provider's system is "totally indifferent to the material's content," whereas courts require "some aspect of volition" directed at the copyrighted material before direct liability may be imposed. The defendant may be held directly liable only if the defendant itself "trespassed on the exclusive domain of the copyright owner." Most of the time that issue will come down to who selects the copyrighted content: the defendant or its customers.

So which is Aereo: the copy shop or the video-on-demand service? In truth, it is neither. Rather, it is akin to a copy shop that provides its patrons with a library card. Aereo offers access to an automated system consisting of routers, servers, transcoders, and dime-sized antennae. Like a photocopier or VCR, that system lies dormant until a subscriber activates it. When a subscriber selects a program, Aereo's system picks up the relevant broadcast signal, translates its audio and video components into digital data, stores the data in a user-specific file, and transmits that file's contents to the subscriber via the Internet—at which point the subscriber's laptop, tablet, or other device displays the broadcast just as an ordinary television would. The result of that process fits the statutory definition of a performance to a tee: The subscriber's device "show[s]" the broadcast's "images" and "make[s] the sounds accompanying" the broadcast "audible." § 101. The only question is whether those performances are the product of Aereo's volitional conduct.

I share the Court's evident feeling that what Aereo is doing (or enabling to be done) to the Networks' copyrighted programming ought not to be allowed. But perhaps we need not distort the Copyright Act to forbid it.

f. Significant focus has been on section 1201 of the Digital Millennium Copyright Act which bans the anti-circumvention of copyright protection systems. "Congress enacted three new anti-circumvention prohibitions.... The first two provisions target circumvention of technological measures that effectively control access to a copyrighted work; the third ... [prohibits] the trafficking in and marketing of devices primarily designed to circumvent the use restriction protective technologies." *United States v. Elcom Ltd.*, 203 F. Supp. 2d 1111, 1120 (N.D. Cal. 2002). *See also DVD Copy Control Assn., Inc. v. Bunner,* 75 P.3d 1 (Cal. 2003); *Universal City Studios, Inc. v. Corley,* 273 F.3d 429 (2d Cir. 2001). These provisions have been generally upheld by the courts and widely criticized by commentators.

g. In *Ellison v. Robertson,* 357 F.3d 1072 (9th Cir. 2004), RemarQ Communities, Inc. and Critical Path, Inc., settled the case with the following joint statement:

The copyright infringement action filed by noted author and literary activist Harlan Ellison against Critical Path, Inc. and its subsidiary RemarQ

Communities, Inc. has been settled. The action stemmed from the unauthorized posting of some of Ellison's most well-known copyrighted stories on the RemarQ service. Ellison's copyright infringement action is continuing against the remaining defendant, America Online, Inc.

Among the terms of the settlement, Critical Path will develop software that allows Ellison immediately to delete unauthorized postings of his works of which he becomes aware. Critical Path will also appoint an employee to be available to Ellison as a back up measure.

Ellison, who has authored 75 books in his distinguished career, noted: "I am pleased to have settled this case with Critical Path and RemarQ and believe we have taken a step forward for writers everywhere in their efforts to protect copyrighted works."

The settlement did not include any admission of liability. Commenting on the settlement, a Critical Path spokesperson said: "We are pleased to reach a settlement in this case that will aid authors in protecting their intellectual property."

h. The reframing of *Grokster* to use the "inducement of infringement" doctrine has the potential to separate out interesting new technologies and well-intended companies from those sham enterprises that provide noninfringing activities as a smokescreen for the business of profiting from other parties' copyright infringement.

i. On remand, the district court applied the "inducement doctrine" to the claim. "Plaintiffs need prove only that StreamCast distributed the product with the intent to encourage infringement. Since there is no dispute that StreamCast did distribute an infringement-enabling technology, the inquiry focuses on the defendant's intent, which can be shown by evidence of the defendant's expression or conduct." The district court found sufficient intent and issued the injunction. *MGM Studios, Inc. v. Grokster Ltd.*, 454 F. Supp. 2d 966, 985 (C.D. Cal. 2006).

j. An example of this attempt to distinguish between infringement and technical copyright noncompliance was demonstrated in *Chamberlain Grp., Inc. v. Skylink Techs., Inc.*, 292 F. Supp. 2d 1040 (N.D. Ill. 2003). Here, a garage door manufacturer used encrypted coding to tie its remote door opener to the door mechanism. The court rejected the tying:

Under Chamberlain's theory, any customer who loses his or her Chamberlain transmitter, but manages to operate the opener either with a non-Chamberlain transmitter or by some other means of circumventing the rolling code, has violated the DMCA. In this court's view, the statute does not require such a conclusion. GDO transmitters are similar to television remote controls in that consumers of both products may need to replace them at some point due to damage or loss, and may program them to work with other devices manufactured by different companies. In both cases, consumers have a reasonable expectation that they can replace the original product with a competing, universal product without violating federal law.

Id. at 1046. The distinction is not grounded in copyright or fair use, but in the reasonable expectations of consumers. While this is a proper outcome, to what extent can consumer expectation provide a guide for common law development of copyright policy?

Problem 16-D

In addition to the issues Bryce raised in Problem 16-B, Bryce also found that two-thirds of Bryce's recorded songs were available free on the Internet. Bryce had originally placed three of those songs on Napster to promote the CD four years earlier, but now wishes to remove them. The other songs were never placed in peer-to-peer networks with permission. To what extent does this information add to the advice you provided pursuant to Problem 16-B?

E. Consumer Services & Electronics

Introduction

Despite headlines which suggest that the primary threat to the entertainment industry is piracy, the true battle for the future of the United States entertainment industry is being waged against the consumer electronic industry and computer industry. Although the income from the consumer electronic industry and computer industry dwarfs that of all the entertainment companies combined, most consumer electronics equipment would be unneeded and unused without the content of the entertainment industries. In industry parlance, music and video is the "killer app" for consumer electronics and many computer upgrades.

This tension between the content industries and the electronic industries is at the heart of the debate for the future of the industries. Sony is the only company to successfully operate within all industries, but private reports suggest that Sony does not operate so much as an integrated company as it does as a balkanized confederation of competing industries — the battle over control is being fought within the corporate, multinational structure. Similarly, the potential of the AOL-Time/Warner merger went largely unrecognized because the merged entity could not take advantage of the integration.

Perhaps ironically, it was *Sony Corp. of America v. Universal City Studios, Inc.*, which began the series of cases that fostered the consumer electronic industry by permitting the consumer electronics industry to rely on fair use rather than licensed content to promote the growth of the VCR.

Given these cases and the track record of both Sony and AOL/Warner, there is perhaps some reason that other large consumer electronics companies have not directly purchased the media companies. Steve Jobs (1955–2011), co-founder and longtime CEO of Apple Computer and co-founder of Pixar, may have best exemplified the potential leadership needed to meld the two industries. It is inevitable that these mergers will eventually take place, if for no other reason than so that key players in the consumer electronics industry can gain control over archival content. The nature of these eventual mergers will dramatically impact each entertainment industry as it is subsumed. Nonetheless, fair use decisions reduce the incentive to buy the media producers.

Indeed, it may be that losing these lawsuits is the most important thing the entertainment industry can do to remain free from merger mania.

Recording Industry Association of America v. Diamond Multimedia Systems, Inc.

180 F.3d 1072 (9th Cir. 1999)

[The Ninth Circuit found that the early digital music players did not violate copyright laws and did not require payments to the copyright holders under the Audio Home Recording Act of 1992.]

Rio's operation is entirely consistent with the Act's main purpose—the facilitation of personal use. As the Senate Report explains, "[t]he purpose of [the Act] is to ensure the right of consumers to make analog or digital audio recordings of copyrighted music for their *private, noncommercial use.*" The Act does so through its home taping exemption, which "protects all noncommercial copying by consumers of digital and analog musical recordings." The Rio merely makes copies in order to render portable, or "space-shift," those files that already reside on a user's hard drive. Such copying is paradigmatic noncommercial personal use entirely consistent with the purposes of the Act.

Even though it cannot directly reproduce a digital music recording, the Rio would nevertheless be a digital audio recording device if it could reproduce a digital music recording "from a transmission." ... The parties do not really dispute the definition of transmission, but rather, whether *indirect* reproduction of a transmission of a digital music recording is covered by the Act....

[T]he Rio is not a digital audio recording device subject to the restrictions of the Audio Home Recording Act of 1992. The district court properly denied the motion for a preliminary injunction against the Rio's manufacture and distribution. Having so determined, we need not consider whether the balance of hardships or the possibility of irreparable harm supports injunctive relief.

UMG Recordings, Inc. v. MP3.com, Inc.

92 F. Supp. 2d 349 (S.D.N.Y. 2000)

The complex marvels of cyberspatial communication may create difficult legal issues; but not in this case. Defendant's infringement of plaintiff's copyrights is clear....
[D]efendant MP3.com, on or around January 12, 2000, launched its "My.MP3.com"
service, which it advertised as permitting subscribers to store, customize, and listen
to the recordings contained on their CDs from any place where they have an Internet
connection.... [A]lthough defendant seeks to portray its service as the "functional
equivalent" of storing its subscribers' CDs, in actuality defendant is re-playing for
the subscribers converted versions of the recordings it copied, without authorization,
from plaintiffs' copyrighted CDs. On its face, this makes out a presumptive case of
infringement under the Copyright Act of 1976 ...

Viacom International, Inc. v. YouTube, Inc.

676 F.3d 19 (2d Cir. 2012)

This appeal requires us to clarify the contours of the "safe harbor" provision of
the Digital Millennium Copyright Act (DMCA) that limits the liability of online
service providers for copyright infringement that occurs "by reason of the storage at
the direction of a user of material that resides on a system or network controlled or
operated by or for the service provider." 17 U.S.C. § 512(c).

... The plaintiffs alleged direct and secondary copyright infringement based on the
public performance, display, and reproduction of approximately 79,000 audiovisual
"clips" that appeared on the YouTube website between 2005 and 2008. They demanded,
inter alia, statutory damages pursuant to 17 U.S.C. § 504(c) or, in the alternative, actual
damages from the alleged infringement, as well as declaratory and injunctive relief.

... [W]e affirm the District Court's holding that three of the challenged YouTube
software functions fall within the safe harbor for infringement that occurs "by reason
of" user storage; we remand for further fact-finding with respect to a fourth software
function.

BACKGROUND

A. The DMCA Safe Harbors

"The DMCA was enacted in 1998 to implement the World Intellectual Property
Organization Copyright Treaty," *Universal City Studios, Inc. v. Corley*, 273 F.3d 429,
440 (2d Cir. 2001), and to update domestic copyright law for the digital age. Title II
of the DMCA, separately titled the "Online Copyright Infringement Liability Limitation Act" (OCILLA), was designed to "clarif[y] the liability faced by service providers
who transmit potentially infringing material over their networks." S. Rep. No. 105-
190 at 2 (1998).... OCILLA established a series of four "safe harbors" that allow qualifying service providers to limit their liability for claims of copyright infringement
based on (a) "transitory digital network communications," (b) "system caching," (c)

"information residing on systems or networks at [the] direction of users," and (d) "information location tools." 17 U.S.C. §§ 512(a)–(d).

To qualify for protection under any of the safe harbors, a party must meet a set of threshold criteria. First, the party must in fact be a "service provider," defined, in pertinent part, as "a provider of online services or network access, or the operator of facilities therefor." 17 U.S.C. § 512(k)(1)(B). A party that qualifies as a service provider must also satisfy certain "conditions of eligibility," including the adoption and reasonable implementation of a "repeat infringer" policy that "provides for the termination in appropriate circumstances of subscribers and account holders of the service provider's system or network." *Id.* § 512(i)(1)(A). In addition, a qualifying service provider must accommodate "standard technical measures" that are "used by copyright owners to identify or protect copyrighted works." *Id.* §§ 512(i)(1)(B), (i)(2).

Beyond the threshold criteria, a service provider must satisfy the requirements of a particular safe harbor. In this case, the safe harbor at issue is § 512(c), which covers infringement claims that arise "by reason of the storage at the direction of a user of material that resides on a system or network controlled or operated by or for the service provider." *Id.* § 512(c)(1). The § 512(c) safe harbor will apply only if the service provider:

> (A) (i) does not have actual knowledge that the material or an activity using the material on the system or network is infringing;
>
> (ii) in the absence of such actual knowledge, is not aware of facts or circumstances from which infringing activity is apparent; or
>
> (iii) upon obtaining such knowledge or awareness, acts expeditiously to remove, or disable access to, the material;
>
> (B) does not receive a financial benefit directly attributable to the infringing activity, in a case in which the service provider has the right and ability to control such activity; and
>
> (C) upon notification of claimed infringement as described in paragraph (3), responds expeditiously to remove, or disable access to, the material that is claimed to be infringing or to be the subject of infringing activity.

Id. §§ 512(c)(1)(A)–(C). Section 512(c) also sets forth a detailed notification scheme that requires service providers to "designate[] an agent to receive notifications of claimed infringement," *id.* § 512(c)(2), and specifies the components of a proper notification, commonly known as a "takedown notice," to that agent. Thus, actual knowledge of infringing material, awareness of facts or circumstances that make infringing activity apparent, or receipt of a takedown notice will each trigger an obligation to expeditiously remove the infringing material.....

B. Factual Background

YouTube was founded in February 2005 by Chad Hurley ("Hurley"), Steve Chen ("Chen"), and Jawed Karim ("Karim"), three former employees of the internet company PayPal. When YouTube announced the "official launch" of the website in December 2005, a press release described YouTube as a "consumer media company" that "allows people to watch, upload, and share personal video clips at www.YouTube.com." Under the slogan "Broadcast yourself," YouTube achieved rapid prominence and profitability, eclipsing competitors such as Google Video and Yahoo Video by wide margins. In November 2006, Google acquired YouTube in a stock-for-stock transaction valued at $1.65 billion. By March 2010, at the time of summary judgment briefing in this litigation, site traffic on YouTube had soared to more than 1 billion daily video views, with more than 24 hours of new video uploaded to the site every minute.

The basic function of the YouTube website permits users to "upload" and view video clips free of charge. Before uploading a video to YouTube, a user must register and create an account with the website. The registration process requires the user to accept YouTube's Terms of Use agreement, which provides, *inter alia*, that the user "will not submit material that is copyrighted ... unless [he is] the owner of such rights or ha[s] permission from their rightful owner to post the material and to grant YouTube all of the license rights granted herein." When the registration process is complete, the user can sign in to his account, select a video to upload from the user's personal computer, mobile phone, or other device, and instruct the YouTube system to upload the video by clicking on a virtual upload "button."

Uploading a video to the YouTube website triggers a series of automated software functions. During the upload process, YouTube makes one or more exact copies of the video in its original file format. YouTube also makes one or more additional copies of the video in "Flash" format, a process known as "transcoding." The transcoding process ensures that YouTube videos are available for viewing by most users at their request. The YouTube system allows users to gain access to video content by "streaming" the video to the user's computer in response to a playback request. YouTube uses a computer algorithm to identify clips that are "related" to a video the user watches and display links to the "related" clips....

We review an order granting summary judgment *de novo*, drawing all factual inferences in favor of the non-moving party.

A. Actual and "Red Flag" Knowledge: § 512(c)(1)(A)

The first and most important question on appeal is whether the DMCA safe harbor at issue requires "actual knowledge" or "aware[ness]" of facts or circumstances indicating "specific and identifiable infringements," *Viacom v. YouTube, Inc.*, 718 F. Supp. 2d at 523. We consider first the scope of the statutory provision and then its application to the record in this case.

1. The Specificity Requirement

"As in all statutory construction cases, we begin with the language of the statute," *Barnhart v. Sigmon Coal Co.*, 534 U.S. 438, 450 (2002). Under § 512(c)(1)(A), safe harbor protection is available only if the service provider:

(i) does not have actual knowledge that the material or an activity using the material on the system or network is infringing;

(ii) in the absence of such actual knowledge, is not aware of facts or circumstances from which infringing activity is apparent; or

(iii) upon obtaining such knowledge or awareness, acts expeditiously to remove, or disable access to, the material....

17 U.S.C. §512(c)(1)(A). As previously noted, the District Court held that the statutory phrases "actual knowledge that the material ... is infringing" and "facts or circumstances from which infringing activity is apparent" refer to "knowledge of specific and identifiable infringements." *Viacom*, 718 F. Supp. 2d at 523. For the reasons that follow, we substantially affirm that holding.

Although the parties marshal a battery of other arguments on appeal, it is the text of the statute that compels our conclusion. In particular, we are persuaded that the basic operation of §512(c) requires knowledge or awareness of specific infringing activity. Under §512(c)(1)(A), knowledge or awareness alone does not disqualify the service provider; rather, the provider that gains knowledge or awareness of infringing activity retains safe-harbor protection if it "acts expeditiously to remove, or disable access to, the material." 17 U.S.C. §512(c)(1)(A)(iii). Thus, the nature of the removal obligation itself contemplates knowledge or awareness of specific infringing material, because expeditious removal is possible only if the service provider knows with particularity which items to remove. Indeed, to require expeditious removal in the absence of specific knowledge or awareness would be to mandate an amorphous obligation to "take commercially reasonable steps" in response to a generalized awareness of infringement. Such a view cannot be reconciled with the language of the statute, which requires "expeditious[]" action to remove or disable "*the material*" at issue. 17 U.S.C. §512(c)(1)(A)(iii) (emphasis added).

On appeal, the plaintiffs dispute this conclusion by drawing our attention to §512(c)(1)(A)(ii), the so-called "red flag" knowledge provision. *See id.* §512(c)(1)(A)(ii) (limiting liability where, "in the absence of such actual knowledge, [the service provider] is not aware of facts or circumstances from which infringing activity is apparent"). In their view, the use of the phrase "facts or circumstances" demonstrates that Congress did not intend to limit the red flag provision to a particular type of knowledge. The plaintiffs contend that requiring awareness of specific infringements in order to establish "aware[ness] of facts or circumstances from which infringing activity is apparent," 17 U.S.C. §512(c)(1)(A)(ii), renders the red flag provision superfluous, because that provision would be satisfied only when the "actual knowledge" provision is also satisfied. For that reason, the plaintiffs urge the Court to hold that the red flag provision "requires less specificity" than the actual knowledge provision.

This argument misconstrues the relationship between "actual" knowledge and "red flag" knowledge.... The phrase "actual knowledge," which appears in §512(c)(1)(A)(i), is frequently used to denote subjective belief. By contrast, courts often invoke the language of "facts or circumstances," which appears in §512(c)(1)(A)(ii), in discussing an objective reasonableness standard.

The difference between actual and red flag knowledge is thus not between specific and generalized knowledge, but instead between a subjective and an objective standard. In other words, the actual knowledge provision turns on whether the provider actually or "subjectively" knew of specific infringement, while the red flag provision turns on whether the provider was subjectively aware of facts that would have made the specific infringement "objectively" obvious to a reasonable person. The red flag provision, because it incorporates an objective standard, is not swallowed up by the actual knowledge provision under our construction of the §512(c) safe harbor. Both provisions do independent work, and both apply only to specific instances of infringement.

The limited body of case law interpreting the knowledge provisions of the §512(c) safe harbor comports with our view of the specificity requirement. Most recently, a panel of the Ninth Circuit addressed the scope of §512(c) in *UMG Recordings, Inc. v. Shelter Capital Partners L.L.C.*, 667 F.3d 1022 (9th Cir. 2011), a copyright infringement case against Veoh Networks, a video-hosting service similar to YouTube. As in this case, various music publishers brought suit against the service provider, claiming direct and secondary copyright infringement based on the presence of unauthorized content on the website, and the website operator sought refuge in the §512(c) safe harbor. The Court of Appeals affirmed the district court's determination on summary judgment that the website operator was entitled to safe harbor protection. With respect to the actual knowledge provision, the panel declined to "adopt[] a broad conception of the knowledge requirement," holding instead that the safe harbor "[r]equir[es] specific knowledge of particular infringing activity." The Court of Appeals "reach[ed] the same conclusion" with respect to the red flag provision, noting that "[w]e do not place the burden of determining whether [materials] are actually illegal on a service provider."

Although *Shelter Capital* contains the most explicit discussion of the §512(c) knowledge provisions, other cases are generally in accord. While we decline to adopt the reasoning of those decisions *in toto*, we note that no court has embraced the contrary proposition—urged by the plaintiffs—that the red flag provision "requires less specificity" than the actual knowledge provision.

Based on the text of §512(c)(1)(A), as well as the limited case law on point, we affirm the District Court's holding that actual knowledge or awareness of facts or circumstances that indicate specific and identifiable instances of infringement will disqualify a service provider from the safe harbor.

2. The Grant of Summary Judgment

The corollary question on appeal is whether, under the foregoing construction of §512(c)(1)(A), the District Court erred in granting summary judgment to YouTube on the record presented. For the reasons that follow, we hold that although the District

Court correctly interpreted §512(c)(1)(A), summary judgment for the defendants was premature.

i. Specific Knowledge or Awareness

The plaintiffs argue that, even under the District Court's construction of the safe harbor, the record raises material issues of fact regarding YouTube's actual knowledge or "red flag" awareness of specific instances of infringement. To that end, the plaintiffs draw our attention to various estimates regarding the percentage of infringing content on the YouTube website. For example, Viacom cites evidence that YouTube employees conducted website surveys and estimated that 75–80% of all YouTube streams contained copyrighted material. The class plaintiffs similarly claim that Credit Suisse, acting as financial advisor to Google, estimated that more than 60% of YouTube's content was "premium" copyrighted content and that only 10% of the premium content was authorized. These approximations suggest that the defendants were conscious that significant quantities of material on the YouTube website were infringing. But such estimates are insufficient, standing alone, to create a triable issue of fact as to whether YouTube actually knew, or was aware of facts or circumstances that would indicate, the existence of particular instances of infringement.

Beyond the survey results, the plaintiffs rely upon internal YouTube communications that do refer to particular clips or groups of clips. The class plaintiffs argue that YouTube was aware of specific infringing material because, *inter alia*, YouTube attempted to search for specific Premier League videos on the site in order to gauge their "value based on video usage." In particular, the class plaintiffs cite a February 7, 2007 e-mail from Patrick Walker, director of video partnerships for Google and YouTube, requesting that his colleagues calculate the number of daily searches for the terms "soccer," "football," and "Premier League" in preparation for a bid on the global rights to Premier League content. On another occasion, Walker requested that any "clearly infringing, official broadcast footage" from a list of top Premier League clubs — including Liverpool Football Club, Chelsea Football Club, Manchester United Football Club, and Arsenal Football Club — be taken down in advance of a meeting with the heads of "several major sports teams and leagues." YouTube ultimately decided not to make a bid for the Premier League rights — but the infringing content allegedly remained on the website.

The record in the *Viacom* action includes additional examples. For instance, YouTube founder Jawed Karim prepared a report in March 2006 which stated that, "[a]s of today[,] episodes and clips of the following well-known shows can still be found [on YouTube]: Family Guy, South Park, MTV Cribs, Daily Show, Reno 911, [and] Dave Chapelle [sic]." Karim further opined that, "although YouTube is not legally required to monitor content ... and complies with DMCA takedown requests, we would benefit from *preemptively* removing content that is blatantly illegal and likely to attract criticism." He also noted that "a more thorough analysis" of the issue would be required.... A reasonable juror could also conclude that Karim believed the clips he located to be infringing (since he refers to them as "blatantly illegal"), and that YouTube did not remove the content from the website until conducting "a more thorough analysis," thus exposing the company to liability in the interim....

ii. "Willful Blindness"

The plaintiffs further argue that the District Court erred in granting summary judgment to the defendants despite evidence that YouTube was "willfully blind" to specific infringing activity. On this issue of first impression, we consider the application of the common law willful blindness doctrine in the DMCA context.

"The principle that willful blindness is tantamount to knowledge is hardly novel." *Tiffany (NJ) Inc. v. eBay, Inc.*, 600 F.3d 93, 110 n.16 (2d Cir. 2010) (collecting cases). A person is "willfully blind" or engages in "conscious avoidance" amounting to knowledge where the person "'was aware of a high probability of the fact in dispute and consciously avoided confirming that fact.'" *United States v. Aina-Marshall*, 336 F.3d 167, 170 (2d Cir. 2003) Writing in the trademark infringement context, we have held that "[a] service provider is not ... permitted willful blindness. When it has reason to suspect that users of its service are infringing a protected mark, it may not shield itself from learning of the particular infringing transactions by looking the other way." *Tiffany*, 600 F.3d at 109.

The DMCA does not mention willful blindness. As a general matter, we interpret a statute to abrogate a common law principle only if the statute "speak[s] directly to the question addressed by the common law." *Matar v. Dichter*, 563 F.3d 9, 14 (2d Cir. 2009) (internal quotation marks omitted). The relevant question, therefore, is whether the DMCA "speak[s] directly" to the principle of willful blindness. The DMCA provision most relevant to the abrogation inquiry is §512(m), which provides that safe harbor protection shall not be conditioned on "a service provider monitoring its service or affirmatively seeking facts indicating infringing activity, except to the extent consistent with a standard technical measure complying with the provisions of subsection (i)." 17 U.S.C. §512(m)(1). Section 512(m) is explicit: DMCA safe harbor protection cannot be conditioned on affirmative monitoring by a service provider. For that reason, §512(m) is incompatible with a broad common law duty to monitor or otherwise seek out infringing activity based on general awareness that infringement may be occurring. That fact does not, however, dispose of the abrogation inquiry; as previously noted, willful blindness cannot be defined as an affirmative duty to monitor. Because the statute does not "speak[] directly" to the willful blindness doctrine, §512(m) limits—but does not abrogate—the doctrine. Accordingly, we hold that the willful blindness doctrine may be applied, in appropriate circumstances, to demonstrate knowledge or awareness of specific instances of infringement under the DMCA....

B. Control and Benefit: §512(c)(1)(B)

...

On appeal, the parties advocate two competing constructions of the "right and ability to control" infringing activity. 17 U.S.C. §512(c)(1)(B). Because each is fatally flawed, we reject both proposed constructions in favor of a fact-based inquiry to be conducted in the first instance by the District Court.

The first construction, pressed by the defendants, is the one adopted by the District Court, which held that "the provider must know of the particular case before he can control it." The Ninth Circuit recently agreed, holding that "until [the service provider] becomes aware of specific unauthorized material, it cannot exercise its 'power or authority' over the specific infringing item. In practical terms, it does not have the kind of ability to control infringing activity the statute contemplates." *UMG Recordings, Inc. v. Shelter Capital Partners L.L.C.*, 667 F.3d 1022, 1041 (9th Cir. 2011). The trouble with this construction is that importing a specific knowledge requirement into § 512(c)(1)(B) renders the control provision duplicative of § 512(c)(1)(A). Any service provider that has item-specific knowledge of infringing activity and thereby obtains financial benefit would already be excluded from the safe harbor under § 512(c)(1)(A) for having specific knowledge of infringing material and failing to effect expeditious removal. No additional service provider would be excluded by § 512(c)(1)(B) that was not already excluded by § 512(c)(1)(A). Because statutory interpretations that render language superfluous are disfavored, we reject the District Court's interpretation of the control provision.

The second construction, urged by the plaintiffs, is that the control provision codifies the common law doctrine of vicarious copyright liability. The common law imposes liability for vicarious copyright infringement "[w]hen the right and ability to supervise coalesce with an obvious and direct financial interest in the exploitation of copyrighted materials—even in the absence of actual knowledge that the copyright mono[poly] is being impaired." *Shapiro, Bernstein & Co. v. H.L. Green Co.*, 316 F.2d 304, 307 (2d Cir. 1963); *cf. Metro-Goldwyn-Mayer Studios Inc. v. Grokster, Ltd.*, 545 U.S. 913, 930 n.9 (2005).... [A] service provider who has knowledge or awareness of infringing material or who receives a takedown notice from a copyright holder is *required* to "remove, or disable access to, the material" in order to claim the benefit of the safe harbor. But in taking such action, the service provider would—in the plaintiffs' analysis—be admitting the "right and ability to control" the infringing material. Thus, the prerequisite to safe harbor protection under §§ 512(c)(1)(A)(iii) & (C) would at the same time be a disqualifier under § 512(c)(1)(B).

Moreover, if Congress had intended § 512(c)(1)(B) to be coextensive with vicarious liability, "the statute could have accomplished that result in a more direct manner." *Shelter Capital*, 667 F.3d at 1045.

> It is conceivable that Congress ... intended that [service providers] which receive a financial benefit directly attributable to the infringing activity would not, under any circumstances, be able to qualify for the subsection (c) safe harbor. But if that was indeed their intention, it would have been far simpler and much more straightforward to simply say as much.

Id. (alteration in original).

... Accordingly, we conclude that the "right and ability to control" infringing activity under § 512(c)(1)(B) "requires something more than the ability to remove or block access to materials posted on a service provider's website." [*Capitol Records, Inc. v.*] *MP3tunes, L.L.C.*, 821 F. Supp. 2d 627, 2011 WL 5104616, at *14. The remaining— and more difficult—question is how to define the "something more" that is required.

To date, only one court has found that a service provider had the right and ability to control infringing activity under § 512(c)(1)(B).[12] In *Perfect 10, Inc. v. Cybernet Ventures, Inc.*, 213 F. Supp. 2d 1146 (C.D. Cal. 2002), the court found control where the service provider instituted a monitoring program by which user websites received "detailed instructions regard[ing] issues of layout, appearance, and content." *Id.* at 1173. The service provider also forbade certain types of content and refused access to users who failed to comply with its instructions. Similarly, inducement of copyright infringement under *Metro-Goldwyn-Mayer Studios Inc. v. Grokster, Ltd.*, 545 U.S. 913 (2005), which "premises liability on purposeful, culpable expression and conduct," *id.* at 937, might also rise to the level of control under § 512(c)(1)(B). Both of these examples involve a service provider exerting substantial influence on the activities of users, without necessarily—or even frequently—acquiring knowledge of specific infringing activity.

In light of our holding that § 512(c)(1)(B) does not include a specific knowledge requirement, we think it prudent to remand to the District Court to consider in the first instance whether the plaintiffs have adduced sufficient evidence to allow a reasonable jury to conclude that YouTube had the right and ability to control the infringing activity and received a financial benefit directly attributable to that activity.

C. "By Reason of" Storage: § 512(c)(1)

The § 512(c) safe harbor is only available when the infringement occurs "by reason of the storage at the direction of a user of material that resides on a system or network controlled or operated by or for the service provider." 17 U.S.C. § 512(c)(1). In this case, the District Court held that YouTube's software functions fell within the safe harbor for infringements that occur "by reason of" user storage. For the reasons that follow, we affirm that holding with respect to three of the challenged software functions—the conversion (or "transcoding") of videos into a standard display format, the playback of videos on "watch" pages, and the "related videos" function. We remand for further fact-finding with respect to a fourth software function, involving the third-party syndication of videos uploaded to YouTube....

The relevant case law makes clear that the § 512(c) safe harbor extends to software functions performed "for the purpose of facilitating access to user-stored material." *Id.* Two of the software functions challenged here—transcoding and playback—were expressly considered by our sister Circuit in *Shelter Capital*, which held that liability arising from these functions occurred "by reason of the storage at the direction of a

---

12. Other courts have suggested that control may exist where the service provider is "actively involved in the listing, bidding, sale and delivery" of items offered for sale, Hendrickson v. eBay, Inc., 165 F. Supp. 2d 1082, 1094 (C.D. Cal. 2001), or otherwise controls vendor sales by previewing products prior to their listing, editing product descriptions, or suggesting prices, *Corbis Corp.* [v. *Amazon.com, Inc.*], 351 F. Supp. 2d at 1110 [(W.D. Wash. 2004)]. Because these cases held that control did not exist, however, it is not clear that the practices cited therein are individually sufficient to support a finding of control.

user." 17 U.S.C. § 512(c). Transcoding involves "[m]aking copies of a video in a different encoding scheme" in order to render the video "viewable over the Internet to most users." The playback process involves "deliver[ing] copies of YouTube videos to a user's browser cache" in response to a user request. The District Court correctly found that to exclude these automated functions from the safe harbor would eviscerate the protection afforded to service providers by § 512(c).

A similar analysis applies to the "related videos" function, by which a YouTube computer algorithm identifies and displays "thumbnails" of clips that are "related" to the video selected by the user. The plaintiffs claim that this practice constitutes content promotion, not "access" to stored content, and therefore falls beyond the scope of the safe harbor.... The record makes clear that the related videos algorithm "is fully automated and operates solely in response to user input without the active involvement of YouTube employees." Furthermore, the related videos function serves to help YouTube users locate and gain access to material stored at the direction of other users. Because the algorithm "is closely related to, and follows from, the storage itself," and is "narrowly directed toward providing access to material stored at the direction of users," we conclude that the related videos function is also protected by the § 512(c) safe harbor.

. . .

The District Court correctly determined that a finding of safe harbor application necessarily protects a defendant from all affirmative claims for monetary relief. For the reasons previously stated, further fact-finding is required to determine whether YouTube is ultimately entitled to safe harbor protection in this case. Accordingly, we vacate the order denying summary judgment to the plaintiffs and remand the cause without expressing a view on the merits of the plaintiffs' affirmative claims.

EMI Christian Music Group, Inc. v. MP3tunes, L.L.C.

844 F.3d 79 (2d Cir. 2016)

In this appeal we principally consider the requirement of the Digital Millennium Copyright Act ("DMCA") safe harbor that an internet service provider "adopt[] and reasonably implement[ ]" a policy to terminate "repeat infringers." 17 U.S.C. § 512. Plaintiffs-appellees-cross-appellants are all record companies and music publishers. They filed this copyright infringement lawsuit against MP3tunes, L.L.C. and its founder and Chief Executive Officer Michael Robertson, alleging that two internet music services created by MP3tunes infringed their copyrights in thousands of sound recordings and musical compositions. The two services are MP3tunes.com, which primarily operated as a locker service for storing digital music, and sideload.com, which allowed users to search for free music on the internet.

BACKGROUND

I. MP3tunes.com and Sideload.com

Robertson founded MP3tunes in 2005. It is undisputed that, by then, Robertson was familiar with both the online music industry and copyright litigation, having previously run the music site MP3.com, against which a copyright infringement judgment was entered in 2000. While recruiting for MP3tunes several years later, Robertson emphasized, "[T]his will be VERY big news. Major labels selling MP3s. MP3.com guy back to rejuvenate MP3 business. Largest copyright infringer of all time back at it again. Lots of juicy press angles."

MP3tunes.com was MP3tunes's first project. Initially, customers could visit MP3Tunes.com and purchase MP3 versions of music created by musicians who were not associated with major record labels. In 2005 MP3tunes.com added a "locker storage" service, which charged users a fee to store music on the MP3tunes server. A user who uploaded songs to her "locker" (through LockerSync, a free plugin on the site) could play the music through other internet-enabled devices.

MP3tunes owned and operated a second website, sideload.com, that allowed users to search for free music on the internet. Sideload.com offered a free plug-in to enable users to "sideload" (or, to use Robertson's definition of "sideload," enabled users to "download[]" directly to their MP3tunes lockers) free songs that they found on the internet. Songs sideloaded into users' lockers were then added to sideload.com's index of searchable songs. This meant that the more songs users sideloaded from the internet, the more free music became available for sideload.com users to stream, download, or sideload into their own lockers. MP3tunes's executives, including Robertson, used their own accounts with MP3tunes to store sideloaded songs.

Users of MP3tunes.com could store a certain amount of music through the service for free and could purchase additional storage space for tiered fees, while storage associated with sideloaded songs did not count against the free storage limit. Partly as a result, sideload.com became "the most effective partner in driving traffic to [MP3tunes's] locker service." At Robertson's direction, MP3tunes strove to expand sideload.com's catalog by encouraging users to upload songs to the sideload.com index. For example, members of MP3tunes's staff were encouraged to upload songs from their own accounts, even when those songs came from websites that appeared to contain infringing material. Robertson directed MP3tunes employee Sharmaine Lindahl to provide MP3tunes employees a list of sites featuring free MP3s "for sideloading purposes." Lindahl observed that one of the sites on the list "look[ed] to be mainly pirated music." MP3tunes also encouraged repeated sideloading among MP3tunes.com users by creating a "Sideload Hall of Fame" consisting of the "top 25 Sideloaders with accounts at MP3tunes.com."

In October 2006 MP3tunes added a cover art feature. When a user began to "sync" or upload a song to her locker and cover art was not part of the music file, MP3tunes's software would "automatically go check for ... cover art" provided on Amazon.com and download the cover art to MP3tunes's servers. Although MP3tunes had two agreements with Amazon, an Amazon operations analyst testified at trial that the copying of cover art violated the agreements. The analyst explained that "there was no reference to Amazon around th[e] cover image[s]" and that the display of the cover art therefore "was not being used for the primary purpose of driving traffic to Amazon," as the agreements required.

DISCUSSION

I. The Plaintiffs' Appeal

The plaintiffs challenge three rulings made by the District Court: first, that MP3tunes reasonably implemented a repeat infringer policy and was eligible for DMCA safe harbor protection for pre- and post-1972 songs; second, that the jury's finding of red-flag knowledge or willful blindness with respect to certain categories of songs was wrong as a matter of law; and third, that the plaintiffs were entitled to only one award of statutory damages for songs where the copyright to the musical composition and the copyright to the sound recording were owned by different holders. We address each of these challenges.

A. "Reasonably Implemented" Repeat Infringer Policy

The DMCA shields a service provider from liability for the infringing acts of its users if the provider satisfies certain conditions. One of those conditions requires that a service provider "adopt[] and reasonably implement[] ... a policy that provides for the termination in appropriate circumstances of subscribers and account holders of the service provider's system or network who are repeat infringers." 17 U.S.C. § 512(i)(1)(A). The plaintiffs argue that MP3tunes never reasonably implemented a repeat-infringer policy because it failed to track users who repeatedly created links to infringing content in the sideload.com index or who copied files from those links, which appeared on multiple takedown notices sent to MP3tunes.

In addressing this argument, we answer two questions: first, whether certain MP3tunes users qualified as "repeat infringers"; and second, if so, whether MP3tunes reasonably implemented a policy directed at them....

Starting with the text, we note that the DMCA does not itself define "repeat infringers." But "where a statute does not define a term, we give the term its ordinary meaning." *Laurent v. PricewaterhouseCoopers LLP*, 794 F.3d 272, 281 (2d Cir. 2015). In this context, we take "repeat" to mean "a person who does something ... again or repeatedly," Oxford English Dictionary (3d ed. 2009), while an "infringer" is "[s]omeone who interferes with one of the exclusive rights of a ... copyright," Infringer, Black's Law Dictionary (10th ed. 2014). Copyright infringement is a strict liability offense in the sense that a plaintiff is not required to prove unlawful intent or culpability, and a user does not have to share copyrighted works in order to infringe a copyright. In the context of this case, all it took to be a "repeat infringer" was to repeatedly sideload copyrighted material for personal use.

We turn next to the structure and context of the DMCA, interpreting the term "repeat infringer" against the backdrop of the statute as a whole. It is important to recall that the DMCA imposes certain requirements on service providers in exchange for limitations on liability. It would make little sense to link that limitation on liability to the knowledge of users.[13] Indeed, the DMCA explicitly relieves service providers from having to affirmatively monitor their users for infringement—something that would likely be required should MP3tunes have to ascertain its users' knowledge....

The Senate and House reports accompanying the DMCA recognize a difference between inadvertent and willful infringement. But both reports also assert that a "repeat infringer" requirement is meant to deter those "who repeatedly or flagrantly abuse their access to the Internet through disrespect for the intellectual property rights of others." In other words, the legislative history of the DMCA indicates that a "repeat infringer" does not need to know of the infringing nature of its online activities....

Our view of what Congress meant by the term "repeat infringer" leads us to conclude that the District Court improperly granted summary judgment. Prior to trial, there was clearly enough disputed evidence relating to MP3tunes's policy regarding infringers to conclude that summary judgment was inappropriate....

Furthermore, the plaintiffs presented evidence that MP3tunes executives were encouraged to and did personally sideload songs from blatantly infringing websites. The same executives made the songs available to sideload.com users. There was also evidence that MP3tunes was capable of cataloging the sideloads of each MP3tunes user. A jury could reasonably infer from that evidence that MP3tunes actually knew of specific repeat infringers and failed to take action.

A reasonable jury alternatively could have determined that MP3tunes consciously avoided knowing about specific repeat infringers using its services, even though the infringement was rampant and obvious. In *Viacom*, we held that "the willful blindness doctrine may be applied, in appropriate circumstances, to demonstrate knowledge or awareness of specific instances of infringement under the DMCA." [*Viacom International, Inc. v. YouTube, Inc.*, 676 F.3d 19 (2d Cir. 2012).] Thus, at trial the plaintiffs could prevail by demonstrating that MP3tunes's failure to track users who created links to infringing content identified on takedown notices or who copied files from

---

13. The Nimmer treatise on copyright law similarly links the term "repeat infringer" more directly to the knowledge of service providers rather than users. *See* 4 Nimmer on Copyright § 12B.10. The treatise defines an "infringer" for the purposes of § 512(i)(1)(A) as follows: "either a party who has been adjudicated to have committed copyright infringement, or a party about whom the service provider has actual knowledge that s/he has engaged in infringement." *Id.* § 12B.10[B][3][c]. The treatise cautions that a service provider has to have done more than just receive a copyright holder's takedown notices in order to be charged with knowledge of infringement. *Id.* In this case, as will become clear, we need not decide whether takedown notices suffice on their own to prove that the provider was aware of infringement.

those links evidenced its willful blindness to the repeat infringing activity of its users. . . .

B. Red-Flag Knowledge and Willful Blindness

We turn next to the District Court's determination that the jury's finding of red-flag knowledge or willful blindness with respect to certain categories of songs was wrong as a matter of law. We start with the proposition that even if a service provider has a reasonably implemented repeat infringer policy, it relinquishes the DMCA's safe harbor if it, first, has "actual knowledge that the material or an activity using the material on the system or network is infringing" or "in the absence of such actual knowledge, is [] aware of facts or circumstances from which infringing activity is apparent," and second, "upon obtaining such knowledge or awareness, [does not] act[] expeditiously to remove, or disable access to, the material." 17 U.S.C. § 512(c)(1)(A); *see also* 17 U.S.C. § 512(d)(1). At trial, the plaintiffs contended that MP3tunes was "aware of facts or circumstances from which infringing activity was apparent" — or in other words had "red-flag knowledge" or willful blindness, with respect to several categories of songs. The jury found that MP3tunes had knowledge as to four categories of files: (1) those stored on domains identified in takedown notices as having ten or more infringing files; (2) sideloads of MP3s before January 2007; (3) certain sideloads by MP3tunes executives; and (4) works by the Beatles. The District Court upheld the jury's finding of red-flag knowledge with respect to certain songs and subsets of songs but granted the defendants judgment as a matter of law as to two categories of songs that are the subject of our review: MP3s from major labels issued before 2007, and all songs by the Beatles.

We have already explained that the DMCA does not impose "an amorphous obligation to take commercially reasonable steps in response to a generalized awareness of infringement." *Viacom*, 676 F.3d at 31 (quotation marks omitted). Accordingly, "[o]n the issue of disqualifying knowledge ... the burden falls on the copyright owner to demonstrate that the service provider acquired knowledge of the infringement, or of facts and circumstances from which infringing activity was obvious, and failed to promptly take down the infringing matter, thus forfeiting its right to the safe harbor." *Capitol Records, L.L.C. v. Vimeo, L.L.C.*, 826 F.3d 78, 95 (2d Cir. 2016). In other words, a copyright owner must point to a defendant's "actual knowledge or awareness of facts or circumstances that indicate specific and identifiable instances of infringement." *Viacom*, 676 F.3d at 32.

With this principle in mind, we conclude that the trial evidence in this case, viewed in the light most favorable to the plaintiffs, showed that MP3tunes and Robertson knew that major music labels generally had not even authorized their music to be distributed in the format most widely available on sideload.com, let alone authorized it to be shared on the internet. In particular, Robertson apparently knew that major record labels had not offered songs in MP3 format until 2007. In January 2007, in connection with MP3tunes's MP3 sale model, for example, Robertson admitted that "popular acts have never before sold tracks in MP3 formats." With respect to MP3s sideloaded before 2007, therefore, the jury reasonably could have concluded that

MP3tunes and Robertson were aware of "facts and circumstances that make infringement obvious." *Vimeo*, 826 F.3d at 98.

What prompted the District Court to conclude otherwise? In granting judgment as a matter of law to the defendants on this issue, the District Court explained that barring MP3tunes from the DMCA safe harbor "would require Defendants to actively conduct routine searches and eliminate material likely to be infringing." *Capitol Records, Inc. v. MP3tunes L.L.C.*, 48 F.Supp.3d 703, 716 (S.D.N.Y. 2014). It therefore understandably concluded that imposing such a duty clashed with the DMCA's "express ... disavowal of a duty to affirmatively monitor." Under the circumstances of this case, we respectfully disagree with the District Court's assessment, primarily for two reasons.

First, the jury was clearly instructed, and we presume it understood, that MP3tunes had no continuing, affirmative duty to monitor its servers for infringement. The jury could comply with that instruction and still find that MP3tunes was required to disable access to pre-2007 songs by "act[ing] expeditiously to remove, or disable access to" the pre-2007 songs "upon obtaining such knowledge or awareness." 17 U.S.C. § 512(c)(1)(A)(iii). There was evidence at trial that MP3tunes could disable access. Indeed, an expert testified that searching through libraries of MP3 songs was a common function of MP3tunes's business. The jury was therefore permitted to conclude that a time-limited, targeted duty—even if encompassing a large number of songs—does not give rise to an "amorphous" duty to monitor in contravention of the DMCA. The same is true of the Beatles songs. The jury heard evidence that Robertson knew there had been no legal online distribution of Beatles tracks before 2010, other than one track used within a video game. Robertson further admitted that he authored a 2009 e-mail that showed he was aware of the plaintiffs' position that "[the] Beatles have never authorized their songs to be available digitally." And MP3tunes was made aware through user emails that Beatles songs such as "Strawberry Fields Forever" were on sideload.com's index. The jury could have reasonably concluded that MP3tunes had red-flag knowledge of, or was willfully blind to, the infringing nature of the Beatles tracks on its servers and failed to "act[] expeditiously" to remove them.

Second, the jury could reasonably have found that MP3tunes conceived of and was designed to facilitate infringement based in part on evidence presented at trial that MP3tunes "actively encourage[d] infringement" and that Robertson and MP3tunes executives "personally used [sideload.com] to download infringing material." *Columbia Pictures Indus., Inc. v. Fung*, 710 F.3d 1020, 1043 (9th Cir. 2013). Although such evidence might not alone support a separate finding of red-flag knowledge or willful blindness as to users, the jury could certainly rely on it in deciding whether MP3tunes was entitled to the DMCA safe harbor. Indeed, the jury could reasonably have understood Robertson to have admitted on cross-examination that sideload.com "was premised on the notion that everything that was on the internet that was not locked down could be sideloaded into the site." And in editing sideload.com's Frequently Asked Questions ("FAQs"), Robertson emphasized that the site should tell users that its music is "legal to download" because "[s]ideload.com does not store any music, but rather links to files publicly available [in] other places on the net."

For these reasons, we reverse the District Court's ruling vacating the jury verdict with respect to red-flag knowledge and willful blindness for pre-2007 MP3s and Beatles songs....

Exemption to Prohibition on Circumvention of Copyright Protection Systems for Access Control Technologies
83 Fed. Reg. 54010, 37 CFR 201 (Oct. 28, 2018)[14]

Congress enacted the DMCA in 1998 to implement certain provisions of the WIPO Copyright and WIPO Performances and Phonograms Treaties. Among other things, title I of the DMCA, which added a new chapter 12 to title 17 of the U.S. Code, prohibits circumvention of technological measures employed by or on behalf of copyright owners to protect access to their works. In enacting this aspect of the law, Congress observed that technological protection measures ("TPMs") can "support new ways of disseminating copyrighted materials to users, and ... safeguard the availability of legitimate uses of those materials by individuals."

Section 1201(a)(1) provides in pertinent part that "[n]o person shall circumvent a technological measure that effectively controls access to a work protected under [title 17]." Under the statute, to "circumvent a technological measure" means "to descramble a scrambled work, to decrypt an encrypted work, or otherwise to avoid, bypass, remove, deactivate, or impair a technological measure, without the authority of the copyright owner." A technological measure that "effectively controls access to a work" is one that "in the ordinary course of its operation, requires the application of information, or a process or a treatment, with the authority of the copyright owner, to gain access to the work."

Section 1201(a)(1) also includes what Congress characterized as a "fail-safe" mechanism, which requires the Librarian of Congress, following a rulemaking proceeding, to publish any class of copyrighted works as to which the Librarian has determined that noninfringing uses by persons who are users of a copyrighted work are, or are likely to be, adversely affected by the prohibition against circumvention in the succeeding three-year period, thereby exempting that class from the prohibition for that period.

Final Regulations: For the reasons set forth in the preamble, 37 CFR part 201 is amended as follows: Section 201.40 is amended by revising paragraphs (b) and (c) to read as follows:

---

14. Exemption to Prohibition on Circumvention of Copyright Protection Systems for Access Control Technologies, 83 Fed. Reg. 54010, 37 CFR 201 (Oct. 28, 2018), http://www.federalregister.gov/documents/2018/10/26/2018-23241/exemption-to-prohibition-on-circumvention-of-copyright-protection-systems-for-access-control.

(b) Classes of copyrighted works. Pursuant to the authority set forth in 17 U.S.C. 1201(a)(1)(C) and (D), and upon the recommendation of the Register of Copyrights, the Librarian has determined that the prohibition against circumvention of technological measures that effectively control access to copyrighted works set forth in 17 U.S.C. 1201(a)(1)(A) shall not apply to persons who engage in noninfringing uses of the following classes of copyrighted works:

(1) Motion pictures (including television shows and videos), as defined in 17 U.S.C. 101, where the motion picture is lawfully made and acquired on a DVD protected by the Content Scramble System, on a Blu-ray disc protected by the Advanced Access Content System, or via a digital transmission protected by a technological measure, and the person engaging in circumvention under paragraph (b)(1)(i) and (b)(1)(ii)(A) and (B) of this section reasonably believes that non-circumventing alternatives are unable to produce the required level of high-quality content, or the circumvention is undertaken using screen-capture technology that appears to be offered to the public as enabling the reproduction of motion pictures after content has been lawfully acquired and decrypted, where circumvention is undertaken solely in order to make use of short portions of the motion pictures in the following instances:

(i) For the purpose of criticism or comment:

(A) For use in documentary filmmaking, or other films where the motion picture clip is used in parody or for its biographical or historically significant nature;

(B) For use in noncommercial videos (including videos produced for a paid commission if the commissioning entity's use is noncommercial); or

(C) For use in nonfiction multimedia e-books.

(ii) For educational purposes:

(A) By college and university faculty and students or kindergarten through twelfth-grade (K-12) educators and students (where the K-12 student is circumventing under the direct supervision of an educator), including of accredited general educational development (GED) programs, for the purpose of criticism, comment, teaching, or scholarship;Start Printed Page 54029

(B) By faculty of massive open online courses (MOOCs) offered by accredited nonprofit educational institutions to officially enrolled students through online platforms (which platforms themselves may be operated for profit), in film studies or other courses requiring close analysis of film and media excerpts, for the purpose of criticism or comment, where the MOOC provider through the online platform limits transmissions to the extent technologically feasible to such officially enrolled students, institutes copyright policies and provides copyright informational materials to faculty, students, and relevant staff members, and applies technological measures that reasonably prevent unauthorized further dissemination of a work in accessible form to others or retention of the work for longer than the course session by recipients of a transmission through the platform, as contemplated by 17 U.S.C. 110(2); or

(C) By educators and participants in nonprofit digital and media literacy programs offered by libraries, museums, and other nonprofit entities with an educational mission, in the course of face-to-face instructional activities, for the purpose of criticism or comment, except that such users may only circumvent using screen-capture technology that appears to be offered to the public as enabling the reproduction of motion pictures after content has been lawfully acquired and decrypted.

(2)(i) Motion pictures (including television shows and videos), as defined in 17 U.S.C. 101, where the motion picture is lawfully acquired on a DVD protected by the Content Scramble System, on a Blu-ray disc protected by the Advanced Access Content System, or via a digital transmission protected by a technological measure, where:

(A) Circumvention is undertaken by a disability services office or other unit of a kindergarten through twelfth-grade educational institution, college, or university engaged in and/or responsible for the provision of accessibility services to students, for the purpose of adding captions and/or audio description to a motion picture to create an accessible version as a necessary accommodation for a student or students with disabilities under an applicable disability law, such as the Americans With Disabilities Act, the Individuals with Disabilities Education Act, or Section 504 of the Rehabilitation Act;

(B) The educational institution unit in paragraph (b)(2)(i)(A) of this section has, after a reasonable effort, determined that an accessible version cannot be obtained at a fair price or in a timely manner; and

(C) The accessible versions are provided to students or educators and stored by the educational institution in a manner intended to reasonably prevent unauthorized further dissemination of a work.

(ii) For purposes of this paragraph (b)(2), "audio description" means an oral narration that provides an accurate rendering of the motion picture.

(3) Literary works, distributed electronically, that are protected by technological measures that either prevent the enabling of read-aloud functionality or interfere with screen readers or other applications or assistive technologies:

(i) When a copy of such a work is lawfully obtained by a blind or other person with a disability, as such a person is defined in 17 U.S.C. 121; provided, however, that the rights owner is remunerated, as appropriate, for the price of the mainstream copy of the work as made available to the general public through customary channels; or

(ii) When such work is a nondramatic literary work, lawfully obtained and used by an authorized entity pursuant to 17 U.S.C. 121.

(4) Literary works consisting of compilations of data generated by medical devices that are wholly or partially implanted in the body or by their corresponding personal monitoring systems, where such circumvention is undertaken by a patient for the sole purpose of lawfully accessing the data generated by his or her own device or monitoring system and does not constitute a violation of applicable law, including without limitation the Health Insurance Portability and Accountability Act of 1996, the Computer Fraud and Abuse Act of 1986 or regulations of the Food and Drug Ad-

ministration, and is accomplished through the passive monitoring of wireless transmissions that are already being produced by such device or monitoring system.

(5) Computer programs that enable the following types of lawfully acquired wireless devices to connect to a wireless telecommunications network, when circumvention is undertaken solely in order to connect to a wireless telecommunications network and such connection is authorized by the operator of such network:

(i) Wireless telephone handsets (i.e., cellphones);

(ii) All-purpose tablet computers;

(iii) Portable mobile connectivity devices, such as mobile hotspots, removable wireless broadband modems, and similar devices; and

(iv) Wearable wireless devices designed to be worn on the body, such as smartwatches or fitness devices.

(6) Computer programs that enable smartphones and portable all-purpose mobile computing devices to execute lawfully obtained software applications, where circumvention is accomplished for the sole purpose of enabling interoperability of such applications with computer programs on the smartphone or device, or to permit removal of software from the smartphone or device. For purposes of this paragraph (b)(6), a "portable all-purpose mobile computing device" is a device that is primarily designed to run a wide variety of programs rather than for consumption of a particular type of media content, is equipped with an operating system primarily designed for mobile use, and is intended to be carried or worn by an individual.

(7) Computer programs that enable smart televisions to execute lawfully obtained software applications, where circumvention is accomplished for the sole purpose of enabling interoperability of such applications with computer programs on the smart television.

(8) Computer programs that enable voice assistant devices to execute lawfully obtained software applications, where circumvention is accomplished for the sole purpose of enabling interoperability of such applications with computer programs on the device, or to permit removal of software from the device, and is not accomplished for the purpose of gaining unauthorized access to other copyrighted works. For purposes of this paragraph (b)(8), a "voice assistant device" is a device that is primarily designed to run a wide variety of programs rather than for consumption of a particular type of media content, is designed to take user input primarily by voice, and is designed to be installed in a home or office.

(9) Computer programs that are contained in and control the functioning of a lawfully acquired motorized land vehicle such as a personal automobile, commercial vehicle, or mechanized agricultural vehicle, except for programs accessed through a separate subscription service, when circumvention is a necessary step to allow the diagnosis, repair, or lawful modification of a vehicle function, where such circumvention does not constitute a violation of applicable law, including without limitation regulations promulgated by the Department of Transportation or the Environmental

Protection Agency, and is not accomplished for the purpose of gaining Start Printed Page 54030unauthorized access to other copyrighted works.

(10) Computer programs that are contained in and control the functioning of a lawfully acquired smartphone or home appliance or home system, such as a refrigerator, thermostat, HVAC, or electrical system, when circumvention is a necessary step to allow the diagnosis, maintenance, or repair of such a device or system, and is not accomplished for the purpose of gaining access to other copyrighted works. For purposes of this paragraph (b)(10):

(i) The "maintenance" of a device or system is the servicing of the device or system in order to make it work in accordance with its original specifications and any changes to those specifications authorized for that device or system; and

(ii) The "repair" of a device or system is the restoring of the device or system to the state of working in accordance with its original specifications and any changes to those specifications authorized for that device or system.

(11)(i) Computer programs, where the circumvention is undertaken on a lawfully acquired device or machine on which the computer program operates, or is undertaken on a computer, computer system, or computer network on which the computer program operates with the authorization of the owner or operator of such computer, computer system, or computer network, solely for the purpose of good-faith security research and does not violate any applicable law, including without limitation the Computer Fraud and Abuse Act of 1986.

(ii) For purposes of this paragraph (b)(11), "good-faith security research" means accessing a computer program solely for purposes of good-faith testing, investigation, and/or correction of a security flaw or vulnerability, where such activity is carried out in an environment designed to avoid any harm to individuals or the public, and where the information derived from the activity is used primarily to promote the security or safety of the class of devices or machines on which the computer program operates, or those who use such devices or machines, and is not used or maintained in a manner that facilitates copyright infringement.

(12)(i) Video games in the form of computer programs embodied in physical or downloaded formats that have been lawfully acquired as complete games, when the copyright owner or its authorized representative has ceased to provide access to an external computer server necessary to facilitate an authentication process to enable gameplay, solely for the purpose of:

(A) Permitting access to the video game to allow copying and modification of the computer program to restore access to the game for personal, local gameplay on a personal computer or video game console; or

(B) Permitting access to the video game to allow copying and modification of the computer program to restore access to the game on a personal computer or video game console when necessary to allow preservation of the game in a playable form by an eligible library, archives, or museum, where such activities are carried out without any purpose of direct or indirect commercial advantage and the video game is not distributed or made available outside of the physical premises of the eligible library, archives, or museum.

(ii) Video games in the form of computer programs embodied in physical or downloaded formats that have been lawfully acquired as complete games, that do not require access to an external computer server for gameplay, and that are no longer reasonably available in the commercial marketplace, solely for the purpose of preservation of the game in a playable form by an eligible library, archives, or museum, where such activities are carried out without any purpose of direct or indirect commercial advantage and the video game is not distributed or made available outside of the physical premises of the eligible library, archives, or museum.

(iii) Computer programs used to operate video game consoles solely to the extent necessary for an eligible library, archives, or museum to engage in the preservation activities described in paragraph (b)(12)(i)(B) or (b)(12)(ii) of this section.

(iv) For purposes of this paragraph (b)(12), the following definitions shall apply:

(A) For purposes of paragraph (b)(12)(i)(A) and (b)(12)(ii) of this section, "complete games" means video games that can be played by users without accessing or reproducing copyrightable content stored or previously stored on an external computer server.

(B) For purposes of paragraph (b)(12)(i)(B) of this section, "complete games" means video games that meet the definition in paragraph (b)(12)(iv)(A) of this section, or that consist of both a copy of a game intended for a personal computer or video game console and a copy of the game's code that was stored or previously stored on an external computer server.

(C) "Ceased to provide access" means that the copyright owner or its authorized representative has either issued an affirmative statement indicating that external server support for the video game has ended and such support is in fact no longer available or, alternatively, server support has been discontinued for a period of at least six months; provided, however, that server support has not since been restored.

(D) "Local gameplay" means gameplay conducted on a personal computer or video game console, or locally connected personal computers or consoles, and not through an online service or facility.

(E) A library, archives, or museum is considered "eligible" when the collections of the library, archives, or museum are open to the public and/or are routinely made available to researchers who are not affiliated with the library, archives, or museum.

(13)(i) Computer programs, except video games, that have been lawfully acquired and that are no longer reasonably available in the commercial marketplace, solely for the purpose of lawful preservation of a computer program, or of digital materials dependent upon a computer program as a condition of access, by an eligible library, archives, or museum, where such activities are carried out without any purpose of direct or indirect commercial advantage and the program is not distributed or made available outside of the physical premises of the eligible library, archives, or museum.

(ii) For purposes of the exemption in paragraph (b)(13)(i) of this section, a library, archives, or museum is considered "eligible" if—

(A) The collections of the library, archives, or museum are open to the public and/or are routinely made available to researchers who are not affiliated with the library, archives, or museum;

(B) The library, archives, or museum has a public service mission;

(C) The library, archives, or museum's trained staff or volunteers provide professional services normally associated with libraries, archives, or museums;

(D) The collections of the library, archives, or museum are composed of lawfully acquired and/or licensed materials; and

(E) The library, archives, or museum implements reasonable digital security measures as appropriate for the activities permitted by this paragraph (b)(13).

(14) Computer programs that operate 3D printers that employ microchip-reliant technological measures to limit the use of feedstock, when circumvention is accomplished solely for the purpose of using alternative feedstock and not for the purpose of accessing design software, design files, or proprietary data.

(c) Persons who may initiate circumvention. To the extent authorized under paragraph (b) of this section, the circumvention of a technological measure that restricts wireless telephone handsets or other wireless devices from connecting to a wireless telecommunications network may be initiated by the owner of any such handset or other device, by another person at the direction of the owner, or by a provider of a commercial mobile radio service or a commercial mobile data service at the direction of such owner or other person, solely in order to enable such owner or a family member of such owner to connect to a wireless telecommunications network, when such connection is authorized by the operator of such network.

Dated: October 19, 2018.

Carla D. Hayden,
Librarian of Congress

Notes and Questions

a. On remand, the district court granted summary judgment to YouTube. *See Viacom Int'l Inc. v. YouTube, Inc.*, 940 F. Supp. 2d 110, 123 (S.D.N.Y. 2013).

b. One of the more challenging aspects of online liability has been the finding of personal liability—both civil and criminal—for individual consumer violations. While the collective impact of the infringement has been significant, the actual damages by any individual consumer for downloading commercially available content has been minor. The highest of these awards were in two notorious cases, *Sony BMG*

Music Entm't v. Tenenbaum, 719 F.3d 67 (1st Cir. 2013), and *Capitol Records, Inc. v. Thomas-Rasset*, 692 F.3d 899 (8th Cir. 2012). *Thomas-Rasset* involved three trials. The initial jury awarded $222,000 for the defendant's activity in downloading music on a peer-to-peer file system, $9,250 for each of the twenty-four infringed songs, for a total of $222,000. The facts included the likelihood that many more songs were collected, and there were severe credibility issues.

> A second jury found Thomas-Rasset liable for willful copyright infringe-ment under a different instruction, and awarded statutory damages of $1,920,000. The district court remitted the award to $54,000, and the com-panies opted for a new trial on damages. A third jury awarded statutory dam-ages of $1,500,000, but the district court ultimately ruled that the maximum amount permitted by the Due Process Clause of the Fifth Amendment was $54,000 and reduced the verdict accordingly.

On appeal, the court upheld a statutory damage award that matched the first trial.

On the question of damages, we conclude that a statutory damages award of $9,250 for each of the twenty-four infringed songs, for a total of $222,000, does not con-travene the Due Process Clause. The district court erred in reducing the third jury's verdict to $2,250 per work, for a total of $54,000, on the ground that this amount was the maximum permitted by the Constitution.

> The Supreme Court long ago declared that damages awarded pursuant to a statute violate due process only if they are "so severe and oppressive as to be wholly disproportioned to the offense and obviously unreasonable." *St. Louis, I.M. & S. Ry. Co. v. Williams*, 251 U.S. 63, 67 (1919)....

Capitol Records, Inc. v. Thomas-Rasset, 692 F.3d 899 (8th Cir. 2012).

One of the largest awards for a peer-to-peer infringer was in *Sony BMG Music Entm't v. Tenenbaum*, 719 F.3d 67 (1st Cir. 2013).

> On appeal, Tenenbaum invites us to assume that he is "the most heinous of noncommercial copyright infringers." We need not go so far as to accept his offer. The evidence of Tenenbaum's copyright infringement easily justifies the conclusion that his conduct was egregious. Tenenbaum carried on his activities for years in spite of numerous warnings, he made thousands of songs available illegally, and he denied responsibility during discovery. Much of this behavior was exactly what Congress was trying to deter when it amended the Copyright Act. Therefore, we do not hesitate to conclude that an award of $22,500 per song, an amount representing 15% of the maximum award for willful violations and less than the maximum award for non-willful violations, comports with due process. For the reasons stated above, the jury's award of $675,000 did not violate Tenenbaum's right to due process. The judgment of the district court is affirmed.

Sony BMG Music Entm't v. Tenenbaum, 719 F.3d at 71.

Following a public outcry about the size of these awards against noncommercial defendants, the industry plaintiffs have sought lower damages. Even in these two cases, the plaintiffs had made efforts to settle for lower amounts rather than going to trial. Following these cases, however, the plaintiffs seem to be seeking more measured damages rather than risk the public backlash for overreaching. Courts are also more sensitive to the equities of these situations. The following is illustrative:

> Plaintiff requests statutory damages in the amount of $9,250.00. In a copyright infringement case, the copyright owner may elect to recover, instead of actual damages, an award of statutory damages for all infringements involved in the action, with respect to any one work, in a sum of not less than $750 or more than $30,000 as the court considers just. Where, as here, willful infringement is alleged, the Court, in its discretion, may increase the award of statutory damages to a sum of not more than $150,000 per violation.

> Under 17 U.S.C. § 504(c)(1), courts have wide discretion in determining the appropriate amount of statutory damages, but are urged to consider three main factors: "the expenses saved and profits reaped by the defendants in connection with the infringements, the revenues lost by the plaintiffs as a result of the defendants' conduct, and the infringers' state of mind whether willful, knowing, or merely innocent." *Gnat Booty Music v. Creative Catering of Wadhams, L.L.C.*, 761 F.Supp.2d 604, 609 (E.D.Mich.2011).

Applying those considerations here, the Court concludes that the damages requested should be reduced. The Court first notes that there are no allegations that Defendant reaped profits as a result of the infringement. And the expense saved by Defendant, the cost of purchasing the Motion Picture for private use, is minimal. The Court further notes that the asserted factual basis for Plaintiff's allegation of willful conduct is less than compelling. Plaintiff's factual allegations provide only that Defendants presumably had notice of Plaintiff's copyright by virtue, "at least," of a copyright notice on the DVD case for the Motion Picture. There are no allegations, however, that this Defendant possessed or saw a DVD cover and the manner in which Defendant allegedly viewed the Motion Picture suggests the contrary. In addition, Plaintiff alleges that notice of the copyright violation was sent to attorneys for the entity hosting the BitTorrent website used by the swarm, but not that Defendant received such notice.

> Taking into account all the factors discussed above, the Court concludes that awarding statutory damages in the amount of $3,250.00 accomplishes the statutory purposes of compensation and deterrence in a proportionate and reasonable manner.

W. Coast Prods., Inc. v. Garrett, No. 4:12CV01551 AGF, 2014 WL 752670, at *2 (E.D. Mo. Feb. 25, 2014). One might ask how likely a user of a bit torrent system to share movies is unaware that the films being shared are protected by copyright. Nonetheless, it shows the willingness of the court to find reasons to lower the statutory damages.

c. Part of the ongoing battle between copyright owners and pirates has been the creation and banning of software designed to circumvent encryption on various products and services. *See, e.g., Universal City Studios, Inc. v. Corley,* 273 F.3d 429 (2d Cir. 2001) (enjoining posting of DVD anti-encryption software); *United States v. Elcom Ltd.,* 203 F. Supp. 2d 1111 (N.D. Cal. 2002) ("Congress banned trafficking in devices that are primarily designed for the purpose of circumventing any technological measure that 'effectively protects a right of a copyright owner,' or that have limited commercially significant purposes other than circumventing use restrictions, or that are marketed for use in circumventing the use restrictions.").

d. In *Universal City Studios, Inc. v. Corley,* 273 F.3d 429 (2d Cir. 2001), the Second Circuit upheld a permanent injunction against Eric Corley, barring him from posting DeCSS, the simple computer program that disabled the encryption software on commercial DVDs. The injunction barred Corley from posting DeCSS on his website or from knowingly linking via a hyperlink to any other website containing DeCSS. Corley was the publisher of "2600: The Hacker Quarterly," and he ran a companion website to the publication. The injunction was largely symbolic since the computer program was widely available on the Internet. Nonetheless, the impact of encryption and decryption software remains one of the most important issues bedeviling the entertainment and software industries.

The movie studios were reluctant to release movies in digital form until they were confident they had in place adequate safeguards against piracy of their copyrighted movies. The studios took several steps to minimize the piracy threat. First, they settled on the DVD as the standard digital medium for home distribution of movies. The studios then sought an encryption scheme to protect movies on DVDs. They enlisted the help of members of the consumer electronics and computer industries, who in mid-1996 developed the Content Scramble System ("CSS"). CSS is an encryption scheme that employs an algorithm configured by a set of "keys" to encrypt a DVD's contents. The algorithm is a type of mathematical formula for transforming the contents of the movie file into gibberish; the "keys" are in actuality strings of 0's and 1's that serve as values for the mathematical formula. Decryption in the case of CSS requires a set of "player keys" contained in compliant DVD players, as well as an understanding of the CSS encryption algorithm. Without the player keys and the algorithm, a DVD player cannot access the contents of a DVD. With the player keys and the algorithm, a DVD player can display the movie on a television or a computer screen, but does not give a viewer the ability to use the copy function of the computer to copy the movie or to manipulate the digital content of the DVD.

The studios developed a licensing scheme for distributing the technology to manufacturers of DVD players. Player keys and other information necessary to the CSS scheme were given to manufacturers of DVD players for an administrative fee. In exchange for the licenses, manufacturers were obliged to keep the player keys confidential. Manufacturers were also required in the licensing agreement to prevent the transmission of "CSS data" (a term undefined in the licensing agreement) from a DVD drive to any "internal recording device," including, presumably, a computer hard drive.

With encryption technology and licensing agreements in hand, the studios began releasing movies on DVDs in 1997, and DVDs quickly gained in popularity, becoming a significant source of studio revenue. By the end of 1997, most if not all DVDs that were released were encrypted with CSS. Moreover, DVD players were projected to be in ten percent of United States homes by the end of 2000. In fact, as of 2000, about thirty-five percent of one studio's worldwide revenues from movie distribution was attributable to DVD sales and rentals.

In 1998, the studios secured added protection against DVD piracy when Congress passed the DMCA, which prohibits the development or use of technology designed to circumvent a technological protection measure, such as CSS....

In September 1999, Jon Johansen, a Norwegian teenager, collaborating with two unidentified individuals he met on the Internet, reverse-engineered a licensed DVD player designed to operate on the Microsoft operating system, and culled from it the player keys and other information necessary to decrypt CSS. The record suggests that Johansen was trying to develop a DVD player operable on Linux, an alternative operating system that did not support any licensed DVD players at that time. In order to accomplish this task, Johansen wrote a decryption program executable on Microsoft's operating system. That program was called, appropriately enough, "DeCSS."

If a user runs the DeCSS program (for example, by clicking on the DeCSS icon on a Microsoft operating system platform) with a DVD in the computer's disk drive, DeCSS will decrypt the DVD's CSS protection, allowing the user to copy the DVD's files and place the copy on the user's hard drive. The result is a very large computer file that can be played on a non-CSS-compliant player and copied, manipulated, and transferred just like any other computer file. DeCSS comes complete with a fairly user-friendly interface that helps the user select from among the DVD's files and assign the decrypted file a location on the user's hard drive. The quality of the resulting decrypted movie is "virtually identical" to that of the encrypted movie on the DVD. And the file produced by DeCSS, while large, can be compressed to a manageable size by a compression software called "DivX," available at no cost on the Internet. This compressed file can be copied onto a DVD, or transferred over the Internet (with some patience).

The history of DeCSS encapsulates the history of digital piracy. Distributors are extremely fearful of releasing products without some promise of anti-theft protection, but those same promises invariably understate the problem or overstate the solution.

e. The 1995 amendments to §§ 106 and 114 were originally written to take advantage of the dramatic changes made in digital radio technology. Three years earlier, in 1992, the FCC had approved the implementation of Digital Audio Radio Services. The 1995 amendments were designed to allow the recording artists to participate in expected technological innovation. It was not until 1997 that the FCC actually approved the licenses for what are now Sirius Satellite Radio and XM Satellite Radio. Although these two services have begun to gain some market share, the bulk of the activity in digital broadcast moved to the Internet. The ability to stream audio files, download files for permanent storage on the listener's machine, and to create interactive uses forced Congress to amend the law in 1998. Continuing controversy over the pricing structure led to a December 2002 compromise and additional statutory changes.

f. To what extent does the subject of an overly aggressive effort to find the IP address of a potential infringer have the power to seek both the dismissal of the lawsuit and an award of attorneys' fees associated with the cost of defending the suit? *See Cobbler Nevada, L.L.C. v. Gonzales*, 901 F.3d 1142, 1149 (9th Cir. 2018) ("The Copyright Act states that a district court 'may … award a reasonable attorney's fee to the prevailing party as part of the costs….' 17 U.S.C. § 505.")"

Problem 16-E

Bryce is trying to promote the musicians who are popular locally by creating a website. Bryce wants the project to be entirely legal and fully licensed. The goal is to acquire the right to post local musicians' songs to a website, sell them for $0.75 per song, and split the income between the artist and Bryce. Bryce will use the income to promote the site. Bands will also be able to announce concerts, sell memorabilia, and operate chat-rooms.

Advise Bryce as to the types of licenses and agreements which will be needed to allow local bands to participate in the project, including both bands with recording contracts and those which do not yet have recording contracts.

F. Bibliography and Links

Yochai Benkler, *The Public Domain: Through the Looking Glass: Alice and the Constitutional Foundations of the Public Domain*, 66 LAW & CONTEMP. PROB. 173 (2003).

Dan L. Burk, *Perverse Innovation*, 58 WM. & MARY L. REV. 1 (2016).

Nicholas C. Butland & Justin J. Sullivan, *Pirate Tales from the Deep (Web): An Exploration of Online Copyright Infringement in the Digital Age*, 13 U. MASS. L. REV. 50 (2018).

Edward L. Carter & Scott Lunt, *Podcasting and Copyright: The Impact of Regulation on New Communication Technologies*, 22 SANTA CLARA COMPUTER & HIGH TECH. L.J. 187 (2006).

Jacqueline C. Charlesworth, *The Moral of the Story: What Grokster Has to Teach About the DMCA*, 2011 STAN. TECH. L. REV. 6 (2011).

James DeBriyn, *Shedding Light on Copyright Trolls: An Analysis of Mass Copyright Litigation in the Age of Statutory Damages*, 19 UCLA Ent. L. Rev. 79 (2012).

Michael M. Epstein, *Social Media and "Flash Infringement": Live Music Culture and Dying Ip Protection*, 3 Belmont L. Rev. 1 (2016).

Robert A. Heverly, *Revisiting "The Information Semicommons,"* 59 IDEA: L. Rev. Franklin Pierce Center for Intell. Prop. 137 (2018).

John T. Holland, *Making Money Instead of Excuses: A Market-based Alternative to the Digital Millennium Copyright Act that Protects Copyrights without Diminishing Expression*, 7 Geo. J.L. & Pub. Pol'y 279 (2009).

Michal Lavi, *Evil Nudges*, 21 Vand. J. Ent. & Tech. L. 1 (2018).

Yafit Lev-Aretz, *Second Level Agreements*, 45 Akron L. Rev. 137 (2012).

Jessica Litman & Pamela Samuelson, *Intellectual Property Law: Toward a "New Deal" for Copyright in the Information Age*, 100 Mich. L. Rev. 1488 (2002).

Joseph P. Liu, *The DMCA and the Regulation of Scientific Research*, 18 Berkeley Tech. L.J. 501 (2003).

Yushan Luo, *Intellectual Property Crimes*, 55 Am. Crim. L. Rev. 1399 (2018).

Gregory N. Mandel, *Institutional Fracture in Intellectual Property Law: The Supreme Court Versus Congress*, 102 Minn. L. Rev. 803 (2017).

Lionel S. Sobel, *DRM As an Enabler of Business Models: ISPs as Digital Retailers*, 18 Berkeley Tech. L.J. 667 (2003).

Peter K. Yu, *The Copyright Divide*, 25 Cardozo L. Rev. 331 (2003).

Peter K. Yu, *Digital Copyright and Confuzzling Rhetoric*, 13 Vand. J. Ent. & Tech. L. 881 (2011).

Websites

Electronic Frontier Foundation, http://www.eff.org/

RIAA, www.riaa.com

MPAA, www.mpaa.com

Federal Bureau of Investigation, www.fbi.gov

FBI Investigative Programs Cyber Investigations, http://www.fbi.gov/cyberinvest/cyberhome.htm

Chapter 17

Publishing

A. Overview

As in every other entertainment industry, the pairing of computers with the Internet has reshaped publishing, an industry which dates back to the invention of the Gutenberg press. As with all other media, there has been significant consolidation into a small group of five major publishing houses. There has also been significant disruption by Amazon.com, which plays a dual role as the leading ebook distributor and as the fifth largest publisher of ebooks.[1] Apple is also a significant alternative for ebooks, though it does serve as a retail outlet for sales of physical books. The "Big Five" primary publishers are Penguin Random House, Hachette Livre (including Little Brown and Co.), HarperCollins, Macmillan Publishers, and Simon & Schuster. Together, they represent slightly more than 80% of the trade book publishing in the U.S.[2] The "Big Three" in educational publishing are Pearson Education, McGraw-Hill Education, and Houghton Mifflin Harcourt, while Springer, Scholastic, and Wiley (John Wiley & Sons) also play very important roles in academic publishing.

At the retail level, the dominance of Amazon.com has fundamentally transformed the publishing industry. Barnes & Noble remains as the only national book chain with a physical retail presence. The quaint, local bookshop has become a new front in the brewing cultural war against overreaching Silicon Valley dominance of the U.S. economy and culture. The local bookstore is seeing a renewed life, but the number of such stores has dropped dramatically in the past two decades.

Amazon and Apple are the leaders in electronic book distribution on the Kindle and iPad formats. Barnes & Noble has struggled with the Nook to remain a relevant competitor in ebooks. Publishing has become easier than ever, and there are even a small group of self-published authors earning salaries that dwarf their commercially published rivals.

Computers have made the production of publications a much less complicated and time-consuming enterprise. The increased pace of production, however, does not necessarily improve the quality of the output. The number of books published

---

1. Authors Earnings report, U.S. Online Book Sales, January 2018.

2. Thad McIllroy, *What the Big 5's Financial Reports Reveal About the State of Traditional Book Publishing*, BOOKBUSINESS, Aug. 5, 2016, https://www.bookbusinessmag.com/post/big-5-financial-reports-reveal-state-traditional-book-publishing/.

has continued to rise steadily in the past few decades, which has added pressure on the publishers to finance and promote an ever-decreasing percentage of the published titles. Just as in other crowded and highly competitive segments of the entertainment industries, publishers have found it is the ability to market and promote that drives success.

Books tend to be perennials. Academic assignments, bibles, Shakespeare, and similar works provide economic balance for publishers and booksellers, which otherwise rely on the hot new books touted on the best-sellers list. As a result, a publisher's "backlist" or catalog of books that are in print from prior years serves as a considerable part the of publisher's revenue. (This is also true in the music recording industry.) New technologies may change this historical balance in two ways. Electronic versions of public domain materials may decrease the value of backlist printings, while efficiencies in print technologies will decrease the manufacturing and distribution costs of copyrighted works. In addition, copyright piracy is eroding the markets for reprints, anthologies, and other secondary sources of author revenues.

1. Bookstores and Ebooks

Throughout the last century, legal issues in publishing tended to focus on chain booksellers such as Barnes & Noble and Waldenbooks. *Publishers Weekly* noted that there were 1,100 fewer bookstores in 2011 than in 1991.[3] Barnes & Noble is now essentially alone. Waldenbooks, Crown Books, Kroch's & Brentano's, Borders Books, and Lauriat's Books are all out of business.

> The number of bookstores at physical locations declined almost every year from 1992 to 2016. For 1992, the Census Bureau reported 13,136 bookstore establishments, consisting of small "independent" stores as well as larger chain stores. As of 2016, the number of stores tallied in the Census Bureau survey had fallen to less than half that figure, to an all-time low of 6,448. According to the American Booksellers Association (ABA), the number of independent bookstores started to fall in the early 1990s due to competition from "superstores" (Borders and Barnes and Noble) and online booksellers (such as Amazon, which was established as an online bookstore in 1994). Since 2011, however, the media and the ABA have reported growth in the number of independent bookstores, even as the large chains have been consolidating stores and going out of business.[4]

Retail has seen a similar decline, with total bookstore revenues dropping from $2.2 billion in 2004 down by 53% to $1.03 by 2018.[5] As the mix of independent stores has

---

3. Jim Milliot, *Tracking 20 Years of Bookstore Chains*, Publishers Weekly, (Aug. 26, 2011), http://www.publishersweekly.com/pw/by-topic/industry-news/bookselling/article/48473-tracking-20-years-of-bookstore-chains.html.

4. *Bookstores: Establishments and Sales*, Human. Indicators, http://www.humanitiesindicators.org/content/indicatordoc.aspx?i=11095#p_en_-1_6, (last updated Apr. 2019).

5. *Id.*

changed and chain stores have closed, the average earning per store has managed to remain stable.

2. Ebooks

What has emerged is a rapidly growing trend for ebooks read on tablets and mobile devices. Although Amazon.com did not create the first ebook reader, Amazon's integration of the Kindle reader with its online bookstore dominated the marketplace. By 2009, Amazon had 90% of the ebook market share. Apple entered the market with the iPad and a strong movement into book sales in the iTunes marketplace. Barnes & Noble offers a competing service through its Nook devices, but has not become a serious competitor to Amazon or Apple. Amazon's share has dropped to approximately 70% as a variety of smaller companies and services have tried to become part of this market. Ebooks represent just under 20% of the trade book publishing industry.

The cost of an ebook can be as little as 10% of a print edition of the same work. Pricing strategies continue to change and evolve. In addition, Amazon has begun to aggressively market unlimited licensing packages, essentially turning Amazon into a public library with a monthly user fee. The blanket licensing model upends the traditional publication sales model.

The battle between print and ebook as well as between Amazon and traditional publishers is fierce. As a result, the Association of American Publishers (AAP), which regularly reports on book and ebook sales, has been reporting a steady decline in ebook sales. But AAP's reports exclude Kindle Unlimited, Amazon Publishing, or Kindle Direct Publishing figures, significantly undervaluing the ebook marketplace. The market competition and lack of transparency among Amazon and the large print publishers means that none of the data being provided to the public is particularly trustworthy. The anecdotal aspects, however, remain that through phones, tablets, ereaders, and computers, access to ebooks has exceeded 95% of the public. At the same time, in addition to buying oneself books to read, books are often purchased either for academic reasons or as gifts, and neither of these markets is particularly well suited to the ebook. As a result, both print and ebooks continue to play a part in the marketplace, and neither is likely to eliminate the other in the next five to ten years.

The sale of ebooks and the aggressive pricing strategy used by Amazon has resulted in changes to standard publishing agreements by the publishers and to antitrust violations between many of the publishers and Apple.

3. Print-on-Demand

A segment of the publishing industry once known as the vanity press served a specialized niche market that enabled individuals to self-publish books. Printing technology has transformed the ability to produce very small quantities of books economically. This technology has transformed the vanity press industry. Combined with ebooks, these services have eliminated virtually all barriers to publishing.

A number of online publishers provide high quality, low volume self-publishing enterprises which are perfect for small projects or those who wish to direct-market their wares. These companies feature the ability to print-on-demand, allowing the books to be created, packaged and shipped individually as orders arrive. These services typically tie closely with ebook publishing so that the author can offer both online and physical distribution without prohibitively high production and warehouse costs.

Ebooks and print-on-demand technology are forcing publishers and authors to redefine the concept of the term "out of print." Books need not ever be unavailable or go out of print. Future agreements may have to redefine reversionary interests based on a book's sales, the promotional activities of the publisher, or other measures relevant to the particular transaction.

4. The Book Tie-In Market: Inter-Media Integration

Increasingly, published works tend to be impacted by film, television and other popular media. The book *Seabiscuit* was propelled to many best-sellers lists because of the success of the motion picture adaptation. Similarly, the success of each film in the *Lord of the Rings* trilogy further propelled the backlist works of Tolkien. The trend towards inter-media integration is perhaps the strongest trend that will be seen over the next decade. Despite poor internal integration in most media conglomerates, the promotional opportunities are maximized when books, comics, and video/computer games are tied directly to television and motion picture production. These combinations will increasingly drive the need to hit "homeruns" to finance entertainment companies.

5. Libraries and Ebooks

Another of the economic pressures on traditional publishers has been the resurgence of library use by the public through lending programs on platforms such as Overdrive and Libby, which allow library patrons to get library books without the need to go to a branch. Publishers report that this is yet another reason for declining royalties.

The Authors Guild has reported that Macmillan, one of the four largest publishers, is changing the licensing terms to the libraries. "Under the new terms, libraries will be able to purchase only a single one-user/one-ebook perpetual license upon publication, and will then have to wait eight weeks to purchase additional metered licenses."[6]

---

6. Matt Enis, *Macmillan Announces Two-Month Embargo on Library Ebooks*, Libr. J. (Jul. 25, 2019), http://www.libraryjournal.com/?detailStory=macmillan-announces-two-month-embargo-on-library-ebooks.

"On that single copy we will cut the price in half to $30 (currently first copies are $60 and need renewal after two years or 52 lends)," Macmillan CEO John Sargent explained in a memo to the publisher's authors, illustrators, and agents. "This change reflects the library request for lower prices and perpetual access. Additional [ebook] copies of that title will not be available for library purchase until eight weeks after publication. All other terms remain in place."

In the memo, Sargent said that the embargo had been tested with the Tor imprint "in response to our growing fears that library lending was cannibalizing sales" and that the company had been "reviewing all the available data, from all sources, to determine the effects of library ebook lending on digital and physical book sales…. One thing is abundantly clear. The growth in ebook lends through libraries has been remarkable. For Macmillan, 45 percent of the ebook reads in the U.S. are now being borrowed for free from libraries. And that number is still growing rapidly.[7]

There is significant disagreement whether library usage has promoted book sales or cut into the revenue for publishers. What remains clear is that the availability of books has only increased while the ability for authors to earn a living at publishing has also become more difficult and more competitive than ever before.

B. Author Agreements and Delivery Requirements

Chodos v. West Publishing Co.

292 F.3d 992 (9th Cir. 2002)

This case presents the question whether a publisher retains the right to reject an author's manuscript written pursuant to a standard industry agreement, even though the manuscript is of the quality contemplated by both parties. In this case, attorney Rafael Chodos entered into a standard Author Agreement with the Bancroft-Whitney Publishing Company under which he agreed to write a treatise on the intriguing subject of the law of fiduciary duty. The agreement is widely used in the publishing industry for traditional literary works as well as for specialized volumes. Bancroft-Whitney thought that the treatise would be successful commercially and that it would result in substantial profits for both the author and the publisher. After Chodos had spent a number of years fulfilling his part of the bargain and had submitted a completed manuscript, Bancroft-Whitney's successor, the West Publishing Company, came to a contrary conclusion. It declined to publish the treatise, citing solely sales and marketing reasons. Like a good lawyer, Chodos responded by suing

---

7. *Id.*

for damages, first for breach of contract, and then, after amending his complaint to drop that claim, in quantum meruit. The district court held that under the terms of the contract West's decision not to publish was within its discretion, and granted summary judgment in West's favor. Chodos appeals, and we reverse.

Rafael Chodos is a California attorney whose specialty is the law of fiduciary duty. His practice consists primarily of matters involving fiduciary issues such as partnership disputes, corporate dissolutions, and joint ventures.... In July, 1995, Bancroft and Chodos entered into an Author Agreement, which both parties agree is a standard form contract used to govern the composition of a literary work for hire.

The Author Agreement provided for no payments to Chodos prior to publication, and a 15% share of the gross revenues from sales of the work. Farber informed Chodos that a typical successful title published by Bancroft grossed $1 million over a five-year period, although Chodos's work, of course, might be more or less successful than the average. Chodos sought publication of the work not only for the direct financial rewards, but also for the enhanced professional reputation he might receive from the publication of a treatise, which in turn might result in additional referrals to his practice and increased fees for him.

From July, 1995 through June, 1998, Chodos's principal professional activity was the writing of the treatise. He significantly limited the time spent on his law practice, and devoted several hours each morning as well as most weekends to the book project. Chodos estimates that he spent at least 3600 hours over the course of three years on writing the treatise and developing the accompanying electronic materials. He did so with the guidance of Bancroft staff. For example, in late 1995 or early 1996, Farber instructed Chodos that because Bancroft viewed the book as a practice aid and not as an academic work, he should delete an introductory chapter that was primarily historical and disperse the historical material throughout the text, in footnote form. As Chodos completed each of the chapters, he submitted them to Bancroft on a CD-ROM; the seventh and final chapter was sent to the publisher in February, 1998. When finished, the book consisted of 1247 pages.

In mid-1996, Bancroft-Whitney was purchased by the West Publishing Group, and the two entities merged at the end of the year. The Bancroft editors, now employed by West, continued to work with Chodos in preparing the work for publication, although West did establish a management position that ultimately had a direct bearing on Chodos's career as a treatise-writer, that of Director of Product Development and Management for the Western Market Center. Between February and June, 1998, after the entire treatise had been submitted, Chodos reviewed the manuscript to ensure that the formatting was consistent and that no substantive gaps existed. In the summer of 1998 the West editors provided him with detailed notes and suggestions, to which he diligently responded. In November, 1998, West again sent Chodos a lengthy letter including substantive editorial suggestions related to the organization of the book. In early December, 1998, West sent Chodos yet another letter, this time apologizing for delays in publication, and assuring him that publication would take place in the first quarter of 1999. Burt Levy, who replaced Farber as Chodos's editor, informed

Chodos that copy editors were preparing the manuscript for release in the early part of that year.

After receiving no communication from Levy in January, 1999, Chodos contacted West to check on the status of his treatise. On February 4, 1999, Chodos received a response from Nell Petri, a member of the marketing department. Petri informed Chodos that West had decided not to publish the book because it did not "fit within [West's] current product mix" and because of concerns about its "market potential." West admits, however, that the manuscript was of "high quality" and that its decision was not due to any literary shortcomings in Chodos's work.

The decision not to publish the treatise on fiduciary duty was made by Carole Gamble, who joined West as Director of Product Development and Management for the Western Market Center at about the same time that Chodos completed the manuscript. In late 1998, West developed new internal criteria to guide publication decisions. Applying these criteria, Gamble decided not to go forward with the publication of the treatise. She did not in fact read what Chodos had written, but instead reviewed a detailed outline of the treatise and the original proposal for it. Gamble did not prepare a business analysis prior to making her decision. After Chodos informed West that in his view the publisher had breached its contract, West did prepare an economic projection that concluded that the publication of Chodos's work would be an unprofitable venture. Thus, this legal action was born....

Chodos makes two alternative arguments: first, that the standard Author Agreement is an illusory contract, and second, that if a valid contract does exist, West breached it. Under either theory of liability, Chodos contends that he is entitled to recover in quantum meruit.

A. The Author Agreement Is Not Illusory.

In support of his first argument, Chodos correctly notes that in order for a contract to be enforceable under California law, it must impose binding obligations on each party. The California Supreme Court has held that "if one of the promises leaves a party free to perform or to withdraw from the agreement at his own unrestricted pleasure, the promise is deemed illusory and it provides no consideration." Chodos contends that because the contract required him to produce a work of publishable quality, but allowed West, in its discretion, to decide unilaterally whether or not to publish his work, the contract violates the doctrine of mutuality of obligation and is therefore illusory.

California law, like the law in most states, provides that a covenant of good faith and fair dealing is an implied term in every contract. Thus, a court will not find a contract to be illusory if the implied covenant of good faith and fair dealing can be read to impose an obligation on each party. The covenant of good faith "finds particular application in situations where one party is invested with a discretionary power affecting the rights of another." It is correct that the agreement at issue imposes numerous obligations on the author but gives the publisher "the right in its discretion to terminate" the publishing relationship after receiving the manuscript and determining that it is unacceptable. However, we conclude that the contract is not illusory because West's duty to exercise its discretion is limited by its duty of good faith and fair dealing. More specifically, because the standard Author Agreement obligates the publisher to make a judgment as to the quality or literary merit of the author's work — to determine whether the work is "acceptable" or "unacceptable" — it must make that judgment in good faith, and cannot reject a manuscript for other, unrelated reasons. Thus, Chodos's first argument fails.

B. West Breached the Agreement.

Chodos's alternative argument — that a contract exists and it was breached — is more persuasive. West contends that the Author Agreement allowed it to decline to publish the manuscript after Chodos completed writing it for *any* good-faith reason, regardless of whether the reason was related to the quality or literary merit of Chodos's manuscript. However, West's right to terminate the agreement is a limited one defined in two related provisions of the agreement. The first, the "acceptance clause," establishes that West may decline to publish Chodos's manuscript if it finds the work to be "unacceptable" in form and content. The acceptance clause, paragraph eight of the agreement, provides that:

> After timely receipt of the Work or any portion of the Work prepared by Author, Publisher shall review it as to both form and content, and notify Author whether it is acceptable or unacceptable in form and content under the terms of this Agreement. In the event that Publisher determines that the Work or any portion of the Work is unacceptable, Publisher shall notify Author of Publisher's determination and Publisher may exercise its rights under paragraph 4.

The second relevant provision (referred to in the acceptance clause as West's "rights under paragraph 4") allows West to terminate the publishing agreement if the author does not cure a failure in performance after being given an opportunity to do so. This provision, numbered paragraph four of the contract and entitled "Author's Failure to Perform," states:

> If Publisher determines that the Work or any portion of it is not acceptable to publisher as provided in paragraph 8 [the acceptance clause] ... after thirty (30) days following written notice to author if Author has not cured such failure in performance Publisher has the right in its discretion to terminate this Agreement.

The district court agreed with West that in determining whether a manuscript is satisfactory in form and content under the acceptance clause of the standard Author Agreement, the publisher may in good faith consider solely the likelihood of a book's commercial success and other similar economic factors. We unequivocally reject the view that the relevant provisions of the Author Agreement may be so construed in the absence of additional language or conditions.

The expansive reading of the acceptance clause suggested by West is inconsistent with the language of the two contract clauses. Under the agreement, the publisher may deem a manuscript unacceptable only if it is deficient in "form and content." Thus, had Chodos submitted a badly written, poorly researched, disorganized or substantially incomplete work to West, the publisher would have been well within its rights to find that submission unacceptable under the acceptance clause—as it would were it to reject any work that it believed in good faith lacked literary merit. A publisher bargains for a product of a certain quality and is entitled to reject a work that in its good faith judgment falls short of the bargained-for standard. Nothing in the contract, however, suggests that the ordinary meaning of the words "form and content" was not intended, and nowhere in the contract does it state that the publisher may terminate the agreement if it changes its management structure or its marketing strategy, or if it revises its business or economic forecasts, all matters unrelated to "form and content".

To the contrary, the fact that the contract required West to afford Chodos an opportunity to cure any deficient performance supports our straightforward reading of the acceptance clause as a provision that relates solely to the quality or literary merit of a submitted work. As noted above, if West determined that Chodos's submission was unacceptable, he was to be given a period of time to cure his failure in performance. The inclusion of this provision indicates that a deficiency in "form and content" is one that the author has some power to cure. Chodos has no power to "cure" West's view that the marketplace for books on fiduciary duty had changed; nor could he "cure" a change in West's overall marketing strategy and product mix; nor, indeed, could he be expected to do much about a general downturn in economic conditions. The text and structure of the contract thus demonstrate that West's stated reasons for terminating the agreement were not among those contemplated by the parties.

The uncontroverted evidence in this case is that Chodos worked diligently in cooperation with West—indeed, with West's encouragement—to produce a work that met the highest professional standard, and that he was successful in that venture. His performance was induced by an agreement that permitted rejection of the completed manuscript only for deficiencies in "form and content." Chodos thus labored to complete a work of high quality with the expectation that, if he did so, it would be published. He devoted thousands of hours of labor to the venture, and passed up substantial professional opportunities, only for West to decide that due to the vagaries of its internal reorganizations and changes in its business strategies or in the national economy or the market for legal treatises, his work, albeit admittedly of high quality, was for naught. It would be inequitable, if not unconscionable, for an author to be forced to bear this considerable burden solely because of his publisher's change in management, its poor planning, or its inadequate financial analyses at the time it entered into the contract, or even because of an unexpected change in the marketplace. Moreover, to allow a publisher to escape its contractual obligations for these reasons would be directly contrary to both the language and the spirit of the standard Author Agreement.

West urges us to affirm the district court's ruling because, in its view, it is well-accepted that, regardless of the contract's failure to mention economic circumstances or market demands, publishers have broad discretion under the acceptance clause of the standard Author Agreement to reject manuscripts for any good faith commercial reason. For this proposition, the district court cited two cases from the Second Circuit involving that same clause. Although at least one of the cases contains dicta that would support the district court's decision, both are distinguishable factually and legally. Moreover, to the extent that either case suggests that a publisher bound by the standard Author Agreement may terminate the contract for *any* reason so long as it acts in good faith, we respectfully reject that view.

In *Doubleday & Co. v. Curtis*, 763 F.2d 495, 496 (2d Cir. 1985), a publisher rejected a manuscript by the well-known actor but neophyte author, Tony Curtis, on the basis of its poor literary quality. There, as here, the publishing agreement allowed the publisher to reject a submission if it was not satisfactory as to "form and content." However, in *Doubleday*, in direct contrast to the circumstances here, it was agreed that the manuscript was *unsatisfactory* in form and content. In *Doubleday*, Curtis's claim was that the publisher had a good-faith obligation under the contract to re-write his admittedly unsatisfactory manuscript and to transform it into one of publishable quality. The Second Circuit held that a publisher's good faith obligation does not stretch that far; thus, the Second Circuit's essential holding in *Doubleday* has no bearing on the present case.

It is true that the Second Circuit appears to have stated its holding in *Doubleday* more broadly than the case before the court warranted. The court said:

> We hold that a publisher may, in its discretion, terminate a standard publishing contract, provided that the termination is made in good faith, and that the failure of an author to submit a satisfactory manuscript was not caused by the publisher's bad faith.

> Still, read in context, the holding does not make it clear whether the court meant that a publisher may reject a manuscript for reasons wholly unrelated to its literary worth or that it may do so only if it determines in good faith that the submitted work is unsatisfactory on its literary merits. If the former is the Second Circuit's view of the law, we respectfully disagree.

The district court also relied on *Random House, Inc. v. Gold*, 464 F. Supp. 1306 (S.D.N.Y. 1979). That case is more apposite than *Doubleday* in that the district court there held that a publisher may consider economic circumstances when evaluating a manuscript's "form and content" under the standard publishing agreement. Although we disagree with that holding for the reasons set forth above, and are certainly not bound by it, we note that even in *Random House* the court did not go so far as to state that economic considerations may be the *sole* reason for a publisher to decline to publish a manuscript that is in every other respect acceptable. In *Random House*, as in *Doubleday*, the submitted manuscript was not of publishable quality. In contrast to Chodos's work, the editor at Random House considered the manuscript at issue to be "shallow and badly designed."

In sum, we reject the district court's determination that West acted within the discretion afforded it by the Author Agreement when it decided not to publish Chodos's manuscript. Because West concedes that the manuscript was of high quality and that it declined to publish it solely for commercial reasons rather than because of any defect in its form and content, we hold as a matter of law that West breached its agreement with Chodos.

C. Chodos May Pursue A Quantum Meruit Claim.

The district court ruled that if West breached the contract, Chodos could proceed in quantum meruit, but only if the damages were not determinable under the contract.... Here, it is impossible to determine even now what those revenues would have been had West not frustrated the completion of the contract. Had West honored its contractual obligations and published the treatise, the revenues would have depended on any number of circumstances, including how West chose to market the book, and how it was received by readers and critics....

It might also be reasonably argued that West's publishing of Chodos's treatise was an additional element of consideration to which Chodos was entitled.... Because West breached its contract with Chodos by rejecting his manuscript for a reason not permitted by the contract between the parties and because Chodos is entitled to recover for the breach in quantum meruit, we REVERSE the district court's grant of summary judgment in West's favor, and REMAND the case to the district court with instructions to enter summary judgment as to liability in Chodos's favor, and for further proceedings consistent with this opinion ...

Helprin v. Harcourt, Inc.

277 F. Supp. 2d 327 (S.D.N.Y. 2003)

Plaintiff Mark Helprin ("Helprin") filed a complaint (the "Complaint") against Defendants Harcourt Brace Jovanovich, Inc. ("HBJ") and Harcourt, Inc. (together with HBJ, "Harcourt") alleging that Harcourt ... breached [a publishing agreement between Helprin and Harcourt the ("Agreement")] by (i) failing to publish Helprin's second work produced pursuant to the Agreement, (ii) improperly accounting for interest that accrued on the unrecouped portion of the advance paid to Helprin under the Agreement (the "Excluded Claim"), and (iii) failing to expend the required amounts for promotion of Helprin's first work produced pursuant to the Agreement....

Both parties acknowledge that Helprin is a world-famous, talented author whose previous works have earned both commercial and critical acclaim. In addition, both parties agree that in 1989, Helprin and Harcourt entered into the Agreement, which obligated Helprin to produce five works (the "Works") over an indefinite time period in exchange for, among other things, a $2,000,000 advance (the "Advance") and royalties from sales of the Works. In conjunction with the signing of the Agreement, Harcourt purchased a $2,000,000 insurance policy (the "Policy") on Helprin's life to protect Harcourt in the event that Helprin died before he was able to fulfill his obligations under the Agreement. Finally, both parties concur that in 1995, Harcourt published the first Work by Helprin under the Agreement, entitled Memoir from

Antproof Case (the "First Work"), and Helprin did not submit a draft of his next Work (the "Contested Work") until October 24, 2002. Past those points of agreement lie the contested issues of the instant litigation.

In the Complaint, Helprin alleges he received no response to his submission of the Contested Work until December 17, 2002, when Dan Farley, president of Harcourt, informed Helprin via letter that Harcourt was rejecting the Contested Work for publication because it was "unacceptable as defined in paragraph 16 of the Agreement." In the Agreement, the standard for determining what constitutes an "acceptable" Work is described as follows:

> "A Work shall be "acceptable" under this Agreement if such Work meets a standard comparable to the literary merit of [Helprin's] previous works."

The Agreement further stated that in the event Harcourt did reject a Work because it was not acceptable, Heplrin would regain all rights with respect to such Work upon notice of the rejection. Helprin then would be obligated to use his best efforts to sell the Work to another publisher, and some of the payments he received from such a deal would first go to Harcourt to reimburse it for certain portions of the Advance that went unrecouped because of the rejection.

Helprin alleges that Harcourt's rejection of the Contested Work was a breach of contract motivated by Harcourt's belief that the Contested Work would not be commercially successful and by Harcourt's desire to avoid spending money on advertising and promoting the Contested Work. Helprin also alleges that Harcourt breached the Agreement by failing to make promotional expenditures for the First Work as required under the Agreement, which states:

> [Harcourt] agrees to allocate a budget of not less than one hundred thousand dollars ($100,000.00) per Work to be used at [Harcourt's] discretion for out-of-house advertising and promotion with respect to first hardcover publication of each Work in the United States, including the costs of [Harcourt's] reimbursement of cooperative advertising expenditures of its wholesalers or dealers.

Moreover, Helprin alleges that Harcourt made intentional misstatements in an effort to conceal this failure to expend the required promotional amounts, thus committing fraud....

Helprin's first claim for relief alleges that Harcourt breached the Agreement when it rejected the Contested Work. Harcourt responds that paragraph 8 of the Agreement prevents Helprin from instigating a lawsuit because it provides that

> if a Work is not published within the time provided in Paragraph 6 ... [Helprin] may thereafter request [Harcourt] by written notice ... to publish such Work within six months after [Harcourt's] receipt of [Helprin's] request. If, after receipt of such notice, [Harcourt] fails to publish such Work within such period, this Agreement will terminate with respect to such Work immediately and automatically at the end of such period, all rights to such Work will revert to [Helprin] on the effective date of termination without further obligation

or liability on the part of [Harcourt], and [Helprin] will have the right to retain any advances previously paid, but will be entitled to no other compensation, remedy, or damages, and [Helprin] will retain the right to sell such Work to another publisher and retain the proceeds. [Harcourt's] failure to publish a Work that it has accepted according to the provisions of paragraphs 16 and 17 hereof will not alter the conditions under which [Helprin] is deemed to have satisfied his obligation in regard to such Work.

Paragraph 6 requires that "within eighteen months after delivery and acceptance of the final revised manuscript of a Work hereunder, [Harcourt] will publish such Work at its own expense," and Harcourt contends that the Contested Work is an acceptable Work for purposes of paragraphs 6 and 8—despite Harcout's rejection of it—because "Helprin has pleaded [in the Complaint] that [the Contested Work] met the standards of paragraph 16(a) and therefore under that paragraph's express terms it is deemed to be accepted by Harcourt."

1. What Constitutes an "Acceptable" Work?

Harcourt's argument raises the crucial question at the heart of Helprin's claim: what constitutes an "acceptable" work under the Agreement? To answer that question, the Court first looks at paragraph 16(a) of the Agreement, which states as follows:

> [Harcourt] recognizes its obligation to give editorial assistance to [Helprin] in order to assist [him] in making the manuscript of each Work hereunder acceptable for publication by [Harcourt]. However, [Harcourt] reserves the right to determine the amount and usefulness of its editorial assistance and whether or not its editorial intervention will result in an acceptable manuscript that merits publication by [Harcourt]. A Work shall be "acceptable" under this Agreement if such Work meets a standard comparable to the literary merit of [Helprin's] previous works. When the manuscript of a Work meets the foregoing standard, [Harcourt] shall notify [Helprin] of its acceptance thereof in accordance with paragraph 17 hereof. [Helprin] recognizes [his] obligation to deliver manuscripts that are complete and acceptable in accordance herewith and to participate in the editorial process for that purpose.

Helprin contends that this paragraph was drafted in a way that "substantially alter[ed Harcourt's] discretion in accepting or rejecting a manuscript." However, in reviewing other cases before this Court involving similar contractual obligations, the Court reaches a different conclusion.

… [T]he ultimate acceptance of a "finally" edited work is to be given "by [Harcourt]." In order for Harcourt to accept a submitted Work, it has to execute a written notice signed by an officer of the company explicitly stating Harcourt's acceptance of the Work. The second sentence's clarification that certain preliminary editorial comments and other communications to Helprin that do not explicitly express Harcourt's acceptance "do not constitute acceptance" demonstrates the intent of the parties to make clear that, as a condition precedent, Harcourt had to determine to unequivocally accept the Work in order for the acceptance to qualify under the Agreement's definition.

Another manifestation of this intent is contained in paragraph 16(c), discussed below, governing the procedure to be followed in the event Harcourt does determine that a manuscript of the Work "is not acceptable to [Harcourt]." As a result, for Harcourt now to contend in its response to Helprin's allegations that paragraph 8 is relevant because Helprin has pleaded that the Contested Work is acceptable invokes a form of circular reasoning that the Court rejects. A contract provision cannot be read to have been fulfilled simply because, in a pleading and without more, one party says so. The claim at issue does not involve Helprin's view of the quality of the Contested Work — which would most likely be favorably biased — but rather Harcourt's assertion in its letter dated December 17, 2002 that the Contested Work was not acceptable. Consequently, paragraphs 6 and 8 are inapplicable to the factual situation as Helprin has pleaded it.

2. Harcourt's Good Faith

Having rejected both Helprin's contention that the acceptability clause is distinct from other such clauses in the publishing industry and Harcourt's assertion that paragraphs 6 and 8 should govern the situation presented here, the Court turns to paragraph 16(c), which contemplates a prospect identical to the factual situation at hand:

> In the event that [Harcourt] determines in accordance with this Agreement that the manuscript of a Work is not acceptable to it, it shall so notify [Helprin] and upon such notice all rights with respect to such Work granted or transferred to [Harcourt] under this Agreement will automatically revert to [Helprin].

The paragraph continues by stating that upon such rejection, Helprin is obligated to use his best efforts to sell the Work to another publisher and, if successful, return some of the profits from that sale to Harcourt so Harcourt could recoup the portion of the Advance that applied to the Contested Work. In light of paragraph 16(c), Harcourt might be inclined to argue that it is under no obligation to publish a submission that it finds unacceptable. Harcourt does not make such an argument, perhaps in part because of the existence of a significant body of precedent in this Court that directly addresses when a publisher is permitted to reject a submitted work from an author who is under contract with that publisher.

In at least six cases in recent years with similar fact patterns to the instant case, the Court has interpreted comparable "acceptability" clauses as granting publishers wide discretion to terminate publishing contracts if the submitted draft is not acceptable, "provided that the termination is made in good faith, and that the failure of the author to submit a satisfactory manuscript was not caused by the publisher's bad faith." The Court reached these holdings based in part on analogous breach of contract cases considered by New York courts where the satisfactory performance of one party was to be judged by another party. In such cases, the New York courts required the party terminating the contract to act in good faith.

In *Curtis*, for example, the Court observed that:

> this principle — that a contract containing a "satisfaction clause" may be terminated only as a result of honest dissatisfaction — would seem especially

appropriate in construing publishing agreements. To shield from scrutiny the already chimerical process of evaluating literary value would render the "satisfaction" clause an illusory promise, and place authors at the unbridled mercy of their editors. [*Doubleday & Co., Inc. v. Curtis*, 599 F. Supp. 779 (S.D.N.Y. 1984).]

Furthermore, testimony at some of the Court's cases established that publishing industry practice has always involved "significant editorial changes, and that it is 'inconceivable'… that a publisher would reject a completed manuscript written under contract, without first offering or providing some editorial assistance to revise it." [S]ee also [*Harcourt Brace Jovanovich, Inc. v.*] *Goldwater*, 532 F. Supp. at 624 [(S.D.N.Y. 1982)] (observing that both parties' witnesses testified that the "custom of the trade" establishes an implied good faith obligation on the part of a publisher to engage in appropriate editorial work with the author).

Thus, in determining whether the publisher in each of the foregoing cases acted in good faith, the Court focused primarily on the amount of editorial assistance the publisher provided. A publisher that provided a "detailed and lengthy editorial analysis of the shortcomings in the plot, characters and pacing of the submitted draft" demonstrated its good faith in offering sufficient editorial assistance. A publisher that did "nothing approaching any [kind of] sensible editorial activity" and failed to provide any "comments of a detailed nature designed to give the author[ ] an opportunity to remedy defects" failed the test and could be considered in possible breach of its agreement.

Based on the Complaint, the Court finds that Helprin has pled sufficient facts to state a sufficient claim at this point in the litigation that Harcourt did not act in good faith when judging the Contested Work unacceptable. Helprin alleges that he sent the Contested Work to Harcourt, and less than two months later received a letter back saying only that the Contested Work was being rejected because it was unacceptable as defined in paragraph 16 of the Agreement. There is no indication at this stage from either party that Harcourt offered any further editorial comments or assistance, nor has it been alleged by either party that Harcourt allowed Helprin an opportunity to cure whatever defects Harcourt found in the Contested Work. As a result, the Court finds that Helprin has met his burden to state a claim with regard to breach of contract based on rejection of the Contested Work....

Helprin [further] alleges that Harcourt breached the Agreement by not expending the required amounts for the promotion of the first hardcover edition of the First Work.... Harcourt's defense raises several issues, some of which are not addressed by either party. First, does the language of the Agreement's promotion paragraph actually create a definitive contractual obligation for Harcourt to spend the entire promotional budget for the First Work (the "Budget")? Paragraph 30 states that, with regard to out-of-house advertising and promotion for the American hardcover edition of each Work, Harcourt "agrees to allocate a budget of not less than one hundred thousand dollars ($100,000.00) per Work to be used at [Harcourt's] discretion...." The Agreement's use of the verb "allocate" — which Miriam-Webster's Dictionary defines as "apportioning for a specific purpose or to particular persons or things,"—implies that, while Harcourt is obligated to reserve or earmark a minimum amount for promotion, it is not necessarily required to fully spend the money. Indeed, use of the Budget is left completely to Harcourt's discretion and the provision specifies no time frame in which Harcourt is required to spend the entire Budget.

Moreover, Harcourt is not obligated to account for the Budget, as it is required to do with respect to Helprin's royalties, nor is Helprin given any right to request an audit of the Budget, as he is allowed to with regard to his royalties. Such circumstances lend support to the interpretation that the Agreement intended to provide Harcourt free reign in utilizing what Helprin himself alleged "was substantially in excess of the average [promotional budget] in the publishing industry in June 1995, and … more than the average for Harcourt at that time as well." However, while Helprin's claim that Harcourt breached the Agreement by not spending the full amount may not be sufficient to state a claim, neither party raises the issue of the interpretation of the promotional paragraph in their briefs on the Motion. Consequently, the Court is not inclined to dismiss the claim out of hand without the benefit of the parties' briefing of the matter. …

[3. Helprin's request for Recission.]

Helprin seeks rescission of the Agreement on the ground that a material breach has occurred. "Under New York law, 'rescission is an extraordinary remedy, appropriate only where the breach is found to be material and willful, or, if not willful, so substantial and fundamental as to strongly tend to defeat the object of the parties in making the contract.'" "Courts generally permit rescission of a contract only when it appears reasonably feasible to return the parties to their respective positions prior to the contract." Harcourt contests Helprin's request, asserting that the alleged breach is not material, willful, substantial or fundamental, that Helprin has not offered to restore the status quo, and that he has an adequate remedy at law. The Court is not persuaded that the alleged breach is not significant enough to qualify for rescission. The test for determining the materiality of a breach for purposes of rescission is whether the alleged breach is "of such nature and such importance that the contract would not have been made without it." Assuming that Helprin's allegation that Harcourt rejected the Contested Work in bad faith is correct, it is fair to conclude that such a rejection could serve to undermine the entire purpose of the Agreement, which was to produce the Works for Harcourt to publish. …

Finally, Harcourt asserts that Helprin's claim for breach of contract based on the rejection of the Contested Work can be adequately remedied by money damages reflecting lost royalties. This argument ignores Helprin's concerns regarding his ability to publish future Works under the Agreement and the possible lost trust between him and Harcourt that could make it difficult for a working relationship to continue in the future. If the trier of fact eventually finds these concerns have merit, money damages may not be sufficient as a remedy. Thus, at this stage of the proceeding, the Court is satisfied that Helprin's allegations on these issues demonstrate that a request for rescission should be maintained as a possible remedy should the instant case be resolved in favor of Helprin. …

Dunn v. CCH Inc.

834 F. Supp. 2d 657, 658 (E.D. Mich. 2011)

This is a contract case. Plaintiff Stephen J. Dunn ("Dunn") is suing defendant CCH Incorporated ("CCH") claiming that CCH breached a Publishing Agreement regarding Dunn's authorship of a treatise on IRS Tax Practice and Procedure to be published by CCH. Dunn says CCH improperly terminated the contract. Dunn claims (1) breach of contract and (2) breach of implied covenant of good faith and fair dealing....

The good faith requirement in publishing contracts comes from the implied covenant of good faith and fair dealing. The covenant of good faith and fair dealing requires a party vested with broad discretion to act reasonably and not arbitrarily or in a manner inconsistent with the reasonable expectations of the parties. It cannot, however, create new terms which do not exist in the contract. Rather, the covenant is used as an interpretative tool by Illinois courts. Under Illinois law, a party cannot be held liable for a breach of the covenant of good faith where it acts pursuant to the terms of the contract. Therefore, the question of CCH's breach of the Publishing Agreement and its obligations under the implied covenant of good faith and fair dealing are one and the same....

2. Interpretation of Paragraph 1

The parties disagree on the interpretation of paragraph 1 of the Publishing Agreement. As set forth above, paragraph 1 provides in relevant part:

> If the Author has not delivered in form and content acceptable to the Publisher a complete manuscript and all permissions by the delivery date herein agreed to, including any delivery date pursuant to paragraph 8 with respects to any new edition of the Work, the Publisher may, if it so chooses, return all of the unpublished materials that have been submitted to the Publisher by the author and, at its sole option, terminate this Agreement by prior written notice to the Author without any liability whatsoever on the Publisher's part. Alternatively, the Publisher may, at its sole option, extend the manuscript delivery date or give the Author a reasonable amount of additional time to make changes or revisions acceptable to the Publisher (although the Publisher shall not be required to do so). Should the Author be unwilling or unable to meet the new delivery date or make changes or revisions acceptable to the Publisher in that time, the Publisher may return all unpublished materials as provided above and, at its sole option, terminate this agreement by prior written notice to the Author, without any liability whatsoever on the Publisher's part.

Dunn says that this paragraph gives CCH the right to terminate the Publishing Agreement only if Dunn fails to deliver a completed manuscript by a deadline that is unsatisfactory to CCH. Dunn says that because it is undisputed that there was no deadline and because it is undisputed that Dunn did not fail to timely submit a "complete manuscript," he is entitled to summary judgment on his breach of contract claim because CCH undisputedly breached the Publishing Agreement.

CCH disagrees with Dunn's interpretation. CCH says there is no temporal requirement and that the question of whether CCH breached the Publishing Agreement depends upon whether CCH acted in bad faith. In other words, CCH focuses on the language that CCH could "at its sole option, terminate this Agreement" if Dunn did not "deliver[] in form and content acceptable to [CCH] …" and that "[s]hould the Author be unwilling or unable to meet the new delivery date or make changes or revisions acceptable to [CCH] in that time," CCH "may … at its sole option, terminate this agreement by prior written notice to the Author, without any liability whatsoever on the Publisher's part." CCH argues that Dunn's interpretation—which essentially is that CCH could not have terminated the Publishing Agreement until Dunn failed to deliver a complete treatise that was unacceptable by the deadline for the completed treatise—contradicts the express terms in the Publishing Agreement.

The Publishing Agreement could be interpreted to link the temporal element—delivery of a competed work by a deadline—with CCH's right to terminate only if the work is not acceptable when delivered by the deadline. Because it is clear that there was no deadline for the completed treatise, and Dunn had only submitted two chapters, it is not unreasonable to argue that CCH breached the Publishing Agreement by terminating Dunn's contract when it did. However, this interpretation gives [too] much leeway to the author than what reasonably could be contemplated. As CCH suggests in its papers, such an interpretation results in the untenable result that CCH could not terminate a contract, no matter how poor of quality an author's work is submitted, until the very end of the completed project. CCH's interpretation makes sense because the Publishing Agreement says that "[s]hould the Author be unwilling or unable to meet the new delivery date or make changes or revisions acceptable to CCH in that time." Under Dunn's interpretation, CCH could not terminate the Publishing Agreement until Dunn finished the entire treatise and turned in unacceptable work, wasting months of time and work. It is more reasonable that the Publishing Agreement allows CCH to terminate it if it receives unacceptable work that it does not believe can be revised to be made acceptable. Overall, Dunn is not entitled to summary judgment based on his interpretation of the Publishing Agreement.[8]

3. CCH's Good Faith

Dunn goes on, however, to argue that summary judgment is still appropriate because there is no genuine issue of material fact that CCH acted in bad faith. CCH says just the opposite—that it is entitled to summary judgment because there is no genuine issue of material fact that it did not act in bad faith. Both parties cite publishing cases from the Second Circuit, applying New York law. According to CCH, the lead case in this area is *Doubleday & Co. v. Curtis*, 763 F.2d 495 (2d Cir. 1985). In *Doubleday*, the contract provided that Curtis would deliver manuscripts "satisfactory

---

8. Part of the problem with the Publishing Agreement as applied to this case is that it appears to be drafted to apply to a single submission, i.e. a single completed manuscript. The nature of the treatise project, as evidenced by the sequence of events, is that there are multiple submissions, *i.e.* chapter by chapter. Although CCH has not so argued, a reasonable interpretation would be each submitted chapter constitutes a "manuscript" within the meaning of the Publishing Agreement.

to the Publisher in content and form," a contract described by the Second Circuit as a "standard industry form." The Second Circuit noted that such contracts, which allow the publisher to terminate if the work is not acceptable as to form or content, have an implied good-faith requirement, which stems from the requirement that a party vested with discretion must exercise that discretion in good faith. The Second Circuit held that "a publisher may, in its discretion, terminate a standard publishing contract, provided that the termination is made in good faith, and that the failure of an author to submit a satisfactory manuscript was not caused by the publisher's bad faith." In other words, the Second Circuit said that so long as the publisher terminates the contract due to its "honest dissatisfaction" with the work, there is no breach.

Assuming that this is the standard of good faith to be applied in publishing cases, the record shows that neither party is entitled to summary judgment. Both parties suggest that the issue boils down to one question—was CCH honestly dissatisfied with Dunn's work on the Tax Returns Chapter? There is a clear dispute of material fact as to whether Dunn was unwilling or unable to revise the chapter he submitted to make it acceptable to CCH. In other words, CCH's honest dissatisfaction is disputed. Dunn revised his first chapter to CCH's satisfaction albeit after having to make substantive revisions. However, Bornstein, apparently did not believe that Dunn was willing and/or capable of making the changes necessary to have the Tax Returns Chapter acceptable to CCH. CCH did not offer Dunn an opportunity to make revisions, as it had done with the Testimonial Privileges Chapter. While Dunn did not ask for an opportunity to revise the chapter, CCH simply told Dunn to stop working on the treatise and later terminated the Publishing Agreement. Under these circumstances, reasonable minds could differ on whether CCH breached the Publishing Agreement when it concluded that Dunn was unwilling or unable to make revisions that would be acceptable to CCH. In other words, there is sufficient doubt as to whether CCH was honestly dissatisfied with Dunn's work such that it had the right to terminate the Publishing Agreement.

B. Dunn's Damages

CCH also argues that summary judgment is appropriate because Dunn cannot establish damages. Damages are an essential element of a breach of contract claim under Illinois law. Dunn is seeking damages for lost royalties and for lost business referrals. Given that liability and damages could be bifurcated at trial, the Court declines to make a ruling on Dunn's damages at this time. However, it offers the following as it may assist the parties in charting the future course of this case, including bringing it to a resolution.

As to lost business referrals, under Illinois law, lost profits may be recovered only when there are "criteria by which they can be estimated with reasonable certainty." *Reliable Fire Equip. Co. v. Arredondo*, 405 Ill. App. 3d 708, 719 (2d Dist. 2010) (finding that plaintiff could not recover lost profits because it failed to prove that lost profits were calculable with reasonable certainty). Indeed, Illinois courts "will reverse damage awards that are based on speculation or conjecture," such as where damages are based on "false assumptions or data." *SK Hand Tool Corp. v. Dresser Indus., Inc.*, 284 Ill. App. 3d 417, 426–27 (1st Dist. 1996)....

[I]t would appear that any possible referrals that he might have received as a result of being a co-author of the P&P Treatise are too speculative to be recoverable as a matter of law. Here, discovery has closed and Dunn has not pointed to any evidence of the quantity or monetary value of his alleged lost business referrals. The only evidence is, in Dunn's words, "speculation." Thus, it seems unlikely Dunn can recover for lost business referrals.

As to his claim for future royalties, CCH says that the P&P Treatise and the Expert Treatise Library is a "new business venture" for the company and that under Illinois law, evidence of projected profits of new business ventures attempted by an established business cannot support a damages award based on lost future profits. CCH explains that the P&P Treatise was an entirely new product for CCH, being built from the ground up and, to this date—much less on August 11, 2010, the date Dunn claims CCH breached the Publishing Agreement—has no record of sales or profits because it has not been released. CCH also says that it is undisputed that the Expert Treatises Library itself was an entirely new business venture for CCH. CCH had never before published treatises and had no track record for the sales or profits associated with treatises of any kind. CCH also says that it is undisputed that Dunn's royalties would have been based exclusively on net sales of the P&P Treatise. The Publishing Agreement provided that the entire author team for the P&P Treatise would have collectively been entitled to royalties of 20% of net sales in the first year of publication and 15% of net sales thereafter. Because there are no established record of sales, CCH argues that royalties dependent upon those sales are too speculative under Illinois' new business rule.

Dunn, however, says that his royalty damages are not speculative. He first relies on historical sales of the Saltzman Treatise as a basis for future sales of the P&P Treatise, [citing cases] which hold that a similarly situated business can be used as a proxy for future profits....

Dunn's argument is not particularly persuasive. As CCH points out, while it may established in the publishing field, the venture into the treatise market was new. Illinois law seems to suggest that the new business rule applies in such a circumstance. Moreover, discovery has closed and Dunn has not designated an expert. Overall, using the Saltzman Treatise as a model for Dunn's damages is problematic....

Moreover, the actual sales of the treatises that have been released are a small fraction of the sales anticipated by the 2009 Projections. Where the 2009 Projections hoped for $494,662 in sales for 2010, the projected first year of publication, actual sales for five months of 2011, the actual first year of production were $5,997.

In the end, even if Dunn is able to establish liability, the amount of damages he would be able to recover is very likely to be far lower than the over $600,000 he is seeking.

V. Conclusion

As explained above, reasonable minds could differ on whether CCH terminated the Publishing Agreement because it was honestly dissatisfied with Dunn's work. Because Dunn was not given an opportunity to revise the second chapter and CCH simply told him to stop working altogether, following up later with a termination letter, reasonable minds could question whether CCH's actions were premature. While a full exposition of the facts at trial may show CCH acted appropriately, there is sufficient doubt in the record so as to prevent summary judgment in CCH's favor.

Notes and Questions

a. One of the more well-known disputes over delivery occurred with film star Tony Curtis, who tried his hand as a novelist. *See Doubleday & Co., Inc. v. Curtis*, 599 F. Supp. 779 (S.D.N.Y. 1984). This dispute originally set the New York standards for good faith and the right to refuse a manuscript.

b. As alluded to in the complaint brought by Helprin, the obligation of the publisher may come in the form of promotional obligations rather than merely an advance. For many authors, publishing income is not the goal but rather a step towards an increase in professional stature or public exposure, both of which afford more lucrative financial opportunities. For nonfiction authors, the opportunities may flow from being perceived as an expert in a field. For fiction writers, the larger income opportunities invariably come from either the motion picture industry or through increased paperback sales.

Rather than merely provide a budget account, authors looking for a meaningful promotional guarantee should seek to be sure that the promotional funds are allocated during a fixed period, actually expended during that period, and accounted for in audits on behalf of the author.

c. In *Zilg v. Prentice-Hall, Inc.*, 717 F.2d 671 (2d Cir. 1983), the Second Circuit rejected a claim for breach of contract when a polemic written about the history and influence of the DuPont family saw its advertising and promotional budget greatly reduced in size and the production run decreased. The Second Circuit found no best-efforts obligation to promote, only an obligation of good faith and fair dealing, so it reversed a finding of breach of contract. While the Court alluded to political influence brought by the DuPont family, it relied more heavily on the publisher's aversion to the book rather than any bad-faith actions.

d. How much work must a publisher do? Is there a minimal level of work that must go into a contractual obligation to promote and distribute a line of books, absent claims of bad faith? *See Proteus Books, Ltd. v. Cherry Lane Music Co.*, 873 F.2d 502 (2d Cir. 1989).

e. With increasing pressure on public personalities to be free of controversy, the use of "morals clauses" are increasingly common in publishing agreements. The Authors Guild has published a position paper opposing such contractual terms.[9] The Authors Guild uses this example:

> In the event that Author is publicly accused of the violation of law, the infringement or invasion of the rights of any third party, inciting infringement or invasion of third-party rights by others, or is otherwise accused of libel, slander, or defamatory conduct, or any other conduct that subjects, or could be reasonably anticipated to subject Author or Publisher to ridicule, contempt, scorn, hatred, or censure by the general public or which is likely to materially diminish the sales of the Work, Publisher may terminate . . .

> Publisher may terminate . . . if Author's conduct evidences a lack of due regard for public conventions and morals, or Author commits a crime or any other act that will tend to bring Author into serious contempt, and such behavior would materially damage the Work's reputation or sales.

> Publisher may at any time prior to publication choose not to publish the Work if past or future illegal conduct of the Author, inconsistent with the Author's reputation at the time this Agreement is executed and unknown to Publisher, is made public and results in sustained, widespread public condemnation of the Author that materially diminishes the sales potential of the Work. Should Publisher elect not to publish the Work pursuant to this section, Publisher shall give the Author timely written notice of such decision, all rights in the Work shall revert to the Author, no further advances shall be payable, and the Author shall not be required to repay any sums paid to date.[10]

This clause highlights the challenges of operating as a celebrity (even a minor one) in an era where ones' reputation can be destroyed through an ill-conceived tweet or because of a past indiscretion. The Authors Guild explains its position by reference to the hysteria of past generations:

> As playwright Lillian Hellman notably wrote in response to a subpoena to testify before the House Un-American Activities Committee, which was investigating Communist infiltratration of Hollywood and other American institutions, "I cannot and will not cut my conscience to fit this year's fashions." Yet, before McCarthyism came to an end in 1954, it destroyed the careers of thousands of writers, filmmakers, artists, academics, and other left-leaning intellectuals. In 1990, before the courts declared it unconstitutional, the NEA, bowing to pressure from cultural conservatives, mandated that grant applicants had to sign "obscenity pledges" promising not to use public funds to create works of a morally questionable nature.

---

9. *Why We Oppose Morals Clauses in Book Contracts*, Authors Guild (Jan. 24, 2019), http://www.authorsguild.org/industry-advocacy/why-we-oppose-morals-clauses-in-book-contracts/.
    10. *Id.*

The morals clause quoted by the Authors Guild only spoke of the obligation to publish. In June 2019, Linda Fairstein, the former New York prosecutor who became a New York Times bestselling crime novelist, was dropped by her publisher in response to the negative press coverage triggered by a documentary about the Central Park Five.

The Central Park Five were young African-American and Hispanic men falsely convicted for a gang rape in Central Park in 1989, despite exonerating DNA evidence and confessions obtained by the minors without any representation by counsel. The actual perpetrator confessed in 2001 while serving a life sentence for murder and other rapes. The wrongful convictions were vacated in 2002, but the city refused to settle until 2014. The pressure on the prosecutor, Linda Fairstein, did not significantly materialize until the 2019 Netflix dramatization, *When They See Us*. Earlier books and documentaries had covered the injustice of the case, but the political context of 2019 significantly changed the public outrage at the prosecutorial insistence of the culpability by the young men initially charged.

To what extent is the economic value of Fairstein as an author changed by the public perception of her prosecutorial career? Should a publisher have the right to walk away from its authors, even if there has been no conviction of a crime or finding of civil liability?

f. The consequences of termination are upsetting to an author, but a clause calling for indemnification could be much more costly. If a contract includes an indemnification clause, could a publisher seek to recover the cost of unsold works because of the public animosity that could arise later in an author's career? Should an author guarantee the litigation costs for the content in a publication? To what extent does such risk-shifting stifle an author's ability to provide investigative journalism?

Problem 17-B

Bryce is working on a new project. Through your work together, Bryce now comes to your office regularly as new deals and opportunities develop. Your association together has taught Bryce to seek advice in the earliest stages of each venture, so that problems are addressed early on in the process.

Bryce's current project is a coffee table book, a photojournalistic exposé. Bryce is supplying much of the editorial content. Jesse Yang is the photographer and photo editor. The project is to photograph the famous and near famous of the city and then write a brief introduction and caption for each picture. Some of the subjects will be asked to pose while those who are more camera shy will be photographed paparazzi-style.

The publisher loves the idea and has approved the concept. Bryce and Jesse submitted a list of probable subjects, but they both clearly explained to the publisher that the final selection of subjects would be based on availability of photographic opportunities and content. Bryce and Jesse will jointly own the copyright in the finished work, sharing royalties evenly and making editorial decisions by mutual consent.

Bryce is concerned that the publisher will not treat the book with the investment it needs. Coffee table books are expensive to produce, and Bryce wants assurances as to the quality of the final product, some guarantee that a reasonable number of books will be published, funds will be spent to promote the book, and that the publisher will not try to shorten the project or later back out of the publishing commitment.

Outline a deal memorandum that Bryce can use as a checklist to finalize negotiations with the publisher regarding the project.

C. Termination and New Technology Issues

Random House, Inc. v. Rosetta Books L.L.C.

150 F. Supp. 2d 613 (S.D.N.Y. 2001),
aff'd 283 F.3d 490 (2d Cir. 2002)

In this copyright infringement action, Random House, Inc. seeks to enjoin Rosetta Books L.L.C. and its Chief Executive Officer from selling in digital format eight specific works on the grounds that the authors of the works had previously granted Random House — not Rosetta Books — the right to "print, publish and sell the work[s] in book form." Rosetta Books, on the other hand, claims it is not infringing upon the rights those authors gave Random House because the licensing agreements between the publisher and the author do not include a grant of digital or electronic rights. Relying on the language of the contracts and basic principles of contract interpretation, this Court finds that the right to "print, publish and sell the work[s] in book form" in the contracts at issue does not include the right to publish the works in the format that has come to be known as the "ebook." Accordingly, Random House's motion for a preliminary injunction is denied.

In the year 2000 and the beginning of 2001, Rosetta Books contracted with several authors to publish certain of their works — including The Confessions of Nat Turner and Sophie's Choice by William Styron; Slaughterhouse-Five, Breakfast of Champions, The Sirens of Titan, Cat's Cradle, and Player Piano by Kurt Vonnegut; and Promised Land by Robert B. Parker — in digital format over the internet. On February 26, 2001 Rosetta Books launched its ebook business, offering those titles and others for sale in digital format. The next day, Random House filed this complaint accusing Rosetta Books of committing copyright infringement and tortiously interfering with the contracts Random House had with Messrs. Parker, Styron and Vonnegut by selling its ebooks. It simultaneously moved for a preliminary injunction prohibiting Rosetta from infringing plaintiff's copyrights.

Ebooks are "digital book[s] that you can read on a computer screen or an electronic device." Ebooks are created by converting digitized text into a format readable by computer software. The text can be viewed on a desktop or laptop computer, personal digital assistant or handheld dedicated ebook reading device. Rosetta's ebooks can only be read after they are downloaded into a computer that contains either Microsoft Reader, Adobe Acrobat Reader, or Adobe Acrobat eBook Reader software....

While each agreement between the author and Random House differs in some respects, each uses the phrase "print, publish and sell the work in book form" to convey rights from the author to the publisher.

1. Styron Agreements

Forty years ago, in 1961, William Styron granted Random House the right to publish The Confessions of Nat Turner. Besides granting Random House an exclusive license to "print, publish and sell the work in book form," Styron also gave it the right to "license publication of the work by book clubs," "license publication of a reprint edition," "license after book publication the publication of the work, in whole or in part, in anthologies, school books," and other shortened forms, "license without charge publication of the work in Braille, or photographing, recording, and microfilming the work for the physically handicapped," and "publish or permit others to publish or broadcast by radio or television ... selections from the work, for publicity purposes...." ...

The publisher agreed in the contract to "publish the work at its own expense and in such style and manner and at such a price as it deems suitable." The contract also contains a non-compete clause that provides, in relevant part, that "the Author agrees that during the term of this agreement he will not, without the written permission of the Publisher, publish or permit to be published any material in book or pamphlet form, based on the material in the work, or which is reasonably likely to injure its sale." Styron's contract with Random House for the right to publish Sophie's Choice, executed in 1977, is virtually identical to his 1961 contract to publish The Confessions of Nat Turner.

2. Vonnegut Agreements

Kurt Vonnegut's 1967 contract granting Random House's predecessor-in-interest Dell Publishing Co., Inc. the license to publish Slaughterhouse-Five and Breakfast of Champions follows a similar structure to the Styron agreements. Paragraph # 1 is captioned "grant of rights" and contains those rights the author is granting to the book publisher. Certain rights on the publisher's form contract are crossed out, indicating that the author reserved them for himself. One of the rights granted by the author includes the "exclusive right to publish and to license the Work for publication, after book publication ... in anthologies, selections, digests, abridgements, magazine condensations, serialization, newspaper syndication, picture book versions, microfilming, Xerox and other forms of copying, either now in use or hereafter developed."

Vonnegut specifically reserved for himself the "dramatic ... motion picture (silent and sound) ... radio broadcasting (including mechanical renditions and /or recordings of the text) ... [and] television" rights. Unlike the Styron agreements, this contract does not contain a non-compete clause.

Vonnegut's 1970 contract granting Dell the license to publish The Sirens of Titan, Cat's Cradle, and Player Piano contains virtually identical grants and reservations of rights as his 1967 contract. However, it does contain a non-compete clause, which provides that "the Author ... will not publish or permit to be published any edition, adaptation or abridgment of the Work by any party other than Dell without Dell's prior written consent."

3. Parker Agreement

Robert B. Parker's 1982 contract granting Dell the license to publish Promised Land is similar to the 1970 Vonnegut contract. Paragraph # 1 contains the "grant of rights," certain of which have been crossed out by the author. The contract does grant Random House the right to "Xerox and other forms of copying of the printed page, either now in use or hereafter developed." Parker also reserved the rights to the "dramatic ... motion picture (silent and sound) ... radio broadcasting ... television ... mechanical or electronic recordings of the text...." There is also a non-compete clause that provides, in relevant part, that "the Author ... will not, without the written permission of Dell, publish or permit to be published any material based on the material in the Work, or which is reasonably likely to injure its sale." ...

Two elements must be proven in order to establish a prima facie case of infringement: "(1) ownership of a valid copyright, and (2) copying of constituent elements of the work that are original." In this case, only the first element—ownership of a valid copyright—is at issue, since all parties concede that the text of the ebook is identical to the text of the book published by Random House.

It is well settled that although the authors own the copyrights to their works, "the legal or beneficial owner of an exclusive right under a copyright is entitled ... to institute an action for any infringement of that particular right committed while he or she is the owner of it." 17 U.S.C. § 501. The question for resolution, therefore, is whether Random House is the beneficial owner of the right to publish these works as ebooks....

[T]his Court finds that the most reasonable interpretation of the grant in the contracts at issue to "print, publish and sell the work in book form" does not include the right to publish the work as an ebook. At the outset, the phrase itself distinguishes between the pure content—i.e. "the work"—and the format of display—"in book form." The Random House Webster's Unabridged Dictionary defines a "book" as "a written or printed work of fiction or nonfiction, usually on sheets of paper fastened or bound together within covers" and defines "form" as "external appearance of a clearly defined area, as distinguished from color or material; the shape of a thing or person."

Manifestly, paragraph # 1 of each contract—entitled either "grant of rights" or "exclusive publication right"—conveys certain rights from the author to the publisher. In that paragraph, separate grant language is used to convey the rights to publish book club editions, reprint editions, abridged forms, and editions in Braille. This language would not be necessary if the phrase "in book form" encompassed all types of books. That paragraph specifies exactly which rights were being granted by the author to the publisher. Indeed, many of the rights set forth in the publisher's form contracts were in fact not granted to the publisher, but rather were reserved by the authors to themselves. For example, each of the authors specifically reserved certain rights for themselves by striking out phrases, sentences, and paragraphs of the publisher's form contract. This evidences an intent by these authors not to grant the publisher the broadest rights in their works.

Random House contends that the phrase "in book form" means to faithfully reproduce the author's text in its complete form as a reading experience and that, since ebooks concededly contain the complete text of the work, Rosetta cannot also possess those rights. While Random House's definition distinguishes "book form" from other formats that require separate contractual language—such as audio books and serialization rights—it does not distinguish other formats specifically mentioned in paragraph # 1 of the contracts, such as book club editions and reprint editions. Because the Court must, if possible, give effect to all contractual language in order to "safeguard against adopting an interpretation that would render any individual provision superfluous," Random House's definition cannot be adopted.

Random House points specifically to the clause requiring it to "publish the work at its own expense and in such a style and manner and at such a price as [Random House] deems suitable" as support for its position. However, plaintiff takes this clause out of context. It appears in paragraph # 2, captioned "Style, Price and Date of Publication," not paragraph # 1, which includes all the grants of rights. In context, the phrase simply means that Random House has control over the appearance of the formats granted to Random House in the first paragraph; i.e., control over the style of the book.

Random House also cites the non-compete clauses as evidence that the authors granted it broad, exclusive rights in their work. Random House reasons that because the authors could not permit any material that would injure the sale of the work to be published without Random House's consent, the authors must have granted the right to publish ebooks to Random House. This reasoning turns the analysis on its head. First, the grant of rights follows from the grant language alone. Second, non-compete clauses must be limited in scope in order to be enforceable in New York. Third, even if the authors did violate this provision of their Random House agreements by contracting with Rosetta Books—a point on which this Court does not opine—the remedy is a breach of contract action against the authors, not a copyright infringement action against Rosetta Books.

The photocopy clause—giving Random House the right to "Xerox and other forms of copying, either now in use or hereafter developed"—similarly does not bolster Random House's position. Although the clause does appear in the grant language paragraph, taken in context, it clearly refers only to new developments in xerography and other forms of photocopying. Stretching it to include new forms of publishing, such as ebooks, would make the rest of the contract superfluous because there would be no reason for authors to reserve rights to forms of publishing "now in use." This interpretation also comports with the publishing industry's trade usage of the phrase.

Not only does the language of the contract itself lead almost ineluctably to the conclusion that Random House does not own the right to publish the works as ebooks, but also a reasonable person "cognizant of the customs, practices, usages and terminology as generally understood in the particular trade or business," would conclude that the grant language does not include ebooks. "To print, publish and sell the work in book form" is understood in the publishing industry to be a "limited" grant.... In fact, the publishing industry generally interprets the phrase "in book form" as granting the publisher "the exclusive right to publish a hardcover trade book in English for distribution in North America." 1 LINDEY ON ENTERTAINMENT, PUBLISHING AND THE ARTS FORM 1.01-1 (2d ed. 2000) (using the Random House form contract to explain the meaning of each clause).

3. Comparison to Prior "New Use" Caselaw

The finding that the five licensing agreements at issue do not convey the right to publish the works as ebooks accords with Second Circuit and New York case law. Indeed, the two leading cases limned above that found that a particular new use was included within the grant language — *Boosey* [*& Hawkes Music Publishers, Ltd. v. Walt Disney Co.*], 145 F.3d 481 (2d Cir. 1998), and *Bartsch* [*v. Metro-Goldwyn-Mayer, Inc.*], 391 F.2d 150 (2d Cir. 1968) — can be distinguished from this case on four grounds.

First, the language conveying the rights in *Boosey* and *Bartsch* was far broader than here. *See Boosey*, 145 F.3d at 486; *Bartsch*, 391 F.2d at 153. Second, the "new use" in those cases — i.e. display of a motion picture on television or videocassette — fell squarely within the same medium as the original grant. *See Boosey*, 145 F.3d at 486 (describing videocassettes and laser discs as "subsequently developed methods of distribution of a motion picture"); *Bourne* [*v. Walt Disney Co.*], 68 F.3d at 630 [(2d Cir. 1995)] ("The term 'motion picture' reasonably can be understood to refer to 'a broad genus whose fundamental characteristic is a series of related images that impart an impression of motion when shown in succession ... Under this concept the physical form in which the motion picture is fixed — film, tape, discs, and so forth — is irrelevant.'").

In this case, the "new use" — electronic digital signals sent over the internet — is a separate medium from the original use — printed words on paper. Random House's own expert concludes that the media are distinct because information stored digitally can be manipulated in ways that analog information cannot. Ebooks take advantage of the digital medium's ability to manipulate data by allowing ebook users to electronically search the text for specific words and phrases, change the font size and style, type notes into the text and electronically organize them, highlight and bookmark, hyperlink to specific parts of the text, and, in the future, to other sites on related topics as well, and access a dictionary that pronounces words in the ebook aloud. The need for a software program to interact with the data in order to make it usable, as well as the need for a piece of hardware to enable the reader to view the text, also distinguishes analog formats from digital formats. *See Greenberg v. National*

Geographic Soc'y, 244 F.3d 1267, 1273 n.12 (11th Cir. 2001) (Digital format is not analogous to reproducing the magazine in microfilm or microfiche because it "requires the interaction of a computer program in order to accomplish the useful reproduction involved with the new medium.")

Therefore, *Boosey* and *Bartsch*, which apply to new uses within the same medium, do not control this case. *See, e.g., Raine* [*v. CBS Inc.*], 25 F. Supp. 2d 434, 445 (S.D.N.Y. 1998) (finding that the right to "television broadcasts" did not include broadcasts on cable television or videocassettes); *General Mills, Inc. v. Filmtel Int'l Corp.*, 195 A.D.2d 251, 252, 599 N.Y.S.2d 820, 821–22 (1st Dep't 1993); *Tele-Pac, Inc. v. Grainger*, 168 A.D.2d 11, 570 N.Y.S.2d 521 (1st Dep't 1991) (distinguishing Second Circuit "new use" doctrine by holding that right to "broadcast[] by television or any other similar device now known or hereafter to be made known" was so dissimilar from display on videocassette and videodisc "as to preclude consideration of video rights as even falling within the 'ambiguous penumbra' of the terms used in the agreement").

The third significant difference between the licensee in the motion picture cases cited above and the book publisher in this action is that the licensees in the motion picture cases have actually created a new work based on the material from the licensor. Therefore, the right to display that new work—whether on television or video—is derivative of the right to create that work. In the book publishing context, the publishers, although they participate in the editorial process, display the words written by the author, not themselves.

Fourth, the courts in *Boosey* and *Bartsch* were concerned that any approach to new use problems that "tilts against licensees [here, Random House] gives rise to antiprogressive incentives" insofar as licensees "would be reluctant to explore and utilize innovative technologies." However, in this action, the policy rationale of encouraging development in new technology is at least as well served by finding that the licensors—i.e., the authors—retain these rights to their works. In the 21st century, it cannot be said that licensees such as book publishers and movie producers are ipso facto more likely to make advances in digital technology than start-up companies....

In *Dresser v. William Morrow & Co.*, 278 A.D. 931, 105 N.Y.S.2d 706 (1st Dep't 1951), aff'd 304 N.Y. 603, 107 N.E.2d 89 (N.Y. 1952), the issue was whether an author could receive additional payments for reprint editions of his book when his publishing contract only provided for an "outright fixed payment." The *Dresser* court found that, under the terms of the contract, he could not. The court relied on the fact that the contract was "at variance with the usual pattern of contracts between author and publisher." Here, although each contract is slightly different, none varies greatly from the usual pattern of contracts between author and publisher; therefore, there is no reason to depart from the usual meaning of such contracts....

HarperCollins Publishers L.L.C. v.
Open Road Integrated Media, L.L.P.

7 F. Supp. 3d 363 (S.D.N.Y. 2014)

Plaintiff HarperCollins Publishers L.L.C. ("HarperCollins") brings this action against defendant Open Road Integrated Media, LLP ("Open Road"), alleging willful infringement of HarperCollins' rights under federal copyright law to the well-known children's novel Julie of the Wolves. Open Road, a digital publisher who has issued an e-book version of Julie of the Wolves, counters that the operative contract, signed in 1971, does not convey exclusive electronic publication rights to HarperCollins. Now pending before the Court are the parties' cross-motions for summary judgment. For the reasons stated herein, this Court grants plaintiff's motion and denies defendant's motion.

BACKGROUND

I. Factual Allegations

The present dispute arises out of a publishing agreement (hereafter the "contract" or the "agreement") executed on April 13, 1971 by the author Jean George and the publishing house Harper & Row, plaintiff's predecessor in interest, which, broadly speaking, gave plaintiff the right to publish George's children's novel Julie of the Wolves. The novel was first published in hardcover format by Harper & Row in 1972. It won the Newbury Medal in 1973 for the most distinguished contribution to children's literature and was a finalist for the 1973 National Book Award. Between 1972 and December 2011, HarperCollins sold more than 3.8 million units of the novel in hardcover and paperback, among other formats. Then and in the years since, Julie of the Wolves has been considered a celebrated title in children's literature.

By the 1971 contract, Ms. George conveyed publishing rights to HarperCollins to publish Julie of the Wolves in exchange for a $2,000 advance and royalty payments of between ten and fifteen percent, depending on number of copies sold. The contract contemplated the sale of paperback editions ("cheap edition") but did not specify the royalty rate for paperbacks, instead indicating that the publisher would pay a paperback royalty "to be mutually agreed."

The contract contains several clauses critical to the outcome of this suit. Paragraph 1 of the agreement grants to HarperCollins "the exclusive right to publish" Julie of the Wolves "in book form" in the English language and within specified territory. In addition to this broad grant language, the contract provided in a paragraph entitled "Disposition of Subsidiary Rights" that "[i]t is understood and agreed that the Publisher shall have the exclusive right to sell, lease or make other disposition of the subsidiary rights in which he has an interest under the terms of clause (subject to the 'consultation' provision in 7f) 19 and 20."

Paragraph 20, in turn, makes the following provision:

> Anything to the contrary herein notwithstanding, the Publisher shall grant
> no license without the prior written consent of the Author with respect to

the following rights in the work: *use thereof in storage and retrieval and information systems, and/or whether through computer, computer-stored, mechanical or other electronic means now known or hereafter invented* and ephemeral screen flashing or reproduction thereof, whether by print-out, phot [o] reproduction or photo copy, including punch cards, microfilm, magnetic tapes or like processes attaining similar results, and net proceeds thereof shall be divided 50% to the Author and 50% to the Publisher. However, such license shall not be deemed keeping the work in print once the work has gone out of print in all editions" (emphasis added).

This clause was inserted at the request of Ms. George's literary agency, Curtis Brown, which negotiated the contract on the author's behalf....

In addition to these critical clauses, the contract also contained other paragraphs pertinent to this action, including Paragraph 19, which gave the Publisher the right "to reprint the said Work in whole or in part in the form of excerpts, digests and selections in one or more issues of a newspaper, magazine, book or anthology," with revenues generally divided evenly between author and publisher. The contract also contained a "Reserved Rights" clause that reserved to the author "[a]ll rights in the Work now existing, or which may hereafter come into existence, not specifically herein granted," including motion picture rights. The contract provided for a New York choice of law.

In the decades that followed, the parties apparently coordinated with regard to the use of the work by third parties in electronic formats. Repeatedly in recent years, HarperCollins forwarded requests to Ms. George "[p]er our agreement," to use text from Julie of the Wolves in CD-Roms, online teaching materials, online examination materials and the like, including in August 1998 a request to include Julie of the Wolves in a test of an early e-book reading device. The record before us indicates that Ms. George generally agreed to these requests, sometimes after negotiating a more favorable royalty. The parties disagree, however, on the implication to be taken from these communications regarding third-party uses. HarperCollins asserts that this course of performance was undertaken pursuant to the requirements of Paragraph 20. Open Road contends that these uses fell under the "permissions" provision set forth in Paragraph 19; and further notes that Ms. George unilaterally granted electronic rights to the Work without HarperCollins's involvement (but apparently also without HarperCollins knowledge or consent).

The events immediately precipitating this lawsuit began in 2010, nearly forty years after the execution of the operative contract, at which point the publishing world featured an e-book market....

In 2010, Open Road approached Ms. George's literary agent Curtis Brown with a proposal to publish an e-book edition of Julie of the Wolves in exchange for a 50% royalty to Ms. George. Preferring initially to pursue an e-book publication with her longtime publisher HarperCollins, Ms. George authorized her agent to contact HarperCollins and suggest the e-book publication, with the proviso that HarperCollins match Open Road's 50% royalty offer. HarperCollins expressed interest in electronic publication; however, they counter-offered only a 25% royalty. Dissatisfied with that offer and expressing her belief that she—not HarperCollins—owned the e-book rights, Ms. George instead contracted in April 2011 with Open Road to publish Julie of the Wolves as an e-book. Before doing so, Ms. George entered an agreement with Open Road, by which the electronic publisher agreed to indemnify Ms. George in the event HarperCollins asserted a claim against the author. Open Road subsequently distributed Julie of the Wolves as an e-book via a number of distribution channels; between October 2011 and March 2012, approximately 1,600 such e-book copies were sold.

Plaintiff HarperCollins filed suit against Open Road on December 23, 2011, alleging willful copyright infringement in violation of 17 U.S.C. § 106 and seeking injunctive relief, statutory or actual damages at its election, and the recovery of Open Road's profits and HarperCollins' costs. Defendant answered on February 16, 2012 and discovery followed. After briefing of the instant cross-motions was completed, oral argument was held on January 30, 2014.

DISCUSSION

...

III. Principles of Contract Interpretation in the Copyright Context

To maintain an action for copyright infringement, plaintiff must establish two elements: "(1) ownership of a valid copyright, and (2) copying of constituent elements of the work that are original." In the case sub judice, the parties dispute only the first element—that is, whether HarperCollins' uncontested publication rights to Julie of the Wolves encompass the exclusive right to publish and license e-book versions of the work. Copyright infringement actions such as this "involving only the scope of the alleged infringer's license present the court with a question that essentially is one of contract: whether the parties' license agreement encompasses the [relevant] activities." *Bourne v. Walt Disney Co.*, 68 F.3d 621, 631 (2d Cir.1995). This case thus turns on the construction of the governing 1971 contract between author Jean George and publisher HarperCollins.

Pursuant to New York law, the interpretation of an unambiguous contract is a question of law to be addressed by the Court. So too is the determination of whether a contract provision is in fact ambiguous. A contract is ambiguous only if "the provisions in controversy are reasonably or fairly susceptible of different interpretations or may have two or more different meanings." *Goldman Sachs Grp., Inc. v. Almah L.L.C.*, 85 A.D.3d 424, 924 N.Y.S.2d 87, 90 (1st Dep't 2011) (internal citation and quotation marks omitted)....

IV. New Use Precedent

In accord with these principles of contract construction, the Second Circuit's "new use" precedent sets forth a procedure for evaluating whether a contract covers later-developed technology. This Court is guided by several leading cases, including *Bartsch v. Metro-Goldwyn-Mayer, Inc.*, 391 F.2d 150 (2d Cir.1968), *Bourne v. Walt Disney Co.*,

68 F.3d 621 (2d Cir.1995), and *Boosey & Hawkes Music Publishers, Ltd. v. Walt Disney Co.*, 145 F.3d 481 (2d Cir.1998), all of which arise in the context of the motion picture industry. Bartsch posed the question of whether an earlier grant of motion picture rights to a play also comprised the right to broadcast that movie on television 28 years later. Bourne and Boosey considered whether the holder of a license to use a piece of music in a motion picture also had the right to use the music in distribution of the movie via videocassette over forty years later. In these three cases, all of which evaluated contracts pursuant to New York law, the initial grant language was found to encompass the later-developed new use.

In a "new use" case, the Court must determine whether the new use "may reasonably be said to fall within the medium as described in the license." *Bartsch*, 391 F.2d at 155. The key interpretive principle to be applied is that the language of the contract itself governs.

In construing the scope of the contractual grant, the Court must apply "neutral principles of contract interpretation" and avoid any "default rule in favor of copyright licensees or any default rule whatsoever." As the Second Circuit instructs, "[i]f the contract is more reasonably read to convey one meaning, the party benefitted by that reading should be able to rely on it; the party seeking exception or deviation from the meaning reasonably conveyed by the words of the contract should bear the burden of negotiating for language that would express the limitation or deviation." *Id....*

Thus, the leading cases discussed here placed primary emphasis on the contractual language. They also considered the "foreseeability" of the new use at the time of contracting, and found, respectively, that "future possibilities of television were recognized by knowledgeable people in the entertainment and motion picture industries," *Bartsch*, 391 F.2d at 154; that "home viewing of motion pictures was within the contemplation of persons in the motion picture industry," *Bourne*, 68 F.3d at 630; and that "a nascent market for home viewing" existed at the time of contracting. *Boosey*, 145 F.3d at 486. Notably, however, and contrary to defendant's contention, the case law did not explicitly treat "foreseeability" of the new use at the time of contract as a sine qua non. Instead, whether foreseeability is required remains an open question.

V. Application

...

Based on a plain reading of the contractual language, we hold that the 1971 contract grants HarperCollins the exclusive right to license third parties to publish e-book versions of Julie of the Wolves. This determination follows from the contract as a whole, and chiefly from Paragraphs 1, 20 and 23.

A. Paragraph 1

Paragraph 1 conveyed to HarperCollins "the exclusive right to publish [Julie of the Wolves] ... in book form." Relying heavily on prior precedent from this district, Open Road argues that this language cannot possibly extend to e-book publication rights. However, the operative contract here differs significantly from its counterpart in Rosetta Books, which was held to be limited to paper book publication. In the instant case, the governing grant conveys the right "to publish ... in book form," whereas in Rosetta Books, the grant was one "to print, publish and sell." As was explicitly argued in the earlier case, the inclusion of the word "print" has a limiting effect and a strong connotation of paper copy. The word "print" is absent from the 1971 contract governing here, thereby distinguishing the case at bar from Rosetta Books.

Nonetheless, given that we must interpret the contract as a whole, we need not reach the issue of whether Paragraph 1 standing alone is sufficient to convey e-book publication rights. With that precept in mind, we turn next to evaluate Paragraph 20, which, by explicitly granting HarperCollins certain rights associated with use by "electronic means," created a critical distinction from Rosetta Books, whose contract made no mention of electronic exploitation at all.

B. Paragraph 20

Paragraph 20, supported by the grant provision in Paragraph 23, enables Harper-Collins to issue licenses, subject to the author's permission, to use the work in "in storage and retrieval and information systems, and/or whether through computer, computer-stored, mechanical or other electronic means now known or hereafter invented." This language, encompassing as it does the forward-looking reference to technologies "now known or hereafter invented," is sufficiently broad to draw within its ambit e-book publication. Although no commercial market for e-books existed at the time of its drafting, e-book technology comprises a later-invented version of the very "computer, computer-stored, mechanical or other electronic means" provided by Paragraph 20.

In light of precedent indicating that broad grant language will extend to later-invented uses, e-book publication "may reasonably be said to fall within the medium as described in the license." *Bartsch*, 391 F.2d at 155. Our conclusion that e-books constitute a permissible new use follows both from the expansive contractual language and from the lens through which the Second Circuit directs us to construe it. The applicable Second Circuit precedent cautions courts not to limit new uses to those that "fall within the unambiguous core meaning of the term" provided by the contract. Rather, the e-book format constitutes a permissible extension of "book form" via "storage and retrieval and information systems, and/or whether through computer, computer-stored, mechanical or other electronic means" just as the television broadcast of a movie and the videocassette constituted a lawful extension of the motion picture form in *Bartsch* and *Boosey*, respectively....

By specifically providing for anticipated electronic means that might be "hereafter invented," the 1971 contract's grant language becomes greater in breadth, at least with respect to new uses, than the analogous contracts in Second Circuit new use precedent, which were themselves found sufficiently broad to encompass an electronic new use. . . .

Indeed, apparently recognizing the breadth of the language in Paragraph 20, Open Road's briefing largely ignored it. Instead, Open Road attempted to redirect the Court's attention to Paragraph 1 and to the Rosetta Books precedent, which, as discussed above, did not directly address the issues present here. To the extent that Open Road did grapple with the implications of Paragraph 20, its strategy has been to attempt to rewrite the provision. Specifically, Open Road entreats the Court to disregard the "and/or" language, thereby converting the latter clause from an independent to a dependent one as follows: "in storage and retrieval and information systems, [and/or] whether through computer, computer-stored, mechanical or other electronic means now known or hereafter invented." In support of this proposed ex post revision, Open Road argues that the "and/or" is "syntactically awkward," that it constitutes an "unnecessary insertion," that it would create meaningless surplusage, and that it would lead to an "absurd result."

Defendant's request to rewrite the contract is at variance with the generally-applied "heavy presumption that a deliberately prepared and executed written instrument manifest[s] the true intention of the parties," and is further unsupported by the "correspondingly high order of evidence [that] is required to overcome that presumption ... show[ing] in no uncertain terms, not only that mistake or fraud exists, but exactly what was really agreed upon between the parties." *Chimart Assocs. v. Paul*, 66 N.Y.2d 570, 498 N.Y.S.2d 344, 489 N.E.2d 231, 234 (1986) (internal quotations and citations omitted). The case law is clear that "the burden of justifying a departure from the most reasonable reading of the contract should fall on the party advocating the departure." *Boosey*, 145 F.3d at 488. Notwithstanding its arguments to the contrary, Open Road has failed to carry that burden. The request is particularly unwarranted in a new use context, where, given the age of the contract at issue, extrinsic evidence is scarce and thus "the parties or assignees of the contract should be entitled to rely on the words of the contract."

Also undermining defendant's argument is the plain fact that the language of Paragraph 20 was inserted verbatim into the contract at the request of Ms. George's agent, a circumstance that defendant tries in vain to reconcile with its litigation position. As a matter of neutral contract interpretation, "New York follows the well established *contra proferentem* principle which requires that equivocal contract provisions are generally to be construed against the drafter." *McCarthy v. Am. Int'l Grp., Inc.*, 283 F.3d 121, 124 (2d Cir.2002). Here, we need not even resort to the use of contra proferentem, because the "and/or" language is not, in the context of this contract, equivocal.

Finally, it is worth noting that, even if the Court were to adopt Open Road's deletion of the "and/or" conjunctive, it is far from clear that this revision would support Open Road's overall position. Given the record before us, this Court finds it plausible that Paragraph 20's "storage and retrieval and information systems" could, pursuant to new use precedent, encompass today's e-book technology. Nevertheless, having found no basis for removing the "and/or" language, we deem it unnecessary to undertake this inquiry or adjudicate the merits of the copious, competing expert material presented on the precise definitional scope of "storage and retrieval and information systems." ...

D. Foreseeability

...

To the extent that foreseeability at the time of the grant is required to extend a copyright to a new use, however, the language of the contract itself provided for foreseeable uses. The reference to electronic means "now known or hereafter invented" anticipated future technological uses for the work, which would one day include e-books. By this logic, the contract here may be said to fulfill the foreseeability standard, to the extent it exists, even without reference to the record evidence. *See, e.g., Reinhardt v. Wal-Mart Stores, Inc.*, 547 F.Supp.2d 346, 354–55 (S.D.N.Y.2008) ("The phrase 'now or hereafter known,' when referring to forms of reproduction, reveals that future technologies are covered by the agreement.... This unambiguous language [inter alia] forecloses other interpretations and the need to consider extrinsic evidence.").

Even if foreseeability were a requirement not satisfied by the contractual language, the record before us, particularly in the context of the new use precedent, would support our decision. Although no commercial e-book market existed at the time of the grant, knowledgeable industry members seem to have contemplated electronic or computer-assisted delivery of book text in much the same way that knowledgeable members of the motion picture industry could contemplate television broadcasts and videocassettes at the time of contracting in *Bartsch, Bourne,* and *Boosey.* Recall too that in those precedential cases, the Circuit did not require that industry participants foresee with specificity actual videocassette technology, for example. Rather, the Courts merely noted that, when the contracts at issue were drafted, industry participants recognized the possibility of a "home viewing" market. If videocassettes can be said to have been in contemplation of members of the motion picture industry in the 1930s, it follows a fortiori that the same can be said for e-books at the time of the 1971 contract. Open Road seemed almost to concede as much at oral argument, indicating that industry participants drafted Paragraph 20 and similar clauses elsewhere against the backdrop of contemporaneous university initiatives "digitizing the libraries, putting on electronic databases [of] books." ...

CONCLUSION

For the foregoing reasons, plaintiff's motion for summary judgment is granted and defendant's cross-motion is denied.

Notes and Questions

a. The common practice in publishing is to allow the publishing rights to revert to the author after the book has gone out of print. In addition to the technical issues involving the concept that a book may no longer ever be out of print due to ebooks and on-demand printing facilities, standard contracts may fail to address the disposition of income received after the date of the reversion based on license agreements entered into prior to the date of reversion. The rights to those proceeds can be extensive if the license is for adaptation into new media.

b. Remedies for breach of contract may have some interesting termination issues. *See Frankel v. Stein & Day Inc.*, 1980 U.S. Dist. LEXIS 11510 (S.D.N.Y. Apr. 24, 1980) (allowing the publisher to retain a one-third interest in license income despite a revision caused by the publisher's breach of contract).

c. How could a publisher today guard against the publisher's fate in *Random House, Inc. v. Rosetta Books L.L.C.*? Is there any contract language that could prevent technological advances from terminating the publisher's copyright? What is the proper balance between the author, publisher, and society?

d. To better understand the economics of the publishing industry, the Court in *Health Communs., Inc. v. Chicken Soup for the Soul Publ'g, L.L.C.*, 2009 Conn. Super. LEXIS 337 (Super. Ct. Feb. 6, 2009) provided a helpful summary of publishing economics:

> [I]t helps to become familiar with what constitutes a "front list" book, and what is a "backlist" book.[11] These concepts are known and used in both the publishing industry in general, and also by these parties in particular. The front list and the backlist must be viewed and analyzed two ways: both in the realities of the Chicken Soup series in the book publishing marketplace, and in the often ambiguous or imprecisely drafted definitions and terms of the various contracts between the parties the court is called upon to construe here.
>
> Front list and backlist are the shorthand terms used in the industry to distinguish the lists of book titles offered for sale each year by any given publisher. A series of newly published books offered for sale to the public each year is known as a publisher's "front list." By contrast, a publisher's "backlist" refers to older books from past seasons still in print; that is, they are books that are yet available for purchase through the publisher, if not always currently stocked in bookstores. Both newly published books (the front list) and older books still in print (the backlist) that are sold by a publisher are known and referenced in the book trade in this fashion. As time goes by, the books on a publisher's front list eventually turn into (and add to the inventory of) a publisher's backlist. Like any other property rights that are alienable pursuant to contract, the court notes that it is not unheard of in the publishing industry for the rights to the backlist and the rights to the front list of a particular book series to be owned by two different companies, as is now the situation in this case.

---

11. Unlike "backlist," accepted English usage requires that "front list" be spelled as two words.

These sales and marketing terms—front list and backlist—are widely used in the book publishing world, and were the subject of testimony by most, if not all, witnesses for both parties at the hearing on this matter. It was covered by extensive (if not exhaustive) questioning by all counsel, both on direct and in cross examination. As to the backlist, the court finds that it is a property interest with somewhat less market value in terms of current sales than the front list catalog. This would seem to be true even with a normal or more typical book cycle, one considered in the absence of litigation such as now clouds the Chicken Soup brand. Backlist titles, by their nature of being on the backlist and with an older date of original publication, are less subject to the current marketing and promotional efforts of a party.

e. The controversy surrounding the *Chicken Soup* book series was likely triggered by too much success rather than too little. Often parties focus too much on the terms for cementing the relationship and too little on the consequences of the post-termination relationships. If a publishing agreement includes a termination provision based on a term of years rather than merely based on the book going out of print, how should the parties treat the rights following publication? *See Health Communs., Inc. v. Chicken Soup for the Soul Publ'g, L.L.C.,* 2009 Conn. Super. LEXIS 337 (Conn. Super. Ct. Feb. 6, 2009).

Problem 17-C

Bryce and Jesse are continuing to work on the coffee table photo-exposé. (*See* Problem 17-B.) Bryce and Jesse understand that this book will not be sold in stores for more than one or two years. If the book somehow becomes popular, there is the opportunity for sequels and updates, but neither Bryce nor Jesse expects this to happen.

Bryce, however, believes that once the book has run its initial course, the material could lend itself very well to a website-based literary project. At the very least, Bryce wants to post the contents of the book on the Internet. Bryce hopes the posting will grow into a viral editing project[12] that will greatly increase exposure for the writers. Bryce also believes posting the book's content online might create a new market for sales of the printed book.

Bryce and Jesse want the opportunity to recapture the rights to the book so that they can create the website marketing. Advise Bryce and Jesse as to what contractual provisions should be in the final agreement to best reflect their interests in a manner that will be acceptable to their publisher.

---

12. By viral, Bryce means a self-propagating editorial project in which the viewers of the work are able to add content and promote the work. *See* Wikipedia.org for an example of the largest viral encyclopedia. ("Wikipedia is a multilingual project to create an accurate and comprehensive free-content encyclopedia.")

D. Ownership of Editorial Content

N.Y. Times Co. v. Tasini

533 U.S. 483 (2001)

JUSTICE GINSBURG delivered the opinion of the Court.

This copyright case concerns the rights of freelance authors and a presumptive privilege of their publishers. The litigation was initiated by six freelance authors and relates to articles they contributed to three print periodicals (two newspapers and one magazine). Under agreements with the periodicals' publishers, but without the freelancers' consent, two computer database companies placed copies of the freelancers' articles—along with all other articles from the periodicals in which the freelancers' work appeared—into three databases. Whether written by a freelancer or staff member, each article is presented to, and retrievable by, the user in isolation, clear of the context the original print publication presented.

The freelance authors' complaint alleged that their copyrights had been infringed by the inclusion of their articles in the databases. The publishers, in response, relied on the privilege of reproduction and distribution accorded them by §201(c) of the Copyright Act, which provides:

> "Copyright in each separate contribution to a collective work is distinct from copyright in the collective work as a whole, and vests initially in the author of the contribution. In the absence of an express transfer of the copyright or of any rights under it, the owner of copyright in the collective work is presumed to have acquired only the privilege of reproducing and distributing the contribution as part of that particular collective work, any revision of that collective work, and any later collective work in the same series."

Specifically, the publishers maintained that, as copyright owners of collective works, *i.e.*, the original print publications, they had merely exercised "the privilege" §201(c) accords them to "reproduce and distribute" the author's discretely copyrighted contribution.

In agreement with the Second Circuit, we hold that §201(c) does not authorize the copying at issue here. The publishers are not sheltered by §201(c), we conclude, because the databases reproduce and distribute articles standing alone and not in context, not "as part of that particular collective work" to which the author contributed, "as part of ... any revision" thereof, or "as part of ... any later collective work in the same series." Both the print publishers and the electronic publishers, we rule, have infringed the copyrights of the freelance authors.

Respondents Jonathan Tasini, Mary Kay Blakely, Barbara Garson, Margot Mifflin, Sonia Jaffe Robbins, and David S. Whitford are authors (Authors). Between 1990 and 1993, they wrote the 21 articles (Articles) on which this dispute centers.... The Authors registered copyrights in each of the Articles. The Times, Newsday, and Time

(Print Publishers) registered collective work copyrights in each periodical edition in which an Article originally appeared. The Print Publishers engaged the Authors as independent contractors (freelancers) under contracts that in no instance secured consent from an Author to placement of an Article in an electronic database.

At the time the Articles were published, all three Print Publishers had agreements with petitioner LEXIS/NEXIS (formerly Mead Data Central Corp.), owner and operator of NEXIS, a computerized database that stores information in a text-only format. NEXIS contains articles from hundreds of journals (newspapers and periodicals) spanning many years. The Print Publishers have licensed to LEXIS/NEXIS the text of articles appearing in the three periodicals. The licenses authorize LEXIS/NEXIS to copy and sell any portion of those texts.

Pursuant to the licensing agreements, the Print Publishers regularly provide LEXIS/NEXIS with a batch of all the articles published in each periodical edition. The Print Publisher codes each article to facilitate computerized retrieval, then transmits it in a separate file. After further coding, LEXIS/NEXIS places the article in the central discs of its database.

Subscribers to NEXIS, accessing the system through a computer, may search for articles by author, subject, date, publication, headline, key term, words in text, or other criteria.

On December 16, 1993, the Authors filed this civil action in the United States District Court for the Southern District of New York. The Authors alleged that their copyrights were infringed when, as permitted and facilitated by the Print Publishers, LEXIS/NEXIS and UMI (Electronic Publishers) placed the Articles in the NEXIS, NYTO, and GPO databases (Databases). The Authors sought declaratory and injunctive relief, and damages. In response to the Authors' complaint, the Print and Electronic Publishers raised the reproduction and distribution privilege accorded collective work copyright owners by 17 U.S.C. § 201(c). After discovery, both sides moved for summary judgment.

Under the Copyright Act, as amended in 1976, "copyright protection subsists ... in original works of authorship fixed in any tangible medium of expression ... from which they can be perceived, reproduced, or otherwise communicated." 17 U.S.C. § 102(a). When, as in this case, a freelance author has contributed an article to a "collective work" such as a newspaper or magazine, the statute recognizes two distinct copyrighted works: "Copyright in *each separate contribution to a collective work* is distinct from copyright in *the collective work as a whole....*" § 201(c) (emphasis added). Copyright in the separate contribution "vests initially in the author of the contribution" (here, the freelancer). Copyright in the collective work vests in the collective author (here, the newspaper or magazine publisher) and extends only to the creative material contributed by that author, not to "the preexisting material employed in the work," § 103(b).

Prior to the 1976 revision ... authors risked losing their rights when they placed an article in a collective work. Pre-1976 copyright law recognized a freelance author's copyright in a published article only when the article was printed with a copyright notice in the author's name. When publishers, exercising their superior bargaining power over authors, declined to print notices in each contributor's name, the author's copyright was put in jeopardy. The author did not have the option to assign only the right of publication in the periodical; such a partial assignment was blocked by the doctrine of copyright "indivisibility." Thus, when a copyright notice appeared only in the publisher's name, the author's work would fall into the public domain, unless the author's copyright, in its entirety, had passed to the publisher. Such complete transfer might be accomplished by a contract, perhaps one with a provision, not easily enforced, for later retransfer of rights back to the author. Or, absent a specific contract, a court might find that an author had tacitly transferred the entire copyright to a publisher, in turn deemed to hold the copyright in "trust" for the author's benefit.

In the 1976 revision, Congress acted to "clarify and improve [this] confused and frequently unfair legal situation with respect to rights in contributions." The 1976 Act rejected the doctrine of indivisibility, recasting the copyright as a bundle of discrete "exclusive rights," each of which "may be transferred ... and owned separately." Congress also provided, in § 404(a), that "a single notice applicable to the collective work as a whole is sufficient" to protect the rights of freelance contributors. And in § 201(c), Congress codified the discrete domains of "copyright in each separate contribution to a collective work" and "copyright in the collective work as a whole." Together, § 404(a) and § 201(c) "preserve the author's copyright in a contribution even if the contribution does not bear a separate notice in the author's name, and without requiring any unqualified transfer of rights to the owner of the collective work."

Section 201(c) both describes and circumscribes the "privilege" a publisher acquires regarding an author's contribution to a collective work:

> "In the absence of an express transfer of the copyright or of any rights under it, the owner of copyright in the collective work is presumed to have acquired *only* the privilege of reproducing and distributing the contribution as part of that particular collective work, any revision of that collective work, and any later collective work in the same series" (emphasis added).

A newspaper or magazine publisher is thus privileged to reproduce or distribute an article contributed by a freelance author, absent a contract otherwise providing, only "as part of" any (or all) of three categories of collective works: (a) "that collective work" to which the author contributed her work, (b) "any revision of that collective work," or (c) "any later collective work in the same series." In accord with Congress' prescription, a "publishing company could reprint a contribution from one issue in a later issue of its magazine, and could reprint an article from a 1980 edition of an encyclopedia in a 1990 revision of it; the publisher could not revise the contribution itself or include it in a new anthology or an entirely different magazine or other collective work."

Essentially, § 201(c) adjusts a publisher's copyright in its collective work to accommodate a freelancer's copyright in her contribution. If there is demand for a freelance article standing alone or in a new collection, the Copyright Act allows the freelancer to benefit from that demand; after authorizing initial publication, the freelancer may also sell the article to others. It would scarcely "preserve the author's copyright in a contribution" as contemplated by Congress, if a newspaper or magazine publisher were permitted to reproduce or distribute copies of the author's contribution in isolation or within new collective works.

In the instant case, the Authors wrote several Articles and gave the Print Publishers permission to publish the Articles in certain newspapers and magazines. It is undisputed that the Authors hold copyrights and, therefore, exclusive rights in the Articles.[13] It is clear, moreover, that the Print and Electronic Publishers have exercised at least some rights that § 106 initially assigns exclusively to the Authors: LEXIS/ NEXIS' central discs and UMI's CD-ROMs "reproduce ... copies" of the Articles, § 106(1); UMI, by selling those CD-ROMs, and LEXIS/NEXIS, by selling copies of the Articles through the NEXIS Database, "distribute copies" of the Articles "to the public by sale," § 106(3); and the Print Publishers, through contracts licensing the production of copies in the Databases, "authorize" reproduction and distribution of the Articles, § 106.

Against the Authors' charge of infringement, the Publishers do not here contend the Authors entered into an agreement authorizing reproduction of the Articles in the Databases. Nor do they assert that the copies in the Databases represent "fair use" of the Authors' Articles. Instead, the Publishers rest entirely on the privilege described in § 201(c). Each discrete edition of the periodicals in which the Articles appeared is a "collective work," the Publishers agree. They contend, however, that reproduction and distribution of each Article by the Databases lie within the "privilege of reproducing and distributing the [Articles] as part of ... [a] revision of that collective work," § 201(c). The Publishers' encompassing construction of the § 201(c) privilege is unacceptable, we conclude, for it would diminish the Authors' exclusive rights in the Articles.

In determining whether the Articles have been reproduced and distributed "as part of" a "revision" of the collective works in issue, we focus on the Articles as presented to, and perceptible by, the user of the Databases. In this case, the three Databases present articles to users clear of the context provided either by the original periodical editions or by any revision of those editions.... One might view the articles as parts of a new compendium—namely, the entirety of works in the Database. In that compendium, each edition of each periodical represents only a miniscule fraction of the ever-expanding Database. The Database no more constitutes a "revision" of each constituent edition than a 400-page novel quoting a sonnet in passing would represent a "revision" of that poem. "Revision" denotes a new "version," and a version is, in this setting, a "distinct form of something regarded by its creators or others as one

13. The Publishers do not claim that the Articles are "works made for hire." 17 U.S.C. § 201(b). As to such works, the employer or person for whom a work was prepared is treated as the author. The Print Publishers, however, neither engaged the Authors to write the Articles as "employees" nor "commissioned" the Articles through "a written instrument signed by [both parties]" indicating that the Articles shall be considered "work[s] made for hire."

work." The massive whole of the Database is not recognizable as a new version of its every small part.

Alternatively, one could view the Articles in the Databases "as part of" no larger work at all, but simply as individual articles presented individually. That each article bears marks of its origin in a particular periodical (less vivid marks in NEXIS and NYTO, more vivid marks in GPO) suggests the article was previously part of that periodical. But the markings do not mean the article is currently reproduced or distributed as part of the periodical. The Databases' reproduction and distribution of individual Articles — simply as individual Articles — would invade the core of the Authors' exclusive rights under § 106.

The Publishers press an analogy between the Databases, on the one hand, and microfilm and microfiche, on the other. We find the analogy wanting. Microforms typically contain continuous photographic reproductions of a periodical in the medium of miniaturized film. Accordingly, articles appear on the microforms, writ very small, in precisely the position in which the articles appeared in the newspaper. The Times, for example, printed the beginning of Blakely's "Remembering Jane" Article on page 26 of the Magazine in the September 23, 1990, edition; the microfilm version of the Times reproduces that same Article on film in the very same position, within a film reproduction of the entire Magazine, in turn within a reproduction of the entire September 23, 1990, edition. True, the microfilm roll contains multiple editions, and the microfilm user can adjust the machine lens to focus only on the Article, to the exclusion of surrounding material. Nonetheless, the user first encounters the Article in context. In the Databases, by contrast, the Articles appear disconnected from their original context. In NEXIS and NYTO, the user sees the "Jane" Article apart even from the remainder of page 26. In GPO, the user sees the Article within the context of page 26, but clear of the context of page 25 or page 27, the rest of the Magazine, or the remainder of the day's newspaper. In short, unlike microforms, the Databases do not perceptibly reproduce articles as part of the collective work to which the author contributed or as part of any "revision" thereof.

Invoking the concept of "media neutrality," the Publishers urge that the "transfer of a work between media" does not "alter the character of" that work for copyright purposes. That is indeed true. But unlike the conversion of newsprint to microfilm, the transfer of articles to the Databases does not represent a mere conversion of intact periodicals (or revisions of periodicals) from one medium to another. The Databases offer users individual articles, not intact periodicals. In this case, media neutrality should protect the Authors' rights in the individual Articles to the extent those Articles are now presented individually, outside the collective work context, within the Databases' new media.

The dissenting opinion apparently concludes that, under the banner of "media-neutrality," a copy of a collective work, even when considerably changed, must constitute a "revision" of that collective work so long as the changes were "necessitated by … the medium." We lack the dissent's confidence that the current form of the Databases is entirely attributable to the nature of the electronic media, rather than the nature of the economic market served by the Databases. In any case, we see no grounding in § 201(c) for a "medium-driven" necessity defense to the Authors' infringement claims. Furthermore, it bears reminder here and throughout that these Publishers and all others can protect their interests by private contractual arrangement....

The Publishers warn that a ruling for the Authors will have "devastating" consequences. The Databases, the Publishers note, provide easy access to complete newspaper texts going back decades. A ruling for the Authors, the Publishers suggest, will punch gaping holes in the electronic record of history.... Notwithstanding the dire predictions from some quarters, it hardly follows from today's decision that an injunction against the inclusion of these Articles in the Databases (much less all freelance articles in any databases) must issue. The parties (Authors and Publishers) may enter into an agreement allowing continued electronic reproduction of the Authors' works; they, and if necessary the courts and Congress, may draw on numerous models for distributing copyrighted works and remunerating authors for their distribution. In any event, speculation about future harms is no basis for this Court to shrink authorial rights Congress established in § 201(c). Agreeing with the Court of Appeals that the Publishers are liable for infringement, we leave remedial issues open for initial airing and decision in the District Court.

We conclude that the Electronic Publishers infringed the Authors' copyrights by reproducing and distributing the Articles in a manner not authorized by the Authors and not privileged by § 201(c). We further conclude that the Print Publishers infringed the Authors' copyrights by authorizing the Electronic Publishers to place the Articles in the Databases and by aiding the Electronic Publishers in that endeavor. We therefore affirm the judgment of the Court of Appeals.

Faulkner v. National Geographic Society
294 F. Supp. 2d 523 (S.D.N.Y. 2003)

The digital revolution has caused substantial growing pains in the law of copyright as the law has sought to adapt to the demands of a new age. This case is yet another example.

Plaintiffs here are freelance photographers or writers who created images or text that originally appeared in the print version of the *National Geographic Magazine* (the "*Magazine*"). While the ownership of the copyrights in their creations in many cases is disputed, all agree that defendant National Geographic Society ("NGS") had the right to publish their works in the *Magazine* regardless of who owns the copyrights.

In the late 1990s, defendants produced and began to market various editions of "The Complete National Geographic" (the "CNG"), a digital archive of all past issues of the *Magazine* on CD-ROM and DVD. Plaintiffs here claim that the production and sale of the CNG infringed their copyrights in and otherwise violated their rights with respect to their contributions to the *Magazine*. The fundamental questions, common to all of the cases, are whether the NGS, as owner of the copyrights in the individual issues of the *Magazine,* is privileged by Section 201(c) of the Copyright Act of 1976 (the "1976 Act") to market the CNG on the theory that it is a reproduction or revision of the *Magazine* and whether NGS is foreclosed from reliance on Section 201(c) by a previous adverse decision in the Eleventh Circuit.

The matter now is before the Court on defendants' motions for partial summary judgment dismissing the copyright infringement and certain other claims and motions by many of the plaintiffs for partial summary judgment determining that defendants are liable for copyright infringement under the 1976 Act.... The principal defendants are NGS and two of its subsidiaries....

The Complete National Geographic

In 1996, NGS developed a proposal to reproduce all issues of the *Magazine* published between 1888 and 1996 in CD-ROM format. The product, now known as the CNG, was produced in significant part through a process of digital scanning. Each issue of the *Magazine* published between 1888 and 1996 was scanned, page by page, into a computer system. The pages were scanned two at a time, so that a user of CNG is presented with the exact same visual experience as if reading from the print version of the *Magazine.* Defendants assert that the scanning process created an "exact image-based reproduction" of each page as it appeared in the *Magazine....*

"The Complete National Geographic: 108 Years of National Geographic Magazine on CD-ROM" ("CD-ROM 108"), which was introduced to the marketplace in 1997, has three components. The first is a multimedia sequence that displays NGS's logo followed by a promotional message for Kodak and a sequence depicting the covers of ten issues of the *Magazine* that transition from one into another (the "Moving Cover Sequence"). The multimedia sequence plays on the first time a user boots up CD-ROM 108 and at the beginning of each subsequent session. In subsequent sessions, however, the user can skip the sequence by clicking on the logo once. The second component, referred to in this opinion as the Replica, consists of the digital reproduction of the pages and issues of the *Magazine.* The third is the computer software that serves as the storage repository and retrieval system for the *Magazine* images.

Since 1997, the NGS has published additional CNG products, principally CD-ROMs and DVDs for the first 109, 110, 111 and 112 years of the *Magazine.* These products have varied slightly from the first with respect to the introductory sequences, which display the NGS's logo, and the Kodak promotional message. Only the 108 and 109 year CD-ROMs contained the Moving Cover Sequence. Beginning with the 110 year product, each version has contained a very short summary of each article that appears on the list of "hits" generated by the search engine in response to user queries. Capabilities have been added to the software. All, however, contain a Replica section....

II. Copyright Infringement

Section 201(c) of the 1976 Act provides:

Copyright in each separate contribution to a collective work is distinct from copyright in the collective work as a whole, and vests initially in the author of the contribution. In the absence of an express transfer of the copyright or of any rights under it, the owner of copyright in the collective work is presumed to have acquired only the privilege of reproducing and distributing the contribution as part of that particular collective work, any revision of that collective work, and any later collective work in the same series.

It thus distinguishes between the "copyright in each separate contribution to a collective work" and the "copyright in the collective work as a whole." The former "vests initially in the author of the contribution." The owner of the copyright in the collective work, barring an express transfer, is presumed to have acquired from the owner of the copyright in each separate contribution only the privilege of "reproducing and distributing the contribution as part of [1] that particular collective work, [2] any revision of that collective work, and [3] any later collective work in the same series."

The parties agree that NGS acquired from the plaintiffs at least the right to publish their contributions in the *Magazine*. Defendants contend that the CNG is a "reproduction" or "revision" of the *Magazine* and, in consequence, that the infringement claims must be dismissed. Plaintiffs, for their part, maintain that NGS litigated and lost precisely this argument in *Greenberg v. National Geographic Society* [244 F.3d 1267 (11th Cir.) (corrected opinion), *cert. denied*, 534 U.S. 951, 151 L. Ed. 2d 262, 122 S. Ct. 347 (2001) (mem.). and that defendants therefore are collaterally estopped from relying on Section 201(c)....

Section 201(c) creates a privilege in the publisher of a collective work for "reproduction" of "that particular collective work, any revision of that collective work, and any later collective work in the same series" but does not define any of those terms. The phrase "that particular collective work" obviously includes "a specific edition or issue of a periodical." The meaning of the remaining terms, however, is far from self evident. Where, as here, the language of the statute is unclear, resort to legislative history is appropriate. The most pertinent indication is in the House Judiciary Committee Report, which states in relevant part:

> Under the language of this clause a publishing company could reprint a contribution from one issue in a later issue of its magazine, and could reprint an article from a 1980 edition of an encyclopedia in a 1990 revision of it; the publisher could not revise the contribution itself or include it in a new anthology or an entirely different magazine or other collective work.

A staff report expressed much the same idea, stating that the privilege did not permit "inclusion of [an author's] contribution in anthologies or other entirely different works."

These comments are instructive. The use of the term "entirely different" to describe a new work not privileged by Section 201(c) suggests that the privilege extends to a collective work that is merely somewhat different from the original in which the contribution appeared. This view is supported strongly by the Judiciary Committee's encyclopedia revision example. An encyclopedia typically is a collective work consisting of individual articles dealing with the various subjects treated. As time goes by, some articles become outdated and new subjects come into being. A revised edition of an encyclopedia thus would contain some articles that have been revised to take account of new learning and some entirely new articles, as well as some articles in precisely their original forms. Each revised and new article would be copyrightable independently. Hence, *Greenberg*'s holding—that the presence of independently copyrightable material is inconsistent with a conclusion that the CNG is a "revision" of the print versions of the *Magazine*—cannot be reconciled with the legislative history. Indeed, it "defies the very legislative history" upon which the Eleventh Circuit relied.

What then distinguishes a "revision" from an "entirely different" work? As the Supreme Court noted in [*New York Times, Inc. v.*] *Tasini*, [533 U.S. 483 (2001),] Section 201(c) was a compromise intended "to adjust the balance between" freelancers and publishers so that "if there is demand for a freelance [work] standing alone or in a new collection, the Copyright Act allows the freelancer to benefit from that demand." In determining whether the freelancer's work is part of a new collection as distinguished from a revision, the focus is on the manner in which it is "presented to, and perceptible by, the user." A critical consideration is whether the original contribution is presented in the same context in which it appeared in the initial collective work, at least to such an extent that the new product "perceptibly presents the author's contribution as part of a revision of the collective work." As the Register of Copyright wrote in a letter discussing *Tasini*:

> "The legislative history of § 201(c) supports this conclusion [i.e., that the NEXIS database at issue in *Tasini* was not a revision]. It offers, as examples of a revision of a collective work, an evening edition of a newspaper or a later edition of an encyclopedia. *These examples retain elements that are consistent and recognizable from the original collective work so that a relationship between the original and the revision is apparent. Unlike NEXIS, they are recognizable as revisions of the originals.* But as the Second Circuit noted, all that is left of the original collective works in the databases involved in *Tasini* are the authors' contributions.
>
> "It is clear that the databases involved in *Tasini* constitute, in the words of the legislative history, 'new,' 'entirely different' or 'other' works. *No elements of arrangement or coordination of the pre-existing materials contained in the databases provide evidence of any similarity or relationship to the original collective works to indicate they are revisions.*"

147 Cong. Rec., E182-02, E183 (daily ed. Feb. 14, 2001) (emphasis added).

In this case, with a few immaterial exceptions, each issue of a regional edition of the *Magazine* was scanned, page by page, into a computer system, creating an exact image of each and every page as it appeared in that edition of the *Magazine*. There are no changes to the content, format or appearance of the issues of the *Magazine* reproduced in the CNG. Each page of each issue appears to the user exactly as it was in the scanned print version of the *Magazine*, including all text, images, advertising and attributions....

The fact that this product appears in a new medium makes no difference, in and of itself, as media neutrality is a fundamental principle of the Copyright Act. So what remains is the contention that the user experience with the CNG—its easy searchability and other attractive software-dependent features—is so different from that with the *Magazine* itself that the CNG should be regarded as an "entirely different" work.

It is difficult to see why this should take the CNG out of Section 201(c). The predominant differences between the *Magazine* and the CNG are the CNG's convenient physical "package" and the software that provides easy searchability, i.e., the animated opening sequence and other such material and the search engine, respectively.... The fact that more purchasers may be interested because the package is more attractive than a library full of more than 112 years of monthly copies of the *Magazine* is immaterial.

As the Supreme Court said in *Tasini,* the accommodation struck by Section 201(c) was to allow a freelancer to benefit where "there is demand for a freelance article standing alone or in a new collection." But the CNG is not a new collection. Nor is it, in words the House Judiciary Committee used to articulate the limits of the Section 201(c) privilege, "a new anthology or an entirely different magazine or other collective work." Rather, it is a package that contains substantially everything that made the *Magazine* copyrightable as a collective work—the same original collection of individual contributions, arranged in the same way, with each presented in the same context. It is readily recognizable as a variation of the original. Accordingly, the Court holds that the CNG is a revision of the individual print issues of the *Magazine*; it respectfully disagrees with so much of *Greenburg* as held otherwise.

B. Effect of Section 201(c) on Pre-1978 Works

The Court's previous opinions determined that the NGS owned copyright in some of the Pre-1978 Works while issues of fact exist concerning ownership of others. NGS argues, however, that these issues are immaterial because Section 201(c) protects the use of the Pre-1978 Works in the CNG.

The NGS at all relevant times owned the copyrights in issues of the *Magazine* published before and after January 1, 1978. In consequence, the privileges conferred upon it by Section 201(c) as the holder of those copyrights govern regardless of when they were published. Accordingly, to whatever extent that Section 201(c) protects publication of the CNG, it does so regardless of whether the NGS or plaintiffs own the copyrights in plaintiffs' individual contributions.

Notes and Questions

a. One of the greatest concerns raised by the dissent in *Tasini* was the fear that large segments of material would become unavailable on the Internet, as well as on Lexis, Westlaw, and similar databases. The Court suggested that there were alternatives to the publisher's losing access to this material. What might some of those options be?

b. The decisions seem to turn on the nature of the display. If the work is reproduced whole, then it is not an infringement. But if the work is disaggregated into individual articles, then the statute does not treat the work as a reprint. Some imaging software does both. The physical pages of a work are photographically reproduced for display.

A copy of the text is dumped into the database so that text-based searches can allow the viewer to call up a page through a keyword search. Does this form of visual representation working in tandem with a searchable database fall outside the statutory definition articulated in *Tasini*? If this is also actionable, then note that Google and other online search engines offer functionality of a similar manner in regards to PDF files posted to the Internet.

c. The case of *Faulkner v. Nat'l Geographic Soc'y.*, 294 F. Supp. 2d 523 (S.D.N.Y. 2003), was affirmed, *Faulkner v. Nat'l Geographic Enters.*, 409 F.3d 26 (2d Cir. 2005), though the ongoing litigation continued through numerous additional opinions. In affirming the district court decision, the Second Circuit explained:

> [W]e hold that, because the original context of the Magazines is omnipresent in the CNG and because it is a new version of the Magazine, the CNG is a privileged revision.

> "'Revision' denotes a new 'version,' and a version is, in this setting, a "'distinct form of something regarded by its creator or others as one work.'" [*N.Y. Times Co. v. Tasini*, 533 U.S. 483, 500 (2001)] (quoting Webster's Third New International Dictionary 1944, 2545 (1976)). "In determining whether the [underlying works] have been reproduced and distributed 'as part of' a 'revision' of the collective works in issue, we focus on the [underlying works] as presented to, and perceptible by, the user of the [CNG]." *Id.* at 499 (citations omitted).

> Moreover, because the Section 201(c) privilege of reproduction and distribution extends to that collective work and any revision of that collective work, a permissible revision may contain elements not found in the original—for example, a collection of bound volumes of past issues with a copyrightable index to the entire collection.... In the case of the CNG, some images found in the original version of the Magazines are blacked out, and it contains additional elements.... However, these changes do not substantially alter the original context which, unlike that of the works at issue in *Tasini*, is immediately recognizable. The presentation does not, therefore, affect the CNG's status as a revision.

Faulkner v. Nat'l Geographic Enters., 409 F.3d 26, 38 (2d Cir. 2005).

The last round of litigation addressed whether there was a breach of contact for failing to compensate the "further uses" of the photographs. In *Faulkner v. Natl. Geographic Soc.*, 452 F. Supp. 2d 369, 379–81 (S.D.N.Y. 2006), *aff'd sub nom. Ward v. Natl. Geographic Socy.*, 284 Fed. Appx. 822 (2d Cir. 2008) (unpublished), the court found little ambiguity in the contracts and a clear course of dealing that demonstrated which further uses entitled plaintiffs to additional payments.

> [B]oth NGS and the plaintiffs rely on extrinsic evidence of the course of dealing between them. Both cite evidence that NGS consistently paid plaintiffs when their contributions to the Magazine were reused in filmstrips, books, slide presentations, and promotional brochures.... [P]laintiffs do not dispute

that they were not paid for use of their work in microform, microfiche, or bound compilations of the magazine. No do they provide any evidence to suggest that they requested payment for such uses from NGS. Unlike the subjective intent or post hoc conclusions of contracting parties, the parties' course of dealing throughout the life of a contract is highly relevant to determining the meaning of the terms of the agreement.

This undisputed evidence of the course of dealing between the parties under the contracts at issue compels the conclusion that the "further use" provisions require additional payments only if a new use presents the contributors' works in a context different than the Magazine article in which they originally appeared.

d. The Supreme Court also returned to the case of *New York Times Co. v. Tasini*. Because of the growing size and complexity of the lawsuit, the [*Tasini*] District Court referred the parties to mediation. For more than three years, the freelance authors, the publishers (and their insurers), and the electronic databases (and their insurers) negotiated. Finally, in March 2005, they reached a settlement agreement that the parties intended "to achieve a global peace in the publishing industry." *In re Literary Works in Electronic Databases Copyright Litigation*, 509 F.3d 116, 119 (2d Cir. 2007).

> The parties moved the District Court to certify a class for settlement and to approve the settlement agreement. Ten freelance authors, including Irvin Muchnick (hereinafter Muchnick respondents), objected. The District Court overruled the objections; certified a settlement class of freelance authors under Federal Rules of Civil Procedure 23(a) and (b)(3); approved the settlement as fair, reasonable, and adequate under Rule 23(e); and entered final judgment.... The Muchnick respondents appealed.... Shortly before oral argument, the Court of Appeals *sua sponte* ordered briefing on the question whether § 411(a) deprives federal courts of subject-matter jurisdiction over infringement claims involving unregistered copyrights. All parties filed briefs asserting that the District Court had subject-matter jurisdiction to approve the settlement agreement even though it included unregistered works.... [T]he Court of Appeals concluded that the District Court lacked jurisdiction to certify a class of claims arising from the infringement of unregistered works, and also lacked jurisdiction to approve a settlement with respect to those claims ...

Reed Elsevier, Inc. v. Muchnick, 559 U.S. 154, 159–60, 173 (2010). The Supreme Court reversed, finding that § 411(a) of the Copyright Act did not require every work in dispute between parties to be a registered work. "Section 411(a) imposes a precondition to filing a claim that is not clearly labeled jurisdictional, is not located in a jurisdiction-granting provision, and admits of congressionally authorized exceptions. Section 411(a) thus imposes a type of precondition to suit that supports nonjurisdictional treatment under our precedents." In so deciding, the Court allowed the hard fought class action settlement to go into effect.

e. The saga continued in *Literary Works in Elec. Databases Copyright Litig. v. Thomson Corp.*, 654 F.3d 242, 254–255 (2d Cir. 2011). The Second Circuit reversed the class action settlement because it found that the various categories of claimants were not adequately represented.

> The Settlement divides the works at issue ("Subject Works") into three categories: A, B, and C. Category A covers works that authors registered with the U.S. Copyright Office in time to be eligible for statutory damages and attorney's fees under the Copyright Act. At the time of the Settlement, registration cost $30 per work or $30 per group registration covering multiple periodical contributions by one individual over a 12-month period. Category B includes works that authors registered before December 31, 2002, but too late to be eligible for statutory damages. These claims are eligible to recover only actual damages suffered by the author and any profits of the infringer that are not duplicative of the actual damages. All other claims fall into Category C and cannot be litigated for damages purposes unless they are registered with the Copyright Office. If registered, however, these claims—like those in Category B—would be eligible for awards based on authors' actual damages and infringers' profits. Category C claims comprise more than 99% of authors' total claims. Many authors hold claims in more than one category, each claim based on a separate freelance article they sold for publication....

> We agree with objectors that the interests of class members who hold only Category C claims fundamentally conflict with those of class members who hold Category A and B claims. Although all class members share an interest in maximizing the collective recovery, their interests diverge as to the distribution of that recovery because each category of claim is of different strength and therefore commands a different settlement value. Named plaintiffs who hold other combinations of claims had no incentive to maximize the recovery for Category C-only plaintiffs, whose claims were lowest in settlement value but eclipsed all others in quantity. The interests of Category C-only plaintiffs could be protected only by the formation of a subclass and the advocacy of independent counsel. We therefore hold that the district court abused its discretion in certifying the class based on its finding that class representation was adequate.

f. To what extent can the sleuthing needed to find previously unpublished works become a part of a compiler's copyright? When Stuart Silverstein published a book of Dorothy Parker's uncollected poems, he did not expect Penguin Books to first reject his manuscript and then publish the same poems in its own anthology. But sleuthing and compiling may not be the same. *See Silverstein v. Penguin Putnam, Inc.*, 368 F.3d 77 (2d Cir. 2004).

g. With the rise of new technology and self-publishing technology, anyone can serve as a publishing house. At what point do the promises of a successful print and promotional campaign become contractual guarantees? For insight into this issue and the risks of interference with an author's rights, *see Lee v. Mt. Ivy Press, L.P.*, 63 Mass. App. Ct. 538 (2005).

Problem 17-D

Bryce and Jesse are continuing to work on the coffee table photo-exposé. (*See* Problem 17-B.) With the book now tentatively entitled *Exposure*, Jesse has photographed 50 subjects. Bryce has written the introduction for the book, photo captions, and a biography for each subject. Because most of the book's subjects know each other, the book has developed a narrative that neither Bryce nor Jesse expected. The book is actually telling the story of an elite subculture in the city.

Bryce and Jesse expected to use only 35 subjects. The publisher is willing to increase the number slightly, but has asked that all 50 of the completed exposés be delivered. It plans to "assist" in the selection process, "subject to the authors' final approval." Based on their working relationship with the publisher thus far, Bryce and Jesse are not concerned about soliciting the advice of the publisher on the selection process. Bryce is concerned, however, that individual exposés are not sold as filler for magazines or used outside of the completed book — at least not without Bryce's and Jesse's approval. Bryce wants to know whether copyright law would allow the publisher to publish the rejected exposés elsewhere and what contractual language should be added to the agreement to stop this from happening.

E. Fair Use in Publishing

Rosemont Enterprises, Inc. v. Random House, Inc.

366 F.2d 303 (2d Cir. 1966)

On May 26, 1966, plaintiff-appellee, Rosemont Enterprises, Inc. (Rosemont) commenced this action in the district court alleging that copyrights which it owned on a series of articles entitled "The Howard Hughes Story" which appeared in Look Magazine in early 1954 were infringed by a book entitled "Howard Hughes — a Biography by John Keats" published on May 23, 1966 by defendant-appellant, Random House, Inc. In June, Rosemont made a motion for a preliminary injunction restraining the sale, publication, distribution and advertisement of the biography pending final determination of the action on the ground that it had made out a prima facie case of infringement. The defendants, Random House, Inc. and John Keats, opposed the motion on the grounds, *inter alia*, that the copying which was done was insubstantial and that, in any event, whatever use was made of the Look articles constituted a fair use and, thus, was privileged. The district court granted the motion for a preliminary injunction and, in rejecting defendants' claim of fair use, narrowly confined the privilege to materials "used for purposes of criticism or comment or in scholarly works of scientific or educational value." In the district court's view, if a work is published "for commercial purposes" and is designed for the popular market, those responsible for its appearance are precluded from invoking the fair use privilege, regardless of the nature of the work involved. Since the court found that the Hughes biography "can scarcely be said to be a scholarly, scientific or educational work," and was designed for the popular market, it concluded that the fair use privilege was inappropriate here. For the reasons set forth below, we reverse.

The only issue presently before this court is: Was the preliminary injunction erroneously issued as a matter of law?

The articles entitled "The Howard Hughes Story" published in three issues of Look Magazine dated February 9, 23 and March 9, 1954, and copyrighted by its publisher, Cowles Communications, Inc., in January and February 1954 and the allegedly offending book, published in 1966, "Howard Hughes—a Biography by John Keats," are before the court. The nature and extent of the infringement, if any, can be gauged by a comparison of the two writings. For the purposes of this appeal, an attempt will be made to restrict the factual statement to those undisputed items which bear upon a preliminary injunction.

The Circumstances Under Which Plaintiff Acquired the Look Copyrights

At the outset, defendants assert that plaintiff's conduct in acquiring the copyrights indicates that they were purchased solely for the purpose of bringing this lawsuit and, hence, plaintiff is deprived "of the right to relief as a matter of law and as a matter of equitable discretion."

From the facts as outlined in the district court's opinion, it appears that for some time prior to 1962 Random House had been considering a biography of Howard Hughes who by reason of his remarkable exploits and achievements, primarily in the aviation and motion picture fields, had become quite a public figure despite a publicized passion for personal anonymity. To prepare such a biography, Random House in September of 1962 engaged the services of Thomas Thompson, a member of the staff of Life Magazine. After submitting his draft manuscript, Thompson for business reasons could not continue with the additional work necessary for its completion. In the latter part of 1964, Random House obtained the services of an author, the defendant, John Keats, who took the Thompson manuscript, news and copyrighted magazine articles, including the 1954 Look articles, and various public documents, and produced the biography now before the court.

Apparently Hughes and/or his attorneys learned of the forthcoming Random House publication, and his attorney warned Random House that Hughes was opposed to the biography "and would make trouble if the book was published." The legal effect of the "trouble" should not be pre-judged at this time, except as certain aspects bear upon the granting of the preliminary injunction. Whether there be any reality to the claim that the plaintiff Rosemont, organized in September 1965 by Hughes' attorney and two officers of his wholly-owned Hughes Tool Company, is engaged in writing a Hughes biography, must await the trial. For the present, it is sufficient to note that in February 1966 plaintiff, having by some means obtained a galley proof of the forthcoming biography, brought an action against defendants in the Supreme Court of New York alleging in substance a plan to exploit commercially the name and personality of Hughes and an invasion of his right of privacy.

On May 20, 1966, plaintiff obtained from Cowles Communications, Inc. (Look), the copyrights to the 1954 Look articles, so advised Random House the next day and brought this suit five days later. Apparently Look had done nothing with the articles since 1954; they had not been compiled into book form or reprinted or offered to the public in any manner except as articles in three February and March 1954 editions of Look. Nor is there any indication that Look, although advised of the proposed Random House biography, intended to bring an infringement action or to seek an injunction. However, whether the "trouble" threatened will have legal consequences sufficient to constitute a defense cannot be determined upon the facts as adduced at this stage. Nevertheless, we have referred with approval to the rule that "'[t]he interference of the court by injunction being founded on pure equitable principles, a man who comes to the court must be able to show that his own conduct in the transaction has been consistent with equity.'"

A Comparison of the 1954 Look
Articles and the 1966 Biography

The three 1954 Look articles contain some 13,500 words and would have, if published in book form (which they were not), filled some 36 to 39 book-size pages. The 1966 biography consists of some 116,000 words and 304 pages. The Look articles do not purport to be a biography in the accepted meaning of the word but narrate certain phases or highlights of Hughes' quite eventful career. Naturally, any writing purporting to deal with the life of a public figure is bound to touch upon the same events as have given rise to the publicity. In addition, various incidents of interest to the reading public can usually be developed from friends, neighbors, teachers, business associates, employees, newspaper and magazine articles and public and private records. And so here the biography gives evidence of such source material. Moreover, there can be little doubt that portions of the Look articles were copied. Two direct quotations and one eight-line paraphrase are attributed to Stephen White, the author of the articles. A mere reading of the Look articles, however, indicates that there is considerable doubt as to whether the copied and paraphrased matter constitutes a material and substantial portion of those articles. On the other hand, the material at most forms an insubstantial part of the 304 page biography. Furthermore, while the mode of expression employed by White is entitled to copyright protection, he could not acquire by copyright a monopoly in the narration of historical events. Finally, in an affidavit submitted to the district court, Thompson asserted that he engaged in extensive research while preparing his manuscript, which included personal interviews with many people familiar with Hughes' activities (fifteen of whom he listed by name) and the employment of a Houston newspaper man to conduct additional interviews for him. There is no dispute that defendant Keats, named as author of the biography, was retained solely to revise Thompson's manuscript which, as described in his contract with Random House, was to include rewriting and reorganization; rechecking facts against the sources used; and such additional research as was necessary to "update the work and fill in facts and events." In any event, the extent of Keats' independent research is of little relevance since Thompson's work, embodied in the manuscript, formed the core of the published biography.

While it is undoubtedly true, as the district court observed, that "the book does rely heavily on previously published newspaper and magazine articles and similar material," that fact does not create a presumption of infringement. At this time, we are not prepared to hold that as a matter of law there has been a clear showing of probable success at a trial with respect to the extent and quality of infringement of the Look articles which warrants the grant of a preliminary injunction.

Fair Use

There is no question that material appearing in the Look articles is contained in the Hughes biography. Appellants contend, however, that the district court erred as a matter of law in refusing to honor their claim of fair use on the ground that the court unjustifiably restricted the privilege to scholarly works written and prepared for scholarly audiences. We agree.

"Fair use" is a "privilege in others than the owner of a copyright to use the copyrighted material in a reasonable manner without his consent, notwithstanding the monopoly granted to the owner...." The fundamental justification for the privilege lies in the constitutional purpose in granting copyright protection in the first instance, to wit, "To Promote the Progress of Science and the Useful Arts." To serve that purpose, "courts in passing upon particular claims of infringement must occasionally subordinate the copyright holder's interest in a maximum financial return to the greater public interest in the development of art, science and industry." Whether the privilege may justifiably be applied to particular materials turns initially on the nature of the materials, e.g., whether their distribution would serve the public interest in the free dissemination of information and whether their preparation requires some use of prior materials dealing with the same subject matter. Consequently, the privilege has been applied to works in the fields of science, law, medicine, history and biography.

Biographies, of course, are fundamentally personal histories and it is both reasonable and customary for biographers to refer to and utilize earlier works dealing with the subject of the work and occasionally to quote directly from such works. This practice is permitted because of the public benefit in encouraging the development of historical and biographical works and their public distribution, e.g., so "that the world may not be deprived of improvements, or the progress of the arts be retarded." Indeed, while the Hughes biography may not be a profound work, it may well provide valuable source material for future biographers (if any) of Hughes or for historians or social scientists....

By this preliminary injunction, the public is being deprived of an opportunity to become acquainted with the life of a person endowed with extraordinary talents who, by exercising these talents, made substantial contributions in the fields to which he chose to devote his unique abilities. Inheriting a small fortune in early youth, Hughes can hardly qualify as a Horatio Alger hero in a "From Rags to Riches" story but a narration of his initiative, ingenuity, determination and tireless work to achieve his conception of perfection in whatever he did ought to be available to a reading public which, even in an affluent society, might well be reminded that affluence usually comes from the work of such entrepreneurs in business and industry.

The Keats biography is laudatory and where critical is critical in an understanding fashion. No claim has been made that the biography contains misrepresentations of fact. Judging by the accounts in the Look articles and the biography, Hughes has almost an obsession as to his privacy and his right thereto. However, when one enters the public arena to the extent that he has, the right of privacy must be tempered by a countervailing privilege that the public have some information concerning important public figures. The district court itself recognized that "Howard Hughes is a rather enigmatic contemporary personality of considerable public interest." ...

Random House, Inc. v. Salinger
811 F.2d 90 (2d Cir. 1987)

This appeal presents the issue whether the biographer of a renowned author has made "fair use" of his subject's unpublished letters. The issue arises on an expedited appeal from an order of the District Court for the Southern District of New York (Pierre N. Leval, Judge) denying a preliminary injunction sought by the well-known writer, J. D. Salinger, against Ian Hamilton and Random House, Inc., the author and publisher, respectively, of a book about Salinger and his writings. For reasons that follow, we conclude that a preliminary injunction should be issued.

The plaintiff J. D. Salinger is a highly regarded American novelist and short-story writer, best known for his novel, *The Catcher in the Rye*. He has not published since 1965 and has chosen to shun all publicity and inquiry concerning his private life. The defendant Ian Hamilton is a well-respected writer on literary topics. He serves as literary critic of *The London Sunday Times* and has authored a biography of the poet Robert Lowell. In July 1983 Hamilton informed Salinger that he was undertaking a biography of Salinger to be published by Random House and sought the author's cooperation. Salinger refused, informing Hamilton that he preferred not to have his biography written during his lifetime. Hamilton nevertheless proceeded and spent the next three years preparing a biography titled *J. D. Salinger: A Writing Life*....

Ian Hamilton located most, if not all, of the letters in the libraries of Harvard, Princeton, and the University of Texas, to which they had been donated by the recipients or their representatives. Prior to examining the letters at the university libraries, Hamilton signed form agreements furnished by the libraries, restricting the use he could make of the letters without permission of the library and the owner of the literary property rights. The Harvard form required permission "to publish the contents of the manuscript or any excerpt therefrom." The Princeton form obliged the signer "not to copy, reproduce, circulate or publish" inspected manuscripts without permission.

By May 1986 Hamilton had completed a version of his biography. Salinger received a set of the galley proofs of this version (the "May galleys") and learned from the galleys and the footnote citations to his letters that the letters had been donated to university libraries. In response, he took two actions. First, he registered 79 of his unpublished letters for copyright protection. Second, he instructed his counsel to object to publication of the biography until all of Salinger's unpublished materials were deleted.

In response to Salinger's objection, Hamilton and Random House revised the May galleys. In the current version of the biography (the "October galleys"), much of the material previously quoted from the Salinger letters has been replaced by close paraphrasing. Somewhat more than 200 words remain quoted. Salinger has identified 59 instances where the October galleys contain passages that either quote from or closely paraphrase portions of his unpublished letters....

On October 3, 1986, Salinger sued Ian Hamilton and Random House, seeking an injunction against publication of Hamilton's biography and damages.... To a large extent the appropriate legal principles are not in dispute on this appeal, though their application is seriously contested. The author of letters is entitled to a copyright in the letters, as with any other work of literary authorship. Prior to 1978, unpublished letters, like other unpublished works, were protected by common law copyright, but the 1976 Copyright Act preempted the common law of copyright, and brought un-published works under the protection of federal copyright law, which includes the right of first publication among the rights accorded to the copyright owner. The copyright owner owns the literary property rights, including the right to complain of infringing copying, while the recipient of the letter retains ownership of "the tan-gible physical property of the letter itself." Having ownership of the physical document, the recipient (or his representative) is entitled to deposit it with a library and contract for the terms of access to it. As with all works of authorship, the copyright owner secures protection only for the expressive content of the work, not the ideas or facts contained therein, a distinction fundamental to copyright law and of special signifi-cance in determining whether infringement has occurred in a work of biography or other account of historical or contemporary events.

Central to this appeal is the application of the defense of "fair use" to unpublished works. Though common law, especially as developed in England, appears to have denied the defense of fair use to unpublished works, the 1976 Act explicitly makes all of the rights protected by copyright, including the right of first publication, subject to the defense of fair use. That fair use applies to unpublished works does not deter-mine, however, the scope of the defense as applied to such works. Whatever glim-merings on that subject have appeared in cases decided before May 20, 1985, our guidance must now be taken from the decision of the Supreme Court on that date in *Harper & Row, Publishers, Inc. v. Nation Enterprises,* 471 U.S. 539, 85 L. Ed. 2d 588, 105 S. Ct. 2218 (1985), the Court's first delineation of the scope of fair use as applied to unpublished works.

The Court begins its discussion of fair use by considering the application of the doctrine to unpublished works. The Court observes that "fair use traditionally was not recognized as a defense to charges of copying from an author's as yet unpublished works," but that this "absolute rule" was "tempered in practice by the equitable nature of the fair use doctrine." The Court notes that, under the Copyright Revision Act of 1976, all of the rights protected by copyright, including the right of first publication, are subject to fair use, but explicitly rejects the contention, advanced by *The Nation* that Congress "intended that fair use would apply *in pari materia* to published and unpublished works." "Under ordinary circumstances," the Court states, "the author's right to control the first public appearance of his undisseminated expression will outweigh a claim of fair use." This proposition was emphasized with respect to unpublished letters. Reckoning with *The Nation's* argument that fair use could permissibly be made of President Ford's unpublished memoirs because the imminent publication demonstrated that the author has no interest in nonpublication, the Court said, "This argument assumes that the unpublished nature of copyrighted material is only relevant to letters or other confidential writings not intended for dissemination," an assumption the Court went on to reject. Pertinent to our case is the fact that the Court underscored the idea that unpublished letters normally enjoy insulation from fair use copying.

After emphasizing the insulation of unpublished works from fair use under "ordinary circumstances," the Court considers in turn each of the four factors identified by Congress as "especially relevant," in determining whether a use is fair. Reflecting its earlier discussion, the Court gives special weight to the fact that the copied work is unpublished when considering the second factor, the nature of the copyrighted work.

Following the Supreme Court's approach in *Harper & Row*, we place special emphasis on the unpublished nature of Salinger's letters and proceed to consider each of the four statutory fair use factors. Application of these four factors points in Salinger's favor.

1. *Purpose of the use.* Hamilton's book fits comfortably within several of the statutory categories of uses illustrative of uses that can be fair. The book may be considered "criticism," "scholarship," and "research." The proposed use is not an attempt to rush to the market just ahead of the copyright holder's imminent publication, as occurred in *Harper & Row*. Whether Random House plans to "exploit the headline value of its infringement," as *The Nation* did, is not clear on the record thus far developed. Though no evidence has yet been presented on the advertising materials Random House plans to use, it is hard to believe that some emphasis will not be placed upon the fact that the book draws generously upon Salinger's unpublished letters.

We agree with Judge Leval that Hamilton's purpose in using the Salinger letters to enrich his scholarly biography weighs the first fair use factor in Hamilton's favor, notwithstanding that he and his publisher anticipate profits. However, we do not agree that a biographer faces a dilemma that entitles him to a generous application of the fair use doctrine.... This dilemma is not faced by the biographer who elects to copy only the factual content of letters.

The biographer who copies only facts incurs no risk of an injunction; he has not taken copyrighted material. And it is unlikely that the biographer will distort those facts by rendering them in words of his own choosing. On the other hand, the biographer who copies the letter writer's expression of facts properly faces an unpleasant choice. If he copies more than minimal amounts of (unpublished) expressive content, he deserves to be enjoined; if he "distorts" the expressive content, he deserves to be criticized for "sacrificing accuracy and vividness." But the biographer has no inherent right to copy the "accuracy" or the "vividness" of the letter writer's expression. Indeed, "vividness of description" is precisely an attribute of the author's expression that he is entitled to protect.

The point is sharply, though unwittingly, made by defendant Hamilton in the course of his deposition in this case. On cross-examination, he is pressed as to why he copied a stylistic device that Salinger had employed in one of the letters. He responds: "I wanted to convey the fact that [Salinger] was adopting an ironic term...." When the cross-examiner asks, "Couldn't you have stated that he had an ironic tone," Hamilton replies, "That would make a pedestrian sentence I didn't wish to put my name to." But when dealing with copyrighted expression, a biographer (or any other copier) may frequently have to content himself with reporting only the fact of what his subject did, even if he thereby pens a "pedestrian" sentence. The copier is not at liberty to avoid "pedestrian" reportage by appropriating his subject's literary devices.

In sum, we agree with the District Court that the first fair use factor weighs in Hamilton's favor, but not that the purpose of his use entitles him to any special consideration.

2. *Nature of the Copyrighted Work.* "The fact that a work is unpublished is a critical element of its 'nature.' " Salinger's letters are unpublished, and they have not lost that attribute by their placement in libraries where access has been explicitly made subject to observance of at least the protections of copyright law. In considering this second factor, we encounter some ambiguity arising from the Supreme Court's observation that "the *scope* of fair use is narrower with respect to unpublished works." This could mean either that the circumstances in which copying will be found to be fair use are fewer in number for unpublished works than for published works or that the amount of copyrighted material that may be copied as fair use is a lesser quantity for unpublished works than for published works. Some support for the latter view can be derived from the statement in *Harper & Row* that, though "substantial" quotations might be used in a review of a published work, the author's right to control first publication weighs against "such use" prior to publication. However, we think that the tenor of the Court's entire discussion of unpublished works conveys the idea that such works normally enjoy complete protection against copying any protected expression. Narrower "scope" seems to refer to the diminished *likelihood* that copying will be fair use when the copyrighted material is unpublished.

The District Judge considered the nature of the copyrighted work, especially its unpublished nature, primarily in rejecting the plaintiff's argument that fair use was inapplicable to unpublished works. However, in analyzing and weighing the fair use factors, Judge Leval gave no explicit consideration to this second factor. Since the copyrighted letters are unpublished, the second factor weighs heavily in favor of Salinger.

3. *Amount and Substantiality of the Portion Used.* It is with regard to this third factor that we have the most serious disagreement with the District Judge's legal analysis, both as to the pertinent standard and its application. As to the standard, we start, as did Judge Leval, by recognizing that what is relevant is the amount and substantiality of the copyrighted *expression* that has been used, not the *factual content* of the material in the copyrighted works. However, that protected expression has been "used" whether it has been quoted verbatim or only paraphrased....

We have carefully analyzed all 59 of the passages from Hamilton's book cited by Salinger as instances of infringing copying from 44 of his letters. Of these 44 letters, the Hamilton biography copies (with some use of quotation or close paraphrase) protected sequences constituting at least one-third of 17 letters and at least 10 percent of 42 letters. These sequences are protected, notwithstanding that they include some reporting of facts and an occasional use of a commonplace word or expression. Hamilton's use of these sequences "exceeds that necessary to disseminate the facts." Judge Leval found that "in the rarest case a complete sentence was taken." That is true only with respect to material directly quoted. The material closely paraphrased frequently exceeds ten lines from a single letter. Even if in one or two instances the portions of the letters copied could be said to lack sufficient creativity to warrant copyright protection, there remains sufficient copying of protected material to constitute a very substantial appropriation.

The taking is significant not only from a quantitative standpoint but from a qualitative one as well. The copied passages, if not the "'heart of the book,'" are at least an important ingredient of the book as it now stands. To a large extent, they make the book worth reading. The letters are quoted or paraphrased on at least 40 percent of the book's 192 pages.

In sum, the third fair use factor weighs heavily in Salinger's favor.

4. *Effect on the Market.* The Supreme Court has called the fourth factor — effect on the market for the copyrighted work — "the single most important element of fair use." As Judge Leval recognized, the need to assess the effect on the market for Salinger's letters is not lessened by the fact that their author has disavowed any intention to publish them during his lifetime. First, the proper inquiry concerns the "potential market" for the copyrighted work. Second, Salinger has the right to change his mind. He is entitled to protect his *opportunity* to sell his letters, an opportunity estimated by his literary agent to have a current value in excess of $500,000.

Proceeding from his conclusion that only a few fragments of the letters have been used in Hamilton's book, Judge Leval expressed the view that such use would have "no effect" on the marketability of the letters. Concluding as we do that substantial portions of the letters have been copied, we do not share the District Judge's view that marketability of the letters will be totally unimpaired. To be sure, the book would not displace the market for the letters. Indeed, we think it likely that most of the potential purchasers of a collection of the letters would not be dissuaded by publication of the biography. Yet some impairment of the market seems likely. The biography copies virtually all of the most interesting passages of the letters, including several highly expressive insights about writing and literary criticism. Perhaps few readers of the biography would refrain from purchasing a published collection of the letters if they appreciated how inadequately Hamilton's paraphrasing has rendered Salinger's chosen form of expression. The difficulty, however, is that some readers of the book will gain the impression that they are learning from Hamilton what Salinger has written. Hamilton frequently laces his paraphrasing with phrases such as "he wrote," "said Salinger," "he speaks of," "Salinger declares," "he says," and "he said." For at least some appreciable number of persons, these phrases will convey the impression that they have read Salinger's words, perhaps not quoted verbatim, but paraphrased so closely as to diminish interest in purchasing the originals. The fourth fair use factor weighs slightly in Salinger's favor.

On balance, the claim of fair use as to Salinger's unpublished letters fails. The second and third factors weigh heavily in Salinger's favor, and the fourth factor slightly so. Only the first factor favors Hamilton. We seriously doubt whether a critic reviewing a published collection of the letters could justify as fair use the extensive amount of expressive material Hamilton has copied. However that may be, if fair use is to have a more "limited scope" with respect to unpublished works, it is not available with respect to the current version of Hamilton's proposed biography.

To deny a biographer like Hamilton the opportunity to copy the expressive content of unpublished letters is not, as appellees contend, to interfere in any significant way with the process of enhancing public knowledge of history or contemporary events. The facts may be reported. Salinger's letters contain a number of facts that students of his life and writings will no doubt find of interest, and Hamilton is entirely free to fashion a biography that reports these facts. But Salinger has a right to protect the expressive content of his unpublished writings for the term of his copyright, and that right prevails over a claim of fair use under "ordinary circumstances." Public awareness of the expressive content of the letters will have to await either Salinger's decision to publish or the expiration of his copyright, save for such special circumstances as might fall within the "narrower" scope of fair use available for unpublished works. Evidently, public interest in the expressive content of the letters of a well-known writer remains substantial even fifty years after his death.

Since we conclude that the record establishes Salinger's entitlement to a preliminary injunction on his copyright claim, we need not consider at this stage of the litigation whether he is also entitled to relief by virtue of the library agreements.

Reversed and remanded with directions to issue a preliminary injunction barring publication of the biography in its present form.

Salinger v. Colting

607 F.3d 68 (2d. Cir. 2010)

Defendants-Appellants Fredrik Colting, Windupbird Publishing Ltd., Nicotext A.B., and ABP, Inc. appeal from an order of the United States District Court for the

Southern District of New York (Deborah A. Batts, Judge) granting Plaintiff-Appellee J.D. Salinger's[14] motion for a preliminary injunction. The District Court's judgment is VACATED and REMANDED.

Salinger published The Catcher in the Rye (hereinafter "Catcher") in 1951.... Catcher was an instant success. It was on the New York Times best-seller list for over seven months and sold more than one million copies in its first ten years. To date it has sold over 35 million copies, influenced dozens of literary works, and been the subject of "literally reams of criticism and comment." ...

Inseparable from the Catcher mystique is the lifestyle of its author, Salinger. Shortly after publishing Catcher, Salinger did what Holden did not do: he removed himself from society. Salinger has not published since 1965 and has never authorized any new narrative involving Holden or any work derivative of Catcher. Other than a 1949 film adaptation of one of his early short stories, Salinger has never permitted, and has explicitly instructed his lawyers not to allow, adaptations of his works. He has, however, remained in the public spotlight through a series of legal actions to protect his intellectual property. Salinger has registered and duly renewed his copyright in Catcher with the U.S. Copyright Office.

Defendant-Appellant Fredrik Colting wrote 60 Years Later: Coming Through the Rye (hereinafter "60 Years Later") under the pen name "John David California." Colting published 60 Years Later with his own publishing company, Defendant-Appellant Windupbird Publishing, Ltd., in England on May 9, 2009. Copies were originally scheduled to be available in the United States on September 15, 2009. Colting did not seek Salinger's permission to publish 60 Years Later.

60 Years Later tells the story of a 76-year-old Holden Caulfield, referred to as "Mr. C," in a world that includes Mr. C's 90-year-old author, a "fictionalized Salinger." The novel's premise is that Salinger has been haunted by his creation and now wishes to bring him back to life in order to kill him. Unsurprisingly, this task is easier said than done. As the story progresses, Mr. C becomes increasingly self-aware and able to act in ways contrary to the will of Salinger. After a series of misadventures, Mr. C travels to Cornish, New Hampshire, where he meets Salinger in his home. Salinger finds he is unable to kill Mr. C and instead decides to set him free. The novel concludes with Mr. C reuniting with his younger sister, Phoebe, and an estranged son, Daniel....

On July 1, 2009, the District Court granted Salinger's motion for a preliminary injunction, barring Defendants from "manufacturing, publishing, distributing, shipping, advertising, promoting, selling, or otherwise disseminating any copy of [60 Years Later], or any portion thereof, in or to the United States." In doing so, it found that (1) Salinger has a valid copyright in Catcher and the Holden Caulfield character, (2) absent a successful fair use defense, Defendants have infringed

---

14. We note that Plaintiff-Appellee J.D. Salinger died during the pendency of this appeal. In a February 18, 2010 order, we granted the motion of Colleen M. Salinger and Matthew R. Salinger, trustees of the J.D. Salinger Literary Trust, to be substituted for Salinger as Appellees. For reasons of convenience, however, we will continue to refer to Salinger as "Plaintiff" or "Appellee" in this opinion.

Salinger's copyright in both Catcher and the Holden Caulfield character, (3) Defendants' fair use defense is likely to fail, and (4) a preliminary injunction should issue....

Having made this determination, the District Court turned to whether a preliminary injunction should issue. According to the Court:

> Under Rule 65, to obtain a preliminary injunction a party must demonstrate: (1) that it will be irreparably harmed if an injunction is not granted, and (2) either (a) a likelihood of success on the merits or (b) sufficiently serious questions going to the merits to make them a fair ground for litigation, and a balance of hardships tipping decidedly in its favor.

Given its findings, the Court deemed the only remaining question to be whether Salinger had shown that he would be irreparably harmed if an injunction was not granted. Because Salinger had established a *prima facie* case of copyright infringement, and in light of how the District Court, understandably, viewed this Court's precedents, the District Court presumed irreparable harm without discussion....

We hold that, although the District Court applied our Circuit's longstanding standard for preliminary injunctions in copyright cases, our Circuit's standard is inconsistent with the "test historically employed by courts of equity" and has, therefore, been abrogated by *eBay, Inc. v. MercExchange, L.L.C.*, 547 U.S. 388, 390 (2006).

The Copyright Act of 1976 authorizes courts to "grant temporary and final injunctions on such terms as [they] may deem reasonable to prevent or restrain infringement of a copyright." 17 U.S.C. § 502(a). And, as the District Court stated, this Court has long issued preliminary injunctions in copyright cases upon a finding of (a) irreparable harm and (b) either (1) likelihood of success on the merits or (2) sufficiently serious questions going to the merits to make them a fair ground for litigation and a balance of hardships tipping decidedly toward the party requesting the preliminary relief.

Thus, once a plaintiff establishes a likelihood of success on the merits, the only additional requirement is a showing that the plaintiff will be irreparably harmed if the preliminary injunction does not issue. And traditionally, this Court has presumed that a plaintiff likely to prevail on the merits of a copyright claim is also likely to suffer irreparable harm if an injunction does not issue....

Defendants do not claim that the District Court failed to apply this Circuit's longstanding preliminary injunction standard. Rather, they argue both that this standard is an unconstitutional prior restraint on speech and that it is in conflict with the Supreme Court's decision in *eBay, Inc. v. MercExchange, L.L.C.*, 547 U.S. 388 (2006). We agree that *eBay* abrogated parts of this Court's preliminary injunction standard in copyright cases, and accordingly, this case must be remanded to the District Court to reevaluate Salinger's preliminary injunction motion. In light of that holding, we need not decide whether the preliminary injunction issued by the District Court constituted an unconstitutional prior restraint on speech.

eBay involved the propriety of a permanent injunction after a finding of patent infringement. The United States District Court for the Eastern District of Virginia had ostensibly applied the traditional four-factor test for determining whether a permanent injunction should issue....

Writing for a unanimous Court, Justice Thomas held that neither the district court nor the Federal Circuit correctly applied the equitable factors:

> According to well-established principles of equity, a plaintiff seeking a permanent injunction must satisfy a four-factor test before a court may grant such relief. A plaintiff must demonstrate: (1) that it has suffered an irreparable injury; (2) that remedies available at law, such as monetary damages, are inadequate to compensate for that injury; (3) that, considering the balance of hardships between the plaintiff and defendant, a remedy in equity is warranted; and (4) that the public interest would not be disserved by a permanent injunction.

eBay, 547 U.S. at 391. Although the courts below had articulated the correct standard, they had both, albeit in different ways, applied "broad classifications" that were inconsistent with traditional equitable principles....

We hold today that *eBay* applies with equal force (a) to preliminary injunctions (b) that are issued for alleged copyright infringement.... Moreover, the Court expressly relied upon copyright cases in reaching its conclusion. In response to the Federal Circuit's reasoning that the Patent Act's right to exclude justifies the preference for injunctive relief, the Court stated that "the creation of a right is distinct from the provision of remedies for violations of that right." In support of this distinction, it noted that "[l]ike a patent owner, a copyright holder possesses the right to exclude others from using his property." It further noted that "[l]ike the Patent Act, the Copyright Act provides that courts 'may' grant injunctive relief 'on such terms as it may deem reasonable to prevent or restrain infringement of copyright.'" *Id.* (quoting 17 U.S.C. §502(a)). Because of these similarities, the Court emphasized that it "has consistently rejected invitations to replace traditional equitable considerations with a rule that an injunction automatically follows a determination that a copyright has been infringed." Whatever the underlying issues and particular circumstances of the cases cited by the Court in *eBay*, it seems clear that the Supreme Court did not view patent and copyright injunctions as different in kind, or as requiring different standards....

The first consideration in the preliminary injunction analysis is the probability of success on the merits. In gauging this, we emphasize that courts should be particularly cognizant of the difficulty of predicting the merits of a copyright claim at a preliminary injunction hearing. *See* [Mark A. Lemley & Eugene Volokh, *Freedom of Speech and Injunctions in Intellectual Property Cases*, 48 DUKE L.J. 147, 201–02 (1998)] ("[When deciding whether to grant a TRO or a preliminary injunction,] the judge has limited time for contemplation. The parties have limited time for briefing. Preparation for a typical copyright trial, even a bench trial, generally takes many months; the arguments about why one work isn't substantially similar in its expression to another, or about why it's a fair use of another, are often sophisticated and fact-intensive, and must be crafted with a good deal of thought and effort."). This difficulty is compounded significantly when a defendant raises a colorable fair use defense. "Whether [a] taking[] will pass the fair use test is difficult to predict. It depends on widely varying perceptions held by different judges." Pierre N. Leval, *Toward a Fair Use Standard*, 103 HARV. L.REV. 1105, 1132 (1990).

Next, the court must consider whether the plaintiff will suffer irreparable harm in the absence of a preliminary injunction, and the court must assess the balance of hardships between the plaintiff and defendant. Those two items, both of which consider the harm to the parties, are related. The relevant harm is the harm that (a) occurs to the parties' legal interests and (b) cannot be remedied after a final adjudication, whether by damages or a permanent injunction. The plaintiff's interest is, principally, a property interest in the copyrighted material. But as the Supreme Court has suggested, a copyright holder might also have a First Amendment interest in *not* speaking. *See Harper & Row Publishers, Inc. v. Nation Enters.*, 471 U.S. 539, 559 (1985). The defendant to a copyright suit likewise has a property interest in his or her work to the extent that work does not infringe the plaintiff's copyright. And a defendant also has a core First Amendment interest in the freedom to express him or herself, so long as that expression does not infringe the plaintiff's copyright.

But the above-identified interests are relevant only to the extent that they are not remediable after a final adjudication. Harm might be irremediable, or irreparable, for many reasons, including that a loss is difficult to replace or difficult to measure, or that it is a loss that one should not be expected to suffer. In the context of copyright infringement cases, the harm to the plaintiff's property interest has often been characterized as irreparable in light of possible market confusion....

After *eBay*, however, courts must not simply presume irreparable harm. Rather, plaintiffs must show that, on the facts of their case, the failure to issue an injunction would actually cause irreparable harm. This is not to say that most copyright plaintiffs who have shown a likelihood of success on the merits would not be irreparably harmed absent preliminary injunctive relief. As an empirical matter, that may well be the case, and the historical tendency to issue preliminary injunctions readily in copyright cases may reflect just that....

But by anchoring the injunction standard to equitable principles, albeit with one eye on historical tendencies, courts are able to keep pace with innovation in this rapidly changing technological area. Justice Kennedy, responding to Justice Roberts, made this very point as to patent injunctions in his *eBay* concurrence. Although the "lesson of the historical practice ... is most helpful and instructive when the circumstances of a case bear substantial parallels to litigation the courts have confronted before[,] ... in many instances the nature of the patent being enforced and the economic function of the patent holder present considerations quite unlike earlier cases." Justice Kennedy concluded that changes in the way parties use patents may now mean that "legal damages [are] sufficient to compensate for the infringement."

Finally, courts must consider the public's interest. The object of copyright law is to promote the store of knowledge available to the public. But to the extent it accomplishes this end by providing individuals a financial incentive to contribute to the store of knowledge, the public's interest may well be already accounted for by the plaintiff's interest.

The public's interest in free expression, however, is significant and is distinct from the parties' speech interests. "By protecting those who wish to enter the marketplace of ideas from government attack, the First Amendment protects the public's interest in receiving information." *Pac. Gas & Elec. Co. v. Pub. Utils. Comm'n of Cal.*, 475 U.S. 1, 8 (1986). Every injunction issued before a final adjudication on the merits risks enjoining speech protected by the First Amendment. Some uses, however, will so patently infringe another's copyright, without giving rise to an even colorable fair use defense, that the likely First Amendment value in the use is virtually nonexistent.

Because the District Court considered only the first of the four factors that, under *eBay* and our holding today, must be considered before issuing a preliminary injunction, we vacate and remand the case. But in the interest of judicial economy, we note that there is no reason to disturb the District Court's conclusion as to the factor it did consider — namely, that Salinger is likely to succeed on the merits of his copyright infringement claim.

Most of the matters relevant to Salinger's likelihood of success on the merits are either undisputed or readily established in his favor. Thus, Defendants do not contest either that Salinger owns a valid copyright in *Catcher* or that they had actual access to *Catcher*. And while they argue only that *60 Years Later* and *Catcher* are not substantially similar, that contention is manifestly meritless. "In considering substantial similarity between two items, we review the district court's findings *de novo* — not on the clearly erroneous standard — because what is required is only a visual comparison of the works, rather than credibility, which we are in as good a position to decide as was the district court." *Folio Impressions, Inc. v. Byer Cal.*, 937 F.2d 759, 766 (2d Cir.1991). And for largely the same reasons as the District Court, we affirm the District Court's finding that *Catcher* and *60 Years Later* are substantially similar.

More serious is Defendants' assertion of a fair use defense. And at this preliminary stage, we agree with the District Court that Defendants will not likely be able to make out such a defense. The District Court in its discussion of fair use focused on the first statutory factor: the "purpose and character of the use." 17 U.S.C. § 107(1). In doing this, the Court found that "[i]t is simply not credible for Defendant Colting to assert now that his primary purpose was to critique Salinger and his persona, while he and his agents' previous statements regarding the book discuss no such critique, and in fact reference various other purposes behind the book." Such a finding is not clear error. It may be that a court can find that the fair use factor favors a defendant even when the defendant and his work lack a transformative *purpose*. We need not decide that issue here, however, for when we consider the District Court's credibility finding together with all the other facts in this case, we conclude, with the District Court, that Defendants are not likely to prevail in their fair use defense.

In this preliminary injunction case, the District Court erred by not applying the equitable standard outlined by the Supreme Court in *eBay, Inc. v. MercExchange, L.L.C.* and *Winter v. Natural Resources Defense Council* [555 U.S. 7 (2008)]. Accordingly, we vacate and remand for further proceedings consistent with this opinion. The preliminary injunction will stay in place for ten days following the issuance of the mandate so that Appellees will have an opportunity to apply for a temporary restraining order pending the rehearing of the motion for a preliminary injunction.

Authors Guild v. Google, Inc.

804 F.3d 202 (2d Cir. 2015)

This copyright dispute tests the boundaries of fair use. Plaintiffs, who are authors of published books under copyright, sued Google, Inc. ("Google") for copyright infringement in the United States District Court for the Southern District of New York (Chin, J.). They appeal from the grant of summary judgment in Google's favor. Through its Library Project and its Google Books project, acting without permission of rights holders, Google has made digital copies of tens of millions of books, including Plaintiffs', that were submitted to it for that purpose by major libraries. Google has scanned the digital copies and established a publicly available search function. An Internet user can use this function to search without charge to determine whether the book contains a specified word or term and also see "snippets" of text containing the searched-for terms. In addition, Google has allowed the participating libraries to download and retain digital copies of the books they submit, under agreements which commit the libraries not to use their digital copies in violation of the copyright laws. These activities of Google are alleged to constitute infringement of Plaintiffs' copyrights. Plaintiffs sought injunctive and declaratory relief as well as damages.

Google defended on the ground that its actions constitute "fair use," which, under 17 U.S.C. § 107, is "not an infringement." The district court agreed. *Authors Guild, Inc. v. Google Inc.*, 954 F.Supp.2d 282, 294 (S.D.N.Y.2013). Plaintiffs brought this appeal.

Plaintiffs contend the district court's ruling was flawed in several respects. They argue: (1) Google's digital copying of entire books, allowing users through the snippet function to read portions, is not a "transformative use" within the meaning of *Campbell v. Acuff-Rose Music, Inc.*, 510 U.S. 569, 578–585 (1994), and provides a substitute for Plaintiffs' works; (2) notwithstanding that Google provides public access to the search and snippet functions without charge and without advertising, its ultimate commercial profit motivation and its derivation of revenue from its dominance of the world-wide Internet search market to which the books project contributes, preclude a finding of fair use; (3) even if Google's copying and revelations of text do not infringe plaintiffs' books, they infringe Plaintiffs' derivative rights in search functions, depriving Plaintiffs of revenues or other benefits they would gain from licensed search markets; (4) Google's storage of digital copies exposes Plaintiffs to the risk that hackers will make their books freely (or cheaply) available on the

Internet, destroying the value of their copyrights; and (5) Google's distribution of digital copies to participant libraries is not a transformative use, and it subjects Plaintiffs to the risk of loss of copyright revenues through access allowed by libraries. We reject these arguments and conclude that the district court correctly sustained Google's fair use defense.

Google's making of a digital copy to provide a search function is a transformative use, which augments public knowledge by making available information about Plaintiffs' books without providing the public with a substantial substitute for matter protected by the Plaintiffs' copyright interests in the original works or derivatives of them. The same is true, at least under present conditions, of Google's provision of the snippet function. Plaintiffs' contention that Google has usurped their opportunity to access paid and unpaid licensing markets for substantially the same functions that Google provides fails, in part because the licensing markets in fact involve very different functions than those that Google provides, and in part because an author's derivative rights do not include an exclusive right to supply information (of the sort provided by Google) about her works. Google's profit motivation does not in these circumstances justify denial of fair use. Google's program does not, at this time and on the record before us, expose Plaintiffs to an unreasonable risk of loss of copyright value through incursions of hackers. Finally, Google's provision of digital copies to participating libraries, authorizing them to make non-infringing uses, is non-infringing, and the mere speculative possibility that the libraries might allow use of their copies in an infringing manner does not make Google a contributory infringer. Plaintiffs have failed to show a material issue of fact in dispute.

We affirm the judgment.

BACKGROUND

I. Plaintiffs

The author-plaintiffs are Jim Bouton, author of Ball Four; Betty Miles, author of The Trouble with Thirteen; and Joseph Goulden, author of The Superlawyers: The Small and Powerful World of the Great Washington Law Firms. Each of them has a legal or beneficial ownership in the copyright for his or her book.[15] Their books have

---

15. The Authors Guild, a membership organization of published authors, is also a plaintiff and appellant, seeking injunctive and declaratory relief on behalf of its members. However, in a separate case, this court found that, under the Copyright Act, the Authors Guild lacks standing to sue for copyright infringement on its members' behalf. Authors Guild, Inc. v. HathiTrust, 755 F.3d 87, 94 (2d Cir.2014). As the three individual author-plaintiffs clearly do have standing, their suit and their appeal are properly adjudicated, notwithstanding the Authors Guild's lack of standing. See Bowsher v. Synar, 478 U.S. 714, 721, 106 S. Ct. 3181, 92 L.Ed.2d 583 (1986) (finding that where one appellee had standing, the court need not consider the standing of other appellees in order to determine the merits of the appeal).

been scanned without their permission by Google, which made them available to Internet users for search and snippet view on Google's website.

II. Google Books and the Google Library Project

Google's Library Project, which began in 2004, involves bi-lateral agreements between Google and a number of the world's major research libraries. Under these agreements, the participating libraries select books from their collections to submit to Google for inclusion in the project. Google makes a digital scan of each book, extracts a machine-readable text, and creates an index of the machine-readable text of each book. Google retains the original scanned image of each book, in part so as to improve the accuracy of the machine-readable texts and indices as image-to-text conversion technologies improve.

Since 2004, Google has scanned, rendered machine-readable, and indexed more than 20 million books, including both copyrighted works and works in the public domain. The vast majority of the books are non-fiction, and most are out of print. All of the digital information created by Google in the process is stored on servers protected by the same security systems Google uses to shield its own confidential information.

The digital corpus created by the scanning of these millions of books enables the Google Books search engine. Members of the public who access the Google Books website can enter search words or terms of their own choice, receiving in response a list of all books in the database in which those terms appear, as well as the number of times the term appears in each book. A brief description of each book, entitled "About the Book," gives some rudimentary additional information, including a list of the words and terms that appear with most frequency in the book. It sometimes provides links to buy the book online and identifies libraries where the book can be found. The search tool permits a researcher to identify those books, out of millions, that do, as well as those that do not, use the terms selected by the researcher. Google notes that this identifying information instantaneously supplied would otherwise not be obtainable in lifetimes of searching.

No advertising is displayed to a user of the search function. Nor does Google receive payment by reason of the searcher's use of Google's link to purchase the book.

The search engine also makes possible new forms of research, known as "text mining" and "data mining." Google's "ngrams" research tool draws on the Google Library Project corpus to furnish statistical information to Internet users about the frequency of word and phrase usage over centuries. This tool permits users to discern fluctuations of interest in a particular subject over time and space by showing increases and decreases in the frequency of reference and usage in different periods and different linguistic regions. It also allows researchers to comb over the tens of millions of books Google has scanned in order to examine "word frequencies, syntactic patterns, and thematic markers" and to derive information on how nomenclature, linguistic usage, and literary style have changed over time. he district court gave as an example "track[ing] the frequency of references to the United States as a single entity ('the United States is') versus references to the United States in the plural ('the United States are') and how that usage has changed over time." *Authors Guild, Inc.*, 954 F.Supp.2d at 287.

The Google Books search function also allows the user a limited viewing of text. In addition to telling the number of times the word or term selected by the searcher appears in the book, the search function will display a maximum of three "snippets" containing it.... A searcher can view more than three snippets of a book by entering additional searches for different terms. However, Google makes permanently unavailable for snippet view one snippet on each page and one complete page out of every ten—a process Google calls "blacklisting."

Google also disables snippet view entirely for types of books for which a single snippet is likely to satisfy the searcher's present need for the book, such as dictionaries, cookbooks, and books of short poems. Finally, since 2005, Google will exclude any book altogether from snippet view at the request of the rights holder by the submission of an online form.

Under its contracts with the participating libraries, Google allows each library to download copies—of both the digital image and machine-readable versions—of the books that library submitted to Google for scanning (but not of books submitted by other libraries). This is done by giving each participating library access to the Google Return Interface ("GRIN"). The agreements between Google and the libraries, although not in all respects uniform, require the libraries to abide by copyright law in utilizing the digital copies they download and to take precautions to prevent dissemination of their digital copies to the public at large. Through the GRIN facility, participant libraries have downloaded at least 2.7 million digital copies of their own volumes.

III. Procedural History

Plaintiffs brought this suit on September 20, 2005, as a putative class action on behalf of similarly situated, rights-owning authors.[16] After several years of negotiation, the parties reached a proposed settlement that would have resolved the claims on a class-wide basis. The proposed settlement allowed Google to make substantially more extensive use of its scans of copyrighted books than contemplated under the present judgment, and provided that Google would make payments to the rights holders in return. On March 22, 2011, however, the district court rejected the proposed settlement as unfair to the class members who relied on the named plaintiffs to represent their interests. *Authors Guild v. Google Inc.*, 770 F.Supp.2d 666, 679–680 (S.D.N.Y.2011)....

DISCUSSION

I. The Law of Fair Use

The ultimate goal of copyright is to expand public knowledge and understanding, which copyright seeks to achieve by giving potential creators exclusive control over

---

16. A year earlier, authors brought suit against the HathiTrust Digital Library, alleging facts that are closely related, although not identical, to those alleged in the instant case. Authors Guild, Inc. v. HathiTrust, 755 F.3d 87, 91 (2d Cir.2014).

copying of their works, thus giving them a financial incentive to create informative, intellectually enriching works for public consumption. This objective is clearly reflected in the Constitution's empowerment of Congress "*To promote the Progress of Science ...* by securing for limited Times to Authors ... the exclusive Right to their respective Writings." U.S. Const., Art. I, §8, cl. 8 (emphasis added). Thus, while authors are undoubtedly important intended beneficiaries of copyright, the ultimate, primary intended beneficiary is the public, whose access to knowledge copyright seeks to advance by providing rewards for authorship.

For nearly three hundred years, since shortly after the birth of copyright in England in 1710, courts have recognized that, in certain circumstances, giving authors absolute control over all copying from their works would tend in some circumstances to limit, rather than expand, public knowledge. In the words of Lord Ellenborough, "[W]hile I shall think myself bound to secure every man in the enjoyment of his copy-right, one must not put manacles upon science." *Cary v. Kearsley*, 170 Eng. Rep. 679, 681, 4 Esp. 168, 170 (1802). Courts thus developed the doctrine, eventually named fair use, which permits unauthorized copying in some circumstances, so as to further "copyright's very purpose, '[t]o promote the Progress of Science and useful Arts.'" *Campbell v. Acuff-Rose Music, Inc.*, 510 U.S. 569, 575 (1994) (quoting U.S. Const., Art. I, §8, cl. 8). Although well established in the common law development of copyright, fair use was not recognized in the terms of our statute until the adoption of §107 in the Copyright Act of 1976. 17 U.S.C. §§101 et seq.

Section 107, in its present form,13 provides:

> [T]he fair use of a copyrighted work ... for purposes such as criticism, comment, news reporting, teaching (including multiple copies for classroom use), scholarship, or research, is not an infringement of copyright. In determining whether the use made of a work in any particular case is a fair use the factors to be considered shall include—
>
> (1) the purpose and character of the use, including whether such use is of a commercial nature or is for nonprofit educational purposes;
>
> (2) the nature of the copyrighted work;
>
> (3) the amount and substantiality of the portion used in relation to the copyrighted work as a whole; and
>
> (4) the effect of the use upon the potential market for or value of the copyrighted work.
>
> The fact that a work is unpublished shall not itself bar a finding of fair use if such finding is made upon consideration of all the above factors.

17 U.S.C. §107. As the Supreme Court has designated fair use an affirmative defense, the party asserting fair use bears the burden of proof.

The statute's wording, derived from a brief observation of Justice Joseph Story in *Folsom v. Marsh*,[17] does not furnish standards for recognition of fair use. Its instruction to consider the "purpose and character" of the secondary use and the "nature" of the copyrighted work does not explain what types of "purpose and character" or "nature" favor a finding of fair use and which do not. In fact, as the Supreme Court observed in *Campbell*, the House Report makes clear that, in passing the statute, Congress had no intention of normatively dictating fair use policy. The purpose of the enactment was to give recognition in the statute itself to such an important part of copyright law developed by the courts through the common law process....

The *Campbell* Court undertook a comprehensive analysis of fair use's requirements, discussing every segment of § 107. Beginning with the examples of purposes set forth in the statute's preamble, the Court made clear that they are "illustrative and not limitative" and "provide only general guidance about the sorts of copying that courts and Congress most commonly ha[ve] found to be fair uses." 510 U.S. at 577–578 (internal quotations and citations omitted). The statute "calls for case-by-case analysis" and "is not to be simplified with bright-line rules." *Id.* at 577. Section 107's four factors are not to "be treated in isolation, one from another. All are to be explored, and the results weighed together, in light of the purposes of copyright." *Id.* at 578. Each factor thus stands as part of a multifaceted assessment of the crucial question: how to define the boundary limit of the original author's exclusive rights in order to best serve the overall objectives of the copyright law to expand public learning while protecting the incentives of authors to create for the public good.

At the same time, the Supreme Court has made clear that some of the statute's four listed factors are more significant than others. The Court observed in *Harper & Row Publishers, Inc. v. Nation Enterprises* that the fourth factor, which assesses the harm the secondary use can cause to the market for, or the value of, the copyright for the original, "is undoubtedly the single most important element of fair use." 471 U.S. 539, 566 (citing Melville B. Nimmer, 3 Nimmer on Copyright § 13.05[A], at 13–76 (1984)). This is consistent with the fact that the copyright is a commercial right, intended to protect the ability of authors to profit from the exclusive right to merchandise their own work.

In *Campbell*, the Court stressed also the importance of the first factor, the "purpose and character of the secondary use." 17 U.S.C. § 107(1). The more the appropriator is using the copied material for new, transformative purposes, the more it serves copyright's goal of enriching public knowledge and the less likely it is that the appropriation will serve as a substitute for the original or its plausible derivatives, shrink-

---

17. 9 F. Cas. 342, 348 (C.C.D.Mass.1841) ("[W]e must often, in deciding questions of this sort, look to the nature and objects of the selections made, the quantity and value of the materials used, and the degree in which the use may prejudice the sale, or diminish the profits, or supersede the objects, of the original work.").

ing the protected market opportunities of the copyrighted work. 510 U.S. at 591 (noting that, when the secondary use is transformative, "market substitution is at least less certain, and market harm may not be so readily inferred.").

With this background, we proceed to discuss each of the statutory factors, as illuminated by *Campbell* and subsequent case law, in relation to the issues here in dispute.

II. The Search and Snippet View Functions

A. Factor One

(1) Transformative purpose. Campbell's explanation of the first factor's inquiry into the "purpose and character" of the secondary use focuses on whether the new work, "in Justice Story's words, … merely 'supersede[s] the objects' of the original creation, … or instead adds something new, with a further purpose…. [I]t asks, in other words, whether and to what extent the new work is 'transformative.'" 510 U.S. at 578–579 (citations omitted). While recognizing that a transformative use is "not absolutely necessary for a finding of fair use," the opinion further explains that the "goal of copyright, to promote science and the arts, is generally furthered by the creation of transformative works" and that "[s]uch works thus lie at the heart of the fair use doctrine's guarantee of breathing space within the confines of copyright." *Id.* at 579, In other words, transformative uses tend to favor a fair use finding because a transformative use is one that communicates something new and different from the original or expands its utility, thus serving copyright's overall objective of contributing to public knowledge.

The word "transformative" cannot be taken too literally as a sufficient key to understanding the elements of fair use. It is rather a suggestive symbol for a complex thought, and does not mean that any and all changes made to an author's original text will necessarily support a finding of fair use. The Supreme Court's discussion in *Campbell* gave important guidance on assessing when a transformative use tends to support a conclusion of fair use. The defendant in that case defended on the ground that its work was a parody of the original and that parody is a time-honored category of fair use. Explaining why parody makes a stronger, or in any event more obvious, claim of fair use than satire, the Court stated,

> [T]he heart of any parodist's claim to quote from existing material … is the use of … a prior author's composition to … *comment[] on that author's works*…. If, on the contrary, the commentary has no critical bearing on the substance or style of the original composition, which the alleged infringer merely uses to get attention or to avoid the drudgery in working up something fresh, the claim to fairness in borrowing from another's work diminishes accordingly (if it does not vanish)…. Parody needs to mimic an original to make its point, and so has some claim to use the creation of its victim's … imagination, whereas satire can stand on its own two feet and so requires justification for the very act of borrowing.

Id. at 580–81, (emphasis added). In other words, the would-be fair user of another's work must have justification for the taking. A secondary author is not necessarily at liberty to make wholesale takings of the original author's expression merely because of how well the original author's expression would convey the secondary author's different message. Among the best recognized justifications for copying from another's work is to provide comment on it or criticism of it. A taking from another author's work for the purpose of making points that have no bearing on the original may well be fair use, but the taker would need to show a justification. This part of the Supreme Court's discussion is significant in assessing Google's claim of fair use because, as discussed extensively below, Google's claim of transformative purpose for copying from the works of others is to provide otherwise unavailable information about the originals.

A further complication that can result from oversimplified reliance on whether the copying involves transformation is that the word "transform" also plays a role in defining "derivative works," over which the original rights holder retains exclusive control. Section 106 of the Act specifies the "exclusive right[]" of the copyright owner "(2) to prepare derivative works based upon the copyrighted work." *See* 17 U.S.C. § 106. The statute defines derivative works largely by example, rather than explanation. The examples include "translation, musical arrangement, dramatization, fictionalization, motion picture version, sound recording, art reproduction, abridgement, condensation," to which list the statute adds "any other form in which a work may be ... *transformed.*" 17 U.S.C. § 101 (emphasis added). As we noted in *Authors Guild, Inc. v. HathiTrust*, "[p]aradigmatic examples of derivative works include the translation of a novel into another language, the adaptation of a novel into a movie or play, or the recasting of a novel as an e-book or an audiobook." 755 F.3d 87, 95 (2d Cir. 2014). While such changes can be described as transformations, they do not involve the kind of transformative purpose that favors a fair use finding. The statutory definition suggests that derivative works generally involve transformations in the nature of changes of form. 17 U.S.C. § 101. By contrast, copying from an original for the purpose of criticism or commentary on the original or provision of information about it,[18] tends most clearly to satisfy *Campbell*'s notion of the "transformative" purpose involved in the analysis of Factor One.

---

18. *See, e.g., HathiTrust,* 755 F.3d at 97–98 (justifying as transformative fair use purpose the digital copying of original for purpose of permitting searchers to determine whether its text employs particular words); A.V. ex rel. Vanderhye v. iParadigms, L.L.C., 562 F.3d 630, 638–640 (4th Cir. 2009) (justifying as transformative fair use purpose the complete digital copying of a manuscript to determine whether the original included matter plagiarized from other works); Perfect 10, Inc. v. Amazon.com, Inc., 508 F.3d 1146, 1165 (9th Cir. 2007) (justifying as transformative fair use purpose the use of a digital, thumbnail copy of the original to provide an Internet pathway to the original); Kelly v. Arriba Soft Corp., 336 F.3d 811, 818–819 (9th Cir.2003) (same); Bond v. Blum, 317 F.3d 385 (4th Cir.2003) (justifying as fair use purpose the copying of author's original unpublished autobiographical manuscript for the purpose of showing that he murdered his father and was an unfit custodian of his children); Nuñez v. Caribbean Int'l News Corp., 235 F.3d 18, 21–23 (1st Cir. 2000) (justifying as transformative fair use purpose a newspaper's copying of a photo of winner of beauty pageant in a revealing pose for the purpose of informing the public of the reason the winner's title was withdrawn).

With these considerations in mind, we first consider whether Google's search and snippet views functions satisfy the first fair use factor with respect to Plaintiffs' rights in their books. (The question whether these functions might infringe upon Plaintiffs' derivative rights is discussed in the next Part.)

(2) Search Function. We have no difficulty concluding that Google's making of a digital copy of Plaintiffs' books for the purpose of enabling a search for identification of books containing a term of interest to the searcher involves a highly transformative purpose, in the sense intended by *Campbell.* Our court's exemplary discussion in *HathiTrust* informs our ruling. That case involved a dispute that is closely related, although not identical, to this one. Authors brought claims of copyright infringement against HathiTrust, an entity formed by libraries participating in the Google Library Project to pool the digital copies of their books created for them by Google. The suit challenged various usages HathiTrust made of the digital copies. Among the challenged uses was HathiTrust's offer to its patrons of "full-text searches," which, very much like the search offered by Google Books to Internet users, permitted patrons of the libraries to locate in which of the digitized books specific words or phrases appeared. (HathiTrust's search facility did not include the snippet view function, or any other display of text.) We concluded that both the making of the digital copies and the use of those copies to offer the search tool were fair uses.

Notwithstanding that the libraries had downloaded and stored complete digital copies of entire books, we noted that such copying was essential to permit searchers to identify and locate the books in which words or phrases of interest to them appeared. We concluded "that the creation of a full-text searchable database is a quintessentially transformative use ... [as] the result of a word search is different in purpose, character, expression, meaning, and message from the page (and the book) from which it is drawn." We cited *A.V. ex rel. Vanderhye v. iParadigms, L.L.C.,* 562 F.3d 630, 639–40 (4th Cir.2009), *Perfect 10, Inc. v. Amazon.com, Inc.,* 508 F.3d 1146, 1165 (9th Cir.2007), and *Kelly v. Arriba Soft Corp.,* 336 F.3d 811, 819 (9th Cir.2003) as examples of cases in which courts had similarly found the creation of complete digital copies of copyrighted works to be transformative fair uses when the copies "served a different function from the original." *HathiTrust,* 755 F.3d at 97.

As with *HathiTrust* (and *iParadigms*), the purpose of Google's copying of the original copyrighted books is to make available significant information about those books, permitting a searcher to identify those that contain a word or term of interest, as well as those that do not include reference to it. In addition, through the ngrams tool, Google allows readers to learn the frequency of usage of selected words in the aggregate corpus of published books in different historical periods. We have no doubt that the purpose of this copying is the sort of transformative purpose described in *Campbell* as strongly favoring satisfaction of the first factor....

B. Factor Two

The second fair use factor directs consideration of the "nature of the copyrighted work." While the "transformative purpose" inquiry discussed above is conventionally treated as a part of first factor analysis, it inevitably involves the second factor as well. One cannot assess whether the copying work has an objective that differs from the original without considering both works, and their respective objectives.

The second factor has rarely played a significant role in the determination of a fair use dispute. The Supreme Court in *Harper & Row* made a passing observation in dictum that, "[t]he law generally recognizes a greater need to disseminate factual works than works of fiction or fantasy." 471 U.S. 539, 563. Courts have sometimes speculated that this might mean that a finding of fair use is more favored when the copying is of factual works than when copying is from works of fiction. However, while the copyright does not protect facts or ideas set forth in a work, it does protect that author's manner of expressing those facts and ideas. At least unless a persuasive fair use justification is involved, authors of factual works, like authors of fiction, should be entitled to copyright protection of their protected expression. The mere fact that the original is a factual work therefore should not imply that others may freely copy it. Those who report the news undoubtedly create factual works. It cannot seriously be argued that, for that reason, others may freely copy and re-disseminate news reports.

In considering the second factor in *HathiTrust*, we concluded that it was "not dispositive," commenting that courts have hardly ever found that the second factor in isolation played a large role in explaining a fair use decision. The same is true here....

C. Factor Three

The third statutory factor instructs us to consider "the amount and substantiality of the portion used in relation to the copyrighted work as a whole." The clear implication of the third factor is that a finding of fair use is more likely when small amounts, or less important passages, are copied than when the copying is extensive, or encompasses the most important parts of the original. The obvious reason for this lies in the relationship between the third and the fourth factors. The larger the amount, or the more important the part, of the original that is copied, the greater the likelihood that the secondary work might serve as an effectively competing substitute for the original, and might therefore diminish the original rights holder's sales and profits.

(1) Search Function.... In *HathiTrust*, our court concluded in its discussion of the third factor that "[b]ecause it was reasonably necessary for the [HathiTrust Digital Library] to make use of the entirety of the works in order to enable the full-text search function, we do not believe the copying was excessive." As with HathiTrust, not only is the copying of the totality of the original reasonably appropriate to Google's transformative purpose, it is literally necessary to achieve that purpose. If Google copied less than the totality of the originals, its search function could not advise searchers reliably whether their searched term appears in a book (or how many times).

While Google makes an unauthorized digital copy of the entire book, it does not reveal that digital copy to the public. The copy is made to enable the search functions to reveal limited, important information about the books. With respect to the search function, Google satisfies the third factor test, as illuminated by the Supreme Court in *Campbell*.

(2) Snippet View.... What matters in such cases is not so much "the amount and substantiality of the portion used" in making a copy, but rather the amount and substantiality of what is thereby made accessible to a public for which it may serve as a competing substitute. In *HathiTrust*, notwithstanding the defendant's full-text copying, the search function revealed virtually nothing of the text of the originals to the public. Here, through the snippet view, more is revealed to searchers than in *HathiTrust*.

Without doubt, enabling searchers to see portions of the copied texts could have determinative effect on the fair use analysis. The larger the quantity of the copyrighted text the searcher can see and the more control the searcher can exercise over what part of the text she sees, the greater the likelihood that those revelations could serve her as an effective, free substitute for the purchase of the plaintiff's book. We nonetheless conclude that, at least as presently structured by Google, the snippet view does not reveal matter that offers the marketplace a significantly competing substitute for the copyrighted work.

Google has constructed the snippet feature in a manner that substantially protects against its serving as an effectively competing substitute for Plaintiffs' books. In the Background section of this opinion, we describe a variety of limitations Google imposes on the snippet function. These include the small size of the snippets (normally one eighth of a page), the blacklisting of one snippet per page and of one page in every ten, the fact that no more than three snippets are shown—and no more than one per page—for each term searched, and the fact that the same snippets are shown for a searched term no matter how many times, or from how many different computers, the term is searched. In addition, Google does not provide snippet view for types of books, such as dictionaries and cookbooks, for which viewing a small segment is likely to satisfy the searcher's need. The result of these restrictions is, so far as the record demonstrates, that a searcher cannot succeed, even after long extended effort to multiply what can be revealed, in revealing through a snippet search what could usefully serve as a competing substitute for the original.

The blacklisting, which permanently blocks about 22% of a book's text from snippet view, is by no means the most important of the obstacles Google has designed. While it is true that the blacklisting of 22% leaves 78% of a book theoretically accessible to a searcher, it does not follow that any large part of that 78% is in fact accessible. The other restrictions built into the program work together to ensure that, even after protracted effort over a substantial period of time, only small and randomly scattered portions of a book will be accessible. In an effort to show what large portions of text searchers can read through persistently augmented snippet searches, Plaintiffs' counsel employed researchers over a period of weeks to do multiple word searches on Plaintiffs' books. In no case were they able to access as much as 16% of the text, and the snippets collected were usually not sequential but scattered randomly throughout the book. Because Google's snippets are arbitrarily and uniformly divided by lines of text, and not by complete sentences, paragraphs, or any measure dictated by content, a searcher would have great difficulty constructing a search so as to provide any extensive information about the book's use of that term. As snippet view never reveals more than one snippet per page in response to repeated searches for the same term, it is at least difficult, and often impossible, for a searcher to gain access to more than a single snippet's worth of an extended, continuous discussion of the term....

D. Factor Four

The fourth fair use factor, "the effect of the [copying] use upon the potential market for or value of the copyrighted work," focuses on whether the copy brings to the marketplace a competing substitute for the original, or its derivative, so as to deprive the rights holder of significant revenues because of the likelihood that potential purchasers may opt to acquire the copy in preference to the original. Because copyright is a commercial doctrine whose objective is to stimulate creativity among potential authors by enabling them to earn money from their creations, the fourth factor is of great importance in making a fair use assessment. *See Harper & Row*, 471 U.S. at 566, 105 S. Ct. 2218 (describing the fourth factor as "undoubtedly the single most important element of fair use").

Campbell stressed the close linkage between the first and fourth factors, in that the more the copying is done to achieve a purpose that differs from the purpose of the original, the less likely it is that the copy will serve as a satisfactory substitute for the original. Consistent with that observation, the *HathiTrust* court found that the fourth factor favored the defendant and supported a finding of fair use because the ability to search the text of the book to determine whether it includes selected words "does not serve as a substitute for the books that are being searched."

However, *Campbell*'s observation as to the likelihood of a secondary use serving as an effective substitute goes only so far. Even if the purpose of the copying is for a valuably transformative purpose, such copying might nonetheless harm the value of the copyrighted original if done in a manner that results in widespread revelation of sufficiently significant portions of the original as to make available a significantly competing substitute. The question for us is whether snippet view, notwithstanding its transformative purpose, does that. We conclude that, at least as snippet view is presently constructed, it does not....

Accordingly, considering the four fair use factors in light of the goals of copyright, we conclude that Google's making of a complete digital copy of Plaintiffs' works for the purpose of providing the public with its search and snippet view functions (at least as snippet view is presently designed) is a fair use and does not infringe Plaintiffs' copyrights in their books.

[The court then ruled against all other theories of liability.]

In sum, we conclude that: (1) Google's unauthorized digitizing of copyright-protected works, creation of a search functionality, and display of snippets from those works are non-infringing fair uses. The purpose of the copying is highly transformative, the public display of text is limited, and the revelations do not provide a significant market substitute for the protected aspects of the originals. Google's commercial nature and profit motivation do not justify denial of fair use. (2) Google's provision of digitized copies to the libraries that supplied the books, on the understanding that the libraries will use the copies in a manner consistent with the copyright law, also does not constitute infringement. Nor, on this record, is Google a contributory infringer.

CONCLUSION

The judgment of the district court is AFFIRMED.

Notes and Questions

a. *Authors Guild v. Google, Inc.* and *Authors Guild, Inc. v. HathiTrust*, represented a decades-long battle between the technology giant and the publishing industry, won convincingly by the technology industry. Despite the clear victory for Google, however, the battle also served to significantly alter the activities conducted by Google, moving them from a predatory consumption of most published books into a much less controversial service for the public. Google, of course, benefitted tremendously by using the scanned books to serve as the basis for its natural language translation services and the heart of its artificial intelligence efforts. Neither of these uses were identified as intermediary copying uses that could have given rise to copyright liability because the confidential nature of such uses in 2004 were not considered by the publishers.

b. Google's book project began with Google's drive to organize all information. The process resulted in an abortive competitive effort from Microsoft, and lawsuits by the Authors Guild and a group of commercial publishers. After three years of negotiations, the litigation resulted in a proposed settlement among the Authors Guild, the Association of American Publishers, and Google. The proposed Amended Settlement Agreement received preliminary approval in 2009. However, in 2011 final settlement approval was denied.

> [C]iting copyright, antitrust and other concerns, Judge Denny Chin said that the settlement went too far. He said it would have granted Google a "de facto monopoly" and the right to profit from books without the permission of copyright owners.

> Judge Chin acknowledged that "the creation of a universal digital library would benefit many," but said that the proposed agreement was "not fair, adequate and reasonable." He left open the possibility that a substantially revised agreement could pass legal muster. Judge Chin was recently elevated to the United States Court of Appeals for the Second Circuit, but handled the case as a district court judge.

The decision is also a setback for the Authors Guild and the Association of American Publishers, which sued Google in 2005 over its book-scanning project. After two years of painstaking negotiations, the authors, publishers and Google signed a sweeping settlement that would have brought millions of printed works into the digital age.

The deal turned Google, the authors and the publishers into allies instead of opponents. Together, they mounted a defense of the agreement against an increasingly vocal chorus of opponents that included Google rivals like Amazon and Microsoft, as well as academics, some authors, copyright experts, the Justice Department and foreign governments.[19]

Had the settlement with the publishers been part of the class action, it would have removed the pricing model and other potentially anti-competitive behavior outside of antitrust scrutiny. The settlement with publishers returns control over publishing distribution largely to the publishers.

c. Amazon.com had entered into an agreement with Borders Books to operate Borders.com, and eventually Waldens.com, because Borders was unsuccessful at running its online book business. Borders hoped to reduce its losses through the Amazon arrangement while maintaining an Internet presence. The district court rejected claims of a *per se* antitrust challenge to the relationship, since the sales prices of the two companies were not fixed by agreement and the pricing was ancillary to the overall legitimate purposes of the agreement. *See Gerlinger v. Amazon.com, Inc.*, 311 F. Supp. 2d 838 (N.D. Cal. 2004). Following the bankruptcy of Borders, the website was purchased by Barnes & Noble.

d. The decision in *Random House, Inc. v. Salinger* set off a controversy over the scope of fair use for unpublished works. L. Ron Hubbard was the subject of much litigation in this regard. *See New Era Publ'ns Int'l, ApS v. Henry Holt & Co.*, 695 F. Supp. 1493 (S.D.N.Y. 1988). The District Court did not appear to think much of the Second Circuit's new jurisprudence:

> As to the book overall, were it not for the ruling of the Court of Appeals in *Salinger*, I would conclude that fair use has been adequately demonstrated.... Many of the takings of Salinger's expression were for the purpose of enlivening that text with Salinger's expressive genius.... Hubbard's expression is taken primarily to show character flaws in a manner that cannot be accomplished without use of his words.

Id. at 1524. The Second Circuit did not appreciate the criticism, but affirmed the decision. *New Era Publs. Int'l v. Henry Holt & Co.*, 873 F.2d 576 (2d Cir. N.Y. 1989). *See also Norse v. Henry Holt & Co.*, 847 F. Supp. 142, 147 (N.D. Cal. 1994); *Wright v. Warner Books, Inc.*, 953 F.2d 731 (2d Cir. 1991) (a slightly more balanced decision

---

19. Miguel Helft, *Judge Rejects Google's Deal to Digitize Books*, N.Y. Times, Mar. 23, 2011, at B1.

making a finding of fair use involving the biography of Richard Wright, author of *Native Son* and *Black Boy*).

Congress finally weighed in on the issue, adding language to § 107 which provides "[t]he fact that a work is unpublished shall not itself bar a finding of fair use if such finding is made upon consideration of all the above factors." As unhelpful as this sentence appears, Congress was correct to add this text to clarify its intent to extend the reach of Fair Use to unpublished works. The legislative history criticized *Salinger* and the Second Circuit, yet it also approved of *Wright*, which was not a particularly broad use of unpublished material. The tone of the legislative hearings may have done more than the text of the statutory amendment to liberalize the courts on the availability of fair use for unpublished material.

e. The Second Circuit continued to struggle with its decision in *Random House, Inc. v. Salinger*. In *Wright v. Warner Books, Inc.*, 953 F.2d 731 (2d Cir. 1991), the Second Circuit appeared to liberalize its analysis somewhat. As the Court explained:

> In the words of the district court: This case presents the next chapter in the continuing narrative of this Circuit's treatment of the fair use defense to a charge of copyright infringement." The principal question presented is whether defendants' sparing use of creative expression from the unpublished letters and journals of the late author Richard Wright constitutes fair use as a matter of law.

By framing the question as "sparing use of creative expression," the court moved the decision factually from *Salinger*. The court continued to apply the full, four-factored fair use analysis, but found that the sparing paraphrasing by Dr. Margaret Walker, an acquaintance and biographer of Richard Wright, was fair use.

It might also be noted that Dr. Walker first tried to gain the estate's permission and, when refused, edited out large portions of the unpublished materials. Despite this, the first two publishers later withdrew the offer of publication, fearing the inevitable litigation.

f. The public importance of material sometimes has significant impact on a court's willingness to find fair use. For example, see *Time, Inc. v. Bernard Geis Assocs.*, 293 F. Supp. 130 (S.D.N.Y. 1968) (upholding fair use for illegal access and copying of 22 frames of the Zapruder film).

One of the few cases to anticipate *eBay, Inc. v. MercExchange, L.L.C.*, 547 U.S. 388 (2006), in the area of copyright was *Suntrust Bank v. Houghton Mifflin Co.*, 268 F.3d 1257, 1265 (11th Cir. 2001).

> The basic framework for our analysis remains, however, the standard test governing the issuance of preliminary injunctions. Suntrust is not entitled to relief in the form of a preliminary injunction unless it has proved each of the following four elements: "(1) a substantial likelihood of success on the merits, (2) a substantial threat of irreparable injury if the injunction were not granted, (3) that the threatened injury to the plaintiff outweighs the

harm an injunction may cause the defendant, and (4) that granting the injunction would not disserve the public interest."

Suntrust Bank v. Houghton Mifflin Co., 268 F.3d 1257, 1265 (11th Cir. 2001), quoting *Am. Red Cross v. Palm Beach Blood Bank, Inc.*, 143 F.3d 1407, 1410 (11th Cir.1998). Here the court found the unauthorized retelling by Alice Randall of Margaret Mitchell's *Gone with the Wind* was fair use. Randall's *The Wind Done Gone* "persuasively claim[ed] that her novel is a critique of [Gone with the Wind's] depiction of slavery and the Civil-War era American South" and as such Randall's novel was not a market substitute for a sequel to *Gone with the Wind*.

g. Which of the two competing demands should hold greater sway: The free speech interests of the biographer or the privacy rights of the original author? *See* Samuel D. Warren & Louis D. Brandeis, *The Right to Privacy*, 4 HARV. L. REV. 193 (1890). This ground-breaking law review article discovered the law of privacy, but careful examination shows the authors relied very heavily on the tort of common law copyright infringement. It was the unauthorized publication of private letters and papers that they relabeled "privacy."

h. Secrecy in publishing is generally inconsistent with copyright registration. In the area of copyrighted test books, the two areas conflict a great deal. To what extent can a newspaper "report" the content of such a copyrighted but nonpublic test book? *See Chi. Bd. of Educ. v. Substance, Inc.*, 354 F.3d 624 (7th Cir. 2003). For a discussion regarding competing test preparation companies, *see Mulcahy v. Cheetah Learning L.L.C.*, 386 F.3d 849 (8th Cir. 2004).

i. Fair use in academic publishing has become much more complex as a result of digital archives and electronic reproductions of course packs. In *Cambridge Univ. Press v. Albert*, the district court has been reversed three times on its application of fair use. *See* 906 F.3d 1290, 1293 (11th Cir. 2018). In the initial 2012 trial, the district court ruled that the publishers established a prima facie case that 48 digital excerpts infringed their copyrights but that the University prevailed on an affirmative defense of fair use on all but five of those excerpts. By the third proceeding, the district court had changed its weighing of the fair use factors for approximately a half dozen more, but its conclusions on the fair use analysis for each of the 48 works has yet to be approved by the appellate court. Compare this with non-digital decisions *Basic Books, Inc. v. Kinko's Graphics Corp.*, 758 F. Supp. 1522 (S.D.N.Y. 1991); *Princeton Univ. Press v. Mich. Document Servs., Inc.*, 99 F.3d 1381 (6th Cir. 1996); and *Am. Geophysical Union v. Texaco Inc.*, 60 F.3d 913 (2d Cir. 1994).

j. In *United States v. Apple, Inc.*, 791 F.3d 290 (2d Cir. 2015), the effort by Apple to collaborate with the major publishers to thwart Amazon.com resulted in a finding of antitrust violations:

> Since the invention of the printing press, the distribution of books has involved a fundamentally consistent process: compose a manuscript, print and bind it into physical volumes, and then ship and sell the volumes to the public. In late 2007, Amazon.com, Inc. ("Amazon") introduced the Kindle,

a portable device that carries digital copies of books, known as "ebooks." This innovation had the potential to change the centuries-old process for producing books by eliminating the need to print, bind, ship, and store them. Amazon began to popularize the new way to read, and encouraged consumers to buy the Kindle by offering desirable books—new releases and New York Times bestsellers—for $9.99. Publishing companies, which have traditionally stood at the center of the multi-billion dollar book-producing industry, saw Amazon's ebooks, and particularly its $9.99 pricing, as a threat to their way of doing business.

By November 2009, Apple, Inc. ("Apple") had plans to release a new tablet computer, the iPad. Executives at the company saw an opportunity to sell ebooks on the iPad by creating a virtual marketplace on the device, which came to be known as the "iBookstore." Working within a tight timeframe, Apple went directly into negotiations with six of the major publishing companies in the United States. In two months, it announced that five of those companies—Hachette, HarperCollins, Macmillan, Penguin, and Simon & Schuster (collectively, the "Publisher Defendants")—had agreed to sell ebooks on the iPad under arrangements whereby the publishers had the authority to set prices, and could set the prices of new releases and New York Times bestsellers as high as $19.99 and $14.99, respectively. Each of these agreements, by virtue of its terms, resulted in each Publisher Defendant receiving less per ebook sold via Apple as opposed to Amazon, even given the higher consumer prices. Just a few months after the iBookstore opened, however, every one of the Publisher Defendants had taken control over pricing from Amazon and had raised the prices on many of their ebooks, most notably new releases and bestsellers.

The United States Department of Justice ("DOJ" or "Justice Department") and 33 states and territories (collectively, "Plaintiffs") filed suit in the United States District Court for the Southern District of New York, alleging that Apple, in launching the iBookstore, had conspired with the Publisher Defendants to raise prices across the nascent ebook market. This agreement, they argued, violated § 1 of the Sherman Antitrust Act, 15 U.S.C. § 1 et seq. ("Sherman Act"), and state antitrust laws. All five Publisher Defendants settled and signed consent decrees, which prohibited them, for a period, from restricting ebook retailers' ability to set prices. Then, after a three-week bench trial, the district court (Cote, J.) concluded that, in order to induce the Publisher Defendants to participate in the iBookstore and to avoid the necessity of itself competing with Amazon over the retail price of ebooks, Apple orchestrated a conspiracy among the Publisher Defendants to raise the price of ebooks—particularly new releases and New York Times bestsellers. *United States v. Apple Inc.*, 952 F.Supp.2d 638, 647 (S.D.N.Y.2013). The district court found that the agreement constituted a per se violation of the Sherman Act and, in the alternative, unreasonably restrained trade under the rule of reason. On September 5, 2013, the district court entered final judgment on the liability finding and issued an injunctive order that, *inter alia*, prevents Apple from entering into agreements with the Publisher Defendants that restrict its ability to set, alter, or reduce the price of ebooks, and requires Apple to apply the same terms and conditions to ebook applications sold on its devices as it does to other applications....

Because we conclude that the district court did not err in deciding that Apple violated § 1 of the Sherman Act, and because we also conclude that the district court's injunction was lawful and consistent with preventing future anticompetitive harms, we affirm.

Problem 17-E

Bryce and Jesse have just received a telephone call from the publisher of *Exposure*. In reviewing the manuscript, the publisher explained it found "a significant number of exposés which pose an editorial problem from a privacy and copyright standpoint." (You shake your head, knowing full well this moment was inevitable, based on the book's premise and structure.) Specifically, the publisher is concerned because (i) twelve of the subjects were photographed without their consent; (ii) three of the photographs depict artists creating their own works, thus publishing the artist's work as background in Jesse's photograph; (iii) four of the narratives written by Bryce include direct quotes from private letters to and from the subject of the exposé; and (iv) one exposé uses the first line and entire rhythm of a poem written by the subject of that exposé.

Bryce wants you to call the publisher's lawyer and explain why this is all fair use and free speech. After a brief discussion with you, Bryce asks that you write an opinion letter explaining that the items objected to above are fair use and therefore not actionable. Explain whether or not you could provide such a letter and the reason for that decision.

Assuming you do not provide an opinion letter to the publisher, draft a letter to Bryce explaining the legal status of the exposés and the options available to both the authors and the publisher.

F. Bibliography and Links

Chris Sagers, United States v. Apple: Competition in America (Harvard University Press 2019).

Daniel J. Coplan, *When Is "Best Efforts" Really "Best Efforts": An Analysis of the Obligation to Exploit in Entertainment Licensing Agreements and an Overview of How the Term "Best Efforts" Has Been Construed in Litigation*, 31 SW. U. L. Rev. 725 (2002).

William M. Cross, *Restoring the Public Library Ethos: Copyright, E-Licensing, and the Future of Librarianship*, 104 LAW LIBR. J. 195 (2012).

Kristelia A. García, *Copyright Arbitrage*, 107 CAL. L. REV. 199 (2019).

Jane C. Ginsburg, *The Author's Place in the Future of Copyright*, 45 WILLAMETTE L. REV. 381 (2009).

Jane C. Ginsburg, *The Right to Claim Authorship in U.S. Copyright and Trademarks Law*, 41 HOUS. L. REV. 263 (2004).

Lina M. Khan, *Sources of Tech Platform Power*, 2 GEO. L. TECH. REV. 325 (2018).

Martin P. Levin, *The Contemporary Guide to Negotiating the Author-Publisher Contract*, 54 N.Y.L. SCH. L. REV. 447 (2009–10).

Jake Linford, *A Second Look at the Right of First Publication*, 58 J. COPYRIGHT SOC'Y U.S.A. 585, 586 (2011).

Jiarui Liu, *An Empirical Study of Transformative Use in Copyright Law*, 22 STAN. TECH. L. REV. 163 (2019).

Orly Lobel, *The Law of the Platform*, 101 MINN. L. REV. 87 (2016).

Stephen M. Maurer, *Digital Publishing: Three Futures (and How to Get There)*, 36 CARDOZO ARTS & ENT. L.J. 675 (2018).

Christina Mulligan, *A Numerus Clausus Principle for Intellectual Property*, 80 TENN. L. REV. 235 (2013).

Guy A. Rub, *Amazon and the New World of Publishing Comments on Chris Sagers, Apple, Antitrust, and Irony (Harvard University Press, 2018)*, 14 I/S: J.L. & POL'Y FOR INFO. SOC'Y 367 (2018).

Pamela Samuelson, *Collective Management of Copyright: Solution or Sacrifice?: Legislative Alternatives to the Google Book Settlement*, 34 COLUM. J.L. & ARTS 697 (2011).

Pamela Samuelson, *The Dead Souls of the Google Book Search Settlement*, 52 COMM. ACM (July 2009).

Websites

Authors Guild, https://www.authorsguild.org/

Amazon.com, https://www.amazon.com

Barnes & Noble, https://www.barnesandnoble.com/

National Writers Union, http://www.nwu.org/

XLibris Publishing, www.xlibris.com/

Chapter 18

Visual Arts and Cultural Artifacts

Although somewhat different than the more commercial areas of entertainment law, fine art, visual arts, sculpture, and cultural artifacts play a similar role in society of entertaining and educating the public. In the same vein, the laws of copyright, trademark, publicity rights, First Amendment law, contract law, and labor law shape the world of art and the operations of museums in much the same way as the other entertainment industries.

Between 2008 and 2012, national rates of attendance at visual and performing arts activities dropped slightly, remaining below 2002 levels. In 2012, one in three U.S. adults (33 percent, or about 78 million) visited an art museum or gallery or attended at least one of various types of performing arts events....

As in prior years, more Americans went to visual arts events and activities than attended most types of arts performance. Between 2008 and 2012, however, rates declined for the following activities:

- Visiting an art museum or gallery (21 percent of adults nationwide, or 49.3 million, did this activity at least once in the 2012 survey year)

- Attending a crafts fair or visual arts festival (22.4 percent, or 52.6 million adults) ...

The share of adults who toured a park, monument, building, or neighborhood for historic or design value remained on par with the 2008 level. In 2012, 23.9 percent of all adults (56.2 million) made these kind of trips.[1]

In 2017, 53.8 percent of U.S. adults (up from 50.2 percent in 2012), or 132.3 million people, attended a visual or performing arts activity at least once in the past 12 months.... Much of that increase is due to greater attendance at art museums or galleries, at outdoor performing arts festivals, at unspecified types of performing arts events, and at parks, monuments, buildings, and neighborhoods visited for their design or historic value. In the past, these types of activity have drawn a broader cross-section of the

---

1. Nat'l Endowment For The Arts, How a nation engages with art — Highlights from the 2012 survey of public participation in the arts Research Report #57 (2013), http://www.arts.gov/sites/default/files/highlights-from-2012-sppa-revised-oct-2015.pdf.

U.S. adult population—one that is demographically more diverse—than have some other types of arts events. So it is fitting that relatively younger adults, those with a modest amount of formal education, and adults belonging to one or more racial/ethnic minority groups, often contributed to those increases in 2017.[2]

This chapter provides an introduction to a group of issues unique to the fields of visual arts and cultural artifacts. The topic is the subject of entire courses, so these materials are designed to illustrate its intersection with entertainment law and to highlight the stark differences which derive from the unique management obligations of museums and the international issues related to art theft, forgery, and trafficking in stolen or illegally obtained artifacts.

A. Overview of Copyright for Pictorial, Graphic, or Sculptural Arts

Bleistein v. Donaldson Lithographing Company
188 U.S. 239 (1903)

Mr. Justice Holmes delivered the opinion of the court.

The alleged infringements consisted in the copying in reduced form of three chromolithographs prepared by employees of the plaintiffs for advertisements of a circus owned by one Wallace. Each of the three contained a portrait of Wallace in the corner and lettering bearing some slight relation to the scheme of decoration, indicating the subject of the design and the fact that the reality was to be seen at the circus. One of the designs was of an ordinary ballet, one of a number of men and women, described as the Stirk family, performing on bicycles, and one of groups of men and women whitened to represent statutes. The Circuit Court directed a verdict for the defendant on the ground that the chromolithographs were not within the protection of the copyright law, and this ruling was sustained by the Circuit Court of Appeals. . . .

We shall do no more than mention the suggestion that painting and engraving unless for a mechanical end are not among the useful arts, the progress of which Congress is empowered by the Constitution to promote. The Constitution does not limit the useful to that which satisfies immediate bodily needs. It is obvious also that the plaintiffs' case is not affected by the fact, if it be one, that the pictures represent actual groups—visible things. They seem from the testimony to have been composed from hints or description, not from sight of a performance. But even if they had

---

2. Nat'l Endowment For The Arts, U.S. Trends in Arts Attendance and Literary Reading: 2002–2017 (2018), http://www.arts.gov/sites/default/files/2017-sppapreviewREV-sept2018.pdf.

been drawn from the life, that fact would not deprive them of protection. The opposite proposition would mean that a portrait by Velasquez or Whistler was common property because others might try their hand on the same face. Others are free to copy the original. They are not free to copy the copy. The copy is the personal reaction of an individual upon nature. Personality always contains something unique. It expresses its singularity even in handwriting, and a very modest grade of art has in it something irreducible, which is one man's alone. That something he may copyright unless there is a restriction in the words of the act.

If there is a restriction it is not to be found in the limited pretensions of these particular works.... We assume that the construction of Rev. Stat. § 4952 ... provides that "in the construction of this act the words 'engraving,' 'cut' and 'print' shall be applied only to pictorial illustrations or works connected with the fine arts." We see no reason for taking the words "connected with the fine arts" as qualifying anything except the word "works," but it would not change our decision if we should assume further that they also qualified "pictorial illustrations," as the defendant contends.

These chromolithographs are "pictorial illustrations." The word "illustrations" does not mean that they must illustrate the text of a book, and that the etchings of Rembrandt or Steinla's engraving of the Madonna di San Sisto could not be protected today if any man were able to produce them. Again, the act however construed, does not mean that ordinary posters are not good enough to be considered within its scope. The antithesis to "illustrations or works connected with the fine arts" is not works of little merit or of humble degree, or illustrations addressed to the less educated classes; it is "prints or labels designed to be used for any other articles of manufacture." Certainly works are not the less connected with the fine arts because their pictorial quality attracts the crowd and therefore gives them a real use—if use means to increase trade and to help to make money. A picture is none the less a picture and none the less a subject of copyright that it is used for an advertisement. And if pictures may be used to advertise soap, or the theatre, or monthly magazines, as they are, they may be used to advertise a circus. Of course, the ballet is as legitimate a subject for illustration as any other. A rule cannot be laid down that would excommunicate the paintings of Degas....

It would be a dangerous undertaking for persons trained only to the law to constitute themselves final judges of the worth of pictorial illustrations, outside of the narrowest and most obvious limits. At the one extreme some works of genius would be sure to miss appreciation. Their very novelty would make them repulsive until the public had learned the new language in which their author spoke. It may be more than doubted, for instance, whether the etchings of Goya or the paintings of Manet would have been sure of protection when seen for the first time. At the other end, copyright would be denied to pictures which appealed to a public less educated than the judge. Yet if they command the interest of any public, they have a commercial value—it would be bold to say that they have not an aesthetic and educational value—and the taste of any public is not to be treated with contempt. It is an ultimate fact for the moment, whatever may be out hopes for a change. That these pictures had their worth and their success is sufficiently shown by the desire to reproduce them without regard to the plaintiffs' rights. We are of opinion that there was evidence that the plaintiffs have rights entitled to the protection of the law.

The judgment of the Circuit Court of Appeals is reversed; the judgment of the Circuit Court is also reversed and the cause remanded to that court with directions to set aside the verdict and grant a new trial.

Mr. Justice Harlan, with whom concurred Mr. Justice McKenna, dissenting.

[Quoting the Court of Appeals] "What we hold is this: That if a chromo, lithograph, or other print, engraving, or picture has no other use than that of a mere advertisement, and no value aside from this function, it would not be promotive of the useful arts, within the meaning of the constitutional provision, to protect the 'author' in the exclusive use thereof, and the copyright statute should not be construed as including such a publication, if any other construction is admissible.... It must have some connection with the fine arts to give it intrinsic value, and that it shall have is the meaning which we attach to the act of June 18, 1874, amending the provisions of the copyright law. We are unable to discover anything useful or meritorious in the design copyrighted by the plaintiffs in error other than as an advertisement of acts to be done or exhibited to the public in Wallace's show. No evidence, aside from the deductions which are to be drawn from the prints themselves, was offered to show that these designs had any original artistic qualities." ... The clause of the Constitution giving Congress power to promote the progress of science and useful arts, by securing for limited terms to authors and inventors the exclusive right to their respective works and discoveries, does not, as I think, embrace a mere advertisement of a circus.

Notes and Questions

a. Initially, the courts must grapple with the definition of art in a number of contexts. As Justice Learned Hand explained, "It is true that 'works of art' is a loose phrase whose perimeter is hard to define; nevertheless ... the mere fact that the meaning of the phrase, 'works of art,' admits of debate does not make it different from many statutes whose interpretation is every day regarded as reviewable by the courts." *Vacheron & Constantin-Le Coultre Watches, Inc. v. Benrus Watch Co.*, 260 F.2d 637, 640 (2d Cir. 1958).

b. Congress and the courts did not hesitate to recognize fine art as within the ambit of copyright protection. The courts extended this protection to artistic photographs as writings within the meaning of the Constitution. *Burrow-Giles Lithographic Co. v. Sarony*, 111 U.S. 53 (1884). Despite this expansion, however, questions remain regarding the scope of this protection and the meaning of "author" for purposes of copyright.

c. To what extent does the reproduction of a public domain work of art entitle the new artist to claim copyright in the completed work? *Compare L. Batlin & Son, Inc. v. Snyder*, 536 F.2d 486 (2d Cir. 1976), *with Durham Indus., Inc. v. Tomy Corp.*, 630 F.2d 905 (2d Cir. 1980), *and Entm't Research Grp., Inc. v. Genesis Creative Grp., Inc.*, 122 F.3d 1211, 1219 (9th Cir. 1997).

B. Artists' Rights to Attribution and Integrity

Introduction

The law protecting visual artists builds on the legal protections afforded to all copyright owners—those protected by § 43(a) of the Lanham Act, as well as the state law protections for publicity rights. In addition to these protections, select works of visual art are protected by the Visual Artists Rights Act, providing protection for an artist's rights of attribution and integrity.

Article 6*bis* of the Berne Convention states the international standard for the protection of moral rights.

> Independently of the author's economic rights, and even after the transfer of the said rights, the author shall have the right to claim authorship of the work and to object to any distortion, mutilation or other modification of, or other derogatory action in relation to, the said work, which would be prejudicial to his honor or reputation.

Berne Convention for the Protection of Literary and Artistic Works, September 9, 1886, art. 6*bis*, S. Treaty Doc. No. 27, 99th Cong., 2d Sess. 41 (1986).

> In the United States, the moral rights of attribution regarding the identity of the author or artist of a work and the moral right of integrity protecting the work from destruction or mutilation are not explicitly recognized under copyright law, except as provided in the Visual Artists Rights Act of 1990, 17 U.S.C. § 106(a) (2000) ("VARA").

> Despite this, courts prior to 1990 and courts adjudicating copyright claims outside the coverage of VARA have sometimes recognized aspects of the moral rights of attribution and integrity through an interpretation of contractual provisions, Lanham Act § 43(a) unfair competition claims, or various state law claims. In a report on VARA, the Register of Copyrights provides a useful history of this litigation:

> Although moral rights were not recognized in U.S. copyright law prior to enactment of VARA, some state legislatures had enacted moral rights laws, and a number of judicial decisions accorded some moral rights protection under theories of copyright, unfair competition, defamation, invasion of privacy, and breach of contract. Such cases have continued relevance, not only for historical interest, but also for precedential value because state and common law moral rights protection was not entirely preempted by VARA. Arguably, state laws of defamation, invasion of privacy, contracts, and unfair competition by "passing off" are not preempted. Further, VARA rights endure only for the artist's life, after which preemption ceases.

> In *Vargas v. Esquire* [164 F.2d 522, 526 (7th Cir. 1947)], artist Antonio Vargas created a series of calendar girl illustrations for *Esquire* magazine, some of which were published without his signature or credit-line. The U.S. Court of Appeals for the Seventh Circuit ruled the rights of the parties were

determined by the contract in which Vargas agreed as independent contractor to furnish pictures and granted all rights in the artwork to *Esquire*. The court rejected theories of implied contract, moral rights, and unfair competition.

In *Granz v. Harris* [198 F.2d 585 (2d Cir. 1952)], a jazz concert was re-recorded with a reduced playing time and content, such that a full eight minutes was omitted. The contract required the defendant to use a credit-line attributing the plaintiff-producer, who sued. The Second Circuit decided that selling abbreviated recordings with the original credit line constituted unfair competition and breach of contract. Whether by contract or by tort, the plaintiff could prevent publication "as his, of a garbled version of his uncopyrighted product."

In *Gilliam v. American Broadcasting Cos.* [538 F.2d 14 (2d Cir. 1976)], ABC broadcast the first of two 90-minute specials, consisting of three 30-minute Monty Python shows each, but cut 24 of the original 90 minutes. Monty Python sued for an injunction and damages. The Second Circuit ruled that ABC's actions contravened contractual provisions limiting the right to edit the program and that a licensee's unauthorized use of an underlying work by publication in a truncated version was a copyright infringement. In a theory akin to moral rights, the court said that a distorted version of a writer's or performer's work may violate rights protected by the Lanham Act and may present a cause of action under that statute. The concurrence cautioned against employing the Lanham Act as a substitute for moral rights, and believed the court should restrict its opinion to contract and copyright issues.

Another case, *Wojnarowicz v. American Family Ass'n* [772 F. Supp. 201 (S.D.N.Y. 1991)], involved a group that protested an artist's work by reproducing 14 fragments in a pamphlet. The U.S. District Court for the Southern District of New York found for the artist under the New York Artists' Authorship Rights Act, but dismissed claims under the Copyright and Lanham Acts.[3]

Carter v. Helmsley-Spear, Inc.
71 F.3d 77 (2d Cir. 1995)

Defendants 474431 Associates and Helmsley-Spear, Inc. (defendants or appellants), as the owner and managing agent respectively, of a commercial building in Queens, New York, appeal from an order of the United States District Court for the Southern District of New York (Edelstein, J.), entered on September 6, 1994 following a bench trial. The order granted plaintiffs, who are three artists, a permanent injunction that enjoined defendants from removing, modifying or destroying a work of visual art that had been installed in defendants' building by plaintiffs-artists commissioned

3. WAIVER OF MORAL RIGHTS IN VISUAL ARTWORKS, EXECUTIVE SUMMARY, REPORT OF THE COPYRIGHT OFFICE (October 1996), *available at* http://www.copyright.gov/reports/exsum.html.

by a former tenant to install the work. *See Carter v. Helmsley-Spear, Inc.*, 861 F. Supp. 303 (S.D.N.Y. 1994). Defendants also appeal from the dismissal by the trial court of their counterclaim for waste. Plaintiffs cross-appeal from the dismissal of their cause of action for tortious interference with contractual relations and from the denial of their requests to complete the work and for an award of attorney's fees and costs.

On this appeal we deal with an Act of Congress that protects the rights of artists to preserve their works. One of America's most insightful thinkers observed that a country is not truly civilized "where the arts, such as they have, are all imported, having no indigenous life." 7 WORKS OF RALPH WALDO EMERSON, SOCIETY AND SOLITUDE, CHAPT. II CIVILIZATION 34 (AMS. ed. 1968). From such reflection it follows that American artists are to be encouraged by laws that protect their works. Although Congress in the statute before us did just that, it did not mandate the preservation of art at all costs and without due regard for the rights of others.

For the reasons that follow, we reverse and vacate the grant of injunctive relief to plaintiffs and affirm the dismissal by the district court of plaintiffs' other claims and its dismissal of defendants' counterclaim for waste.

BACKGROUND

Defendant 474431 Associates (Associates) is the owner of a mixed use commercial building located at 47-44 31st Street, Queens, New York, which it has owned since 1978. Associates is a New York general partnership. The general partners are Alvin Schwartz and Supervisory Management Corp., a wholly-owned subsidiary of Helmsley Enterprises, Inc. Defendant Helmsley-Spear, Inc. is the current managing agent of the property for Associates.

On February 1, 1990 Associates entered into a 48-year net lease, leasing the building to 47-44 31st Street Associates, L.P. (Limited Partnership), a Delaware limited partnership. From February 1, 1990 until June 1993, Irwin Cohen or an entity under his control was the general partner of the Limited Partnership, and managed the property through Cohen's SIG Management Company (SIG). Corporate Life Insurance Company (Corporate Life) was a limited partner in the Limited Partnership. In June 1993 SIG ceased its involvement with the property and Corporate Life, through an entity controlled by it, became the general partner of the Limited Partnership. The property was then managed by the Limited Partnership, through Theodore Nering, a Corporate Life representative. There is no relationship, other than the lease, between Associates, the lessor, and the Limited Partnership, the lessee.

Plaintiffs John Carter, John Swing and John Veronis (artists or plaintiffs) are professional sculptors who work together and are known collectively as the "Three-J's" or "Jx3." On December 16, 1991 SIG entered into a one-year agreement with the plaintiffs "engaging and hiring the Artists ... to design, create and install sculpture and other permanent installations" in the building, primarily the lobby. Under the agreement plaintiffs had "full authority in design, color and style," and SIG retained authority to direct the location and installation of the artwork within the building.

The artists were to retain copyrights to their work and SIG was to receive 50 percent of any proceeds from its exploitation. On January 20, 1993 SIG and the artists signed an agreement extending the duration of their commission for an additional year. When Corporate Life became a general partner of the Limited Partnership, the Limited Partnership assumed the agreement with plaintiffs and in December 1993 again extended the agreement.

The artwork that is the subject of this litigation is a very large "walk-through sculpture" occupying most, but not all, of the building's lobby. The artwork consists of a variety of sculptural elements constructed from recycled materials, much of it metal, affixed to the walls and ceiling, and a vast mosaic made from pieces of recycled glass embedded in the floor and walls. Elements of the work include a giant hand fashioned from an old school bus, a face made of automobile parts, and a number of interactive components. These assorted elements make up a theme relating to environmental concerns and the significance of recycling.

The Limited Partnership's lease on the building was terminated on March 31, 1994. It filed for bankruptcy one week later. The property was surrendered to defendant Associates on April 6, 1994 and defendant Helmsley-Spear, Inc. took over management of the property. Representatives of defendants informed the artists that they could no longer continue to install artwork at the property, and instead had to vacate the building. These representatives also made statements indicating that defendants intended to remove the artwork already in place in the building's lobby.

As a result of defendants' actions, artists commenced this litigation. On April 26, 1994 the district court issued a temporary restraining order enjoining defendants from taking any action to alter, deface, modify or mutilate the artwork installed in the building. In May 1994 a hearing was held on whether a preliminary injunction should issue. The district court subsequently granted a preliminary injunction enjoining defendants from removing the artwork pending the resolution of the instant litigation.

A bench trial was subsequently held in June and July 1994, at the conclusion of which the trial court granted the artists the permanent injunction prohibiting defendants from distorting, mutilating, modifying, destroying and removing plaintiffs' artwork. The injunction is to remain in effect for the lifetimes of the three plaintiffs. Plaintiffs' other claims, including their cause of action for tortious interference and a request for an award of costs and attorney's fees and that they be allowed to continue to add to the artwork in the lobby, as well as defendants' counterclaim for waste, were all dismissed with prejudice. This appeal and cross-appeal followed.

DISCUSSION

I. Artists' Moral Rights

A. History of Artists' Moral Rights

Because it was under the rubric of the Visual Artists Rights Act of 1990 that plaintiffs obtained injunctive relief in the district court, we must explore, at least in part, the contours of that Act. In doing so it is necessary to review briefly the concept of artists' moral rights and the history and development of those rights in American jurisprudence, which led up to passage of the statute we must now examine.

The term "moral rights" has its origins in the civil law and is a translation of the French *le droit moral*, which is meant to capture those rights of a spiritual, non-economic and personal nature. The rights spring from a belief that an artist in the process of creation injects his spirit into the work and that the artist's personality, as well as the integrity of the work, should therefore be protected and preserved. Because they are personal to the artist, moral rights exist independently of an artist's copyright in his or her work.

While the rubric of moral rights encompasses many varieties of rights, two are protected in nearly every jurisdiction recognizing their existence: attribution and integrity. *See* Art Law at 420. The right of attribution generally consists of the right of an artist to be recognized by name as the author of his work or to publish anonymously or pseudonymously, the right to prevent the author's work from being attributed to someone else, and to prevent the use of the author's name on works created by others, including distorted editions of the author's original work. The right of integrity allows the author to prevent any deforming or mutilating changes to his work, even after title in the work has been transferred.

In some jurisdictions the integrity right also protects artwork from destruction. Whether or not a work of art is protected from destruction represents a fundamentally different perception of the purpose of moral rights. If integrity is meant to stress the public interest in preserving a nation's culture, destruction is prohibited; if the right is meant to emphasize the author's personality, destruction is seen as less harmful than the continued display of deformed or mutilated work that misrepresents the artist and destruction may proceed.

Although moral rights are well established in the civil law, they are of recent vintage in American jurisprudence. Federal and state courts typically recognized the existence of such rights in other nations, but rejected artists' attempts to inject them into U.S. law. Nonetheless, American courts have in varying degrees acknowledged the idea of moral rights, cloaking the concept in the guise of other legal theories, such as copyright, unfair competition, invasion of privacy, defamation, and breach of contract.

In the landmark case of *Gilliam v. American Broadcasting Companies, Inc.*, 538 F.2d 14 (2d Cir. 1976), we relied on copyright law and unfair competition principles to safeguard the integrity rights of the "Monty Python" group, noting that although the law "seeks to vindicate the economic, rather than the personal rights of authors ... the economic incentive for artistic ... creation ... cannot be reconciled with the inability of artists to obtain relief for mutilation or misrepresentation of their work to the public on which the artists are financially dependent." Because decisions protecting artists rights are often "clothed in terms of proprietary right in one's creation," we continued, "they also properly vindicate the author's personal right to prevent the presentation of his work to the public in a distorted form."

Artists fared better in state legislatures than they generally had in courts. California was the first to take up the task of protecting artists with the passage in 1979 of the California Art Preservation Act, Cal. Civ. Code § 987 et seq. (West 1982 & Supp. 1995), followed in 1983 by New York's enactment of the Artist's Authorship Rights Act, N.Y. Arts & Cult. Aff. Law § 14.03 (McKinney Supp. 1995). Nine other states have also passed moral rights statutes, generally following either the California or New York models.

B. Visual Artists Rights Act of 1990

Although bills protecting artists' moral rights had first been introduced in Congress in 1979, they had drawn little support. The issue of federal protection of moral rights was a prominent hurdle in the debate over whether the United States should join the Berne Convention, the international agreement protecting literary and artistic works. Article 6*bis* of the Berne Convention protects attribution and integrity, stating in relevant part:

> Independently of the author's economic rights, and even after the transfer of the said rights, the author shall have the right to claim authorship of the work and to object to any distortion, mutilation or other modification of, or other derogatory action in relation to, the said work, which would be prejudicial to his honor or reputation.

Berne Convention for the Protection of Literary and Artistic Works, September 9, 1886, art. 6*bis*, S. Treaty Doc. No. 27, 99th Cong., 2d Sess. 41 (1986).

The Berne Convention's protection of moral rights posed a significant difficulty for U.S. adherence. *See* Copyright Law at 1022 ("The obligation of the United States to provide *droit moral* ... was the single most contentious issue surrounding Berne adherence."); NIMMER at 8D-15 ("During the debate over [the Berne Convention Implementation Act], Congress faced an avalanche of opposition to moral rights, including denunciations of moral rights by some of the bill's most vociferous advocates."); H.R. Rep. No. 514, 101st Cong., 2d Sess. 7 (1990), reprinted in 1990 U.S.C.C.A.N. 6915, 6917 ("After almost 100 years of debate, the United States joined the Berne Convention.... Consensus over United States adherence was slow to develop in large part because of debate over the requirements of Article 6*bis*.").

Congress passed the Berne Convention Implementation Act of 1988, Pub. L. No. 100-568, 102 Stat. 2853 (1988), and side-stepped the difficult question of protecting moral rights. It declared that the Berne Convention is not self-executing, existing law satisfied the United States' obligations in adhering to the Convention, its provisions are not enforceable through any action brought pursuant to the Convention itself, and neither adherence to the Convention nor the implementing legislation expands or reduces any rights under federal, state, or common law to claim authorship of a work or to object to any distortion, mutilation, or other modification of a work.

Two years later Congress enacted the Visual Artists Rights Act of 1990 (VARA or Act), Pub. L. No. 101-650 (tit. VI), 104 Stat. 5089, 5128–33 (1990). Construing this Act constitutes the subject of the present appeal. The Act protects both the reputations of certain visual artists and the works of art they create. It provides these artists with the rights of "attribution" and "integrity." ...

These rights are analogous to those protected by Article 6*bis* of the Berne Convention, which are commonly known as "moral rights." The theory of moral rights is that they result in a climate of artistic worth and honor that encourages the author in the arduous act of creation.

H.R. Rep. No. 514 at 5 (internal quote omitted). The Act brings to fruition Emerson's insightful observation.

Its principal provisions afford protection only to authors of works of visual art—a narrow class of art defined to include paintings, drawings, prints, sculptures, or photographs produced for exhibition purposes, existing in a single copy or limited edition of 200 copies or fewer. 17 U.S.C. § 101 (Supp. III 1991). With numerous exceptions, VARA grants three rights: the right of attribution, the right of integrity and, in the case of works of visual art of "recognized stature," the right to prevent destruction. 17 U.S.C. § 106A (Supp. III 1991). For works created on or after June 1, 1991—the effective date of the Act—the rights provided for endure for the life of the author or, in the case of a joint work, the life of the last surviving author. The rights cannot be transferred, but may be waived by a writing signed by the author. Copyright registration is not required to bring an action for infringement of the rights granted under VARA, or to secure statutory damages and attorney's fees. 17 U.S.C. §§ 411, 412 (1988 & Supp. III 1991). All remedies available under copyright law, other than criminal remedies, are available in an action for infringement of moral rights. 17 U.S.C. § 506 (1988 & Supp. III 1991). With this historical background in hand, we pass to the merits of the present litigation.

II. Work of Visual Art

Because VARA is relatively new, a fuller explication of it is helpful. In analyzing the Act, therefore, we will follow in order the definition set forth in § 101, as did the district court when presiding over this litigation. The district court determined that the work of art installed in the lobby of Associates' building was a work of visual art as defined by VARA; that distortion, mutilation, or modification of the work would prejudice plaintiffs' honor and reputations; that the work was of recognized stature, thus protecting it from destruction (including removal that would result in destruction); and that Associates consented to or ratified the installation of the work in its building. The result was that defendants were enjoined from removing or otherwise altering the work during the lifetimes of the three artists.

[] The Statutory Definition

A "work of visual art" is defined by the Act in terms both positive (what it is) and negative (what it is not). In relevant part VARA defines a work of visual art as "a painting, drawing, print, or sculpture, existing in a single copy" or in a limited edition of 200 copies or fewer. 17 U.S.C. § 101. Although defendants aver that elements of the work are not visual art, their contention is foreclosed by the factual finding that the work is a single, indivisible whole. Concededly, considered as a whole, the work is a sculpture and exists only in a single copy. Therefore, the work satisfies the Act's positive definition of a work of visual art. We next turn to the second part of the statutory definition — what is not a work of visual art.

The definition of visual art excludes "any poster, map, globe, chart, technical drawing, diagram, model, applied art, motion picture or other audio-visual work." 17 U.S.C. §101. Congress meant to distinguish works of visual art from other media, such as audio-visual works and motion pictures, due to the different circumstances surrounding how works of each genre are created and disseminated. *See* H.R. Rep. No. 514 at 9. Although this concern led to a narrow definition of works of visual art,

> the courts should use common sense and generally accepted standards of the artistic community in determining whether a particular work falls within the scope of the definition. Artists may work in a variety of media, and use any number of materials in creating their works. Therefore, whether a particular work falls within the definition should not depend on the medium or materials used.

Id. at 11.

"Applied art" describes "two- and three-dimensional ornamentation or decoration that is affixed to otherwise utilitarian objects." Defendants' assertion that at least parts of the work are applied art appears to rest on the fact that some of the sculptural elements are affixed to the lobby's floor, walls, and ceiling — all utilitarian objects. Interpreting applied art to include such works would render meaningless VARA's protection for works of visual art installed in buildings. A court should not read one part of a statute so as to deprive another part of meaning.

Appellants do not suggest the entire work is applied art. The district court correctly stated that even if components of the work standing alone were applied art, "nothing in VARA proscribes protection of works of visual art that incorporate elements of, rather than constitute, applied art." VARA's legislative history leaves no doubt that "a new and independent work created from snippets of [excluded] materials, such as a collage, is of course not excluded" from the definition of a work of visual art. H.R. Rep. No. 514 at 14. The trial judge correctly ruled the work is not applied art precluded from protection under the Act.

III. Work Made for Hire

Also excluded from the definition of a work of visual art is any work made for hire. A "work made for hire" is defined in the Copyright Act, in relevant part, as "a work prepared by an employee within the scope of his or her employment." Appellants maintain the work was made for hire and therefore is not a work of visual art under VARA. The district court held otherwise, finding that the plaintiffs were hired as independent contractors.

A. *Reid* Tests

The Copyright Act does not define the terms "employee" or "scope of employment." In *Community for Creative Non-Violence v. Reid*, 490 U.S. 730 (1989), the Supreme Court looked to the general common law of agency for guidance. It held that a multifactor balancing test was required to determine if a work was produced for hire (by an employee) or was produced by an independent contractor. The Court elaborated 13 specific factors:

> the hiring party's right to control the manner and means by which the product is accomplished.... the skill required; the source of the instrumentalities and tools; the location of the work; the duration of the relationship between the parties; whether the hiring party has the right to assign additional projects to the hired party; the extent of the hired party's discretion over when and how long to work; the method of payment; the hired party's role in hiring and paying assistants; whether the work is part of the regular business of the hiring party; whether the hiring party is in business; the provision of employee benefits; and the tax treatment of the hired party.

Reid, 490 U.S. at 751–52. While all of these factors are relevant, no single factor is determinative. Instead, the factors are weighed by referring to the facts of a given case.

The district court determined that the sculpture was not "work for hire" and therefore not excluded from the definition of visual art. The *Reid* test is a list of factors not all of which may come into play in a given case. The Reid test is therefore easily misapplied. We are usually reluctant to reverse a district court's factual findings as to the presence or absence of any of the *Reid* factors and do so only when the district court's findings are clearly erroneous. By contrast, the ultimate legal conclusion as to whether or not the sculpture is "work for hire" is reviewed *de novo*. The district court correctly stated the legal test. But some of its factual findings, we think, were clearly erroneous.

B. Factors Applied

The district court properly noted that *Aymes* established five factors which would be relevant in nearly all cases: the right to control the manner and means of production; requisite skill; provision of employee benefits; tax treatment of the hired party; whether the hired party may be assigned additional projects. Analysis begins with a discussion of these factors. [*Aymes v. Bonelli*, 980 F.2d 857, 861 (2d Cir. 1992).]

First, plaintiffs had complete artistic freedom with respect to every aspect of the sculpture's creation. Although the artists heeded advice or accepted suggestions from building engineers, architects, and others, such actions were not a relinquishment of their artistic freedom. The evidence strongly supports the finding that plaintiffs controlled the work's "manner and means." This fact, in turn, lent credence to their contention that they were independent contractors. While artistic freedom remains a central factor in our inquiry, the Supreme Court has cautioned that "the extent of control the hiring party exercises over the details of the product is not dispositive." *Reid*, 490 U.S. at 752. Hence, resolving the question of whether plaintiffs had artistic freedom does not end the analysis.

The district court also correctly found the artists' conception and execution of the work required great skill in execution. Appellants' contention that the plaintiffs' reliance on assistants in some way mitigates the skill required for this work is meritless, particularly because each of the plaintiffs is a professional sculptor and the parties stipulated that professional sculpting is a highly skilled occupation. The right to control the manner and means and the requisite skill needed for execution of this project were both properly found by the district court to weigh against "work for hire" status.

The trial court erred, however, when it ruled that the defendants could not assign the artists additional projects. First, the employment agreement between SIG Management Company and the artists clearly states that the artists agreed not only to install the sculpture but also to "render such other related services and duties as may be assigned to [them] from time to time by the Company." By the very terms of the contract the defendants and their predecessors in interest had the right to assign other related projects to the artists. The district court incorrectly decided that this language supported the artists' claim to be independent contractors. While the artists' obligations were limited to related services and duties, the defendants nonetheless did have the right to assign to plaintiffs work other than the principal sculpture.

Further, the defendants did, in fact, assign such other projects. The district court concedes as much, explaining that "plaintiffs did create art work on the property other than that in the Lobby." The record shows the artists performed projects on the sixth floor of the building, on the eighth floor, and in the boiler room. Thus, on at least three different occasions the plaintiffs were assigned additional projects, which they completed without further compensation....

We must also consider factors the district court correctly found to favor finding the sculpture to be work for hire. Specifically, the provision of employee benefits and the tax treatment of the plaintiffs weigh strongly in favor of employee status. The defendants paid payroll and social security taxes, provided employee benefits such as life, health, and liability insurance and paid vacations, and contributed to unemployment insurance and workers' compensation funds on plaintiffs' behalf. Moreover, two of the three artists filed for unemployment benefits after their positions were terminated, listing the building's management company as their former employer. Other formal indicia of an employment relationship existed. For instance, each plaintiff was paid a weekly salary. The artists also agreed in their written contract that they would work principally for the defendants for the duration of their agreement on a 40-hour per week basis and they would only do other work to the extent that it would not "interfere with services to be provided" to the defendants. All of these facts strongly suggest the artists were employees....

C. Employee Status

Our review of the legal conclusion drawn from balancing the various *Reid* factors persuades us that the factors that weigh in favor of finding the artists were employees outweigh those factors supporting the artists' claim that they were independent contractors.... These factors, properly considered and weighed with the employee benefits granted plaintiffs and the tax treatment accorded them, are more than sufficient to demonstrate that the artists were employees, and the sculpture is therefore a work made for hire as a matter of law.

IV. Defendants' Counterclaim and Plaintiffs' Cross-appeal

Finally, since we have determined that the work is one made for hire and therefore outside the scope of VARA's protection, we need not discuss that Act's broad protection of visual art and the protection it affords works of art incorporated into a building. Also, as plaintiffs' sculpture was not protected from removal because the artists were employees and not independent contractors, we need not reach the defendants' Fifth Amendment takings argument.

Moreover, because the sculpture is not protected by VARA from removal resulting in its destruction or alteration, we do not address plaintiffs' contentions that VARA entitles them to complete the "unfinished" portion of the work, that they are entitled to reasonable costs and attorney's fees, and that appellants tortiously interfered with the artists' contract with SIG and the Limited Partnership. Finally, the district court dismissed defendants' counterclaim against the artists for waste, finding, *inter alia*, that such a cause of action under New York law may only be brought by a landlord against a tenant. Appellants have failed to persuade us that it was error to dismiss this counterclaim.

CONCLUSION

Accordingly, the district court's order insofar as it held the work was one not made for hire is reversed and the injunction vacated. In all other respects, the order of the district court is affirmed. Each party to bear its own costs.

Martin v. City of Indianapolis

192 F.3d 608 (7th Cir. 1999)

We are not art critics, do not pretend to be and do not need to be to decide this case. A large outdoor stainless steel sculpture by plaintiff Jan Martin, an artist, was demolished by the defendant as part of an urban renewal project. Plaintiff brought a one-count suit against the City of Indianapolis (the "City") under the Visual Artists Rights Act of 1990 ("VARA"), 17 U.S.C. § 101 *et seq*. The parties filed cross-motions for summary judgment. The district court granted plaintiff's motion and awarded plaintiff statutory damages in the maximum amount allowed for a non-willful statutory violation....

Plaintiff is an artist, but in this instance more with a welding torch than with a brush. He offered evidence to show, not all of it admitted, that his works have been displayed in museums, and other works created for private commissions, including a time capsule for the Indianapolis Museum of Art Centennial. He has also done sculptured jewelry for the Indiana Arts Commission. In 1979, at the Annual Hoosier Salem Art Show, plaintiff was awarded the prize for best of show in any medium. He holds various arts degrees from Purdue University, the Art Institute of Chicago and Bowling Green State University in Ohio. Plaintiff had been employed as production coordinator for Tarpenning-LaFollette Co. (the "Company"), a metal contracting firm in Indianapolis. It was in this position that he turned his artistic talents to metal sculpture fabrication.

In 1984, plaintiff received permission from the Indianapolis Metropolitan Development Commission to erect a twenty-by-forty-foot metal sculpture on land owned by John LaFollette, chairman of the Company. The Company also agreed to furnish the materials. The resulting Project Agreement between the City and the Company granted a zoning variance to permit the erection of plaintiff's proposed sculpture. An attachment to that agreement and the center of this controversy provided as follows:

> Should a determination be made by the Department of Metropolitan Development that the subject sculpture is no longer compatible with the existing land use or that the acquisition of the property is necessary, the owner of the land and the owner of the sculpture will receive written notice signed by the Director of the Department of Metropolitan Development giving the owners of the land and sculpture ninety (90) days to remove said sculpture. Subject to weather and ground conditions.

Plaintiff went to work on the project and in a little over two years it was completed. He named it "Symphony # 1," but as it turns out in view of this controversy, a more suitable musical name might have been "1812 Overture." Because of the possibility that the sculpture might someday have to be removed, as provided for in the Project Agreement, Symphony # 1 was engineered and built by plaintiff so that it could be disassembled for removal and later reassembled. The sculpture did not go unnoticed by the press, public or art community. Favorable comments admitted into evidence and objected to by the City are now an issue on appeal and their admissibility will be considered hereinafter.

The trouble began in April 1992 when the City notified LaFollette that there would be public hearings on the City's proposed acquisition of various properties as part of an urban renewal plan. One of the properties to be acquired was home to Symphony # 1. Kim Martin, president of the Company and plaintiff's brother, responded to the City. He reminded the City that the Company had paid for Symphony # 1, and had signed the agreement with the Metropolitan Development Corporation pertaining to the eventuality of removal. Martin stated that if the sculpture was to be removed, the Company would be willing to donate it to the City provided the City would bear the costs of removal to a new site, but that plaintiff would like some input as to where his sculpture might be placed. Plaintiff also personally appeared before the Metropolitan Development Commission and made the same proposal. This was followed by a letter from plaintiff to the Mayor reiterating the removal proposal. The Mayor responded that he was referring plaintiff's proposal to his staff to see what could be done.

The City thereafter purchased the land. At the closing, plaintiff again repeated his proposal and agreed to assist so Symphony # 1 could be saved and, if necessary, moved without damage. The City's response was that plaintiff would be contacted in the event the sculpture was to be removed. Shortly thereafter, the City awarded a contract to demolish the sculpture, and demolition followed, all without prior notice to plaintiff or the Company. This lawsuit resulted in which summary judgment was allowed for plaintiff. However, his victory was not entirely satisfactory to him, nor was the City satisfied. The City appealed, and plaintiff cross-appealed.

VARA seems to be a stepchild of our copyright laws, but does not require copyright registration. Some remedies under the Copyright Act, however, including attorney's fees, are recoverable. 17 U.S.C. §§ 504–05. VARA provides: "The author of a work of visual art ... shall have the right ... to prevent any destruction of a work of recognized stature, and any intentional or grossly negligent destruction of that work is a violation of that right." The district court considered Symphony # 1 to be of "*recognized stature*" under the evidence presented and thus concluded that the City had violated plaintiff's rights under VARA. That finding is contested by the City.

"Recognized stature" is a necessary finding under VARA in order to protect a work of visual art from destruction. In spite of its significance, that phrase is not defined in VARA, leaving its intended meaning and application open to argument and judicial resolution. The only case found undertaking to define and apply "recognized stature" is *Carter v. Helmsley-Spear, Inc.*, 861 F. Supp. 303 (S.D.N.Y. 1994), *aff'd in part, vacated in part, rev'd in part,* 71 F.3d 77 (2nd Cir. 1995). Involved was an unusual work of art consisting of interrelated sculptural elements constructed from recycled materials, mostly metal, to decorate the lobby of a commercial building in a borough of New York City. Part of the work was "a giant hand fashioned from an old school bus, [and] a face made of automobile parts...." Although the Second Circuit reversed the district court and held that the work was not a work of visual art protected by VARA, the district court presented an informative discussion in determining whether a work of visual art may qualify as one of "recognized stature." That determination is based greatly on the testimony of experts on both sides of the issue, as would ordinarily be expected.

The stature test formulated by the New York district court required:

> (1) that the visual art in question has "stature," i.e. is viewed as meritorious, and (2) that this stature is "recognized" by art experts, other members of the artistic community, or by some cross-section of society. In making this showing, plaintiffs generally, but not inevitably, will need to call expert witnesses to testify before the trier of fact.

Carter I, 861 F. Supp. at 325.

Even though the district court in this present case found that test was satisfied by the plaintiff's evidence, plaintiff argues that the *Carter v. Helmsley-Spear* test may be more rigorous than Congress intended. That may be, but we see no need for the purposes of this case to endeavor to refine that rule. Plaintiff's evidence, however, is not as complete as in *Carter v. Helmsley-Spear,* possibly because Symphony # 1 was destroyed by the City without the opportunity for experts to appraise the sculpture in place.

The City objects to the "stature" testimony that was offered by plaintiff as inadmissible hearsay. If not admitted, it would result in plaintiff's failure to sustain his burden of proof. It is true that plaintiff offered no evidence of experts or others by deposition, affidavit or interrogatories. Plaintiff's evidence of "stature" consisted of certain newspaper and magazine articles, and various letters, including a letter from an art gallery director and a letter to the editor of *The Indianapolis News*, all in support of the sculpture, as well as a program from the show at which a model of the sculpture won "Best of Show." After reviewing the City's objection, the district court excluded plaintiff's "programs and awards" evidence as lacking adequate foundation, but nevertheless found Martin had met his "stature" burden of proof with his other evidence.

Included in the admitted evidence, for example, was a letter dated October 25, 1982 from the Director of the Herron School of Art, Indiana University, Indianapolis. It was written to the Company and says in part, "The proposed sculpture is, in my opinion, an interesting and aesthetically stimulating configuration of forms and structures." *The Indianapolis Star*, in a four-column article by its visual arts editor, discussed public sculpture in Indianapolis. This article included a photograph of Symphony # 1. The article lamented that the City had "been graced by only five pieces of note," but that two more had been added that particular year, one being plaintiff's sculpture. It noted, among other things, that Symphony # 1 had been erected without the aid of "federal grants" and without the help of any committee of concerned citizens. Other public sculptures came in for some criticism in the article. However, in discussing Symphony # 1, the author wrote: "Gleaming clean and abstract, yet domestic in scale and reference, irregularly but securely cabled together, the sculpture shows the site what it might be. It unites the area, providing a nexus, a marker, a designation, an identity and, presumably, a point of pride." ...

Next the City claims that the Project Agreement entered into pre-VARA by plaintiff and the City encompassed many of plaintiff's rights under VARA. Therefore, the City argues, that whereas plaintiff failed to remove his work within the time allowed in the contract, plaintiff waived any cause of action he might have had under VARA. That failure was the City's, not plaintiff's, as under the Agreement the City was obligated to give the owners of the land and the sculpture ninety days to remove the sculpture. The City, after discussing with the Company and plaintiff possible other uses for the tract and the removal proposal, failed to give the required notice and went ahead and demolished the sculpture. Nothing had happened between the parties prior to that which could constitute a waiver of any rights by the Company or plaintiff. Plaintiff had no notice of the City letting a contract for Symphony # 1's demolition and no notice when that demolition would actually occur. After the preliminary and ongoing discussions plaintiff and the Company had with the City, when there was no immediate threat of imminent demolition, plaintiff had the right to continue to rely on the specific notice provided in the Agreement, unless it had been waived, which it was not.

Plaintiff and the Company had proposed a solution if the sculpture was to be moved. That proposal was still pending when the surprise destruction of Symphony # 1 occurred. Prior to the demolition, nothing more had been heard from anyone, including the Mayor. Bureaucratic ineptitude may be the only explanation. Under 17 U.S.C. § 106A(e)(1), an artist may waive VARA rights "in a written instrument signed by the author," specifying to what the waiver applies. There is no written waiver instrument in this case which falls within the VARA requirements. We regard this argument to be without merit.

In spite of the City's conduct resulting in the intentional destruction of the sculpture, we do not believe under all the circumstances, particularly given the fact that the issue of VARA rights had not been raised until this suit, that the City's conduct was "willful," as used in VARA, 17 U.S.C. § 504(c)(2), so as to entitle the plaintiff to enhanced damages. This appears to be a case of bureaucratic failure within the City government, not a willful violation of plaintiff's VARA rights. As far as we can tell from the record, those VARA rights were unknown to the City. The parties proceeded under their pre-VARA agreement which the City breached. However, plaintiff retained his VARA rights. As unfortunate as the City's unannounced demolition of Symphony # 1 was, it does not qualify plaintiff for damages under VARA....

Being fully satisfied with the district court's careful resolution of these unique issues and the resulting judgment, the district court's finding is affirmed in all respects.

MANION, *Circuit Judge*, concurring in part and dissenting in part.

Like my colleagues, I am not an art critic. So I begin with the well-worn adage that one man's junk is another man's treasure. No doubt Jan Martin treasured what the city's bulldozers treated as junk. At this point in the litigation this court is not in a position to attach either label (or perhaps one falling somewhere in between) to Symphony # 1. For the Martin sculpture to receive protection under the Visual Arts Rights Act (VARA), it has to rise to the statutory level of "recognized stature." Because at this summary judgment stage, at least, it has clearly not merited the protection that goes with that description, I respectfully dissent.

Another well-worn adage advises that you should never look a gift horse in the mouth. Of course anyone who has ever accepted a gift horse that turns out to be lame or otherwise infirm quickly understands the error of that advice when the feed and veterinary bills arrive. When the City acquired several tracts of land for urban renewal, Martin's Symphony # 1 remained in place on one of the tracts. Martin offered to donate the sculpture to the City if it would remove and relocate it to another site. The City examined this "gift" and determined it would have cost it $8,000 to relocate, so it declined the offer. But it did agree to notify Martin in advance of any renewal project so he could remove Symphony # 1 if he so chose. Although it appears that Martin was fully aware that the sculpture's days were numbered, the City did not send him an official notice before the bulldozer moved in. If this were a simple breach of contract claim (albeit not a federal case), damages could well be in order. Instead, this is a federal claim under VARA, and different standards apply.

I dissent, however, because summary judgment is not appropriate here. A plaintiff cannot satisfy his burden of demonstrating recognized stature through old newspaper articles and unverified letters, some of which do not even address the artwork in question. Rather, as the district court stated in *Carter*, in "making this showing [of recognized stature] plaintiffs generally, but not inevitably, will need to call expert witnesses to testify before the trier of fact." Instances where expert testimony on this point is not necessary will be rare, and this is not one of those exceptional cases where something of unquestioned recognition and stature was destroyed. Furthermore, where newspaper articles are admitted into evidence only to acknowledge recognition but not for the truth of the matter asserted (that the art in question was good or bad), a plaintiff needs more to overcome *a defendant's* motion for summary judgment on a VARA claim, much less prevail on his own summary judgment motion. While the very publication of newspaper articles on a work of art may have bearing on the "recognized" element, there has to be some evidence that the art had stature (i.e., that it met a certain high level of quality)....

For now, however, those who are purchasers or donees of art had best beware. To avoid being the perpetual curator of a piece of visual art that has lost (or perhaps never had) its luster, the recipient must obtain at the outset a waiver of the artist's rights under VARA. Before awarding building permits for erection of sculptures, municipalities might be well advised to obtain a written waiver of the artist's rights too. If not, once destroyed, art of questionable value may acquire a minimum worth of $20,000.00 under VARA.

Cohen v. G & M Realty L.P.

320 F. Supp. 3d 421 (E.D.N.Y. 2018)

This marks the latest chapter in the ongoing saga of what has commonly become known as the 5Pointz litigation. Plaintiffs, 21 aerosol artists, initiated this lawsuit over four years ago by seeking a preliminary injunction under the Visual Artists Rights Act of 1990 ("VARA"), 17 U.S.C. § 106A, against defendants Gerald Wolkoff ("Wolkoff") and four of his real estate entities to prevent the planned demolition by Wolkoff of his warehouse buildings in Long Island City and consequent destruction of plaintiffs' paintings on the walls of the buildings....

On November 12, 2013, after a hearing, the Court issued an order denying preliminary injunctive relief and stating that "a written opinion would soon be issued." Rather than wait for the Court's opinion, which was issued just eight days later on November 20th, Wolkoff destroyed almost all of the plaintiffs' paintings by whitewashing them during that eight-day interim.

In its extensive opinion the Court initially noted that Wolkoff's buildings "had become the repository of the largest collection of exterior aerosol art ... in the United States" and that this litigation "marks the first occasion that a court has had to determine whether the work of an exterior aerosol artist—given its general ephemeral nature—is worthy of any protection under the law." *Cohen v. G & M Realty L.P.*, 988 F.Supp.2d 212, 214 (E.D.N.Y. 2013) ("*Cohen I*").

Given the abject nature of Wolkoff's willful conduct, the Court awards the maximum statutory damages under VARA for each of the 45 works of art wrongfully and willfully destroyed in the combined sum of $6,750,000....

... The Witnesses and Evidentiary Landscape

Each of the 21 plaintiffs/artists testified; they were respectful, articulate and credible. Folios for each were admitted into evidence collectively containing their professional achievements and recognition in the form of an impressive array of fellowships, residences, public and private commissions, teaching positions, media coverage, and social media presence. Not surprisingly, each of the 21 Folios contained beautiful color prints of the artists' respective aerosol works of art which are the subject of the lawsuit. They are appended to this opinion. It is apparent that they reflect striking technical and artistic mastery and vision worthy of display in prominent museums if not on the walls of 5Pointz. The Folios also contain photos showing how almost all of these works of art were partially or wholly whitewashed by Wolkoff.

5Pointz was an egalitarian place. The artists came from many backgrounds. Some of the plaintiffs testified via Skype from international residences. Many who live in New York had immigrated from other countries to join the 5Pointz community. One artist flew from London to testify; another came of age in rural West Virginia. Some artists came from highly prestigious art schools; others were self-taught. Some were fixtures in elite, traditional art circles; others were simply dedicated to street and community art. The Court was impressed with the breadth of the artists' works and how many of the works spoke to the social issues of our times.

The principal testimony about the advent, evolution and demolition of 5Pointz came from plaintiff Jonathan Cohen, one of the world's most accomplished aerosol artists. Wolkoff had designated Cohen as 5Pointz's de facto curator, appointing him to run the site and pick the works he thought were of merit: "I gave him permission, plain, Jonathan, you are in charge, bring whoever you think is right to come and display their work on my building."

In addition to the artists, three experts testified for the plaintiffs. Renee Vara, a certified art appraiser, former head fine art expert at Chubb Insurance and art professor at New York University, testified to the quality and recognized stature of the works; Elizabeth Littlejohn, an art appraiser certified through the Appraisers Association of America, testified to their appraisal value; and Harriet Irgang Alden, the chief paintings conservator at Art Care NYC, testified as to the removability of each of the artworks from the 5 Pointz walls.

... The Advent and Evolution of 5Pointz

What became 5Pointz originated as Phun Phactory in the early 1990s. The warehouses were largely dilapidated and the neighborhood was crime infested. There was no control over the artists who painted on the walls of the buildings or the quality of their work, which was largely viewed by the public as nothing more than graffiti. This started to change in 2002 when Wolkoff put Cohen in charge. Cohen and several other artists also rented studio space in the warehouse buildings. Collectively, they worked to improve conditions. As Cohen explained:

> We took it upon ourselves to clean the loading dock.... The dumpsters were
> overflowing. We took it upon ourselves, we hired his employees, we paid for

the lighting. We put motion sensors up so that when you came to the loading dock it was inviting. It actually drew you in as opposed to scaring you away.

Wolkoff recognized the merit of the art. As he acknowledged: "I liked it and they did more and more and I thought it was terrific. They were expressing themselves." And he approved of the job Cohen did in curating the art: "I have no feelings even today against Jonathan Cohen. I thought he was terrific handling my building.... Anything to do with art I left up to Jonathan. He had good taste in the artists that came there."

Until Wolkoff decided over a decade later that the economic climate was ripe to convert the site into luxury condos, he and Cohen had a copacetic relationship.

But nothing was ever reduced to writing and Wolkoff only verbally laid out three rules for what could be put on the walls: no pornography, no religious content, and nothing political. In his role, Cohen established a system of rules for both the creation and curation of the art, spending seven days a week without pay to bring 5Pointz to fruition.

Cohen oversaw the site, kept it clean and safe, allotted wall space, and explained the site's rules and norms to new artists. Over time, crime in the neighborhood dropped and the site became a major attraction drawing thousands of daily visitors, including busloads of tourists, school trips, and weddings. Movie, television, and music video producers came; it was used for the 2013 motion picture Now You See Me, starring Jesse Eisenberg and Mark Ruffalo, and was the site of a notable tour for R & B singer Usher.

As the plaintiff Castillo explained, "street art became a new form," which "now has become an industry." And 5Pointz became "this outdoor museum where kids can touch the wall, and ... you can't do that at a museum. You can't go and touch a Van Gogh or like a Mona Lisa."

Wolkoff had nothing to do with day-to-day operations. Under Cohen's control, he witnessed his buildings emerge as a mecca for the world's largest collection of quality outdoor aerosol art....

5Pointz was organized into short-term rotating walls and long-standing walls. The short-term walls would change on a daily or weekly basis. As Cohen explained: "There were allocated spaces that were for straight beginners that had no idea how to paint. And those, I would say you could utilize the space, but it more than likely will be gone tomorrow or the next day or whatever." "Short-term rotating walls, it was communicated up front so they'd know you could have several weeks or whatever."

... The Planned Demolition

Starting in 2011, rumors that Wolkoff had plans to shut down 5Pointz and turn it into luxury condos began to concern the artists. In May 2013, the rumors became reality: Cohen learned that Wolkoff had started to seek the requisite municipal approvals for his condos.

Hoping to save 5Pointz, Cohen filed an application with the City Landmark Preservation Commission to preserve the site as one of cultural significance. It was denied because the artistic work was of too recent origin. *See* Letter from NYC Landmarks Preservation Commission, August 20, 2013. Cohen also sought funding to buy the property, which had been valued at $40 million. However, this fell through in October 2013 when Wolkoff obtained a necessary variance, instantly raising the property value to more than $200 million. The higher price was out of reach of Cohen's potential investors. Plaintiffs then initiated this litigation to enjoin Wolkoff from destroying 5Pointz.

... The Whitewashing

As soon as the Court denied the plaintiffs' application for preliminary injunction, Wolkoff directed the whitewashing of virtually all the artwork on the 5Pointz site with rollers, spray machines, and buckets of white paint ... [N]one of the covered works was salvageable. And plaintiffs were no longer allowed on the site, even to recover the scattered remnants of their ruined creations. Since their works were effectively destroyed,8 plaintiffs were relegated to seeking monetary relief under VARA.

IV

A. Temporary Works of Art

Defendants' overarching contention is that plaintiffs knew that the day would come when the buildings would be torn down and that, regardless, the nature of the work of an outdoor aerosol artist is ephemeral. They argue, therefore, that VARA should not afford plaintiffs protection for their temporary works.

VARA does not directly address whether it protects temporary works. However, in the context of works on buildings, it is clear from 17 U.S.C. § 113(d) that temporary works are protected. Moreover, relevant case law conceptually supports this conclusion. In short, there is no legal support for the proposition that temporary works do not come within VARA's embrace.

First, § 113(d)(1) specifies that an unremovable work incorporated in a building is protected by VARA unless the artist waives his or her rights in a writing signed by both the artist and the building owner. If the building owner could orally inform the artist that the building is coming down someday, and thereby convert the work into an unprotected temporary work, the written consent provision would be rendered nugatory. As the House Judiciary Committee Report explains: "The purpose of [the written waiver] is to ensure that the author is made fully aware of the circumstances surrounding the installation and potential removal of the work and has nevertheless knowingly subjected the work to possible modifications that would otherwise be actionable under section106A." H.R. Rep. No. 101-514, at 21. And as Patry adds: "In light of this provision's purpose of ensuring that artists be made aware fully of the circumstances surrounding installation and potential destructive removal, it should be strictly construed." Patry [on Copyright] § 16:33.

Second, § 113(d)(2), specifying that artists are entitled to 90 days' written notice to allow them to salvage their removable works, contemplates that such works may be temporarily on the side of a building. Thus, VARA resolves the tension between the building owners' rights and the artists' rights through § 113(d), not by excluding temporary works from protection.

Analogy to traditional copyright law is also relevant. Under the Copyright Act— of which VARA is a part—a work is "'created' when it is fixed in a copy or phonorecord for the first time[.]" 17 U.S.C. § 101. And a work is "'fixed' in a tangible medium of expression when its embodiment in a copy or phonorecord, by or under the authority of the author, is *sufficiently permanent or stable to permit it to be perceived … for a period of more than transitory duration.*" *Id.* (emphasis added). For copyright protection, therefore, fixation for even a short period will suffice.

Thus, in *Cartoon Network LP, LLLP v. CSC Holdings, Inc.,* 536 F.3d 121 (2d Cir. 2008), the Second Circuit held that copies of television programs were not capable of being perceived "for a period of more than transitory duration" when they existed in the defendant's data buffers for only 1.2 seconds. However, the court suggested that a work would exist for "more than transitory duration" if it was embodied in the data buffers for "at least several minutes." *Id.* at 128. With no indication to the contrary, it is reasonable to assume that Congress intended to apply the same minimal fixation requirement to works of visual art under VARA.

In sum, § 113(d) contemplates temporary works, § 106A(c) excludes only a narrow category of temporary works unrelated to this case, and analogous case law is consistent with the conclusion that temporary works are protected under VARA.

B. Works of Recognized Stature

As the Court stated in *Cohen I,* the district court's decision in *Carter v. Helmsley-Spear, Inc.,* 861 F.Supp. 303 (S.D.N.Y. 1994) ("*Carter I*"), aff'd in part, vacated in part, rev'd in part, 71 F.3d 77 (2d Cir. 1995) ("*Carter II*") remains the seminal case interpreting the phrase "recognized stature"—which is not defined in VARA—to require "a two-tiered showing: (1) that the visual art in question has 'stature,' i.e. is viewed as meritorious, and (2) that this stature is 'recognized' by art experts, other members of the artistic community, or by some cross-section of society." 861 F.Supp. at 325.

The Second Circuit on appeal never had occasion to address the correctness of this formulation since, in reversing, it held that the work did not qualify for VARA protection because it was made for hire. *Carter II,* 71 F.3d at 85–89. But one circuit court did thereafter embrace and apply the district court's standard for evaluating whether a work of visual art is of "recognized stature."

As explained in *Cohen I,* the Seventh Circuit in *Martin v. City of Indianapolis,* 192 F.3d 608, 612 (7th Cir. 1999), noted that the *Carter I* test "may be more rigorous than Congress intended," but nonetheless affirmed the district court's grant of summary judgment and its award of damages for a sculpture that had been destroyed, under the *Carter I* test utilized by the district court. In doing so, it noted that "plaintiff offered no evidence of experts or others by deposition, affidavit or interrogatories," but nonetheless established the work's recognized stature via "certain newspaper and magazine articles, and various letters, including a letter from an art gallery director and a letter to the editor of The Indianapolis News, all in support of the sculpture."

The circuit court's decision in *Martin* appropriately recognizes, therefore, that expert testimony is not the *sine qua non* for establishing that a work of visual art is of recognized stature, and indeed the district court in *Carter I* cautioned that plaintiffs need "not inevitably … call expert witnesses to testify before the trier of fact." This is in keeping with Congress's expansive recognition of the moral rights of attribution and integrity of the visual artist and the consequent need to create "a climate of artistic worth and honor that encourages the author in the arduous act of creation." The Second Circuit noted in *Carter II*, therefore, the courts "should use common sense and generally accepted standards of the artistic community in determining whether a particular work" is a work of visual art since "[a]rtists may work in a variety of media, and use any number of materials in creating their works."

The same common sense should be utilized in assessing whether the visual work is of recognized stature since "[b]y setting the standard too high, courts risk the destruction of the unrecognized masterwork; by setting it too low, courts risk alienating those … whose legitimate property interests are curtailed." Christopher J. Robinson, *The "Recognized Stature" Standard in the Visual Artists Rights Act*, 68 FORDHAM L. REV 1935, 1968 (2000). Thus, as one court has held, even inferred recognition from a successful career can be considered in determining whether a visual artist's work has achieved recognized stature. *See Lubner v. City of Los Angeles*, 45 Cal. App. 4th 525, 531, 53 Cal.Rptr.2d 24 (1996).

In the present case, the Court need not dwell on the nuances of the appropriate evidentiary standard since the plaintiffs adduced such a plethora of exhibits and credible testimony, including the testimony of a highly regarded expert, that even under the most restrictive of evidentiary standards almost all of the plaintiffs' works easily qualify as works of recognized stature.

To begin, that Jonathan Cohen selected the handful of works from the thousands at 5Pointz for permanence and prominence on long-standing walls is powerful, and arguably singular, testament to their recognized stature. They were walls that spanned multiple stories, walls visible to millions on the passing trains; walls near the entrances. Many of these works had survived for years. As 5Pointz's curator, Cohen considered them outstanding examples of the aerosol craft. And as Wolkoff himself acknowledged, Cohen was qualified to assess the artistic merits of the works since "he had good taste in the artists that came there." They were 5Pointz's jewels.

Wolkoff's faith in Cohen was not unwarranted. The multitude of artists painting on the walls marched to Cohen's beat. He called the shots and had the respect of his artistic community. That it was he who chose the works that are worthy of VARA protection in this litigation speaks volumes to their recognized stature.

But there is so much more. All of the plaintiffs had also achieved artistic recognition outside of 5Pointz. And in their Folios they collectively presented over a thousand exhibits in support of their claims that their works at 5Pointz had achieved recognized stature. The Folios covered the highlights of their careers, as well as evidence of the placement of their works at 5Pointz in films, television, newspaper articles, blogs, and online videos, in addition to social media buzz.

And plaintiffs' highly qualified expert, Vara, provided detailed findings as to the skill and craftsmanship of each of the 49 works, the importance of 5Pointz as a mecca for aerosol art, the academic and professional interest of the art world in the works, and her professional opinion that they were all of recognized stature. The Court finds Vara highly credible and affords great weight to her testimony, although, as explained infra, it finds that four of the 49 works do not qualify as having achieved recognized stature.

Defendants' expert Thompson's testimony had two fatal flaws: First, she used an unduly restrictive interpretation of recognized stature that was more akin to a masterpiece standard. Second, she relied heavily on her inability to find the works on social media or in academic databases; but, as effectively drawn out by plaintiffs' counsel on cross-examination, her search methodology was unduly restrictive and almost designed to avoid finding results. Tellingly, her searches did not even uncover many of plaintiffs' social media exhibits, demonstrating the weakness of her approach. Her final conclusion that none of the works had achieved recognized stature defies credibility. If not a single one of these works meet the recognized stature standard, it is hard to imagine works that would, short of a Caravaggio or Rembrandt. . . .

2. The Statutory Factors

"When determining the amount of statutory damages to award for copyright infringement, courts consider: (1) the infringer's state of mind; (2) the expenses saved, and profits earned, by the infringer; (3) the revenue lost by the copyright holder; (4) the deterrent effect on the infringer and third parties; (5) the infringer's cooperation in providing evidence concerning the value of the infringing material; and (6) the conduct and attitude of the parties." *Bryant v. Media Right Prods.*, 603 F.3d 135, 144 (2d Cir. 2010). Wolkoff rings the bell on each relevant factor. . . .

3. The Statutory Damages Award

Collectively, all five relevant factors support the maximum award of statutory damages. Therefore, the Court awards $150,000 for each of the 45 works, for a total statutory damages award of $6,750,000.

If not for Wolkoff's insolence, these damages would not have been assessed. If he did not destroy 5Pointz until he received his permits and demolished it 10 months later, the Court would not have found that he had acted willfully. Given the degree of difficulty in proving actual damages, a modest amount of statutory damages would probably have been more in order.

The shame of it all is that since 5Pointz was a prominent tourist attraction the public would undoubtedly have thronged to say its goodbyes during those 10 months and gaze at the formidable works of aerosol art for the last time. It would have been a wonderful tribute for the artists that they richly deserved.

Cheffins v. Stewart

825 F.3d 588 (9th Cir. 2016)

Plaintiffs Simon Cheffins and Gregory Jones, along with a number of volunteers, built the La Contessa, a replica of a 16th-century Spanish galleon for use at the Burning Man Festival. Cheffins began his creation by acquiring a used school bus. He and Jones then designed and constructed the galleon facade, including a hull, decking, masts, and a hand-crafted figurehead. These elements and the bus were then transported to the Black Rock Desert in northern Nevada, the site of Burning Man, and assembled. When completed, the La Contessa was approximately sixty feet wide and sixteen feet long with a mast over fifty feet tall....

After the 2002 Festival, Cheffins and Jones stored the La Contessa on property owned by Festival organizers. After the 2003 and 2005 Festivals, Cheffins and Jones stored the La Contessa on land in Nevada held in life estate by one Joan Grant, who had given them permission to do so. In late 2005, however, Grant's home burned down, causing her to abandon the life estate. Thereafter, defendant Michael Stewart took possession of the land in fee simple through a limited liability company.

Cheffins and Jones did not relocate the La Contessa after the change of property ownership. Rather, it sat unmoved on Stewart's land until December 2006. Sometime during that month, Stewart intentionally burned the wooden structure of the La Contessa so that a scrap metal dealer could remove the underlying school bus from his property....

On summary judgment, Stewart asserted, and the trial court subsequently concluded, that the La Contessa was not a "work of visual art" because it was "applied art." Whether the trial court properly granted summary judgment on the VARA claim turns on whether the La Contessa was a "work of visual art." The parties assert that this question, in turn, depends on whether it was applied art.

The VARA does not define the term "applied art," and federal courts have rarely had occasion to interpret its meaning. In *Carter v. Helmsley-Spear, Inc.*, 71 F.3d 77 (2d Cir. 1995), the Second Circuit held that a sculpture constructed of portions of a school bus and affixed to a wall in a building lobby was not "applied art." It explained that the term "applied art" means "two-and three-dimensional ornamentation or decoration that is affixed to otherwise utilitarian objects." The court further explained that the sculpture was not "applied art" simply because it was affixed to "the lobby's floor, walls, and ceiling" because "[i]nterpreting applied art to include such works would render meaningless VARA's protection for works of visual art installed in buildings."

The Second Circuit provided an additional gloss on what constitutes a "work of visual art," and by extension what constitutes "applied art," in *Pollara v. Seymour*, where it explained that the "VARA may protect a sculpture that looks like a piece of furniture, but it does not protect a piece of utilitarian furniture, whether or not it could arguably be called a sculpture." 344 F.3d 265, 269 (2d Cir. 2003). The court went on to hold that an elaborate painted banner was not a "work of visual art" eligible for protection under the VARA.

We agree in large part with the Second Circuit's analysis. As the Second Circuit suggested, the focus of our inquiry should be on whether the object in question originally was—and continues to be—utilitarian in nature. Such a focus comports with dictionary definitions of the term "applied art." For example, Webster's Dictionary defines "applied art" as "employed in the decoration, design or execution of *useful* objects." The Merriam Webster Dictionary 105 (3d ed. 1974) (emphasis added). Similarly, the Oxford English Dictionary explains that one definition of "applied" is "put to practical use" and lists "applied arts" as a frequent application of the term. The Oxford English Dictionary (2d ed. 1989). These definitions suggest that, in its ordinary meaning, applied art consists of an object with a utilitarian function that also has some artistic or aesthetic merit.

Further, this approach makes sense in the statutory context in which "applied art" is used in 17 U.S.C. § 101. "Applied art" is enumerated in a list that also contains, inter alia, maps, globes, charts, technical drawings, diagrams, models, newspapers, periodicals, data bases, and electronic information services. The fact that the other items in the list are utilitarian objects leads us to conclude that the listed items are related by their practical purposes and utilitarian functions, requiring a focus on utility when construing the term "applied art."

We therefore hold that an object constitutes a piece of "applied art"—as opposed to a "work of visual art"—where the object initially served a utilitarian function and the object continues to serve such a function after the artist made embellishments or alterations to it. This test embraces the circumstances both where a functional object incorporates a decorative design in its initial formulation, and where a functional object is decorated after manufacture but continues to serve a practical purpose. Conversely, "applied art" would not include a piece of art whose function is purely aesthetic or a utilitarian object which is so transformed through the addition of artistic elements that its utilitarian functions cease.

McKEOWN, Circuit Judge, concurring:

I write separately to express my concern with the majority's definition of applied art, which centers on whether an object has or retains a utilitarian function. This focus runs the risk of unduly narrowing the protections of artists under the Visual Artist Right's Act of 1990, 17 U.S.C. § 106A ("VARA"), and not focusing on the work as a whole. Although the majority's formulation may protect the clearest cases—those works that are "purely aesthetic" or "so transformed through the addition of artistic elements that [their] utilitarian functions cease"—it leaves other cases—such as works of art that incorporate utilitarian elements, or that could be put to practical purposes—out in the cold. To better effectuate the purpose of VARA, we need a more nuanced definition of "applied art" that balances between the risk of unduly restricting VARA's reach and the risks of turning judges into art critics or consigning to litigation every work of art that includes some utilitarian function. In determining whether a work is "applied art," the right question to ask is whether the primary purpose of the work as a whole is to serve a practical, useful function, and whether the aesthetic elements are subservient to that utilitarian purpose....

To effect the purpose of VARA and provide guidance for the art community, I believe courts should evaluate the work as a whole, asking whether its primary purpose is to serve a useful function and whether the artistic creation is subservient to that purpose. If the primary purpose is for the work to be viewed and perceived as art, then any incidental utilitarian function will not push it outside the scope of VARA. If a work's primary purpose is functional, however, no amount of aesthetic appeal will transfer it into visual art subject to VARA's protections. Determining a work's primary purpose need not constitute a judicial inquiry into the nature of art. Rather, as in other legal contexts, courts should ask whether "a reasonable observer" would "consider [the work] designed to a practical degree" for a utilitarian or artistic purpose. *See Lozman v. City of Riviera Beach*, [568 U.S. 115], 133 S. Ct. 735, 741 (2013) (articulating a "primary purpose" test for determining whether an object is a "vessel").

[Because the bus/Spanish galleon La Contessa is applied art under either standard, I concur in the judgment as well as parts I, II, IV, and V of the panel opinion.]

Report Waiver of Moral Rights in Visual Artworks

Executive Summary, Report of the Copyright Office (October 1996)[4]

On June 10, 1992, eighteen months after VARA's enactment, the [Copyright Office (Office)] published a Request for Information in the Federal Register seeking comments on artists' bargaining power relative to that of commercial users of artworks, on parties' awareness of the VARA rights and their inclusion of waiver provisions in contracts, on the contractual compliance with the law's requirements that works and uses subject to waivers be specifically identified, on the actual exercise of waivers, and on the relative numbers of waivers granted for rights of attribution and integrity for moveable works of visual art and for art works incorporated into buildings. We asked for empirical evidence on the kinds of contracts that include waivers and on the economic impact of those waivers; and we requested parties' assessment of whether the artist's renown affected his or her waiver of rights, and on what factors influence artists' decisions to waive rights. Finally, we asked for comments on possible constitutional problems that might arise if waivers were prohibited....

More than 1,000 persons filed written responses to the survey. Responses were received from 47 states and the District of Columbia, and 955 respondents were self-described visual artists. Most artists grossed less than $10,000 annually from their artwork and most had multiple sources of income.

About three-fourths of the respondents claimed awareness of moral rights, although many who elaborated in written comments stressed the need for more education of artists. Fewer than half knew that moral rights could be waived. Seven percent of

---

4. Waiver of Moral Rights in Visual Artworks, Executive Summary, Report of the Copyright Office (October 1996), available at http://www.copyright.gov/reports/exsum.html.

those who answered the question said waiver clauses were routinely included in artists' contracts, but nearly 40 percent said waiver clauses were part of contracts for commissioned works.

Nearly one quarter of artists covered by VARA knew of artists who had been asked to waive their moral rights. Thirteen percent of artists covered by VARA said they had refused contracts because they included waivers and a similar number had insisted that a waiver clause be struck from a contract. These artists were generally those who earned more than $25,000 annually from their art or who were represented by an agent. More than half of those who had rejected a request for waiver said such rejection voided the deal. In general, those participants who filed written commentary believe that VARA does little to enhance the artist's inferior bargaining position relative to the buyer.

More than half of the respondents who had experienced waivers said they complied with the specificity requirements of VARA, and about one-third said contracts contained a separate price for the waiver of moral rights. However, most art contracts continue to be oral and therefore cannot contain valid waiver clauses under the terms of VARA. Many artists decried the complexity of art contracts and stated that legal requirements were too burdensome and legal advice too costly....

On June 21, 1995, the Copyright Office held a public hearing to solicit comments on the effect of the waiver of moral rights provision of VARA.... Most saw the need for the sec. 113 waiver provisions for works incorporated into buildings. For one attorney, however, the fact that most contracts for major commissions will now routinely require waivers means that the sec. 113 waiver provision should be tightened, if not repealed....

Many panelists believed that repeal of sec. 113 waiver would result in a chilling effect on creation of art, since property owners may be unwilling to commit to a permanent structure. On the other hand, there may be a chilling effect even if building owners have secured a waiver: several artists reported that, had they been operating under a waiver, they would have undertaken the project, but with a different scale and design. Some predicted a standard term in landlord-tenant contracts requiring tenants to get waivers or refrain from installing art.

Other recommendations were made for VARA. For example, several parties agreed that one joint author should not have the ability to waive for all co-authors. Others believed VARA should apply to print or broadcast reproductions of works, thus covering distortions in books, magazines and electronic media....

Close v. Sotheby's, Inc.
894 F.3d 1061 (9th Cir. 2018)

The California Resale Royalties Act ("CRRA") grants artists an unwaivable right to 5% of the proceeds on any resale of their artwork under specified circumstances. To that end, the CRRA requires the seller of the artwork or the seller's agent to withhold 5% of the resale price and pay it to the artist or, if the artist cannot be found, to the California Arts Council. If the seller or the seller's agent fails to pay the 5% resale royalty, the artist may bring an action for damages.

Plaintiffs are artists and their successors in interest seeking resale royalties under the CRRA from the statute's effective date of January 1, 1977, to the present. The issue in this case is whether plaintiffs' claims are preempted by federal copyright law. The district court held that they are, as a matter of both express and conflict preemption.

We affirm in part and reverse in part. Plaintiffs' CRRA claims covered by the 1976 Copyright Act—i.e., those concerning sales postdating the 1976 Act's effective date of January 1, 1978—are expressly preempted by 17 U.S.C. § 301(a). We therefore affirm dismissal of those claims.

The 1909 Copyright Act, however, has no express preemption provision. As such, plaintiffs' CRRA claims covered only by the 1909 Act—i.e., those concerning sales that occurred between the CRRA's effective date of January 1, 1977, and the 1976 Act's effective date of January 1, 1978—cannot be expressly preempted. Nor are they preempted by conflict preemption. Accordingly, we reverse dismissal of those claims and remand them to the district court for further proceedings.

I. LEGAL AND FACTUAL BACKGROUND

A. The Droit de suite

Many nations recognize the *droit de suite*, under which artists receive a royalty each time the original, tangible embodiment of their work is resold. The practice was first recognized in France in 1920 and then adopted in other civil-law jurisdictions. More recently, a number of common-law jurisdictions have adopted some form of the *droit de suite*. In those countries that recognize it, the *droit de suite* is considered a moral right, albeit one with economic value.

The *droit de suite* protects visual artists, who face particular difficulty in capitalizing on their work. Literary and recording artists can generally profit from their efforts by controlling the reproduction of books or music. For visual artists such as painters and sculptors, however, the right to control reproduction is often not their principal source of income. Rather, it is often the sale of their original work that allows them to make a profit. The *droit de suite* gives these artists an economic interest in subsequent sales of their original work, thereby allowing them to capture some of its appreciation in value after the first sale.

The *droit de suite* also appears in international copyright law. Since 1948, the Berne Convention has recognized that artists possess an "inalienable right to an interest in any sale of the work subsequent to the first transfer by the author of the work." Berne Convention for the Protection of Literary and Artistic Works art. 14*ter*(1), Sept. 9, 1886, as amended Sept. 28, 1979, S. Treaty Doc. No. 99-27 (1986). Nevertheless, the Berne Convention does not obligate its signatories to adopt the *droit de suite*. Instead, the Berne Convention makes the recognition of such rights optional, but rewards such recognition with reciprocity: countries recognizing the right will protect the right of each others' artists.

The United States became a signatory to the Berne Convention in 1989, but to date, it has not adopted the *droit de suite*. As early as the 1970s, Congress considered adopting the *droit de suite* as part of U.S. copyright law, but those efforts have never proved successful. A *droit de suite* provision made its way into an early version of the Visual Artists Rights Act of 1990 ("VARA"), but was removed from the bill that Congress ultimately enacted.

In 1992, the Copyright Office issued an extensive report concluding that there was insufficient economic or copyright-policy justification to adopt the *droit de suite* in the United States. *See generally* 1992 Copyright Report. The report recommended that "[g]iven potential problems of preemption, enforcement, and multiple application, any *droit de suite* that is enacted in the United States should be at the federal level." Two decades later, members of Congress requested that the Copyright Office revisit the issue, and the Copyright Office issued a second report. *See generally* 2013 Copyright Report. This time, in light of "the adoption of resale royalty laws by more than thirty additional countries since the Office's prior report," the Copyright Office endorsed "implementation of a resale royalty right in the United States ... as one alternative to address the disparity in treatment of artists under the copyright law." *Id.* at 1, 3. Congress has not acted on the Copyright Office's recommendation.

B. The California Resale Royalties Act of 1976 ("CRRA")

The CRRA is "the first, and thus far only, American recognition of the *droit de suite*." NIMMER § 8C.04[B]. Under the CRRA, the seller of "a work of fine art"[5] or the seller's agent must withhold 5% of the sale price and pay it to the artist. Cal. Civ. Code § 986(a). If the seller or agent is unable to locate and pay the artist within 90 days, the 5% royalty goes to the California Arts Council. *Id.* § 986(a)(2). In that event, the California Arts Council must attempt to locate and pay the artist. *Id.* § 986(a)(5). If the artist has not been located after seven years, the Council may then use the funds to acquire fine art for public buildings. If the seller or agent fails to pay the 5% royalty, the artist may bring an action for damages and attorneys' fees. *Id.* § 986(a)(3). Notably, the artist's right to the 5% royalty may not be waived or reduced by contract. *Id.* § 986(a).

As originally enacted, the CRRA applied to sales of fine art in California or by a California seller (whether inside California or not). But, as discussed in greater detail below, we have since limited the statute to regulate only sales in California. *Sam Francis Found. v. Christies, Inc.*, 784 F.3d 1320, 1322 (9th Cir. 2015) (*en banc*). Other conditions to the CRRA's application include, inter alia, that the artist must be a citizen of the United States or resident of California; the sale must occur after the initial sale by the artist (i.e., it must be a resale); the sale must be for $1,000 or more; the sale cannot be for less than the purchase price paid by the seller; and the sale must occur during the artist's life or within 20 years of his death. Cal. Civ. Code § 986(a)–(c)....

---

5. "Fine art" is defined as "an original painting, sculpture, or drawing, or an original work of art in glass." Cal. Civ. Code § 986(c)(2).

II. ANALYSIS

"It is well-established that Congress has the power to preempt state law." *Montalvo v. Spirit Airlines*, 508 F.3d 464, 470 (9th Cir. 2007) (citing U.S. Const. art. VI, cl. 2). In general, there are three forms of preemption: express preemption, conflict preemption, and field preemption. *Arizona v. United States*, 567 U.S. 387, 398–400 (2012). Because Congress has not preempted the field in copyright law, only two forms of preemption are at issue here: express and conflict. Below, we first hold that plaintiffs' claims arising under the 1976 Act are expressly preempted by 17 U.S.C. § 301(a). We then consider whether what remains of plaintiffs' claims conflicts with the 1909 Act. We conclude that *Morseburg* [*v. Balyon*, 621 F.2d 972 (9th Cir. 1980)] controls our conflict preemption analysis and that plaintiffs' claims arising under the 1909 Act are therefore not preempted. Finally, we consider defendants' alternative argument based on the Takings Clause.

A. Express Preemption

The 1976 Copyright Act adopted, for the first time, an express preemption provision in § 301(a) and thereby accomplished a sea change in the relative powers of the states vis-à-vis the federal government over copyright protection. The House of Representatives anticipated that the preemption provision "would accomplish a fundamental and significant change in the present law." H.R. Rep. No. 94-1476, at 129 (1976). "By substituting a single Federal system for the present anachronistic, uncertain, impractical, and highly complicated dual system, the bill would greatly improve the operation of the copyright law and would be much more effective in carrying out the basic constitutional aims of uniformity and the promotion of writing and scholarship." *Id*. Section 301(a) states:

> On and after January 1, 1978, all legal or equitable rights that are equivalent to any of the exclusive rights within the general scope of copyright as specified by section 106 in works of authorship that are fixed in a tangible medium of expression and come within the subject matter of copyright as specified by sections 102 and 103, whether created before or after that date and whether published or unpublished, are governed exclusively by this title. Thereafter, no person is entitled to any such right or equivalent right in any such work under the common law or statutes of any State.

17 U.S.C. § 301(a).

In accordance with § 301(a), we have adopted a two-pronged test to determine whether a state law claim is preempted by the 1976 Act. *Maloney v. T3Media, Inc.*, 853 F.3d 1004, 1010 (9th Cir. 2017). "First, we decide whether the subject matter of the state law claim falls within the subject matter of copyright as described in 17 U.S.C. §§ 102 and 103." "Second, assuming it does, we determine whether the rights asserted under state law are equivalent to the rights contained in 17 U.S.C. § 106, which articulates the exclusive rights of copyright holders."

With respect to the first prong, the subject matter of copyright encompasses "original works of authorship fixed in any tangible medium of expression, now known or later developed, from which they can be perceived, reproduced, or otherwise communicated, either directly or with the aid of a machine or device." 17 U.S.C. § 102(a). This includes, for example, "pictorial, graphic, and sculptural works." There is no doubt that plaintiffs' claims under the CRRA for resale royalties on works of "fine art"—defined as original paintings, sculptures, drawings, or works in glass, Cal. Civ. Code § 986(c)(2)—fall within the subject matter of copyright. Plaintiffs do not dispute this prong of the test.

The second prong is also satisfied—that is, plaintiffs' state law claims assert rights "equivalent to rights within the general scope of copyright as specified by section 106 of the Copyright Act." *Maloney*, 853 F.3d at 1019. To explain why this is so, we begin with a short history of the first sale doctrine. The Copyright Act of 1891 provided that the copyright owner had "the sole liberty of printing, reprinting, publishing, completing, copying, executing, finishing, and vending" the copyrighted work. Copyright Act of 1891, § 4952, 26 Stat. 1106, 1107 (1891). In *Bobbs-Merrill Co. v. Straus*, the Supreme Court construed the right to "vend" as being limited to the first sale. Bobbs-Merrill Company owned the copyright to the novel The Castaway, each copy of which stated that its retail price was $1 and that a retail sale at any lesser price would be treated as copyright infringement. R.H. Macy & Company purchased copies of the book from wholesalers and retailed them for less than $1, and Bobbs-Merrill sued for infringement. The Court held that Bobbs-Merrill could not control Macy & Company's resale of the purchased copies: a copyright owner "who has sold a copyrighted article, without restriction, has parted with all right to control the sale of it."

Congress codified the first sale doctrine in the 1909 Copyright Act and later retained it in the 1976 Act. Today, § 109(a) provides that "the owner of a particular copy or phonorecord lawfully made under this title, or any person authorized by such owner, is entitled, without the authority of the copyright owner, to sell or otherwise dispose of the possession of that copy or phonorecord." "The practical effect of this language is to significantly circumscribe a copyright owner's exclusive distribution right 'only to the first sale of the copyrighted work' because 'once the copyright owner places a copyrighted item in the stream of commerce by selling it, he has exhausted his exclusive statutory right to control its distribution.'" *Adobe Sys. Inc. v. Christenson*, 809 F.3d 1071, 1076–77 (9th Cir. 2015) (quoting *Quality King* [*Distribs., Inc. v. L'anza Research Int'l, Inc.*], 523 U.S. at 141). One purpose of the first sale doctrine is to effect the "common law's refusal to permit restraints on the alienation of chattels." *Kirtsaeng v. John Wiley & Sons, Inc.*, 568 U.S. 519, 538 (2013). Another purpose is to "free[] courts from the administrative burden of trying to enforce restrictions upon difficult-to-trace, readily movable goods" and "avoid[] the selective enforcement inherent in any such effort." *Id.* at 539.

In this case, plaintiffs' CRRA claims assert rights equivalent to the federal distribution right codified in § 106(3), as limited by the first sale doctrine codified in § 109(a). Section 106(3) grants copyright holders the exclusive right "to distribute copies or phonorecords of the copyrighted work to the public by sale or other transfer of ownership, or by rental, lease, or lending," while the first sale doctrine circumscribes that right by limiting it to the first sale of a copyrighted work.

Although the CRRA's resale royalty right and § 106(3)'s distribution right are not coextensive, they are equivalent. The two rights differ in that one grants artists the right to receive a percentage payment on all sales of artwork after the first, while the other grants artists the right to receive full payment on the first (and only the first) sale. But, at root, both concern the distribution of copies of artwork and define artists' right (or lack thereof) to payment on downstream sales of those copies.

The equivalence of the two rights is further underscored by the manner in which the CRRA both expands and restricts the federal distribution right. The CRRA expands the federal distribution right because, whereas the first sale doctrine limits artists' right to payment to the first sale, the CRRA grants artists an unwaivable right to a 5% royalty on all downstream sales. Indeed, the CRRA is designed precisely to alter the first sale doctrine by affording artists a right to at least some measure of payment on every sale after the first. At the same time, the CRRA also restricts the federal distribution right by forbidding artists from fully alienating copies of their artwork. In effect, the CRRA creates an inalienable restraint on alienation.

In short, the CRRA does not merely grant an additional right beyond what federal copyright law already provides but fundamentally reshapes the contours of federal copyright law's existing distribution right. This runs counter to § 301(a), which precludes "all legal or equitable rights that are equivalent to any of the exclusive rights within the general scope of copyright," even if they are not precisely within the contemplation of the Copyright Act.

Plaintiffs raise a number of arguments in response. First, they argue that the CRRA cannot be expressly preempted because it creates a monetary, not a distribution, right. According to plaintiffs, the CRRA governs proceeds on the sale of art, not the distribution of art itself; a seller need only pay the artist a royalty, not obtain the artist's permission to make a sale. But plaintiffs' attempted distinction between monetary and distribution rights takes an unduly narrow view of § 106(3). That provision represents not merely copyright holders' ability to choose when to sell a copy of their work and to whom. It also represents copyright holders' ability to receive payment for selling copies of their work. Even though there are differences in how the CRRA and § 106(3) affect artists' right to payment—one requires a royalty on all sales after the first, and the other contemplates full alienation upon the first sale—there is significant overlap between the two for the reasons explained above.

Second, plaintiffs argue that the CRRA's resale royalty right cannot be expressly preempted because artists can create a similar right by contract. Plaintiffs have misunderstood the difference between a law that permits an act and a law that compels an act....

Third, plaintiffs argue that *Morseburg* should control our express preemption analysis. Acknowledging that *Morseburg* did not address the preemptive effect of the 1976 Act, plaintiffs argue that *Morseburg*'s reasoning is nevertheless dispositive of the present case. But "we emphasize[d] that this case concern[ed] the preemptive effect of the 1909 Act only." *Morseburg*, 621 F.2d at 975. We noted that the 1976 Act became effective after the sales at issue in Morseburg's suit. . . .

Finally, plaintiffs point to the legislative history of VARA. In enacting VARA in 1990, the House of Representatives indicated that: "State artists' rights laws that grant rights not equivalent to those accorded under the proposed law are not preempted, even when they relate to works covered by H.R. 2690. For example, the law will not preempt a cause of action for a misattribution of a reproduction of a work of visual art or for a violation of a right to a resale royalty." H.R. Rep. No. 101-514, 1990 U.S.C.C.A.N. 6915, 6931 (1990). This brief statement postdates the 1976 Copyright Act by over a decade, and at best, represents the House's understanding—right or wrong—of how existing law might intersect with the changes proposed in VARA. It is not legislative history of the preemption clause adopted in the 1976 Act. Nor are we aware of any similar statement in the actual legislative history of the 1976 Act. VARA's legislative history does not alter our analysis regarding the equivalence of the state and federal rights at issue. *See, e.g., Bruesewitz v. Wyeth L.L.C.*, 562 U.S. 223, 242 (2011) ("Post-enactment legislative history . . . is not a legitimate tool of statutory interpretation;" rejecting the use of subsequent legislative history as a test for interpreting a preemption clause).

In short, the CRRA falls within the subject matter of the Copyright Act and asserts rights equivalent to those found in § 106(3) of the Copyright Act. The CRRA is therefore expressly preempted by § 301(a). Plaintiffs' CRRA claims arising after the effective date of the 1976 Act—January 1, 1978—are barred.

B. Conflict Preemption

Unlike the 1976 Act, the 1909 Act contained no express preemption provision. Our holding on express preemption therefore does not account for plaintiffs' claims, if any actually exist, that arose between the CRRA's effective date of January 1, 1977, and the 1976 Act's effective date of January 1, 1978. This remaining sliver of claims is preempted only if it conflicts with the 1909 Act. Our decision in *Morseburg*, which likewise addressed sales of fine art occurring in 1977, is squarely on point. Its holding that the CRRA does not conflict with the 1909 Act therefore controls our analysis of plaintiffs' remaining claims. *Morseburg*, 621 F.2d at 977–78. . . .

III. CONCLUSION

Our decision today means that the CRRA had a short effective life. California's statute permissibly coexisted for exactly one year alongside the 1909 Act. Once the 1976 Act took effect, however, the balance of state versus federal copyright protection shifted and the CRRA was preempted by § 301(a). . . .

Notes and Questions

a. To what extent do the cases identified by the Register of Copyright regarding U.S. moral rights law compare to the treaty obligation to adhere to Article 6*bis* of the Berne Convention?

b. The Supreme Court has significantly revised the role the Lanham Act § 43(a) can play with regard to protection for the attribution of a motion picture video cassette, providing that the source of goods is the distributor of those cassettes. Does the same source of goods analysis apply to the creation of a work of art? Does it matter whether the work is incorporated into a utilitarian object (such as the base of a lamp or a piece of jewelry) or if the work is a more traditional oil painting or photograph? *See Dastar Corp. v. Twentieth Century Fox Film Corp.*, 539 U.S. 23 (2003).

c. When an artist's clay model for a sculpture is left outdoors, does this constitute a violation of VARA? In this case the model was a 35-foot clay model for a statue's head made for the "purpose of memorializing the life of Catherine of Braganza, Princess of Portugal and Queen of England in the mid-seventeenth century and namesake of the borough of Queens." The statue was to become "a monument to Queen Catherine to be installed at a prominent place within the Hunters Point Redevelopment Project in Queens." *See Flack v. Friends of Queen Catherine, Inc.*, 139 F. Supp. 2d 526 (S.D.N.Y. 2001).

d. What attributes constitute the artwork? Often, sculptural works are designed for particular locations. To what extent does the spatial environment define the work and become part of the installation for purposes of VARA protection? *See Phillips v. Pembroke Real Estate, Inc.*, 459 F.3d 128 (1st Cir. 2006).

e. What constitutes a work of art of a sufficiently recognized stature to gain VARA protection? *Compare Pollara v. Seymour*, 344 F.3d 265 (2d Cir. 2003), *and Martin v. City of Indianapolis*, 192 F.3d 608 (7th Cir. 1999), *with Scott v. Dixon*, 309 F. Supp. 2d 395 (E.D.N.Y. 2004).

f. A church mural depicting a very masculine Christ met with increasing consternation by the congregation, which had the mural covered over. The artist sued under Article 6*bis* of the Berne Convention but could not establish that the treaty applied to New York real property law. *See Crimi v. Rutgers Presbyterian Church*, 194 Misc. 570 (Sup. Ct. 1949).

g. In addition to VARA, states including California, New York, and Massachusetts have state legislation involving the protection of moral rights for authors. Some states also provide ongoing economic rights to artists such as *droit de suite* (a royalty for visual artists). *See Phillips v. Pembroke Real Estate, Inc.*, 459 F.3d 128 (1st Cir. 2006); Massachusetts Art Preservation Act, Mass. Gen. Laws ch. 231, § 85S (1984); California Art Preservation Act, Cal. Civ. Code § 987 (West 1979).

h. To what extent does VARA preempt the previous state statutes that provide moral rights or economic resale rights? *See Bd. of Managers of Soho Int'l Arts Condo. v. City of N.Y.*, 2003 U.S. Dist. LEXIS 10221 (S.D.N.Y. June 17, 2003) (unreported) (reviewing N.Y. Arts & Cult. Aff. Law § 14.03 (McKinney 1984)). The court explains the standard copyright preemption standard: a "statute pre-empts a state law if two conditions are met: 1) if the work to which the rights under the state statute falls within the 'subject matter' of copyright as specified in 17 U.S.C. §§ 102 and 103 and 2) if the right is the same or 'equivalent' to those granted by [the state law]." *Id.* (internal citations omitted).

More recently, the Ninth Circuit found the California Resale Royalties Act, Cal. Civ. Code §986 (West 2007), to be preempted by the 1976 Copyright Act. Copyright royalties after the effective date of the Copyright Act, January 1, 1978 are therefore preempted and invalid. *See Close v. Sotheby's, Inc.*, 894 F.3d 1061 (9th Cir. 2018). The 1909 Copyright Act, however, did not have the same preemptive effect. As a result, the Ninth Circuit found that claims for works sold during the period following the effective date of the California Resale Royalties Act of January 1, 1977 and the effective date of the Copyright Act of January 1, 1978 were not preempted.

i. Another challenge to the scope of VARA involves unfinished works. In an unfortunate case involving the Massachusetts Museum of Contemporary Art, a large installation went unfinished amid claims of vague instructions, corner-cutting, and a lack of written instructions. Among the legal issues was the extent to which VARA applied to works that had yet to be completed. Reviewing the question for the first time, the First Circuit found unfinished works are covered. "Reading VARA in accordance with the definitions in section 101, it too must be read to protect unfinished, but 'fixed,' works of art that, if completed, would qualify for protection under the statute." *See Mass. Museum of Contemporary Art Found., Inc. v. Buchel*, 593 F.3d 38 (1st Cir. 2010).

j. Yet another challenge to the scope of VARA involves nontraditional media. To what extent is a park design, including its floral decoration, protected by the statute? *See Kelley v. Chi. Park Dist.*, 635 F.3d 290 (7th Cir. 2011).

k. Graffiti art has its own subculture and communal importance. In Los Angeles, the city has responded to the need for art preservation and community building with an ordinance on the subject. *See L.A., Cal., Code §§14.4.2, 14.4.3, and 14.4.20 (all as amended), L.A., Cal., Admin. Code §22.119, available at http://clkrep.lacity.org/onlinedocs/2011/11-0923_ord_182706.pdf. See also* Eric Bjorgum, *Los Angeles Gets A New Mural Ordinance*, L.A. Law. Jan. 2014, at 36.

l. Art storage is often another area of tension between artists and commercial vendors. Christian Narkiewicz-Laine, an artist, stored his artwork and other belongings in a space in Galena, Illinois that he rented from the defendants. Years into the lease, the defendants emptied the unit, destroying the majority of Narkiewicz-Laine's property. He responded by suing to recover for the loss of his property under VARA as well as his common law claims of trespass, conversion, and negligence. A jury awarded him $300,000 for the loss of all of his property discarded from the rental unit and $120,000 in statutory and/or actual copyright damages. The judge found the two awards were duplicative, and set the total award at the $300,000 amount. What was the likely result on appeal? *See Narkiewicz-Laine v. Doyle*, 930 F.3d 897 (7th Cir. 2019).

Problem 18-B

Bryce has been in pre-production for a feature-length film. The director of photography hopes to shoot a location that is described in the screenplay and based on a true historical story. To shoot the location, a mural painted in 2001 would need to be covered during the shooting. Bryce has been assured by the set designer that the mural can be covered with a paint that can easily be removed. Bryce has contacted the building owners for permission to temporarily cover the mural in order to make the film. Because of the historical importance of the location and potential marketing opportunities, the building's owners would like the film to be shot, but they are concerned that the temporary covering of the mural would interfere with the artist's rights under VARA. Please advise Bryce on the obligations the mural owners have to the artist under VARA. If Bryce were to remove the image in post-production rather than by covering it, explain any VARA or other copyright issues.

C. Government Regulation of Content in the Visual Arts

National Endowment for the Arts v. Finley

524 U.S. 569 (1998)

JUSTICE O'CONNOR delivered the opinion of the Court.

The National Foundation on the Arts and Humanities Act, as amended in 1990, requires the Chairperson of the National Endowment for the Arts (NEA) to ensure that "artistic excellence and artistic merit are the criteria by which [grant] applications are judged, *taking into consideration general standards of decency and respect for the diverse beliefs and values of the American public.*" 20 U.S.C. § 954(d)(1). In this case, we review the Court of Appeals' determination that § 954(d)(1), on its face, impermissibly discriminates on the basis of viewpoint and is void for vagueness under the First and Fifth Amendments. We conclude that § 954(d)(1) is facially valid, as it neither inherently interferes with First Amendment rights nor violates constitutional vagueness principles.

With the establishment of the NEA in 1965, Congress embarked on a "broadly conceived national policy of support for the … arts in the United States," pledging federal funds to "help create and sustain not only a climate encouraging freedom of thought, imagination, and inquiry but also the material conditions facilitating the release of … creative talent." The enabling statute vests the NEA with substantial discretion to award grants; it identifies only the broadest funding priorities, including "artistic and cultural significance, giving emphasis to American creativity and cultural diversity," "professional excellence," and the encouragement of "public knowledge, education, understanding, and appreciation of the arts."

Applications for NEA funding are initially reviewed by advisory panels composed of experts in the relevant field of the arts. Under the 1990 Amendments to the enabling statute, those panels must reflect "diverse artistic and cultural points of view" and include "wide geographic, ethnic, and minority representation," as well as "lay individuals who are knowledgeable about the arts." The panel reports to the 26-member National Council on the Arts (Council), which, in turn, advises the NEA Chairperson. The Chairperson has the ultimate authority to award grants but may not approve an application as to which the Council has made a negative recommendation.

Since 1965, the NEA has distributed over three billion dollars in grants to individuals and organizations, funding that has served as a catalyst for increased state, corporate, and foundation support for the arts. Congress has recently restricted the availability of federal funding for individual artists, confining grants primarily to qualifying organizations and state arts agencies, and constraining sub-granting. By far the largest portion of the grants distributed in fiscal year 1998 were awarded directly to state arts agencies. In the remaining categories, the most substantial grants were allocated to symphony orchestras, fine arts museums, dance theater foundations, and opera associations.

Throughout the NEA's history, only a handful of the agency's roughly 100,000 awards have generated formal complaints about misapplied funds or abuse of the public's trust. Two provocative works, however, prompted public controversy in 1989 and led to congressional revaluation of the NEA's funding priorities and efforts to increase oversight of its grant-making procedures. The Institute of Contemporary Art at the University of Pennsylvania had used $30,000 of a visual arts grant it received from the NEA to fund a 1989 retrospective of photographer Robert Mapplethorpe's work. The exhibit, entitled *The Perfect Moment*, included homoerotic photographs that several Members of Congress condemned as pornographic. Members also denounced artist Andres Serrano's work *Piss Christ*, a photograph of a crucifix immersed in urine. Serrano had been awarded a $15,000 grant from the Southeast Center for Contemporary Art, an organization that received NEA support.

When considering the NEA's appropriations for fiscal year 1990, Congress reacted to the controversy surrounding the Mapplethorpe and Serrano photographs by eliminating $45,000 from the agency's budget, the precise amount contributed to the two exhibits by NEA grant recipients. Congress also enacted an amendment providing that no NEA funds "may be used to promote, disseminate, or produce materials which in the judgment of [the NEA] may be considered obscene, including but not limited to, depictions of sadomasochism, homoeroticism, the sexual exploitation of children, or individuals engaged in sex acts and which, when taken as a whole, do not have serious literary, artistic, political, or scientific value." The NEA implemented Congress' mandate by instituting a requirement that all grantees certify in writing that they would not utilize federal funding to engage in projects inconsistent with the criteria in the 1990 appropriations bill. That certification requirement was subsequently invalidated as unconstitutionally vague by a Federal District Court, and the NEA did not appeal the decision.

In the 1990 appropriations bill, Congress also agreed to create an Independent Commission of constitutional law scholars to review the NEA's grant-making procedures and assess the possibility of more focused standards for public arts funding. The Commission's report, issued in September 1990, concluded that there is no constitutional obligation to provide arts funding, but also recommended that the NEA rescind the certification requirement and cautioned against legislation setting forth any content restrictions. Instead, the Commission suggested procedural changes to enhance the role of advisory panels and a statutory reaffirmation of "the high place the nation accords to the fostering of mutual respect for the disparate beliefs and values among us." ...

Ultimately, Congress adopted the Williams/Coleman Amendment, a bipartisan compromise between Members opposing any funding restrictions and those favoring some guidance to the agency. In relevant part, the Amendment became §954(d)(1), which directs the Chairperson, in establishing procedures to judge the artistic merit of grant applications, to "take into consideration general standards of decency and respect for the diverse beliefs and values of the American public."[6]

The NEA has not promulgated any official interpretation of the provision, but in December 1990, the Council unanimously adopted a resolution to implement §954(d)(1) merely by ensuring that the members of the advisory panels that conduct the initial review of grant applications represent geographic, ethnic, and aesthetic diversity. John Frohnmayer, then Chairperson of the NEA, also declared that he would "count on [the] procedures" ensuring diverse membership on the peer review panels to fulfill Congress' mandate.

The four individual respondents in this case, Karen Finley, John Fleck, Holly Hughes, and Tim Miller, are performance artists who applied for NEA grants before §954(d)(1) was enacted. An advisory panel recommended approval of respondents' projects, both initially and after receiving Frohnmayer's request to reconsider three of the applications. A majority of the Council subsequently recommended disapproval, and in June 1990, the NEA informed respondents that they had been denied funding. Respondents filed suit, alleging that the NEA had violated their First Amendment rights by rejecting the applications on political grounds, had failed to follow statutory procedures by basing the denial on criteria other than those set forth in the NEA's enabling statute, and had breached the confidentiality of their grant applications through the release of quotations to the press, in violation of the Privacy Act of 1974, 5 U.S.C. §552(a). Respondents sought restoration of the recommended grants or reconsideration of their applications, as well as damages for the alleged Privacy Act violations. When Congress enacted §954(d)(1), respondents, now joined by the National Association of Artists' Organizations (NAAO), amended their complaint to challenge the provision as void for vagueness and impermissibly viewpoint based.

The District Court denied the NEA's motion for judgment on the pleadings, and, after discovery, the NEA agreed to settle the individual respondents' statutory and

---

6. Title 20 U.S.C. §954(d) provides in full that:

"No payment shall be made under this section except upon application therefor which is submitted to the National Endowment for the Arts in accordance with regulations issued and procedures established by the Chairperson. In establishing such regulations and procedures, the Chairperson shall ensure that—

"(1) artistic excellence and artistic merit are the criteria by which applications are judged, taking into consideration general standards of decency and respect for the diverse beliefs and values of the American public; and

"(2) applications are consistent with the purposes of this section. Such regulations and procedures shall clearly indicate that obscenity is without artistic merit, is not protected speech, and shall not be funded."

as-applied constitutional claims by paying the artists the amount of the vetoed grants, damages, and attorney's fees.

The District Court then granted summary judgment in favor of respondents on their facial constitutional challenge to §954(d)(1) and enjoined enforcement of the provision. The court rejected the argument that the NEA could comply with §954(d)(1) by structuring the grant selection process to provide for diverse advisory panels. The provision, the court stated, "fails adequately to notify applicants of what is required of them or to circumscribe NEA discretion." Reasoning that "the very nature of our pluralistic society is that there are an infinite number of values and beliefs, and correlatively, there may be no national 'general standards of decency,'" the court concluded that §954(d)(1) "cannot be given effect consistent with the Fifth Amendment's due process requirement." Drawing an analogy between arts funding and public universities, the court further ruled that the First Amendment constrains the NEA's grant-making process, and that because §954(d)(1) "clearly reaches a substantial amount of protected speech," it is impermissibly overbroad on its face. The Government did not seek a stay of the District Court's injunction, and consequently the NEA has not applied §954(d)(1) since June 1992. A divided panel of the Court of Appeals affirmed the District Court's ruling.... We granted certiorari and now reverse the judgment of the Court of Appeals.

Respondents raise a facial constitutional challenge to §954(d)(1), and consequently they confront "a heavy burden" in advancing their claim. Facial invalidation "is, manifestly, strong medicine" that "has been employed by the Court sparingly and only as a last resort." To prevail, respondents must demonstrate a substantial risk that application of the provision will lead to the suppression of speech.

Respondents argue that the provision is a paradigmatic example of viewpoint discrimination because it rejects any artistic speech that either fails to respect mainstream values or offends standards of decency. The premise of respondents' claim is that §954(d)(1) constrains the agency's ability to fund certain categories of artistic expression. The NEA, however, reads the provision as merely hortatory, and contends that it stops well short of an absolute restriction. Section 954(d)(1) adds "considerations" to the grant-making process; it does not preclude awards to projects that might be deemed "indecent" or "disrespectful," nor place conditions on grants, or even specify that those factors must be given any particular weight in reviewing an application. Indeed, the agency asserts that it has adequately implemented §954(d)(1) merely by ensuring the representation of various backgrounds and points of view on the advisory panels that analyze grant applications.

We do not decide whether the NEA's view—that the formulation of diverse advisory panels is sufficient to comply with Congress' command—is in fact a reasonable reading of the statute. It is clear, however, that the text of §954(d)(1) imposes no categorical requirement. The advisory language stands in sharp contrast to congressional efforts to prohibit the funding of certain classes of speech. When Congress has in fact intended to affirmatively constrain the NEA's grant-making authority, it has done so in no uncertain terms.

Furthermore, like the plain language of § 954(d), the political context surrounding the adoption of the "decency and respect" clause is inconsistent with respondents' assertion that the provision compels the NEA to deny funding on the basis of viewpoint discriminatory criteria. The legislation was a bipartisan proposal introduced as a counterweight to amendments aimed at eliminating the NEA's funding or substantially constraining its grant-making authority. The Independent Commission had cautioned Congress against the adoption of distinct viewpoint-based standards for funding, and the Commission's report suggests that "additional criteria for selection, if any, should be incorporated as part of the selection process (perhaps as part of a definition of 'artistic excellence'), rather than isolated and treated as exogenous considerations." In keeping with that recommendation, the criteria in § 954(d)(1) inform the assessment of artistic merit, but Congress declined to disallow any particular viewpoints. As the sponsors of § 954(d)(1) noted in urging rejection of the Rohrabacher Amendment, "if we start down that road of prohibiting categories of expression, categories which are indeed constitutionally protected speech, where do we end? Where one Member's aversions end, others with different sensibilities and with different values begin." 136 Cong. Rec. 28624 (statement of Rep. Coleman); *see also id.*, at 28663 (statement of Rep. Williams) (arguing that the Rohrabacher Amendment would prevent the funding of Jasper Johns' flag series, "The Merchant of Venice," "Chorus Line," "Birth of a Nation," and the "Grapes of Wrath"). In contrast, before the vote on § 954(d)(1), one of its sponsors stated: "If we have done one important thing in this amendment, it is this. We have maintained the integrity of freedom of expression in the United States."

That § 954(d)(1) admonishes the NEA merely to take "decency and respect" into consideration, and that the legislation was aimed at reforming procedures rather than precluding speech, undercut respondents' argument that the provision inevitably will be utilized as a tool for invidious viewpoint discrimination. In cases where we have struck down legislation as facially unconstitutional, the dangers were both more evident and more substantial. In *R.A.V. v. St. Paul*, 505 U.S. 377 (1992), for example, we invalidated on its face a municipal ordinance that defined as a criminal offense the placement of a symbol on public or private property " 'which one knows or has reasonable grounds to know arouses anger, alarm, or resentment in others on the basis of race, color, creed, religion, or gender.' " That provision set forth a clear penalty, proscribed views on particular "disfavored subjects," and suppressed "distinctive ideas, conveyed by a distinctive message."

In contrast, the "decency and respect" criteria do not silence speakers by expressly "threatening censorship of ideas." Thus, we do not perceive a realistic danger that § 954(d)(1) will compromise First Amendment values. As respondents' own arguments demonstrate, the considerations that the provision introduces, by their nature, do not engender the kind of directed viewpoint discrimination that would prompt this Court to invalidate a statute on its face. Respondents assert, for example, that "one would be hard-pressed to find two people in the United States who could agree on what the 'diverse beliefs and values of the American public' are, much less on whether a particular work of art 'respects' them"; and they claim that "'decency' is likely to mean something very different to a septuagenarian in Tuscaloosa and a teenager in Las Vegas." The NEA likewise views the considerations enumerated in §954(d)(1) as susceptible to multiple interpretations. Accordingly, the provision does not introduce considerations that, in practice, would effectively preclude or punish the expression of particular views. Indeed, one could hardly anticipate how "decency" or "respect" would bear on grant applications in categories such as funding for symphony orchestras.

Respondents' claim that the provision is facially unconstitutional may be reduced to the argument that the criteria in §954(d)(1) are sufficiently subjective that the agency could utilize them to engage in viewpoint discrimination. Given the varied interpretations of the criteria and the vague exhortation to "take them into consideration," it seems unlikely that this provision will introduce any greater element of selectivity than the determination of "artistic excellence" itself. And we are reluctant, in any event, to invalidate legislation "on the basis of its hypothetical application to situations not before the Court." *FCC v. Pacifica Foundation*, 438 U.S. 726, 743, 57 L. Ed. 2d 1073, 98 S. Ct. 3026 (1978).

The NEA's enabling statute contemplates a number of indisputably constitutional applications for both the "decency" prong of §954(d)(1) and its reference to "respect for the diverse beliefs and values of the American public." Educational programs are central to the NEA's mission. And it is well established that "decency" is a permissible factor where "educational suitability" motivates its consideration.

Permissible applications of the mandate to consider "respect for the diverse beliefs and values of the American public" are also apparent. In setting forth the purposes of the NEA, Congress explained that "it is vital to democracy to honor and preserve its multicultural artistic heritage." The agency expressly takes diversity into account, giving special consideration to "projects and productions ... that reach, or reflect the culture of, a minority, inner city, rural, or tribal community," §954(c)(4), as well as projects that generally emphasize "cultural diversity," §954(c)(1). Respondents do not contend that the criteria in §954(d)(1) are impermissibly applied when they may be justified, as the statute contemplates, with respect to a project's intended audience.

We recognize, of course, that reference to these permissible applications would not alone be sufficient to sustain the statute against respondents' First Amendment challenge. But neither are we persuaded that, in other applications, the language of §954(d)(1) itself will give rise to the suppression of protected expression. Any content-based considerations that may be taken into account in the grant-making process are a consequence of the nature of arts funding. The NEA has limited resources and it must deny the majority of the grant applications that it receives, including many that propose "artistically excellent" projects. The agency may decide to fund particular projects for a wide variety of reasons, "such as the technical proficiency of the artist, the creativity of the work, the anticipated public interest in or appreciation of the work, the work's contemporary relevance, its educational value, its suitability for or appeal to special audiences (such as children or the disabled), its service to a rural or isolated community, or even simply that the work could increase public knowledge of an art form." As the dissent below noted, it would be "impossible to have a highly selective grant program without denying money to a large amount of constitutionally protected expression." The "very assumption" of the NEA is that grants will be awarded according to the "artistic worth of competing applications," and absolute neutrality is simply "inconceivable."

Respondent's reliance on our decision in *Rosenberger v. Rector and Visitors of Univ. of Va.*, 515 U.S. 819 (1995), is therefore misplaced. In *Rosenberger*, a public university declined to authorize disbursements from its Student Activities Fund to finance the printing of a Christian student newspaper. We held that by subsidizing the Student Activities Fund, the University had created a limited public forum, from which it impermissibly excluded all publications with religious editorial viewpoints. Although the scarcity of NEA funding does not distinguish this case from *Rosenberger*, the competitive process according to which the grants are allocated does. In the context of arts funding, in contrast to many other subsidies, the Government does not indiscriminately "encourage a diversity of views from private speakers." The NEA's mandate is to make aesthetic judgments, and the inherently content-based "excellence" threshold for NEA support sets it apart from the subsidy at issue in *Rosenberger*—which was available to all student organizations that were "'related to the educational purpose of the University,'"—and from comparably objective decisions on allocating public benefits, such as access to a school auditorium or a municipal theater, or the second class mailing privileges available to "'all newspapers and other periodical publications.'"

It is so ordered.

Justice Scalia, with whom Justice Thomas joins, concurring in the judgment.

"The operation was a success, but the patient died." What such a procedure is to medicine, the Court's opinion in this case is to law. It sustains the constitutionality of 20 U.S.C. § 954(d)(1) by gutting it. The most avid congressional opponents of the provision could not have asked for more. I write separately because, unlike the Court, I think that § 954(d)(1) must be evaluated as written, rather than as distorted by the agency it was meant to control. By its terms, it establishes content- and viewpoint-based criteria upon which grant applications are to be evaluated. And that is perfectly constitutional.... One can regard [the statute] as either suggesting that decency and respect are elements of what Congress regards as artistic excellence and merit, or as suggesting that decency and respect are factors to be taken into account *in addition to* artistic excellence and merit. But either way, it is entirely, 100% clear that decency and respect are to be taken into account in evaluating applications....

This is so apparent that I am at a loss to understand what the Court has in mind (other than the gutting of the statute) when it speculates that the statute is merely "advisory." ... The statute requires the decency and respect factors to be considered in evaluating *all* applications—not, for example, just those applications relating to educational programs, *ante*, at 13, or intended for a particular audience....

Section 954(d)(1) is no more discriminatory, and no less constitutional, than virtually every other piece of funding legislation enacted by Congress. "The Government can, without violating the Constitution, selectively fund a program to encourage certain activities it believes to be in the public interest, without at the same time funding an alternative program...." *Rust v. Sullivan*, 500 U.S. 173 (1991). As we noted in *Rust*, when Congress chose to establish the National Endowment for Democracy it was not constitutionally required to fund programs encouraging competing philosophies of government—an example of funding discrimination that cuts much closer than this one to the core of *political* speech which is the primary concern of the First Amendment. It takes a particularly high degree of chutzpah for the NEA to contradict this proposition, since the agency itself discriminates—and is required by law to discriminate—in favor of artistic (as opposed to scientific, or political, or theological) expression. Not all the common folk, or even all great minds, for that matter, think that is a good idea. In 1800, when John Marshall told John Adams that a recent immigration of Frenchmen would include talented artists, "Adams denounced all Frenchmen, but most especially 'schoolmasters, painters, poets, &C.' He warned Marshall that the fine arts were like germs that infected healthy constitutions." Surely the NEA itself is nothing less than an institutionalized discrimination against that point of view. Nonetheless it is constitutional, as is the congressional determination to favor decency and respect for beliefs and values over the opposite. Because such favoritism does not "abridge" anyone's freedom of speech....

JUSTICE SOUTER, dissenting.

The question here is whether the italicized segment of this statute is unconstitutional on its face: "artistic excellence and artistic merit are the criteria by which applications [for grants from the National Endowment for the Arts] are judged, *taking into consideration general standards of decency and respect for the diverse beliefs and values of the American public.*" 20 U.S.C. § 954(d) (emphasis added). It is.

The decency and respect proviso mandates viewpoint-based decisions in the disbursement of government subsidies, and the Government has wholly failed to explain why the statute should be afforded an exemption from the fundamental rule of the First Amendment that viewpoint discrimination in the exercise of public authority over expressive activity is unconstitutional. The Court's conclusions that the proviso is not viewpoint based, that it is not a regulation, and that the NEA may permissibly engage in viewpoint-based discrimination, are all patently mistaken. Nor may the question raised be answered in the Government's favor on the assumption that some constitutional applications of the statute are enough to satisfy the demand of facial constitutionality, leaving claims of the proviso's obvious invalidity to be dealt with later in response to challenges of specific applications of the discriminatory standards. This assumption is irreconcilable with our long standing and sensible doctrine of facial overbreadth, applicable to claims brought under the First Amendment's speech clause. I respectfully dissent....

One need do nothing more than read the text of the statute to conclude that Congress's purpose in imposing the decency and respect criteria was to prevent the funding of art that conveys an offensive message; the decency and respect provision on its face is quintessentially viewpoint based, and quotations from the Congressional Record merely confirm the obvious legislative purpose. In the words of a cosponsor of the bill that enacted the proviso, "works which deeply offend the sensibilities of significant portions of the public ought not to be supported with public funds." ... In the face of such clear legislative purpose, so plainly expressed, the Court has its work cut out for it in seeking a constitutional reading of the statute....

Because "the normal definition of 'indecent'... refers to nonconformance with accepted standards of morality," restrictions turning on decency, especially those couched in terms of "general standards of decency," are quintessentially viewpoint based: they require discrimination on the basis of conformity with mainstream mores. The Government's contrary suggestion that the NEA's decency standards restrict only the "mode, form, or style" of artistic expression, not the underlying viewpoint or message, may be a tempting abstraction (and one not lacking in support). But here it suffices to realize that "form, mode, or style" are not subject to abstraction from artistic viewpoint, and to quote from an opinion just two years old: "In artistic ... settings, indecency may have strong communicative content, protesting conventional norms or giving an edge to a work by conveying otherwise inexpressible emotions.... Indecency often is inseparable from the ideas and viewpoints conveyed, or separable only with loss of truth or expressive power." *Denver Area Ed. Telecommunications Consortium, Inc. v. FCC*, 518 U.S. 727, 805 (1996) (concurrence)....

Brooklyn Institute of Arts & Sciences v. New York & Rudolph W. Giuliani
64 F. Supp. 2d 184 (E.D.N.Y. 1999)

The Mayor of the City of New York has decided that a number of works in the Brooklyn Museum's currently showing temporary exhibit "Sensation: Young British Artists from the Saatchi Collection" are "sick" and "disgusting" and, in particular, that one work, a painting entitled "The Holy Virgin Mary" by Chris Ofili, is offensive to Catholics and is an attack on religion. As a result, the City has withheld funds already appropriated to the Museum for operating expenses and maintenance and, in a suit filed in New York State Supreme Court two days after the Museum filed its suit in this court, seeks to eject the Museum from the City-owned land and building in which the Museum's collections have been housed for over one hundred years.

The Museum seeks a preliminary injunction barring the imposition of penalties by the Mayor and the City for the Museum's exercise of its First Amendment rights.... For the reasons that follow, defendants' motion is denied, and plaintiff's motion is granted....

Upon completion of construction of a wing of the new building, the City of Brooklyn entered into a building lease and contract (the "Contract") [in 1893, under a 100-year lease] with the Institute, for a term coextensive with the Lease, to house the Institute's collections. The City of New York is the successor to the City of Brooklyn under the Lease and the Contract. The parties agree that, upon the expiration of the original term of the Lease agreement in December 1993, the Museum remained a tenant in possession of the land and the building on the same terms and conditions as contained in the Lease and Contract.... The Contract provides that "[the City] shall pay to the [Institute] each year such sum as may be necessary for the maintenance of said Museum Building, or as may be authorized by law or be apportioned or appropriated by [the City]." The Contract specifically defines "maintenance" to include: (1) repairs and alterations; (2) fuel; (3) waste removal; (4) wages of employees providing essential maintenance, custodial, security and other basic services; (5) cleaning and general care; (6) tools and supplies; and (7) insurance for the building, furniture and fixtures.

Consistent with the applicable statutes, the Lease, and the Contract, as well as with historical practices, the City's Procedures Manual specifies that public funds are provided to designated cultural institutions to help meet costs for general maintenance, security and energy, and in some instances to support education programs. City funds generally "are not used for direct curatorial or artistic services." The City also approves certain capital expenditures as part of its program "to protect and ensure the continued existence of New York City's most precious assets, its cultural institutions, for local communities, the general public and the artistic community." The City's Fiscal Year 2000 appropriation of approximately $5.7 million to the Museum specifies that the funding contributes to "maintenance, security, administration, curatorial, educational services and energy costs." The City was not asked to fund the controversial exhibit giving rise to this action. The City's Fiscal Year 2000 appropriation to the Brooklyn Children's Museum is approximately $1.6 million.

Nothing in the City's lengthy annual final report and budget request form, which each institution must supply, asks for detailed information concerning the individual works in exhibits. Instead, the form is designed to determine, among other things: the general purposes and plans of the institution; "*brief* descriptions" (emphasis in original) of immediate past and future programming; accomplishments and plans for educational programs for children, educators and the general public; and detailed financial information.

The Sensation Exhibit was first shown in 1997 at the Royal Academy of Art in London, where it drew record crowds for a contemporary art exhibit and generated controversy and some protest demonstrations.... Mr. Lehman's efforts to bring the Exhibit to Brooklyn continued through 1998, and plans were finalized in April 1999....

The Exhibit was scheduled to open to the public at the Museum on October 2, 1999. City officials first began raising objections to the Exhibit on September 22. On that date, Commissioner Chapin, stating that he was acting on behalf of the Mayor, advised Mr. Lehman by telephone that the City would terminate all funding to the Museum unless it canceled the Exhibit. Commissioner Chapin specifically referred to the fact that the Mayor found objectionable "The Holy Virgin Mary" by Chris Ofili. (All of the five Ofili works in the Exhibit use elephant dung together with other materials. In addition, on the painting entitled "The Holy Virgin Mary," there are

small photographs of buttocks and female genitalia scattered on the background.)
The Mayor explained his position publicly that day, taking particular exception to
"The Holy Virgin Mary." The Mayor stated that this work "offends me" and "is sick,"
and he explained his decision to terminate City funding as follows:

> You don't have a right to a government subsidy to desecrate someone else's
> religion. And therefore we will do everything that we can to remove funding
> from the [Museum] until the director comes to his senses. And realizes that
> if you are a government subsidized enterprise then you can't do things that
> desecrate the most personal and deeply held views of the people in society.

The Mayor also referred to a Hirst work of two pigs in formaldehyde as "sick stuff"
to be exhibited in an art museum.

The following day, the Mayor accused the Museum of violating the Lease by mount-
ing an exhibit which was inaccessible to schoolchildren and by failing to obtain his
permission to restrict access to the Exhibit, which he made clear he would not give
because of his view that taxpayer-funded property should not be used to "desecrate
religion" or "do things that are disgusting with regard to animals." In a letter from
New York City Corporation Counsel Michael D. Hess to Mr. Lehman, dated September 23, 1999, Mr. Hess stated that "the Mayor will not approve a modification
of the Contract to allow [the Museum] to restrict admission to the museum. In light
of the fact that [the Museum] has already determined that it would be inappropriate
for those under 17 years of age to be admitted to the exhibit without adult supervision
(a determination with which the City does not disagree), [the Museum] cannot proceed with the exhibit as planned."

The Mayor and other senior City officials continued, and escalated, their attacks
on the Exhibit and their threats to the Museum, vowing to cut off all funding, including construction funding, to seek to replace the Board of Trustees, to cancel the
Lease, and to assume possession of the Museum building, unless the Exhibit were
canceled. The Mayor asserted on September 24 that he would not "have any com-
punction about trying to put them out of business, meaning the board." On September
28, the Mayor publicly stated that taxpayer dollars should not "be used to support
the desecration of important national or religious symbol, of any religion." A City
press release that day denounced "an exhibit which besmirches religion and is an
insult to the community." The press release announced that, in response to the Museum Board's formal decision that day to proceed with the Exhibit, the City would
end its funding of the Museum immediately. In his deposition, Deputy Mayor Joseph
Lhota acknowledged that he had earlier told the Chairman of the Museum's Board
of Trustees, Robert Rubin, that all City funding to the Museum would be canceled
unless the Museum agreed to remove "The Holy Virgin Mary" from the Exhibit.

In response to the City's threats, including explicit statements by senior officials
that the City would withhold its monthly payment of $497,554 due on October 1,
1999, the Museum commenced this action against the City and the Mayor on September 28, 1999, pursuant to 42 U.S.C. § 1983, seeking declaratory and injunctive
relief, to prevent the defendants from punishing or retaliating against the Museum

for displaying the Exhibit, in violation of the Museum's rights under the First and Fourteenth Amendments, including cutting off funding, terminating the lease, seizing the building or attempting to fire the Board of Trustees. The City has in fact withheld the scheduled October payment to the Museum. Plaintiff filed an amended complaint on October 1, 1999, adding claims for damages against the defendants, and claims of violation of the Equal Protection Clause and state and local law.....

THE FIRST AMENDMENT CLAIM: THE MUSEUM'S MOTION FOR A PRELIMINARY INJUNCTION

A party seeking a preliminary injunction must ordinarily demonstrate (a) irreparable harm and (b) either (1) likelihood of success on the merits or (2) sufficiently serious questions going to the merits to make them a fair ground of litigation and a balance of hardships tipping decidedly in its favor.... In any event, as will be seen, the Museum easily establishes a likelihood of success on the merits.

The Museum is suffering and will continue to suffer irreparable harm if an injunction is not granted. "The loss of First Amendment freedoms, for even minimal periods of time, unquestionably constitutes irreparable injury." Because of this, it is sometimes said that "when an injunction is sought to protect First Amendment rights, likelihood of success on the merits and irreparable harm merge into a single threshold requirement."

The City and the Mayor argue that there is no irreparable injury because the Museum has not shown that the withholding of funding prevented it from showing the Sensation Exhibit or that the loss of its operating and maintenance subsidy will force the imminent closing of the Museum. Counsel for defendants further stated at oral argument that the City's own ejectment suit cannot be a sound basis for a preliminary injunction motion because the suit has just begun and, "in the event that that particular action gets to a critical stage," the motion can be renewed. These arguments ignore the very reason that interference with First Amendment rights constitutes irreparable injury.

This is not a case involving the mere assertion of an incidental infringement of First Amendment rights insufficient to establish irreparable harm. Nor does the Museum rely on remote or speculative fears of future retaliation. The Museum has already suffered direct and purposeful penalization by the City in response to its exercise of First Amendment rights. First, the City has cut off appropriated funding. Second, the City has sued in state court to evict the Museum from the property which it has occupied for over one hundred years and in which it houses its enormous collections of ancient and modern art.... [T]he City asks the court to treat its ejectment suit as brought in good faith, that is, as brought with the goal of ejecting the Museum. It cannot on the one hand seek so serious a penalty (it could, after all, have brought only a declaratory judgment action) and on the other hand claim that no harm is imminent. For a museum of the magnitude of the Brooklyn Museum, planning for a move of one and a half million art objects would obviously be a monumental task. Given the finding of a likelihood of success on the merits of the Museum's claim of a First Amendment violation, the Museum should not have to wait until a City sheriff is at the door to seek equitable relief....

In keeping with that principle, the First Amendment bars government officials from censoring works said to be "offensive," *Texas v. Johnson*, 491 U.S. 397 (1989), "sacrilegious," *Joseph Burstyn, Inc. v. Wilson*, 343 U.S. 495 (1952), "morally improper," *Hannegan v. Esquire*, 327 U.S. 146 (1946), or even "dangerous," *Regan v. Taxation with Representation of Washington*, 461 U.S. 540, 548 (1983). "If there is a bedrock principle underlying the First Amendment, it is that the government may not prohibit the expression of an idea simply because society finds the idea itself offensive or disagreeable."

In *Hannegan*, for example, the Supreme Court held that the Postmaster General could not deny second-class postal privileges to a magazine, admittedly not containing material that was obscene and therefore illegal, because it was found by him not to be conducive to the "public good." In *Joseph Burstyn, Inc.*, the Supreme Court found the First Amendment violated by a New York statute authorizing denial of a license to motion pictures found to be "sacrilegious." ...

Similarly, in *Spence v. Washington*, 418 U.S. 405 (1974), the Supreme Court struck, on First Amendment grounds, a flag misuse statute as applied to a college student who hung an American flag with a peace symbol on it upside down out of his window. Among the grounds considered and rejected for upholding the judgment against the student, the Court noted: "that the State may have desired to protect the sensibilities of passersby" is not a basis for suppressing ideas, and that "anyone who might have been offended could easily have avoided the display." *Spence*, 418 U.S. at 412. Thus, "under our system of government there is an accommodation for the widest varieties of tastes and ideas. What is good literature, what has educational value, what is refined public information, what is good art, varies with individuals as it does from one generation to another."

The City and the Mayor acknowledge that the art being shown at the Museum and the ideas which they find that art to express are within the protections of the First and Fourteenth Amendments. Contrary to their assertions, however, although they did not physically remove the art objects from the Museum, they are not insulated from a claim that they are violating the overwhelming body of First Amendment law establishing that government cannot suppress ideas indirectly any more than it can do so directly....

In many different contexts, then, the Supreme Court has made clear that, although the government is under no obligation to provide various kinds of benefits, it may not deny them if the reason for the denial would require a choice between exercising First Amendment rights and obtaining the benefit. That is, it may not "discriminate invidiously in its subsidies in such a way as to 'aim[] at the suppression of dangerous ideas.'"

...

The reliance of the City and the Mayor on *National Endowment for the Arts v. Finley*, 524 U.S. 569 (1998), as support for their claim that viewpoint discrimination in arts funding is permissible, is misplaced. In *Finley*, the Supreme Court rejected a facial challenge to a provision adding "general standards of decency and respect for the diverse beliefs and values of the American public" to the "considerations" to be applied by the NEA in the awarding of grants to individual artists and arts organizations. The Court described the provision's legislative history, including Congress's rejection of language that would have prohibited awards of grants that would have the purpose or effect of denigrating particular religions, or of denigrating people on the basis of race, sex, handicap, or national origin. It noted that, ultimately, "the legislation was a bipartisan proposal introduced as a counterweight to amendments aimed at eliminating the NEA's funding or substantially constraining its grant-making authority." The Court also noted that "Congress declined to disallow any particular viewpoints," and it went on to hold the challenged provision facially constitutional upon finding that it "[did] not preclude awards to projects that might be deemed 'indecent' or 'disrespectful' nor place conditions on grants ..." and, further, because the Court did "not perceive a realistic danger" that it will be used "to effectively preclude or punish the expression of particular views." Thus, even in *Finley*, where the issue was the "considerations" that could apply in the awarding of grants, unlike here, where funding has already been appropriated for general operating expenses, the Supreme Court upheld the "decency" and "respect" considerations only by reading them, on their face, as not permitting viewpoint discrimination.

When questioned on oral argument whether the City could direct a publicly supported library to remove particular books on pain of a loss of financial support, counsel for defendants responded that the visual art in the Exhibit has a greater impact than do books. Counsel for the Museum, in reply, noted that books like *Mein Kampf* have done enormous harm, but are still protected by the First Amendment. The relative power of books and visual art is of course immaterial. The communicative power of visual art is not a basis for restricting it but rather the very reason it is protected by the First Amendment. As recently stated by the Court of Appeals for the Second Circuit, "visual art is as wide ranging in its depiction of ideas, concepts and emotions as any book, treatise, pamphlet or other writing, and is similarly entitled to full First Amendment protection." ...

The City's motion to dismiss is denied. As the Museum has established irreparable harm and a likelihood of success on its First Amendment claim, its motion for a preliminary injunction is granted.

Trebert v. City of New Orleans

2005 U.S. Dist. LEXIS 1560 (E.D. La. Feb. 1, 2005)

Plaintiff, Marc C. Trebert, sued the City of New Orleans pursuant to 42 U.S.C. § 1983, asserting that §§ 110–121 through 110–132 of the City's Municipal Code violate his constitutional rights of free speech under the First Amendment.... Trebert takes digital photographs, prints them and colors them with pastels. The City granted

Trebert a "Jackson Square A" permit dated January 6, 2004, which was to expire on December 31, 2004 …"to paint and sell works of art in that area defined as 'the Jackson Square set-up area.'" "Permit A" allows its holder "to manually paint, sketch or draw on plain surfaces only in … the Jackson Square artist set-up area." Trebert intends to make and sell art produced by digital technology, i.e., digital photographs that are colored with pastels.… On January 14, 2004, the Municipal Court temporarily enjoined Trebert "from selling [presumably within the Jackson Square A area only] any paintings, sketches or drawings produced by or with the assistance of a mechanical devices [sic] and with the use of any process used to duplicate an existing image," until February 3, 2004.

The Municipal Code provides that artists may create and sell only "original" art along the Jackson Square fence. "Original means only those works produced and for sale by the artist which have been accomplished essentially by hand and precludes any mechanical or duplicative process in whole or part." The ordinance prohibits plaintiff from selling, at his Jackson Square site [e.g., the French Quarter], digital photographs that have been printed and colored because they are not within the law's definition of "original" art. The City agreed to dismiss the criminal citation against Trebert and to refrain from enforcing the ordinance against him until the instant lawsuit is resolved.…

Trebert and the City agree that the ordinance at issue is content neutral and that it regulates the time, place and manner of display and sale of the works it defines as art. They also agree that "preserving the distinctive charm, character and tout ensemble of the [French] Quarter" is a significant governmental interest.…

The City has presented no evidence to sustain its burden to show that the ordinance is narrowly tailored to serve the City's significant interest in preserving the French Quarter's charm and authenticity. The City merely speculates that any less burdensome alternative would result in its interests being achieved less effectively and that "the obvious effect of lifting the restriction would be the prospect that the area surrounding Jackson Square would become one big photography studio, with cardboard images of President Clinton and faux backgrounds of French Quarter scenes."

The City also asserts that the law is narrowly tailored because "it does not prohibit duplicative processes by brush, charcoal, airbrush, finger-paint, etc." Arguably, the ordinance does prohibit such processes, inasmuch as it "precludes any mechanical or duplicative process in whole or part," and an airbrush is clearly a mechanical tool. One could also argue that an artist who churns out repetitive, albeit handmade, paintings or drawings of the same familiar French Quarter scenes for sale to tourists uses "duplicative" processes. These ambiguities in the ordinance undermine the City's argument that it is narrowly tailored to its purpose.

In *Bery*, the Second Circuit Court of Appeals invalidated the City of New York's licensing requirement for visual artists who wished to sell their works in public spaces. Despite the City's significant interest in keeping its public spaces safe and congestion-free, the court found that the law was not narrowly tailored because it effectively barred artists from selling their work on the streets. The City produced no evidence to justify such a sweeping bar on an entire category of expression. *Bery v. City of New York*, 97 F.3d 689, 697 (2d Cir. 1996)....

In contrast to these cases, the First Circuit upheld an ordinance that prohibited licensed commercial activity (including plaintiff's business of motion picture exhibition) between the hours of 1:00 a.m. and 6:00 a.m., based on the town's substantial interest in minimizing traffic, noise, litter and security problems in residential areas around the movie theater. *National Amusements, Inc. v. Town of Dedham*, 43 F.3d 731 (1st Cir. 1995). The court found that the town's avowed purposes were strongly supported by an evidentiary showing, including the records of numerous citizen complaints and the records of town meetings that led to passage of the ordinance.

The First Circuit held that the ordinance was narrowly tailored because it promoted the substantial governmental interest in preserving peace and tranquility, which could not be achieved as effectively absent the regulation, and that plaintiff had ample alternative means of reaching its intended movie-going audience during the remaining 19 hours of the day....

The City of New Orleans indisputably has a significant interest in preserving the authenticity and charm of the French Quarter. In this case, the City bears the burden to establish that its ordinance is narrowly tailored to achieve its interest. However, ... the City has produced no evidence to support its speculative assertion that any less burdensome alternative than the challenged ordinance would result in its interests being achieved less effectively. "We have never accepted mere conjecture as adequate to carry a First Amendment burden." Display of plaintiff's works does not detract from the ambiance of the French Quarter any more than electric lights do.

In the absence of any evidence submitted by the City, this court cannot find that the ordinance is narrowly tailored to serve a significant government interest. Because the City has failed to carry its burden to show that the ordinance is narrowly tailored to achieve its interest, Trebert is entitled to partial summary judgment in his favor.

Because that ruling forecloses a finding of constitutionality, the court need not address whether the ordinance leaves open to Trebert ample alternative avenues of expression. Nonetheless, for purposes of any further review of this ruling, I will analyze that prong of the constitutional test as well.

It is well established that Trebert is "entitled to a public forum for [his] expressive activities." The City argues that Trebert may sell his work from tables outside of events inside the City's Convention Center, inside the Superdome, inside arenas where concerts are held or at other events or festivals throughout the New Orleans area. Defendant contends that Trebert has failed to show that these alternative venues are inadequate. The City misconceives the evidentiary burden in this regard. It is not Trebert's burden to show that alternatives are inadequate; it is the City's burden to show that they are ample....

None of the City's proposed alternative venues for Trebert's work is Jackson Square. The City has not demonstrated that events in the Convention Center, the Superdome, other arenas or festivals are as easily accessible to plaintiff and/or his intended audience as the fence area of Jackson Square, which is a unique venue for the display and sale of works like Trebert produces to passersby.

Sports events, conventions, concerts and festivals are episodic. Many sports events and concerts occur at night, as compared to plaintiff's daily, daytime access to Jackson Square. The City has not shown that Trebert could obtain access to the inside areas of the Convention Center, the Superdome, the New Orleans Arena or Kiefer UNO Lakefront Arena as simply and cheaply as he is able to obtain a one-year permit from the City for a nominal fee....

Trebert [also] argues that the ordinance is unconstitutionally overbroad both on its face and as applied to him. In his motion for partial summary judgment, he asks that the court enjoin enforcement of the ordinance against him and any other person.

"[A] statute or ordinance may be considered invalid 'on its face' — either because it is unconstitutional in every conceivable application, or because it seeks to prohibit such a broad range of protected conduct that it is unconstitutionally 'overbroad.'" ... In the instant case, Trebert has "failed to identify any significant difference between [his] claim that the ordinance is invalid on overbreadth grounds and [his] claim that it is unconstitutional when applied to [his photographically originated work]." ...

I find that the ordinance is unconstitutional only as applied to Trebert and his activities at Jackson Square that are the subject of this lawsuit. There has been no showing that his pastel-colored, digitally initiated photographs, produced on Jackson Square, interfere with or detract from the "distinctive charm, character and tout ensemble of the [French] Quarter" or that a ban on the type of work he produces would advance protection of that interest.

This does not mean, however, that the City might not be able to show in a different case that a different type of operation than plaintiff's might be banned consistently with the First Amendment. For example, the feared prospect of a commercial photography business, featuring life-sized cardboard cutouts of presidents or other celebrities and faux backgrounds of French Quarter scenes (ironically set against the actual historic backdrop of Jackson Square) with which tourists might pose, or other similar ventures not in keeping with the unique character of Jackson Square, should they materialize, could very well be subject to prohibition under the ordinance without offending the First Amendment. In such a case, it is conceivable that the City and its lawyers might rouse themselves to develop and submit to the court evidence sufficient to bear the burden imposed by the law. In Trebert's particular case, however, they have not done so, and the ordinance unconstitutionally applies to him. Accordingly, appropriate declaratory and injunctive relief will be awarded, limited to Trebert's activities that are the subject of this lawsuit.

City of New Orleans v. Clark

251 So. 3d 1047 (La. 2018)

Defendant, Lawrence Clark, was issued a citation for displaying his art for sale on the neutral ground at Decatur Street and Esplanade Avenue in New Orleans, in violation of New Orleans Municipal Code § 110-11. Mr. Clark moved to quash the charging affidavit, asserting the ordinance is unconstitutional. We granted this writ application to consider whether New Orleans Municipal Code § 110-11, which regulates the outdoor retail sale of art, is unconstitutional as a violation of Mr. Clark's First Amendment rights. For the following reasons, we find the ordinance is unconstitutional. Therefore, we reverse the lower courts' rulings and grant the motion to quash the charging affidavit against Mr. Clark....

The New Orleans Municipal Code regulates outdoor retail sales conducted on city property. In general, Section 110-11, entitled "Prohibited street vendors," provides:

> (a) It shall be unlawful for any person to engage in any retail sales or permit any displays, signs, or advertisements for retail sales outside of any enclosed building within the city, unless expressly provided in another section of the Code of the City of New Orleans.

> (b) Whoever violates the provisions of this section shall be punished by a fine not exceeding $500.00 or by imprisonment for not more than six months, or both such fine and imprisonment.

Pursuant to the directive of subsection (a), the Municipal Code expressly provides for the sale of art in other sections. *See* New Orleans, La., Municipal Code §§ 110–121 to 110–132. Specifically, through a series of ordinances, the City of New Orleans provides a permitting process that allows artists to sell their work in certain defined areas: an "A" permit allows the "permittee to paint and sell original works of art in that area defined as 'the Jackson Square setup area.'" ... A "B" permit allows artists to "paint and sell works of art in that area defined as the 'vicinity of Jackson Square.'" ... Artists holding "A" or "B" permits can also apply to the French Market Corporation "for permission to manually paint, sketch or draw on plain surfaces only" within the French Market promenades and parks. New Orleans, La., Municipal Code § 110–130. In addition to the explicit provision for "A" and "B" permits in the ordinances, the City of New Orleans also provides for an artist "C" license for the sale of art in Edison Park, located off of Bourbon Street in the French Quarter. Although "C" permits are not specifically described in the Municipal Code, the City provides for type "C" permits (Edison Park) in its master application for occupations/general business license. The parties do not dispute the availability of this type of permit. The Municipal Code provides that "A" permits are limited to 200, but provides no cap for "B" or "C" permits. New Orleans, La., Municipal Code § 110–127.

Mr. Clark argues the cumulative effect of these ordinances (collectively, "the ordinance") is a blanket prohibition on the outdoor sale of art in New Orleans other than in these narrowly defined spaces in the French Quarter. He argues this sweeping

ban on a core form of artistic expression violates the fundamental free speech guarantees of the First Amendment of the United States Constitution and Article I, Section
7, of the Louisiana Constitution. By contrast, the State of Louisiana and the City of
New Orleans (collectively, "the City") argue the ordinance sets forth constitutional
regulations on commercial speech. The City also argues the regulations are constitutionally permissible as time, place, and manner regulations on speech.

The determination of the constitutionality of a statute presents a question of law,
which is reviewed by this court de novo. *State v. Webb*, 13-1681 (La. 5/7/14), 144
So.3d 971, 975. "This court interprets a municipal or City ordinance using the same
guidelines as those used in construing a statute. An ordinance, like a state statute, is
presumed to be constitutional. Whoever attacks the constitutionality of an ordinance
bears the burden of proving his allegation." *Rand v. City of New Orleans*, 17-0596
(La. 12/6/17), 235 So.3d 1077, 1082 (internal citations removed).

The First Amendment prohibits the enactment of laws "abridging the freedom of
speech." U.S. Const., amend. I.2 In a series of decisions beginning with *Gitlow v. New
York*, 268 U.S. 652, 45 S. Ct. 625 (1925), the Supreme Court has held and reaffirmed
"that the liberty of speech ... which the First Amendment guarantees against abridgment by the federal government is within the liberty safeguarded by the Due Process
Clause of the Fourteenth Amendment from invasion by state action." *First Nat. Bank
of Boston v. Bellotti*, 435 U.S. 765, 779 (1978) (citing *Joseph Burstyn, Inc. v. Wilson*,
343 U.S. 495, 500–01 (1952)). The Supreme Court has further stated that the Constitution looks beyond written or spoken words as mediums of expression:

> Noting that symbolism is a primitive but effective way of communicating
> ideas, our cases have recognized that the First Amendment shields such
> acts as saluting a flag (and refusing to do so), wearing an armband to protest
> a war, displaying a red flag, and even marching, walking or parading in
> uniforms displaying the swastika. As some of these examples show, a nar-
> row, succinctly articulable message is not a condition of constitutional pro-
> tection, which if confined to expressions conveying a "particularized
> message," would never reach the unquestionably shielded painting of Jack-
> son Pollock, music of Arnold Schöenberg, or Jabberwocky verse of Lewis
> Carroll.

Hurley v. Irish-Am. Gay, Lesbian & Bisexual Grp. of Boston, 515 U.S. 557, 569 (1995)
(internal quotes and citations removed). It is undisputed that the speech or expression
involved in this case is protected by the First Amendment. Although the factual record
is limited, based on the summons issued to Mr. Clark and the contentions of the
parties, it is apparent that Mr. Clark was selling his artwork from a display table on
the neutral ground at Esplanade Avenue and Decatur Street in New Orleans. "It goes
without saying that artistic expression lies within this First Amendment protection."
Nat'l Endowment for the Arts v. Finley, 524 U.S. 569, 602 (1998).

Moreover, the fact that Mr. Clark was selling his art for profit does not change the
First Amendment analysis. "It is well settled that a speaker's rights are not lost merely

because compensation is received; a speaker is no less a speaker because he or she is paid to speak." *Riley v. National Fed'n of the Blind of N.C., Inc.*, 487 U.S. 781, 801 (1988). Speech is protected even though it is carried in a form that is sold for profit and even though it may involve a solicitation to purchase. *Virginia State Bd. of Pharmacy v. Virginia Citizens Consumer Council, Inc.*, 425 U.S. 748, 761 (1976). Thus, contrary to the City's assertion, we do not find Mr. Clark's action of selling his artwork to be commercial speech. Commercial speech is defined as speech that solely proposes a commercial transaction, not speech for profit. *Bd. of Trustees of State Univ. of New York v. Fox*, 492 U.S. 469, 482 (1989); *Virginia Pharmacy Board*, 425 U.S. at 761. There is nothing in the record to suggest Mr. Clark's work proposed a commercial transaction. Rather, he was selling his artwork for profit.

The application of the ordinance to Mr. Clark's expressive activity undoubtedly raises the question of whether the ordinance abridges his freedom of speech and expression within the meaning of the First Amendment. However, the fact that the ordinance presents a First Amendment issue does not necessarily mean it constitutes a First Amendment violation. *See Members of the City Council of City of Los Angeles v. Taxpayers for Vincent*, 466 U.S. 789, 808-04 (1984). The Supreme Court has explained:

> To ascertain what limits, if any, may be placed on protected speech, we have often focused on the "place" of that speech, considering the nature of the forum the speaker seeks to employ. Our cases have recognized that the standards by which limitations on speech must be evaluated differ depending on the character of the property at issue. Specifically, we have identified three types of fora: the traditional public forum, the public forum created by government designation, and the nonpublic forum.

Frisby v. Schultz, 487 U.S. 474, 479–80 (1988) (internal citations removed). Public places historically associated with the free exercise of expressive activities, such as streets, sidewalks, and parks, are generally considered to be traditional public forums. We recognize, and the City does not dispute, that the neutral ground where Mr. Clark was selling his artwork is a public forum for First Amendment purposes.

The government's ability to prohibit expressive activity in public forums is limited. However, it is well settled that the First Amendment does not guarantee the right to communicate one's views at all time and places or in any manner that may be desired. The Supreme Court has long held that even in a public forum the government may impose reasonable restrictions on the time, place, or manner of protected speech, provided the restrictions are content neutral, narrowly tailored to serve a significant governmental interest, and leave open ample alternative channels for communication of the information. *See, e.g., Ward v. Rock Against Racism*, 491 U.S. 781, 791 (1989); *Clark v. Community for Creative Non-Violence*, 468 U.S. 288, 293 (1984). The City's ordinance must be examined in the context of this framework.

The first criterion for a valid time, place, and manner restriction is that the ordinance be "content neutral." This determination is essential because regulations that burden speech, but that are unrelated to the speaker's viewpoint or to the content of the speech, are subject to an intermediate level of judicial scrutiny, rather than the strict level of scrutiny that is applicable to content based regulations that suppress, disadvantage, or impose differential burdens on speech because of its content. Strict scrutiny makes it less likely that a regulation will clear the constitutional hurdle because the operative test is whether a regulation "is necessary to serve a compelling state interest and is narrowly drawn to achieve that end." *Arkansas Writers' Project, Inc. v. Ragland*, 481 U.S. 221, 231, 107 S. Ct. 1722, 95 L.Ed.2d 209 (1987). However, under intermediate scrutiny, the test is less exacting and requires only that the restriction be narrowly tailored to serve a significant governmental interest, and that it leaves open ample alternative channels for communication of the information.

"The principal inquiry in determining content neutrality, in speech cases generally and in time, place or manner cases in particular, is whether the government had adopted a regulation of speech because of disagreement with the message it conveys." *Rock Against Racism*, 491 U.S. at 791. A regulation that serves purposes unrelated to the content of expression is deemed neutral, even if it has an incidental effect on some speakers or messages but not others. *Rock Against Racism*, 491 U.S. at 79. In this case, the ordinance regulates the outdoor locations where artists can sell their artwork. The ordinance is equally applicable to all artists, regardless of medium or message. Thus, we find the ordinance satisfies the content neutrality requirement.

To pass constitutional muster, the ordinance must also serve a significant governmental interest. The City asserts an interest in preserving the "tout ensemble" of the French Quarter and advancing its substantial economic interest by promoting tourism, and an interest in keeping its streets and neutral grounds open and available for movement in a manner that advances public safety. We accept that the City has stated a legitimate and significant interest in preserving the distinct charm, character, and economic vitality of the French Quarter. In enacting the ordinance, the New Orleans City Council recognized the Supreme Court's decision in *City of New Orleans v. Dukes*, which noted "[t]he Vieux Carre of the city of New Orleans is the heart of [the] city's considerable tourist industry and an integral component of the city's economy." 427 U.S. 297, 299 (1976). The regulation of sales of merchandise on city property within city limits is part of a city's traditional municipal police powers, and the City has a legitimate interest in controlling commerce on city streets and other public property. The City has made the considered decision to promote its economy by driving outdoor art sales to the heart of the City's tourism industry—the French Quarter—thereby "enhancing the vital role of the French Quarter's tourist-oriented charm in the economy of New Orleans." We find that decision advances the City's significant economic and cultural preservation interests. The Supreme Court has recognized that the government may exercise its police powers to advance esthetic values, reasoning the "concept of public welfare is broad and inclusive. The values it represents are spiritual as well as physical, aesthetic as well as monetary." *Taxpayers for Vincent*, 466 U.S. at 805. Further, there is no question that "[g]overnmental authorities have the duty and responsibility to keep their streets open and available for movement." *Cox v. Louisiana*,

379 U.S. 536, 554–55 (1965). The neutral grounds between the streets should be treated no differently. We find the City has the right to regulate the use of its streets, neutral grounds, and other facilities to assure the safety and convenience of the people in their use of the property.

In addition to serving a significant governmental interest, the ordinance must be narrowly tailored to serve that interest. The means chosen by the City to achieve the desired end need not be the least intrusive or least restrictive means of doing so. The Supreme Court has clearly held that "restrictions on the time, place, or manner of protected speech are not invalid 'simply because there is some imaginable alternative that might be less burdensome on speech.'" *Rock Against Racism*, 491 U.S. at 797. Allowing some forms of expression, while denying others, does not signify a violation of the First Amendment. The sale of art in outdoor public spaces invites patrons not only to observe the artwork, but also to stop for longer periods of time to conduct a sales transaction. As the Court explained in *Kokinda*:

> Solicitation impedes the normal flow of traffic. Solicitation requires action by those who would respond: The individual solicited must decide whether or not to contribute (which itself might involve reading the solicitor's literature or hearing his pitch), and then, having decided to do so, reach for a wallet, search it for money, write a check, or produce a credit card. As residents of metropolitan areas know from daily experience, confrontation by a person asking for money disrupts passage and is more intrusive and intimidating than an encounter with a person giving out information. One need not ponder the contents of a leaflet or pamphlet in order mechanically to take it out of someone's hand, but one must listen, comprehend, decide, and act in order to respond to a solicitation. Solicitors can achieve their goal only by "stopping [passersby] momentarily or for longer periods as money is given or exchanged for literature" or other items.

[*United States v. Kokinda*,] 497 U.S. at 733–34, 110 S. Ct. 3115 (internal citations removed). The outdoor sale of art raises the same concerns. Notably the ordinance does not purport to regulate display of art, or other forms of communication. The act of displaying art does not require action by anyone, whereas the sale of art requires action—someone stopping to make a transaction. Art purchases are more time-consuming and more absorbing than observing a display and moving on. Limiting outdoor sale of art to designated areas of the city and prohibiting general retail sale of art on sidewalks and neutral grounds allows drivers to have clear visuals of the roads and pedestrians without distractions and delays, and allows for the free flow of pedestrian and vehicular traffic within the city.

The City maintains that absent the ordinance, unlimited artists could set up shop and conduct retail sales on the neutral grounds, sidewalks, or other public areas throughout the city. Unquestionably, crowds of artists selling their work would affect the City's ability to control public safety and regulate sales on its property. While the ordinance does impose some burden on speech, the ordinance does not prohibit all speech on public property, including the neutral ground chosen by Mr. Clark. The City asserts that restricting outdoor sales of art to its highest tourism area serves its significant governmental interests of public safety and economic benefit, and, without the regulation, it could not effectively accomplish its goals.

Mr. Clark concedes that the City has a valid interest in regulating the conduct of art vendors and that narrowly tailored regulations that ensure safety of drivers and pedestrians comport with the First Amendment. However, he argues, the City has taken no measures to tailor its regulation of the sale of art in public places such as the neutral ground to avoid impermissibly burdening protected speech. Rather, the City has completely banned the sale of art in every public space in New Orleans save the Jackson Square area and Edison Park in the French Quarter.

The decision in *ACORN v. City of New Orleans*, 606 F.Supp. 16 (E.D.La. 1984), provides guidance on permissible regulations on speech in the neutral ground and other public fora. In *ACORN*, a non-profit organization challenged a New Orleans city ordinance that prohibited persons from standing in a roadway or on the neutral ground for the purpose of soliciting funds. The court found the total ban on soliciting funds in roadways or on neutral grounds to be an unconstitutional restriction of expression and enjoined its enforcement. The court held that while the City had a valid interest in promoting safety and convenience by enacting time, place, and manner restrictions on expressive activity on the neutral ground, a complete ban was overbroad. Specifically, the court found the City had not taken into account factors such as "the part of town, the number of cars passing, the speed of traffic, the width of the neutral grounds, the presence of a stop sign or traffic signal, or the color of the light ... the number of solicitors, their visibility, the size of their signs, the time of day or the day of the week."

The record before us indicates the City has taken no measures to tailor its regulation of the sale of art in public places to avoid impermissibly burdening protected speech. In fact, Municipal Code § 110–11 is not even limited to areas next to roadways or solicitation of motorists. Rather, it extends to all outdoor sales to all individuals, including pedestrians. The City could have made "an earnest attempt to accommodate legitimate speech interests through careful drafting" by adopting "less restrictive methods" to ensure public safety—for example, by regulating the distance between an artist and the roadway or by prohibiting artists from distracting behavior. We find neither of the purported interests identified by the City—public safety and economic benefit—justify the significant burden on speech created by Municipal Code § 110–11. Both of these interests can be achieved by far less restrictive means than the ordinance's citywide prohibition on outdoor sales of art, save the Jackson Square area and Edison Park in the French Quarter. Thus, we conclude the ordinance is overly broad and not narrowly tailored to serve the City's substantial interests.

Furthermore, we find the ordinance does not allow ample alternative channels for artists to communicate their message. The City's ordinance offers no alternative geographic channel for selling art; such sales are completely banned outside the French Quarter.

The guarantee of the right to expression under the Louisiana Constitution must be at least equal — if not greater — to that of the First Amendment. However, owing to a ban on artistic expression that is geographically broad in scope, there is no ample alternative channel for artistic expression. In a city with allegiances to neighborhoods spanning generations, the people who populate Central City, the Garden District, the Irish Channel, Broadmoor, Hollygrove, Gert Town, Mid-City, Treme, City Park, Lakeview, Gentilly Woods, Faubourg Marigny, St. Roch, the Lower Ninth Ward, Little Woods, Village de L'est, Lake Catherine, Algiers Point and English Turn, among other neighborhoods, have limitations imposed on their constitutionally-protected artistic expression. Thus, we find the City's ordinance violates the First Amendment, and the lower courts erred by holding otherwise.

DECREE

Accordingly, we hold New Orleans Municipal Code § 110–11 is unconstitutional. We reverse the lower courts' rulings and grant the motion to quash the charging affidavit against Mr. Clark.

Notes and Questions

a. The strong support of the New York courts against Mayor Giuliani's religious outrage suggests rather unbridled control by the curators of government sponsored art exhibits. To what extent is the variation in outcome based on the independence of the museum (or its statute) and the right of the government to select which speech to adopt? *Compare Esperanza Peace and Justice Ctr. v. City of San Antonio*, 316 F. Supp. 2d 433 (W.D. Tex. 2001), *with Piarowski v. Ill. Comm. Coll. Dist.*, 759 F.2d 625 (7th Cir. 1985).

b. Mayor Giuliani is not the only political figure who may be offended. The Second City, never to be outdone by New York, had its own controversy. When the Chicago Art Institute displayed a student's painting entitled "Mirth and Girth" depicting deceased former Mayor Harold Washington in a bra, g-string, stockings, and garter belt (based on a rumor he had woman's underwear on when admitted to the hospital), local officials attempted to withhold funding and to physically remove the work. *See Nelson v. Streeter*, 16 F.3d 145 (7th Cir. 1994).

c. To what extent can a jurisdiction use the power to speak for itself and to be selective in financing under *Rust v. Sullivan* and *Finley v. NEA* to choose whether or not to provide a lease for a museum? *See Cuban Museum of Arts and Culture, Inc. v. City of Miami*, 766 F. Supp. 1121 (S.D. Fla. 1991).

d. The categorization of speech will often determine the outcome. *Pulphus v. Ayers*, 249 F. Supp. 3d 238, 247 (D.D.C. 2017), provides an interesting example. After a student had his artwork removed from an area near the Capitol, he brought a First Amendment action. But the artwork was displayed as part of a heavily regulated congressional art competition:

> Plaintiffs contend that the government engaged in viewpoint discrimi-
> nation when it removed Pulphus's painting from display, which, if the com-

petition is a limited or non-public forum, would likely violate plaintiffs' First Amendment rights. But if the art competition is government speech, then plaintiffs have no First Amendment rights at stake and forum analysis does not apply; therefore, it does not matter if the government engaged in viewpoint discrimination. *See, e.g., Walker v. Sons of Confederate Veterans,* 135 S. Ct. 2239, 2245, 192 L.Ed.2d 274 (2015) ("When government speaks, it is not barred by the Free Speech Clause from determining the content of what it says."); *People for the Ethical Treatment of Animals v. Gittens,* 414 F.3d 23, 30 (D.C. Cir. 2005) (noting that when the government is acting as an arts patron, it is "free to communicate some viewpoints while disfavoring others").

The government speech doctrine is still evolving, and it is not entirely clear how courts should distinguish between non-public forums and government speech. *See, e.g.,* [*Pleasant Grove City, Utah v. Summum,* 555 U.S. 460, 470 (2009)] ("There may be situations in which it is difficult to tell whether a government entity is speaking on its own behalf or is providing a forum for private speech."). *Walker* and *Summum* discuss three factors relevant to identifying government speech: (1) whether the medium at issue has historically been used to communicate messages from the government; (2) whether the public reasonably interprets the government to be the speaker; and (3) whether the government maintains editorial control over the speech.

e. Many controversies involving public museums also involve works that have a religious or anti-religious theme. To what extent may a governmental museum or government-funded organization present such art? Is religious and anti-religious art subject to the same standard? *See Lynch v. Donnelly,* 465 U.S. 668 (1984). *See also Santa Fe Indep. Sch. Dist. v. Doe,* 530 U.S. 290 (2000) (student led prayers deemed governmental speech); *O'Connor v. Washburn Univ.,* 416 F.3d 1216 (10th Cir. 2005).

f. In some cases, the municipalities wish to promote art and culture. If a city were to adopt the following ordinance, would it survive constitutional attack from those claiming that it discriminated on the basis of speech or viewpoint?

WHEREAS, The City Council wishes to foster the production of live performances that offer theatrical, musical, or cultural enrichment to the city's residents and visitors; and

WHEREAS, Small theaters and other small venues often promote the local production of new and creative live cultural performances, and often have the most difficulty absorbing or passing on any additional costs; and

WHEREAS, Costs faced by those who produce live theatrical, musical, or other culturally enriching performances at smaller venues are substantial, and such performances often require governmental support since they could not otherwise flourish.

NOW THEREFORE, the admissions fees charged for a live theatrical, live musical, or other live cultural performance shall be exempt from sales tax that take place in a space with a maximum capacity of not more than 750 people. For purposes hereof, a "live cultural performance" shall be deemed to be a live performance in any of the disciplines which are commonly regarded as part of the fine arts, such as live theater, music, opera, drama, comedy, ballet, modern or traditional dance, and book or poetry readings. This term does not include such amusements as athletic events, races, or performances conducted at adult entertainment cabarets [as defined elsewhere in the ordinance].

See *Pooh-Bah Enters. v. Cty. of Cook*, 232 Ill. 2d 463, 467 (Ill. 2009).

Problem 18-C

As part of Bryce's current project, Bryce has been working with a local city-owned community center to produce an exhibit of 1950s works of art that were created by local artists of the neighborhood. The board of directors for the community center was supportive of the exhibit and approved the event. Bryce also has permission to film the exhibit and possibly release a documentary about finding the works and presenting them.

Bryce now learns that the neighborhood had a much more vibrant and controversial debate during the 1950s that ended with fears from the anti-communist congressional hearings. The works Bryce has collected include both highly religious works that combine U.S. military images with religious iconography and works that depict workers chained to burning crosses. Although the approval for the exhibit had not included any approval rights over the works in the collection, word has spread regarding the works in the collection. The mayor has called the community center president and asked that the exhibit be cancelled. The city has also refused to provide Bryce a filming permit or parking permits necessary to park electrical generators for the lighting equipment that had been planned. Bryce calls you for help to stop the city and community center from frustrating the exhibit and the documentary.

D. Art Fraud & Trafficking in Art & Artifacts

United States v. An Antique Platter of Gold
184 F.3d 131 (2d Cir. 1999)

Michael H. Steinhardt appeals from Judge Jones's ordering of the forfeiture of a "Phiale," an antique gold platter. The district court held that false statements on the customs entry forms and the Phiale's status as stolen property under Italian law rendered its importation illegal. As such, the Phiale was subject to forfeiture.

Steinhardt contends that: (i) the false statements on the customs forms were not material under 18 U.S.C. §542, (ii) stolen property under the National Stolen Property

Act ("NSPA") does not encompass property presumed to belong to the state under Italian patrimony laws, (iii) both statutes afford him an innocent owner defense, and (iv) the forfeiture violates the Eighth Amendment. We hold that the false statements on the customs forms were material and, therefore, need not reach issue (ii). We further hold that there is no innocent owner defense and that forfeiture of the Phiale does not violate the Eighth Amendment.

At issue is a Phiale of Sicilian origin that dates from the 4th Century B.C. Its provenance since then is largely unknown, other than its possession by Vincenzo Pappalardo, a private antique collector living in Sicily, who traded it in 1980 to Vincenzo Cammarata, a Sicilian coin dealer and art collector, for art works worth about $20,000. Cammarata sold it in 1991 to William Veres, the owner of Stedron, a Zurich art dealership, for objects worth about $90,000.

Veres brought the Phiale to the attention of Robert Haber, an art dealer from New York and owner of Robert Haber & Company. In November 1991, Haber traveled to Sicily to meet with Veres and examine the Phiale. Haber informed Steinhardt, a client with whom he had engaged in 20–30 previous transactions, of the piece. Haber told Steinhardt that the Phiale was a twin to a piece in the Metropolitan Museum of Art in New York City and that a Sicilian coin dealer (presumably Cammarata) was willing to guarantee the piece's authenticity.

On December 4, 1991, Haber, acting for Steinhardt, finalized an agreement to purchase the Phiale for slightly more than $1 million—plus a 15% commission, making the total price paid by Steinhardt approximately $1.2 million. Haber and Veres also agreed to a "Terms of Sale," which stated, *inter alia*, that "if the object is confiscated or impounded by customs agents or a claim is made by any country or governmental agency whatsoever, full compensation will be made immediately to the purchaser." It further provided that a "letter is to be written by Dr. [Giacomo] Manganaro that he saw the object 15 years ago in Switz." In fact, Dr. Manganaro, a professor of Greek history and Numismatics, had examined the Phiale in 1980 in Sicily and had determined thereafter that it was authentic and of Sicilian origin.

On December 10, 1991, Haber flew from New York to Zurich, Switzerland, and then proceeded to Lugano, near the Italian border, where he took possession of the Phiale on December 12. The transfer was confirmed by a commercial invoice issued by Stedron, describing the object as "ONE GOLD BOWL—CLASSICAL ... DATE— C. 450 B.C.... VALUE U.S. $250,000." The next day, Haber sent a fax to Jet Air Service, Inc. ("Jet Air"), Haber's customs broker at John F. Kennedy International Airport in New York, which included a copy of the commercial invoice. Jet Air prepared an Entry/Immediate Delivery form (Customs Form 3461) to obtain release of the Phiale prior to formal entry. This form listed the Phiale's country of origin as "CH," the code for Switzerland. In addition, Jet Air prepared an Entry Summary form (Customs Form 7501), which also listed the country of origin as "CH" and stated the Phiale's value at $250,000, as Haber's fax had indicated. Haber was listed as the importer of record.

On December 15, Haber returned to the United States from Zurich with the Phiale and later gave it to Steinhardt. Before completing the purchase, Steinhardt had the piece authenticated through a detailed examination by the Metropolitan Museum of Art. Thereafter, the Phiale was displayed in his home from 1992 until 1995.

Under Article 44 of Italy's law of June 1, 1939, an archaeological item is presumed to belong to the state unless its possessor can show private ownership prior to 1902. On February 16, 1995, the Italian government submitted a Letters Rogatory Request to the United States seeking assistance in investigating the circumstances of the Phiale's exportation and asking our government to confiscate it so that it could be returned to Italy. In November 1995, the Phiale was seized from Steinhardt pursuant to a warrant. Soon thereafter the United States filed the present *in rem* civil forfeiture action. The government claimed that forfeiture was proper under 18 U.S.C. § 545 because of false statements on the customs forms. It also claimed that forfeiture was proper under 19 U.S.C. § 1595a(c) because the Phiale was stolen property under the NSPA as a result of Article 44 of Italy's patrimony laws.

Steinhardt entered the proceeding as a claimant, and he and the government moved for summary judgment. In granting judgment for the government, the district court held that the misstatement of the country of origin was material, and, alternatively, that the Phiale was stolen property under Italian law. The court also held that an innocent owner defense was not available under either statute, and that the forfeiture did not violate the Excessive Fines Clause. This appeal followed....

Section 545 prohibits the importation of merchandise into the United States "contrary to law" and states that material imported in such a manner "shall be forfeited." 18 U.S.C. § 545.[7] The government claims that the importation of the Phiale was illegal because it violated 18 U.S.C. § 542, which prohibits the making of false statements in the course of importing merchandise into the United States. Steinhardt claims, however, that an element of a Section 542 violation is that such a false statement must be material and that the government has failed to show materiality in the instant case, at least for purposes of summary judgment....

Section 542 states in pertinent part:

> Whoever enters or introduces ... into the commerce of the United States any imported merchandise by means of any fraudulent or false invoice, declara-

---

7. Section 545 reads, in relevant part:
   Whoever fraudulently or knowingly imports or brings into the United States, any merchandise contrary to law, or receives, conceals, buys, sells, or in any manner facilitates the transportation, concealment, or sale of such merchandise after importation, knowing the same to have been imported or brought into the United States contrary to law [shall be subject to criminal penalties.] ... Merchandise introduced into the United States in violation of this section, or the value thereof, to be recovered from any person described in the first or second paragraph of this section, shall be forfeited to the United States.
18 U.S.C. § 545.

tion, affidavit, letter, paper, or by means of any false statement, written or verbal, ... or makes any false statement in any declaration without reasonable cause to believe the truth of such statement, or procures the making of any such false statement as to any matter material thereto without reasonable cause to believe the truth of such statement [shall be guilty of a crime].

8 U.S.C. §542. There can be no dispute that the designation of Switzerland as the Phiale's country of origin and the listing of its value of $250,000 were false. Haber had examined the Phiale in Sicily about a month before the sale to Steinhardt, and that sale was for $1 million plus 15% commission....

The dispute pertinent to this appeal concerns the proper test for materiality. Steinhardt argues for a "but for" test of materiality, i.e., a false statement is material only if a truthful answer on a customs form would have actually prevented the item from entering the United States. The district court, however, employed a "natural tendency" test, asking whether the false statement would have a natural tendency to influence customs officials. The circuits are divided as to the proper test. The Fifth and Ninth Circuits have adopted a but for test, while the First Circuit has come down in favor of the natural tendency test. We adopt the natural tendency test.

The statutory language, caselaw, and the statutory purpose lead us to this conclusion. First, the statute prohibits importations "by means of" a false statement. Although there is overlap, this language is not synonymous with "because of," and ought not be read so narrowly. Instead, the ordinary meaning of the statutory language requires only that the false statements be an integral part of the importation process. In this case, the false statements were on custom forms and thus easily meet the by means of requirement.

Second, the Supreme Court has noted that "the most common formulation of [materiality] ... is that a concealment or misrepresentation is material if it 'has a natural tendency to influence or was capable of influencing, the decision of' the decision-making body to which it was addressed." *Kungys v. United States*, 485 U.S. 759, 770 (1988). Both the Supreme Court and this circuit have employed such a standard in numerous contexts....

Finally, the natural tendency approach is far more consistent with the purpose of the statute — to ensure truthfulness of representations made during importation — than is a but for test. Under a but for test, lying would be more productive because the government would bear the difficult burden of proving what would have happened if a truthful statement had been made. Moreover, under such a test, liability would not attach for misstatements in cases where truthful answers would still have enabled the goods to enter the United States. Importers have incentives to lie for reasons not related to achieving actual entry of the goods — e.g., to reduce the duties payable or to obtain expeditious customs treatment. The statutory purpose would thus be frustrated by the narrow reading suggested by appellant.

We therefore hold that "a false statement is material under Section 542 if it has the potential significantly to affect the integrity or operation of the importation process as a whole, and that neither actual causation nor harm to the government need be demonstrated." For a trier of fact to determine whether a statement can significantly affect the importation process, it need ask only whether a reasonable customs official would consider the statements to be significant to the exercise of his or her official duties. This analysis is analogous to the securities context, where a statement (or omission) is material if there is a "substantial likelihood" that a reasonable investor would view it as "significantly altering the 'total mix' of information made available." Moreover, this test of materiality applies not only to the decision to admit an item but also decisions as to processing, e.g., expediting importation. With this test in mind, we turn to the misstatements on the Phiale's entry form.

Steinhardt contends that even under a natural tendency test, the misstatements are immaterial. He claims that the customs officials lacked statutory authority to seize the Phiale and that it was customs policy not to review information about the country of origin of such an object. He further argues that the statement of the Phiale's value was relevant only to the imposition of the processing fee, which was unaffected by the misstatement. Because the misstatement of the country of origin was material as a matter of law and thus proper grounds for summary judgment, we need not examine the misstatement of value.

Customs Directive No. 5230-15, regarding the detention and seizure of cultural property, fatally undermines Steinhardt's contention that listing Switzerland as the country of origin was irrelevant to the Phiale's importation. The Directive advised customs officials to determine whether property was subject to a claim of foreign ownership and to seize that property. An item's country of origin is clearly relevant to that inquiry....

The Directive provides a basis for seizing cultural property under the NSPA in the seizure provisions of 19 U.S.C. § 1595a(c). Seizure of the Phiale would clearly be authorized by this provision under *United States v. McClain*, 545 F.2d 988 (5th Cir. 1977), which held that violations of a nation's patrimony laws are covered by the NSPA. Because Steinhardt asserts that *McClain* was improperly decided, he claims that the customs officials lacked a statutory basis to seize the Phiale.

This argument, however, misperceives the test of materiality. Regardless of whether *McClain*'s reasoning is ultimately followed as a proper interpretation of the NSPA, a reasonable customs official would certainly consider the fact that *McClain* supports a colorable claim to seize the Phiale as having possibly been exported in violation of Italian patrimony laws. Indeed, the Directive explicitly references the *McClain* decision and informs officials that if they are unsure of the status of a nation's patrimony laws, they should notify the Office of Enforcement. Knowing that the Phiale was from Italy would, therefore, be of critical importance....

Eighth Amendment

While Steinhardt raised an Eighth Amendment claim in the district court [that] the forfeiture violates the Excessive Fines Clause of the Eighth Amendment [in violation of *United States v. Bajakajian*, 524 U.S. 321 (1998)]. We disagree. [The] instant case ... bears all the "hallmarks of the traditional civil *in rem* forfeitures." First, the forfeiture here was not part of a criminal prosecution. While Section 545 is part of the criminal code, this fact alone does not render the forfeiture punitive. Although the question whether a proceeding is civil or criminal is certainly relevant, it is not dispositive. Thus, the fact that the present action is a civil *in rem* proceeding weighs against a finding that it is punitive.

Even more important to the inquiry is the nature of the statute that authorizes forfeiture. As opposed to Section 982(a), the provisions at issue in *Bajakajian*, Section 545 is a customs law, traditionally viewed as non-punitive. The Phiale is thus classic contraband, an item imported into the United States in violation of law.... It is forfeiture of the former that *Bajakajian* continues to recognize as nonpunitive and outside the scope of the Excessive Fines Clause.

We therefore affirm.

United States v. Austin

54 F.3d 394 (7th Cir. 1995)

FLAUM, *Circuit Judge.*

Defendant Donald Austin was convicted and sentenced to 8 1/2 years for knowingly buying and selling counterfeit works of art. Although we uphold his conviction, the denial of his motion for a new trial, and all but one of the trial court's sentencing determinations, we remand for a reconsideration of whether Austin deserved a sentencing enhancement under the Guidelines for being an "organizer or leader."

Donald Austin owned and operated Austin Galleries, a chain of art galleries in Chicago, Detroit, and San Francisco. Austin, whose business grew from one Chicago gallery in the mid-1960s to over thirty galleries in the mid-1980s, was a "hands-on" manager who took an active interest in all facets of his business and in each of his galleries. Austin Galleries specialized in modern and contemporary artists, including Salvador Dali, Joan Miro, Pablo Picasso, and Marc Chagall, and sold mostly lithographic and serigraphic prints of their works. Although the individual galleries had prints on hand, many customers purchased prints on a "to ordered" basis; a customer would see a copy in a gallery, and order the actual print from Austin's headquarters in Palatine, Illinois.

Lithographic and serigraphic prints can be divided into three categories for the purposes of this opinion. Lithographs and serigraphs are most valuable when they are part of an "original" limited edition print, a "category 1." Art industry standards require that an original be prepared under the artist's supervision. The artist signifies his acceptance of the edition by signing and numbering them. The artist may also reserve a small percentage of the edition for his own use or that of the publisher. Called "artist's proofs," such works are identified by the designation H.C., E.A., or A.P., usually in place of the edition number. Less valuable than originals are "afters" or "category 2" prints. Afters are copies of an original work made by others with the artist's permission; these copies have nominal value in the decorative art market. Finally, there are "category 3" prints: unauthorized reproductions of an artist's work (or independent works made to look like something the artist might have created), made without the artist's involvement or approval. These works do not have an established market, and if they carry an artist's signature, they are forgeries.

Austin sold most of his art as signed original limited edition prints. His customers thought they were buying originals. The customers were wrong; most of what Austin sold were forgeries. Several of Austin's employees recalled that they never seemed to run out of any print and that there was never a time when a customer requesting a specific edition number was told that the number had been sold or was otherwise unavailable. Others noticed that a number of works they were selling were obvious forgeries and brought this to Austin's attention, to no avail. Two employees even tried removing what they thought were frauds from the walls of one gallery, but when Austin learned of this he merely became angry and ordered them to place the prints back on display.

Acting on complaints, the Federal Trade Commission ("FTC") brought suit against Austin in May, 1988. A district court placed a temporary restraining order on Austin on May 5, 1988, restricting Austin's sales of Dali, Picasso, and Chagall prints and permitting the FTC to enter Austin's galleries to inspect his prints and documents. The inspection yielded widespread evidence of forgeries among Austin's inventory and prior sales. One expert who examined 490 prints, including 387 in current inventory and 103 sold to customers, did not find a single authentic original. Records also revealed that Austin had been able to acquire prints in suspiciously large quantities, some quantities even exceeding the number in the actual edition of the print. The results of the investigation also raised concerns about the authenticity of Austin's Miro prints, and the court, after the FTC amended its complaint, added Miro's works to the list of those Austin could not sell.

Following the investigation, in April, 1990, Austin entered into a settlement agreement with the FTC. The agreement, as approved by the court, forbade Austin from making misrepresentations in the sale of artwork. Austin also agreed to surrender all of his pencil-signed Miros, Chagalls, and Picassos. Austin was allowed to sell Dalis so long as he did not represent them as authentic works of art. Additionally, the court ordered Austin to pay $625,000 into a consumer redress fund to be administered by the FTC, with the condition that if he did not pay the entire sum by January 1, 1991, or if he declared bankruptcy before that day, the amount would increase to $1.5 million. As a final part of the settlement, Austin signed a stipulation for judgment admitting the allegations of fraud contained in the complaint. The stipulation was to be filed only in the event Austin went into bankruptcy or defaulted on his payments to the FTC.

The FTC settlement failed to deter Austin. Austin did not turn over all of the Chagalls, Miros, and Picassos as required. He also attempted to sell several Chagalls to one of his art suppliers, Michael Zabrin, and to sell to another supplier, Phillip Coffaro, a "package" of Chagalls and Miros, although both men turned him down. Most significant, Austin sold nine Chagall prints to a customer, Merlin Hanson, for

$50,000, with an option to repurchase within six months. Austin originally had requested only a loan from Hanson and had offered the prints as collateral, but Hanson's financial advisor had insisted on the buy-back arrangement to avoid any losses should Austin enter bankruptcy. Austin represented the prints as having a value of $70,000 wholesale and $140,000 retail. Prior to the sale, which was made eleven days after the FTC settlement, an FTC expert had informed Austin's attorney that at least one of the prints sold to Hanson was a fake.

Following these events, the government initiated criminal proceedings against Austin, and a grand jury indicted him on March 11, 1993. Counts I through VII of the indictment alleged violations of the mail and wire fraud statutes, 18 U.S.C. §§ 1341 & 1343, while Count VIII charged Austin with causing money he knew to have been taken by fraud to be transmitted in interstate commerce, 18 U.S.C. § 2314. The first five counts related to transactions prior to the FTC proceeding, while the last three concerned the Hanson sale. In the course of its investigation, the grand jury subpoenaed Austin's records for sales of Chagalls after 1988. In response, Austin did not turn over information regarding the Hanson sale; Austin testified at trial that he thought the sale was a loan and did not have to be reported.

The government, which relied heavily on the information produced by the FTC investigation, introduced at trial extensive evidence of fraud against Austin. A jury returned guilty verdicts against Austin on all counts, and the trial judge sentenced him to 102 months imprisonment to be followed by two years supervised release. The court also ordered Austin to pay into the FTC's compensation fund $505,000, which was the difference between the restitution he had already made, about $120,000, and the original sum stipulated in the FTC settlement, $625,000.

On appeal, Austin raises several challenges to his conviction. He contends that double jeopardy barred his conviction because of the earlier FTC suit and settlement and that the trial court erred in admitting much of the government's evidence....

Austin first maintains that the FTC settlement had placed him once in jeopardy for any fraud he might have perpetrated on his customers. Austin does not argue that the $625,000 he was initially required to pay into a "consumer redress fund" constituted a punishment for his actions; he admits that that sum was a remedial payment. Rather, Austin submits that when he defaulted on the $625,000 installment plan and his liability jumped to $1.5 million, the $875,000 increase constituted a punishment above and beyond his agreement to return his customers' money. This civil sanction, he suggests, placed him once in jeopardy, thereby rendering the criminal trial an unconstitutional proceeding.

Austin is correct that "punitive" civil sanctions can constitute punishment for the purposes of the double jeopardy clause. Austin is also correct that even where a civil punishment precedes a criminal trial, jeopardy may attach. Austin's argument falters, however, when he asserts that if $625,000 satisfied the FTC's remedial interests, any payment above that amount is properly categorized as "a deterrent or retribution." The FTC accepted $625,000 initially because it feared that the defendant might go into bankruptcy. The FTC's offer amounted to a discount for prompt and early payment of the total loss Austin had caused, a sum the FTC estimated to be in excess of $3.8 million. When Austin violated the terms of the settlement and the amount he owed increased, the FTC was still only holding Austin liable for an amount less than that it thought his fraud had caused. Thus, the net consequence of the FTC's actions was still remedial. Such circumstances do not implicate the Double Jeopardy Clause.

Second, Austin objects to the trial court's admission of extensive evidence relating to the FTC settlement, including the terms of the consent decree and Austin's stipulation in the settlement admitting to the allegations in the FTC's complaint. He asserts that this evidence was unfairly prejudicial because it likely led the jury to think that "the same issues had already been determined in the civil action." We review the admission of this evidence for abuse of discretion.

Austin's contentions on this point are equally unavailing. Prior to trial, the government informed Austin that it would introduce the consent decree in order to show Austin's criminal intent in subsequently violating its conditions. While Federal Rule of Evidence 408 prohibits the admission of statements made in the course of settlement to prove liability and Rule 404(b) prohibits the admission of other wrongs in order to show action in conformity therewith, both rules allow the admission of such evidence when offered for another purpose. The evidence from the civil suit served a number of alternative purposes. First, it showed that Austin was on notice when he subsequently sold other prints that those prints were forgeries. It also demonstrated Austin knew he could not sell those prints without reporting the sale to the FTC. Moreover, the facts from the FTC case both provided the background for Austin's indictment and laid the evidentiary foundation for many of the governments exhibits in the criminal proceeding. Finally, the stipulation itself constituted a direct judicial admission to the accusation of fraud in the conduct underlying the indictment. These purposes provided sufficient bases to introduce this evidence against Austin.

We also do not think that the evidence, in light of its relevance, was so "unfairly prejudicial" that the trial court should have excluded it under Fed. R. Evid. 403....
[W]e affirm Austin's conviction ...

Notes and Questions

a. Defendant Michael Steinhardt continues to have legal issues with his collectibles. Most recently, the Republic of Turkey has challenged the legality of his sale of a rare idol that "Republic contends was illicitly removed from the Republic." Steinhardt and Christie's, Inc. sought a protective order prohibiting the Republic "from pursuing certain deposition testimony, documents and written discovery from Steinhardt, his wife and his employee regarding Steinhardt's experience and practices in acquiring antiquities." *See Republic of Turkey v. Christie's, Inc.*, 312 F. Supp. 3d 385 (S.D.N.Y. 2018).

b. In *United States v. Schultz*, 333 F.3d 393 (2d Cir. 2003), the Second Circuit formally addressed the application of the National Stolen Property Act (NSPA), 18 U.S.C.

§ 2315, to antiquities that are not stolen from a private owner, but, rather, are excavated in violation of state law. Many countries have laws which provide for state ownership of excavated antiquities. The court reaffirmed the position that these patrimony laws provide sufficient ownership of the property to allow for enforcement of the NSPA. *See also United States v. McClain*, 545 F.2d 988 (5th Cir. 1977).

c. Other federal statutes provide criminal sanctions, including theft of major artwork, 18 U.S.C. § 668 (to obtain by theft or fraud any object of cultural heritage from a museum); interstate or foreign shipments by carrier; state prosecutions, 18 U.S.C. § 659 (to steal or obtain by fraud anything from a conveyance, depot, or terminal, any shipment being transported in interstate or foreign commerce); fraud and swindles, 18 U.S.C. § 1341 (to cause anything to be sent through the U.S. mails in furtherance of a scheme to defraud); fraud by wire, radio, or television, 18 U.S.C. § 1343 (to cause any electronic signal to cross state lines in furtherance of a scheme to defraud); interference with commerce by threats or violence (Hobbs Act), 18 U.S.C. § 1951 (to obstruct interstate commerce by robbery, extortion, threat of violence, or actual violence); and illegal trafficking in Native American human remains and cultural items, 18 U.S.C. § 1170 (discussed below).

d. One analogy to the NSPA for intellectual property applies to the transportation and sale of bootleg records. Is there a sufficient ownership in the copyright underlying the bootleg records or the public performance of the artist to give rise to a cause of action? *See Dowling v. United States*, 473 U.S. 207 (1985).

e. The treatment of Native American sacred sites and gravesites has been one of the many troubling aspects of expropriated art and artifacts. In 1990, Congress enacted The Native American Graves Protection and Repatriation Act, codified at 25 U.S.C. §§ 3001–3013 and 18 U.S.C. § 1170.

The bill summary provides a simple outline of the legislation:

- Clarifies the right of ownership of Indian, Alaska Native, and Native Hawaiian (Native American) human remains and artifacts, including funerary objects, religious artifacts, and objects of cultural patrimony, found on Federal or tribal lands.

- Establishes conditions for the excavation or removal of Native American human remains or cultural artifacts, including the consent of the appropriate tribe or Native American organization.

- Establishes notification requirements for the inadvertent discovery of Native American human remains or cultural artifacts on Federal or tribal lands.

- Establishes criminal penalties for the sale, purchase, or transport of Native American human remains or cultural artifacts without a legal right of possession.

- Directs Federal agencies and museums receiving Federal assistance to identify the geographic and tribal origins of human remains or cultural artifacts in their collections, and require the return of the remains or artifacts to the appropriate tribe or Native American organization upon request.

- Establishes a Department of Interior advisory committee to review the identification and repatriation processes for Native American human remains and cultural artifacts held by Federal agencies and federally assisted museums.

- Establishes civil penalties for museums failing to comply with requirements of this act.

f. Another difficult issue in theft and misappropriation of art and cultural artifacts stems from the atrocities of the Nazi regime during its reign through the end of World War II. Limited legal activity continues today, and new evidence provides a better historical record, if not any meaningful measure of legal relief. *See Alperin v. Vatican Bank*, 410 F.3d 532 (9th Cir. 2005).

A group of twenty-four individuals and four organizations (the "Holocaust Survivors") claim that the Vatican Bank, known by its official title Istituto per le Opere di Religione, the Order of Friars Minor, and the Croatian Liberation Movement (Hrvatski Oslobodilacki Pokret), profited from the genocidal acts of the Croatian Ustasha political regime (the "Ustasha"), which was supported throughout World War II by Nazi forces. That profit allegedly passed through the Vatican Bank in the form of proceeds from looted assets and slave labor. The Holocaust Survivors brought suit in federal court claiming conversion, unjust enrichment, restitution, the right to an accounting, and human rights violations and violations of international law arising out of the defendants' alleged involvement with the Ustasha during and following World War II....

> The viability of the Holocaust Survivors' claims apart from the issue of the political question doctrine is not before us. Nevertheless, looking ahead, we note that the statutory grounds on which the Holocaust Survivors base their claims have, for the most part, not fared well in recent litigation. Just last term, the Supreme Court limited the [Alien Tort Statute (ATS)] in *Sosa v. Alvarez-Machain*, 542 U.S. 692 (2004) (curtailing the scope of actionable international norms under the ATS but explaining that "the door is still ajar subject to vigilant doorkeeping"); *see also Weiss v. Am. Jewish Comm.*, 335 F. Supp. 2d 469 (S.D.N.Y. 2004) (dismissing claim under the ATS for injunctive relief in connection with the construction of a Holocaust memorial in light of the Court's holding in Sosa).

> The contours of the [Foreign Sovereign Immunities Act (FSIA)] have also changed with the Supreme Court's holding in Republic of *Austria v. Altmann*, 541 U.S. 677 (2004), that the FSIA applies retroactively. *See also Abrams v. Societe Nationale des Chemins de Fer Francais*, 389 F.3d 61, 64–65 (2d Cir. 2004) (dismissing case for lack of subject matter jurisdiction because the French government's acquisition of defendant railroad company immunized it from suit under the FSIA). In *Deutsch v. Turner Corp.*, 324 F.3d 692, 719 (9th Cir. 2003), we held that a California statute on which the Holocaust Survivors' claims are based in part, Cal. Civ. Proc. Code § 354.6, unconstitutionally intruded on the foreign affairs power of the fed-

eral government. We leave the district court to determine in the first instance to what extent the Holocaust Survivors have correctly invoked these and other jurisdictional bases.

A similar result resulted five years later in *Von Saher v. Norton Simon Museum of Art at Pasadena*, 592 F.3d 954 (9th Cir. 2010).

Marei von Saher ("Saher") seeks the return of two paintings alleged to have been looted by the Nazis during World War II. The paintings were purchased in or around 1971 by the Norton Simon Museum of Art in Pasadena, California ("the Museum"), and are now on display there. Saher brought this claim against the Museum under § 354.3 of the California Code of Civil Procedure, which extends the statute of limitations until 2010 for actions for the recovery of Holocaust-era art. The primary issue on appeal is whether § 354.3 infringes on the national government's exclusive foreign affairs powers. The district court held that it does. We agree, and affirm the district court's holding that § 354.3 is preempted.

Is the current trend against enforcement of claims for property stolen by Nazi governments consistent with the NPSA or the Native American Graves Protection and Repatriation Act? Should the provenance of stolen art or cultural artifacts be subject to a statute of limitations? Does it matter whether the work has religious significance, and if so, significance to whom?

g. Can there be an innocent art dealer in the chain of title for stolen art and artifacts? Again, does the answer change if the works are religious in nature, or if they were stolen as part of an occupational government or during the commission of human rights violations? *See Autocephalous Greek-Orthodox Church v. Goldberg & Feldman Fine Arts, Inc.*, 917 F.2d 278 (7th Cir. 1990).

Problem 18-D

As Bryce has worked in the neighborhood on the feature film, art exhibit, and documentary (*see* Problems 18-B, 18-C), Bryce has gained the trust and respect of many of the elderly artists in the area. Alice McGreevy, one of the artists, gave Bryce a group of five oil paintings that she had made in 1952. McGreevy explained that she had sold the paintings to a collector in 1952, but then found out that the collector was planning to destroy the work out of fear that the pieces would result in his identification as a Communist sympathizer. (The collector, in fact, had attended Communist political party meetings twice in the 1930s.) McGreevy explained that she "took the artwork back" from the unnamed collector—but kept the payments.

Bryce accepted the gift, but is now worried. The exhibit and the associated publicity have generated a great deal of interest in these works. The children of the collector have contacted Bryce claiming ownership of the five works and demanding their return. McGreevy says that the family has no claim over the works, so she can dispose of them however she wants. Bryce requests your advice and guidance.

E. Bibliography and Links

Amy M. Adler, *Against Moral Rights*, 97 Calif. L. Rev. 263 (2009).

Genevieve Blake, *Expressive Merchandise and the First Amendment in Public Fora*, 34 Fordham Urb. L.J. 1049 (2007).

Sonya G. Bonneau, *Honor and Destruction: The Conflicted Object in Moral Rights Law*, 87 St. John's L. Rev. 47 (2013).

Richard Chused, *Moral Rights: The Anti-Rebellion Graffiti Heritage of 5pointz*, 41 Colum. J.L. & Arts 583 (2018).

Patty Gerstenblith, *Acquisition and Deacquisition of Museum Collections and the Fiduciary Obligations of Museums to the Public*, 11 Cardozo J. Int'l & Comp. L. 409 (2003).

Jennifer Anglim Kreder, *Analysis of the Holocaust Expropriated Art Recovery Act of 2016*, 20 Chap. L. Rev. 1 (2017).

Jennifer Anglim Kreder, *The Public Trust*, 18 J. Const. L. 1425 (2016).

Tzu-I Lee, *A Battle Between Moral Rights and Freedom of Expression: How Would Moral Rights Empower the "Charging Bull" Against the "Fearless Girl"?*, 17 J. Marshall Rev. Intell. Prop. L. 672 (2018).

Lydia Pallas Loren, *Law, Visual Art, and Money*, 22 Lewis & Clark L. Rev. 1331 (2018).

Naomi Mezey, *The Paradoxes of Cultural Property*, 107 Colum. L. Rev. 2004 (2007).

Brandon J. Pakkebier, *Form over Function: Remedying VARA's Exclusion of Visual Art with Functional Qualities*, 103 Iowa L. Rev. 1329 (2018).

Kurt G. Siehr, *Globalization and National Culture: Recent Trends toward a Liberal Exchange of Cultural Objects*, 38 Vand. J. Transnat'l L. 1067 (2005).

Brian Soucek, *Aesthetic Judgment in Law*, 69 Ala. L. Rev. 381 (2017).

Ryan C. Steinman, *Taking a Mulligan: Moral Rights and the Art of Golf Course Design*, 51 IDEA 47 (2011).

Drew Thornley, *The Visual Artists Rights Act's "Recognized Stature" Provision: A Case for Repeal*, 67 Clev. St. L. Rev. 351 (2019).

Stephen K. Urice, *Between Rocks and Hard Places: Unprovenanced Antiquities and the National Stolen Property Act*, 40 N.M.L. Rev. 123 (2010).

Websites

Art and Cultural Property Law, http://www.hg.org/art.html

California Arts Council, http://www.cac.ca.gov

Federal Bureau of Investigation, Art Theft Program, http://www.fbi.gov/hq/cid/art theft/arttheft.htm

Publication 557 (3/2005), Tax-Exempt Status for Your Organization, http://www.irs. gov/publications/p557/index.html

United States Department of State Bureau of Educational and Cultural Affairs, http:// exchanges.state.gov/culprop/index.html

United Nations Educational, Scientific and Cultural Organization, www.unesco.org

F. Epilogue

The battle over the publication of *Exposure* grew as Bryce began to write letters to the editor decrying the censorship by the subjects of the book. (*See* Problems 17-B, 17-E.) Bryce also created and operates a website about the controversy surrounding the book. The website continues to grow in popularity.

Eventually the book was published with only five of the exposés removed. Out of sheer spite, Bryce and Jesse added a very unflattering exposé of the publisher's attorney. Although the attorney had planned to sue, she found that she had assigned her copyright and publicity rights to her employer under the terms of the employee handbook she had helped author. The law firm owning the copyright and publicity rights did not have an interest in pursuing the claims; Bryce does not believe the content is defamatory or inaccurate.

Bryce followed up the publication of *Exposure* with a stage musical tribute to the book and the tribulations of getting it into print. *Exposure—The Musical* is scheduled to premiere at the State Theatre and then move to an Off-Broadway venue for an indefinite run. Bryce has also arranged to cut a cast album, to film a making-of documentary, and to option the film rights to the musical.

Bryce calls you for advice. Evidently, the city council is upset because two of the photographs in the book were of nudes. To celebrate these photographs, Bryce has written a production number entitled "Warm Your Hands Before You Shoot." The city council is not amused and has told the State Theatre officials to cancel the production.

Bryce wants advice.

Seems like old times.

Index